The Oxford
Companion to
Local and Family
History

THE OXFORD COMPANION TO LOCAL AND FAMILY HISTORY

Edited by David Hey

Oxford   New York
OXFORD UNIVERSITY PRESS
1996

Oxford University Press, Walton Street, Oxford OX2 6DP

Oxford New York
Athens Auckland Bangkok Bombay
Calcutta Cape Town Dar es Salaam Delhi
Florence Hong Kong Istanbul Karachi
Kuala Lumpur Madras Madrid Melbourne
Mexico City Nairobi Paris Singapore
Taipei Tokyo Toronto
and associated companies in
Berlin Ibadan

Oxford is a trade mark of Oxford University Press

First Published by Oxford University Press 1996

British Library Cataloguing in Publication Data
Data available

Library of Congress Cataloging in Publication Data
The Oxford companion to local and family history
edited by David Hey.
p.   cm.
Includes Index.
1. Genealogy—Methodology. 2. History, Local—Methodology.
I. Hey, David.
CS9.094 1996 929'.1'072041—dc20 95—43895
ISBN 0-19-211688-6

1 3 5 7 9 10 8 6 4 2

Typeset by Interactive Sciences Ltd., Gloucester
Printed in Great Britain
on acid-free paper by
The Bath Press
Bath, Avon

PREFACE

The Oxford Companion to Local and Family History is conceived as a reference book that presents a complete view of the related subjects of Local and Family History. It is intended as a starting point for those professional scholars and amateur researchers who are working in these fields, and serves as a valuable source of information for the general reader. The entries summarize present knowledge and academic debate and point to research priorities where both amateurs and professional historians can make a real contribution. Books and articles are suggested for further reading. The *Companion* provides information on archives, how to use them and where they can be found, and defines terms commonly used in Local and Family History research. The *Companion* covers a broad time span and geographical area. It looks at the whole of the British Isles from prehistory to the present day, concentrating on the period after the Norman Conquest.

A volume which attempts to review such a wide range of work needs to draw upon the expertise of leading scholars. I have been fortunate in having the ready and enthusiastic co-operation of sixteen colleagues who together have contributed nearly a quarter of the book. Local and Family History are subjects whose practitioners are generally known for their friendly assistance and mutual high regard. The contributors are listed on pages vii–ix and each contribution is attributed.

A very special mention must be made to Dr Joan Thirsk, FBA, CBE, who has not only contributed a pioneering piece on women writers of Local and Family History, but who has commented constructively on the entire text, offering numerous suggestions and correcting errors. She has approached this task with her customary thoroughness and generosity and I am deeply indebted to her. The *Companion* is as much her view of the subject as it is mine. We are conscious, however, that others will wish to approach the subject differently and that new developments will in time make our interests seem old-fashioned. If the *Companion* helps in that process, we shall have served our purpose.

I also wish to thank the editorial and production staff at Oxford University Press for all their help in planning and producing this volume. In particular, I thank Pam Coote for all her helpful suggestions and encouragement and Alysoun Owen for dealing with all the problems of production so pleasantly and efficiently.

DAVID HEY
January 1995

CONTRIBUTORS

Dr Malcolm Airs is a Fellow of Kellogg College, Oxford, and University Lecturer in Historic Conservation. He is a Commissioner of the Royal Commission on the Historical Monuments of England and a member of the Historic Buildings and Areas Advisory Committee of English Heritage. He has written extensively on the buildings of the Tudor and Jacobean period, and his publications include *The Making of the English Country House, 1500–1640* (1975) and *The Tudor and Jacobean Country House* (1995).

Professor J. V. Beckett is Professor of English Regional History at the University of Nottingham. He has written extensively on landed estates and their owners, and his publications include *The Aristocracy in England 1660–1914* (1986), and *The Rise and Fall of the Grenvilles: Dukes of Buckingham and Chandos, 1710–1921* (1994).

Anthony Camp joined the staff of the Society of Genealogists in 1957 and became Director in 1979. He was elected to Honorary Fellowship for very distinguished services to the Society in 1982. Currently the President of the Hertfordshire Family & Population History Society, a Vice-President of the Association of Genealogists & Record Agents, he has the Order of Merit of the National Genealogical Society. His books include *Tracing your Ancestors* (1964), *Wills and their Whereabouts* (1963, 1974), *Everyone has Roots* (1978), *My Ancestors came with the Conqueror* (1988), *My Ancestors Moved* (1994), and six volumes of an *Index to P.C.C. Wills 1750–1800*.

Dr H. S. A. Fox is Senior Lecturer in English Topography in the Department of English Local History at the University of Leicester. He is the author of numerous essays on agrarian history, landscape history, and demographic history and specializes in the counties of Devon, Somerset, and Cornwall. His current work is on aspects of Somerset's population, including the labouring poor in the early middle ages, and on the origins of fishing villages in Devon.

Dr Margaret Gelling embarked on place-name studies in 1946, when she became Research Assistant to the English Place-Name Society, of which she is now President. She is Honorary Reader in English Place-Name Studies at Birmingham University and her publications include *Signposts to the Past* (2nd edn. 1988), *Place-Names in the Landscape* (repr. 1993), and *The West Midlands in the Early Middle Ages* (1993).

John L. Halstead teaches at the Division of Adult Continuing Education of the University of Sheffield. He is editor of *Labour History Review* and his published work on historical and adult education topics include 'The Voice of the West Riding: Promoters and Supporters of a Provincial Unstamped Newspaper, 1833–34'. He is currently working on a history of labour periodicals.

Professor David Hey (General Editor) is Professor of Local and Family History and Dean of the Faculty of Educational Studies at the University of Sheffield. His recent publications include *The Oxford Guide to Family History*

(1993), Family History and Local History in England (1987), *Yorkshire from AD 1000* (1986), and *The Fiery Blades of Hallamshire: Sheffield and its Neighbourhood, 1660–1740* (1991).

Dr Ralph Houlbrooke, Reader in History at the University of Reading, is the author of *Church Courts and the People during the English Reformation* (1979), *The English Family 1450–1700* (1984), and editor of *Death, Ritual and Bereavement* (1989). He has nearly finished a book on the social history of death in early modern England.

Dr R. W. Hoyle is Senior Lecturer in History at the University of Central Lancashire where he teaches early modern Economic History and Local History. His publications include *The Estates of the English Crown, 1558–1640* (1992), and *Tudor Taxation Records: A Guide for Users* (1994).

David Moody is a librarian with East Lothian District Library and author of three books in the Batsford Local History series, *Scottish Local History* (1986), *Scottish Family History* (1988), and *Scottish Towns* (1992). He is currently editor of the *Transactions of the East Lothian Antiquarian and Field Naturalists' Society.*

Dr D. Huw Owen is Keeper of Pictures and Maps at the National Library of Wales. A professional archivist, he previously taught at the College of Librarianship Wales, Aberystwyth, and at University College, Cardiff. His recent publications include *Settlement and Society in Wales* (1989) [contributor and editor] and three regional chapters on Wales and the Marches in *The Agrarian History of England and Wales*, vol. iii, *1349–1500* (1991). He is a member of the Council of the British Association for Local History.

Professor David M. Palliser is Professor of Medieval History at the University of Leeds. His main research interests are in medieval urban, demographic, and settlement history, and he also has a special interest in Northern and regional history. His numerous publications include *Tudor York* (1979), *Recent Archaeological Research in English Towns* (ed. with John Schofield, 1981), and *Domesday York* (1990). He is a member of the Council of the Royal Historical Society and of the Research Committee of the Society of Antiquaries.

Professor Charles Phythian-Adams is Head of the Department of English Local History at the University of Leicester, which he first joined under W. G. Hoskins in 1966. His publications include *Desolation of a City* (1979) and *Re-Thinking English Local History* (1987). His *Land of the Cumbrians: A study in British provincial origins* is to be published soon.

Dr N. L. Ramsay is a curator in the Department of Manuscripts, British Library, and an Honorary Research Fellow, University of Kent, Canterbury. He has written on the history of Canterbury Cathedral's library and archives for *A History of Canterbury Cathedral* (1995), of which he was a joint editor and has co-edited *English Medieval Industries: Craftsmen, Techniques, Products* (1991) and *St Dunstan: His Life, Times and Cult* (1992).

Dr Brian M. Short is Senior Lecturer in Geography and Dean of the School of Cultural and Community Studies, University of Sussex. His interests include the changing rural society, economy, and landscape of Britain from 1650 to the present. His publications include *The English Rural Community: Image and Analysis* (1992), *South East England from AD 1000* (1990) in the Longman Regional History of England series, and *The Geography of England and Wales in 1910: An Evaluation of Lloyd George's 'Domesday' of Landownership.*

Dr Joan Thirsk is a historian of English agriculture, who worked for thirteen years in the Department of English Local History at the University of Leicester. All her writing is coloured by strong perceptions of local differences. She was President of the British Association for Local History from 1986 to 1992, and has been President of the Kent History Federation since 1990. Her numerous books include *Economic Policy and Projects: The Development of a Consumer Society in Early Modern England* (1978), and *The Rural Economy of England: Collected Essays* (1989). She is General Editor and part-author of the multi-volume *Agrarian History of England and Wales*.

Professor Kevin Whelan is Professor at the Royal Irish Academy, Dublin and is Burns Library Visiting Scholar in Irish Studies at Boston College 1995–6. He has published extensively on eighteenth- and nineteenth-century Ireland. His most recent publications include *The Tree of Liberty. Radicalism, Catholicism and the Construction of Irish Identity 1760–1830* (1995) and *Endurance and Emergence. Catholics in Ireland in the Eighteenth Century* (co-editor, 1990).

NOTE TO READER

ENTRIES are arranged in strict letter-by-letter alphabetical order up to the first punctuation in the headword. Cross-references are indicated by an asterisk or by the use of 'see' followed by the entry headword in small capitals. 'See also' is also used to inform the reader of related subjects which may be of interest. *The Companion* does not include entries on living historians.

An appendix at the back of the book lists national and major county and local record offices along with special collections of national interest.

A

abbey. A major *monastery, ruled over by an abbot. The *Cistercian and *Premonstratensian foundations were abbeys, whereas the *Cluniac and *Carthusian houses were *priories dependent on the original monastery of their order. The *Benedictines, *Augustinians, and *Gilbertines had both abbeys and priories. In practice, the greatest priories were as large as many of the abbeys. See Glynn Coppack, *The English Heritage Book of Abbeys and Priories* (1990).

abstract. A summary of a document.

accompt. Archaic form of 'account'.

accounts, medieval. The survival rate of annual accounts for medieval estates varies from one part of the country to another. For Norfolk alone almost 2,000 accounts are extant for the period 1238–1450, representing some 219 different *demesnes, 60 per cent of them with fewer than five *compotus rolls. On the other hand, in the remote north-west and south-west of England hardly any accounts survive.

achievement of arms. The complete representation of the heraldic insignia of a family, including the *coat of arms, crest, helmet, mantling, torse, and motto. The achievement of a peer also includes chapeau, coronet, supporters, and compartment.

acre. Derived from *Old English *aecer* or Old Norse *akr*, 'plot of cultivated land'. Originally an approximate measure of land which a yoke of *oxen could plough in a day, it was standardized by Edward I (1272–1307) as a unit of 4,840 square yards. However, in northern and western England, and in Scotland and Ireland, the customary acre remained much larger. The Cheshire acre, for example, was about twice the size of the statute acre. Yorkshire is still known as 'the county of the broad acres'. In these parts it is often difficult to judge whether acres recorded in *surveys, *rentals, etc. refer to customary or statutory units.

act books. Records which summarize the procedure in a case before an *ecclesiastical court, particularly during the second half of the 16th century and much of the 17th century. See J. S. Purvis, *Tudor Parish Documents of the Diocese of York* (1948). Chapter act books are of use for the building history and furnishing of a *cathedral. See S. Bond, 'Chapter Act Books', *History*, 54 (1969). See also PROBATE COURTS.

Acts of Parliament. Statute Rolls, which contain all Acts of Parliament since 1500, are housed in the *House of Lords Record Office. Acts which have not been printed may also be seen there. Public Acts from 1485 to 1702 have been printed as *Statutes of the Realm*, and from 1702 as *Statutes at Large*. Local, Personal and Private Acts from 1797 are kept among the Parliament Rolls in the *Public Record Office. Printed sets of Local and Personal Acts are available at the *British Library. Many local *record offices and libraries have printed copies of local Acts, e.g. those relating to parliamentary *enclosure, *turnpike roads, etc. See HOUSE OF COMMONS JOURNALS; HOUSE OF LORDS JOURNALS; PARLIAMENTARY PAPERS.

Adams, John: *Index Villaris*. A list of the market towns of England and Wales, compiled by John Adams (*fl.* 1680). The second edition, published in London in 1690, is the more useful.

Addy, S. O. (1848–1933). Antiquarian and folklorist. A Sheffield solicitor who contributed numerous articles on medieval *charters, *place-names, *dialect, *folklore, material culture, etc. to the *Derbyshire Archaeological Journal*, the *Transactions of the Hunter Archaeological Society*, the *Yorkshire Archaeological Journal*, *Notes and Queries*, etc., Addy is best remembered as the author of *The Evolution of the English House* (1898, revised edn. 1933), the pioneering work on *vernacular architecture. He also wrote a *Glossary of Words Used in the Neighbourhood of Sheffield* (1888) for the English Dialect Society, *The Hall of Waltheof* (1893), and *Household Tales* (1895).

administration, letters of and bonds. When a person died without making a *will, or if the named executors were unavailable, the next-of-kin, a friend, or a creditor could apply to a *probate court for letters of administration of the estate. The applicant had to swear that he would discharge all funeral expenses and debts and would submit a true and perfect *inventory and an account of his stewardship. He was sometimes required to enter into a *bond.

Administration Acts (the records of the above, known as Admons.) are kept with wills in diocesan *record offices. They were written in Latin until 1733. A probate inventory is often attached.

Admiralty, High Court of. The court with jurisdiction in cases involving piracy, privateering, and other offences committed on the high seas. It developed into the court which heard all matters relating to the high seas and business abroad. Its records—especially for the period from 1525—are kept at the *Public Record Office under HCA 13 (examinations), 15–20 (instance papers), 23 (interrogatories), 24 (libels and answers), and 30 (miscellenea). See the lists under LIS 45, 46, 93, 112, 180, 183, 184, and 194, and *Records of the High Court of Admiralty*, published by the *List and Index Society, vol. xxvii (1967). See also D. O. Shilton and R. Holworth (eds.), *High Court of Admiralty Examinations, 1637–8* (1932), and R. G. Marsden (ed.), *Select Pleas in the Court of Admiralty* (Selden Society, vi and xi, 1892, 1897).

adoption. A register of adoption from 1927 onwards is kept at the *General Register Office, St Catherine's House, London. No formal mechanism was available previously, unless the parties drew up a *deed. Birth certificates obtained via the Adopted Children's Register at the General Register Office give the dates of birth and adoption and the names of the adopting parents, but not the child's original surname or the names of the natural parents.

The Children Act, which came into force on 12 November 1975, allows an adopted person over the age of 18 to apply for his or her original birth certificate at the General Register Office or by writing to the General Register Office (CA side), PO Box 7, Titchfield, Fareham, Hampshire PO15 5RU. An applicant who was adopted before 12 November 1975 will be interviewed by an experienced social worker before a certificate is issued. A person adopted after that date can decide whether or not to be interviewed.

Adoption was not recognized in Scottish law until 1930. Records of adoption in the Court of Sessions and Sheriff Court are kept in the *Scottish Record Office, but information is supplied (by order of the court) only if the adopted child has reached the age of 17.

Advent. In the ecclesiastical calendar, the season immediately preceding the festival of the Nativity, including the four Sundays before Christmas. Because it was regarded as a time for fasting and repentance, this was a prohibited season for marriages.

advertisements in early provincial *newspapers are a prime source of local information, especially about the sale of properties, which are sometimes described in detail, e.g. they may list the stock of a business.

advowson. The right to appoint a priest to a *benefice, especially a parish *church. This right might be held by an individual (often a *lord of a manor) or an institution (e.g. an Oxford or Cambridge college or a *monastery). Upon the *dissolution of the monasteries many such rights were purchased by individuals from the Crown. The descent of the advowson is often traced in detail in the older county histories and in the *Victoria County History*.

aerial archaeology. Photographs taken from a light aircraft flying at a height of one or two thousand feet can reveal ancient remains that are invisible or barely visible on the ground. These remains are often in the form of *crop marks or soil marks that can be seen from the air only in certain conditions, at the right time of day and year. Shadows cast in low sun at an angle pick out the lines of old mounds, banks, and ditches, or the remains of ruined walls that were grassed over centuries ago. Aerial photographs have pinpointed the sites of previously unknown *Neolithic henges, *Iron Age farmsteads, Roman villas and forts, Romano-British *field systems, linear earthworks, medieval planned villages and towns, *deserted medieval villages, decayed *monasteries, the buried remains of early industries, and many other aspects of *landscape history. An aerial photograph can act as a blueprint of, for example, the playing-card shape and internal divisions of a Roman fort, when taken from directly above, and can thus be a great aid to excavation. In other cases, the discovery of a new site by means of an aerial photograph can lead to intensive fieldwork and documentary research, e.g. the correlation of *ridge-and-furrow patterns with 16th-century maps showing *strips in *open-fields. Aerial photographs are now a major tool for landscape studies.

The first archaeological air photographs were taken between the two world wars, but it was not until after the Second World War that systematic aerial exploration and recording began. The major collections of photographs of historical sites are those of the University Committee for Aerial Photography in Cambridge (which was founded by Professor J. K. St Joseph) and of the Air Photography Unit of the National Monuments Record (Royal Commission on *Historical Monuments). See M. W. Beresford and J. K. St Joseph, *Medieval England: An Aerial Survey* (2nd edn., 1979), E. R. Norman and J. K. St Joseph, *The Early Development of Irish Society: The Evidence of Aerial Photography* (1969), D. R. Wilson, *Air Photo Interpretation for Archaeologists* (1982), and Richard Muir, *History from the Air* (1983). Many local *record offices or public libraries have collections of aerial photographs that were taken for other purposes but which are now of historic value, e.g. in showing the construction of new housing estates, or in demonstrating the physical patterns of towns before redevelopment.

affinity. Relationship through marriage, not through blood, e.g. son-in-law, stepdaughter. The table of affinities in the *Book of Common Prayer lists the relationships within which marriage was forbidden until the 20th century. These included 'deceased wife's sister' and 'deceased husband's brother'.

aftermath (agricultural). Grass that sprouts anew after the cutting of a crop of hay, suitable for grazing.

agent. See STEWARD.

agger. The raised foundations and drainage ditches of a *Roman road.

agistment. 1. The right to graze livestock on the *commons in the summer.

2. The rate levied or profit made on the grazing of pastures.

agnate. A relative descended from a common male ancestor.

Agnus Dei (Lat. 'Lamb of God'). The Christian symbol of Christ as the Paschal Lamb, which is shown with a halo and usually bearing a cross or flag. Part of the mass begins with these words.

Agrarian History of England and Wales. An eight-volume survey under the general editorship of H. P. R. *Finberg and Joan Thirsk, published by Cambridge University Press. This work of co-operative scholarship was planned in 1956 and was due to be completed by 1996–7. It is essential background reading for rural historians.

Agricultural Depression, the. This term may refer to the 1930s but more usually relates to the late 1870s. The belief that British agriculture suffered a deep decline from the 1870s onwards has been much refined. The importation of American cereals certainly forced many farmers into bankruptcy during the last quarter of the 19th century and the early years of the 20th century. The effects on corn growers were real enough, but farmers in pastoral regions were not similarly affected. T. W. Fletcher, 'The Great Depression of English Agriculture, 1873–96', *Economic History Review*, 2nd ser., 13/3 (1961) first suggested that the depression was not general across the whole country and that some farmers did well during these years. He showed that in Lancashire those who grew corn suffered but that others who concentrated on livestock prospered. See also P. J. Perry (ed.), *British Agriculture, 1875–1914* (1974), and F. M. L. Thompson, 'An Anatomy of English Agriculture, 1870–1914' in B. A. Holderness and Michael Turner (eds.), *Land, Labour and Agriculture, 1700–1920: Essays for Gordon Mingay* (1991), ch. 11, which concludes that the idea that there was a general depression in English agriculture in the last quarter of the 19th century must be abandoned. The worst effects of the depression were felt in Berkshire, Buckinghamshire, Herefordshire, Hertfordshire, Huntingdonshire, Northamptonshire, Nottinghamshire, Oxfordshire, Rutland, and Surrey.

agricultural history. The study of agricultural history became a serious academic concern in the late Victorian period. J. E. Thorold-Rogers, *History of Agriculture and Prices in England, 1259–1793*, the seventh and last volume of which was published in 1887, was of lasting influence in stressing the importance of trends in the economy. Frederic *Seebohm, *The English Village Community* (1883), which was immediately hailed as a pathfinding work, emphasized the value of local studies and initiated a long debate on the origins of the *manor, which was taken up by F. W. *Maitland, *Domesday Book and Beyond* (1897), and by P. *Vinogradoff in two works, *The Growth of the Manor* (1904), and *English Society in the Eleventh Century* (1908).

The *Agricultural Depression of the last quarter of the 19th century, following a long period of prosperity, turned attention to the past. A debate about the condition of the small farmer after parliamentary *enclosure began with the publication of G. Slater, *The English Peasantry and the Enclosure of the Common Fields* (1907), A. H. Johnson, *The Disappearance of the Small Landowner* (1909), and E. C. K. Gonner, *Common Land and Inclosure* (1912). In 1911 the appearance of John and Barbara *Hammond's

The Village Labourer inflamed the discussion and drew public attention to the fate of the rural poor. The book has remained controversial and a stimulus to enquiry to the present day. Meanwhile, George Sturt, writing under the pen-name of George *Bourne, studied the effects of enclosure in one Hampshire community in *Change in the Village* (1912). R. H. Tawney's *The Agrarian Problem in the Sixteenth Century* (1912) examined similar problems in an earlier age.

This productive period saw the publication of the first comprehensive survey of English agricultural history, R. E. Prothero (later Lord Ernle), *English Farming Past and Present* (1912), which eventually ran into six editions. About the same time, the American historian, H. L. Gray, published a massive amount of evidence on the origins and nature of *open-field systems, which is still of value, in *English Field Systems* (1915). The study of *field systems received fresh stimulus from C. S. and C. S. *Orwin, *The Open Fields* (1938). Here again a subject that interested these early scholars remains a matter of lively debate to this day.

But after the First World War interest waned and few scholars turned their attention to agricultural history. George *Fussell (1889–1990) had a remarkable encyclopaedic knowledge of contemporary printed literature, which he used to good effect in more than 20 books and 600 articles published between 1922 and his centenary year. Others, notably G. H. *Tupling, J. D. *Chambers, and W. G. *Hoskins, turned their attention to detailed regional and local studies which challenged the conclusions of earlier scholars who had attempted national surveys. The opening of county *record offices in many parts of England, making accessible much new archival material, encouraged the local and regional approach which has been so important since the Second World War. The expansion of the national higher education system and in particular the establishment of university departments of economic history brought many new scholars into the field. By 1953 there were sufficient of these to launch the *British Agricultural History Society and its journal, The *Agricultural History Review, which contains an annual bibliography of current writing. Three years later The *Agrarian History of England and Wales (ed. H. P. R. Finberg and later Joan Thirsk) was launched as an authoritative work in eight volumes, covering all periods of time from *prehistory to the Second World War. The publication of the final volume, scheduled for 1996–7, will set the seal on a remarkable co-operative enterprise that has established

agricultural history as a major scholarly activity. The series provides an indispensable base for further advances in the subject.

What are the major concerns of agricultural historians now that more than a century has passed since Thorold-Rogers and Seebohm were publishing their findings? Medieval historians have shifted their attention from the history of the manor to the origins of the village and its associated field systems. The old belief that the village was imported by the first *Anglo-Saxons in the 5th century has been abandoned. A degree of continuity between the Roman and medieval countryside is now accepted, and archaeologists have concluded from the absence of Anglo-Saxon deposits below *deserted medieval villages, and the discovery of small, scattered sites elsewhere, that the village was a later form of settlement. Some villages were formed through the coalescing of independent farmsteads, others were deliberately planned. No agreement has been reached on the firm dating of planned villages, though it is accepted that they were created between the 9th and the 13th centuries.

Archaeological, topographical, and documentary research has shown that communal farming in open-field systems began not with the arrival of the Anglo-Saxons, but with the later creation of villages. Emphasis is now placed on the Anglo-Scandinavian period, for similar systems can be observed in many other parts of Europe from the 9th century onwards. Their original layouts became obscured over time to allow complex and flexible arrangements, with the *furlong rather than the field being the usual cropping unit. *Population pressure is thought to have been the instrument for change. A much greater understanding of the function and the transformation of field systems and of their regional diversity has now been achieved.

The attention that has been paid to open-field systems, together with the concentration of research on the large, *cereal-growing estates of lowland England, has underplayed the role of pastoral farming. The importance of *wool-growing has long been accepted, but less emphasis has been placed on the raising and fattening of *cattle, which is now recognized to have been the mainstay of the agrarian economy in many parts of northern and western England and much of the rest of the British Isles. By the early 13th century the documentary evidence is sufficient to enable historians to study regions and to observe changes in their economy over time.

A recent reappraisal has recognized the role

of the market in medieval agriculture. Farmers were partly restricted by soils, *climate, manorial structure, and field systems, but by the second half of the 13th century market forces were influencing the choice of crops and livestock and decisions on the intensity of production. The growth of *London and, to a less extent, the regional capitals, together with the success of many of the *medieval new towns, stimulated the exchange of goods between town and country. Towns were larger and more numerous, and the countryside more open to commercial influences, than was once thought. Detailed regional studies have shown that *lords and *peasants alike responded to the new opportunities by changing their methods of production. See, for instance, B. M. S. Campbell, 'Agricultural Progress in Medieval England: Some Evidence from Eastern Norfolk', *Economic History Review*, 2nd ser., 36/1 (1983), and B. M. S. Campbell and M. Overton, 'A New Perspective in Medieval and Early Modern Agriculture: Six Centuries of Norfolk Farming, *c.*1250–*c.*1850', *Past and Present*, 141 (1993).

Although a number of important studies have dealt with the economy of large lay and ecclesiastical estates, few attempts have been made to analyse the social structure of *lordship. New work is needed on the origins of the manor, the power of lords, and the status of the peasantry. The period 1250–1420 is well documented quite far down the social scale, but is under-researched. Previous estimates of population levels are now considered to be too low. A figure of five to six million for England *c.*1300 is now considered likely. Our view of this period has been dominated by the argument of M. M. *Postan that population growth necessitated more intensive cultivation, an expansion of arable production onto marginal areas, and the subdivision of peasant holdings until grain yields diminished and a crisis of subsistence occurred long before the *Black Death. His ideas have subsequently been refined, but they still provide the framework for debate on medieval agriculture. See H. E. Hallam (ed.), *The Agrarian History of England and Wales*, ii: *1042–1350* (1988), and Edward Miller (ed.), *The Agrarian History of England and Wales*, iii: *1350–1500* (1991).

The Black Death and later epidemics, which reduced the population substantially, had profound consequences for agriculture. In lowland England, particularly in the 15th century, a great deal of land was converted from cereal-production to pasture. Faced with a shortage of labour, *landowners turned from farming their *demesne to leasing their land to *graziers and *butchers or to enterprising peasant farmers. This long period of economic decline or stagnation provided opportunities for some families to increase their wealth by *engrossing the farms that others had abandoned. *Wood-pasture regions were less affected by decay during the 15th and early 16th centuries than were the cereal-growing areas, where many villages were gradually deserted and open-fields were converted into sheep-runs or cattle pastures. In Warwickshire, for example, the success of the cattle-raisers of the Forest of Arden is in marked contrast with the failure of the Fielden economy.

The abandonment of demesne farming has made the hundred years or so from the 1420s a difficult period to study because of the lack of demesne accounts. The lessees employed labour on a substantial scale to farm much larger holdings than before. Many of them rose from the ranks of the peasantry to *yeoman or even *gentry status; others came as wealthy outsiders. At the same time, more modest advancement was achieved by tenants who took over an extra customary holding. The social distinctions between various types of *tenure declined, but the stratification of the peasantry became more marked. See, for example, Christopher Dyer, *Lords and Peasants in a Changing Society: The Estates of the Bishopric of Worcester, 680–1540* (1980).

Until recently, much of what was written about medieval agriculture was concerned with the demesne, particularly those large ecclesiastical estates which are abundantly recorded. A much wider social and geographical coverage was achieved by John Langdon, *Horses, Oxen and Technological Innovation: The Use of Draught Animals in English Farming from 1066–1500* (1986), which used a national sample of the thousands of manorial *accounts that were drawn up each *Michaelmas by the *reeve or *bailiff of a manor. These demesne accounts can be supplemented by the inventories, *lay subsidies, *heriots, maintenance agreements, *surveys, *tithe returns, and *extents that provide information about peasant agriculture. Two outstanding studies of the social and economic relations of the medieval peasantry are Zvi Razi, *Life, Marriage and Death in a Medieval Parish: Economy, Society and Demography in Halesowen, 1270–1400* (1980), and Margaret McIntosh, *Autonomy and Community: the Royal Manor of Havering, 1200–1500* (1986).

Historians of the early modern period have much richer sources with which to study the farming practices of individual yeomen and *husbandmen in all parts of the country. In particular, the tens of thousands of probate *inventories that have survived provide a firm statistical basis for establishing the varied emphases of regional husbandry and the gradual acceptance of new methods. Their analysis has underpinned much of the writing of volumes iv and v of *The Agrarian History of England and Wales*, ed. Joan Thirsk, which cover the period 1500–1750. These two volumes demonstrate the huge advances that have been made in our understanding of the early modern period. Growing regional specialization within an integrated national economy is now seen as having been facilitated by the development of more sophisticated marketing methods and structures and by improvements in transport. An apt illustration is the rapid growth of *market gardening during the 17th century, especially in the vicinity of London, which provided ready sales and supplies of *manures; many of the new crops which eventually transformed farming practices were introduced in this way. During the 17th and 18th centuries England became agriculturally the most advanced country in Europe. It remained largely self-sufficient in food despite a substantial growth of the urban and industrial population, for gains were made in agricultural productivity per head and in yields per acre.

Commercial agriculture diversified considerably in response to market opportunities. Between 1500 and 1640 the general level of agricultural prices increased sixfold. Thereafter, sheep-and-corn farmers fared badly, but men who concentrated on *dairying and meat production continued to do well. For example, the pastoral farmers of Durham and Northumberland profited from feeding the large number of *coal miners who worked in the vicinity. In the Cheshire Plain and the Dove Valley farmers abandoned cereals to become specialist *cheese-producers serving many parts of the country; their profits enabled them to import the cereals they needed.

The empirical methods that were applied to agriculture by enterprising tenants on land held in *severalty formed part of the intellectual movement of the 16th and 17th centuries. From about the 1470s onwards landowners returned to farming their own demesnes. In part this was due to the influence of classical writers such as Cato, Varro, and Columella, whose works were appearing in print; surviving copies are underlined and well-thumbed. The first English book on agriculture—*Fitzherbert's *Book of Husbandry*—appeared in 1523. The gentry were urged to see themselves as responsible, patriarchal figures. This advice became all the more attractive when food prices began their steady upward trend from about 1515 and farming became more profitable.

Many of the technological improvements that earlier writers saw as determinants of an *Agricultural Revolution after 1750 have been dated to much earlier periods. In *The Agricultural Revolution* (1967) Eric Kerridge argued that the floating of water-meadows, the substitution of *convertible husbandry for permanent tillage and permanent grass or for shifting cultivation, the introduction of new *fallow and other crops, roots, and selected grasses, fen drainage, manuring, and stock breeding were practices that could be dated to the 16th and 17th centuries. Other historians have agreed on the dating of the beginnings of these changes, but they have stressed the slow diffusion of ideas and have argued that these new methods had little quantitative effect on the early modern economy.

It is clear, however, that the 16th and 17th centuries saw dramatic improvements in the quality of livestock. In 1500 cattle, *sheep, and *pigs still had to scavenge for food upon bits and pieces of land and were badly provided for in winter. On mixed farms stock fed upon the stubble of arable crops and whatever land could be spared for grazing. In those parts of the country where rearing was the speciality large tracts of land had to be set aside to provide fodder. The next two centuries saw great improvements as land was earmarked for grazing, fertilized regularly, ploughed, and sown with *clovers, for both summer and winter feeding. The same period saw a much greater use of convertible husbandry, in which land that had previously been used solely for cereals was rotated between arable and pasture, with the elimination of the fallow. During the second half of the 17th century clovers were commonly used. Rising prices for livestock products as the national population increased encouraged farmers in this direction.

A great deal is also now known about landlords and estates, the size of holdings, the various methods of tenure, dual occupations, farmhouses, different field systems, and the enclosure of fields and commons. Much enclosure took place in the 16th and 17th centuries. In counties such as Oxfordshire, Leicestershire, and Northamptonshire, parliamentary enclosure can now be seen as merely the last and most intense phase of a very protracted process which had been going on for centuries.

The drop in population levels in the late Middle Ages left some landlords with no option but to enclose. Decay of tillage and conversion to pasture, leading to deserted villages, unemployment, poverty, and *vagabondage, were already evident by the late 15th century, but government attempts at controlling the problem were ineffective. Meanwhile, much enclosure took place by the agreement of all those involved. Only when there was disagreement was it necessary to obtain a private Act of Parliament to enclose. The gradual process of enclosure became much more intense during the period 1750–1850, when over 4,000 private Acts of Parliament were passed to permit the enclosing of at least 6.8 million acres. During the 1760s and 1770s most of the surviving open-field parishes of the Midlands were enclosed, so as to allow farmers to shift their attention to animal husbandry. A new wave of activity took place during the French Revolutionary and *Napoleonic wars of 1793–1815, when food prices rose rapidly. Much of this was concerned not with reorganizing open-fields but with bringing the poorer-quality land of the wastes and commons into arable production. The resulting changes in both types of landscape were profound.

If the broad picture of enclosure is now clear, debate still rages over its social consequences. Passions run high when post-enclosure living standards, the *Poor Law, and rural riots are discussed. Neither the proponents nor the opponents of enclosure doubted that enclosure turned commoners into *labourers. Many people felt that they had suffered by the substitution of small *allotments for their rights on the *commons and wastes. Nationally, 36 per cent of the enclosure bills were opposed at some stage of their progress through Parliament. Although the debate has not been resolved, it has become clear that only one in four or five of the rural population was directly affected by enclosure, that experience differed from region to region, and that the great growth of the national population produced unprecedented numbers of landless people regardless of the enclosure movement.

By the late 19th century the vast majority of the land in Britain was held in large estates. Studies of different areas have destroyed the view that the period from 1688 to 1750 was particularly important in the creation of large estates, for they have revealed a variety of consolidation patterns over the two centuries after 1660. See F. M. L. Thompson, *English Landed Society in the Nineteenth Century* (1963), and J. V. Beckett, *The Aristocracy in England, 1660–1914* (1986). For a regional study over nearly four centuries, see Barbara English, *The*

Great Landowners of East Yorkshire, 1530–1910 (1990). It remains uncertain whether enclosure led to a consolidation of individual farms. A gradual increase in farm size occurred during the 18th and the first part of the 19th century, especially in the south Midlands, East Anglia, and the southern counties, so that by 1851 just over half the farmed land of England and Wales was contained in holdings of 200 or more acres, and four-fifths was in farms exceeding 100 acres. However, small farms remained important in many parts of the north and west, even after enclosure. Nor does it appear to be true that the larger farms employed more capital per acre and were therefore more productive.

The achievements of the 1750–1850 period were considerable. At the very time that *Malthus was making his gloomy prophecies, the direct link between population and prices was broken for the first time in British history. Net food imports rose by about a third, but were paid for by increased exports of manufactured goods. A falling proportion of the national work-force was able to produce most of the food that was necessary to sustain a population that was increasingly divorced from the land. Agricultural output doubled and labour productivity rose as the national population tripled. This was a considerable achievement, but did it amount to a revolution?

The concept of an Agricultural Revolution in the 70 years between 1760 and 1830, which was advanced by Lord Ernle in *English Farming Past and Present* (1912), still has popular appeal, though it has been either discarded or altered out of recognition by academics. Ernle's arguments were substantially modified in J. D. Chambers and G. E. Mingay, *The Agricultural Revolution, 1750–1880* (1966), and then eroded by much detailed archival research. Present opinion holds that agricultural change was a long and complex process that varied considerably from one region to another. The concept of an Agricultural Revolution has been diluted so much as to have become unsustainable. G. E. Mingay, the editor of *The Agrarian History of England and Wales, vi. 1750–1850* (1989) now concludes: 'Given the many persistent obstacles which lay in the path of agricultural progress, the achievements of the hundred years after 1750 were remarkable. It could hardly be said that they amounted to an agricultural revolution.' See J. V. Beckett, *The Agricultural Revolution* (1990) for a summary of the debate.

The 'capitalist agriculture' of the era of parliamentary enclosure, culminating in the *High Farming of the first half of Victoria's reign, produced the threefold division of landowner, tenant farmer, and labourer in the cereal-growing regions, while small family farms continued elsewhere in time-honoured fashion. Regional variety is as much a feature of Victoria's reign, whether in prosperity or in the prolonged agricultural depression of the last quarter of the century, as it was of earlier times. It is this variety of experience that agricultural historians have come to recognize whatever their subject of enquiry. The simple generalizations of the past have been rejected.

The achievements of the agricultural historians associated with the British Agricultural History Society and *The Agrarian History of England and Wales* have been considerable. Scotland and Ireland have not been so well served, largely because of the paucity of records for the pre-modern era. See, however, Cormac Ó Gráda, 'Irish Agricultural History: Recent Research', *Agricultural History Review*, 38/2 (1990), for an account of current scholarship, particularly on the 19th century. Jonathan Bell and Mervyn Watson, *Irish Farming, 1750–1900* (1986) is one of the few general surveys, but many detailed studies have appeared in Irish journals. Some of the best research is on the first half of the 19th century, that critical period between Union and the *Famine. On the eve of the *potato famine output per male Irish worker was about half the British level. Despite the over-reliance on the potato, there was nothing inevitable about the crisis that struck in 1846. Research on the period 1850–1920 has concentrated on tenurial relations and on farming techniques, output, and prices. In Scotland, the best work has been done on the Highland *Clearances.

Scholarly debate now centres on how far an emphasis on economic history, viewed through estate records and official publications, has produced an optimistic picture that obscures the sufferings of the rural poor. The developing interest in social history has led some historians—notably those associated with the journals *History Workshop* and *Rural History*—to offer a different picture, focused on rural protest. It is argued that too much stress on the achievements of agriculture in feeding the rapidly growing industrial population overlooks the periods of famine and starvation suffered by the rural poor. The debate is particularly concerned with the late 18th and 19th centuries. The questions raised by George Bourne and the Hammonds are still not resolved to everyone's satisfaction. See, for example, K. D. M. Snell, *Annals of the Labouring Poor: Social Change and Agrarian England, 1660–1900* (1985), M. Reed

and R. Wells (eds.), *Class, Conflict and Protest in the English Countryside, 1700–1880* (1990), and Alun Howkins, *Poor Labouring Men: Rural Radicalism in Norfolk, 1870–1923* (1985). For similar concerns amongst Welsh historians see, for example, REBECCA RIOTS.

For the modern period, see P. J. Perry (ed.), *British Agriculture, 1875–1914* (1974), F. M. L. Thompson, 'An Anatomy of English Agriculture, 1870–1914', in B. A. Holderness and Michael Turner (eds.), *Land, Labour and Agriculture, 1700–1920: Essays for Gordon Mingay* (1991), Richard Perren, *The Meat Trade in Britain, 1840–1914* (1978), M. E. Turner, 'Rural Economies in Post-Famine Ireland, c.1850–1914', in B. J. Graham and L. J. Proudfoot (eds.), *An Historical Geography of Ireland* (1993), P. E. Dewey, *British Agriculture in the First World War* (1989), E. H. Whetham (ed.), *The Agrarian History of England and Wales*, viii: *1914–1939* (1978), and B. A. Holderness, *British Agriculture Since 1945* (1985). For the social history of the countryside, see Alun Howkins, *Reshaping Rural England: A Social History, 1850–1925* (1991), and Anne O'Dowd, 'Women in Rural Ireland in the Nineteenth and Early Twentieth Centuries: How the Daughters, Wives and Sisters of Small Farmers and Landless Labourers Fared', *Rural History*, 5/2 (1994). See also TWENTIETH CENTURY and ORAL HISTORY.

Agricultural History Review. The journal published twice a year by the *British Agricultural History Society since 1953. It deals with all aspects of agrarian society, particularly with farming practices, landscapes and the farming economy. An index to volumes 1–35 (1953–87) is available.

agricultural labourers. The distinction between a farm labourer and a *farm servant was that a servant was hired on a yearly basis from about the age of 14 and lived on the farm, whereas a labourer was usually a married man, employed on either a regular or a casual basis, who lived elsewhere. (See TIED HOUSING.) In the Tudor and early Stuart period the labouring population of England and Wales probably formed about one quarter or one third of the entire population of the countryside. The figure varied considerably from region to region. It was lowest in *moorland areas, a little higher on *wolds and *downs, and much higher in fertile corn-growing districts and in unenclosed *heath- and *forest-lands. As the population recovered to its medieval level, so the proportion of labourers grew. By the end of the 17th century labourers, cottagers, and paupers formed nearly half the entire population. Landless, migrant labourers were far more numerous than before. See Alan Everitt, 'Farm Labourers', in Joan Thirsk (ed.), *The Agrarian History of England and Wales, iv. 1500–1640* (1967), ch. 7. (See also COTTAGES; COMMONS AND WASTES; WAGES; and BY-EMPLOYMENTS.)

The great increase in the national population from the mid-18th century onwards meant that more and more families had to seek employment as wage labourers. Meanwhile, the fashion for living-in servants declined, especially in southern England. In arable areas, a threefold division between landlords, tenant farmers, and labourers became commonplace. The 1851 census for England and Wales suggests that the ratio of labourers to all farmers was 3:1, and of labourers to those farmers who were employers was 5:1. See G. E. Mingay (ed.), *The Agrarian History of England and Wales, vi: 1750–1850* (1989). The term 'labourer'—the 'ag. labs' of *census returns and *parish registers—covered a wide variety of conditions. The labourer was usually far removed from the 'Hodge' stereotype of his social superiors, for he had to possess a variety of skills. See J. G. O'Leary (ed.), *The Autobiography of Joseph Arch* (1966), the champion hedge-cutter who became a *trade union leader; M. K. Ashby, *Joseph Ashby of Tysoe, 1859–1919* (1961); and George Sturt, *Change in the Village* (1912). Some labourers had a little land or at least a cottage garden, but for many the opportunities for work were uncertain. Bad weather meant that many were 'laid off', and the chances of work varied according to the seasons. Groups of migrant seasonal workers were a common sight, e.g. in the *hop fields of Kent. Farmers throughout England were dependent upon Irish, and to a much less extent Scottish, workers for getting in the harvest. From the mid-18th century Irish labourers worked on farms in Lowland Scotland, but in the 19th century they spread into most parts of England. The great majority of these temporary migrants were adult men seeking to earn sufficient cash to pay the rent on their Irish farms. The number of men who during their lifetime went to work on an English or Scottish farm was very large. Numbers peaked during the 1840s and 1850s. See E. J. T. Collins, 'Migrant Labour in British Agriculture in the Nineteenth Century', *Economic History Review*, 2nd ser., 29/1 (1976). (See also GANGS, LABOUR.)

The 'regular' outdoor labourers nevertheless formed the main group of farmworkers, accounting for 65 per cent of the farm labourers of England and Wales in 1851, when the agricultural work-force was at its peak. The conditions experienced by labouring families varied from region to region. The worst conditions were found in southern England, especially in Dorset, Somerset, and Wiltshire. In northern England the industrial wages that were on offer pulled up those that were paid to farm labourers in nearby villages. Rural discontent was therefore much more evident in the south. See Andrew Charlesworth, *An Atlas of Rural Protest in Britain, 1548–1900* (1983), Alun Howkins, *Poor Labouring Men: Rural Radicalism in Norfolk, 1870–1923* (1985), G. E. Mingay (ed.), *The Victorian Countryside*, 2 vols. (1981), K. D. M. Snell, *Annals of the Labouring Poor: Social Change and Agrarian England, 1660–1900* (1985), and Harold Newby, *The Deferential Worker* (1977). See also SWING, CAPTAIN; REBECCA RIOTS; POACHING; GAME LAWS; and EMIGRATION.

The number of people earning their living from the land has declined steadily from its high point in the middle years of the 19th century to a very small percentage of the total British work-force by the late 20th century. See Alan Armstrong, *Farmworkers: A Social and Economic History, 1770–1980* (1988) and D. W. Howell, *Land and People in Nineteenth-Century Wales* (1978). For graphic accounts of the lives of late 19th- and early 20th-century farmworkers see the books of George Ewart *Evans, Stephen Caunce, *Amongst Farm Horses: The Horselads of East Yorkshire* (1991), Fred Kitchen, *Brother to the Ox* (1942), and W. H. Hudson, *A Shepherd's Life* (1910).

agricultural returns. See CROP RETURNS and AGRICULTURAL STATISTICS.

agricultural societies. The *Royal Society, founded in 1660, made enquiries into agriculture during its early years. Agriculture was among the chief concerns of the Society of Improvers, founded in Scotland in 1723, the Dublin Society, formed in 1731, and the Society of Arts (1754). The Smithfield Club (1798) was established to promote the improvement of livestock. At the annual dinner of the Smithfield Club in 1837 the third Earl Spencer proposed the formation of the Royal Agricultural Society of England, which was founded the following year. It was concerned to show how scientific discoveries could help the advancement of agriculture and it quickly attracted the support of influential *landowners. The Farmers' Club, founded in London in 1842, was another influential body. Some local societies came into existence, inspired by the Society of Arts; the first was the Brecknockshire Society

(1755). Numerous local societies were founded in many parts of Britain during the period 1750–1850; about 400 were in existence by 1840. See Nicholas Goddard, 'Agricultural Literature and Societies', in G. E. Mingay (ed.), *The Agrarian History of England and Wales*, vi: *1750–1850* (1989). See also SHOWS, AGRICULTURAL.

agricultural statistics were first kept in the late 18th century. (See BOARD OF AGRICULTURE; SINCLAIR, SIR JOHN; and *General Views of Agriculture*. See also A. H. John, 'Statistical Appendix', in G. E. Mingay (ed.), *The Agrarian History of England and Wales*, vi: *1750–1850* (1989); and TITHE AWARDS AND MAPS.) The 1801 *crop returns, which are housed in the *Public Record Office under HO 67, are responses on printed forms to government enquiries sent to local clergymen. They are arranged by dioceses and parishes and note the acreages devoted to specific crops, often including general remarks. See, for example, W. G. Hoskins, 'The Leicestershire Crop Returns for 1801', *Transactions of the Leicestershire Archaeological Society*, 24 (1948). From 1866 to the present day annual summaries of the livestock kept and crops grown in each parish have been returned to the central government. Those from 1866 to 1963 are kept at the PRO under MAF 68. The early returns must be treated cautiously, for until 1917 the information was provided voluntarily. See J. T. Coppock, 'The Agricultural Returns as a Source for Local History', *The Amateur Historian*, 4/2 (1958–9). See also TWENTIETH CENTURY, THE.

ague. Archaic term for acute fever, with cold, hot, and sweating stages. It is also used for malaria, caught in *fens and marshes.

aid. 1. A tax or subsidy paid to the Crown.

2. A feudal due paid by a tenant to a lord. It was limited by *Magna Carta (1215) to ransom, the knighting of the lord's eldest son, and the marriage of the lord's eldest daughter. Feudal aids were abolished in 1660.

aisled hall. A superior form of medieval *open hall, where the roof-truss is extended to the wall-plates of aisles so as to provide extra space. They have been identified in south-east England and in west Yorkshire. See F. Atkinson and R. W. McDowall, 'Aisled Houses in the Halifax Area', *Antiquaries Journal*, 47 (1967).

alabaster. A translucent white or nearly-white form of gypsum (sulphate of lime), sometimes flecked with red, and much used in the past, particularly in England, for statuary and other decorative purposes. It is found in various parts of the country, but was quarried mainly in the Trent valley, from where it could be transported along the river. The best quarries were at Chellaston (Derbyshire), Tutbury (Staffordshire), and Red Hill (Nottingham), and the finest carvers worked in Nottingham, Derby, and Burton-on-Trent. Alabaster can be dressed smoothly and given a high polish, and was therefore much favoured for medieval and 16th- and 17th-century monuments inside churches, which were originally coloured and gilded. English churches contain 342 surviving alabaster monuments, with Yorkshire (34), Derbyshire (29), Nottinghamshire (20), and Lincolnshire (20) heading the list.

Alabaster was also used for busts, vases, and ornaments, and for the columned halls at Holkham (Norfolk) and Kedleston (Derbyshire). Victorian church architects were fond of red and white—'streaky bacon'—alabaster for interiors.

alchemy. The chemistry of the Middle Ages and throughout the 16th century, concerned especially with the attempt to transmute base metal into gold.

alderman. 1. The *Old English title (*ealdorman*) for a royal official comparable with the post-Conquest *sheriff.

2. A senior member of a medieval *guild or, by extension, *borough, elected by his fellows. This system was also used by 19th- and 20th-century *county or borough councils.

alehouses. Information about medieval alehouses is hard to come by, but much is now known about those of the early modern period. See Peter Clark, *The English Alehouse: A Social History, 1200–1830* (1983). The government was concerned to know what facilities were available for quartering troops in the event of war, and therefore made enquiries from time to time, notably in 1577 and 1686. (See INNS.) It also tried to control the numbers of alehouses through a system of licensing by the *Justices of the Peace, which is still in existence. Alehouses received much hostile publicity in the late 16th and early 17th century, not only from *Puritans, but from the upper ranks of society who were fearful of political and religious dissent. Pamphleteers saw the alehouse as an ungodly rival to the church or chapel.

The licensing system began in 1495, but most licences were issued after the passing of another Act in 1552. Amongst the records of *quarter sessions are those of special sittings known as *brewster sessions, when each *constable had to present a list of the names of licensed innkeepers and alehouse keepers in his *township. In these records, alehouse keepers are often listed as 'tipplers', without the modern connotation of the word. An Act of 1753 required all *clerks of the peace to keep registers of licensed victuallers. Not all clerks complied with this Act, but where they did the amount of information about alehouses increases substantially.

Alehouses were found particularly in towns, including the *suburbs. In 1693 Derby had 120 inns and alehouses to 684 houses, a proportion of 1 to 5.7. In the 1670s Sheffield had an inn or alehouse for every six or seven households; alehouses probably outnumbered inns by three to one. At the same time, most rural parishes had only a few alehouses and hardly any inns. Many alehouses did not last very long. They were a valued extra source of income for a family, since the man was more likely to have another job, while his wife brewed ale and served customers. Women often ran alehouses as widows. Brewing was strongly associated with immigrants from the Low Countries. Alehouse-keepers are much more difficult to identify than the more prosperous innkeepers, but the names recorded in the brewster sessions can sometimes be matched to names recorded in *parish registers and other sources, though the licensee of the alehouse, being the male head of household, is usually described by his other occupation. The brewhouses that are named in probate *inventories often provide a clue, together with stocks of ale in cellars and occasional references to signs.

At first, alehouses were ordinary dwelling-houses, providing drink, food, and sometimes lodging. After the *Restoration the lowly alehouse gradually provided better facilities, partly as a result of tight magisterial control. By the middle years of the 18th century larger alehouses were becoming common. The term 'alehouse' was gradually replaced by 'public house' during the course of the 18th century. From the 1810s and 1820s purpose-built public houses were erected in London and the larger provincial towns. See Mark Girouard, *Victorian Pubs* (1975). The Beer Act (1830) brought free trade to the brewing industry (see BREWERIES). The rise in the living standards of the working classes from the mid-19th century was reflected in the improved standard of Victorian public houses. These can be identified by their names and those of their publicans in trade and commercial *directories.

ale-taster. A manorial officer responsible for the taste and correct measurement of ale.

alias (Lat. 'otherwise'). Aliases were used in cases of illegitimacy, upon the remarriage of a parent, upon inheriting property from a female relative, etc. In some cases the alias form was inherited for several generations and was thus similar to a double-barrelled surname. See also DEED POLL.

alienation (legal). The transfer of ownership.

aliens, returns of. The *Public Record Office Records Information leaflet no. 10, 'Immigrants: Documents in the Public Record Office' gives full details of the available public records concerning aliens. See also J. S. Burn, *The History of the French, Walloon, Dutch and Other Protestant Refugees Settled in England from the Reign of Henry VIII to the Revocation of the Edict of Nantes* (1846) for general background. Settlers from France and the Low Countries in the 16th century, in southern and eastern England, can sometimes be identified by subsidy rolls (E 179) which record the payment of a special tax on aliens. See R. E. G. Kirk, *Returns of Aliens in London, 1523–1603* (Huguenot Society, 10, in 4 parts, 1900–8); W. D. Cooper (ed.), *Lists of Foreign Protestants and Aliens Resident in England, 1618–1688, from Returns in the State Paper Office* (Camden Society, 82, 1862); and Brian G. Awty, 'Aliens in the Ironworking Areas of the Weald: The Subsidy Rolls, 1524–1603', *Bulletin of the Wealden Iron Research Group*, 2nd ser., 4 (1984).

In 1793 the Home Office took responsibility for regulating aliens. Certificates of aliens (1836–52) are housed in the Public Record Office under HO 2; these are arranged by port of arrival in England and Scotland and record date of entry, nationality, the last country visited, occupation, and signature. For further details, see Stella Colwell, *Dictionary of Genealogical Sources in the Public Record Office* (1992). See also DENIZATION and NATURALIZATION.

allegations, marriage. A statement made on oath, or affidavit, in order to obtain a *marriage licence.

allotment. 1. A piece of land awarded by commissioners under the terms of an Act of *Enclosure.

2. A plot of land for growing vegetables. A few allotments were provided for *agricultural labourers in the late 18th century, but the impetus to provide such plots grew after the *Napoleonic wars. Radicals urged the provision of allotments to give working men some independence. Others thought that allotments would promote habits of industry and help to keep down the rates, but many farmers feared

that the principal efforts of their labourers might be reserved for cultivating their own plots. An enquiry in 1833 showed that 42 per cent of *parishes had some allotments. The Allotments Act (1887) enabled local authorities to purchase land for allotments. The voluntary provision of allotments by landowners grew at the same time, so that by 1900 there were nearly half a million allotments in England and Wales. The number increased during the First World War and reached one and a quarter million in the 1920s. The 'Dig for Victory' campaign of the Second World War led to a further increase, but after 1945 the number of allotments began to decline.

almanac. Almanacs were very popular from the 17th century onwards. By the 1660s some 400,000 were being sold every year, enough to provide a copy to 40 per cent of the households of the kingdom. They generally cost between 2*d.* and 6*d.* and included a calendar, information on *fairs, *roads, and posts, advice on farming, historical and scientific information, comments on political and religious matters, sensational news, and astrological predictions. See Bernard Capp, *Astrology and the Popular Press: English Almanacs, 1500–1800* (1979). In Victorian times, many small towns published their own annual almanac, keeping much of the old format but adding short articles and poems, often written in dialect. Some of these were published into the second half of the 20th century.

alms-giving. The medieval church taught the value and necessity of giving alms. After the *Reformation bequests to the poor continue to feature prominently in *wills. See W. K. Jordan, *The Charities of Rural England, 1480–1660* (1961). Parish churches had a poor box for donations to the poor, which was chained to a post or pillar near the door.

almshouse. A charitable foundation for the care of the poor, especially the elderly. In the Middle Ages almshouses were known alternatively as hospitals or *maisons dieu*. They were supervised by a warden or master and contained an infirmary hall and a chapel. Many were dissolved at the *Reformation. The Elizabethans re-established some of the old almshouses and founded many new ones by private benefaction. Many examples survive from the 17th and 18th centuries, particularly in south-western England. See B. Bailey, *Almshouses* (1988). The benefactor usually stated the number of places that were to be provided. Sometimes, almshouses were restricted to a single sex, but often they accommodated equal numbers of old men and old women. Those who qualified for admission had to be of good character and were sometimes restricted to infirm members of a particular craft, or their widows. In some cases, inmates had to wear clothes that were provided to a specified design and colour. A body of trustees or 'feoffees' were appointed as managers and a chaplain was usually paid to conduct services in the chapel.

Each inmate normally had private accommodation, often in the form of a single apartment. A common chapel and a dining hall acted as a visual focus in a symmetrical composition, sometimes as the centrepiece of a long, low range, sometimes in a courtyard. Almshouses can usually be recognized immediately from their architecture, even though numerous different designs were used and many are idiosyncratic. The donor was normally commemorated by an inscribed tablet and sometimes by a bust or a *coat of arms. A large number of early modern almshouses still perform their original function; others have moved to new premises but are still administered by the trust established by the founder. Many more almshouses were founded on traditional lines during the 19th century.

altar. The focal point of a church for the celebration of the mass or communion. In the earliest years of Christianity free-standing wooden altars were used. Early Saxon churches placed the high altar at the west end of the *chancel, but in time it came to be fixed in a raised position at the east end. The chancel was partly hidden from view from the *nave by a *rood screen. The altar took the form of a stone slab, with four small incised crosses in each corner, and another in the centre, supported on a rectangular stone base. Some were covered with decorative cloths, upon which were placed a cross and candles. Other altars were placed in *chantry chapels. At the *Reformation it was ordered that altar stones should be removed and destroyed; nevertheless, a considerable number survive. Some have been converted into gravestones, but can be recognized by their crosses. See Eamon Duffy, *The Stripping of the Altars: Traditional Religion in England, 1400–1580* (1992). See also COMMUNION TABLES and HIGH CHURCH MOVEMENT.

alternate husbandry. See CONVERTIBLE HUSBANDRY.

alum was used by dyers and tanners as a binding agent. Until the 16th century it was imported, particularly from Spain and Italy. The first patent to dig for alum in Devon and Cornwall was granted in 1562, but from 1611 the main centre of the industry was on the cliffs of the North Sea coast in north Yorkshire, at Mulgrave, Asholme, and Sandsend. By the 1660s alum was being exported to Ireland, Scotland, and the Continent, the East Indies, and the colonies. George Walker, *The History of Yorkshire Costume* (1814) contains an illustration of the alum works in north Yorkshire. The industry decayed during the 19th century.

Amateur Historian. The journal for local historians set up by the *Standing Conference for Local History, and first published in August–September 1952. In 1968 it became The *Local Historian*.

amen ('so be it'). Until the 19th century *wills normally started: 'In the Name of God Amen'.

amercement. The fine for an offence at a manorial *court leet. The jurors presented the offender, the steward declared him to be 'in mercy' of the court, and the amount of the amercement was then decided.

America. About 20 per cent of the inhabitants of the United States of America are of English descent and about 16 per cent have Irish ancestors. The Elizabethan attempts to colonize the New World failed. The first successful plantation was that at Jamestown in 1607. (See VIRGINIA.) After the arrival of the *Mayflower* at Plymouth in 1620 the New England colony, 200 miles to the north of Virginia, attracted further settlers who turned it into a *Puritan stronghold. See C. E. Banks and E. E. Brownell, *Topographical Dictionary of 2885 English Emigrants to New England, 1620–1650* (1912) for the names of these early emigrants. Roger Thompson, *Mobility and Migration: East Anglian Founders of New England, 1629–1640* (1994) has traced the movement of 934 emigrants from Norfolk, Suffolk, Cambridgeshire, Essex, and Lincolnshire to New England. In the 17th century settlers were attracted to the *West Indies, *Chesapeake Bay, and New England, in that order of popularity. The 'Great Migration' of the 1630s was important from an American perspective, but represented less than half of 1 per cent of the population of England and made little impact in the home country. See David Cressy, *Coming Over: Migration and Communication between England and New England in the Seventeenth Century* (1987). See also David Dobson, *Directory of Scottish Settlers in North America, 1625–1825* (1984).

Most emigrants travelled in family groups to New England. The core consisted of people in middling occupations—*yeomen, *artisans, etc. The Chesapeake colony had many more *indentured servants who worked for a fixed term on the *tobacco plantations in order to pay for their passage and board, before obtaining their freedom. Others went as convicts, for until the War of Independence America was the destination for those sentenced to *transportation. Over 30,000 convicts were sent to America and the West Indies between 1615 and 1775. See P. W. Coldham, *The Complete Book of Emigrants in Bondage, 1614–1775* (1987). Many of the earliest settlers continued to move their home upon arrival, either to better themselves or to find work, spreading out along the Atlantic seaboard and inland to Pennsylvania. See James Horn, *Adapting to a New World: English Society in the Seventeenth-Century Chesapeake* (1994). A substantial number returned to Britain, for they had never thought of emigration as being permanent.

About three-quarters of the population of colonial America were descended from British settlers, but in the 19th century vast numbers of emigrants from many parts of Europe changed the composition of the population radically. The population of the USA rose from about 4 million in 1790 to 23 million in 1850. See Charlotte Erickson, *Emigration from Europe, 1815–1914* (1976). Some 10 million people are thought to have left the British Isles during the course of the 19th century, most of them for America. The emigrants came from all sorts of backgrounds, both industrial and agricultural, attracted by the availability of cheap land, regular employment, and relaxed social relations. Numbers increased once steamships began to operate in the 1840s, but it was another 20 years before sailing ships were abandoned. Most people travelled steerage, the cheap rate offered to those who were crammed together below deck. Two-thirds of the British emigrants embarked at Liverpool, their numbers hugely inflated after the failure of the *potato crop in Ireland in the mid-1840s. See C. J. Houston and W. J. Smyth, 'The Irish Diaspora: Emigration to the New World, 1720–1920', in B. J. Graham and L. J. Proudfoot, *An Historical Geography of Ireland* (1993). Between 1870 and 1920 some 2.5 to 3 million English, well over half a million Scots, and approaching 100,000 Welsh people settled in the USA, but they were soon to be heavily outnumbered by immigrants from other parts of Europe. As many as one in four eventually returned to Europe, however. Restrictions on immigration imposed during the 1920s brought this mass movement of population to the United States of America to an end. See also CANADA.

Anabaptist. Originally, a name given to several unorthodox *Protestant sects in Europe, who shared in common a rejection of infant baptism. In the British Isles the term was used in a derogatory way in the 16th and 17th centuries for a *Baptist and, more loosely, for other Protestant dissenters.

ancestry. Many false claims concerning descent have been made, both in the past and at the present day. Each link in a chain has to be proved convincingly. Most people will not be able to prove ancestry further back than the 16th or 17th centuries. Only the Ardens and the Berkeleys can prove descent from a pre-Conquest Englishman, and only a few families can trace their families back to pre-Conquest Normandy.

angel (monetary). A gold coin bearing the image of St Michael the Archangel slaying the dragon, introduced in the reign of Edward IV (1461–83), and valued at 6s. 8d. It was known originally as the angel-noble, being a new issue of the *noble. It ceased to be legal tender in the reign of Charles I (1625–49). It was the coin given to those who were touched for the *King's Evil.

Anglo-Saxons. The first Anglo-Saxon settlers arrived in Britain peacefully during the later stages of the *Roman Empire. The military conquest of the *Lowland zone followed the withdrawal of the Romans. The earliest kingdoms were in the east and the south-east (Lindsey, *East Anglia, Essex, Kent, and Sussex), but expansion to the north and west was achieved under the powerful kingdoms of *Northumbria, *Mercia, and *Wessex. By the end of the 8th century Anglo-Saxon colonists controlled all of the area south of the Forth and as far west as Wales and Cornwall. The colonists were Germanic peoples from different parts of north-west Europe. These different origins are reflected in the separate characters of the various kingdoms that comprised England, 'the land of the Angles'. See Steven Bassett (ed.), *The Origins of the Anglo-Saxon Kingdoms* (1989). Although the various peoples known as the Anglo-Saxons shared a common culture and basic language, they were not a unified group. Occasionally, the ruler of the most powerful kingdom of the time acquired the title *Bretwalda*, but Anglo-Saxon England was never a unified political force. Thus, the use of the term 'Saxon' to include the Angles of Northumbria is misleading. Sir F. M. *Stenton's classic work, *Anglo-Saxon England* (2nd edn., 1947) is still an excellent introduction to the study of the separate peoples who formed the Anglo-Saxons.

Historians and archaeologists now stress continuity rather than a clean break with the past upon the arrival of the Anglo-Saxons. See Alan Everitt, *Continuity and Colonization: The Evolution of Kentish Settlement* (1986). The old view that the original Anglo-Saxons settled in villages surrounded by *open-fields has been abandoned because of the mounting archaeological evidence for dispersed settlement in the early period. It is now believed that nucleated villages and open-field systems were not created until much later, in the Anglo-Scandinavian period. (See LANDSCAPE HISTORY and FIELD SYSTEMS.) *Place-names shed much light on Anglo-Saxon settlement, but the evidence has been reinterpreted to match the archaeological discoveries and old views have been discarded. The numerous charters that survive from the later Anglo-Saxon period for parts of southern England (and occasionally in the north) have been the subject of much scholarly investigation, particularly concerning *boundaries. See P. H. Sawyer (ed.), *Anglo-Saxon Charters* (1986), which provides an annotated list and bibliography.

Many of the traditions of the settlers were preserved in verse, oral genealogies of kings, and ecclesiastical memoranda, and set down as a series of annals in Wessex in the mid-9th century in the work known as the *Anglo-Saxon Chronicle*. This was subsequently kept up to date by later monks and is a useful source up to and beyond the *Norman Conquest. At first, the Anglo-Saxons were pagans, but during the 7th and 8th centuries they became converted to Christianity. (See BEDE and CELTIC CHRISTIANITY.) A substantial body of *churches retain some Anglo-Saxon architecture. See H. M. Taylor and Joan Taylor, *Anglo-Saxon Architecture*, 3 vols. (1980). A monastic revival after the destruction of *monasteries by the *Vikings began in 10th-century Wessex, but did not extend north of the Trent.

The Anglo-Saxons also built *towns as fortified trading centres. The topography of some modern towns still reflects the original plans. In Wareham (Dorset) the late Saxon walls survive. See Barry Cunliffe, *Wessex to A.D. 1000* (1993), Martin Welch, *Anglo-Saxon England* (1992), and Richard Hodges, *The Anglo-Saxon Achievement* (1989).

annuity. An annual sum of money, payable for either a fixed term, or for life, or in perpetuity. The first state life annuities were granted in the 1690s; see F. L. Leeson, *A Guide to the Records of British State Tontines and Life Annuities of the Seventeenth and Eighteenth Centuries* (1968). The records, which are kept at the *Public Record Office under NDO 1–3, give names, addresses, ages at entry, and the dates of last payments, together with some marriages, deaths, and wills. See Stella Colwell, *Dictionary of Genealogical Sources in the Public Record Office* (1992). Most of the annuitants who are recorded as such in *census returns, *parish registers, etc. received their annuities from private settlements.

antiquarian tradition, the. Britain has a long tradition of antiquarian writing, stretching from the Middle Ages to the 20th century, which has formed the basis of many of the modern concerns of local historians. The first attempts in this genre were topographical descriptions allied to the study of genealogy and *heraldry. During the 16th century, scholars influenced by their European counterparts placed the study of antiquities on a firm footing. Their works and approaches remained deeply influential over the next three centuries. A change of emphasis occurred during the second half of the 17th century, under the influence of Baconian empiricism, when the study of natural history was combined with that of antiquities. Meanwhile, an interest in urban history, and to a lesser extent in the history of rural parishes, was beginning to grow. The 19th century saw a flowering of the antiquarian tradition, with the publication of many substantial works and the establishment of numerous record societies. However, the social backgrounds of the writers meant that although they did much scholarly work on manorial and ecclesiastical history, and on the genealogies of the landed families, they largely ignored the history of ordinary people. In the second half of the 20th century this balance was redressed.

An interest in British antiquities is evident in the works of the earliest writers—the monks Gildas, Nennius, and *Bede—and in the chronicles of the Anglo-Norman monks. In his *Gesta Pontificum Anglorum* ('History of the Prelates of England') of 1125, *William of Malmesbury used topographical and antiquarian approaches in surveying the ecclesiastical history of England. *Gerald of Wales's works included one of the first attempts at a description of Ireland and the Irish, *Topographia Hibernica* (1187); also the *Itinerarium Cambriae*

(1188), a travel diary of a preaching tour through Wales; and his *Descriptio Cambriae* (1191), which combined personal observation and *folklore in a description of the geography, social life, popular customs, antiquities, and some of the natural history of Wales. Other religious writers turned to more local subjects; for example, Gervase made a study of the architectural history of Canterbury Cathedral, and Matthew Paris researched the antiquities of St Albans.

In the 14th and 15th centuries a few writers who were neither monks nor clerics completed descriptive works that acquired the genre name of chorographies. Ranulph Higden's *Polychronicon* (completed in 1327) was translated into English in 1387, and the topographical part was published by Caxton in 1480 as *The Discrypcion of Britayne*. Between 1478 and 1480 *William of Worcester (1415–82) travelled through Norfolk, Bristol, and south-west England collecting materials for a chorographic description of Britain. This was never completed, but his daily journal is now a valuable historical source. Worcester knew many of the leading Continental humanists, though he never achieved their level of scholarship.

By 1500 these early studies had created something of a tradition. They included descriptions of a county, of cities, and of ruins. But they did not have a common sense of purpose and cannot be regarded as a unified whole. Some were in the form of annals, and most relied uncritically on previous narratives. During the 16th century, the Italian Renaissance became a European movement that inspired English writers to attempt something more rigorous. A large amount of manuscript material became available upon the *dissolution of the monasteries, and ruined monastic buildings stimulated curiosity about the past. Further stimuli to historical enquiry came from the Tudor myth that Henry VIII was descended from King Arthur and from the desire to prove that the Protestant form of religion had acceptable antecedents. This new sense of purpose was inspired not only by intellectual curiosity, but by a fierce patriotism. Scholars began to discover the whole of England.

John *Leland (1506?–52), who was appointed the official 'King's Antiquary' in 1533, was England's first great topographer. Leland spent nearly ten years travelling and collecting materials for a chorography of Britain. He never completed it, but the copious rough notes made during his journeys formed the basis of much later scholarship. Now known as Leland's *Itinerary*, these notes still provide valuable information about Tudor England. They also established that the topographer should not rely upon previous chronicles but must base his writing on personal observation and first-hand research. Upon completing his journeys, he settled in London and planned a history of every county, but the project was too immense and he ended his days insane.

A new generation of scholars built on Leland's foundations in the middle and later years of Elizabeth I's reign. William *Lambarde's A Perambulation of Kent (1576) was the first chorography of a single county and an impressive standard for others to follow. It copied Leland's example in dealing with both the past and the present, but differed in concentrating on the *gentry families, especially on their genealogies. The following year saw the publication of William *Harrison's Description of England, and Raphael *Holinshed's Chronicle of England, Scotlande and Irelande. Meanwhile, Christopher *Saxton was producing his county *maps; between 1574 and 1579 a complete set for England and Wales was published. By the end of Elizabeth's reign it was said that Saxton's maps were 'usual with all noblemen and gentlemen, and daily perused by them'. Lord Burghley kept a framed set hanging in his house.

English historical scholarship was established during this period. Its chief flowering was the publication of William *Camden's Britannia (1586, with revised editions in 1587, 1590, 1594, and 1600). Written in Latin, as a conscious contribution to the wider world of European scholarship, it was principally concerned to show that Britain had a Roman heritage that could stand comparison with that of its continental neighbours. Camden stated his aims as: 'That I would restore antiquity to Britaine, and Britaine to . . . antiquity . . . that I would renew ancientrie, enlighten obscuritie, cleare doubts, and recall home Veritie by way of recovery.' The classical heritage also led Camden and other topographers to draw upon the writings of Ptolemy, Strabo, and others in their descriptions of the countryside and its people.

William Camden (1551–1623) was known to Continental scholars as 'the British Strabo', but he was as familiar with the native tradition of topographical-historical scholarship as he was with the classical achievement. A friend of Lambarde's and a member of the Society of *Antiquaries, he had contacts all over Britain. His Britannia was immediately popular. The sixth (1607) edition was substantially revised and enlarged and was published as a large folio volume with maps by John *Norden and Christopher Saxton. In 1610 Philemon Holland translated the work into English; by 1806 seven posthumous editions, notably those of Edmund *Gibson and Richard *Gough, had been published.

The growing interest in antiquarian subjects led to the foundation of the Society of Antiquaries in 1585. Outside London, Oxford became a centre for antiquarian and historical research, especially after the opening of Sir Thomas *Bodley's library in 1602. Groups of like-minded scholars also gathered at the University of Cambridge and at the *Inns of Court. The Inns provided not only a practical training in the law, but also a general humanistic education. Many a future writer had his interests awakened as a young man at one of the universities or inns.

The Elizabethan antiquaries had employed a multi-disciplinary approach to their studies, using whatever material was available. Although they turned to written records such as *chronicles, they relied much more on the evidence of ruins, relics, coins, and other non-literary sources of information. They were less concerned with causes or personalities than with topography. Camden explained that: 'neither is it any part of my meaning now to write an Historie, but a Topographie'. Lambarde was 'specially' concerned 'to write a Topographie, or description of places'.

In the first edition of the Perambulation Lambarde appealed for others to complete the description of the rest of the counties of England and Wales. His example was, indeed, soon followed. One of the most readable and informative of the early chorographies was Richard *Carew's Survey of Cornwall (1602). John Norden planned to write a series of county chorographies, illustrated by small maps, but he was frustrated by the lack of a patron. He managed to publish his descriptions of Middlesex (1593) and Hertfordshire (1598), but his accounts of Essex, Surrey, Sussex, Hampshire, the Isle of Wight, the Channel Islands, Kent, Northamptonshire, Cornwall, and possibly Norfolk and Suffolk never got further than manuscript form.

John *Speed had access to many of Norden's manuscripts and printed works. His series of 54 county maps, completed between 1605 and 1610, were published in a large folio volume, Theatre of the Empire of Great Britaine (1611), with a descriptive chorographic text. By this time, chorography had become popular throughout the country. Much of it, however, such as Robert Reyce's Breviary of Suffolk, remained unpublished. William Burton's

Description of Leicester Shire (1622) was the only county chorography to be printed between 1602 and 1656.

A growing interest in genealogy and heraldry, partly to suit the demands of local readers, is evident in the first half of the 17th century. Increasing attention was also being devoted to the etymology of *place-names. Sir William *Dugdale's interest in these matters is evident in *The Antiquities of Warwickshire* (1656), one of the most scholarly of the old chorographies. Here, and in *Monasticon Anglicanum* (1655–73), a history of the *abbeys, Dugdale set a new standard in the systematic and critical use of documentary sources. In his *Warwickshire* he followed Camden in dividing the county into its *hundreds and then proceeding along the rivers and streams in order to describe each parish. He anticipated 20th-century interests in identifying deserted settlements, but he showed little interest in the new approaches of his day, such as the detailed investigation of individual sites or the whole field of natural history. As a member of the College of *Arms, his principal concern was with genealogy and heraldry. His example was closely followed by Robert *Thoroton, *The Antiquities of Nottinghamshire* (1677), which is largely genealogical and heraldic in character, but not by other writers. His principal legacy was his rigorous treatment of documentary material.

Meanwhile, a parallel interest in natural history had been growing since the publication of William Turner's *New Herball* (1551) and John Gerard's *Herball* (1597). A few other publications, such as William Bourne's *A Booke called the Treasure for Traveilers* (1578), contained material on natural history for the observant layman. Gerald of Wales and William of Worcester had included natural history in their descriptions in earlier times, but an unbroken succession of active field naturalists can be traced only from Turner. Like the antiquaries, the naturalists were part of a wider European fraternity. During the second half of the 17th century the interests of antiquarians and naturalists converged. Sir Francis Bacon (1561–1626) argued that in human and natural history the value of any work depended on its use of measurement and induction. Bacon's empirical approach, which was based on the close observation and description of nature, was adopted by the members of the *Royal Society in the 1660s.

Irelands Naturall History (1645), written by the Dutchman Gerard Boate, from information provided by his brother and other planters, was the first study of natural history to make careful and exact observations of a particular part of Britain. The Baconian approach also liberated archaeological studies from a dependence on literary sources. John *Aubrey (1626–97), a Fellow of the Royal Society who had begun collecting observations on antiquities and natural history in the 1630s, and who made a famous survey of Stonehenge, illustrates this new method of study, though he was notoriously disorganized and credulous. In 1685 he compiled a *Naturall Historie of Wiltshire*, whose emphasis on describing and arranging natural phenomena was in marked contrast to the concerns of the earlier chorographers.

The *Natural History of Oxfordshire* (1677), written by Aubrey's friend, Robert *Plot, firmly established local natural history and was an immediate success. Plot was particularly concerned with natural features and practical problems, so he surveyed the county in this way rather than parish by parish. He used the same method later in *The Natural History of Staffordshire* (1686). His successor as Keeper of the Ashmolean Museum, Edward *Lhuyd (1660–1709), acquired a reputation as a natural historian (especially as a palaeontologist), antiquary, and comparative philologist. The interests of such men were very wide. The regional studies of the second half of the 17th century became more realistic once they were dominated by an interest in natural history. The study of weather and *climate, of earth formations and fossils, of flora and fauna, and so on, showed others how to use non-literary evidence. See Stan A. E. Mendyk, 'Speculum Britanniae': Regional Study, Antiquarianism, and Science in Britain to 1700 (1989).

Meanwhile, a flourishing tradition of regional studies had developed in Scotland. Robert Sibbald (1641–1722) personifies the links with Oxford and with the Low Countries that underpinned these studies. He and Edward Lhuyd were among the many scholars who helped Edmund Gibson (1669–1748) to publish a revised edition of Camden's *Britannia* in 1695, which provided a new impetus to antiquarian studies in many parts of Britain.

Such writing continued to flourish in the 18th century and was given a new stimulus in the later decades by the *Romantic Movement. However, the most popular 18th-century works were sometimes more akin to the early chorographic studies than to the new natural histories. The finest included John *Hutchins, *The History and Antiquities of the County of Dorset* (1774), Edward *Hasted, *The History and Topographical Survey of the County of Kent* (1778–99), John *Nichols, *History and Antiquities of the*

County of Leicester (1795–1815), Sir Richard Colt *Hoare, *The Ancient History of South Wiltshire* (1812), and Robert Surtees, *The History and Antiquities of the County Palatinate of Durham* (1816–40). These should be set alongside the two volumes of *British Topography* (1768 and 1780) by Richard Gough, the same author's *The Architectural Antiquities of Great Britain* (1805), and his edition of Camden's *Britannia* (1789).

The approach adopted by these antiquarians is very limited by modern standards, for they ignored the history of the ordinary families who formed the majority of the population. But present-day historians working on counties not possessing such scholarly works realize that they lack the essential spadework on the descent of feudal and ecclesiastical properties which forms the basis of so many other enquiries.

A similar stream of publications from Elizabethan times onwards dealt with the individual histories of English towns and cities. Medieval authors had attempted only chronicles and annals. London's chronicles had been written in English from about 1414 and by the 1430s were being brought up to date each year; Bristol had its mayor's kalendar, compiled by Robert Rickart, the town clerk, during Edward IV's reign (1461–83). The three earliest urban histories were written in the last years of the 16th century. Pride of place must go to John *Stow, a member of the circle of antiquaries centred on Camden and Lambarde, who completed his *Survey of London* in 1598; three further editions were issued by 1640. Stow wrote that he had 'attempted the discovery of London'. John *Hooker's *Description of the Citie of Excester*, finished in the same year, was not published in full until the 20th century. Hooker was Exeter's first chamberlain and was an exact contemporary of Stow, for both were born in 1525. The third volume was Thomas Nash's *Nashes Lenten Stuffe, containing the description and first procreation and increase of the towne of Great Yarmouth in Norfolk* (1599).

After this auspicious start, no further urban histories appeared until the 1640s. That decade saw the publication of William Somner, *Antiquities of Canterbury* (1640), Richard Butcher, *The Survey and Antiquitie of the Towne of Stamford* (1646), and William Gray, *Chorographia: A Survey of Newcastle upon Tyne* (1649). But the standards of the English urban historians fell far below those of their counterparts in the wealthier and more populous towns of Germany and Italy. Only 12 histories of English towns are known to have been published before 1700,

though others circulated in manuscript form. During the 18th century, however, a further 116 were printed. See Peter Clark, 'Visions of the Urban Community: Antiquarians and the English City before 1800' in D. Fraser and A. Sutcliffe (eds.), *The Pursuit of Urban History* (1983).

The new authors were largely gentry and professional men, especially the clergy and lawyers. Most had been to one of the universities or the Inns of Court. One of the best was Ralph *Thoresby, whose topographical survey of Leeds was published in 1715 as *Ducatus Leodiensis* and whose first part of a projected history was published nine years later as *Vicaria Leodiensis*. Most English towns, even ancient cities like York and Norwich, did not have their history written until much later. York actually got two in the 1730s; Thomas Gent, *The Antient and Modern History of the Famous City of York* (1730), and Francis Drake, *Eboracum: Or the History and Antiquities of the City of York* (1736). Gent was a printer who went on to publish histories of Ripon and Hull. Drake came from a clerical family and was a surgeon, an FRS, and an FSA. Most of the towns that received early histories were the seats of bishops, so the emphasis was on ecclesiastical matters rather than on municipal development. Like the county histories, their scope was limited. They presented materials for a history, but made little attempt to fashion them.

The second half of the 18th century saw a threefold increase in the number of published town histories and a greater range of towns that were covered. William *Hutton published his history of Birmingham in 1781, and Manchester, Liverpool, Halifax, Derby, Nottingham, and Leicester soon had their own histories. Even small towns such as Whitby, Hinckley, Nantwich, Tewkesbury, and Leominster received attention. All over England community pride was being expressed in this way.

Meanwhile, a handful of men were writing the history of the small rural parishes to which they were connected in some way or other. The first parish history to be published was The Revd White *Kennett's *Parochial Antiquities Attempted in the History of Ambrosden, Burcester and Other Adjacent Parts* (1695), which concentrated almost exclusively on ecclesiastical and legal matters. A unique parish history was written a few years later, though it was probably intended only for a circle of friends and was not published until the 19th century. Richard *Gough was a member of a long-established yeoman family in the Shropshire parish of Myddle, and a former clerk to the leading gentleman in the county. His *Antiquityes and Memoyres of the Parish of Myddle* (1700) was inspired by Camden's *Britannia* (perhaps the new edition of 1695); it was concerned with the church and the descent of the manor, with local administration and disputes, with topography and place-names. But when he had finished, Gough went on to write *Observations Concerning the Seates in Myddle and the Familyes to which They Belong* (1701–2). The seating arrangements in the church provided the shape for a history of all the families in the parish. Gough used the parish register, manorial records, and the oral memories of his neighbours to write the most detailed account that we have of the lives of all the inhabitants of one rural parish in late Stuart England. The manuscript was not published until 1834, when Sir Thomas Phillips, an antiquarian book-collector, brought it out under the title *Human Nature Displayed in the History of Middle, by Richard Gough*. Phillips described it as 'one of the most extraordinary topographical and genealogical works ever written'.

In the lowland part of south Yorkshire, The Revd Abraham de la *Pryme, the grandson of a Flemish immigrant who had settled in Hatfield Chase upon its partial drainage by Cornelius Vermuyden, started a history of his parish in the late 1690s. It never saw the light of day, but is useful now for its description of Hatfield at that time and for its comments on recent changes, such as the replacement of the old *timber-framed houses by *brick buildings roofed with *pantiles. A history of the remote north Lancashire parish of Warton is also useful in a similar way. John *Lucas was a Leeds schoolmaster who was born in Warton and who spent much of his spare time between 1710 and 1740 in writing its history and jotting down everything that came into his head, whether it was relevant to his parish or not. It was not published until 1931, when the editors pruned the manuscript drastically, leaving out a great deal of material of local interest.

Few parish histories were written during the 18th century. Parsons were the scholars most likely to attempt the task, often combining an interest in antiquities with a passion for natural history. The Revd Gilbert *White, the most famous English naturalist of the 18th century, is known throughout the world for *The Natural History of Selborne* (1789), but little attention is now paid to the second part of his original volume, which was published as *The Antiquities of Selborne*. White's *Antiquities* traced the history of the area from Roman times, but most of the text was devoted to the history of the parish

church and its associated priory. It is of interest as an early example of a parish history, based on much first-hand research, but it has hardly anything to say about the local inhabitants. The *Antiquities* was included in many of the Victorian editions of the *Natural History*, but was omitted after the first decade of the 20th century.

The scholar-parson who studied both natural history and local history remained a typical figure in later centuries. The Revd W. Keble Martin achieved national fame with the publication of *The Concise British Flora in Colour* (1965), whereas his *History of the Ancient Parish of Wath-upon-Dearne* (1920) is hardly known outside south Yorkshire, though it is a worthy example of the local histories of that period. The Revd Alfred Gatty, vicar of the neighbouring parish of Ecclesfield from 1839 to 1903, was another outstanding local scholar, and the head of a family that distinguished itself in the fields of children's literature, theology, history, archaeology, heraldry, painting, music, and natural history. The country parish where they lived was the focal point for much of this multifarious activity.

The major Victorian figure in the distinguished line of scholar-parsons who were interested in all aspects of their parish was Canon J. C. *Atkinson, the incumbent of Danby on the North York Moors from 1847 to 1900. Atkinson calculated that he had walked over 70,000 miles in the course of his clerical duty. During these long walks he developed his keen powers of observation. Cut off from other scholars, he nevertheless published an impressive variety of books and articles during the last four decades of the 19th century. Atkinson had immense intellectual curiosity. Coming as a young parson from the south of England to one of the wildest parts of the country, he became interested not only in documentary and topographical research, and in natural history and archaeology, but in the lives of his parishioners: their homes, their speech, their customs, beliefs, and superstitions. His knowledge of Scandinavian and other languages convinced him that 'to all practical intents and purposes, the people of [this] district continued for ages to be a Danish-speaking people'. His studies of *folklore brought him a sympathetic understanding of tales of *witchcraft, *wisemen, *fairies, and hobgoblins, and the customs surrounding weddings, births, and *burials. His archival searches and observations as a field archaeologist provided him with the perspective to view continuity and change. He was different from earlier scholars in his breadth of outlook and in his concern with the ordinary families of his parish. His *Forty Years in a Moorland Parish* (1891) can be classified as social anthropology, anticipating many of the concerns of the local historians of the late 20th century.

The 18th and 19th centuries saw the formation of local historical societies in many parts of the land. The Spalding Gentleman's Society, which was interested in historical as well as other matters, was founded as early as 1710. The Society of Antiquaries was re-formed in London, along the lines of its Elizabethan predecessor, in 1717. From 1731 the *Gentleman's Magazine* regularly included contributions on the topography and antiquities of places from correspondents all over the country. The Society of Antiquaries of Scotland was founded in Edinburgh in 1780, the Society of Antiquaries of Newcastle-upon-Tyne in 1813. Some of these societies concentrated on publishing articles and scholarly editions of local records. The first volume of the *Surtees Society appeared in 1835; the Chetham Society (Lancashire and Cheshire) began publishing in 1844; the Sussex Archaeological Collections, 'illustrating the history and antiquities of the county', started in 1848; the Yorkshire Archaeological Society, which grew out of meetings held in Huddersfield from 1863, issued its first journal in 1869 and began its record series in 1885; the Bristol and Gloucestershire Archaeological Society began publishing in 1876; the Thoresby Society in 1889; and the Thoroton Society in 1897. By contrast, some counties, such as Derbyshire, were badly provided for, and the national coverage was very patchy. See E. L. C. Mullins (ed.), *Texts and Calendars: A Guide to the Historical and Archaeological Publications of Societies in England and Wales, 1901–33* (1968).

The official printing of records started in 1783 with an edition of the *Domesday Book. During the early 19th century a series of royal commissions began the work of publishing texts and calendars of public records. Then, in 1838, the *Public Record Office was set up to take over this work. By the later 1850s the PRO had begun its monumental series of *Calendars of State Papers. Between 1857 and 1900 the *Rolls Series published 250 volumes of records relating to the Middle Ages. The Royal Commission on *Historical Manuscripts was established in 1869 and the *British Record Society in 1888; the Index Library of the BRS began immediate publication with a calendar of Northamptonshire and Rutland wills, and in the following year with the first of many volumes relating to the records in the Public Record Office. The Rolls Series, the *Camden Society, the

*Hakluyt Society, the *Harleian Society, the *Pipe Roll Society, the *Selden Society, and the *Huguenot Society, together with the county record-publishing societies, printed large collections of records during these years, many of them of great value to the local historian. See G. H. Martin and P. Spufford (eds.), *The Records of the Nation: The Public Record Office, 1838–1988: The British Record Society, 1888–1988* (1990).

A major landmark at the end of the century was the establishment of *The *Victoria History of the Counties of England*. The *VCH*, as it is commonly known, began as a private enterprise in 1899. It aimed to be a comprehensive work of reference, an authoritative work of scholarship, and a starting-point for future research for all the counties of England. The influence of the old county histories is reflected in the plan of the general volumes, which cover natural history and earthworks and a transcript of the Domesday Book entries, as well as chapters on administrative history, ecclesiastical history and religious houses, agriculture and industries, population, endowed schools, and sport. The accompanying topographical volumes treat each hundred or *wapentake parish by parish. A section on the topography of the parish is followed by chapters on *manors and other estates, economic history, *local government, church, *Nonconformity, *education, and charities for the poor. Nearly 100 years later, over 200 volumes of the *VCH* have been published, but the original scheme is far from complete. The *VCH* provides a link between the best scholarship of the antiquarian tradition and that of the local historians of the 20th century. It is fitting that a *Festschrift* for the general editor, C. R. Elrington, should be published as C. R. J. Currie and C. P. Lewis (eds.), *English County Histories: A Guide* (1994). See also WOMEN LOCAL AND FAMILY HISTORIANS.

Antiquaries of London, Society of. Founded in 1585 to further the study of antiquities, but banned as a possible political threat in 1604 by James I, the society was revived in 1707 and formally re-established ten years later; in 1751 it received a charter from George II. Regular publications began in 1747; *Archaeologia* started in 1770. The society is based at Burlington House, London, where it has a fine library, open only to its fellows.

Antonine wall. A Roman wall constructed from *c*.AD 140, on the order of Emperor Antonius Pius. It ran for 37 miles, between the Firth of Forth and the Firth of Clyde, so as to allow the re-occupation of Lowland Scotland beyond

*Hadrian's Wall. It was constructed of turf on a stone base and was defended by a deep ditch and a series of forts and outposts. The wall was abandoned c.163.

apothecaries. The London Company of Apothecaries, incorporated in 1606, was empowered in 1815 to license apothecaries throughout England and Wales and to enforce a five-year *apprenticeship. The records of the Company date from 1670 and are kept at the *Guildhall Library, London. The apprenticeship records usually give not only the date of the *indenture, the name and residence of the lad's father, and the name of the master, but also the date of the lad's baptism. The apothecary may be seen as the forerunner of the general practitioner in medicine.

Probate *inventories are a major source of information about the provincial apothecary, for they provide detailed lists of his stock of medicines, perfumes, spices, herbs, comfits, antidotes, aphrodisiacs, antiseptics, tonics, purgatives, laxatives, emetics, astringents, and general cure-alls. They include foreign drugs such as Peruvian bark and quinine and exotically named items such as Spanish Juice and Dragon's Blood. See J. G. L. Burnby, *A Study of the English Apothecary from 1660 to 1760* (1983).

apparitor. The messenger who summoned people to appear before an *ecclesiastical court.

appraiser. A valuer of property, e.g. one who drew up a probate *inventory.

apprenticeship. It was the normal practice in the Middle Ages and the early modern period for boys (and to a much lesser extent girls) who wished to learn a trade to be formally apprenticed for a period of seven years or more. The Statute of Apprentices of 1563, which forbade anyone to enter a trade without serving an apprenticeship, remained on the statute book until 1814, though it was modified by later Acts and by legal judgements. Apprenticeship served the purpose not only of teaching a trade but of helping to ensure a supply of labour and keeping adolescents under control. The apprenticeship indenture was a legal document which bound a boy to a master, with a premium paid to the master by the boy's parents (or, in the case of paupers, by the overseer of the *poor). The boy received board and lodging and his training. He was forbidden to marry or to set up his own business until the completion of his term. Relations between masters and boys varied considerably. Indentures could be broken only by the decision of *Justices of the Peace;

the records of *quarter sessions include cases of absconding, ill-treatment, disputes over the placing of pauper apprentices, etc. In practice, however, large numbers of apprentices either failed to complete their training or did not become masters at the end of their term. Dropout rates of 50 per cent have been noted in 16th- and 17th-century London and Bristol; see Ilana Krausman Ben-Amos, 'Failure to Become Freemen: Urban Apprentices in Early Modern England', *Social History*, 16 (1991). The great growth of the *population in the second half of the 18th and early 19th centuries increased demand for goods and manufactures, and opportunities for employment elsewhere brought about the collapse of the system, except in certain trades.

Large numbers of apprenticeship indentures survive in assorted collections in county *record offices. At the Society of *Genealogists 'Crisp's Bonds' lists some 18,000 apprenticeships between 1641 and 1888. In some towns, registers of apprentices and grants of freedom upon the completion of an apprenticeship are a prime source of both local and family history. In Sheffield, for example, the registers of the Cutlers' Company, covering the period 1624–1791, have been published. They give the name, place of residence, and occupation of the master, the boy's name, and the name, residence, and occupation of his father. They can thus be used not only for genealogical purposes but for studies of migration and occupational structure. See, for example, E. J. Buckhatzsch, 'Places of Origin of a Group of Immigrants into Sheffield, 1625–1799', *Economic History Review*, 2nd ser., 2/2 (1950).

An Act of 1710 made stamp duty payable on indentures of apprenticeship. Registers of money received were kept from 1710 to 1811. These 'Apprenticeship Books' may be consulted at the *Public Record Office, where they are classified as IR 1. They record the names, addresses, and trades of the masters, the names of the apprentices, and the dates of the indentures. Until 1752 the names of the parents of the apprentices are also given. Indexes of masters' names, 1710–62, and of apprentices' names, 1710–74, are available at the Society of Genealogists, and at the Public Record Office under IR 17. Some county indexes have been published by local record societies, e.g. in Surrey, Sussex, and Wiltshire. The duty was not paid by all apprentices, e.g. those who worked for their father or those who did not enter into any formal agreement. Many industries were excluded by the ruling that the Statute of Apprentices did not extend to trades which did not exist when it was passed in 1563. Indentures involving pauper children were exempt from the payment of duty. For the decline of apprenticeship, see K. D. M. Snell, *Annals of the Labouring Poor: Social Change and Agrarian England, 1660–1900* (1985), which includes a chapter on the apprenticeship of women.

appropriation (in church documents). The transfer to a monastic house or other religious institution of the *tithes and other endowments of a *parish.

appurtenances. The rights and duties appended to an agreement over holding land, especially within a *manor. These included rights of grazing, other rights on the *commons and wastes, and the obligation to abide by the customs and regulations of the manor. *Copyhold or *leasehold property was often described as 'a messuage or tenement with appurtenances'.

apse. A semi-circular or polygonal recess, with an arched or domed roof, especially at the eastern end of the *chancel of a church. This feature was characteristic of the Kentish churches of *c.*600 associated with Augustine of Canterbury and of Norman churches of the late 11th and 12th centuries. Many small Norman churches, which were not subsequently enlarged, retain their apse, e.g. Kilpeck (Herefordshire) and Steetley (Derbyshire).

aqueduct. The Roman method of conveying a channel of water over a river or dry valley was used by the *canal builders of the 18th and 19th centuries. The most famous British example is Pontcysyllte on the Ellesmere canal, near Llangollen, designed by Thomas Telford and completed in 1805. It crosses the river Dee by a cast-iron trough supported by 19 stone piers at a height of 121 feet.

arable farming. The growing of *cereals has naturally been the mainstay of farming in lowland Britain, other than in areas of *marsh, *fen, or *wood. Many former corn-growing districts have been converted to pasture, though some have since reverted to cereals as farmers have responded to different market demands, but changing levels of demand for cereals have at different times caused arable to be converted to pasture and back again. See FIELD SYSTEMS and AGRICULTURAL STATISTICS.

archaeological and historical societies. The Society of *Antiquaries, which was founded in London in 1585, was the first society whose purpose was the study of antiquities, but it was far in advance of its time. The Society was re-formed in 1717, from which time it has had a continuous history. A great surge of interest led to the formation of numerous provincial societies in the 19th century. (See ANTIQUARIAN TRADITION, THE.) Many societies have published *journals* or *transactions* on an annual basis since their foundation, and some have printed much valuable material from local and national archives in their *record series*. These can usually be found on the shelves of public reference libraries and in local studies collections. They continue to form an essential starting-point for much local research. Some counties and cities are very well served, but others have started record societies only in the last quarter of the 20th century. *Local History Magazine* prints occasional directories of local history societies operating at the county level under *County-FILE*, together with news and information about county events. This gives the aims and objectives of county societies and lists their latest publications. See also David Hayns, 'County Local History Organisations: A Report on the Recent B.A.L.H. Survey', *The Local Historian*, 22/2 (1992). See also E. L. C. Mullins (ed.), *Texts and Calendars: A Guide to the Historical and Archaeological Publications of Societies in England and Wales, 1901–33* (1968).

archbishopric. The Archbishop of Canterbury is Primate of All England and is senior to the Archbishop of York. The Archbishopric of Wales was established in 1920. The Archbishop of Armagh has primacy in Ireland; Dublin became an Archbishopric in 1152. In England, the modern Roman Catholic Church is under the spiritual leadership of the Archbishop of Westminster.

archdeaconries and deaneries. The large *dioceses of the medieval church were subdivided into smaller administrative units, some of which survive to this day. A bishop delegated administrative authority over parts of his diocese to a number of archdeacons. In turn, an archdeaconry was subdivided into rural deaneries, each of which comprised a group of *parishes. The archdeacon was charged with visiting each of his parishes from time to time in order to ensure that churches were kept in good repair, that services were being conducted upon approved lines, and that scandalous behaviour was being punished. (See E. R. Brinkworth, *The Archdeacons' Court* (1942), and ECCLESIASTICAL COURTS.) Visitations by an archdeacon, or more rarely by a bishop, were sometimes preceded by articles of enquiry, to which ministers and churchwardens were expected to provide a written response. The records of such visitations are kept in diocesan *record offices. They are often informative about the condition of the church fabric, the income of the living, the frequency of services and numbers of attenders, and sometimes provide information on religious dissent, schools and charities. (See also LICENCES.)

*Wills and probate *inventories were processed through the tiers of administration, rising from parish to deanery and archdeaconry. Probate records are filed under deaneries in diocesan record offices, except for those which were proved by *peculiar jurisdictions. Deaneries were created in the Norman period, but their territories were often much older political or administrative units.

archery. In late medieval England practice with the longbow was a statutory requirement. Fear of French invasion prompted the revival of the statute in 1543. Men in every town and village were required to practice at the *butts after attending church on Sundays and holidays. The statute fell into abeyance during the 17th century.

Arches, Court of. The provincial court of appeal of the Province of Canterbury acquired its popular name from being held in the *peculiar jurisdiction of Bow, in the church of 'Blessed Mary of the Arches'. The records of this court are kept at *Lambeth Palace Library. Few survive before 1660 and many are in a poor condition from having been stored in a well in St Paul's Churchyard. Many of the 10,000 records are concerned with disputed *wills and letters of *administration from the *Prerogative Court of Canterbury or with applications for separation and nullity of marriage. The *British Record Society has published an index and *calendar, *Cases in the Court of Arches, 1660–1913*. See also ECCLESIASTICAL COURTS.

architectural styles. Buildings designed in the style of the Romans continued to be erected in western Europe until the end of the 12th century. In Britain, this *Romanesque style is divided into the Saxon and Norman periods, allowing for the *Saxo-Norman overlap of the 11th century. Churches were modelled on ancient Roman *basilicas, with rows of round arches providing access from the *nave to the aisles in the largest examples, e.g. Brixworth (Northamptonshire). The *Anglo-Saxons favoured tall, rather narrow, rectangular buildings with small, splayed windows, e.g. Escomb (County Durham), sometimes with *porticus* or side-chapels, e.g. Bradford-upon-Avon (Wiltshire). Towers were not buttressed, and had large quoins arranged in a side-alternate man-

ner, or in the long-and-short work favoured by the Mercians in the 10th and 11th centuries. The largest of these Mercian churches, e.g. Earls Barton (Northamptonshire) and Barton-on-Humber (Lincolnshire), used pilaster strips for decorative and structural purposes. Most Anglo-Saxon churches should be thought of as samples of *vernacular architecture, reflecting local traditions, and using local building materials.

The Normans built in the same tradition. Their early secular and ecclesiastical buildings were austere, but grander in scale than what had been built before. (See CASTLE; MANOR HOUSE; CATHEDRAL; and MONASTERY.) The Normans used thick walls and rounded arches that seem earthbound in slow, solid rhythms. The nave of Durham Cathedral is the finest example in Britain. From the middle of the 12th century parish *churches became much more decorative, with larger windows and carvings on capitals, doors, tympanum, arches, string courses, and corbel tables. Outstanding examples include Barfreston (Kent), Iffley (Oxfordshire), Kilpeck (Herefordshire), and Steetley (Derbyshire). The styles of decoration allow fairly precise dating for the first time, e.g. the use of water-leaf on capitals between 1175 and 1190.

The *Gothic style was introduced from France for use in monasteries and cathedrals in the last decades of the 12th century. The cathedrals at Canterbury and Wells are early examples from the 1170s. Based on knowledge of geometry gained from the Arabs, with thrust and counter-thrust obtained through the use of buttresses and pointed arches, these buildings soared to new heights. The style was soon taken up by parish churches and secular halls. The window styles of the *open hall of Stokesay Castle (Shropshire), for example, are similar to those in contemporary late 13th-century churches. Window styles are the first point of reference for dating. The English Gothic styles are divided into three main phases: *Early English (1170–1300), *Decorated (1300–50), and *Perpendicular (1350–1550).

The grandest secular buildings continued to use Gothic forms throughout the 16th century. The Tudor-Court Gothic style of Hampton Court influenced building in the provinces. See Maurice Howard, *The Early Tudor Country House: Architecture and Politics, 1490–1550* (1987). The *prodigy-houses of Elizabeth's reign, e.g. Hardwick Hall (Derbyshire), owed more to the native tradition than to the influence of the Italian Renaissance. See Mark Girouard, *Robert Smythson and the Elizabethan Country House* (1983). These buildings were much admired by Sir John Vanbrugh and influenced the design of some of his early 18th-century buildings.

The ideas of the Italian Renaissance were known to the Elizabethans principally through translations, notably that of Sebastiano Serlio, *L'Architettura* (1567). Such works were treated as *pattern books which provided ideas for particular features, but there was little understanding of the principles of classical architecture. The ruined Kirkby Hall (Northamptonshire) is a rare example of an Elizabethan building which has a whole range built in the Renaissance style. Inigo Jones was the only architect who travelled abroad and enthusiastically adopted the Italian approach, but his commissions were restricted to the Court circle. New ideas from the Continent, e.g. the *strapwork designs and curving gables of the Low Countries, came into Britain via the Court, the capital, the universities, and trading ports such as Topsham (Devon). The diffusion of ideas is seen in the way that Robert Lyminge, the architect of Robert Cecil's house at Hatfield (Hertfordshire), was employed to build Blickling Hall (Norfolk) for Sir Henry Hobart, the Lord Chief Justice, using many of the same features, or in the way that John Smythson was sent to sketch the finest new houses in London before designing a range at Bolsover Castle (Derbyshire) for Sir William Cavendish. The new style was often not understood, with local builders merely picking and choosing designs from pattern books without a knowledge of the whole (see ARTISAN MANNERISM).

The Royalist *nobles and *gentry who returned from France and the Low Countries after the *Civil War and *Commonwealth determined to build in the compact, classical style that they had become accustomed to during their exile. See Mark Girouard, *Life in the English Country House* (1978). The example of Versailles and other French buildings was a source of inspiration into the 18th century. See James Lees-Milne, *Baroque, 1685–1715* (1970). The great country houses that were erected after the *Glorious Revolution were largely the products of native architects—Wren, Talman, Vanbrugh, and Hawksmoor—who were deeply influenced by past and contemporary buildings on the Continent. Foreign craftsmen employed in the rebuilding of Hampton Court were commissioned for the paintings, woodwork, sculpture, ironwork, etc. at Chatsworth, Castle Howard, Blenheim, and the other great houses of the *baroque era.

The fashion for young nobles to make a Grand Tour of the Continent, with Rome as the ultimate destination, brought them into contact with the buildings of antiquity and the villas, churches, town halls, etc. of Andrea Palladio (1508–80) of Vicenza and Venice. Palladio's *The Four Books of Architecture* (1570, transl. 1715) enabled them to reflect on what they had seen when they returned home. The Earl of Burlington led the *Palladian movement which sought to build according to the purest principles of classical architecture. The extravagances of the baroque style were abandoned in favour of Palladian villas such as that built by Lord Burlington at Chiswick as a centre for the arts, or huge Whig palaces such as Wentworth Woodhouse (Yorkshire). During the second quarter of the 18th century the Palladian style was the only one considered for country houses. The inevitable reaction took the form of the Rococo designs of Robert Adam, but Palladio's works remained very influential, in Edinburgh and other cities as well as for country houses, and in America as well as in Britain and Ireland.

The town houses and public buildings of the Georgian age were built in simple classical styles, with symmetrical frontages, but in a variety of local materials. See Kerry Downes, *The Georgian Cities of Britain* (1979). Places such as Bath and Stamford owe a great deal of their character to the use of good-quality local limestone; others, such as Ashbourne (Derbyshire), to the use of hand-made *bricks. (See also REGENCY.) Meanwhile, the Gothic style had not disappeared entirely. Church towers were built in the Perpendicular tradition in the 17th and 18th centuries long before the 'Gothic Revival' of the early 19th century; *'Gothick' windows were used both in churches and in secular buildings; Gothic *follies were a feature of 18th-century *parks; and old *abbeys such as Lacock (Wiltshire) and Newstead (Nottinghamshire) were given a romantic, Gothic feel. 'Gothic survival' and 'Gothic revival' are shorthand terms that obscure a continuing affection for the style throughout the centuries.

The Victorians were eclectic in their choice of styles. The Gothic triumphed as the choice for Anglican churches (see PUGIN; SCOTT; and HIGH CHURCH MOVEMENT). Some notable Catholic churches, e.g. Brompton Oratory, also favoured Gothic. Gothic was much less popular amongst *Nonconformists, who favoured the classical style for their *chapels. The public buildings, ranging from town and city halls to cotton, wool, and *corn exchanges, theatres, concert halls, libraries, *market halls and shopping arcades, warehouses, offices, mills and *factories, railway stations, and Board schools, used every style that was on offer, from neo-classical and neo-Gothic designs to Tudor and Jacobean and 'Queen Anne'. Local building firms, such as Lockwood and Mawson, who were largely responsible for the best buildings in Victorian Bradford, turned their hand to a variety of styles to suit the commission. Much work remains to be done by local historians on the records and surviving buildings of provincial architectural practices. Meanwhile, the country houses abandoned the strict proportions of their predecessors in favour of huge, rambling, idiosyncratic designs, notably Harlaxton (Lincolnshire), Cragside (Northumberland), and Carlton Towers (Yorkshire). See Mark Girouard, *The Victorian Country House* (1979). Smaller houses designed by Lutyens and Voysey and by local architects all over the country also sought individuality, expressed in the choice of details.

The 'modern' and 'post-modern' styles of the 20th century have an international flavour much wider than the western European context of earlier centuries. Thus, Le Corbusier's concept of 'streets in the air' influenced post-war municipal housing in the form of high-rise flats, American skyscrapers have been copied by office buildings, and the ideas of Walter Gropius and the German Bauhaus have been instrumental in the planning of schools. The influence of new materials, especially concrete, is seen everywhere. The uniformity of the design of shop frontages has reduced the individual character of British towns that was such a marked feature of previous centuries. The buildings of the 20th century do not have the regional characteristics that were such a pronounced feature of the past.

Sir Nikolaus *Pevsner's The Buildings of England* series, arranged in county volumes, some of which are being revised, is the indispensable starting-point. See also John G. Dunbar, *The Architecture of Scotland* (1978). For general background see Sir John Summerson, *Architecture in Britain, 1530 to 1830* (1969), Anthony Quiney, *Period Homes: A Guide to Authentic Architectural Features* (1989), and J. C. Curl, *Encyclopaedia of Architectural Terms* (1993). Alec Clifton-Taylor, *Buildings of Delight* (1986) provides a readable introduction to the varied range of interesting buildings. For a fine regional study, see Derek Linstrum, *West Yorkshire: Architects and Architecture* (1978).

archive. A historical document. The plural form is also applied to the place where such documents are housed, e.g. a county *record office.

Archivists, Society of. The professional body for archivists, archive conservators, and records managers, which co-ordinates responses to issues of public concern relating to the keeping of archives and their accessibility to the public. The Society's *Journal*, which has appeared twice a year since 1980, publishes articles on the use and interpretation of records together with reviews of scholarly works, many of which are relevant to the interest of local and family historians.

aristocracy. The definition of an aristocrat has been contentious. Many have agreed with Dr Johnson that the *gentry should not be included within the meaning of this term, yet others have insisted that the gentry were thought of as being *noble in the Middle Ages, and should therefore be included even though a gentleman had no title. Some 19th-century gentlemen, however, had no landed estate, which seemed an essential requirement of an aristocrat. See J. V. Beckett, *The Aristocracy in England, 1660–1914* (1986). These problems troubled the compilers of Victorian publications such as the successive editions of *Burke's Landed Gentry*, but are of little concern in the late 20th century.

The problem of definition is made more difficult by the unstable composition of the membership. The aristocratic families of Victoria's reign were rarely descended from the richest and most powerful families in the early Middle Ages. In England, in contrast to the usual practice on the Continent, a title descended only in the eldest male line, so that younger members of aristocratic families often did not retain their nobility. The frequent failure of male lines has meant that many peerages have become extinct. In many other cases, titles and estates have passed to such distant branches of the family that any continuity of an aristocratic line is largely illusory. It has been a common practice for men to change their *surname as a condition of inheriting property. This fluidity of membership does not mean that British aristocracy has been readily open to newcomers, however. Entrance into the ranks of the aristocracy has always been difficult and slow. First-generation entry was always exceptional, for an aspirant had to establish his pedigree as well as to purchase a suitable landed estate. It was commonly held that it took three generations to become accepted.

The change in the composition of Britain's landowning élite has been achieved in a piecemeal way over the centuries as the result of thousands of varying individual fortunes. The membership has not undergone sudden and radical change since the *Norman Conquest. Serving the Crown was always the quickest way to a title, especially under monarchs who were liberal in their favours or who needed the money that title-seekers would offer. (See DUKE; EARL; MARQUESS; and BARONET.) Most modern peers have titles of no great antiquity and many have no landed estate. A sharp decline in the political power of the aristocracy occurred during the half-century after the First World War. Politics no longer revolve around the great country houses which were once the seats of Prime Ministers and members of the Cabinet. See David Cannadine, *The Decline and Fall of the British Aristocracy* (1990), and four Presidential Addresses, published as F. M. L. Thompson, 'English Landed Society in the Twentieth Century', *Transactions of the Royal Historical Society*, 5th ser., 40 (1990), and 6th ser., 1–3 (1991–3).

armiger. Someone who is entitled to bear a *coat of arms, an *esquire.

Arminianism. The theological views of James Arminius, a 17th-century Dutch Protestant theologian, who rejected the predestination beliefs of Calvinism in favour of free will. John *Wesley was influenced by Arminius.

armory. *Heraldry; armorial bearings. See Sir Bernard Burke, *General Armory of England, Ireland, Scotland and Wales* (1842).

Arms, College of. The corporation of heralds, founded in 1483–4. The College is situated in Queen Victoria Street, London EC4. Its registers include grants made or confirmed to English and Welsh families from the 15th century to the present day. See COAT OF ARMS.

army records. England had no regular standing army until the outbreak of the *Civil War in 1642. When regiments were formed in previous times, of necessity they took the names of the colonels who raised them. No systematic records relating to such troops survive. The officers alone of the armies of the Civil War and *Commonwealth are listed by regiment and indexed in Edward Peacock, *The Army List of Roundheads and Cavaliers* (2nd edn., 1874). Upon the *Restoration, a Secretary at War with responsibility for army administration was appointed; from 1660 the records therefore become more abundant. See the *Public Record Office Records Information leaflet no. 59, 'British Army Records as Sources for Biography and Genealogy', the PRO Readers' Guide, *Army Records for Family Historians* (1992), and Stella Colwell, *Dictionary of Genea-*

logical Sources in the Public Record Office (1992).

Personal information about officers should be first sought in the published *Army Lists*, which are available from 1754 in the larger public reference libraries. Manuscript lists of army officers from 1702 to 1752 (with an index) are kept in the Public Record Office under WO 64. Genealogical information about officers was seldom recorded by the army before the early 19th century, from which time several series of records, especially those kept under WO 25 and WO 76, are more informative. These give date and place of birth, and the dates of marriage and the births of children.

Knowing the name of the regiment in which an ancestor served saves a great deal of time in searching the many and varied records concerning other ranks of soldiers. The attestation and discharge documents in WO 97 provide a detailed record of service, nearly always with the place of birth, age on enlistment, and a physical description. From 1833 they also note details of next-of-kin, wives, and children. Three series deal with soldiers discharged from 1756 to 1872, 1873 to 1882, and 1883 to 1913. Unfortunately, the records of soldiers who died whilst serving have been destroyed. Regimental pay lists and *muster rolls are available in annual bound volumes from 1732 to 1878 under WO 12 and from 1878 to 1898 under WO 16. Description books, which give a physical description of a soldier, together with his age, place of birth, trade, and length of service, are available for the period 1756–1900 under WO 25, though many regiments have records only for the first half of the 19th century.

Soldiers who completed their term of service or who became invalids received a pension or institutional care in the Royal Hospitals at *Chelsea and Kilmainham. Admission books for out-pensioners in the 18th and 19th centuries are housed under WO 116 to 118. Records of in-pensioners are kept under WO 23. See the PRO Records Information leaflet no. 123. See also leaflet no. 84 for court-martial records.

The *General Register Office at *St Catherine's House, London stores the regimental registers of 1761–1924, which record the births, marriages, and deaths of soldiers who were stationed in the United Kingdom. The marriage records also note the names, births, and baptisms of any children who were born to a given marriage. The Army Register Book (1881–1959) notes genealogical details of the families of those serving overseas. From 1959 the entries of births, marriages, and deaths of the members of the families of those serving in all three forces—Army, Navy, RAF—are combined. Certified copies of these entries may be obtained at the same cost as certificates of *civil registration.

Background knowledge of the regiment in which an ancestor served can be obtained from the large collection of regimental histories that have been published. These may be consulted at the National Army Museum, Royal Hospital Road, Chelsea, London SW3, or they may be seen at large public reference libraries. Regimental museums provide additional background and may be able to help with old *photographs. See G. Hamilton-Edwards, *In Search of Army Ancestry* (1977), and Norman Holding, *World War One Army Ancestry* (1991). Scottish soldiers formed part of the British Army after 1707 and are therefore recorded as above, but for additional information see Cecil Sinclair, *Tracing Your Scottish Ancestors: A Guide to Ancestry Research in the Scottish Record Office* (1990), ch. 15. Irish Army records since 1922 are housed at the Public Record Office, Dublin. See also MILITIA RECORDS; WORLD WARS, RECORDS OF; and EAST INDIA COMPANY.

Array, Commission of. In the late 13th century, in order to raise an army from each *shire in times of emergency, Edward I appointed commissioners from the ranks of the *barons, *knights of the shire, and officers of the royal household to choose from the *muster rolls the required number of men from each *township. Musters of males aged between 15 and 60 were held twice a year in every *hundred or *liberty. Wages were paid to men who had to serve abroad, but each man was expected to provide his own equipment. This system of providing against emergency survived until 1551, when the commission was replaced by *lords lieutenant.

arrowsmiths. The making of arrows was a medieval trade which lingered on until the 17th century.

Arthurian legends. Arthur was supposedly a Celtic soldier who led the resistance to the Anglo-Saxon invasions in the early decades of the 6th century. A Welsh bard, Aneurin, wrote about him in *Gododin* (*c*.600) and his supposed exploits were described by another Welshman, Nennius, in *Historia Britonum* towards the end of the 8th century. Many parts of western and northern Britain have legends and place-names associated with Arthur, but he remained an obscure figure until *Geoffrey of Monmouth's fanciful *Historia Regium Britanniae* (*c*.1138). This formed the basis of verse and prose romances that became popular in the age of chivalry, notably the anonymous *Sir Gawain and the Green Knight* (1360s) and Malory's *Morte d'Arthur* (1469).

From Edward I (1272–1307) onwards the kings of England encouraged these legends, especially that of the Knights of the Round Table. The Order of the Garter was founded in 1346; Henry Tudor claimed descent from Arthur; Henry VIII (1509–47) repaired and repainted the Round Table which hangs in Winchester Castle, and which has been dated by *dendrochronology to the middle years of the 13th century.

Artificers, Statute of (1563). An Act which ordered that the level of wages should be determined by *Justices of the Peace, that the hours of labour should be limited to 12 in the summer and to daylight in the winter, that servants should be hired for at least a year, and that *apprentices should serve seven years. Some of its provisions were difficult to enforce.

artisan. A skilled craft worker. The term was used particularly in the 19th century. Artisans provided the leadership of working-class political reform groups. They had higher incomes, better houses, and more independence than less-skilled workers, and are sometimes referred to as the labour aristocracy.

Artisan Mannerism. A term coined by Sir John Summerson to describe architectural features on small or medium-sized houses in the mid- and late 17th century, which were taken from foreign *pattern books and applied without any real understanding of the principles of Renaissance architecture by local builders. These included door surrounds, pediments over windows, pilasters, etc.

Ashkenazic Jews. Those Jews who came from Germany and other parts of eastern, central, and northern Europe. (See JEWISH IMMIGRANTS.) They spoke Yiddish, a form of German written in Hebrew characters. In the late 19th century thousands of poor Ashkenazic Jews fled the Russian Empire, many of them settling in the East End of London and other industrial cities such as Leeds and Manchester. In Britain they are far more numerous than *Sephardic Jews.

ashlar. Freestone; smoothly cut stone for building purposes, introduced into Britain by the Normans.

assart. A piece of land, often of irregular shape, brought into cultivation from the waste, especially woodland. The term is usually applied to a medieval clearance.

assembly rooms. Some 17th-century examples of rooms being provided for younger members of the *gentry to dance have been noted at York, Tunbridge Wells, and Buckingham, but the fashion did not take hold until after 1700. *Defoe's *Tour through the Whole Island of Great Britain* (1724–6) comments on their modernity. By the middle of the 18th century most towns of a reasonable size had their assembly rooms. In York, Lord Burlington designed an 'Egyptian hall', which was opened as the assembly room in 1732. Bath had a series of rooms which provided improved facilities as the century progressed. The county towns and the *spas led the way. The regular assemblies formed the weekly basis of the social round, but others were held on special occasions, e.g. at the meetings of *quarter sessions, or during race week. Some assemblies were not held in specially designed buildings, but in guildhalls, *market halls, *theatres, *inns, schools, etc. Some new *town halls were provided with a ballroom for this purpose. The fashion declined in the 19th century. See Peter Borsay, *The English Urban Renaissance: Culture and Society in the Provincial Town, 1660–1770* (1989).

Assize, Courts of. Sessions of courts presided over by judges on circuit in England and Wales which tried capital and other serious offences, including homicide, infanticide, rape, robbery, burglary, *larceny, and arson, offences which were too serious to be tried at *quarter sessions. The assize judges also tried a variety of civil cases. Convicted criminals were executed in public spaces close to the court. The visits of the assize judges were amongst the social highlights of the year and brought in much business to an assize town.

The assize circuits that remained in use until 1876 had been defined by the 14th century. England was divided into six circuits beyond London and Middlesex: the Home, Midland, Western, Oxford, Norfolk, and Northern. These were modified between 1876 and 1893 but were subsequently unaltered until the merger of assize and quarter-sessions courts in 1971. After the Union with England in 1536, Wales was divided into four assize circuits: Chester, North Wales, Brecon, and Carmarthen. (For the separate Scottish system see HIGH COURT OF JUSTICIARY.)

The records of the assize courts are held in the *Public Record Office under Assi. 44, etc. They are amongst the most difficult to use for the purpose of a local study. Few finding aids are available, except for the Home Circuit. The records are poorly preserved. Only the Home

Circuit has any 16th-century documentation, and the Midland Circuit has nothing before 1818. The records of the other circuits have large gaps. For details, see Stella Colwell, *Dictionary of Genealogical Sources in the Public Record Office* (1992). See also J. S. Cockburn, *A History of English Assizes, 1558–1714* (1972), and his article 'Early-Modern Assize Records as Historical Evidence', *Journal of the Society of Archivists*, 5 (1974–7). For wider background, see J. M. Beattie, *Crime and the Courts in England, 1600–1800* (1986).

Assize of Mort D'ancestor. A court for determining a claim to inheritance, founded in 1176 and abolished in 1833. Most cases were brought by manorial lords in order to repossess property upon the death of a tenant.

Assize of Novel Disseisin. A procedure established in 1176 and abolished in 1833, whereby a tenant who had been removed from his holding could have his case dealt with speedily.

Association Oath rolls. After a plot to assassinate William III in 1696, an Act of Association required all office-holders to take a solemn oath of association by which they vowed to help preserve King William III's person and government. The names of the oath-takers in each *parish, and in the *livery companies of the City of London, are recorded under C 213 at the *Public Record Office.

astrology. The belief in the influence of the planets and stars on human behaviour. Astrology was based on an ancient body of learning and was intellectually respectable until the end of the 17th century. It was not regarded as necessarily in conflict with Christian teaching. An élite group of astrologers attracted a wealthy clientele in London. In the countryside, local conjurors or *wisemen were called upon for predictions and advice about missing persons, stolen goods, the causes of misfortune, etc. *Almanacs containing astrological predictions had an enormous sale. See Keith Thomas, *Religion and the Decline of Magic* (1971). The decline in belief in astrology as an intellectual pursuit was not matched at the popular level: it is taken half-seriously by millions of people to this day.

asylum, lunatic. The earliest asylums were private or charitable institutions, though pauper lunatics were sometimes housed in parish or union *workhouses or given outdoor relief. An Act of 1828 empowered *Justices of the Peace to erect and maintain asylums from county rates; another Act of 1845 compelled them to do so. Records of this period will be found amongst those of the *quarter sessions. In 1888 responsibility was transferred to county and borough *councils, until the establishment of the National Health Service in 1948.

For England and Wales few records of a personal nature appear to survive; others are unavailable until they are 100 years old. Even the *census enumerators used only the initials of inmates in their returns (whereas they listed the names of those in workhouses and gaols in full). If the approximate date of admission to an asylum is known, it is worth searching the registers compiled by the Lunacy Commissioners, and from 1913 the Board of Control, for the whole of England and Wales. These are arranged chronologically from 1846 to 1960, and are housed at the *Public Record Office under MH 94. Correspondence and papers under MH 51 include files on individual asylums and gaols with insane prisoners.

Class MH 83 contains the building records of the county pauper asylums which were erected under the terms of the 1845 Act. Many of these buildings are major Victorian monuments of considerable architectural merit. Characteristically, they stand in their own grounds outside towns with accommodation for about 300 inmates. Locally, their names have often become synonymous with madness. Many were demolished in the 1960s, but others were converted into *hospitals or put to new purposes. A number of histories of local asylums have been written in the 1980s and 1990s: see, for example, Bernard Cashman, *A Proper House: Bedford Lunatic Asylum, 1812–1860* (1992).

Scotland has few records of asylums before 1858, though the Aberdeen Sheriff Court records include registers of lunatics in asylums between 1800 and 1823 and between 1855 and 1857. From 1857 Scottish asylums were regulated by the General Board of Commissioners in Lunacy, whose archives are kept at the *Scottish Record Office. These are available only after 75 years. The general register (MC 7) of all lunatics in asylums notes name, date of admission, which asylum, date of discharge or death, and whither removed (if relevant); an index is provided. Notices of Admission (MC 2) record name, age, marital status, previous place of abode, nearest relative, and observations on the mental and physical health of the patient.

Atkinson, J. C. (1814–1900). John Christopher Atkinson was Vicar of Danby on the North York Moors from 1847 to his death, and a Canon of York Cathedral. He was one of the most remarkable local historians of Victorian

England, with a wide range of interests, including natural history, *folklore, speech, *vernacular architecture, and archaeology, as well as documentary research. His major publications were *British Birds' Eggs and Nests* (1861), *Sketches in Natural History* (1861), *A Glossary of the Cleveland Dialect* (1868), *A Glossary of the Dialect of The Hundred of Lonsdale* (1869), *The History of Cleveland, Ancient and Modern* (1872), *The Whitby Chartulary* (edited for the Surtees Society, 2 vols., 1879–81), *North Yorkshire Quarter Sessions Records* (edited vols., 1883 and 1892), *The Coucher Book of Furness Abbey* (edited for the Chetham Society, 3 vols., 1886), *The Chartulary of Rievaulx Abbey* (edited for the Surtees Society, 1889), *Forty Years in a Moorland Parish* (1891), *Scenes in Fairyland* (1892), *Memorials of Old Whitby* (1894), and numerous other writings, including sermons and contributions to *Notes and Queries*.

His lasting fame is due to his account of his lengthy incumbency at Danby, *Forty Years in a Moorland Parish*, parts of which have been reprinted in a paperback edition as *Countryman on the Moors*. This ranks as one of the finest books on rural England in the 19th century.

attainder. A person condemned to death or outlawry for treason or *felony forfeited both his real and personal estate and, by 'corruption of blood', his right to inherit or transmit property. Attainder was ordered either by judicial judgement or, from 1539, by an Act of Parliament (an Act of Attainder). For most crimes attainder was ended by the Forfeiture Act of 1870, but for outlawry it lasted until 1938. Inventories of the goods and chattels of attainted persons are found in the *Public Record Office, mainly under E 154.

attorneys. In no other profession in late 17th- and early 18th-century Britain did so many men make so much money, or make it so quickly, as in the law. By the second half of the 17th century attorneys were found occupying important positions in British towns. See G. Holmes, *Augustan England: Professions, State and Society, 1680–1730* (1982). They were able to make a handsome living from drafting and executing *wills, drawing up deeds and *settlements, arranging mortgages and loans, giving advice on investments, and by acting as stewards, estate managers, and rent-collectors. They spent much time travelling up to London to attend the Crown courts and journeying to meetings of the *assizes and *quarter sessions. Their legal expertise made them valuable members of town corporations and other governing bodies. Many were younger sons of *gentry families who were trained at one of the *Inns of Court. Some were able to retire to a rural property which they had purchased from the profits of their business. Since 1875 attorneys have been called solicitors. See Stella Colwell, *Dictionary of Genealogical Sources in the Public Record Office* (1992) for central records of the activities of attorneys.

Aubrey, John (1626–97). Antiquarian and Fellow of the *Royal Society, whose ambitious projects remained uncompleted. He is now best remembered for his *Brief Lives* of his contemporaries and of famous people of the previous century. His fine studies of Avebury and Stonehenge (he was the first to observe what are now known as the 'Aubrey holes') were meant to be part of a *Monumenta Britannica*, which he did not finish. He nearly completed an account of his native county, *The Natural History of Wiltshire*. His only published work was the *Miscellanies* (1696), a book of superstitions and strange happenings. See the Folio Society editions of *Aubrey's Brief Lives* (1975) and *The Worlds of John Aubrey* (1988), edited by Richard Barber.

auditor. The Office of the Auditors of Land Revenue formed a sub-department of the *Exchequer from the abolition of the Court of *Augmentations in 1554 until 1832. Its records are kept at the *Public Record Office under E 299 to 330 and LR 1 to 16.

Augmentations, Court of. Formed in 1536 upon the *dissolution of the monasteries to administer the monastic properties and revenues confiscated by the Crown, the Court was amalgamated with the *Exchequer in 1554. Its records are housed in the *Public Record Office under E315 and E321. Some of these have been calendared by the *List and Index Society. See W. C. Richardson, *History of the Court of Augmentations, 1536–1554* (1961).

Augustinians. Religious communities of regular canons organized according to the rule of St Augustine of Hippo (354–430), which emphasized poverty, celibacy, and obedience. The order was founded in Italy and France in the mid-11th century; the first community in Britain was that of St Botolph's Priory, Colchester, established in 1103. The order was known in Britain as the Austin Canons (after St Augustine) or the Black Canons (from their black outdoor cloaks). They were popular in lay society and had over 200 houses in England, Scotland, and Wales by 1350, and many others in Ireland, where they vied with the *Cistercians in popularity. Many of their houses

were small, but some *priories—Bolton-in-Wharfedale, Bridlington, Carlisle, Cirencester, Colchester, Guisborough, Haughmond, Jedburgh, Kirkham, Lanercost, Lilleshall, Llanthony, Merton, St Andrew's, St Frideswide's (Oxford), Thornton, Ulverscroft, and Walsingham—were large and famous. The Austin Canons sometimes shared their church with the parishioners. At Cirencester the canons built a separate parish *church, in splendid style, at the *abbey gates. Some canons were seconded to be *vicars of parish churches that were under the patronage of the priory. The order also founded hospitals, including St Bartholomew's and St Thomas's in London. See H. M. Colvin, *The White Canons in England* (1951), and J. C. Dickinson, *The Origins of the Austin Canons* (1950).

aulnage. Edward I (1272–1307) appointed aulnagers to give their seal of approval to cloths manufactured to standard sizes and quality. Aulnage was extended to knitted goods in the 16th century. The regulations on size were repealed in 1381, but those on quality remained in force until 1699. The earliest surviving rolls at the *Public Record Office give the names of clothiers and the numbers of cloths produced. See J. Lister, *The Early Yorkshire Woollen Trade* (Yorkshire Archaeological Society Record Series, 64, 1924).

Austin Canons. (See AUGUSTINIANS.)

Australia. A penal colony was founded in Australia in 1788, after the American War of Independence had brought to an end the previous policy of transporting convicts to the New World. See P. G. Fildon and R. J. Ryan (eds.), *The First Fleeters* (1981), for the names of the 1,493 passengers, including 586 male and 192 female convicts, who set sail from Portsmouth to Botany Bay; the others on board were members of the Royal Navy, or *merchant seamen and their families. The policy of *transportation brought convicts to New South Wales until 1840, to Van Diemen's Land (renamed Tasmania in 1856) and Norfolk Island until 1853, and to Western Australia until 1868. Some 162,000 people were transported during these 70 years.

Nevertheless, the convicts were always outnumbered by 'free settlers' attracted by cheap passages, often sponsored by landlords, *workhouses, or central government, and by the opportunity of acquiring land on which to raise sheep. The journey to the other side of the world took three months. The number of emigrants increased considerably in the second quarter of the 19th century: by 1851 Australia's population had risen to 437,665. Hopes of finding gold lured others across the seas. The population reached 1 million in 1858, 2 million in 1877, and 3 million in 1889. The census of 1861 noted that of those who had been born in the *United Kingdom, 56.3 per cent came from England and Wales, 15.48 per cent from Scotland, and 28.19 per cent from Ireland. These proportions remained roughly identical for the rest of the 19th century. Few Irish people had emigrated to Australia before the *famine, but then many took advantage of subsidized schemes. In all, about 300,000 Irish emigrants settled in Australia during the 19th century; perhaps about one-eighth of these were transported. See Patrick O'Farrell, *The Irish in Australia* (1987), and Colin Kiernan (ed.), *Ireland and Australia* (1984). See also E. Richards, A. Howe, I. Donnachie, and A. Graves, *That Land of Exiles: Scots in Australia* (1988).

David T. Hawkings, *Bound for Australia* (1987) describes the range of sources that are available for the study of this emigration. See also the *Public Record Office Records Information leaflet no. 94, 'Australian Convicts: Sources in the Public Record Office'. The PRO has no lists of passengers who sailed as ordinary emigrants until 1890, but it has the New South Wales Original Correspondence, 1784–1900 (CO 201), Entry Books, 1786–1873 (CO 202), and Registers, 1849–1900 (CO 360 and 369), which give names of settlers and convicts. For a regional study using the records relating to one county, see Irene Wyatt, *Transporters from Gloucestershire to Australia, 1783–1842* (1988).

The Archives Authority of New South Wales has listed many details of the early convicts and free settlers. For those who were transported, there are details about the date and place of trial, which leads to information about the age and place of birth of the convict. The records of pardons (absolute or conditional) give the place and year of birth, the name of the ship in which the convict sailed, the year of arrival, the convict's occupation, sentence, and physical description, and the date of the pardon. Other records include lists of convicts, tickets of leave, and certificates of freedom. The (incomplete) records of assisted emigration give the age, education, and occupation of the migrant, his birthplace or place of residence, his mother's name and maiden surname, and her father's occupation and often the maiden surname of her mother. Testimonials required under the government's bounty scheme of 1835, which paid the passage of emigrants of good character, usually have baptismal certificates attached. The registration of births, marriages, and deaths in the Australian states began at various times between 1841 and 1856. The early census returns have been destroyed, except for the census of New South Wales of 1828, which has been published by the Library of Australian History. This gives the name, age, year of birth, and religious affiliation of every person in the colony, together with the name of the ship and the year of arrival, occupation, place of residence, amount of land and stock, and (if the individual was a convict) his sentence.

Emigration to Australia continued in the 20th century and reached new heights in the 1950s and 1960s before restrictions were imposed. The Dominions Office correspondence at the Public Record Office (DO 35/3366–3443) contains information on assisted passages in this period.

avenue. In the British Isles the fashion for formal avenues of trees at the approach to a country house began in the 17th century, following French and Italian examples. Avenues were intended to add to the dignity of a place and to heighten the sense of expectation as the visitor entered the estate. This is particularly well achieved at Castle Howard (Yorkshire). Some civic authorities began to adorn their towns in this way during the 18th century. The tree-lined Walks in Dorchester (Dorset), which followed the lines of the old Roman walls, are a notable example. The fashion remained popular throughout Victorian times into the 20th century.

average. The three most commonly used averages in the statistical analysis of historical data are the mean, the median, and the mode. The mean is the arithmetical average; the median is the middle value when all items in a distribution are arranged in order of size; and the modal value is that for which the frequency is greatest.

B

back lane. A lane still found in many villages and small towns, which separates the *tofts behind the houses from the fields beyond. It provided ready access from the farmsteads to the fields.

back-to-back housing. Once the typical working-class accommodation in the industrial towns of northern England. See M. W. Beresford, 'The Back-to-Back House in Leeds, 1787–1939; in *Time and Place: Collected Essays* (1984), ch. 25. In Leeds, back-to-backs were first erected by workers' building-clubs, but they soon became the high-density housing favoured by speculators. They consisted of one room on the ground floor and one room above. Their walls were shared by three other houses, and as back doors and back windows could not be provided the houses lacked through ventilation. Their numbers can be assessed from local maps, especially the large-scale sheets of the *Ordnance Survey. They were condemned by reformers, and in the middle decades of the 19th century most towns passed by-laws forbidding future erections. In Leeds, however, back-to-backs continued to be built until 1937. They were thus a major part of the post-war housing problem. Most back-to-back were demolished during the clearance schemes of the 1950s and 1960s.

badger (historical). A dealer in meal, malt, dairy produce, eggs, etc. Badgers had to be licensed at the *quarter sessions under an Act of 1563, though those who lived in the northern counties of England were exempt. In time, badgers became general dealers or middlemen.

badging. Under an Act of 1697 those in receipt of poor relief were supposed to have a letter P and the initial of the parish sewn on to their clothes. Many parishes did not insist on this humiliation. Badging was abolished in 1782.

bailey. An enclosure within a *castle, beyond the *keep, containing accommodation, service buildings, etc., and defended by a ditch, rampart, and wall. The larger castles had both an inner and an outer bailey. See MOTTE-AND-BAILEY.

bailie. In Scotland, originally the chief magistrate of a *barony or part of a county, equivalent to an English *sheriff. Later, a municipal magistrate, equivalent to the English *alderman.

bailiff. 1. The holder of a public office in a certain district, e.g. a *sheriff or mayor. Thus, William Shakespeare's father was Bailiff of Stratford. The usage survives in some places. 2. The agent of the *lord of the manor responsible for administering the estate, collecting rents, etc. 3. A court official responsible for executing writs and distraining goods.

bailiwick. A district or place under the jurisdiction of a *bailiff or *bailie.

balk. An unploughed piece of land which formed a boundary between, and provided access to, the *furlongs of *open-fields. Grass balks did not serve as boundaries between individual *strips, as historians once believed, but were sometimes valued as grazing.

ballads. A high proportion of surviving ballads can be dated, on internal evidence, to the second half of the 16th century and the first part of the 17th century. The old oral tradition faded with the publication of printed *broadsides because the printed text came to be regarded as the sole authentic version. The tune to which the ballad was set likewise became the accepted one, though previously ballads had been set to different tunes at various times. See Geoffrey Grigson, *The Penguin Book of Ballads* (1975), Margaret Spufford, *Small Books and Pleasant Histories: Popular Fiction and Its Readership in Seventeenth-Century England* (1981), and Tessa Watt, *Cheap Print and Popular Piety, 1550–1640* (1991). Thousands of ballads were enrolled by the Company of Stationers during this period. Ballads formed a large proportion of the stock of London booksellers; they were sold throughout the land by thousands of *pedlars and petty *chapmen. Professional troupes of interlude players who travelled from one noble household to another were responsible for many compositions. For a case study of the historical events which furnished the material for a ballad see David Hey, 'The Dragon of Wantley: Rural Popular Culture and Local Legend', *Rural History*, 4/1 (1993). In Scotland, Ireland, and Wales the oral tradition lasted much longer. See D. Buchan, *Ballad and the Folk* (1972).

banking and finance. Until the late 17th century businessmen raised money on *bills of exchange which were due to be paid to them at a later date. *Attorneys, scriveners, and London goldsmiths were prominent in arranging *credit. According to Clarendon, writing in Charles II's reign, 'Bankers were a tribe that had risen and grown up in Cromwell's time, and never even heard of before the late troubles, till when the whole trade of money had passed through the hands of the scriveners; they were for the most part Goldsmiths.' Between 1640 and 1670 the City of London developed the three essential functions of the banker: to take deposits, to discount bills, and to issue notes. This movement culminated in the foundation of the Bank of England in 1694, the foundation of the Bank of Scotland in the following year, the emergence of the Stock Exchange, and the reform of the coinage. See Eric Kerridge, *Trade and Banking in Early Modern England* (1991), and Charles Wilson, *England's Apprenticeship, 1603–1763* (1965). During the 18th century local savings banks were established in most provincial towns, though failure was a regular occurrence. In 1828 the central government appointed a barrister to certify the rules of saving banks. Such banks became prominent High Street institutions during the Victorian era, their architecture conveying their supposed solidity and trustworthiness as they developed from being family firms into joint stock companies.

See the *Survey of the Records of British Banking* (Royal Commission on *Historical Manuscripts, 1980). Bank records have been used in C. W. Chalklin, *The Provincial Towns of Georgian England: A Study of the Building Process, 1740–1820* (1974) to provide evidence of loans to builders and craftsmen.

bankruptcy. Records of bankruptcy proceedings are housed at the *Public Record Office. From 1571 some conveyances of bankrupts' property can be found in the *Close rolls. The Court of Bankruptcy's records are available from 1710, under a 75-years rule. Class B 3, which has been indexed by name, place, and occupation, contains the files of examinations and depositions from 1780 to 1842. B 1 contains the order books from 1710 to 1877, B 6 contains the registers from 1733, and B 7 the minute books from 1714. Some *Chancery and

*Exchequer records contain information about bankruptcy in law cases. G. Elwick, *The Bankrupt Directory, 1820–43* (1843) lists insolvents of that period. Notices of adjudications were, and still are, published in the *London Gazette* and advertised in local *newspapers. See Sheila Marriner, 'English Bankruptcy Records and Statistics before 1850', *Economic History Review*, 2nd ser., 33/3 (1980). In Scotland, bankruptcy papers prior to 1839 are among the Court of *Session records in the *Scottish Record Office; a 'Guide to Scottish Sequestrations, 1839–1913' is available in the Search Room. (See SEQUESTRATION.) In 1883 the Government created a Bankruptcy Department with responsibility for investigating and administering the affairs of insolvent individuals and firms; its records are housed at the Public Record Office under B 11 and 12. For further details, see Stella Colwell, *Dictionary of Genealogical Sources in the Public Record Office* (1992).

banksman. The man in charge of the winding gear at a *coal mine.

banns of marriage. The proclamation in church of an intended wedding, in order that those who know of any impediment may object. The banns are read on three successive Sundays in the *parish churches of both the bride and the bridegroom. The procedure can be avoided by obtaining a *marriage licence.

Between 1653 and 1660, when marriages were civil contracts under the authority of a *Justice of the Peace, banns were read either in church on three consecutive Sundays or in the *market-place on three successive weekly market days. These banns were sometimes recorded in a separate book and sometimes in the *parish register, with the letter M (for market) added.

Lord Hardwicke's *Marriage Act (1753) regularized the keeping of registers of banns, but only a few books survive. The registering of banns was stopped in 1812 by *Rose's Act.

banqueting-house. In Elizabethan times, a place for an intimate meal. These were special-purpose buildings, sometimes in the form of rooftop towers, e.g. at Lacock Abbey (Wiltshire), sometimes as garden buildings, e.g. at Weston Hall, Wharfedale (Yorkshire). They range considerably in size. Many are delicately carved and highly decorated.

baptism customs. Baptism was held to be essential to salvation in the Middle Ages and was therefore performed as soon as possible after birth. After the *Reformation the *Book of Common Prayer recommended that baptism should be performed upon a Sunday or holy day, unless it was feared that the infant might die. The interval between birth and baptism varied from parish to parish and over time, but was normally only a few days and rarely more than a fortnight. (See GODPARENT.) A celebration at the parents' home or in a nearby *alehouse was held afterwards. Traditional gifts included apostle spoons, porringers, bowls, and mounted coral for the baby to cut his or her teeth on and for protection from *witchcraft. See Ralph A. Houlbrooke, *The English Family, 1450–1700* (1984). In the early modern period the custom grew up amongst the *gentry of private baptism at home. (See HALF-BAPTIZED.) For the church ceremony by which the mother was welcomed back to church after giving birth, see David Cressy, 'Purification, Thanksgiving and the Churching of Women in Post-Reformation England', *Past and Present*, 141 (1993).

baptistery. The part of a church, or a separate building to the west, where the rite of baptism is, or was, administered.

Baptists. The English Baptist movement was founded in exile in Amsterdam in 1611 by a group of Separatists from the *Church of England led by John Smith. The following year Thomas Helwys returned to London to establish the first Baptist church in England. Infant baptism was rejected in the belief that baptism should be administered only to believers and by full immersion.

In 1633 a group in Southwark who believed in Calvinistic predestination broke away to form the Particular Baptist Church. Those who remained with the original body became known as the General Baptists. Both were derided by opponents as *Anabaptists. By the late 17th century the Particular Baptists had become the more numerous body. Many General Baptist churches eventually became *Unitarian; those that remained formed the General Baptist New Connection in 1770. Splinter groups like the *Scotch Baptists continued to form and reform. In 1891 the General and Particular Baptists united in the Baptist Union of Great Britain and Ireland.

The Baptist Union Library, 4 Southampton Row, London WC1, incorporates the Baptist Historical Society Library. Other relevant archives are kept at Dr *Williams's Library, Gordon Square, London WC1. Registers before 1837 are kept with other *Nonconformist records at the *Public Record Office.

barbican. An outer fortification or first line of defence, especially at an entrance to a walled city or a *castle, or a temporary wooden tower

or bulwark. These structures strengthened defences at weak points, served as watch-towers, and were intended to dictate the approach of enemy forces. They usually date from the 13th or 14th century. Few barbicans survive intact. Lewes Castle (Sussex) has a fine example. At York, Walmgate Bar is the only one of the four entrances to the city to retain its barbican. A barbican at the north-western edge of the walls of the city of London has given its name to the theatre and music complex known as the Barbican Centre.

bargain and sale. A 16th-century method of conveying property by a private agreement drawn up by a lawyer, which was gradually replaced by that of *lease and release.

Barley, M. W. (1909–91). Archaeologist and local historian, who for many years was an adult education lecturer at the Universities of Hull and Nottingham. In 1971 he became Professor of Archaeology at Nottingham University. He was Secretary, then President, of the Council for British Archaeology, President of the York Archaeological Trust, Vice-President of the Society of *Antiquaries, Member of the Royal Commission on *Historical Monuments, and editor of the *History of Lincolnshire* series. He wrote on a wide variety of topics, but his major works are concerned with houses: *The English Farmhouse and Cottage* (1961), *The House and Home* (1963), and *Houses and History* (1986). His autobiography, *The Chiefest Grain*, was published posthumously in 1993.

barmote court. In the Peak District of Derbyshire all *lead mining in the King's Field was controlled by barmote courts, which date from at least the 13th century. The laws of both the High and Low Peak were affirmed by Act of Parliament in 1554. The courts met twice a year, under a barmaster appointed by the Crown, in order to solve disputes, enforce customs, and receive duties. The only courthouse to survive—that at Wirksworth—is a rebuilding of 1814. It contains an oblong measuring vessel, containing 14 pints, dating from 1509–10.

Barnardo homes, Dr. Thomas John Barnardo (1845–1905) founded his first home for destitute children at Stepney in 1870. The archives of this and many subsequent foundations are kept at the University of Liverpool, where those over 100 years old may be consulted, by arrangement. Between 1874 and 1905 the photographic department of Dr Barnardo's Homes took over 55,000 photographs of nearly all the children in the homes, many of whom emigrated to *Australia and *Canada. See John Kirkham, 'Barnardo's Photographic and Film Archive', *Local History Magazine*, 41 (1993).

barns are not simply for storing crops that have been harvested, but for any agricultural equipment. Hand *threshing by *flail was performed on the floor between doors in opposite walls, which when opened allowed sufficient draught for *winnowing. (See also WHEELHOUSES; TITHE BARNS; and FARM BUILDINGS.) In the Lake District barns were built on a slope to allow access at a lower level to a cart-shed flanked by a cowhouse and stable, and at the upper level (by a ramp on the opposite side of the building) to the storage area for crops. Fodder was dropped from the upper part, though hatches, to the manger. Another regional type is the small field-barn found in the Pennine fields that were formed by parliamentary *enclosure. They provided storage for crops and shelter for a few animals. (See also LONGHOUSE and LAITHE HOUSES.) Some of the finest *timber-framed medieval buildings are barns. See Cecil A. Hewett, *English Historic Carpentry* (1980).

baron. The lowest rank of the peerage; originally, a rank held by military or other honourable service from the king. The term was introduced after the *Norman Conquest to signify a *tenant-in-chief of the king below the rank of *earl. By the 13th century it was applied only to those lords who were summoned to Parliament. The Great Barons attended the king's Great Council. Most modern titles are not ancient; in 1956 only 144 of the 550 baronies went back beyond 1832. Since 1958 non-hereditary peerages with the rank of baron (or baroness) have also been conferred.

baron and feme. A legal term. In common law, a man and his wife were considered as one person. (Feme is derived from French *femme*.) Thus, upon marriage, a woman's personal property became her husband's. For the ways in which some women nevertheless acted independently, see Mary Prior, 'Wives and Wills, 1558–1700' in John Chartres and David Hey (eds.), *English Rural Society, 1500–1800: Essays in Honour of Joan Thirsk* (1990).

baronet. The hereditary rank created by James I in 1611 to raise money for troops in *Ulster, the fee being £1,095. Baronets are styled 'Sir' and take precedence over *knights. Separate baronetcies of Ireland (1619) and Nova Scotia (1625) were also created. Of the 1,226 baronetcies created between 1611 and 1800 only 295 (24 per cent) survived in 1928. Nearly 22 per cent of all baronetcies failed in the first

generation. For a study of prominent families of this rank in the 17th and 18th centuries, see Peter Roebuck, *Yorkshire Baronets, 1640–1760* (1980).

barony. The domain of a *baron. In Ireland, the division of a county. In Scotland, a large *freehold estate or *manor.

baroque. The term is used on the Continent for a florid architectural style that originated during the late Italian Renaissance and which became widely used, particularly for churches, in Catholic Europe during the 17th and 18th centuries. Classical elements were used for dramatic frontages topped with statues, and for rich internal decoration, including altar-pieces, gilded woodwork, and painted ceilings. (See ORGANS.) In Britain, the term is used in a more restricted sense and is applied particularly to country houses erected between 1685 and 1715. English baroque was never a unified style, but embraced a variety of individual designs that were classical in their inspiration. The greatest houses had painted ceilings by Varrio and Laguerre, carved woodwork by Grinling Gibbons and Samuel Watson, wrought-iron work by Jean Tijou, and decorative plasterwork by Italian artists. The *Palladians considered Vanbrugh, Hawksmoor, Talman, Archer, and other baroque architects to be undisciplined. Thus, Castle Howard was criticized for having the Corinthian order on one side of the house and the Ionic on the other. The stricter rules of the Palladians made the baroque style unfashionable during the reign of George I (1714–27).

barrow. A prehistoric burial mound, found in many parts of Britain, dating from the *Neolithic period and the *Bronze Age. The earliest are the long barrows of Wiltshire, Gloucestershire, and Dorset. The round barrows of the Bronze Age are more widespread. Some can now be identified only as *crop marks on aerial photographs.

barton. The word is used especially in southwest England, to mean either the home farm of a *lord of a manor, a monastic farm or *grange, or simply a barley farm. In modern times the word normally means a farmyard.

basilica. The principal civic buildings of ancient Rome were the models for early *churches. The basilica plan consisted of an oblong, with double colonnades and a semicircular apse at the end. See H. M. Taylor and Joan Taylor, *Anglo-Saxon Architecture* (3 vols., 1980).

bastardy papers. Parish records of the 16th to the 19th century kept by the overseers of the *poor concerning the parentage of illegitimate children and efforts to make the fathers responsible for maintenance.

bastides. The medieval planned towns of France, which have many points of comparison with those of Britain. These include grid patterns, town walls, market squares, and *burgage plots. See Maurice Beresford, *New Towns of the Middle Ages* (1967), which has a chapter on Gascony.

bastle. A fortified farmhouse of a type found in the Scottish borders, especially Northumberland, dating from the 16th and 17th centuries, and providing protection from raiders for livestock and people. Cattle were accommodated on the ground floor and the inhabitants occupied an upper room which was reached by an outside staircase. See H. Ramm, R. W. McDowall, and E. Mercer, *Shielings and Bastles* (1970).

bathrooms. As early as the mid-13th century the Palace of Westminster had bathrooms for the king and queen. In 1351–2 the king's bath was fitted with 'two large bronze taps . . . to bring hot and cold water to the bath'. The majority of medieval *castles and *manor houses had no bathrooms. Baths were installed in the great country houses of the late 16th and 17th centuries, after Queen Elizabeth I had started the fashion of having a bath once a month, 'whether she needed it or no'. Well into the 19th century, however, most country houses relied on hip baths and basins fitted in bedrooms. The Victorian villas of the middle classes had bathrooms, and towards the end of the 19th century so did the terraced houses of the lower-middle classes. The *council houses of the 20th century were generally fitted with bathrooms, but the tin bath-tub in front of the fire remained the normal method of bathing for many working-class families for much of the first half of the 20th century and sometimes later. The shower bath, which was invented early in the 19th century, became available to most sections of society during the last third of the 20th century.

battlefields, historic. Britain has relatively few historic battlefields compared with the Continent of Europe. The country has not been invaded since 1066, so the battlefields since then are those of civil wars. The site of the battle of Hastings on Senlac Hill (Sussex) is the best known. The exact sites of earlier battles is often a matter of dispute. Even the site of the battle of Bosworth (1485) remains controversial. Battles were fought during a campaigning season which lasted from May to October. They rarely lasted more than a day. Full-scale battles were the exception; the usual form of warfare involved raids and sieges and innumerable skirmishes. (See WARS OF THE ROSES.) The major battles of the *Civil War, notably those at Edgehill (Oxfordshire), Marston Moor (Yorkshire), and Naseby (Northamptonshire), are well known, but local historians still have plenty of scope to describe the military activities within a local area. (See MONMOUTH'S REBELLION; the GLORIOUS REVOLUTION for the battle of the Boyne (1690); and JACOBITES for the battle of Culloden (1746).) See also *The Ordnance Survey Complete Guide to the Battlefields of Britain*, A. Baker, *The Battlefields of the English Civil War* (1986), J. Kinross, *Walking and Exploring the Battlefields of Britain* (1987), and W. Seymour, *Battles in Britain*, i: *1066–1547*, and ii: *1547–1746* (1975).

battlement. An indented parapet along the top of a wall, used originally in fortified buildings, but by the 15th and 16th centuries for ornamentation in major houses and *Perpendicular Gothic churches. The fashion was revived in the 19th century.

bawn. A fortified farm or walled cattle enclosure in Ireland, especially one in the *Ulster plantations of the early 17th century. The word is incorporated in minor place-names, e.g. Seamus Heaney's childhood home Mossbawn.

bay. 1. The area between two sets of principal posts or dividing walls in a building. Early *surveys record buildings as being of so many bays.
   2. A recess in a room with a projecting window. In large houses these were often attractive architectural features.

beacon. In the age before modern communications technology the most rapid means of alerting people to danger from invasion was by the lighting of hill-top beacons. These were not simply bonfires, but were often stone-built structures which were maintained regularly through county rates. A network of beacons was developed in the Middle Ages. The Tudors maintained beacons along the south coast and the Severn estuary to guard against invasion from France and Spain. The method was also used to alert the *militia and volunteer companies during the *Napoleonic wars. A number of false alarms are recorded in local accounts. Many hill-top sites are commemorated by the place-name 'Beacon'.

beadle. 1. A town-crier or a crier in a law court.

2. A minor parish official responsible for keeping order; sometimes the equivalent of the *constable.

3. Someone who walks in front of dignitaries in a procession.

Beaker culture. So-called from the characteristic drinking vessels found in graves known as round *barrows in many parts of Britain and Europe dating from the late *Neolithic and early *Bronze ages, c.2800–1500 BC. Old ideas concerning the spread of this culture by invasion have been discarded.

bear- and bull-baiting. Cruel sports which were commonly practised in market towns and at country feasts until they were prohibited in the first half of the 19th century. Bulls were tied to a post and attacked by a group of bulldogs (bigger and fiercer than the modern breed); part of the attraction was the gambling on which dog was judged the bravest. In Birmingham the sport is commemorated by the street-name Bull Ring. A Sheffield map of 1771 marks 'Bull Stake' in the 'Beast Market'. As bears were in shorter supply they were baited less often than bulls. Bears which were trained to dance to music were made to perform in the streets well into the 20th century.

beast gate. The right to pasture an animal on the *commons and wastes was regulated by the manorial *courts, which imposed a stinting system of so many 'gates' per holding.

Bede, the Venerable (c.673–735). A monk who spent his life at the *Benedictine monasteries of Monkwearmouth and Jarrow (County Durham), and who became the greatest scholar in *Anglo-Saxon England. The most important of his many written works is his *History of the English Church and People*, which is the basic source for the ancient history of England to the year 731.

bederoll. (also bead-roll). The list of persons to be specially prayed for, which was read out from the pulpit each Sunday and at Christmas and *Michaelmas; these persons usually comprised the benefactors of the church.

bedesman. (also beadsman). A man who prayed for the soul or spiritual welfare of others, usually in a paid capacity. The term might be applied to the inmate of an *almshouse who was charged with praying for his benefactor.

Bedlam. Shortened form for the Hospital of St Mary of Bethlehem, in London, which was founded as a *priory in 1247 and became a hospital for lunatics, the oldest in England. The modern sense of the word was in use by the 16th century.

bees were the source of the main sweetener in cooking until sugar-cane was grown more abundantly in the Mediterranean in the 16th century and imported into northern Europe. In the early modern period bees were kept on estates in bee-boles, which are recesses built into a south-facing wall in which a straw hive could be protected from rain. Samuel Hartlib, *The Reformed Common-wealth of Bees* (1655) advocated the widespread keeping of bees. See Michael Leslie and Timothy Raylor (eds.), *Culture and Cultivation in Early Modern England: Writing and the Land* (1992). Many superstitions were associated with beekeeping. See, for example, J. C. *Atkinson, *Forty Years in a Moorland Parish* (1891).

beggars. The Elizabethan *Poor Law Acts of 1597–1601 ordered that beggars should be punished by whipping. Examples of such punishment being meted out can be found in *quarter sessions and *parish records. The Elizabethan authorities were much concerned with the problem of menacing bands of 'sturdy and idle' beggars, the memory of which survives in the nursery rhyme, 'Hark, hark! The dogs do bark, the beggars are coming to town'. In reality, most beggars operated in ones or twos, not in bands; they tended to be young, single men, and most of those who were brought before the *Justices of the Peace had travelled less than 40 miles. They were often seeking work or the assistance of relatives. See Paul Slack (ed.), *Rebellion, Popular Protest and Social Change in Early Modern England* (1984), and A. L. Beier, *Masterless Men: The Vagrancy Problem in England, 1560–1640* (1965). In the second half of the 17th century strident complaints about beggars ceased to be heard. This may have been partly the result of the Act of *Settlement (1662), which restricted movement, but, more positively, it was probably caused by the easing of population pressure and an increase in the general standard of living. The harshness of the law was often mitigated by individual acts of charity. Begging has remained a social problem, but not on the scale experienced during the 16th century.

Beguines. The lay sisterhoods which began in the Low Countries in the 12th century. They pursued a religious life but did not bind themselves to a strict vow, and sometimes left upon marriage. See Carol Neel, 'The Origins of the Beguines' in Judith M. Bennett *et al.*, *Sisters and*

Workers in the Middle Ages (1976). Some modern Anglican sisterhoods have a similar form of organization.

Belgae. Late *Iron Age Celtic immigrants from Belgium and northern France who settled in south-east England *c.*100 BC.

bell-founding. In the Middle Ages bells were cast using alloys of *copper and *tin. Bell-founding was an urban craft in the early modern period, when it was often combined with that of the brazier or potter. Bells were cast in pits containing bell-moulds next to a reverberatory furnace. Sometimes, bells were recast in pits dug into the *naves of churches.

bell pit. A pit for the extraction of *iron ore and *coal. Although the technique was a medieval one, it was still used in the 19th century where coal or iron ore were found near the surface. A vertical shaft was dug to the seam, which was then worked in all directions, thus producing a bell shape. Fear of roof collapse would then lead to the pit being abandoned and the digging of a new shaft alongside. Pits are thus arranged in rows, marked by the spoil which was deposited around the head of the shafts. They appear as a dramatic landscape feature in aerial photographs.

bell-ringing. Inside the towers of parish churches can often be found notices of marathon bell-ringing feats, with details of the changes that have been rung. Otherwise, information about local bell-ringers is hard to come by. The *calendar custom known as the Castleton Garland (Derbyshire) appears to have originated as the entertainment provided by the bell-ringers at the local May games.

belvedere. A turret-room, often glazed on all sides, at the top of a house or tower, providing distant views across the countryside; a summer-house. The name is derived from Italian words for a pleasant view or fair prospect. Introduced into Britain during the 16th century, e.g. the belvedere tower at Melbury House (Dorset), which dates from the 1530s, the fashion flourished in the late 18th and early 19th centuries.

bench end. Benches were introduced into the *naves of parish *churches towards the end of the 15th century. The earliest ones were very simple, but in time it became the practice to carve bench ends with tracery designs or with heraldic or allegorical subjects. The best and most numerous examples from the 15th and 16th centuries are in Somerset and Devon and in Norfolk and Suffolk. A famous group at Brent Knoll (Somerset) ridicules a mitred abbot, who is shown as a fox preaching to pigs and geese, then in the stocks, and finally hanging from the gallows.

bench mark. Mark used by surveyors of the *Ordnance Survey to provide a 'bench' or support for a levelling staff in order to determine altitude above mean sea-level. Below the horizontal notch is the broad arrowhead that was used from the Middle Ages onwards to mark the property of the sovereign. Bench marks are found on the Ordnance Survey's trigonometrical pillars and on prominent buildings such as *church towers.

Benedictines. The largest monastic order in Britain, based on the rule of St Benedict (d. 543). The early foundations of the black monks, including *Bede's monasteries at Monkwearmouth and Jarrow, were destroyed in the 9th century by the *Vikings. The Benedictines were re-established in southern England in the 10th century; in 943 Dunstan, with the support of the Wessex king Edmund, restored the Benedictine rule to Glastonbury, where he was abbot. By the middle of the 12th century southern England had about 50 Benedictine *monasteries and 12 *nunneries, most of which were wealthy. During the reigns of William I and II (1066–1100) many important monasteries were founded or re-established, including Selby and Whitby in the north of England. Some were situated in towns, notably those that were associated with *cathedrals. In the later Middle Ages the Benedictines had 245 houses in England, Wales, and Scotland, but the movement had lost its impetus before the Anglo-Norman settlement of Ireland.

Other famous Benedictine monasteries include Abbotsbury, Bath, Bury St Edmunds, Canterbury, Chester, Crowland, Dunfermline, Durham, Ely, Gloucester, Lindisfarne, Norwich, Peterborough, Ramsey, Rochester, St Albans, Sherborne, Tavistock, Tewkesbury, Tynemouth, Westminster, Winchester, Worcester, and York. All were secularized or destroyed at the *dissolution of the monasteries. In the 19th century new Benedictine houses were established at Ampleforth and Downside.

benefice. An ecclesiastical living.

benefit club. See FRIENDLY SOCIETY.

benefit of clergy. In the Middle Ages the Common Law courts substituted a minor punishment for the death penalty for some of the less serious capital crimes when the convicted person was a clerk (clergyman). In 1305 this benefit was extended to secular clerks who were able to read and understand Latin. The first verse of the 50th Psalm in the Vulgate version of the *Bible was used as the test. After the *Reformation this was replaced by the ability to read, in English, the same verse in the Authorized Version of the Bible (where it was the 51st Psalm). It read, 'Have mercy upon me, O God, according to thy loving kindness; according unto the multitude of thy tender mercies, blot out my transgressions.' It became known popularly as the 'Neck Verse'. Anyone convicted of a capital offence who could read this verse was not hanged, but merely branded on his thumb. In practice, benefit of clergy had become a useful legal fiction to mitigate the severity of the law for first offenders. The formality of the test was abandoned in 1705. Benefit of clergy was abolished in 1827.

berewick. A dependent settlement within a *manor. The term is used in the *Domesday Book.

Best, Henry. Substantial East Riding farmer, whose account of his farming practices is one of the most detailed sources for the agricultural history of the 17th century. See Donald Woodward (ed.), *The Farming and Memoranda Books of Henry Best of Elmswell, 1642* (1984). His house at Elmswell on the Yorkshire Wolds is still standing.

bestiary. A moralizing treatise on beasts, written during the Middle Ages. Real and imaginary beasts were thought to have medicinal powers and spiritual qualities which the reader was urged to emulate. Bestiaries were a source of inspiration for the sculptors who adorned Norman churches (especially the tympanum and corbel tables) with carvings of animals. A famous example is Kilpeck Church (Herefordshire).

betrothal. Up to the early 17th century a betrothal before witnesses, followed by consummation, was considered a valid marriage. This explains why some *baptisms recorded in early *parish registers follow shortly after a church wedding. The Church had a long struggle to enforce its view that marriages were valid only after a church ceremony. Betrothals gradually declined in status to that of the engagement, which could be broken.

bibles. The Vulgate bible, which was based on that prepared by St Jerome *c.*400, and revised in 1592, is the official text of the Roman Catholic church. It takes its name from the Latin *vulgare*, 'make public'. The first translation of the Bible into English was made in 1382 by John Wycliff and his associates. The first printed English bible was that translated by William Tyndale, starting with the New Testament in 1526 and followed by the Pentateuch and the Book of Jonah in 1530–1. A complete English bible, edited by Miles Coverdale, was published on the Continent in 1535. Various other editions extended Tyndale's work. The Geneva Bible of 1560 was popularly known as the Breeches Bible, for it translated the aprons of Genesis 3: 7 as breeches. It became immensely popular during the reign of Elizabeth and ran to over 150 editions. The Authorized or King James Bible was published in 1611. See Christopher Hill, *The English Bible and the Seventeenth-Century Revolution* (1993), which emphasizes the important influence of the translation of the Bible into the vernacular on the events that culminated in the *Civil War. The revised version of the King James Bible was published in 1881–5. It has been largely replaced in *Protestant churches in Britain during the later 20th century by the New English Bible (1961–70).

bidding. A custom which survived in Wales until the late 19th century, whereby close friends and relatives of a bride and groom were bidden by word of mouth or letter to a festivity at which they were expected to make a gift of money towards the setting-up of the new home. The contributions ranged from 6d. to 2s. 6d., the most common being 1s. These payments were regarded as 'marriage dues', for the contributors had received, or would hope to receive, such gifts themselves. In effect, the bidding acted as a sort of savings club. See David Jenkins, *The Agricultural Community in South-West Wales at the Turn of the Twentieth Century* (1971). A large number of printed bidding-letters survive from the 19th century for Carmarthenshire and parts of Cardiganshire and Pembrokeshire. These often append the names and relationships of both families. See John Rowlands *et al.* (eds.), *Welsh Family History: A Guide to Research* (1993).

bierlow. The *Viking word for a *township, retained in some place-names, e.g. Brightside Bierlow and Ecclesall Bierlow in Sheffield.

bill, hedging. The hook-shaped tool with a sharp cutting edge, used by hedge-layers in the late 18th and 19th centuries.

bill of exchange. A method of payment much used to obtain *credit before the system of bank cheques was devised. It took the form of a written order by the writer (the 'drawer') to the person to whom it was addressed (the 'drawee') to pay to the 'drawer' or to a named third person (the 'payee') a stated sum of money on a certain date. Over time it aquired a looser meaning of a promissory note.

bird scaring. An immemorial job for boys. For the great damage to crops done by birds, and their slaughter as pests, see E. L. Jones, 'The Bird Pests of British Agriculture in Recent Centuries', *Agricultural History Review*, 20/2 (1972).

birth-rates. The 'crude' birth-rate is the number of births in a given year, expressed as so many per thousand. Since the only evidence in quantity of births before 1837 is the record of baptisms in *parish registers, such figures have to be converted to birth-rates corrected for under-registration. Birth-rates can only be approximations before reasonably accurate population figures are available from *census returns.

bishopric. See DIOCESES.

bishops' registers. Volumes recording the administrative acts of bishops in their *dioceses. They date from the 12th and 13th centuries onwards, but are less useful after the *Reformation. Such registers record the ordination of clergy and their institution to livings, the *appropriation of *benefices to religious houses, etc. See D. M. Smith (ed.), *Guide to Bishops' Registers of England and Wales: A Survey from the Middle Ages to the Abolition of Episcopacy in 1646* (1981).

bishops' transcripts. In 1598 it became the practice for each parish in England and Wales to copy the entries made the previous year in the *parish register and to forward this transcript (signed by the incumbent and the churchwardens) to the bishop of the *diocese or to the head of the relevant *peculiar jurisdiction. These records are now kept in diocesan *record offices or the National Library of *Wales. They are invaluable where an original register has been destroyed or where there are gaps or passages that are difficult to read. On the whole, the transcripts have not been as well preserved as the originals. The copyists frequently lacked care.

Few transcripts were made during the *Commonwealth period, but the practice was revived at the *Restoration. It petered out during the 19th century at times which differed from diocese to diocese. See J. S. W. Gibson, *Bishops' Transcripts and Marriage Licences, Bonds and Allegations: A Guide to Their Location and Indexes* (1981).

Black Death. The first outbreak of *plague, which affected almost the whole of Europe, occurred between 1348 and 1352. In Britain, its main effects were felt in 1348–9. A third or more of the population died as a result of this epidemic. The clergy suffered death rates of 40 to 45 per cent, judging by the number of vacant *benefices. Manorial records indicate that between one-third and two-thirds of tenants on *manors in different parts of England died at this time. Further epidemics occurred in 1360–2 and 1369, and plague remained endemic in Britain until the mid-1660s. The Black Death had a great effect on the popular imagination, as evidenced in painting, sculpture, and literature. It also had important social and economic consequences, relieving *population pressure and creating opportunities for the economic advance of all classes. See Rosemary Horrox, *The Black Death* (1994), John Hatcher, *Plague, Population and the English Economy, 1348–1530* (1977), Christopher Dyer, *Lords and Peasants in a Changing Society: The Estates of the Bishopric of Worcester, 680–1540* (1980), Zvi Razi, *Marriage and Death in a Medieval Parish: Economy, Society and Demography in Halesowen, 1270–1400* (1980), L. R. Poos, *A Rural Society after the Black Death: Essex, 1350–1525* (1991), and John Hatcher, 'England in the Aftermath of the Black Death', *Past and Present*, 144 (1994).

Blome, Richard. 17th-century mapmaker. His world map, *Cosmography*, went through various editions from 1669. His *Britannia* (1673) was a series of county maps and included a map of Ireland. The maps have little geographical merit but are decorative.

Blomefield, Francis (1705–52). Clergyman, and author of the *History of Norfolk* (1739–75).

blood groups and DNA. The work of geneticists on mapping blood groups is of great interest to local and family historians in confirming the evidence of *surnames and studies of *communities and societies that most families remained attached to their neighbourhoods or '*countries' over long periods of time. The study of blood groups points, for instance, to a genetic divide which still exists in Northumberland between the people who inhabit the western hills and those who live in Tyneside. It also confirms that the original border between Wales and Herefordshire was a barrier to migration. See E. Sunderland, 'Comment on "History and Blood Groups in the British Isles" by W. T. Potts' in P. Sawyer (ed.), *Medieval Settlement* (1976).

Geneticists have extended this work to the sampling of DNA structures. It was reported at the 1992 Summer Meeting of the British Association for the Advancement of Science that such research suggests that the descendants of *Vikings continue to occupy the central Lake District, the Conway valley in north Wales, Pembrokeshire, the north-east coast of Scotland, and the Shetland Islands. People living in the central areas of the Lake District have genes similar to those of present-day Norwegians, but different genes from those of their neighbours in the Cumbrian lowlands. A genetic dividing-line roughly separates Norfolk from Suffolk, even though there is no physical barrier to movement between the two counties. The inhabitants of the Orkneys are genetically quite distinct from the rest of Britain, and even parts of Europe; their relative isolation has meant that they have preserved links with the *Neolithic settlers of 5,000 BC.

bloomery. A *forge in an ironworks where the melted ore is hammered into bars of *iron known as blooms, so as to remove the slag. Sites are often located by the presence of slag and by place-names such as Cinder Hill or Smithies. Units of production were small and often short-lived. From the 14th century *water power was used for bellows and hammers. Powered bloomeries remained important in many parts of the country until the middle of the 17th century. On average, a bloomery produced 20 to 30 tons of iron a year. Some powered bloomeries were converted into finery forges or into other forms of mill. Only three water-powered bloomeries have been excavated in Britain. See D. W. Crossley and D. Ashurst, 'Excavations at Rockley Smithies, a Water-Powered Bloomery of the 16th and 17th Centuries', *Post-Medieval Archaeology*, 2 (1968).

blowing house. The term used on Dartmoor and in Cornwall for the *water-powered smelting works of the *tin industry. The technique was well established by the end of the Middle Ages and continued in use into the 19th century, even though the reverberatory *furnace had been introduced by 1702. Many of these granite-built works survive in a ruinous condition.

blue books. The official series of *parliamentary papers from the late 18th century onwards. The most important ones have been reprinted by the Irish Universities Press and are available in large public libraries, university libraries, and the official publications room of the *British Library. They are often difficult to locate because their lengthy titles are cited in different ways and they are unindexed. They include House of Commons Sessional Papers and Reports of Select Committees and Royal Commissions. The evidence of witnesses called

before committees and commissions can provide vivid local detail, e.g. on the employment of *children in *coal mines or *factories. The local historian needs to be aware that the questions that were asked were often designed to lead a witness to the answer that was wanted, and that replies were not necessarily recorded verbatim.

Board of Agriculture. Founded in 1793, with Sir John *Sinclair as President and Arthur *Young as Secretary, and an annual parliamentary grant of £3,000. Its founders hoped that it would become a department of state, but it was never more than a private society which spread useful knowledge and encouraged agricultural improvements. Its earliest and most important task was to commission a series of county reports, known as the *General Views of Agriculture*. These are now a major source for agricultural historians. The Board was less successful in its attempts to encourage *agricultural societies and to award premiums. However, it did sponsor a series of lectures by Humphrey Davy which became famous as the *Elements of Agricultural Chemistry* (1813). Replies to a circular letter asking questions about the extent of the post-*Napoleonic war depression were published as the *Agricultural State of the Kingdom* (1816). The government grant was withdrawn in 1820. The Board sponsored livestock shows in London in 1821 and 1822, but these were unsuccessful. Attempts to keep the Board in operation by private subscription failed, and it was dissolved in 1822, two years after Young's death. Although it was judged a failure by contemporaries, the Board paved the way for the foundation of the Royal Agricultural Society in 1838.

boatmen. The classic study of boatmen in a local context is Mary Prior, *Fisher Row: Fishermen, Bargemen and Canal Boatmen in Oxford, 1500–1900* (1982). The families that lived in a row of fishermen's houses between two streams in Oxford formed an occupational community in the 16th century. They were joined by bargemen in the 17th century and canal boatmen after the opening of the Oxford Canal in 1790. Fisher Row was a tight-knit community in which occupations were inherited. A stable group of families, linked closely through intermarriage, provided the core of the community, in contrast to the comings and goings of others. The canal boatmen who came to live in Fisher Row in the 1790s had distinctive dress, customs, and styles of boat decoration. See also Harry Hanson, *The Canal Boatmen, 1760–1914* (1975), and Sheila Stewart, *Ramlin Rose: The*

Boatwoman's Story (1993), which deals with the horse-drawn narrow boats on the Oxford Canal in the first half of the 20th century.

Bodleian Library. Copyright library at the University of Oxford, which contains thousands of rare volumes and large manuscript collections in the Department of Western Manuscripts. When it was founded in 1598 by Sir Thomas Bodley it attracted the attention of scholars all over Europe because of its novelty. It served at first almost as a national library. Bodley spent £8,000 on the repair and extension of the building which had once housed the 15th-century University Library of Humphrey, Duke of Gloucester. He and his friends spent another £11,000 on fitting it out. By 1620 the library had 16,000 volumes and soon it became a rich repository of manuscript materials.

Boer War. The war in *South Africa (1899–1902) between Great Britain and the Afrikaner republics of Transvaal and the Orange Free State. 'Boer' is the Dutch word for countryman or farmer. Many British towns have streets named after the battles at Mafeking and Ladysmith. The steep terraces of some football grounds were named Spion Kop after the hill near Ladysmith.

bole hill. *Lead-smelting site on the Pennines and the Mendips dating from the period before the adoption of bellows-blown hearths in the 16th century. The sites, which occupied windy escarpments, are often commemorated by the place-name Bole Hill, but remains are difficult to identify. The bole consisted of a stone-walled enclosure up to 5 or 6 yards in diameter, open on the side of the prevailing wind. The ore was stacked in the hearth and covered with brushwood and thicker wood. The molten lead was directed into a pig-mould. See David Kiernan, *The Derbyshire Lead Industry in the Sixteenth Century* (1988).

bona notabilia. These Latin words ('considerable goods') are noted in the records of *probate courts of the 16th to the 18th centuries when an estate was valued at £5 or more.

bond. 1. A deed by which a person binds himself to pay a certain sum of money, or a document issued by the government or a public company promising to repay borrowed money at interest. Bonds recorded as credits in probate *inventories were of this sort.

    2. An agreement with a penalty for non-performance. A bond deed consists of two parts: the *obligation* (which before 1733 was in Latin) states the penalty; the *condition* (written in English) describes the commitment. These bonds could be private agreements or a necessary response to the law, e.g. to obtain a licence as a *drover, *badger, etc.

bond, marriage. An obligation entered into by a groom or someone acting on his behalf that the particulars in a marriage *allegation were true and that there was no impediment to the marriage. The practice was discontinued in 1823.

bondage system. A system of tenure with defined services, common in Northumberland and south Scotland in the 18th and 19th centuries, designed to provide casual labour in times of need. *Farm servants who were hired annually were provided with a house, specified quantities of food and coals, and the keep of a cow or a pig. In return the servant contracted to supply a woman labourer (usually his wife or daughter) to work for his employer for cash wages when required. These female workers performed all the jobs on the farm except ploughing and ditching. The system had virtually died out by the 1890s.

bonding. The arrangement of *bricks in distinctive courses in a wall. As continuous vertical joints are structurally unsound, various types of bonds were evolved. The normal method in the Middle Ages was the English bond, by which courses were arranged alternately in stretchers (bricks laid at length along the face of the wall) and headers (bricks laid at right angles to the face of the wall). Flemish bond (alternate stretchers and headers in the same course) became popular in the 17th century. There are several variations on these two basic types.

bondman. A *villein or *serf.

bookland. The *Old English name for land obtained by 'book' or written *charter, hence the place-name Buckland.

Book of Common Prayer. This prayer book, which was the sole legal form of worship in England and Wales from Whit Sunday 1549, was the first to set out the liturgy of the *Church of England. Written in English and largely the work of Archbishop Cranmer, it was revised in 1552, 1559, and by James I. The final text is that of 1662.

Book of Hours. A personal devotional book for the rich medieval laity, containing prayers for each of the eight times of prayer of the daily liturgy. They were often beautifully illuminated. See John Harthan, *Books of Hours and Their Owners* (1977).

booksellers. London was the early centre of the book trade. The publisher-booksellers were especially found in St Paul's Churchyard and on London Bridge. They had thousands of books in their warehouses, ranging from substantial theological, historical, and literary works down to *chapbooks and *ballads. See Margaret Spufford, *Small Books and Pleasant Histories: Popular Fiction and Its Readership in Seventeenth-Century England* (1981). The links between the capital and the provinces are shown in the case of the Simmons family, who moved from Kidderminster to London before the *Civil War. They are known to have published 250 titles between 1635 and 1724, including the works of John Milton and Richard Baxter. By 1687 Nevill Simmons had left London to establish a business as a stationer and bookseller in the Market Place at Sheffield, specializing in *Nonconformist literature, and publishing the sermons of local preachers. In 1692 he held an auction at a nearby inn of 'Excellent English and Latin Books, On most Subjects', ranging from substantial theological works to twopenny and fourpenny sermons. He held similar sales in Leeds and York and had a government licence to hawk his books in the neighbouring villages. It has been estimated that by 1700 about 200 booksellers were operating from 50 different towns. By the mid-1740s this number had grown to 381 booksellers in 174 towns. See J. Feather, *The Provincial Book Trade in Eighteenth-Century England* (1985).

boon work. A manorial duty to do such seasonal work as ploughing and harvesting. The original sense of the word was 'favour', but such tasks became compulsory.

Booth, Charles (1840–1916). English social reformer, whose *Labour of the People in London* (1903) was the forerunner of the modern social survey.

bordar. A term frequently found in the *Domesday Book, meaning a smallholder who farmed *assarted land on the edge of settlements.

Border marriage. Lord Hardwicke's *Marriage Act, which came into force in 1754, made marriages in England and Wales legal only if they were performed in a building licensed for that purpose. Runaway couples therefore crossed the border into Scotland, where marriage could take place by mere consent, in the presence of witnesses, without even a priest. Gretna Green is the best-known of these places, but businesses whose sole purpose it was to perform such ceremonies were set up by men in various border settlements, including Alison's Toll Bar, Lamberton Toll Bar, Sark Toll Bar,

Springfield, and Coldstream. Some of the marriage registers of these places have survived. See G. S. Chrichton, 'Irregular Border Marriages', *The Genealogists Magazine*, 20/8 (1981).

Lord Brougham's Marriage Act (1856) made it necessary to obtain a licence to marry if neither partner had been resident in the proposed place of marriage during the preceding 21 days. From 1878 marriages in Scotland could be performed only in buildings licensed for that purpose. Marriage by consent was abolished in 1940.

borough. Many English boroughs were recorded as such in the *Domesday Book. The major medieval towns and cities obtained royal *charters which granted or confirmed their privileges. These are kept at the *Public Record Office, mostly in the *Charter rolls or *Patent rolls. They have been listed in A. Ballard, *British Borough Charters, 1042–1216* (1913), J. Tait, *British Borough Charters, 1216–1307* (1923), and M. Weinbaum, *British Borough Charters, 1307–1660* (1943). (For Scotland see BURGH.) Some of the chartered towns did not prosper and remained small settlements or even disappeared completely. See Susan Reynolds, *An Introduction to the History of English Medieval Towns* (1975), and Colin Platt, *The English Medieval Town* (1976). (See also MEDIEVAL NEW TOWNS.) As an introduction to the early modern period, see Peter Clark and Paul Slack, *English Towns in Transition, 1500–1700* (1976). Many old boroughs took the precaution of renewing their charters during the reigns of Charles II and James II. A list of charters granted between 1680 and 1688 is published in the *Historical Manuscripts Commission, Twelfth Report*, appendix, part VI (1889).

A great number of towns were *seigneurial boroughs, which had a certain amount of independence from their *lord of the manor, but which did not have corporate status. The leading townsmen were called *burgesses, but they administered their affairs through an institution (often a *guild) which was recognized by the lord, but which did not have the same powers as a corporation. The lord of the manor usually retained his manorial courts. For example, Chesterfield was a seigneurial borough from an unknown date in the 12th century; the town's privileges were based on charters granted by its lords in 1204, 1232, and 1294, but it did not become a corporation until 1598. The move to complete independence was delayed much longer in Sheffield, whose burgesses had received a charter from their lord in 1297, but who did not achieve corporate status until 1843.

The *municipal corporations which were reformed in 1835 and 1882 can claim continuity from medieval institutions, but their previous experience of local government was varied.

The mayor of a corporation was normally the *ex officio* *Justice of the Peace for the borough. The mayor and corporation were sometimes lords of the manor and usually had jurisdiction over *markets and fairs. Borough records, therefore, are often not confined to minutes of corporation meetings, orders, by-laws, lists of admissions to the corporation and mayoralty, etc., but contain *deeds to land, the records of the *quarter sessions, and a great deal of information about the sites of markets and fairs and the attempts to regulate the commercial activities there. (See also FREEMAN ROLLS.) Many towns have published some of their records (which are now housed in the appropriate local *record office). See, for example, M. D. Harris (ed.), *The Coventry Leet Book, 1420–1555* (4 vols., 1907–13), and G. A. Chinnery (ed.), *Records of the Borough of Leicester*, vi: *The Chamberlains' Accounts, 1688–1835* (1967). See also C. Gross, *A Bibliography of British Municipal History including Guilds and Parliamentary Representation* (1897), and G. H. Martin and S. McIntyre, *A Bibliography of British and Irish Municipal History*, i: *General Works* (1972).

Corporate towns had the right to elect Members of Parliament. Where a borough decayed, e.g. Old Sarum (Wiltshire), the owner of the site retained the right to choose MPs. Such 'rotten' boroughs, together with many 'pocket' boroughs which were under the control of a landowner because the electorate was so restricted in size, were disenfranchised by the Parliamentary Reform Act (1832).

Borough English. The *inheritance custom in certain medieval *boroughs and *manors, notably in the south of England, whereby the youngest son was the heir to his father's lands and tenements.

Borthwick Institute of Historical Research, York. A department of the University of York, specializing in the ecclesiastical history of the province of York, with search facilities (by appointment only) for members of the public in the medieval St Anthony's Hall. The institute houses the diocesan archives, including *wills and *inventories, *parish registers, *bishops' transcripts, *tithe awards, and *ecclesiastical court records. The records of most of the *peculiar jurisdictions within the province of York are also kept there. The parish registers and some other records are on microfilm. See

C. C. Webb, *A Guide to Genealogical Sources in the Borthwick Institute of Historical Research* (1983), and C. C. Webb, *A Guide to Parish Records in the Borthwick Institute of Historical Research* (1987).

bote. The common right to take timber from the manorial wastes in order to repair houses, hedges, or fences, or for firewood and the making of tools.

bothy. A hut or cottage in Ireland or Scotland with stone or turf walls and roofs, used as a summer residence by farmers pasturing their livestock or as a one-roomed communal dwelling for servants or other workmen.

boundaries. The study of boundaries involves a combination of fieldwork and documentary research. Old maps, place-names such as Meersbrook, Anglo-Saxon and medieval *charters, law suits, and *perambulations need to be compared with the visual evidence in the form of boundary stones, wells, watercourses, embankments, etc. See Maurice Beresford, *History on the Ground* (1957) and Angus Winchester, *Discovering Parish Boundaries* (1990). Wherever possible, boundaries were marked by natural features, especially watercourses. Natural boulders were inscribed with *crosses, the initials of the *lord of the manor, or those of the name of the *township, a practice that survived from the Middle Ages into the 19th century. Some stones have been marked also by later graffiti, and others have been used as *Ordnance Survey *bench marks. Where no natural boulders were available, upright stones or poles were erected. Many different boundaries were marked in this way: *parish; township, manor, or other estate; divisions of woodland, etc. Before large-scale maps became available in the 19th century, such stones were particularly necessary in moorland areas, particularly in parts which were featureless. The grazing and other rights were often disputed between townships, so markers and regular perambulations were needed to preserve rights and counter the claims of others. Sometimes, the inscriptions on boundary stones have been defaced to challenge the claim of a rival.

Stanage Pole, which divides Yorkshire and Derbyshire, consists of a wooden pole, which has been replaced from time to time, set in a natural boulder which is marked by graffiti going back to the 17th century. It served many purposes, for it also divided the *lordship and parish of Sheffield from those of Hathersage, separated the province of York from that of

Canterbury, and thus the *diocese of York from that of Lichfield and Coventry, and in earlier times acted as the boundary between *Northumbria and *Mercia. It stands on the skyline in the midst of *moors and can be seen for miles around. The relatively undisturbed character of moors means that many old boundary stones survive there, though many of them are now hard to find. Boundary stones are notoriously difficult to date. Even if they have a date inscribed, it may not be that of the year in which the stone was erected but may have been cut during a *Rogationtide perambulation or on some other occasion. Documentary references to stones with particular names, e.g. Lady Cross, help with the date, though sometimes a new stone has replaced the original, and in other cases the stone has acquired a new name. Some of the medieval stones are set in stone bases whose edges have been chamfered; many no longer resemble a cross but may well have done so before the *Reformation. Some boundary stones have a dual purpose as waymarkers.

The antiquity of certain boundaries has been a matter of considerable interest. Some appear to go back to prehistoric times. See Desmond Bonney, 'Early Boundaries in Wessex' in P. J. Fowler (ed.), *Archaeology and the Landscape* (1972), Andrew Fleming, *The Dartmoor Reaves* (1988), and C. H. E. Jean Le Patourel, Moira H. Long, and May F. Pickles, *Yorkshire Boundaries* (1993). Prehistoric linear earthworks can sometimes be shown to be ancient boundaries. Certain *Roman roads act as boundaries between townships for many miles, but other Roman roads are ignored by boundaries. May Pickles has shown that the topography and underlying geology of the Roman roads (many of which were older roads taken over by the Romans) are of crucial importance in determining whether they were used as lengthy boundaries. Those which act as watersheds and divide resources because they form natural ridges, however slight, are the ones that have served as boundaries from very early times.

See also DETACHED PORTION.

bourgeoisie. The prosperous middle class.

Bourne, George (1863–1927). The pen-name of George Sturt of Farnham (Surrey), author of *The Bettesworth Book* (1901), *Memoirs of a Surrey Labourer* (1907), *Change in the Village* (1912), *The Wheelwright's Shop* (1923), and other sympathetic accounts of the lives, work, and thoughts of the people of his village during a period of profound change.

bovate. An oxgang, one-eighth of a ploughland or *carucate, varying in size from 10 to 18 *acres according to the condition of the land.

Bowen, Emanuel. 'Engraver of Maps' for both George II of Great Britain and Louis XV of France. With Thomas Kitchin, he produced some of the finest county maps of the 18th century, between 1750 and 1780. These were unusual in devoting a great deal of space to a descriptive text in the form of historical notes. His *Complete System of Geography* (1744–7), illustrated with 70 maps, the *Complete Atlas or Distinct Views of the Known World* (1752), which had 68 maps, and *The Royal English Atlas* (1762, and later editions), with 44 maps, were his major works.

Boyd's Marriage Index. Percival Boyd's compilation of marriage entries in English *parish registers for 16 counties from the beginning of registration in 1538 up to the year 1837. The entries are copied mainly from printed registers and the coverage is not complete. The index may be consulted at the Society of *Genealogists (which has published a *Key*) or at the *Guildhall Library, London.

The counties included in the index are as follows: (the number of parishes covered, at least in part, is given in brackets): Cambridgeshire (169), Cornwall (202), Cumberland (34), Derbyshire (80), Devon (169), Durham (72), Essex (374), Gloucestershire (121), Lancashire (101), London and Middlesex (160), Norfolk (146), Northumberland (84), Shropshire (125), Somerset (120), Suffolk (489), Yorkshire (174).

brass, memorial. The practice of commemorating individuals by a figure and inscription on a flat metal plate fixed to the floor or wall of a church began in West Germany and the Low Countries in the 13th century. About 7,500 memorial brasses survive in England alone, more than in any other country. The earliest English brasses were imported from Flanders, but by the 14th century workshops had been set up in London, Norwich, and York. Purchasers normally chose from a series of standard designs, to which was added a personal inscription; but a few were special commissions to the customer's specifications. Brasses were not intended to be accurate portraits. The use of figures declined in the late 16th century in favour of armorial designs or inscriptions. The fashion disappeared during the second half of the 17th century but was revived in the 19th century as part of a renewed interest in the Middle Ages. See J. Coales (ed.), *The Earliest

English Brasses, 1270–1350 (1987), and M. Norris, *Monumental Brasses: The Craft* (1978).

brass bands. Most of the famous brass bands are or were associated with *factories or collieries, especially in the North of England, e.g. Black Dyke Mills or Grimethorpe Colliery. Brass bands were formed in rural areas in the later 19th century. In *Progress in Pudsey* (1887, 1978 reprint), Joseph Lawson (born 1821) described the Pudsey Old Reed Band of his childhood and youth in the West Riding. The band played clarinets, trumpets, bugles, trombones, French horns, brass horns, serpents, bassoons, fifes, and big drum, but their performance was 'child's play' compared with the standards of later bands.

brass-making. Most brass used in Britain before the 18th century was imported, despite the efforts of the Mineral and Battery Company, which had been granted a monopoly in 1567 to use Coniston *copper and Somerset zinc. From the 16th century onwards decorated brass guns were made in London and nearby in Kent, and brass *wire was used for *pin-making. Bristol became the centre of production of brass following the foundation of Baptist Mills in 1702; William Champion's works and housing at Warnley were erected from 1740 onwards. Another *water-powered site that has been investigated is that at Holywell (Flintshire), established in 1765.

breckland, brecks. That part of west Norfolk and Suffolk which is characterized by *heaths and light sands in the driest part of the British Isles. The term 'Breckland' was coined by a journalist in 1894, but 'breck' was a medieval term for a tract of land which was cultivated for a few years at a time and left for several years to recover. The open heaths, sheepwalks, and rabbit *warrens were managed in a way that enabled farmers to obtain a satisfactory living. See Mark Bailey, *A Marginal Economy? East Anglian Breckland in the Later Middle Ages* (1989). Since the 1920s the character of the area has been altered by the large coniferous plantations of the Forestry Commission.

breweries. The history of the brewing industry is covered in two volumes: Peter Mathias, *The Brewing Industry in England, 1700–1830* (1959), and T. R. Gourvish and R. G. Wilson, *The British Brewing Industry, 1830–1980* (1994). For Scotland and Ireland see I. Donnachie, *A History of the Brewing Industry in Scotland* (1979), and P. Lynch and J. Vaizey, *Guinness's Brewery in the Irish Economy, 1759–1876* (1960).

The early history of brewing was much associated with immigrants from the Low Countries, especially to London. The rise of the 'common brewery', as the large production unit was known in order to distinguish it from the numerous domestic breweries, began in the 18th century. By 1830 production of beer in London, Liverpool, Edinburgh, and Norwich was almost entirely in the hands of common brewers, but in the midlands, Manchester, and the West Riding of Yorkshire the publican-brewer was dominant. Nation-wide, private and publican-brewing accounted for half the production of beer. The Beer Act (1830) created a free trade in the sale of beer. *Inns, taverns, and *alehouses (which possessed no spirit licence) were still controlled by magistrates, but now a fourth type of public house—the beer house—came on the scene. Any householder who paid rates could apply for a two-guinea excise licence to brew and sell beer on his premises. Within eight years almost 46,000 beer houses were added to the stock of 51,000 licensed premises. The centuries-old industry was shaken up. Alarm at the 'evils of drink' made teetotalism a national issue from the 1840s onwards. (See TEMPERANCE MOVEMENT, and B. Harrison, *Drink and the Victorians* (1971).)

London was the great focus of commercial brewing, but several businesses that were to become of national importance were based in the provinces. The rise of Burton-upon-Trent as a brewing centre was spectacular; see C. C. Owen, *The Development of Industry in Burton-upon-Trent* (1978). Changing fashions meant that brewers had to be adaptable. For example, between 1830 and 1860 the London market, which traditionally favoured the drinking of porter, turned increasingly to the consumption of mild ales. The great Victorian breweries existed alongside thousands of small firms, but in the second half of the 20th century the trade became increasingly concentrated in the hands of half a dozen large companies. For examples of the histories of individual firms see Richard G. Wilson, *Greene King: A Business and Family History* (1983), and John Chartres, 'Joshua Tetley and Sons, 1890s to 1990s: A Century in the Tied Trade' in John Chartres and Katrina Honeyman (eds.), *Leeds City Business, 1893–1993* (1993), ch. 5. See also L. Richmond and A. Tuton (eds.), *The Brewing Industry: A Guide to Historical Records* (1990).

brewster session. A special meeting of the *quarter sessions at which *Justices of the Peace licensed the keepers of *inns and *alehouses. The parish *constable had to provide lists of the names of applicants for licences. The names of inns and alehouses are not recorded.

brick was much used by the Romans, whose forts and villas were quarried by later builders, e.g. for many of the medieval churches of Essex. It was once thought that the art of brick-making was unknown to the *Anglo-Saxons, but detailed investigations of major churches, notably Brixworth (Northamptonshire), have revised that view. Brick was not widely used by the Normans, though examples of 12th-century brickwork are known at Polstead Church and Little Coggeshall Priory (Essex). The example of the Low Countries led builders in East Yorkshire to use brick extensively in the 14th century for the *town walls and gates of Hull and Beverley, and the large church of Holy Trinity, Hull. Brick became a prestigious building material in the 15th century, particularly in the Humber basin and other parts of eastern England where no local *building stone was available, and sometimes further west because of its rarity value. It was used for *colleges such as Eton (Buckinghamshire), *castles such as Tattershall (Lincolnshire) and Herstmonceux (Sussex), gate-towers such as Oxburgh Hall (Norfolk), and bishops' *palaces such as Bishopthorpe (Yorkshire). *Perpendicular churches in eastern England used brick extensively, particularly for new towers and porches.

Brick was much favoured for the great houses of the Tudor period, including Hampton Court Palace, Layer Marney (Essex), and places as far west as Compton Wynyates (Warwickshire). Fantastic brick chimney-stacks became popular, even in smaller houses. During the 17th century curved and stepped Dutch gables became fashionable in East Anglia and the south-east. Great country houses such as Hatfield (Hertfordshire) and Blickling (Norfolk) were built mostly in brick. The fashion spread down the social scale during the 17th century, as *yeomen and *husbandmen in districts devoid of suitable stone rebuilt their old *timber-framed houses in brick, often with *pantile roofs. The Great Fire of London (1666), and provincial fires in towns such as Warwick and Blandford Forum (Dorset), convinced urban authorities that brick was safer than wood. Brick became a very fashionable material for the houses and public buildings of Georgian towns. On the stone belts brick remained unusual well into the 18th century; houses which chose this material often got the name of Red House because they were so distinct.

Bricks were almost invariably made close to the building site. Their variety of colours arises not just from the nature of the local clays but from the firing process that was adopted. Medieval brick-makers knew how to fire bricks to produce a black finish which could then be used to pick out patterns, such as the large St Andrew's crosses on the tower and porch of St Andrew's Church, Sandon (Essex). See Alec Clifton-Taylor, *The Pattern of English Building* (1972), ch. 9, Maurice Barley, *Houses and History* (1986), Jane A. Wight, *Brick Building in England* (1972), and R. W. Brunskill and A. Clifton-Taylor, *English Brickwork* (1977). The British Brick Society publishes new information in its bulletin. (See also BONDING.)

Before the 19th century, brick buildings harmonized with the local landscape. The *canals, and then (especially) the *railways, enabled mass-produced, machine-made bricks of regular size to be transported from large brickfields e.g. in Bedfordshire to all parts of Britain. Row upon row of terraced houses, built of standard bricks, and usually roofed with equally regular Welsh blue *slates, were monotonously different from the houses built with handmade bricks, whose imperfections added to their beauty; but they were economical and therefore much favoured, even by middle-class owners who faced the fronts of their houses with stone or *stucco.

Bridewell. A *house of correction for prisoners, originally *vagabonds who were set to hard labour. It was named after Bride Well in London, where Henry VIII had a *lodging, which was given by Edward VI to the City and made into a house of correction in 1552. By the 1630s every county in England and Wales had a similar institution for petty offenders.

bridges. A large number of medieval bridges survive. They can be recognized by their pointed, ribbed arches, but are difficult to date precisely. Sometimes they can be recognized only from underneath, for they have been partly rebuilt and widened. They are marked on Christopher *Saxton's county maps of the 1570s. These medieval bridges were built by local authorities, such as *boroughs or *manors, or by monastic institutions or private individuals. In the Middle Ages they normally had a chapel attached, for the saying of a prayer for safe delivery on a journey and for the paying of what amounted to a toll. These chapels were often placed on the bridge itself but were sometimes built on one of the banks. They were dissolved as *chantry chapels in 1547, but many were converted to other purposes, such as small *almshouses, lock-ups, or warehouses. The only survivors are at Rotherham and Wakefield

(Yorkshire), St Ives (Huntingdonshire), Bradford-upon-Avon (Wiltshire), and Derby. The bridge at Cromford (Derbyshire) has a ruined chapel on an adjoining bank; the bridge (which replaced an earlier ford, judging by the place-name), has pointed arches on its downstream side, but round arches upstream from when it was widened. Medieval bridges were rarely more than 12 to 15 feet wide, and most have been widened to cater for an increased volume of traffic in later centuries. The widening almost invariably took place on the upstream side; straight joints which reveal the extent of the widening can usually be seen underneath the bridge. Lady's Bridge, Sheffield, has a history that is typical of many. The original wooden bridge was replaced in 1486, when William Hill, mason, contracted with the townsmen to build a stone bridge, whose pointed, ribbed arches can still be seen underneath, despite the fact that the bridge has been considerably widened on four occasions to cater for the present heavy traffic. The chapel of 'Our Blessed Lady of the Bridge', which stood on the southern bank, survived until 1767, having been used after its dissolution as an almshouse for poor widows and then as a wool warehouse.

During the 16th and 17th centuries the *Justices of the Peace took over responsibility for the major bridges, which were designated 'county bridges'. *Quarter sessions records note the money spent on repairing them from time to time. They also note the smaller 'packhorse bridges' which were in need of repair, when local overseers of the *highways were admonished for not performing their duty. Packhorse bridges are not as old as the larger 'county bridges'. They date from the second half of the 17th century and the first half of the 18th. A number of contracts survive in local *record offices (in miscellaneous collections), which show that old wooden bridges were replaced by stone structures during this period. They were sometimes built by private individuals, but more often were the responsibility of a *parish or *township, or the joint responsibility of such bodies where they crossed boundary streams. (See PACKHORSES.) Place-name references from the Middle Ages often show that bridges crossed streams or rivers at the point where a bridge now stands, but they do not help to date the present structure. The simplicity of the design of packhorse bridges should not confuse the investigator into thinking that such structures are medieval. Even some of the *clapper bridges on Dartmoor are no older than the 18th or 19th centuries.

Many packhorse bridges were demolished when roads were *turnpiked in the 18th and early 19th centuries, to be replaced by bridges that were wide enough to take wheeled vehicles. Packhorse bridges survive only on the minor routes or near a later diversion. Some of the most beautiful 'county bridges' date from this period. For a study which relates bridges to the local economy and other features of the old transport system, see David Hey, *Packmen, Carriers and Packhorse Roads: Trade and Communications in North Derbyshire and South Yorkshire* (1980).

bridleway. A right of way for those travelling on horseback, as distinct from a footpath.

brief, church. A royal mandate authorizing a collection for some deserving cause, addressed to the incumbent and churchwardens of a parish and read from the pulpit. The collection was made at the end of the service by the *parish clerk, who handed the money to the official travelling collector. The brief was endorsed with the amount raised and the sum entered in the *parish register or *churchwarden's account.

Britain, Great. The whole island, including England, Wales, and Scotland. The term was used by the early *antiquarians only in a historical context, with particular reference to *Roman Britain (Latin *Britannia*). Scotland was referred to as North Britain. Upon the accession of James I (James VI of Scotland) in 1603 he was proclaimed 'King of Great Britain'. The two kingdoms were united as Great Britain in 1707. In 1801 the *United Kingdom of Great Britain and Ireland was formed. Since 1922 the Irish part of the UK has consisted only of Northern Ireland.

British Agricultural History Society. The society was founded in 1953 to promote the study of all aspects of the history of the countryside by holding conferences and publishing *The *Agricultural History Review* twice yearly from the *Rural History Centre, University of Reading, Reading RG6 2AG.

British Association for Local History. The society which was founded in 1982 to promote the interests of local historians at national level continued the work of the *Standing Conference for Local History. It organizes conferences in various parts of Britain and publishes *The *Local Historian*, handbooks, and *Local History News*, which contains news of local societies, *record offices, libraries, *museums, and issues that concern local historians. It is based at Shopwyke Manor Barn, Chichester, PO20 6BG.

British Library. A group of libraries that was formed in 1973 out of a merger of the national lending, patent and science reference libraries with the collections of the printed-book and manuscript departments of the British Museum. The latter collections are the two largest of their kind in the British Isles; they have always been freely accessible to anyone who can show reasonable need (bringing with them proof of identity and two passport-size colour photographs, and, for the Department of Manuscripts, a letter of recommendation at their first visit). The reading rooms will be relocated in a new building beside St Pancras railway station, London, but for the present they remain in the British Museum building in Bloomsbury. The collections of the former National Lending Library now form part of the British Library's stock of books that is housed at Boston Spa in Yorkshire but is available through the inter-library loans system. Yet a further British Library resource is the National Sound Archive, which incorporates the BBC Sound Archive and has about two million items. The NSA is computerizing its catalogues, so they will be searchable by locality (county or place), dialect, and subject.

The manuscript collection includes about 75,000 Additional Manuscripts and a similar number of Additional Charters. For the local historian its greatest riches, however, are perhaps the Cotton and Harleian collections: the former comprises about 1,000 volumes, including many medieval *chronicles and more than 150 medieval *cartularies, collected by Sir Robert Cotton (d. 1631); while the 7,600 Harleian manuscripts, which were collected by Robert Harley (d. 1724) and his son Edward (d. 1741), successive earls of Oxford, include many heraldic volumes besides more chronicles, cartularies, and a wide range of historical and other texts. Until the setting up of county *record offices, the Department of Manuscripts actively collected manuscripts and charters that were primarily of local interest, while it was also building up its matchless holdings of political and literary papers. Its various published catalogues are listed in M. A. E. Nickson, *The British Library: Guide to the Catalogues and Indexes of the Department of Manuscripts*, 2nd edn. (1982).

For the early stages of an enquiry involving manuscripts, the most useful starting-point is likely to be the amalgamated index to persons and places, the *Index of Manuscripts in the British Library*, 10 vols. (1984–6), formed by bringing together into one sequence the various indexes to all the published catalogues of manuscripts acquired down to 1950, including the two volumes of the *Index to the Charters and Rolls in the Department of Manuscripts, British Museum* (2 vols., 1900, 1912). A subject-based approach, such as to *heraldry, is best begun through the multi-volume Class Catalogue (comprising catalogue descriptions, cut up and mounted on a subject basis), of which the sole copy is in the Department's reading room, the Students' Room. The Class Catalogue has not been added to since about 1950, but its topographical volumes (59–62) may also still be found useful (despite the availability of the much fuller *Index of Manuscripts*) for a county-by-county or intra-county search.

The collections of the former Department of Printed Books can be accessed via catalogues in printed form, compact disk, or on-line computer (the latter gradually becoming available in universities through JANET). They comprise about 12 million volumes, and include various English royal libraries (those of the monarchs down to 1757, as well as that formed by George III), and other special collections rich in early materials. Their greatness lies in the fullness of the holdings of British works, thanks to the effective working of the Copyright Acts (especially those of 1775, 1814, and 1842), which required the British Museum to be given one free copy of every book published in the British Isles, combined with what has at times been a substantial annual expenditure on privately printed, antiquarian, and other books that had escaped the copyright net. Other than by searching for a particular author, title, or place-name, the researcher is likely to find it most effective to master the different tricks of catalogue searching—by the most fruitful keyword combinations, on the computer, or through the printed (latterly, also microfiche) subject catalogues, as well as through the printed author / title catalogue, *British Library General Catalogue of Printed Books to 1975*, 366 vols. (1979–88), and subsequent continuations. For genealogical enquiries, guidance is given in the Library's free pamphlet, Reader Guide no. 10, *British Family History: Printed Sources in the Department of Printed Books*, comp. Mary S. Hurworth (1981).

Among the printed-book collections is that of official publications, which has its own reading room in the British Museum building. This contains an exceptionally full set of all British official publications—notably the HMSO's Command Papers and printed parliamentary bills and statutes, including the various governmental commission reports and the like that are often known as *blue books.

The map library has been a separate unit since 1867, and has its own reading room: it contains the fullest sets in existence of *Ordnance Survey and other published maps of the British Isles (these having come within the scope of the copyright legislation), as well as a major collection of early printed maps. Useful introductions are the Library's free pamphlet, *The Map Collections of the British Library* (1989, revised 1993), and the entry on the Map Library in Helen Wallis and Anita McConnell (eds.), *Historians' Guide to Early British Maps. A Guide to the Location of pre-1900 Maps of the British Isles preserved in the United Kingdom and Ireland* (Royal Historical Society, Guides and Handbooks, no. 18, 1994), 111–14. Manuscript maps have always been held in the Department of Manuscripts, with the two exceptions of the maps in the King's Topographical Collection and maps preparatory to the English Ordnance Survey and to other printed maps. The department's accessions down to 1841 were described by Sir F. Madden, *Catalogue of the Manuscript Maps, Charts, and Plans, and of the Topographical Drawings in the British Museum*, 3 vols. (1844–61); and summarized by the complete and up-to-date listing by Tony Campbell, 'Indexes to Material of Cartographic Interest in the Department of Manuscripts and to Manuscript Cartographic Items elsewhere in the British Library', 3 vols. (1992; not printed, but available in the Map Room and in the Students' Room of the Department of Manuscripts). The Map Library's printed materials down to 1974 are catalogued in *The British Museum: Catalogue of Printed Maps, Charts and Plans . . . to 1964*, 15 vols. (1967) and supplement, 1965–74 (1978); since then, they have been catalogued on microfiche and computer (available on-line and on disk).

*Topographical drawings and prints are not necessarily easy to locate within the British Museum building. Original drawings and views have mostly gone to the Department of Manuscripts since 1845 (when the then Keeper of Manuscripts persuaded the Trustees of the British Museum that all drawings of documentary rather than artistic interest belonged to his department); they are catalogued and indexed in the same way as the rest of that department's holdings. For overviews of the most important groups of drawings in the department, such as those by S. H. Grimm (d. 1794), John Carter (d. 1817), the Buckler family (principally John Buckler, d. 1851, and his son John Chessell

Buckler, d. 1894), and Edward Blore (d. 1879), see C. E. Wright, 'Topographical Drawing in the Department of Manuscripts, British Museum', *Archives*, 3 (1957–8), and M. W. Barley, *A Guide to British Topographical Collections* (Council for British Archaeology, 1974). Sir F. Madden's *Catalogue of Manuscript Maps*, mentioned above, remains useful, not least because it covers material in the Map Room and the Museum's Print Room as well as in the Department of Manuscripts; see the 'Explanation of the references used', in vol. 3, pp. vii–ix.

No department of the British Museum was ever outstanding in its holding of topographical prints. If these were issued with a printed title-page, they were counted as printed books, and were placed in that department. In that case, of course, the individual prints would never be catalogued. There is a considerable number of topographical prints in the Department of Prints and Drawings, which remains part of the British Museum: these are mostly arranged by artist, not location, and there is no overall topographical index. There is, however, an admirable introductory guide: Antony Griffiths and Reginald Williams, *The Department of Prints and Drawings in the British Museum: User's Guide* (1987). Topographical prints in the Map Library as well as some in the former Department of Printed Books are included in the *Catalogue of Printed Maps*.

Newspapers are divided between the former Department of Printed Books' collections in Bloomsbury and a separate reading room and store at Colindale, in Hendon, north-west London; only those published before 1801 are at Bloomsbury (and listed among Periodical Publications in the main *British Library Catalogue to 1975*). English newspapers of all dates, and in whatever libraries, are now most conveniently located in either of the complementary but overlapping series that is in course of publication by the British Library: the Newsplan series, of *Reports of the Newsplan Project* (volumes for the East Midlands, West Midlands, North Western Region, Yorkshire & Humberside, and Northern Region so far published since 1989), or the more detailed *Bibliography of British Newspapers* (Cornwall & Devon, Derbyshire, Durham & Northumberland, Kent, and Nottinghamshire, published since 1982).

Seal impressions in the Department of Manuscripts were carefully described by W. de G. Birch, *Catalogue of Seals in the Department of Manuscripts in the British Museum*, 6 vols. (1887–99); this is arranged on a systematic basis, but for personal seals it is generally necessary to turn to the unprinted Index of Seals, 3 series in 6 volumes, covering accessions down to 1910, and kept in the Department's Students' Room, pressmark 29e. The metal (or, just occasionally, bone or ivory) matrices from which seals were cast are kept in the British Museum's Department of Medieval and Later Antiquities: see A. B. Tonnochy, *Catalogue of British Seal-Dies in the British Museum* (1952).

The librarian's dream of a single catalogue for all the collections of the British Library is being brought nearer to reality by the computerization of the existing printed catalogues. To imagine that this would result in an evenness of treatment of the holdings would be an illusion, however, since the various catalogues have been issued over a period of more than two centuries. For practical, researching purposes it will remain best to bear in mind the separate history of each of the multifarious collections, for it is only in that way that their strengths and weaknesses can be assessed. Help may be found in such books as A. J. K. Esdaile's *The British Museum Library: A Short History and Survey* (1946), or Edward Miller's *That Noble Cabinet: A History of the British Museum* (1973).　　　N. L. RAMSAY

British Record Society. Founded in 1888 as the Index Society, it publishes indexes of historical records, such as *Chancery proceedings, *inquisitions post mortem, *wills, and marriage licences. See G. H. Martin and Peter Spufford (eds.), *The Records of the Nation: The Public Record Office, 1838–1988; The British Record Society, 1888–1988* (1990).

broadcasting (agricultural). The casting of seed by hand from a basket, alternatively to the right and to the left, an ancient method of sowing which lasted in some districts into the 20th century.

broadcloth. A fine woollen cloth of the Middle Ages and early modern period.

broadside. A printed, popular *ballad of the 16th to the 19th century. See, for instance, Peter Carnell (ed.), *Broadside Ballads and Song-Sheets from the Hewins Mss Collection in Sheffield University Library* (1987).

Bronze Age. The prehistoric era between the *Stone Age and the *Iron Age, lasting from c.2,500 BC to c.800 BC. This was the era of the great *henge monuments. See, for example, Barry Cunliffe, *Wessex to A.D. 1000* (1993), chs. 3 and 4.

brother. The term was often used to mean a brother-in-law.

Brown, 'Capability'. Lancelot Brown (1716–83), the most famous landscape gardener of the 18th century and the designer of numerous schemes for British country houses. Brown got his nickname from his habit of saying that an estate looked capable of improvement. He swept away the formal gardens of previous generations and provided instead an open, 'natural' look, with rolling pastures, clumps of mature trees, and wide expanses of water.

Brownists. The earliest *Puritan sect in England, founded in the 1580s by Robert Browne. Members were also known as Separatists (from the *Church of England). They were forerunners of the *Congregationalists or *Independents.

Buck, Samuel and Nathaniel. As a young man, Samuel Buck (1696–1779) was commissioned to draw views of towns and country houses in Yorkshire for an uncompleted project of John Warburton's. His sketchbook of 1719–23 has been published as *Samuel Buck's Yorkshire Sketchbook* (1979). He and his brother Nathaniel later achieved fame through their prints, made over a period of 30 years, which they assembled in their *Antiquities* (2nd edn., 1774). These careful engravings are now a major source for the study of *urban topography and of buildings.

buckwheat. Known alternatively as French wheat, it was grown on barren, sandy ground and was prized as fodder for *pigs and *poultry. The largest acreages devoted to buckwheat from the 16th century onwards were on the sands and *brecklands of East Anglia, where it was grown for feeding *turkeys, *geese, chickens, and *ducks. It was also grown on the Bagshot heaths (Surrey), the Hampshire downlands, and in Essex.

Builder, The. Founded in 1834, this journal contains numerous articles which provide information about public buildings and houses erected in many parts of Britain during the Victorian period. It is particularly useful for the period 1844–83, when George Goodwin was editor.

buildings, domestic. Shelter is a fundamental requirement of human beings and the archaeological evidence for the ways by which this basic need has been met extend far back into the prehistoric period. However, it is only in the centuries following the *Norman Conquest that the house as a standing structure survives in sufficient numbers to enable its three-dimensional history to be written. Wealth and social rank are the major distinguishing features which have shaped the architectural forms taken by buildings with a predominantly domestic function, and these have played a significant part in the historiography of the subject. The study of the house until comparatively recently has been largely the history of the high-status dwelling, strongly influenced by considerations of architectural aesthetics, and mainly written by the landowning classes and their professional advisers. It is only in the twentieth century that the houses lived in by the vast majority of the population have been studied in a systematic and scholarly way, and that the evidence provided by housing in general has been seen to have an importance for social, economic, and cultural history as well as simply for the evolution of particular architectural styles. Accordingly, the country houses belonging to the rich and the powerful will be considered first in this account, if only because the documentation which provides the main material for the history of the house survives in far greater quantities for these houses and their families than it does for dwellings of lower status.

An admirably concise introduction to the architectural sources is provided for England by H. M. Colvin, *English Architectural History: A Guide to the Sources* (2nd edn., 1976), and for Scotland by J. G. Dunbar, 'Source Materials for Scottish Architectural History', *Art Libraries Journal*, 4/3 (1979). The estate papers of landed families are the primary material for the study of the country house. These often contain building accounts and contracts as well as letters, bills, maps, diaries, architectural drawings, and a wide variety of other written material relating to the building and remodelling of the family house and the ancillary buildings that made up the estate. Some builders, with a conscious eye to posterity, left detailed manuscript accounts of their building activities, which provide invaluable evidence for contemporary attitudes and practices. A highly readable example of this is the 'Cursory Notes of Building occasioned by the Repair, or rather Metamorfosis, of an old house in The Country, Reserved for Private Reflection, if not Instruction, to such as succeed in it', compiled by Roger North in 1698 and first published in an edition edited by Howard Colvin and John Newman in 1981 under the shorter title *Of Building*; its value is greatly enhanced by the survival of 13 personal notebooks on architectural matters compiled in the 1660s by Sir

Roger Pratt, published as *The Architecture of Sir Roger Pratt* by R. T. Gunther in 1928. Taken together, the writings of these two cultivated, landed gentlemen give a vivid and complementary picture of the practicalities involved in the building of country houses in the second half of the 17th century which can hardly be matched for any other period.

Both these manuscripts are directly concerned with architecture; but the family histories which were sometimes compiled by descendants working through the documents in the estate muniment room can be an equally rewarding source for the social history of the country house. Alice T. Friedman, in *House and Household in Elizabethan England* (1989), demonstrates how such a history—in this case 'The Account of the Willughby's [*sic*] of Wollaton taken out of the Pedigree, old letters, and old Books of Accounts in my brother Sir Thomas Willoughby's study, Dec A. D. 1702', written by Cassandra Willoughby, Duchess of Chandos—can be used to illuminate, in her own words 'the day-to-day activities, attitudes, and social customs which underlay decisions about the planning of Wollaton Hall and buildings like it'.

Documents like this, originally kept in the muniment rooms of the houses themselves, are now scattered in a wide variety of repositories. Some remain with the families who originally compiled them, others are held by the family solicitors. But, increasingly, the majority of them have been deposited in county and university *record offices and the great national collections in the *British Library and the *Bodleian Library. *Researching the Country House: A Guide for Local Historians* (1992) by A. Elton, B. Harrison, and K. Wark contains a select list of country houses open to the public in England, Wales, Ireland, Northern Ireland, and Scotland with the location of their archives, as well as offering practical advice on other potential sources.

The private bank accounts of the very wealthy can often provide important information on the dates and costs of building works, and help to identify the individual architects and craftsmen involved. Coutts', Drummonds, Glyn Mills, Hoare's, and the Bank of England all have records dating back to the 18th century. *Fire insurance records can also be of assistance in charting the history of houses of a variety of sizes. From the early 18th century major works of alteration or new building were likely to be followed by the prudent owner taking out an insurance policy which would have been marked by the attachment of a company plate to the building. Some companies incorporated the policy number on the plate, and these can be used to refer to the original policy, where this survives. The policy-books of the Sun Fire Office, founded in 1710, for example, are deposited in the *Guildhall Library, London, and contain information on the form and materials of the individual properties as well as the name of the policy-holder and the date that it was taken out.

A major primary source for the study of the high-status house is provided by plans, drawings, and other graphic material. Purely architectural designs are likely to be found together with the family papers as already described, or in a select number of other collections. The Drawings Collection of the *Royal Institute of British Architects is the most important repository, with a published catalogue in 19 volumes which can be accessed through the *Catalogue of the Drawings Collection of the Royal Institute of British Architects: Cumulative Index* (1989). But most of the major national institutions have collections of architectural drawings, and some private bodies, such as Sir John Soane's Museum in London and Worcester College, Oxford, have remarkably rich collections of original designs.

Topographical views have always provided important visual evidence for the history of the house. Their picturesque qualities have meant that some quite humble dwellings have attracted the eye of the artist, but it remains a field that is largely the preserve of the grander house. M. W. Barley published *A Guide to British Topographical Collections* in 1974, and John Harris in *The Artist and the Country House* (1979) embraced the world of fine art with his copiously illustrated history of country-house and garden-view painting in the period between 1540 and 1870. Engraved views of individual country seats in their landscaped settings were popular from the late 17th century onwards, and these were often published in book form. Amongst the most attractive early examples is *Britannia Illustrata or Views of Several of the Queens Palaces also of the Principal Seats of the Nobility and Gentry of Great Britain* drawn by Leonard Knyff and engraved by Jan Kip, which was first published in 1707. A two-volume edition was published in 1715 which included the additional plates that Kip had drawn for Sir Robert Atkyn's *Gloucestershire*. Later examples of the same genre include W. Angus, *The Seats of the Nobility and Gentry in Great Britain and Wales* (1787), W. Watts, *The Seats of the Nobility and Gentry* (1779), and R. Ackerman's *Views of the Country Seats of the Royal Family, Nobility,*

and Gentry in England (1830). John Harris has published *A Country House Index* (2nd edn., 1979) which lists over 2,000 country houses illustrated in 107 books of country views published between 1715 and 1872, together with a list of British country-house guides and catalogues issued between 1726 and 1880. A more comprehensive index to the literature on over 4,000 country houses in England, Wales, Scotland, and Ireland, which covers general books on architecture and county histories as well as guides to individual country houses and sale catalogues, was published in 1986 by Michael Holmes under the title of *The Country House Described*. This is the essential starting-point for researching the history of an individual country house.

Another indispensable index is the monumental *The Literature of British Domestic Architecture, 1715–1842* by John Archer (1985), which catalogues all the printed books containing original designs for residential structures published in the period between Colen Campbell's first volume of *Vitruvius Britannicus* (1715) and the first additional supplement of J. C. Loudon's *Encyclopedia of Cottage, Farm and Villa Architecture* (1842). It is complemented for the earlier period by *British Architectural Books and Writers 1556–1785* (1990) by Eileen Harris, assisted by Nicholas Savage, which deals with books relating to architecture and the building trades published between those dates.

It is not without significance that the earliest known photographic negative is of one of the windows at Lacock Abbey, Wiltshire, taken by its owner, William Henry Fox Talbot, in August 1835. *Photographs have ever since played an important role in documenting the changing appearance and social life of the 19th- and 20th-century country house. *Country House Album* (1989) by Christopher Simon Sykes is one of a number of recent books that have explored the historic potential of this medium to good effect. The National Monuments Record Centre at Swindon holds the largest collection of relevant photographs in England. The collection is fully described in Stephen Croad, 'Architectural Records in the Archive of the Royal Commission on the Historical Monuments of England', *Transactions of the Ancient Monuments Society*, 33 (1989). The equivalent repositories for Scotland and Wales are in Edinburgh and Aberystwyth.

The journals and *diaries of travellers are an entertaining source for contemporary attitudes and comments on domestic architecture. Their observations are usually confined to high-status houses, but the best of them can often provide more general evidence for the quite humble buildings in both town and countryside that they encountered in their journeys. The tradition begins with John *Leland in the 16th century and was continued through subsequent centuries by writers such as Celia *Fiennes, Daniel *Defoe, and Lord *Torrington. *The Discovery of Britain* (1964) by Esther Moir provides the best introduction to this category of evidence. The diaries and reminiscences of James Lees-Milne, who represented the National Trust when they were acquiring the bulk of their country-house estate in the 1940s and 1950s, were published too late to be included in her compendium, but they offer a vivid account of the declining years of the traditional country-house way of life. *Another Self* was published in 1970, *Ancestral Voices* in 1975, *Prophesying Peace* in 1977, and the sequence was concluded with *Caves of Ice*, published in 1983. Works of fiction, too, can offer perceptive insights to the mores of country house society, and novelists from Jane Austen to Aldous Huxley, Evelyn Waugh, and Kazuo Ishiguro should properly be considered as primary sources.

The secondary literature on the high-status house is vast and can be treated only in a perfunctory manner here. Until relatively recently, much of it was written by architects or art historians, and concentrated on developments in architectural style which reflected contemporary perceptions of aesthetic value, often with an underlying polemical message for current practice. Thus the needs of the *Gothic Revival in the 19th century prompted the publication of *Domestic Architecture of the Middle Ages* by T. Hudson Turner and J. H. Parker in four volumes between 1851 and 1859, and Joseph Nash's *The Mansions of England in the Olden Time* (3 vols., 1839–49) stimulated a revival in Elizabethan design. In Scotland a similar interest in the revival of the *tower house was fostered by the publication of the magisterial volumes on *The Castellated and Domestic Architecture of Scotland* (1887–92) by D. MacGibbson and T. Ross. The weekly magazine *Country Life*, which commenced publication in January 1897, promoted the architecture of Wren and the 18th century through its advocacy of the designs of Edwin Lutyens and the interests of its staff writers, particularly Christopher Hussey. It set new standards of architectural scholarship in its articles on individual houses, and its annual cumulative index provides an essential gazetteer to the study of the country house. For the first 60 years of its existence *Country Life* also functioned as a

publishing house, and the two major series of books on the country house that it issued are a good indication of changing attitudes to the study of the subject in the present century. Under the general title of *English Homes* it published 10 volumes (1921–37), written by H. Avray Tipping and covering the period between 1066 and 1820, which were largely descriptive and lavishly presented in a format appropriate to the adornment of a gentleman's library. The second series, called *English Country Houses*, reflected the more seriously historical approach which had developed in the period after the Second World War and, although some of the details have been challenged by subsequent research, the individual volumes still offer a convenient summary of the architectural development of the post-medieval English country house. Starting with *Caroline, 1625–1685* by Oliver Hill and John Cornforth (1966), the chronological sequence continues with *Baroque, 1685–1715* (James Lees-Milne, 1970), and concludes with three volumes by Christopher Hussey on *Early Georgian, 1715–1760* (revised edn., 1965), *Mid-Georgian, 1760–1800* (revised edn., 1963), and *Late Georgian, 1800–1840* (1958). The spirit of the series was continued with different publishers to include *The Victorian Country House* (revised edn., 1979) by Mark Girouard, and *The Last Country Houses* (1982) by Clive Aslet, with a postscript by John Martin Robinson called *The Latest Country Houses* (1984), which brings the story into the post-war period. Complementing this series for the earlier period is Margaret Wood's *The English Mediaeval House* (1965), and mention must be made of John Summerson's *Architecture in Britain, 1530–1830* (9th edn., 1993), in which the country house plays a prominent role.

All of these books are essentially concerned with the architecture of the country house, but in recent years the study of the subject has been widened to consider its social and cultural context. The pioneering *Life in the English Country House* (1978) by Mark Girouard has profoundly changed the way in which historians view these monuments to privilege and power, and *The Servants' Hall* by Merlin Waterson (1980) has indicated the need to rescue the contribution of the working household for a proper understanding of the functional history of the house. The actual processes of building, including design, organization of the building operation, labour relations, and building materials, as well as economics and transport, remains a curiously neglected area of research. L. F. Salzman showed the potential in *Building in England down to 1540* as long ago as 1952, and

Malcolm Airs applied a similar approach to the Tudor and Jacobean period in *The Making of the English Country House, 1500–1640* (1975); but apart from the study of a single house by Charles Saumarez Smith in *The Building of Castle Howard* (1990), no other historian has explored the practices of more recent centuries, and the subject remains a fruitful area for future work. The application of archaeological techniques to the surviving fabric of country houses is another recent development which promises to expand our understanding of individual buildings and to modify some of the conclusions drawn by architectural historians on the basis of stylistic evidence alone. So far the results have been published mainly in academic journals, such as the pioneering studies by Paul Drury of Hill Hall and Audley End, both in Essex, but the forthcoming monograph on Acton Court, Avon, by Rob Bell and Kirsty Rodwell will demonstrate the full potential of this approach to a more general readership.

Some of the primary sources, such as estate records, topographical views, maps, and old photographs which have been cited for the country house can also be used in the study of rural *vernacular housing, but they rarely allow more than a general impression and the opportunities for documentary research at this social level are very much more restricted. Court rolls and other manorial records are sometimes helpful, and probate *inventories have been a well-used source for the period from the 16th to the 18th centuries, although they present a number of difficulties of interpretation. The *hearth tax returns of 1662 to 1688 and the *census returns for the 19th century can provide supplementary evidence of great value, and *glebe terriers and *Faculties are informative on *parsonages and other domestic buildings belonging to the church. *People at Home* (1993) by N. W. Alcock demonstrates how this sort of evidence can be used in conjunction with the surviving buildings to recreate a plausible picture of housing conditions in a Warwickshire village in the period between 1500 and 1800. On very rare occasions, building accounts or contracts for individual houses survive, and *The Building Accounts of Mapperton Rectory, 1699–1703* have been published by the Dorset Record Society (Publication No. 8, 1983) with a perceptive introduction by R. Machin. Contemporary accounts of local communities can also offer incidental evidence on housing which can supplement these meagre sources of information. The Revd William *Harrison's *Description of England*, first published in 1577 and expanded in 1586–7, has long been recognized as a classic source for Essex houses at a period of major change, and there are other accounts, such as Richard *Gough's *The History of Myddle* (1701), which could prove almost as fruitful for the analysis of other areas.

But the fundamental evidence for the history of the vernacular house is provided by examination of the fabric itself, either in the form of upstanding buildings or as below-ground archaeology; and in consequence it is to the secondary literature that the student must turn for guidance in this rapidly developing field. The tradition of this line of enquiry was established only in the last years of the 19th century, and the early scholars were amateurs in the best sense of that word. From the very beginning it was recognized that a regional approach was necessary to chronicle the separate development of the smaller house in different parts of the kingdom, where local craft traditions responded to climate, topography, available building materials, farming practices, and economic prosperity, to create local solutions to the housing needs of the local population. The two pioneering studies both came from Yorkshire. In 1898 S. O. *Addy, a Sheffield solicitor and prolific antiquary on subjects ranging from dialect to cutlery, published *The Evolution of the English House*, and in 1916 C. F. Innocent, an architect and another native of Sheffield, published *The Development of English Building Construction*. Both books drew on local examples and remain invaluable because they record rural houses at a period before the radical alterations demanded by changing perceptions of public hygiene and domestic comfort had obliterated much of the evidence for their original forms. In Wales, Harold Hughes and Herbert North published *The Old Cottages of Snowdonia* in 1908, and the Principality remained in the forefront of regional studies with the publication of *The Welsh House* (1940) by I. C. Peate, written from the point of view of folk culture, and the three volumes on *Monmouthshire Houses* (1951–4) by Sir Cyril Fox and Lord Raglan, which established the basis of the archaeological approach to the analysis of standing buildings and first formulated the concept of a *Great Rebuilding in the 16th and early 17th centuries. This concept was developed and given a national perspective for England by W. G. *Hoskins in a seminal essay on 'The Rebuilding of Rural England, 1570–1640', first published in the academic journal *Past and Present* in 1953 and later reprinted in *Provincial England* (1964). Although its central thesis has been refined by the detailed regional studies which Hoskins encouraged to test the validity of his generalizations, the essay had a significant impact on bringing the study of vernacular buildings into the mainstream of serious history, and was an astringent antidote to the popular concentration on the aesthetic charm of the country cottage, which had been fostered by a whole series of books from publishers like Batsford in the decades on either side of the Second World War. Regional studies and accounts of individual buildings have proliferated since the 1950s, and the details of their publication are comprehensively indexed in the excellent bibliographies published by the Vernacular Architecture Group, beginning with *A Bibliography on Vernacular Architecture* (ed. R. de Z. Hall, 1972), and continuing with *A Current Bibliography of Vernacular Architecture 1970–1976* (ed. D. J. H. Michelmore, 1979) and *A Bibliography of Vernacular Architecture 1977–1989* (eds. I. R. Pattison, D. S. Pattison, and N. W. Alcock, 1992). The bibliographies cover Ireland, Scotland, and Wales as well as England, but the Scottish Vernacular Buildings Working Group has published additional bibliographies for Scotland in 1985 and 1987.

A national account for England, based on wide fieldwork and judiciously using both documentary and physical evidence, had been published as early as 1961 under the title of *The English Farmhouse and Cottage* by M. W. *Barley. R. W. Brunskill encouraged a whole generation of local historians to study the buildings of their locality when he published the methods for systematic and extensive surveys devised at the Manchester School of Architecture in his *Illustrated Handbook of Vernacular Architecture* (1970). The success of this slim volume was a measure of the increasing popular interest in the subject, and it was followed in 1975 by a major review of the current state of knowledge by Eric Mercer in *English Vernacular Houses*, the first thematic volume by the Royal Commission on the *Historical Monuments of England. In the same year Peter Smith published a comprehensive volume on the *Houses of the Welsh Countryside* for the Royal Commission on Ancient and Historical Monuments in Wales, whose sub-title, *A Study in Historical Geography*, indicates his particular approach to the subject. General accounts also appeared for Scotland with A. Fenton, B. Walker, and G. Stell, *Building Construction in Scotland: Some Historical and Regional Aspects* (1976) and, more particularly, *The Rural Architecture of Scotland* (1981), also by Fenton and Walker. *Ireland's Vernacular Architecture* is covered by C. Danachair (1975), and A. Bailey published *Rural Houses of the North of Ireland* in 1984. The most

recent synthesis for England is the attractively illustrated *The Traditional Buildings of England* (1990) by A. P. Quiney, who has also documented the development of the academic study of the subject in a detailed paper on 'Medieval and Post-Medieval Vernacular Architecture' in Blaise Vyner (ed.), *Building on the Past* (1994), which fully acknowledges the importance of the work of scholars such as J. T. Smith, in establishing the typology of built forms, and Cecil Hewett, in the study of joinery. Quiney's extensive bibliography is an accessible point of entry for further study of the subject, although it ignores the recent trend by a new generation of scholars who are bringing the tools of anthropological analysis to bear on the physical and documentary evidence. This is likely to prove a fruitful area in the future, although its protagonists will need to improve their methods of communication if they are to reach the wider audiences that studies such as Matthew Johnson's *Housing Culture* (1993) deserve.

Urban housing is another area with potential for further research and publication. In addition to the general documentary sources already discussed, certain classes of records are peculiar to towns and cities, particularly those that are associated with the development of public supervision over urban activities. A system of building control had been established in many cities by the 18th century; the returns of the District Surveyors survive in London from 1774 and in Bristol from 1788. By the 19th century the records of the Boards of Works and the gas and sewer companies are a particularly valuable source in conjunction with other administrative records such as parish *rate books and *registries of deeds. *Exploring Urban History* (1990) by Stephen Porter is a useful introduction to the available sources, and the chapter by D. M. Palliser on sources in *The Plans and Topography of Medieval Towns in England and Wales*, ed. M. W. Barley (1976) should also be consulted.

The secondary literature is diverse and voluminous, and most major cities and many towns have extensive bibliographies. However, few of the books deal specifically with housing as a discrete subject in the manner of John Summerson's classic *Georgian London* (3rd revised edn., 1978) and A. J. Youngson's *The Making of Classical Edinburgh* (1966). The vernacular buildings of King's Lynn were analysed by Vanessa Parker in *The Making of King's Lynn* (1971), and those of Exeter in D. Portman's *Exeter Houses 1400–1700* (1966), but recent scholars have largely avoided this difficult area where much of the structural evidence is frag-

mentary and often obscured by later alterations. The post-medieval town has been more
extensively treated, and mention should be
made of the pioneering architectural studies by
Walter Ison of *The Georgian Buildings of Bath*
(1948) and its companion volume on *The Georgian Buildings of Bristol* (1952). *Bristol, An Architectural History* (1979), by A. Gomme, M.
Venner, and B. Little covers a wider historical
period, as does *The Architecture of Glasgow*
(revised edn., 1987) by A. Gomme and D.
Walker. *The English Town* (1990) by Mark
Girouard is a highly stimulating introduction to
the theme.

In *London: The Art of Georgian Building*
(1975), Dan Cruickshank and Peter Wyld
attempt to explain the construction of houses of
the period as well as their architectural development; and *Life in the Georgian City* (1990) by
Dan Cruickshank and Neil Burton expands on
that theme with a more general account of
domestic conditions in the houses of the period.
The planning of cities has usually been tightly
controlled either by private landowners or public authorities, and the profound influence that
this has exercised over housing conditions in
London is clearly documented in Donald J.
Olsen's *Town Planning in London: The Eighteenth and Nineteenth Centuries* (1964), and *The
Growth of Victorian London* (1976). The classic
study of the development of a London suburb is
Victorian Suburb: A Study of Camberwell (1961)
by H. J. Dyos, and *The English Terraced House*
(1982) is broadly covered by Stefan Muthesuis.
J. N. Tarn's *Five Per Cent Philanthropy* (1973)
describes the measures taken to provide cheap
housing for the working classes in urban areas
between 1840 and 1914, and the story is taken
up to the very recent past in *Tower Block:
Modern Public Housing in England, Scotland,
Wales and Northern Ireland* (1994) by Miles
Glendinning and Stefan Muthesius.

There is probably more literature on the
housing of London than for any other city in
the kingdom. It has also been more extensively
illustrated, and a thorough index to topographical books with London views is provided in
London Illustrated, 1604–1851 (1983) by Bernard
Adams. Certainly, nowhere else has anything to
compare with the Survey of London, which was
established in 1894 and which since 1900, has
published 44 volumes of the architectural history of numerous parishes in inner London,
together with 17 monographs on individual
buildings. The full list of parishes together with
a history of the project is set out in Hermione
Hobhouse, *London Survey'd* (1994).

Since 1986 the Survey of London has been
part of the responsibility of the Royal Commission on the Historical Monuments of England.
The three Royal Commissions for England,
Scotland, and Wales were founded in 1908 and,
although they deal with architectural and
archaeological monuments of all types, domestic buildings have featured prominently in the
county inventories that they have published
regularly ever since. The English Commission
has now abandoned the inventory series in
favour of a thematic approach. J. T. Smith's
*The English House 1200–1800: The Hertfordshire
Evidence* (1992) was prepared under the traditional policy, but the volumes on the smaller
medieval houses of Kent (1994) and a national
survey of the gentry house reflect the new
approach. Other national surveys which are
relevant for the study of housing include the
*Victoria County Histories for England, which
began publication in 1904 and, of course, the
monumental architectural gazetteer which Sir
Nikolaus *Pevsner created for Penguin Books
under the title of *The Buildings of England* in
1951. All the English counties had been covered
by 1974, and the greatly expanded revised
editions have been appearing since that date
under the general editorship of Bridget Cherry,
who published a fascinating history and bibliography of the series in 1983. The first volume of
The Buildings of Scotland was published in 1978,
and *The Buildings of Wales* and *The Buildings of
Ireland* followed in 1979, although it will be
many years before these latecomers provide full
coverage for their respective countries. In 1994
*A Compendium of Pevsner's Buildings of England
on Compact Disc* provided the researcher with
electronic access to an architectural database of
300,000 entries, and this is likely to prove an
indispensable reference tool for future work.
The statutory lists of buildings of special architectural or historic interest are legal documents
compiled for the purposes of planning control,
but they also represent a national inventory
which was mainly drawn up by historians and
which contains a great deal of essential information on historic housing. They can be consulted in the offices of the local planning
authority as well as the national record repositories.

Housing of any status was often designed by
professional architects, and biographical dictionaries provide the basic information on their
lives and works. John Harvey's *English Mediaeval Architects* (revised edn., 1984, supplement
1987) covers the period down to 1550 and Sir
Howard Colvin deals with the period from 1600
to 1840 in his *Biographical Dictionary of British
Architects* (1978; new edn., 1995). For

Ireland there is *A Biographical Dictionary of Architects in Ireland, 1600–1720* (1981) by Rolf Loeber, and the architects of the Victorian period are listed in A. Felstead, J. Franklin, and L. Pinfield, *Directory of British Architects, 1834–1900* (1993). For the early years of the twentieth century *Edwardian Architecture: A Biographical Dictionary* (1985) by A. Stuart Gray is highly readable.

Predictably, the study of the interior of the domestic house has been mainly concentrated on the homes of the élite. The magnificent aquatints that W. H. *Pyne published in three volumes between 1816 and 1820 under the title of *The History of the Royal Residences of Windsor Castle, St James's Palace, Carlton House, Kensington Palace, Hampton Court, Buckingham House, and Frogmore* are an opulent testament to royal taste in the Regency period and a valuable historical record in their own right. Inventories provide an important source for understanding the interiors of the early country house, and the publications of the Furniture History Society such as *The Hardwick Hall Inventories of 1601* (ed. Lindsay Boynton, 1971) and *The Furnishing and Decoration of Ham House* (Peter Thornton and Maurice Tomlin, 1980) explore their potential as a primary record. *Seventeenth Century Interior Decoration in England, France & Holland* (1978) by Peter Thornton uses a full range of documentary evidence and surviving examples to explore the fashionable interior, and Geoffrey Beard in *Craftsmen and Interior Decoration in England, 1660–1820* (1981) provides an appropriate emphasis on the workmen and their various crafts. The pioneering study on the more transitory aspects of decoration, such as the uses of colour and the arrangement of rooms, was published by John Fowler and John Cornforth in 1974 as *English Decoration in the 18th Century*, and this was followed by John Cornforth, *The Quest for Comfort: English Interiors 1790–1848* (1978). The invention of *photography in the 19th century provided a new medium for documenting changing tastes in interiors, and the work of H. Bedford Lemere is celebrated by Nicholas Cooper in *The Opulent Eye: Late Victorian and Edwardian Taste in Interior Design* (1976). John Fowler was perhaps the most influential designer in the evolution of country-house taste in the 20th century, and his contribution is fully acknowledged by John Cornforth in *The Inspiration of the Past* (1985).

The publications of Margaret Jourdain in the 1920s did much to establish the scholarly basis for the study of interior decoration and *furni-ture. Although they were mainly concerned with houses of high status, she ventured further down the social scale with *English Interiors in Smaller Houses from the Restoration to the Regency, 1660–1830* (1923); but the middle-class home remains an area that continues to be neglected. Despite the difficulties of the evidence, the vernacular interior has been bravely covered by James Ayres in *The Shell Book of The Home in Britain* with its more informative subtitle of *Decoration, Design and Construction of Vernacular Interiors, 1500–1850* (1981).

British and Irish Architectural History: A Bibliography and Guide to Sources of Information (1981) by Ruth Kamen has been partially superseded by later work, and it was never as comprehensive as the title suggested. Nevertheless, it remains the single most valuable introduction to the study of domestic buildings. *Houses and History* (1986) by Maurice Barley most nearly gives an overview. It contains a number of insights but the struggle to compress so much information into a mere 290 pages is ultimately disappointing. Anyone embarking on this field for the first time is urged to read David Watkins's *The Rise of Architectural History* (1980) in order to understand the motives and prejudices of all those who have written on the subject.   MALCOLM AIRS

building societies were originally small clubs of 20 to 50 people who paid regular subscriptions which enabled the society to build houses. These were then allotted by ballot. Many of these societies were wound up when all the members were housed. (See FREEHOLD LAND SOCIETIES.) Such societies were formed from the late 18th century onwards, especially in northern industrial towns. Thus, the Halifax Permanent Building Society began as the Loyal Georgian Society in 1779. The earliest building society in the West Midlands was formed in Birmingham in 1775, and others were soon established at Dudley, Wolverhampton, Burslem, Handsworth, and Coventry. Some societies, such as the Halifax, developed wider interests, eventually becoming societies that invested shareholders' money in *mortgages for house purchasers. Until the last decade of the 19th century, however, owner-occupancy was regarded as a minority interest of thrifty and respectable artisans and lower-middle-class families.

Most societies remained purely local, but some became household names. Many lost their identity in the third quarter of the 20th century upon merger with a larger institution. Their annual reports (which were often reported in local *newspapers) and rule books have often been deposited in local *record offices and are informative about the development of local housing. See E. J. Cleary, *The Building Society Movement* (1965), S. J. Price, *Building Societies: Their Origin and History* (1958), and Martin Gaskell, 'Self-Help and House Building in the Nineteenth Century', *The Local Historian*, 10/2 (1973). For an example of a local study see Michael Collins, 'The History of the Leeds Permanent Building Society, 1893–1993' in John Chartres and Katrina Honeyman (eds.), *Leeds City Business, 1893–1993* (1993), ch. 3.

building stones. Until the late 16th and 17th centuries the houses of most British people were *timber-framed. Most medieval *castles, *cathedrals, *monasteries, *churches, and many *manor houses were, however, built of stone. The Romans had used stone where it was available, and the Anglo-Saxons had used it for their major buildings. Stone replaced timber as the building material for the houses of the *yeomen, *husbandmen, and craftsmen in the *Great Rebuilding of the early modern period, wherever it was available; otherwise *brick was used. As transporting stone was difficult and costly, local stone was used wherever possible. The geological structure of Britain, particularly England, is immensely varied, so the use of local materials adds greatly to the interest and appeal of *vernacular architecture.

The problems and cost of moving stone from the quarry to the building site were largely overcome if transport could be arranged along navigable rivers and down the coast. See L. F. Salzman, *Building in England Down to 1540* (1952), which provides much documentary evidence, and David Parsons (ed.), *Stone: Quarrying and Building in England, AD 43–1525* (1990). Caen stone from Normandy was brought economically across the English Channel for prestige buildings; *Portland stone and *Purbeck marble quarries had immediate access to the sea; the oolitic limestone quarries within a 25-mile radius of Stamford provided high-quality building stones, which were taken down the Welland and the Ouse for the building of Ely and Peterborough cathedrals and many of the Cambridge colleges; and magnesian limestone was transported up the Yorkshire rivers towards York, and down the rivers and via the east coast to Cambridge and London. See Alec Clifton-Taylor, *The Pattern of English Building* (1972) for the major quarries and for discussions of the merits of different stones.

Much remains to be learned from detailed investigations of the building stones of individual buildings, particularly medieval parish *churches. Thus St John the Baptist, Alkborough (Lincolnshire) is, as might be expected, largely built of local oolitic limestones and ironstones, but its Anglo-Saxon quoins are of coal-measure sandstone, and millstone grit is used in the buttresses. The tombstones inside the church are Pennine flagstones. Alkborough stands by the Trent and the Humber, so these stones could have been brought from the west at cheap rates. St Peter's, Howden, is another church in the Humber basin which uses small quantities of millstone grit, though the immediate impression is of a building constructed of magnesian limestone which has been brought much shorter distances.

The choice of building material often reflects the prosperity or otherwise of a parish during a particular phase of church construction. Local *rubble may have sufficed in early periods, but imported *ashlar was sometimes afforded later on. (See FLINT for the way in which splendid churches could be built with inferior material where good-quality stone was not available locally.) Since the coming of the *railways, brick has been a more economical material and the use of stone has declined. By the late 20th century stone was a costly building material, used largely as a veneer.

building trades. The fortunes of the building industry have usually provided a sound indication of the health of both the national and the local economy. The medieval masons were often itinerant workers whose trade was controlled through a system of lodges. (See MASONS' MARKS.) However, the most important medieval towns had various craftsmen's *guilds which regulated the building trades. The characteristic unit long remained that of the small master, with perhaps a man or two and a lad, who had contacts with other skilled craftsmen, e.g. glaziers, plasterers, and plumbers. See Donald Woodward, *Men at Work: Labourers and Building Craftsmen in the Towns of Northern England, 1450–1750* (1994). In the 1840s and 1850s carpenters and masons were affected by competition with machine-made products, but most work was carried on as before. The building industry was little affected by technological change before the 20th century. Large employers were a rarity before the 1960s.

Because of the small scale of business units the history of the building trades in the 19th century is not well recorded. See, however, H. J. Dyos, *Victorian Suburb: A Study of the Growth of Camberwell* (1961), which notes the numerous small variations in house type in this south London suburb because so many different builders were at work. Between 1878 and 1880, at the height of the building boom, some 416 firms or individual builders erected 5,670 houses in Camberwell. Over half the builders constructed no more than six houses during these three years, and nearly three-quarters built no more than 12. Many of these small firms went bankrupt. On the other hand, nearly one-third of the houses were built by the 15 largest firms, each of which constructed between 75 and 230 buildings. Some attempt at planning control was made by local authorities under powers obtained from national legislation. See Martin Gaskell, *Building Control: National Legislation and the Introduction of Local Bye-Laws in England* (1983).

Bunyan, John (1628–88). Author of *The Pilgrim's Progress* (1678, with additions in subsequent editions), once one of the most widely read books in the English language. Bunyan was a Bedfordshire tinker and *Nonconformist *pastor, who spent over 12 years in gaol because of his religious beliefs. See Christopher Hill, *A Turbulent, Seditious and Factious People: John Bunyan and His Church* (1989).

burgage plot. The property owned by a *burgess in a medieval town. As burgesses congregated around the *market place and main streets, space at the front was at a premium. Burgage plots are therefore characteristically long and narrow, with a row of outbuildings stretching to the rear of the house and shop. The pattern of burgage plots is often evident from old maps and sometimes can still be discerned on the ground.

burgess. 1. A citizen or *freeman of a *borough, especially a member of the governing body of a town.
2. A member of parliament for a borough, corporation, or university.

burgh. A Scottish town which had a measure of self-government and defined trading privileges. The most important were the royal burghs which were founded by royal charter and whose lands were held directly from the Crown. Burghs founded by *barons often had no elected council or access to foreign trade. A large number of 'burghs of barony' were created in the 16th and 17th centuries, but most remained very small. The royal burghs had their own courts, many of whose records—particularly in the form of minute-books—have been published by the Scottish Burghs Records Society (1868–1908). The oldest records are those of Aberdeen (from 1398), Edinburgh (1403), Peebles (1456), and Lanark (1488). See A. J. Mill, *Inventory of the Records of the Older Scottish Burghs* (1923), D. Robertson and M. Wood, 'Burgh Court Records' in *Sources and Literature of Scots Law* (1936), and W. M. MacKenzie, *The Scottish Burghs* (1949).

Burghal Hidage. The date of this document is debatable, but it is generally agreed that it refers to the defensive system created by King Alfred of *Wessex at the time of the Danish invasions. The document lists the *burhs, or fortified places, in a clockwise order, starting in the east. An area of land, measured in *hides, was allocated to each stronghold. See D. H. Hill, 'The Burghal Hidage: The Establishment of a Text', *Medieval Archaeology*, 13 (1969).

burh. A fortified place of the late 9th and 10th centuries, constructed by the kings of *Wessex to resist the Danish invaders. Several towns in south-western England retain part of the street plan and defensive walls of this period. Wareham (Dorset) is an outstanding example. The *burh* element is incorporated in some placenames. (See BURGHAL HIDAGE.) As the kingdom of Wessex expanded, so new burhs were erected well north of the former boundaries, e.g. at Bakewell (Derbyshire).

burial customs. The funerals of monarchs and *nobles were arranged by the heralds of the College of *Arms in the Middle Ages and for much of the early modern period, until the rise of undertakers in the 18th century. A long, formal procession, led by conductors, included large numbers of poor people and a choir, followed by gentlemen, officers, heralds, and the corpse, then by the chief mourners and their principal guests. The interior of the church was hung in black cloth, with heraldic displays around the hearse. (See HATCHMENT.) A number of funeral invitation cards, inviting mourners to 'accompany the corpse', and bordered with pictorial *memento mori*, survive from the 17th century. These great occasions influenced the form of funeral—led by 'plumes and horses'—which were favoured by the Victorian middle classes. See Julian Litten, *The English Way of Death: The Common Funeral since 1450* (1991).

The *Reformation removed the sustained intercession on behalf of the dead man's soul that was central to Catholic practice before, during, and after the interment of the body, for the Protestant conviction was that prayers for the dead were useless. Older practices nevertheless continued well into the 17th century.

John *Aubrey remembered that when he was a boy in Wiltshire a penny would be placed in the mouth of the deceased before interment, as a gift for St Peter; he thought that this custom was still current in Wales and the north of England. He also noted that in Yorkshire 'they continue the custome of watching and sitting up all night till the body is interred', during which time 'some kneel down and pray (by the corps), some play at cards, some drink and take tobacco; they have also mimicall playes and sportes'. Funerals might still be accompanied by 'sin-eating', in which one of the poor of the parish, in return for food, drink, and money, would offer to assume the responsibility for the sins of the deceased. It remained the usual practice for death to be followed by a formal period of mourning. See Clare Gittings, *Death, Burial and the Individual in Early Modern England* (1984), and Stephen Porter, 'From Death to Burial in Seventeenth-Century England', *The Local Historian*, 23/4 (1993).

The survival of old customs and superstitions on the North York Moors is recorded in J. C. *Atkinson, *Forty Years in a Moorland Parish* (1891). Funerals attracted a wide range of kin, who were afterwards given a meal, which traditionally included ham and cakes ('funeral biscuits'). The funeral wakes of Ireland were traditionally celebratory rather than mournful occasions. In the 19th and early 20th centuries the working classes made small weekly payments to burial clubs (often a *friendly society, or a national body such as the Ancient Order of Foresters), for a decent funeral was thought necessary to preserve a family's standing in a community. A pauper burial was considered the ultimate disgrace. (See also FUNERARY MONUMENTS; LYCH-GATE; CORPSE WAY; and CEMETERIES AND CREMATORIA.) A particular custom is observed in Gwen Davies, 'Stockings Prepared for Laying Out and Burial Held by Museums in the UK', *Textile History*, 23/1 (1992).

Burke, John (1787–1848). Burke's *Peerage* was first published in 1826. It was an annual publication from 1847 to 1940, except for the years 1918–20. Occasional editions have appeared since 1949. Burke's *Landed Gentry* was first published in 1837 as *A Genealogical and Heraldic History of the Commoners of Great Britain and Ireland, Enjoying Territorial Possessions or High Official Rank; but Uninvested with Heritable Honours*. Although it did not become an annual publication, many subsequent editions appeared under the title of *Burke's Genealogical and Heraldic History of the Landed Gentry*. The word 'gentry' did not replace 'commoners'

until the 1840s. By then, families that had acquired land through fortunes made in industry or trade were being included. The ownership of a substantial landed estate was considered a necessary condition of entry until the outbreak of the First World War, when men 'who have never owned land, but have won their way to distinction and position in the service of the King and in other ways' were also included. In 1877 Professor E. A. *Freeman dismissed the pedigrees published in Burke's *Landed Gentry* as 'much wild nonsense'.

John Burke wrote several other books on heraldry and genealogy. He was succeeded as editor of the *Peerage* and the *Landed Gentry* by his son Sir John Bernard Burke (1814–92) and his grandsons.

business records. As British governments have not interfered much with the running of most businesses, other than those which have been nationalized, few public records are available for study. The records of individual firms have often been deposited at local *record offices. They include board minutes, accounts, and correspondence, but on the whole they are not as well preserved as *deeds and other *estate records. Annual reports and unusual activities are reported in local *newspapers. The histories of many individual businesses have been published. See the articles and reviews in the journals *Business History* and *Business Archives*. See also Royal Commission on Historical Manuscripts, *Guides to Sources for British History, 8. Records of British Business and Industry, 1760–1914: Textiles and Leather* (1990). For studies of a range of local businesses see John Chartres and Katrina Honeyman (eds.), *Leeds City Business, 1893–1993* (1993). For general background see Julian Hoppit, *Risk and Failure in English Business, 1700–1800* (1987), and Peter L. Payne, *Studies in Scottish Business History* (1967).

butchers. Butchers were concentrated in a single street near the *market place in medieval towns, e.g. the *Shambles in York. The London butchers obtained supplies from Midlands *graziers. Here, and perhaps in the larger provincial cities, butchers were retailers. Elsewhere, however, they operated on a smaller scale and obtained their supplies directly from the farm. In the early 19th century, although some butchers killed as many as 20 or 30 beef cattle a week, most slaughtered an average of only one cow and perhaps two sheep a day, even in busy times. The hides were purchased by the *tanners. In the 19th century, butchers can be identified from trade *directories. See

Roger Scola, *Feeding the Victorian City: The Food Supply of Manchester, 1770–1870* (1992).

butt. 1. A shooting target, a mound for *archery practice. Edward IV (1461–83) made shooting practice compulsory on Sundays and feast days. Every man between the ages of 16 and 60 was expected to own a bow of his own height, and every township was ordered to set up its own butts. Games that might prove counter-attractions, such as *football, were designated 'unlawful sports'. The longbow ceased to be an important weapon during the reign of Elizabeth I.

2. Grouse butts, a hideout from which *grouse are shot.

3. A shorter or irregularly shaped *selion, in an *open-field, or one that abuts at right angles upon other selions.

button-making. Buttons were made of a variety of materials, including silver, alcomy (a base metal that resembled gold), brass, horn, and cloth. Button-making originated as an urban craft that required no *apprenticeship and was therefore attractive as an occupation to the poor. It became an important trade in Birmingham and the Black Country and in Sheffield in the late 17th century. Old Sheffield Plate began as a new industry in 1743 when Thomas Bouls-over discovered how to plate copper buttons with silver.

by-employments. The occupational descriptions of people in the past often obscure the fact that they obtained their living in a variety of ways. (See DUAL ECONOMY for the families which combined a craft with the running of a farm or smallholding.) In the summer months the carriage of goods was a frequent source of extra income. The poorer classes sought work wherever it was available. In addition to their gardens or *allotments, *agricultural labourers often turned to wood or textile crafts, or to work in sand-pits, quarries, lime kilns, etc. when the opportunity arose. Much work was of a seasonal nature.

bylawman. Alternative name for a *constable.

by-names. Before *surnames became fixed and hereditary, the narrow range of forenames that were in use meant that people had to be distinguished by a by-name, which might be a *nickname, an occupation, a reference to one or other of the parents, or an association with a place. Many of these by-names became hereditary surnames, but in documents of the 13th and 14th centuries it is not usually possible to be certain of this.

byre. A term used in some regions for a cowshed. See LONGHOUSE.

C

cadet. A younger son or brother; a younger branch of a family.

cairns. 1. Piles of stones marking *Bronze Age graves or field clearances.
2. Stones piled as waymarkers on *moors and fells.

calendar. 1. In 1752 Britain changed from the inaccurate *Julian calendar to the *Gregorian calendar, which had been used in Catholic countries since 1582. The eleven days' discrepancy between the two calendars meant that 2 September 1752 was followed after the change by 14 September. At the same time the old custom of starting the official year on *Lady Day (25 March), which the *Book of Common Prayer 'supposed to be the first day upon which the world was created and the day when Christ was conceived in the womb of the Virgin Mary', was abandoned in favour of the year beginning on 1 January.

As 1 January had long been regarded by most people as the true beginning of the year, regardless of official reckoning, dates between 1 January and 25 March were often written as e.g. 1688/9. To avoid confusion, it is a useful practice for local and family historians to follow this convention and to refer to dates before 1752 as Old Style and those after 1752 as New Style. In many places annual *fairs and other customary events continued to be held on the Old Style date long after 1752. A curious survival of the old system is the starting of the official financial year on 6 April, which is Old Lady Day, eleven days after the present 25 March.

Before 1752 September, October, November, and December were often referred to in written records as 7ber, 8ber, 9ber, and 10ber. *Quakers called all the months by numbers; before 1752 March was their First Month, afterwards it was the Third Month. This Quaker practice continued into the 20th century.

In the Middle Ages documents were dated not by calendar years but by *regnal years starting from the time that a monarch ascended the throne. In the early modern period documents give regnal years alongside calendar ones.

2. A catalogue summarizing what the editor deems to be the essential data contained in a series of documents. Calendars of State Papers vary greatly in the amount of information contained in their summaries. Sometimes they are almost full transcripts of the original text; sometimes they omit to mention information which the present-day local or family historian considers to be of prime significance.

calendar customs. Calendar customs are cultural expressions of repetitive seasonal rhythms, and as such have continuously evolved and accumulated over centuries in particular localities. Although geographically specific, however, such calendars always simultaneously respect yet wider, culturally defined contexts, from the cycles of agriculture or industry on the one hand to the routine rounds of church, state, and regional administration on the other. When all such relevant rhythms are taken together in individual places, customary calendars may be seen to represent the extraordinarily varied ways in which different localities structure their social time. It is thus essential to understand such calendars as far as possible as wholes.

All that may safely be claimed about the origins of calendrical patterns in Britain is that they were structured broadly according to earlier perceptions of the solar year. These seem to have reflected regionally variable divisions of the seasons (whether for geographical or cultural reasons it is not clear) by symbolically marking the beginning and end of summer with observances which were probably concerned with first-fruits and harvest. In the pastoral Celtic areas of Ireland, Scotland, and Wales, for example, the feasts of Beltane (*May Day eve) and Samhaim (1 November), the Celtic New Year, included the lighting of fires at dawn in the case of the former and at dusk in the case of the latter. It is notable that other pasture-farming areas in England similarly not only emphasized May Day (which was associated with increased milk production) but also later timed their *hiring fairs to fall around either early May or early November, whereas arable or mixed-farming areas in England held their hirings around *Michaelmas (29 September) after an earlier harvest.

In these generally more southerly climes, and probably under Anglo-Saxon influence, greater emphasis seems to have been placed on the midwinter and midsummer solstices (thus emphasizing by contrast the longest night and the longest day). The deliberate policy of the early church to accommodate its observances to established pre-Christian rhythms thereafter ensured a division of the year at *Christmas— the start of a twelve-day New Year interval, often taken to presage the fortunes of the ensuing 12 months—and at *Midsummer. With the subsequent determination in AD 664 of the way in which the date of Easter, itself apparently named after a heathen goddess, might be calculated (as the first Sun-day after the first full moon after the spring equinox on 21 March), the whole liturgical cycle attached to that feast moved backwards and forwards with it in a highly significant manner. Easter could now fall as early as 22 March or as late as 25 April; in the latter case the final feast in the two-month movable cycle (that of *Corpus Christi, established in England in 1318) coincided precisely with Midsummer Day.

Also attached to the liturgical high points between Christmas and Midsummer, from at least the days of Alfred's *Wessex, were the traditional three extended breaks in the year at Christmas, Easter, and Whitsuntide, not to speak of single holy-days in between which, like St George's Day, for example, might themselves eventually become occasions for public rituals. Because of this division of the medieval year, it has been suggested that the heightened symbolic content of the period between Christmas and Midsummer—which included all the great liturgical celebrations of Christ's life and resurrection through to and even beyond Pentecost, as well as the more important popular customary occasions which they had been designed to supplant—justifies its description as the 'ritualistic' half. This then may be seen to contrast with the six months between Midsummer and Christmas which, being devoted largely (though not exclusively) to observances arising from work, like the harvest and fairs, might more appropriately be labelled 'secular'; see Charles Phythian-Adams, *Local History and Folklore* (1975). Such a division does provide a measure against which may usefully be set the decline of spectacular religious occasions in the 'ritualistic' half after the *Reformation, together with the subsequent tilting of ever more nationalistically inspired observances and holidays, such as parish wakes, Guy Fawkes, the August Bank Holiday, and Harvest Festival, towards the later 'secular' part of the year.

The two halves together, however, are best regarded as what may most fittingly be thought of in each local place as the 'communal year' since, as is discussed under *customs, it was on fixed, annually repetitive, calendrical occasions that the most public 'customs' (and especially *civic ritual) which related to a whole local society or the formal relationships between its component groups were formerly observed. Such occasions marking the status quo (in contradistinction to *ad hoc* rites of passage) may thus be seen as thereby gaining added public significance from the symbolic associations of their timing. The regular punctuation of normal working life by such ritualized customary activity, finally, clearly helped also to highlight whatever element of the local social structure was then being given prominence.

At the popular level, it is the fleeting relics of association between the seasons and the more basic aspects of social structure, the 'ages of man'—birth at Christmas, death at Halloween—that have survived to this day, even when, as has so often been the case, the customs in question are perpetuated eventually for or by children; see I. and P. Opie, *The Lore and Language of Schoolchildren* (1959). See also Ronald Hutton, *The Rise and Fall of Merry England: The Ritual Year 1400–1700* (1994), and David Cressy, *Bonfires and Bells: National Memory and the Protestant Calendar in Elizabethan and Stuart England* (1989).

CHARLES PHYTHIAN-ADAMS

Cambridge University archives. The Cambridge University Library, Department of Manuscripts and University Archives, West Road, Cambridge CB3 9DR houses the archives of the University. The various colleges also have archive collections. The older colleges often have *estate records that are of interest to local historians in the various parts of the country where the colleges were landlords.

Camden, William (1551–1623). Author of *Britannia* (1586), a milestone in the development of historical studies. The first (Latin) edition was an immediate success; five enlarged editions were published during his lifetime and a further seven posthumously, notably those by Edmund *Gibson (1695) and Richard *Gough (1789). Camden's motives were patriotic; he wished to establish the importance of the Roman antiquities of Britain. In so doing, he won the respect of Continental humanist scholars, who called him 'the British Strabo'. Camden was familiar with Continental writings and with the native *antiquarian tradition. He drew upon the work of *Leland and *Lambarde and was well-served by correspondents from different parts of the country, especially his friends in the Society of *Antiquaries. His *Britannia* covered history, geography, topography, anthropology, and antiquarianism, often in great detail. Although his primary concern was Roman antiquities, he depended on literary sources rather than archaeological evidence. Nevertheless, he toured the country and his work is now valuable for its contemporary descriptions and observations. He adopted Lambarde's plan of proceeding, with a long introductory essay. Additional material, including the first study of the etymology of *surnames, was brought together in his *Remaines of a Greater Worke Concerning Britaine* (1605).

Camden Society. Named after William *Camden, the antiquary, the Camden Society was formed in Cambridge in 1839 to further the cause of ecclesiology. It was enormously influential, through its journal, *The *Ecclesiologist*, in determining the style of church building and restoration. The society also published edited historical texts, with introductions. In 1897 it was amalgamated with the Royal Historical Society and represents their series of edited historical texts on extremely varied subjects. Five series have been published on an annual basis.

Camping Closes. *Field names such as Camping Close indicate the places where the game of camping (a mixture of *football and handball) was played from the Middle Ages through to the 19th century. It was particularly popular in Norfolk, Suffolk, Cambridgeshire, and Essex. See David Dymond, 'A Lost Social Institution: The Camping Close', *Rural History: Economy, Society, Culture*, 1/2 (1990).

CAMPOP. The Cambridge Group for the Study of Population and Social Structure. This group of researchers, based at Cambridge University and drawing on the labours of local historians throughout England, has since the 1960s placed the study of historical demography on a sound footing. They were the first to use *parish registers to reconstitute families. The major publication of the group is E. A. Wrigley and R. S. Schofield, *The Population History of England, 1541–1871: A Reconstruction* (1981), which is dedicated 'To the local population historians of England'. Members of the group have published several other important books and numerous essays on historical demography and have contributed regularly to the journal *Local Population Studies*. See

POPULATION LEVELS AND TRENDS; HOUSEHOLD; FAMILY AND SOCIETY.

Canada. The French were the more numerous settlers in the 17th century: by 1660 the colony of New France had attracted nearly 3,000 inhabitants. They fished for cod off Newfoundland and traded for furs along the St Lawrence. This colony was ceded to Britain after a military victory in 1763, by which time Canada's European population had reached 60,000. British colonial plantation had begun in the 17th century, e.g. in Nova Scotia. (See HUDSON'S BAY COMPANY.) After 1763 migration was on a larger scale, especially after the British defeat in the American War of Independence (1775–83). A large proportion of these 18th-century migrants were Scottish Highlanders. The Irish, too, emigrated in considerable numbers even before the *famine. They settled in the river valleys and the Great Lake lowlands of eastern and central Canada, especially in the second quarter of the 19th century.

Canada was the cheapest destination in the New World because of the passages provided in the numerous *ships that brought timber to England and which had to find a return cargo. These ships left from many small ports in the spring, so as to arrive as the ice was breaking in the St Lawrence. Steamships offered a quicker and safer passage from the 1840s, but wooden ships were not replaced until the late 1860s. Assisted passages were provided by government grants, poor law *guardians, and charities. Between 1825 and 1851 some 834,306 British people emigrated to Canada; indeed, during the 19th century Canada was the second most popular choice for migrants from the British Isles, except for a 15-year period after the discovery of gold in *Australia in 1852.

The Dominion of Canada was formed in 1867 (though Newfoundland did not join until 1949). The 1871 census revealed that 850,000 people, amounting to a quarter of the population of the new nation, claimed Irish ancestry; they were outnumbered only by the French Canadians who mostly resided in Quebec. Ontario and New Brunswick, and to a lesser extent Prince Edward Island and Nova Scotia, had a high proportion of Irish. See Cecil J. Houston and William J. Smyth, *Irish Emigration and Canadian Settlement: Patterns, Links and Letters* (1990), and Donald MacKay, *Flight From Famine: The Coming of the Irish to Canada* (1990). The 1881 Canadian census showed that 33 per cent of the English- and Gaelic-speaking population were Irish by ancestry, 30 per cent were English, 25 per cent were Scottish (mainly

Highlanders), but less than 0.5 per cent were Welsh. The rapid pace of emigration continued, and by the early 20th century more English and Scots emigrants went to Canada than to the United States of *America.

The Colonial Papers (CO 5) in the *Public Record Office include records of emigration from before 1782 for the former French colony of Canada, Hudson's Bay, Newfoundland, Nova Scotia and Cape Bretton Island, and Prince Edward Island. See R. B. Pugh, *The Records of the Colonial and Dominions Offices* (P.R.O. Handbook, no. 3, 1964). (See also PASSENGER LISTS.)

canals. During the late 17th and early 18th centuries the navigability of major rivers had been improved by a series of local schemes authorized by private Acts of Parliament. Some of these had involved the digging of 'cuts'. The construction of artificial canals to link industrial districts to markets and to navigable *rivers was the next logical improvement, for water transport for heavy, bulky goods of low value was much cheaper than road transport. The first important British canal was that which brought *coal from the Duke of Bridgewater's mines at Worsley (Lancashire) to Manchester. This was authorized by an Act of Parliament in November 1758 and completed by 1761 under the supervision of the Duke's agent, John Gilbert, and his engineer, James Brindley. The canal began in the depths of the mine, crossed the river Irwell by the Barton aqueduct, and ran through the unstable district of Trafford Moss; by 1780 the Duke was selling 400 tons of coal a week in Manchester. Meanwhile, a passenger service had been opened and a network of rivers and canals provided access all the way down to Bristol.

Within two generations the industrial districts of Britain were connected by a system of canals that involved some amazing technical feats. The Pennines were crossed by tunnels and flights of locks, deep valleys were negotiated by *aqueducts and huge embankments, and in 1832 Thomas Telford's great Caledonian Canal provided access from the North Sea to the Atlantic via a series of interconnected lochs from Inverness to Fort William. See Jean Lindsay, *The Canals of Scotland* (1986), Nigel Crowe, *Canals* (1994), and the various regional studies of canals by Charles Hadfield, e.g. *The Canals of the West Midlands* (1969). The back carriage of goods such as lime formed an important part of the economy of the canal system and led to the rapid growth of canal ports, notably Ellesmere Port, Goole, Runcorn,

and Stourbridge. See J. D. Porteous, *Canal Ports: The Urban Achievement of the Canal Age* (1977). Canals gradually declined with the coming of the *railways, but in the late 20th century many have been partly restored for leisure purposes. Some small canal settlements, e.g. Stoke Bruerne (Northamptonshire) or Shardlow (Derbyshire), retain much of their former character. See Eric de Maré, *The Canals of England* (1991).

The passage of the private Acts of Parliament which authorized canals can be followed in the *House of Commons and the *House of Lords Journals. The sponsors of local canals can be identified and any opposition noted. *Parliamentary papers include the Report of the Select Committee on Canals (1883), the returns made to the Board of Trade of canal statistics (1888), and the 12-volume Report of the Royal Commission on Canals of 1906–11, which contains a great deal of information, including maps. The *Public Record Office has papers and correspondence concerning individual canals, including much information on proposed closures, under MT 52. Local *record offices have minute books, correspondence, engineers' reports, etc. See Charles Hadfield, 'Sources for the History of British Canals', *Journal of Transport History*, 2/2 (1955). See also BOATMEN.

Candlemas. The feast of the Purification of the Virgin Mary (2 February; 14 February *old style), traditionally celebrated with a display of candles. See Eamon Duffy, *The Stripping of the Altars: Traditional Religion in England, 1400–1580* (1992). Bargains to take effect on *Lady Day were often made at Candlemas fairs.

canons. 1. (historically). Priests who lived according to a strict, almost monastic rule. The *Augustinian and *Premonstratensian orders arrived from France in Britain during the early 12th century. The *Gilbertines (founded 1131) were the only native order. The houses generally smaller than *monasteries, though some impressive churches survive as ruins. (See DISSOLUTION OF THE MONASTERIES.) The canons preached in local parish *churches and were expected to combine manual labour with their devotions and studies.

2. (present-day). Member of a cathedral *chapter in the *Church of England.

capite, tenant in. The holding of land in *feudal tenure direct from the monarch; cf. TENANT-IN-CHIEF.

cap money. A statute of 1571, repealed in 1598, enforced the wearing of caps of English wool on

Sundays and holy days. Cap money was the fine of 3s. 4d. for non-observance.

cardmaker. A maker of a wooden instrument which was shaped like a square bat with raised iron spikes and held in the hand in order to card wool in preparation for spinning.

Carew, Richard (1555–1600). Author of *Survey of Cornwall* (1602), member of a leading Cornish family, JP, High Sheriff, and, in 1584 and 1597, an MP. He was a member of the Society of *Antiquaries and a friend of *Camden.

carrier. Much carriage of goods for market in the Middle Ages and the early modern period was undertaken on a part-time basis by farmers in the summer months. The distances travelled were relatively short, to the nearest inland port or market town. The long-distance professional carrier operated in the Middle Ages under a variety of names, e.g. salter or *jagger. The numbers of long-distance carriers grew in the later 16th and 17th centuries, by which time regular services to London had been established from all parts of the provinces. (See *Carriers' Cosmographie*.) Local records from this period occasionally identify someone based in a market town as a 'London Carrier'. Those carriers who travelled long distances, e.g. the 'Kendal men' from north-west England, used teams of *packhorses, but by the 1560s *waggons were being used by the carriers of East Anglia and parts of southern England. Services to and from London grew quickly in the later 17th and 18th centuries. See J. A. Chartres, 'Road Carrying in England in the Seventeenth Century: Myth and Reality', *Economic History Review*, 30/1 (1977), and G. L. Turnbull, 'Provincial Road Carrying in England in the Eighteenth Century', *Journal of Transport History*, 2nd ser., 4/1 (1977).

The London carriers are easier to identify than the carriers who offered local services or connections to other provincial centres. Information about local carriers is hard to come by until the publication of trade and commercial *directories in the late 18th and 19th centuries, which show that a network of routes linking the whole of the country was well established by that time. Directories normally give full details of carriers' services, including starting points and destinations, times of departure and arrival, and connections with distant places. This information demonstrates that, collectively, the provincial carriers far outnumbered their London counterparts. For example, in 1787 Sheffield had 42 services linking the town directly or through connections with most parts of England, Scotland, and Wales. See David Hey, *Packmen, Carriers and Packhorse Roads: Trade and Communications in North Derbyshire and South Yorkshire* (1980). Some firms expanded their activities to include water transport, but few seem to have lasted for more than one generation. Pickfords are the great exception in being able to prove continuity in the carrying business from at least the 18th century and possibly the 17th. See Gerard L. Turnbull, *Traffic and Transport: An Economic History of Pickfords* (1979).

The local carrier who took passengers and goods to the nearest market town survived the coming of the *railways for he was able to provide services from railway stations to remote places. The activities of such humble carriers are not well recorded, though they figure in the works of Thomas *Hardy and a few other 19th-century authors. See Alan Everitt, 'Country Carriers in the Nineteenth Century' in *Landscape and Community in England* (1985), ch. 11, which shows the important role of village carriers in Victorian times. See also INNS, and MARKETS AND FAIRS.

Carriers' Cosmographie (1637). A publication of John Taylor (known as the water-poet), naming the London *inns which were the destinations of provincial *carriers, and giving the days and times of arrival and departure. This establishes that all parts of provincial England and Wales were connected by weekly services with the capital.

Cartae Antiquae rolls. A series of 46 rolls at the *Public Record Office, containing transcripts of documents from 1189 to 1327, which renewed or confirmed privileges, e.g. *charters. The first 10 were published by the *Pipe Roll Society, new series, 17.

Carthusians. A monastic order, The Poor Brothers of God of the Charterhouse, founded in 1084 in France, but not officially an order until 1142. The Carthusian monks modelled their way of life on that of the desert hermits of early Christian Egypt. This was deliberately harsh, involving the wearing of rough hair shirts and the eating of coarse food in slender portions. The monks were housed in separate cells with a small garden to the rear, arranged around a central courtyard. They accepted a vow of silence, except during the singing of offices (kept to the minimum of *Matins, Lauds, and Vespers) and on feast days when they shared a communal meal. Their lives were devoted to prayer and study. Numbers at each Charterhouse were restricted to a prior, 12 monks, and 18 *lay brothers.

The first British Carthusian priory was founded in 1178 by Henry II at Witham (Somerset). The number of foundations was much smaller than those of the other monastic orders. However, the Carthusians won great respect for maintaining their standards, and after the *Black Death they were the only order to create new houses. They attracted the enthusiastic support of the royal family and members of the nobility. The London Charterhouse was founded by 1370 and other major houses were established by nobles at Hull, Coventry, Epworth (Nottinghamshire), and Mount Grace (north Yorkshire). Mount Grace Priory (now owned by the National Trust) is the best-preserved Charterhouse in Britain. The austere standards of the Carthusians were maintained right through to the *dissolution of the monasteries.

cartulary, or chartulary. A register of the *charters, *deeds, grants of property, etc. of a *monastery. See G. R. C. Davis, *Medieval Cartularies of Great Britain: A Short Catalogue* (1958), which covers England, Wales, and Scotland.

carucate. The term used in the *Danelaw, comparable to the Saxon *hide, for a unit of taxation, originally the amount of land that a team of eight *oxen could plough each year. This varied according to the quality of the land but was about 120 *acres. The carucate or hide was the basic unit of taxation in the *Domesday Book.

Cary, John (*c.*1754–1835). A prolific maker of high-standard maps, which rank in accuracy with those of the *Ordnance Survey. His *New and Correct English Atlas* (1787), *Cary's Travellers' Companion* (1790), *Cary's New Itinerary* (1798), and *New British Atlas* (1805) were constantly updated in later editions. He also published maps of foreign countries and the *New Universal Atlas* (1808).

castellany. A large *lordship centred on the castle of one of the Norman *barons, especially in the border areas of northern and western England.

castle. The purpose of a castle was to dominate an area, rather than to act merely as a place of refuge, and to provide accommodation on a grand scale for the monarch or a *baron. The earliest castles were private forts, erected by forced labour. As such, they differed from the communal forts of the *Iron Age and the Saxon *burhs which served a whole neighbourhood. Some of these earlier forts are commemorated by minor place-names such as Castle

Hill, but the term 'castle' is used by historians to refer to fortified buildings erected after the *Norman Conquest.

Hundreds of *motte-and-bailey castles were erected in Britain by the Normans. They were a recent invention which had spread rapidly in Normandy. A few had been erected in England in Edward the Confessor's reign, but the majority were constructed hastily immediately after the Norman Conquest. Others may date from the civil wars of Stephen's reign (1135–54). The documentary record for this period is too poor for these castles to be dated precisely. The *Anglo-Saxon Chronicle* said of William I: 'Castles he caused to be made, and poor men to be greatly oppressed', and of Stephen's reign: 'They filled the whole land with these castles. They sorely burdened the unhappy people of the country with forced labour on the castles. And when the castles were made they filled them with devils and wicked men.'

Most motte-and-baileys were subsequently abandoned, but during the second quarter of the 12th century the most important ones were converted into stone castles, surrounded by huge ditches, ramparts, and a curtain wall, and entered by a *gatehouse. They became the seats of the monarch and the barons and were fortified to withstand long periods of siege. Most have been substantially altered over time to take account of new standards of accommodation and the changing technologies of warfare. For example, the curtain walls were raised to new heights in the 1160s and 1170s to protect the castles from new trajectory missiles, and towers were built with round instead of square sides. (See BARBICAN and SHELL KEEP.) Some castles have been rebuilt many times over.

Some early Norman castles had never been motte-and-baileys but were formidable stone castles from the start. The Tower of London and Colchester Castle are early examples, dating from the 1070s, which were conceived as defensive *palaces. The Crown and the greater barons spent an enormous amount of money on castles during the third quarter of the 12th century. See M. W. Thompson, *The Rise of the Castle* (1991), and Derek Renn, *Norman Castles in Britain* (1973). Some castles, e.g. Richmond (Yorkshire), did not conform to the usual plans but were built on hill-top sites chosen for their natural strength. The central feature of the castles of the second half of the 12th century and the first three decades of the 13th century is the stone *keep, a strongly defended tower which contained the domestic apartments of the owner. The ground floor was a vaulted chamber used for storage, e.g. Ludlow (Shropshire), not, as is popularly supposed, for a dungeon. An entrance chamber provided access, via a barbican and a staircase in the thickness of the wall. For reasons of defence, the staircases were placed on opposite sides at different levels. They led to the great hall and to the *solar above. The solar was a private apartment, used as a retiring room and bedroom; the chapel was usually on the same level. At the top of the keep were a variety of buildings, ranging from guard towers to water tanks, ovens, and *dovecotes.

In the courtyard of some Norman castles was a second hall, which was sometimes larger than the great hall in the keep. A remarkably well-preserved example of an *open hall with aisles is that built by Walklin de Ferrers at Oakham Castle (Rutland) in the last quarter of the 12th century. Scolland's Hall, Richmond (Yorkshire), is another example, though it is in a ruinous state.

Major changes in the design of castles came in the later 13th century, particularly with the building of Edward I's castles in north Wales at Beaumaris, Caernarvon, Conway, Harlech, etc. These perimeter-defence castles were influenced by designs that originated in the Middle East and spread through Europe via Italy and France. These castles had huge walls, powerful gatehouses, and a number of defensive buildings in the courtyard which had to be captured one by one. The costs were astronomical. By the 1380s such castles were becoming redundant in warfare, in face of cannon that were increasingly effective. At the same time, royal government was becoming more centralized, thus reducing the need for regular progressions with large retinues from one mighty castle to another. Royal palaces became increasingly concentrated within reasonable travelling distance of London.

Meanwhile, the number of licences to *crenellate reached a peak in the second quarter of the 14th century as magnates throughout the country topped their curtain walls and residential buildings with *battlements. Late medieval castles were very different from their Norman predecessors. By the early 14th century the keep had been abandoned. Smaller baronial castles, such as Castle Bolton and Sheriff Hutton (Yorkshire), used high walls and massive square corner towers to enclose a courtyard. Although the fear of attack was still there, and such buildings were designed to endure a siege, they were less concerned with defence than before. By the second half of the 14th century two-thirds of the expenditure on a typical castle was spent on the private apartments rather than on defence, reversing the proportions of earlier expenditure.

Throughout the Middle Ages defence remained a consideration for builders. (See TOWER HOUSES and PELE-TOWERS.) In the more settled times under the Tudors castles fell out of fashion. Those which were refortified by Royalists in the *Civil War of the 1640s were dismantled after the Parliamentarian victory. Others were allowed to decay gradually until serious interest in their preservation began in the 19th century. See R. Allen Brown, *English Castles* (1970) and J. R. Kenyon, *Medieval Fortifications* (1990).

cathedral. (See DIOCESES.) The derivation of cathedral is from the Latin *cathedra*, meaning a chair, or throne, the chair of office of a bishop.

Catholic Emancipation Act (1829). Roman Catholics were prohibited from membership of the House of Commons, even after the inclusion of Ireland in the *United Kingdom in 1801. The election of Daniel O'Connell for Clare, in 1828, dramatized the situation and led to the cancelling of this disqualification.

Catholic Record Society. A society housed at 114 Mount Street, London WC2Y 6AH, which was founded in 1905 to publish historical records concerning Roman Catholicism in Britain, including registers of baptisms, burials, and marriages from the later 18th century, Recusant Rolls (1592–1691) kept at the *Public Record Office, monographs, etc. *Recusant History* (from 1951) is the historical journal of the society.

cattle. Cattle have been the mainstay of British farming over the centuries (see the volumes of *The* AGRARIAN HISTORY OF ENGLAND AND WALES and the bibliographies contained therein). Cattle were valued for their meat and milk and as draught animals (see OXEN). They were often the first item to be listed in 16th-century probate *inventories. In the Middle Ages young cattle were reared in the moorland *vaccaries of large *lordships before being fattened on lusher pastures in the lowland vales. This tradition of upland breeding was continued during the early modern period in the Scottish Highlands and Islands, the mountains of Wales, and the upland parts of northern and south-western England (see DROVERS; FAIRS; GRAZIERS; and BUTCHERS). Irish cattle were exported to England in large numbers; see D. M. Woodward, 'The Anglo-Irish Livestock Trade in the Seventeenth Century', *Irish Historical Studies*, 18 (1973).

In the later 17th century certain agricultural regions began to specialize (see DAIRYING). The extensive trade in cattle meant that most herds were a motley collection. Regional types could nevertheless be recognized, principally the black longhorns of Yorkshire, Derbyshire, Lancashire, and Staffordshire, the pied cattle of the Lincolnshire *fens and *marshes, and the red cattle of Somerset and Gloucestershire, but many local breeds could also be seen in the fields. Rinderpest was a major problem; see John Broad, 'Cattle Plague in Eighteenth-Century England', *Agricultural History Review*, 31/2 (1983). Few attempts at controlled breeding were made before the mid-18th century, when Robert Bakewell began to improve his longhorns. See R. J. Moore-Colyer's account of breed improvements in G. E. Mingay (ed.), *The Agrarian History of England and Wales*, vi, *1750–1850* (1989), and the *General Views of Agriculture*, which reported on the state of farming in each English county in the late 18th and early 19th centuries. Most breeds were not established until well into the 19th century, e.g. the Hereford herd book was opened in 1846. Friesian-Holsteins and other Continental breeds became popular in the second half of the 20th century. (See AGRICULTURAL HISTORY for the literature on the modern period.)

causewayed enclosures. Earthworks in southern England dating from the 4th and 5th millenia BC, whose purpose remains mysterious. Some appear to have been fortified, others to have been used for ceremonial or ritual purposes.

causey, causeway. A series of flagstones laid down on wet or soft terrain to prevent the formation of *holloways. Causey is derived from a Norman French word meaning 'trodden' and is not a shortening of causeway, which comes from a similar root. Causey is still used in the speech of northern and midland England to mean 'pavement', usually in the form of 'causey edge' alongside a road. Causeys were horse and foot paths associated with the *packhorse era. Individual causeys cannot be dated on stylistic grounds. Documentary evidence points to the use of causeys in the Middle Ages, but most surviving examples are probably from the 17th, 18th, and 19th centuries. Some were constructed by private enterprise, many by parish authorities. Long stretches survive in some moorland districts, but many are now overgrown or have been replaced by modern surfaces. See David Hey, *Packmen, Carriers and Packhorse Roads: Trade and Communications in North Derbyshire and South Yorkshire* (1980).

caveat. A legal process to suspend proceedings.

caves in the limestone parts of Britain have yielded much evidence of human occupation from the earliest times, e.g. remains from the Upper *Palaeolithic at Cresswell Crags (Derbyshire). *Folklore and place-names suggest the fear that later people had for caves. Such fears did not prevent some caves from being used for industrial purposes, e.g. *rope-making at Castleton (Derbyshire), or the *smelting of iron ore in the Forest of Dean.

cell. A small dwelling used by a *hermit, or an apartment in a *monastery.

cellars were an essential feature of the medieval town houses of *merchants and craftsmen. Surviving examples, e.g. at Chester, show that they were stone vaulted and approached via a short flight of steps. These cellars were used for storing and displaying goods for sale, and as workshops. Cellars were not normally a feature of rural *vernacular architecture before the 18th century, unless the lie of the land favoured such constructions. In the 19th century cellar accommodation became a notorious method of housing the poorest sections of society in the largest industrial towns. Such rooms were entered by a flight of external steps, which descended past a window. In the worst cases, an entire family was accommodated in a single room in a cellar.

Celtic Christianity. Christianity was established in Britain during the time of the Roman Empire. It retained its hold in Ireland, Wales, and parts of Scotland after the pagan *Anglo-Saxons had destroyed most of the churches in what was to become England. The first missionaries from Gaul arrived in Ireland in the late 4th or early 5th centuries; others soon followed from other parts of Britain. St Patrick, the greatest of the missionaries in Ireland, came from Wales in the early or the mid-5th century. Little is known about the organization of the missionary church, but an austere monasticism was well established by the 6th century. Armagh, which claimed St Patrick as its founder, became the greatest ecclesiastical centre in Ireland. In the late 6th century St Columba established a *monastery on the island of Iona to serve as a base for a mission to Scotland. See Charles Thomas, *Christianity in Roman Britain to AD 500* (1981), and Donnchadh Ó Corráin, 'Prehistoric and Early Christian Ireland', in R. F. Foster (ed.), *The Oxford Illustrated History of Ireland* (1989), ch. 1.

The slow conversion of the pagan Anglo-

Saxons came partly from St Augustine's mission from Rome to Kent in 597, and partly from the work of Celtic missionaries based at Iona. *Bede acknowledged the role of Irish monks in the conversion of *Northumbria after King Oswald encouraged missionaries from Iona to settle at Lindisfarne off the Northumberland coast. Three of the first four bishops of *Mercia were either Irish-born or Irish-trained, and another Irish monk, St Fursey, was active in *East Anglia. The question of which form of Christian organization—the Celtic or the Roman—should be accepted in England was determined in favour of the Roman model in 664 at the *Synod of Whitby. See Richard Morris, *Churches in the Landscape* (1989).

Celtic fields. The name given to prehistoric fields whose outline is preserved on the ground or can be seen from aerial photographs. Such fields are best preserved in limestone or chalk districts, e.g. Grassington (Yorkshire Dales) or Dorset, which have long been laid down to pasture and have not therefore had their archaeological features destroyed by ploughing. Celtic fields are roughly square or rectangular in shape and underlie later *field systems. (See also LYNCHET.)

cemeteries and crematoria. (See CAIRNS and TUMULUS for prehistoric cremation practices.) The Romans buried their urban dead in extramural cemeteries. The pagan *Anglo-Saxons practised cremation, but the Christian church insisted on burial. Cremation was not used again in Britain until the late 19th century. Early *churches were often sited by burial grounds or over the tomb of a martyr. (See CHURCHYARDS.)

The idea of landscaped public cemeteries came from Italy, France, and Sweden. The winding, tomb-lined avenues and well-contrived vistas of the landscaped cemetery at Père-Lachaise in Paris was widely admired. See J. S. Curl, *A Celebration of Death: An Introduction to Some of the Buildings, Monuments, and Settings of Funerary Architecture in the Western European Tradition* (1980). The Clifton Graveyard, Belfast, dates from 1774, and Calton Hill, Edinburgh, from the late 18th century, but England did not follow the fashion until the severe overcrowding of churchyards made them a health risk. Liverpool led the way in England, with the opening of the Necropolis in 1825 and the much larger St James Cemetery four years later. The St James Cemetery was in a redundant quarry, which was landscaped and provided with processional ramps for funeral carriages and with catacombs cut out of the quarry face. London acquired its first public cemetery in 1827 at Kensal Green, a 79-acre site, which had separate chapels for Anglicans and Dissenters. Other landscaped public cemeteries were soon opened at Norwood (1837), Highgate (1839), Nunhead (1840), Abney Park, Stoke Newington (1840), and Tower Hamlets (1841). Before the middle of the 19th century such cemeteries were generally established and run as commercial ventures, but after the passing of legislation in the 1850s and 1860s enforcing the closure of urban churchyards, municipal cemeteries became the rule. J. C. Loudon, *On the Laying Out, Planting, and Managing of Cemeteries* (1843) was widely influential and also led to improvements in the design of churchyards, with the construction of *lych-gates and new paths and the planting of yews, cypresses, and junipers, alongside native species like lime and elm. Such ideas also influenced the layout of public crematoria after the practice of cremation was ruled legal in 1884. The public crematorium at St John's, Woking (Surrey), opened the following year, was one of the first.

Cemetery records have sometimes been deposited at local *record offices, but others are still kept at the office on the site. They usually give the name, address, age, and occupation of the deceased, the date of death and of burial, and the position of the grave. These records are arranged chronologically, and are not indexed alphabetically.

censuses, local. For most places in England, Scotland, and Wales the national census of 1801 is the first count of the population; for Ireland it is 1821. However, individual places sometimes held a local census for a particular reason. Thus, the *township of Sheffield had 2,207 inhabitants in 1616, when a count was made on behalf of the *lord of the manor who was preparing a charitable bequest, and 10,121 people in 1736, when a case was being made for the opening of a new *chapel-of-ease. The records of local censuses appear in miscellaneous collections in local *record offices. Those that have come to light are listed in Colin R. Chapman, *Pre-1841 Censuses and Population Listings* (1990), and M. Medlycott, 'A Survey and Guide of Listings of Inhabitants', *Local Population Studies*, 46 (1991). (See also ECCLESIASTICAL CENSUSES.) Some of these local censuses are much more than a simple count of heads; they are listings by name of the inhabitants. See P. Laslett and J. Harrison, 'Clayworth and Cogenhoe' in H. E. Bell and R. L.

Ollard (eds.), *Historical Essays Presented to David Ogg* (1963) for an analysis of listings in two East Midlands parishes in the late 17th century.

census returns. The first census for the whole of Britain, except Ireland, was taken in 1801, but no central archival material survives from that exercise or from the following censuses of 1811, 1821, and 1831. A few schedules compiled by the census takers have come to light in local *record offices, but the great bulk of this material was destroyed once the official statistical tables had been published as *Parliamentary papers. These tables are a basic source for the study of *population levels and trends in the 19th and 20th centuries. They are available in the larger public reference libraries. Figures from at least the 19th-century returns for some counties may be more readily available in the relevant volumes of the *Victoria County History*. See the Office of Population Censuses and Surveys, *Guide to Census Reports, Great Britain, 1801–1966* (1977).

From 1841 the census has been collected by the office of the *Registrar-General. A number of enumerators were appointed for each sub-district, to issue forms and collect them the day after census night, and to copy the information into books. The transcriptions, or 'enumerators' returns', for 1841–91 survive. Those for England and Wales are available for consultation in microfilm form at the *Public Record Office Census Rooms, Chancery Lane, London, WC2. A leaflet explaining 'How to Use the Census Rooms' is available, but learning how to use the place indexes is a time-consuming task. No indexes of surnames are available, but the *Mormon Church, in co-operation with *family history societies, is preparing a national index of the 1881 census. Many family history societies have also made indexes of the personal names in the census returns for their area. Microfilm copies of the returns for particular districts are often available at public *libraries and local record offices or at *Mormon branch libraries. The Scottish system of enumeration differed in minor ways. In 1861 the Registrar-General for Scotland assumed responsibility for the Scottish census. The records are kept in the New Register House of the *Scottish Record Office, Edinburgh, and are now subject to the same *one hundred years' confidentiality rule as those for England and Wales. The Irish census records are discussed below.

The enumerators' districts of 1841 were retained, as far as possible, up to at least 1891, so that comparisons with previous data could be made. The aim was to make the districts of a roughly standard size and to create them from administrative units, or parts of units, such as *parishes or *townships, that were meaningful to local people. The rapid growth of the population of Victorian Britain meant that some districts eventually had to be altered. The alterations are noted in the printed summaries of the returns.

The information provided by the 1841 census enumerators' returns is not as full as that given in later years. The arrangement is by *households (or by institutions, e.g. *workhouse or *prison), but the relationship of each member to the head of the household is not recorded. The ages of people over 15 were rounded down to the nearest five, so that the population could be classified in age-bands. Thus, someone whose age is recorded as 40 could have been 41, 42, 43, or 44. (This leaves aside the consideration that the age might not be accurate even within this band.) The occupation of each person is then noted; this is necessarily a succinct description that takes no account of dual occupations or *by-employments. The final column does not record the birthplace, but merely notes whether the person was born in the same county as his or her present residence, or whether the place of birth was in Scotland, Ireland, or 'foreign parts'. The 1841 census was taken on 6 June, but as some itinerant harvest workers were sleeping rough and were therefore not recorded, it was decided in future to hold the census on a Sunday at the beginning of spring. The days on which the census was taken for the rest of the 19th century were 30 March 1851, 7 April 1861, 2 April 1871, 3 April 1881, 5 April 1891, and 31 March 1901.

From 1851 onwards the enumerators' returns provide fuller information. Nightworkers who were not at home on census night but who returned the following morning were now listed with other members of their household. The relationship of each person with the head of household was noted. The returns purport to record the exact age and place of birth, but this information needs to be handled cautiously. It is a common experience to find that a person had apparently not aged 10 years by the time of the next census and to discover that the birthplace was no longer the same. The recorded birthplace may have been the nearest town, or perhaps the place where the person had lived as a child.

Despite the inclusion of Ireland within the *United Kingdom in 1801, the procedure for making a census of the Irish population was quite different. After an abortive attempt in

1813, the first official census was taken in 1821. It gave names, ages, occupations, and relationships to heads of household, also the acreages of land and the number of storeys in the house. The Irish census returns for 1861, 1871, 1881, and 1891 were destroyed by government order; those for 1821, 1831, 1841, and 1851 were destroyed in an explosion and fire in Dublin in the time of the Civil War (1922). The few fragments that were saved are listed in James G. Ryan, *Irish Records: Sources for Family and Local History* (1988). The 1901 and 1911 census returns were stored locally and were thus preserved from destruction in 1922. They are now available for inspection at the National Archives, Dublin. Although the enumerators' returns do not survive, published reports from 1841 to 1911 give the acreage, population, number of houses, and valuation of each individual townland. The 1851 report is of particular interest for it gives the 1841 figures as well, and thus allows comparison of the pre- and post-famine population. It is published as *British Parliamentary Papers, 1851, Census Ireland Population* by the Irish Universities Press. (See EMIGRATION; and IRISH EMIGRATION.)

Edward Higgs, *Making Sense of the Census: The Manuscript Returns for England and Wales, 1801–1901* (1988), supplemented by the same author's article, 'The 1891 Census: Continuity and Change', *The Local Historian*, 22/4 (1992), provides a full guide to the administrative background of the census returns of England and Wales and the interpretation of the data, e.g. the practical problems in deciding what was meant by 'household' in towns where subletting was widespread and lodgers were numerous. Identifying a particular family from a census return is not much of a problem in a rural parish, but it can be a time-consuming task in a city, particularly in London. The boundaries of the enumerators' districts sometimes ran down the middle of a street, and even in the large towns houses were rarely numbered before the 1850s, and often much later. Some Victorian towns expanded so rapidly that the address system was chaotic. Street indexes exist in many record offices to help the researcher. For an example of the ways in which the different social classes were segregated into different residential districts, see J. Foster, *Class Struggle and the Industrial Revolution: Early Industrial Capitalism in Three English Towns* (1974).

The genealogical information provided by the enumerators' returns is of great value. For example, the information about age and birthplace can often lead the researcher to an entry in a baptism register. If a person appeared in the 1851 census for a particular place but was not there in 1861, then the period of migration or the search for a death certificate is narrowed to a decade. Similarly, the age of the eldest child will narrow the period for which a search is made for a marriage certificate. However, it must be remembered that the people who supplied the information to the census enumerators were sometimes confused and that, although the falsification of census returns was a criminal act, some replies were untruthful.

A particular problem concerns the casual or part-time nature of much women's work, for this was often not recorded, particularly as the home was the usual place of work. See Edward Higgs, 'Women, Occupations and Work in the Nineteenth-Century Censuses', *History Workshop Journal*, 23 (1987), and Elizabeth Roberts, *Women's Work, 1840–1940* (1988). The same problem of identification occurs with children's employment: see A. Davin, 'Working or Helping? London Working-Class Children in the Domestic Economy' in J. Smith, I. Wallerstein, and H. Evers (eds.), *Households and the World Economy* (1984). See also R. Lawton (ed.), *The Census and Social Structure: An Interpretative Guide to Nineteenth-Century Censuses for England and Wales* (1978). Two detailed local studies are Michael Anderson, *Family Structure in Nineteenth-Century Lancashire* (1971), which investigates Preston, and Alan Armstrong, *Stability and Change in an English Country Town: A Social Study of York, 1801–51* (1974).

The computer analysis of the census enumerators' returns for one rural parish is reported in John Beckett and Trevor Foulds, 'Beyond the Micro: Laxton, the Computer and Social Change Over Time', *The Local Historian*, 16/8 (1985). This analysis demonstrated the high turnover of names between 1851 and 1861, but the underlying stability of a core group of households. Laxton's population fell from 534 to 500 during this decade, and only 247 people appeared in both returns; on the other hand, no fewer than 75 of the 99 households recorded in 1861 had been there 10 years earlier. Half the population of the parish had changed, but the family structure was not much different. In his study of Preston, Michael Anderson found that in 1851 about 80 per cent of the town's population had been born within a 30-mile radius. He showed that, far from destroying *kinship links, the *Industrial Revolution actually strengthened them, for migrants retained their connections with their former homes and clustered in family and neighbourhood groups (including the lodgers) in their new town.

Census returns are therefore a prime source for local and family historians. They provide much information about household structure, occupations, stability and migration, and genealogical connections.

central government. Central government may be readily defined as the central executive of government (the council or cabinet), the revenue and disbursing departments, parliament, the government departments concerned with defence, and the law courts. Until the 18th century the royal household ought to be included as an additional element. Generally, central government was located in Westminster, but it has also had its provincial off-shoots—in York and Ludlow before 1640, in Dublin, Edinburgh, and latterly in Cardiff. Indeed, it is all too easy for an English audience to forget that England was only one of the nations for which the Westminster Government was responsible. At its early 14th-century apogee, Westminster governed an area between Kent and County Kerry, after 1707 between Cornwall and Caithness, and, until recent memory, much of Africa, Asia, and the Antipodes. Again, the English are prone to overlook the fact that a disproportionate preoccupation of central government between the 16th and the early 20th century was the maintenance of order in Ireland. Local circumstances, both there and in Scotland, necessitated policies which diverged significantly from those employed in England itself. The 20th century has seen the loss of some areas (the Irish Republic), the establishment of satellite government in another (Northern Ireland), and the delegation of powers to regional offices in Scotland and Ireland. 'Central government' means markedly different things from different regional perspectives.

A section on central government may seem out of place in a companion to local and family history, but this is not so. What we can discover of the past is determined (or circumscribed) by the documents which survive or, more crucially, which were created in the first place. A large proportion of the materials available to us were made for (or by) central government. What it is possible for us, as historians, to know about the past is conditioned, in ways which we might prefer to ignore, by the preoccupations of central government. When government started to take *censuses, instituted a system of *civil registration, or began to collect data on crops or *Poor Law expenditure, it was for their purposes and not ours. We are prisoners of that essential truth.

Here we have to recognize that the purposes of central government were, before the 19th century, limited by a narrow concept of what government could (and could not) attempt. One need be neither Marxist nor cynical to recognize that the central purpose of government was to perpetuate its own existence and to protect the interests of a property-owning class. This purpose took several forms. Obviously, government was concerned with the defence of the borders of the realm and to this end maintained armed forces, voluntary militias, and a navy. But government was also anxious to protect itself against the enemy within: its own subjects, or sections of them. Here we have to recognize that the military power available to English government before the 19th century was extremely limited in scale. Indeed, in the 16th century the repression of *rebellions was undertaken by recruiting into armies people directly equivalent to those rebelling in neighbouring districts. The preservation of public order before modern times was undertaken by government anticipating and ameliorating grievances, especially those concerning the distribution of foodstuffs. The government's preoccupation with *enclosure derived not from any desire to retard economic change, but from a belief, confirmed by events in Oxfordshire in 1596 (where a small revolt was launched and failed), or in the Midlands in 1607 (where more serious riots against enclosures took place), that the public associated enclosure with high prices and so empty bellies, and that this could lead to breakdowns in public order. Likewise, social stability was encouraged by the provision of a stable currency and a system of *courts—both central and local—for the resolution of public and private grievances. Central government therefore supplied services to its citizens in order to maintain civil order and stability, the touchstone of which was the continuance of government. (The caveat might be added that English government in Ireland has never been entirely consensual, with the result that civil administration there has always been much more militaristic in character.)

The capacity of government was, however, limited. Here, two points need to be made. First, despite the *Councils in the North and Wales, or the chief deputy's office in Dublin, government was highly centralized in Westminster. Given the slow speed of communications before the 19th century, it was not possible for any central authority, especially one located so far from the geographical centre of the British Isles, to control in detail the actions of its local agents. Council or Cabinet could therefore find themselves trailing behind decisions taken in the field, of which they might not approve but could do nothing to alter. And, as we shall see, it was quite possible for the government's local agents to conceal from Westminster inconvenient facts or to supply favourable accounts of events.

Secondly, government had not the manpower to deal with the queries and requests which would inevitably have flowed to the centre if Westminster had tried to regulate the actions of its officers in greater detail. Enclosure is a typical instance of this. Whilst the legislative framework against enclosure remained basically unaltered over long periods, government was generally inactive until disturbances or high prices forced the matter on to its agenda. Then, and only then, were commissions established to gather details of the scale of the problem, and prosecutions launched against offenders; but interest soon waned when the immediate social problems disappeared and government turned its attention to more pressing matters.

The majority of the government's employees were concerned with the collection of revenue as *customs officials, rent collectors, or excise men. For the early modern period, it is impossible to produce accurate figures of how large the central establishment was for much government work was carried out not by its own salaried officers but by clerks and deputies employed by them and paid out of the officers' own salaries, fees, and *pourboires*. (In time the most successful of these deputies might become officers in their own right.) Dr Penry Williams has estimated the number of formal government servants in the late 16th century at around 600 administrators of the crown lands (mostly stewards and bailiffs) and a further 600 in all other departments, and goes on to suggest that, proportionately, this was only a tenth of the numbers employed in France, whose officials, in the eyes of a contemporary, lay 'as thick as the grasshoppers in Egypt' (P. Williams, *The Tudor Regime* (1979), 107). The Privy Council was serviced by either one or two principal secretaries and a clerk to the Council, all aided by a handful of clerks—the majority of whom were probably only copyists who took no role in the decision-making process—supported by around 30 messengers. This was little changed by the end of the 18th century. Even then, the Home Office had a staff of less than two dozen (the Secretary of State, two permanent under-secretaries, a dozen clerks, and 'various cleaning and janitorial staff'). 'The size of the office was reflected in the quality of its administration. It did not, indeed, could not, administer

programmes or policies: it dealt with individuals' (C. Emsley, 'The Home Office and its sources of information and investigation', *English Historical Review*, 94 (1979), 532). Or, as Dr Eastwood has written, it monitored and advised. By comparison, in 1690 the excise establishment had 1313 employees and by 1779 it had 5778, but by 1783 this had been reduced to 4910 (J. Brewer, *The Sinews of Power* (1989), table 4.1). Other than its excise men, central government had no salaried officials in the counties. It therefore relied on its local correspondents to bring matters to its notice. These informers were mostly *Justices of the Peace over whom the centre had little real control. Government could select the individuals to be named to the Commission of the Peace; but it could not ensure that they would serve, nor could it prevent them placing local solidarities and interests above the needs of their counties. JPs in the 1530s rushed to tell Cromwell and the Council of potentially treasonable gossip out of fear that their negligence might be discovered and found culpable. At other periods the desire to avoid central interference led JPs to keep the centre ignorant of their actions: in 1793 the magistrates in Bristol chose not to tell the Home Office of riots in which the militia had shot rioters.

Until the early 19th century the English had laws rather than government, hence the information that central government required was limited. It was concerned to hear about—and punish—outrages, but it had no interest in, say, the local operation of the Poor Law other than ensuring that the appropriate statutes were implemented. For these various reasons central government was rarely in control of events.

The expansion of government over the past 200 years reflects the enormous increase in the range of activities in which it has been thought necessary for government to be involved. In turn, this has required an enormous expansion in the information required by central government to allow it to undertake the effective and efficient administration of the provinces. The first indications of this urge to control and regulate may be found in the decades of the *Napoleonic wars (it being a rule of history that external emergencies lead to extensions in government powers and competences). It is no coincidence that government was more or less simultaneously seeking information on the state of agriculture through *crop returns and holding the first decennial census in 1801. After this time, central government came to require ever more detailed information about circumstances in the counties, sometimes gathered by circulars directed to the local authorities and sometimes by a commission or inquiry specially set up to undertake investigations. The need for fuller and better information grew as central government came to have fingers in more and more local pies. The commission established to supervise the local administration of the New Poor Law was only the first of a whole series of boards designed to shadow local government, either compelling local authorities to implement new statutory provisions (often by offering grants in aid) or attempting to restrain them from profligate expenditure (a theme as much of the 1820s and 1830s as of the 1980s and 1990s). And despite the Victorian commitment to *laissez-faire*, it quickly became obvious that both industry and the privately owned infrastructure needed to be supervised. Again, the answer was the creation of boards out of which the modern ministries have developed. In the 20th century the collection of statistics and the need for local authorities to seek central government sanction for local initiatives meant that all the business of the localities was known to, and approved by, London. The growth of central government was mirrored by the progressive emasculation of *local government.

The increased regulation of local government was only one dimension of the growth of central government in the 20th century. It was matched by the development of interventionist economic policies, a great expansion of public welfare provision, and the nationalization (for doctrinaire as well as economic reasons) of key industries. The taste for centralized planning meant that decisions over, say, road development were taken in London. The changing concerns of government are reflected in the range and content of the government archives available to the historian and many are highly informative on local and family history. By using the public records it is possible, in the 19th and 20th centuries, to describe aspects of life which are invisible for earlier periods, and often to hear individual voices which earlier are lost to us. The great expansion in the range of government activity is therefore a blessing for the historian: the sheer volume of materials available for exploration means that it is also a curse.   R. W. HOYLE

centres of local and regional history. A number of British universities, e.g. East Anglia, Keele, Lancaster, and Nottingham, have centres which offer lectures, seminars, research classes, and postgraduate study on the region which they serve. The Centre for English Cultural Tradition and Language at the University of Sheffield provides for the study of *folklore, language, *surnames, and local and family history. The University of Edinburgh has a School of Scottish Studies, and the University of Strathclyde has a Research Centre in Scottish History. (See also LEICESTER, DEPARTMENT OF ENGLISH LOCAL HISTORY.)

centuriation. The laying out of roads and fields in a regular pattern by the Romans. Some of these patterns survive in the present English landscape, notably in south-east Essex. They are particularly well observed from aerial photographs.

ceorl. The lowest class of *Old English freeman; the origin of 'churl', though without the later associations.

cereals. An outline of those areas which have traditionally been farmed for cereals is provided in Joan Thirsk, *England's Agricultural Regions and Agrarian History, 1500–1750* (1987), S. J. Graham and L. J. Proudfoot (eds.), *An Historical Geography of Ireland* (1993), G. Whittington and I. D. Whyte (eds.), *An Historical Geography of Scotland* (1983), and the various volumes of The *Agrarian History of England and Wales*. See also Alan R. H. Baker and Robin A. Butlin (eds.), *Studies of Field Systems in the British Isles* (1973).

Wheat and barley were dominant over much of southern England, whereas oats was the chief crop north of the Trent. The 1801 *crop returns reveal that wheat was grown on 33 per cent of the arable land of England, oats on 26 per cent, and barley on 19 per cent, but that in all counties north of the Trent oats accounted for over 50 per cent. In the midland shires of England *peas and beans ranked as the second or third crops. During the first half of the 19th century wheat began to be grown more extensively in northern England. (See TITHES, and AGRICULTURAL STATISTICS.) In Wales, oats covered 38 per cent of the arable land, barley 29 per cent, and wheat 22 per cent, but most land was used for pastoral farming. In Scotland, wheat was grown in the most favoured areas, with some barley, peas, and beans, but the arable land was mainly given over to oats. In Ireland, on the eve of the Famine, wheat accounted for 11.5 per cent of agricultural output by value, barley 4 per cent, and oats 19 per cent; the *potato was, of course, the chief crop.

certificates of residence. See SETTLEMENT, ACT OF; and POOR LAW.

chain. A linear measure of 22 yards used in surveying, which remains in use as the length of a cricket pitch.

chain-making. A West Midlands industry established in the 19th century. The heaviest chains were made in a few large workshops by the 1830s, but most chains were made in about 300 small workshops in Cradley and neighbouring settlements.

chalkland. The chalk *Downs of southern England and the *Wolds of Lincolnshire and Yorkshire are distinctive landscapes, now largely devoid of trees, populated only thinly, with little or no signs of rural industry. They were once, however, lightly wooded; see Alan Everitt, 'River and Wold: Reflections on the Historical Origin of Regions and *Pays*' in *Landscape and Community in England*, ch. 3 (1985). They provide archaeological evidence of former arable cultivation, and since parliamentary *enclosure have partly reverted to the growing of crops, but essentially these poor, thin soils are used for sheep grazing. See, for example, W. H. Hudson, *A Shepherd's Life* (1910), which deals with Wiltshire.

chambered tomb. *Neolithic tomb from the 4th millennium BC.

Chambers, J. D. (1898–1971). Professor of Economic History, University of Nottingham, and outstanding regional historian. His research interests were centred on population, agriculture, and industry from the late 17th century to the mid-19th century. Much of his evidence was taken from his native Nottinghamshire. (He was the younger brother of Jessie Chambers, the friend of D. H. Lawrence.) His work on Nottinghamshire led to the publication of *Nottinghamshire in the Eighteenth Century* (1932) and *The Vale of Trent, 1670–1800: A Regional Study of Economic Change* (1957), a pioneering analysis of demographic evidence from *parish registers. This interest culminated in the writing of *Population, Economy and Society in Pre-Industrial England* (1972).

David Chambers's farming background led him to consider the effects of *population and parliamentary *enclosure on the rural economy in 'Enclosure and Labour Supply in the Industrial Revolution', *Economic History Review*, 2nd ser., 5/3 (1953). This famous article challenged the views of the *Hammonds on the social effects of enclosure. He went on to join G. E. Mingay in writing *The Agricultural Revolution, 1750–1880* (1966).

champion land. A term used in the early modern period to denote land given over to cereals in *open-fields as distinct from *wood pasture, *fens, *moors, etc. The term conjures up a picture of a certain kind of landscape with large fields, few hedges, and little timber. It also implies the settlement of people in *villages rather than *hamlets or scattered farms.

chancel. The eastern part of a church (now known as the sanctuary) containing the high *altar and reserved for the clergy and choir. Until the *Reformation it was usually divided from the *nave and partly hidden from public view by a *rood screen across the chancel arch. At the Reformation in England most rood screens were taken down and the congregation admitted into the chancel for the celebration of the eucharist. The maintenance of the chancel was the responsibility of the *tithe owner; for this reason the architecture of the chancel is often different from that of the rest of the church. The tombs and monuments in the chancel are normally of tithe owners. William Shakespeare is buried in the chancel of Holy Trinity, Stratford-on-Avon, not because of his fame but because he had purchased the right to collect the local tithes.

Chancellor. An official secretary, e.g. of the *chapter of a *cathedral. The Chancellor of England (Lord Chancellor or Lord High Chancellor) became the highest officer in medieval England; he presides over the House of Lords and remains a member of the Cabinet and the highest judicial officer. The Chancellor of the Exchequer became the highest finance minister.

Chancery, Court of. In the early Middle Ages the decisions of the king's council were put into effect through the Chancery, under the direction of the *Chancellor. The records of the Chancery date from the beginning of the reign of King John in 1199 (see CHARTER ROLLS; PATENT ROLLS; and CLOSE ROLLS). The Chancery became a court of law about 1348, during the reign of Edward III. It acted as a court of *equity to deal with cases for which there was no provision under Common Law, and later with cases where the plaintiff might have been at a disadvantage. In 1873 all equity jurisdiction passed to the Chancery Division of the Supreme Court of Judicature. See E. F. Garrett, *Chancery and Other Legal Proceedings* (1968), W. J. Jones, *The Elizabethan Court of Chancery* (1967), and Dorian Gerhold, *Courts of Equity: A Guide to Chancery and other Legal Records for Local and Family Historians* (1994).

The Court of Chancery has extensive records, which are housed at the *Public Record Office. All records before 1873 begin with the letter C, afterwards with the letter J. See the Public Record Office Records Information leaflet, no. 30, 'Chancery Proceedings (Equity Suits)', which includes a list of published and unpublished finding aids. The various classes are described in the *Guide to the Contents of the Public Record Office*, 3 vols. (1963–8). The records of cases include pleadings (statements made by parties to a case; known collectively as Chancery Proceedings), evidence in the form of affidavits (statements on oath) and depositions (examinations of witnesses), and court decisions and opinions, though these last are the most difficult documents to locate in the archive. Cases were mostly in English. No records of the oral proceedings at court survive, but the written depositions of witnesses are a rich source of information for local and family historians. Families of middling means often used the court, and the witnesses were drawn from all sections of local society. Most of the records are indexed only by the name of the plaintiff. The finding aids, which are arranged chronologically, give names of plaintiffs (sometimes called the *orator) and defendants, but there is no index of the names of those who were called upon to be witnesses. Most indexes are unpublished and are available only on the shelves of the search rooms at the Public Record Office. See Stella Colwell, *Dictionary of Genealogical Sources in the Public Record Office* (1992).

chantry chapel. A private chapel, normally attached to a parish *church or a *chapel-of-ease, with an *altar for the celebration of mass for the souls of the founder and his or her nominees, or for the souls of the members of *guilds and fraternities who had erected such a chapel. The system began in the 13th century, but became fashionable in the later Middle Ages, particularly after the *Black Death, when the number of endowments to *monasteries declined sharply. Chantry chapels were built at the end of the aisles of the *nave, extending along the side walls of the *chancel, or within the transepts of cruciform churches. They were dedicated to the saints nominated by the founders. (See LADY CHAPELS.) Some of the chantry chapels founded by members of the royal family and the nobility are major works of architecture, with fan-vaults, carved and gilded woodwork, and *stained glass windows. One of the most substantial is that at St Mary's, Warwick, which was built in the 1440s to house the tomb of Richard Beauchamp, Earl of Warwick. The endowment of a chantry chapel allowed for the employment of a priest who received either

a money payment or land to farm or rent. These properties were confiscated when Edward VI dissolved all chantries in 1547. See G. H. Cook, *Medieval Chantries and Chantry Chapels* (1947), and A. Kreider, *English Chantries: The Road to Dissolution* (1979).

chapbook. Cheap popular books, published in London from the 16th to the 18th centuries and sold by *book sellers, *chapmen, or *pedlars throughout the land. The texts consisted of traditional stories and *ballads, histories, and moral and religious tales. The chapbooks collected by Samuel *Pepys in the 1680s (held at Magdalene College, Cambridge) are the major source. See Margaret Spufford, *Small Books and Pleasant Histories: Popular Fiction and its Readership in Seventeenth-Century England* (1981).

chapel, domestic. The *palaces of the *Anglo-Saxons incorporated private chapels. They were the forerunners of domestic chapels that were built by rich *landowners throughout the Middle Ages and after, down to the 19th century. In medieval palaces and *castles chapels were normally sited on the same floor as the private chambers. Some developed into parish *churches or *chapels-of-ease, but at Haddon Hall (Derbyshire) the reverse process can be seen, by which the parish church was incorporated within the manorial complex after the village that it had once served had disappeared. A lord who maintained a chapel and a priest had to obtain a licence from the bishop (see BISHOPS' REGISTERS). After the *Reformation, *Roman Catholic landowners were forced to keep such activities secret (see PRIEST HOLES). The *Protestant chapels of 16th-century country houses, e.g. Hardwick Hall (Derbyshire), are plain, rather modest structures, but in the last decade of the 17th century the family that owned Hardwick built an ornate chapel in *baroque style at their larger property at Chatsworth, employing craftsmen from the King's Works and abroad. Richly decorated and furnished chapels remained in vogue in country houses for the next two centuries, an outstanding example being that at Castle Howard (Yorkshire), which was redecorated in the 1870s by William Morris and Edward Burne-Jones.

chapel, Nonconformist. The word 'chapel' was originally applied to a Roman Catholic place of worship. (See CHAPEL-OF-EASE.) During the 17th century *Puritan landowners, concerned to increase facilities for organized religion along lines of which they approved, revived the medieval tradition of endowing places of worship in remote areas distant from parish churches. Chapels thus acquired a connection with a form of religion that after 1662 became classified as *Nonconformity or Protestant Dissent. Early chapels were plain, rectangular, single-storey structures in *vernacular styles, whose interiors were focused on the pulpit, which stood in a prominent position either at one end or at the centre of one side. Even when much larger buildings, two storeys high and fitted with galleries, were erected, they retained a barn-like appearance. The early Wesleyan preaching houses that favoured an octagonal shape, e.g. Heptonstall (Yorkshire), were exceptional in favouring a different design. Many 19th-century chapels were small and simple; the humblest earned the nickname of tin-tabernacles. However, those denominations which attracted wealthy congregations rebuilt their chapels, first in classical and then in *Gothic styles. The Gothic was long resisted as representing medieval Roman Catholicism, but in the Victorian period some Wesleyan, *Congregational, and *Unitarian congregations announced their respectability by choosing this style. Rectangular buildings with a classical front remained the preferred form, however. Such chapels are a distinctive feature of the Welsh landscape; many have a prominent inscription giving the name, date of foundation, and a biblical text. Large numbers of Nonconformist chapels became redundant in the last third of the 20th century. Many have been demolished, others have been taken over by different bodies (both religious and secular). See Christopher Stell, *An Inventory of Nonconformist Chapels and Meeting Houses in Central England* (1986), . . . *South-West England* (1991), and . . . *the North of England* (1994).

chapel-of-ease. A term used to indicate a building used for religious worship that was created for the ease of the inhabitants of an outlying part of a *parish. These included the places of worship in many of the *medieval new towns. Thus, the large church of Holy Trinity, Hull, was a chapel-of-ease of the parish of Hessle. The *tithes of the inhabitants of a *chapelry went to the *rector of the parish; the chapels were served by curates. Many chapels-of-ease obtained rights of baptism, marriage, and burial. Most were made into parish churches during the 19th century. See Paul Hair, 'The Chapel in the English Landscape', *The Local Historian*, 21/1 (1991).

chapelry. The area served by a *chapel-of-ease.

chaplain. A priest serving a private individual or family, a private body, e.g. a *hospital, or a public institution, e.g. the army.

chapman. A middleman. The term is derived from *Old English *chepe*, meaning market, which has given place-name forms such as Chipping and Cheapside. It has also given rise to an occupational *surname. The commercial activities of a chapman might have been extensive, but a petty-chapman was no more than a *pedlar.

chapter. 1. The governing body of a *cathedral or a *collegiate church.
2. The daily assembly of the members of a religious house. The name is derived from the practice of reading a chapter from the rule of the order of that assembly.

chapter house. The building used for the meetings of a *chapter. At first these were rectangular in shape, but during the 13th century the polygonal form was adopted because of its superior acoustics and the opportunities it afforded for architectural display. The chapter houses at Wells, Southwell, and York cathedrals are particularly fine examples. See also DEAN.

charcoal was used for a range of industrial activities, but especially as fuel in the *water-powered blast *furnaces of the 16th to the 18th centuries. It was obtained from the underwood of *coppices, which was charred in hearths that did not admit air, so preventing rapid combustion. The process lasted for several days in order to get rid of moisture in the wood. Charcoal burners were referred to as colliers and are thus often confused with coal miners. Leases allowed the 'coaling' of coppiced wood. Whilst the job was under way, the charcoal burners lived in temporary huts constructed of poles and turf sods: an example may be seen at the open-air Weald and Downland Museum at Singleton (Sussex). The evidence of former hearths is often hard to find as they are now overgrown, but clues are provided by blackened soils in circles of about 15 feet diameter, often burrowed into (because of their softness) by *rabbits. By the late 19th century charcoal burning was considered a suitably quaint subject for photographers to record. It is reviving again because of the popularity of barbecues.

charity boards. Lists of the charitable endowments within a parish, painted on boards which normally hang inside the tower or porch of the parish *church. They usually date from the 18th and 19th centuries.

Charity Commissioners. The Charity Commission for England and Wales was established in 1853, following the recommendation of a royal commission of 1849, to oversee the accounts and activities of registered charities. Previous inquiries into charities had been conducted on an *ad hoc* basis. The Charitable Trusts Act (1860) empowered the commission to appoint or remove trustees and to change the purpose of a trust if the original purpose was outdated. See R. Tompson, *The Charity Commission and the Age of Reform* (1979). The Charities Act (1960) provides the basis for the work of the present Charity Commission, which maintains a central register of charities at 14 Ryder Street, London SW1 (for national charities and those in southern England) and Graeme House, Derby Square, Liverpool (for northern England and Wales). Documents over 30 years old are open to public inspection.

charivari. See ROUGH MUSIC.

charnel house. Before the practice arose in the 17th century of marking graves with permanent *gravestones, churchyard graves were often reused. The bones from previous burials were collected together in a charnel house next to the church or at the edge of the churchyard. *Crypts were sometimes used for the same purpose.

charter. A document granting rights or privileges. Thus, a *lord of a manor who wished to create a *market or to hunt in a *park or *chase had to obtain a royal charter. (See CHARTER ROLLS.) Anglo-Saxon charters are a major source for the study of ancient *estates and *boundaries.

chartered company. A company of *merchants, e.g. the Merchant Adventurers', the *East India Company, and the *Hudson's Bay Company, which were incorporated by royal or parliamentary *charter, and received certain monopoly privileges.

Charter rolls. Records from the Court of *Chancery, dating from 1199 to 1517, of royal grants of land or rights, and confirmations of such grants. They are housed at the *Public Record Office under C 53 and have all been published. Those for the reign of King John (1199–1216) were printed by the Record Commissioners in 1837, the rest in six volumes in the PRO's *Calendar of Charter Rolls* (1903–27). They are particularly important for the study of the history of *boroughs.

Chartism. The Chartist movement acquired its name from the six points of the charter published in 1838 by the London Working Men's Association. The Charter demanded universal male suffrage, equal electoral districts, annual Parliaments, payment of members, secret ballots, and no property qualifications for MPs. All this was eventually achieved, except for annual Parliaments, but at the time it was considered revolutionary.

The Chartist movement grew from earlier agitation, going back to the constitutional societies of the 1790s, but is regarded as the first genuinely working-class mass political movement. It was fuelled by disappointment over the 1832 Reform Act, which had left the majority of the population disenfranchised, and by other Radical causes such as opposition to the new Poor Law. At first, it attracted much Radical middle-class support, for it was seen as growing naturally from the Radical programme, but the middle classes were soon put off by the associated ideas of social change and what they saw as the threat of mob rule. Chartist meetings drew large crowds in 1838, until they were made illegal. By 1840 the Chartists were in retreat. Their revival in 1841–2 saw a gradual shift to more extreme demands. In 1848, the year of revolutions in Europe, the Chartists presented a huge national petition to Parliament. Their support was greatest in the manufacturing districts, where they were able to get many of their members elected to local councils. Their activities are well recorded in local *newspapers. But their failure in 1848 heralded their decline in a subsequent period of prosperity.

The original six points of the charter were widened to include other social reforms. See Malcolm Chase, 'The Chartist Land Plan and the Local Historian', *The Local Historian*, 18/2 (1988). For a detailed study of a region that was not at the forefront of Chartist activity, see Roger Wells, 'Southern Chartism', *Rural History: Economy, Society, Culture*, 2/1 (1991). See also Asa Briggs (ed.), *Chartist Studies* (1959), J. T. Ward, *Chartism* (1971), D. Thompson, *The Chartists: Popular Politics in the Industrial Revolution* (1984), and J. F. C. Harrison and D. Thompson, *Bibliography of the Chartist Movement, 1837–1976* (1978).

chase. A hunting area allowed by royal *charter, the private equivalent of a royal *forest. Chases were larger than *deer parks and were not enclosed by ditches and palings. Even when chases such as Hatfield Chase (Yorkshire) reverted to the Crown they were not normally subject to forest law.

chattel. Personal property that is not real estate or *freehold. Chattel is derived, via Norman

French, from the same Latin word as is cattle: thus, confusion arises when *wills and probate *inventories refer to 'catell'.

cheap. Old English *chepe*, meaning market, has given rise to street names in many parts of England. In provincial towns the name 'Cheapside' was often adopted in imitation of the London name. Chipping Camden, Chipping Sodbury, and other market towns have acquired their names in this way.

cheese trade. In the 17th century, particularly after 1660, certain areas began to acquire a national reputation for the quality of their cheese. Farmers found that they could afford to concentrate on cheese production and buy what *cereals they needed at market out of their profits. Thus, the Cheshire cheese trade expanded rapidly in the late 17th century. The natural quality of the grass in the *meadows and pastures of the Cheshire Plain, even before the introduction of *clovers and improved grasses, together with the local availability of *salt, enabled farmers with only small or medium-sized herds to produce cheese for factors who saw to its export by river and along the coast to London and the naval ports, or overland to market towns and *fairs. In Cheshire between 1660 and 1740 five out of every six farmers' probate *inventories record cheese, sometimes in special cheese chambers. North Shropshire, Gloucestershire, Warwickshire, Leicestershire, Suffolk, and the Dove Valley (separating Staffordshire and Derbyshire) prospered in a similar manner, but the prices obtained for Cheddar cheeses show that they were considered the best. By 1750 all the cheese-producing areas that were of national importance in Victorian times were already sending their cheese to market in London. The coming of the *railways enabled the cheese-producers of remoter areas, e.g. Wensleydale, to compete nationally. The late 20th century has seen the disappearance of farm-made cheeses in favour of factory products and a greatly increased import trade in Continental cheeses, though English farmhouse cheeses show signs of returning. A Specialist Cheesemakers' Association was formed in 1989.

Chelsea Hospital. A retirement home in south-west London for army pensioners, founded by Charles II in a building designed by Wren, and completed in 1692. Its registers of baptisms (1691–1812), marriages (1691–1765), and burials (1692–1856) can be consulted at the *General Register Office, St Catherine's House, London.

chemical industry. The major centres of the chemical industry since its rapid growth in the 19th century have been Merseyside and Teesside. The towns in both these districts were created largely by *immigration. The *soap and *glass manufacturers were British, but the entrepreneurs who established the heavy chemicals and dyestuff industries in south Lancashire were men from the Continent, such as Alfred Mond, who was born in Germany, or men who had been trained there. Towns such as Runcorn and Widnes, which grew quickly in the desolate landscape around the alkali works, had little in common with the neighbouring textile towns. Good wages for heavy, dirty jobs, including night shift work, attracted immigrants, particularly from Ireland and Wales. Industrial relations were generally peaceful. See T. C. Barker and J. R. Harris, *A Merseyside Town in the Industrial Revolution: St Helens, 1750–1900* (1959). Meanwhile, Manchester became a noted centre for *dyeing and, to a lesser degree, a chemical industry developed in Glasgow to serve the local textile industries. In the 20th century Teesside became the other major centre of the chemical industry and the headquarters of Imperial Chemical Industries (ICI). See W. G. Reader, *Imperial Chemical Industries: A History*, 2 vols. (1970, 1975).

Chesapeake Bay. The arrival of three ships belonging to the Virginia Company of London in Chesapeake Bay in 1607, and the foundation of Jamestown, marks the beginning of permanent British settlement in America. After the first two years, only 38 of the original 105 settlers were still alive. The colony eventually prospered through the cultivation and sale of *tobacco. About 75 per cent of the names of those who settled in the Chesapeake during the 17th century are recorded in the Land Office at Richmond, Virginia, but only a small proportion have been traced to their origins in Britain. The settlers did not always stay in their new abode, but moved on to new sites. See J. P. R. Horn, 'Moving on in the New World: Migration and Out-Migration in the Seventeenth Century Chesapeake' in P. Clark and D. Souden (eds.), *Migration and Society in Early Modern England* (1987).

chevage. A payment made to a lord by a *villein who wished to move from one *manor to another.

chief rent. Formerly, rent paid by a *tenant-in-chief; now *quit rent.

children. An adequate history of children has not been written. For the Middle Ages, see

Barbara A. Hanawalt, *Growing Up in Medieval London: The Experience of Childhood in History* (1993). Many generalizations have been advanced without the support of empirical evidence. For example, it has been claimed that the high level of *infant mortality in earlier centuries prevented the development of warm emotional relationships between parents and children. The evidence that exists in the form of *diaries, autobiographies, *wills, etc. indicates that such a claim is wildly mistaken. The 17th-century diary of Ralph *Josselin is typical of such evidence that survives in depicting great parental care and warm emotional bonding, and prolonged parental anxiety for the physical, material, and moral welfare of children. For balanced reviews of the evidence and summaries of published work, see Keith Wrightson, *English Society, 1580–1680* (1982), ch. 4, Ralph A. Houlbrooke, *The English Family, 1450–1700* (1984), chs 6 and 7, for the early modern period, and F. M. L. Thompson, *The Rise of Respectable Society: A Social History of Victorian Britain, 1830–1900* (1988), ch. 4, for the 19th century.

In the centuries before adequate methods of *contraception were available, child-bearing began in the first year or two of marriage and continued at regular intervals. The dangers of childbirth, followed by high rates of infant mortality, were constant sources of anxiety. Despite the high death rates amongst the youngest section of society, it has been estimated that about 40 per cent of the population of early modern England consisted of dependent children living at home with their parents. Evidence for the rearing of children is very thin. Discipline was probably not enforced as harshly as is popularly believed. Conduct books stress the authority of parents but also their responsibilities. Children were usually regulated and disciplined, but also cherished. Most children were probably engaged in some kind of work by the age of 7 during the early modern period, well before they entered *farm or *domestic service or *apprenticeship in adolescence. Children therefore commonly worked for small wages or in assisting their parents long before the late 18th and early 19th centuries, when children were employed (most notoriously as poor *orphan apprentices) in the *cotton mills and *coal mines. See Hugh Cunningham, 'The Employment and Unemployment of Children in England, c.1680–1851', *Past and Present*, 126 (1990). During the 19th century government legislation gradually prohibited the worst instances of child labour by enforcing a minimum age at which children could be employed in mines and factories and by raising the school-leaving age. (See EDUCATION.)

The history of childhood during the 19th century needs to be considered according to class, occupation, and region, for there were enormous differences of experience. Even when dealing with just the working-class section of the population simple generalizations are unlikely to be correct. See Eric Hopkins, *Working-Class Children in Nineteenth-Century England* (1994), John Burnett, *Destiny Obscure: Autobiographies of Childhood, Education and Family from the 1820s to the 1920s* (1982), Pamela Horn, *The Victorian Country Child* (1974), Flora *Thompson, *Lark Rise* (1939), and Iona and Peter Opie, *The Lore and Language of Schoolchildren* (1959), and *Children's Games in the School and Playground* (1969).

chimney. The term was originally applied to a fireplace, hence the alternative name for the *hearth tax was the chimney tax. During the 16th century the term was applied to the flue and surmounting pot, which were replacing the old open hearths and louvres. In his *Description of England* (1577) William *Harrison commented that chimneys were one of the improvements that old people remembered as happening during their lifetime. Chimney pieces and chimney pots became an art form from the Tudor period onwards. The use of *coal rather than wood fuel encouraged the adoption of chimneys. The widespread use of central heating systems in the later 20th century has removed the need for chimneys in new houses.

Chinese immigrants. In the late 20th century most British towns have some Chinese residents because of the popularity of Chinese restaurants since the 1950s. The Chinese population in Britain has grown from less than 5,000 in 1946 to about 250,000 in 1993, mostly as a result of immigration from Hong Kong. About 70,000 live in the Greater London area. In earlier times the Chinese population was largely concentrated in London, though small colonies were also found in some other ports, e.g. Cardiff and Liverpool; these colonies consisted of seamen who worked for the *East India Company and other shipping firms. White sailors regarded them as cheap and docile labour, and much hostile propaganda about 'opium dens' fuelled occasional violence. By the 1880s a Chinese quarter had been created in Limehouse, centred on just two streets. Work was at first confined to the docklands, but in 1901 the first Chinese laundry was established. By 1931 there were over 800 such laundries in

Britain, but the advent of automatic washing machines and launderettes brought about their decline. The depression in the *shipping industry in the 1930s caused many Chinese to return to China. Most of the old Chinatown in Limehouse was destroyed during the Blitz in the Second World War. A second Chinatown developed in Soho during the 1960s, with numerous restaurants, shops, and businesses. Nearly half the Chinese population in late 20th-century Britain is British-born. See Anthony Shang, 'The Chinese in London' in Nick Merriman (ed.), *The Peopling of London* (1993), and Colin Holmes, *John Bull's Island: Immigration and British Society, 1871–1971* (1988).

Chivalry, High Court of. The court within the College of *Arms which has jurisdiction over armorial matters in England, Wales, and Northern Ireland.

choir. That part of a medieval *cathedral, *monastery, or *collegiate church, between the high *altar and the pulpitum, which was occupied by the stalls of the monks, minor clerics, and boys, who sang the music of divine services. Victorian clergy began the practice of introducing choir stalls for lay singers in the *chancels of parish *churches.

cholera. A water-borne disease endemic in India, which struck Britain in 1831–2 and again in 1848. It caused violent vomiting and was very often fatal. About 53,000 people in England and Wales died in the 1831–2 outbreak; the victims were mostly from the poorest section of the population in the insanitary districts of industrial towns. Official and popular reactions were very similar to those in the 16th and 17th centuries in the face of bubonic *plague. The authorities enforced some measures of quarantine, but were reluctant to be very strict because they feared the extent of popular opposition. See Asa Briggs, 'Cholera and Society', *Past and Present*, 19 (1961), R. J. Morris, *Cholera 1832* (1976), M. Durey, *The Return of the Plague: British Society and the Cholera, 1831–2* (1979), and M. Pelling, *Cholera, Fever and English Medicine, 1825–1865* (1978).

chrisom. 1. The images of dead infants on tombs and memorial *brasses, showing children wrapped in the white chrisom cloths that were commonly worn for a month after baptism, and used as a shroud if they died within the month.
2. (or chrism). The mixture of olive oil and balsam used in baptism, confirmation, and consecration services.

Christian names. The personal names that had been used by people of Anglo-Saxon and Scandinavian descent mostly fell rapidly out of fashion after the *Norman Conquest. Edward remained popular because Edward the Confessor was held in high repute by the Normans, but otherwise the Norman kings and barons bore names of Germanic origin or Celtic names if they came from Brittany. Such names were soon adopted by the rest of the male population. To this day the most popular names have been those of monarchs and other members of the royal family. The New Testament name of Elizabeth would not have been so popular had it not been for Queen Elizabeth I. Most English royal names, including William, Henry, Richard, and Charles, are not Biblical in origin but go back to the pagan Germanic period.

The range of new names did not match that of the old ones which had disappeared. The proportion of men bearing the five names Henry, John, Richard, Robert, and William rose steadily from 38 per cent of recorded masculine names in the 12th century to 64 per cent in the 14th century. It is probably for this reason that so many diminutives were formed. (See WELSH NAMES and IRISH NAMES for naming customs in the other parts of the British Isles.)

Biblical names became fashionable during the 12th and 13th centuries, especially those of the apostles and the evangelists. During the 13th and 14th centuries a number of names taken from the Old Testament began to be chosen. The popularity of the medieval *mystery plays may have helped in this process. Girls, too, were baptized with Biblical names; Joan and Agnes are first recorded in England in 1189, Catherine in 1196, Mary in 1203, Elizabeth in 1205, and Anne in 1218. Biblical names eventually became the most widespread of all first names. Some very obscure ones were chosen by 16th- and 17th-century *Puritans, and Biblical names such as Amos, Ebenezer, and Noah were revived by 19th-century *Nonconformists, together with names which expressed Christian virtues such as Faith, Hope, and Charity.

Names of classical antiquity, such as Horace or Julius, also became fashionable amongst the educated classes in the 16th and 17th centuries, but they never became as popular as those derived from the Bible. Most of the Roman names that were chosen were those possessed by some early saint or martyr. In the 18th century upper-class families began the fashion of using Latin forms of girls' names, e.g. Anna or Maria. Towards the end of the 18th century, and especially during the following century under the influence of Tennyson and the pre-Raphaelites, some Anglo-Saxon or medieval names were revived: they included Alfred, Edwin, Guy, Nigel, Quentin, Roland, and Walter for boys and Alice, Amy, Audrey, Edith, and Mabel for girls. The names of early Christian saints or martyrs such as Aidan, Alban, Benedict, Bernard, and Theodore were chosen under the influence of the *Oxford Movement. Many other names which had once been fashionable fell into disuse and were never revived.

Aristocratic families began the practice of using surnames as Christian names in the 16th century. During the following two centuries it became increasingly common to preserve surnames on the female side in this way. Surnames which have been adopted as Christian names include Douglas, Dudley, Keith, Neville, Sidney, Stanley, and Stuart. Families further down the social scale rarely followed this practice before the 18th century, though occasional exceptions can be found. The fashion became increasingly popular in Victorian times, as did the practice of using hyphenated surnames to preserve the name of the female line. During the 20th century it has become common to use the mother's maiden name as a second Christian name. (See also ALIAS.)

Many female names are derived from male names, e.g. Paula, Petra, or Patricia. A few Christian names, e.g. Evelyn or Hilary, have been used by either sex. Some, e.g. Francis and Frances, or Jesse and Jessie, are spelt in different ways. Some female names which were popular in the Middle Ages acquired different forms, such as Elizabeth and Isobel, Ann and Agnes, Joan and Jane, or Marion and Mary Ann. These may be written in either form in *parish registers. Pet forms, such as Nancy for Ann, Polly for Mary, and Sally for Sarah may appear in more intimate written records such as letters. The practice of shortening names, sometimes with the addition of a suffix such as -cock or -kin, is an ancient one going back to the Middle Ages. (See also GODPARENTS for their role in choosing Christian names.)

In the 20th century the number of first names has grown considerably. Many can no longer be classified as Christian names for they have been given without baptism or have been chosen by people of different religions. Modern names include those taken from flowers and plants or gemstones and other desirable objects, foreign names such as the Russian Tanya and Natasha, and those of film stars and pop stars. See E. G. Withycombe, *The Oxford Dictionary of English* *Christian Names* (1977), and Patrick Hanks and Flavia Hodges, *A Dictionary of First Names* (1990), which includes a comparative survey of the names found in various European languages.

Christmas. The modern forms of celebration at Christmas are largely Victorian, including the emphasis on the Christmas tree (which was imported from Germany by Prince Albert), the sending of Christmas cards, and the use of holly for decoration. Christmas had replaced an older mid-winter festival in which excessive eating and drinking was an essential feature. In the Middle Ages and beyond Christmas was followed by 12 days of celebration during which activities which at other times of the year would have been suppressed were tolerated. (See LORDS OF MISRULE and MUMMERS.) Church services at Christmas were simple affairs before the 19th century. Although carols had been popular since the Middle Ages, church carol services are Victorian and 20th-century inventions.

chronicles. The keeping of chronicles of important events was an ancient monastic tradition, going back to the *Anglo-Saxon Chronicle*. Chronicles written by laymen were published in the 16th century. Edward Hall's *The Union of the Two Noble and Illustre Families of Lancaster and York* (1548) was much used by *Holinshed, the best-known chronicler of the Elizabethan period. (See also STOW.) A number of towns kept chronicles of important local events. See Alan Dyer, 'English Town Chronicles', *The Local Historian*, 12/6 (1977).

church ales. A common form of fund-raising for the maintenance of parish *churches and the poor in the Middle Ages. On special occasions home-brewed ales were sold either in the *nave of the church or in an adjacent churchhouse. Some 16th-century examples of churchhouses survive. After their suppression at the *Reformation some became secular *alehouses. See Judith Bennett, 'Conviviality and Charity in Medieval and Early Modern England', *Past and Present*, 134 (1992), and Ronald Hutton, *The Rise and Fall of Merry England: The Ritual Year, 1400–1700* (1994).

church dedications. The starting point for an inquiry into the meaning of church dedications remains Frances Arnold-Forster, *Studies in Church Dedications, or England's Patron Saints*, 3 vols. (1899). The subject is fraught with difficulty for there are too many exceptions to any general rules which may be formulated. However, it is accepted that certain dedications tended to be fashionable in certain periods and that some are associated with very early churches or even with pre-Christian sites. The only attempt to analyse the entire body of dedications within a county and to use them for an understanding of historical development is Alan Everitt, *Continuity and Colonization: The Evolution of Kentish Settlement* (1986), ch. 9, which studies 540 dedications throughout the county of Kent to show a striking contrast between the early dedication patterns and that of the later churches and chapels.

The first problem to be faced is that of the authenticity of the dedication, for in many places the original dedication is known to have been changed. Often, there is no early evidence, but medieval *wills can be informative. Everitt concludes that the great majority of Kentish dedications go back to the early medieval period and in all probability earlier still. Very few were altered at the *Reformation. Where changes have occurred the new name is often paired with the old, e.g. St Mary and St Eanswythe, Folkestone, or St Mary and St Ethelburga, Lyminge.

Comparative figures from the rest of the country reveal which saints were particularly popular in the chosen area of study. Thus, in Kent, St Augustine, St Mildred, St Dunstan, and St Alphege formed a higher proportion of the total than in the country at large. In England as a whole the most popular dedications were to St Mary (2,094), All Saints (1,097), St Peter (760), St Michael (623), St Andrew (595), St John the Baptist (458), and St Nicholas (393). Many of the churches in Wales and Cornwall are dedicated to local saints, some of whom received only one dedication; in most cases, such local cults are very early. In Suffolk, for example, St Gregory dedications relate to early church foundations. See D. W. Rollason, *The Mildrith Legend: A Study in Early Medieval Hagiography in England* (1982). Sometimes, pre-Christian cults are disguised by dedications to saints with similar names. It is likely, for instance, that many of the St Helen dedications in Yorkshire and neighbouring counties were originally to Elen, a Celtic goddess associated with wells.

A complicating factor is that some churches were deliberately given the same dedication as their mother church. Indeed, such dedications are often valuable clues to former links between such churches. Elsewhere, particular circumstances often accounted for the choice of patron saint: St Michael is associated with hill-top sites, St Nicholas was the choice of fishermen, and St James the patron of travellers. The difficulties of interpretation are illustrated by the three medieval churches in south Yorkshire which were dedicated to St Nicholas; those at Thorne and Bawtry served inland ports and fall neatly into the broader pattern of such dedications, but the third example is at Bradfield, high on the Pennines and about as far from the sea as it is possible to be in England.

churches, architectural styles. The earliest surviving structures are in the *Romanesque style. Those erected before the *Norman Conquest can rarely be dated by written records. Scholars have developed a method of dating such buildings by the styles of their features: see H. M. Taylor and Joan Taylor, *Anglo-Saxon Architecture*, 3 vols. (1980). The architectural features which are characteristic of pre-Conquest buildings include double belfry windows with a mid-wall shaft supporting a through-stone slab, triangular-headed windows or doorways, strip-work panelling of wall surfaces, and the use of large stones arranged in a 'side-alternate' or 'long-and-short' manner. There are numerous other minor features described by the Taylors, who divide these early churches into three periods: group A (AD 600–800), group B (800–950), and group C (950–1100). The third group is the most numerous. The style continued to be used by local builders after 1066 in what is termed the '*Saxo-Norman overlap'.

Large numbers of churches were built, or rebuilt, by the Normans, who continued to use the Romanesque style. The semi-circular *apse at the eastern end of the church had gone out of fashion in England after the 7th century, but was revived by the Normans. During the middle and later years of the 12th century Norman churches became much more decorative, both externally and internally. Characteristic mouldings, e.g. beakhead or chevron patterns, were used on doorways, windows, capitals, and arches. Some of these stylistic features provide firm dating evidence, e.g. the use of water-leaf designs on capitals was restricted to the period 1175–90. In some churches, notably Kilpeck (Herefordshire), carved heads of fantastic and often grotesque design form a corbel table at the top of the external walls. A tympanum over the main door was frequently carved with a serpent or some other imaginative beast. See G. Zarnecki, *Later English Romanesque Sculpture, 1140–1210* (1953). Where aisles were needed to accommodate the growing population, the columns in the *nave were thick, solid, and rounded. Norman walls were thicker than those constructed by the Anglo-Saxons, being over three feet wide. The finest examples of Norman churches include Melbourne (Derbyshire), Iffley (Oxfordshire), and Barfreston (Kent).

The Norman style continued in use to c.1200. The *Gothic style had been imported from France in the 1170s for the greatest *cathedrals and *monasteries, but it took a generation or so for the new techniques to be used at parish church level. The term 'Transitional' is used for the overlap period. The Gothic style was based on knowledge of geometry and used thrust and counter-thrust. The Normans had used slim pilaster-buttresses on some of their later buildings, but most Norman churches had been unbuttressed. Gothic buildings soared to unprecedented heights, with tall, pointed arches supported on slim columns. The splayed windows of the earlier churches were replaced by windows with the simple Y-tracery of the *Early English style and the geometric and exuberant designs of the *Decorated style during the 13th and early 14th centuries. English styles had until then copied the French, but from the middle years of the 14th century until the *Reformation and later a native style known as *Perpendicular Gothic was developed. This is named after the perpendicular lines of the mullions in the windows (which were enlarged until they filled all the available space in the walls), but the style includes much more than that, e.g. flat lead roofs hidden behind *battlements and pinnacles, long ranges of clerestory windows, and carved wooden roofs. See John Harvey, *The Perpendicular Style, 1330–1485* (1978). In Ireland, Scotland, and Wales there are far fewer examples of fine medieval churches. For Scotland, see Richard Fawcett, *Scottish Medieval Churches* (1985), and D. MacGibbon and T. Ross, *The Ecclesiastical Architecture of Scotland*, 3 vols. (1896–7).

The Gothic style of architecture continued in use during the later 16th and 17th centuries. St John's, Leeds (1632–4) is a complete Gothic building, both externally and internally. Towers, in particular, continued to be built in the old fashion. The Gothic style was never completely abandoned and was revived in the 19th century, when new buildings were deliberately designed to look medieval and many old buildings were 'improved' with new Gothic features. The use of Classical architecture for parish churches is largely restricted to the later 17th, 18th, and early 19th centuries. After the Fire of London (1666) Wren and Hawksmoor built a remarkable series of churches, whose designs influenced builders in other towns and in parts of the countryside where new accommodation

was needed or where a great landowner rebuilt a church on his estate. In the Victorian period such estate churches were invariably Gothic. In the second half of the 20th century a wide range of modern styles have been used.

churches, parish. Parish churches range in size from St Mary Redcliffe, a church built in the late Middle Ages by Bristol merchants and described by Queen Elizabeth I as 'the fairest, goodliest, and most famous parish church in England', to tiny Norman structures such as Winterborne Tomson (Dorset), or Adwick-upon-Dearne (Yorkshire), which was described in a guidebook of 1911 as a 'humble, unrestored little church . . . pink-washed, mouldy and not worth a visit'.

Some remarkably early churches survive in part. They include St Martin, Canterbury, which *Bede knew as the ruined Roman church that Queen Bertha restored in the mid-6th century and which St Augustine used as his base upon his mission to reChristianize Britain in 597; the present *chancel wall incorporates part of the Roman *nave. The churches at Jarrow and Monkwearmouth (County Durham), where Bede spent his life, retain some masonry and architectural features which date back to his time in the early 8th century. In the same county a complete Anglo-Saxon church survives at Escomb.

Most parish churches were built by local lords close to their *castle or *manor house. Where a manor house has been extended and the village has disappeared, e.g. Neville Holt (Leicestershire), the church has subsequently been incorporated within the manorial complex. The enlargement of country houses and the removal of villages to create landscaped *parks in the 18th century sometimes resulted in the church being left alongside the hall, as at Kedleston (Derbyshire), and sometimes in the building of a new church at the edge of the park, as at Allerton Mauleverer (Yorkshire). In many other cases, the manor house has disappeared, making the reason for the siting of the church less obvious. In Norfolk and other counties where settlements were dispersed, the church may now be standing next to a manor house, or all alone, for the small village or hamlet that was associated with it has gone. When villages decayed, the parish church, being built of sturdier materials, was the last building to survive. Ruined or heavily restored churches which stand in isolation are usually an immediate indication of a *deserted medieval village. (See CHURCH SITES.)

However, some churches occupy unusual

positions because the early Christians took over pagan sites and adapted them for their own purposes. In 597 Pope Gregory instructed Augustine's mission not to alienate the native population by the wholesale destruction of their religious buildings but rather to convert heathen temples to Christian use. Four years later, Gregory wrote to Abbot Mellitus: 'Destroy the idols; purify the buildings with holy water; set relics there; and let them become temples of the true God. So the people will have no need to change their place of concourse, and where of old they were wont to sacrifice cattle to demons, thither let them continue to resort on the day of the saint to whom the church is dedicated, and slay their beasts no longer as a sacrifice, but for a social meal in honour of Him whom they now worship.' It is impossible to know how many churches are on old pagan sites. (See also CHURCH DEDICATIONS.)

Many early churches were wooden and have been replaced. The oldest surviving timber-framed church is at Greensted-juxta-Ongar (Essex), where the nave walls have been dated to the mid-9th century, with the reuse of some 7th-century timbers. *Bricks and stones from nearby Roman forts were used extensively. Many other Anglo-Saxon churches were built with new stones, however, and a detailed investigation of the famous church at Brixworth (Northamptonshire) has revealed that building took place over a long period of time and that new bricks were used; see Diana Sutherland and David Parsons, *The Petrological Survey of All Saints' Church* (Brixworth Archaeological Research Committee, interim reports, 1985). It is common to find that early medieval churches used whatever local building materials were available, but those parishes which became wealthy rebuilt with imported stone in the later Middle Ages. Proximity to the coast or a navigable river enabled stone to be brought long distances. In East Anglia the great churches that were built out of the profits of the cloth trade were constructed of *rubble, with a veneer of knapped *flints and imported limestone for the quoins and dressings. The humblest materials could be used to construct some very fine buildings.

The earliest churches cannot be dated precisely, except in unusual circumstances: thus, a dedication stone at St Gregory, Kildale (Yorkshire) dates the church to 1055–65. Only a handful of Anglo-Saxon churches can be dated from written evidence. One is St Laurence, Bradford-upon-Avon (Wiltshire), which was recognized as an Anglo-Saxon church only in 1856, as it had been converted into cottages. An architectural survey has confirmed *William of Malmesbury's account that it was erected by Aldhelm in the early 8th century, though it was much adapted in the later *Anglo-Saxon period. Dating Anglo-Saxon churches is hazardous and depends on the construction of typologies. Fortunately, the stylistic features that have been accepted as being pre-Conquest are not repeated in the later Middle Ages. Churches of similar architectural styles are of the same approximate date. In the later Middle Ages, dates can be ascribed more confidently for the chances of finding confirmation from written records are much greater.

As the responsibility for building and maintaining the nave, tower, and porch lay with the parishioners, whereas the *tithe owners were responsible for the chancel and private individuals or *guilds for any *chantry chapels that were attached, complete rebuilding in any one period was comparatively rare; piecemeal additions and reconstruction were more usual. Parish churches are therefore usually built in a mixture of styles. Even if they look to be of one build externally, earlier work is often found inside. The stripping of plaster from the interior walls during the *High Church movement of Victorian times encouraged much architectural and archaeological investigation. Indeed, early histories of parish churches concentrate excessively on styles and use technical language that is forbidding to the beginner. A basic knowledge of architectural development is necessary if a local historian is to relate periods of building, rebuilding, and decline to the general economic and social history of the community that was served by the church. The failure to complete the tower at East Bergholt (Suffolk) demonstrates the collapse of the woollen cloth trade in the 1520s. Even churches which had wealthy benefactors, such as the Earl of Oxford and the Spring family at Lavenham (Suffolk), were dependent also on the contributions of the other parishioners; an inscription at Long Melford (Suffolk) speaks of the contributions of 'all the well-disposed men of this town'. Regular fund-raising events were held, such as *church ales and May games.

*Church interiors have traditionally been studied for their collection of curiosities, e.g. a rare sedilia, a unique *Doom painting, or some famous *alabaster monument. Much pleasure can be derived from such pursuits, which are particularly worthwhile when the investigation of particular topics is conducted on a regional basis, but church interiors need also to be studied as a whole to illustrate changes in liturgy and to shed light on social and economic developments over the centuries. The parish church was not only a place of worship, but in most cases the only public building available for social purposes. For centuries, the parish church served also as a village hall, a centre of social life, and the administrative centre for much *local government. (See PARISH; CHAPEL-OF-EASE; PARISH REGISTERS; CHURCHWARDENS' ACCOUNTS; and POOR, OVERSEER OF, and HIGHWAYS, OVERSEERS OF.)

The problem of restoration on a large scale was tackled by the Victorians. In many cases, the restoration was heavy-handed, but there is no doubt that it was necessary. Steetley Church (Derbyshire) was a roofless barn until J. L. Pearson's restoration in 1880. It is shown as a ruin in Samuel Lysons, *Magna Britannia* (1817), in illustrations which also reveal how much of the present church is a genuine survival from the mid-12th century and how much was added by Pearson. A great deal of work remains to be done on diocesan and parish records and on locating and studying old prints, paintings, and photographs before the full extent of the Victorian contribution to the present appearance of parish churches can be assessed. The modern work of such bodies as the Redundant Churches Fund is much better recorded.

See Richard Morris, *Churches in the Landscape* (1989), J. H. Bettey, *Church and Parish: An Introduction for Local Historians* (1987), and Colin Platt, *The Parish Churches of Medieval England* (1981).

church interiors. The interiors of medieval parish churches were very different in appearance from what they are now. The first impression upon entering would have been of a blaze of colour. Instead of being bare stone, the walls would have been plastered over and decorated with paintings which were used both for devotional purposes and as visual aids to the story of Christianity as depicted in the Bible and the lives of saints. (See WALL PAINTING.) Over the chancel arch would have been a representation of the Day of Judgement. Images of the Virgin Mary and other saints, *stained glass windows, painted screens, roof bosses, and memorials all added to the display of colour. Most of this was swept away at the *Reformation. In his *Description of England* (1577) William *Harrison wrote: 'As for churches themselves, belles and times of morning and evening prayer remain as in time past, saving that all images, shrines, tabernacles, rood loftes and monuments of idolatrie are removed, taken down and defaced: Onlie the stories in glasse windowes excepted, which,

for want of sufficient store of new stuffe, and by reason of extreme charge that should grow by the alteration of the same into white panes throughout the realme, are not altogether abolished in most places at once, but by little and little suffered to decaie that white glass may be set up in their roomes.' The paintings which have been rediscovered under layers of whitewash survive in sufficient numbers to demonstrate the medieval practice.

Many ancient parish churches would have been darker in the Middle Ages than they are now, not only because of the modern use of electric lights but because many churches have lost most, if not all, of their medieval stained glass, which has not always been replaced by Victorian glass. Candles would have been burning at more altars than are usual at present, for the *chantry chapels that were dissolved in 1547 were more numerous than the present *Lady chapels. The *nave was cut off from the *chancel by a screen and *rood loft, so as to create a sense of mystery around the high *altar. Aisles were separated from the chantry chapels, which were commonly sited at their eastern ends, by parclose screens. Surviving examples, e.g. at Kimbolton (Huntingdonshire) and Southwold (Suffolk), show that screens were painted with images of saints, who are identifiable by their special symbols. In the first half of the 17th century some churches returned to the former practice of having elaborate screens. See Eamon Duffy, *The Stripping of the Altars: Traditional Religion in England, 1400–1580* (1992). St Mary, Croscombe (Somerset) has an unusually complete interior from this period, with an elaborate rood screen surmounted by the *royal arms, a pulpit donated by the Bishop of Bath and Wells, box pews, and chandeliers. (See CHURCH SEATING PLANS.) Under the influence of Archbishop Laud, many churches attempted to restore 'the beauty of holiness', but this movement came to an end with the defeat of the Royalists in the *Civil War.

During the later 17th, 18th, and early 19th centuries the interiors of churches became increasingly cluttered with box pews and galleries. The outstanding surviving example of a Georgian interior is St Mary, Whitby (Yorkshire), where every available bit of space is taken with pews and galleries, the squire's pew across the chancel arch, a three-decker pulpit, chandeliers, and a stove whose flue rises through the ceiling. Churches at that time were cold and often damp. Tobias Smollett wrote satirically in *Humphry Clinker* (1771): 'When we consider our ancient churches . . . may we not term them so many magazines of rheums, created for the benefit of the medical faculty? And may we not safely aver that, in the winter especially (which may be said to engross eight months in the year), more bodies are lost, than souls saved, by going to church?' Heating was much improved in the 19th century by the use of boilers.

From the 1840s onwards the *High Church movement dictated how the interiors of churches should be arranged. The present internal appearance of most ancient parish churches dates from the period 1840–90. Walls were stripped bare, and box pews, galleries, and three-decker pulpits were removed. Only about 140 Georgian interiors survive reasonably intact: they are described and illustrated in Mark Chatfield, *Churches the Victorians Forgot* (1979). See also Alec Clifton-Taylor, *English Parish Churches as Works of Art* (1974). For guidance on how to study church interiors, see Thomas Cooke, *Recording a Church: An Illustrated Glossary* (1984).

Church in Wales. In 1920 the four dioceses of Bangor, Llandaff, St Asaph, and St David's were formed into a disestablished and separate province of the Anglican communion, with its own archbishop. The Department of Manuscripts and Records in the National Library of *Wales, Aberystwyth, is the approved repository for non-parochial records; parish records may be deposited locally or at the Library.

Church of England. The Church of England was created by a series of Acts of Parliament between 1529 and 1559. (See REFORMATION.) The Elizabethan Settlement of 1559 provided the framework for the Anglican Church (its alternative name) in succeeding centuries. The monarch replaced the Pope as the head of the Church of England, which became (and has remained) the official religion of the state. Most of the clergy who had been parish priests before the Reformation remained in office and the medieval buildings which had long served as parish *churches were simply adapted to the new liturgical requirements. (See BOOK OF COMMON PRAYER.) Moreover, the Church of England was governed on similar lines to its Catholic predecessor, with two archbishops and 24 bishops. The *dioceses consisted of the medieval sees and the five new ones created by Henry VIII. Each diocese was divided into *archdeaconries, *deaneries, and *parishes.

See PURITAN for developments in the later 16th and early 17th centuries, culminating in the *Civil War and *Commonwealth, and NONCONFORMITY for the split which occurred in 1662. From 1689 Protestant Nonconformists were allowed to worship in their own meeting houses according to their own beliefs. During the 19th century the Church of England attracted only a minority of the population to its services and, in many places, had smaller congregations than those in the Nonconformist chapels. See J. Walsh, C. Haydon, and S. Taylor (eds.), *The Church of England, c.1689–c.1833: From Toleration to Tractarianism* (1993), and A. D. Gilbert, *Religion and Society in Industrial England: Church, Chapel and Social Change, 1740–1914* (1976). Rivalry between the Anglican Church and Nonconformity had political overtones during the 19th century, the 'C. of E.' being associated with the *Tory Party and the Nonconformists with the *Liberals. A campaign to disestablish the Church of England proved unsuccessful, however. The *High Church movement greatly influenced the interior arrangements of parish churches during the half-century after 1840, but elsewhere (especially in the industrial towns and cities) Low Church evangelicals were dominant (see CHURCH INTERIORS).

During the 20th century membership of the Church of England has continued to decline, though its services continue to be widely used for baptisms, marriages, and burials. The average attendance at services on Sundays in 1992 was 1,122,600, or 2.3 per cent of the national population. The 'C. of E.' remains a 'broad church' of people with many different shades of persuasion. The decision in 1993 to ordain women priests revealed deep divisions. The Anglican church continues to flourish in Britain's former colonies and dominions. It remains the official religion of the state (but see CHURCH OF SCOTLAND; CHURCH OF IRELAND; and CHURCH IN WALES).

Church of Ireland. The Anglican Church in Ireland since the 16th century. The Church was badly in need of reform in the 18th and 19th centuries, when many of its bishops and clergy were non-resident. It was disestablished in 1869. Some *parish registers exist from the middle of the 17th century onwards; they are housed in the *Public Record Office in Dublin.

Church of Scotland. At the *Reformation the Catholic Church was replaced by *Presbyterianism as the official state religion of Scotland. A new hierarchical structure was created, headed by an annual General Assembly in Edinburgh, and descending through synods, presbyteries, and kirk sessions, all of which were courts as well as administrative bodies.

Nearly all the records of the Church of Scotland are kept at the *Scottish Record Office. See *Records of the Church of Scotland Preserved in the Scottish Record Office and General Register Office* (1967).

The Church of Scotland has experienced many schisms since the 18th century. The main division occurred in 1843, when a long-standing dispute over patronage came to a head with the withdrawal of 474 ministers, a third of the total, to form the Free Church of Scotland. A third Presbyterian body, the United Presbyterian Church, was formed in 1847.

church rates. Until 1868 churchwardens were allowed to levy a rate on all householders in a *parish in England and Wales (regardless of whether or not they attended the services of the *Church of England) in order to help maintain the parish *church and *churchyard. Such rates were known in the Welsh Borders as leawans.

church seating plans. In the Middle Ages most people stood in the *nave during church services. The expression 'the weak to the wall' comes from the practice of providing a stone bench around the wall of the nave and its aisles, such as the surviving example at Gaddesby (Leicestershire). Wooden benches were introduced in the first half of the 14th century, but few early examples survive. Many churches have a few pews from the late Middle Ages. Launcells (Cornwall) has 60 benches with carved ends dating from the 15th or early 16th century. In most churches only the better-off inhabitants constructed their own seats; most parishioners remained standing well after the *Reformation.

During the 17th century churches became filled with pews. The inevitable disputes which broke out over their positioning were settled at parish meetings. It became the custom in most places, particularly in the countryside, for the right to sit in a pew to be regarded as part of the property of a farm or *cottage; in this way, the social structure of a parish was formalized during a church service. The owners or tenants of the largest farms sat at the front, the smallholders were seated in the middle, and the cottagers occupied the seats to the rear. See David Hey (ed.), *Richard *Gough: The History of Myddle* (1981) for an example from Shropshire, where the seating plan of 1701 was used as the basis of a history of all the families in the parish. Disputes arose when families owned more than one property and allowed their servants to sit in pews in front of others. In towns, the most prominent pews were set aside for the mayor and *aldermen. Few seating plans survive from the 17th century, but a number of later ones are displayed in churches or are occasionally found in the records of *ecclesiastical courts.

The growth of the *population in the 18th century caused many parishes to fit galleries in their churches. The *High Church movement of the Victorian period considered these unsightly and had them removed. The marks on pillars and walls and the unusual position of small windows provide clues as to where they were fitted. The present seating arrangements commonly date from the period 1840–90. Photographs of church interiors before Victorian restoration survive for many parishes.

church sites. Most parish churches were sited near the *castle or *manor house of the *lord of the manor. Some now appear isolated because the lord's residence, and even the village that lay alongside it, have decayed and disappeared. Thus, the church of St Giles, Great Stretton (Leicestershire) now stands alone, and that at Ketsby on the Lincolnshire Wolds is almost as ruined as the *deserted medieval village that it once served. If a church stands oddly in relation to a village or town, it is likely that the main focus of settlement has altered over the centuries, sometimes by deliberate replanning. The church of St Nicholas, Bawtry (Yorkshire), for example, stands by the former wharf on the river Idle, for it originally served a small trading settlement; it cannot be seen from the huge, rectangular market place that was laid out at the centre of the new town at the end of the 12th century.

But some churches occupy what now appear to be strange sites because they were deliberately sited to convert adherents from pagan forms of religion. At All Saints, Rudston (Yorkshire) a prehistoric monolith, which dates from the late *Neolithic or *Bronze Age, stands over 25 feet high in the churchyard, 10 metres from the chancel. The place-name has led to the suggestion that a Christian cross, or rood, was attached to the top of the stone. A local legend maintained that the stone was a javelin hurled in anger by the Devil at this desecration of his site, but that it was deflected by divine intervention. Such folk-tales often preserve a memory of the Christian conversion of a pagan site.

The word 'pagan' is derived from the Latin *paganus*, meaning a 'country dweller'. It is likely that pagan beliefs long persisted in a rural context. The popularity of St Michael dedications speaks of the battle to replace pagan beliefs. He had many attributes, but was generally portrayed in medieval art fighting the Devil, often on a hill top. In the dioceses of Hereford and Exeter he was even more popular. See the distribution map of Michael dedications in Richard Morris, *Churches in the Landscape* (1989), p. 54 and the ensuing discussion. Morris concludes that: 'Faced with such a jumble of cults and observances, almost all ill understood, the question of possible relationships between pre-Christian sacral places and later parish churches becomes bewilderingly complicated.' How far the pagan veneration of trees, stones, and springs is responsible for the siting of particular churches is a question that cannot be answered with certainty, although there is no doubt that in general such beliefs took a long time to eradicate. That conversion, rather than replacement, of previous holy sites was the usual policy is well attested in surviving letters, in *Bede's writings, and in other contemporary accounts. For a study of the limited evidence for pagan religion, see Ronald Hutton, *The Pagan Religions of the Ancient British Isles* (1991).

The time-scale of conversion was long and the persistent strength of pagan beliefs, reinforced by the *Viking invaders, must not be underestimated. Pagan sites of regional or tribal significance would have been the first to be converted. Some local sanctuaries may have retained their hold until the 11th century. Very many parish churches were founded in the period 850–1050, at a time when pagan ideas were still flourishing; the siting of at least some of these local churches may therefore have been a deliberate act of conversion of a place that had already been regarded as holy for centuries.

church towers and spires. In 9th-century Italy the casting of bells heavier than hitherto necessitated the construction of separate belfry towers either of timber or of stone. By the 10th century the fashion had spread to England. In some surviving *Anglo-Saxon churches, e.g. Monkwearmouth (County Durham) or Deerhurst (Gloucestershire), earlier western porches were heightened into towers. Over 70 Anglo-Saxon towers are still standing. Nearly all are at the west end of the nave, for the skills required to construct central towers in churches of a cruciform plan were beyond those possessed by most masons at that time. Some towers, most notably that at Sompting (Sussex), with its famous 'Rhenish helm' roof, were clearly influenced by the Carolingian style of the Rhineland. Northamptonshire has some very fine examples of Anglo-Saxon towers at Barnack, Brigstock, Brixworth, and Earls Barton.

Another outstanding tower is that at Barton-on-Humber (Lincolnshire), which has pilaster strips, long-and-short quoins, belfry openings with a mid-wall shaft, and triangular-headed windows similar to those at Earls Barton.

Norman towers were generally capped with low pyramidal roofs of timber and shingles, though few original examples survive. Some towers near the borders of Scotland and Wales were used for shelter against raiders. Great Salkeld (Cumberland) has a door to the tower which is strongly barred on the inside and iron-plated on the nave side, and the tower staircase at Bedale (Yorkshire) is protected by a *portcullis. The *round towers of East Anglia and Sussex were not constructed for defence, however, but were built in this style because the *flint (which was the only building material available) could not be shaped into quoins. Some Norman towers, e.g. Clun (Shropshire), are massive, with very thick walls, but others, e.g. Campsall (Yorkshire) are elegant. A lot of Norman towers are known to have collapsed; others have been replaced by later towers, particularly in the period of *Perpendicular Gothic. The smaller Norman churches had no towers; a rare example of a Norman bell-cote can be seen at Adwick-upon-Dearne (Yorkshire).

*Gothic towers soared to new heights. A famous example from the second quarter of the 13th century at West Walton (Norfolk) is detached from the rest of the church because of uncertainty over the foundations in the former marshland. East Anglia contains some of the finest church towers, notably at Lavenham and Southwold, using imported limestone for quoins and dressings and a veneer of dressed flints. Herefordshire has a number of sturdy timber-framed towers, e.g. at Bromsbarrow. The finest group of Perpendicular towers are those erected in oolitic limestone in Somerset. Towers of this period can often be dated closely by bequests in *wills, though they normally took many years to complete. The fashion for building towers in the Perpendicular style continued long after the *Reformation.

Spires were introduced in the *Early English period of Gothic architecture and were sometimes added to earlier towers. They are a particular feature of the band of oolitic limestone, especially in Lincolnshire and Rutland and adjacent counties, where the stone is suited to slender structures which are pierced by openings relieving an otherwise heavy appearance. The problem of fitting an eight-sided spire on to a four-sided tower was first solved by the use of broaches in the form of half-pyramids at the joint. Broach spires were less successful in buildings where sandstone was used, e.g. in the Derbyshire Peak District, at Baslow, Hope, and Old Brampton. They date from the 13th and 14th centuries, before the use of recessed spires, where the joint was masked by *battlements and pinnacles. The contrast in styles can be observed at Stamford, where St Mary's has a broach spire and All Saints has a spire that is both recessed and crocketed. The ornamental 'crown' of the later towers became a decorative feature of distinction in the finest Perpendicular churches. Counties such as Essex, which lacked suitable stone, erected wooden spires on top of wooden towers: notable examples range from the 13th-century spire at Stock to the 15th-century example at Blackmore. The shingles have to be replaced every 70 years or so. Chesterfield's famous crooked spire has become twisted as a result of the fracture of the supporting king-post and the heavy weight of the lead covering. It was not until the late 18th century that travellers began to comment on its misshapen appearance.

churchwardens' accounts. A few accounts survive from the 14th century; others become much more plentiful in later years. See J. C. Cox, *Churchwardens' Accounts from the Four-teenth Century to the Close of the Seventeenth Century* (1913); for an example, see Thomas Wright (ed.), *Churchwardens' Accounts of the Town of Ludlow, in Shropshire, from 1540 to the End of the Reign of Queen Elizabeth* (Camden Society, CII, 1869). Until 1868 the churchwardens were allowed to levy a rate on all parishioners, regardless of whether or not they attended the *Church of England. The accounts note expenditure on the maintenance, cleaning, and decoration of the parish church and provision for the services. Those that survive from the 15th and 16th centuries are an important source of information about changes associated with the *Reformation, e.g. the removal of *rood screens and gilded images. See the monumental study by Ronald Hutton, *The Rise and Fall of Merry England: The Ritual Year, 1400–1700* (1994), which located nine accounts from the 14th century, 33 from the period 1400–49, 75 for 1450–99, and 196 for 1500–49; they were overwhelmingly from the southern two-thirds of the country. In an appendix he lists all the accounts that are available for study before the year 1690, arranged by county.

In addition to their responsibilities for the parish church, the churchwardens often paid for the shooting of birds and vermin, gave relief to the itinerant poor, and paid the ringers for celebrating national events. Their account books are therefore a mine of miscellaneous local information. Structural changes to a church required the grant of a *faculty from the bishop. (See also ECCLESIASTICAL COURTS.)

churchyards are normally larger on the south side than on the north, though 19th- and 20th-century enlargements may have obscured this arrangement. This was because well into the 18th century (and sometimes beyond) the north side was regarded as the Devil's side, where excommunicants, the unbaptized, suicides, etc. were buried. The main public entrance to a church was normally on the south side of the *nave, except where considerations of local topography and convenience dictated otherwise.

The earliest *gravestones in churchyards date from the 17th century and are normally found near the south door of the church. Before this fashion arose, previous graves were often cleared to make way for new burials and the bones collected in a *charnel house. The present appearance of most churchyards dates from the Victorian period, when the erection of gravestones prevented further burials and the laying out of general cemeteries made clergymen and churchwardens think about tidiness and design. *Lych-gates, paths, and many of the trees (including imported species such as cypresses and cedars) that now adorn churchyards date from that period. Some churchyard yews are ancient, but many are Victorian.

Raised churchyards have been a matter for much speculation. Where they are no higher than the foundations of the church, they cannot be the result of generations of burials. Raised churchyards are often of a distinctive circular or oval shape. These may have been holy sites even before the introduction of Christianity.

cider. The fermented juice of apples, made into an often staple drink on farms in southwest England and the Welsh border counties. The word is French in origin and cider mills are thought to have been introduced by the Normans. The variability of cider yields in English orchards did not encourage large-scale production. Cider was the product of medium-sized and small, mixed farms until modern times. See John Chartres, 'No English Calvados? English Distillers and the Cider Industry in the Seventeenth and Eighteenth Centuries' in John Chartres and David Hey (eds.), *English Rural Society, 1500–1800: Essays in Honour of Joan Thirsk* (1990), ch. 13. See also J. Williams-

Davies, 'The Travelling Cidermaker', *Folk Life*, 29 (1991).

cinemas. The Lumier brothers showed the first programme of films, projected by their Cinematographe, in Paris in 1895. The first public film show in the United Kingdom followed a few weeks later. For the early history of the cinema see Kevin Brownlow, *The Parade's Gone By*... (1968), a study of the silent cinema between 1916 and 1928. The cinema buildings of the inter-war years followed the tradition of the music hall and the popular theatre in having exotic names and decorative frontages. Many fell into disuse in the 1960s. For an example of a local study see Doris Johnson, *The Cinemas of South Tyneside* (1992).

Cinque ports. The south-eastern ports of Dover, Hastings, Hythe, Romney, and Sandwich (and, later, Rye and Winchelsea) which in the Middle Ages enjoyed trading privileges in return for their contributions to naval defence. These privileges were mostly abolished in the 19th century.

Cistercians. Monastic order founded at Cîteaux in Burgundy in 1098 in an attempt to return to the original simplicity of the *Benedictines, from whom they were immediately distinguished by their white habit. By the 15th century they had established 750 *monasteries throughout western Europe. Regularity of observance was achieved through the legislation passed by the annual meeting of abbots at Cîteaux and by frequent visitations by the abbot of the house from which a daughter *abbey had been founded.

The first Cistercian house in Britain was established at Waverley (Surrey) in 1128; by the end of the century over 100 Cistercian houses had been settled in England and Wales. The greatest houses were those founded in Yorkshire. In March 1132 Walter L'Espec, lord of Helmsley, allowed 13 monks from Clairvaux (a great French Cistercian house) to settle on his land in the remote Rye Valley, on the edge of the North York Moors. By the middle of the 12th century Rievaulx (as the site became known in the Norman-French manner) had 140 monks and over 500 *lay brothers, with a wide reputation for their spirituality. The contemporary house at Fountains was settled by a breakaway group from the Benedictine abbey of St Mary's, York. Harsh winters nearly destroyed the early community, but the abbey eventually matched that at Rievaulx in size and fame.

The early Cistercians sought remote sites and renounced the lavish buildings and ritual of the *Cluniacs. They refused gifts other than stretches of uncultivated land which they could improve. Early Cistercian architecture, best seen at another Yorkshire site at Kirkstall, was deliberately simple and devoid of decoration; towers were forbidden. Each abbey was laid out to a standard plan. The Cistercian ideal was the frugal, devotional, and meditative life, but the monks relied on the manual labour of large numbers of lay brothers. The wealth of their monasteries came from the farming and industrial activities of the lay brothers, many of whom worked at outlying *granges. The Cistercians acquired huge tracts of moorland which they converted into sheep pastures to produce wool to sell to Italian merchants. They were also instrumental in developing the *iron and *lead industries.

The Cistercian abbeys in northern England founded daughter houses in Scotland, e.g. Rievaulx was responsible for Melrose, Newbattle, Kinloss, and Dundrennan. The order penetrated central and north Wales, with endowments from Welsh princes. In both Scotland and Wales the monks exploited the sheep pastures. Large numbers of Cistercian houses were also established in Anglo-Norman Ireland in the 12th and early 13th century; see Roger Stalley, *The Cistercian Monasteries of Ireland* (1987).

As they became wealthier, the Cistercians quickly adopted the new *Gothic style; an early example from the 1170s is the transept of the church at Roche (Yorkshire). Soon, they were accepting gifts of properties that their predecessors had refused. They became very wealthy, their buildings were more lofty and grand, and in the 16th century the abbot of Fountains built a tower alongside the nave of the abbey church. The remoteness of Cistercian sites such as those at Fountains, Rievaulx, Byland, Tintern, etc. ensured that even after the *dissolution of the monasteries the monastic buildings were not razed to the ground. They are now amongst the most spectacular ruined medieval sites in Europe. Some were partly landscaped in the 18th century.

civic ritual. The changing pattern of public urban ritual has to be understood as crystallizing much wider processes, because cities and large towns were so central to the regionalized nature and development of traditional popular culture. Towns, and hence their annual cycles of set civic rituals, stood between the popular usages of their surrounding countryside and the wider, more formalized, expectations of the State.

Probably at most periods, rural popular customs have tended to be perpetuated most closely in the larger towns at the level of the street neighbourhood, whether that was expressed institutionally either by wards or *parishes (or, for different purposes, both). Between them, the street and the parish church with its yard provided both the backing and the public venues for many aspects of such medieval calendrical occasions as *Christmas, *Shrovetide, *Hocktide, *May Day, Whitsuntide, or *Midsummer (the 'ritualistic' half-year discussed under *calendar customs), quite apart from *ad hoc* recreations like animal-baiting or *football. As in the country, some of these activities might be deliberately organized so as to raise funds for the fabrics of churches, *roads, or *bridges. Clearly urban populations were too large for the purposes of mounting such customary practices spontaneously across an entire city.

What does seem to have occurred in some cases during the Middle Ages, nevertheless, was the overlaying—rather than the exclusion—of such activities by 'formal' observances, organized at municipal level, which involved the provision of an elaborate spectacle for the whole community on those occasions when popular licence might otherwise be perceived as posing a threat to public order. These included the Christmas procession of Yule and his wife at York; the Shrovetide procession of the King of Christmas at Norwich (the nearest that England gets to Continental carnival); and the Midsummer-eve and St-Peter's-eve torchlight-marching watches (often with 'giants') at London, Bristol, or Coventry, for example.

Medieval cities also added supra-parochial levels of performance to established or new observances of the church, especially in those cases where superior socio-religious *guilds (containing the more powerful official elements in civic society) took responsibility for open-air spectacles to mark major feasts. The three most common of these were the processions associated with St George's Day (with the dragon), Whitsunday, and *Corpus Christi. This last occasion dominated urban spectacle during the final two centuries of the Middle Ages, not only because of the elaborate play-cycles associated with it, but also because the parading through the streets of the consecrated host—the body of Christ—with all the craft guilds in due order of precedence, and the leading *burgesses in close attendance, vividly expressed the contemporary ideal of urban 'common wealth' in which all might regard themselves as part of one supernaturally sanctioned body politic; see Mervyn James, 'Ritual, Drama and Social Body in the Late Medieval English Town' in James (ed.), *Society, Politics and Culture: Studies in Early Modern England* (1986).

At every period, *towns contained approved structures of authority responsible to the Crown. Solemn emphasis was therefore laid on the ceremonies surrounding the annual elections and public oath-swearings for positions in the magistracy and that of mayor in particular; on the regular public appearance in their red robes of the *aldermen on set occasions; and on the public show of precedence that marked their presence in great processions like the armed marching of the 'King's' Watch at Midsummer and St Peter's. Conversely, when a sovereign came on progress, the civic officials would surrender their symbols of office, like the mace, at the boundary so that these might be returned to them by the monarch as a visual reminder of the royal authority bestowed upon them. Special tableaux or pageants, replete with learned or not-so-learned (but certainly not popular) allusions were increasingly provided on such occasions; see D. M. Bergeron, *English Civic Pageantry 1558–1642* (1971).

Of the three levels of activity described, what was almost wholly swept away at the *Reformation were the great civic spectacles that had functioned on behalf of a city as a whole—for either popular or ecclesiastical festival purposes—and which in so doing had often, complementarily, traversed civic space to its outer limits. In some cases a similar residual activity like the Shrewsbury Show survived or was reflected in new observances like the London Lord Mayor's Show. Such customary days could be deliberately contrived to attract rural customers to an annual *fair, as was the clear intention at late 17th-century Coventry, when it initiated the unprecedented Godiva procession. But such commercially manipulative occasions had by then, of course, been removed from their special calendrical positions in the symbolically rich 'ritualistic' half of the old 'communal' year as had been widely observed in the greater towns. In its stead was emerging a new 12-monthly calendar of individual observances commemorating a range of national celebrations (whether royal or martial) which gave yet more opportunity for public appearances by magisterial élites, those whose existing ceremonializations of the royal authority delegated to them had in any case been least affected by the changes eroding other urban rituals. See Peter Borsay, '"All the Town's a Stage": Urban Ritual and Ceremony, 1660–1800' in Peter Clark (ed.), *The Transformation of English Pro-

vincial Towns, 1600–1800 (1984), and Charles Phythian-Adams, 'Ceremony and the Citizen: The Communal Year at Coventry, 1450–1550' in P. Clark and P. Slack (eds.), *Crisis and Order in English Towns, 1500–1700* (1972).

CHARLES PHYTHIAN-ADAMS

civil registration. From 1 July 1837 the state took responsibility for the registration of all births, marriages, and deaths in England and Wales. Civil registration began in Scotland on 1 January 1855 and in Ireland on 1 January 1864. The system continues to this day. The indexes of the events registered in England and Wales are kept at the *General Register Office, St Catherine's House, 10 Kingsway, London WC2B 6JP. Those for Scotland are kept at the General Register Office, New Register House, Edinburgh EH1 3YT. Irish records are kept at the Office of the Registrar General, Joyce House, 8–11 Lombard Street, Dublin 2, and the General Register Office, Oxford House, 49–55 Chichester Street, Belfast BT1 4HL. All these places are open to the public free of charge. Microfiche copies of indexes are also available at major public *libraries and some *record offices, the Society of *Genealogists, the research centres of the *Mormon Church, and various *family history societies.

The indexes are kept in bound volumes on open shelves, in sections arranged according to births, marriages, and deaths. The earliest ones have handwritten entries and are therefore particularly bulky. Each of the three sections is arranged chronologically, with the years divided into quarters labelled March, June, September, and December. The indexes for each quarter are arranged alphabetically by surname, and then under each surname by first name. The next column notes the name of the Superintendent Registrar's District where the event was registered. The final column contains a reference giving a volume and page number. All this information (including the year and quarter on the spine of the index) should be entered on an application form for a certificate and presented at the counter with the fee. The certificate is not immediately available, but can be collected after four working days, or it may be posted in a week or two's time at no extra charge. The cost of applying by post, even if full details are provided on an application form, is far higher than the cost of applying at the counter.

A great deal of information may be obtained freely from the bound indexes without the cost of applying for a certificate. For example, knowing that a boy's birth was registered in the quarter ending in September 1861 in a certain registration district will prompt a search of the relevant enumeration district in the 1861 census and the baptism registers of local churches. The registration districts were based on the *Poor Law Unions that were created in 1834, but some changes were made from 1 January 1852. The local and family historian has always to be aware of the boundaries of the various administrative units such as *township, *parish, or *Poor Law union. Difficulties arise when an ancestor is being sought in an unfamiliar district. The *Institute of Heraldic and Genealogical Studies has published two small-scale maps that mark the approximate positions, but not the boundaries, of the registration districts of England and Wales, 1837–51 and 1852–1946. Location books are available at St Catherine's House and the other Register Offices. A list of the 650 or so original registration districts in England and Wales is provided in Ray Wiggins, *St Catherine's House Districts*, a booklet which is available from the Society of Genealogists.

Local Register Offices do not have the staff or facilities to deal with general enquiries, and indexes are not available there for public consultation, but specific requests can be dealt with if the information about name, place, and date of event is already known. See Victor J. Price, *Register Offices of Births, Deaths, Marriages in England, Scotland, Wales and Ireland* (1993), which is a checklist of addresses.

Birth certificates give the precise date of the event, followed by the place of birth. Until streets were numbered, the place was normally given as a street name in a town or the name of the village, hamlet, or farmhouse in the countryside. The next columns give the name and sex of the child, the father's forename and surname (or a blank space for an illegitimate child), and the mother's forename, surname, and maiden name. The occupation of the father is then recorded, followed by the signature, description, and residence of the informant (usually the mother). It is very common in the early decades of registration to find that the informant signed with a mark. The final columns contain the date of registration and the signature of the registrar. Birth certificates are therefore a rich source of genealogical detail. They also provide new leads in tracing ancestry back into the previous generation.

The indexes of marriages are arranged in the same way as those of births. From March 1912 onwards the name of the spouse was entered in the index alongside that of the bride or groom. Marriage certificates give the date of the event and the name of the church, chapel, or register office where the ceremony was performed. They then record the names of both partners, their ages, and their 'condition' as bachelor, spinster, widower, or widow. Before 1870 many marriage certificates did not note precise ages but record that the person was 'of full age'. This does not mean that the person was at least 21, for some registrars took the wording to mean the age of consent, which until 1929 might have been even less than 16. The next columns note the 'rank or profession' of each partner, their places of residence at the time of marriage, and the full names and ranks or professions of their fathers. It is sometimes not clear from this information that a father may be deceased. The names of the witnesses who signed the certificates often provide clues to family connections.

From 1866 the indexes of death give an extra piece of information, namely the age at death. The death certificates record the date and place of death, the forename(s) and surname of the deceased, and his or her sex, age, and occupation. The next columns note the cause of death and give the signature, description, and residence of the informant, followed by the date of registration and the signature of the registrar.

The Irish certificates of births, marriages, and deaths from 1864 are similar in form to those for England and Wales. As in England and Wales, the 163 Poor Law unions formed the registration districts. These can be identified from the 1877 edition of the *Alphabetical Index to the Townlands and Towns of Ireland*. Records for each superintendent's district are held locally as well as centrally. Scottish certificates give more information than the English, Welsh, and Irish ones. The birth certificates note the date of marriage of the parents; marriage certificates record the names of both parents of each partner; and death certificates note the names of both parents. From 1929 onwards birth certificates also note the mother's maiden surname. Between 1855 and 1865 married women are indexed under their married name (with their maiden name added), but from 1866 there are separate entries in the marriage indexes under married name and maiden name. As in other parts of Britain, age at death is recorded from 1866 onwards. The indexes are available on microfiche and computer program. See Cecil Sinclair, *Tracing Your Scottish Ancestors: A Guide to Ancestry Research in the Scottish Record Office* (1990).

The registration system was not completely effective in its early years. It has been estimated that in some parts of England and Wales, particularly in Surrey, Sussex, Middlesex,

Essex, and Shropshire, up to 15 per cent of births were not registered between 1837 and 1860. Parents were not penalized for failing to register a birth until 1875. Nor was there any way of ensuring that the information supplied was accurate. Misinformation may have been deliberate or simply caused through forgetfulness. The recorded age at death is particularly suspect, though it is unlikely to be wildly inaccurate. The information provided should therefore be treated warily. Nevertheless, civil registration is one of the most important sources for the family historian.

The cost of obtaining certificates has largely restricted their use to family historians pursuing individual pedigrees. However, marriage certificates have formed the basis of three studies of the social and economic composition of Victorian society. Analyses have been made of about 11,000 marriages in Northampton, Oldham, and South Shields for the period 1846–56 by John Foster, *Class Struggle and the Industrial Revolution* (1974); over 8,000 marriages in Deptford, Greenwich, and Woolwich, 1851–3 and 1873–5 by Geoffrey Crossick, *An Artisan Elite in Victorian Society* (1978); and about 2,000 marriages in Edinburgh for 1865–9 and 1895–7 by Robert Gray, *The Labour Aristocracy in Victorian Edinburgh* (1976). The data provided by the indexes of births, marriages, and deaths are also invaluable in plotting the distribution of *surnames at various times. A *Special Report on Surnames in Ireland*, prepared by Robert E. Matheson and issued as an appendix to the 1894 report of the Registrar-General, lists every surname for which five or more births were recorded in the year 1890. See Donal F. Begley (ed.), *Irish Genealogy: A Record Finder* (1981), ch. 10.

civil service. Government posts were filled by patronage until well into the reign of Victoria. The Northcote–Trevelyan report (1854) recommended changes, including entry to a civil service by competitive examination, promotion by merit, improved pay and pensions, and the division of the service into administrative, executive, and clerical grades. The incompetence revealed by the *Crimean War hastened the implementation of these reforms, which were largely complete by 1870.

Civil War. The English Civil War of 1642–6 has attracted a great deal of scholarly research and continues to provoke debate. Amongst the numerous contributions, see Anthony Fletcher, *The Outbreak of the English Civil War* (1985), Robert Ashton, *The English Civil War* (1989), and Peter R. Newman, *A Companion to the*

English Civil Wars (1990). Much remains to be done on local sources and in analysing regional support for one side or the other. See G. E. Aylmer and J. S. Morrill, *The Civil War and Interregnum: Sources for Local Historians* (1979) and, as an example of a regional approach, B. G. Blackwood, 'Parties and Issues in the Civil War in Lancashire and East Anglia', *Northern History*, 29 (1993). The local approach was first used by Alan Everitt, *Suffolk and the Great Rebellion, 1640–1660* (1960) and *The Community of Kent and the Great Rebellion, 1640–60* (1966). See also Anthony Fletcher, *A County Community in Peace and War: Sussex, 1600–1660* (1975). The damage caused by the opposing armies is assessed in Stephen Porter, *Destruction in the English Civil Wars* (1994). (See also LEVELLERS and CLUB MEN.) The second Civil War of 1648 was a short-lived, uncoordinated series of revolts, which led to the execution of Charles I on 30 January 1649.

clandestine marriage. Until Lord Hardwicke's *Marriage Act came into force in 1754 it was possible to be married without the calling of *banns or the obtaining of a marriage licence. Certain clergymen got the reputation of being willing to perform such ceremonies. Prison chapels, most notoriously the Fleet, where 217 marriages were performed on the day before Hardwicke's Act came into operation, were commonly used. The *Public Record Office holds about 300 registers of clandestine marriages. See Tony Benton, *Irregular Marriage in London before 1754* (1993), and Jeremy Boulton, 'Clandestine Marriages in London: An Examination of a Neglected Urban Variable', *Urban History*, 20/2 (1993).

clans, Scottish. Since the late 18th century much romantic nonsense has been written about clans. The popular concept of Highland clans is largely the invention of Sir Walter Scott and other romantic writers and businessmen who have profited from the sale of supposed clan tartans and kilts. See Hugh Trevor-Roper, 'The Invention of Tradition: The Highland Tradition of Scotland' in Eric Hobsbawm and Terence Ranger (eds.), *The Invention of Tradition* (1983), which shows that the kilt was invented by a Lancashire ironmaster, Thomas Rawlinson, in the late 1720s, that clans were not distinguished by their own tartans before the 1745 rebellion, that the tradition of wearing a distinctive tartan grew up with the Highland regiments that were formed in the second half of the 18th century, and that the occasion of George IV's celebrated visit to Edinburgh in 1822 was responsible for many clans first adopting their own tartan.

It is easier to strip the myths of their romantic excesses than to determine the true nature of the pre-1745 clan system, for written records, especially in the Middle Ages, are scarce and a knowledge of the *Gaelic language is essential. The consensus of opinion is that clans developed from the kin groups of the Picts and the Scots but that the system acquired some feudal characteristics. The chief was a military lord (laird), who could be replaced if he proved ineffective. He was normally a *tenant-in-chief of the Crown, but the physical isolation of his territory meant that he had a great deal of independence. An inner core of kinsmen, the gentry of the clan, known as 'tacksmen', organized the clan as a fighting force. The small tenants and sub-tenants were the *crofters and *cottagers who had fixed obligations, including military service. Geography was more important than *kinship in determining the territory over which a chief ruled. These territories varied over time, for chiefs, like the barons of England, were indifferent to whether or not the people over whom they ruled shared the same name and blood.

The chiefs of clans were mostly known by the name of their estates. It is debatable whether Highland surnames were distinguished by clan or whether a variety of names could be found within a clan. A clan was a unit which contained families of different lineages; common descent is often assumed but it cannot be demonstrated. See R. W. Munro, 'The Clan System: Fact and Fiction' in Loraine Maclean, *The Middle Ages in the Highlands* (1981), Audrey Cunningham, *The Loyal Clans* (1932), and T. M. Devine, *Clanship to Crofters' War: The Social Transformation of the Scottish Highlands* (1994).

clapper bridges consisting of long slabs of stone, or sometimes just a single slab, are found in south-western England and the Pennines. Their age is often greatly exaggerated, for despite their primitive appearance many are 18th-century.

Clare, John (1793–1864). English poet, the son of a farm labourer from Helpstone, near Peterborough. His works are of great interest to social and economic historians for their attitudes to changes in the countryside, particularly those resulting from *enclosure, and for presenting the point of view of *agricultural labourers. See, in particular, *The Mores* and *The Parish*, which deal with enclosure, and his account of the farming year in *The Shepherd's Calendar*.

Clarenceux King of Arms. The second rank-ing King of Arms in England.

class, social. The term was not widely used until the 19th century, though examples of its usage can be found from the 17th century onwards. In the early modern period com-mentators spoke of orders of society rather than classes. Class is a basic tool of Marxist histori-ans, even when dealing with earlier periods. It offers a wide analysis of society and historical events but has not been much employed by historians concerned with local societies. For examples of this approach, see Mick Reed and Roger Wells (eds.), *Class, Conflict and Protest in the English Countryside, 1700–1880* (1990), and Brian Harrison, 'Class and Gender in Modern British Labour History', *Past and Present*, 124 (1989).

Asa Briggs, 'The Language of "Class" in Early Nineteenth-Century England' in A. Briggs and J. Saville (eds.), *Essays in Labour History* (1960), showed how people came to speak of 'class' rather than 'classes'. E. P. *Thompson, *The Making of the English Working Class* (1965), argued that the historical phe-nomenon of a working class appeared in the late 18th and early 19th centuries as a con-sequence of industrialization. Most *labour his-torians now argue that the working class was formed at a much later period: see John Ben-son, *The Working Class in Britain, 1850–1939* (1989). Other historians have argued that the various occupational groups amongst the work-ing classes never formed a cohesive entity that can be regarded as a single class. The term *middle class is likewise too wide and elusive to be more than a convenient shorthand descrip-tion. The concept of class is therefore con-troversial. Most local historians prefer to adopt an empirical approach to their evidence.

clay tobacco pipes. The presence or absence of pipes is a crucial aid to dating archaeological sites at the end of the 16th and the beginning of the 17th century, when *tobacco smoking was introduced into Britain. The changing styles and decoration of pipes provides broad dating for later periods. See David Crossley, *Post-Medieval Archaeology* (1990) and Edward Fletcher, *Clay Pipes* (1977). In 1619 a company of pipemakers was established in London; pro-vincial manufacture began during the first half of the 17th century. York and Bristol had pipemakers' guilds by the 1650s. The Gates-head pipemakers' guild, established in 1675, sold their wares over much of north-eastern England and into Scotland. Most production centres catered for local markets, though they

were said in 1677 to have a great export trade. Pipes made in the Shropshire parishes of Brose-ley, Benthall, and Much Wenlock were carried down the Severn and along the coast to Lon-don, and some found their way to America. Many pipes can be dated by makers' marks by the mid-17th century. A wide variety of local clays were suitable for pipe manufacture, par-ticularly those on the coalfields. Many local industries have been studied: see, for example, Peter J. Hammond, 'The Clay Tobacco-Pipe Making Industry of Newark', *Thoroton Society Transactions*, 89 (1985).

Clearances, Highland. After the defeat of Bonnie Prince Charlie's rebellion at Culloden in 1746, the Highland chiefs lost many of their former powers. Many of them left the High-lands and Islands to live in Edinburgh or Lon-don and ceased to speak the *Gaelic language. Their commitment to the former semi-feudal society based on the *clan system was weak-ened. It became obvious that their estates could be run more profitably by the grazing of *sheep and *cattle than by farming the land in small crofts. Their agents pursued a policy of clearing the cottages of the *crofters, by raising rents and sometimes by violent methods. Between 1763 and 1775 about 20,000 inhabitants of the Highlands and Islands emigrated to *America and *Canada. The scale of emigration was already a matter of concern when Samuel John-son and James Boswell made their tour of the Highlands and Islands in 1773. The numbers of emigrants grew enormously during the 19th century. The present loneliness of much of the Highlands and Islands landscape is a result of the clearances of this period.

The history of the clearances has received scholarly treatment in Eric Richards, *A History of the Highland Clearances*, vol. i: *Agrarian Transformation and the Eviction, 1746–1886* (1982), and vol. ii: *Emigration, Protest, Reasons* (1985). Richards shows that the expansion of large-scale sheep farming through the High-lands was responsible for the widespread evic-tions, but that it should not be assumed that the previous era was a golden one. He argues for root and branch transformation of the region in the later 18th and early 19th centuries, based on the cultivation by crofters of the *potato. See also T. M. Devine, *The Great Highland Famine* (1988), which reveals that 62 of the 86 estates had acquired new owners since 1800; the lim-ited importance of rentals as a source of income for landowners, and the weakness of the croft-ing region during the 1820s and 1830s, are seen as making the clearance policy attractive to these new owners, who were not bound by the old feudal ties of loyalty to their tenants. See also T. M. Devine, *Clanship to Crofters' War: The Social Transformation of the Scottish Highlands* (1994).

clergy, Church of England. The *Reformation reduced the number of English clergy by about a half. The *Church of England suffered a severe shortage of manpower until well into Elizabeth's reign, and many livings remained vacant. For a local study, see Martha C. Skeeters, *Community and Clergy: Bristol and the Reformation, c.1530–c.1570* (1993). The standard of education of the average clergyman was low; when 396 clergymen in the Archdeaconries of Stow and Lincoln were tested on their knowledge of the Scriptures in 1576, only 123 were judged adequately qualified to fulfil their duties. Similar investigations elsewhere came up with similar results. Inadequate stipends failed to attract an educated clergy. In 1585 Archbishop Whitgift estimated that only 600 of the 9,000 or so livings were adequately provided; as a consequence, pluralism and non-residency were rife. The *Puritans sought to improve the educational qualifications of ministers and to make them 'painful and laborious' preachers. By the 1630s the majority of parishes had a resident, graduate clergy. See Rosemary O'Day, *The English Clergy: The Emergence and Consolidation of a Profession, 1558–1642* (1979).

During the *Commonwealth, many ministers who were judged inadequate by the Puritans were ejected from their livings. In 1662 many Puritan ministers were ejected in their turn (see NONCONFORMITY). For an investigation of the Church of England's ministers at a county level see John H. Pruett, *The Parish Clergy Under the Later Stuarts: The Leicestershire Experience* (1978). The most revealing clergyman's diary in the 17th century is that of the Essex parson Ralph *Josselin: see Alan MacFarlane (ed.), *The Diary of Ralph Josselin, 1616–1683* (1976), and MacFarlane's study, *The Family Life of Ralph Josselin, a Seventeenth-Century Clergyman: An Essay in Historical Anthropology* (1970).

Clergymen continued to be educated at the universities of Oxford and Cambridge during the 18th century, but standards were lower than previously. Three diaries that are revealing about the life of rural clergymen are John Beresford (ed.), *The Diary of a Country Parson, 1758–1802 by James Woodforde* (1978), G. M. Ditchfield and Bryan Keith-Lucas (eds.), *A Kentish Parson: Selections from the Private Papers of The Revd Joseph Price, Vicar of Bradbourne,* *1767–1786* (1991), and Jack Ayres (ed.), *Paupers and Pig Killers: The Diary of William Holland: A Somerset Parson, 1799–1818* (1984).

Endowments were made more equal by a series of reforms in the 1830s, and the Church of England belatedly began to tackle the problems of the industrial towns. Ministers belonged to either the High Church, which emphasized liturgy and ritual, or the Low Church, which was evangelical. The Tractarian movement (see OXFORD MOVEMENT) helped to improve the educational standards of clergymen, many Victorian parsons becoming noted scholars, especially in the fields of local and natural history. Many clergymen were now trained in theological colleges rather than at the ancient universities. Crockford's *Clerical Directory*, which has appeared regularly since 1858, is the prime source of information about clergymen in the 19th and 20th centuries, but much information can be found in parish magazines, local *newspapers, and diocesan records. In 1993 the General Synod of the Church of England voted to admit women priests.

clerical subsidy. In the Middle Ages religious bodies paid taxes separately from lay people. The records are kept in the *Public Record Office under E 179. Names of priests appear only in the *poll tax returns of 1377–81 and in the early 16th century; names of chaplains only in 1450 and 1468.

clerk, parish. Originally, a man who was appointed to assist the parish priest and who held his office for life. He was paid from church funds. His duties included making arrangements for services and leading the responses. The civil parishes which were created in 1894 have a parish clerk as their administrative officer.

clerk of the peace. The principal officer who kept the records of the *quarter sessions and the lieutenancy.

climate. The official recording of rainfall, temperature, and air pressure at the Royal Observatory, Greenwich, began in 1840. For earlier periods, information about climate can be gathered from *newspapers, *diaries, *chronicles, letters, etc. and by scientific methods such as pollen analysis and the study of tree-rings.

The last great Ice Age came to an end about 10,000 years ago. The *Stone and *Bronze Ages were warmer than now, but much of the *Iron Age was colder. A warmer period followed until the early 13th century, when colder weather, marked by violent storms, was responsible for much *coastal erosion and flooding of reclaimed *marshland. From the second quarter of the 14th century to the end of the 15th century temperatures rose, but this period was followed by cooler weather from about 1540 to around 1700. During this time the Thames frequently froze over. Between 1550 and 1620 bad harvests were more common and good harvests more rare than in the previous 70 years. The mid-1590s was a period of terrible weather in many parts of western Europe. The 16th and 17th centuries have been called a 'Little Ice Age', but this is an exaggeration. These two centuries did not form a period of continuous cold, for accounts speak of occasional warm winters and sultry summers leading to drought. Nevertheless, winters were generally harsher than the average winter in later times. The Thames has not frozen over since 1814.

See H. H. Lamb, *Climate, History and the Modern World* (1982). The Climate Research Unit at the University of East Anglia is studying the history of climate.

clipping. 1. A church ceremony, often held on *Shrove Tuesday, whereby parishioners held hands to form a chain around the parish *church to ward off evil spirits. The term comes from an *Old English word meaning embracing. The custom has been revived at some churches, e.g. Tankersley (Yorkshire).

2. The clipping of coins was a capital offence tried at the *assizes during the 16th, 17th, and 18th centuries. Coins became worn and varied in weight and so clipping of silver or gold coins could be a profitable business.

cloister. A covered way in a *monastery, for walking and recreation, enclosing a usually quadrangular area, and with a number of cubicles for private study or meditation leading off. They were usually placed on the south side of the church. English medieval cloisters did not normally enclose herb and vegetable gardens as is commonly believed. Delicate window tracery and fan-vault roofs adorn many a cloister, notably that at Gloucester Cathedral.

close 1. (cathedral). The enclosed area around a cathedral, which contains the houses and offices of the principal officers: dean, treasurer, chancellor, and precentor, and the bishop's *palace, forming a separate jurisdiction. See Royal Commission on Historical Monuments, *Salisbury: The Houses of the Close* (1993).

2. (field). A small, hedged or walled field, either at the edge of cultivation or taken in ('enclosed') from the *open-fields, and so not subject to rights on the *commons and wastes.

Close rolls. Records of the Court of *Chancery, housed in the *Public Record Office under C 54, so called because registered copies of private letters and documents were closed with a seal. Further copies were written on sheets of parchment which were stitched together and stored in rolls. The enrolment of private transactions was a safety measure for the parties involved. The rolls record large numbers of *bargains and sales of land, including sales of confiscated land during the *Interregnum.

close studding. The method of arranging vertical timbers close together in the walls of a *timber-framed building. This method was usual in eastern and south-eastern England, in contrast to the *square panelling of the western half of the country, but it was also favoured elsewhere in towns.

clothiers. The term covered a wide range of activities in the cloth trade. The wealthiest merchants of medieval and early modern England were often described as clothiers, e.g. the three generations of the Springs of Lavenham (Suffolk). The term continued in use to mean those engaged in selling cloth, but it was also used from the 16th to the 19th century to describe those men whose families manufactured pieces of cloth, from the preparation and carding of the wool and the *spinning, through to the *weaving. In the West Riding of Yorkshire *wills and *inventories show that such clothiers were smallholders who produced a piece of cloth each week to sell at the *Piece Halls in the neighbouring towns. The term was still used in the early 19th century to distinguish such farmer-manufacturers from those men who were by then full-time weavers.

clover was introduced from the Low Countries into East Anglia in the early 17th century, but it was not until the 1650s that agricultural writers began to speak of its merits in the *meadow and the grass *ley. Imported seed was expensive and some early experiments failed. By the 18th century it had become recognized that the value of clover lay not so much in improving traditional meadows, but in its use in an arable rotation on otherwise bare *fallows, on suitable soils in a dry climate.

club men. In the *Civil War farmers armed with clubs tried to protect their crops and livestock against plundering armies. They were active in Dorset, Hampshire, Gloucestershire, Wiltshire, and Somerset in 1645–6 and 1648. See David Underdown, 'Clubmen in the Civil War', *Past and Present*, 85 (1979), and the same author's *Revel, Riot and Rebellion: Popular Politics and Culture in England, 1603–1660* (1985).

Cluniacs. Monastic order founded at Cluny in Burgundy in 910 and much favoured by the Norman kings and barons. It placed great emphasis on liturgy. More time was devoted to the singing of the Office, to psalms and prayers, ceremonies, intercessions, and masses than was usual among other orders. Cluny's most influential period was during the long abbacy of St Hugh (1049–1109). The first Cluniac priory in England was founded at Lewes (Sussex) in 1077 by William de Warenne, who had received lavish hospitality at Cluny. Ten years later, Alwin Child, a London merchant, founded another Cluniac house at Bermondsey, which was subsequently endowed by William II. In 1080 Roger Montgomery refounded Much Wenlock Priory as a Cluniac house. William de Warenne II founded Castle Acre (Norfolk) in 1089; Robert de Lacy founded Pontefract Priory (Yorkshire) about 1090, from which sprang Monk Bretton (1154, later Benedictine); Roger Bigod endowed Thetford (Norfolk) in 1103–4, and Gervase Paganel founded Dudley (Worcestershire) in 1160. The rest of the 36 Cluniac priories in England were small establishments. Only three Cluniac houses were built in Scotland and none at all in Wales and Ireland.

coaches. According to John *Stow, 'In the yeare 1564 Guilliam Boonen, a Dutchman, became the Queene's Coachman, and was the first that brought the use of coaches into England . . . within twenty years began a great trade of coach making.' At first the use of coaches was confined to the London area, but by the end of the century noblemen were using them in other parts of the country. Some regarded this method of travelling as unmanly and insisted on riding on horseback, but by the 1630s public stage-coaches provided links with London within a 30-mile radius of the capital. By 1658, if not before, places as far north as Doncaster and Wakefield could be reached by stage-coaches from the capital in four days. A more comfortable ride was made possible by the use of steel springs in coaches from 1754. Many more stage-coach routes were opened once the principal highways were *turnpiked in the 18th century. Provincial *directories from the late 18th and early 19th centuries are a major source of information about routes and coach proprietors. *Newspapers often contain advertisements of the services that were available, and private letters and journals give other details. See also CARRIERS.

coal has been mined in Britain since at least Roman times. Those coalfields which had seams near the surface have documentary evidence of small-scale mining since the 13th century. The first coalfield to be developed in a major way was that in Durham and Northumberland, which had the inestimable advantage of being near the sea and therefore able to export its products at prices that could not be matched by its landlocked competitors. 'Carrying coal to Newcastle' became a popular phrase for a useless activity. The term 'sea-coal' was widely used, even in places far distant from the sea, as a generic word for coal, to distinguish it from *charcoal and the white-coal of the *lead smelters. The north-eastern coalfield was exploited on a massive scale from the second half of the 16th century onwards. See David Levine and Keith Wrightson, *The Making of an Industrial Society: Whickham, 1560–1765* (1991), an outstanding local study set in a regional and national context, which links the social history of this community to technological developments. Elizabethan Whickham had many of the characteristics that are normally associated with coalfield settlements in the 19th century.

The *canals and, especially, the *railways enabled the landlocked coalfields to compete on a national scale. It has been estimated that there were about 50,000 coalminers in Britain by 1800; by 1914 the number had risen to well over 1 million. Coal mining had become a major source of employment and coal was the basis of Britain's rapid industrial development. The Yorkshire, Derbyshire, and Nottinghamshire coalfield, for example, produced 8 million tons of coal in 1851 and 73 million tons in 1913. The South Wales and Central Scotland coalfields, and to a lesser extent those in Lancashire, Staffordshire, and other Midland counties, witnessed similar massive developments. For a general introductory view see A. R. Griffin, *The British Coalmining Industry: Retrospect and Prospect* (1977). An authoritative five-volume history, commissioned by the National Coal Board, has been published as *The History of the British Coal Industry*; (1) J. Hatcher, *Before 1700* (1993); (2) M. W. Flinn, *1700–1830* (1984); (3) R. Church, *1830–1913* (1986); (4) B. Supple, *1913–1946* (1987); (5) W. Ashworth, *1946–1982* (1986).

What has come to be regarded as the 'traditional' pit village rarely lasted for more than 100–120 years and often had a much shorter life-span of two or three generations. The earliest miners did not form a distinctive group, for they were not numerous and, like many other craftsmen, they often combined their work with the running of a smallholding. During the 19th century, however, some old villages and market towns were transformed by coalmining and some entirely new communities were formed near the pits, beyond the older settlements. Sometimes, these new places were no more than a row of houses, but elsewhere they grew into sprawling villages that were as large as towns but which lacked the usual range of urban amenities. Much work remains to be done on the various types of coalmining settlements that grew up in the 19th and early 20th centuries. A few, notably Elsecar (Yorkshire), were planned by paternalistic landowners who provided adequate housing, schools, village halls, churches, etc. Some, e.g. Denaby Main (Yorkshire), were company towns, full of immigrant workers who rented terraced houses from the coalowners and who used the pub, shops, church, and school built by their employers. Other settlements consisted merely of rows of speculative building on former *commons, close to the mine. In South Wales the mining towns and villages were strung out along the valleys, totally transforming the landscape. Those villages which housed the much deeper mines in the 20th century were often more spacious, on the lines of later council estates.

Early studies of coalmining concentrated on the role of *trade unions, whose leaders were often cast in a heroic mould. A much wider interest in the social history of mining communities is now evident: see, for instance, Raphael Samuel (ed.), *Miners, Quarrymen and Saltworkers* (1977), which includes a chapter by Dave Douglas on 'Pit Talk in County Durham', and John Benson, *British Coalminers in the Nineteenth Century: A Social History* (1993). In *Pit-Men, Preachers and Politics: The Effects of Methodism in a Durham Mining Community* (1974) Robert Moore analyses four small and relatively isolated mining villages in the period 1870–1926; Methodism is seen here as a binding social force which cut across class divisions in the period before the General Strike. For an example of a study of the people who came to live in the new pit villages, see A. G. Walker, 'Migration into a South Yorkshire Colliery District, 1861–1881', *Northern History*, 29 (1993), which makes effective use of the *census returns. *Newspapers can provide a great deal of information about strikes and accidents and about the range of social activities in mining areas. The rapid decline of coalmining in the late 20th century has resulted in most coalfields being abandoned. Pits villages can now be seen as a historical phenomenon that lasted a relatively short period of time. This sense of an era

which has passed away should encourage local historians to study these mining communities in the same detailed and comparative ways in which the rural communities of the early modern period have been analysed.

coastal erosion. The relative level of the sea to the land has varied over the centuries. It rose in the late Roman period, receded in the Anglo-Saxon period, and rose again from about 1250 onwards. Huge banks have been constructed since at least Roman times in attempts to prevent the flooding of coastal areas, but these have often been destroyed by the power of the sea when whipped up by gale force winds. See J. A. Steers, *The Sea Coast* (1969).

Coastal areas like Romney Marsh (Kent), the Lancashire dunes, the Culbin Sands (Nairnshire), and the salt marshes of Essex and the Wash are the result of accretion over the centuries. Orford Beach (Suffolk), 10 miles long and at its neck less than 100 yards wide, is the most dramatic example of the results of contrasting phases of accretion and erosion; it reached approximately its present shape in the mid-16th century. Other places which were once flourishing settlements on the eastern or southern coasts of England have been completely destroyed. In the East Riding of Yorkshire 16 places which were recorded in the *Domesday Book, in a strip about 35 miles long and two-thirds of a mile wide, were lost to the sea in the later Middle Ages: see T. Sheppard, *Lost Towns of the Yorkshire Coast* (1912). The Norfolk parishes of Happisburgh and Eccles have lost their medieval churches to coastal erosion, and at least half a mile of parts of the Suffolk coast has gone, including almost all the town and port of Dunwich. At the mouth of the Humber, the shingle strip known as Spurn Head has often changed shape. It was once stable enough to support settlements. In about 1235 fishermen began to dry their nets on an area of sand and stones accumulated from the North Sea; houses were soon built at three separate places, one of which—Ravenser Odd—prospered and became a *borough before disappearing under the sea in the middle years of the 14th century. As the *climate deteriorated and sea levels rose, much of the land that had been laboriously reclaimed was lost. In the 20th century the North Sea has caused renewed concern, especially during the serious flooding of 1953, but large sums of money have been spent on coastal defences and the damage has been limited. Research on the long history of one coastal area, by an interdisciplinary team, is being coordinated by The

Romney Marsh Research Trust: see Jill Eddison and Christopher Green (eds.), *Romney Marsh: Evolution, Occupation, Reclamation* (1988).

The fall in the relative level of the land to the sea began in the second half of the 13th century and continued well into the 15th century. It was associated with a worsening climate characterized by increasing storminess and more frequent and longer spells of foul weather. The southern coast of England was as badly affected as the eastern one. In 1287 Old Winchelsea was destroyed. Major flooding was reported on a number of occasions in the early 14th century, but the worst floods of all came in the first and third decades of the 15th century. See Peter Brandon and Brian Short, *The South East From AD 1000* (1990).

coat of arms. Distinctive heraldic bearings. The name is derived from the 13th-century fashion of applying armorial bearings to a surcoat. See Thomas Woodcock and John Martin Robinson, *The Oxford Guide to Heraldry* (1988).

cob. A traditional building material, especially in Devon, Dorset, and Cornwall, consisting mostly of mud, with pebbles, straw, or horse hair for binding. A firm foundation and an overhanging thatched roof keeps rain water out of buildings; thick walls make them warm in winter and cool in summer. Surviving farmhouses and outbuildings date mostly from the 17th to the early 19th centuries.

Cobbett, William (1763–1835). Writer and politician. Cobbett was at first a 'King and Country' man, but after his return from a prolonged stay in the United States of America in the 1790s, he became a champion of the *agricultural labourers. He was a prolific writer; in 1802 he started his *Weekly Political Register*, which he continued until his death. A lover of the country who was concerned about the changes that were occurring, he is best remembered for his *Rural Rides* (1830), which were passages reprinted from the *Register*. This now has historical value for its descriptions of many parts of southern England in the early 19th century. See Ian Dyck, *William Cobbett and Rural Popular Culture* (1992).

cock fighting was originally an outdoor 'sport' held in circular pits dug into the ground. Throwing stones at cocks was a traditional pastime of *apprentices on *Shrove Tuesday. During the 17th and 18th centuries smaller cockpits were constructed indoors. A wide section of society was attracted by the violence and by gambling on the winner. Cock fights were frequently depicted in satirical cartoons. The 'sport' was largely suppressed in the first half of the 19th century.

codicil. An addition to a *will that seeks to explain or alter previous provision.

coffee house. The first coffee house in England was reputedly established in London in 1650 at the Angel. They became popular after the *Restoration and remained so during the 18th century. The fashion spread quickly to provincial towns. Coffee houses provided informal meeting places for gossip and serious discussion, with *newspapers provided, and formal settings for meetings of local officers and clubs. They also acted as venues for auctions. They thus served many of the functions of *inns, with which they were often closely associated.

cognate. Related on the mother's side.

coinage. The Romans were the first to use coins in the British Isles. The Anglo-Saxons and Vikings minted coins in several places, though by the late 9th century London had become the principal mint. The Normans continued to use the same mints, whose principal output was silver pennies and half-pennies. The range of coins was increased in the late 13th, 14th, and 15th centuries. (See ANGEL; FARTHING; FLORIN; GROAT; and NOBLE.) The Tudors added the *sovereign and the *crown, the *shilling, sixpence, and threepenny piece. From the middle of the 16th century coins frequently bore their minting date, but this did not become accepted practice until the later 17th century. After the *Restoration some new coins were minted, including the *guinea. The abbreviated Latin inscriptions on coins refer to the monarch's role as 'Defender of the Faith' and head of the *Church of England. From 1877 to 1947 the inscription also noted that the monarch was emperor of India. Until 1971, when decimal coinage was introduced, coins were valued as 12 pence (*d.*) = 1 shilling (*s.*), 20 shillings = 1 pound (£). See H. Seaby, *The Story of British Coinage* (1985).

college. The colleges that were founded in the Middle Ages by members of royal or aristocratic families or great church dignitaries were intended as residences and places of prayer and study for priests. Some were for the priests of *collegiate churches. Some, e.g. the mid-15th-century St William's College, York, provided accommodation for chantry priests, or in the case of the Bedern, York, for the *vicars-choral of the cathedral. Some were primarily educational institutions, e.g. Eton College founded by Henry VI in the mid-15th century, or the colleges of the universities at Oxford and Cambridge, which were organized like great medieval households, with a porter's lodge, domestic accommodation around courtyards, a chapel, and a communal dining hall that was arranged in a similar manner to those of great manor houses. Many colleges were dissolved in 1547, for they were regarded in the same light as *chantry chapels, but those whose purpose was principally educational survived. The word 'college' thus became applied to institutions of higher education.

collegiate church. Some of the largest parish *churches in the Middle Ages were endowed by rich benefactors who made provision for them to be served by a college of priests who were not bound to any specific monastic rule. (See COL-LEGE.) The medieval diocese of York had 21 such colleges, including pre-Conquest examples at Beverley, Ripon, and Southwell (Nottinghamshire) and the 13th-century foundation at the Bishop of Durham's manor at Howden. Each was associated with a market town. Other collegiate churches were established in rural parishes, especially in eastern England during the 14th and 15th centuries. They normally had endowments for a provost or master and up to 12 priests, but a few were much larger, e.g. the royal foundation at Fotheringay (Northamptonshire) had 34 members. Collegiate churches can often be recognized by their grand *chancels, which retain stalls with *misericords. The constitutions of priestly colleges varied considerably, but from the middle of the 14th century the great majority, including almost all those associated with parish churches, were *chantry foundations, and as such were dissolved in 1547. Sometimes, as at Fotheringay, the chancel was demolished following the *dissolution of the Monasteries. At Howden, the chancel decayed through neglect and is now a spectacular ruin.

collier. The term has come to be used exclusively for a coal miner, particularly one who works at the coal face, but before the 19th century it included wood-colliers or charcoal burners. Place-names such as Colliers End (Hertfordshire) can be found well away from coal-mining districts.

colonia. Roman Colchester, Gloucester, Lincoln, and York had areas set aside for families (especially those of former soldiers) who had full rights of Roman citizenship. The medieval walls at York preserve the territory of the colonia south of the Ouse.

Combination Acts. The Acts of 1799 and 1800 prohibited combinations of workers in *trade unions. They were passed during the *Napoleonic wars, when fear of revolution after the French example was at its height. They were repealed in 1824.

comes. A Latin word which was Anglicized as count.

commerce. See INDUSTRY AND TRADE.

Commissary Court. An *ecclesiastical court presided over by a commissary acting on behalf of a bishop where the area served by the court lay well away from the bishop's residence. See, for example, F. G. Emmison, *Essex Wills: The Bishop of London's Commissary Court, 1558–1569* (1993), which contains abstracts of 1,065 wills. In Scotland the Edinburgh Commissary Court assumed responsibility for the proving of Scottish wills, the taking of oaths, the trying of cases of slander, and for dealing with marriage contracts, divorce, separation, and bastardy. The records have been indexed as 'The Commissariot of Edinburgh: Consistorial Processes and Decrees, 1630–1800' (Scottish Record Society, 1909). In 1823 most of the jurisdiction of the Commissary Court was transferred to the *sheriff courts.

Common Pleas, Court of. A royal court of justice sitting at Westminster, whose origins go back to the reign of Henry II (1154–89). From the reign of Edward I (1272–1307) its work became restricted to common law actions between private subjects. It became a division of the High Court in 1873. The records are kept at the *Public Record Office under CP. The archives of most use to local and family historians are the *final concords which end fictitious suits, whose real purpose was to transfer property. See FEET OF FINES.

commons and wastes. The common was once an integral part of the farming economy of a *manor. In *open-field villages the manorial tenants had the right to graze livestock not only on the common at the edge of the settlement, but on the *fallow field, and on the other openfields after harvest. (See also GREEN.) Settlements on the edges of the *moors, *woods, or *fens often had rights over extensive commons and wastes. Some of these areas were intercommoned by neighbouring manors. (See also DETACHED PASTURE.) Common rights were vital to the ability to survive on a small farm; in *deeds they are referred to as the '*appurtenances' of a property. The right to graze a few animals on the commons in summer was particularly important. Common rights were basically those of pasture (for cattle, sheep, and horses), pannage (for pigs), turbary (peat), estovers (wood), piscary (fish), and common in the soil (sand, stone, gravel, etc.), but they varied from manor to manor. Occasionally, the jury of a manor court noted the customs of the manor and the rights which could be claimed by the tenants; e.g. in the 17th century the copyholders of Wirksworth (Derbyshire) claimed common of pasture for all manner of cattle, liberty to get turves, peats, clods, limestone, clay, marl, sand, gravel, slate, stone, heath, fern, furze, and gorse, and to fell or cut for reasonable estovers any hollies or underwoods on the wastes. Commons in the Peak District were graded best, middle, and worst; e.g. in the 17th century Castleton (Derbyshire) had 732 acres of the best sort, 150 acres of the middle sort, and so much of the worst kind that the inhabitants could not estimate them or define the bounds accurately.

Manorial *courts insisted that only those tenants of 'ancient enclosures' had rights over the common and that these rights were in direct proportion to the size of the holding. This was crucial to the question of compensation for the loss of rights at the time of *enclosure. Common rights did not imply common ownership; they are best regarded in the same way as the right to use a footpath over somebody else's land. Manorial juries often found it was necessary to limit common rights so as to prevent overstocking of the commons. The rights were therefore 'stinted' to so many 'cow gates', etc., according to the size of the holding. The poor inhabitants of a manor had a different view of the common from that expressed by the manorial courts and they felt dispossessed by enclosure: see the discussion of 'Custom, Law and Common Right' in E. P. Thompson, *Customs in Common* (1991), ch. 3, and Jean M. Neeson, *Commoners: Common Right, Enclosure and Social Change in England, 1700–1820* (1993). The nature of common rights is still a matter of debate amongst historians, often passionately so. For a local study see C. E. Searle, 'Customary Tenants and the Enclosure of the Cumbrian Commons', *Northern History*, 29 (1993).

Thousands of acres of commons and wastes survived the period of parliamentary enclosure and continue to be administered by local authorities: see W. G. Hoskins and L. Dudley Stamp, *The Common Lands of England and Wales* (1963). Under the Commons Registration Act (1965) a national register has been made of these commons, whose main use is now for recreational activities.

Commonwealth, the (historical). The period of republican government following the execution of Charles I in 1649 until the *Restoration of Charles II in 1660. In 1653 the Rump Parliament was dissolved by the army and Oliver Cromwell became Lord Protector. He was succeeded upon his death in 1658 by his son Richard.

Commonwealth immigrants. A small number of African, Caribbean, and South Asian people lived in London during the 17th and 18th centuries, as a result of the *slave trade and employment as *merchant seamen. The number of seamen who came from distant parts of the British Empire to settle in various ports, e.g. Cardiff, increased in the 19th and early 20th centuries, but there were few well-defined communities of emigrants from these countries in Britain until after the Second World War. Immigration on a large scale began on 8 June 1948 when 492 passengers sailed from Kingston, Jamaica, to settle in Britain. Many more West Indians, predominantly Jamaicans, followed during the 1950s and 1960s in the knowledge that jobs were available. Some British employers, e.g. London Transport, actively recruited workers from the New Commonwealth countries. Another large group of immigrants came from the Indian sub-continent; in the 1950s Sikhs came from eastern Punjab, and smaller numbers of Hindus, Muslims, and Parsees came from other parts of India. The majority of Muslims came from Mirpur and Sylhat in rural Pakistan to settle in Bradford and other textile towns where the demand for labour was high. The newcomers settled mainly in the large conurbations which were losing population and where there was prospect of work: London, Birmingham, Leicester, Nottingham, and Derby, and the textile towns of Lancashire and Yorkshire were the main centres of New Commonwealth settlement. Scotland, Wales, and those parts of England where unemployment was high were generally avoided. See Colin Holmes, *John Bull's Island: Immigration and British Society, 1871–1971* (1988).

The rush to arrive in England reached its height before the Commonwealth Immigrants Act (1962) restricted entry to dependants and skilled workers. Many of the early immigrants were young men who had originally intended to return to their native country after saving sufficient money, but during the 1960s increasing numbers of wives and children arrived to set up homes. The variety of New Commonwealth immigrants increased during the 1960s and 1970s with the arrival of refugees from Kenya (1967) and Uganda (1972), who were mainly business and professional people with family roots in India. Other refugees arrived later, e.g. Malawis in the mid-1970s and Somalis in the 1980s. A series of Acts passed between 1968 and 1981 imposed further restrictions on entry.

The numbers of immigrants from the New Commonwealth countries are difficult to measure precisely. The 1951 census recorded only 138,072 people in Britain who had been born in the Caribbean and the Indian sub-continent, including an uncertain number of whites. By 1971 there were 633,100 people whose parents had both been born in the Caribbean or South Asia and another 35,490 with one parent born there. The immigrant population has remained youthful: in the late 1980s over half the 150,000 Africans and 456,000 Caribbeans in Britain were under 30 years of age. The New Commonwealth immigrants have remained concentrated in several distinct areas within the conurbations in which they have settled. In London, for example, the West Indian population is largely concentrated in Brixton, Shepherds Bush, and north and east London, whereas people from the Indian sub-continent and other parts of South Asia are found especially in Hounslow, Tower Hamlets, and Newham. In 1991 London had 521,900 of the 1,476,900 South Asians living in Britain: see Nick Merriman (ed.), *The Peopling of London* (1993). The techniques of *oral history are particularly appropriate to the recording of the history of New Commonwealth immigration.

communion tables. The medieval church used stone *altars, inscribed with small crosses at each corner and in the middle. In 1550 wooden communion tables replaced stone altars as part of the liturgical rearrangements of the *Reformation. See Eamon Duffy, *The Stripping of the Altars: Traditional Religion in England, 1400–1580* (1992). Parishioners were given freer access to the area where the eucharist was performed, but because of the problem of stray dogs it became usual to fence off the area around the communion table with low rails. During the 1630s Archbishop Laud tried to introduce more ritual into church services, including the installation of permanently placed east altars beyond the communion rail, at which communicants could kneel. In 1643 Parliament abolished all east altars and communion rails. However, a lot

of pre-*Commonwealth rails survived to be reused after the *Restoration. See Mark Chatfield, *Churches the Victorians Forgot* (1979).

communities and local societies. The study of local communities has been the major academic concern of local historians since the 1950s, particularly those connected with, or influenced by, the *Leicester University Department of English Local History. In *The Local Historian and His Theme* (1952) H. P. R. *Finberg defined the 'business of the local historian' as the study of 'the Origins, Growth, Decline and Fall of a local community'. This was soon followed by an exemplary study: W. G. *Hoskins, *The Midland Peasant: The Economic and Social History of a Leicestershire Village* (1957). The works of rural sociologists such as W. M. Williams, *The Sociology of an English Village* (1957), which studied Gosforth (Cumberland), and David Jenkins, *The Agricultural Community in South-West Wales at the Turn of the Century* (1971), which analysed Troedyraur (Cardiganshire), together with a new interest in social history, influenced the next generation of rural community studies: Margaret Spufford, *Contrasting Communities: English Villagers in the Sixteenth and Seventeenth Centuries* (1974), a study of Chippenham, Orwell, and Willingham, three contrasting Cambridgeshire parishes; David Hey, *An English Rural Community: Myddle Under the Tudors and Stuarts* (1974), a study of a Shropshire parish; and Keith Wrightson and David Levine, *Poverty and Piety in an English Village: Terling, 1525–1700* (1979), a study of an Essex community. This approach was particularly congenial to rural historians of the early modern period, but was just as applicable to the study of medieval and Tudor towns, as in Alan D. Dyer, *Worcester in the Sixteenth Century* (1973), David Palliser, *Tudor York* (1979), and Charles Phythian-Adams, *Desolation of a City: Coventry and the Urban Crisis of the Later Middle Ages* (1979). A different sort of community was studied in depth in Mary Prior, *Fisher Row: Fishermen, Bargemen and Canal Boatmen in Oxford, 1500–1900* (1982). In the 1980s and 1990s the study of both urban and rural communities continued to flourish; see, for example, Marjorie Keniston McIntosh, *Anatomy and Community: The Royal Manor of Havering, 1200–1500* (1986), and *A Community Transformed: The Manor and Liberty of Havering-atte-Bower, 1500–1620* (1991), and David Levine and Keith Wrightson, *The Making of an Industrial Society: Whickham, 1560–1765* (1991). The 19th century has not attracted many community studies: see, however, J. Robin, *Elmdon:*

Continuity and Change in a North-West Essex Village, 1861–1964 (1980). See also Brian Short (ed.), *The English Rural Community: Images and Analysis* (1992), and Claire Jarvis, 'The Reconstitution of Nineteenth-Century Rural Communities', *Local Population Studies*, 51 (1993).

The concept of a 'community' has been attacked by sociologists on the grounds that its meaning varies too much to allow comparisons and because it implies an enclosed group unaffected by the wider world. Local historians, however, have always been well aware that the parish boundary, while defining a unit that can be studied in practical terms, did not restrict movement in and out of the parish. See Alan MacFarlane in collaboration with Sarah Harrison and Charles Jardine, *Reconstructing Historical Communities* (1977), and J. D. Marshall, 'The Study of Local and Regional "Communities": Some Problems and Possibilities', *Northern History*, 17 (1981).

The need for a framework wider than that of a town or a rural community defined by the parish has been a matter of academic debate amongst local historians. (See LOCAL AND REGIONAL HISTORY, and PAYS.) Charles Phythian-Adams, *Re-Thinking Local History* (1987), advocated the need to study local societies which could be defined in four ways: (1) as an inhabited territory with a fair degree of geographic coherence, (2) by enduring features of societal organization, (3) by shared cultural associations, and (4) by the presence of a body of indigenous families. The old concept of *'country' is useful in recognizing these local societies. In 'Local History and National History: The Quest for the Peoples of England', *Rural History*, 2/1 (1991), Charles Phythian-Adams showed how local historians should be concerned with identifying and analysing such societies and with the ways in which they relate to the wider world, illustrating his theme by the example of the broad rhythms of experience of the people of northern Cumbria. In Charles Phythian-Adams (ed.), *Societies, Cultures and Kinship, 1580–1850: Cultural Provinces and English Local History* (1993), he offered an agenda for local historians by dividing England into 14 cultural provinces based on river-drainage patterns. Three other essays in the same volume studied local societies in south-west Nottinghamshire, south-east Surrey, and that based on St Ives (Huntingdonshire). See also David Hey, *The Fiery Blades of Hallamshire: Sheffield and its Neighbourhood, 1660–1740* (1991). The new local history looks outwards as well as inwards and attempts to relate the experiences of local societies to those of the nation as a whole.

commutation. The change from paying *tithes in kind to a fixed money payment. The Tithe Commutation Act (1836) made this change compulsory.

comperta. 'Things discovered' at an *ecclesiastical visitation of a parish by a bishop or archdeacon.

Compotus rolls. Accounts of royal and seigneurial estates. The records of royal *escheators are kept in the *Public Record Office under E 136 and 357. The compoti of manorial lords are mostly housed in local *record offices.

Compton ecclesiastical census. An *ecclesiastical census, taken in 1676 for the *Provinces of Canterbury and York and named after Henry Compton, Bishop of London. The returns have been published as Anne Whiteman (ed.), *The Compton Census of 1676: A Critical Edition* (1986). The answers given by the incumbents of parishes were recorded in three columns, which gave the total number of Conformists, Papists, and Nonconformists. In perhaps the majority of parishes the number listed under Conformists is in fact probably the total number of inhabitants over the age of 16 in the parish, including Papists and Nonconformists. The difficulties in interpreting the returns and converting the figures into population totals are set out in Anne Whiteman, 'The Compton Census of 1676' and Tom Arkell, 'A Method for Estimating Population Totals from the Compton Census Returns' in Kevin Schurer and Tom Arkell (eds.), *Surveying the People: The Interpretation and Use of Document Sources for the Study of Population in the Later Seventeenth Century* (1992). Part of the problem is that the form of questions differed from *diocese to diocese and sometimes from *archdeaconry to archdeaconry. Another problem concerns the proportion of the population that was under 16; estimates range from 30 to 40 per cent. Correlations of the population figures derived from the Compton census with those derived from the *hearth tax returns are variable, and occasionally poor. Despite all the problems of interpretation, the Compton census is seen as a major source for estimating the size of local populations, as well as being of fundamental importance in assessing the strength of *Nonconformity and *Roman Catholicism in the reign of Charles II. The number of Nonconformists may have been understated, but no systematic distortion is apparent.

compurgation. The process whereby an accused person could call upon 12 people to swear to his innocence or the truth of his statement. It was abolished in 1833.

computers, use of. Many aspects of history are suitable for quantitative analysis and therefore lend themselves readily to the use of computers. Historical demography is the outstanding example (see POPULATION LEVELS AND TRENDS). For a computer analysis of the *ecclesiastical census of 1851 see K. D. M. Snell, *Church and Chapel in the North Midlands: Religious Observance in the Nineteenth Century* (1991). See also P. Denley, S. Fogelvich, and C. Harvey (eds.), *History and Computing, II* (1989), and Evan Mawdsley and Thomas Munck, *Computing for Historians: An Introductory Guide* (1993). For the use of computers in the field of local history see Christopher Harrison, 'Computing for Local and Regional Historians', *The Local Historian*, 20/3 (1990), and Stephen J. Page, 'Researching Local History: Methodological Issues and Computer-Assisted Analysis', *The Local Historian*, 23/1 (1993). The creation of a computer database allows the stored information to be sorted quickly in many different ways. For example, the *apprenticeship records of the Cutlers' Company of Hallamshire are available in print, arranged alphabetically by the names of the apprentices. The creation of a computer database allows these lists to be rearranged in alphabetical order of the masters' names, or by the trade of the master, the trade of the father of the apprentice lad, the specific locality of the master or of the father, and by periods. In other words, the same information can be reshuffled quickly in many different ways.

Family historians include among their numbers many people who are skilled users of computers. For beginners, the Society of *Genealogists offers a *Computers in Genealogy Beginner's Pack*, which gives advice on PCWs, programs, and the creation of records for each person on a family tree. The Society issues a quarterly newsletter, *Computers in Genealogy*, to members of the Genealogists Computer Interest Group. See also the *Family Tree Computer Magazine*, which is also published quarterly and which offers hints for beginners as well as articles on more advanced techniques. Many family history societies have their own computer group. The Genealogical Society of Utah acquires and computerizes genealogical information from around the world, which it makes freely available to anyone who is interested (see MORMON BRANCH LIBRARIES). It has also developed Personal Ancestral File, a personal computer software package.

coney, or cony. The original English name for *rabbit. Minor place-names frequently commemorate 'coney-garths' or 'conigers'.

Conference of Regional and Local Historians. Founded in 1978 to promote regional and local history among teachers in higher and further education, CORAL holds regular conferences and has published some of the papers, sometimes in conjunction with the *Journal of Local and Regional Studies* published by the University of Humberside.

confirmation rolls. Records of the renewal of privileges by the Crown from 1483 to 1625, housed at the *Public Record Office under C 56. The *Calendar of Letters and Papers, Henry VIII* includes those for 1509–14.

Congregationalists. The Congregationalists originated as a *Puritan sect led by Robert Browne in the 1580s. They were known at first as Brownists and, until well into the 18th century, also as *Independents. Their distinguishing feature was their insistence on the independence of each congregation. Their theological views in the 17th century were similar to those of the *Presbyterians, with whom they were often associated, differing chiefly in the method of church organization. Many, though not all, Congregational congregations were affected by the evangelical movement of the late 18th and 19th centuries. The Congregational Union of England and Wales was formed in 1831. Congregationalism proved particularly attractive to the middle classes in both small and large towns. In 1972 the Congregationalists and English Presbyterians joined together to form the United Reformed Church. The Congregational History Society and the United Reformed Church History Society have published some of their records.

consanguinity. Blood-relationship; descent from a common ancestor.

consecration cross. When a bishop consecrated a new church he anointed each of the 24 crosses marked high on the walls, half of which were on the outside. Each cross was painted red and enclosed in a small circle. Many churches have a few surviving crosses. Edington (Wiltshire) is exceptional in having 11 in the interior and 10 on the outer face of the walls.

Conservative Party. Sir Robert Peel, *Prime Minister 1834–5 and 1841–6, is recognized as the first leader of the Conservative Party, which grew out of the *Tory Party of the late 17th and

18th centuries. The Conservatives and the *Liberals (who grew out of the other old party, the *Whigs) alternated in government during the second half of the 19th century and the first quarter of the 20th century, when the *Labour Party replaced the Liberals as the main opposition to the Conservatives. The Conservatives have been the dominant political force in the 20th century in terms of the number of years during which they have held power.

consistory court. See ECCLESIASTICAL COURTS.

constable. The office was manorial in origin; the constable was the link between the lord and his tenants, the keeper of law and order. He was appointed by the jury of the *court leet. Where manors decayed during the 17th and 18th centuries, the appointment was made by the parish *vestry meeting. The constable served for one year and was usually elected on a rotation basis from the farmers and craftsmen, the better-off members of the community. The office was unpaid and no expenses were given for loss of earnings. The constable raised taxes, kept accounts, and presented these for approval at the end of his year of office. He was also responsible to the Head Constable of the *hundred or *wapentake for certain duties and to the *Justices of the Peace for others. Daniel *Defoe remarked in his *Parochial Tyranny* (1714) that the office of constable was one of 'insupportable hardship . . . it takes up so much of a man's time that his own affairs are frequently totally neglected, too often to his ruin', but others regarded the position as an honour which gave them status in the community. See Joan R. Kent, *The English Village Constable* (1986).

In dealing with petty law and order the constable was responsible for the *stocks, *pillory, and village lock-up. He raised the *hue and cry, saw to the *whipping of vagrants, and secured prisoners and escorted them to the *quarter sessions or *assizes. Most troubles were dealt with informally or by arbitration, but a constable could find himself in situations where his responsibilities to the Justices of the Peace conflicted with a communal sense of good neighbourliness. His other duties included the collection of county rates which paid for the *house of correction, *roads, and *bridges, lame soldiers, travellers with passes, and the assizes, etc., and of national taxes such as the *poll tax, *hearth tax, and *land tax. His military duties included the raising of the local *militia, the provision of accommodation and transport for armed forces, and the lighting of *beacons. He was responsible also for weights and measures and the supervision of *alehouses, including the provision of lists of alehouses for licensing at the *brewster sessions. Surviving constables' accounts in local *record offices and the records of quarter sessions reveal the variety of tasks that fell to the constable during his year of office. The office was replaced by the establishment of a national police force in the mid-19th century.

constitutional societies. In the early 1790s, under the influence of the French Revolution and Tom Paine's *Rights of Man*, constitutional or 'corresponding' societies were set up by working men in London, Sheffield, Derby, and Manchester. They were suppressed by the end of the decade, but have come to be regarded as the first working-class political organizations. See E. P. *Thompson, *The Making of the English Working Class* (1965).

consumer revolution. It is clear from the analysis of probate *inventories and other records that the general standard of living rose considerably in the early modern period, particularly after the *Restoration. See Lorna Weatherill, *Consumer Behaviour and Material Culture in Britain, 1660–1760* (1988), and Peter Earle, *The Making of the English Middle Class: Business, Society and Family Life in London, 1660–1730* (1989). (See also STANDARD OF LIVING DEBATE.) For the even greater changes since the late Victorian period see John Benson, *The Rise of Consumer Society in Britain, 1880–1980* (1994).

contraception. Condoms made from animal intestines were used from at least the early 18th century by upper-class men who were more worried about venereal disease than contraception. Rubber sheaths replaced skins in the 1870s. By the 1890s several firms were supplying the market and barbers' shops had become the main retail outlet. Knowledge of contraception became much more widespread through the pioneering work of Marie Stopes and when the army distributed condoms on a massive scale during the First World War in order to limit venereal disease. In the later 20th century contraception techniques have become more varied and reliable. The social consequences have been immense.

contumacy. Refusal to appear before an *ecclesiastical court or to accept its authority.

conventicle. The term used in the late 17th century for a meeting of religious Dissenters. *Quarter sessions licensed conventicles during periods when they were tolerated and prosecuted those who attended conventicles when they were not.

conventionary tenure. A system of tenure peculiar to Cornwall and parts of Devon, by which tenants obtained a seven-year lease at a negotiated rent, with no automatic right of renewal.

convertible husbandry. Also known as alternate, or up-and-down husbandry, this method of farming allowed the temporary conversion of arable strips in the *open-fields into grass *leys. Some leys remained under grass for up to 10 years; others became permanent grass. This system enabled sufficient grass to be grown to feed livestock (for *meadows and pasture were always at a premium under the *open-field system) and it gave the arable land a period in which to recover. The system was in use in parts of the Midlands by the 15th century, was widely employed in the early modern period, and was revived in the 1930s through the advocacy of Sir George Stapledon.

conveyance. See DEED, TITLE. The present form of conveyance document became standard in 1840.

co-operative societies. Many 19th-century industrial towns had a co-operative society, founded on the principles of Robert Owen, by which the profits of an enterprise were shared out amongst the members. See R. G. Garnett, 'Records of Early Co-operation with Particular Reference to Pre-Rochdale Consumer Co-operation', *Local Historian*, 9/4 (1971). The library of the Co-operative Union Ltd is at Holyoake House, Manchester. The movement was non-political until just before the First World War, when Co-operative MPs and councillors were affiliated to the *Labour Party. The 'Co-op' was often the largest shop in a town or village until the 1960s, since when the decline of such enterprises has been dramatic. See Johnston Birchall, *Co-op: The People's Business* (1994) and G. D. H. Cole, *A Century of Co-operation* (1944).

copper. A monopoly organization, the Company of Mines Royal, was founded in 1567 to locate and mine metals, including copper. German workers were employed by the Company in the Coniston area during the late 16th century. Many disputes over the Company's rights arose where copper was found in association with other metals. The Company lost its monopoly in 1689, after which a major growth in copper production occurred. Production in Cornwall increased enormously, particularly after the sinking of deep mines drained by *steam pumping engines; Cornwall's most productive years were between 1820 and 1870. In 1768 enormous deposits of low-grade copper ore were discovered at Parys Mountain, Anglesey, where proximity to an adequate harbour and sea routes allowed rapid expansion; extensive physical evidence survives in the form of open-cut workings and the remains of tanks and other works connected with dressing ore. A number of other places, e.g. Alderley Edge (Cheshire) and Llanberis (north Wales), mined and smelted copper. Extensive copper mines dating from the Bronze Age have been discovered at Great Ormes Head, Llandudno.

coppice and coppicing. Most native species of deciduous trees (unlike the pine) will grow again if cut down to a stump. The following spring young shoots will appear to form a stool, from which a succession of poles can be cropped at frequent intervals of years. The art of coppicing has been practised since prehistoric times. (See WOODS.) Most surviving broad-leaved woods were coppiced for centuries up to about the First World War. Such woods had a different appearance from today, for they were characteristically managed for underwood rather than mature trees. The cycle of years varied according to the product that was required; on average, it was seven years in the Middle Ages, but by the 19th century the average length had doubled. Some underwood was cut in the first year of growth, but for pit props the cycle was over 30 years. See E. J. T. Collins, 'The Coppice and Underwood Trades' in G. E. Mingay (ed.), *The *Agrarian History of England and Wales*, vi, *1750–1850* (1989). See also CHARCOAL.

copyhold tenure. A form of customary tenure by which a tenant held a copy of the entry in the rolls of the manorial *court baron which recorded his or her possession of a holding on agreed terms. In the early Middle Ages the tenant performed services to the lord, but by the 16th century services had generally been converted into money payments, involving large entry *fines and nominal annual rents. During the same century copyhold began to be replaced by *leasehold agreements. Copyhold was abolished in 1922. With a good series of manorial records, a family historian can trace the descent of a family holding over several generations. The date of death of a tenant can often be inferred and relationships between different members of a family deduced.

cornet. The lowest commissioned rank in a cavalry regiment; the man who carried the colours, traditionally the youngest in the regiment.

corn exchange. During the second and third quarters of the 19th century the corporations of the more substantial market towns such as Doncaster built large, imposing corn exchanges for trading in samples. These were often built on the site of the old *market place. Surviving examples are amongst the largest Victorian public buildings.

Cornish language. A Celtic language which ceased to be spoken in the 18th century. Cornish was more closely related to the Breton tongue than to any other Celtic language. See O. J. Padel, *Cornish Place-Name Elements* (1985), and G. P. White, *A Handbook of Cornish Surnames* (1984). Cornish place-names have given rise to a large number of locative *surnames.

corn laws. From at least the 12th century, the English government attempted to regulate the export and import of grain. (See CORN TRADE.) The laws became controversial at the end of the *Napoleonic wars. The supply of imported grain from Continental Europe had been severely affected by the long war with France, so British farmers had been encouraged by government bounties to increase their production. The onset of peace made farmers fearful of bankruptcy. The government therefore agreed to a policy of protection which prohibited imported corn under a certain price. Sliding scales of prices were introduced in 1828 and adjusted in 1842, but the corn laws were not repealed until 1846 after much public pressure from the Anti-Corn Law League.

corn trade. The export of grain from Britain, particularly barley and wheat, was an intermittent trade in the Middle Ages and the early modern period, depending on abundance and scarcity at home and regulated by the *corn laws. These laws obstructed the export of corn for longer periods than they allowed it. The most important granary was East Anglia, and the largest foreign market was the Netherlands. King's Lynn and Yarmouth were the principal ports which supplied London, the North, and the Midlands. The East Anglian export trade was occasionally allowed by special licences and at other times was the result of *smuggling. Other parts of eastern and southern England which were important exporters of grain were the East Riding of Yorkshire, Lincolnshire, the Downs of Kent and Hampshire, and south Devon. The efficiency of the distribution system allowed some farming regions to import all their corn and thus to concentrate on the production of their own specialities, e.g. *cheese. (See MARKETS AND FAIRS.) The govern-

ment encouraged corn exports from 1654 and helped the growers of grain by the payment of bounties from 1674. The export trade in grain expanded remarkably in the first half of the 18th century. See David Ormrod, *English Grain Exports and the Structure of Agrarian Capitalism, 1700–1760* (1985). From the late 1760s, however, Britain became a net importer of foreign grain. The war with France from 1793 to 1815 caused hardship. The corn laws kept prices high until their repeal in 1846. American grain began to be imported into Britain in large quantities in the 1870s. See the volumes of *The* AGRARIAN HISTORY OF ENGLAND AND WALES.

Cornwall, Duchy of. The oldest duchy, founded in 1337. The estates of the Duchy are chiefly, but not exclusively, in Cornwall, Devon, and Somerset. A few records are kept at the *Public Record Office, but most are available for consultation at the Duchy's own estate office in Buckingham Gate, London.

coroner. The office was created in 1194, when coroners were appointed to enquire into cases of sudden or unexplained death. They gradually acquired other functions, including confiscating property from *outlaws. Records survive from the 14th century under 'Justices Itinerant' at the *Public Record Office. The Coroners Act (1887) and the Coroners Amendment Act (1926) created the modern office. Coroners' inquests are usually reported in local *newspapers, but the official records are closed to public inspection for 75 years.

corporations. See BOROUGH.

Corpse Way. In large parishes coffins sometimes had to be carried several miles for burial in the *churchyard. Burial parties followed traditional routes, fearing that if they deviated from the 'corpse way' the ghost of the deceased would rise to haunt them. A graphic account of such burial customs on the North York Moors in the 19th century is given in J. C. *Atkinson, *Forty Years in a Moorland Parish* (1891).

Corpus Christi. The Body of Christ, or the Feast of the Blessed Sacrament, on the Thursday after Trinity Sunday. Corpus Christi is a movable feast that depends on the day of Easter; it falls between 21 May and 24 June. Established in England in 1318, until the *Reformation this was the day on which the *guilds of the major cities performed their *mystery plays, telling the Biblical story from the Creation to the Day of Judgement. See Miri Rubin, 'Corpus Christi Fraternities and Late Medieval Piety' in W. J. Sheils and Diana Wood (eds.),

Voluntary Religion (1986), and Ronald Hutton, *The Rise and Fall of Merry England: The Ritual Year, 1400–1700* (1994).

cottages / cottagers. The term 'cottage' has come to be widely applied to any small or medium-sized domestic building, but most of the older structures that are now referred to as cottages were originally the houses of *yeomen, *husbandmen, and craftsmen. Thus, 'Willy Lott's Cottage' at Flatford Mill (Suffolk), which was featured in some of John Constable's paintings, was actually a farmhouse known as Gibeon's Gate. Cottages were smaller, inferior buildings inhabited by the poorest sections of society. Many were only a single room, open to the rafters. The great majority of the cottages of the labourers of the early modern period do not survive. Those 16th- and 17th-century cottages which do remain in use have often been extended. They are found particularly in Shropshire and Herefordshire, and in neighbouring counties, where the standard of building at this social level was perhaps better than elsewhere. In the rest of Britain cottages rarely survive from before the end of the 18th century.

The families which lived in cottages during the early modern period are the most elusive social group to study. They tended to be more mobile than other groups and to have left fewer records. At the parish level, it is difficult to find sufficient information to analyse their activities in detail. See, however, David Hey, *An English Rural Community: Myddle Under the Tudors and Stuarts* (1974), ch. 5, which makes use of a unique source. Cottages appear in manorial records, often as *encroachments upon the *commons and wastes. The fines that were levied were a roundabout way of charging rent. Manorial surveys sometimes describe cottages, e.g. as 'one-bay thatched'. An Act of 1589 insisted that new cottages should have at least four acres of land attached, but this legislation was not enforced consistently. Increasing numbers of poor cottagers led to decisions being taken at some manor courts and parish *vestries to restrict further building and sometimes to demolish recently constructed cottages. Disputed cases ended up at the *quarter sessions. Encroachments for cottages are normally identified in *enclosure awards, for the cottagers' rights on the commons were often disputed. See J. M. Neeson, *Commoners: Common Right, Enclosure and Social Change in England, 1700–1820* (1993). Most parishes had to balance the shrinking of their resources on the commons against the need for housing for younger members of local families and for immigrants who supplied necessary labour on local farms and industrial sites. In the early modern period the scale of immigration into *lead mining areas was such that whole new communities of cottagers were created on the wastes. *Coal mining attracted similar new settlements in the 19th century. See also AGRICULTURAL LABOURERS.

cottar. The term used in the *Domesday Book and other medieval records for *cottagers.

cotton. Raw cotton originally came to Britain from the Levant into London, then during the second quarter of the 17th century it came from the East and West Indies. By the early 18th century American and West Indian cotton was being imported through Bristol, Lancaster, and Liverpool; after 1750 Liverpool became the leading port for this trade and Manchester became the chief market. Eli Whitney's invention of the cotton gin was crucial in making the southern states of the USA the major producer of raw cotton. Lancashire had the advantage of coal, soft water for bleaching, dyeing, and printing, a damp climate that helped the fibres to cling together (thus reducing the strain put on them by machinery), cheap land, and ample *water power.

By the end of the 18th century all the processes for making cotton goods had been brought into *factories. The *spinning process was the first to be mechanized. James Hargreaves's jenny (1767) was a hand-powered machine, but in 1771 Richard Arkwright moved from Nottingham to Cromford to establish the first water-powered cotton spinning mill, using his water frame. See S. D. Chapman, *The Early Factory Masters* (1967). Samuel Crompton's mule (1779) and Edmund Cartwright's loom (1785) were other crucial inventions which were much modified and improved over time. The early industry was concentrated in Derbyshire, in the wake of Arkwright and the Strutts, but it soon moved to Lancashire, where the first Arkwright mills were built in 1777; many more mills were erected after the expiry of his patent in 1785. By 1787, out of 143 cotton mills in Great Britain, 41 were in Lancashire, 22 in Derbyshire, and eight in Cheshire. The earliest cotton mills were water-powered and therefore sited in remote valleys, such as that at Styal (Cheshire) or New Lanark (Scotland). See Mary B. Rose, *The Gregs of Quarry Bank Mill: The Rise and Fall of a Family Firm, 1750–1914* (1986). These mills depended largely on the labour of children and made much use of pauper *apprentices; from the 1770s until the passing of the Factory Act (1833) several thousand children grew up in apprentice houses. During the 1780s *steam power began to be used to raise water for the wheels which powered cotton mills; soon they were used directly for driving machinery. Mules and power-looms operated by men increasingly replaced the labour of children. Water and steam power long existed side by side, but many of the remoter valleys were derelict by the later 19th century. See S. D. Chapman, *The Cotton Industry in the Industrial Revolution* (1987).

The factory-based cotton industry was created by self-made men during the two generations from 1770 to 1840. By 1803 cotton had overtaken *wool as Britain's leading export, a position which it kept until 1938. Many Lancashire towns became dominated by their cotton mills: see M. Williams, *Cotton Mills in Greater Manchester* (1992). By 1830 sales of cotton yarn and goods accounted for just over half of Britain's overseas earnings, a proportion that had declined to a quarter by the First World War. Cotton was the first industry to make the whole world its market. A period of spectacular growth came to an end during the early 1860s, when the American Civil War prevented supplies of raw cotton from reaching Britain. Growth resumed immediately afterwards and reached a peak in 1912. Competition from Asian countries began to affect the industry during the 1920s and 1930s, and in 1958 Britain became a net importer of cottons. During the 1960s and 1970s most of the Lancashire cotton mills were closed. For overviews of the industry see C. B. Phillips and J. H. Smith, *Lancashire and Cheshire from AD 1540* (1994), and Chris Aspin, *The Cotton Industry* (1981). For the decline of the industry see John Singleton, *Lancashire on the Scrapheap: The Cotton Industry, 1945–1970* (1991).

council housing. A few local authorities, e.g. Liverpool in 1869, obtained local powers to build houses for rent by working-class tenants before the Housing of the Working Classes Act (1890), which authorized the building of such houses by public subsidies, but it was this Act which led to the appearance of 'council houses' in significant numbers. The new powers were taken up mainly by urban authorities in order to clear slums and rehouse families that were living in insanitary conditions. The Housing, Town Planning, Etc. Act (1909) was another important step forward in that it gave local authorities planning powers over land for development. The first major Scottish programme followed the report of the Royal Commission on the Housing of the Industrial Population of Scotland (1917). A succession of Housing Acts after the First World War, beginning in 1919, led to the creation of large council estates on the edges of towns and the building of smaller estates alongside villages in many parts of Britain. Together with the creation of private suburban housing, they transformed the appearance of many urban and rural settlements. The minutes of the relevant housing committees, which are kept at local *record offices, are the major source of information, though local *newspapers are also informative. Council estates were built to low densities, on lines pioneered by philanthropic projects such as Port Sunlight. They continued to be built until the 1980s, when the withdrawal of central government subsidies made further building impractical. At the same time, central government policy also encouraged sales of existing houses to tenants.

Council in the Marches of Wales. 'The Lord President and Council of the Dominion and Principality of Wales and the Marches of the Same' was created in the late 15th century but acquired much greater powers upon the Union of Wales and England (1536–43), with a headquarters eventually settled at Ludlow Castle. Its civil and criminal jurisdiction extended over the whole of Wales and the English border shires. It was abolished during the *Civil War but revived at the *Restoration until 1689. See P. H. Williams, *The Council in the Marches of Wales under Elizabeth I* (1958), and R. Flenley (ed.), *A Calendar of the Register of the Queen's Majesty's Council in the Dominion and Principality of Wales and the Marches of the Same, 1569–1591* (1916).

Council in the North. 'The King's Council in the Northern Parts' was established at York in 1537 in order to counter the threat of rebellion. The Lord President was seated at the King's Manor, a rebuilding of the former house of the Abbot of St Mary's, a dissolved *Benedictine monastery. The Council was abolished in 1641. Surviving records are fragmentary. See F. W. Brooks, *The Council of the North* (1966).

counties, origins of. The word 'county' is derived from the Norman French *comté*, but most of the English counties of the post-Conquest period covered the same area as the Anglo-Saxon shires. Some of these shires were based on ancient tribal divisions. Kent, Cornwall, and Devon are named after Celtic tribes, and Berkshire and Dorset have names with Celtic roots. Norfolk and Suffolk were the districts populated by the north folk and the south folk of the kingdom of *East Anglia; the east, middle, and south Saxons settled in Essex, Middlesex, and Sussex; and Dorset and Somerset are early folk names. The other Anglo-Saxon shires were not necessarily based on tribal divisions but were created for military reasons around a town or royal estate. The earliest shires were Berkshire, Dorset, Hampshire, Somerset, and Wiltshire, which were formed in 8th- and 9th-century *Wessex. The west midland counties were created during the 10th-century campaigns of Edward the Elder into the kingdom of *Mercia; for example, Shropshire was formed by the union of two tribal districts and named after its capital, Shrewsbury. The east midland shires were created under the *Danelaw during the 10th century and were named after the military centres that became their county towns: Derby, Nottingham, Leicester, Northampton, Huntingdon, Bedford, and Cambridge; Lincolnshire united the two Danish armies based on Lincoln and Stamford. Rutland was the only county south of the Humber that had not come into existence by the time of the *Norman Conquest. The complex reasons for the origins of this small county are discussed in Charles Phythian-Adams, 'Rutland Reconsidered' in A. Dornier (ed.), *Mercian Studies* (1977).

North of the Humber the only county that was in existence before the Norman Conquest was Yorkshire, the area occupied by the Danish army at Jorvik (York). After the Conquest, Lancashire was created from territories which had previously formed part of Cheshire and Yorkshire, but which by the 12th century were grouped together as the Honour of Lancaster. Cumberland and Westmorland were also created in the late 12th century, though they were based on older territories. County Durham was that area which formed the central part of the lands of the prince bishops of Durham. Northumberland was the shrunken remnant of the ancient kingdom of *Northumbria. Manchester University Press are publishing a series of volumes on the Origins of the Shire, starting with Denise Kenyon, *The Origins of Lancashire* (1991), Michael Costen, *The Origins of Somerset* (1992), N. J. Higham, *The Origins of Cheshire* (1993), and Tom Williamson, *The Origins of Norfolk* (1993).

The Scottish Lowland counties were created by Malcolm II in the 11th century on similar lines to those south of the border. Those in the Highlands date from the 16th and 17th centuries. The Welsh counties were created after the Act of Union with England (1536), on the

English model. During the second half of the 16th century Ireland's four provinces of Ulster, Connacht, Leinster, and Munster were divided into 32 counties, which were based on older *lordships.

country. The word 'country' was used not only for describing the whole of England, Scotland, Ireland, and Wales, etc., but more imprecisely to convey a sense of a district much wider than that of a town or rural parish, but smaller than that of a county. Daniel *Defoe used the word in a variety of ways. Sometimes he simply meant the district around a town; at other times he spoke of an agricultural area as 'a corn country' or 'an inclosed country', and elsewhere he used the phrase 'a manufacturing country', which could range in size from the neighbourhood of Tiverton to the clothing region that included much of Somerset, Dorset, Wiltshire, and Gloucestershire. Occasionally, he applied the word 'country' to a named district, such as the Rodings (in Essex) or 'the country called Hallamshire', the metal-working district around Sheffield. The identity of a 'country' was determined largely by topography and the nature of the work, but also by the residential persistence of a group of core families. It is a useful concept for local and family historians in defining the wider district to which people felt that they belonged. (See PAYS.)

Some of the 'countries' of Britain are no longer as readily identifiable as they used to be, but elsewhere the term long continued in use in local speech. When The Revd Francis Kilvert recorded his impressions of the Hay Flower Show of August 1870, he wrote, 'The whole country was there'. The Black Country survives as a district name that is known nationally.

country leisure pursuits. In the Victorian period the country leisure pursuits of the aristocratic families and local squires became organized on an unprecedented scale. (See GROUSE; PHEASANT SHOOTING; FOX HUNTING; GAME LAWS; and HORSE RACING.) Certain wild parts of Britain, especially in the Scottish Highlands, became the exclusive preserve of the wealthy hunters, shooters, and fishermen, who arrived in well-defined seasons. Huge bags of game were recorded as gun technology improved. Such activities were socially exclusive and created tensions between hunters and farmers and between landowners and those who wanted access to wild places on ancient rights of way which had been closed. Other country sports such as hare coursing were popular at a lower social level. *Cricket came to be seen as a social unifier in many an estate *village, a game that could be played by all men and boys.

county councils. Elected county councils, together with county borough councils for towns with a population of over 50,000, were created in 1888 and abolished in 1974. They took over the administrative responsibilities of the county *quarter sessions and were empowered to appoint medical officers. Outside the county boroughs, however, *public health remained the responsibility of urban and rural sanitary authorities, which in 1894 became *Rural and *Urban District Councils. County councils acquired housing and planning powers from 1890 onwards. In 1902 county councils took over responsibility for elementary and secondary *education from the school boards. The minutes and other records of the council and its committees, the letter books and files of the clerk, and the treasurer's accounts are deposited in local *record offices.

court, central. Contemporaries used the Westminster courts to resolve conflicts within families, between neighbours, amongst trading partners, or between landlords and tenants; in short, conflicts about every dimension of human experience. We, however, approach the central courts with a quite different aim: to obtain from their records some understanding of the historical human experience. This might be objected to as a form of historical ambulance-chasing, history as individual or collective misfortune: but the records of the central courts are too large, too rich, too compelling to be ignored. Their language (frequently Latin before 1733), their sheer volume and frequent lack of serviceable indices deter, and, because in some courts the records were designed to track the litigant's passage through the court rather than outline the circumstances which brought him to law, the records are terse, intractable, and unyielding.

Medieval and early modern men thought in legal terms to a degree alien to ourselves. The law was the most usual type of education for those not destined to become clergy. Political discourse often took the form of legal argument, especially over the prerogative: political engagement often took the form of jury service. Our ancestors were readier to turn to law than we are. This willingness to commence litigation was tempered by a readiness to discontinue a suit if it had satisfied its purpose without coming to trial. Only a small proportion of suits commenced reached a verdict; recent work has shown how many of those which apparently peter out ended in arbitration or private settlement. (It might be added that there was never any problem securing either legal advice in the shires or counsel in London even in the 13th century. The social range of the individuals launching litigation is impressively wide.)

None the less, litigants were confronted by an immediately confusing plethora of courts, local and central, royal and ecclesiastical. Business commenced in a local court could ultimately be decided in a central court, either by the record of the case being transferred, or by appeal, or by the case being recommenced elsewhere. It was appreciated that, whilst each court could offer specific remedies, a single grievance could be fought through a number of courts at the same time, either to wear down an opponent or to gain some advantage. A Welsh vicar took his revenge on a parishioner by launching 26 suits in six years, seven in the local *consistory or the Court of *Arches, seven in the *Council in the Marches of Wales, two in *Star Chamber, one in *Chancery, four in *Common Pleas, and five in *King's Bench (L. Stone, *The Crisis of the Aristocracy*, 1965). This is exceptional only in the number of courts used. It was quite normal in the 16th and early 17th centuries for a defendant in a suit in one court to commence a suit in another to inhibit, by injunction, the litigation commenced against him in the first.

The wide range of courts available to litigants has deep historical origins. It arises from the conservatism of individual courts and their unwillingness to extend new remedies to litigants by modifying their procedures. The pattern, which is repeated over a long period of time, was for litigants to find that the procedures or rules of the existing courts offered them no remedy for their individual grievances. They therefore petitioned the king, his council, or one of his senior councillors (often the Chancellor), asking that justice should be done them. Over a period of years, essentially informal means of dealing with petitioners were elaborated into courts with their own staff and rules; but the institutionalization of procedure again left some petitioners without redress as their needs altered.

It has to be acknowledged, though, that whilst the courts portrayed themselves as being rooted in tradition and precedent, they were not wholly immutable. Courts were placed under a constant pressure from litigants and their counsel looking for new remedies. And they were in a competitive situation. Their officers lived on the fees which litigants paid for process. The profitability of legal office was related to the volume of business passing through the court. There was, therefore, an obvious incentive to meet the needs of both litigants and office-holders through the evolution of procedure, and instances can be offered of this being done. The most notorious was the Bill of Middlesex, devised to expedite the business of King's Bench (and described below). In terms of extending new remedies to litigants, one of the most familiar (though hotly debated by modern historians) was the extension of common-law remedies to the copyholder, probably between 1560 and 1580, which involved a redefinition of his legal status.

The basic distinction is between the *common law* courts, in which the plaintiff instituted proceedings by the purchase of a *writ, and where pleadings were conducted orally before a jury; and the *equity courts* employing English bill procedure in which the plaintiff came into the court and laid before it a bill or petition of grievances (normally in English) which, after the collection of written evidence, was finally determined by a judge. Common-law procedure was concerned with the facts, equity much more about reconciling the parties. These distinctions divide the first generation of common law courts from those which followed.

The writ was a licence which allowed the plaintiff to sue for a certain kind of justice. The early writs were flexible in that the clerks who drafted them could tailor them to the plaintiff's circumstances, but by the mid-13th century the range of writs, and their wording, was settled by precedent. The litigant therefore had to discover which writ (out of the precedent writs available) fitted his particular condition. If none sufficed his needs, then he was without remedy.

Three courts, the Exchequer of Pleas, Common Pleas, and King's Bench used writs, Common Pleas and King's Bench developing out of the undifferentiated *Curia Regis after 1234. The Exchequer of Pleas was used to bring actions against crown officials, including *sheriffs, and whilst its jurisdiction was widened by the fiction of allowing suits from crown debtors, it was never a busy jurisdiction. Common Pleas was the busiest court, having in the late 15th century between 70 and 80 per cent of the total common-law business (E. W. Ives, *The Common Lawyers of Pre-Reformation England*, 1983, 199). In theory it dealt with actions in which the king had no interest: in practice it was the court to which litigants turned in disputes over property, and overwhelmingly in those over debt. King's Bench, on its crown side, was essentially a criminal jurisdiction, whilst its plea side dealt with trespass, appeals of *felony, and suits

brought to correct errors in other courts. In the late 15th century the business of King's Bench was substantially enlarged by the introduction of the Bill of Middlesex which, by incorporating a range of legal fictions into process, allowed cases to be begun without the plaintiff securing a writ. This brought more but also a wider range of business to the court, with the consequence that where the functions of the three courts were once fairly clearly differentiated, they tended, in the 17th century, to develop similar jurisdictions over common pleas, although the character of their procedures, their expedition, and so the cost to litigants were far from the same.

Procedure by writ remained substantially unaltered between the 13th and the 19th centuries; but the rigidity of the course of the common law forced the development of new courts. Frustrated litigants who were unable to find a common-law remedy were always prone to petition the king and his council asking for justice to be done them. By the mid-14th century bills directed to the king were normally dealt with by the *Chancellor. This responsibility led to the development of a court which conducted its business in English. The compliance of litigants was secured by the use of the subpoena. Evidence was gathered by interrogatory and deposition. When enough information had been gathered, cases were determined by the chancellor rather than a jury. Chancery was therefore the litigant's friend in circumstances where the common law failed to provide a suitable writ; where it did not recognize a specific type of property (uses, copyhold, the equity of redemption of a mortgage, for instance); or where the plaintiff lacked the appropriate evidence to prove his case (lost deeds, uncancelled bonds, and so on). These were all instances where the plaintiff deserved to be relieved in *equity*.

Whilst it was once fashionable to see Chancery as a challenge to older courts, it is now more common to see it as an overflow which dealt with forms of business which they could not handle. The numbers of cases going into Chancery, even at its busiest, were only a small proportion of those going through Common Pleas. (Ives estimates 360 petitions in Chancery per year against 700 pleadings *per term* in Common Pleas in the late 15th century; *Common Lawyers*, 199.) Chancery, though, underwent the same process of growing rigidity which affected the common-law writs in the 13th century. Where in the 15th and 16th centuries it heard cases on their own merits, in the 17th century it increasingly judged cases according to rules and precedent, and so lost the flexibility and expedition which had first made it attractive to litigants.

The delegation of a class of conciliar business to the Chancellor did not, though, stop plaintiffs laying bills before the council, and the need to deal with these petitions led to the appearance of additional courts in the early 16th century. The most important of these, the courts of Star Chamber and *Requests, were dimensions of the council's judicial function. Here it must be appreciated that the early Tudor council was a large body of men, whose common feature was they had sworn the councillor's oath. Like the broomstick of the sorcerer's apprentice, the council still functioned no matter how small the pieces. Those councillors around the king (the 'council attendant') received petitions for justice. From around 1517–20 this work was given to a small panel of junior councillors who sat in the White Hall in the palace of Westminster. This court was reconstituted in 1529 and again in 1538. It became known as the Court of Requests, and specialized in poor men's suits. The council itself, which sat in the Star Chamber, a room in the Palace of Westminster, also received petitions for justice. So far as the surviving manuscript evidence allows, it appears that the numbers were small in Henry VII's reign (perhaps one a month): but Wolsey, in particular, encouraged suitors to complain to the council and the volume of business increased tenfold. Inevitably this swamped the council. The immediate reaction to this problem was to deal with litigants only on certain days, but the longer-term solution was to withdraw the council's administrative work to an inner group (the *Privy Council, certainly in existence in 1536), leaving the council sitting in Star Chamber to deal with the judicial business. (Another device to reduce the workload was the establishment of councils in Wales and Northern England; after 1536 these were administrative bodies which also sat as both criminal and equity courts.)

Star Chamber came to deal with essentially criminal business—riot, unlawful assembly, assault, corruption of officers, the impediment of justice, perjury—but also such varied civil matters as breach of contract, debt, defamation, and so on. A proportion of the cases of riot which came before it were actually about title although, in theory, real property cases were barred to the court, a rule which was restated in 1552 and then adhered to. The majority of cases were between parties; relatively few were inspired by the state, but a handful of cases

from the 1630s have coloured the whole history of the court. It was abolished in 1642 as an abuse of power; the Court of Requests and the *Councils in the North and Wales withered away at around the same time.

It might be added that the Tudor revenue courts all had equitable jurisdictions using English bill procedure. All were loosely modelled on the Duchy of *Lancaster, whose equitable jurisdiction mostly dealt with matters between its tenants (although the duchy's officers or the attorney-general could appear as plaintiffs). The courts of General Surveyors, *Augmentations, *First Fruits, and *Wards all had equitable jurisdictions dealing with matters within their ambit, and much of this litigation dealt with the management of estates under their control. The busiest of these courts was the equitable jurisdiction of the *Exchequer. This developed rapidly in the 1550s, and whilst a great deal of its business concerned the Crown lands, it also specialized in the trial of commercial and tithe cases.

The 1640s saw the last wholesale alterations in the legal system before the 19th century. The Exchequer (whose business had more or less run out) was abolished in 1841; Chancery, King's Bench, and Common Pleas were all merged into a single High Court of Justice with several divisions in 1875.

It is paradoxical that the courts about which historians habitually enthuse were the ones whose business was only a small proportion of that going through Common Pleas. The records of the common-law courts, however, for reasons which relate to their procedures, are dry and relatively uninformative. Their arrangement in termly files or rolls, which generally lack modern indices to their contents, has discouraged their use. The attraction of Chancery, Star Chamber, and Requests is their use of English bill procedure. This allowed both plaintiffs and defendants to lodge with the court colourful, anecdotal, and often tendentious accounts of their mishaps, frequently at great length. These are then enlarged upon by copious depositions and examinations. Although some of their records are lost (the decree and order books of Star Chamber, together with virtually all the records of the regional councils), the body of surviving records is enormous and the modern lists of their pleadings in the *Public Record Office make them relatively accessible to historians. See J. H. Baker, *An Introduction to English Legal History* (3rd edn., 1990); C. W. Brooks, *Petty-foggers and Vipers of the Commonwealth: The 'Lower Branch' of the Legal Profession in Early*

Modern England (1986); W. H. Bryson, *The Equity Side of the Exchequer* (1975); M. S. Giuseppi, *Guide to the Contents of the Public Record Office* (3 vols., revised edn. 1960–8), i. (continued in the typescript *Current Guide*, produced by the PRO); J. A. Guy, *The Cardinal's Court: The Impact of Thomas Wolsey in Star Chamber* (1977); J. A. Guy, *The Court of Star Chamber and Its Records to the Reign of Elizabeth I* (1985); J. A. Guy, 'The Privy Council: Revolution or Evolution' in C. Coleman and D. Starkey (eds.), *Revolution Reassessed: Revisions in the History of Tudor Government and Administration* (1986); H. Horwitz, *A Guide to Chancery Equity Records and Proceedings, 1600–1800* (Public Record Office, 1995); W. J. Jones, *The Elizabethan Court of Chancery* (1967); and A. W. B. Simpson, *A History of the Land Law* (2nd edn., 1986).   R. W. HOYLE

court, manorial. Early manorial courts used oral procedures. Although *custumals and *surveys survive in a written form from *c*.1180 to *c*.1240, records of manorial courts do not start until the mid-13th century. The earliest surviving original court roll is for the English manors of Bec Abbey and dates from 1246. In the second half of the 13th century, especially in the 1270s and 1280s, the practice of keeping manorial records became widespread as landlords copied the example of the king's courts.

Zvi Razi, *Life, Marriage and Death in a Medieval Parish: Economy, Society and Demography in Halesowen, 1270–1400* (1980) argues that the range of activities recorded in the manorial court rolls of the best documented manors is so wide that the adult male population could hardly avoid being noted. A great deal of reliable genealogical information can be obtained from such rolls. L. R. Poos and R. M. Smith, ' "Shades still on the window" . . . A Reply to Zvi Razi', *Law and History Review*, 3 (1985) challenge Razi's belief that court rolls may provide a complete enumeration of the adult male population of a particular village; they quote wider documentation from two Essex manors which demonstrates that nearly a quarter of all male tenants did not appear in the courts at all. The tenants of the smallest holdings were the ones most likely to be unrecorded. Women, servants, children, and poor people are less well documented.

Every lord of a manor had the right to hold a court for his tenants. Whether or not *freeholders attended depended on local practice. In some manors of the Abbot of Ramsay in the 13th century all the freemen attended, but in other manors only some of them did so. This example is typical of the confused practices of law and custom, which varied over time and from one part of the country to another. (See COURT BARON and COURT LEET for the responsibilities of these two branches of the manorial court, though in practice the functions were not always distinct.) The courts were presided over by the lord's steward. Manorial juries, consisting of 12 *homagers, were sworn in. Their first duty was to deal with the lord's financial interests in his manor. They then appointed officers, e.g. the *constable, judged pleas brought by individuals, and laid *pains or fixed penalties on categories of petty offences. Decisions were not imposed by the lord or his steward but were made by the jury, who were selected from the chief tenants of the manor. Freeholders played little part in the administration of the manor. (See also RESIANTS.)

By the early modern period many manorial courts had declined and some had disappeared. Nevertheless, some others continued to thrive. A few survive, mainly to supervise remaining common lands, to the present day. Some manors have long runs of records from the 13th to the 19th or 20th centuries, but the records of many smaller manors have been lost or destroyed. Surviving manor court rolls are normally housed at local *record offices or in national collections at the *Public Record Office, *British Library, etc. Except for the period of the *Commonwealth, records were normally written in Latin until 1733. See P. D. A. Harvey, *Manorial Records* (1984), Nathaniel Hone, *The Manor and Manorial Records* (1906), Denis Stuart, *Manorial Records: An Introduction to their Transcription and Translation* (1992), and Mary Ellis, *Using Manorial Records* (1994). See also MANOR.

court baron. The manorial *court which dealt with the transfer of *copyhold land, upon inheritance or sale, which determined the customs of the manor, and which enforced payment of services which were due to the lord. It was normally held every three weeks.

court leet. The manorial *court which dealt with petty law and order and the administration of communal agriculture. By the late Middle Ages the court leet and the view of *frankpledge came to be treated as alternative names for the same jurisdiction. Rolls were often headed: 'The Court Leet with View of Frankpledge'. It was normally held every six months. See W. J. King, 'Untapped Resources for Social Historians: Court Leet Records', *Journal of Social History*, 15 (1982). For an example of a printed series of leet records see J. G. de T. Mandley (ed.), *The Portmote or Court Leet Records of the Borough or Town and Royal Manor of Salford from the Year 1597 to the Year 1669 Inclusive*, 2 vols. (1902).

courtyard house. A distinctive type of late medieval *manor house, arranged around a rectangular open space which was entered by a broad arch. Some were planned in that form, in imitation of contemporary *castles, but others grew into that shape by extensions over the centuries. Many, e.g. Ightham Mote (Kent), were surrounded with a *moat.

credit was widely available in the early modern period. Probate *inventories regularly note the debts that were due to the deceased, and sometimes the debts that he himself had incurred. These included bills and *bonds on which interest was paid. A network of kin and neighbours could be drawn upon when credit was needed, and women especially relied on their income from loans. See B. A. Holderness, 'Credit in English Rural Society before the Nineteenth Century', *Agricultural History Review*, 24/2 (1976), and Amy Louise Erickson, *Women and Property in Early Modern England* (1993). Businessmen allowed their customers credit long before banks were founded, and many commercial and industrial enterprises were founded on credit. See, for example, Pat Hudson, *The Genesis of Industrial Capital: A Study of the West Riding Wool Textile Industry, c.1750–1850* (1986). See also BANKRUPTCY.

creek. Small harbours which came under the jurisdiction of neighbouring ports.

crenellate, licence to. A royal licence was necessary before a house could be fortified. The records of such licences, dating from the 12th to the 16th century, are kept mostly in the *Patent rolls at the *Public Record Office.

cricket. The origins of the game are traced back to 18th-century Hampshire and Kent. The professional game began with teams playing for wagers and with challenge matches such as those featuring a top-hatted All England XI, which toured the country and played up to 40 matches a season, often against twice as many opponents. *Newspapers are the major source of information about matches and venues. Old *photographs show players in a variety of dress even when playing in the county championship, which developed in the second half of the 19th century and which attracted large crowds to permanent grounds. See Keith A. P. Sandiford, *Cricket and the Victorians* (1994).

crime, associations for the prevention of. In the late 18th and early 19th centuries, before the establishment of a local police force, property owners commonly formed a local organization that was pledged to bring offenders before the courts. These bodies had names such as Association for the Prosecution of Felons. Printed handbills declaring the intentions of such bodies and offering rewards for information leading to an arrest are sometimes found in local *record offices, and notices of the activities of such associations are reported in local *newspapers.

Crimean war. Fought by British, French, and Turkish troops against the Russians, 1854–6, with heavy losses on both sides. The major battles—Alma, Inkerman, Sebastopol—are often commemorated in street names. Florence Nightingale's work in the military hospitals was an important influence on the development of professional nursing.

croft. 1. An enclosed piece of land by a dwelling.
   2. In the Scottish Highlands and Islands, a smallholding centred on a *cottage.

crofter. The Scottish crofters held a small area of arable land and grazing rights on the *commons and wastes. They supplemented their income by *weaving, fishing, and the burning of seaweed (*kelp). Many were driven out of their holdings by the *landowners of great estates during the 18th and 19th centuries, whereupon thousands emigrated to *Canada and the United States of *America. Security of tenure was achieved by the Crofters Act of 1886. (See CLEARANCES, HIGHLAND.) Present-day crofters are smallholders. See J. Hunter, *The Making of the Crofting Community* (1976), and T. M. Devine, *Clanship to Crofters' War: The Social Transformation of the Scottish Highlands* (1994).

crop marks. On intensively cultivated land, where ancient sites have been obliterated by the plough, crop marks seen from aeroplanes can give remarkably accurate indications of the ground plans of former structures. (See AERIAL ARCHAEOLOGY.) Crop marks are best seen in barley and wheat, but they can also be observed in sugar beet and sometimes in other crops. Their principal cause is differences in soil depth; they therefore demonstrate the filling-in of ancient ditches and pits. Crop marks show best during dry weather in early summer, especially on thin soils above gravel or chalk.

cropper. A skilled craftsman who cropped the imperfections in a piece of finished cloth with a large pair of shears. See LUDDITES.

crop pests. Until the development of agricultural chemistry in the late 19th and 20th centuries farmers expected to lose part of their crops to attacks by fungi and insects. The adoption of more intensive farming practices had increased the likelihood of crop disease. The *potato blight epidemic of 1845–6 had horrendous consequences. Methods of combating pests and diseases were then still in their infancy. Mildew frequently destroyed whole crops of *cereals; the turnip fly and the carrot fly were major problems. The main preventive method tried by farmers was to steep seed in solutions, using soot, oil, etc., prior to sowing. Most remedies relied on *folklore and on trial and error. How effective they were and how much was lost to blight remains problematical.

crop returns. The Home Office files at the *Public Record Office (H.O. 67) contain the returns of a national survey of 1801, arranged by *diocese and *parish. The ministers of each parish in England and Wales were asked to complete printed forms by noting the acreages devoted to wheat, barley, oats, potatoes, peas and beans, and turnips and rape. Some correspondents also noted rye, lentils, and flax. The returns were not concerned with pasture or meadow and therefore vary in importance from one farming region to another. Space was left for comments, many of which are revealing about local farming practices. Returns do not survive for all parishes and the minister was not always well informed. See M. E. Turner's edition of the returns in *List and Index Society, 189, 190, 195, and 196 (1982–3), and his article 'Arable in England and Wales: Estimates from the 1801 Crop Returns', *Journal of Historical Geography*, 7 (1981).

In 1854 Parliament ordered the gathering of information from 11 representative counties—Berkshire, Breconshire, Denbighshire, Hampshire, Leicestershire, Norfolk, Shropshire, Suffolk, Wiltshire, Worcestershire, and the West Riding of Yorkshire—on crops, livestock, grassland, and waste. See *British Parliamentary Papers: Reports by Poor Law Inspectors on Agricultural Statistics (England): House of Commons Sessional Papers, 1854–5*. For a discussion of the reliability of these returns see J. P. Dodd, 'The Agricultural Statistics for 1854: An Assessment of their Value', *Agricultural History Review*, 35/2 (1987).

From 1866 agricultural returns have been collected each March for livestock and each June for crops (except for certain years). (See AGRICULTURAL STATISTICS.) These returns are housed at the Public Record Office under M.A.F. 68. See the Public Record Office Records Information leaflet, no. 14, 'Agricultural Statistics: Parish Summaries'. Farmers were wary of the purpose of the returns and the figures for the earliest years undoubtedly under-represent the actual amount that was grown. The problems of analysing the returns are discussed in J. T. Coppock, 'The Agricultural Returns as a Source for Local History', *The Amateur Historian*, 4/2 (1958–9).

crosses. Intricately carved crosses, standing several feet high, in *churchyards or in isolation, survive in many parts of the British Isles, but mainly in northern England and Ireland from the era of the *Celtic church or from the *Anglo-Saxon and *Viking periods. Their purpose has never been explained convincingly. Some may have marked preaching sites, but others were personal memorials. They first appeared in 7th-century Northumbria. Their designs follow regional patterns and sometimes incorporate pagan motifs. See R. N. Bailey, *Viking Age Sculpture in Northern England* (1980). The Normans often reused old crosses as common building stone for their churches.

The tradition of erecting wayside crosses, such as are still seen in the Republic of Ireland or in Catholic countries in Europe, ceased in England, Scotland, and Wales upon the *Reformation. Some survive in mutilated form. (See also ELEANOR CROSSES.) Crosses of a simple form which survive in churchyards usually served as markers in churchyard processions; they are similar in form to crosses which marked the *boundaries of *parishes, *townships, *manors, or monastic estates. In *moorland areas such markers were essential before large-scale maps were available. (See PERAMBULATIONS.) Some are now little more than stumps, but often they are inscribed with the initials of the parish or manor. Crosses consisting of a square base and short shaft continued to be erected in the early 19th century to mark township boundaries. See also MARKET CROSSES.

crown (coin). Gold crowns and half-crowns were first issued in 1526. After 1551 they were minted in silver and a crown was worth 5 *shillings.

crown estates. The crown estates were one of several sources of income used to support the monarch, his household, and the machinery of government. The earliest statement of the extent of the estates can be found in the *Domesday Book, which identifies both the lands of Edward the Confessor and William I.

By 1130 the estate of the first Norman king had been considerably reduced by grant, and contributed slightly less than a half of the income recorded in the *Pipe Roll of that year. This figure includes income from the *fee-farm of towns as well as the income from rural *manors: it was (even in the 17th century) collected by the *sheriffs and paid to the Clerk of the Pipe.

It was only in the later Middle Ages that the Crown's landed interest grew. Successive monarchs (Edward III in particular) had tended to fracture the crown lands to provide for their children, but inheritance and usurpation together worked to the advantage of the crown after 1399. The deposition of Richard II by Henry IV joined the Duchy of Lancaster to the crown. Likewise, the deposition of Henry VI by Edward IV brought the lands of the Duchy of York. Henry VII secured all this and, in addition, Richard III's estates as Duke of Gloucester, further acquiring by inheritance the lands of the earldoms of Richmond and Pembroke, and yet more lands by *attainder. To this conglomeration Henry VIII added the monastic lands and a large number of private estates, including the estates of the Duke of Buckingham, the lands of Cardinal Wolsey, the lands of the Northern Rebels of 1536–7, the lands of the Marquess of Exeter, all confiscated; and (in rather strange circumstances) the earldom of Northumberland. 1540 marks the apogee of the royal landed interest. From that time onwards the sale of the estates was the irresistible means by which war and overspending on the current account was subvented. In 1627–8 Charles I conveyed most of what was left to the City of London in settlement of mortgages ('the Royal Contract Estate'): by 1640 it had virtually all gone, although the practice of selling land in fee-farm (with a reserved rent) meant that income remained high. The residual crown estate was sold during the *Interregnum and resumed after 1660. By the later 17th century, with the development of new sources of income, it ceased to be of financial importance. The remaining lands were indifferently supervised until 1783, when a commission was appointed to discover their extent. In 1810 their management was committed to a board (the 'Commissioners of Woods, Forests and Land Revenues'), which in 1832 also became responsible for the Scottish land revenues. There is from then a continuity to the present administrative arrangements.

As an investigation into the crown estate in 1994 reported: 'The crown estate is part of the hereditary possessions of the crown. It is not owned by the government, nor does it form part of the private estate of the monarch . . . [it] consists of a wide range of property spread throughout Great Britain, including Regent Street in central London, retail centres, business parks and offices, housing, farms, and approximately half the foreshore and seabed lying below low water and the limit of territorial waters' (National Audit Office, *The Performance of the Crown Estate*, House of Commons Paper, 1993–4, 622.) The estates were valued at £1,947m in 1994 and paid £78.9m to the Exchequer in 1993–4. In 1981 the estate acquired the *Laxton (*open-field) estate: as the historian of Laxton comments, '[m]anaging Laxton is almost impossible to square with their statutory duty to increase income and enhance the capital value of properties under their control on behalf of the Chancellor of the Exchequer' (J. V. Beckett, *A History of Laxton*, 1989, 319).

The financial contribution of the crown estates was, for a short period of English history, extremely important. But the lands were also of much greater utility than merely a source of income. Firstly they provided an income (and a territorial base) for members of the royal family, either the eldest son (Duke of Cornwall from 1337), or royal wives and dowagers (when the alienation was temporary), or for the endowment of younger children (in which case inheritance might finally bring the lands back into the main family line). The crown estates must therefore be seen not as a single entity, but one which could be divided several ways as required.

Secondly, the estates were an important source of patronage. Grants might be made outright, or as leases for terms of years (in Elizabeth's reign sometimes as leases in reversion). Offices on the estates were also highly valued. The estates enabled the crown both to reward service and also to encourage service in the future.

Administratively, the crown estate fell into distinct parts. The first were those rents collected by *sheriffs. The main estates were, for much of Henry VII's and Henry VIII's reigns, in the hands of bodies collectively called General Surveyors. The former monastic lands (and the other lands which came to the crown in the 1530s) were administered by the Court of *Augmentations established for that purpose. In 1547 General Surveyors and Augmentations were merged; and in 1554 the 'second court of Augmentations' became part of a reconstructed Exchequer. The Duchy of *Lancaster was (and remains) a separate element, with its own legal status, management, and tradition of record-keeping. The Duchy of *Cornwall was administered by the Exchequer when there was no duke, but this practice was not restored when Charles I became king in 1625 (possibly to save it from sale), since when the Duchy has had a continuous existence. The queen's dowager estates had their own administrations which terminated on the death of the queen.

It will already be clear that the estates were not a body of land with a continuous existence, but a portfolio of estates into which manors passed by inheritance, exchange, or political misfortune, often to be granted or sold after a period of time. Whilst some places have remained 'crown estates' over long periods (notably Windsor), an enormous area of the country has been part of the estate at one time or another. The progressive liquidation of the estates between 1540 and 1640 and their reputation for lax management has led many historians to view them as no more than a capital reserve to be liquidated when necessary. More recent work has revealed a logical (though cumbersome) organization. The records of the crown administration are now mostly in the Public Record Office, although the fact of sale and the habit of officials on the estates of treating the records as a private possession has brought both dispersal and loss. See R. W. Hoyle (ed.), *The Estates of the English Crown, 1558–1640* (1992), R. B. Pugh, *The Crown Estate: An Historical Essay* (1960), R. Somerville, *History of the Duchy of Lancaster* (2 vols., 1953, 1970), B. P. Wolffe, *The Crown Lands 1461–1536: An Aspect of Yorkist and Early Tudor Government* (1970), and B. P. Wolffe, *The Royal Demesne in English History: The Crown Estate in the Government of the Realm from the Conquest to 1509* (1971). R. W. Hoyle

crucks. A distinctive method of supporting the roof of a *vernacular building was the cruck frame. A pair of curving timbers, known as cruck blades, were hoisted on to stone footings by means of poles inserted into holes near the bases of the blades, so as to provide a secure foundation, prevent rising damp, and sometimes to acquire extra height. At mid-level the two blades were joined by a tie-beam and at the top by a collar-beam and by a variety of techniques. Sometimes, the two cruck blades were split from the same tree. Pairs of crucks were then connected by ridge-poles, purlins, and wall-plates in order to form a bay. Cruck buildings could be several bays long, but were commonly of only two or three bays.

Early writers assumed that this primitive form of building must be very early, but *dendrochronology dates show that surviving examples date mostly from the 13th to the 17th centuries, and that some are later. The earliest known examples are *cottages in the Oxfordshire villages of Harwell Steventon and Radley, which are 13th century in part, and a complete example at Mapledurham in the same county, dated 1335. Long Crendon (Buckinghamshire) has six cruck-framed buildings that pre-date 1500 and at least another three that are early 16th century; a further seven have not been dated precisely but were probably erected during the 15th or 16th century. The problem of dating cruck buildings is complicated by variant forms; the base-cruck type can sometimes be dated to the 14th century, whereas raised-crucks and upper crucks may be as late as the 19th century. Cruck frames are not found in eastern or south-eastern England, but are common in central and northern England, much of Wales and parts of Scotland. Cruck frames were commonly used for small farmhouses, cottages, barns, and other outbuildings. See N. W. Alcock (ed.), *Cruck Construction: An Introduction and Catalogue* (1982), and Eric Mercer, *English Vernacular Houses* (1975).

Crusades. Western Christendom organized several Crusades between 1095 and 1269 to capture the Holy Land from the Muslims. The first Crusade was initially successful and Jerusalem was captured in 1099. The kingdom of Jerusalem, which was established as a result of this victory, survived until 1187. The popular enthusiasm of the first Crusade was never repeated in subsequent endeavours. During the 13th century Muslim armies recaptured all their lost territories. (See HOSPITALLERS; TEMPLARS.) See also Sir Steven Runciman, *A History of the Crusades*, 3 vols. (1952, 2nd edn., 1978), and J. Riley-Smith, *What Were the Crusades?* (1977).

crypt. A vaulted chamber below the *chancel of a medieval parish *church, or beneath the *choir of a *cathedral or *abbey, containing the tomb or relics of a saint or martyr, and sometimes an *altar. Some of these shrines attracted *pilgrims. A good example of an Anglo-Saxon crypt is that which contains the tomb of St Wystan at Repton (Derbyshire).

cucking stool. A wooden contraption whereby a woman was ducked in a pool or a river as a punishment for *scolding, etc., during the early modern period. The evidence is stronger from the towns than from the countryside; see J. A. Sharpe, *Judicial Punishment in England* (1990).

Curia Regis. The king's council, established by William I, out of which in the 13th century grew the courts of *Exchequer, *Common Pleas, and *King's Bench. Records dating from the late 12th and the 13th centuries are kept in the *Public Record Office under KB 26.

cursing. It was widely believed in the Middle Ages and beyond that physical injury could be caused by cursing. The *ecclesiastical courts of the 16th and 17th centuries frequently presented offenders for cursing. The curses of the poor and the injured were thought to be particularly effective. See Keith Thomas, *Religion and the Decline of Magic* (1971), ch. 16.

curtilage. A legal term for the land on which a dwelling and outbuildings are situated.

customs. Set customary practices, or 'customs' in the plural, have to be understood as expressions of what formerly was regarded as 'custom' in the singular. For both individuals and communities in 'traditional' society, custom itself represented the proper local way of 'doing', as that was established by precedent. The precedents in question were either the ancient inherited tenets of *'folklore' in the context of the supernatural or, at the more practical everyday level, were reflected in usages in all areas of social life that had survived, apparently continuously and unchallenged, 'so long as the memory of man runneth not to the contrary'. Current practice was thereby legitimized through its appeal to a theoretically stable past. (This might nevertheless be creatively *re*interpreted when preferred precedents were sought, especially if common rights or shop-floor usages were threatened.) At one extreme, therefore, custom would be regarded as having virtually the force of local law, while at the other it represented effectively a firm set of expectations passed on by the older generation. Accordingly, 'customs' ranged all the way through from private rituals in face of the supernatural, and expressions of, or restraints on, personal conduct whether sexual or social, via communal observances marking the local social structure as a constantly renewing process in a specific environment, to more formal matters concerned with access to property. These last might be personal, in terms of local tenure or *post mortem* arrangements (e.g. *Borough English or *freebench), or communal, in organizing agricultural routines, apportioning rights of common, and defending the rights of a community in the face of its lord.

Together, the body of customs thus combined to comprise a locally approved (but certainly not unalterable) framework of secular rules and expectations within which, to a greater or lesser degree of compliance, individuals conducted their social lives. The formal aspects of this framework, of course, might be codified in the rolls of the appropriate local lordly court (with specified penalties for breaching the rules), or, when urgent need arose, vouched for orally through the testimony of the more elderly residents in their capacity as custodians of the collective memory. The more informal aspects of the customary framework, by contrast, were perpetuated simply by constant reiteration, whether judgementally in the form of *ad hoc* comment or gossip, or routinely through repetitive ritual. In either case, custom carried moral obligation, any serious anti-social deviation from which furnished an equally 'moral' justification for the mounting of communal, as opposed to officially approved, sanctions. This might be by *'rough music' in the case of marital mistreatment, or, when the moral right to survival itself was threatened by excessively high grain prices or mechanization, for example, through riotous and sometimes destructive collective action; see E. P. Thompson, *Customs in Common* (1991). It is important, therefore, to appreciate that attached to every single aspect of 'custom'—even riot—were what we now think of as 'customs', or at least customary ways of behaving (e.g. in the case of riot, men wearing women's clothes), even if sometimes such customs did little more than mark the timing of an occasion. The customs discussed here have, consequently, to be understood as no more than a few representative fragments removed from what, in each different locality, was formerly a coherent social and cultural process.

The social customs in question involved abnormal ways of 'doing' in isolated circumstances, whether these were specific moments in a personal, social, or seasonal cycle, or of an *ad hoc* emergency nature. At the core of each set customary observance, and so representing the essence of it, lay some form of ritual, although the more elaborate occasions were often surrounded by ancillary activities like dancing, sports, or feasting as well; see Charles Phythian-Adams, *Local History and Folklore: A New Framework* (1975). Ritual openly mobilized quite specific participants and different symbolic objects through a conventionalized series of actions in a range of locations that varied according to the nature of the occasion. Ritual 'moved' people out of their usual stations in the life-cycle, either for the purposes of irreversible change, or in order temporarily to exaggerate status, or, for no longer than the duration of an observance, when normality was being temporarily reversed and the world turned upside down. Ritual also frequently and deliberately 'moved' objects out of their 'proper' place and then usually returned or discarded them within the time-span of the observance; for example, the consecrated wafer, the host, was taken out of the church into the streets at the medieval feast of *Corpus Christi; one tree and masses of branches were brought out of the woods and into human settlements at *May Day; a hare's paw was often hung on the human person as a specific against cramp or rheumatism. Ritual was something to be understood through performance rather than by description, its symbolism becoming to a degree transparent because of the nature of the occasion. Ritual thus expressed itself through clusters of signals and meanings and so metaphorically rather than directly. Since such clusters could be rearranged as need arose, moreover, ritual was flexible enough to evolve both its content and its meanings over time, not least when traditional rural practices had to be adapted to unprecedented urban conditions; see Charles Phythian-Adams, 'Milk and Soot: The Changing Vocabulary of a Popular Ritual in Stuart and Hanoverian London' in D. Fraser and A. Sutcliffe (eds.), *The Pursuit of Urban History* (1983).

Social customs may be broadly categorized according to their personal, group, or communal observance. Personal or interpersonal customs clearly tended to involve (at least at core) one or two individuals only, and were usually invoked privately and *ad hoc* as need arose. At one extreme such needs could involve an individual in observing the customary techniques of a craft, or in the propitiatory, defensive, or curative actions that might be required in the face both of the supernatural and of illness, or the correct ways of divining or interpreting signs about the future. At the other, more humdrum extreme were the customary ways in which the conduct of two people might be formalized for such purposes as simple etiquette, striking a bargain, courtship rituals, plighting troth, or even face-to-face confrontation; see Charles Phythian-Adams, 'Rituals of Personal Confrontation in Late Medieval England', *Bulletin of the John Rylands University Library of Manchester*, 73 (1991).

Group customs may have had overt purposes like the election of *guild officers or the parochial assertion of *boundaries, but in doing so they also related individuals to wider social contexts by publicly advertising personal belonging to, or exclusion from, an established body (a congregation, a guild, a club, a regiment, or a family). The invocation of the supernatural through the swearing of an oath underlined the solemnity that marked admission to membership, and helps to explain, conversely, the theoretical completeness of total exclusion in traditional society, as exemplified in abjuring the realm, *outlawry, *excommunication, 'discommoning' from the freedom of a city, or even *wife-selling. To avoid expulsion when it was threatened or to earn readmission to society therefore involved a range of exaggerated rituals: from the body language customarily expected in public when someone cravenly begged for their life, through the humiliating performance of exemplary *penance, to the manner of openly witnessed punishment. It is these considerations that lend significance to the oath-swearings that attended nearly all public rites of passage from one social condition to another, not only at *baptism and *marriage, but also at the successive levels of official standing that contributed to the overall status of an individual.

Customs which variously marked the stages of individual life-cycles in relation to a whole range of component groupings in society have to be contrasted with customary occasions which aspired to communal inclusiveness (at least to the point where even non-participants acknowledged the existence of the observance). The cycle here was (and is) the annual cycle peculiar to the rhythm of each local society, with all that that implied for the extra meanings to be attached to a custom by the precision of its timing. With the exception of the election or inauguration of official figureheads, such *calendar customs therefore concentrated not on 'passage', but on the variable interrelationships one to another of already constituted formal groups or identifiable categories of people by age, sex, marital status, institutional membership, or office. Such observances might range, therefore, from the informal activities of May Day to the solemn, hierarchically organized processions on, for example, St George's Day. Whereas rites of passage defined new positions, communal customs expressed ritualized versions of the established status quo, either by magnifying hierarchy, or by inverting normal status relationships such as, down to the 16th century, winter or summer *lords of misrule, boy bishops or abbots of misrule, or *Hocktide wives.

On communal occasions in particular the ancillary activities surrounding the central ritual often complemented it. Where status was emphasized, for example, some reciprocity was expected of superiors, especially in the form of customary hospitality from lords at *Christmas, wealthy urban neighbours at *Midsummer, or farmers at sheep-shearing or harvest. Other expressions of superior obligation included non-prosecution for the appropriation by customary 'right' from private woodlands of trees or boughs for the construction of maypoles or summer bowers. At harvest the very poor could claim rights of *gleaning off the land even of small-farming neighbours. In post-*Restoration times, finally, obligation was met through payments made by the spectators into a collecting ladle in return for the performance of a ritual (as though by actors). Such central and ancillary activities together, therefore, formerly combined to comprise a custom as a whole.

At some periods customary and ritual practices seem to accrete, while at others they are either transformed or leave but a husk behind. The later Middle Ages, for example, appear to have seen the addition of a number of new observances: the feast of Corpus Christi, Robin Hood plays, lords of misrule, *morris dancing. The later 19th century, by contrast, witnessed the pressing-back of customary activities to more remotely situated communities at the margins of cultural regions or 'provinces', or the transfer of communal customary observances to the economically less fortunate, the labourers, women, apprentices, and children who, to enhance their earnings, might sometimes perform a *mummers' play, mobilize an animal disguise (E. C. Cawte, *Ritual Animal Disguise*, 1978), or parade a May Day garland. What more usually vanished in such cases, however, was the central ritual itself (though sometimes this was artificially revived). What tended to remain were what we today tend to regard as 'customs': the foods, decorations, or sports which, if nothing else, at least conspire to ensure the continuing recognition of each special day, albeit at the expense of an appreciation of any earlier meaning. See Margaret Bennett, *Scottish Customs from the Cradle to the Grave* (1992), and Bob Bushaway, *By Rite: Custom, Ceremony and Community in England, 1700–1880* (1982).   CHARLES PHYTHIAN-ADAMS

customs and excise. From the reign of King John (1199–1216) duties have been payable on certain imported goods, and customs men have been employed by the government to collect the duties and prevent *smuggling. In 1643 excise duties were introduced on certain home-produced goods and a Board of Excise set up for their collection. It was not until the creation of the Board of Customs and Excise in 1909 that the two collecting bodies were amalgamated. See the *Public Record Office Records Information leaflet, no. 106, 'Customs and Excise Records as Sources for Biography and Family History'. Customs records include pay lists for the period 1675–1829 (CUST 18 and 19), an incomplete series of staff lists, 1671–1922 (CUST 39), and superannuation registers, 1803–1922 (CUST 39; closed for 75 years). See CUST 20 and 39 for the Irish Board of Customs. The excise records of particular use are classified under CUST 39, 47, 48, and 116. Local collectors sometimes appear in *parish registers as 'Officer of the Excise'.

Custos rotulorum. The principal *Justice of the Peace who was responsible for the safeguarding of the records of the *quarter sessions.

custumal. A record of the customs of a *manor, drawn up by the manorial jury.

cutlery. London was the ancient centre of the manufacture of high-class cutlery. By the 16th century superior grinding facilities had enabled Sheffield to triumph over its provincial rivals such as Thaxted and Salisbury. At first, Sheffielders concentrated on the cheaper end of the market, but from the late Elizabethan period onwards they increasingly made high-quality knives. The Cutlers' Company of Hallamshire was founded in 1624 for makers of knives, *scissors, shears, and *sickles; in the later 17th century the Company admitted makers of files, awl blades, and *scythes. During the 18th century Sheffield overtook London as the leading centre of cutlery manufacture. Competition from Solingen (Germany), Thiers (France), etc. prevented much penetration of the Continental market, but America became an important outlet for sales. The industry was characterized by numerous small workshops and independent craftsmen; *factories did not appear until well into the 19th century. From the 1970s onwards competition from East Asia forced the closure of many Sheffield firms and automation led to the loss of jobs and the virtual disappearance of the 'little mester', or independent craftsman. Nevertheless, the level of production remains as high as before.

cypher. A personal monogram, popular in the 18th and 19th centuries.

dairying became an increasingly important sector of the agricultural economy in the later 17th century. (See CHEESE TRADE.) Joan Thirsk, *England's Agricultural Regions and Agrarian History, 1500–1750* (1987), indicates the specialist dairying areas at that time. See G. E. Mingay (ed.), *The *Agrarian History of England and Wales*, vi: *1750–1850* (1989) for further growth in sales of butter, cheese, and liquid milk from town dairies. Many farms in the neighbourhood of industrial towns began to specialize in milk production. The *railways had an enormous influence on liquid milk sales. See Christine Hallas, 'Supply Responsiveness in Dairy Farming: Some Regional Considerations', *Agricultural History Review*, 39/1 (1991), which discusses the impact of the railway in Wensleydale in the late 19th century. See also D. Taylor, 'Growth and Structural Change in the English Dairy Industry, c.1860–1930', *Agricultural History Review*, 35/1 (1987). Joanna Bourke, 'Dairywomen and Affectionate Wives: Women in the Irish Dairy Industry, 1890–1914', *Agricultural History Review*, 38/2 (1990), demonstrates the importance of milking and butter-making in the rural Irish economy, and shows how work that was once everywhere in the hands of women became dominated by men working in creameries. See also Deborah Valenze, 'The Art of Women and the Business of Men: Women's Work and the Dairy Industry, c.1740–1840', *Past and Present*, 130 (1991).

Dame. The form of address for a woman of rank or position.

Danegeld. A payment made to the Danes by the *Anglo-Saxon kingdoms to prevent invasion in the 10th and 11th centuries. The money was raised by a tax on land. Similar taxes were raised later by Cnut and the early Norman kings to pay for national defence. Danegeld was abolished in 1162.

Danelaw, the. A collective term for those shires which were ruled by the Danes from the 9th to the 11th centuries. The Danelaw comprised four areas: *Northumbria; the territory of the *Five Boroughs; *East Anglia; and the south-eastern midlands. Its southern boundary was Watling Street, the *Roman road whose line is largely followed by the present A5 road from London to Chester.

Dark Ages. An old-fashioned term for the period beginning with the withdrawal of the *Romans in the 5th century to the later *Anglo-Saxon period of the 8th century onwards, for which there is relatively little evidence.

datestones. A fashion which began in the second half of the 16th century for *gentlemen and *yeomen farmers to carve a date on the stone of their door lintel, or perhaps on the chimney breast. The date was often combined with the initials of the forenames of husband and wife and of their surname placed centrally above. A datestone usually commemorates the completion of a building, but the evidence should be handled with care; it may refer to the addition of a wing or some other improvement; it may have been carved much later; or it may have come from another building. The recording of all datestones in a region helps to identify particular phases of building activity.

daughter. The term could include a daughter-in-law.

day labourer. A labourer paid by the day, and not living in the farmer's household.

deacon. 1. A clerk in holy orders who assists a priest.

2. An officer of the Presbyterian and *Congregational churches.

dean. The head of a *chapter of a *cathedral or of a body of *canons in a *collegiate church. A rural dean heads a *deanery.

deanery, rural. A group of *parishes that form a subdivision of an *archdeaconry. Although deaneries are Anglo-Scandinavian in origin, they often did not achieve their final form until after the *Norman Conquest. Within the *Danelaw, deaneries normally had the same *boundaries as the secular *wapentakes.

death duty. The Legacy Duty Act (1796) imposed a tax on certain types of bequests and residues of the personal estate of deceased persons. These duties were extended by further Acts in 1805 and 1815. A duty on succession has been payable since 1853. Registers from 1796 to 1903 record bequests chargeable with these duties. They list the name of the deceased, the date of the *will, the place and date of probate, the names and addresses of executors, and details of estates, legacies, trustees, legatees and their degree of *consanguinity, *annuities, and the amount of duty paid. They are kept in the *Public Record Office under IR 26 and 27 and are indexed in the *List and Index Society's volume 177. See the Public Record Office Records Information leaflet no. 66, 'The Death Duty Registers'. The registers serve as a finding aid to the court where a will was proved or an administration granted.

death rates. The number of deaths in a year expressed as a rate per thousand of the total population. As the number of burials in *parish registers is under-recorded, a correction factor is used to produce estimated death rates. See E. A. Wrigley and R. S. Schofield, *The Population History of England, 1541–1871: A Reconstruction* (1981).

Debrett, John, Peerage and Baronetage. John Debrett (d. 1822) published the first edition of his *Peerage* in 1802 and that of his *Baronetage* in 1808. The *Peerage* went through 15 editions in his lifetime and was continued by others after his death. It was eventually combined with the *Baronetage* in an annual volume. See also BURKE, JOHN.

Decorated architecture. A style introduced in major religious and secular buildings in the late 13th century and characteristic of parish *churches in the first half of the 14th century, replacing the *Early English style of *Gothic architecture. The Decorated style involved the use of flowing window tracery and ogee-arches, and a delight in decorative sculpture. The *chapter house at Southwell Cathedral (Notts.) is an outstanding example. The style was admired and imitated by the Victorians.

decoy. A trap for *ducks and other wildfowl in *forests, *chases, *parks, and especially in *fens. The birds were enticed into funnel-shaped arms of pools or rivers and caught in nets. The word is of Dutch origin and the use of decoys seems to have originated in the early 17th century. Duck-decoys became increasingly complex during the late 17th and 18th centuries. Tame ducks and dogs assisted in the trapping.

decree. A judgement of a court; a judicial decision; an edict.

deed, title. A legal document which transfers property or rights from one person (or institu-

tion) to another. The Law of Property Act (1925) abolished the necessity of proving the title back more than 30 years. Since then, huge collections of title deeds that were formerly held by solicitors have been deposited at local *record offices; most of these have been *calendared. See Stella Colwell, *Dictionary of Genealogical Sources in the Public Record Office* (1992), and *registries of deeds. The deeds give information about vendors and purchasers, the agreed price, some description of the property, and (from 1840) a plan. They sometimes record previous transactions, which may be summarized as 'abstracts of title'. See N. W. Alcock, *Old Title Deeds: A Guide for Local and Family Historians* (1986). See also BARGAIN AND SALE; FEET OF FINES; and LEASE AND RELEASE.

deed poll. A deed involving only one person or body, e.g. for changing a *surname.

deer park. It has been estimated that at least 1,900 deer parks were created in England alone during the Middle Ages, particularly in the midlands and the south, though they were not all in existence at the same time. A few were recorded in the *Domesday Book, but most were created during the 12th and 13th centuries. The fashion declined during the 15th and 16th centuries, but enjoyed a brief revival during the reign of Charles II. As deer were the property of the Crown, a lord was supposed to obtain a royal *charter to empark. However, there are many well-documented parks for which no royal licence exists. It has been suggested that a licence may not have been sought if the park lay well away from a royal *forest. Many of the smaller manorial parks have left little or no written evidence. They may sometimes be identified from surviving earthworks or from a field- or farm-name incorporating 'park' on the first edition of the six-inch *Ordnance Survey map.

The management of a deer park was a task for the specialist. Deer require a varied environment, including open grassland, *wood, and *coppice. The national distribution of parks corresponds closely with areas where woodland was recorded in the Domesday Book. Enclosed tracts of wild, semi-wooded country, sometimes taken in from waste ground on the edge of a *manor, were especially favoured. Often, parks encroached on former *commons and wastes, or on to the *open-fields, but they were rarely responsible for the complete disappearance of a village.

The main types of deer which were kept in parks in the Middle Ages were the native red and roe deer, and fallow deer, which are thought to have been introduced by the Normans. Although venison was not produced for the market, it was highly valued in great houses and as gifts. Parks were not just status symbols for occasional hunting; they were economic assets. Only the larger parks were used for hunting; in the smaller ones the keeper culled the deer as demand for venison arose. Parks were also a valuable source of pasture for domestic animals and of timber and coppiced wood. In the 16th century some parks were converted to cattle grazings, when meat was more profitable. In the late 16th and 17th centuries others were converted into woods, when better prices could be obtained for coppice and timber.

Parks were enclosed by an oak palisade, or a fence or stone wall on the top of a high earthen bank, surrounded by a deep ditch. These barriers were costly and troublesome to maintain. The optimum shape of a park was circular as this reduced the amount of fencing, but local conditions often dictated other shapes. The keeper and tenants who paid a money rent for *agistment were allowed to graze cattle, sheep, horses, and pigs in parts of a park which were defined by internal barriers. Winter fodder for the deer took the form of hay and browsewood and holly leaves. See Martin Spray, 'Holly as a Fodder in England', *Agricultural History Review*, 29/2 (1981).

*Manor houses were not usually sited within parks, but the hunting lodges which were provided for keepers were sometimes converted into country houses during the 16th century, e.g. Sheffield Manor Lodge and Tankersley Hall (Yorkshire). In the 18th century deer were often kept to adorn landscaped parks. See Susan Neave, *Medieval Parks of East Yorkshire* (1991) and Jean Birrell, 'Deer and Deer Farming in Medieval England', *Agricultural History Review*, 40/2 (1992). (See also CHASE.) On deer stalking in the Scottish Highlands, see W. Orr, *Deer Forests, Landlords and Crofters* (1982).

defaulter. In the Middle Ages, an absentee who was fined for not attending a manorial *court.

Defoe, Daniel (1660–1731). A prolific and versatile writer whose works are of great importance in the development of the novel and journalism. For local historians his most important work is *A Tour through the Whole Island of Great Britain* (1724–6), a record of journeys undertaken over many years which provides a vivid and informed account of Britain in the first quarter of the 18th century.

deforciant. A defendant.

de-industrialization. Economic historians have pointed out that those parts of Britain which first underwent an *industrial revolution had experienced a long period of growth prior to the spectacular advances of the late 18th and 19th centuries. (See PROTO-INDUSTRIALIZATION.) However, the process of continuous development was not inevitable. Some parts of Britain which had industries in the Middle Ages and/or the 16th and 17th centuries comparable to those which became heavily industrialized not only failed to develop but lost their industries entirely. There is now little industry in the Weald, the Cotswolds, the Stour Valley, and some other districts that were once noted for their industries. Explaining the decline of an industry is often more difficult than explaining its rise. See, for example, Michael Zell, *Industry in the Countryside: Wealden Society in the Sixteenth Century* (1994).

Delft ware. Blue-and-white pottery, originally from Delft (Holland). The first Delft ware factory in England was established in Norwich in 1567 by two Dutchmen, who in 1570 moved to London to start the industry in Southwark and Lambeth. Delft ware was popular throughout the country in the 17th and early 18th centuries and was often recorded in probate *inventories.

demesne. Land on a *manor that was reserved for the lord's own use, as distinct from land held by tenants. The demesne was effectively the same as the so-called 'home farm' of 18th-, 19th-, and 20th-century estates. The term 'ancient demesne' was used to describe manors held by the king at the time of the *Norman Conquest. In the Middle Ages the labour was provided by *famuli and by the *boon work of the tenants. (See DOMESDAY BOOK; INQUISITION POST MORTEM; and ACCOUNTS, MEDIEVAL.) Lords no longer found it profitable to farm their demesne after the *Black Death, but were content to lease their lands to others. There was a revival of interest from the late 15th century onwards, when *population increase once more raised the price of *cereals and encouraged large-scale farming by *gentry.

demise. To convey property by *will or *lease for a term of years or for life.

dendrochronology. The technique of dating timbers by their annual growth rings. Large databases of computerized information have been compiled and some remarkably accurate results have been achieved. The dating of *timber-framed buildings has thus been placed on a much firmer footing. In many cases it has been possible to fix the year that particular timbers were felled for building. The practice of using timbers from an old building in a new one causes difficulties in interpretation, however. In other cases, the removal by carpenters of the outer rings makes dating imprecise. See J. Fletcher, M. Bridge, and J. Hillam, 'Tree-Ring Dates for Buildings with Oak Timber', *Vernacular Archaeology*, 12 (1981).

denization. A grant by letters patent by which an *alien was allowed some of the privileges of naturalization, e.g. the buying and devising of land. The records, from c.1400 to 1844, are kept in the *Public Record Office under C 66 and 67. They are useful in naming an immigrant's place of origin. See also the Parliament Rolls for the same period (C 65), and the *Close Rolls (C 54), which have enrolments of Naturalization Certificates, 1844–73. See W. Page, *Denizations and Naturalizations of Aliens in England, 1509–1603* (Huguenot Society, viii, 1893), and W. A. Shaw, *Letters of Denization and Acts of Naturalization for Aliens in England, etc., 1603–1800* (Huguenot Society, xviii, xxvii, and xxxv).

deodand. A legal term for the instrument which caused a person's death.

deponent. One who makes an oral or written statement (deposition) on oath in a court of law. It was usual in civil cases in the 16th and 17th centuries for both sides to present supporting statements of this sort, often in the form of answers to leading questions. The records of quasi-judicial enquiries under special commissions initiated by the Exchequer are kept at the *Public Record Office under E 133, 134, and 178.

deposition. See DEPONENT.

deserted medieval villages. Over 3,000 deserted villages in England alone have now been identified, yet until the 1940s, when M. W. Beresford and W. G. *Hoskins began to survey sites and to research their history, the existence of such a phenomenon was disputed. The publication of Beresford's *The Lost Villages of England* (1954) established the importance of the subject and demonstrated how topographical and documentary evidence could be combined to elucidate the histories of individual villages and to offer a broad explanatory framework. Meanwhile, Beresford had begun to excavate Wharram Percy on the Yorkshire Wolds, a site that is now presented by English Heritage as the deserted medieval village (DMV) about which we know most. See M. W.

Beresford and J. G. Hurst (eds.), *Deserted Medieval Villages* (1971), M. Aston, D. Austin, and C. Dyer (eds.), *The Rural Settlements of Medieval England: Studies Dedicated to Maurice Beresford and John Hurst* (1989), and Richard Muir, *The Lost Villages of Britain* (1984).

The original emphasis was on discovering the date of and explaining the reasons for desertion. It has become recognized that desertion was a long-drawn-out process, stretching from the 11th to the 18th centuries. See Stuart Wrathmell, 'Village Depopulation in the 17th and 18th Centuries: Examples From Northumberland', *Post-Medieval Archaeology*, 14 (1980), and Susan Neave, 'Rural Settlement Contraction in the East Riding of Yorkshire Between the Mid-Seventeenth and Mid-Eighteenth Centuries', *Agricultural History Review*, 41/2 (1993). In Ireland the 17th century was the period of greatest desertion of rural settlements, at least in the east and south of the country.

The period of desertion can be judged from taxation returns, starting with the *lay subsidies and *poll taxes of the 14th century and leading on to the *hearth tax returns of the 1660s and 1670s, but much detailed work on individual cases has to be done on *estate records and maps, and on *parish registers. Place-names are sometimes suggestive, and obvious gaps in the settlement pattern can quickly be spotted from *Ordnance Survey maps. Investigation on the ground involves the recognition of earthworks such as house platforms and abandoned holloways amidst the *ridge-and-furrow patterns of the former arable fields. An isolated church, often abandoned and in ruins, but sometimes heavily restored by a Victorian squire, is frequently an immediate clue.

The Medieval Village Research Group has recognized that deserted sites provide unequalled opportunities to study many aspects of the development and workings of English rural life. Their work has significantly changed our understanding of the history of the countryside. (See MEDIEVAL PEASANT HOUSES.) The excavations at Wharram Percy, for instance, have shed light on settlement that goes back beyond the *Anglo-Saxons, the *Romans, and the *Iron Age to *Neolithic farmers. See Maurice Beresford and John Hirst, *Wharram Percy* (1990).

detached pasture. In areas of *intercommoning of a *moor, *marsh, *wood, etc., the inhabitants of some *manors had common rights on pastures that were physically detached from the rest of the fields and commons. These detached pastures could be several miles away from the homes of the farmers, e.g. the 'dens' or swine pastures of the Kentish Weald, which belonged to farmers from further north in the county.

detached portion. Many *parishes were not compact entities, but had detached portions that were surrounded by the lands of neighbouring parishes. Such arrangements reflect ancient tenurial history, often from before the *Norman Conquest. In some cases, adjacent *strips in *open-fields belonged to different parishes. Detached portions could also result from the division of a 'mother' parish, or *minster territory, into 'daughter' parishes and *chapels-of-ease. The parish system has been reorganized in modern times so as to create compact units.

devise. To convey or bequeathe land, as distinct from personal property.

dew pond. A familiar sight on *chalklands and limestone since the 17th century, such ponds were used to collect rain-water for cattle. They were usually lined with clay and straw, though some now have a concrete base. The piping of water into troughs has brought about their decline.

dialects and accents. Accent refers to pronunciation, dialect to vocabulary, grammar, and idiom as well. Medieval England had an enormous variety of dialects as Middle English developed out of *Old English, with influences from Scandinavian languages and Norman French. In the 12th century *William of Malmesbury wrote that the speech of northern England was incomprehensible to those who lived in the south. (See also GAELIC LANGUAGE; WELSH LANGUAGE; and CORNISH LANGUAGE.) Standard English developed from a south midlands dialect, the speech of a particular social group in and around the Court. By the 16th century courtiers such as Sir Walter Raleigh (who spoke in the broad accents of his native Devon) were exceptional.

A scholarly interest in local speech began in the later 17th century. The first dialect dictionary was John Ray's *Collection of English Words* (1674). In Lincolnshire, Sarah Sophia Banks compiled 'Glossaries in Lincolnshire Dialect, 1778–83' (*British Library, Add. MS 32,640), with additions up to 1841. In *The Hallamshire Glossary* (1829) Joseph *Hunter made the point that many dialect words were in fact archaic survivals which had been in more widespread use in earlier times and could be found in the works of Chaucer and Shakespeare. The 19th century saw the publication of much dialect writing, especially in *almanacs. Interest was at its height in the late 19th century, when it was

thought that compulsory elementary education would eradicate dialects. One of the earliest serious investigators was Georgina Jackson, *Shropshire Word-Book: A Glossary of Archaic and Provincial Words . . . Used in the County* (1879). J. C. *Atkinson recorded the speech of his parishioners on the North York Moors in a sympathetic way and sought parallels with the speech of Scandinavia. This scholarly interest culminated in the publication of Joseph Wright, *The English Dialect Dictionary* (6 vols. 1898–1905). In the second half of the 20th century a survey of English dialects has been conducted from the Universities of Leeds and Sheffield. See Clive Upton, David Parry, and J. D. A. Widdowson, *Survey of English Dialects: The Dictionary and Grammar* (1994). See also Martyn F. Wakelin, *English Dialects: An Introduction* (1977), A. Hughes and P. Trudgill, *English Accents and Dialects* (1979), and Peter Trudgill (ed.), *Language in the British Isles* (1984).

The debate about the decline of dialects as modern communications reduce the differences between one part of the country and another continues. It is now appreciated that dialects have never been static and that the loss of vocabulary is a natural process. This process has been hastened, however, by the decline of handcrafts whose specialized terms have disappeared. Accents, as distinct from dialect, remain as local as ever. It is still possible to place speakers within a small district—what would once have been called a *country—and not just within a broad region. The phonetic spellings used in local records, especially in probate *inventories, provide the local historian with much material for a study of local speech, but few attempts have been made to use such sources in this way. See Edmund Weiner, 'Local History and Lexicography', *The Local Historian*, 24/3 (1994).

diaries. The keeping of diaries as a record of personal experience and development began in the 17th century and in most cases was inspired by piety. (See, in particular, JOSSELIN, RALPH.) The diaries of Adam Eyre (a captain in the parliamentary army) and of John Shaw (a *Nonconformist minister) have been published in *Four Yorkshire Diaries* (Surtees Society, lxv, 1875). (See also HEYWOOD, OLIVER.) The keeping of a diary appealed particularly to earnest men and women of religion, but the finest diary of all is that of Samuel *Pepys, who gave a complete picture of his life, including work, amusements, amorous involvements, domestic concerns, worries, etc. in the midst of stirring national events. (See also the diary of his friend EVELYN, JOHN.) Some people combined the keeping of a diary with the writing of a brief autobiography. They included men of different background from most diarists, such as the Quaker shopkeeper William *Stout. Diaries such as these provide much information on *kinship, contacts, travel, and local events which would otherwise be difficult to obtain, especially in the early modern period. Women's diaries show different preoccupations, but shed much light on local and family life. See, for example, D. M. Meads (ed.), *Diary of Lady Margaret Hoby, 1599–1605* (1930), and Mary Carbery (ed.), *Mrs Elizabeth Freke, Her Diary, 1671 to 1714* (1913).

Clergymen are again well represented in the 18th and 19th centuries. See John Beresford (ed.), *The Diary of a Country Parson, 1758–1802 by James Woodforde* (1978), and Jack Ayres, *Paupers and Pig Killers: The Diary of William Holland, A Somerset Parson, 1799–1818* (1984). In the 19th and 20th centuries working-class people began to keep diaries and to record their memories in the form of an autobiography. See J. Burnett, 'The Autobiography of the Working Class', *Labour History Review*, 55/1 (1990), which gives an account of a survey of over 1,000 autobiographies written by working-class men and women from 1790 to 1900 and a further thousand written between 1900 and 1945. See also W. Matthews, *British Diaries: An Annotated Bibliography of British Diaries Written Between 1442 and 1942* (1980).

Dictionary of National Biography. The *DNB*, edited by Leslie Stephen and published by George Smith, was launched in 1882. It included short biographies of notable British people from earliest times up to 1900. Supplements have been published every 10 years. Since 1917 the *DNB* has been published by Oxford University Press. A *New Dictionary of National Biography* was started in 1994.

diet. *Famine was an ever-present threat in the Middle Ages and later, but when the harvest was average or good smallholdings provided families with sufficient calories throughout the year. In the early modern period the rich ate well in terms of bulk, but their diet was unbalanced, showing over-reliance on meat and cereals, though more varied vegetables and *fruit were introduced by *gentry and *French and *Dutch immigrants at this time. Information on the diet of ordinary families is hard to come by, but they seem to have eaten a lot of bread and stews based on cereals or legumes, such as pease pudding, some fish, and much beer, with garden crops and fruit according to season. The farming systems of the various regions had an important bearing on local diets. In pastoral areas oatcakes, porridge, and rye bread formed the mainstay, though more dairy products were available than elsewhere until the development of better marketing systems and rapid communications. During the second half of the 18th century the general standard of diet improved, accompanied by the more widespread popularity of wheaten bread. (See CEREALS; DAIRYING; and FOOD SUPPLY. See also EDEN, SIR F. M. for *workhouse menus in the 1790s.) An interest in regional recipes developed in the 19th century. See, for example, Peter Brears, *Traditional Food in Yorkshire* (1987). For renewed interest nowadays in dietary history, see Hans J. Teuteberg, *European Food History: A Recent Review* (1992).

dioceses. A diocese is an ecclesiastical administrative territory under the jurisdiction of a bishop.

The medieval English dioceses were created as follows: Canterbury (AD 597), London (604), Rochester (604), York (625), Winchester (662), Lichfield (669), Hereford (676), Worcester (c.680), Bath and Wells (909), Durham (995), Exeter (1050), Lincoln (1072), Chichester (1075), Salisbury (1078), Norwich (1091), Ely (1109), and Carlisle (1133). Six new dioceses were created by Henry VIII in the 1540s, following the *dissolution of the monasteries: Chester, Peterborough, Gloucester, Bristol, Oxford, and Westminster (which lasted only a decade). No further *Church of England dioceses were created until 1836, since when 20 have been founded in response to population changes; the cathedrals of these new dioceses are often enlarged versions of medieval parish *churches. The older cathedrals are the chief glory of English *Gothic architecture. See Alec Clifton-Taylor, *The Cathedrals of England* (1967).

The Welsh dioceses of Bangor, St Asaph, St David's, and Llandaff were created in the mid-6th century, and that of Sodor and Man in the 11th century. The Irish dioceses were mostly created in the *Viking period, e.g. the diocese of Cork was essentially the territory of the Mac Carthaigs. However, these territories were based on even older units. By the early 14th century Ireland was divided into four provinces and 35 dioceses: Armagh (11), Dublin (6), Tuam (8), and Cashel (10). The 13 medieval dioceses of Scotland were swept away at the *Reformation. The new *Church of Scotland established a structure consisting of General

Assembly, synod, presbytery, and kirk session. However, the *Scottish Episcopal Church and the *Roman Catholic Church are administered through dioceses.

For administrative purposes dioceses are divided into *archdeaconries, rural *deaneries, and *parishes. The records of the diocese are available for public consultation at the various diocesan *record offices, some of which are amalgamated with county or city record offices.

diphtheria was a winter disease which mainly attacked children under the age of five. In the early modern period it could kill up to 40 per cent of those affected. It remained a major cause of *infant mortality in the 19th century and the first part of the 20th century. During the 1950s and 1960s the disease was controlled by *vaccination.

directories. Trade and commercial directories are a major source of information for all parts of Victorian and Edwardian Britain, and for certain places from much earlier. The first London directory was Samuel Lee's list of the City merchants in 1677, but this was not followed until 1734 with the publication of Brown and Kent's London directory, which was subsequently published in annual revised versions by Kent up to 1771, and by others until 1826. The industrial towns took the lead in the provinces, with Sketchley's Birmingham (1763), Raffald's Manchester (1772), Sketchley's Sheffield (1774), etc. These early publications contain far less information than the directories of the Victorian era, but they arrange the names of people in each trade in alphabetical order and give their addresses, together with details of postal, coach, and carrying services. See Jane E. Norton, *A Guide to National and Provincial Directories* (1984), Gareth Shaw and Allison Tipper, *British Directories: A Bibliography and Guide to Directories Published in England and Wales, 1850–1950, and Scotland, 1775–1950* (1988), and P. J. Atkins, *The Directories of London, 1677–1977* (1990). A full series of local directories is usually available at local reference libraries and local *record offices.

In the late 18th century a number of directories covering much wider areas than single towns were published, e.g. William Bailey's *Northern Directory* (1781–7) and John Wilkes, *The Universal British Directory* (issued in 69 parts, comprising 5 volumes, 1790–9). It proved more economical and useful, however, for publishers to issue detailed local directories. The first national series was that of James Pigot, published between 1814 and 1853, after which the firm was taken over by Francis Kelly, who had begun to expand his London business in 1845 by publishing provincial directories for the south of England. Kelly's became the most famous series of directories up to the middle of the 20th century, though there were other well-known names, such as William White. In contrast, many other publishers of directories did not remain in the business very long.

The general trade directories acquired a common style. They began each entry with brief notes on the history and topography of the settlement, with some account of recent economic developments, and with notes on land-ownership, tenures, and the administrative details of *townships, *parishes, and *manors. They then listed the 'principal inhabitants' and arranged the names of professionals, businessmen, and tradesmen in alphabetical order under different occupations. Even the best directories are not comprehensive in their listings, nor did they record labourers, *domestic servants, and other employees. They do, however, give a good indication of the commercial life of a town and the names of farmers and craftsmen in a village. They are useful to family historians in recording the names and addresses of people (though the information was slightly out of date by the time of publication). This helps to refine the search in *census returns or *civil registration records. Directories may also help to date *photographs, for many photographers did not stay in business very long.

disafforestation. The process by which some of the royal *forests were sold and converted to other agricultural purposes, particularly during the reigns of James I (1603–25) and Charles I (1625–49), when the Crown was attempting to rule without revenue authorized by Parliament. This process was resisted by local people who feared the loss of common rights. See CROWN ESTATES.

disease. The impact of infectious disease on early modern society has been the subject of much scholarly work. See E. A. Wrigley and R. S. Schofield, *The Population History of England, 1541–1871: A Reconstruction* (1981), and John Walter and Roger Schofield (eds.), *Famine, Disease and the Social Order in Early Modern Society* (1989). For a detailed study of the effects of disease on an urban community see David Palliser, 'Epidemics in Tudor York', *Northern History*, 8 (1973). Paul Slack, *The Impact of Plague in Tudor and Stuart England* (1985) deals not only with the spread of disease but with attitudes and actions and social repercussions. See also POPULATION LEVELS AND

TRENDS, and articles in the journal *Local Population Studies*.

Interpreting the entries of burials in *parish registers is basic to the study of disease in the early modern period. Contemporaries often did not know the exact nature of an epidemic and used vague descriptions such as 'a sort of rambling, feverish distemper'. It is, nevertheless, sometimes possible to identify a particular disease from the pattern of recorded burials. Bubonic *plague, for instance, struck in the summer months and lay dormant during winter. The '*sweating sickness' of the late 1550s is now thought to have been a virulent form of *influenza. (See SMALLPOX; DIPHTHERIA; DYSENTERY; TYPHOID; TYPHUS; CHOLERA; TUBERCULOSIS; and MEASLES.)

Wrigley and Schofield have concluded that by the 17th century the state of the harvest rarely had dire consequences in England, and that periods of high mortality were not usually related to economic conditions. They argue that independent and unpredictable outbreaks of infectious disease were responsible for the exceptional numbers of burials that occur in parish registers. In their sample of 404 English parishes they found that local crises were overwhelmingly of short duration and that although they occurred throughout the year they were generally much more frequent in late summer and autumn, in contrast to the normal seasonality of burials which peaked in the spring. August and September were the peak months of crisis mortality in their sample of parishes. This points to diarrhoeal infections such as dysentery as the major killer. Much local research needs to be done on the lines pioneered by Wrigley and Schofield and the other members of *CAMPOP, for 404 parishes are only a small proportion of the whole. Sheffield, for instance, does not fit the crisis pattern of the majority of the 404 parishes. On the other hand, it does offer support for the suggestion that killer epidemics were isolated, summer visitations. In 1715 the Sheffield parish register recorded 104 burials in the first five months, but in June the number of deaths started to rise. During the four months from July to October 224 people were buried, of whom 185 (82.6 per cent) were children. The vulnerability of children to this particular epidemic is made clear by the burial entries for August, when only one of the 54 recorded deaths was that of an adult. No clues to the precise nature of this deadly infection were given.

The pattern of burials recorded in parish registers certainly supports the claim that infectious disease rather than *famine was responsible for the unusual numbers of deaths that occurred from time to time. See, however, A. P. Appleby, *Famine in Tudor and Stuart England* (1978). Malnutrition rather than famine may have contributed to outbreaks of dysentery and *agues. Bubonic plague disappeared after the 1660s, but most of the other killer diseases remained major health hazards throughout the 19th century and well into the 20th century. (See PUBLIC HEALTH; VACCINATION; and INOCULATION.) The local historian has much more reliable information for later periods, including government inquiries, the reports of local medical officers, and *newspapers.

dispensaries. A charitable provision in many 18th- and 19th-century towns, whereby poor people nominated by the subscribers were able to get free medical treatment.

disseisin. Forcible eviction.

dissenting academies. In the later 17th century various *Nonconformist preachers started to provide education for those who wished to enter the ministry and for the sons of members of their congregations. These academies became leading educational institutions after the Toleration Act of 1689, but gradually declined in the middle and later years of the 18th century. Thus the Attercliffe Academy, on the outskirts of Sheffield, lasted from 1686 to 1750. For a time the best academies were regarded as superior to the universities, so that they attracted some pupils whose parents conformed to the *Church of England. Famous dissenting academies included those at Hackney and Warrington, and Phillip Doddridge's academy at Northampton.

dissolution of the monasteries. By the beginning of the 16th century the number of monks and nuns was far lower than it had been 200 years previously. Many *monasteries and convents, especially the smaller establishments, had insufficient numbers to run efficiently. Conditions and standards varied widely from monastery to monastery, though they were never as lax as the propagandists for dissolution made out. Confessions of sinful conduct and incompetent management, which were made at the time of surrender, should not be taken at face value. The *Valor Ecclesiasticus* identified half the monasteries of England as having incomes of less than £200 a year, whereas 4 per cent had more than £1,000 per annum.

Henry VIII's government did not have a clear policy of wholesale destruction when it began to dissolve the smaller monasteries in 1536. It started with those institutions which had fewer than a dozen monks or nuns and an endowment of less than £200 per annum. In the first year 374 were dissolved, 90 of them in Yorkshire and Lincolnshire. (See PILGRIMAGE OF GRACE for the subsequent revolt that broke out in those counties.) The attack on the greater monasteries began with the looting of the treasures of Bury St Edmunds early in 1538. In the first nine months of that year 38 monasteries were induced to surrender. During 1539–40 Thomas Cromwell sent his commissioners to all parts of the country to enforce systematically the surrender of all the remaining houses, county by county. In the five years between 1536 and 1540 all 650 monasteries in England and Wales were dissolved. About a third of them have left no physical remains, and another third have only insubstantial ruins. The monks were dispossessed and scattered. The pensions that were given to the monks varied in value from house to house but were assessed fairly and were paid over the succeeding years. The commissioners rarely met with resistance, for the memory of the punishments handed out to the rebels after the failure of the Pilgrimage of Grace was fresh in people's minds. The last monastery to fall was Waltham Abbey (Essex) on 23 March 1540.

Once a monastery had surrendered to the commissioners it was ransacked, so that the Crown could maximize its profits from the plunder and in order to prevent reoccupation of the site by the monks. Chattels and movables were auctioned on the site. Lead roofs were stripped and building stone was carted away. Livestock and crops were confiscated and *granges converted to farms. A new ministry, known as the Court of *Augmentations, had been established at the beginning of dissolution in March 1536 in order to deal with the newly acquired spoils. Only about 2.5 per cent of the plunder was given away, and sales started almost immediately. Groups of London speculators were prominent purchasers, but they bought simply in order to resell at a profit. Lawyers, government officials, and merchants also did well, and so did the commissioners. Some of the rich landed families of later years began to accumulate their estates in this way; these included the Cavendishes, the Russells, and the Thynnes. The *aristocracy added to their possessions through purchases at bargain prices (for the market was flooded with property as Henry VIII desperately tried to finance his wars), but local studies in Devon, Lincolnshire, Norfolk, and Yorkshire have shown that local *gentry were the ones who benefited most in the long run. Those families which did not

scruple to take their share of the spoils were able to increase their property substantially, for this was the greatest transfer of land since the *Norman Conquest. Some monasteries were converted into residences for *noble and gentry families. A few monastic churches were retained as parish churches, but most were despoiled. (See also TITHES.) See Joyce Youings, *The Dissolution of the Monasteries* (1971), J. H. Bettey, *The Suppression of the Religious Houses in Bristol* (1989), and W. G. Hoskins, *The Age of Plunder: The England of Henry VIII, 1500–1547* (1976).

distilling. A science learned from the Arab world which was carried on in the Middle Ages mainly by *apothecaries, and in *monasteries and noblemen's houses, but which became a subject of considerable interest among *gentry and their wives from the 16th century onwards, as a result of the publication of many books of instruction and possibly some simplification or cheapening of the equipment required. The distillation of the oils of plants as medicines and for cooking made the 'still house' an essential room in *manor houses. Some households, like Elizabeth Freke's (see DIARIES), had hundreds of bottles in store. The domestic history of distillation awaits an author among local historians. See C. Anne Wilson, 'Burnt Wine and Cordial Waters: The Early Days of Distilling', *Folklife*, 13 (1975). The distillation of alcohol was better understood in Britain after the migration to England of *Dutch and *Flemish refugees after the 1560s. They were masters of the art, and popularized spirit drinking, at first as a medicine, then for seamen and workers in cold, wet conditions, and then as a pleasure. The Distillers' Company of London was formed in 1629. See also CIDER and WHISKY.

distraint. Originally the seizure of livestock or other possessions for a breach of *feudal dues, the term came to be used for the seizure of goods to compensate for unpaid rent.

ditches were dug for defence or, more commonly, to mark the boundary of an estate. The *dykes of the *Roman and *Anglo-Saxon periods were immense linear earthworks running for miles. Smaller ditches were dug along the *boundaries of *manors and estates, around the perimeters of *open-fields, or to separate *woods or *deer parks from cultivated land. They can sometimes be traced as landscape features or on a large-scale map with the assistance of minor place-names.

divorce. Before the *Reformation marriages could not be dissolved by formal procedures.

By the end of the 16th century all the *Protestant countries except England had divorce laws. In Scotland, by the mid-16th century, divorce was permitted on the grounds of adultery or desertion and the innocent party was allowed to remarry. In England and Wales no changes in the law of divorce were made before the *Matrimonial Causes Act (1857). This Act was never extended to Ireland. In practice, however, the ending of unsatisfactory marriages was possible through the common law and the *ecclesiastical courts and by Act of Parliament. See Lawrence Stone, *Road to Divorce: England, 1530–1987* (1990), *Uncertain Unions: Marriage in England, 1660–1753* (1992), and *Broken Lives: Separation and Divorce in England, 1660–1857* (1994). See also the *Public Record Office Records Information leaflet no. 127, 'Divorce Records in the Public Record Office', which also outlines the further legislation of 1873–1969. For the poorer classes from the 16th to the 19th century there was the option of *wife-selling, which followed customary rules in a public place. See E. P. *Thompson, 'The Sale of Wives', in *Customs in Common* (1991), ch. 7.

The Matrimonial Causes Act (1937; extended to Northern Ireland, 1939) broadened the grounds of divorce in England and Wales to include desertion and cruelty, unsoundness of mind, rape, sodomy, and bestiality. The Divorce Reform Act (1969) made the irretrievable breakdown of marriage the sole ground of divorce in Britain; this was taken to have occurred if there was adultery, unreasonable behaviour, desertion for at least two years, or if the parties had been living apart for five years. In the Republic of Ireland, however, an Act of 1937 forbade the dissolution of marriage. See David Fitzpatrick, 'Divorce and Separation in Modern Irish History', *Past and Present*, 114 (1987).

docks, dockyards. The Pool of London was by far the most important ancient centre of trade in Britain. By the late 18th century London accounted for 75 per cent of all British imports and exports. Deptford, Greenwich, and other settlements on the Thames were also the main naval centres. In the early 19th century London's docking facilities were greatly extended in the East End and the area was transformed as thousands of immigrants came to live and work there. The West India Dock, which was opened on the Isle of Dogs in 1802, was half a mile in length and accommodated up to 600 ships. It was soon followed by the London Docks on the north bank of the

Thames at Wapping, the East India Dock at Blackwall, and St Katherine Docks by the Tower, so that by 1828 London possessed by far the largest dock system in the world. Huge warehouses which enclosed the docks housed exotic goods from all over the Empire. Work for dockers was irregular and insecure, however, especially in winter time. See Gavin Weightman and Steve Humphries, *The Making of Modern London, 1815–1914* (1983).

Liverpool and Bristol began to grow in the 18th century, but the pace of development there and in Glasgow, Hull, etc. increased enormously when the *railways provided quick and cheap connections. Nearly eight miles of the Liverpool seashore were eventually fronted by docks and basins. See Peter Aughton, *Liverpool: A People's History* (1990). Maps, prospects, and *travellers' accounts, notably those of *Defoe, are useful sources for the 18th century. The construction of a dock sometimes required a private Act of Parliament; maps and plans deposited prior to an application, together with records of naval dockyards, are found in the *Public Record Office under WORK 41 to 44. Other records are kept under MT 19 (1848–63, arranged by harbour), and MT 10 (from 1864, arranged chronologically). See also MT 21, 22, and 26 for individual ports. Large redevelopment schemes for many of Britain's 19th- and early 20th-century docklands took place in the 1980s.

doctors. Early medical practitioners included *apothecaries, barber-surgeons, and physicians. See Margaret Pelling, 'Appearance and Reality: Barber-Surgeons, the Body and Disease' in A. L. Beier and Roger Finlay (eds.), *London, 1500–1700: The Making of the Metropolis* (1986), and M. Pelling and C. Webster, 'Medical Practitioners' in Charles Webster (ed.), *Health, Medicine and Mortality in the Sixteenth Century* (1979). In the 18th century medical training was still largely by apprenticeship, except for those who graduated at Edinburgh University or who had studied at Leiden. From the late 18th century onwards a number of provincial medical schools were established. In 1858 medical education came under the authority of the General Medical Council.

Dodsworth, Roger. Early 17th-century Yorkshire antiquary whose manuscripts are kept in the *Bodleian Library. His 'Yorkshire Church Notes, 1619–31' have been edited by J. W. Clay and published in the *Yorkshire Archaeological Society Record Series*, 34 (1904). His research underpins William *Dugdale's *Monasticon*, a history of the *monasteries. See ANTIQUARIAN TRADITION, THE.

dole. **1.** A donation to charity. These are often recorded on charity-boards in the towers or porches of parish *churches. Some churches retain their dole-cupboards in which bread was kept for distribution to the poor. This sense is preserved in the expression 'on the dole'.

2. A division of the common *meadows, shared out annually by rotation or by lot. The name is sometimes preserved in minor place-names and in the expression 'to dole out'.

dolmen. An old term for *Neolithic burial chambers whose stones have been exposed.

Domesday Book. In 1085 William the Conqueror, meeting with his Council at Gloucester, decided on a survey of all his new lands in England to determine who owned what both before and after the *Norman Conquest and what each of their holdings was worth. The whole of England, except Cumberland and northern Westmorland, was surveyed during 1086. The survey was organized by county, under the headings of the *tenants-in-chief of each county. The Domesday Book is the most remarkable early source in Europe, a unique portrayal of England 20 years after the Norman Conquest. It is, however, a very difficult document to interpret. It contains many pitfalls for the unwary.

The returns from each county were gathered at Winchester, where they were recorded (in abbreviated Latin) in two volumes, now housed at the *Public Record Office. The volume that contains the unabridged returns for Essex, Norfolk, and Suffolk is the most detailed; the other volume has clearly lost much of the original material through editing. The greatest loss is that the surveys of County Durham and Northumberland and of major towns, including London and Winchester, were not transcribed. Some surviving contemporary surveys, notably the *Exon Domesday, may have been preliminary work for the compilation of the Domesday Book. The name of the completed work arises from the unprecedented and comprehensive nature of the enquiry, which was compared by contemporaries with Domesday, the Last Day of Judgement. The information contained in the Domesday Book is available in several printed forms, either as a whole or as extracts published on a county basis. These include full translations for separate counties, published by Phillimore, and the entries in the general volumes of the *Victoria County History.

In many cases, the Domesday Book reference is the earliest documentary source of information about a place and the first recorded spelling of its name. In some cases the Norman clerks had difficulty in pronouncing (and thus spelling) a name. Not all places known from other sources to have been in existence by the 11th century are recorded in the Domesday folios. The purpose of the survey was to record properties, not settlements; those places which were dependencies of large *estates were therefore ignored. Some villages or *hamlets can be assumed to be silently included under another *manor. The Domesday Book is therefore a misleading guide to the extent and character of rural settlements. See, for example, Alan Everitt, *Continuity and Colonization: The Evolution of Kentish Settlement* (1986). (See also 'WASTE' IN DOMESDAY BOOK.) On the other hand, it is possible in some areas of scattered settlements to identify individual farms from entries in the Domesday Book. See W. G. Hoskins, 'The Highland Zone in Domesday Book', in *Provincial England* (1963), ch. 2, which examines some of the evidence for Devon.

The only people to be named in the Domesday Book are the tenants-in-chief and their *sub-tenants, both before and after the Conquest. The *villeins, *cottars, *bordars, freemen, *sokemen, and slaves are simply numbered. Some social groups are significantly under-recorded, so any estimates of *population based on the Domesday Book have to be treated cautiously. The Domesday Book is not an accurate guide to the early Norman landscape. The only buildings mentioned are *churches and *mills, and even those figures are minimal; a number of churches with surviving Anglo-Saxon features, or which are known from other records to have been in existence by the 11th century, are not recorded, and some places have priests but no churches mentioned. Historians are divided on the accuracy of the figures for woodland. The importance of livestock in the economy is largely ignored, for the compilers were chiefly concerned with arable land. They noted the number of plough-teams that were in use and how many were ideally necessary, but were reticent when it came to noting pasture and meadow. They therefore underplayed the importance of mixed farming in arable regions and distorted the nature of the economy in pastoral districts, as the figures from the Exon Domesday make clear. Nor were they usually concerned with crafts and industries; a number of smiths and saltworkers, etc. are recorded, but only one carpenter (in Herefordshire) was noted for the whole of England. The information about *towns was unsystematic and incomplete. It is usually difficult to assess the population of a town from the Domesday reference and impossible to ascertain the economic activities which sustained the urban economy.

The Domesday Book is nevertheless important as the earliest systematic survey of land-ownership in England. It is a description of rights, charges, customs, duties, and titles. It is clear from its pages that England was already an old country and that the Norman Conquest represented a clean break only in terms of the personnel who were the major *landowners. Despite the great difficulties of interpretation, an edifice of scholarly work has been erected since the publication of F. W. Maitland, *Domesday Book and Beyond* (1897). A great advance was made in the five regional volumes which analysed the Domesday Book geographically and presented the information in maps, edited by H. C. Darby and his collaborators between 1952 and 1967. The whole is summarized in H. C. Darby (ed.), *Domesday England* (1977), though many of the interpretations are now out of date. See R. W. Finn, *An Introduction to Domesday Book* (1963), and Edward Miller and John Hatcher, *Medieval England: Rural Society and Economic Change, 1086–1348* (1978).

Domesday of Inclosures. Most of the findings of a Commission of Inquiry, which was set up by Wolsey in 1517 to investigate the *enclosure of arable land and its conversion to pasture, were published under this title, in two volumes, by I. S. Leadham in 1897. The findings provide vivid accounts of enclosure in various parts of the country.

domestic economy. The term is used to describe the system of manufacture which was in widespread use before the *factory system was developed in the late 18th and 19th centuries. The place of work was the home, and much manufacture was combined with farming. Each member of the family had particular tasks. The term is applied particularly to the textile industries which were carried on in rural areas. The system was abandoned only gradually; for example, hand-loom *weaving survived well into the 19th century, long after the *spinning of yarn had been mechanized.

domestic servant. Entering domestic service as a young teenager and continuing in such employment until marriage was the normal expectation of girls from farming, craft, and labouring families in the early modern period, and probably had been in the Middle Ages. Most girls did not travel far, but some ventured to London or the nearest provincial city. In the later 19th and the first half of the 20th century domestic servants sometimes moved much further away, though most stayed near to home. Domestic servants were found not only in upper-and middle-class households, but on farms and in working households where help was needed in the shop or workplace; they did not simply perform household chores. The 1851 census return recorded 1 million female domestic servants; by 1901 there were 1.4 million. Although many employers still preferred country girls, an increasing proportion were urban-born. The wealthiest households had a hierarchy of servants, but the one-servant family was the most common.

doom painting. The public part of a medieval church (the *nave) was separated from the priest's part (the *chancel) by a stone arch and a wooden *rood screen which supported an image of Christ on the cross. A painting of the Last Judgement (a 'doom') often occupied the space above the arch. This depicted Christ in majesty and the weighing of the souls of the dead. Good Christians are shown ascending to heaven, sinners as descending into hell. The fine example at St Thomas's, Salisbury, shows the sinners in the mouth of the great whale or the Leviathan of the Book of Job. These dooms were painted over at the *Reformation, but over 60 have been restored.

doomsman. A juryman of a manorial *court. See HOMAGERS.

dorse. The reverse side of a sheet of paper or parchment. Any writing on that side 'endorsed' a document.

dorter. The monks' dormitory, usually on the first floor of the building on the south side of the *cloister and connected by a stair to the church. Few survived the *dissolution of the monasteries.

dovecotes. The Romans bred pigeons, but surviving dovecotes date from the 12th to the 18th century. They are built of stone, brick, or timber and are difficult to date, though most were built in periods when grain was more plentiful. Some contained more than 1,000 nesting holes. They were originally confined to the *demesne lands of manorial lords and *monasteries, but ordinary farmers broke down this monopoly in the 17th and early 18th centuries. Pigeons were valued for their meat, eggs, feathers, down, and dung. The cost of their upkeep was small, as pigeons forage for food and have a strong homing instinct. Birds mate for life and produce numerous offspring. Architectural interest in dovecotes has lately increased. See, for example, Peter Jeevar, *Dovecotes of Cambridgeshire* (1977), John Severn, *Dovecotes of Nottinghamshire* (1986), and Peter and Jean Hansell, *Doves and Dovecotes* (1989).

dowager. A widow whose title is derived from her late husband.

dower. The widow's third; that part of an estate which by common law passed to a widow on the death of her husband for the duration of her lifetime or until she remarried. This might include a residence known as a dower house. Manorial law governed a widow's claim to *copyhold estate on her husband's death but it was called *freebench. It varied, but could be much more generous than dower, allowing her a half, sometimes even the whole, of her husband's estate.

Downs. A word derived from Old English *-dun*, meaning a hill. In southern England it came to mean the chalk uplands used as sheep-pastures.

dowry. Property that a wife gave to her husband on the day of their marriage; also known as 'a marriage portion'.

dozener. A name derived from the head of the dozen or jury, applied to the *constable or other officer in some *boroughs.

drainage. Some of the *fens and *marshlands were partly drained in Roman times or in the Middle Ages. Major schemes were undertaken, particularly by Dutch and Flemish 'adventurers' in parts of eastern England during the 17th century, using new 'cuts' and wind-pumps; but it was not until the use of *steam pumping engines in the 19th century that the most difficult areas could be tackled successfully. See, for example, Michael Williams, *The Drainage of the Somerset Levels* (1970). (See also UNDERDRAINAGE of farmland.) Drainage also became a major concern of urban public health authorities in Victorian times. Efficient sewage-disposal systems were not installed until late in the 19th century.

dreng. A Scandinavian word for a well-to-do farmer. Drengs generally disappeared after the *Norman Conquest. The Yorkshire place-names Dringhoe and Dringhouses are derived from this word.

dress, regional styles of. The so-called 'traditional' costumes of Wales and the Highlands of Scotland are not as ancient as is often claimed. They are the joint invention of romantics and commercial interests in the early 19th century. Tourists and artists who visited Wales in the late 18th century did not note a national dress,

though they did observe that women in the mountains often wore large blue or red tweed cloaks and tall black hats of the type that had gone out of fashion in lowland England in the first half of the 17th century. These had survived in remote parts of Wales simply through conservatism. The cloak and tall hat were deliberately turned into a national costume for women in the 1830s by the leaders of the picturesque romantic Welsh revival. See Prys Morgan, 'From Death to a View: The Hunt for the Welsh Past in the Romantic Period' in Eric Hobsbawm and Terence Ranger (eds.), *The Invention of Tradition* (1983), ch. 3. In the same volume see ch. 2, Hugh Trevor-Roper, 'The Invention of Tradition: The Highland Tradition of Scotland', which shows that the kilt was designed by a Lancashire Quaker, Thomas Rawlinson, in the late 1720s for the Highlanders who worked at his furnace near Inverness. The kilt was an improved version of the belted plaid that had been used previously by the poorer Highlanders, though some preferred trews. At this time, *clans did not wear distinctive tartans. The idea that a certain design of tartan identified a particular group originated with the Highland regiments that were formed after the defeat of the 1745–6 rebellion. A romanticized picture of the Highlanders was gradually created by writers, notably Sir Walter Scott and Colonel David Stewart, the author of *Sketches of the Character, Manners and Present State of the Highlanders of Scotland* (1822). The publicity given to George IV's visit to Edinburgh in 1822, when he was portrayed wearing a kilt, had an enormous impact. Local businesses seized the opportunity to invent distinctive clan tartans for the occasion and to create the full Highland dress that is now regarded as traditional.

A suitable analogy is provided by the costume of Brittany. Old theories about the ancient origins of the distinctive dress that is worn on special occasions have been shown to be wrong. Instead, R. Y. Creston, *Le Costume Breton* (1974), has established beyond doubt that Breton costume, like other regional styles of dress in France, originated in fashions that were disseminated from Paris and the court, from the 17th century onwards, but particularly after the Revolution of 1789. A few older influences can be discerned, but Brittany did not possess a distinctive local costume before the Revolution. The elaborate costumes worn now at festivals were unknown; feminine costumes were completely plain and strictly utilitarian. After the Revolution peasants all over France adopted costumes imitating those of the ruling classes. Only gradually did regional styles develop from these. See *Costume*, the annual journal of the Costume Society (founded 1965).

drinking fountains. The thousands of surviving public drinking fountains in towns and villages and water troughs for livestock date from the Victorian period, when there was great concern about the quality of drinking water. Some were provided by local authorities, but many were philanthropic gifts. One at Low Bradfield (Yorkshire) is inscribed: 'In memory of Mary Ann Smith: God's gift to man'.

drovers. The droving of *cattle and *sheep is an ancient activity that goes back to prehistoric times. (See TRANSHUMANCE.) During the Middle Ages flocks of sheep and herds of cattle were driven long distances from vast monastic and manorial pastures to market. The poor, wetter pastures of the *Highland zone were adequate for the raising of young livestock, but beasts and sheep could be fattened only on the lusher pastures of the lowlands. The droving trade grew considerably during the early modern period and was at its peak from the 17th century to the railway era. Cattle were brought from Scotland and Wales to the lowland pastures of midland, southern, and eastern England. Most sheep also came from Wales. They walked along traditional routes, grazing at the roadside and in rented pastures. Other routes covered much shorter distances, linking the various *fairs and market towns. The most important droving routes became *turnpike roads, but drovers who wished to avoid the payment of tolls created an independent network, twisting around the countryside. Old drove-roads are now difficult to identify in the lowlands, but many survive as 'green roads' in highland areas. See A. R. B. Haldane, *The Drove Roads of Scotland* (1952), K. J. Bonser, *The Drovers* (1970), Arthur Raistrick, *Green Roads in the Mid-Pennines* (1978), Richard Colyer, *Roads and Trackways of Wales* (1984), F. Godwin and S. Toulson, *The Drovers' Roads of Wales* (1977), and Brian Paul Hindle, *Roads, Tracks and Their Interpretation* (1993).

The Scottish drovers began their journeys either in the far north or from the west coast and Skye. They converged on Crieff until 1770, and then on Falkirk, where the cattle were bought by English dealers and then driven hundreds of miles south. By the middle of the 18th century 80,000 cattle crossed the border every year. The Welsh drovers headed towards Shrewsbury, Leominster, Hereford, or Monmouth, and then proceeded towards London or the towns of southern and midland England. A number of Drovers' Inns mark the routes.

The documentation for the history of droving is meagre. From 1552 to 1772 drovers and *badgers were expected to be licensed at *quarter sessions (except in the six northern counties of England). A drover had to be a married householder of at least 30 years of age. Some drovers were dealers of considerable standing. See Richard Colyer, *The Welsh Cattle Drovers* (1976).

drunkenness. Richard *Gough, *The History of Myddle* (written 1701–2) is one of the few sources from the early modern period which reveals how families could be ruined by the alcoholism of the head of household. He quotes several examples of men and women who squandered their estate in the *alehouse. Drunkenness was a major social problem in the Victorian period, in both the towns and the countryside. The *temperance movement failed to prohibit the sale of alcohol and the pub remained central to working-class culture.

drystone walls. Field walls built without the use of mortar. Most are a product of the period of parliamentary *enclosure of the *commons and wastes in the 18th and 19th centuries, though walls close to villages and farmsteads may be earlier. The oldest walls use upright boulders—'orthostats'—but they are difficult to date. Field walls help to determine the character of a region, for their construction depends on the nature of the local stone. Walls are significantly broader at their base than at the top. Smaller stones are used in the higher reaches, though large 'through stones' are used for binding. In some regions the top course is laid upright and bonded by mortar. Sheep are sometimes allowed to pass through specially constructed gaps. Lowland areas favour hedgerows rather than walls.

dual economy. A term used to describe the combination of farming a smallholding (or sometimes a larger property) with another employment, e.g. *weaving, metalworking, woodworking, fishing, etc. To have a dual occupation was a common way of life in many parts of the British Isles until the *population explosion of the 18th and 19th centuries, the mechanization of industry, and the growth of towns. In the 17th century perhaps half the land in England was farmed by families who had another occupation to supplement their living. In some parts of the country, e.g. the West Riding of Yorkshire, this was the normal way of life in the countryside. The work was divided amongst members of the family and varied according to season; for example, work at a craft was abandoned during harvest. Information on how the work was divided on a daily basis is lacking. See David Hey, *The Rural Metalworkers of the Sheffield Region* (1972), and Pauline Frost, 'Yeomen and Metalsmiths: Livestock in the Dual Economy of South Staffordshire', *Agricultural History Review*, 29/1 (1981). Documentary evidence for dual occupations comes from *wills and *inventories and from descriptions of buildings in manorial *surveys. Some farmhouses retain former workshops amongst their outbuildings or rows of weavers' windows in an upper storey. The importance of dual occupations is obscured by descriptions of individuals in *parish registers, *census returns, and other lists which note only the major occupation. Many men who were described as *yeoman, *husbandman, etc. can be seen from other evidence to have been metalworkers or weavers as well. See also DOMESTIC ECONOMY and PROTO-INDUSTRIALIZATION.

ducks were fattened in Norfolk and Suffolk for sale in London during the early modern period, but not on the same scale as *geese and *turkeys. Elsewhere, they were kept only in small numbers. See DECOY.

Dugdale, William, Sir (1605–86). Warwickshire country gentleman, antiquary, and distinguished member of the College of *Arms. His *The Antiquities of Warwickshire* (1656) is one of the finest of the old county histories; it set new standards of scholarship in the interpretation of historical documents. His *Monasticon Anglicanum* (1655–73) owed much to the copious notes of Roger *Dodsworth. His other works were *The History of St Paul's Cathedral* (1658), *The History of Imbanking and Drayning of Diverse Fenns* (1662), *Origines Juridiciales* (1666), and *The Baronage of England* (1675–6). He was appointed *Garter King of Arms in 1677. See ANTIQUARIAN TRADITION, THE.

duke. A title created in England by Edward III in 1337 as the most senior rank of the peerage. The title had been used previously by the kings of England, but only for their possessions in France; thus, William the Conqueror was known as Duke of Normandy and King of England.

Durham Ox. A famously huge Shorthorn bred by Charles Colling in 1796, which was exhibited at numerous *fairs. A number of pubs were named after this amazing animal.

Dutch immigrants. The term 'Dutch' was used in England not only for the people of Holland, but also those of Flanders, Brabant, and sometimes Germany ('Deutsch'). Large numbers of immigrants from the Low Countries settled in London, Norwich, Colchester, Sandwich, and other south-eastern towns during the second half of the 16th century. Many came as religious refugees, particularly during the Duke of Alva's persecution of *Protestants in the Spanish Netherlands in 1567, but others came to practise their trades or business skills. Together with French *Huguenot immigrants they introduced the *New Draperies. They were also largely responsible for the development of *market gardening around the capital city. As well as this, they were noted potters, glass-makers, brick-makers, tailors, haberdashers, and craftsmen in leather, printing, brewing, goldsmithing, and the making of clocks and spectacles. They established a centre of tapestry-making at Mortlake in 1619. See Andrew Pettegree, ' "Thirty Years On": Progress towards Integration Amongst the Immigrant Population of Elizabethan London' in John Chartres and David Hey (eds.), *English Rural Society, 1500–1800: Essays in Honour of Joan Thirsk* (1990), ch. 12. (See also FLEMISH IMMIGRANTS and ALIENS, RETURNS OF.) Almost all the early drawings showing prospects of London were by Dutchmen; on these can be seen the 'Dutch church', the former monastery at Austin Friars which was granted to the Dutch immigrants by Edward VI in 1550. During the 17th century Dutch engineers drained large areas of eastern England. Other Dutch immigrants, notably merchants and financiers, were attracted to London upon William of Orange becoming king of England in 1689.

dyeing. Concern over the high prices of imported dyes in the 1570s and 1580s led to the Elizabethan government actively encouraging the cultivation of *woad, *madder, *saffron, and *weld for use in the textile industries. Vegetable dyes, together with those obtained from insects and lichens, remained the major sort until well into the 19th century. Mills for grinding logwood and other dyewoods were erected in east Lancashire. Manchester and the Merseyside towns became the leading centres of the production of coal-based dyes in the mid-19th century (see CHEMICAL INDUSTRY). The German contribution to the development of this industry was crucial. See C. B. Phillips and J. H. Smith, *Lancashire and Cheshire from AD 1540* (1994).

dykes. Linear earthworks dating from the *Bronze Age to the *Anglo-Saxon period, constructed as *boundaries. They are often major structures running for many miles across the countryside, notably Offa's Dyke, the 8th-century boundary between *Mercia and Wales. Folk memory has often attributed them to the Devil or to the ruler of the gods known to the *Vikings as Grim and to the *Anglo-Saxons as Woden.

Dyos, H. J. (1921–78). Professor of Urban History in the Department of Economic History at the University of Leicester, and the leading figure in the establishment of urban history as a discipline in the 1960s and 1970s. His *Victorian Suburb: A Study of the Growth of Camberwell* (1961) is an exemplary study. With M. Wolff, he edited *The Victorian City: Images and Realities*, 2 vols. (1973).

dysentery. A disease which inflames the mucous membrane and glands of the large intestine, thus causing severe pain and loss of blood. It was transmitted by impure drinking water, and malnutrition weakened resistance. Outbreaks were common amongst armies and in sieges. In the 19th century it remained a major concern of the *public health authorities, particularly in the industrial towns.

E

ealdorman. The chief royal official of a county in Anglo-Scandinavian England; cf. the post-Conquest *sheriff.

earl. Derived from Scandinavian *jarl*, earl is the oldest English title and rank. Later in the Middle Ages it was placed below the new ranks of *duke and *marquess. An earl's wife is a countess.

Earl Marshall. The officer responsible for state ceremonies. This has long been a hereditary role of the Duke of Norfolk.

Early English architecture. The earliest of the *Gothic styles, introduced into England from France in the third quarter of the 12th century for *cathedrals (e.g. Canterbury and Wells) and *abbeys (e.g. Roche, Yorkshire). The style subsequently replaced the Norman form of *Romanesque for parish *churches and remained popular throughout the 13th century. Windows designed as single lancets or as Y-tracery are the most readily identified feature of this style. By the end of the 13th century the geometric and flowing designs of *Decorated architecture had replaced the earlier, simpler patterns. The style was revived in some 19th-century churches.

East Anglia, kingdom of. The *Anglo-Saxon kingdom of East Anglia comprised most of present Norfolk and Suffolk. It was conquered by the Danes in 869 and became part of the *Danelaw. The Devil's Dyke and other linear earthworks marked its boundary in the south-west.

Easter book. A list of householders in a parish, compiled as a record of those liable to pay personal *tithes on the profits of trade, crafts, wages, and other dues to the incumbent at Easter. Such books date from the second half of the 16th century until the Tithe Commutation Act (1836). Where they survive, they can be used to estimate the total population of a parish. They are also an important source for family historians. See S. J. Wright, 'Easter Books and Parish Rate Books: A New Source for the Urban Historian', *Urban History Yearbook* (1985), and 'A Guide to Easter Books and

Related Parish Holdings', *Local Population Studies*, 42 (1988) and 43 (1989).

East India Company. Incorporated on 31 December 1600, this joint-stock company established trading stations in India and the East Indies and served as the agent of British administration there. By the later 17th century the members of the company were very wealthy. Many middle-class families prospered through membership over three or four generations. After the Indian Mutiny of 1857 the company was taken over by the Crown. See Philip Lawson, *The East India Company: A History* (1993).

The Company's archives can be consulted at the India Office Library, Orbit House, Blackfriars Bridge Road, London SE1. The records of baptism, marriage, and burial in India date from the late 17th century. From 1803 annual printed lists name all the Company's workforce. The records of the London office and of the various stations abroad complement those of the armed forces and the merchant ships in Asia.

ecclesiastical censuses. On two occasions in 1563 and 1603 the *Privy Council required bishops to make returns of the number of people in the *parishes and *chapelries of their *dioceses. These are found in the Harleian manuscripts 280, 594, 595, and 618 at the *British Library. Returns survive for 12 dioceses in England and Wales. The return of the number of householders in 1563 is an important source for assessing local and national *population totals close to the beginning of Elizabeth I's reign; a multiplier of 4.75 is commonly used, though the range, when tested alongside other evidence, can be shown to vary from 3.7 to 5.2. It has been argued that, in reality, the figures were slightly lower than this, for the population had not recovered to its normal level from the '*sweating sickness' of 1557–9. The return is nevertheless the best basis for estimating population at that time. See Alan Dyer, 'The Bishops' Census of 1563: Its Significance and Accuracy', *Local Population Studies*, 49 (1992). The returns of 1603 survive for only seven dioceses. They record numbers of communicants, Protestant dissenters, and Roman Catholics. Converting them into population totals is more difficult. The number of communicants probably inflates the number of committed Anglicans by including sporadic attenders. See D. M. Palliser and L. J. Jones, 'The Diocesan Population Returns for 1563 and 1603', *Local Population Studies*, 30 (1983). (See also COMPTON ECCLESIASTICAL CENSUS.) Other ecclesiastical censuses were taken which were peculiar to individual dioceses. See, for example, *Bishop Secker's Visitation Returns* (Oxford Record Society, xxxviii, 1957) for a census of 1738.

The only census of attendance at religious worship ever taken by the state was that for England and Wales on Sunday 30 March 1851, the same date as the *census of the entire population. The returns were collected and examined by a local census officer. They provide detailed information, parish by parish, on the places of worship of each denomination, on the number of sittings available, and the numbers attending the morning, afternoon, and evening services that were held by different denominations during that day. These returns are kept at the *Public Record Office under HO 129. Some Anglican vicars refused to complete the forms on the grounds that the state had no right to enquire into such matters. There is no indication in the returns of how many people attended more than one religious service that day, so one cannot arrive at an accurate total for the number who attended. Some people attended the service of one denomination in the morning and another in the afternoon or evening. Some returns have been printed. See R. W. Ambler (ed.), 'Lincolnshire Returns of the Census of Religious Worship, 1851', *Lincoln Record Society*, 72 (1979), Kate Tiller (ed.), *Church and Chapel in Oxfordshire, 1851: The Return of the Census of Religious Worship* (1987), and D. W. Bushby (ed.), 'Bedfordshire Ecclesiastical Census, 1851', in *Bedfordshire Historical Record Society*, 54 (1975). See also I. G. Jones and D. Williams (eds.), *The Religious Census of 1851: A Calendar of the Returns Relating to Wales*, i: *South Wales* (1976).

The problems of interpretation do not detract from the usefulness of the census in establishing the relative strengths of the various denominations. See Alan Everitt, *The Pattern of Rural Dissent: The Nineteenth Century* (1972), D. G. Hey, 'The Pattern of Nonconformity in South Yorkshire, 1660–1851', *Northern History*, 80 (1973), D. M. Thompson, 'The Religious Census of 1851' in R. Lawton (ed.), *The Census and Social Structure: An Interpretative Guide to*

Nineteenth-Century Censuses for England and Wales (1978), and K. D. M. Snell, *Church and Chapel in the North Midlands: Religious Observance in the Nineteenth Century* (1991). The consensus of opinion is that the returns were made conscientiously and that they have a fair degree of general accuracy.

The returns also note the number of children who attended Sunday School in the morning or afternoon. The foundation date of a particular meeting or of the place of worship was often recorded. Many small groups met in cottages, barns, warehouses, etc. It is clear from the returns that well over half the national population did not attend any form of religious service on that day. In some industrial cities the proportion was as little as one in ten. About half of those who did attend chose a *Nonconformist meeting. In some areas, such as the West Riding of Yorkshire, the proportion of Nonconformists was much higher.

ecclesiastical courts. During the Middle Ages the Church exercised jurisdiction over matters which were dealt with by ecclesiastical law rather than by common law. The system of ecclesiastical courts was therefore distinct from that of the civil courts. At the *Reformation ecclesiastical authorities tackled administration with a new zeal, partly under the influence of the new *dioceses that were created by Henry VIII. The highest ecclesiastical court in the land was the High Court of Delegates, beneath which sat the Court of *Arches and its northern equivalent and the *prerogative courts of Canterbury and York. Below these were the bishops' and archidiaconal courts. The records of ecclesiastical courts are a major source of information for local and family historians for the 16th, 17th, and 18th centuries. During the 19th century ecclesiastical courts withered as the state took over many of their powers (notably, in 1858, their jurisdiction over probate) and as the *Church of England no longer tried to enforce public morality or to suppress dissent in this manner.

The records of the consistory courts of bishops and archdeacons are notoriously difficult to read and interpret, because of their use of technical terms and scribbled abbreviations. The more legible ones include cause papers, which contain details of arguments and evidence in particular cases, and *Act books which summarize the procedure of a case. The number of surviving records increases from the late 16th century onwards. A particularly fruitful source for local and family historians are the depositions of witnesses in such cases. These begin with a note of the witness's name, occupation, age ('or thereabouts'), residence, etc. and sometimes an account of previous jobs and places of residence. Many cases deal with church matters such as the conduct of the minister, *plurality, the state of the church fabric and furniture, *Roman Catholicism or Protestant *Nonconformity, non-attendance at services and sacraments, the payment of dues, etc. Disputes over the non-payment of *tithes were frequently contested; amongst other matters of interest tithe cases sometimes provide information about the growing of new crops and whether these were subject to the payment of tithes. For a practical guide to the records, see Ann Tarver, *Church Court Records* (1994).

The officers of the consistory courts also saw themselves as the guardians of public morality. They became known in some places as 'bawdy courts' because they dealt with sexual misconduct and defamation. Public *penance was imposed on those guilty of adultery, fornication, slander, etc. See Martin Ingram, *Church Courts, Sex and Marriage in England, 1570–1640* (1987). Such records may be consulted at diocesan *record offices. See also COMMISSARY COURT.

ecclesiastical visitations. Bishops were supposed to visit all parts of their diocese every three years and archdeacons to visit their archdeaconries annually. Ministers and churchwardens would travel to a nearby town to answer questions about attendances at services, the state of the church as a building, the conduct of their parishioners, the names of Recusants and Nonconformists, etc. These records are available at diocesan *record offices. Some county history societies have published the detailed investigations that were made from time to time in the 18th and early 19th centuries and which give information on other topics, e.g. schools and *almshouses. For instance, the Yorkshire Archaeological Society has published Archbishop Herring's visitation returns of 1743 in its record series.

Ecclesiologist, The. Published by the *Camden Society between 1841 and 1868, this journal greatly influenced the course of church building and restoration in the Victorian period. Its pages are now an important source of information about Victorian church architecture.

Economic History Review. A quarterly journal, first issued in 1927, which contains articles and reviews on economic and social history.

Eden, Sir Frederick Morton (1766–1809). Eden's enquiry into *The State of the Poor* (3 vols., 1797) is a major source of information about the *workhouses that were set up under the Old Poor Law before the *Poor Law Amendment Act (1834). The abridged (single-volume) version of his report contains descriptions of a selection of workhouses throughout England.

education. The history of education at a local and regional level has attracted a great deal of attention, ranging from booklets on small schools to specialist articles and lengthy monographs. Much of the local research has been of an antiquarian nature. For a pioneering and stimulating general survey which relates the history of education to the political, social, and economic history of the nation at large, see W. H. G. Armytage, *Four Hundred Years of English Education* (1964).

A number of present-day schools can trace their history back to the later Middle Ages, but the connection is usually a tenuous one, for the character of the institution has altered out of all recognition, the original buildings have gone, and the site has often been changed. Opportunities for elementary education for the richer and middle classes, down to the level of the sons of the more prosperous farmers, were widespread, and the constitutions, curricula, facilities, and aims of the schools were reasonably consistent nation-wide. See, for example, H. M. Jewell, ' "The Bringing up of Children in Good Learning and Manners": A Survey of Secular Educational Provision in the North of England, *c.*1350–1550', *Northern History*, 18 (1982). Many of these medieval schools were taught by a clergyman in a *chantry within the parish church. These chantries were dissolved in the 1540s, but many parishes managed to retain the chantry funds to refound a school, usually at the edge of the churchyard or nearby. A. F. Leach, *English Schools at the Reformation, 1546–8* (1896) lists all the schools mentioned in the chantry certificates of 1546 and 1548, and derivative documents. For an overview, see Nicholas Orme, *Education and Society in Medieval and Renaissance England* (1989).

The *Victoria County History* is invaluable in tracing the history of individual schools in counties which have been covered by that enterprise, for educational provision is one of the subsections of the parish entries in the topographical volumes. For individual school histories see P. J. Wallis, *Histories of Old Schools: A Revised List for England and Wales* (1966), though many more histories have been published subsequently. The works of W. K. Jordan, *Philanthropy in England, 1480–1660* (1959), *The Charities of London, 1480–1660* (1960), and *The Charities of Rural England, 1480–1660* (1961), together with Joan Simon, *Education and Society in Tudor England* (1966), laid the foundations for the intensive local and regional work on late medieval and early modern schools, which has considerably revised the conclusions of earlier authors. Much of this research has been published in the journals of local historical societies and of the History of Education Society.

A number of schools retain a Tudor or Stuart building that was erected by the munificence of a local lord, or perhaps a local man who had made his fortune in London and who remembered his place of birth when he came to make his will. Such buildings were constructed in the *vernacular style of the region and were commonly adorned with the *coat of arms of the founder and with an inscription. See Malcolm Seaborne, *The English School: Its Architecture and Organization, 1370–1870* (1971). During the 16th and 17th centuries England became a semi-literate society, where even some of the humblest members were able to read. A school was available within walking distance for most of the boys and some of the girls whose parents had the means and the desire to seek such opportunities. Intensive research in many parts of England has located references to schools of various types, or at least to schoolmasters who were licensed by the *Church of England to ensure conformity with Anglican beliefs. It is clear from this work that an expansion in educational provision began in Elizabethan times, though in many regions it did not reach its peak until after the *Restoration. In Cambridgeshire, for instance, one-fifth of the villages, mainly the larger ones, and the minor market towns, had masters licensed continuously from 1570 to 1620. In Cheshire, 132 places had masters at some point between 1547 and 1700. Proving continuity of educational provision is an elusive task, but in all parts of England where a thorough search has been made, a large number of masters have been found. Many of these men no doubt taught in unendowed village schools rather than grammar schools, but it was possible for a boy to progress from one school to another and sometimes to go on to university, provided his parents had the means to support him. See David Cressy, *Literacy and the Social Order: Reading and Writing in Tudor and Stuart England* (1980), Margaret Spufford, *Small Books and Pleasant Histories: Popular Fiction and Its Reader-*

ship in Seventeenth-Century England (1981), ch. 2, and Rosemary O'Day, *Education and Society, 1500–1800: The Social Foundations of Education in Early Modern England* (1982).

In Wales, too, the provision of grammar and other schools was generous in the second half of the 16th and the 17th centuries. See Malcolm Seaborne, *Schools in Wales, 1500–1900: A Social and Architectural History* (1992). Meanwhile, Scotland had its parish and *burgh schools. See James Grant, *History of the Burgh Schools in Scotland* (1876). The minutes of burghs or town councils record the appointment of schoolmasters. In rural districts masters were nominated by the *heritors (landowners) and the minister of the parish, and were then examined by the presbytery. See the Heritors' Records and the records of the parish and the presbytery, class CH 2 in the *Scottish Record Office. Ireland was much less well-endowed with schools.

During the early modern period the status of schoolmasters was low compared to that of other professions. Many of them taught no more than reading and writing and simple accounts, but in the grammar schools the emphasis of the teaching was on the classics and the Latin language. Those boys who wished to pursue a legal career went on to the *Inns of Court. The earliest admission books of the various Inns of Court have been published: see, for instance, R. J. Fletcher, *The Pension Book of Gray's Inn, 1669–1800* (1910). The main role of the universities was to qualify young men for the church ministry, but they also attracted the sons of the *aristocracy and *gentry who did not have that vocation in mind. Oxford had become a university gradually during the early 12th century. The university at Cambridge began in the early 13th century but did not seriously rival Oxford for another 200 years. See Christopher Brooke and Roger Highfield, *Oxford and Cambridge* (1988) and the bibliography therein. J. Foster, *Alumni Oxonienses, 1715–1886*, 4 vols. (1888), and J. and J. A. Venn, *Alumni: Alumni Cantabrigienses*, 2 parts (to 1751, 1752–1900), 4 and 6 vols. (1922–54), list the students of those periods. The next four British universities were all founded in Scotland: at St Andrews (1410), Glasgow (1451), Aberdeen (1494), and Edinburgh (1582); these were followed by Trinity College, Dublin (1591). From its foundation in 1571, Jesus College, Oxford was the main institution of higher education for Welsh students.

The names of the earliest alumni of the Scottish universities are published in: P. J.

Anderson and J. F. K. Johnstone, *Fasti Acade-miae Mariscallanae Aberdonensis, 1593–1860*, 3 vols. (1889–98), P. J. Anderson, *Officers and Graduates of University and King's College, Aberdeen, 1495–1860* (1893), W. I. Addison, *A Roll of the Graduates of the University of Glasgow from 1727 to 1897* (1898), J. M. Anderson, *Early Records of the University of St Andrews: The Graduate Roll, 1413–1579 and the Matriculation Roll, 1473–1579* (1926), and J. M. Anderson, *The Matriculation Roll of the University of St Andrews, 1747–1897* (1905). The only other British universities that were founded before the civic universities of the late 19th and early 20th centuries were London (1826) and Durham (1837). During the late 17th and the 18th centuries, however, a broader education (including science) was available at some of the *dissenting academies, notably those at Northampton and Warrington. Many students went on from these academies to Scottish or Continental universities, especially Leiden.

Concern over the lack of educational provision for the children of the poor led to the formation of charity schools. See M. G. Jones, *The Charity School Movement* (1938). The *Society for the Promotion of Christian Knowledge, founded in 1698, was the first national body in England to build and manage elementary schools for children aged 7 to 11 or over. In its first 35 years it helped form, or re-form, over 1,500 schools. The society erected 96 schools in Wales before 1740, of which 79 were founded between 1705 and 1718, mostly in the four counties of the South Wales coast. Although it began as an interdenominational body, the SPCK soon became specifically Anglican. Its schools provided a basic education for thousands of children, including girls. The printed reports of the SPCK, 1705–32, list the schools that were connected with the society; the manuscript records of the society include correspondence, minutes, etc. Much evidence relating to charity schools is to be found in local *record offices, and it is worth looking at *wills for generous bequests at this time to set up village schools, e.g. Lady Joanna Thornhill of Wye (Kent), leaving in 1708 part of her estate for the education of poor children, and so being responsible for a school which had 100 boys and girls c.1780. In Scotland the Scottish Society for the Promotion of Christian Knowledge erected and maintained schools in the remotest parts of the Highlands and Islands, where 'popery and ignorance' did 'much abound'. Their records are housed under GD. 95 at the Scottish Record Office. Meanwhile, in Ireland 'Charter schools' were established from 1731 to teach the rudiments of the English language, with a similar concern to combat 'popery'.

Sunday schools were started by Robert Raikes in Gloucester in 1785. The movement spread rapidly amongst Anglicans and *Nonconformists alike, and by 1795 Sunday schools were providing a basic education for three-quarters of a million children. By 1851 Sunday schools had nearly 2.5 million pupils, that is nearly two-thirds of the 5 to 14 age range; at their peak in 1906 they had over 6 million pupils, more than 80 per cent of the age range. Unfortunately, few Sunday schools have left adequate records. In both charity and Sunday schools monitors were employed to cope with the large numbers of pupils. The system began as an expedient, but was soon thought of as a virtue; the great increase in the child population could be dealt with only by mass instruction. Credit for starting the monitorial system is divided between Dr Andrew Bell, an Anglican chaplain to the Indian Army who publicized his method in 1797, and Joseph Lancaster, who began on similar lines in 1801 in Borough Road, London. Lancaster was sponsored by two *Quakers who formed a society in 1808 which was renamed the British and Foreign Schools Society six years later. The Anglican response was almost immediate. In 1810 the SPCK reported that two-thirds of the children of the poor had no schooling at all. In the following year members of the SPCK formed the National Society for the Education of the Poor in the Principles of the Established Church throughout England and Wales; this society was incorporated in 1817. The National Society took over the 230 schools and 40,000 pupils of the SPCK and, after 1845, issued its own books and school material. Its archives are kept at Church House, Dean's Yard, London. The two societies competed to build schools, especially in the manufacturing towns, but the National schools had a head start. From 1833 the efforts of the two societies were supported by government grants, for at this time the state did not provide schools of its own; but this first venture of the state into the provision of education made religious control of schools a matter of great controversy throughout Britain for the rest of the century. From 1839 the state appointed school inspectors to advise and to spread good practices. The 'Revised Code' of 1862 introduced 'payment by results', by which the size of the annual grant depended on inspectors' reports. The need to train monitors also forced the two societies to launch a programme of teacher training. From 1846 certain schools became training centres for pupil teachers, selected at the age of 13. In this way a new career path was opened to thousands of young women as well as men.

Other schools of this period include the Ragged Schools (charitable foundations which provided a basic education and industrial training for the urban poor), schools run by the *Poor Law guardians after the passing of the Poor Law Amendment Act (1834), and schools which *factory and colliery owners were obliged to keep (after the Acts of 1833 and 1842) in order to provide two hours of schooling six days a week for their child workers aged 9 to 13. The numerous private schools were often ephemeral, many of them dismissed contemptuously as 'dame schools', for they were little more than child-minding establishments, though the more successful ones were listed as 'private academies' in trade and commercial *directories. The emergence of a sizeable middle class created a demand for superior private schools, especially for girls. The churches were active in promoting both day proprietary schools and proprietary boarding schools. Standards were improved immeasurably by such headmasters as Thomas Arnold of Rugby (1828–42), with an emphasis on 'muscular Christianity'. The coming of the *railways enabled the better 'public schools' to attract boarders over long distances. Much information on the nine big public schools is contained in the report of the Clarendon Commission, which met from 1861 to 1864, and which published its findings as a *parliamentary paper.

Meanwhile, adult members of the working classes tried self-improvement with *mechanics' institutes and various colleges, institutes, and Owenite halls of science. The first mechanics' institute was founded at Chester in 1810, followed by that at Perth in 1814 and by a surge of interest in 1823 with foundations at Glasgow, Kilmarnock, Greenock, Liverpool, and Sheffield. By 1826 there were over 104 others. The movement was particularly important in the industrial areas of the West Riding and Lancashire, which together contained 27 per cent of all the British institutes. These mechanics' institutes formed the first important national movement in adult education, a term which in the 19th century included elementary education for those who had had little or no opportunity to study as children. They were the forerunners of the University extension movement (from 1867 onwards) and the Workers' Educational Association (founded in 1903). At the same time in towns throughout Britain the middle classes formed musical, scientific, philosophical, and literary societies, and circulating libraries and book clubs.

Despite all this activity, educational provision was unable to keep pace with *population growth. For example, in 1840 an official enquiry estimated that two-thirds of Sheffield's working-class population were growing up in ignorance, that only one-third were able to read 'fairly', and that not more than 50 per cent attended school regularly. The burgeoning industrial towns posed unique problems; elsewhere, the situation was more promising. In 1843 it was estimated that two-thirds of the national male population and nearly 50 per cent of females were basically literate.

At a local level, much information about 19th-century schools can be gleaned from *newspapers, including advertisements, parish magazines, and local reports. A great deal of local information is tucked away in various national journals, periodicals, parliamentary papers, and annual reports, e.g. those of the two voluntary societies, the National and the British and Foreign. A thorough search of all these can be very rewarding. Among the parliamentary papers are the volumes of the *Reports of the Charity Commissioners* (1819–40), which contain information on charity schools. Later investigations into charities (1896–1907) add to this information for certain places.

Parliamentary papers are a fruitful source of information for the history of elementary education in every part of Britain throughout the 19th century. Places can readily be identified in the various indexes, including those of reports concerned with industry. Some large towns had their own special enquiries. The relevant reports start with the *Abstract of the Answers and Returns Relative to the Poor* (1803–4), which notes the number of children in schools of industry in each parish and gives information on the state of parochial schools. A *Digest of Parochial Returns* (1819) includes statements of the educational provision of every parish in England, Scotland, and Wales. Further official surveys in the 1830s produced indexed volumes of evidence and an *Abstract of Education Returns: 1833*. A survey of 1851 provides a detailed analysis of numbers and types of schools, the attendance and age of pupils, the capacity and religious affiliation of schools, etc. arranged by registration districts of Poor Law unions.

National reports on the grammar schools start with Nicholas Carlisle, *Concise Description of the Endowed Grammar Schools in England and Wales*, 2 vols. (1818), which includes replies from correspondents to his 18 questions. The

Reports of the Charity Commissioners of the earlier 19th century, often known as the reports of the Brougham Commission, were published from 1819 in 32 volumes. The *Reports of the Schools Inquiry Commission* (the Taunton Commission, 1868-9) and the *Reports of the Royal Commission on Secondary Education* (Bryce Commission, 1895) are a major source of information on the grammar and other secondary schools of the period. See John Roach, *A History of Secondary Education in England, 1800-1870* (1986).

The Newcastle Commission (1857) surveyed elementary schools in Great Britain and abroad. After three years one of its recommendations was the need for 'a searching examination by competent authority of every child in every school to which grants are to be paid'. Two other general surveys are in print for 1846-7 and 1866-7, but only on a county rather than a parish basis. A survey of Roman Catholic voluntary schools returned in 1845 was published as an appendix to the *Report of the Catholic Poor School Committee* for 1849. Parliamentary papers also include three later surveys: for 1871, 1893, and 1899. These and other reports are listed in W. B. Stephens, *Sources for English Local History* (3rd edn., 1994), ch. 7. For Scotland, two volumes of reports to the Department of Education by school inspectors for the years 1859 and 1866-7 are kept at the Scottish Record Office under ED. 16/13 and 14. Only a selection of schools were visited, and these are indexed. See also James Craigie, *A Bibliography of Scottish Education Before 1872* (1970).

The voluntary societies had expanded rapidly since the 1840s, so that by the 1860s they had 1.5 million pupils on roll, with a normal attendance of *c*.900,000 in nearly 7,000 schools. But they could not keep pace with population growth, and half the children of Britain did not attend day-school. It was clear that the state had to intervene. The Education Act of 1870, followed two years later by a similar one for Scotland, brought the state firmly into the educational arena by providing for the election of school boards with power to build and manage schools where the provision by the two voluntary bodies was inadequate. This threat stimulated the Anglican squires of many a village to improve the educational opportunities of the poor by building or rebuilding a National school before the local board could take responsibility. In the largest cities splendid Victorian Gothic board schools were erected to cater for over 1,000 pupils each; in these cities and in many a smaller settlement the board

school remains in use to this day. Equally importantly, all schools were subject to government inspection to ensure adequate standards, and once schools were provided attendance was made compulsory. In 1880 all children were compelled to attend school up to the age of 10. The leaving age was raised to 11 in 1893 and to 12 (except for those employed in agriculture) in 1899. Fees for poor children were paid by the boards from 1876 until all fees were abolished in 1891. As with all Acts, there was a time-lag between what was intended and what happened, but the establishment of board schools had a revolutionary effect on elementary education.

From the beginning of the 19th century the bulk of elementary teaching was undertaken by children under a certificated head teacher, few of whom were college-trained. Most heads were ex-pupil teachers who had secured a certificate through part-time study. The minimum age for apprenticeship as a pupil teacher was not raised to 14 until 1877, and the system lasted until 1906. The adult assistants employed by the board schools were outnumbered by pupil teachers. A parliamentary paper of 1897, *Return of the Pupils in Public and Private Secondary and Other Schools in England*, provides a great deal of information on the numbers of schools and pupils, on the ages of pupils, and on the qualifications of teachers.

Board school records are kept at county or county borough *record offices, together with whatever records have survived at individual schools. The school log-books which were first kept in the 1840s contain much miscellaneous information. Admission registers from 1870 onwards name the child and give the date of admission, the father's name and address (and sometimes the mother's name), the child's date of birth, the name of his or her previous school, and the date of leaving. Some registers also record when a child left school and the destination. School photographs and leaving certificates (from 1908) are more likely to survive in individual family collections. The *Public Record Office has copious records of schools from 1870 onwards. See the *List and Index Society volumes 21, 48, 55, 71, 78, 94, 102, and 111, and the classes of files on individual schools, numbered Ed. 144 onwards, listed in Philip Riden, *Record Sources for Local History* (1987), ch. 5. The PRO also has 6,700 files on endowed schools, which were revitalized under the Endowed Schools Act of 1869. These are kept under Ed. 27 and cover the period 1850-1903. See also the *Reports of the Endowed School Commissioners* for 1872 and 1875, etc.

The late 19th century saw a decline in the number of voluntary schools, which were unable to compete with the board schools, but which nevertheless remained a vital part of educational provision. Some of the best schools became higher-grade elementary schools, which were in fact public secondary schools. The Technical Instruction Act (1889) allowed the newly established county and county borough councils to provide a variety of teaching, from elementary work to post-school training for trades and crafts. See John Roach, *Secondary Education in England, 1870–1902* (1991).

The educational system was completely reorganized in 1902 when responsibility for providing elementary, secondary, and technical education was given to 330 local education authorities (LEAs) under a central Board of Education. The Elementary School Code of 1904 provided the rationale of the educational system until the 1960s. The 'board' schools became 'council' schools, and a new emphasis was placed on extending provision for secondary education. From 1906 the LEAs provided school meals, and from 1907 a school medical service. In 1918 the school-leaving age was raised to 14. The annual reports of the Education Committees of the LEAs provide much detailed information about the building of new schools, the struggle to reduce class sizes and enforce attendance, and plans to provide special schools for handicapped children.

A great deal of statistical information is available for the 20th century in the form of parliamentary papers and Board of Education records. See P. H. and J. H. Gibson, 'Twentieth-Century Archives of Education as Sources for the Study of Education Policy and Administration', and G. Sutherland, 'A View of Education Records in the Nineteenth and Twentieth Centuries', both in *Archives*, 15 (1981–2). See also James Craigie, *A Bibliography of Scottish Education, 1872–1972* (1974).

Further reorganization took place after the passing of the Education Act (1944), which replaced the Board with a Ministry of Education and established a tripartite system of secondary education: grammar, technical, and secondary modern. The school-leaving age was raised to 15 in 1947 and to 16 in 1965. Lack of resources after the Second World War meant that all-age schools, catering for those aged from 5 to 15 who were not 'selected' for grammar or technical schools, were not phased out until the mid-1960s, by which time comprehensive schools, which took all children of secondary age, were becoming common. In 1965 the comprehensive system was adopted as official national policy.

Under the Education Act (1944) LEAs were also given responsibility for further education. They took over existing provision, which in some cases dated back to the 19th century, and built further education colleges which specialized in technology, commerce, and art. They also assumed responsibility for teacher training colleges. From this background emerged the first polytechnics in 1969, which played a significant part in the expansion of higher education. The polytechnics achieved university status in 1992. Meanwhile, the university system had been expanded by enlarging the older universities and creating several new ones. The Open University, which provides long-distance education for people studying at home, awarded its first degrees in 1973. By the last quarter of the 20th century the number of people in higher education was far higher than it had been two decades earlier.

Ekwall, Eilert. Once the leading figure in the study of *place-names, his *The Concise Oxford Dictionary of English Place-Names* (1936; 4th edn. 1960) has been superseded by later reinterpretation. His other works include *The Place-Names of Lancashire* (1928), *Street Names of the City of London* (1954), and *English River Names* (1960).

Eleanor crosses. Memorial crosses erected at resting places along the route by which the body of Queen Eleanor, wife of Edward I, was brought from Nottinghamshire for burial at Westminster in 1290. Three of the 11 crosses survive, at Geddington and Hardingstone (Northamptonshire) and Waltham Cross (Essex). Charing Cross, London, is named after a former Eleanor cross.

electoral register. The Parliamentary Reform Act of 1832 required the publication on a *parish basis of lists of persons eligible to vote. As the franchise has been gradually extended, so the lists have become more comprehensive. Since 1928 (when the age that women were allowed to vote was lowered to 21) they list the names and addresses of all adults who have registered. Copies may be seen at county and borough *record offices and public libraries. They are an important 20th-century source for family historians.

electricity. Michael Faraday's publications led to the use of electrical lighting in lighthouses and street lamps in the 1860s and 1870s. In 1880 Sir William Armstrong, the Tyneside armaments manufacturer, made his home at

Cragside (Northumberland) the first house in the world to be lit by hydro-electric power, using the light bulbs patented by another Newcastle man, Joseph Swan. The first municipal power station was built at Bradford (Yorkshire) in 1889. Electric lighting in the home or at work did not become widely used until the 1930s. See L. Hannah, *Electricity before Nationalisation: A Study of the Development of the Electricity Supply Industry in Britain* (1979).

emigration. Small numbers of people left the British Isles to settle in the Low Countries and other parts of the Continent during the Middle Ages and later, but it was not until the early 17th century that emigration became significant. The principal destination at first was *Ulster, but from the 1630s the *plantations in *America and the *West Indies became increasingly favoured. No firm figures are available, but it is estimated that about 540,000 people left England between 1630 and 1700, of whom roughly 380,000 went to the New World. (See VIRGINIA and PLYMOUTH COLONY.) Many went to Virginia as indentured servants, and between 1615 and 1775 more than 30,000 were *transported as convicts. See P. W. Coldham, *The Complete Book of Emigrants in Bondage, 1614-1775* (1987).

Emigrants from Britain formed only a small proportion of the population before the 19th century. Former estimates that 60 million people left Europe between the end of the *Napoleonic wars in 1815 and the Wall Street Crash of 1929 are now considered to be too high, but the scale of emigration in that period was nevertheless totally different from before. About 10 million people left Britain on a permanent basis; see Dudley Baines, *Emigration From Europe, 1815-1930* (1991) and Nicholas Canny (ed.), *Europeans on the Move: Studies on European Migration, 1500-1800* (1994) for the European context. The number of emigrants is uncertain because of deficiencies in the records, but as the population of the United States of America rose from about 4 million in 1790 to 23 million in 1850, the figure is clearly huge. In the early 19th century most emigrants to America came from Britain and Ireland. They came from every occupation and social class. The volume and the rate of emigration from Europe rose until the First World War and continued at a lower rate in the 1920s, but collapsed in the international depression of the 1930s. (See also CANADA; AUSTRALIA; NEW ZEALAND; and SOUTH AFRICA.)

*Passenger lists are the most useful source for tracing individual emigrants. In some cases these lists give the age, occupation, and marital condition of emigrants, and the name of the community they have just left. Most of the lists of immigrants to the United States have survived and some have been analysed. See Charlotte Erickson, 'Emigration to the USA from the British Isles, part I: Emigration from British Isles; part II: Who Were the English Emigrants?', *Population Studies*, 43 (1989) and 44 (1990), and Charlotte Erickson, *Emigration from Europe, 1815-1914: Select Documents* (1976).

Estimating the scale of emigration is complicated by the fact that large numbers eventually returned home. Some were failures, but most never intended to settle overseas on a permanent basis. The best estimate is that more than a quarter of all emigrants from Europe eventually returned. The earliest emigrants were the most likely to stay, if only because of the rigours of the voyage. The Irish who left in the wake of the *famine of 1846-8 also stayed. On the other hand, nearly 40 per cent of the English and Welsh who emigrated between 1861 and 1913 did not settle permanently. Most migrants expected to return once they had made sufficient money. In the earlier part of the 19th century the typical emigrants were a young family. By the later 19th century, however, typical emigrants were young single adults, males outnumbering females by two to one (except the Irish). Most of the earlier emigrants (again, with the exception of the Irish) worked on the land, but later ones were more likely to enter urban and industrial occupations and to return home. This change in attitude was brought about largely because of the reduction in cost and sailing-time of the voyage, with the advent of steamships on the North Atlantic route in the 1860s, linked at both ends of the journey by *railways. The cheapest individual fare from Liverpool to New York before steamships reduced costs was about a month's income for a skilled worker and two months' income for an unskilled worker (plus no income during the voyage). The creation of shipping lines that catered for the emigrant trade, with regular timetabled departures, greatly facilitated the emigration process.

The great majority of emigrants paid their own fares. Perhaps a quarter were helped by friends or relatives and another 10 per cent received official assistance. Between 1846 and 1869 some 339,000 emigrants from Britain and Ireland were aided by government schemes, but this was only 7 per cent of emigrants at the time. See K. A. Miller, *Emigrants and Exiles: Ireland and the Irish Exodus to North America*

(1985), Donald Whyte, 'Scottish Emigration: A Select Bibliography', *Scottish Genealogist*, 21 (1974), the *Public Record Office Records Information leaflet no. 71, 'Emigrants: Documents in the Public Record Office', and the survey in David Hey, *The Oxford Guide to Family History* (1993).

enclosure, parliamentary. Parliamentary enclosure was the last stage of a process that was centuries old. It occurred where an agreement to enclose by all the owners of land in a *parish or *township could not be obtained; a hostile minority could be overruled by a private or public Act of Parliament. The first Act was that for Radipole (Dorset) in 1604, but it was well into the 18th century before this method became common and not until after 1750 that it became dominant. Over 85 per cent of parliamentary enclosure was completed or on the statute book by 1830; the rest was finished within the next 40 years, except for Elmstone Hardwicke (Gloucestershire), which was not enclosed until 1914. In all, 5,341 awards were made for England and 229 for Wales. These were of two types: those which dealt with both *open-fields and common pastures, and those which were concerned only with *commons and wastes. In Scotland, most enclosure was enacted under legislation that predated the Union with England in 1707 (even though the timing of enclosure was much later).

The impact of enclosure was first quantified by G. Slater, *The English Peasantry and the Enclosure of Common Fields* (1907) and E. C. K. Gonner, *Common Land and Inclosure* (1912). The discussion of the impact of parliamentary enclosure has been placed on a much firmer statistical basis during the last quarter of the 20th century. See Michael Turner, *Enclosures in Britain, 1750–1830* (1984). The same author's edition of W. E. Tate, *A Domesday of English Enclosure Acts and Awards* (1978) and John Chapman, *A Guide to Parliamentary Enclosures in Wales* (1992) provide details of all the parliamentary awards for England and Wales.

The sponsors of individual Acts of parliamentary enclosure are named in the petition and bill, and in the subsequent Act and award. The progress of the bill through Parliament can be followed in the journals of the *House of Commons and *House of Lords. The size of any opposition was noted at the Report Stage in both Houses. It was accepted that if the bill had the support of the owners of 75–80 per cent of the land then it could proceed. (These owners did not necessarily form a numerical majority of all the landowners in the parish or township.)

The Act named the commissioners and surveyors, who proceeded to survey the land, consider claims, and award allotments in proportion to the size of the common rights of the property owners. (See ENCLOSURE AWARDS AND MAPS, and ENCLOSURE ROADS.) General Enclosure Acts of 1836, 1840, and 1845 eased the procedure, though it was still necessary to obtain a separate Act.

In England and Wales 38 per cent of all Acts were passed in the first main period of activity between 1755 and 1780. During the 1770s 321 Acts were passed, reaching a peak of 92 in the year 1777. These early Acts were concerned mainly with the heavy soils of the midland clay belts in Northamptonshire, Warwickshire, Leicestershire, and adjoining parts, together with the lighter clays of much of Lincolnshire and the East Riding. A second wave of activity from the 1790s to the mid-1830s was at its height during the French Revolutionary and *Napoleonic wars, when grain prices were high and farming prosperous. Indeed, the war years accounted for 43 per cent of all parliamentary enclosures. During this time, the rest of the heavier soils, together with the lighter soils of East Anglia, Lincolnshire, and the East Riding and the marginal soils of the Pennine uplands, the Lake District, and the *heaths of Surrey, Berkshire, and Middlesex were enclosed by stone walls or hawthorn hedges. The Welsh uplands were enclosed a little later, half of them after 1840, though local and regional variations in chronology are marked. Wales had long had a tradition of enclosing by agreement, and although common grazing was now abolished, the effects of parliamentary enclosure on what had always been a pastoral farming system were less pronounced than in the open-field areas of England. Chapman concludes that 525,880 acres were enclosed in Wales by the 229 acts of Parliament.

The area of open-field arable that was enclosed by Acts of Parliament measured almost double the area covered by commons and wastes. The enclosure of arable land allowed owners to exchange and consolidate their scattered strips in order to create square or rectangular fields of manageable size within separate ring-fence farms. The abolition of communal rights and obligations, especially the regulations that allowed all commoners to graze their cattle and sheep together over arable land after harvest, enabled farmers to choose their own courses of cropping and to sow, harvest, or leave their land fallow as they wished. Much of the heavier soils were converted to pasture. On light soils the *fallow was abolished. As for the unimproved commons and wastes above 800 feet, which were enclosed during and after the Napoleonic wars, much was left for rough grazing or for *grouse shooting; but wherever practicable the rest was converted into pastures and hill-meadows, or brought into temporary cultivation.

In Scotland enclosure brought about a rapid and major transformation of the agricultural economy. Enclosures of any type had hardly been known before the late 17th century. At first, they were on a small scale (rarely more than 250 to 350 acres) and were associated with the desire to fix boundaries around country houses; they had little economic or social impact on the tenantry. Two Acts of 1695 facilitated the legal process through the Court of *Session. Over 650,000 acres were enclosed between 1720 and 1850, a much smaller area than in England. Scottish enclosures replaced the *infield / outfield system by regular-shaped fields and obliterated *runrig. The main period of activity in the lowlands was in the 1760s and 1770s and in the uplands at the end of the 18th century.

The richer farmers of England and Wales did well out of parliamentary enclosure, but there were wider benefits to the nation in that agricultural productivity increased. The economic and social effects on smallholders and *cottagers are hotly debated. See AGRICULTURAL HISTORY.

enclosure, private and piecemeal. 'Enclosure' was a general term which differed in its impact according to time and place. The enclosure of land in the *open-fields in the midlands aroused strong opposition, culminating in the Midland Revolt of 1607, but elsewhere enclosure could be carried out amicably and by agreement, with none of the evil social consequences so evident in Leicestershire and Warwickshire and adjacent counties. When *commons and open-fields were enclosed by a hedge, fence, or wall, common rights over them were extinguished. A typical prelude to enclosure was the amalgamation of a holding by the exchange or purchase of *strips. In some parishes all the land came under the ownership of a single individual or a small group of farmers. In such cases enclosure by agreement was easy; hedges or walls were simply planted around blocks of strips, following their ancient curving patterns. Numerous examples of such walls survive in the limestone part of the Peak District, where they form a sharp contrast with the rectangular fields of parliamentary enclosure. The agreements that were drawn up often do

not survive, but some can be found amongst parish records, *estate papers, and solicitors' collections in local *record offices. An alternative method was to contest a fictitious suit in the Court of *Chancery, so that a binding legal judgement resulted. See M. W. Beresford, 'The Decree Rolls of Chancery as a Source for Economic History, 1547–c.1700', *Economic History Review*, 2nd ser., 32/1 (1979).

The piecemeal enclosure of the wastes by *assarting had proceeded in fits and starts during the Middle Ages. *Manors with large commons and wastes continued to allow small enclosures in this way up to the time of parliamentary enclosure. Thus, in the huge manor of Wakefield, which stretched on to the Pennines, the graveship of Holme had 14,280 acres of commons and wastes in 1709 but only 9,200 acres at the time of the *enclosure award of 1834. Such enclosures were allowed because they brought in extra rent to the lord and sufficient common grazing survived. They did not arouse opposition because nobody's interests were harmed. Those parts of Britain which had plenty of moorland, woodland, or marshland had little cause for concern. Pastoral farming took precedence over cereals in these parts. Relatively little land was farmed in open-fields, and enclosure was agreed readily when it became possible to buy in sufficient corn for local needs at market. By the 16th century the open-fields of the counties of Cornwall, Devon, Somerset, Worcestershire, Herefordshire, Shropshire, Kent, Essex, Suffolk, and Hertfordshire had been either completely or largely enclosed.

In those parts of England where commons were much smaller and the farming was organized communally in large open-fields the implications of enclosure were very different. The growth of *population in the 16th century created new tensions, not only between neighbouring *townships which shared a common, but within townships between the occupiers of ancient holdings and new enclosures, especially if the newcomers were poor *cottagers. Smallholders who were dependent upon their rights on the *commons in order to make ends meet became anxious about the increased demands on grazing land. The farmers of the populous open-field parishes of the midland counties found themselves in a particularly critical situation, in which the private benefits of any act of enclosure were bound to hurt someone else. When the consolidation of strips and a withdrawal from communal husbandry in the open-fields went hand-in-hand with piecemeal enclosure of the wastes the farming routine of the whole township was disrupted. However, Robert C. Allen, *Enclosure and the Yeoman: The Agricultural Development of the South Midlands, 1450–1850* (1992) has argued that early enclosure, particularly that of open-fields in the 17th century, brought great gains in productivity, and that this achievement contrasts with the social losses sustained by later parliamentary enclosure.

Rising prices for meat tempted farmers to convert arable land into pasture. Although this conversion could be achieved by using strips as temporary grass *leys, the freedom to farm as one pleased in enclosed fields without the restrictions of communal decisions led many individuals to press for enclosure. Powerful landowners could force weaker neighbours into submission, even forcing them off the land. Many *deserted medieval villages were created in the late 15th and early 16th centuries, when it was said that 'sheep ate men'; and other settlements were fatally weakened, shrinking and sometimes disappearing generations later. By the early 16th century the central government was taking the problem seriously. In 1517 Cardinal Wolsey set up a royal commission to enquire into how many houses had been demolished, how much land had been converted from arable to pasture, and how many *parks had been enclosed since Michaelmas 1488. See I. S. Leadham (ed.), *The *Domesday of Inclosures, 1517–1518* (1897). The enquiry did not reveal the full extent of enclosure. Further commissions reported in 1545, 1566, and 1607. This last enquiry was prompted by the widespread violent resistance to enclosure in Leicestershire, Warwickshire, Northamptonshire, and Bedfordshire. Although acreages affected by enclosure were recorded precisely, it is clear that much was missed by the commissioners, who recorded hardly any enclosure by agreement, and reported only that which was contentious.

Pamphleteers who advocated the benefits of enclosure stressed that increased yields and thus higher rents would ensue. Henry *Best in the early 17th century believed that enclosed lands were worth three times as much as lands farmed in open-fields. However, the initial costs, e.g. fencing, were high. Enclosure was attractive only when livestock prices were high and a quick return seemed likely. In Leicestershire about half the total area of the county was enclosed between 1607 and 1730, far more than in the contentious Tudor period and rather more than that which was enclosed later by Act of Parliament. Very often a township was enclosed in stages, so that open-fields appeared

increasingly truncated. Thus, W. G. *Hoskins has shown that it took nearly 200 years to enclose all of the 700 acres of the small parish of Great Stretton. Enclosure continued after the 1650s without causing any further outcry in the 17th century. Agreements were either reached amicably by a small group of farmers or a single owner acquired all of the land. It is clear that parliamentary enclosure, which was necessary when complete agreement could not be reached, was merely the final stage of a process which had been in operation for centuries.

enclosure awards and maps. The parliamentary *enclosure of *open-fields and *commons and wastes in England and Wales was achieved through thousands of private Acts of Parliament. The commissioners appointed under the terms of these Acts conducted a thorough survey and considered claims based on ownership of land in the open-fields and of certain rights over the commons. This process took several years in the largest parishes. Thus, the enclosure of the Pennine townships and hamlets of Hallam, Fulwood, Stannington, Storrs, and Dungworth took 14 years between the passing of the Act in 1791 and the award in 1805.

The new *allotments were set out in an award which contained a schedule and an accompanying map. The copy of the award that was deposited in the parish chest is now normally kept at the appropriate county *record office, though a large number are housed at the *Public Record Office. See *Maps and Plans in the Public Record Office, c.1410–1860* (1967), and the various county lists available at local record offices. Awards and maps are frequently consulted to settle current disputes over boundaries, rights of way, and ownership. In open-field parishes awards and maps deal with all the land. Elsewhere they are concerned only with the former commons and wastes, except in parishes where the opportunity was taken to commute the *tithes at the same time. The map is often the earliest one available for a particular *township or *parish.

Awards describe the position and acreage of the new allotments and list their owners and tenants. As such they are a major source of information about open-field parishes in the late 18th or early 19th centuries. Some allotments were granted to parish bodies, e.g. quarries, and gravel- or sand-pits that were placed under the supervision of the overseers of the *highways. The awards also set out public roads, bridleways and footpaths, watercourses and drains, and other conveniences such as public wells. The maps mark (with a letter T on the inside boundary) which owners were responsible for the maintenance of walls. Enclosure maps make interesting comparisons with the present landscape. The pattern of fields and roads laid out two centuries or so ago is still evident on the ground in many places.

The award was made available for public inspection. Complaints were considered at the *quarter sessions. Exchanges were normally allowed if written consent was given, and sometimes the commissioners oversaw these arrangements. The expenses of enclosure were determined by the commissioners and, if necessary, payment was enforced by law.

enclosure roads. The commissioners responsible for individual Acts of parliamentary enclosure had, as one of their tasks, to define public rights of way, including roads, bridleways, and footpaths. These were described in their *enclosure award and set out on the accompanying map. Some of the roads followed the lines of ancient highways, but others were new routes across former *open-fields, *commons, and wastes. They were given standard widths, e.g. of 30 or 40 feet, and were enclosed with hedges or walls. They are characteristically long and straight. Even some of the new *turnpike roads were improved in this way where they crossed former common land. The widths were generous to allow grazing and to enable travellers to circumvent holes. Modern surfacing methods have created relatively narrow strips down the middle of many of these roads, leaving wide verges which are generally a good guide to parliamentary enclosure.

encroachment. The extension of a piece of private property so as to enclose part of a *green or *common or someone else's land. See ENCLOSURE, PRIVATE AND PIECEMEAL.

end. A part of a *village, sometimes detached from the rest of the settlement, or a *hamlet. These distinctive parts often use the suffix -end in their place-name, e.g. Townend (of which there are numerous instances), or Silver End (Essex).

endogamy. The practice of marrying within a *clan or local society. The term is used by social historians when discussing the geographical origins of marriage partners.

enfeoffment. The surrender of property to a group of trustees.

enfranchisement. The conferring of freedom, e.g. making land *freehold.

engineering. In the Middle Ages an engineer was a military man. During the *Industrial Revolution civil projects, notably the construction of *canals, led to the formation of the Society of Civil Engineers (1793) and the Institute of Civil Engineers (1818). The invention of *steam engines and *railway locomotives by a new type of engineer led to the formation of the Institute of Mechanical Engineers (1847), of which George Stephenson was the first President. Several other institutes, e.g. for chemical engineers, electrical engineers, or gas engineers, were formed later in the century. Agricultural engineering became an important industry in many market towns (see THRESHING). About a quarter of the industrial work-force was employed in engineering in the second half of the 19th century, but the term 'engineer' was applied not only to inventors and skilled craftsmen but also to relatively unskilled workers in the engineering industry. The *Great Exhibition of 1851 demonstrated the great variety and complexity of the products of engineering, which made Britain the 'workshop of the world'.

In 1994 the Institute of Civil Engineers began to publish a series of volumes on civil engineering heritage, starting with E. A. Labrum (ed.), *Eastern and Central England*, and R. A. Otter (ed.), *Southern England*.

English Place-Name Society. Founded in 1923, the society has published surveys of *place-names for many English counties and its work continues. Its volumes record place- and *field-names, *parish by parish, and explain, where possible, their meaning. They form the essential starting-point for local studies of settlement, even though those published before the 1960s were compiled before the modern advances in the subject.

engrossing. The amalgamation of two or more farms into one. This led to the abandonment of superfluous farmhouses, or their conversion into *cottages with small pieces of land attached. The term is applied particularly to the Tudor period, when engrossing was often associated with *enclosure and with the conversion of arable land to pasture, which required less labour. Engrossing was therefore regarded as part of the general evil of depopulation. It was a particular problem in the midland counties of England during the late 15th and 16th centuries.

Government concern is evident from 1488, when an Act was passed against engrossers in the Isle of Wight, who converted arable land into sheep and cattle pastures. National defence was uppermost in government minds when measures were taken against engrossing, for they feared the consequences of the decay of population. A general statute of 1489 quickly followed, but proved ineffectual. The problem was tackled again by Acts of 1515 and 1536, which tried to prevent further engrossing. However, the machinery for enforcing such legislation was largely ineffective.

An Act of 1597 ordered that all houses with 20 acres or more of land which had been allowed to fall into decay during the past seven years should be rebuilt and between 20 and 40 acres of land attached to them. Half the houses decayed for more than seven years were to be treated in the same way. The connection between engrossing and *enclosure was obvious to the legislators, who passed another Act in the same year ordering that lands in the *open-field counties which had been converted since 1588 into sheep or cattle pastures, and which had previously been tilled for arable for at least 12 years, should be restored to their former use. All these Acts recognized the variety of farming systems in England and Wales and so restricted their penalties to those who engrossed holdings in open-field districts. Engrossing did not cause the same social problems in other parts of Britain which had long been devoted to the rearing and fattening of livestock rather than the growing of cereals.

ensign. The lowest commissioned rank in an infantry regiment; the man who carried the flag.

entail. To bequeath an estate in a named sequence of succession. The *Scottish Record Office has a Register of Entails or Tailzies from 1685. In 1914 the creation of new entails was prohibited.

ephemera. Handwritten or printed papers which were not meant for posterity but which are now often valuable historical sources.

epitaphs. Inscriptions on monuments or *gravestones commemorating the deceased. The Elizabethans started the fashion for lengthy epitaphs, often in verse, which described a man's family background and his achievements and extolled his virtues. The style degenerated into ridiculous flattery and bad verse during the 18th century. An epitaph in St Thomas, Salisbury, starts by saying that the rhymer did not have space to do justice to the deceased's many virtues, which were then lauded in 42 lines.

Epitaphs reveal the social attitudes of the age. At Kedleston (Derbyshire) the grandiose mon-uments of the Curzon family are inside the parish church next to the hall, whereas the tomb of James Field is in the churchyard by the south door. His gravestone reads: 'Beneath lie the remains of JAMES FIELD who was for 36 years a Confidential Domestic of the late LORD SCARSDALE. He died April the 17th 1813, Aged 69. His spotless integrity gained him the esteem of the Noble family with whom he resided, and the Evening of his days Closed amidst the calm enjoyments of retirement and Social Happiness.'

equity. 1. (legal) General principles of justice used to correct or supplement common and statute law.

2. (commercial) Stocks and shares which do not have a fixed interest.

escheat. Escheated property reverted to a lord when a tenant was guilty of a *felony or when he died without adult heirs. The term will often be found in manorial records.

espousal. A betrothal, which until the 17th century was considered almost as valid as marriage. This practice sometimes explains why a child was baptized less than nine months after a marriage.

esquire. Originally the shield-bearer to a *knight, by the 16th century an officer of the Crown, and in the following two centuries a man with a *coat of arms who was a superior *gentleman. In the 19th century 'esquire' became more widely used as a style when addressing letters to a gentleman, and later to all men.

essoin. An acceptable excuse for absence from a manorial *court. Lists of names and the fines charged for absence commonly appear at the beginning of records of the proceedings of manor courts. Essoins were the equivalent of the modern 'apologies for absence' which are recorded at the beginning of minutes of meetings.

estate, early or multiple. The work of G. R. J. Jones and others in proposing that territorial estates in medieval England and Wales demonstrate remarkable continuity from Roman, and possibly even earlier, times has gained wide acceptance. See G. R. J. Jones, 'Multiple Estates and Early Settlement' in P. H. Sawyer (ed.), *Medieval Settlement: Continuity and Change* (1976). A summary of the various writings on the subject is given in N. Gregson, 'The Multiple Estate Model: Some Critical Questions', *Journal of Historical Geography*, 11 (1985), and in Jones's response, 'Multiple Estates Perceived', in the same issue. The model defines the archetypal land-management units of early England and Wales, showing that they had a religious as well as a secular focus, and a *hill fort for refuge in times of danger; hence their description as 'multiple' estates. Their descent from the Roman period is observable in the form of the continuity of estates rather than of settlements on unchanging sites. They covered a variety of terrain, so as to include arable, meadow, wood, and waste. A multiple estate formed the framework for the evolution of settlement.

Some multiple estates, such as Hallamshire, remained intact for centuries. (See LATHE; SHIRES; and SOKE.) Others became fragmented, but their original territory can sometimes be pierced together. (See MINSTER CHURCHES and DETACHED PORTION.) See also the discussion of the *regio* of Milton Regis in Alan Everitt, *Continuity and Colonization: The Evolution of Kentish Settlement* (1986), ch. 11.

estate records. In the post-medieval period archivists often catalogue records that were previously described as manorial accounts and rolls as 'estate papers'. These include correspondence, accounts of the management of the estate, maps, *surveys, *leases, and *rentals. Most of these records have now been deposited at county *record offices. They are a major source for the study of agricultural and industrial developments and they contain copious information of interest to family historians. It is usually far easier to trace ancestors who lived and worked on a great estate than it is to trace freeholders. Estate records are also indispensable for a study of the building of the great house, its *gardens and *park, and of lesser buildings such as farmhouses, *cottages, and *barns. Many great landowners owned land on the edge of towns which was developed in the late 18th and 19th centuries as building land for housing and industry; their records are therefore an important source for the study of urban development.

estover, right of. The right to take timber, brushwood, bracken, etc. from *commons for use in building, repairing fences, or as fuel etc.

estreat. An extract from a list of *fines, returned to the *Exchequer.

evangelical revival. A Protestant movement in the late 18th and 19th centuries, which included 'Low Church' members of the *Church of England and most of the *Nonconformist sects, and which emphasized salvation by faith alone.

Philanthropic campaigns included an effective one against cruel sports such as *bear-baiting or *cock fighting.

Evans, Emyr Estyn (1905–89). A pioneer of folk-culture studies in the British Isles, Professor of Irish Studies and first Director of the Institute of Irish Studies, Queen's University, Belfast. His books *Irish Heritage* (1942), *Mourne Country* (1951), *Irish Folk Ways* (1957), and *The Personality of Ireland: Habitat, Heritage and History* (1973) were highly influential in interesting others in archaeology, social anthropology, and material culture. He was instrumental in founding the Ulster Open-Air Folk Museum in 1958.

Evans, George Ewart (1909–88). In a series of readable books written since 1956 Evans established the value of *oral history. His *Ask the Fellows Who Cut the Hay* (1956) centred on the Suffolk village of Blaxhall, using the memories of people born in the last quarter of the 19th century. His next books, *The Horse in the Furrow* (1960), *The Pattern Under the Plough* (1966), and *The Farm and the Village* (1969) also dealt with the 'prior culture' (as he termed it) of farming communities in the age of horse power and hand tools. The value of the oral-history approach to a wider variety of topics was shown in later books: *The Days that We Have Seen* (1975), *From Mouths of Men* (1976), and *Where Beards Wag All* (1977). His continued interest in folk-life studies is evident in *The Leaping Hare* (1974), which was written with David Thompson, and *Horse Power and Magic* (1979). He reflected on his early life in South Wales and on his work in Suffolk in his autobiography, *The Strength of the Hills* (1983), and in *Spoken History* (1987). A posthumous collection of his writings, *Crooked Scythe: An Anthology of Oral History*, was edited by David Gentleman in 1993. See Gareth Williams, *Writers of Wales: George Ewart Evans* (1991), which also deals with his poetry and fiction.

Evelyn, John (1620–1706). Diarist, author, and prominent member of the *Royal Society, who spent most of his life at Wotton (Surrey) or in London, except for a period starting in 1642 when he travelled on the Continent. Apart from his diary, his best-known work is *Silva, or a Discourse on Forest Trees* (1664), which was very influential in reviving a professional interest in silviculture. His contribution to horticulture was just as substantial, though his manuscript on the subject, *Elysium Britannicum*, was not published, and part is now lost. But some parts appeared as *Gard'ners Almanack* and a *Discourse on Sallets*.

eviction. Families living in *tied houses or *cottages could be summarily evicted by the owner. *Newspapers sometimes reported evictions, but often the only information about such events is through *oral history. The threat of eviction was often sufficient to enforce the wishes of an owner.

Exchequer, Court of. The administrative body that collected royal revenue and the court which originally dealt with fiscal matters, but which became an ordinary court of justice. The records are kept at the *Public Record Office under class E; many have been printed. The court was merged with the High Court of Justice in 1880. In Scotland, after the Act of Union (1707), a remodelled Exchequer was responsible for forfeited estates, particularly after the failure of the rebellions of 1715 and 1745. The records are kept at the *Scottish Record Office, which has published extracts and summaries.

excommunication. The exclusion of a person from the communion of the Church, imposed by an *ecclesiastical court for offences ranging from non-attendance at church to heresy. Christian burial was denied to ex-communicants.

execution, public. Capital punishment was normally performed in public throughout the Middle Ages and the early modern period. Successive Tudor governments turned it into street theatre, with set-piece executions for high-born traitors and later for common felons. The offender was led through the streets to the place of execution and was there expected to show obedience and contrition in a highly structured ritual which was designed to impress on witnesses the authority of the state. The offender often made a full public confession on the gallows.

The number of capital offences increased greatly during the second half of the 17th century and the first part of the 18th century. See J. M. Beattie, *Crime and the Courts in England, 1660–1800* (1986). The most infamous gallows was at *Tyburn, which was approached on a 'hanging day' by a long procession through the streets of London. See Peter Linebaugh, *The London Hanged: Crime and Civil Society in the Eighteenth Century* (1991) and V. A. C. Gatrell, *The Hanging Tree: Execution and the English People, 1770–1868* (1994). The last hanging at Tyburn was in 1783; later hangings in London took place instead within the confines of Newgate Prison, but many sentences were commuted to *transportation. Public executions were abolished in 1868. Capital punishment within prisons was abolished in 1965.

Exon Domesday. A survey of the south-western counties, preserved in Exeter Cathedral and printed in volume iv of the Record Commission edition of the *Domesday Book. It includes a count of farm stock, which is not given in the final version of the Domesday Book.

expectation of life. The average expectation of life before the 20th century was lowered considerably by the high rate of *infant mortality. In the Elizabethan period, for instance, if a person survived childhood he or she could expect to live into what is now called middle age (though sudden death at all ages was a common experience) and some lived as long as the oldest people of today. The great difference between the present age and the past is that a high proportion of the population are now elderly. Society was formerly much more youthful in its composition. See E. A. Wrigley and R. S. Schofield, *The Population History of England, 1541–1871: A Reconstruction* (1981).

exports. In the Middle Ages and the early modern period the English export trade was dominated by *wool and woollen cloth. In the 16th century *lead was also an important export. Government efforts to stimulate local industries reduced the number of *imports by the later 17th century. At the same time, the colonial market became increasingly important for the sale of British goods, including metalware. See Ralph Davis, *English Overseas Trade, 1500–1700* (1973). Overseas trade, particularly with the American colonies, was the responsibility of a series of committees of the *Privy Council from 1621 until 1784, when the Board of Trade was established. (See CUSTOMS AND EXCISE; PORT and SHIPS.) See also Ralph Davis, 'Shipping Records', *Archives*, 7 (1965–6) and P. Mathias and A. W. H. Pearsall (eds.), *Shipping: A Survey of Historical Records* (1971).

During the late 18th and 19th centuries Britain became a major exporting nation, especially to the various parts of the British Empire. The fortunes of the Lancashire *cotton industry, the *steel industry, and other important sectors of the economy were dependent on the export trade. See, for example, Geoffrey Tweedale, *Sheffield Steel and America: A Century of Commercial and Technological Interdependence, 1830–1930* (1987). Foreign competition caused the rapid decline of manufacturing exports in the later 20th century.

extent. A detailed *survey and valuation of an estate, especially a manorial one. It records the names of tenants, the size and nature of their holdings, and the form of their tenure.

extra-parochial. An area outside the jurisdiction of an ecclesiastical or civil *parish. The inhabitants of such places therefore paid no *church or poor rates, and their *tithes were supposed to go to the Crown but were often not collected. In 1894 all such areas were incorporated into parishes or made into new ones.

eyre, in. A system of justice introduced in 1166 by which the king's justices travelled on circuits to county sessions. General eyres were replaced by *assizes in the late 13th century.

factor. An agent, dealer, or middleman. The term was used in overseas trade and in the Birmingham and Sheffield metal trades.

factory. The original meaning was trading station, the place of work of a company's *factors. The change took place in the 19th century when *cotton 'manufactories' became known by the shortened form. The local usage, however, was more often *mill, which had evolved from the use of *water power for milling corn. The prototype of the cotton factories was the Derby Silk Mill, built by George Sorocold for the Lombe brothers in 1718–21. This was 500 feet long, five storeys high, with 460 windows, and all the machines were worked by a huge water-wheel. It employed 300 people, chiefly women and children, and was the model for Richard Arkwright's first mill at Nottingham (1769) and those at Cromford (from 1771), which in turn were widely copied elsewhere, especially in Derbyshire, during the age of water power. Quarry Bank Mill, Styal (Cheshire), now a National Trust property, is a uniquely preserved cotton mill of this type. See Stanley D. Chapman, *The Early Factory Masters: The Transition to the Factory in the Midlands Textile Industry* (1993 reprint).

In the 19th century the cotton industry moved from rural Derbyshire to Lancashire as water-powered mills were replaced by *steam-driven factories. Lancashire became the most urbanized county in Britain. Factories brought a complete change in the nature of work, for employees were now tied to regular hours at routine tasks under supervision. Men were put in charge of the *spinning mules, while women were relegated to inferior work such as carding, and the children were employed at piecing. The *Factory Acts restricted child labour, but families and neighbours continued to operate as working units within a factory. Women and children continued to outnumber men, and for the first three-quarters of the 19th century the majority of factory workers were first-generation incomers, often from a rural background. *Weaving did not become factory-based until the widespread adoption of the power-loom in the 1830s and 1840s: the Lancashire cotton industry again led the way. In times of full employment factory work was relatively well-paid, and in no other industry did women fare so well. Throughout the 19th century female weavers did the same job as men, in equal numbers and for the same pay. The West Riding woollen and *worsted industry adopted weaving machines some decades later than the Lancashire cotton factories. Although the Crossleys and Akroyds of Halifax and Titus Salt of Saltaire built factories of a comparable size to those across the Pennines, the average West Riding mill was much smaller. See Colum Giles and Ian H. Goodhall, *Yorkshire Textile Mills, 1770–1930* (1992).

The decline of the Lancashire and West Riding textile industries in the second half of the 20th century has left a legacy of abandoned or converted factories, which now attract interest as important monuments of industrial archaeology. For social and economic background see C. B. Phillips and J. H. Smith, *The Lancashire / Cheshire Region from AD 1540* (1994). See also M. B. Rose, *The Gregs of Quarry Bank Mill: The Rise and Fall of a Family Firm, 1750–1914* (1986).

Factory Acts. The Factory Act (1819) prohibited children under 9 from working in *cotton mills and restricted older children to a 12-hour day. The Factory Act (1833) reduced the daily hours of children under 12 working in textile mills to nine, with a maximum of 48 hours a week, and those aged 13–18 to 12 hours a day, with a maximum of 69 hours a week; children at these mills were obliged to have two hours' schooling a day; and factory inspectors were appointed to enforce these regulations. The Factory Act (1844) ordered that women were not to work more than 12 hours a day in textile mills and that children were to spend half their day at school. Further reforms were passed by the Factory Acts of 1853, 1867, 1874, 1891, 1901, and 1937.

faculty. A licence from a bishop to alter or add to church buildings or a *churchyard.

fairies, belief in. The fairies that were widely believed in during the Middle Ages and beyond were very different from the fairies of children's stories in modern times. They were not thought of as small, kindly people, but as bitter, malevolent spirits to beware of. John Bunyan's 'hobgoblin nor foul fiend' was something to guard against with ritual precautions. After the *Reformation belief in harmful elves, goblins, and fairies declined; Shakespeare treats them humorously. Fairy lore became a matter of mythology amongst educated people, but it long remained accepted literally at a populist level. See Keith Thomas, *Religion and the Decline of Magic* (1971).

The best contemporary account of fairy and associated beliefs in 17th-century Britain is Robert Kirk, *The Secret Common-Wealth & A Short Treatise of Charms and Spels*, ed. Stewart Sanderson (1976). This was written near the end of the 17th century by a scholarly, *Gaelic-speaking minister of the *Church of Scotland. Kirk recognized that many of his parishioners believed in fairies, 'second sight', and other supernatural phenomena, and so set out to record the evidence in the spirit of scientific enquiry. He held that belief in fairies was not inconsistent with belief in Christianity; the crafty, bitter, menacing fairies could be regarded as the agents of the Devil. Fairies had to be placated and their unpredictable and sinister powers counteracted. Kirk described the ways in which people visualized the physical appearance of the fairy folk, their dress and weapons, and concepts of their social organization and domestic economy. Other contemporary accounts support his findings, as do the legends and traditions of Scotland and Ireland.

Much evidence of living fairy-beliefs was collected by 19th-century folklorists. The pioneers were Georgina F. Jackson and Charlotte Burne, who collected material from Shropshire and the Severn Valley respectively in the 1870s. (See also ATKINSON, J. C) Here and in later works, notably C. M. Armstrong, *The Irish Countryman* (1937), the social function of such beliefs is stressed. Domestic untidiness was punished, a code of conduct was enforced (fairies were said to hate lust and lechery), and the virtues of neighbourliness were upheld. The cruel pranks of fairies accounted for mysterious happenings, ill fortune, and unsatisfactory situations. Fraudsters and tricksters could exploit these beliefs to their own advantage, but on the whole a fear of fairies in all their various forms helped to reinforce communal values and to offer comfort in distressing circumstances.

fairs. From the late 12th century onwards the right to hold a fair was granted by a royal *charter. Fairs already in existence were claimed by prescriptive right; some probably go back to prehistoric times. The greatest period of creation, as with *markets, was between the *Norman Conquest and the *Black Death. See Ellen Wedemeyer Moore, *The Fairs of Medieval England: An Introductory Study* (1985). The major fairs before the Black Death were at Boston, Stamford, King's Lynn, St Ives, Bury St Edmunds, Northampton, Winchester, and Westminster. The rapid methods of communication in modern times have destroyed the great majority of fairs; there are a few famous survivals, e.g. the Appleby (Westmorland) *horse fair, and others that continue merely as pleasure fairs on the traditional days. Before the 19th century numerous fairs were held in all parts of the country. Somerset, for example, held 180 fairs every year in the 18th century, most of which were in existence by 1600. Many of these were held in one or other of the 39 market towns in the county, but others were held in places which had no market rights. Some lasted several days; many were held on the eve, day, and morrow of the patron saint of the local parish church; others were one-day affairs devoted to a particular commodity. The grant specified the day(s) on which the fair could be held. The largest market towns had three or four fairs a year, though one of these was usually thought of as the chief fair.

In a report of 1889 on market tolls and rights, the Government published a list of markets and fair charters down to 1483. This was compiled from the grants recorded in the Letters Patent at the *Public Record Office. These lists have been extended in *The *Agrarian History of England and Wales*, vols. iv and v, to include fairs held by prescriptive right and later creations. See also *Owen's *Book of Fairs*, whose various editions list the fairs that were being held in the second half of the 18th century. Some of these continued to be held according to the *Julian calendar long after the change to the *Gregorian calendar in 1752.

The staple commodity of most fairs was *cattle, followed by *sheep, then horses. The major fairs catered for a variety of commerce, including *pedlars' goods, but those held at remote country sites were limited to one speciality. The most famous fair in Britain was that held in a field at Stourbridge on the outskirts of Cambridge, which *Defoe described in his *Tour Through the Whole Island of Great Britain*, ii (1726) as the greatest in the world: 'the shops are placed in rows like streets, wherof one is call'd Cheapside; and here, as in several other streets, are all sorts of trades, who sell by retale, and who come principally from London with their goods; scarce any trades are omitted, goldsmiths, toyshops, brasiers, turners, milliners, haberdashers, hatters, mercers, drapers, pewtrers, china-warehouses, and in a word all trades that can be named in London; with coffee-houses, taverns, brandy-shops, and eating-houses, innumerable, and all in tents, and booths, as above.' The fair was particularly noted for its *wool and its *hops. It was attended by traders from many different parts of the land.

At the great majority of fairs vendors had rarely travelled more than 20 or 25 miles. Regional differences in density were marked. The seasonal peak was in May and June, with another peak in October for autumn cattle-fairs. At some of the remote country sites several thousand sheep were sold at a time, but most rural fairs were modest in scale. In towns, fairs were increasingly moved out of the market-place to a suitable space at the edge of the settlement. Such places are often commemorated by street names such as Horse Fair Green. See also HIRING FAIRS.

falling sickness. Epilepsy.

fallow. Arable land which is left unploughed for a year in order to recuperate. In *open-field systems an entire field was left fallow in rotation. The jurors of the manorial *court determined when and how the fallow could be grazed in common.

families, core. The population of medieval and early modern Britain was far more mobile than was once realized. Movement beyond the *parish boundary was commonplace. Nevertheless, most movement was restricted to a radius of between 20 and 25 miles, within an area bounded by the nearest *market towns. Past and present distributions of *surnames show that, on the whole, people did not travel very far, unless they were attracted to *London, and to a lesser extent to other cities.

Much of the movement in and out of parishes was by young *farm and *domestic servants and *apprentices. Young people often returned upon inheriting the family farm or *cottage. Studies of *communities and local societies in many different parts of the country have emphasized the contrast between this mobility and the stability of core groups of families over the generations. See, for example, W. G. Hoskins, *The Midland Peasant: The Economic and Social History of a Leicestershire Village* (1957), David Hey, *An English Rural Community: Myddle Under the Tudors and Stuarts*

(1974), and Anne Mitson, 'The Significance of Kinship Networks in the Seventeenth Century: South-West Nottinghamshire', in Charles Phythian-Adams (ed.), *Societies, Cultures and Kinship, 1580–1850: Cultural Provinces and English Local History* (1993).

Sometimes, as with the Widdowsons of Trowell (Nottinghamshire), a core family remained largely confined to a single parish over several generations. More often, the dynastic network was likely to spread over a group of adjacent parishes in a neighbourhood area. The study of such families involves an intensive search of *parish registers, *wills, *hearth tax returns, etc. The neighbourhood can often be defined as that from which marriage partners were drawn. The bonds which united a neighbourhood were strengthened by the frequent intermarriage of the core families.

The members of core families feature large in the lists of local officials, e.g. *churchwardens, *constables, overseers of the *poor and of the *highways, witnesses to wills, and appraisers of probate *inventories. They were the people who were most often asked to be the witnesses whose depositions helped to resolve local disputes, for they had access to communal memories that stretched far back in time. The core families were the ones who set the standards of behaviour and preserved the traditions of local communities and societies. The local peculiarities of speech, for instance, were transmitted by these groups.

The core families which remained in a particular locality for at least a century or two were largely drawn from the middle ranks of society. The *gentry had wider contacts, including a bigger circle from which they drew marriage partners, and more opportunities to move on. At the other end of the social scale the poor labourers often sought to try their luck elsewhere. The *yeomen, *husbandmen, and craftsmen were the most likely to stay, for they had sufficient resources to survive in reasonable comfort but few opportunities to better themselves by moving.

The importance of core families was not restricted to rural areas. It was equally evident in the early modern metalworking district centred on Sheffield, for example. Thus, the *scythe-makers of Norton parish, the *sickle-makers of Eckington parish, and the *cutlers and *scissor-smiths of Attercliffe township were as residentially stable as were the farmers of Wigston or Myddle. Even in the town of Sheffield itself the continuity of cutlery families was remarkable. See David Hey, *The Fiery Blades of*

Hallamshire: Sheffield and Its Neighbourhood, 1660–1740 (1991).

Families were loyal over long periods of time even to certain districts within a town, especially one devoted to a particular occupation. In *Fisher Row: Fishermen, Bargemen and Canal Boatmen in Oxford, 1500–1900* (1982) Mary Prior showed how a group of families who were united by occupation and *kinship formed a remarkably stable group by the riverside, while transient and seasonal workers such as carters and drovers were constantly moving in and out. Family continuity is equally evident in trades requiring fixed capital, such as *milling, *malting, *tanning, or *brewing.

Historians of the early modern period have been concerned with identifying core families, but the later period has not attracted as much attention. See, however, Alan Everitt's essay on 'Dynasty and Community since the Seventeenth Century', in his *Landscape and Community in England* (1985), which is concerned with the growth of dynastic connection in provincial society and the rise of family networks, drawing particularly from the evidence of Victorian Kent. It is clear from present distributions of surnames, patterns of local speech, and strong loyalties to localities, that core families still play their traditional role in cementing the bonds of local societies.

family and society. In Britain, the first serious attempts to write a rounded history of the family as a social institution have been made since the 1970s. The most useful studies of different aspects of family life from various vantage points (legal, ideological, sociological, demographic, and economic) are also recent ones, though a few much older works may be mentioned. F. W. Maitland's chapters on family law in *The History of English Law* (1895, 1968) are still indispensable reading. Among the many books devoted to *marriage and *divorce are G. E. Howard, *A History of Matrimonial Institutions* (1904), R. H. Helmholz, *Marriage Litigation in Medieval England* (1974), Martin Ingram, *Church Courts, Sex and Marriage in England* (1987), and Lawrence Stone, *Road to Divorce* (1990). Lloyd Bonfield's is the most authoritative account of *Marriage Settlements, 1601–1740: The Adoption of the Strict Settlement* (1983). Amy Louise Erickson, *Women and Property in Early Modern England* (1993) is the first comprehensive treatment of its subject, overlapping chronologically with Susan Staves, *Married Women's Separate Property in England, 1660–1833* (1990), while Lee Holcombe's is the best account of *Wives and Property: Reform of the*

Married Women's Property Law in Nineteenth-Century England (1983).

Works dealing with ideologies of the family include C. L. Powell, *English Domestic Relations, 1487–1653* (1917), L. L. Schücking, *The Puritan Family: A Social Study from the Literary Sources* (1969), and Susan Dwyer Amussen, *An Ordered Society: Gender and Class in Early Modern England* (1988). The changing forms and meanings of family rites of passage and the beliefs and assumptions which underlay them are the main concerns of John Gillis, *For Better, for Worse: British Marriages, 1600 to the Present* (1985), and Clare Gittings, *Death, Burial and the Individual in Early Modern England* (1984).

Historical sociologists have investigated such topics as household structures and *kinship networks. Peter Laslett, the foremost of them, has published the fruits of his work on household structure as revealed by local population listings in a series of books, including *The World We Have Lost* (1965), *The World We Have Lost Further Explored* (1983), *Household and Family in Past Time* (with Richard Wall, 1972), and *Family Life and Illicit Love in Earlier Generations* (1977). Two innovative investigations of the importance of ties with a larger kin-group can be found in Alan MacFarlane, *The Family Life of Ralph Josselin, a Seventeenth-Century Clergyman: An Essay in Historical Anthropology* (1970), and Michael Anderson, *Family Structure in Nineteenth-Century Lancashire* (1971). These topics also bulk large in community studies (see below).

Historical demography has been placed on a new footing by the Cambridge Group for the Study of Population and Social Structure (*CAMPOP). The group has systematically applied the technique of *family reconstitution to the study of *parish registers in order to investigate such matters as the age at marriage, completed family size, and child and *infant mortality . 'Aggregative back projection', which uses the aggregated totals of vital events calculated from hundreds of registers to trace the course of English population change backwards from the *census era, provided the foundation for E. A. Wrigley and R. S. Schofield, *The Population History of England, 1541–1871: A Reconstruction* (1981). Three shorter surveys which between them cover a longer time-span and compare English developments with those in other countries of the British Isles are N.L. Tranter, *Population and Society 1750–1940* (1985), Theo Barker and Michael Drake, *Population and Society in Britain 1850–1980* (1982), and R. A. Houston, *The Population History of Britain and Ireland, 1500–1750* (1992).

Economic historians have long been concerned with the role of the family and the *household in the organization of production. But the transformation of demographic studies by the Cambridge Group has made possible a much fuller integration of the family into economic history. The closely connected subjects of youth employment, family formation, *inheritance, and the organization of local economies are explored in David Levine's *Family Formation in an Age of Nascent Capitalism* (1977) and *Reproducing Families: The Political Economy of English Population History* (1987), Anne Kussmaul's *Servants in Husbandry in Early Modern England* (1981) and *A General View of the Rural Economy of England, 1538–1840* (1990), and R. M. Smith (ed.), *Land, Kinship and Life-Cycle* (1984).

All these works, and especially perhaps the last, take careful account of the variety of local conditions. Community studies offer one of the best ways of setting families in a larger context. It is above all the concern with such things as fertility, mortality, inheritance, links with kin and neighbours, and the continuity or disappearance of family lines, which distinguishes the best of recent community studies from older works of local history. They include (in order of the chronological span covered) Margaret McIntosh, *Autonomy and Community: The Royal Manor of Havering, 1200–1500* (1986), Zvi Razi, *Life, Marriage and Death in a Medieval Parish: Economy, Society and Demography in Halesowen 1270–1400* (1980), Cicely Howell, *Land, Family and Inheritance in Transition: Kibworth Harcourt 1280–1700* (1983), David Hey, *An English Rural Community: Myddle Under the Tudors and Stuarts* (1974), Margaret Spufford, *Contrasting Communities: English Villagers in the Sixteenth and Seventeenth Centuries* (1974), and two studies by Keith Wrightson and David Levine, *Poverty and Piety in an English Village: Terling 1525–1700* (1979) and *The Making of an Industrial Society: Whickham 1560–1765* (1991).

Surveys of *classes or social groups offer another means of setting the family in a larger context. Some outstanding examples are S. L. Thrupp, *The Merchant Class of Medieval London, 1300–1500* (1948), Lawrence Stone, *The Crisis of the Aristocracy, 1558–1641* (1965), Peter Earle, *The Making of the English Middle Class: Business, Society and Family Life in London 1660–1730* (1989), and Keith Snell, *Annals of the Labouring Poor: Social Change and Agrarian England 1660–1900* (1985).

Several historians have looked at the family through the eyes of women and *children, and some of them have emphasized the repressive aspects of the institution. See, for example, Mary Prior (ed.), *Women in English Society, 1500–1800* (1985), and Valerie Fildes (ed.), *Women as Mothers in Pre-Industrial England* (1990), which develops the innovative work of Dorothy McLaren on lactation and breastfeeding and its effects on family size. (See also WIDOW.) The importance of women's work and of their contribution to the household economy was underlined by Alice Clark, *Working Life of Women in the Seventeenth Century* (1919, 1982, and 1992), and Ivy Pinchbeck, *Women Workers and the Industrial Revolution 1750–1850* (1930). A more critical post-1960s feminism informs (to varying degrees) Bridget Hill, *Women, Work and Sexual Politics in Eighteenth-Century England* (1989), Leonore Davidoff and Catherine Hall, *Family Fortunes: Men and Women of the English Middle Class, 1780–1850* (1987), and Jane Lewis, *Women in England, 1870–1950: Sexual Divisions and Social Change* (1984). The body of recent studies of women's lives is enormous. Of all the books written about children's experience, the most influential was Philippe Ariès, *Centuries of Childhood* (1962). His argument that adult attitudes towards children changed fundamentally in early modern times has been challenged, especially by Linda Pollock, *Forgotten Children: Parent/Child Relations from 1500 to 1900* (1983), though she in turn perhaps emphasized continuity rather too strongly.

Lawrence Stone, *The Family, Sex and Marriage in England, 1500–1800* (1977) was the first attempt to describe the institution's development over a long period of time. It remains the most popular account of its subject, despite being criticized for its highly schematic approach, excessive pessimism concerning the emotional climate of the pre-17th-century family, and relative neglect of the middling and lower ranks of society. The alternative model of family history offered by Alan MacFarlane in *Marriage and Love in England 1300–1840* (1986) corrected some of Stone's mistakes, but presented too static a picture and paid insufficient attention to class differences. An interpretation between these two was offered by Ralph Houlbrooke, *The English Family, 1450–1700* (1984). In 1980 Michael Anderson published a broad historiographical survey setting out three fruitful *Approaches to the History of the Western Family, 1500–1914*, through 'sentiments', demography, and household economics.

The family in Britain had certain enduring characteristics, some of them shared with most of north-western Europe, for hundreds of years before 1900. The most important of these was that the nuclear family was founded on a marriage which was normally expected to be for life. Many marriages were cut short by death long before old age, and remarriage was very common. Yet the majority of unions lasted a long time. Secondly, England shared in a north-west European pattern of relatively late marriage, usually several years after puberty. At any one time a sizeable minority of the adult population was single, and lifetime celibacy was a fairly common lot. In England this pattern was probably established by the close of the Middle Ages, in Lowland Scotland by the eighteenth century, but in both cases it may go much further back. Thirdly, English kinship terminology has always been vague, and despite the patrilineal descent of *surnames, no clearly defined group of kinsfolk outside the nuclear family has had special claims on the individual. Loyalty to the name was far stronger in Scotland. But there too, at any rate in the Lowlands, households seem to have been economically independent. Finally, English households were normally based on a nuclear family, and numbered between four and five persons on average from the 16th century until the beginning of the 20th. The same was probably true of Lowland Scottish ones.

The medieval sources which tell us most about the family are those concerned with property, such as manorial records, testaments, and *wills. The most important of the rules of succession to land established in Anglo-Norman England was *primogeniture: the succession of the eldest son. Primogeniture was generally adopted by the upper classes and established as the main rule of succession for manorial tenants. But in certain parts of the country different rules survived. Kent, with its custom of *gavelkind (equal division among all sons), was the most notable of these. The common law allowed the alienation of land *inter vivos* (between living people), and a vigorous land market existed by the 13th century. The right to bequeath movable goods by testament was established by this time, strongly upheld by the church. Land, with some exceptions such as *burgage tenements, could not be devised by testament or last will. Yet various procedures of *surrender and regrant, surrender to the use of the will, and *feoffment to uses, eventually gave landholders at most levels some freedom to decide what should happen to their land after their deaths, while continuing to enjoy the income from it till then. This freedom was not absolute, however. Many men did not use it at all, and one of the main aims of those who did was to make better provision for younger sons and daughters than was otherwise possible.

There is a continuing debate between historians who emphasize freedom of alienation, notably R. M. Smith, and Alan MacFarlane in his *The Origins of English Individualism: The Family, Property and Social Transition* (1978) and Zvi Razi, who insists upon the strength of feelings of solidarity and obligation among kinsfolk, as in 'The Myth of the Immutable English Family', *Past and Present*, 140 (1993).

Freedom of alienation was limited by (among other things) the widow's right to a *dower in a third of her husband's land. In the later Middle Ages, dower was gradually replaced, in the upper classes, by *jointure, the income from specified land held jointly by husband and wife, and after the husband's death by the widow for life. In propertied families, marriage was in part a financial transaction, in which the dowry or cash portion paid with the bride secured her future maintenance in marriage and widowhood. (In the absence of sons, daughters inherited land, and these heiresses were regarded as desirable brides. The practice of giving land with non-inheriting daughters had all but died out by 1300.) Marriage gave control over the wife's property to her husband, except that he could not alienate her land without her consent. Married women could not make wills without their husband's permission.

In canon law, only the free and mutual consent of the partners could make a valid marriage. In practice, the *nobility tended to arrange marriages for their heirs when they were still young. Property holders generally expected that their children would, in return for any material help given, take their views into account before choosing a partner. Yet young people in the middle and lower ranks of society had considerable freedom in courtship. The church, while accepting that a couple could marry by means of a spoken contract without its blessing, strongly discouraged the consummation of such marriages before the service. The common law, representing the interests of the propertied classes, came to insist during the later Middle Ages that the widow's dower rights depended on words of endowment publicly spoken by the husband at the church door before the service.

Later medieval high mortality, especially after 1348, had profound effects. The greater mobility of tenants seeking more favourable terms loosened the ties between families and land. Enterprising peasant farmers building up substantial holdings were better able to pass them on intact, because high infant and child mortality drastically reduced the numbers of children surviving to adulthood. The greatly reduced supply of workers encouraged employers to retain young people in service and to offer work to women, possibly helping to delay marriage and put a brake on demographic recovery, as argued by Jeremy Goldberg in *Women, Work and Life Cycle in a Medieval Economy* (1992).

The first signs of demographic recovery, hesitant at first, are apparent from the late 15th century. From the 1520s *population growth was stronger, and after 1538 early parish registers point to a regime of high fertility and of mortality lower than in the preceding era. They also reveal that relaxed attitudes to antenuptial consummation were widespread: one bride in three was probably pregnant at marriage in the second half of the 16th century. A narrowing of economic opportunities for the majority, one sign of which was a marked decline in real *wages, largely due to the rapid population growth of the 16th century, formed the backdrop to an increasingly widespread concern about premature and improvident marriages as a cause of poverty. Legislative attempts were made to delay marriage (e.g. through standard *apprenticeship terms ending in the twenties, laid down in the 1563 Statute of *Artificers, and a 1604 canon which required those under 21 to gain parental consent before marrying). In 1576, *Justices of the Peace were empowered to punish the parents of illegitimate children. In the early 17th century, clergy and overseers of the *poor in many *parishes co-operated to prevent the settlement and marriage of incomers whose families might become a burden on the rates. It seems likely that an increasing proportion of the population—perhaps as many as a fifth of those reaching marriageable age in the years immediately before the *Civil War—never married at all.

Parish registers reveal, during the first century after their inception, levels of infant and child mortality almost certainly lower than those of the 150 years after the *Black Death. Infant mortality ranged from less than one in nine of those born in one remote rural parish to one in three in a crowded London suburb in non-plague years; nationally the figure may have been one in six or seven. A fairly long period of maternal breastfeeding, which prolonged intervals between births and improved babies' chances of survival, seems to have been normal in England. During later childhood, from 6 or 8 onwards, girls and boys increasingly helped to earn their keep in domestic industry and on the farm, as they were drawn into *spinning, *knitting, and the lighter agricultural tasks. But longer-term provision for increasing numbers of surviving children was a costly business for parents squeezed by rent and price increases. The more successful landholders, traders, and professional people were able to raise cash portions to pay their daughters' dowries and educate their younger sons for a business or professional career. But the need to bring up larger numbers of offspring placed heavy burdens on those tenants whose holdings were too small to allow them to exploit the opportunities presented by the market.

How deeply the 16th-century *Reformation influenced the family is a much-debated question. The reduction of the prohibited degrees of marriage was probably not a momentous development for most people. In England, expectations of major divorce-law reform were disappointed; see E. J. Carlson, *Marriage and the English Reformation* (1994). In their teaching on the family, based firmly on the Bible, the *Protestant reformers emphatically upheld the authority of husbands, fathers, and parents. It was the duty of superiors in the family to rule firmly but with love. Books of advice for family use were printed in large numbers. Much of what they contained was far from original, but, written as many of these books were by married clergy, they benefited from a fuller and more intimate personal experience of family life than that enjoyed by Catholic writers. Protestant authors, many of whom belonged to the *Puritan wing of the Church, also laid greater emphasis on family prayers, Bible reading, and household Sabbath observance.

Reforming (Protestant and humanist) hopes of a well-ordered society also affected the family. In Scotland, the leaders of the new kirk aimed (1561) to provide for both *education and poor relief. In educational provision, Lowland Scotland may have been ahead of England, though south of the border too there was a great increase in the number of schools during and after the Reformation. More children, especially from the middle ranks of society, were going to school, and those who went were tending to stay on longer. But in poor relief Scotland lagged far behind England with its system based on statutory parish rates (installed between 1563 and 1601). For the first time there was in principle a nation-wide safety-net beneath those who had no family help or could not discharge their familial obligations: the disabled, the unemployed, the poor wage-earner overburdened with children, widows, orphans, and the enfeebled aged.

The Puritans at last gained political power in the 1640s only to see their own ranks fragment, and to face a task of imposing moral discipline made all the more difficult by the collapse of the church courts. Adultery became a capital offence in 1650, but the ordinance remained little more than a dead letter. Civil marriage, introduced in 1653, lasted only until the *Restoration. But Parliament's victory in the Civil War brought, in 1646, one of the most fundamental changes ever to take place in the family life of the upper classes, the abolition of feudal *wardship. Some of its worst abuses had already been removed under the early Stuarts, but its abolition removed for good the fear that predatory guardians might choose unsuitable marriage partners for orphaned heirs. Minorities now became opportunities for beneficial retrenchment. It was also during the 1640s that the mechanism of the 'strict *settlement' was perfected, the best device ever developed for combining the orderly transmission of the upper classes' landed property from one generation to the next with provision for non-inheriting children.

The century or so after the Civil War was a demographic plateau between two periods of steep growth. The sometimes terrible pressures of the era before 1650 eased off; real wages began to recover. Favourable service terms offered by employers anxious to secure labour (as after the Black Death) may have helped to delay marriages and thus limit fertility, but this was offset by a fall in the proportion of the population which remained permanently celibate. See Roger Schofield, 'English Marriage Patterns Revisited', *Journal of Family History*, 10 (1985), which corrects earlier accounts. Higher mortality was the most important underlying cause of the halt in population growth. *Smallpox, in particular, was a terrible scourge of the young. *London grew prodigiously; its high death-rates mopped up many of the young immigrants who settled in its *suburbs. Yet the metropolis also had a liberating influence. The London marriage market was just one example of this process. It catered both for the upper classes, whose life now centred on the capital to a greater extent than ever before, and for the huge numbers of young immigrants seeking betterment. The Fleet and other London liberties met the needs of those who wanted speedy and private marriages. London was the great centre of *clandestine marriage facilities, but they were available in many other places. Individual marriage decisions increasingly escaped the supervision of the local community and the weakened church courts. Young heirs and heiresses were now married later than in the 16th century, and were allowed more freedom of choice. But the wise did not marry for love alone. Financial con-

siderations were possibly more important than ever before. Divorce by Act of Parliament was introduced (1670–1700), allowing a failed marriage to be dissolved. But this remedy remained for a long time a luxury which only the rich could afford.

For the first time, female authors published books in some numbers. One of the most famous, Mary Astell (1668–1731), while not advocating women's participation in public life, claimed that education made them better mothers and wives. Yet there was also some deterioration in the position of women relative to their husbands. Statutes passed after the Restoration whittled down widows' property rights. During the 18th century the court of *Chancery, which had protected the wife's separate estate, became so costly as to be inaccessible to all save the very rich. Changes in the law made it harder to establish a separate estate. Parliamentary divorce overwhelmingly favoured men whose wives had been unfaithful.

Between 1751 and 1850, the population of Britain nearly tripled. The greater part of this growth resulted from the facts that a high proportion of the population was entering marriage and that the age of marriage was falling. These in turn were probably due, above all, to the rapid growth of the wage-earning workforce with the development of manufacturing and commercial agriculture and the decline of apprenticeship and service in husbandry. Paid employment, and the opportunity of engaging in forms of domestic industry which required little capital, lessened the dependence of prospective marriage partners on inheritance and other forms of assistance from the previous generation. Hardwicke's *Marriage Act (1753), designed to prevent the abduction and clandestine marriage of heirs and heiresses, tried to stamp out irregular marriages. But, it has been claimed, it did little to check the spread of unsolemnized 'common-law' unions among the poorer classes. *'Wife-selling' as a form of divorce was commonest (though never very frequent) in this period. By the later 18th century bridal pregnancy and *illegitimate birth rates stood at a higher level in England than ever before. They may point either to exceptional sexual freedom, or the vulnerability of poor girls in an age of unprecedented change and uncertainty.

Among upper-class families affection was accepted as a normal element in the choice of marriage partners. Aristocratic parents were having more children towards the end of the 18th century than at any previous time since the early 17th; upper-class infant mortality also fell sharply during the second half of the 18th century, and Randolph Trumbach, *The Rise of the Egalitarian Family: Aristocratic Kinship and Domestic Relations in Eighteenth-Century England* (1978), argued that parents were taking a closer and more affectionate interest in the welfare of their children than ever before.

The Agricultural and *Industrial Revolutions took much production out of the home and reduced the importance of the small-scale family enterprise in the national economy. The growth of the *factory, the large commercial farm, and bigger distributional enterprises, separated the worlds of home and 'gainful' employment for an increasing proportion of the population. The lives of women were profoundly affected by this change. During the phase of *proto-industrialization domestic industry expanded rapidly, and some 18th-century technological innovations created short-lived economic opportunities for women. But Bridget Hill (see above) thinks that there had already been a net loss in employment opportunities for women before the end of the 18th century. Work had always been largely separate from the domestic sphere for the professional classes. Business people, and eventually also the better-paid manual workers, aspired to fulfil the breadwinning role themselves and to keep their wives at home. The proportion of married women in full-time work fell by nearly half between 1851 and 1901, from 25 per cent to 13 per cent, and continued to decline, albeit more slowly, till the 1930s. Wives deprived of paid employment and confined to a narrower sphere became more dependent on their husbands. The rule of the Victorian patriarch could be suffocatingly protective or tyrannically overbearing. But happy marriages were nevertheless common in Victorian England, and attitudes to female sexuality in particular have been grotesquely caricatured by some historians.

There were also gains for women during this period. The Divorce Reform Act of 1857 made divorce more accessible and did something to right the previous bias in favour of men in the administration of the law. It also protected the property of wives who had been deserted or who had obtained separations or divorces. The Married Women's Property Act of 1882 (improving on a measure of 1870) protected the wife's control over all property which she brought to a marriage or acquired after it.

Victoria's reign also brought changes in the lives of children. Between 1833 and 1874, legislation curbed their employment. The conditions under which some children worked in factories and mines in the second quarter of the 19th century scandalized many observers, but their employment had probably been more widespread, and in many cases its nature had been as bad or worse, during the earliest stages of industrialization. The proportion of children aged 10 to 14 described as being in employment was 30 per cent in 1851, 17 per cent in 1901. (Very few children under 10 were involved). Already in 1851 41 per cent of the 10-to-14 age group were said to be scholars; and in 1870, when the first Education Act provided for universally available elementary education, the figure was 53 per cent.

The century between 1851 and 1951 saw mortality and fertility both fall. In each case the trends had begun before 1900 but became much more marked during the 20th century. Children and young adults were the first to benefit from falling mortality and infants and the elderly were the last, benefiting only after 1900. The improvement in life expectancy was most dramatic in the case of newly born babies. In England and Wales, infant mortality fell by nearly a quarter in the first decade of the 20th century. Such a reduction is more likely to have resulted from better care of babies than any improvement in the environment. A gradual if uneven rise in lifetime celibacy, and a rise in the age at marriage, put a brake on population increase in the late 19th century. Not until the last quarter of the 19th century was deliberate family limitation widely practised, first by the *middle classes, then by manual workers some decades later. The reasons probably included better prospects of survival for children and infants, the expense of bringing up larger numbers of surviving children, especially after women and children had largely been removed from the labour market, and higher material aspirations on the part of parents.

The welfare state was set up during the first half of the 20th century. Through the *old age pension, sickness and unemployment benefits, and the National Health Service, the state (using tax payments and National Insurance contributions) underpinned the family at moments of crisis and lightened its load. Support for the aged was particularly important. Between 1901 and 1951 the proportion of the population of England and Wales aged 65 and over more than doubled, from 4.7 per cent to 11 per cent.

The salient features of family life in the 1960s included individual longevity, a high incidence of marriage, the concentration of childbearing in the early years of marriage, and the widespread experience of retirement and grandparenthood. Shorter working hours, fewer children, and a longer life together made companionship more important for married couples. The home became for many people a haven of comfortable domesticity from which 'gainful employment' had been removed, and where the pressures of childbearing and rearing had been greatly reduced. Family life was more stable and more predictable than it had ever been before. The likelihood of early bereavement or a sudden slide into destitution had receded.

Since the 1960s, however, in a period of very rapid social change, the family as an institution has had to face a series of fundamental challenges. One of these has been posed by the return of married women to employment, but outside the home, rather than, as in pre-industrial times, in a family enterprise. The proportion of married women recorded as being in work rose from 10 per cent in 1931 to 22 per cent in 1951 and 49 per cent in 1976. Now the situation is fast approaching where as many women as men will be employed, and in many families women are already the chief or even sole breadwinner. Even though average female pay still falls far short of male, women are now for the first time taking over traditionally male jobs in large numbers.

The widespread adoption of much more effective means of *contraception, together with the continuing decline of the authority of the churches, a greater independence on the part of women, and the promotion of the ideal of self-fulfilment, have all played their part in the so-called 'sexual revolution' since 1960. Higher individual expectations in marriage, the reluctance of husbands to accept a changed role, the greater opportunities open to divorced women to support themselves, easier access to the courts through legal aid, and successive reforms of the law, have produced an unprecedented and marked increase in divorce cases. Britain has one of the highest divorce rates in Europe; for every two marriages in 1991 there was one divorce. Despite the availability of reliable contraception, births outside marriage have also increased very rapidly, reaching 30 per cent of the total in 1992. Reluctance to take precautions, the inexperience of adolescents engaging in sexual experiments at ever younger ages, and the failure of expected marriages to materialize, have all contributed to this result.

A new development has been a growing readiness to substitute the idea of 'partnership' for 'marriage', with its connotations of permanence, formal obligation, and tradition. It remains to be seen whether the British family can survive in anything like its traditional form.

The story of the family is one with substantial gaps in it. We need to know much more about the family economy, especially in the centuries before industrialization. There is considerable scope for further investigation of the lives of children and adolescents within the family since the Middle Ages. Attitudes, expectations, and the emotional climate of the family have been the subjects of some wild generalizations. There is a mass of letters, *diaries, and biographies which await careful analysis, an endeavour in which especial attention must be paid to the changing meanings of words.

RALPH HOULBROOKE

family bibles. In the 19th century popular editions of the Bible left several preliminary sheets blank to allow the insertion of genealogical details. Some give information that starts with the owner, others go further back in time (and need to be checked); many were brought up to date by later owners.

Family Division, Principal, Registry of. Since 1858 all *wills in England and Wales have been proved at the registry in Somerset House, Strand, London. The annual indexes, which name the testator and (until 1967) executor(s), can be consulted free of charge. A fee is payable to see the will. The indexes to letters of *administration may also be consulted; before 1870 these are indexed in separate volumes.

family history. The exploration of documentary sources by which to establish and prove the relationships set out in a *pedigree (in earlier times usually for legal purposes), the later development of the writing of family history, and more recently the relating of that history to the social and economic history of the time, has been a slow process over a long period.

Although the Saxons produced fictitious pedigrees linking Irish and British traditional genealogies with those of the Bible and classical antiquity, whose fullest development was seen in the British history of *Geoffrey of Monmouth written about 1135, there is little other evidence of Anglo-Saxon concern with genealogy. After the *Norman Conquest it was the legal aspect of individual pedigrees for particular purposes, as in the lengthy statements of descents on the *Plea rolls, which was pre-eminent for some centuries. Most of these statements were probably based on orally transmitted knowledge, though some of the longer ones may have been compiled from written evidence, as in the Scrope versus Grosvenor case of 1378, when *charters were produced in evidence.

It was not until the 15th century, with the development of other antiquarian and topographical studies, that collections of pedigrees were made. Old men were interviewed and searches were carried out in local *Chronicles and deeds and in *Chancery and *Exchequer records. By the end of the 14th century the heralds had assisted with peerage claims, but the oldest books of pedigrees which are known to be the work of heralds date from about 1480.

The rise in the 16th century of many new families to wealth and station, in a society where the prestige of ancient blood was great, produced, as it did in the 19th century, a market for deplorable concoctions as well as for genuine research. The series of heralds' visitations made in the 1560s recorded many lengthy but doubtful pedigrees as well as some fabrications, and it was not until those in the 1580s that Robert Glover (d. 1588) began to illustrate the principle that pedigrees should, if possible, be founded on record evidence.

The pedigree form with radiating lines (the *pied de grue* or crane's foot) derives from that given to the Genealogy of Christ or Tree of Jesse and to the Table of Kindred and Affinity. The oldest example of a Tree of Jesse is thought to be that in the Gospel of the Coronation of Wratislaw, King of Bohemia, dated about 1285, its earliest use by a European family being in a pedigree of Guelph, now at Fulda in Germany, dated about 1180–1225. Sir Thomas Wriothesley (d. 1534), *Garter King of Arms, was the first to use the rectilinear or drop-line pedigree. Robert Glover employed it regularly in the 1570s and by 1618 it had superseded the older forms.

Augustine Vincent (d. 1626), a pupil of William *Camden, who entered the College of *Arms in 1597, was the first to bring a knowledge of the public records to genealogy, having worked at the Tower Record Office. The first family history to have been compiled seems to be that by John Smyth (d. 1640), of Nibley in Gloucestershire, steward of the Berkeley family, who wrote their history and genealogy partly out of public records and partly from their family papers and charters at Berkeley Castle; but the first to be published did not appear until 1685.

Sir William *Dugdale (d. 1686), in his *Antiquities of Warwickshire* (1656) and *Baronage of England* (1675–6), displayed his superiority over earlier antiquarians by the skill with which he marshalled his evidence and drew conclusions from it, citing contemporary record evidence for every statement made.

Peter le Neve (1661–1729), Norroy King of Arms, showed that by the end of the century the Pedigrees of some knights needed something more than a knowledge of the records of land tenure. He therefore began to use *parish registers. Church monuments had always been used, but half a century later the importance of those in *churchyards for humbler families was also recognized. Two Garter Kings of Arms, Ralph Bigland (1711–84) and Sir Isaac Heard (1730–1822), were notable for their able use of available material in the construction of pedigrees for their numerous new clients.

Peerage writers of the 18th century, Arthur Collins (1682–1760) and Joseph Edmondson (d. 1786), almost exhausted that side of the market, but the local historians of the 18th and early 19th centuries wrote county histories containing pedigrees of the landed *gentry, many embodying fabulous material as the price of a subscription, for, as Thomas Whitaker wrote, 'in the genealogies of old families there are many vestiges of error, and some of fraud, which time and vanity have rendered sacred'.

However, the movement at the end of the 18th and in the 19th century toward the publication and arrangement of the public records had a beneficial influence on the study and literature of genealogy, and the peerage claims of the 1830s produced considerable genealogical activity, much of it fine work.

The 19th century, with its great growth in the *middle class, saw the development of several large commercial genealogical practices. The Burke family, of which John *Burke (1787–1848), his son Sir Bernard Burke (1814–92), and grandson Henry Farnham Burke (d. 1930) were the chief members, conducted a very considerable practice in research and publishing, and is well known for the production of Burke's *Peerage* (from 1826), the *Commoners* and *Landed Gentry* (from 1837), the *General Armory* (several editions, 1842–84), and numerous other works. The *Peerage* was based on the earlier work of Arthur Collins, and not only perpetuated the myths which Collins accepted, but added more from information supplied by the families and from other sources. The newly compiled *Landed Gentry* contained even more unreliable matter.

It was the critical genealogist Horace *Round (1854–1928) who, by his attacks from about 1893 onwards on these fabulous pedigrees, 'preserved like flies in amber the follies and errors which he chose to castigate'. He was by no means their first critic. The historian Edward Augustus *Freeman (1823–92), and others earlier, had fiercely attacked the 'monstrous fictions' to be found in Burke's quasi-official compilations. Round's attacks, with those of his friend Oswald Barron (1868–1939), were a potent influence in raising critical standards.

The vehicles used by these critics were various popular genealogical periodicals. John Gough *Nichols (1806–73), the editor of the *Gentleman's Magazine, published three: Collectanea Topographica et Genealogica (1834–43), The Topographer and Genealogist (1846–58), and The Herald and Genealogist (1863–74). Following his death, George William Marshall (1839–1905) founded The Genealogist (1877–1922) and Joseph Jackson Howard (1827–1902) founded Miscellanea Genealogica et Heraldica (1866–1938). Barron was himself the editor of The Ancestor (1902–5).

Of the family histories published in the 19th century, few have much merit. Among the best are R. E. Chester Waters's Genealogical Memoirs of the Extinct Family of Chester of Chicheley (1878), Falconer Madan's The Gresleys of Drakelowe (1899), and A. L. Reade's The Reades of Blackwood Hill (1906). Some of the best-researched and -arranged chart pedigrees are, however, to be found in the 35 volumes published between 1893 and 1921 by J. J. Howard and Frederick Arthur Crisp under the title Visitation of England and Wales.

The first guide to the subject was the peerage lawyer Stacey Grimaldi's Origines Genealogicae; or the Sources whence English Genealogies May Be Traced (1828). In their days, Richard Sims's Manual for the Genealogist (1856 and 1888), Walter Rye's Records and Record Searching (1888 and 1897), and William Phillimore's How to Write the History of a Family (1887 and 1900) and Pedigree Work (3rd edn., revised by Bower Marsh, 1936) were much respected.

Not all the large commercial genealogical practices at the end of the century were associated with the College of Arms, and several others were noteworthy, though their records have not always survived. Charles Allan Bernau (1878–1961) established a successful Genealogical Co-operative Research Club, which abstracted and indexed various classes of record at the *Public Record Office which were too large to be tackled by individuals.

It was C. A. Bernau who, on the suggestion of William Blyth Gerish (1864–1921) and with the co-operation of E. F. Briggs, Gerald Fothergill, F. K. Hitching, and a group of other middle-class and professional people, founded the Society of *Genealogists in the London office of the professional genealogist George Frederick Tudor Sherwood (1867–1958) in 1911, 'to promote, encourage and foster the study, science and knowledge of genealogy by all lawful means'.

One of the Society's aims was to bring together in one place the various indexes and transcripts which were then being made; it continues to do this, and a remarkable collection has been built up. It also greatly strengthened co-operation amongst genealogists. Following the failure of The Genealogist in 1922 it commenced to publish The *Genealogists' Magazine in 1925.

There was still undoubtedly a considerable element of snobbery in much of the work that was done, with an accent on 'good' lines and royal descents. In general, no necessity was seen to link the history of the families researched to the histories of the times in which they lived. However, the first competent history of a *yeoman family was probably William Miller Higgs's A History of the Higges or Higgs family (1933).

New records were being explored, and following the great social upheavals in the first half of the 20th century more people began to take an interest in the subject. The first of the new generation of basic guides for family historians was Arthur Willis's Genealogy for Beginners (1955). With the subsequent growth of the subject, elementary guides have become legion.

In 1961 the Society of Genealogists staged an exhibition on the theme 'The Ancestry of the Common Man'. The position at this time is surveyed in the writings of Anthony Richard Wagner (1908–95), Garter King of Arms from 1961 to 1978. His English Genealogy (1960) reflects the basic desire of the genealogist to extend his or her pedigree further, and this is taken to its limits in Pedigree and Progress (1975) with its tentative lines into antiquity; but Wagner also took considerable interest in social demography.

Wagner's Pedigree and Progress came at the time of an explosion of interest in genealogy. Every type of ancestor, good or bad, came to be pursued, a process no doubt assisted by a generally more relaxed attitude to illegitimacy, lack of marriage, and the breakdown of family life itself. Indeed, an inverted snobbery of descent from convicts became fashionable. At the same time an interest in medieval genealogy fell by the wayside in England, its last great flowering being probably the production of the Complete Peerage (14 vols., 1910–59).

Genealogy at this time developed also into something which its devotees began to call 'family history'. This term, not without argument, is frequently used instead of 'genealogy'. The latter term can be defined as 'the study of a technique establishing, with documentary evidence, the details of the relationships between generations', whereas the history of the family relates the grouping of people to their environmental and socio-economic surroundings. The introduction of the term 'family history', however, undoubtedly helped to give the subject some further academic respectability.

The catalyst in a world-wide process seems to have been the publication and filming of Alex Haley's *Roots* (1st edn. in Great Britain, 1977). Several local family history societies had been founded in the 1970s, and much publicity had been given to the subject during a widespread press campaign against the proposed removal of the *Registrar-General's search room to Southport in 1974–5. An International Congress had been held in London in 1976; the Parochial Registers and Records Measure was passed in 1978; a popular BBC television series 'Family History' was first transmitted in March 1979, and several very cheap and popular handbooks appeared. About the same time the Children Act (1975) had given adopted people the right to obtain a copy of their original entry in the register of births, a right which (if they fail to make application in their lifetimes) is sadly not transmitted to their descendants. The first history of a working-class family was probably Peter Sanders's *The Simple Annals* (1989). A *Dictionary of Genealogy* by T. V. F. FitzHugh had been first published in 1985.

The Society of Genealogists remained the only society catering for the subject in the British Isles until the Birmingham and Midland Society for Genealogy and Heraldry was founded in 1963. In the 1970s, with the great increase in interest in the subject, societies were founded in every county, many in time acquiring numerous branches. Their members, often without any formal academic background or training, were encouraged to trace their ancestors. These societies have brought like-minded people together and have shown that they are frequently tracing the same ancestors. They have also become important for their project work and publications. A *Federation of Family History Societies, to which all these societies and many overseas belong, was founded in 1974, and has itself done much to publicize and assist the subject through its twice-yearly conferences and a notable series of publications. The varied interests and objectives of family historians have also, since 1984, been reflected in the pages of the popular commercial magazine *Family Tree.

These co-operative movements in family history have taken place not only in Britain but over all the English-speaking world. In Europe also there has been a similar grassroots development in family history, except in Spain, Italy, and Greece, where family ties, it seems, have remained stronger and many families are still rooted in the soil.

C. A. Bernau had published the first directory of the names of families which people were researching. Such *surnames have come to be called the 'interests' of family historians. Recent directories, the *National Genealogical Directory* (published between 1979 and 1993) and the larger *Genealogical Research Directory* (published annually since 1981), have between them contained many hundreds of thousands of names. Similar directories are published by many local societies and by the Federation of Family History Societies (the latter being called the *British Isles Genealogical Register* or 'BIG-R').

The part played by the Genealogical Society of Utah in the development of genealogy in the British Isles is a considerable one. It has microfilmed great numbers of records in Britain since the Second World War and many of these are now available through the 35 Family History Centres which have been established in England. As mentioned below, its *International Genealogical Index became available in England in 1977, and in 1985 the British Genealogical Record Users' Committee was organized to support its microfilming programme and has since become an active forum for organizations representing users and keepers of archives.

A few genealogists in the past were sufficiently dedicated to trace everyone with their particular surname, and with the growth of the subject such 'one-name studies' have become much more common. With the passage of time they will become more so, and the bodies of information being collected are already showing the wider demographic uses of pure genealogy. A number of one-name studies are being made by associations of people with the same surname. A Guild of *One-Name Studies was established in 1979.

In Australia, New Zealand, and America, where it is possible to identify the original immigrant, many associations of descendants have been formed and regular reunions take place. The publication of books containing the complete descendants of particular people in both male and female lines is frequent in these countries, and has been popular in Europe, but seems much less popular in England. Similarly, books showing the complete ancestries of individuals in all their lines are rare in England, but are more common in Europe.

With the steady increase in the numbers of people interested in the subject and the demand for professional assistance the need for professional standards came to be recognized. An *Institute of Heraldic and Genealogical Studies was formed at Canterbury in 1961, and the process was given greater strength from 1968 onwards by the annual publication of a list of competent record agents and professionals by the Association of *Genealogists and Record Agents formed that year 'to promote and maintain high standards of professional conduct and expertise within the spheres of genealogy, record searching and associated disciplines'. However, the subject continues to produce numerous part-time researchers, many far from competent. Since the 1970s many classes for family historians have been organized by the various societies involved, and others have been provided by the WEA and university extramural departments. These have all assisted in the process of improving the standards of the work done.

The transcription, calendaring, and indexing of documents on a large scale by local family history societies and by some individuals, and the collection of large quantities of data by genealogists, particularly those interested in one-name studies, has in turn fuelled an interest in *computers and in computer programs specifically designed for recording pedigrees.

A computer group was formed within the Society of Genealogists, and in 1982 the Society started its quarterly journal *Computers in Genealogy* to report progress in the application of computers in genealogy. The management and arrangement of genealogical information, whether by drop-line chart pedigree, indented narrative, printed card or form, punched card or computer, is undoubtedly one of the attractions of the subject, and the two disciplines go well together.

The speed with which information can be transmitted by computers has, however, inherent dangers for the genealogist. Without proper referencing incorrect or fraudulent information is easily propagated, and a more strict attention to the quotation of sources is now constantly urged.

The Public Records Act (1958) embodied the principle that, in the words of the Grigg Committee (1954), 'no attempt should be made to keep in the Public Record Office things which would not otherwise be preserved solely because they contained information which might be useful for genealogical or biographical purposes'. However, a generation later the Wilson Committee's *Report on Modern Public Records* (1981) noted that the older genealogical or antiquarian uses of records had been 'absorbed into a richer and far wider study of family history, local history and military history', and concluded: 'We consider that these widespread interests in the history of the nation, the family, locality and other groups . . . are an important and wholly desirable development in national cultures.' Since then there appears to have been some attention to the needs of genealogists when the preservation or destruction of records is being considered, but much remains to be done.

Throughout the period under discussion the main sources used by genealogists slowly became accessible and more widely available. The value of *parish registers as a genealogical source for those families which did not own land began to be realized at the end of the 17th century, but it was not until the 19th century that genealogists began to transcribe and publish them in a systematic way.

The *Harleian Society, founded in 1869 to print 'the Heraldic Visitations of Counties and any manuscripts relating to genealogy, family history, and heraldry', established in 1877 a Register Section which continues to publish parish registers, the great majority relating to London. At the turn of the century, societies for the publication of registers were established in several counties, including Lancashire, Shropshire, Staffordshire, Surrey, and Yorkshire, and a general Parish Register Society was formed in 1896 and flourished for two or three decades. Most registers were transcribed from their commencement to 1812 or 1837 only. The first county to have all its parish registers up to 1837 in print was Bedfordshire, a task which was commenced in 1934 and completed in 1992.

In 1894 William P. W. Phillimore (1853–1913), believing that 'one of the chief obstacles to the completion of a pedigree, is the difficulty of obtaining the names of the wives', produced the first of 233 volumes containing transcripts of the marriage registers of about 1,650 parishes, the success of the scheme owing much to his partner Thomas Matthews Blagg (1875–1948).

The Society of Genealogists, founded in 1911, made one of its principal objects the collection of printed, manuscript, and typescript copies of registers. Its work was given urgency by the Second World War, and there was impetus through the Committee for Microfilming Parish Registers, which was active between 1939 and 1952.

Using the transcribed registers then available at the Society of Genealogists, Percival *Boyd (1866–1955) worked for 30 years at compiling a consolidated typescript index (by county) to marriages in England from 1538 to 1837. This contains about seven million entries, perhaps 13 per cent of the marriages which took place in that period. An old firm of record agents, Messrs. *Pallots, had already compiled a marriage index for much of London from 1800 to 1837 (now at the Institute of Heraldic and Genealogical Studies, Canterbury), in this instance working from the centrally deposited *bishops' transcripts of parish registers, the registers themselves in parish churches being difficult and costly of access.

Following the Parochial Registers and Records Measure (1978) the majority of parish registers over 100 years old have been deposited in county *record offices, where they have been the subject of much transcription work by the local family history societies. In two or three counties all the registers have been transcribed, and many societies have compiled county marriage indexes, supplementing or superseding Boyd's work, some going on to compile local burial indexes.

G. W. Marshall published the first list of transcripts of registers in public collections in 1900. This list was brought up to date by the Society of Genealogists in 1939 and again, under the title *National Index of Parish Registers*, in 1966, though so far the details for only 27 counties and Wales have been published. Regularly revised catalogues of the copies in its own possession, now relating to some parts of the registers of about 8,000 parishes, have also been published by the Society.

In 1938 the Genealogical Society of the Church of Jesus Christ of Latter-Day Saints (the *Mormons) commenced microfilming records and after the Second World War started a programme to microfilm parish registers in the British Isles. Using computers and volunteer church members in America, it has compiled from these microfilms one of the genealogist's major tools, the International Genealogical Index. First made available in Britain on microfiche in 1977, and now on CD-ROM, the Index, which is generally limited to the period 1538–1875, has gone through several editions, the most recent containing about 80 million entries of baptism and mar-

riage for the British Isles and about 200 million entries worldwide.

As most county record offices do not charge for access to the records in their custody, and as parish registers are often available there up to quite recent dates, family historians tend when possible to use them (despite their increasingly incomplete coverage) in preference to the records of *civil registration, information from the latter being available only on payment of fees for certified copies. These lengthy, and where marriages are concerned frequently abortive, searches (marriages in Register Offices being permitted from 1837) have increased the pressure of genealogists on some record offices.

Ralph Bigland wrote the first book on the genealogical value of parish registers, *Observations on Marriages, Baptisms and Burials, as Preserved in Parochial Registers* (1764), but recognizing also the importance of tombstone inscriptions as an important source for those below gentry status, he was also the first person to copy them systematically, as his history of Gloucestershire (posthumously published in 1791–2) shows. In this he was followed by numerous 19th-century antiquaries and local historians, though many copied only a proportion of the inscriptions found.

By the turn of the century several genealogists were copying all the stones in their areas, the work of William Blyth Gerish, who copied all the inscriptions in Hertfordshire, being a notable example. With the advent of the local family history societies in the 1970s much more organized transcription has taken place, and several counties have been completely or almost completely covered.

Problems of access to the probate records created by the *ecclesiastical courts prior to the Court of Probate Act in 1858 were long a major deterrent to their exploration and publication. The abstracts of *wills 'of the northern counties of England' published from 1835 onwards by the Surtees Society were a notable exception. In the twentieth century several indexes to the wills proved in the Court of Canterbury have been published.

Although some calendars of testators have been published by local record societies, the Yorkshire Archaeological Society, for instance, publishing those of the *Prerogative Court of York for the period 1388–1688, most work of this nature has been carried out by the *British Record Society. Through its Index Library series, started in 1888, that Society, having filled the gaps in the indexes to the wills of the

Prerogative Court of Canterbury 1383–1700, has turned its attention to providing indexes for the local courts. The process was made easier with local assistance, following the transfer of the early probate records from probate registries to county record offices in the 1950s, though funds for publication remain obstinately difficult to find.

It was not until 1862, following the foundation of the New England Historic Genealogical Society in Boston in 1845, that American genealogists—notably Joseph Lemuel Chester (1821–82) and Henry FitzGilbert Waters (1823–1913)—searching for the origins in England of early emigrants to America, began a systematic exploration of probate records, mostly in those of the Prerogative Court of Canterbury.

The publication of full extracts from the wills themselves has proceeded rather haphazardly, but F. G. Emmison's series of volumes for Essex, extracting all the local wills prior to 1603, form a model for further work of this kind.

The opening of the 1841 and 1851 *census returns to public scrutiny in 1912 gave an impetus to the searches of those who knew little about their immediate ancestry, and in the 1920s Alfred Trego Butler (1880–1946) at the College of Arms and others began to collect trade and commercial *directories as a ready means of identifying the appropriate streets and houses in which the families sought might be found. The 1861 returns did not become available until 1962, and apart from the street indexes compiled at the Public Record Office little systematic indexing by surname took place until the 1970s, since when many surname indexes, particularly to the 1851 returns, have been compiled. The decision, taken by the Genealogical Society of Utah in association with the British Genealogical Record Users' Committee in 1988, to transcribe and index the whole of the 1881 census returns for England, Wales, and Scotland, is already revolutionizing much 19th-century research and giving greater impetus to those having problems in the identification of their families in the centralized indexes of civil registration.

The centralized civil registration of births, marriages, and deaths had been introduced in England in 1837, and already by the turn of the century George Sherwood, a professional, was making general searches in its indexes in order to localize surnames in England and Wales. The original certificates, however, which had previously been open to search, were closed to public access in 1898. Copies are available only on the payment of heavy fees for certificates. This lack of free access to the genealogist's basic records remains a major deterrent to the aspiring genealogist, though the distribution of copies of the indexes on microfilm and then on microfiche in 1990 gave some assistance to local researchers.

The present situation in the British Isles to some extent mirrors that in America, where easy access to transcribed and indexed documents often means that only a limited knowledge of social history or *palaeography is necessary for the construction of a pedigree. Its practical effect is that most work by the local societies in Britain concentrates on the modern period, and Americans coming to Britain to search for ancestors in the 17th century find any work in original records doubly difficult.

As an interest in the subject has gone further down the social scale, an interest in and the exploration of more recent records of every description has grown apace. For many genealogists, for instance, access to First *World War soldiers' records is now of more vital importance than access to those of the 18th century or of earlier periods.

The modern family historian has shown that the past does not belong only to the professional and to the scholar. However, one has to recognize that many think of the subject merely as an amusing and absorbing hobby. They have no interest in producing a documented family history and do not see their work as having any lasting value. The energy, industry, and determination which family historians bring to their subject is, however, proverbial. The challenge, perhaps, is to channel some of that energy and to preserve the best of their work for future generations. For overviews, See A. R. Wagner, *English Genealogy* (3rd edn., 1983) and A. J. Camp, *Everyone has Roots* (1978). See also WOMEN LOCAL AND FAMILY HISTORIANS.   ANTHONY CAMP

family history societies. Until the 1960s the Society of *Genealogists was the only society for family historians. In the 1960s various provincial societies were formed and during the 1970s and 1980s the movement expanded so rapidly that every part of Britain was catered for. Many people join more than one society: the one nearest their home, and others in areas where their ancestors lived. Societies normally hold monthly meetings, organize visits, publish a journal, provide a library, and undertake tasks such as recording monumental inscriptions, or transcribing and indexing *census returns. They have been crucial to the great growth of interest in family history in the last three decades of the 20th century.

family reconstitution. The technique of compiling family trees for as many people as possible in a chosen area of study, e.g. a *parish, so as to obtain detailed demographic data on matters such as age at *marriage, or *expectation of life. In practice, only a minority of families can usually be studied in this way.

family tree. The traditional method since the Middle Ages of summarizing and displaying information about the ancestors of an individual. The earliest ones show the first-known ancestor at the root or trunk of a tree, with his descendants on the branches, but it soon became the custom to reverse the image by showing descendants below the earliest-known member. A modern method is to lay out the information horizontally with a chronological progression from left to right. The early family trees sometimes make spurious claims about the antiquity of a line. They are frequently casual, or totally uninterested, in following the descendants of the women and of younger sons.

Most families cannot prove continuous descent beyond the 16th or 17th century because of the lack of records. The information that has been gathered is so varied that family trees have to be tailored to meet individual requirements. They are merely summaries which should be fully supported by references to the evidence on which they are based. A modern method is to name only the parents, going back four generations to the 16 great-great-grandparents. The lack of adequate space to include all members of a family means that various overlapping trees have to be constructed. It is advisable to try to keep all those of a particular generation on the same level. See the STANDARD ABBREVIATIONS which are used.

Family Tree Magazine. Founded in 1984, this magazine aims at a popular market and is published bi-monthly.

famine. As the population grew rapidly during the 13th and 14th centuries chroniclers bemoaned the famines that resulted from spectacularly bad harvests. The great dearth of 1258 was the worst in the 13th century, but it was far surpassed in severity by the succession of harvest failures and livestock epidemics between 1315 and 1322, which brought a long period of *population growth to an end. See Ian Kershaw, 'The Great Famine and Agrarian Crisis in England, 1315–22', *Past and Present*, 59 (1973). In some parts of Britain, especially the more populous regions, famine conditions had become endemic even before this disaster. Such conditions persisted until the *Black Death of 1348–50. (See POSTAN THESIS.)

The gradual recovery of the population to its medieval level during the late 16th and 17th centuries was not accompanied by a re-emergence of famine, except in the most unfavoured parts. French demographic historians have demonstrated the continued severity of 'subsistence crises', marked by at least a doubling of the mortality rate and a drop of at least one-third in the number of conceptions leading to live births. When comparative demographic techniques were applied to the study of the population history of England, it was expected that a similar picture would be found. However, it is now clear that early modern England did not suffer from famines on a major scale. Mortalities rarely reached the levels that had been discovered in France. Such was the progress that had been made in agriculture that the country was normally able to feed itself, while in bad times corn imported from continental Europe, e.g. Danzig (Gdansk), could be quickly made available at town markets.

This positive picture needs to be qualified in three ways. First, there was undoubtedly hardship on occasion, which led to *food riots directed against profiteers. Second, in certain years the harvests were so bad that some people did die for want of food; three widespread dearths occurred in 1586–8, 1596–8, and 1622–3. Third, the pastoral and upland areas fared worse than the corn-growing lowlands. Cumbria was certainly badly affected during these three crises. See A. P. Appleby, *Famine in Tudor and Stuart England* (1978), R. B. Outhwaite, *Dearth, Public Policy and Social Disturbance in England, 1550–1800* (1991), and John Walter and Roger Schofield (eds.), *Famine, Disease and the Social Order in Early Modern Society* (1989).

Demographic historians now argue that unusual periods of high mortality were the result not of bad harvests but of epidemic *disease. There remains some uncertainty about a supposed connection between malnutrition and disease; did lack of food lower resistance to infection? See E. A. Wrigley and R. S. Schofield, *The Population History of England, 1541–1871: A Reconstruction* (1981), which argues that the seasonal patterns of burials resulting from famine are different from those caused by epidemics. Famine conditions are identified by the unusually high price of grain combined with a high mortality (as revealed by burial registers) in the 'harvest year' beginning on 1 August following (i.e. planted the previous autumn or spring). After 1623 famine conditions seem to have disappeared in England, though it has been argued that dearth was partly responsible for the high mortalities of 1723–30.

Comparable work on the same scale has not been attempted for the other countries of Britain, where the demographic data is far inferior. In the 1840s Ireland experienced a disaster comparable in its effects to the Black Death. See Cormac Ó Gráda, *Ireland Before and After the Famine: Explorations in Economic History, 1800–1825* (1988), Cormac Ó Gráda, *The Great Irish Famine* (1989), and P. M. Solor, 'The Great Irish Famine was no Ordinary Subsistence Crisis' in E. M. Crawford (ed.), *Famine: The Irish Experience, 900–1900* (1989). See also IRISH EMIGRATION. Ireland is seen as a classic *Malthusian country. *Potato failures were not uncommon before the mid-1840s, when exceptional hardship was caused by three failures in a row. However, population growth had slowed down before the Famine and agricultural output had increased by 80 to 100 per cent since 1800. See also T. M. Devine, *The Great Highland Famine* (1988), which deals with the repeated failure of the potato crop between 1846 and 1855 in the Highlands of Scotland. The famine was a demographic turning-point in the Highlands.

famuli. Workers on medieval estates who were paid, as distinct from those tenants who provided *boon labour.

farm, model. In the late 18th and early 19th centuries great landowners such as the Cokes of Holkham (Norfolk) employed architects to design farm buildings that were aesthetically pleasing as well as being an efficient use of space. They hoped to influence neighbouring landlords by their example. See M. Robinson, *Georgian Model Farms: A Study of Decorative and Model Farm Building in the Age of Improvement, 1700–1846* (1983).

farm buildings. The study of *vernacular architecture at first concentrated on farmhouses, but this has developed into a wider appreciation of the part played by all the buildings on a farm. The redundancy of many of these buildings because of modern farming methods has increased the concern to record and analyse in the face of the threat of demolition. See R. W. Brunskill, *Traditional Farm Buildings of Britain* (1982), E. W. Wiliam, *The Historic Farm Buildings of Wales* (1986), and the surveys of the Royal Commission on *Histor-

ical Monuments. Much work has been done on medieval *barns and the survival of the *timber-framed tradition in the post-medieval period. (See also LONGHOUSE and LAITHE HOUSES.) Interest has shifted to the farm buildings of the period 1750 to 1850, especially those associated with parliamentary *enclosure. In areas such as the Lake District traditional building materials continued in use, but in many parts of the country *brick was increasingly favoured. A pioneering survey was J. E. C. Peters, *The Development of Farm Buildings in Western Lowland Staffordshire* (1969), which showed how traditional designs of barns were adapted to store a greater volume of corn and hay. Waggon entries and first-floor storage became standard, and new courtyard layouts incorporated farmhouse, large, well-ventilated barns, *stables, dairies, stock-yards, cart-sheds, and stores for machines and tools. Scottish lowland designs described in Loudon's *Encyclopaedia* were widely followed in England. Great estates, e.g. those of the Sutherlands in Shropshire, led the way. The era of parliamentary enclosure also produced many new farm buildings at a lower social level, including the field barns in the new enclosures. See Nigel Harvey, *A History of Farm Buildings in England and Wales* (1970) and Susanna Wade-Martins, *Historic Farm Buildings* (1991). The Centre for East Anglian Studies, University of East Anglia, is conducting a thorough survey of farm buildings in Norfolk; see Alan Carter and Susanna Wade-Martins (eds.), *A Year in the Field: The Norfolk Historic Farm Buildings Project* (1987). The Historic Farm Buildings Group has an annual conference.

farmer. 1. A collector of taxes, who paid the Crown an agreed sum and made a profit on the collection.

2. In its modern sense, conveying no idea of acreage farmed or social status, the word began to replace *yeoman and *husbandman during the 18th century. It is derived from the Latin *firma*, meaning a fixed money rent.

farming clubs. The earliest farming club was established at Faversham (Kent) in 1727, but its character seems to have been largely social. A number of clubs were formed from the late 18th century onwards, with numbers reaching their peak in the 1830s. They met for regular discussion of farming practices, and some had libraries and organized visits to well-known farms. They were formed under the patronage of local landowners and their paternal character is revealed by the awards made to labourers and servants for loyal service. See AGRICULTURAL SOCIETIES.

farm servants. The distinction between a farm servant and a farm labourer was that a servant was an adolescent boy or an unmarried man who was hired for a year and who lived on the farm, whereas an *agricultural labourer was usually a married man who lived elsewhere (often in a *tied cottage) and who was paid a daily or weekly wage for the job that he performed. Farm service was the normal career expectation of teenage boys from about the age of 14 during the medieval and early modern period, and in some parts of Britain during much of the modern era. See Anne Kussmaul, *Servants in Husbandry in Early Modern England* (1981), which provides a general survey of a poorly recorded topic. Boys were contracted at *hiring fairs at an agreed wage, with board and lodging. At first they chose farms that were near to home, but it was usual for lads to move on at the end of the year to farms that were more distant but still located within a radius of 20 to 25 miles of the boy's home. Farm service, together with *domestic service and the *apprenticeship system, was well suited to an age when most work was performed at the place of residence. Farmers and other employers whose own children were not of the appropriate age were able to find young workers who could not be offered employment at home. Dr Kussmaul estimates that servants supplied between one-third and one-half of the hired agricultural labour-force of the early modern period.

Farm service reached a high point in the mid-18th century, but in the south of England it soon began to decline as farming families ceased to regard their young servants as members of the family. In other parts of Britain, however, the system survived throughout the 19th century, and in some cases up to the Second World War. See Stephen Caunce, *Amongst Farm Horses: The Farm Lads of East Yorkshire* (1991) for an analysis of how the system worked for the benefit of both employers and employees. See also Fred Kitchen, *Brother to the Ox* (1940) for the personal reminiscences of a farm servant and farm labourer. For general background, see Alan Armstrong, *Farmworkers: A Social and Economic History, 1770–1980* (1988), and T. M. Devine (ed.), *Farm Servants and Labour in Lowland Scotland, 1770–1914* (1984), which is concerned with the survival of antique forms of labour alongside technical modernization.

farm sizes. In the early Middle Ages most families earned a living farming a customary *bovate or *carucate of 10 to 15 *acres of arable land with grazing and other rights on the *commons. A few wealthier families had managed to accumulate a number of such holdings, and at the opposite end of the social scale an increasing number of *cottagers had to struggle to survive with less than 5 acres of land. The shortage of land ended with the *Black Death, after which a wealthier peasantry with larger holdings emerged. (See ENGROSSING.)

The renewed growth of *population in the Tudor and early Stuart period again produced a situation where small holdings were characteristic of most areas, but *cottages were becoming numerous. *Copyhold tenure was increasingly converted to *leasehold at this time. After the *Restoration large landowners began to build considerable estates through marriage, purchase, and the application of strict rules of *inheritance. They favoured the letting of farms in much larger units than before. This process gathered pace in much of southern and eastern England during the 18th and 19th centuries, as leases fell in. Nevertheless, small holdings remained characteristic of other parts of Britain.

It was once held that parliamentary *enclosure was a major cause of the decline of the *smallholder, but this picture has been radically revised. Studies of the *estate records of great landowners have shown that even before 1750 the general trend towards larger units was evident, and that this trend continued in corn-growing regions whether or not a particular parish was enclosed or remained under the *open-field system. Other studies have demonstrated the remarkable persistence of small holdings elsewhere.

Large farms of 500 acres or more became the usual type of holding in Northumberland and Norfolk, the *chalklands of southern England, and the chalk and limestone districts of the midlands and the East Riding of Yorkshire. Farms were much smaller on the heavy soils of the midlands, in north-west England, in Devon and Cornwall, close to London, and in Ireland, Scotland, and Wales. The contrasts were marked between different *pays within certain counties, e.g. in Lincolnshire small farmers survived in the *fens and *marshlands, but some very large farms were created on the *wolds. In Wiltshire during the 19th century small owners declined rapidly in chalk areas but continued to predominate in cheese districts. Even Norfolk and Northumberland, which were famous for their large farms and progressive husbandry, also had numerous small holdings on heavier soils and in infertile areas.

David Grigg, 'Farm Size in England and Wales, from Early Victorian Times to the Present', *Agricultural History Review*, 35/2 (1987) shows that before the 1870s larger farms were formed at the expense of smaller ones but that this pattern was reversed in the 1880s, and until the 1920s smaller farms increased absolutely and proportionately whilst larger farms declined. Since then larger farms have again been formed, though it was not until the mid-1960s that farms of 300 acres or more occupied the same proportion of crops and grass as they had in 1851. By 1983, 13 per cent of holdings accounted for over half the total land occupied by farms in England and Wales. Despite the concentration of land in fewer and fewer hands during the 20th century, however, in certain districts, e.g. the Pennines, small holdings remain the characteristic farm unit.

farthing. A quarter-penny. Until 1279 it was formed by cutting a penny into four quarters. The farthing ceased to be legal tender in 1956.

father-in-law. The term was often used to mean stepfather, i.e. a mother's second husband. A father-in-law in the modern sense was often termed 'father'.

fealty. An oath of allegiance to the king, given when a new tenant paid homage to the lord who was his immediate superior, thus recognizing his obligations.

Federation of Family History Societies. Founded in 1974 to co-ordinate the activities of the growing number of *family history societies, the federation publishes *Family History News and Digest* twice a year and a series of booklet guides to the availability and use of records. Conferences are held twice a year under the auspices of member societies. The federation represents the points of view of family historians to official bodies.

fee-farm. An annual rent paid by chartered *boroughs to the Crown in the Middle Ages.

fee simple. *Freehold land which can be disposed of according to the wishes of the owner.

feet of fines. Fine is derived from the Latin *finis*, meaning 'end'. The term came to be applied to a judgement concerning a title to land. From the late 12th century until 1834 a record of title (usually made after a purchase) was written out three times on a single sheet of parchment. The three copies were then cut apart along wavy lines to prevent forgery. Two parts were given to the parties involved, and the

copy at the foot of the fine was filed among the rolls of the Court of *Common Pleas, now kept at the *Public Record Office under the references CP 25 and 27. Until 1688 the rolls were arranged under counties; this has enabled several county record societies to publish editions. See Jonathan Kissock, 'Medieval Feet of Fines: A Study of Their Uses with a Catalogue of Published Sources', *Local Historian*, 24/2 (1994).

felony. Crimes such as murder, rape, arson, robbery, burglary, etc. were regarded (except in Scottish courts) as being more serious than *misdemeanours. The penalties included forfeiture of land and goods. Forfeiture was abolished in 1870.

female descent. Any line of descent through a woman.

fens. Fen is an *Old English word to describe the low-lying, waterlogged areas of eastern England, particularly those draining into the Wash or the Humber. From the early Middle Ages onwards, if not before, man attempted to drain the fens, culminating in the great engineering schemes of the 17th and 19th centuries. Hardly any fenland has not been reclaimed. Wicken Fen (Cambridgeshire), a 600-acre reserve owned by the National Trust, is the finest remnant of the great fens of East Anglia, rich in plant and insect life and a habitat for a wide variety of birds.

Drainage of the fens by high dykes and seawalls proceeded on an irregular basis, with many failures, through the early Middle Ages. Some major projects were supervised by monastic landowners, but piecemeal communal reclamation was more typical. The decline of the national *population after the *Black Death eased the pressure for reclamation, but once the population had recovered to its medieval levels fresh attempts were made. In the 1630s the most spectacular scheme was the reclamation of 190,000 acres of the Bedford Level (named after the owner, the 4th Earl of Bedford) between Cambridge, Peterborough, and Wisbech, involving the Dutch and Flemish company headed by Cornelius Vermuyden. In 1631 what is now called the 'Old Bedford' river was completed, 70 feet wide and 21 miles long. The project was continued after the *Civil War by the cutting of the 'New Bedford' river and other massive drains. See S. Wells, *The History of the Drainage of the Great Level of the Fens, Called Bedford Level* (1830). The shrinkage of the peat on drying was an unforeseen difficulty which had to be tackled by water pumps operated by wind*mills, and in later centuries by pumps driven by *steam and *electricity. In some places the reclaimed fens are now several feet below the level of a road or adjacent fields.

Large blocks of reclaimed land were allotted to the 'adventurers' who had put their money into this scheme. Here, and elsewhere, e.g. Hatfield Chase and the Isle of Axholme, the local smallholders who had managed to earn a sufficient living before drainage were now faced with the loss of valuable rights on the *commons. Rioting and the destruction of some of the new works ensued. In *Fenland Farming in the Sixteenth Century* (1953), *English Peasant Farming: The Agrarian History of Lincolnshire from Tudor to Recent Times* (1957), and *The *Agrarian History of England and Wales, iv: 1500–1640* (1967) Joan Thirsk altered previous perceptions of the farming economy by a sympathetic understanding of the smallholders' complaints against the drainers. Fen parishes were large and populous and geared to raising livestock, especially cattle, rather than the growing of corn. Their vast commons helped to support numerous families, few of whom were rich but most of whom enjoyed a comfortable standard of living. Numerous small farmers continued to earn a satisfactory living during the 19th century. See Adrian Hall, *Fenland Worker-Peasants: The Economy of Smallholders at Rippingale, Lincolnshire, 1791–1871* (1992).

feodary. A survey of the obligations of tenants of the Crown; the officer who enforced such obligations.

feoffee. One of a group of trustees appointed to manage an endowed institution, e.g. a charity school.

feoffment. The original form of conveyance by a symbolic handover known as livery of *seisin.

ferries across rivers were a feature of *Roman roads, notably the crossing of the Humber by Ermine Street. The word is derived from Old Norse. Ferrybridge (Yorkshire) is a name which reveals the way that many of the ancient ferries became redundant.

fertility rates. These are measured in various ways, so the precise method in use needs to be stated. Fertility rates refer to the number of births per female of reproductive age in the population under scrutiny, normally expressed as so many per thousand. Sometimes age-specific rates are used.

feudal aids were originally gifts from a free tenant to his lord, but the system was abused. *Magna Carta (1215) insisted that a lord might exact an aid on only three occasions: to pay a ransom for the lord, upon the lord's eldest son becoming a *knight, and upon the marriage of the lord's eldest daughter.

feudalism. A term used to describe the political and economic system in European countries during the Middle Ages, by which land was held on condition of homage and service to a superior lord. The nobility held their estates in return for military service to the Crown; the peasantry farmed their holdings under the protection of a *lord of the manor in return for *boon work, customary payments, and military service when required. In England the system broke down during the 13th and 14th centuries as services and obligations were commuted to money payments. In the later 13th century Edward I, finding that his feudal levies provided an inadequate force for his Scottish and Welsh campaigns, turned instead to the recruitment of troops by indenture. Historians use the term 'bastard feudalism' to describe conditions in the later Middle Ages, when the system was breaking down. Feudal tenure was abolished in 1660, long after it had ceased to operate in practice. Old notions of feudalism have been challenged in Susan Reynolds, *Fiefs and Vassals: The Medieval Evidence Reinterpreted* (1994).

fief. A hereditary estate held under a superior lord on condition of homage and service. See FEUDALISM.

field books. The notebooks used 'in the field' by surveyors. These working notes and sketches were later converted into maps and plans. Field books form an important part of the Fairbank papers at Sheffield Archives, the best-preserved collection of surveyors' records, extending over four generations from the mid-18th to the mid-19th century.

field-names. Collecting all the field-names of a parish from every available source, from earliest times to the present day, is a worthwhile task for a local historian or a *group project. Unlike the study of *place-names, specialist linguistic knowledge is rarely needed, for few field-names go back so far in time as to hinder interpretation. Every parish has sufficient records to make this task plausible; even towns and cities have records of field-names from earlier times and street-names that commemorate former fields. In some parishes field-names changed considerably over time, but elsewhere the names have remained remarkably consistent over centuries. See John Field, *A History of English Field-Names* (1993).

field systems. Fields help to define the character of the many different regions of Britain. The regularly shaped fields of the Midland Plain, bounded by hawthorn hedges, immediately speak of a different agrarian history from that of the irregular fields and substantial stone walls of the Lake District. Present and past field systems, including regulations imposed by manorial *courts or village meetings, provide much detailed evidence of agricultural practices and communal activities down the ages. Agrarian historians, historical geographers, and archaeologists have all contributed to our understanding of the origins and functions of field systems, and detailed local case-studies have added a great deal of empirical evidence. After more than a century of scholarly activity, the complexity and variety of regional field systems is now well understood, but the debate on origins and development is still not concluded.

Archaeologists and historians now emphasize the enduring influence of the environment on farming systems and other human concerns. A stress on continuity and gradual evolution over long periods of time has replaced older assertions that changes were brought about by invaders bringing a different culture from the Continent. *Population growth and climatic change, new technology, and new management systems are now included among the catalysts for change, and theories about the importance of the ethnic origin of the population have been much modified. It is now accepted that the *prehistoric and Romano-British contribution to the evolution of the historical landscape was immense. The survival of prehistoric and Romano-British field *boundaries into the modern landscape indicates that the *Anglo-Saxons inherited and continued to cultivate an organized agrarian system. (See CELTIC FIELDS.) Christopher Taylor, *Fields in the English Landscape* (1975), summarizes the change of perception by claiming that 'even before 1000 BC much of England was occupied and farmed on a large scale and in a well-organized pattern'. He goes on to demonstrate that evidence of farming activities in the Romano-British period have been discovered 'on every type of soil, in every conceivable situation'.

The major debate on field systems has concerned the origins and nature of the English *open-fields. H. L. Gray, *English Field Systems* (1915), a remarkable pioneering work, remains a valuable introduction to the subject, even though it is now realized that field systems were much more varied and complex than he thought. Gray observed that the two- and three-field system was not ubiquitous, but was most widespread and characteristic in central England. He distinguished the Midland field system from different systems in East Anglia, the Lower Thames Basin, and Kent, and from what he described as the Celtic system. He offered two explanations for these differences: ethnic factors and the restraints imposed by the physical environment. Gray believed that the common-field system had been imported to England from the Continent by the Anglo-Saxons. Irregular field systems were the result of adaptations to physical features and to the presence of extensive wastes, e.g. in *forest areas where the initially small populations were concentrated in *hamlets. Gray's emphasis on the variety of field systems and his map showing the parts of the country where common-fields were characteristic have formed the basis of subsequent research, but his emphasis on ethnic origins has been revised, especially as German scholars now argue that the first complete common-field systems in their country developed during a period of growing population some time between the 10th and 13th centuries and long after the Anglo-Saxon emigrations. English archaeologists have noted, moreover, that many early Anglo-Saxon sites have no relation to patterns of *strips, and have concluded, therefore, that the open-field system came later, when nucleated villages were first formed.

C. S. and C. S. *Orwin, *The Open Fields* (1938) has also been influential in its imaginative reconstruction of the labours of the first open-field farmers. The Orwins saw the open-field system as a sensible method of co-operation that insured against *famine. Strips were long so that a plough-team of *oxen did not have to be turned too often, and they were narrow because that was all that could be ploughed in a day's work. The joint nature of the enterprise was necessary because resources like ploughs and oxen were scarce; co-operation meant that all the land was shared out. The practical approach of the Orwins has been influential, but it assumes, wrongly, that the open-field system was fully fledged from the start.

Joan Thirsk, 'The Common Fields', *Past and Present*, 29 (1964) put forward a new view. Starting from the premiss that the classic common-field system represented an intensive system of farming for corn which was characteristic of all well-populated villages in plain and valley locations whereas, in pastoral areas, arable fields were a subsidiary element in a farming system which was based on the rearing of livestock, she argued that those fields which were parcelled into strips were sometimes subject to common rules of cultivation, sometimes not. This distinction between common-fields and open-fields was not just spatial; open-fields were seen in some areas as an immature common-field system. Thirsk argued that the common-field system developed slowly and did not reach maturity until the 13th century.

A new synopsis was attempted by a team of historical geographers in A. R. H. Baker and R. A. Butlin (eds.), *Studies of Field Systems in the British Isles* (1973), which contained a number of detailed regional studies, including Wales, Scotland, and Ireland. The volume emphasized the considerable variety of field systems, both spatially and temporally, and stressed how they evolved as a response to population growth. It concluded that the so-called Midland field system was more adaptable to change than was once believed, for *leys and complex rotations were used much earlier than was once thought, and as the *furlong, not the field, was often the cropping unit, the distinction between two- and three-field systems is blurred. The varied terminology and the uneven survival of records made regional comparisons difficult. Indeed, the problem of when and how open-field systems began is bedevilled by the lack of documentary evidence. Baker and Butlin argued in general that British field systems after the *Norman Conquest became increasingly varied, both in terms of the farming methods and of the systems of organization being practised. They noted that an early and basic form of settlement and agrarian organization throughout much of western and central Europe, including the British Isles, was the hamlet and its associated *infield / outfield system, and they suggested that field systems evolved from this basic model.

The belief that open-fields evolved from simpler forms has become widely accepted, but an earlier chronology is now preferred. See R. T. Rowley (ed.), *The Origins of Open-Field Agriculture* (1981). Mary Harvey, 'Planned Field Systems in Eastern Yorkshire: Some Thoughts on Their Origin', *Agricultural History Review*, 31/2 (1983) drew attention to the marked regularity of fields over a wide district and suggested that they were deliberately planned by powerful lords. These fields were laid out in long, parallel *lands, which were often over 1,000 yards long, and in some *townships over a mile long. The system was arranged in only two fields, which acted as the cropping units. The furlongs into which the fields were divided

were few and large and of identical structure. Each furlong had the same number of lands and each contained a similar proportion of broad and narrow lands, which lay in the same relative position to each other. Other work has shown that villages themselves, especially in the north of England, were measured out according to a preconceived plan, presumably at the same time as the field systems. Such planning may have been done by Danish overlords, or it may have been a long-drawn-out process stretching into Norman times.

Field work and documentary research into Northamptonshire fields shows that the eastern Yorkshire system was not unique, but that long lands were an early feature of even those midland townships which by the 12th century had developed a classic open-field system. See David Hall, *Medieval Fields* (1982), which argues for an 8th- or 9th-century origin for subdivided fields laid out in a deliberate act of planning. Furlong boundaries often survive in lowland England where the rest of the system has gone. The original plan was drastically modified over time. Only a few two-field systems survived in Northamptonshire until the 18th century; most of the county was farmed on a three-field system by the 15th century. There is no doubt that the open-field systems of the early modern period, here and elsewhere, had become complex and adaptable, as has been demonstrated in volumes iv and v of *The *Agrarian History of England and Wales*, but as yet there is no consensus about the timing of planning and its importance relative to maturation. The variety of regional experience is emphasized, in terms of social structure as well as soil types; did strong lordship produce common fields? Unfortunately, documentary evidence is weakest (and often non-existent) for the period when the open-field system began. The debate over origins cannot be resolved by the use of later historical evidence.

The study of Scottish field systems is hampered by the lack of pre-18th-century maps and associated documents. Much of Lowland Scotland was enclosed after 1695 by gradual consolidation, individual planning, private agreement, and legal action. On the whole, the Scottish landscape is the product of evolutionary rather than revolutionary change, but enclosure brought about rapid change in some areas. Historians and historical geographers have paid most attention to the archaic practices of the Western Highlands and the Outer Isles. (See RUNRIG.) See also R. A. Dodgshon, *Land and Society in Early Scotland* (1981). Here and elsewhere Dodgshon argues that field systems were not consciously designed, nor were they considered responses to the desire for a communal system of farming, but were makeshift in character and origin, an amalgamation of responses to diverse influences. Field systems should be investigated as part of the total history of rural communities. He suggests that subdivided fields originated as the sharing out of *assarts, and that communal agriculture began as a response to logistical problems. Scattered parcels of land were subsequently formalized into shared holdings. He also argues that the significant distinction between infield and outfield land was tenurial rather than practical.

The infield / outfield system was also widely practised in Ireland. See R. H. Buchanan, 'Field Systems of Ireland' in A. R. H. Baker and R. A. Butlin (eds.), *Studies of Field Systems in the British Isles* (1973). Writers in the 19th century used the term 'rundale' to describe surviving field systems which incorporated small gardens, infield, outfield, common meadow, and rough grazing beyond. Arthur *Young, *Tour in Ireland* (1780) and the county statistical accounts of 1802–32 sponsored by the Royal Dublin Society are major sources of information about agricultural practices during the period when rundale was beginning to decline.

It is clear from the intensive studies that have been made of field systems that generalized statements may bear little resemblance to local practices. These practices vary not only spatially but over time. H. L. Gray's belief in the plurality and regional variety of English field systems has been vindicated by detailed studies from all over the British Isles. Works of synthesis are a necessary starting-point, but the local historian should not be surprised if his or her locality pursued its independent methods. In many parts of Britain the arable fields formed a relatively small part of a farming system that was geared more to pastoral farming than the growing of crops. In such places, the agricultural historian needs to turn his attention to *meadows and pastures and the common wastes.

Fiennes, Celia (1662–1741). Her account of journeys undertaken at various times in the later 17th and early 18th centuries is a marvellously rich source of observations on society and the developing economy of late Stuart England. She is particularly informative on the fashionable towns and *spas, industrial enterprises, and the country houses and *inns that she stayed at. Her endless curiosity and eye for human detail endears her to her readers. See

Christopher Morris (ed.), *The Illustrated Journeys of Celia Fiennes, c.1682–c.1712* (1984).

Fifth Monarchy men. A millenarian *Puritan group that emerged during the *Civil War. Their name was taken from the Book of Daniel, which foretold the rise and fall of four successive monarchies, to be followed by a fifth monarchy which would last for ever. This fifth monarchy was identified as the rule of Jesus Christ and his saints. The group was influential in the Barebones Parliament of 1653. After the *Restoration they attempted a rising in London, in January 1661, which failed. They quickly declined as a creditable movement thereafter. See Bernard Capp, *The Fifth Monarchy Men: A Study in Seventeenth-Century Millenarianism* (1972).

final concord. An agreement drawn up at the conclusion of a fictitious suit, whose true purpose was to convey real estate.

Finberg, H. P. R. Herbert Finberg (1900–74) was Head of the Department of English Local History at the University of *Leicester, first as Reader and then as Professor, from 1952 to his retirement in 1965. His first book, *Tavistock Abbey: A Study in the Social and Economic History of Devon* (1951) was published at the end of his previous career as a publisher and printer. In 1952 he and W. G. *Hoskins brought out a collection of essays, *Devonshire Studies*, which did much to establish the new techniques, insights, and approaches of the local historian.

At Leicester his department became recognized as the only centre for postgraduate studies in the subject. The series of *Occasional Papers* which he edited became widely influential, starting with his own paper, *The Local Historian and His Theme* (1952), in which he suggested that local historians should be concerned with the origins, growth, and decline of *communities. This concept proved to be enormously stimulating in the development of local history as an academic discipline. His paper on *Roman and Saxon Withington: A Study in Continuity* (1955) challenged the conventional wisdom that a clean break occurred between the withdrawal of the Romans and the coming of the Saxons. Meanwhile, his work on Anglo-Saxon *charters led to the publication of *The Early Charters of Devon and Cornwall* (1953), *The Early Charters of the West Midlands* (1961), and *The Early Charters of Wessex* (1964). In 1955 he contributed the volume on *Gloucestershire* in the *Hodder and Stoughton landscape history series, and two years later he edited *Gloucestershire Studies*.

In 1953 he became the first editor of *The *Agricultural History Review* and was instrumental in setting the high academic standards of this new venture. But his greatest enterprise was initiating and taking responsibility for *The *Agrarian History of England and Wales*, a massive undertaking that has taken 40 years to complete, but which covers the entire timespan from prehistory to 1939 in eight thick volumes. Finberg was general editor for the whole series and took particular responsibility for the first volume, to which he contributed a lengthy chapter on 'Anglo-Saxon England to 1042'.

A Festschrift, *Land, Church and People*, edited by Joan Thirsk, was published by the *British Agricultural History Society in 1970, in his honour.

Fine Rolls. Records of payments to the Crown for writs, grants, privileges, and pardons, of appointments of royal officials, and of orders sent to sheriffs, etc. The rolls are kept at the *Public Record Office. A published *calendar covers the period 1272–1509.

fines and rents. In the late medieval and early modern period tenants who held their property by *copyhold or *leasehold paid an entry fine upon acquiring a holding through *inheritance or purchase. This fine was a lump sum, which might be either 'certain', that is, fixed by custom, or 'arbitrary', that is, open to negotiation. In an inflationary age tenants who paid 'certain' fines benefited at the expense of their lords. There were therefore many battles in court as to whether or not fines were fixed by custom. The records of such cases—in *Chancery, *Exchequer, etc.—are very informative about local practices and the struggles between lords and tenants. A series of legal decisions in the Court of Chancery and other courts established the principle that arbitrary fines must be 'reasonable'; in other words, manorial lords could not pitch their demands so high that the custom of inheritance was defeated. In practice, therefore, even 'arbitrary' fines were rarely set at more than one year's—or at most two years—improved rental value of a holding. Those 'certain' fines that had been fixed by the 15th century were usually very much less. (See LEASE; RENTAL; and HERIOT.)

Copyholders and leaseholders also paid low annual rents, which were known variously as rents of assize, quit rents, reserved rents, or by some other local name. These rents may once have been set at the full value of the land, but as they were fixed by custom which the manorial lord could not change, they represented, by the 17th century, only a very small proportion of its value. However, the money rent by itself does not reveal the full picture. The landlord was able to shift some of the burden of taxation on to the tenant and to insist that the tenant shared the costs of repair and maintenance. Local customs varied considerably, but in general the common practice was for poor rates and other parish and county dues to be paid by the tenant, whilst parliamentary taxes were paid by the owner. Tenants were also compelled to maintain soil fertility by *manuring with dung, *lime, or *marl, and sometimes to pay for repairs. Fluctuations in 'real' or total rents were therefore greater than the slight upward or downward movement of money rents. The legal position and the reality of the situation were not necessarily the same. Landlords did not always have the advantage even where local custom was weak. In times of depression they had little alternative to treating leniently those tenants who fell behind with their payments; at other times, competition for holdings was never so intense as to drive rents to heights beyond which tenants were unwilling to pay.

During the second half of the 17th and the 18th centuries the system of levying fines on the grant or renewal of leases was gradually abandoned in favour of *rack rents. The fine system declined slowly, but survived on ecclesiastical property well into the 19th century.

firebacks and fireplaces. Cast-iron firebacks, designed to protect the stone wall at the rear of a fire and reflect the heat, were a popular product of 16th- and 17th-century ironworks. Some were decorated with scrolls and floral motifs, with the initials of the householders and the date of manufacture, and sometimes with the royal arms.

The word *chimney was originally used for a hearth or fireplace. The central hearths of medieval *open halls began to be replaced by huge fireplaces set in a side wall during the 16th century; earlier fireplaces can be seen in Norman *castles and other major buildings. In the largest houses of the Elizabethan and early Stuart era elaborate fireplaces were constructed of stone (including local 'marbles') and brick. They were usually supported by classical columns and *strapwork designs taken from *pattern books, and were surmounted by the *coat of arms of the family and sometimes also by the royal arms. Bolsover Castle (Derbyshire) has an outstanding set of fireplaces individually designed by John Smythson. See Mark Girouard, *Robert Smythson and the Elizabethan Country House* (1983). The fashion for such fireplaces spread amongst the *gentry and the wealthier industrialists, e.g. *clothiers or iron-masters; see, for instance, Colum Giles, *Rural Houses of West Yorkshire, 1400–1830* (1986). The *baroque period also favoured elaborate decoration, particularly carvings in wood by Grinling Gibbons, Samuel Watson, etc. During the 18th and early 19th centuries a restrained classical style was preferred. The Victorians were eclectic in their choice of styles, many of the grander houses returning to the fashions of the Tudor and Jacobean era. In the later 20th century central heating has reduced the role of the fireplace in new houses to the purely decorative.

firebote. The right to remove wood from the *commons for fuel.

fire insurance. Fire was a major hazard when buildings were normally constructed of timber and roofed with *thatch. The Great Fire of London (1666) was the worst disaster, but other towns, e.g. Warwick and Blandford Forum (Dorset), were devastated by fire. See the articles by Stephen Porter on local fires, e.g. 'The Oxford Fire of 1644', *Oxoniensia*, 49 (1984). Building regulations insisting on the use of *brick and tiles became increasingly common. In the early 18th century several fire insurance companies started business, at first for London and then for provincial customers. Some metal badges bearing the trade mark of the company are still fixed to 18th- and 19th-century buildings; these were used for identification and as advertisements. The insurance companies had their own primitive fire engines.

The *Guildhall Library, London, has a collection of fire insurance records. These start with the Sun Fire Office and the Hand in Hand in 1710, the London Assurance from 1720, and the Royal Exchange Assurance (whose earlier records are lost) from 1773. The registers note the address of the insured property, the owner's name and occupation, and any transfer of ownership, and give a brief description of the structure, including its building materials. They are an important source for industrial history. Fire insurance plans have been described as a major cartographic source for considering the development of the major British towns and cities and industrial districts, *c*.1885–*c*.1970; See Gwyn Rowley, 'Fire Insurance Plans' in Helen Wallis (ed.), *Historians' Guide to Early British Maps* (1994).

fire service. The leather or canvas buckets, hooks, and grappling irons that sometimes survive in parish churches give a clear idea of the primitive nature of fire-fighting before Victorian times. The earliest municipal fire brigades included those at Edinburgh (1824) and Manchester (1828). In London the *fire insurance companies amalgamated their fire brigades in 1833, but it was not until 1866 that the municipal London Fire Brigade was established. It quickly became the best-equipped and best-trained in the world. Steam-driven engines began to replace the old hand-pumps in the 1850s, and motorized rather than horse-drawn engines appeared in the first years of the 20th century. An Act of 1938 established Fire Authorities throughout Britain and forced municipal authorities to provide a free fire-fighting service.

First Fruits and Tenths, Court of. The profits of a *benefice during the first year after the death or resignation of an incumbent, originally made to the see of Rome, were confiscated by Henry VIII in 1523, together with a payment equal to one-tenth of the value of each benefice. (See *Valor Ecclesiasticus*.) A new court to administer this revenue was set up in 1541, but was abolished in 1553 upon the accession of Mary Tudor. (See QUEEN ANNE'S BOUNTY.) The records of the court are kept at the *Public Record Office under E 331–47.

fish. In the Middle Ages fish formed a major part of everyone's *diet, especially during Lent and other religious festivals. *Fish ponds were therefore a common feature on manorial *demesnes, and *monasteries constructed complex breeding-tanks. Specialist fishermen (who are often named in the *freeman rolls of major towns) used nets to catch bream, pickerel, pike, etc. and vast quantities of eels in rivers and *meres. This diet of freshwater fish was supplemented by herring, haddock, cod, and skate. By the 15th century many a small coastal settlement consisted chiefly of fishermen and their families. Some vessels were already sailing as far as Iceland in search of herring. The mid-16th-century household accounts of Sir George Vernon of Haddon Hall (Derbyshire) show that even in the most landlocked parts of Britain it was possible to obtain a regular supply of both salted and fresh fish from local *fairs and markets. Fresh fish were carried long distances in water-tanks on carts or horses. The high price of fish in the 17th and 18th centuries created a new interest amongst the *gentry in ponds, especially for carp, but also for pike, perch and tench, etc. At the same time, the appearance of Isaak Walton's *The Compleat Angler* (1653) extolled the virtues of fishing as a sport and for relaxation.

The 18th and 19th centuries saw a great development of deep-sea fishing and the rise of large fishing-ports. In the 18th century Hull became the major British whaling-port. One of its rivals was Whitby, where blubber-houses were built alongside the inner harbour. After 1870, when the *railway system allowed ready access to markets as far away as London, Aberdeen turned from inshore herring-fishing to deep-sea trawling. In 1911, with some 200 trawlers operating out of its harbour, Grimsby was another North Sea port from which trawlers sailed and where many found jobs in food processing and freezing. Grimsby had over 5,000 fishermen in 1881, but 70 years later 3,200 fishermen landed nearly four times the catch. The industry declined rapidly from the 1960s after the Icelandic cod war.

Meanwhile, fishing had become a popular sport. Coarse fishing was available to working men once cheap railway fares enabled them to leave the industrial cities at weekends to fish, for example, in the rivers and drains of the Lincolnshire fens. Angling clubs proliferated. Fly fishing, on the other hand, became increasingly expensive in terms of both tackle and rents. The very rich went to Scotland to catch salmon.

fish ponds. In the Middle Ages fish ponds were a normal feature of both lay and ecclesiastical estates, for the consumption of red-blooded meat was forbidden during Lent and at other times. Ponds were sited close to domestic buildings to prevent *poaching; often a surrounding *moat was used. Most ponds have long been abandoned, but their outlines are often still discernible. They were typically rectangular and flat-bottomed, with raised embankments. Young fish were raised nearby in 'stews'. When regularly drained and cleaned, residual deposits were valued for fertilizing fields. In post-medieval times some fishponds (especially for carp) were incorporated into *garden schemes.

Fitz-. From the French *fils*, meaning 'son of'. It was not associated with illegitimacy until Charles II named his bastards in this manner.

Fitzherbert, Master. The author of the earliest English book of advice on farming, published as Revd W. W. Skeat (ed.), *The Book of Husbandry, by Master Fitzherbert, 1534* (1882). He was once thought to have been Sir Anthony Fitzherbert, a lawyer of Norbury (Derbyshire), but it is now believed that the author was his brother John or that the book is a collaborative work by the two brothers.

Five Boroughs. The Five Boroughs of the *Danelaw were Nottingham, Derby, Leicester, Lincoln, and Stamford. They originated as the bases of five armies, which settled upon the land and shared a general assembly. Stamford was the only one of the five that did not develop into a shire town.

Five Mile Act. An Act of 1665 which forbade clergymen who had been ejected from their livings for refusing to subscribe to the Act of Uniformity (1662) from dwelling within five miles of a corporate town. Such towns had been *Puritan strongholds during the *Civil War and *Commonwealth. The Act was repealed after the *Glorious Revolution of 1688.

flail. A hand-tool for threshing corn, consisting of two wooden rods tied together by leather thongs.

flatt. A term used in the north of England for a *furlong, a block of *strips in an *open-field.

flax. In the 17th to 19th centuries flax was grown as a specialist crop in certain areas, e.g. the West Riding of Yorkshire and East Anglia. It had been more widespread when flax-dressing and *linen-weaving were common rural by-employments. A parliamentary bounty had encouraged its growth during the *Napoleonic wars. See Patricia Baines, *Flax and Linen* (1985).

fleet. An Old English word for a channel or stream, especially along the south-eastern and southern coast.

Flemish immigrants came from Flanders and Brabant and spoke a Dutch dialect. They were therefore sometimes confused with *Dutch immigrants. Flemish weavers were encouraged to settle in England by Edward III (1327–77). A second wave came to escape the Spanish occupation of the Low Countries in Elizabeth I's reign. They settled principally in London, Norwich, Canterbury, and other south-eastern towns, where they found employment as *silk weavers, as craftsmen who introduced the *New Draperies, and as *market gardeners. Others came with Dutch settlers upon the 17th-century drainage of the *fens.

flint was used in the *Stone Age for tools and weapons. The most spectacular site is Grimes Graves (Norfolk), which was mined by deep shafts in prehistoric times. Flint has been used as a building material in chalk districts from the Iron Age to the present day. The finest flint buildings are the medieval churches of East Anglia, which used dressed ('knapped') flints as a veneer for walls constructed of *rubble and lime mortar, with imported freestone used for quoins, lintels, window mouldings, etc. The technique is readily observed at the unfinished tower of East Bergholt Church (Suffolk). Knapped flints were set flush with freestone in attractive designs known as flushwork. Flint was also a common material in the *vernacular buildings of eastern England and Sussex.

florin. A gold coin issued by Edward III (1327–77), worth 6 shillings or 6s. 8d.; the name given to various continental gold coins; a silver coin, first minted in 1849, worth two shillings.

foldcourse. The practice of grazing sheep in a restricted area so that *manure could be collected to improve arable land. It was an important element in East Anglian field systems, being originally a lord's monopoly which worked to the disadvantage of peasants, but it underwent changes as the balance of power shifted. See Mark Bailey, 'Sand into Gold: The Evolution of the Foldcourse System in West Suffolk, 1200–1600', *Agricultural History Review*, 38/1 (1990).

folio. A leaf of parchment or paper, either loose or in a book, numbered only at the front.

folklore. 'Folk-lore'—a term coined in 1846 by William John Thoms to describe the 'lore of the people'—is most usefully thought of as comprising that body of pre- (or nowadays 'non-') scientific beliefs through which humanity seeks to explain (and, when need arises, to exploit) its place in relation to the forces of nature and the supernatural. The antiquity of such beliefs is not in doubt, but it is difficult precisely to prove their prehistoric origins in the way so much beloved of the earlier folklorists, beyond acknowledging the probability that belief in the existence of planetary influences and the worship of trees and wells antedated the conversion to Christianity. What matters more to the historian, however, are the continuities of popular beliefs and the ways in which these expressed a fusion of the pagan and the Christian. In Anglo-Saxon charms, for example, frequent reference is made to the baleful effects of 'elf-shot' on the health of farm animals. It is remarkable, therefore, that flint arrowheads or flakes were still being described in this way earlier this century. More broadly, it was the church itself that, from the beginning, deliberately turned a blind eye to the overlap of the least objectionable pagan practices with Christian ideas. The pre-*Reformation church thus simply perpetuated an existing blend of magical and religious beliefs; see Keith Thomas, *Religion and the Decline of Magic* (1971). Even for the

19th century, James Obelkevich has been able to describe the surviving complementarities of paganism and Christianity in his *Religion and Rural Society: South Lindsey 1825–1875* (1976).

Folkloric beliefs reflected every aspect of man's relation to life, death, and the environment. Despite the regional diversity of these superstitions and ritual practices, and although such knowledge was only drawn upon piecemeal by contemporaries as need or custom dictated, unpublished research does seem to show that a coherent underlying structure is broadly reconstructable from 19th-century examples (an impressive proportion of which being also evidenced three or four centuries earlier), even if its non-Christian outlines have to be given undue prominence in the space available. The basic principle behind this structure, however, was an essentially medieval appreciation of, and a need for, order and harmony. Everything in the scheme of things had its correct place, its appropriate connections, and its proper uses. Anything out of place—like a snake on the doorstep—could only be interpreted (unless ritually 'moved', as in certain *customs) to be a pessimistic portent for the future. In a world devoid of modern medical and veterinary knowledge, misfortune might not only be explained but even foretold as a result of disharmonies in nature.

At the terrestrial level, there can be little doubt that there was a traditionally perceived division between the natural world, as the repository for those aspects of the supernatural which existed *outside* the physical being of humankind, and human 'culture' itself. A range of devices (from horseshoes to rowan twigs) was employed, either permanently or at different calendrical moments in separate regions, to 'defend' the garden gate, the foundations of the house, the outer doors, the roof, the hearth, the head of the bed, or the cattle byre, quite apart from amulets used to protect the human person. On certain occasions, especially over the New Year period, *Plough Monday bonfires on *headlands in the *open-fields, the wassailing of fruit trees, or other communally ritualized protective measures might similarly be taken against potential dangers to human cultivation. At the other extreme were the locations from which the supernatural might emanate, the world of 'nature' itself: the fields (reflected in the potency associated with the last sheaf cut), plants known for their specific curative properties (usually according to the 'logic' of sympathetic magic), 'sacred' trees, and wildlife.

What is clear in such cases, however, is that classically educated contemporaries were erroneous in assuming from what they witnessed that country folk were in some sense thus recognizing tutelary deities, like Ceres or Pomona. More probably in question here were the forces seen to have been inherent in different elements of nature (as these may have been portrayed anthropomorphically, for example, in the medieval carvings of the so-called *'Green Man') and forces that had thus to be dealt with correctly. The human body itself was likewise regarded as a repository of forces peculiar to it. Leaving aside the power of saints' relics or the ability of monarchs to heal by touching, even the unconsecrated hand of a newly drowned or hanged man might be wiped across someone's face to cure swellings or eye troubles.

The 'horizontal' dichotomy between 'culture' and 'nature' at the plane of human existence was complemented by a 'vertical' positional hierarchy of elements that linked the heavens and the earth. Albeit removed from the 'scientific' *astrology of the Middle Ages, popular belief consistently interconnected the sun and the moon (and only by implication some of the other planets) with the earth. Sun and moon indeed were integral to the definition of time itself as witnessed in the rhythms of *calendar customs. The sun was ritually propitiated in a south-facing world by observances involving processing clockwise and thereby observing the daily course of the sun, rather than 'withershins' (and even in turning over farm implements or boats in like manner). Sunrise remained an important moment for effecting certain ritual cures. The moon, by contrast, was regarded more ambivalently. A bounteous outcome might result from planting or plucking at the time of the waxing moon, but ill would befall if a new moon became visible on the fourth as opposed to the third day of an interlunar gap; if there were two moons in the already unlucky month of May (a 'month' being named from but one lunar cycle); or if the full moon was seen reflected—and therefore out of place—in water or glass. The different spheres of heaven and earth were further connected by lightning, celestial fire, the potency of which was acknowledged by blacksmiths who carefully reserved the rain water resulting from a thunderstorm.

Between the heavens and earth were specific airborne creatures—real or (like dragons or the Seven Whistlers) imagined—which might be associated in quite different ways with misfortune, death, or the souls of the dead (e.g. unbaptized children). This, after all, was the intermediate sphere through which, before the Reformation, the transmigrating soul was believed to pass. On the one hand were particularly 'sacred' birds like robins or wrens, the killing of which (other than ritually) or the destruction of whose nests or eggs would bring misfortune on the offender. On the other were defined groups of flying creatures the behaviour of which could be interpreted as signals to humanity: rooks evacuating a rookery, variable numbers of magpies, the so-called 'Gabriel Hounds' and 'Wild Hunt', quite apart from *bees that needed to be informed of a death in the house if they were to be prevented from swarming.

At the terrestrial plane itself what was 'above', 'below', or on the same plane as society were equally clearly demarcated. 'Above' were trees with special qualities under different planetary influences yet associated with both lightning and ritual fires at, for example, Christmas: ash (under the sun), oak, hawthorn and holly in England; hazel in Ireland; rowan in Scotland. At Midsummer, the Nativity of St John the Baptist, certain ritual plants connected heaven and earth, especially St John's Wort (under the Sun) and together, in the fabrication of special garlands, marigolds (sun) and orpine (moon). Equally, these were plants that could be picked as protection against lightning and raised up over the lintel of the door. Other plants, like the house leek anciently under Jupiter, the god of thunder) or the fern (also used at midsummer), could actually be planted on a thatched roof to defend the house against lightning strikes. (Yet further species could not be picked at all lest this caused lightning: white campion, poppy, or the greater stitchwort.) 'Below' the surface, by contrast, were the major antidotes to evil and to witchcraft in particular: running spring-water (and thus also holy wells), rocksalt, silver, iron, and coal (all three of which last, of course, required transmutation by fire). Appropriately, and 'in between', it was, lastly, on the plane of human existence itself that there existed the creatures most usually associated with the shape-changes of witches, furtive noctural creatures that might secretly 'milk' the farmer's cows: hares, hedgehogs, cats, bats, and nightjars (which nest on the ground). Not unconnected, therefore, was the further terrestrial association between the Devil and the black dog. At the same level, too, were to be discovered the physical relics of previous onslaughts of evil: hag-shot and elf-shot.

Access to, and the exploitation of, the forces abroad in the world for either medical, practical (e.g. recovering lost property), or evil purposes required special magical abilities, which at these popular levels tended to be restricted to limited categories of person defined either, in the case of women, by the stage in their cycle of fertility, or, more frequently in the case of men, the closeness of their relationship to nature. In the former instance it is noticeable that magical powers are not usually associated with married women of childbearing age and who are still thus theoretically active sexually. Power *against* evil is certainly regarded as a property of virginity in folktales, while both witches and wise women tend to be old and thus post-menopausal. It cannot be accidental that, in later folk-tales, it is often a spayed bitch that is set to catch the witch transformed into a hare. In the case of males, while the erstwhile celibate status of the priesthood may partially explain the power ascribed to the clergy even in post-Reformation times, it is also noticeable that *wisemen were frequently single. Such 'cunning men', however, were simultaneously also the primitive vets of their time and therefore in close contact with animals, as were also blacksmiths and horsemen, who similarly were regarded as capable of at least limited magical prowess; see George Ewart *Evans, *The Horse in the Furrow* (1960).

Variations on the human shape were projected onto the supernatural. Ghosts of the already dead and wraiths of the future dead were commonplace elements in popular apprehension, while fantastical, distorted versions of human society in the forms of giants, *fairies, boggarts, or mermaids and mermen, for example, all helped to supplement an ever-present, supernaturally defined sense of 'parallel' time (in a context which was eternal) as opposed to that modern perception of historical time as time which is always past. Closely connected, therefore, is the fact that traditional society constantly sought as well to read the future, not only in terms of 'accidental' omens or portents, but also in terms of private rituals, especially those of young girls who, through a variety of divinatory devices, hoped to foretell—or even influence—the identity of their future husbands.

Even so brief a sketch demonstrates a complex structure of interconnections and coexistences: past and future, dead and living, supernatural and cultural, man and nature, earth and heaven. What now seem like colourful scraps of superstition in fact once comprised a system of belief by which men and women could occupy and explain an environment which they did not understand scientifically and to which their fate and therefore a good deal of their behaviour (as that might be delimited by custom) was seen to be intimately linked. Understanding the regional variations of folklore (and, indeed, modern industrial versions of it), therefore, deserves to lie more closely than it now does at the very heart of local history. In the meantime, local historians are in as good a position as anyone to emulate George Ewart Evans in seeking to record now the vanishing remnants of what he called 'the prior culture' (*Where Beards Wag All: The Relevance of the Oral Tradition* (1970)). See also Geoffrey Grigson, *The Englishman's Flora* (1958), and Iona Opie and Moira Tatem (eds.), *A Dictionary of Superstitions* (1989).

CHARLES PHYTHIAN-ADAMS

folly. A general term for the romantic structures built in Classical, *Gothick, or Chinese styles in landscaped *parks during the 18th and 19th centuries. Some were eye-catchers, others memorials or imitations of famous structures elsewhere. Few served any practical purpose other than that of a summerhouse.

fonts. The earliest surviving fonts are late-Saxon and Norman. A large number of beautifully carved *Romanesque fonts survive from the 12th century, when many new parish churches were built. Some, e.g. at Thorpe Salvin (Yorkshire), depict baptismal scenes; others, notably Castle Frome (Herefordshire), are an exuberant display of carving. Later fonts can be dated on stylistic grounds and sometimes by *heraldry. From 1236 covers were compulsory; some later covers were very elaborate canopies.

food riots. E. P. *Thompson, 'The Moral Economy of the English Crowd in the Eighteenth Century', *Past and Present*, 50 (1971) has stimulated a great deal of academic research and debate on 18th-century food riots. See the references in 'The Moral Economy Reviewed' which Thompson published alongside a reprint of his original article in *Customs in Common* (1991). He was concerned with the *mentalité* of the risings of 1709, 1740, 1756–7, 1766–7, 1773, 1782, and, above all, 1795 and 1800–1, and showed that 'what is remarkable about these "insurrections" is, first, their discipline, and, second, the fact that they exhibit a pattern of behaviour for whose origin we must look back several hundreds of years'. He observed that it was the restraint, rather than the disorder, that was remarkable, and that the central action was focused on setting a just price in times of dearth. The initiators of the riots were very often women. See also Andrew Charlesworth, *An Atlas of Rural Protest in Britain, 1548–1900* (1983), and Roger Wells, *Wretched Faces*

(1988), a detailed study of the riots of the 1790s based on archival evidence.

food supply. In the Middle Ages and the early modern period markets and *fairs were the major source of food other than that produced at home. Sellers and purchasers were prepared to travel long distances to the *cattle and *sheep fairs. (See DROVERS and BADGER.) A survey of London's food supply in the Middle Ages is being conducted by the Centre for Metropolitan History at the University of London. The ancient market towns had rigorous regulations about trading in agricultural produce which tried to restrict activity to the market square and neighbouring streets. Corn was sold by bulk in the open market until the building of *corn exchanges. The livestock market was held in a central place, close to the slaughterhouses and butchers' *shambles. The growth of *population and of market activity caused increasing congestion, so that during the 18th and early 19th centuries most towns removed their livestock markets and slaughterhouses to new sites at the edges of settlements.

Private bargains beyond the market place became commonplace despite the attempts of the toll-owners to prohibit them. During the 16th and 17th centuries the practice of selling by sample rather than bulk became common. Many of these bargains were struck in *inns or *shops around the market place. The majority of countryfolk made their small purchases in the time-honoured manner, but middlemen of substance—*butchers, *maltsters, *graziers, etc.—made private bargains here or at the farmhouse. These private agreements created work for lawyers, not only in drawing up contracts, but in the large amount of litigation that ensued in the courts of *Chancery, *Requests, *Star Chamber, and *Exchequer as the old protective barriers were broken.

The 17th century saw the emergence of specialized agricultural regions, e.g. the Cheshire cheese district, as farmers found it more profitable to concentrate on certain products and import what they did not produce themselves. The spectacular rise of *London and the more modest growth of other towns stimulated this specialization, which was underpinned by transport improvements. See F. J. Fisher, 'The Development of the London Food Market, 1540–1640', *Economic History Review*, 2nd ser., 5/2 (1935). As private enterprise grew the state became more passive, and toll-owners found that it was increasingly difficult to enforce local restrictions. See The *Agrarian History of England and Wales*, vols. iv, v, and vi (1500–1850).

The growth of the national population from the late 18th century onwards meant not only that more mouths had to be fed, but that large numbers of people in towns and industrial villages were not engaged in food production. This had obvious effects on the agricultural hinterland of towns, e.g. on milk production and on *market gardening. The only detailed study of how an urban population in this period obtained its food is Roger Scola, *Feeding the Victorian City: The Food Supply of Manchester, 1770–1870* (1992), which deals with meat, dairy products, corn and flour, fruit and vegetables, and fish. Numerous separate trades and networks were established. An analysis of debt showed that most customers lived close to shops, but the scale of enterprises grew (especially after the coming of the *railways) with town dairies, wholesale butchers, etc., and a greater seasonal stability to prices. Population growth also meant more reliance on imported grain (except during the *Napoleonic wars). After the protective *Corn Laws were repealed in 1846, American grain was imported in huge quantities. Refrigeration also made possible imports of Australian and New Zealand lamb in the last quarter of the 19th century. The food supply was increasingly international.

football. Although it was an ancient pastime, the game had few rules before the Victorian period. Surviving *calendar customs, e.g. the *Shrove Tuesday football match at Ashbourne (Derbyshire), suggest numerous participants and matches that lasted several hours. The Sheffield Football Club, founded in 1857, is recognized as the oldest in the world. The National Football Association was founded in 1863 as the result of public-school interest (Rugby football was 'rugger', Association football 'soccer'); the FA Cup was first contested in 1871. The Football League, established in 1888, reflected working-class interest in the game and the desire of supporters for regular entertainment. See Tony Mason, *Association Football and English Society, 1863–1915* (1980).

footpath. Public footpaths are marked on definitive maps at county planning offices and on *Ordnance Survey 1:25,000 maps. Some are probably ancient, but many were established in the 18th and 19th centuries as convenient ways of getting to work. *Enclosure awards and maps are useful in confirming or establishing rights of way.

ford. The use of numerous fords before *bridges were built is demonstrated by place-names throughout the land, including *wath* (the Old Norse word), *rhyd* (the Welsh word), etc. Many of these had become settlement names by the time of the *Domesday Book. Place-names can give a broad indication of when a ford was replaced by a bridge; e.g. Grindleford (Derbyshire) has several 14th-century references, but by 1577 it had become Grindleford Bridge.

foreign church. A church established in a town by a group of foreign immigrants in the 16th and 17th centuries, e.g. the Dutch Church (London), or St Julian's, the Walloon church in Southampton.

foreshore. That part of a beach that stretches between the medium low-tide mark and the medium high-tide mark and which belongs to the Crown or its grantee. A long-drawn-out dispute between the Crown and coastal land-owners concerning ownership of land reclaimed from the sea began in Elizabeth I's reign and became more acrimonious under James I and Charles I. It produced many surveys of coastal lands. See Joan Thirsk, 'The Crown as Projector on Its Own Estates from Elizabeth I to Charles I' in R. W. Hoyle (ed.), *The Estates of the English Crown, 1558–1640* (1992), and Joan Thirsk, 'Agrarian Problems and the English Revolution' in R. C. Richardson (ed.), *Town and Countryside in the English Revolution* (1992). The dispute was not resolved until the late 19th century. See S. A. Moore, *A History of the Foreshore* (3rd edn., 1888), which elucidated the current situation at the end of the 19th century when every landowner had to find documentary evidence to support an individual claim against the Crown.

forest. The popular sense of the word is of a dense wood, but medieval forests were never more than partly wooded and often covered *moors, *heaths, and *fens rather than woodland. The Peak Forest in the High Peak of Derbyshire was very different from Wychwood Forest (Oxfordshire) or from the Forest of Dean (Gloucestershire). The term 'forest' had a legal meaning; it referred to an area that was under forest law (with its own courts and officials, known as verderers), in which deer and other game could be killed only by the forest owner, usually the king. See Cyril Hart, *The Verderers and Forest Laws of Dean* (1971), which serves as a guide to the records which may be consulted for other forests. Parts of forests were set aside for grazing other livestock, either by being let out to rent or by the exercise of rights on the *commons. Forests were not devoid of settlement, but could contain villages as well as hamlets, farmsteads, and cottages within their bounds.

Although *Anglo-Saxon kings had hunted in some of the areas which became forests after the *Norman Conquest, it was the Norman kings who introduced forest law into Britain. The New Forest (Hampshire), which was created shortly after the Norman Conquest, is the only forest to survive in a recognizable form, with its court and officials. The small forest at Hatfield (Essex) is a unique survival, for it still has deer, cattle, coppice-woods, pollards, scrub, timber trees, grassland, fen, and a 17th-century lodge and rabbit *warren. See Oliver Rackham, *The History of the Countryside* (1986). At least 143 forests were created in England before the declaration of new ones was prohibited by *Magna Carta. The Anglo-Norman kings established well over 100 forests in Wales, mainly in the south, about half of which were wholly or mainly moorland. The system was briefly extended to Ireland by Henry III (1216–72). The earliest record for Scotland dates the creation of Paisley Forest to 1110. New Scottish ones were declared throughout the Middle Ages. By 1500 there had been about 180 forests in existence at one time or another, about half of them royal. The earlier ones were confined to eastern Scotland; forests did not spread into the Western Highlands (where they are operated to this day) until after 1600. See M. L. Anderson, *A History of Scottish Forestry* (1967), and J. M. Gilbert, *Hunting and Hunting Reserves in Medieval Scotland* (1979).

Many forests were 'disafforested' in the first half of the 17th century, when James I and Charles I attempted to rule without Parliament and were forced to sell off some of their possessions. See Joan Thirsk (ed.), *The *Agrarian History of England and Wales*, iv. *1500–1640* (1967), and P. A. J. Pettit, *The Royal Forests of Northamptonshire: A Study in Their Economy, 1558–1714* (1968). (See also CROWN ESTATES.) Some forests were attractive to *squatters, and in the early modern period gained a reputation for the independence in religion and politics of the inhabitants of their scattered settlements. Forest dwellers were generally believed by outsiders to be rogues, if not criminals. See V. H. T. Skipp, *Crisis and Development: An Ecological Case Study of the Forest of Arden, 1570–1674* (1978).

The Forestry Commission was established in 1919 to restore the losses to native woodlands which occurred during the First World War. The department now adminsters about 3 million acres of land, of which some 2 million are planted (mainly with conifers). The records are kept at the *Public Record Office under F 3 to F 13. See N. D. G. James, *A History of English Forestry* (1981) and *An Historical Dictionary of Forestry and Woodland Terms* (1991).

forestalling. The practice of trading before the ringing of the market bell in order to avoid tolls.

forfeiture. The Crown received the possessions of those who were convicted of high treason. The possessions of other offenders who were sentenced to death or banishment went to the Crown for one year and then to the *lord of the manor.

forge. The term includes a variety of structures from a blacksmith's shop to a large ironworks. In the early 16th century conversion forges were established near charcoal blast-*furnaces in the Weald by immigrant workers, mainly from France. By the late 16th century similar forges had been erected in other iron-working areas. *Water power was used for reheating and to work heavy tilt hammers. The number of water-powered forges increased during the 17th and 18th centuries; a few remained in production until the early years of the 20th century.

forks were introduced from Italy early in the 17th century, but remained rare until Charles II popularized their use. The fashion spread slowly down the social scale, but single knives, kept in sheaths fastened to a belt around the waist, continued to be manufactured well into the 18th century.

fortified houses. Medieval houses were commonly fortified by *moats, *gatehouses, first-floor *halls, and defensive towers. Markenfield Hall (Yorkshire), where the family received a licence to *crenellate in 1310, has all four elements. See PELE-TOWERS and TOWER-HOUSES.

forts, coastal. In 1539 Henry VIII, concerned about the alliance between France, Spain, and the Holy Roman Empire, began a programme of coastal defences involving the construction of artillery forts and the strengthening of urban fortifications from the Thames estuary to Cornwall. The resources were made available from the profits of the *dissolution of the monasteries. Camber Castle (Sussex) is a fine surviving example whose evolution has been traced through excavation. Fear of Scottish attacks led to similar defensive work at Hull and Tynemouth. The Earl of Derby, meanwhile, constructed defensive works on the Isle of Man. Similar considerations in Elizabeth's reign led to further strengthening of south-coast forts and to major defences at Portsmouth and Ber-

wick. See David Crossley, *Post-Medieval Archaeology in Britain* (1990).

foss(e). From the Latin *fossa*, meaning a ditch or trench. The word is usually found in connection with *castles or other fortifications. The Foss Way, which was ditched on either side, marked the limit of Roman occupation by the mid-1st century. It ran from Axminster through Bath to Leicester and Lincoln.

foundlings. Abandoned infants, mostly illegitimate, upon being found became the responsibility of the parish overseers of the *poor. Some were given surnames that were derived from the place where they were found and Christian names from the saint whose festival occurred on the day of discovery. Some given names were decidedly whimsical.

In 1741 Thomas Coram opened his Foundling Hospital in Guildford Street, London. Infants were placed in a basket outside the door, which was connected to a bell; no attempt was made to trace the mother. The government gave the hospital an annual grant from 1756 to 1771, which led to branches being opened at Ackworth (Yorkshire), Aylesbury (Buckinghamshire), Barnet (Middlesex), and Westerham (Kent). The system was abused by parents bringing in dying children to be buried at the hospital's expense or by sending infants via *carriers from the provinces. The rules were changed to admit only infants brought personally by mothers of previous good character.

The hospital gave the child a number and name. Even when the infant's name was known it was changed. Many children were sent outside London for nursing. Eventually, only two districts were so used, Chertsey (Surrey) and East Peckham (Kent). The children were eventually *apprenticed or became *domestic servants. The records are kept at the Greater London *Record Office.

foundries for casting metal in moulds were in use in China long before they were introduced into western Europe in the early 18th century. References to 'air furnaces' or 'cupolas' for the remelting of pig *iron are first found in London and Shropshire. At first, objects such as *firebacks and *gravestones were cast in shallow open moulds. Other small goods were moulded in movable 'flasks' or frames, into which iron was poured from ladles. Larger objects, such as the engine cylinders which the Darbys were making at Coalbrookdale in 1718, were cast in a deep floor of sand. The foundries of the 18th century cast engineering and structural parts, pipes, cannon-balls, railings, pans, and flat-irons. During the 19th century moulding and casting plants became increasingly mechanized, and during the 20th century largely automatic.

Foxe's Book of Martyrs. The popular title of John Foxe's *History of the Acts and Monuments of the Church*, first published in Latin in 1554, and translated into English in 1563. Its vivid (and often inaccurate) account of the lives of *Protestant martyrs quickly became popular and its numerous editions long remained influential.

fox hunting. The first reference to fox hunting is from a Belvoir Castle (Leicestershire) account book of 1539; hare coursing dates from about the same time. Fox hunting did not become a popular organized sport until the 17th and 18th centuries, after the decline of *deer hunting. Hitherto, the fox had been despised as vermin; parish records frequently record payments for fox heads. The strict rules of the organized fox hunt were made by Hugo Meynell, the first master of the Quorn Hunt (Leicestershire), in the second half of the 18th century, at a time when *aristocratic and *gentry families were beginning to finance and organize packs of foxhounds. The rolling pastures of the midland shires, especially Leicestershire, acquired a national reputation as the prime hunting districts. The novels of R. S. Surtees capture the spirit of fox hunting in the days when it attracted supporters from across a wide social spectrum. In the early 19th century squires throughout the land turned to foxes rather than hares. By mid-Victorian times fox hunting had become an influential public institution, an expensive sport that was restricted to the upper and middle classes, whose gamekeepers had to preserve foxes in special coverts to meet the demands of the hunters. The campaign to make fox hunting illegal has gathered increasing support in the last quarter of the 20th century.

framework knitting. Stockings, socks, shirts, gloves, handkerchiefs, underwear, and other fabrics were knitted by men, women, and children in their own home, or in a small workshop, in the towns and villages of Nottinghamshire, Leicestershire, and south Derbyshire from the second half of the 17th century to the beginning of the 20th century. The basic frame had been invented in 1589 by William Lee of Calverton (Nottinghamshire), but the craft was practised at first in London, and did not become established in the midlands until after the *Restoration of Charles II. *Apprenticeship indentures amongst the *inland revenue records at the *Public Record Office show that by the second decade of the 18th century the craft had gained

a foothold in nearly all the places where it was subsequently to prosper. At first, the frame was so heavy it was used only by men, though later it may have been used by women; children worked at associated jobs. In the 17th and early 18th centuries framework knitters were often part-timers who also farmed a small holding, but in the late 18th and 19th centuries, as the *population rose to unprecedented heights, the rural craft became a poor cottage industry. *Parish registers (which often used the abbreviation FWK) show that in many midland villages for much of the 19th century the majority of the inhabitants were working at this trade. Frames and raw materials were supplied by middlemen known as 'bag-hosiers', who worked for a firm in one of the nearby towns, from Mansfield in the north to Hinckley in the south. See John Millington and Stanley Chapman (eds.), *Four Centuries of Machine Knitting* (1989), and David L. Wykes, 'The Origins and Development of the Leicestershire Hosiery Trade', *Textile History*, 23/1 (1992).

franchise court. A *liberty exempt from normal jurisdiction.

frankalmoign. Land granted to an ecclesiastical body by a lay person in return for prayers for the souls of the donor, his family, and his descendants.

franklin. A medieval term for a substantial *freeholder below the rank of gentleman; cf. Chaucer's 'The Franklin's Tale'.

frankpledge. A system of suretyship and mutual responsibility for bringing criminals to justice. In much of medieval England every householder formed part of a group of 10 or 12 known as a *tithing, who were responsible for the good behaviour of one another and for bringing members to a manorial *court leet to face charges. From time to time a manorial court would hold a view of frankpledge to make sure that every man and boy was included. In theory every male over the age of 12 should have been listed, except for lords, knights, and clergy. By the end of the Middle Ages the term 'frankpledge' was synonymous with court leet. True frankpledge never existed in the six northern counties of England or in Cheshire, Shropshire, Herefordshire, or Wales. See D. A. Crowley, 'The Later History of Frankpledge', *Bulletin of the Institute of Historical Research*, 48 (1975). For the use of frankpledge call-lists, see W. A. Champion, 'The Frankpledge Population of Shrewsbury, 1500–1720', *Local Population Studies*, 41 (1989).

freebench. The custom on some manors whereby the widow of a *copyholder retained between a third and all (usually, in practice, a half or more) of her late husband's land until her death or until she remarried. See Barbara Todd, 'Freebench and Free Enterprise: Widows and Their Property in Two Berkshire Villages' in John Chartres and David Hey (eds.), *English Rural Society, 1500–1800: Essays in Honour of Joan Thirsk* (1990).

freehold. A tenurial status for property which was not subject to manorial customs, as were *copyhold or *leasehold. A freehold was originally held either in *knight service or in *socage. (See FEE SIMPLE and ENTAIL.) Men aged between 21 and 70 with freehold property worth at least 40 shillings a year could vote at local and parliamentary elections. Such people were eligible for *jury service and therefore (from 1696) lists were drawn up for each *parish. These are kept amongst the *quarter sessions records at county *record offices. From 1832 the addresses of freeholders were included.

freehold land societies were formed by the lower-middle and working classes in the 19th century to acquire plots of land on which to build good-quality houses. The combined funds of such enterprises were made available to individual members by ballot. Payment was by instalments over many years. Each member was responsible for his own building, so the different characters of the houses were a far cry from the uniform terraces nearby. Many of these early societies failed, but the successful ones have left a number of interesting mid-19th-century *suburbs in our great Victorian towns and cities. See also BUILDING SOCIETIES.

Freeman, E. A. (1823–92). Regius Professor of Modern History, Oxford University, and author of a *History of the Norman Conquest* (1867–76). He was instrumental in setting rigorous standards for research into genealogy.

freeman rolls. Admission to the freedom of a corporate city allowed a man to practise his trade and to vote at elections. Freedom was achieved either upon the completion of an *apprenticeship or through following a father's trade to adulthood, or more rarely by order of the mayor and corporation. The names of freemen were registered annually on a series of rolls. These are now kept at local *record offices, and some have been published; see, for instance, M. M. Rowe and A. M. Jackson (eds.), *Exeter Freemen, 1266–1967* (1967), F. Collins (ed.), *Register of the Freemen of the City of York* (Surtees Society, 96 and 102; 1896 and 1899), which covers the period 1272–1759, and Stella Corpe and Anne M. Oakley (eds.), *The Freemen of Canterbury, 1800–1835* (1990). Such rolls become less valuable from the 18th century onwards.

At their best, the registers note the date of admission, the name of the freeman, the name and occupation of his father, and (where the freedom has been obtained through the completion of an apprenticeship) the name and occupation of the master. They are therefore a prime source for an analysis of the occupational structures of towns and of the social and geographical background of freemen. See, for example, the use to which they are put in David Palliser, *Tudor York* (1979). However, strong reservations about the reliability of freemen rolls have been expressed, e.g. R. B. Dobson, 'Admissions to the Freedom of the City of York in the Later Middle Ages', *Economic History Review*, 2nd ser., 26/1 (1973). Some men evaded the expensive honour of freedom; the variations in the annual numbers of enrolled freemen cannot be relied on. Even when recording was accurate, the freemen probably accounted for only about half the adult male labour-force. They excluded servants, apprentices and casual labourers and, of course, women or children. Although incomplete, they are nevertheless an important source for urban history and for the family historian.

freemason. Originally, a mason who worked the best-quality freestone. A system of lodges was developed to suit the itinerant nature of the job. By the 17th century these lodges had ceased to have any connection with the craft, but had become fellowships acknowledging God as the Great Architect of the Universe. The United Grand Lodge of England (founded in 1717) has records of members' names, their lodge, and the date of entry. Some masonic halls are of historic and architectural interest.

free miner. A miner born in the *hundred of St Briavels in the *Forest of Dean, who upon reaching the age of 21 has worked for a year and a day in a coal or iron-ore mine in the hundred and who is thus entitled to own up to three mines. The rights go back to at least the 13th century, were confirmed by the Dean Forest Mines Act of 1838, and pertain to this day.

free warren. The sole right (granted by royal *charter to a *lord of the manor) to hunt certain beasts and fowls—the pheasant, partridge, hare, and rabbit—within a given area, such as a *chase. Most charters were granted between the late 12th and the early 14th centuries.

French origin, families of. In the Middle Ages and early modern period France provided more immigrants to Britain than any other country. The chief *landowners after the *Norman Conquest were from Normandy and Brittany. They founded dynasties which long remained powerful. Norman French was the language spoken at court and in *castles, *cathedrals, and *monasteries, but the smallness of the body of *place-names which are derived from Norman French suggests that the turnover of personnel at the aristocratic level was not accompanied by large-scale settlement of French soldiers and farmers, as had happened previously with the *Vikings. Between 1066 and 1200 numerous landed families took *surnames which were derived from French place-names, but which have subsequently been Anglicized. The fact that the new rulers of England continued to rule large parts of France encouraged movement across the Channel. Other settlers arrived long after the Conquest, some of them with district names such as Burgin (Burgundy) or Gascoigne (Gascony). *London was their principal destination.

During the early 16th century French *ironworkers and *glass-makers introduced new technology into southern England. Some of these craftsmen, or their descendants, subsequently moved to other parts of the country. Their distinctive surnames can be traced in *parish registers. They were followed by Protestant (*Huguenot) refugees, who were persecuted in their home country from the 1560s onwards, culminating in the treacherous massacre on the eve of the feast of St Bartholomew in 1572. They included French-speaking Walloons from the Low Countries, who were escaping from Spanish rule. French, *Flemish, and *Dutch settlers were welcomed by the government for their craft skills, in textiles, gold- and silver-smithing, enamelling, clock-making, bookbinding, etc. Others were bankers, businessmen, scientists, and academics. Most settled in towns, with about half going to London, particularly to Spitalfields and Soho. Other Huguenots fled to England in the 17th century, particularly in the troubled times of the 1680s. 'Refugee' is a word that has passed into the English language from the French.

A much smaller group of refugees were the landed families who fled the French Revolution, some of whom never returned. In the first half of the 19th century Soho continued to attract French settlers.

friary. The various mendicant orders of friars were founded in the early 13th century in Spain, Italy, and the Holy Land. They arrived in Britain only a few years later, starting with the Dominicans in 1221. Dominic of Osma (Spain) and St Francis of Assisi (Italy) were the most influential founders. The men who joined the Dominicans (black friars), Franciscans (grey friars), or the Friars Minors (the 'little brothers' of Francis) were not originally attached to any particular house, but were free to move around preaching and evangelizing. Great emphasis was placed on sermons, for the whole purpose of the friars was a mission to the laity, including the stamping-out of heresy. Many became scholars of wide repute. About 100 friaries were founded by the early 14th century. The order of Austin Friars eventually had 34 houses, the Carmelites (white friars) had 37, and a number of smaller orders such as the crutched friars and the friars of the sack had a few more.

The friars were welcomed by bishops and lay lords, and received generous gifts from members of the royal family. All the orders were based in towns, and were therefore far removed in spirit from monastic orders such as the *Cistercians, who sought rural solitude. The friars did not possess properties other than their churches and conventual buildings, and even those were held in trust by bodies of lay trustees. At first, the friars deliberately chose discomfort and poverty, but in time they came to build large, attractive buildings. Unfortunately, no complete friary survives in Britain. The only complete church is that of the Dominicans at Norwich, now known as St Andrew's Hall. A few bell-towers survive elsewhere, e.g. the Greyfriars' Tower at Richmond (Yorkshire) and the belfries of both the Franciscan and its Dominican orders at Coventry, but in most cases remains are only fragmentary. It is clear from surveys and excavations that the conventual buildings and *cloisters were not laid out to a standard plan.

The early friars lived on alms, but would not accept money. The Dominicans were famous as scholars and preachers. The Franciscans were dedicated to absolute poverty. Each Franciscan friar was dressed like a beggar, with only one habit, girdled with a cord, and one pair of breeches. They were not allowed shoes, and even in winter weather they travelled barefoot. Once they stopped being itinerants, however, they had problems receiving sufficient alms. Instead, they received offerings at sermons, confessions, and burials, and legacies in *wills. By the late 13th century their way of life was being criticized as not meeting the austere standards of old. Numbers had declined long before 1538, when all orders were dissolved in a single operation. The friars were scattered without pensions, and forbidden to enter parish *churches to hear confessions or to say masses unless licensed by the local bishop. See C. H. Lawrence, *The Friars: The Impact of the Early Mendicant Movement in Western Society* (1994).

The 'Poor Clares' were a sisterhood founded at Assisi *c.*1212, which adopted the Franciscan rule and habit. See Rosalind B. Brown and Christopher N. L. Brooke, 'St Clare' in Derek Baker (ed.), *Medieval Women: Dedicated and Presented to Professor Rosalind M. T. Hill on the Occasion of Her Seventieth Birthday* (1978), Brenda M. Bolton, 'Mulieres sanctae' in Derek Baker (ed.), *Studies in Church History*, x: *Sanctity and Secularity: The Church and the World* (1973), and Margaret L. King, *Women of the Renaissance* (1991).

friendly societies. A few friendly societies were formed in the early 18th century, but most date from the late 18th or 19th centuries. Their heyday was during the Victorian and Edwardian era. They declined gradually during the first half of the 20th century and rapidly during the second half. Friendly societies have been undeservedly neglected by historians, for they played an important role in the lives of the majority of working-class families. See P. H. J. H. Gosden, *The Friendly Societies in England, 1815–1875* (1961). The only serious regional study is David Neave, *East Riding Friendly Societies* (1988). On female friendly societies see Dot Jones, 'Self-Help in Nineteenth-Century Wales: The Rise and Fall of the Female Friendly Society', *Llafur*, 4/1 (1984).

The main purpose of a friendly society was to act as a benefit club in times of sickness and death, but some societies built halls to provide social and educational facilities, and some lent money for *mortgages. They provided many working-class men with their first opportunity to hold public office. The annual club feast was often the social highlight of the year in villages and market towns. Many old photographs survive of feast-day processions, with bands and banners. Some local societies were autonomous, but a large number were affiliated to national organizations with strange names such as the Independent Order of Oddfellows, the Ancient Order of Foresters, the Loyal Order of Ancient Shepherds, the United Ancient Order of Druids, the Independent Order of Rechabites, or the Sons of Temperance. As many branches survived until the second half of the 20th century, local records are often still in private possession. An Act of 1793 provided for the registration of friendly societies with the Clerk of the Peace. Much information relating to this and later Acts, in the form of club rules, membership lists, etc., is therefore available at county *record offices and at the *Public Record Office under FS 1 to FS 23.

Friends, Society of. See QUAKERS.

fruit. Fresh fruit was not grown on a commercial scale in Britain before the 16th century, but was imported from the Low Countries and France by London factors. Kentish apples and cherries were rivalling foreign produce by Elizabeth I's reign. (See MARKET GARDENING for the influence of foreign immigrants and the growing of fruit and vegetables in and around London, and later close to other towns.) From the end of May strawberries, raspberries, currants, and gooseberries provided employment for women pickers, many of whom travelled long distances for the season. The picking and carriage of fruit was labour-intensive. The mid-17th-century enthusiasm for planting fruit trees (Hartlib, *Evelyn, etc.) was maintained after the *Restoration. (See ORCHARDS.) The *railways transformed the distribution system. By the last quarter of the 20th century an increasing variety of fruit from all over the world was available in supermarkets. See F. A. Roach, *Cultivated Fruits of Britain, Their Origin and History* (1985).

Fuller, Thomas (1608–61). Clergyman and antiquarian. His first major work was a *Church History of Britain, with the History of the University of Cambridge and the History of Waltham Abbey* (1655), but he is best known as the author of *The History of the Worthies of England* (1662), which was uncompleted at his death despite nearly 20 years' work on it. This book is arranged by counties and, in a strange miscellany, deals with natural resources, manufactures, wonders, proverbs, and notable people. See ANTIQUARIAN TRADITION, THE.

fulling mills. Before the invention of scribbling and *spinning mills in the late 18th century, fulling was the only mechanical process in the manufacture of cloth. After a piece of cloth had been woven it was taken to a *water-powered fulling mill, where wooden hammers would pound it with fuller's earth in order to scour and cleanse it. The cloth was then hung on *tenter frames to be stretched back to its original size. Fulling mills were known in northern England as walk mills (after the earlier practice of trampling fuller's earth into the cloth) and in the south-west as tuck mills. The surnames

Fuller, Walker, and Tucker, or Tooker, are derived from this occupation. A great deal of documentary evidence survives from the Middle Ages and the early modern period, and from minor place-names, but very few sites have been excavated. This is partly because many fulling mills were converted into larger enterprises including scribbling and spinning, or put to different milling uses, and as a result their original form has been obscured.

funerary monuments. Stone or wooden figures representing a dead person were first placed in churches during the 12th century, when ecclesiastics were commemorated in this way. From the 13th century onwards local lords were depicted in a reclining position clad in armour, often with their feet resting on some mythical animal. They are the subjects of numerous folk-tales, e.g. at Barnburgh (Yorkshire) a knight and the 'wild cat' at his feet are said to have killed each other in mortal combat. The figures can often be identified by *heraldry and sometimes by inscriptions, or placed within a certain period by the style of dress or ornamentation. A lord or knight is sometimes shown lying next to his wife (or wives if he remarried), with representations of his children (including dead ones) on the sides or at the base of the tomb. Some churches contain a succession of family monuments, e.g. of the Fitzherberts at Norbury (Derbyshire). (See also INCISED SLABS; ALABASTER; and BRASS, MEMORIAL.)

From the 16th century these figures are often portraits. Thus, when Sir Richard Scott of Ecclesfield (Yorkshire) died in 1638, it was ordered that his alabaster monument should be 'like his favor, simily, and likeness'. The figures were shown either lying flat, looking up, with hands closed as if in prayer, or reclining upon one elbow. The design of tombs containing effigies in the Elizabethan and Stuart era was influenced by the Italian Renaissance, many ideas being taken from 'emblem' books. Indeed, some figures were represented as Roman soldiers. See Bernard Denvir, *From the Middle Ages to the Stuarts: Art, Design and Society before 1689* (1988). From the later 17th century full figures in an upright position or busts in a classical style were favoured. These were carved in marble and were lifelike or idealized representations. The Victorian fashion was for large monuments in a variety of styles; see GRAVESTONES.

funfairs. The towns led the way to converting the ancient annual livestock *fairs into pleasure fairs. By the 1820s and 1830s Easter and Whit-suntide funfairs were being held in, or close to, major centres of population. London had large funfairs at Shoreditch, Edmonton, Greenwich, Stepney, and Hampstead Heath. The latter was one of the new fairs that were created simply for recreation. Local residents were alarmed by the size of the crowds, and at first the police tried to restrict such activities, but the relaxed holiday mood of the visitors soon persuaded the authorities that boisterous funfairs did not lead to violence. The fairs soon became run by showmen with considerable capital and organization skills. By the last quarter of the 19th century steam roundabouts and steam organs were an essential part of the attraction. By then many old rural 'feasts' and *hiring fairs had been converted into pleasure fairs, and steam traction was bringing travelling funfairs and circuses into the countryside. See S. Alexander, *St Giles Fair, 1830–1914: Popular Culture in the Industrial Revolution in Nineteenth-Century Oxford* (1970). Funfairs declined in popularity from the 1960s onwards. Their place in London has been taken by the Notting Hill Carnival.

furlong. Originally, the length of a furrow in an *open-field, 220 yards. The term was also used for a block of *strips within an open-field (see FLATT and SHOT, SHUTT). Such blocks were often sown with different crops from the rest of the field and were subject to piecemeal *enclosure.

furnaces. The change from the *bloomery method of smelting iron occurred gradually during the 16th and 17th centuries. The charcoal blast-furnace was introduced into southeastern England by French ironworkers. The first furnace was built at Newbridge, in Ashdown Forest, in 1496. The most intensive fieldwork by archaeologists has taken place in the Weald, where numerous blast-furnaces were built half a century or so before the technology spread to other parts of the country. See H. F. Cleere and D. W. Crossley, *The Iron Industry of the Weald* (1985). Some iron was cast in a blast-furnace in the form of artefacts, but most was taken as pig iron, to be converted into wrought iron at a neighbouring *forge. *Charcoal from *coppiced wood was used as fuel, and the blast was provided by bellows worked by a water wheel. In the 1560s blast-furnaces were built at Cleobury Mortimer and Shifnal (Shropshire), Goodrich (Herefordshire), and Cannock Chase (Staffordshire), and soon afterwards in Montgomeryshire and Glamorgan, Derbyshire, and south Yorkshire. The main expansion outside the Weald began in the 1580s, spreading eventually to the Forest of Dean, Cumbria, west Scotland, etc. Meanwhile, output at each furnace was increased considerably. Whereas a late medieval bloomery produced 20 to 30 tons per annum, the average output of a late 17th-century blast furnace was 400 tons. The earliest successful use of coke was at Coalbrookdale in 1709. The use of coke was slow to spread beyond Shropshire, and it was not until the mid-18th century that charcoal was generally replaced as the fuel.

See STEEL for an account of how steel manufacture progressed from cementation and crucible furnaces, to Bessemer converters and Siemens open-hearth furnaces, to modern electric-hearth furnaces.

furniture. The history of high-quality furniture has attracted an extensive scholarly literature, but much work remains to be done at the local level in identifying craftsmen, in describing their tools and skills, and in noting changing styles and tastes. See Bernard Price, *The Story of English Furniture* (1978) for an introductory survey. Probate *inventories are a major source of information for the early modern period which have not yet been analysed in detail for this purpose, nor compared with surviving pieces of furniture in local collections other than for the purpose of providing glossaries of terms. For the range of hand *tools that was available at the end of the 18th century, see Jane and Mark Rees (eds.), *The Tool Chest of Benjamin Seaton* (The Tools and Trades History Society, 1994). Christopher Gilbert, *English Vernacular Furniture, 1750–1900* (1991) is required reading for the later period.

Fussell, G. E. (1889–1990). George Fussell was a prolific writer on agricultural history, who published over 20 books and more than 600 articles from 1922 right up to his centenary year. He developed his literary interests as a civil servant in what became the Ministry of Agriculture and Fisheries. Without any formal academic training, he became an authority on agricultural history at a time when little had been written on the subject. He edited the farm accounts of Robert *Loder in 1936, but most of his vast output was concerned with contemporary printed sources. His pioneering works included *The English Rural Labourer* (1949), *The English Countryman* (1953), *The English Countrywoman* (1955), both with his wife, K. R. Fussell, and *The English Dairy Farmer, 1500–1900* (1966). He was one of the founder members of the *British Agricultural History Society.

Gaelic language. The Celtic language of Ireland, the Isle of Man, and of the Highlands and Islands of Scotland. In Ireland, English speech became dominant in the *Ulster plantations, in and around Dublin, and in other towns and ports, so that by the 18th century the Gaelic language was already in decline. By the mid-19th century Gaelic was largely the language of the poor, especially those in the countryside; it is now largely confined to western parts of Ireland. See W. J. Smyth, 'The Making of Ireland: Agendas and Perspectives in Cultural Geography' in B. J. Graham and L. J. Proudfoot (eds.), *An Historical Geography of Ireland* (1993), ch. 12. The Gaels of Scotland are descendants of settlers from Ireland. Scots Gaelic had begun to differ from the Irish language by the 10th century. It became the language of the whole of Scotland except for the border region and the Norse-speaking districts in the north and west. By the 14th century the Lowlands had become Anglicized and most of its inhabitants had ceased to speak Gaelic. See Charles W. J. Withers, *Gaelic Scotland: The Transformation of a Culture Region* (1988). About 200,000 inhabitants of the Highlands and Islands were still monoglot Gaelic speakers in the 1880s; today, the number of Gaelic speakers is about 80,000, most of whom are bilingual. See V. E. Durkacz, *The Decline of the Celtic Languages* (1983).

Galilee. A vestibule at the western end of a *cathedral or monastic church, used as a *chapel for penitents. Durham Cathedral has a beautiful Norman example.

gallery. 1. Elizabethan *prodigy-houses started the fashion for a long gallery on the top storey. Outstanding examples designed by Robert Smythson can be seen at Haddon Hall and Hardwick Hall (Derbyshire). They provided space for exercise, commanded wide views, and served as a status symbol (for glass was expensive). Even the timber-framed Little Moreton Hall (Cheshire) was provided with a gallery when John Moreton built a new range in Elizabeth I's reign.

2. In the 17th and 18th centuries churches and chapels provided extra seats in upper galleries. St Mary's, Whitby (Yorkshire) is the outstanding example. In most Anglican churches these were removed in the *High Church movement of the 19th century as they were thought to lack dignity and to give a church a cluttered appearance.

galleting. From the French *galet*, meaning a pebble. The practice of placing pebbles in the mortar of *vernacular buildings was common in parts of south-eastern England and East Anglia.

gallows. Minor place-names, e.g. Gallows Hill, frequently commemorate the sites of manorial gallows. Public *executions in *assize towns were abolished in 1868. See TYBURN.

game laws. The strict preservation of game became a concern of *landowners from the second half of the 17th century onwards. In 1671 the property qualification for taking game was set at £100 a year for *freeholders and £150 for *leaseholders; this was enforced by a £5 fine or three months' imprisonment. After 1707 the possessors of illegally acquired game or of 'engines' to kill game faced the same penalty. An Act of 1770 threatened with a year's imprisonment those who took game at night. The laws became increasingly severe in the first half of the 19th century. In 1800 a single JP was empowered to punish poachers with imprisonment and hard labour; in 1803 armed resistance to arrest was punishable by death; and in 1817 armed poachers caught at night were transported for seven years. In the years after the *Napoleonic wars committals for *poaching increased substantially. At the same time, the use of spring-guns to catch poachers was at its peak. The ferocity of the game laws was to some extent counter-productive, however, for some judges and juries preferred to dismiss charges rather than impose harsh penalties. See P. B. Munsche, *Gentlemen and Players: The English Game Laws, 1671–1831* (1981), and E. P. Thompson, *Whigs and Hunters: The Origins of the Black Act* (1975).

The systematic preservation of game, involving the employment of large numbers of keepers charged with the rearing of birds and the provision of coverts, with formal seasons for shooting, was a Victorian development that reached its peak in the early years of the 20th century. It has been estimated that by this time in East Anglia there were three or four game-keepers in every village. Other counties with a large number of keepers included Hampshire, Hertfordshire, Surrey, Sussex, Berkshire, Dorset, Kent, and Shropshire. Elsewhere, the rural population never came across a gamekeeper. In many parts of Britain the game laws caused great bitterness and provoked heated debate. The Ground Game Act of 1881 eased this tension by allowing tenants to shoot *rabbits and hares on their own holdings. See also GROUSE; PHEASANT SHOOTING.

gangs, labour. A system in the eastern counties of England, especially Lincolnshire and East Anglia, whereby gangs of people, especially women and children, under the direction of a gang master, moved from farm to farm to meet seasonal demands for labour. About half the work-force consisted of children aged 7–13. The *Poor Law Amendment Act (1834), which led to the pulling down of *cottages in order to reduce the poor rates, encouraged the spread of this system. A farmer seeking a temporary work-force paid an agreed sum to a gang master, who then directed the work and paid the workers. The profits went to the gang master. The *Report on the Employment of Women and Children in Agriculture* (1843) provides a great deal of information on the hardships endured under this system. It showed how the inhabitants of an open *village such as Castle Acre (Norfolk) met the labour requirements not only of local farmers but of 22 farms, totalling 17,000 acres, in 11 adjacent places.

Gang labour continued throughout the middle decades of the 19th century. A further report of 1867 led to some controls: no child under eight years of age was allowed to work; no women or girls could work in gangs that included men; and gang masters were licensed by the *Justices of the Peace. The Gangs Act (1867) did not, however, prohibit other forms of child employment.

gaol delivery. A Commission of Gaol Delivery ordered *sheriffs to bring prisoners awaiting trial before specially appointed justices. The records are kept at the *Public Record Office under JUST.ITIN. 3 and PL. 25. See also OYER AND TERMINER.

Garden City movement. A new direction in town planning to create an environment that was midway between town and country. Industrial buildings were placed on the perimeter and the town was surrounded by a 'green belt'. The movement began with the publication of Ebenezer Howard, *Tomorrow: A Peaceful Path to Real Reform* (1898), which led to the formation of The Garden City Association in 1899 and four years later to the first scheme at Letchworth; by 1961 this new town had over 25,000 people. Emphasis was placed on the provision of low-density housing (including three-bed-roomed 'cottages' for the working class) in a pleasant environment, with curving streets rather than a grid pattern. Hampstead Garden Suburb was founded in 1907 after a long campaign led by Dame Henrietta Barnett. In 1920 Welwyn Garden City was begun on the same principles and with more pleasing results, with a variety of harmonious accommodation, but it became socially divided by the railway line. After the Second World War the new towns of Stevenage, Hemel Hempstead, and Hatfield were built nearby. See Lionel M. Munby, *The Hertfordshire Landscape* (1977), ch. 10, Mervyn Miller, *Letchworth: the First Garden City* (1989), Mervyn Miller and A. Stuart Gray, *Hampstead Garden Suburb* (1992), and Derick Deakin (ed.), *Wythenshawe: The Story of a Garden City* (1989).

gardens. Roman, Anglo-Saxon, and medieval gardens are not well recorded, but by the Middle Ages both kitchen and flower gardens were prominent features of towns and villages, *monasteries, *castles, and *manor houses. See Teresa McLean, *Medieval English Gardens* (1989). (See also ORCHARDS and VINEYARDS.) The Italian Renaissance inspired the design of gardens as an art form and introduced the idea of botanic gardens: see Roy Strong, *The Renaissance Garden in England* (1979). The Elizabethans favoured formal gardens with symmetrical and knot patterns, observed from mounds, such as those at Little Moreton Hall (Cheshire), or raised terraces. Such gardens were enclosed by a wall, which incorporated towers, e.g. Montacute (Somerset), or seats, e.g. Bolsover Castle (Derbyshire). Bowling greens and garden houses, e.g. Melford Hall (Suffolk), and terraces, e.g. Haddon Hall (Derbyshire), were also fashionable. (See also MARKET GARDENING.)

After the *Restoration French and Dutch garden designs were widely used for country and town houses. They made much use of water in the form of fountains, canals, and ornamental pools and of classical statuary, and introduced the idea of segregated garden areas. Most of these gardens were swept away in the landscape gardening movement of the 18th century, but they can be observed in the bird's-eye views of Knyff and Kip, published as *Britannia Illustrata* (1707), and some are described in the journals of Celia *Fiennes. The Royal Commission on *Historical Monuments has reconstructed the original form of some 16th- and 17th-century gardens, notably in Northamptonshire, by archaeological methods: see Christopher Taylor, *The Archaeology of Gardens* (1983). The reigns of William III and Queen Anne were the apogee of formal gardens, with parterres of box, evergreen hedges and clipped specimens, gravel paths, *avenues, and follies. Bramham Park (Yorkshire) is a rare surviving example from this period.

The 18th century rejected the formal garden and favoured a more 'natural' design. At Castle Howard (Yorkshire) Vanbrugh and Hawksmoor invented an idyllic classical landscape of the type depicted in the paintings of Claude Lorraine. At Studley Royal (Yorkshire) John Aislabie created a series of lakes and woods adorned with classical statuary, temples, and follies leading towards a sudden view of the ruined Fountains Abbey. At Rousham (Oxfordshire) William Kent placed temples and statuary informally in lawns and woods. At Stourhead (Wiltshire) from 1741 onwards Henry Hoare created a complete Virgilian landscape with a chain of lakes, three classical temples, a bridge, a grotto, and a rock arch. The fashion now was to obliterate the avenues, straight paths, and canals in favour of sinuous walks, meandering streams and rivers, and clumps of mature trees set in rolling parkland. (See BROWN, 'CAPABILITY', and REPTON, HUMPHRY.) The impact of classical landscapes seen on the Grand Tour and in the paintings of Claude and Poussin is evident not only in the design of country houses but in that of their surrounding grounds.

Eighteenth-century gardens were also influenced by Chinese designs and by a delight in the *Gothick and the Picturesque. The 19th century saw a huge influx of new trees and shrubs from all over the world. Sir William Armstrong's gardens at Cragside (Northumberland) and the sixth Duke of Devonshire's gardens (including an arboretum and a pinetum) on the hillside above Chatsworth are outstanding examples of informal, almost wild, gardens of this period. Rich men such as these employed large numbers of gardeners and the latest technology, including the lawn mower (invented in 1832) and heated conservatories. Meanwhile, the great walled gardens were brought to a high state of cultivation and all styles of garden layout were attempted, including the reintroduced formal Italianate garden,

e.g. Cliveden (Berkshire), and gardens to show off plants. William Robinson, *The English Flower Garden* (1883), and Gertrude *Jekyll were enormously influential, not only in the layout of the gardens of great houses, but in those of modest properties in the *suburbs. For overviews, see Christopher Thacker, *The History of Gardens* (1979), and A. Taigel and T. Williamson, *Parks and Gardens* (1993). Specialist articles are published in the journal *Garden History*.

garderobe. A latrine in a medieval *castle or house, placed within the thickness of a wall, with a shaft descending to a cesspool or *moat.

Garter King of Arms. The principal King of Arms at the College of *Arms.

garth. From an Old Norse word meaning an enclosure. In northern England garth is still used as a field name, but its derivative 'yard' has a more general meaning of a small, enclosed space, as in *churchyard, courtyard, farmyard. 'Garden' is also derived from the same word.

gas. Gas extracted from coal was first used in Britain in 1792 to light the offices of the Scottish engineer William Murdock. In 1807 Pall Mall, London, became the first thoroughfare in the world to be lit by gas. In the early 19th century towns were supplied with gas for lighting by small private companies which operated over a limited area. From the mid-Victorian period up to nationalization in 1949 the provision of gas was a municipal responsibility. From the 1860s gas was also used for heating and cooking. During the 1920s and 1930s gas lighting was generally replaced by *electricity. See T. Williams, *A History of the British Gas Industry* (1981). For a local study see Sue Bowden, Ronald Crawford, and Graham Sykes, 'The Public Supply of Gas in Leeds, 1818–1949' in John Chartres and Katrina Honeymen (eds.), *Leeds City Business, 1893–1993* (1993), ch. 4.

gate / yat. In areas of Scandinavian settlement in northern and eastern England 'gate' meant a road. Thus, many of the streets of York, e.g. Stonegate, Petergate, Micklegate, have this suffix. The Old English *geat*, meaning 'pass' or 'gap', has sometimes developed into *yat*, as in Symonds Yat in the Wye Valley.

gatehouses. The gatehouses of medieval *castles were strong defensive structures. As the need for defence receded, gatehouses became increasingly decorative. The early 17th-century timber-framed gatehouse at Stokesay Castle

(Shropshire) is ornamental and not at all defensive. Tudor and Jacobean gatehouses (including the porters' lodges of Oxford and Cambridge colleges) sought to impress visitors with heraldic devices and a *Gothic style that suggested past glories. That at Burton Agnes (Yorkshire) is three storeys high, with battlements and corner turrets topped by ogee-shaped domes; it was built in 1610 at the same time as the house. Gatehouses fell out of fashion in the second half of the 17th century, but later enjoyed renewed popularity. See T. Mowl and B. Earnshaw, *Trumpet at a Distant Gate* (1985).

gavelkind. A system of *inheritance, particularly in Kent, and anciently in Wales, whereby estates were equally divided amongst sons, and in the absence of male heirs equally amongst daughters. The system was abolished in Wales by Henry VIII, elsewhere not until 1925.

geese were kept in small numbers except in Norfolk. In his *Tour through the Whole Island of Great Britain* (1724–6) Daniel *Defoe observed that geese and *turkeys were driven in 'prodigious numbers' from 'the farthest parts of Norfolk' to London. He had met droves of 1,000–2,000. 'They begin to drive them generally in August, by which time the harvest is almost over, and the geese may feed in the stubbles as they go. Thus they hold on to the end of October, when the roads begin to be too stiff and deep for their broad feet and short legs to march in.' He also noted that geese were carried on carts 'with four stories or stages'. Nottingham's Goose Fair remains a major annual festival.

geld. A tax calculated upon the holding of land. See DANEGELD.

Genealogists, Society of. Founded in 1911, the Society is based at 14 Charterhouse Buildings, London EC1M 7BA, where it has the largest specialized library of books, journals, manuscripts, indexes, and microfiche and computer databases on genealogy. (See BOYD'S MARRIAGE INDEX and APPRENTICESHIP.) The Society holds regular lecture meetings and publishes guides to records, as well as the quarterly *Genealogists' Magazine*, and a quarterly newsletter *Computers in Genealogy*.

Genealogists and Record Agents, Association of. Founded in 1968, the association aims to preserve professional standards. It is managed by an elected Council.

Genealogists' Magazine. The quarterly journal of the Society of *Genealogists, published since 1925, which contains articles on genealogy and reviews of books on the subject.

General Register Office. Currently at *St Catherine's House, London, where indexes of birth, marriage, and death certificates from 1 July 1837 to the present day may be consulted. See CIVIL REGISTRATION.

General Views of Agriculture. The series of county reports published by the *Board of Agriculture from the 1790s to the early 19th century. The reporters travelled widely and made informed judgements on the state of agriculture, noting best practices, and on the wider economy. They provide many local details and are a basic source for the study of the rural economy at the time. A good example is C. Vancouver, *General View of the Agriculture of Devonshire* (1808).

generation. An imprecise reckoning, roughly 30–40 years.

Gentleman's Magazine. Published from 1731 until 1868, this monthly magazine is a mine of miscellaneous information. Particularly valuable are the topographical descriptions of provincial towns and villages sent in by readers. These describe local antiquities and give a contemporary account that is now of historical interest. G. L. Gomme edited this material for a series of county volumes published about the turn of the 20th century by Elliot Stock of Paternoster Row, London. Two general indexes covering the period 1731–1810, an index of marriages 1731–68, and indexes of obituaries and biographies 1731–80, have also been published. Complete series of the volumes are available at the *British Library and the *Public Record Office. The collection at the Society of *Genealogists is incomplete.

gentry. Although the word 'gentil' originally meant 'noble', by the 15th century a gentleman was one who was superior to a *yeoman but inferior in status to a *baron. Between 1530 and 1688 the heralds attempted to restrict the use of the term gentleman to those who could prove a legal claim to a coat of *arms, but they were unable to enforce their decisions, for in popular usage the term was applied loosely to one who did not work with his hands. Both the richer members of rural society and the urban professionals were known to their neighbours as gentry. This vagueness of definition contrasted sharply with Continental practice. The debate as to whether or not the gentry were members of the nobility continued in the 19th century. (See BURKE, JOHN.) By then, however, public speakers commonly addressed any audience as 'Ladies and Gentlemen'.

For an overview from the Middle Ages to the 20th century, see G. E. Mingay, *The Gentry: The Rise and Fall of a Ruling Class* (1976). The few county studies that are available for the Middle Ages include N. Saul, *Knights and Esquires: The Gloucestershire Gentry in the Fourteenth Century* (1981), Susan M. Wright, *The Derbyshire Gentry in the Fifteenth Century* (1983), and M. J. Bennett, 'A County Community: Social Cohesion amongst the Cheshire Gentry, 1400–1425', *Northern History*, 8 (1973).

The debate as to whether the gentry were rising or falling as a class in the first half of the 17th century, and interest in the role of the gentry in *local government during the *Civil War, stimulated a number of county studies, including Alan Everitt, *The Community of Kent and the Great Rebellion, 1640–1660* (1966), J. T. Cliffe, *The Yorkshire Gentry from the Reformation to the Civil War* (1969), J. S. Morrill, *Cheshire, 1630–1660: County Government and Society during the English Revolution* (1974), and Anthony Fletcher, *A County Community in Peace and War: Sussex, 1600–1660* (1975). For Wales, see Philip Jenkins, *The Making of a Ruling Class: The Glamorgan Gentry, 1640–1790* (1983), and David W. Howell, *Patriarchs and Parasites: The Gentry of South-West Wales in the Eighteenth Century* (1986). The rest of the British Isles is less well served with detailed regional studies. For the 19th century, see D. C. Moore, 'The Gentry' in G. E. Mingay (ed.), *The Victorian Countryside*, vol. ii (1981), and F. M. L. Thompson, *English Landed Society in the Nineteenth Century* (1963).

Geoffrey of Monmouth (*c*.1100–54). Welsh ecclesiastic whose *Historia regum Britanniae* (*The History of the Kings of Britain*), though of little value as a work of history, was influential in popularizing legends involving Arthur, Merlin, Lear, and Cymbeline.

geological surface maps. The Institute of Geological Sciences has published a series of maps of drift geology, based on the *Ordnance Survey 1:63,360 (one inch to one mile) maps for practically the whole of Great Britain, but many of the early ones are no longer in print. This series is being replaced by a new one using the scale of 1:50,000. Sheets are also available on larger scales for much of Great Britain. Other series show the solid geology of Britain.

Georgian architecture. The four Georges ruled from 1714 to 1830, when interest in classical architecture was at its height, but the style continued to be popular for another two or three decades. (See BAROQUE and PALLADIAN for country houses, etc.) The term 'Georgian' is used for plain, symmetrical farmhouses and the town houses and public buildings that survive in most market towns. Blandford Forum (Dorset), which was rebuilt after the fire of 1731, is an outstanding example of a market town where houses were built for all classes by the family firm, the Bastards, in the classical style. Dublin, Edinburgh, Bath, and Stamford retain a great deal of their Georgian buildings. Many of the London squares were laid out and the surrounding houses built during the Georgian period. Other towns commonly have a Georgian development, consisting perhaps of a square and a few streets. See Peter Borsay, *The English Urban Renaissance: Culture and Society in the Provincial Town, 1660–1770* (1989), Kerry Downes, *The Georgian Cities of Britain* (1979), and C. W. Chalklin, *The Provincial Towns of Georgian England: A Study of the Building Process, 1740–1820* (1974).

Gerald of Wales, otherwise Giraldus Cambrensis (*c*.1145–1223), a well-connected Welsh churchman born at Manorbier (Pembrokeshire). His *Topographia Hibernica* and *Expugnatio Hibernica* are accounts of the natural history and the people of Ireland and the conquest of that country by Henry II. Notes made when accompanying the Archbishop of Canterbury on a visit to Wales in 1188 to urge support for the third *Crusade formed the basis of his famous work, *Itinerarium Cambriae* (*The Journey through Wales* and *The Description of Wales*). This is a readable and detailed picture of 12th-century Wales, with many observations on everyday life.

German immigrants. London was the destination of 16th- and 17th-century German immigrants who were *Protestant refugees. They included successful businessmen, particularly from Hamburg. With the accession of the Hanoverian kings more German merchants and craftsmen were attracted to London, though some moved on to *America. A number of German churches were founded in London. In the 19th century German businessmen were also attracted to the industrial towns, notably Manchester and Bradford. Over 50,000 Germans were living in Britain on the eve of the First World War, just over half of them in London. See Panikos Panayi, 'Germans in London' in Nick Merriman (ed.), *The Peopling of London* (1993). See also JEWISH IMMIGRANTS.

gibbet. The post from which the corpse of an executed criminal was hung in chains at prominent crossroads to deter others. Medieval *lords of the manor often had powers of execution. In the early modern period criminals executed at an *assize court were subsequently gibbeted at the scene of their crime. Place-names such as Gibbet Hill commemorate such sites, which have often attracted folk tales and superstitions. Broughton Lane, Sheffield, passes the site where Spence Broughton was gibbeted in 1792, after being hanged at York for highway robbery. His remains were removed in 1827.

Gibson, Edmund (1669–1748), church jurist and antiquary. Editor of the *Anglo-Saxon Chronicle* and of an influential enlarged and corrected edition and translation of *Camden's *Britannia* (1695), and author of *Codex iuris ecclesiastici Anglicani* (1713). He became Bishop of Lincoln in 1716 and Bishop of London in 1720.

Gilbertines. The only religious order to originate in England. Founded in 1131 by Gilbert, the parish priest of Sempringham (Lincolnshire), 12 *monasteries were soon established in his native and neighbouring counties. Ten of these monasteries were double houses for *canons and *nuns. The order had a reputation for high standards and for its charity, but its membership declined rapidly in the 14th century. It was extinguished at the *dissolution of the monasteries.

Gilbert's Act (1782). A reform of the *Poor Law which restricted indoor relief to the impotent poor and allowed the able-bodied to obtain employment outside the *workhouse. Children under seven years were not separated from their parents, orphans were boarded out, the use of the pauper's badge was abandoned, and paupers were sent to workhouses no more than 10 miles away. Inspectors were appointed to enforce these laws and the building of workhouses by unions of parishes was encouraged.

gin. 1. A spirit distilled from malted grain and originally flavoured by juniper berries. The name is contracted from 'geneva' (from the Dutch for juniper). It became a cheap, mass-market drink in the early 18th century and its abuse rapidly turned it into a major social problem, especially in London.
2. A short form for 'engine', used for example in horse-gin.

glass. Glass was used sparingly in most domestic buildings in the Middle Ages because of the cost, but it was used on a lavish scale in major secular and ecclesiastical buildings. The builders of *Perpendicular *Gothic churches filled as much wall space as possible with (*stained) glass, a fashion that was imitated in Elizabethan *prodigy-houses such as 'Hardwick Hall / more glass than wall'. Until the second half of the 16th century better quality glass was imported from the Continent, for windows, bottles, wine glasses, etc.; glass made in the Weald or the forests of Staffordshire was inferior.

In the reign of Elizabeth I the quality of English glass was improved by immigrant French glassworkers, particularly from Lorraine, who settled in the Weald and later moved to other parts of the country. They can be traced over several generations by their distinctive names, even in Anglicized forms, such as Pilmay or Fenny. After 1610 *coal rapidly replaced wood as the fuel in the manufacturing process, and so the industry was re-sited in the coalfields by wealthy landowners who employed the descendants of the Lorrainers. The great conical furnaces which became typical of the industry were introduced around 1700. A cone erected at Catcliffe (Yorkshire) in 1740 is the best surviving example. For a summary of the archaeological and historical evidence for the early modern period see David Crossley, *Post-Medieval Archaeology in Britain* (1990), ch. 11.

Some old glassworks specialized not in 'crown' window glass but in the more mundane production of bottles, jars, jugs, etc. The range of colours varied from deep blue to green, amber, red, mauve, and black. In the 19th century the expansion of the national population and improved communications created a much bigger demand for glass products, which in turn led to larger glassworks and improved technology and the creation of new industrial communities. However, many small firms survived until the first half of the 20th century.

By the mid-19th century bottle, plate, crown, and flint glass were being produced on a large scale in Lancashire. Pilkington's of St Helens had imported Belgian workers and new techniques; by 1900 Pilkington's were the chief manufacturers of window glass in Britain and the only producers of plate glass. See T. C. Barker and J. R. Harris, *A Merseyside Town in the Industrial Revolution: St Helens, 1750–1900* (1959). For a good local study of the industry and its workers from earliest times to the present day see Denis Ashurst, *The History of South Yorkshire Glass* (1992).

gleaning. The practice of collecting stray ears of corn and straw from a field after reaping was an ancient custom (see, for example, the Old

Testament Book of Ruth). It was popularly supposed that a landowner had no right to prevent the practice. In numerous court cases in the 19th century farmers tried to restrict gleaners, or at least to enforce regulations. In many parishes the start and finish of the time allowed for gleaning was announced by the church bells. The contribution that gleaning made to the income of a labouring family was variable: in *Lark Rise to Candleford* (1945) Flora *Thompson reckoned that an industrious family could glean two bushels or more. See Peter King, 'Gleaners, Farmers and the Failure of Legal Sanctions in England, 1750–1850', *Past and Present*, 125 (1989), and 'Customary Rights and Women's Earnings: The Importance of Gleaning to the Rural Labouring Poor, 1750–1850', *Economic History Review*, 2nd ser., 44/3 (1991).

glebe. Land farmed (or leased out) by a *parish priest. Over the centuries parishioners bequeathed small portions of land, e.g. a *strip or two in an *open-field, to their minister, though the major part of his income came from the *tithes. The amount of glebe land varied considerably from parish to parish. In some places sufficient was amassed to create a Glebe Farm. Such land was rarely sold and thus maintained its identity over time.

An *ecclesiastical visitation commonly produced a glebe terrier which gave an account of the *parsonage and the land that belonged to the incumbent. These terriers are preserved amongst diocesan records or in parish records deposited at county *record offices. Where the glebe land was within one or more open-fields they are a useful guide to the timing of *enclosure by agreement in the 16th and 17th centuries, for they will indicate whether the land was held in strips or in hedged closes. They record field and *furlong names, *boundaries, and the names of adjoining property owners. See M. W. Beresford, 'Glebe Terriers in Open-Field Leicestershire', *Transactions of the Leicestershire Archaeological Society*, 24 (1948).

Glorious Revolution. The name given to the events of 1688, whereby James II, the Roman Catholic king, was deposed and William of Orange, the Protestant ruler of the Netherlands, became joint ruler of England, Scotland, Ireland, and Wales with his wife Mary, the daughter of the deposed king. The revolution brought constitutional government and toleration for *Nonconformists. (See WHIGS and TORIES.) William's victory over James's forces at the Battle of the Boyne (1690) is commemorated annually by the Orange Order.

gloss. A marginal commentary on a text.

goats have not been kept in large numbers in the British Isles, even in the upland parts of Wales, since the time of the *Anglo-Saxons. Instead, they have usually been kept in twos or threes by smallholders, primarily as a source of cheese. Larger herds were occasionally found in the Scottish Highlands. See, for instance, Samuel Johnson, *A Journey to the Western Islands of Scotland* (1775).

godparent. A family friend who sponsors a child at baptism. The ancient practice was for a child to have two godparents of his or her own sex and one of the other. Godparents had an important influence on choosing the name of their godchild.

gold. Although gold was mined in parts of Wales (modern Dyfed) by the Romans, mining was conducted on a small scale and was rarely economic.

golf. A game which originated in Scotland in the Middle Ages. The Victorian middle classes formed private clubs or played on municipal courses, which in the 20th century widened the appeal of the game to working-class people. The topography of golf courses may be of interest to local historians, especially courses which were once *deer parks or part of the landscaped park of a country house. Some club houses are the former halls or *manor houses of local *gentry families.

Goodwife. A form of address in the Middle Ages and early modern period for the mistress of a house, below the status of a gentlewoman. The term is sometimes found in records as a prefix to a *surname.

gore. A triangular piece of land.

gorse was collected from the *commons and wastes for fuel. See Alan Harris, 'Gorse in the East Riding of Yorkshire', *Folk Life*, 30 (1992).

Gospel Oak / Gospel Thorn. A place-name on a parish *boundary where a passage from the Gospels was read at the annual *Rogationtide *perambulation or 'beating of the bounds'.

Gothic. Originally a term of abuse coined in the 17th century by admirers of classical architecture, who compared the replacement of the *Romanesque style from the late 12th century onwards with the destruction of ancient Rome by the Goths. The Gothic style was introduced from France for *monasteries and *cathedrals and was used subsequently for parish *churches and secular buildings. Thomas *Rickman divided the Gothic ecclesiastical styles into *Early English, *Decorated, and *Perpendicular. The term 'Tudor Court Gothic' is used to describe Hampton Court and other royal palaces and the Elizabethan *prodigy-houses which were influenced by them. The Gothic style never completely disappeared, though historians speak of 'Gothic survivals' in the 18th century and the 'Gothic revival' of the 19th century; thus, it has become clear from scholarly work in recent years that church towers in the Perpendicular style continued to be built in the later 16th and 17th centuries. Most of the new Anglican and Catholic churches of the 19th century, and some of the later Nonconformist *chapels, were Gothic, but contemporary secular public buildings were designed in a variety of styles.

Gothick. The term is used for architectural features in buildings erected in the 18th and early 19th centuries which were loosely based on medieval *Gothic designs. Such buildings were often romanticized or given a fake air of antiquity. In literature the term is used to describe novels with improbable dramatic plots set in ruined *abbeys, decayed *manor houses, etc. Houses which incorporated medieval abbeys, such as Newstead (Nottinghamshire) or Lacock (Wiltshire), had their medieval features enhanced by Gothick extensions and the erection of *follies in the grounds.

Gough, Richard. 1. (1735–1809). Antiquarian and collector. A man of independent fortune who travelled widely in England in search of antiquities. (See ANTIQUARIAN TRADITION.) His vast collection of antiquarian material—maps, plans, prints, drawings, notes, coins, and medals—is kept in the *Bodleian Library and other repositories. A regular correspondent to the *Gentleman's Magazine, he was made a Fellow of the *Royal Society in 1775. Gough was Director of the Society of *Antiquaries of London from 1771 to 1797. He is best known as the author of *British Topography*, 2 vols. (1768, 2nd ed. 1780), and of *Sepulchral Monuments of Great Britain* (1768), and as the editor of *Camden's *Britannia* (1789 and 1806).

2. of Myddle (1635–1723). The author of *Antiquityes and Memoyres of the Parish of Myddle* (1700), and *Observations concerning the Seates in Myddle and the Familyes to which They Belong* (1701–2), a remarkable account of all the families of this Shropshire parish. Gough took the *church seating plan in the parish church and wrote the intimate family history of each pewholder in turn. His manuscript was not published until 1834 (and then imperfectly). See David Hey (ed.), *Richard Gough: The History of Myddle* (1981).

granary. A place to store grain. Special-purpose buildings were raised on staddle stones to allow air to circulate and to hinder the depredations of rats and mice.

grange. *Monasteries were often given land which was situated too far away to be worked from the monastery itself. The *Cistercians therefore developed a system of granges, which were outlying farms worked by *lay brothers and hired labourers. Such granges were used particularly as arable holdings in the lowlands, but were also used for other purposes, e.g. as a base for the mining and smelting of *iron. Granges varied considerably in size and were distinguished from ordinary farms only by their chapels. See Colin Platt, *The Monastic Grange in Medieval England* (1969). Many farmhouses are built on the sites of former granges, but 'grange' became a popular choice of name for a Victorian house with no monastic connections, especially if neighbours had already named their properties (accurately or inaccurately) 'hall' or 'manor house'.

grave, greave. A person chosen by the tenants of a *manor to act as their representative in dealings with the lord.

gravestones. The earliest inscribed gravestones are those placed within a church by the wealthier inhabitants during the 16th century. Earlier fashions were for effigies, monuments, and memorial *brasses. Graves in parish *churchyards were originally unmarked, or were perhaps marked by an impermanent wooden cross. It was common practice to clear graves from time to time and to stack bones in *charnel houses so that fresh burials could take place. During the 17th century the *yeomen and better-off *husbandmen and craftsmen began to erect tombstones in churchyards in imitation of their social superiors who were buried inside the church. In most parishes the earliest tombstones date from the late 17th century. Some tombstones with 17th-century dates were erected by a later generation; for instance, when a son was buried in the same grave as his parents the tombstone that was erected in his memory might record the ages and deaths of his parents. If all the lettering is in the same style it is likely that the date of the tombstone is that of the last recorded event; in other cases later additions can be readily observed.

The earliest churchyard gravestones are found on the south side, near to the church porch. The north side was regarded as the 'Devil's side' and was used for the burials of excommunicants, suicides, and the unbaptized. This ancient superstition was gradually abandoned during the first half of the 18th century, but to this day the northern sides of churchyards are usually much smaller than those to the south.

The poorer sections of the community long continued to be buried in unmarked graves. Even if a person is known through the evidence of a *parish register to have been buried in a churchyard, a gravestone may not be found. The practice of erecting tombstones became so widespread, however, and the national population increased so much, that in Victorian times churchyards had to be extended and eventually public *cemeteries had to be created.

Gravestones were made from local stones or from materials that could be imported at low cost, e.g. along a navigable river. Some of these stones have weathered so badly that the inscriptions are now illegible. Others are as crisp as when they were new. Some are marked not only with personal information about the deceased but by symbols of death and resurrection. The inscribed side of the tombstone faces the east. Designs are often restricted to a particular region, e.g. gravestones with a heart symbol are common in the Calder Valley (Yorkshire) and are scattered thinly in neighbouring parishes. Gravestones made from *Swithland slate in the East Midlands are distinguished by their flowing letters and the maker's practice of inscribing his name at the bottom. A great deal of work remains to be done on these regional styles.

In recent years many *family history societies and other groups have done valuable work in recording the inscriptions on gravestones before they become too faint or are destroyed. Gravestones are a major source for family historians and some provide considerable detail. See Jeremy Jones, *How to Record Gravestones* (Council for British Archaeology, 1979), and Betty Willsher, 'Scottish Churchyard Memorials in the Eighteenth Century', *The Local Historian*, 23/2 (1993). Sheila and John Mitchell recorded the pre-1855 inscriptions on gravestones in eight counties in Central Scotland and published them in 12 volumes with the aid of the Scottish Genealogical Society.

graziers supplied towns with butcher's meat. Most offered a simple service and operated on a small scale, but the major graziers who leased extensive pastures in the marshes and lowland clays of southern and midland England were substantial men with contracts to provide regular supplies of meat to London. See DROVERS and BUTCHERS.

great chambers were a feature of the *prodigy-houses and other substantial halls and *manor houses of the Elizabethan and Jacobean period. They acted as upper-floor retiring or withdrawing rooms for the owner and his family and guests away from the communal life of the open hall below. An outstanding example at Gilling Castle (Yorkshire) shows how these chambers were decorated with *plasterwork, marquetry, painted friezes, *stained glass, and elaborate chimney pieces, and adorned with heraldic insignia.

Great Exhibition. Held in 1851 at the Crystal Palace, London (an iron and glass structure designed for the exhibition by Joseph Paxton) to display the manufactured goods of industrial Britain. The Crystal Palace was re-erected at Sydenham and burnt down in 1936.

Great Rebuilding. In a pioneering aricle, 'The Rebuilding of Rural England, 1570–1640', *Past and Present*, 4 (1953), W. G. *Hoskins argued that agricultural prices increased so much during the Elizabethan and early Stuart period that 'no yeoman with his wits about him could fail to accumulate money savings on a scale hitherto unknown' and that this led to much rebuilding of houses and a great increase in the standards of domestic comfort. Hoskins used contemporary literary evidence, household accounts, probate *inventories, and above all the visual evidence of rural buildings with *datestones to argue for 'a revolution in the housing of a considerable part of the population'. He accepted that in some parts of the country, notably the four most northerly counties, active rebuilding occurred later, but he assembled an impressive amount of evidence for new houses or extensions, with better-furnished interiors, that could be dated securely within the 70 years after 1570.

His essay—which was reprinted in his *Provincial England* (1964)—was immediately influential and inspired much of the early work of the newly formed Vernacular Architecture Group. The essay remains a useful starting-point in the study of *vernacular architecture, but the ideas have now been considerably refined, almost to the point of outliving their usefulness. In 'The Great Rebuilding: A Reassessment', *Past and Present*, 77 (1977) Robert Machin emphasized the wide variations in the dates of new buildings in the different regions of England; the period 1570–1640 does not look as special as Hoskins had argued, except perhaps in certain restricted areas. More recent work, e.g. at the *deserted medieval village of Wharram Percy (Yorkshire), has undermined the thesis further by demonstrating that the stock of late medieval houses was not of the poor quality that had been supposed and that many of the design features of later houses had already been adopted. It is now thought better to speak of a continuum of improvement from the late 15th century onwards, with much regional variation.

Great Reclothing. Margaret Spufford's book *The Great Reclothing of Rural England: Petty Chapmen and Their Wares in the Seventeenth Century* (1984) examines the evidence for the activities of *pedlars and petty *chapmen throughout England in selling cheap consumer goods, including clothing, all over the kingdom, in the early modern period. Much information is drawn from probate *inventories.

Great Seal. A seal depicting the sovereign on horseback on one side and enthroned on the other, which was used to authenticate important documents issued by the Crown.

green. A large number of medieval villages had a small green, often in a central position, perhaps with a duck pond. These greens were used for recreation and some rough grazing. Many disappeared through *encroachments or at the time of parliamentary *enclosure. In some villages the central green is a larger, planned space of regular shape; they originated in the Anglo-Scandinavian or Norman periods, occasionally later. They are found in all English counties, but Durham has an unusually large number. See B. K. Roberts, *Rural Settlement in Britain* (1977).

Greens are also the focal points of hamlets in areas of scattered settlement, particularly East Anglia. Many place-names in different parts of England incorporate the 'green' element. Peter Warner, *Greens, Commons and Clayland Colonization: The Origins and Development of Greenside Settlement in East Suffolk* (1987) argues that such greens are an ancient feature of the East Anglian countryside that survived from *Anglo-Saxon times through to the parliamentary enclosures of the 19th century. He charts the process of colonization and of desertion to explain the complex settlement patterns that can be found from the *Domesday Book onwards as new tenements 'leap-frogged' over older ones to encroach further on to the small *commons. His analysis of topographical and documentary evidence and his stress upon the role of numerous small freeholders have clear implications for the study of 'green' hamlets elsewhere.

green lane. A popular term for unmetalled tracks in the countryside. Many are of great antiquity and were long used for moving livestock over short, or long, distances, but those that run for miles across the moors take their present form from the period of parliamentary *enclosure.

green men. The carved figures known as green men are of two types. Some are doleful or grimacing faces peering through foliage, others have leaves sprouting from their mouths and ears, or even from their nostrils or eyes. They are often discovered in the stonework or woodwork of medieval churches throughout Europe, especially as roof bosses. They may have been demons or pagan symbols of spring that have been adapted to Christian usage as representations of the festival of Easter, or various other fancies that had a remarkably tenacious hold on popular consciousness. See Kathleen Basford, *The Green Man* (1978), and Roy Judge, *The Jack in the Green* (1979). A large number of pubs are known as The Green Man. However, W. T. Fernie, *Herbal Simples, Approved for Modern Uses of Cure* (2nd edn., 1897) noted that, in the early 19th century, purveyors of medicinal and savoury herbs wandered over England in quest of simples. They were known as 'green men'. They carried portable apparatus for distilling essences and preparing herbal extracts. Fernie believed that inn signs such as 'The Green Man and Still' in London and elsewhere were named after such men.

Greenwood, Charles and James. Publishers of a beautifully engraved *Atlas of the Counties of England* (1834), mostly from their own surveys. They also published large-scale maps of 33 English counties.

Gregorian calendar. Introduced in Catholic Europe in 1582 by Pope Gregory XIII to replace the old *Julian calendar. Britain did not change until 1752, when 11 days between 3 and 14 September were lost to bring the country into line. At the same time the start of the official year was changed from 25 March to 1 January.

gressom. A fine paid to a *feudal lord upon entering a property.

Grim. One of the names of the Anglo-Saxon god Woden; cf. the Scandinavian Grimr for Odin. In the southern part of England massive linear earthworks acquired names such as Grim's Dyke.

grinding. The superiority of its grinding facilities largely explains Sheffield's triumph over its rivals as the place where *cutlery and edge *tools were made. The local sandstone was ideal for grinding and the rivers and streams fell quickly off the Pennines and could be dammed at frequent intervals. Grinding was a specialist craft in the production of *scythes by the 16th century but not in the cutlery trades until the 18th century. With the introduction of *factories and workshops driven by *steam power in the 19th century grinding became a notoriously unhealthy occupation; grinders were well-paid but died young of a form of silicosis, or 'grinders' asthma'. See David Crossley (ed.), *Water Power on the Sheffield Rivers* (1989).

grisaille. Silvery-grey *stained glass used from the 12th to the 14th centuries, e.g. in the 'Five Sisters' window in York Cathedral. This glass was favoured by the *Cistercians in their desire for an austere appearance.

groat. A coin in circulation between 1351 and 1662, worth four pence.

grottoes. Architectural features at the edges of lakes in 18th-century landscaped *parks, imitating water-filled limestone caves and including nymphs, dryads, and often the figure of Neptune. Stourhead (Wiltshire) has a fine example.

group projects. Groups of adult students meeting in classes organized by university adult education departments and the Workers' Educational Association have produced numerous local histories and editions of records, some of them of a high standard. See, for example, Bernard Jennings, *A History of Nidderdale* (1967), one of the first group projects, and Joan Wayne (ed.), *A Foot on Three Daisies: Pirton's Story* (1987). Alan Rogers (ed.), *Group Projects in Local History* (1977) suggests topics that classes might tackle. Since then, other groups have begun to computerize records as an aid to analysis, e.g. at Sheffield University the Fairbank Collection of surveyors' papers, the Cutlers' Company apprenticeship, freemen, and mark books, and local surnames have been computerized and studied in a way that a single individual would find impossible. A national survey in 1992 showed that Local History was by far the most popular subject for this sort of activity. See Joan Unwin, 'Local History Group Research Projects in Adult Continuing Education', *The Local Historian*, 24/1 (1994).

grouse. Although grouse and other game birds had been shot on the wing in earlier times it was only after parliamentary *enclosure divided the *commons and wastes in the late 18th and early 19th centuries that large tracts of moorland came under private ownership. Aristocratic and other owners often preferred to use these moors for shooting rather than for growing timber. Gamekeepers were employed to rear grouse and to maintain shooting cabins and butts, and to keep out trespassers. Some of these moors are still used for shooting in a season that begins on 12 August (the 'Glorious Twelfth'), but public access has been gained to many of them during the second half of the 20th century.

guardians. The *Poor Law Amendment Act (1834) took away parish responsibility for the poor and created instead Boards of Guardians for the management of poor relief through unions of parishes. These guardians were elected by local landowners and rate-payers. Their records are kept at local *record offices and include *workhouse admission registers, accounts, day books, minute books, general ledgers, and correspondence. The Local Government Board Act (1871) created a central government department with responsibility for poor relief and public health. In 1919 its functions were taken over by the newly created Ministry of Health.

guide stoops. Inscribed waymarkers erected by order of *Justices of the Peace under the terms of an Act of 1697. They are similar in size and shape to farm gateposts. Directions are often indicated by pointing hands. Many have been moved from their original position, but it is clear from *in situ* examples that travellers found their way by turning to the right of the inscription. See David Hey, *Packmen, Carriers and Packhorse Roads: Trade and Communications in North Derbyshire and South Yorkshire* (1980), ch. 2. The Derbyshire part of the Peak District has many examples dating from 1709, which mark the directions to the nearest market town, but do not record the mileage; a few more stoops were erected in 1737. The West Riding stoops date from 1733; after 1738 these note customary *miles, often to small settlements. See W. B. Crump, *Huddersfield Highways Down the Ages* (1949). The North York Moors also has stoops from this period. Stoops were necessary only 'upon large moors and commons where intelligence is difficult to be had' and therefore were not erected in many counties where settlements were close together. They provide testimony to the increasing volume of traffic at this period, which also saw the provision of *packhorse bridges and *causeways.

guild. The term 'guild' or 'gild' was used loosely in the Middle Ages to mean any kind of urban religious fraternity or craft organization. Guilds originated in the 12th century as supportive religious societies, offering mutual charitable help and composed of men and women working at a common craft, and living at close quarters in a single parish. See Caroline M. Barron, 'The Parish Fraternities of Medieval London' in Caroline M. Barron and Christopher Harper-Bill, *The Church in Pre-Reformation Society: Essays in Honour of F. R. H. Du Boulay* (1985). They came to be hierarchical trade organizations, with power to control entry into a trade through *apprenticeship and the enrolling of freemen, and power to insist on common standards for goods through the appointment of searchers. They were also mutual protection societies which provided for the poor, sick, and needy, and social organizations devoted to feasting and ornate processions, especially at *Corpus Christi. (See MYSTERY PLAYS.) They obtained their authority through the grant of a royal charter. (See LIVERY COMPANIES.) In small towns the guild fulfilled the role of the *borough until a charter of incorporation was obtained, often in the post-*Reformation period.

For the importance of guilds in medieval cities, see the two great socio-religious fraternities of Coventry, the Guilds of Holy Trinity and Corpus Christi, described in C. V. Phythian-Adams, *Desolation of a City: Coventry and the Urban Crisis of the Late Middle Ages* (1979), ch. 8. This discusses the progression through the ranks of office-holders of the more ambitious and prosperous citizens. The Reformation severely curtailed the roles of the guilds, particularly after the suppression of *chantry chapels in 1547.

The four surviving guildhalls at York illustrate the changing purposes of the guilds. The Guildhall, or 'Commonhall', was built on the north bank of the river Ouse in 1449–54 by the corporation but was also used by two guilds. Just inside the north-eastern corner of the city, St Anthony's Hall was built in 1446–53 as the meeting house of a large religious fraternity, but in 1554 the corporation handed it over as a common hall for the smaller guilds. It has two parallel first-floor halls, which are timber-framed, over a stone and brick ground floor, which contained the chapel and hospital. Nearby, the Merchant Taylors' Hall was built c.1400 for the drapers and tailors, but the oldest building in this group is the Merchant Adventurers' Hall of 1357–61, which has a chapel and hospital on the ground floor and a communal hall above. The company which met here originated as a religious fraternity of men and women, established in honour of Christ and the Virgin Mary. Alongside this fraternity developed the Mystery of Mercers, dedicated to the Holy Trinity and incorporated by royal charter in 1430. In 1581 another royal charter transformed the mystery into the Society or Company of Merchant Adventurers, consisting of the wealthiest merchants who controlled overseas trade. Each of these guilds was a business organization with a strong religious character and an emphasis on charitable works and social activities.

A number of early works on guilds remain useful, including J. Toulmin Smith, *English Gilds* (1870), C. Gross, *The Gild Merchant* (2 vols., 1890), H. F. Westlake, *The Parish Gilds of Medieval England* (1919), and S. Kramer, *The English Craft Gilds* (1927). For guilds as landowners, see Philip Riden and John Blair (eds.), *History of Chesterfield*, v (1980), ch. 2. The range of records that are available for the study of guild activities is outlined in C. V. Phythian-Adams, 'Records of the Craft Guilds', *The Local Historian*, 9/6 (1971).

Guildhall Library and Record Office. Located in central London by the Guildhall, and open to the public since 1873, the Library is a major source of printed historical and genealogical material, despite the losses sustained during the Second World War. It is particularly strong in all aspects of the history of London. The Record Office houses the archives of the City of London, including parochial records, ward *rate books, the records of the City's *livery companies, and the archives of various *fire insurance companies, individual families, estates, businesses, societies, schools, and other institutions, including the Diocese of London and St Paul's Cathedral. The records range in date from the 11th century to the present day. The Print Room has an unrivalled collection of prints and drawings relating to London and south-east England.

guinea. A coin introduced in 1663 and named after the Guinea Coast of Africa, from where gold was obtained for minting. Initially valued at 20 shillings, from 1717 it was valued at 21 shillings. The last guineas were struck in 1813, but the fashion for charging fees in guineas continued until the introduction of decimal coinage.

gunpowder was first used in England during the late 13th or 14th centuries, but guns and cannon remained primitive until the 15th century. Gunpowder was made from a mixture of charcoal, sulphur, and saltpetre, crushed by grindstones. Mills worked by *water power were in use by the 16th century, e.g. at Faversham (Kent), which has the best-preserved remains. The number of such mills expanded during the wars of the later 17th and 18th centuries, even to places as far from London as the Lake District.

gunsmiths. London was the early centre of gun manufacture, specializing in highly decorated guns made of imported *brass. The trade of making guns developed rapidly in Birmingham and neighbouring parishes at the end of the 17th century in order to meet the demands of William III's armies. The subsequent expansion of the British Empire, frequent wars, and an increasing use of guns for sporting purposes created a steady demand that led to the development of some large firms in the West Midlands.

Guppy, H. B. Author of a pioneering work, *Homes of Family Names in Great Britain* (1890), which drew attention to the striking geographical distributions of British *surnames. The surname Guppy, for instance, is largely confined to south-western England, close to the Devonshire place-name from which it is derived.

gypsies. The name originates from the mistaken belief that the first groups to arrive in England in the 16th century came from Egypt. The Romany language shares some characteristics with Sanskrit and later Indian languages and contains some loan words that suggest a migration via the Middle East into south-eastern Europe. References to their being moved on can be found in *parish and *quarter sessions records. See D. Mayall, *Gypsy Travellers in Nineteenth-Century Society* (1988), and Angus Fraser, *The Gypsies* (1992). See also the publications of the Gypsy Lore Society.

habeas corpus. A writ requiring the bringing of a person under arrest before a court to ensure a legal hearing. This ancient right, which pre-dates *Magna Carta, was sometimes abused before it was guaranteed by the Act of 1679.

Hadrian's wall. When the Emperor Hadrian visited Britain in AD 122–3, having served in other borderland parts of the Roman Empire, he ordered the construction of a coast-to-coast wall, 76 miles long, from Bowness-on-Solway to Wallsend, with fortlets every mile. From the beginning, the eastern and central sections were of stone, but the western part was initially of turf. The wall was built to control native movements across the frontier and for surveillance. Major design changes were made during construction and a massive ditch with a double bank was constructed on the northern side. In its final form the wall had 16 forts and a garrison of *c.*9,500 men. The best preserved section runs along the Whin Sill towards the fort at Housesteads. See ANTONINE WALL.

ha-ha. A landscape feature introduced in the early 18th century, which remained popular until Victorian times. The desire to have an uninterrupted view from a house was balanced by the need to keep livestock out. This was achieved by a sunken ditch supported by a wall that did not rise above ground level. The origin of the term is uncertain.

Hakluyt, Richard (*c.*1552–1616). Author of *Divers Voyages touching the Discovery of America* (1582), *Discourse concerning Western Discoveries* (1584), and *Principal Navigations, Voyages, and Discoveries of the English Nation* (1598–1600). The Hakluyt Society was formed in 1846 to publish historical accounts of voyages and journeys of discovery, etc.

half-baptized. Term describing someone baptized at a private christening, as distinct from a service in a church.

hall. In the Middle Ages and later the largest room in both great and small houses was the *open hall. In large houses this served as the communal dining room and fulfilled many other purposes. It was gradually replaced in the later 17th and 18th centuries by a large reception hall, some of which, e.g. Kedleston (Derbyshire), were even greater and much more splendid than their medieval predecessors. In smaller houses during the later Middle Ages and the early modern period the hall was chambered over and a *parlour and service rooms were provided at either side, to form a characteristic three-unit plan. The central room in such buildings retained the name hall, but was known in the north of England as the house, fire-house, or house-body. As the internal designs of houses have changed since the 18th century, the term 'hall' has been relegated to mean the small entrance space.

hallmark. A mark used at Goldsmiths Hall, London, and by provincial assay offices to approve the standard of the gold and silver articles on which it is engraved. An Act of 1300 required the Goldsmiths' Guild to use a leopard's head hallmark to indicate quality. Edinburgh and several English cities also had their goldsmiths' *guilds. In 1700 assay offices were re-established in York, Exeter, Bristol, Chester, and Norwich, followed two years later by Newcastle-upon-Tyne, and in 1773 by Birmingham and Sheffield.

hamlet. The hamlet and the isolated farmstead were the normal forms of settlement in early times. Nucleated *villages were not created until the late *Anglo-Saxon or *Viking period. See Christopher Taylor, *Village and Farmstead: A History of Rural Settlement in England* (1983). Hamlets and isolated farmsteads have remained the norm in the *Highland zone of Britain. They are also the result of secondary settlement in the *Lowland zone, e.g. in woodland areas, or around *greens. Others are the result of the shrinkage of villages, so that only a *manor house, a parish *church, and sometimes a few other buildings remain.

hammer pond. The mill pond of an iron *forge, particularly in the Weald, where they flourished during the 16th and 17th centuries. These often survive, or can be traced in outline, even when little other evidence of former industry remains.

Hammond, J. L. (1872–1949) **and B.** (1873–1961), social historians. In 1911 the publication of *The Village Labourer* started a debate on the social consequences of parliamentary *enclosure that is not yet over. The Hammonds concluded that 'enclosure was fatal to three classes: the small farmer, the cottager, and the squatter. To all of these classes their [rights on the *commons and wastes] were worth more than anything they received in return.' This view was challenged by J. D. *Chambers, 'Enclosure and Labour Supply in the Industrial Revolution', *Economic History Review*, 2nd ser., 5/3 (1953), who stressed instead the role of *population growth in the creation of a wage-dependent labour force. It has become widely accepted that the Hammonds' account was based on selective evidence, but K. D. M. Snell, in *Annals of the Labouring Poor* (1985), has reopened the question of the effects of enclosure on the poorest classes of society, and Jean Neeson, *Commoners: Common Right, Enclosure and Social Change in England, 1700–1820* (1993), has reiterated the vital role of common rights in offering them a livelihood. The Hammonds went on to publish *The Town Labourer* (1917).

Hansard. The official record of the proceedings of the two houses of Parliament since 1803. The first three series (1803–91) were published by the firm of Hansard, whose name was restored to the title pages in 1943. Verbatim reports of debates provide useful background for an understanding of legislation.

harden cloth. Coarse, hard cloth, often of *hemp, recorded in probate *inventories for use on beds and tables.

hardwareman. A term used in the early modern period for an ironmonger or a *chapman specializing in iron wares.

Hardy, Thomas (1840–1928). Dorset novelist and poet. In his work Hardy made a conscious effort to record folk tales, superstitions, and customs, many of which had already passed out of use by the time that he was writing. In the preface to *The Trumpet Major* he wrote: 'The external incidents which direct [the course of the present tale] are mostly an unexaggerated reproduction of the recollections of old persons well known to the author in childhood, but now long dead, who were eye-witnesses of those scenes.' He claimed that the legendary matter and *folklore of his books were not invented and that he was careful not to falsify local beliefs and customs. Hardy's tales have nevertheless to be handled with care; his use of a *wife-selling story in *The Mayor of Casterbridge*, for example, differs in some points from the customary ritual in order to assist the development of the plot.

Harleian Society. Founded in 1869 to publish records relating to *heraldry and genealogy, notably the pedigrees approved at the Heralds' Visitations of various English counties, and many of the *parish registers of London.

harness. Each part of the harness of a draught animal had its name, many of which are noted in probate *inventories: see Rosemary Millward, *A Glossary of Household and Farming Terms from Sixteenth-Century Probate Inventories* (1977). These parts were mostly of leather and were supplied by the saddler, but some pieces were of metal and in the 19th century were increasingly used as decorative 'horse brasses'. See T. Keegan, *The Heavy Horse, its Harness and Harness Decoration* (1973).

Harrison, William (1534–93). Clergyman and antiquarian. His *Description of England* (1577), which used *Leland's notes, was one of the earliest topographical descriptions of the country, but was soon superseded by *Camden's *Britannia*. Students of *vernacular architecture have found it of interest for its comments on changing fashions in building and domestic comfort.

harrow. A heavy frame with iron teeth for breaking down the clods of freshly ploughed land and for removing weeds. Probate *inventories refer to ox-harrows and horse-harrows.

harvest customs. In *Ask the Fellows Who Cut the Hay* (1956), ch. 11, George Ewart *Evans shows that the gathering of the harvest was the climax of the rural year, an event involving all the villagers. The traditional largesse distributed by farmers to their work-force at this time was seen by the labourers as part of their earnings, but by some farmers as a costly business. In 1783 Sir Joseph Banks of Revesby (Lincolnshire) wrote: 'according to ancient custom I am to feed and make drunk everyone who chooses to come, which will cost me in beef and ale near 20 pounds.' See R. W. Ambler, 'The Transformation of Harvest Celebrations in Nineteenth-Century Lincolnshire', *Midland History*, 3 (1976). The Victorian squires and clergy changed the old, disorderly suppers into monster tea parties with speeches. From the 1860s many parishes had a day of harvest thanksgiving with a special church service known as the harvest festival. This became an annual highlight of the church's year.

harvesters, combined. Mechanical mowers and reapers began to replace the *scythe and *sickle in the 1860s, but the old methods long continued in use. The reaper-binder was invented in the 1880s but was not used on some farms even in the 1920s.

harvest fluctuations. The state of the harvest was a matter of annual concern even though bad years rarely resulted in *famine. The weather caused considerable fluctuations in yields from year to year, from crop to crop, and from region to region. See W. G. Hoskins, 'Harvest Fluctuations and English Economic History, 1620–1759', *Agricultural History Review*, 16/1 (1968), and C. J. Harrison, 'Grain Price Analysis and Harvest Qualities, 1465–1634', *Agricultural History Review*, 19/2 (1971).

Hasted, Edward (1732–1812). Kent *antiquarian. His *History and Topographical Survey of the County of Kent*, which was published in four volumes between 1778 and 1799, was one of the outstanding county histories of the old antiquarians. It remains a valuable reference work. See Joan Thirsk, 'Hasted as Historian', *Archaeologia Cantiana*, III (1993).

hatchment. Derived from the heraldic term 'achievement', a display of the arms and other heraldic insignia upon a person's death. The diamond-shaped hatchments, painted on wood or canvas, which can be found in churches, date from the mid-17th to the mid-19th centuries. In some parts of the country such hatchments were placed in the church after a period of mourning at home. The common practice in Scotland was to have one hatchment for the house and another for the church. See the 10 volumes of P. G. Summers, *Hatchments in Britain* (completed 1994), which record 4,500 examples.

haybote. The right to collect wood from the *commons in order to erect and maintain fences.

hayward. The manorial officer responsible for hedges and fences and for preventing cattle from straying.

headborough. Originally, the man at the head of a *tithing or *frankpledge. The term came to

be applied in some places to the *constable or his deputy.

headland. The untilled land at the end of a block of *strips in an *open-field, which allowed access and room for the plough-team to turn. In time, headlands became raised by the accumulation of soil, so they now sometimes appear as linear earthworks. As such, they are valuable archaeological evidence of the extent of former open-fields.

hearth tax. The hearth tax returns of the 1660s and 1670s are a major source of information for local and family historians in England and Wales. For family historians they provide lists of names half-way between the period of *surname formation in the Middle Ages and the present day, and often suggest a line of enquiry when constructing a family tree by pinpointing parishes with appropriate surnames. For local historians they can be used to study social structure and *population and to assist a study of *vernacular architecture.

The tax was levied twice a year—at *Lady Day and *Michaelmas—between 1662 and 1688. During this time the tax was the government's major source of revenue. Its unpopularity led to its abolition after the *Glorious Revolution of 1688. The tax returns are kept at the *Public Record Office under E 179; some counties have copies of individual returns in local *record offices. The coverage is uneven and in a few counties, e.g. Wiltshire, the survival rate is disappointing. An increasing number of counties now have at least one return in print.

The hearth tax was introduced in 1662, 'it being easy to tell the number of hearths, which remove not as heads or polls do'. Each hearth was taxed at the rate of 2 shillings a year, payable in two instalments. Those people who were too poor to be rated to church and poor rates, or who occupied premises worth less than 20 shillings a year, or who possessed property worth not above £10 were exempt, as were charitable institutions such as *hospitals and minor *almshouses. Those who qualified for exemption had to petition the *Justices of the Peace or the commissioners for taxation; some of these petitions have survived amongst *quarter sessions records, but more commonly a marginal note in a list of householders will indicate a certificate of exemption. Some lists simply note 'Poor' in the margins, others list the poor at the end. In other cases, however, the poor are not recorded or the lists are incomplete. See Tom Arkell, 'Printed Instructions for Administering the Hearth Tax' in

Kevin Schurer and Tom Arkell (eds.), *Surveying the People: The Interpretation and Use of Document Sources for the Study of Population in the Later Seventeenth Century* (1992), which details the inconsistencies in the returns that sprang from the muddled instructions to collectors.

The regulations changed from time to time and interpretations made by collectors were challenged by the tax payers. Thus, the cutlers and other metalworkers of Hallamshire resisted the demand that they should pay tax on their smithies as well as on their domestic hearths; in some returns the smithies were therefore listed separately, thus enabling the historian to assess the extent of the metal trades at that time. Problems also arose when houses were empty (in which case the landlord was liable for tax) or when they were being extended or demolished.

The task of assessing and collecting the tax began at the *township level with the *constable, who forwarded the money to the high constable and so to the *sheriff and then to the *Exchequer. Difficulties experienced in collection led to an alternative system in 1664, whereby sheriffs and high constables were replaced by county receivers and sub-collectors who accompanied the constables who collected the tax from the householders of their township. Between 1666 and 1669 the government farmed out the collection to three City of London merchants; there are therefore no surviving returns for these years. Direct collection was the method used for the next five years, but after 1674 no returns survive because once again the collection was farmed out. The surviving returns therefore relate only to 1662–6 and 1669–74.

The returns for each county are arranged by *hundreds or *wapentakes, which in turn are divided into townships. The name of each householder was recorded, together with the number of hearths that he or she possessed. As the number of hearths is usually an indication of wealth, a social pyramid with a broad base of people with one or two hearths, tapering to a few households with a large number of hearths can be constructed. The returns give a general indication of wealth, but of course individuals of similar social status may have lived in houses of different sizes depending on personal preference and regional attitudes. The number of hearths does not necessarily indicate the number of rooms, some of which were unheated. A complicating factor is that *inns had a large number of hearths. Attempts to correlate hearth tax returns with the evidence of probate

*inventories demonstrate the general pattern that higher numbers of hearths indicate wealth, but also show much overlapping of categories. The returns are no more than a rough guide. The varied social structure of English and Welsh communities is nevertheless made clear from a study of the returns. Some rural parishes were dominated by a squire, others had numerous households of modest or poor means. Neighbouring parishes could be very different. See Chris Husbands, 'Hearths, Wealth and Occupations: An Exploration of the Hearth Tax in the Later Seventeenth Century' in Kevin Schurer and Tom Arkell (eds.), *Surveying the People: The Interpretation and Use of Document Sources for the Study of Population in the Later Seventeenth Century* (1992).

The hearth tax returns have been used to estimate total population at township and county level. The mean size of households during the early modern and modern periods is reckoned at 4.75, but it may have been slightly lower in the reign of Charles II. Tom Arkell, 'Multiplying Factors for Estimating Population Totals from the Hearth Tax', *Local Population Studies*, 28 (1982) argues for a mean household size in both rural and urban areas outside London of 4.3, but within a range of 3.7 to 5.2. Estimating the number of unrecorded poor is a major problem. Clearly, precise figures cannot be obtained, but fair approximations can nevertheless be arrived at. These can be compared with estimates based on the *Compton ecclesiastical census of 1676. The hearth tax returns usually provide the best base for assessing population levels before the first *census of England and Wales in 1801.

The returns are of great interest to students of vernacular architecture as they indicate the complete range of houses at a fixed point in time. They also provide information about individual houses (including demolished examples); thus the progress of the rebuilding of Stainborough Hall (Yorkshire) can be inferred from the marginal note that five of the 11 hearths were 'not yet finished'. *Parsonages can often be identified from the returns and, in some cases, the information can be compared with that obtained from *glebe terriers. Many surviving halls and farmhouses can be placed in a contemporary context by comparison with their neighbours.

The Introduction by J. V. Beckett and M. W. Barley to W. F. Webster (ed.), *Nottinghamshire Hearth Tax, 1664 : 1674* (1988) is the best modern study of the administration of the hearth tax and the use to which the returns may be put by local and architectural historians. Most editions of hearth tax returns ignore or underplay their usefulness to family historians. See David Hey, *The Oxford Guide to Family History* (1993), ch. 2, on the use of hearth tax returns for the study of regional surnames.

In Scotland a hearth tax was levied on several occasions between 1691 and 1695. The surviving returns are kept at the *Scottish Record Office under E 69. They list householders and are arranged by counties and parishes, though as in England and Wales the data are not uniform and the problems of interpretation are the same. In Ireland the hearth tax was introduced in 1662 and continued to be levied until the Act of Union (1800). The original rolls were destroyed by fire in 1922, but copies exist for some areas. Hearths were consistently under-recorded through both legitimate exemption and evasion, though the extent of this under-recording is uncertain. See D. Dickson, C. Ó Gráda, and S. Daultrey, 'Hearth Tax, Household Size and Irish Population Change, 1672–1821', *Proceedings of the Royal Irish Academy*, 82/6 (1982).

heathen sites. Pope Gregory advised Augustine and his fellow missionaries who arrived in Kent in 597 not to destroy idol temples but to convert them to Christian usage. The sites of many *cathedrals and parish *churches may therefore have been used for religious purposes from pre-Christian times. Pagan festivals such as Easter or Midsummer were likewise not suppressed but were taken over by the new religion: see Ronald Hutton, *The Pagan Religions of the Ancient British Isles* (1991). Features of pagan belief survived alongside Christianity into modern times: see, for instance, James Obelkevich, *Religion and Society: South Lindsey, 1825–1875* (1976).

Early Christian writers, notably *Bede, make clear the strength of paganism in the *Anglo-Saxon period. This was reinforced in the 9th–11th centuries by *Viking settlers in many parts of Britain and Ireland. However, the archaeological evidence for pagan practices is negligible, for heathen sites were focused on trees (especially oak, yew, and ash), stones, and springs. Many pagan sanctuaries appear to have had only local significance. In some cases, place-names point to their former existence, e.g. at Harrow (Middlesex), Wednesbury (Staffordshire), or Thundersley (Essex), or the numerous Holywells.

The conversion of heathen sites to Christian usage is sometimes indicated by the choice of patronal saint. For example, St Michael the Archangel, slayer of the dragon in medieval art and protector of high places, was commonly chosen for churches or chapels built on hill tops. Churches dedicated to St Helen may, in some cases, have replaced a heathen site dedicated to the Celtic goddess Elen. The presence of wells in *churchyards may indicate a previous *holy well; in Wales many chapels were built over a well. Yew trees are a common feature of churchyards; those of enormous girth, as at Darley (Derbyshire), must be ancient. There is room for much speculation here, but little hard evidence. The presence of megalithic stones close to churches, most famously at Rudston (Yorkshire), is more convincing proof of continuity with a heathen past. The church at Stanton Drew (Somerset) stands close to a stone circle; that at Avebury (Wiltshire) encroaches on the *Bronze Age *henge monument. At Breedon-on-the-Hill (Leicestershire) the church stands high above the surrounding plain, inside an *Iron Age fort. These examples could be multiplied, but the conversion of such sites took place without any written record. The long time-scale of conversion must be emphasized, as must the way this was achieved; kings were converted first, while the ordinary inhabitants of the countryside clung on to many of their old beliefs. See Richard Morris, *Churches in the Landscape* (1989), ch. 2. See also MAGIC, BELIEF IN.

heaths. Low-lying, dry areas of acid soil, whose characteristic vegetation is undershrub, including ling, furze, and *gorse. They are a distinctive feature of the landscape of Lowland England and Lowland Scotland. Pollen analysis has shown that in prehistoric times present-day heathlands were lightly covered with trees, which were subsequently cleared. Some place-name elements incorporating 'heath' are *Anglo-Saxon, but others are much later. It is clear, however, that heathland was extensive well before the *Norman Conquest: see Oliver Rackham, *The History of the Countryside* (1986), ch. 13. In the Middle Ages much heathland was *common land, valued for its furze and its bracken. (See also RABBITS.)

The agricultural writers of the late 18th century were much concerned with the reclamation of 'dreary' and 'barren' heaths and their conversion to arable land. This happened in many areas after parliamentary *enclosure, notably on the *Wolds of Lincolnshire and the East Riding of Yorkshire, where heaths disappeared completely. Such changes brought a recognition of the natural beauty of heaths by writers such as William Gilpin and a demand for their conservation. The encroachment of

London suburbs on Hampstead Heath, Wimbledon Common, etc. led to a campaign for preservation from about 1840.

hedges. The hawthorn hedges that mark the boundaries of the rectilinear fields of the English midlands are the product of parliamentary *enclosure of *open-fields and *commons of c.1750–1850. Where these hedges have been grubbed up in recent decades it can be argued that farmers were re-creating an older form of landscape. However, the removal of hedges elsewhere, e.g. in Suffolk, has destroyed features that were often several centuries old. In many parts of Britain, including highland and woodland areas, hedged *closes have been the normal type of field from prehistoric times onwards. Anglo-Saxon England had numerous hedgerows, but fewer free-standing trees (which were sufficiently uncommon to serve as landmarks in the *boundaries attached to charters). See Oliver Rackham, *The History of the Countryside* (1986), ch. 9. These hedges were valued as a source of wood and were not simply to fence in livestock. Maps which survive from the 16th and 17th centuries show that many present-day field systems are much older than the era of parliamentary enclosure. See Christopher Taylor, *Fields in the English Landscape* (1975), and John Field, *A History of English Field-Names* (1993). Modern concern at the removal of hedges centres not just on their visual attraction but on the loss of habitat for wildlife: see Richard and Nina Muir, *Hedgerows, Their History and Wildlife* (1987).

A method of dating hedges was suggested by Max Hooper: see E. Pollard, M. Hooper, and N. Moore, *Hedges* (1974), and W. G. *Hoskins, *Fieldwork in Local History* (1967). The number of species of trees and shrubs in a sample 30-yard length of hedgerow was said to increase with the age of the hedge, at the rate of one new shrub every 100 years. This dating method has been much criticized; general opinion now holds that a large number of shrubs does indeed indicate an ancient hedge (except where there has been a conscious effort to plant several species) but that the date cannot be estimated with any degree of accuracy. The method must be used with particular caution in northern England and Scotland because the number of possible species diminishes.

heir. One who has inherited a title or property. An *heir apparent* is one whose right to succeed is inalienable; an *heir presumptive* is one who does not have inalienable rights.

hemp. An industrial crop. It requires a rich alluvial soil, so it was grown particularly in the *fens and along rivers. The best seed was imported from Holland. Hemp was never a major field crop but in the early modern period it was grown in small *crofts attached to *cottages and farmhouses. As such, it provided a useful source of extra income for poor families. After harvest, women were employed in curing and spinning and the men in weaving hempen cloth and the manufacture of strong *ropes. Surplus seed was fed to poultry.

henge. A modern term for circular monuments of the *Neolithic period and early *Bronze Age.

Heptarchy. The seven separate kingdoms of *Anglo-Saxon England: *Wessex, Sussex, Kent, Essex, *East Anglia, *Mercia, and *Northumbria.

heraldry. The origins of heraldry are obscure but can be dated to the second quarter of the 12th century in different parts of western Europe. The adoption of colourful devices on shields can best be regarded as a military status symbol that was popularized by the pageantry of *tournaments. The first documentary evidence for the practice comes from the knighting of Geoffrey Plantagenet, Count of Anjou, in 1127.

The simple patterns of the 12th century became increasingly complex in later times. The rules and terminology of heraldry were laid down during the 13th century. By the early 15th century the Crown was attempting to control the use of arms that did not date from *time immemorial. The Heralds formed part of the Royal Household and were incorporated as a College of *Arms by Richard III in 1484. Their county surveys—known as Heralds' Visitations—began in 1530 and continued until the *Glorious Revolution of 1688. Major surveys were made in c.1580, 1620, and 1666 and minor ones at other times. Many of the records of county visitations have been published by the *Harleian Society or by county record societies. These are a useful source for pedigrees of families claiming the right to bear arms. The Ulster King of Arms conducted visitations between 1568 and 1649. In Scotland Lord Lyon King of Arms conducted visitations only for specific purposes.

Arms are hereditary and therefore of great use to genealogists in elucidating family trees. See, for example, Philip H. Blake, 'The Early Derings', *Archaeologia Cantiana*, 112 (1993). However, the mistaken or unauthorized use of arms causes confusion. A common mistake is to assume that all people with the same surname are entitled to the same coat of arms. A knowledge of heraldry is indispensable when studying *funerary monuments, *stained glass windows, bosses in church roofs, etc. See Thomas Woodcock and John Martin Robinson, *The Oxford Guide to Heraldry* (1988).

herbals. The use of herbs for culinary and medicinal purposes led to the collection of 'herbals'. In the 16th century these began to appear in print. John Gerard's *Herbal* of 1597 is the best-known of the early works, though its reputation depends on the improved edition by Thomas Johnson in 1663. A classic study of *Herbals, Their Origin and Evolution* was made by Agnes Arber in 1912, when the full dimensions of the literature were unknown. A complete analysis up to 1800 is now available in Blanche Henrey, *British Botanical and Horticultural Literature before 1800* (1975).

Herbert, George (1593–1633). *Church of England clergyman of the Laudian persuasion, whose poetry (collected together in *The Temple* in the year of his death) was widely appreciated because of its homely imagery.

hereditament. Anything that can be inherited. The term is commonly used in *deeds to include anything not specifically mentioned.

heriot. A payment (often the best beast) from an incoming tenant to the *lord of the manor.

heritor. A Scottish term for the landowners in each *parish, who until 1845 were responsible for the local poor and until 1925 for the maintenance of the church, *manse, and school. Valuations made of parishes (mainly in the 19th century), known as heritors' records, are kept at the *Scottish Record Office.

hermits. Individuals who pursued a solitary, reclusive life for religious purposes. Hermits often served as guides or ferrymen; their hermitages were therefore sited by river crossings or alongside thoroughfares. Sometimes, as in the 14th-century example at Warkworth (Northumberland), hermitages were carved out of a cliff or were developed from natural caves. They sometimes had a chapel attached, but most hermitages were probably only temporary shelters. One near Huddersfield gave rise to a minor place-name which, in turn, was the source of the surname Armitage.

herringbone. A distinctive pattern of courses of *rubble stone, used by masons in the late Saxon and early Norman period in the erection of *churches and *castles.

Heywood, Oliver (1630–1702). *Nonconformist preacher from Coley, Halifax, whose published journals are a major source for the religious history of Yorkshire and adjoining counties in the second half of the 17th century. See J. H. Turner (ed.), *The Rev. Oliver Heywood, BA, 1630–1702: His Autobiography, Diaries, Anecdote and Event Books* (1881).

hide. An area of land, varying according to the quality of the soil and the nature of the terrain, which a team of eight *oxen could plough in a year, sufficient to support a family. It normally covered about 120 *acres. The hide became a unit of tax assessment in southern England and was used as such in the *Domesday Book. Its equivalent in the *Danelaw was the *carucate.

High Church movement. A section of the *Church of England emphasizing the importance of sacraments, the apostolic succession, and use of ritual. Its prominence in early Victorian times led ministers of many Anglican churches to restore ritual to a degree unknown since Archbishop Laud in the 1630s. This led to profound and lasting changes to the physical appearance of churches and the arrangements for worship. Walls were stripped of their paint, box *pews and *galleries were removed, *pulpits and *lecterns of a medieval design were installed in the *nave, and *rood screens were reinstalled. Musicians and choirs were banned from west galleries and were replaced by an organist or harmonium player and by surpliced choirs seated in the *chancel between the congregation and the high *altar. Medieval *Gothic styles of architecture were favoured for the building of new churches and the restoration and extension of old ones.

High Commission, Court of. The highest *ecclesiastical court in England from 1570 to 1641 and from 1686 to 1689. The records of the Province of Canterbury are kept at the *Public Record Office under SP, those for the Province of York at the *Borthwick Institute of Historical Research, York.

High Court of Justiciary. The supreme criminal court in Scotland. See Cecil Sinclair, *Tracing Your Scottish Ancestors: A Guide to Ancestry Research in the Scottish Record Office* (1990).

High Farming. A phrase coined in the 1840s, made popular by Lord Ernle, whose *English Farming Past and Present* (1912) described the epoch of prosperity between 1837 and 1873 as the Age of High Farming. 'High' was used in the sense of 'excellent' or 'superior', but it was a complex expression meaning different things to different users. It included 'high feeding' as well as increased cereal production. The period saw much agricultural investment in buildings, machinery, *underdrainage, the use of phosphates, etc. See B. A. Holderness, 'The Origins of High Farming' in B. A. Holderness and Michael Turner (eds.), *Land, Labour and Agriculture, 1700–1920: Essays for Gordon Mingay* (1991), which discusses the various meanings of the term and which argues that improvements in intensive mixed husbandry in east Norfolk exemplify the advances in agriculture that were made during this period.

Highland zone. In *The Personality of Britain* (1932) Sir Cyril Fox applied the concept of a Highland zone and *Lowland zone, long used by geographers, to the study of *prehistory. The concept was used to good effect by W. G. *Hoskins in his studies of the English landscape; see, for instance, his essay on 'The Highland Zone in Domesday Book' in *Provincial England* (1963). The frontier of the two zones in England is drawn from the mouth of the Tees in the north-east to the mouth of the Exe in the south-west. The distinction between lowland and highland Scotland is clear-cut. The lowland zones of Britain have always been more densely populated (in nucleated rather than dispersed settlements), richer and more powerful, and more receptive to new ideas. This broad concept needs to be refined by the division of such zones into *pays*.

High Sheriff. By the 17th century the ceremonial duties of the *sheriff's office were performed by a high sheriff, while the administrative tasks were undertaken by an under-sheriff.

highwaymen. The danger of being robbed on the public highways was not as great as is sometimes supposed. Reports of highway robbery in 18th-century provincial *newspapers or travellers' journals are infrequent. But the dangers were very real in certain parts of the country, notoriously on the roads leading in and out of London. See Peter Linebaugh, *The London Hanged* (1991), ch. 6.

highways, overseers of. An Act of 1555 required the annual appointment at Easter of a 'Surveyor of the Highways' for each *parish or *township. Like the overseer of the *poor, this officer was empowered to raise local rates; his accounts had to be approved at the end of his term of office, and he was answerable to the *Justices of the Peace. A particular responsibility was the supervision of *statute labour, whereby local people were called upon to maintain their roads. The office of overseer was unpaid and was usually filled by rotation. Accounts of the overseers of the highways do not survive in the same bulk as do the accounts of the overseers of the poor; most date from the late 18th and early 19th centuries. In 1835 a new system was introduced whereby JPs appointed paid surveyors for groups of parishes.

Hill, Sir Francis (1899–1980). Author of a four-volume history of Lincoln (1956–74), whose work is often cited as an outstanding example of the achievement of an amateur historian.

hill forts. Prehistoric hill-top enclosures were fortified long before the *Iron Age, but from the 4th century BC a large number were abandoned and others were greatly strengthened. At Maiden Castle (Dorset), the best-known example, the area that was defended was more than doubled in size and massive ditches and ramparts were constructed. See Barry Cunliffe, *Wessex to AD 1000* (1993).

hiring fairs. Martinmas hiring fairs were known as 'statute' or 'stattis' fairs because an Act of Parliament of 1677 endorsed the yearly bonds that were made at that time. Contracts between farmers and their servants expired on Old Martinmas Day (23 November), the end of the farming year. The practice of holding such fairs survived in market towns until Edwardian times, but rarely beyond the First World War; they are listed for the early modern period in Ann Kussmaul, *Servants in Husbandry in Early Modern England* (1981). In this way, all the farmers and servants of a district came together to negotiate new contracts. Farm servants liked to move to a new place every year. They spoke freely amongst themselves about their experiences and warned others about poor employers who offered inadequate food and harsh treatment; they were not afraid to refuse offers and were in a position to choose. Bargains were clinched with a 'fastening-penny' which was worth much more than the term implies; in the late 19th century, for instance, a head-waggoner was usually given five shillings, a seconder half-a-crown, and lads a shilling. The associated *funfairs were greatly enjoyed by young people, at what was often a dreary time of year; most had a reputation for rowdiness. See Stephen Caunce, *Amongst Farm Horses: The Horselads of East Yorkshire* (1991).

Historical Association. The association which promotes the teaching of history in schools and universities, through conferences, lectures, its quarterly journal, *Teaching History*, and its Short Guides to Records series. Its headquarters is at 59A Kensington Park Road, London SE11 4JH.

Historical Manuscripts, Royal Commission on. This permanent body was first appointed in 1869 to locate and make accessible records in private ownership. In the following year it began to publish reports on the most important collections in the British Isles. In 1945 it set up the *National Register of Archives to collate information about historical manuscripts and to make this available to researchers. In 1959 a new Royal Warrant revised and enlarged the Commission's powers and made it the United Kingdom's central advisory body on all matters concerning the location, preservation, and use of historical manuscripts and archives outside the public records. It also became responsible for the Manorial Documents Register previously maintained by the *Public Record Office. Its address is Quality House, Quality Court, Chancery Lane, London WC2A 1HP.

The series of Reports and Calendars, begun in 1870, now contains 238 volumes describing material in 624 collections of privately owned papers of leading families and institutions. A select bibliography has been published as *Surveys of Historical Manuscripts in the United Kingdom* (1989); this is accompanied by *Record Repositories in Great Britain: A Geographical Directory* (1991). The Commission also publishes Guides to Sources for British History, e.g. no. 7, *Papers of British Politicians, 1782–1900* (1989), and no. 8, *Records of British Business and Industry, 1760–1914: Textiles and Leather* (1990).

Historical Monuments, Royal Commission on. The Commission has been surveying ancient and historical monuments since the beginning of the 20th century. Separate branches deal with England, Wales, Scotland, and Northern Ireland. In 1994 the RCHM (England) completed a move to the converted premises of the Great Western Railway's General Office in Kemble Drive, Swindon SN2 2GZ. These premises house the National Monuments Record Centre (NMR), which combines the National Archaeological Record, the National Buildings Record, and the National Library of Air Photographs. Information is made available to the public in a searchroom and a comprehensive reference library, with computer-aided access to archive material. The NMR has over 3 million records and photographs relating to historic buildings, data on over 150,000 archaeological sites, air photographs covering the whole of England, and definitive data on listed buildings and sched-

uled monuments. The Centre can be visited without an appointment, but a telephone call in advance (01793 414617) saves time.

The Commission has a number of regional offices, which are responsible for surveying and for publishing complete inventories of earthworks and monuments from prehistoric times up to the year 1850, county by county. Only a few counties, e.g. Dorset, Cambridgeshire, and Northamptonshire, have been well covered so far. Five volumes on the city of York were published between 1962 and 1981. During the 1980s and 1990s the Commission extended its remit by publishing a Supplementary Series of volumes, sometimes in co-operation with local authorities, on a variety of topics and often extending beyond the 1850 time limit. These include studies of rural houses in Lancashire, West Yorkshire, and North Yorkshire, an archaeological atlas of Northamptonshire, an archaeological and architectural study of Beverley, and thematic volumes on *chapels, potworks, the buildings of London Zoo, and buildings and structures associated with *coal mining, etc.

history societies. See ARCHAEOLOGICAL AND HISTORICAL SOCIETIES.

History Workshop. Based at Ruskin College, Oxford, the History Workshop are a group of historians whose principal concern is the history of working-class men and women from the 18th century onwards. The group have published *The History Workshop*, a 'journal of socialist and feminist historians', twice yearly since 1976. A number of influential monographs written by members of the group and those who sympathize with its aims have been published by Routledge, starting with Raphael Samuel (ed.), *Village Life and Labour* (1975), and Raphael Samuel (ed.), *Miners, Quarrymen and Saltworkers* (1977).

Hoare, Sir Richard Colt (1758–1838). Wiltshire landowner and *antiquarian, Fellow of the *Royal Society and of the Society of *Antiquaries. His *Ancient History of North and South Wiltshire*, 2 vols. (1812–21) was followed by his *History of Modern Wiltshire*, 6 vols. (1822–44). He spent much time on the gardens at Stourhead and also published many minor works.

Hocktide. The second Monday and Tuesday after Easter, when church fund-raising activities took the form of binding people with ropes until they had paid a ransom for their release. The custom originated in the 15th century and soon became widespread before its demise at the

*Reformation. See Ronald Hutton, *The Rise and Fall of Merry England: The Ritual Year, 1400–1700* (1994).

Hodder and Stoughton landscape histories. The publication of W. G. *Hoskins, *The Making of the English Landscape* (1955), was intended as a general introduction to the subject, to be followed by a series of books on the counties of England, under the general editorship of Hoskins (and later Roy Millward). Volumes on Cornwall, Lancashire, Leicestershire, and Gloucestershire followed quickly. The format changed in 1970 with the appearance of the volumes on Dorset and the West Riding of Yorkshire. Eighteen volumes were published in all. They were intended to make the research of scholars accessible to a wider public and to provide a general survey from prehistoric times to the present day.

hoes. Although hoes were used to destroy weeds in earlier times and Jethro Tull was experimenting with horse-drawn cultivators in the 1720s, hoeing either by hand or by horse-drawn machine was not a widespread practice in the fields until the second quarter of the 19th century, though it was usual much earlier in *market gardens and when growing special crops like *woad. During the 19th century hoeing gradually became normal for wheat, beans, and roots in spring and early summer.

holding. A term for a farmer's landed property, as in smallholding.

holidays. The long working hours, six days a week, that were normal in the Middle Ages and later would have been unbearable without the frequent public 'holy-days', the enforcement of periods of idleness by *guilds, and the casual nature of much employment. A regular cycle of saints' days was celebrated before the *Reformation, in both the towns and the countryside. See Charles Phythian-Adams, 'Ceremony and the Citizen: The Communal Year at Coventry, 1450–1550' in Peter Clark and Paul Slack (eds.), *Crisis and Order in English Towns, 1500–1700* (1972). Many of these festivals, notably that at *Corpus Christi, were abolished in the middle decades of the 16th century; others such as *May Day games and maypole dancing were suppressed by *Puritans in the *Commonwealth period. See Ronald Hutton, *The Rise and Fall of Merry England: The Ritual Year, 1400–1700* (1994). An effect of the Protestant work ethic was that fewer holidays were taken than before, though the conclusion to the Bib-

lical injunction that 'Six days shalt thou labour and do all thy work' was strictly observed by the enforcement of rest and church attendance on Sundays.

In the countryside the holiday calendar was largely determined by the seasonal rhythms of agriculture and the church festivals which had survived the Reformation: *Christmas, *Shrovetide, Easter, May Day, *Whitsuntide, the *harvest festival, the Martinmas *hiring fair, together with the individual parish feasts and country *fairs. In the towns too, customary fairs, including the famous St Giles Fair at Oxford and the Nottingham Goose Fair, continued as popular holidays, and new traditions arose such as *horse-racing week. Men who had some control over their working week, e.g. the 'little mesters' of the Sheffield *cutlery trades, continued to celebrate what they jokingly referred to as 'Saint Monday' and sometimes 'Saint Tuesday' as well. Even in the second half of the 19th century owners of the new *factories had a long battle to enforce regular working hours in place of the old flexible arrangements. The new work discipline led *trade unionists to agitate for a half-holiday on Saturday; this was achieved in 1850 in the textile industries, and soon after in other trades. As Saturday afternoon became the accustomed time for popular sporting events the importance of Saint Monday declined. See E. P. *Thompson, 'Time, Work-Discipline and Industrial Capitalism' in *Customs in Common* (1991), ch. 6, and D. A. Reid, 'The Decline of Saint Monday, 1766–1876', *Past and Present*, 71 (1976).

The coming of the *railways changed the whole concept of what a holiday should be. Families could now travel cheaply to *seaside resorts for a day or even a week. See John K. Walton, *The English Seaside Resort: A Social History, 1750–1914* (1983). Thomas Cook of Leicester began the first successful travel agency, with trips to the Paris International Exhibition in 1855; by the 1880s Cook's were organizing excursions to Egypt and the Nile. Factories found it efficient to close everything down for a week or a fortnight in summer. The Wakes weeks of the Lancashire *cotton industry evolved from a public holiday associated with a rush-bearing ceremony for the reflooring of parish *churches; by the 1840s the cotton-masters had accepted that it had become a time for purely secular holidays. The tradition of works' holiday weeks has survived in some places to the present. Bank holidays began for bank clerks in 1871 but the days when banks were closed quickly became public holidays.

Holinshed, Raphael (d. *c*.1580). Author of *The Chronicles of England, Scotland, and Ireland* (2 vols., 1577), a historical work which Shakespeare used as a basis for his plays. Holinshed drew on the notes of *Leland and was assisted in his compilation by William *Harrison, John *Hooker, and others.

Hollar, Wenceslaus (1607–77). Bohemian engraver who spent much of his career at the English court. He is best known for his panoramic view of London from Bankside (1647), which provides a valuable topographical record, and for his plan of London, which was published in *Blome's *Britannia* (1673).

holloways are an ancient feature of the landscape, which are found, for instance, at the sites of *deserted medieval villages. Settlements named Holloway or Hollowgate are recorded in the Middle Ages. However, most sunken lanes owe their present form to the increase in traffic in the early modern period; the deepest ones were created by the passage of wheeled vehicles rather than *packhorses. Some moorland holloways were dug out to facilitate the movement of *millstones. The age of a holloway cannot be estimated from its depth, as sunken lanes could be formed rapidly if they were heavily used, e.g. upon the opening of a coal pit or a lead-smelting works.

Holloways are often conspicuous where they descend steep hills. They have cut deep into the sub-soil and now serve as natural drains. Samuel Smiles (1812–1904) described them as horse tracks in summer and rivulets in winter. As the rain washed away the loose soil, horses and wheeled vehicles churned up the wet surface and the ways became deeper and deeper. Some were eventually abandoned and a new track was created alongside. Many holloways are now overgrown, but others have been given a modern surface and are still in use as country lanes. Gilbert *White has a graphic description of Hampshire holloways in *The Natural History of Selborne* (1788).

holograph. A deed, letter, or document wholly written by the person under whose name it appears.

holy well. Pagan wells were normally converted to Christian usage by a dedication to a saint and sometimes by the building of a chapel. Their reputation for healing and for divining the future was thus preserved, and their water was considered particularly suitable for baptism. The most famous wells, especially St Winifred's at Holywell (Wales), attracted pilgrims from far away. Pins, ribbons, yarn, and thread were thrown into the wells. The patron saints were usually female; some, such as St Anne and St Helen, were probably direct substitutes for Celtic goddesses. Other wells commemorate minor saints who are often otherwise unknown. For an archaeological investigation of a well at Minster Abbey, Isle of Sheppey, see Brian Slade, *The Well of the Triple Goddess: Minster Abbey* (1993). At the *Reformation Protestants dismissed the magical properties that were claimed for holy wells as mere Roman Catholic superstition. Nevertheless, St Winifred's well continued to attract pilgrims well into the 17th century and belief in the curative powers of such wells remained strong in the 19th century.

The origins of well-dressing in certain villages in the Peak District of Derbyshire are unknown. The present method of dressing these wells by constructing a picture and a religious text from flower petals, leaves, moss, pebbles, etc. pressed into clay owes much to the *evangelical revival and the Sunday school movement of the 19th century, though 'green issues' have been highlighted in recent times. The wells are blessed by the local minister at a Sunday service and the picture remains in place for a week. The custom is strongest at Ashford, Tideswell, Tissington, and Youlgreave, but in recent years has spread from the limestone district to some villages on the sandstones.

homagers. The twelve jurors of a manor *court.

homilies. Official sermons of the second half of the 16th century. As many ministers of the new *Church of England lacked the ability to preach, and as the church authorities wished to enforce conformity, official homilies were prepared, to be read from the *pulpit. Each ended with a prayer for Queen Elizabeth I and for the security of the realm. It has been shown that William Shakespeare's works were influenced by such homilies.

honour. A term used by the Normans for the large *lordships that were centred on *castles, e.g. Richmond (Yorkshire), which had 440 dependent manors in many parts of England.

Hooker, John (1554–1600). Antiquary, friend and helper of *Holinshed, and chamberlain of Exeter, whose *The Description of the Citie of Excester* is an important source for the 16th-century history of the city.

hops. The fruits of a climbing plant, used for flavouring beer. They were first grown in England for this purpose in the mid-16th century in those counties which were nearest France and the Low Countries, stretching from Hampshire round the coast to Norfolk. In time, Kent and Herefordshire became the renowned centres of production. Most early hop growers operated on a small scale of an acre or less, for larger undertakings required capital and labour. The ground had to be dug and spread with manure, poles bought and put up, the plants tied and pruned, the crop picked, dried in *oasthouses, and bagged, and the poles taken down and stacked. Harvesting was by migrant labour, often women. See Christine Faulkner, 'Hops and Hop Pickers of the Midlands', *Folk Life*, 30 (1992), and, for Kent, Margaret Lawrence, *The Encircling Hop* (1990).

horse fairs and dealers. Many towns have a street name indicating the former position of a horse fair. These were commonly moved out of the central market area to a new site on the edge of the town as trade increased during the 18th century. Much information can be obtained from toll books, which were introduced by Act of Parliament in 1555 to reduce the amount of horse stealing. Numerous horse fairs in northern and midland England gained a wide reputation; for example, Penkridge (Staffordshire) was noted for saddle horses, and the horse fair at Horncastle (Lincolnshire) lasted three weeks in August and attracted dealers from all over the country. There were two classes of specialized dealers in the early modern period: the 'jockey' or 'jobber' who purchased colts from northern breeders (either at the stable or at a fair) and sold them to south-country farmers, and the dealer in the neighbourhood of London or other large cities, who operated on a much larger scale, especially from the mid-18th century onwards. Horse dealers had a poor reputation, but only a minority indulged in sharp practices. See Peter Edwards, *The Horse Trade of Tudor and Stuart England* (1988). Horse fairs declined with the coming of the *railways, though that at Appleby (Westmorland) is a notable survival.

horse racing. The early Stuart kings made Newmarket famous by their patronage. It became the seat of the ruling body, the Jockey Club, yet like every other racecourse it attracted all classes. The 18th century saw the laying out of courses and the building of grandstands in or near towns and the holding of small meetings in the countryside. Towns such as Doncaster attracted *aristocratic and *gentry support and much trade during their special race weeks. Racecourses were established at Epsom and Cheltenham in the 19th century to improve the

*spas, and some municipal authorities followed suit. Other meetings, e.g. at Aintree, were the result of individual enterprise which then attracted patrons. The Derby, the major classic which was sponsored by Lord Derby, was first run in 1780. The first Grand National was held in 1839 though the name did not become official until 1847. With the coming of the *railways working-class enthusiasts were able to get to courses all over the country. Certain areas, notably parts of Ireland, became famous for their jockeys and horses. Gambling was always part of the appeal of the sport. *Newspapers, and later radio and television, enabled bookmakers to set up business in towns as well as on courses.

horses. The growing importance of the horse in the medieval economy has been shown by John Langdon, *Horses, Oxen and Technological Innovation* (1986). At the time of the *Domesday Book horses provided only 5 per cent of the total animal draught force on manorial *demesnes, and never more than 10 per cent in any of the regions for which there is evidence. By 1300, however, horses provided at least 20 per cent of the animal draught force on demesnes and almost 50 per cent on peasant farms. In some regions these figures exceeded 50 per cent and 75 per cent, respectively. By then horses were normally preferred to *oxen for the carriage of goods by vehicle, but less so for ploughing. These changes were pioneered in East Anglia, where the horse had been in widespread use from the first half of the 12th century, then by the counties near London and the east midlands. Peasant farmers, who together cultivated most of the land, were particularly strong in their preference for the speedier horse to the sturdier ox.

The rise in trade during the early modern period brought an increased demand for *packhorses and horse-drawn vehicles. The steady increase in the standard of living also meant more riding horses. Most probate *inventories record at least one horse, mare, or nag. Horses were also needed for service in war; the first book on horsemanship to be published in England, *c*.1560, was concerned with horses for war service. See Joan Thirsk, 'Horses in Early Modern England: For Service, For Pleasure, For Power' (1978, reprinted in *The Rural Economy of England*, 1984). Horses were bred in *woodpasture areas and on the edges of *moors and *fens. Some regions began to specialize, e.g. north Yorkshire gained a reputation for saddle, coaching, hunting, and race horses. See HORSE FAIRS AND DEALERS and Peter Edwards, *The*

Horse Trade of Tudor and Stuart England (1988).

By the end of the 18th century the famous breeds—the Clydesdale, Suffolk Punch, and the Black (later the Shire)—had emerged. The art of breeding declined in the early 19th century, but recovered in the 1830s. However, stud books were not kept for Shire horses until the 1870s. Meanwhile, the demand for horses grew enormously. According to William *Marshall, 100,000 horses were bred each year in the late 18th century; a horse was reckoned to have a working life of 10 years. F. M. L. Thompson, 'Nineteenth-century Horse Sense', *Economic History Review*, 2nd ser., 29/1 (1976), has estimated that 800,000 horses were working on the farms of Great Britain in 1811; another 487,000 were used for profit and pleasure. Great numbers were used for transport in the towns of Victorian Britain. See F. M. L. Thompson (ed.), *Horses in European Economic History: A Preliminary Canter* (1983). See also John Singleton, 'Britain's Military Use of Horses, 1914–1918', *Past and Present*, 139 (1993). For farm horses in the 20th century see George Ewart *Evans, *The Horse in the Furrow* (1960), and Stephen Caunce, *Amongst Farm Horses: The Horselads of East Yorkshire* (1991).

hosiery. See KNITTING and FRAMEWORK KNITTING.

Hoskins, W. G. (1908–92). William Hoskins was the great popularizer of local history and, at the same time, the leading academic figure in the subject. He was descended from a long line of Devon yeomen and Exeter bakers. His MA thesis at Exeter University was turned into his first book, *Industry, Trade and People in Exeter, 1688–1800* (1935). After teaching for a short time at Bradford Technical College, he lectured at the University College of Leicester from 1931 and taught extramural courses at Vaughan College, Leicester, where he tried out many of his influential ideas. He wrote most of his earliest articles—on farming, on *yeomen families such as the Humberstones, on *deserted medieval villages—for the *Transactions of the Leicestershire Archaeological and Historical Society*. The contrasts between Leicestershire and his native Devon set him thinking about the historical landscape and the value of visual evidence. Hoskins combined the traditional eclectic approaches of the old antiquaries with the concerns of the new social and economic historians, in, for example, his editorship of the *Victoria County History*'s Leicestershire volumes. He was a man who read widely, not only in the classics and many of the minor works of English literature, but also the writings of contemporary sociologists, especially Lewis Mumford.

Hoskins's renowned study of Wigston Magna—*The Midland Peasant* (1957)—was conceived and written before and during the Second World War, long before its publication after he had become famous through other works. The influence of Mumford's concept of a 'cultural humus' of layers of the past, and of the condemnations of the effects of parliamentary *enclosure in the poems of John *Clare and George *Bourne's *Change in the Village* (1912) is evident in his vision of a stable, sane peasant society that was destroyed by the parliamentary enclosure Act of 1766 for Wigston. 'The reconstruction of this former society is the principal theme', he wrote. The story had two distinctive threads: a village with a large and persistent class of free peasant *landowners without any resident *lord of the manor; and a village which maintained unimpaired its traditional *open-field husbandry when so many other villages in Leicestershire, and in the Midlands generally, were being enclosed and depopulated for sheep and cattle pastures in the 15th, 16th, and 17th centuries. Hoskins did not intend his study to be local history *per se*; he saw it rather as 'a study of the Midland peasant-farmer and of the open-field system in which he worked all his life . . . a study of a peasant culture, of the way it was built up (as far as we can discover it), of the way it worked, and of the way in which it was finally dissolved' (pp. xviii–xxix). Nevertheless, *The Midland Peasant* showed local historians a way of studying the local community of a single parish by taking into account topography, population, family history, vernacular building, the farming and craft economy, and the wider concerns of the inhabitants.

In 1948 he was made Reader and Head of the newly formed Department of English Local History at the University College of *Leicester. In 1951 he moved to Oxford as Reader in Economic History, returning to his old department at Leicester as Professor in 1965 until his retirement three years later. Amongst the books which came from his lectures at these two institutions were *Local History in England* (1959), *Fieldwork in Local History* (1967), and *The Age of Plunder: The England of Henry VIII, 1500–1547* (1976). His most important essays were collected together in *Provincial England* (1964).

His interest in the history and topography of his native county came to fruition in 1954 with the publication of *Devon*. This led to his most popular book, one that ranks with the most influential historical works of the 20th century, *The Making of the English Landscape* (1955). In this he emphasized the importance of visual evidence, interpreted by fieldwork and the study of original documents. He claimed that: 'The English landscape itself, to those who know how to read it aright, is the richest historical record we possess. There are discoveries to be made in it for which no written documents exist, or have ever existed. To write its history requires a combination of documentary research and of fieldwork' (p. 14).

Hoskins came to realize that in this book he had underplayed the importance of the prehistoric and Roman contributions to the making of the landscape. The revised edition (by Christopher Taylor) corrects this view. As Hoskins recognized, the fate of the pioneer is to be overtaken by fresh studies, many of them made by former pupils.

The success of the book led to his editorship of the *Hodder and Stoughton series of county landscape histories, to which he contributed the volume on Leicestershire. Hoskins had always been concerned to make local history and British social and economic history accessible to all, for example through his *Shell Guides* to Rutland and Leicestershire and his talks on BBC Radio 3. The BBC TV series *Landscapes of England* (1976–8) made his a household name and helped to stir an interest in the precious value of the environment and its importance as evidence of man's activities in the past.

Hoskins is hailed as a pioneer not only by local historians, but by historical geographers, urban historians, and students of *vernacular architecture. His essay on 'The Rebuilding of Rural England, 1570–1640' appeared in 1953 just as the Vernacular Architecture Group was being formed, and though it has been subsequently refined it proved to be enormously stimulating. (See GREAT REBUILDING.) His later interests were in demography and the perennial problem of the harvest, in the ways that human communities reacted to their environments. In his inaugural lecture at Leicester, published as *English Local History: The Past and The Future* (1966), he claimed: 'We should be studying living communities and their reaction to their environment, and to change in that environment over the past 2,000 years.' Local history should be, he thought, 'a science of Human Ecology'.

He was made a Fellow of the British Academy in 1969 and was awarded the CBE for 'services to local history' in 1971.

hospice (historical). A lodging for travellers, maintained by a religious order.

Hospitaller, Knights. The Knights of the Hospital of St John of Jerusalem were a military-religious order founded after the capture of Jerusalem from the Turks in the *Crusade of 1099. They provided accommodation and care for the sick, the poor, and pilgrims, and built and garrisoned castles against the Turks. They attracted substantial endowments of land which they administered from their headquarters at St John's Priory, Clerkenwell, London, and from about 50 'preceptories' in various parts of Britain. Their local influence on settlement and farming deserves investigation. See, for example, F. C. Rimington, *The History of Ravenscar and Staintondale* (1988). The order was dissolved in 1540. The preceptories are frequently commemorated by place-names.

hospitals and infirmaries. Medieval hospitals were charitable institutions founded by religious bodies, *guilds, *livery companies, and private individuals. One of the greatest English medieval hospitals was St Leonard's, York, which housed 229 sick inmates in 1280; part of the large infirmary hall, with its vaulted undercroft, and a first-floor chapel remain, albeit in a ruined condition. In the same city the surviving guildhalls of the Merchant Adventurers, the Merchant Taylors, and the crafts which met at St Anthony's Hall retain lower storeys which served as hospitals. Browne's Hospital, Stamford, is an outstanding example of a 15th-century hospital founded by a rich merchant, which still provides sheltered accommodation.

Most medieval hospitals were dissolved at the *Reformation. The numerous *almshouses and small hospitals of the early modern period were founded privately, often by a bequest made in a will. The 18th century saw a great growth in the provision of hospitals. London's famous hospitals mostly date from 1720 to 1745, though St Bartholomew's and St Thomas's were medieval foundations. (See also BEDLAM and CHELSEA HOSPITAL.) By 1800 or shortly afterwards most large provincial towns had opened infirmaries and *dispensaries as a result of voluntary contributions. Thus, in the East Midlands county infirmaries were built in Lincoln and Leicester in the 1760s, Nottingham completed its general hospital in 1781, and Derby's infirmary was opened in 1810. See J. Walter and R. Schofield (eds.), *Famine, Disease and the Social Order in Early Modern Society* (1989).

A striking development of the second half of the 19th century was the creation of infirmaries from the sick wards of *workhouses. London had Poor Law infirmaries from 1867, and other towns soon afterwards. Some hospitals grew on sites that had formerly been occupied by workhouses. They were a valuable addition to the charity hospitals and the civic hospitals of the large boroughs. For example, by 1900 Sheffield had two hospitals that had grown from workhouse provision, an infirmary built by public subscription, a women's hospital donated by a private benefactor, a civic hospital, and an asylum for the mentally ill. Its 17th-century almshouses still functioned alongside later foundations, but the site of its medieval isolation hospital was known only from the place-name Spital Hill. See J. Foster, 'An Introductory Guide to Hospital Records', *Local Population Studies*, 45 (1990).

hotel. The first hotel in England was built in Exeter in 1768. It was known at first simply as 'The Hotel', but it took the name of the Royal Clarence Hotel when it was extended to its present form in 1827. Margate (Kent) had a 'New Inn, Tavern, and Hotel' by 1774, but the term remained rare before 1800. In the 19th century only large establishments were described as hotels, but in the second half of the 20th century the term passed into widespread use amongst smaller properties.

House of Commons Journals. Records of the proceedings of the House of Commons, including the receiving of petitions and the passage of bills. The journals do not summarize debates, though diaries of MPs sometimes shed light on these. (See *Hansard*.) The Journals have been published from 1547. See D. Menhennet, *The Journal of the House of Commons: A Bibliographical and Historical Guide* (1971), which lists libraries that have copies of the journals. The passage of bills through the House of Commons can be followed from the formal procedure and the presentation of petitions. They are useful, for instance, in tracing the history of *enclosure or *turnpike roads.

house of correction. In the early modern period *Justices of the Peace established houses of correction for those found guilty of offences at the *quarter sessions. See Anthony Fletcher, *Reform in the Provinces: The Government of Stuart England* (1986). A master was authorized to maintain discipline in the house by *whipping and by setting the inmates to work. Such places developed into county gaols at a later period. See also BRIDEWELL.

House of Lords Journals. Records of the proceedings of the House of Lords, including the receiving of petitions and the passage of bills. They give no clue to the tenor of debates. The Journals have been published from 1510. The passage of public and private bills can be followed from the indexes.

House of Lords Record Office. The collections in this office which are of most use to local and family historians are the original texts of public and private bills and Acts of Parliament and their associated petitions and papers. They cover such topics as *railways, *canals, *turnpike roads, *enclosure, *reservoirs, etc. See M. F. Bond, *The Records of Parliament: A Guide for Genealogists and Local Historians* (1964), and H. S. Cobb, *A Guide to the House of Lords Papers and Petitions* (1959). See also PROTESTATION RETURNS.

house platform. A feature of *deserted and shrunken villages, marking the slightly raised foundations of former houses.

housebote. The right to take wood from the *commons to repair houses.

household. Demographic historians have shown that the nuclear household of parents and children (including *apprentices and *domestic or *farm servants) was the norm from the Middle Ages to the 20th century. Old notions of extended families living under one roof have been discarded. The majority of households contained fewer than five persons. Grandparents lived with younger generations only if they were infirm; *widows and widowers commonly lived alone, though often close to their offspring. See Peter Laslett, 'Mean Household Size' in Peter Laslett and Richard Wall (eds.), *Household and Family in Past Time* (1972).

Tax lists that record the heads of households, notably the *hearth tax returns of the 1660s and 1670s, may be used to estimate the population of a *parish or *township. Tom Arkell, 'Multiplying Factors for Estimating Population Totals from the Hearth Tax', *Local Population Studies*, 28 (1982), suggests a mean household size in both rural and urban areas outside London of 4.3, within a range of 3.7 to 5.2. Individual households, of course, varied considerably in size; richer families tended to have more offspring and more servants, and the possibility of variations over time and by regions must be kept in mind. Nevertheless, multipliers within this range are generally accepted as providing reasonable estimates.

Kevin Schurer, 'Variations in Household Structure in the Late Seventeenth Century: Toward a Regional Analysis' in Kevin Schurer and Tom Arkell (eds.), *Surveying the People: The Interpretation and Use of Document Sources for the Study of Population in the Later Seventeenth Century* (1992) uses returns of the *Marriage Duty Act (1695) for six areas in order to investigate household structure in a geographical context. He notes the disparities within, rather than homogeneity across, the different regions and concludes that it is difficult to make any case for distinct patterns of regional identity at the close of the 17th century. Geographical patterns in this, as in other matters, are not necessarily constant over time. The regional variations that can be seen in household structure from the 19th century onwards were less a product of underlying geographical factors than of the processes of industrialization and *de-industrialization.

For a discussion of how the term 'householder' implied a status superior to that of *cottager see Charles Phythian-Adams, *Desolation of a City: Coventry and the Urban Crisis of the Late Middle Ages* (1979), ch. 6.

hoy. A small, rigged ship for conveying passengers and goods along a coast. For illustrations and a local history, see John Whyman, 'The Significance of the Hoy to Margate's Early Growth as a Seaside Resort', *Archaeologia Cantiana*, III (1993).

huckster. A hawker.

Hudson's Bay Company. Founded by English royal charter in 1670 with a grant of all the land within Hudson's Bay not already belonging to others and a monopoly of the fur trade there. The Company built forts, established settlements, and became highly profitable. In 1869 the Company ceded its lands to the Canadian government. Microfilm copies of its records are kept at the *Public Record Office, but permission to see them must be obtained from Hudson's Bay & Annings Ltd, 77 Main Street, Winnipeg, Manitoba R3C 2RI, Canada.

hue and cry. A parish responsibility, whereby victims of, or witnesses to, a *felony had to shout an alarm and all who heard this were obliged to pursue the felon.

Huguenot immigrants. The term Huguenot, denoting a French *Protestant of Calvinistic persuasion, is of disputed origin, but it was in use in France by 1560. After the Massacre of St Bartholomew in 1572 many Huguenots fled to Protestant countries such as England. English people tended to use the word Huguenot also to describe Walloon refugees who emigrated from the Low Countries to avoid Spanish control. French Protestants were granted religious freedom by the Edict of Nantes (1598), but this was revoked in 1685, provoking further emigration.

The Huguenots and Walloons settled principally in London and the towns of eastern and south-eastern England, notably Norwich, Canterbury, Sandwich, Maidstone, and Southampton. They made a significant contribution to the introduction of new craft skills, particularly in the *New Draperies. These early settlers founded their own churches, but in time the immigrants, or their descendants, became assimilated in the native population. See Andrew Pettegree, 'Thirty Years On: Progress towards Integration amongst the Immigrant Population of Elizabethan London' in John Chartres and David Hey (eds.), *English Rural Society, 1500–1800: Essays in Honour of Joan Thirsk* (1990).

On arriving in England, a Huguenot refugee had to apply for *naturalization or *denization. The records of this process, and many other records, have been published by the Huguenot Society in numerous volumes of *Proceedings*, *Church Registers*, *Returns of Aliens*, etc. The Huguenot Society was founded in 1885; it is an essential point of contact for enquiries into French Protestant or Walloon ancestry. Some modern surnames are still recognizable as being of Huguenot origin; others have been changed to English forms. Claiming Huguenot descent has a romantic appeal which has led to many false claims being made. See Noel Currer-Briggs and Royston Gambier, *Huguenot Ancestry* (1985).

hundred. Hundreds were subdivisions of counties, from the 10th century onwards, in those parts of England that lay south of the *Danelaw. They had military, judicial, and administrative functions, some of which they retained well into the modern period. Thus, *hearth tax returns and 18th- and early 19th-century *militia records are arranged by hundred (or by *wapentake in the former Danelaw).

In the late *Anglo-Saxon period hundreds probably consisted of 100 *hides, a unit of taxation. Their names were taken from their original meeting-places, which were usually remote from settlements, often at a river crossing or by a major highway. The site was often marked by a stone, tree, or tumulus.

Hundred Rolls (1279). The operation of local government through *hundreds was investigated at Edward I's command in 1274–5. As a result, in 1278 all holders of franchises, such as the right to hold courts or markets, or the right to hunt, were made to justify their claims at

*Quo Warranto enquiries. The surviving records are not comprehensive; they were published in two volumes as *Rotuli Hundredorum* in 1812 and 1818. See Helen Cam, *The Hundred and the Hundred Rolls* (1976 reprint).

These rolls have been used to investigate *feudalism by P. *Vinogradoff, *Villeinage in England* (1892), and E. A. Kosminsky, *Studies in the Agrarian History of England in the Thirteenth Century* (1956). Kosminsky demonstrated that the way in which *manors varied in size and number from place to place had considerable implications for regional agriculture and agrarian institutions. He showed that *freehold land was already of major importance and that half of it was rented by *sub-tenants. Later studies have suggested that these sub-tenants included *gentry, ecclesiastics, urban tradesmen, and craftsmen, as well as peasants.

Hunter, Joseph (1783–1861). *Antiquarian. The son of a Sheffield cutler, Hunter was adopted by a Unitarian minister and himself became the minister of Trim Street Chapel, Bath. There he wrote the history of his native district in *Hallamshire* (1819) and the two volumes of *South Yorkshire: The History and Topography of the Deanery of Doncaster* (1828–31). Further works included *A Hallamshire Glossary* (1829), and an edition of *The Diary of Ralph Thoresby* (1830) for the *Camden Society. In 1833 he became sub-commissioner, and five years later assistant keeper, at the newly established *Public Record Office. There he was responsible for editing *Pipe Rolls, *feet of fines, and the *Valor Ecclesiasticus*. He also made the first serious study of the Robin Hood legends and wrote about early English literature and the first emigrants to America.

Huntingdon Connexion, Countess of. Selina Hastings, Countess of Huntingdon (1707–91), financed the Calvinist branch of the *Methodist movement, led by George Whitefield, whom she appointed her chaplain in 1751. She built chapels in London and at fashionable Bath, Brighton, and Tunbridge Wells, and in 1767 founded a theological college in Breconshire. Services were conducted in conformity with the *Church of England, even after the Methodist break with the Anglican church in 1779. At the time of the *ecclesiastical census of 1851 the Connexion had over 100 chapels. Their registers are kept at the *Public Record Office.

husbandman. The old word for a farmer below the rank of *yeoman. A husbandman usually held his land by *copyhold or *leasehold tenure and may be regarded as the 'average farmer in his locality'. The words 'yeoman' and 'husbandman' were gradually replaced in the later 18th and 19th centuries by 'farmer'.

hut circle. *Bronze Age or early *Iron Age remains of prehistoric dwellings.

Hutchins, John (1698–1773). Clergyman and antiquary, whose four-volume *The History and Antiquities of the County of Dorset* was published from 1773.

Hutton, William (1723–1815). Stationer and author of a *History of Birmingham* (1783), one of the best early town histories.

hydropath. Hydropathy was the name given to the treatment of illness by hot and cold water used both outwardly and inwardly. Formerly used in the classical world, it was reintroduced into Britain in the 1840s. The most famous hydro was that started by John Smedley on Matlock Bank (Derbyshire) in 1853 and extended on a grand scale in the 1880s. Concerts, theatrical performances, dances, and games were provided as well as treatment. It attracted visitors from all over Britain and abroad and remained popular until the Second World War. Several smaller and cheaper hydros were built nearby.

hypocaust. A Roman method of heating buildings by circulating hot air beneath floors and within walls.

ice houses. Introduced from France in the 17th century and much used on country estates until the invention of refrigerators, ice houses had a domed roof and were approached via a short tunnel. Ice was packed with straw in winter, kept as airtight as possible, and used for summer drinks and for preserving meat and vegetables. An urban example can be seen by the northern city wall at York. See Tim Buxbaum, *Ice Houses* (1992).

illegitimacy. Illegitimate births are recorded in *parish registers by such comments as 'base', 'bastard', 'spurious', or a capital letter B, or by some Latin equivalent. From such information it is possible to calculate the percentage of those who were born out of wedlock. Illegitimacy rates were not high during the early modern period: for most of the time illegitimate children accounted for no more than 1 or 2 per cent of baptisms. At their highest between 1590 and 1610 rates reached 3 per cent, but they then declined to their usual lower figure and did not reach 3 per cent again until the 1750s. It may be argued that parish registers are an unreliable guide, in that some pregnant girls may have run away, but the pattern is consistent nation-wide. Evidence derived from the two counties that have been studied in most detail—Somerset and Essex—suggests that the mothers of illegitimate children were very often *domestic servants. Pre-marital pregnancy was common and many illegitimate births were probably the result of abandoned or delayed marriage plans. See, for example, G. R. Quaife, *Wanton Wenches and Wayward Wives: Peasants and Illicit Sex in Early Seventeenth-Century England* (1979).

Illegitimacy rates were at their highest in the second quarter of the 19th century, when national *population growth reached unprecedented levels. From 1837 the information provided by parish registers can be supplemented by that from the *civil registration of births. Illegitimacy rates reached a high point of 7 per cent, but then gradually declined to 4 per cent by the 1890s. As the size of the national population was greatly increased, the actual number of illegitimate births was much higher than before.

The last third of the 20th century has seen very different attitudes to marriage and births emerge, so that it is no longer realistic to speak of illegitimacy rates.

immigration. The British population is largely descended from successive waves of invaders and settlers from the Continent, i.e. *prehistoric people, Celts, *Anglo-Saxons, and *Vikings. The *Norman Conquest brought a total change of landownership, but did not lead to large-scale settlement of French families at lower social levels. The striking regional distribution patterns of *surnames to the present day, the survival of local *dialects and accents, and the restricted geographical spread of *blood groups point to the remarkable continuity of local populations within a restricted area.

Nevertheless, immigrants have played a major part in shaping British society. In *London and in certain other towns they formed substantial groups long before modern times. In *The True-Born Englishman* (1701) Daniel *Defoe ridiculed claims of a 'pure English' ancestry and satirized the mongrel breed that he observed; his remarks were true of the cosmopolitan society of London, but not of most of the rest of Britain. London was always the great magnet for immigrants from overseas, as well as from other parts of Britain, and was exceptional.

In the Middle Ages foreign immigrants came in relatively small numbers from the Continent, principally from France and the Low Countries, but also from the Mediterranean. The *Jews formed a distinctive group in some large towns. *Flemish weavers were welcomed by Edward III (1327–77). Immigration on a much larger scale started in the 16th century, when French *Huguenots came to escape religious persecution and *Dutch, Flemish, and Walloon refugees fled from Spanish oppression. Between 1540 and 1600 over 50,000 men, women, and children crossed the Channel or the North Sea to settle in Britain, mostly in the towns of south-eastern England. (See ALIENS.) The influx continued during the 17th century, with fresh waves of Huguenots in the 1680s and smaller groups of German miners and Dutch drainers in the countryside. (See also GYP-SIES.)

The 18th century saw a continued flow of individuals and small groups. Increased international trade brought immigrants from further and further afield. One of the side effects of the triangular *slave trade, centred on Liverpool and Bristol, was the presence of black servants, as stable boys, grooms, valets, or butlers, particularly in London. But there was no further influx of immigrants on a large scale until the *Irish started to settle in England, Wales, and Scotland from the late 18th century, and especially after Ireland had been incorporated in the *United Kingdom in 1801. The Irish provided the labour force for the construction of *canals, and later the *railways, in the *docks and *factories, and as seasonal labourers getting in the harvest on farms. They had arrived in thousands even before the mass emigration from Ireland from 1846 onwards, when they settled in London, Lancashire, and in and around Glasgow in particular, in surroundings very different from their rural homelands. The first stages of this mass movement have been well recorded, but the available information for the later 19th century is thinner and no satisfactory general historical survey has yet been written. The Irish continued to arrive in significant numbers, but the United States of *America proved an increasingly attractive alternative.

Colin Holmes, *John Bull's Island: Immigration and British Society, 1871–1971* (1988) traces the history of each group of immigrants since mid-Victorian times. See also Nick Merriman (ed.), *The Peopling of London: Fifteen Thousand Years of Settlement from Overseas* (1993), for the special circumstances of the capital city. In 1871 Britain was the world's major industrial power, with a large empire. It therefore attracted foreign businessmen, such as the *Germans who settled in Bradford and Manchester, and immigrant *merchant seamen and labourers. It was also widely known for its liberal policy towards political refugees. The Russian pogroms from 1881 onwards caused thousands of Jews to flee from Poland, Lithuania, and other parts of the Russian Empire. They settled particularly in the East End of London, Leeds, Manchester, and Glasgow; Scotland attracted 7,000 Lithuanians compared to England's 4,000. The numbers of poor Jewish immigrants became so large that in 1905 severe restrictions were placed on their entry. This was the first change in Britain's traditional open-door policy. Other Jewish refugees fled from Hitler's Germany in the 1930s, to be followed after the Second World War by Ukrainians, Poles, and (later) Hungarians fleeing from Russian occupation (see POL-ISH IMMIGRANTS).

A characteristic feature of immigration is that at first immigrant groups cluster in certain areas: thus, in 1902 a London journalist coined the name 'China Town' for Limehouse and 'Little Italy' for Clerkenwell. Although Britain has never had any laws defining areas of residence, in practice certain districts have attracted different groups. This is partly because of available housing and employment, but is also largely a matter of group communication and support. Over the centuries many parts of London have been associated with immigrant groups. The East End attracted Flemish weavers in the 14th century, Dutch and Walloon craftsmen and traders in the 16th century, French Huguenots in the 17th century, the Irish in the 18th and early 19th centuries, then the Eastern European Jews, and later the Bengalis, as well as a host of others. In the West End Soho has attracted *Chinese, *French, Cypriot, and *Italian immigrants. The docklands have provided work and homes for Chinese, Indians, Malayans, Yemenis, Somalians, and people from West Africa. In the late 20th century the population of London is drawn from all over the world; Londoners speak nearly 200 languages and practise all of the world's major religions. Cultural diversity in London is greater than ever before, but then the city has always been cosmopolitan, ever since its foundation by the Romans.

Many immigrants were forced, at first, to work long hours at jobs that nobody else wanted, but those who eventually prospered moved elsewhere, taking their successful neighbours with them. Their original settlements then became vacant for fresh waves of immigrants. The classic example is that of the Jews who moved from the East End to north London, especially to the substantial middle-class district of Golders Green, leaving behind their less successful compatriots and space for newcomers. The same social and geographical mobility can be seen with Italians and Greek Cypriots. Though it is most evident in London, this movement can also be traced in other towns.

The reception afforded to immigrants has always been mixed. The Jews were victims of xenophobia in the late 12th century and Flemish weavers were attacked in the *Peasants' Revolt of 1381. All immigrant groups have had to face negative stereotyping and racial prejudice. Nevertheless, Britain was more welcoming than other countries until the scale of immigration forced a change of policy. The Aliens Act (1905) restricted the entry of Jews from the Russian Empire. The Aliens Restriction Act (1914) was passed because of scares about German spies; its requirement that aliens must register with the police remains in force. The Aliens Act (1919) gave immigration officers the power to refuse entry, restricted the employment of aliens, and allowed the Home Secretary to deport those he saw fit. On the other hand, the British Nationality and Status of Aliens Act (1914) conferred the status of British subject on all inhabitants of the British Empire; this principle was reinforced by the British Nationality Act (1948). During the 1950s members of the Commonwealth from the West Indies, Africa, and Asia took advantage of these Acts to enter Britain in large numbers. At first, they were encouraged by the Government, for Britain was short of labour in certain jobs such as nursing, or in transport or the textile industries. These newcomers followed the traditional choices of immigrants in heading for the cities and towns, notably London, Birmingham, Leicester, and Bradford, and in living in certain districts, such as Brixton in south London, or Handsworth in Birmingham. Public hostility to the large numbers of immigrants of a different colour from the majority of the native population led to restrictions on entry being imposed by the Commonwealth Immigrants Act (1962), which introduced a system of employment vouchers. The door was closed tighter in 1968, after the immigration of Asians expelled from Kenya, by restricting entry to UK passport-holders who had a parent or grandparent born in Britain. Further Acts in 1971 and 1981 reduced future immigration to small numbers.

In the late 20th century Britain is a much more cosmopolitan society than before, though people in rural areas rarely come across immigrants except upon a visit to a town. Descendants of immigrants hold some of the most important political offices and are prominent members of British society. This social mobility has been a recurring feature of British history; the kings of England have included men born in France, Wales, Scotland, Holland, and Germany, and their spouses have often been foreigners.

Imperial Gazetteer. The six volumes of J. M. Wilson's *The Imperial Gazetteer of England and Wales* (1870) are a reliable source of statistical and other information for *towns, *parishes, and rural *townships. They are noted for sig-

nalling, in parishes, whether land was 'much subdivided' or 'divided among a few'.

imports. Britain has always been a trading nation, dependent for much of its goods on imports. A group of 'Commonwealth men' who were very influential in government in the mid 16th century were concerned to reduce England's dependency on imports, particularly of consumer goods; they therefore initiated a successful policy of encouraging projects to establish rural industries and reduce the overseas trading deficit. See Joan Thirsk, *Economic Policy and Projects: The Development of a Consumer Society in England* (1978). Certain goods, including groceries and drink, that could not be produced in Britain were made available to the remotest regions through ports and market towns. For an overview see Ralph Davis, *English Overseas Trade, 1500–1700* (1973). (See also PORT; CUSTOMS AND EXCISE; and SHIPS.)

As Britain became the world's first industrial nation, it was able to import much of its food. See the statistical appendix in G. E. Mingay (ed.), *The *Agrarian History of England and Wales*, vi, 1750–1850 (1989). The colonies of the British Empire provided raw materials for many British industries in the 19th and early 20th centuries. In the second half of the 20th century the trading deficit (imports exceeding exports) caused concern as Britain's share of international markets declined and as foreign imports of *coal, *steel, *cutlery, *cotton and *woollen goods, etc. severely affected traditional industries.

impropriation of parishes. The annexation of a *benefice, and thus of the great *tithes of a *parish, especially by a *monastery or a *college, which would then appoint a *vicar to serve the parish. If the minister of a church is known as a vicar rather than a *rector, then it means that impropriation will have taken place during the Middle Ages. See BISHOPS' REGISTERS.

improvement commissioners. In the 18th and early 19th centuries private Acts of Parliament established 'improvement' or 'street' commissioners in towns. These bodies used their powers of administration to perform many of the tasks of *local government. They are regarded as forerunners of municipal authorities. Their records, which include minute books, *rate books, and building plans, should be sought in local *record offices.

incised slabs. Medieval slabs shaped like coffins and incised with crosses, and occasionally with human figures, laid into church floors as personal memorials. Many have been removed from their original positions.

inclined plane. A method of raising boats from one level of water to another on the smaller *canals of western England, either hydraulically or by *steam power or water wheels.

income tax. Introduced during the *Napoleonic wars. Returns for 1799–1816, giving the names of individual taxpayers on a parish basis, are kept in the *Public Record Office under E 182. See A. Hope-Jones, *Income Tax in the Napoleonic Wars* (1939). Individual tax assessments do not survive for the 19th century, but some returns on a *parish and county basis survive in the Public Record Office class I.R. 14. See also VALUATION OFFICE.

indenture. A formal agreement, so-called from the practice of separating two identical texts by cutting along an irregular line, to prevent forgery. Indentures were used for title *deeds and for contracts, e.g. with *domestic servants or *apprentices.

  In the 17th century a high proportion of emigrants to America, especially to *Virginia, went as indentured servants, who worked for a fixed term on a *plantation in return for their board and passage. See David Souden's study of the records of over 10,000 indentured servants who sailed from Bristol between 1654 and 1679, in P. Clark and D. Souden (eds.), *Migration and Society in Early Modern England* (1987).

Independent Labour Party. Founded in 1893 in Bradford under the leadership of Keir Hardie, the ILP retained its identity after its merger with other bodies in 1900 to form the Labour Representation Committee, the forerunner of the *Labour Party. See David Howell, *British Workers and the Independent Labour Party, 1888–1906* (1983).

Independents. The 17th-century *Nonconformists who rejected national organization in favour of loose affiliations of independent congregations. From the 18th century they were generally known by their alternative name of *Congregationalists.

India Office Library and records. The archives of the *East India Company and the India Office, from 1600 to 1947, are kept at Orbit House, Blackfriars Road, London SE1.

indictment books. The record of charges brought before the *Justices of the Peace at *quarter sessions. These are kept with the order books from the same sessions at county *record offices. Some county record societies have published editions of records from the 16th and 17th centuries.

indulgence. A system begun at the time of the first *Crusade whereby repentant sinners who prayed for forgiveness and made a personal commitment were offered relief from suffering in purgatory. Much revenue for the church was raised in this way, but the system became abused and was scathingly attacked by Martin Luther.

Industrial Revolution. A term coined by Arnold Toynbee in *Lectures on the Industrial Revolution in England* (1884) to describe the period of massive industrial change from the middle of the 18th century onwards, and particularly during the two generations from c.1780. Change was manifest in large-scale production, steam power, the use of machinery, the employment of large numbers of people under one roof, and the expansion of markets. These changes were associated with *population growth and urbanization. The term was widely used by historians until the last quarter of the 20th century, but the concept of a swift and fundamental transformation of the British economy has been so refined that the phrase is now little more than short-hand for the many changes that took place in industry during the period from the mid-18th to the late 19th centuries. The idea that the Industrial Revolution represented a sudden break with the past has been replaced by an emphasis on gradual, incremental change that differed in its pace and nature from one region to another. Stress is now placed on continuity with earlier developments, stretching back to the 16th and 17th centuries. Moreover, the changes that occurred during the second half of the 18th century are now considered modest when compared with those that took place after the ending of the *Napoleonic wars in 1815. See David Cannadine, 'The Past and the Present in the English Industrial Revolution, 1880–1980', *Past and Present*, 103 (1984). For a response, see Maxine Berg and Pat Hudson, 'Rehabilitating the Industrial Revolution', *Economic History Review*, 2nd ser., 45/1 (1992).

  The leading role of *cotton in the development of Britain as the first industrial nation in the world has long been recognized. In Manchester and other parts of east Lancashire (rural as well as urban) large-scale factories, full of machines worked first by *water power, then by *steam engines, set the pace. See S. D. Chapman, *The Cotton Industry in the Industrial Revolution* (1987). In the *woollen and *worsted industries across the Pennines, however, *weaving long remained a domestic craft, moreover one that expanded to match the output of the *spinning mills. Even in the textile industries, therefore, the pace of change was uneven. The East Midlands hosiery industry was not turned into a factory-based system until the second half of the 19th century. The nature of the changes in the metal industries was very different from those in the textile trades; in and around Birmingham and Sheffield expansion occurred through the multiplication of small units of a traditional kind rather than by factories, and in Sheffield water remained a more important source of power than steam until well into the 19th century.

Industrial change also took place in the countryside. Many industrial villages grew quickly, none more so than the Welsh pit villages and slate quarry settlements. Lowland Scotland was transformed, especially in the western parts in and around Glasgow. In Northern Ireland Belfast grew rapidly, mainly because of the *linen industry and *shipbuilding. Most of the burgeoning industrial cities in England had already had a long history as small market towns, but some new towns grew from almost nothing, notably Middlesbrough and Barrow-in-Furness. Cumulatively, these changes were revolutionary, but they differed in so many ways and over such a long period of time that it has to be accepted that the term 'Industrial Revolution' does not have a precise meaning, but can be used only as a convenient general description. Nor must it be forgotten that hand crafts survived well into Victorian times and that large parts of Britain were never affected by industrial change.

industry and trade. The literature on the history of technology is considerable. See, for instance, T. K. Derry and T. I. Williams, *Short History of Technology* (1960), R. A. Buchanan, *Industrial Archaeology in Britain* (1972), R. F. Tylecote, *A History of Metallurgy* (1976), A. E. Musson and E. Robinson, *Science and Technology in the Industrial Revolution* (1969), and articles in the journals *Medieval Archaeology*, *Post-Medieval Archaeology*, and *Industrial Archaeology Review*. Aerial photographs have helped to demonstrate the effects of industry on the *landscape since the Middle Ages. See M. W. Beresford and J. K. St Joseph, *Medieval England: An Aerial Survey* (1979), part 4. Much of the published work on the history of industry, especially that revealed by archaeology, is specialized and makes no attempt to set findings against the wider background of landscape studies and general economic history, but there

is a growing awareness of the need to combine documentary research with the techniques of the archaeologist, particularly in the post-medieval period. See David Crossley, *Post-Medieval Archaeology in Britain* (1990).

For the medieval period, see L. F. Salzman, *English Industries of the Middle Ages* (1913), and John Blair and Nigel Ramsay (eds.), *English Medieval Industries: Craftsmen, Techniques, Products* (1991). Particular industries have been studied in depth at a regional level, especially the important woollen cloth trade. See, for example, W. B. Crump and G. Ghorbal, *History of the Huddersfield Woollen Industry* (1935), and Herbert Heaton, *The Yorkshire Woollen and Worsted Industries from Earliest Times up to The Industrial Revolution* (1920). Here, and elsewhere, the medieval origins of major industries have been explored, both in the towns and in the countryside. An earlier emphasis on craft associations, i.e. *guilds, has been replaced by attempts to study the entire occupational structures of medieval towns and to ascertain the extent and nature of rural industry. See, for instance, John Hatcher, *Rural Economy and Society in the Duchy of Cornwall, 1300–1500* (1970). On medieval trade, see R. H. Britnell, *The Commercialisation of English Society, 1000–1500* (1993). Earlier local studies include E. M. Carus Wilson (ed.), *The Overseas Trade of Bristol in the Later Middle Ages* (1937), and O. Coleman, *The Brokage Book of Southampton, 1443–4*, 2 vols. (1960–1). (See MARKETS AND FAIRS, and PORT.) The wealth generated by industry and trade is an important consideration in the study of *buildings. See Alec Betterton and David Dymond, *Lavenham: Industrial Town* (1989). For a major city that was hit severely by recession in the late medieval period, see Charles Phythian-Adams, *Desolation of a City: Coventry and the Urban Crisis of the Late Middle Ages* (1979).

The pioneering article by W. G. *Hoskins, 'An Elizabethan Provincial Town: Leicester' (1955, reprinted in *Provincial England*, ch. 5, 1964) showed how local historians in the early modern period could use a range of sources to analyse urban occupational structures. Instead of concentrating on one industry, the whole economy was revealed by an examination of Leicester's clothing, food and drink, leather, textile, household goods, building, and distributive trades. Alan D. Dyer, *The City of Worcester in the Sixteenth Century* (1973), and David Palliser, *Tudor York* (1979) incorporated chapters on industry and trade in full studies of provincial cities. Some early modern towns were nevertheless reliant on a particular industry: see

David Hey, *The Fiery Blades of Hallamshire: Sheffield and Its Neighbourhood, 1660–1740* (1991) for the importance of the *cutlery industry and Sheffield's triumph over its provincial rivals. For a new industrial town of this period, see Sylvia Collier and Sarah Pearson, *Whitehaven, 1660–1800* (1991).

The rural industries of the early modern period have attracted much attention. Early regional studies include G. H. Tupling, *The Economic History of Rossendale* (1927), A. P. Wadsworth and J. de L. Mann, *The Cotton Trade and Industrial Lancashire, 1600–1780* (1931), W. H. B. Court, *The Rise of the Midland Industries, 1600–1838* (1938), and G. D. Ramsay, *The Wiltshire Woollen Industry* (1943). Joan Thirsk, 'Industries in the Countryside' (1961, reprinted in *The Rural Economy of England*, 1984) sparked off a new generation of regional studies, including David Hey, *The Rural Metalworkers of the Sheffield Region* (1972), and Marie Rowlands, *Masters and Men in the Small Metalware Trades of the West Midlands* (1975). An overview is provided in D. C. Coleman, *Industry in Tudor and Stuart England* (1975). Joan Thirsk, *Economic Policy and Projects: The Development of a Consumer Society in Early Modern England* (1978) provided a national framework that emphasized the role of central government in actively sponsoring rural industries, through the granting of monopolies and by encouraging foreign craftsmen to settle. (See NEW DRAPERIES.) This intervention helps to explain the local concentration of certain industries, which had previously been scattered. The availability of raw materials does not by itself explain why certain places became industrial centres, for by the 16th century some successful centres were importing their materials over long distances. See David Hey, 'The Origins and Early Growth of the Hallamshire Cutlery and Allied Trades' in John Chartres and David Hey (eds.), *English Rural Society, 1500–1800: Essays in Honour of Joan Thirsk* (1990). For the role of *landowners in industrial development, see J. V. Beckett, *Coal and Tobacco: The Lowthers and Economic Development of West Cumberland, 1660–1760* (1981).

The relationship between rural industry and agriculture has proved a fruitful topic for investigation. (See DUAL ECONOMY and DOMESTIC ECONOMY.) Such studies have made good use of probate *inventories and manorial *surveys and have investigated the surviving material culture. The debate on the origins of the *Industrial Revolution has drawn extensively on studies of rural industries which grew enormously in the early modern period. (See PROTO-INDUSTRIAL-IZATION; see also FRAMEWORK KNITTING for an example of a thriving industry that grew into a modern one.) A full study of a rural parish in County Durham, which became industrialized at an exceptionally early period through the exploitation of its coal reserves, is provided by David Levine and Keith Wrightson, *The Making of an Industrial Society: Whickham, 1560–1765* (1991). Some industries failed to expand, however; see, for example, Michael Zell, *Industry in the Countryside: Wealden Society in the Sixteenth Century* (1994), which is concerned with the decline of a once-thriving textile industry. (See DE-INDUSTRIALIZATION.)

Historians of the early modern period have also reconstructed much of the network of inland trade. T. S. Willan's books, starting with *River Navigation in England, 1600–1750* (1936), and culminating in *The Inland Trade* (1976), were the pioneer works. See David Hey, *Packmen, Carriers and Packhorse Roads: Trade and Communications in North Derbyshire and South Yorkshire* (1980), which relates the evidence on the ground to general economic development, and John Chartres, *Internal Trade in England, 1500–1700* (1977), which provides an overview. For exports, see Ralph Davis, *The Rise of the English Shipping Industry* (1962). (See also ROADS; PACKHORSES; CARRIERS; TRADE, INLAND; TRADE, COASTING; and EXPORTS.)

Daniel *Defoe, *A Tour Through the Whole Island of Great Britain* (2 vols., 1724–6) is a lively and well-informed account of local economies in the early 18th century. Historians no longer regard the Industrial Revolution as a clean break with the past, but emphasize instead the considerable continuity and the gradual mechanization of most industries. There is a vast literature on the industries of the 18th and 19th centuries and numerous local and regional studies. (See COTTON; WOOL; WORSTED; COAL; IRON; STEEL; LEAD; TIN; QUARRYING; CHEMICAL INDUSTRY; GLASS; POTTERY; WATER POWER; STEAM ENGINES; and FACTORY.)

Starting-points for local and regional historians are provided by Barrie Trinder, *The Making of the Industrial Landscape* (1988 reprint), Pat Hudson (ed.), *Regions and Industries: A Perspective on the Industrial Revolution in Britain* (1989), and the Longman Regional History of England series, especially David Hey, *Yorkshire from AD 1000* (1986), Marie B. Rowlands, *The West Midlands from AD 1000* (1987), J. V. Beckett, *The East Midlands from AD 1000* (1988), and C. B. Phillips and J. H. Smith, *Lancashire and Cheshire from AD 1540* (1994). The ways in which altered contexts can illuminate the study of a regional economy are explored in J. D. Marshall and J. K. Walton, *The Lake Counties from 1830 to the Mid-Twentieth Century: A Study in Regional Change* (1981). The rural setting of many industries in the 19th century is explored in David Hey, 'Industrialized Villages' in G. E. Mingay (ed.), *The Victorian Countryside*, vol. i (1981). For the industrial history of a Victorian and 20th-century city, see J. C. Binfield and others (eds.), *The History of the City of Sheffield, 1843–1993* (1993).

Much of the work on the Industrial Revolution by scholars since the 1960s has looked at a large canvas using econometric models, but a renewed emphasis on the importance of detailed local and regional studies was evident in the 1980s with the publication of Pat Hudson, *The Genesis of Industrial Capital: A Study of the West Riding Wool Textile Industry, c.1750–1850* (1986) and Michael Atkinson and Colin Baber, *The Growth and Decline of the South Wales Iron Industry, 1760–1880* (1987). Historians of the 20th century have had to explain how continued prosperity was followed by the rapid decline of major industries in face of international competition. See R. H. Campbell, *The Rise and Fall of Scottish Industry, 1707–1939* (1980), and Philip Jenkins, *A History of Modern Wales, 1536–1990* (1992).

infangentheof. The right of a manorial or borough *court to try and punish a thief arrested within its jurisdiction.

infant mortality. More than one-fifth of all children born in England during the reign of Elizabeth I, and about one-quarter of those born during the 17th century, died before the age of ten. Well over half of these deaths, and almost two-thirds of those in Elizabeth's reign, occurred during the child's first year. Indeed, many infants did not survive their first month. Perhaps half of these deaths were due to the effects of difficult births and congenital defects and not a few were caused by babies being overlain in bed. Infectious diseases largely accounted for the rest, judging by the seasonal and geographical variations revealed by the study of burials in *parish registers. Infant mortality was far higher in the towns than in the countryside, except for notoriously unhealthy spots such as the *fens. It is impossible to determine the level of infanticide, but it is not thought to have been high and was used rather to conceal pregnancy than deliberately to limit the population. See Ralph A. Houlbrooke, *The English Family, 1450–1700* (1984).

Infant mortality remained high in Victorian England, at 150 per thousand live births, which is more than ten times the rate in the late 20th century. The rate for 1899 was 163 per thousand, the highest figure since the *Registrar-General had begun to collect figures 60 years earlier. By 1914 the rate went below 100 per thousand in one year for the first time and by the 1920s it was less than half its 1890s level. These crude national figures mask the differences between social groups and different countries. The Irish rate of infant mortality was about 40 per cent below that of the English, and the Scottish rate was 20 per cent below. Living in the countryside was clearly healthier than living in a town, in terms of both greater expectation of life and lower death rates. See F. M. L. Thompson, *The Rise of Respectable Society: A Social History of Victorian Britain, 1830–1900* (1988).

infield / outfield system. A common response to the cultivation of poor soils in places where plenty of land was available. Such a system was used in many parts of the British Isles. The infield (which was referred to variously as 'croftland', 'inbyland', and 'mucked land') was the inner circle of land around a settlement, which was farmed in common (in *strips) on a rotation that included a *fallow every third year. The infield received all the *manure. Its area, layout, and method of cropping varied over time, and according to location and population density. The food and brewing grains were grown in this part of the system. The outfield lay in irregular patches beyond the settlement. It varied in size, according to local conditions, but was generally about three times as large as the infield. It was poorer in fertility and drainage. The outfield was also farmed in common, but less intensively. Parts would revert to natural grass and weeds for several years at a time to allow recovery. Before the outfield was ploughed, the cattle were folded on it during the nights of the summer months. Oats were then grown for two years, followed by another two years when the crop was left as straw, but the land was not manured. When yields declined, the outfield was allowed to regenerate for five years or more.

Beyond lay the moorland or other wastes, which were used for communal grazing. The system was abandoned first in England, though it survived in some areas, e.g. the *breckland of East Anglia, until the era of parliamentary *enclosure. It was in widespread use in the Highlands and Islands of Scotland and in Ireland, though the antiquity of the system there is doubtful due to lack of medieval references. The terms 'infield / outfield' were generally used in documents, though alternatives such as 'in-bye / out-bye' were sometimes preferred. See A. R. H. Baker and R. A. Butlin (eds.), *Studies of Field Systems in the British Isles* (1973).

infirmary. See HOSPITALS AND INFIRMARIES.

inflation. The three greatest periods of inflation have been those of 1180–1220, when food prices doubled or trebled, the late 15th to the mid-17th centuries, when prices rose four- or fivefold, and that of the later 20th century, when prices rose tenfold between 1960 and 1990. In between these periods have been centuries of steady prices, with slight rises and falls. Historians have little data for the earliest period of inflation, but are aware that the one which lasted throughout the 16th century and beyond was a European-wide phenomenon. See David M. Palliser, *The Age of Elizabeth: England Under the Later Tudors, 1547–1603* (1983), ch. 5. Inflation became a matter of public concern from the end of the reign of Henry VIII, but successive governments were unable to do much to stem the rise in prices. The reasons for inflation in this period are still debated by historians; the causes are generally recognized to be excessive demand for goods over supply, frequently accompanied by government tinkering with the money supply. Thus *population growth and quantities of gold and silver in circulation stood out as prime causes in the 16th century. It is difficult, however, to separate the social effects of inflation from those resulting from population growth and other changes.

influenza. Virulent forms of influenza have been amongst the greatest killers in the past. Influenza was probably the epidemic which *parish registers in the 1550s describe as the '*sweating sickness' or the 'new *ague', and which was particularly virulent in 1557–9. See E. A. Wrigley and R. S. Schofield, *The Population History of England, 1541–1871: A Reconstruction* (1981). The worst international outbreak of influenza ever recorded was that which killed millions of people immediately after the First World War.

Inghamites. A *Nonconformist sect founded in 1754 by Benjamin Ingham, after a break with the *Moravians. Its strength lay in Yorkshire and Lancashire.

ingle-nook. A seat in a recess by the fireplace.

ings. Low-lying meadows and pastures, liable to floods.

inheritance customs. The inheritance customs of the British Isles have varied considerably from region to region and over time. The basic distinction between *primogeniture and *partible inheritance was blurred by customs which ensured that younger children obtained a share of the patrimony and which enabled women to protect their own property and the interests of children by a previous marriage through formal or informal marriage settlements. See Cecily Howell, *Land, Family and Inheritance in Transition* (1983), J. Goody, E. P. Thompson, and J. Thirsk (eds.), *Family and Inheritance: Rural Society in Western Europe, 1200–1800* (1975), and Amy Louise Erickson, *Women and Property in Early Modern England* (1993). Property was subject to several different jurisdictions—the common law, ecclesiastical law, and manorial and borough customs—which did not take a united view. (See also GAVELKIND; BOROUGH ENGLISH; BARON AND FEME; FREEBENCH; HEIR; and ENTAIL. On administration, see WILLS; PROBATE COURTS; PROBATE ACCOUNTS; and ADMINISTRATION, LETTERS OF.) See also Barbara English and John Saville, *Strict Settlement: A Guide for Historians* (1983).

Agrarian historians have long been interested in inheritance customs. See the volumes of *The Agrarian History of England and Wales* and Joan Thirsk's influential article of 1961, 'Industries in the Countryside' (reprinted in her *The Rural Economy of England*, 1984), which demonstrated the importance of inheritance patterns in creating a labour force for rural industries in pastoral areas (see DUAL ECONOMY). Inheritance has also been a major interest of historians of the *family and society, particularly in the early modern period: see, for example, Ralph A. Houlbrooke, *The English Family, 1450–1700* (1984), ch. 9. It has become clear that studies of inheritance should not be concerned simply with bequests in wills, but with the transmission of property at various stages in the life-cycle, particularly when children married and set up home and upon retirement.

inhumation. Burial, as opposed to cremation.

inland revenue records. Housed at the *Public Record Office under IR. (See APPRENTICESHIP; INCOME TAX; TITHES; and VALUATION OFFICE.)

inn names and signs. In an illiterate age each tradesman found it necessary to advertise his business by hanging a sign outside his premises. Most of these have long since been abandoned, though the barber's pole and the three balls of the pawnbroker are remembered. Inns and even the lowliest pub have retained their signs and their distinctive names to allow for easy differentiation. Many of these names are medieval in origin, though they remained popular and were used by much later premises. Inn names have sometimes been changed, not just in recent years; the commercial and trade *directories of the late 18th and 19th centuries are useful for checking old names.

Many names are taken from the local landowner or from a badge or crest taken from his coat of *arms. In the Peak District, for example, the family at Haddon Hall is commemorated by the inn names: Duke of Rutland, Marquis of Granby (the title of the eldest son), and the Peacock, while the family at Chatsworth is linked to inns with such names as the Duke of Devonshire, the Cavendish Arms, and the Snake. Across the county boundary, the territory of another landowner is immediately signalled by the nine pubs in Sheffield that bear the name Duke of Norfolk. Elsewhere, the King's Arms, the Queen's Head, the Crown, the Prince of Wales, etc. may signify a crown estate or simply loyalty to the monarch.

Many pubs have the names of particular occupations, e.g. the Blacksmith's Arms, the Woolpack, or the Plough, or are connected with travel, e.g. the Coach and Horses. Some names have changed over time through a later misunderstanding of local speech, e.g. the Sheep Inn might have become the Ship. One local explanation of the strange name Flouch Inn on the south Yorkshire Pennines is that the sign proclaiming the Plough lost part of its first and fifth letters and the jocular literal pronunciation stuck. Some other inn names refer to legends, notably those concerning Robin Hood, or to such pagan figures as the *Green Man. See Barrie Cox, *English Inn and Tavern Names* (1994).

inns. Alan Everitt's essay 'The English Urban Inn', in his *Landscape and Community in England* (1985), accurately describes most of the previous literature on the subject as 'a wretched farrago of romantic legends, facetious humour and irritating errors'. Everitt's essay is the starting-point for modern studies.

Medieval England had some extensive and important inns, like the George at Glastonbury and the Angel at Grantham. One of the largest was the Chequers at Canterbury, which had 100 beds for pilgrims; the buildings have been subdivided but still stretch along the length of Mercer Lane. Inns increased in number with the growth of *population and trade in Eliz-

abethan times. By 1577 England had nearly 20,000 *alehouses, inns, and taverns, though only 2,000–3,000 of these were inns and most of those were no doubt small. During the 17th century facilities were greatly increased. (See the *Carriers' Cosmographie* (1637) and the account of guest beds and stabling in towns and villages throughout England and Wales in 1686 (*Public Record Office, WO 3/48) and the lists of innkeepers and alehouse keepers licenced at the '*brewster sessions' by *Justices of the Peace.) Inns grew in size and splendour, especially those situated alongside the major highways, during the coaching era. (See TRAVELLERS' ACCOUNTS.) Fine Georgian inns are found in thoroughfare towns such as Stamford, Grantham, Newark, and Bawtry on the Great North Road. Inns declined with the coming of the *railways and with the transfer of many of their functions to the new *town and county halls, *corn exchanges, auction rooms, banks, etc., and with the rise of *hotels. The great age of the inn lasted from the reign of Queen Elizabeth I to that of Queen Victoria.

The position of an inn was important in determining its success. A *market place site was attractive; most historic towns have *Georgian and older inns fronting on to the market square. But such a position was sometimes inconvenient for a large coaching inn, which needed space at the back for extra chambers and warehouses and a back entrance to enable waggons and coaches to enter and leave without turning or backing. Some of the finest coaching inns are therefore by the main road in extra-mural *suburbs. Many inns were no larger than village pubs, but a considerable number up and down the land were remarkable for their scale and splendour. The evidence of surviving buildings can be supplemented by probate *inventories of innkeepers and by *newspaper *advertisements. It was not uncommon for an 18th-century inn to have stabling for 40 or 50 horses; some had stables for well over 100 horses.

Inns did not simply provide accommodation for visitors: they were often the social, intellectual, and commercial centres of the neighbourhood. The principal urban landlords were important figures with flair and the ability to organize activities and events. Before the building of public halls, inns were centres of local administration and politics, the places where feasts and banquets were held, and where the county and urban *gentry met for social and intellectual activities, ranging from *cock fighting to lectures and debates. Inns were also centres of commercial activity, where corn was sold by sample, contracts drawn up, *credit provided, and rooms let out for book auctions and sales of specialist wares or goods brought by *carriers. Some were posting inns, or stages where the horses that pulled coaches or waggons were changed, or were regular stops for *drovers. Some landlords were socially and geographically mobile, always on the look-out for a better position; others established dynasties that remained influential in urban society for two or three generations or more.

Inns of Court. Gray's Inn, Lincoln's Inn, and the Inner and Middle Temple are the surviving Inns of Court in London at which barristers-at-law have been trained since the Middle Ages. The admission books record the name and date of entry of a student, together with the name, status, and residence of his father. These have been printed as Inner Temple, *Students Admitted to the Inner Temple, 1547–1660* (1877), Lincoln's Inn, *Records of the Honorable Society of Lincoln's Inn (Admissions, 1420–1893)* (1893), Gray's Inn, *Register of Admissions to Gray's Inn, 1521–1889* (1889), and Middle Temple, *Register of Admissions* (1949).

inoculation against *smallpox was practised in the eastern Mediterranean and parts of Asia during the 17th century and was first reported in England in 1701. It received widespread publicity after Lady Mary Wortley-Montagu (who had suffered from smallpox) inoculated her son in 1716 while in Turkey. Inoculation with a milder form of the disease was the favoured method of protection until *vaccination with cow-pox was introduced at the end of the 18th century.

Inquisition of the Ninths (1341). An assessment of the agricultural value of each parish in most of the area covered by 27 English counties, published by the Record Commission as *Nonarum Inquisitiones in Curia Saccarii* (1807). Local juries had to explain the discrepancies between the valuation and that of Pope Nicholas of 1291. Their comments refer to land no longer cultivated, the lack of seed, flooding, etc. See A. R. H. Baker, 'Evidence in the "Nonarum Inquisitiones" of Contracting Arable Land in England during the early 14th century', *Economic History Review*, 2nd ser., 19/3 (1966).

inquisition post mortem. An inquest held by the king's *escheator or his deputy after the death of a *tenant-in-chief of the Crown to establish the extent of the estate and to confirm the rightful heir. A jury of 12 local men of high repute gave information under oath. Records

from the 13th century onwards are kept at the *Public Record Office, under C 133–142 and E 149–150. *Calendars and indexes are available for many reigns, and some county record societies have published detailed calendars. Such records survive in large numbers, especially for the period 1270–1350. They are arranged to a fairly consistent format, and as well as showing what estates were held in chief by an individual, they can be used to illustrate broad contrasts between places and regions.

Institute of Heraldic and Genealogical Studies. Housed at Northgate, Canterbury, the institute was founded in 1961 to provide study, research, and training facilities in family history. It has a large library, and publishes aids to study and the journal *Family History*.

Institute of Historical Research. A research institute of the University of London, on the ground floor of the Senate House in Malet Street, WC1. It houses a substantial Local History library (with national coverage) and the headquarters of the *Victoria County History*.

intakes. Irregular-shaped fields enclosed from the edges of *commons.

intercommoning. A system whereby several settlements around a *marsh, *wood, or *moor had rights on the *commons within that area. Where the boundaries of several parishes meet at a point, it is worth looking for evidence of past intercommoning practices.

International Genealogical Index. This microfiche and CD-ROM index of births / baptisms and marriages covering most of the world has been compiled by amateur researchers who are members of the Church of Jesus Christ of the Latter Day Saints (the *Mormon Church). The entries from Britain comprise baptism and marriage entries in *parish and *Nonconformist registers (including those kept at the *Public Record Office) and miscellaneous other sources up to 1885. The IGI has been made widely available for public consultation in *record offices and public libraries, and in the record-searching facilities created by the Mormons in various parts of the country. Many *family history societies have copies for their members to consult. The index is constantly growing and new editions are published at frequent intervals. The entries are arranged under (pre-1974) counties, in alphabetical order of surnames, and then of forenames (in chronological order). There are separate indexes for the Channel Islands and the Isle of Man. Wales and Monmouth are indexed not just by surname but (separately) by forename, to take account of the 'ap' system of naming. A typical entry gives name, name of parents (for baptism) or spouse (marriage), type of event (birth, baptism, marriage), date of event, and place of event. The coverage is uneven, largely because some Anglican bishops or incumbents are hostile to the idea that ancestors identified by Mormon believers may be baptized by proxy and received posthumously into membership of the Mormon Church. The index is a useful starting-point for genealogical research, but entries should be checked against the originals.

interred. Cremated, rather than buried.

Interregnum. The period between the execution of Charles I in 1649 and the restoration of his son, Charles II, in 1660.

intestate. A person who died without making a *will. The next-of-kin had to apply to a *probate court for letters of *administration to distribute the deceased's estate.

inventories, probate. From the early 16th century to the mid-18th century (and in some districts until much later) it was the custom of the *ecclesiastical courts that proved *wills in England and Wales to insist that the executors should appoint three or four local men to make 'a true and perfect inventory' of the personal estate of the deceased, so that any dispute over the will could be more easily settled. The inventory was filed with the will, or where a person died intestate with the letters of *administration. The appraisers, or valuers, swore a solemn oath that they would carry out their duty truthfully. They proceeded to list every item of furniture and utensils in the house, then they noted the livestock, crops, and equipment or the tools and finished goods in workshops, and whatever else was movable and therefore constituted personal estate, as distinct from real estate, i.e. the value of the house, land, etc. The small items that were too troublesome to list were given a nominal value under such terms as 'huslement'.

Tens of thousands of probate inventories survive for most parts of England and Wales. They are mostly kept with wills at the *record offices of the ancient dioceses, except for the period 1653-60, when all wills and inventories for England and Wales were proved at the *Prerogative Court of Canterbury; these are now kept at the *Public Record Office under PROB 3. (See also PECULIAR JURISDICTION.)

Various collections of inventories have been published. See, for example, Michael Havinden (ed.), *Household and Farm Inventories in Oxfordshire, 1550–1590* (1965), Barrie Trinder and Jeff Cox, *Yeomen and Colliers in Telford* (1980), J. S. Moore (ed.), *The Goods and Chattels of Our Forefathers* (1976), F. W. Steer (ed.), *Farm and Cottage Inventories of Mid-Essex, 1635–1749* (1969), Lionel Munby (ed.), *Life and Death in King's Langley: Wills and Inventories, 1488–1659* (1981), and J. M. Bestall and D. V. Fowkes (eds.), *Chesterfield Wills and Inventories, 1521–1603* (1977). These, and the various published analyses of inventories, are listed in Mark Overton, *A Bibliography of British Probate Inventories* (1983).

Many of the words used by the appraisers are archaic terms, often of a technical kind, and frequently employing dialect forms. Little work has yet been done on their value as a source for the study of regional speech. (See DIALECTS AND ACCENTS.) See Edmund Weiner, 'Local History and Lexicography', *The Local Historian*, 24/3 (1994). Helpful glossaries include Rosemary Milward, *A Glossary of Household and Farming Terms from Sixteenth-Century Probate Inventories* (1977), and Susan Needham, *A Glossary for East Yorkshire and North Lincolnshire Probate Inventories* (1984). The difficulties of reading documents that use archaic language are compounded by eccentric spellings, lack of punctuation, and indiscriminate use of capital letters. Nevertheless, probate inventories are a rewarding source of historical information, both at an individual level and when used in bulk. For the family historian they are of great interest when they list the personal estate, room by room, of an ancestor, particularly when the building survives.

Probate inventories were first studied in bulk by agricultural historians. The study of farming history in the early modern period has been transformed by the use made of inventories. The pioneering studies were W. G. *Hoskins, *Essays in Leicestershire History* (1950), and Joan Thirsk, *Fenland Farming in the Sixteenth Century* (1953). Thousands of inventories were analysed for *The *Agrarian History of England and Wales*, vol. iv, *1500–1640* (1967) and vol. v, *1640–1750* (1985) in order to identify the farming systems of different agricultural regions. When used in large numbers inventories give a clear indication of whether farmers followed a mixed form of husbandry or whether they specialized in, say, *dairying. See, for example, P. R. Edwards, 'The Development of Dairy Farming on the North Shropshire Plain in the Seventeenth Century', *Midland History*, 3 (1978). They also provide statistical information about crop yields: see Mark Overton, 'Estimating Crop Yields from Probate Inventories: The Case of East Anglia', *Journal of Economic His-*

tory, 39 (1979) and P. Glennie, 'Continuity and Change in Hertfordshire Agriculture, 1550–1700: II—Trends in Crop Yields and Their Determinants', *Agricultural History Review*, 36/2 (1988), which demonstrates that post-*Restoration crop yields improved dramatically. The introduction of new crops, such as *turnips, *clover, or *potatoes, can also be determined within a decade or two by references in inventories.

Inventories have also been used with profit for the study of *vernacular architecture. Some inventories can be identified with standing buildings and used for determining the uses to which rooms were put, or for showing how a building has been altered over time. Inventories have been used in bulk to demonstrate how living standards varied not only over time but from region to region, and between different social groups within a particular locality. The pioneering work was M. W. Barley, *The English Farmhouse and Cottage* (1961). Amongst later studies, see in particular Barry Harrison and Barbara Hutton, *Vernacular Houses in North Yorkshire and Cleveland* (1984), and N. W. Alcock, *People at Home: Living in a Warwickshire Village, 1500–1800* (1993), both of which combine the surveying of surviving buildings with the study of inventories and other documents, such as *hearth tax returns and *estate records. For a detailed analysis of rooms in urban houses, see U. Priestley, P. J. Corfield, and H. Sutermeister, 'Rooms and Room-Use in Norwich Housing, 1580–1730', *Post-Medieval Archaeology*, 16 (1982).

Probate inventories are an unrivalled source for the study of furnishings and for demonstrating the rise in standards of domestic comfort. See Margaret Spufford, *The Great Reclothing of Rural England: Petty Chapmen and Their Wares in the Seventeenth Century* (1984), and Lorna M. Weatherill, *Consumer Behaviour and Material Culture in Britain, 1660–1760* (1988). See also U. Priestley and A. Fenner, *Shops and Shopkeepers in Norwich, 1660–1730* (1985), and B. A. Holderness, 'Credit in a Rural Community, 1600–1800: Some Neglected Aspects of Probate Inventories', *Midland History*, 3 (1976), which show how inventories reveal many aspects of the history of commerce (see INDUSTRY AND TRADE).

The writers of histories of early modern rural communities, starting with W. G. Hoskins, *The Midland Peasant: The Economic and Social History of a Leicestershire Village* (1957), have used probate inventories to great effect, but urban historians have not used them to the same extent. However, see Alan D. Dyer, *The City of Worcester in the Sixteenth Century* (1973), and David Hey, *The Fiery Blades of Hallamshire: Sheffield and Its Neighbourhood, 1660–1740* (1991), which makes particular use of cutlers' inventories. The full potential of craftsmen's inventories has not yet been realized in the same way as farmers' inventories have for agricultural history.

There are many problems to be faced in interpreting individual inventories and in the statistical analysis of inventories in bulk. The major omission is that of real estate, whether *freehold or *copyhold property. A person whose personal estate was modest may have been living in retirement, having already passed on most of his estate. A widow's property or a wife's dowry may not be included in a man's inventory. Some goods were omitted for legal reasons. The other major item which is often omitted is that of the debts which were owed by the deceased. See Margaret Spufford, 'The Limitations of the Probate Inventory' in John Chartres and David Hey (eds.), *English Rural Society, 1500–1800: Essays in Honour of Joan Thirsk* (1990).

For the different system in Scotland, see Cecil Sinclair, *Tracing Your Scottish Ancestors: A Guide to Ancestry Research in the Scottish Record Office* (1990). The practice of attaching inventories of personal estate to wills was not usual in Ireland.

Irish emigration. The population of Ireland rose from over 4 million in 1781 to over 8 million in 1841. Long before the *famine years of the late 1840s Irish men and women emigrated to England and south Wales, and to a lesser extent to Scotland, in search of work. Both men and women were conspicuous as seasonal harvesters in many rural parts of the 'mainland'. The Irish formed a significant proportion of the *navvies who constructed the *canals and *railways. Numbers of emigrants increased after the formation of the *United Kingdom in 1801; the 1841 *census returns for England and Wales listed 289,404 Irish-born residents, and that for Scotland recorded 126,321.

The famine years from 1846 onwards saw massive emigration from Ireland to the rest of the United Kingdom and to the United States of *America. By 1870 the Irish formed about one-third of the foreign-born population of the USA. The number of Irish-born residents in England and Wales rose to 601,634 in 1861; in Scotland the number peaked 20 years later at 218,745. Of course, these figures do not include the children of Irish-born parents who had emigrated earlier. The total number of Irish immigrants to England, Scotland, and Wales may eventually have reached 1 million. By the end of the 19th century the population of Ireland had dropped to half the size it had attained by 1851. The favourite destinations for those who crossed the Irish Sea were London, Liverpool and other Lancashire towns, and parts of Lowland Scotland. By 1851 many Lancashire towns had large numbers of Irish; 22 per cent of Liverpool's population and 13 per cent of Manchester's was Irish-born. Ulster families tended to head further north: about 1,000 immigrants a week arrived in Glasgow in 1848. Although the number of Irish who chose England or Wales was two or three times as great as those who preferred Scotland, the lower population of Scotland meant that the proportion of immigrants was higher; it has been estimated that in 1851 Irish-born inhabitants formed 7.9 per cent of the population of Scotland, compared with 2.9 per cent of England and Wales. In western towns like Glasgow, Paisley, and Kilmarnock the Irish-born amounted to between 10 and 18 per cent of the population, and in the east Dundee had 18 per cent.

These Irish immigrants met with suspicion and often downright hostility. See Alan O'Day (ed.), *H. Heinrick: A Survey of the Irish in England, 1872* (1990). The Irish were poor, unskilled, often regarded as inferior colonials, and usually *Roman Catholic. Irish demands for Home Rule increased tensions. Moreover, the immigrants usually clustered in the poorer districts of their adopted towns, with smaller groupings based on their counties of origin. They were a clearly defined group that could be subject to violent attacks, as happened in Glasgow, Partick and other Scottish towns, at Tredegar in south Wales, and in Liverpool and other parts of Lancashire. In 1871 the Census of Scotland commented: 'It is painful to contemplate what may be the ultimate effect of this Irish immigration on the morals and habits of the people and on the future prospects of the country.' Most Irish families remained poor and lived in squalid conditions. The 1881 census revealed that 82 per cent of Irish-born immigrants were *day labourers. See Roger Swift and Sheriden Gilley (eds.), *The Irish in the Victorian City* (1985) and *The Irish in Britain, 1815–1939* (1989), L. H. Lees, *Exiles of Erin: Irish Migrants in Victorian London* (1979), J. A. Jackson, *The Irish in Britain* (1963), J. Handley, *The Irish in Modern Scotland* (1947), and S. Gilley, 'English Attitudes to the Irish in England,

1789–1900' in Colin Holmes (ed.), *Immigrants and Minorities in British Society* (1978).

The Irish continued to arrive in considerable numbers during the later decades of the 19th century, particularly in the late 1870s and 1880s when farming was particularly depressed. The creation of an independent southern Ireland in 1922 and the long depression in Great Britain during the inter-war years reduced the flow of Irish immigrants, but after the Second World War and the revival of the British economy in the 1950s and 1960s large numbers of new Irish settlers arrived in search of work. In 1969 it was estimated that there were c.750,000 immigrants from the Irish Republic in the United Kingdom, as well as many thousands from Northern Ireland. These were larger numbers than at any time since the 1880s. The 'New Irish' did not head for the same towns as before, for Liverpool and Glasgow were depressed; instead they headed for London (especially Kilburn), Bristol, and Birmingham.

Irish local and family history. Despite its small size, Ireland is a remarkably variegated country, where the fusion of a diverse environmental base and a complex array of historical experiences has generated a variety of regions, each with a distinctive historical trajectory and inherited character. Because Ireland has only slowly become urbanized and industrialized, and because of the enduring role of its historical experience at the centre of its cultural and political life, Irish people remain intensely territorial. The sense of place and of *kinship remains strong, reflected not least in a warm interest in local and family history. Currently, both of these are in a thriving state, helped by increasing freedom of access to sources, new technologies in information gathering and retrieval, and a renewed interest in both the diaspora and the university world. This resurgence has intersected with the vibrant consciousness of local history within specific communities, which has been transmitted traditionally. The sense of place remains strong and is reflected in the diverse regional styles of traditional and popular music, in painting, and in literature. Irish writers' work remains embedded in their regions—for example, Seamus Heaney in Derry, Brian Friel in Donegal, John McGahern in Leitrim, Roddy Doyle in Dublin.

Among the earliest strands of Irish literature, originating in the early medieval period, the *dinnseanchas* (the lore of places) had an honoured role, as had genealogical learning. The ligatures of myth that tied lords to their lands and people to their places was highly valued and transmitted (albeit embellished and customized to fit current exigencies) from generation to generation. The Gaelic manuscripts recording the *dinnseanchas* contain some of the earlier place-descriptive material in the European literary tradition. As in Europe generally, the 18th-century Enlightenment facilitated a quickening interest in national culture in Ireland. The Royal Irish Academy, founded in 1785, became the focus of this interest, sponsoring the first serious publishing programme in the English language on Irish history, centred especially on Irish antiquities and linguistics. Special emphasis was laid on proving the distinctiveness of pre-conquest Ireland.

In the 19th century, as cultural nationalism developed, and as separatist politics strengthened in Ireland, this initial scholarly emphasis became heavily politicized; energies were devoted both to extolling the pre-eminent cultural values of pre-conquest Ireland (as an implicit—and frequently explicit—rebuke to the ravages of English colonialism), and in an effort to recover those values as the basis for the construction of a distinctive Irish identity in the modern world. Therefore, within this colonial context, the Irish past never entered totally into history, because it never passed totally out of politics.

The 19th-century flurry of activity did, however, encourage the establishment of libraries, the publication of source materials (especially in translation), and the detailed mapping, recording, and collection of antiquities. By the 1870s, a national museum, a national library, and a record office had all been established, and Ireland also possessed a precociously detailed coverage in maps of the 1830s and 1840s by the *Ordnance Survey. This project also generated some superb antiquarian scholars, who developed an unrivalled knowledge about the local history of Ireland—notably John O'Donovan, Eugene O'Curry, and George Petrie. The O'Donovan-inspired Ordnance Survey *Namebooks* and *Letterbooks*, arranged by county, remain one of the outstanding sources of Irish local history, containing a cornucopia of material collected just before the cataclysmic catastrophe of the Great Irish *famine of the 1840s.

With these new scholarly resources and libraries at their backs, and inspired by the *Victoria County History* series in England, the last quarter of the 19th century and the first decades of the 20th century witnessed the first serious efforts to write sustained Irish local histories. Pre-eminent among these was Philip

Hore's six-volume history of County Wexford (1901–11); W. P. Burke's *Clonmel* (1907); John Gleeson's *Ely O'Carroll* (north Tipperary and south Offaly), and the histories of County Monaghan by E. P. Shirley and D. C. Rushe. This period also saw the foundation of the first local history societies and publication of journals, among the best of which were the *Waterford and Southeast of Ireland*, the *Louth*, the *Cork*, and the *Kildare*. These were frequently founded and financed by leading figures from the Anglo-Irish gentry, like Walter Fitzgerald, an indefatigable researcher on County Kildare. As political tensions increased, and as Irish history once more began to be seen in adversarial British–Irish and Protestant–Catholic terms, a faith-and-fatherland approach to local history was promoted by Catholic nationalists. This led to a wave of Catholic diocesan histories, written by priests or zealous laymen. Among the best of these were Carrigan's four volumes on Ossory, Healy's three volumes on Meath, Comerford's three volumes on Kildare and Leighlin, Power on Waterford and Lismore, and Grattan—Flood on Ferns.

Whether written from an Anglo-Irish or Catholic-nationalist perspective, all these books and journals were soon to acquire an added veneer of importance, because of the destruction of the Irish Record Office in 1922 during the Civil War, and with it the annihilation of the richest sources of Irish history from the medieval period onwards. Antiquarians working prior to 1922 had transcribed, consulted, or published some of these documents, and their books or papers are now the sole source for them. In Ireland, therefore, these early local histories have a permanent significance as a primary source: the papers of Hore, Carrigan, and Burke are equally important.

With the creation of two separate states in Ireland after 1921, and with the continuing political difficulties in the Anglo-Irish relationship, the writing of Irish history assumed a heavily politicized and nationalist dimension; the emphasis shifted to creating an old history for a new state, to moulding a shared nationalist inheritance which would bind its citizenry together. In these circumstances, little encouragement was given in government, education, or professional circles to local history. In response to the resurgence of political violence in Northern Ireland after 1969, a new wave of Irish history writing—known as revisionism—gained popularity. Revisionism attacked the nationalist bias of the prevailing historical consensus in Ireland, accusing it of lending legitimacy to those who used violence as a political weapon. It tried to strip nationalist emotion out of history writing through a clinical, detached professionalism; it attempted to orient Ireland towards a modernist Europeanist identity, away from what revisionism saw as its unhealthy obsession with the past, place, territory, identity, and belonging. In this sense, revisionism was opposed to local history, which it saw as force-feeding the atavistic appetite of tradition, whose emphasis on inherited rather than acquired identities did not suit the modernist project in Ireland. Local history, the revisionists argued, was inherently emotional and conservative in an Irish context, and accordingly should be abandoned in favour of a rational and progressive stance.

However, this curious complicity between nationalist and revisionist history in writing out the region and ignoring local history has not been entirely successful in suppressing them. The emphasis on a historical narrative in which high politics has priority, agreed on by both the nationalist and the revisionist projects, has been increasingly challenged by regional and local perspectives, where social, cultural, and economic issues are set equally centre-stage with politics. This post-nationalist, post-revisionist perspective has turned once more towards local studies, which contest the centralized orthodoxy in the name of a more genuine pluralism. In these circumstances, local history has been a growth area in both quantitative and qualitative terms. One can see how the disintegration of the prevailing historical consensus, the pace and direction of cultural change, the agonized questionings generated by the northern crisis, all worked together to clear spaces which local history could inhabit. Local history could provide an anchoring free of the freight of the politics of identity. With its diverse micro-narratives, local history acted as a defence mechanism against both the ruthless totalizing claims of historical meta-narratives and against the rootless blandness of mainstream Anglo-American consumer culture.

In practical terms, the strident and increasingly repetitive revisionist debate had become locked into the stereotyping of national identities and into exclusivist claims on ownership of the past. This has encouraged some to seek alternative modes of understanding, which step outside the narrow ground of politics and a politicized historiography. The historians' monopoly of the past has been implicitly challenged at both the academic and the popular level. Within mainstream academic history, one can also see evidence of disaffection from the imperialist claims of political history. Those

marginalized within these parameters of power—women, minorities, the undocumented—have begun to undermine this conservative bastion. The new local history looks at histories, not history, at real people in specific contexts, not at dehumanized abstractions; it explores the close-up perspective, not the potentially misleading national panorama. It tries to recapture the diverse histories of past generations as they lived and loved, worked and played, in small places through time. In sensitive hands, local history probes the domestic interior of the past, not its public political façade. By reconnecting present communities to their past, local history takes its place alongside literature, music, architecture, and environment as an integral element in a vibrant culture, a living stream flowing from older fountains. Precisely by remaining faithful to the local and familiar, the best local history attaches us to the authentic, and therefore to the universal. Framed in these perspectives, the cultural significance of local history becomes apparent. Local history helps nurture the sense of a shared historical experience which is pivotal to a sense of place and ultimately of community. Nowhere is this more highly visible and insistent than in the Irish context.

These developments impacted on the practice of local history at ground level. A new self-confidence and professionalism became evident in the 1980s, marked by the creation of federations of local history societies in both Northern Ireland and the Republic of Ireland. There was an efflorescence of new societies and journals, and a flood of books, better written and technically well produced. Archives and universities became more aware of the needs of local history, making its practice much easier. While a national phenomenon, the proliferation of new local history societies was most in evidence in the hinterland of the big cities—Dublin, Belfast, and Cork—where there has been a fruitful alliance of native and newcomer. The presence of committed individuals within local communities provided the necessary dynamism and organizational energy to give coherence and continuity to the new interest. Examples would include Margaret Phelan in Kilkenny, Noel Ross and Moira Corcoran in Louth, Jack Magee in Down, Michael Byrne in Tullamore, George Cunningham in Roscrea, Victor Hadden in Carlow, Brian Trainor in Belfast, George Hadden and Nicholas Furlong in Wexford, Muiris Ó Rochain in Clare, and Joe O'Halloran in Galway. The creation of local *museums was another facet of this dynamism, of which the superb restoration of Rothe House by the Kilkenny Archaeological Society might be the best example. New journals were another development, adding to the consistent excellence of the long-established *Cork* and *Louth* journals, *Seanchas Ardhmhacha* (Armagh), and the *Clogher Record* (Monaghan, Fermanagh, Tyrone). Among the best of the new journals were the *Kerry* (1968), *Wexford* (1968), and *Tipperary* (1989). While the county and diocesan journals have in general maintained a high standard, there has been a tremendous proliferation of parish, town, and community-based journals and newsletters, facilitated by desk-top publishing enterprises. This new wave has not always attained the high quality of the bigger journals, although some (those produced in Westport and Bandon, for example) are very good, and all contain at least some material that is valuable.

Another development has been the creation of umbrella bodies which link the work done by the different societies, or which provide for dialogue between professional and local historians. Both the Federation of Ulster Local History Societies (based at the Institute of Irish Studies, Queens University, Belfast), and the Federation of Local History Societies (based at Rothe House, Kilkenny) produce useful newsletters, which list member societies and their activities; they also act in a co-ordinating, policy-setting, and monitoring capacity. The Group for the Study of Irish Historic Settlement (established 1971) has also maintained a dialogue with local history societies, through an annual rotating conference. A further distinctively Irish mode of exchange has been the phenomenally successful Summer Schools; notable among those which encourage the input of local historians are the Merriman (Clare), Parnell (Wicklow), Hewitt (Antrim), Carleton (Fermanagh), Kickham (Tipperary), and the Norman Connection (Wexford). An even more recent development was the establishment in 1993 of a very successful popular illustrated magazine, *History Ireland*, which acts as a broker between professional and local historians. It also has detailed listings of the activities of local societies, and a sources section designed to be helpful to local historians. As yet, however, despite this ferment, local history does not have a secure footing in the universities, with the exception of a diploma course in St Patrick's College, Maynooth, and various extramural activities. This is now one of the biggest unresolved issues confronting local history practitioners in Ireland.

As tourism became increasingly a major industry and as heritage was recognized and marketed as a crucial component of Ireland's appeal, local history, heritage, and genealogy were no longer seen as esoteric or trivial by policy-makers, but as marketable resources. As unemployment rose, schemes were developed which trained young people in computer skills by processing historical and genealogical data. These developments helped to create a more positive profile for local history among policy-makers and administrators. In Northern Ireland, in the context of a divided society, local history was seen by educators as a valuable non-contentious meeting ground for the two traditions, more conductive to creating a healthy sense of a shared past than an adversarial political history, with its insistent emphasis on divisive issues. Thus, in Northern Ireland, local history has been incorporated into school curricula, notably in the Education for Mutual Understanding programme.

Professional historians have also turned to local and regional history to test and subvert the validity of national generalizations. The pioneer here has been Louis Cullen of Trinity College, Dublin, the most respected and prolific historian of his generation; his 1981 book *The Emergence of Modern Ireland* showed in a sophisticated way how local, regional, and national levels interacted in the evolution of Irish society, culture, and politics. Cullen has subsequently applied similar regional approaches to the 1798 Rebellion, whose cumulative effect has been to demolish the received wisdom about this event. Another pioneer was James Donnelly, both in his landmark book *The Land and the People of Nineteenth-Century Cork* (1975), and his subsequent work on popular protest. In Ulster, W. H. Crawford's detailed studies of economy and society have always insisted on the primacy of local contexts; over four decades in different institutions, he has championed the role of local history. Other leading scholars who have accomplished breakthroughs in local history, or been especially alert to the significance of regional pespectives in understanding Irish history, include Kevin O'Neill on pre-famine demography, David Fitzpatrick on local politics, David Dickson on economic history, and David Miller on social history. Another by-product of this strand of scholarship has been the publication of excellent monographs on individual communities or regions; the best include Thomas Power's on Tipperary, Donald Jordan on Mayo, and Robert Scally on Ballykilcline in Roscommon. There have also been some helpful explications of sources and their utilization in local contexts; good examples are

Nicholas Canny on the 1641 depositions, Willie Smyth on the 1660 poll tax, Raymond Gillespie on estate rentals, Patrick Hickey on famine records, and John Mannion on emigration.

Other co-operative ventures in local history also emerged in the 1980s, of which the most important was the *Irish County History* series, under the auspices of William Nolan and Kevin Whelan. These multi-authored, multi-disciplinary volumes assembled a wide-ranging panel of about 20 contributors to deal with the history of individual counties from prehistory to the modern period. The teams involved a mixture of local, national, and international experts and the resulting volumes offer a state of the art view of Irish local history, as well as an invaluable source guide (running to 2,000 footnotes per volume.) To date, Tipperary (1985), Wexford (1987), Kilkenny (1990), Dublin (1992), Waterford (1993), Cork (1993), and Wicklow (1994) have been published. Two smaller volumes on Longford and Cavan have been published under the direction of Raymond Gillespie.

Another significant co-operative venture has been the publication of the 31 volumes of the Ordnance Survey Memoirs (1830–39) by the Institute of Irish Studies in Belfast, edited by Angelique Day and Patrick MacWilliam. Covering large parts of Armagh, Antrim, Derry, Down, Tyrone, and Fermanagh, these memoirs provide a freeze-frame view of Ulster on the eve of the Great Famine and are of paramount importance as a local history source.

Beyond history, other disciplines have increasingly applied local perspectives in their interrogation of the Irish past. *Folklore has been intensely aware of its value, as seen, for example, in the work of Caoimhín Ó Danachair, Alan Gailey, Philip Robinson, and Henry Glassie. Glassie's intelligent piece of Fermanagh-based social anthropology, *Passing the Time* (1982), is already a classic, noted for its respectful treatment of *oral history, so often derided by revisionist historians. Ireland possesses an unusually rich oral history record, in the three-million-plus pages of the Irish Folklore Commission Archive at University College, Dublin, which contains a wealth of material systematically collected since the 1930s. As a discipline, folklore has also engaged with the material base of Irish local life, as for example in the superb books by Alan Gailey on rural housing and Claudia Kinmonth on furniture. The Ulster Folk and Transport Museum at Cultra outside Belfast is one of Ireland's best interpretative facilities, whose open-air exhib-

its, at once attractive and authoritative, are welded to an impressive scholarly base.

Archaeology has also been very active at the local level. Its sharpening profile in the popular consciousness has much to do with the fact that wedge tombs and *Beaker folk inhabit a world beyond history, and therefore beyond politics, and yet they also allow for a sense of continuity and antiquity. One result of this new surge of interest in archaeology has been the compilation of detailed regional and county surveys—notably on Ikerrin (Tipperary), the Dingle peninsula, and Donegal. These have been joined by computerized databases, compiled by the Sites and Monuments Records Office under the direction of Geraldine Stout and Michael Gibbons; the Office of Public Works has also published a series of county inventories (Louth, Meath, Monaghan, Carlow, Cork) under the editorship of David Sweetman. The successful launch of an illustrated magazine, *Archaeology Ireland*, in 1987 marked this new popular awareness of archaeology. This was signalled also in the heritage industry, which moved to 'interpret' spectacular excavated sites like the fossilized landscape under the peat bog at Céide in Mayo, the great Boyne Valley megaliths, and the bog trackways at Corlea in Longford. Archaeological theme parks have been built at Ferrycarrig (Wexford), Cragganowen (Clare), and at the Ulster American Folk Park near Omagh.

As with archaeology, the rise of environmental history provided a different lens for looking at the past, a lens whose perspective was longer and radically different from those used in history. The inanimate world of stone and pollen, bog and tree, offered a sympathetic engagement with a past beyond political contestation, of an enduring bedrock beneath history, a silent witness under the competitive cacophony of historical voices. This Irish movement gained impetus from the deepening global environmental consciousness, offering the possibility of an ethic at once scrupulously local and yet engaged with the wider world, securely rooted in the present and yet with a satisfying sense of age-old continuities in time and tide, bird and blossom, rock and rain. Such engagements were lovingly rendered in fine books like Frank Mitchell's *The Irish Landscape* (1976), Tim Robinson's *Stones of Aran* (1986), and in John Feehan's television series.

Besides environmental and archaeological perspectives, a further impetus for growth in local history came from historical geography. In a curious way, both nationalist and revisionist projects in Irish history have operated within an essentially English historiographical tradition. Both have remained hermetically sealed from developments in the non-anglophone world, notably that in France which hosted arguably the most significant experiments in history-writing in the second half of the 20th century, led by the Annales school and the historians F. Braudel and E. Le Roy Ladurie. In a roundabout way, historical geography has managed to smuggle some of these French concepts into Ireland. Its two most significant practitioners, Estyn *Evans in Queens and Tom Jones Hughes in U.C.D., were both trained in the French *geographie humaine* with its emphasis on the dialectic between history and environment, between *la longue durée* and *les evénements*, and on the interpretation of the cultural landscape as a text to be decoded. In this perspective, existing cultural landscapes are seen as the cumulative creation of centuries of experience in which human desires and needs have transformed the natural environment. They are communal archives, *palimpsests created by the sedimentation of cultural experience through time. The cultural landscape is, therefore, potentially a democratic document from which can be recovered the history of the undocumented. In this approach, history is reconstructed by seeing the landscape through the eyes of those who made it. This generates a broader sense of the past than can be derived from the circumscribed and narrow perspective of documents in isolation. Under the tutelage of Evans and Jones Hughes, landscape became a braille over whose surface the geographical mind passed the sympathetic tips of its understanding to arrive at a reading of what lay behind the landscape. Such perspectives succeeded in revealing a rich mosaic of regional diversity, even in the relatively confined space of a small island. Some of the best writing in Irish local history has come from the historical geographers. Estyn Evans's *Mourne County* (1951) is the classic example and is a compelling expression of how a well-developed sense of place can enrich the historical consciousness. Noticeable recent practicioners include Willie Smyth (on Tipperary), Patrick O'Connor (on Limerick), and Paddy Duffy (on Monaghan).

One area in which the Irish local historian is well served is in guides to the source material. The bible remains the two multi-volume compilations originated by R. J. Hayes. His *Manuscript Sources for the History of Irish Civilisation* was published in 11 volumes, in 1965, with a three-volume supplement in 1975. This lists in meticulous detail, under person, subject, and place headings, material of Irish interest both in the main Irish repositories and in those overseas. A companion set, *Periodical Sources for the History of Irish Civilisation*, appeared in 1970 and performed a similar function for material appearing in Irish journals. While both compilations urgently require updating to incorporate the wealth of new material which has been accessioned or written since 1970, they still remain the essential starting-point for research in Irish local history. For example, *Periodical Sources* lists 2,500 entries for County Antrim (including Belfast), 1,150 for Galway city and county, 600 for County Wexford, and 500 for County Armagh. To keep abreast of more recent publications, one should consult the comprehensive annual bibliography published in the journal *Irish Economic and Social History*. For manuscript material, the only available source is the annual reports of the major repositories—the National Library, National Archive, and Public Record Office of Northern Ireland. As a guide to the archives and the sources, the standard book is William Nolan's *Tracing the Past. Sources for Local Studies in the Republic of Ireland* (1985).

More detailed accounts exist for particular archives; especially useful are Margaret Griffith's *A Short Guide to the Public Record Office* (National Archives since 1985) (1964); Peter Fox (ed.), *Treasures of Trinity College Library* (1986), and Noel Kissane (ed.), *Treasures of the National Library of Ireland* (1994). The National Library and the National Archives have also produced leaflets which list in summary fashion material in their collection which is likely to be of interest to local historians. There are also guides to special collections, such as Rena Lohan's splendid guide to the Board of Works material recently deposited in the National Archives. Among its one million books and 40,000 manuscripts, the material in the National Library most useful to local historians includes microfilm of Catholic *parish registers; estate papers and maps; *parliamentary papers; prints and drawings; tour books; and three principal photographic collections—the Lawrence (40,000 negatives, 1880–1914), the Eason (4,000 negatives, 1900–40), and Valentine collections (3,000 negatives, 1903–60). The National Archives has detailed records of education, the great Irish famine of the 1840s, the 1901 and 1911 manuscript censuses, Tithe Applotment Books (1820s–1830), *Church of Ireland parish registers; will abstracts, police records, and prison registers. Trinity College, Dublin has the Congested Districts Boards' *Baseline Reports* (1890–4); the 1641 depositions; court-martial records of 1798; 1,600 broadsheet *ballads; 200 Gaelic manuscripts, and a vast array of Irish-interest material in its 3 million volumes, including 80,000 journal titles.

Other archives which contain material of interest to the local historian include the *Registry of Deeds, with records from 1708 onwards of land sales, assignments and *conveyances, rent charges, leases, *mortgages, marriage settlements, *wills, and discoveries. The Royal Irish Academy has a rare-books library of 30,000 volumes with special interests in antiquities, archaeology, and the Irish language. A particularly valuable source is the Halliday collection of pamphlets which cover a date-span from 1682 to 1859, and run to about 29,000 items. The Irish Architectural Archive has a large collection of materials, with a strong visual emphasis. The Representative Church Body Library is the official archive of the Church of Ireland, including parish records, vestry books, episcopal visitations, and ecclesiastical correspondence.

Family history has also undergone a marked metamorphosis in recent years. The initial momentum was driven by the diaspora but has increasingly gained local impetus, albeit uneasily cohabiting with commercial exploitation, with all its necessary compromises. The 1980s saw a mushrooming of local genealogical centres, aimed at tapping this perceived roots market by indexing and marketing local records. The earliest and best of these was the Clare Heritage Centre at Corofin, inspired by Naoise Ó Cléirigh, who kept a tight eye on quality control and was himself a respected expert on the history and genealogy of his native county. From these early initiatives, efforts were made to co-ordinate and rationalize the services provided in the 1990s, and to develop a network which would provide centralized marketing. The government-sponsored Irish Genealogical Project (IGP) has been set up to investigate and co-ordinate the plethora of county, diocesan, and local centres which now exist. In Northern Ireland, the Ulster Historical Foundation is the principal genealogical society. The standard and service provided by the genealogical centres remains uneven; the best of them, like the Waterford Heritage Centre, are highly professional in their work. Others are small-scale, run by voluntary labour, and with a relatively limited access to records. The same patchiness is true of individuals offering genealogical services. The Association of Professional Genealogists in Ireland does monitor quality and its members can be assumed to be competent and reliable researchers.

Genealogy remains poorly served by state institutions and record repositories. The understaffed and underfunded Genealogical Office does provide (for a fee) a consultancy service, and has a valuable manuscript collection. The National Library, National Archives, General Registry of Births, Marriages, and Deaths, Valuation Office, and Registry of Deeds all carry essential genealogical records, as does the Public Record Office of Northern Ireland in Belfast. All these institutions have, however, other priorities, but are as co-operative as time and staffing levels permit. For those living outside Ireland who wish to pursue Irish genealogical research, the best advice remains to do as much as possible of the research in one's own country prior to consulting Irish records; without establishing a county of origin at a minimum, Irish research is likely to prove tedious and difficult. Armed with a county of origin (even more preferably, of a *parish or *townland), the research is likely to be much quicker and more productive. It should be possible to trace well back towards the early 19th century a 'standard' Irish family. One should also visit the place of origin of the ancestor, where there is quite likely to be an active local historian, society, or genealogist who can expedite a search.

The best genealogical guidebook is John Grenham, *Tracing Your Irish Ancestors* (1992), while for those more advanced, the essential volume is Donal Begley (ed.), *Irish Genealogy: A Record Finder* (1981). The bibliographies of Irish family history by Edward MacLysaght and Brian de Breffny are useful, as are MacLysaght's various guides to *Irish (sur)names. Among the essential Irish genealogical sources are the 1901 and 1911 manuscript *census returns; parish registers; registers of births, marriages, and deaths; Griffiths valuation, *c.*1850; and Tithe Applotment Books (*c.*1820–30). While Irish genealogical records can be difficult to trace (due to the Record Office fire), sources do exist in abundance, and time and diligence can accomplish a great deal.

Local history and family history, then, have become exciting and challenging pursuits in Ireland, contributing to the striking cultural efflorescence at regional level in that country. The necessity remains for scholars to engage with the material, contingent world, and to engage with it at the local level at which people's lives are essentially lived. Only if the meta-narratives by which intellectuals structure their concepts are in dialogue with the micro-narratives by which people understand their lives will there be fruitful co-operation. Thus, those engaged in local history have to be equipped with a bifocal vision—the eye of the mammoth and the eye of the microbe. KEVIN WHELAN

Irish names. First names such as Brian, Neil, and Sheila, which are now in common use in many parts of the English-speaking world, are Irish in origin. Many Irish names are known from Anglicized versions, but in Gaelic-speaking parts of rural Ireland ancient names such as Aodh, Meadhbh, and Naoise continue in use. Others have been revived in modern times in their original form. The phonology and spelling system of the *Gaelic language is very different from that of English, and Irish personal names have been derived from an independent *folklore tradition. For example, Meadhbh, Deirdre, Connor, and Naoise are names in a story that dates from around the time of Christ. As elsewhere, the influence of Christianity on naming patterns has been profound. The names of Irish saints, especially Patrick, Calum, and Bridget, have been widely adopted. See Donnchadh Ó Corráin and Fidelma Maguire, *Gaelic Personal Names* (1981), and Patrick Hanks and Flavia Hodges, *A Dictionary of First Names* (1990).

Edward MacLysaght's *The Surnames of Ireland* (1980) provides the foundation for studies of Irish surnames. This contains an introduction to the subject, a dictionary of names, and a bibliography of Irish family histories. See also Robert Bell, *The Book of Ulster Surnames* (1988) for commentaries on the most common names of that province. Many hereditary surnames were formed in Ireland before the Anglo-Norman invasion of the 12th century. These were normally created by prefixing Mac to the father's name or Ó (anglicized as O') to that of a grandfather or earlier ancestor. Ó names are more numerous than Mac or Mc names (which were indistinguishable in origin). Later Mac or Ó was prefixed to occupations or nicknames, but these are small in number compared to the patronymics. The prefixes Mac and Ó were commonly dropped from the early 17th century onwards, during the long period of tighter English rule, but they were reintroduced in the late 19th and 20th centuries, particularly after the foundation of the Gaelic League in 1893. Curiously, some well-known Irish names, e.g. Connolly, Donnelly, Doyle, Foley, Hogan, Kennedy, Murphy, Nolan, Quinn, and Sheridan seldom, if ever, use O' today. Nor has Mac been restored to such names as Brady, Clancy, Egan, or Keogh. On the other hand, the stock of Mac names has been replenished with those brought by Scottish settlers, particularly in *Ulster.

These early surnames were mainly derived from the Irish (Gaelic) language, though a few were formed from *Viking personal names. The Anglo-Normans brought a new stock, many of which are now rightly regarded as essentially Irish surnames, e.g. Burke, Cruise, Cusack, Dillon, Nagle, Power, Roche, etc. Some of these were Welsh in origin, brought by members of the army of 'Strongbow', Earl of Pembroke. Taafe, for instance, is probably derived from a Welsh river name. Some of these names have become completely Gaelicized, e.g. Costello, the first Norman name to assume the Mac prefix. Several Irish names introduced by the Normans begin with *Fitz-, e.g. Fitzgerald.

A number of English names entered Ireland in the Middle Ages, but almost all of them have been assimilated over the centuries. The English names that survive date from the *Plantations of the early 17th century and the Cromwellian Settlement of the 1650s. Until 1600 Ulster was the most completely Irish part of Ireland; then it became the province most subject to English and Scottish settlement. However, English and Scottish names now predominate only in Antrim and Down, two counties which were not among the 'planted'; these surnames therefore appear to be the result of modern commercial infiltration. The Cromwellian Settlement was different in dispersing immigrants across the country. It is not now possible to determine the proportion of English names in the modern population. Much further research is necessary before the history of surnames in Ulster is understood, particularly at the local level. It is already clear that many Border Scots, persecuted by James I, who wished to reduce their power, settled in Fermanagh; they are the major source of the Ulster names Johnson, Armstrong, Elliott, Irvine, Nixon, Crozier, etc. The *Huguenot names which have attracted attention were distinctive, but uncommon.

Another difficulty faced by the student of Irish surnames is the widespread practice of translating or altering names into an English form. Many of the MacGowans, O'Gowans, and Gows took the English name Smith, which has the same meaning. Mistranslation was more common than correct translation. Other names were abbreviated or distorted by the duplication of consonants, the use of short internal vowels, and the alternative use of gh and h. MacCathmhaoil, once one of the most common names in Tyrone, has disappeared in favour of a number of Anglicized forms, e.g. Callwell and Cowell. Ó Dubhthaigh became O'Duffy, then Duffy. Rare names have grad-

been absorbed by better-known ones, e.g. Sullahan changed to Sullivan, Blowick to Blake. The Registrar-General's report of 1909 gives as synonyms of Cullen: Colins, Collen, Collins, Colquhoun, Culhoun, Culleeny, Cullinane, Cullion, Culloon, Cully, Quillan, and Quillen.

The study of the derivation of old surnames of Gaelic origin is further complicated by the difficulties of the language at the time of surname formation. Much work remains to be done on past and present surname distributions, though it is clear that despite modern mobility Gaelic surnames are still mainly to be found in the part of the country in which they arose. Thus, nearly all the Conneleys and Keadys come from County Galway, the Teahans and Sugrues from Kerry, and the Lehanes and Riordans from County Cork. This even applies to names which have become numerous and are found in Dublin and other large towns, e.g. the Moriartys and MacElligotts are still mainly concentrated in Kerry, and the O'Mahonys and O'Driscolls are still mostly found in County Cork.

iron. The making of iron goes back to prehistoric times (see IRON AGE). Iron was mined in shallow pits and smelted on windy escarpments (see BELL PIT; BOLE HILL; and BLOOMERY). The ancient system of manufacture, which persisted up to the 18th century, involved the production of an iron bloom, which the smith wrought directly into a finished article in his forge, using a coal-fired hearth and bellows, anvil and hammers, chisels, files, and tongs. The quality and quantity of wrought iron improved during the Middle Ages. *Water-powered bloomeries were in use in England from the 14th century and remained important in some regions until the middle of the 17th century. This method was capable of producing 20–30 tons of iron in a year. From the 16th century onwards better quality ores were imported, first from Spain, then down the Rhine, and by the late 17th century from Sweden.

David Crossley, *Post-Medieval Archaeology in Britain* (1990), ch. 7, provides a survey of the excavations and fieldwork that have increased our knowledge of the early modern iron industry. See also Henry Cleere and David Crossley, *The Iron Industry of the Weald* (1985) for a detailed regional study of the ore-bearing areas of Sussex, Kent, and Surrey, where the majority of the streams were dammed to power *furnaces and *forges. The iron industry grew considerably in the 16th and 17th centuries in response to increased demand for iron in building, agriculture, shipping, and the arms trades.

This growth involved changes in method and an expansion in the number of ironworks. The most radical change, albeit a gradual one, was the abandonment of the bloomery process, in which wrought iron was produced on a small scale direct from the ore, in favour of the production of cast iron in the blast furnace, which was introduced into England by French ironworkers at Newbridge, in Ashdown Forest, in 1496. The Wealden industry grew quickly in the next 50 years, supplying the Crown with arms and also catering for general trade. See B. G. Awty, 'The Continental Origins of Wealden Iron Workers', *Economic History Review*, 2nd ser., 34/4 (1981). The new technology arrived in the midlands and the north of England in the 1560s. The main period of expansion in these regions began in the 1580s; by the 1630s the total production of the Weald had been overtaken by the rest of the country. The era of the charcoal blast furnace lasted until the mid-18th century. The great majority of these early furnaces have since been demolished, but many sites have been identified in valley bottoms through the remains of storage ponds and deposits of slag. On the relationship between the charcoal iron industry and *coppiced woodland see G. F. Hammersley, 'The Charcoal Iron Industry and Its Fuel', *Economic History Review*, 2nd ser., 26/4 (1973).

Some of the pig iron that was smelted at the blast furnace was cast into artefacts, but most was converted into wrought-iron bars in the finery forge, where tilt hammers were worked by water power. The number of tilts on the Sheffield streams rose considerably from the second quarter of the 18th century. Long after Nasmyth's invention of the steam-powered hammer in 1839, water power continued to be important in forging iron. At Wortley Top Forge (Yorkshire) the early 18th-century tilt hammers remained in use until 1910. At such forges, associated *slitting mills produced rod iron for making into *nails or *wire. Water power was also developed for blade forging and *grinding.

Some of the wide range of objects which were made from wrought iron included a proportion of *steel, especially *tools which required a cutting edge. The variety and sophistication of the goods produced in the secondary metal trades for use in the house, farm, or workshop increased over the post-medieval period: they included chisels, axes, wedges, files, locks, keys, awls, flat irons, scissors, knives, nails, etc. See Marie Rowlands, *Masters and Men in the Small Metalware Trades of the West Midlands* (1975). (See also DUAL ECONOMY.)

A major development in the 18th century was the transition to the use of coke fuel in the smelting and refining processes. In 1709 Abraham Darby's works at Coalbrookdale (Shropshire) was the first to use coke successfully, but practical difficulties prevented widespread conversion to the new fuel beyond Shropshire until after 1750. In the later 18th century the design of coke-fuelled furnaces changed rapidly and Henry Cort's puddling process was widely adopted. The production of iron increased considerably and the industry entered into a boom period which lasted for much of the 19th century. See H. R. Schubert, *History of the British Iron and Steel Industry* (1957), T. S. Ashton, *Iron and Steel in the Industrial Revolution* (1993 reprint), and Barrie Trinder, *The Industrial Revolution in Shropshire* (1981).

The 19th-century iron industry was far more complex and varied than its 18th-century predecessor. It was common for a company to own and operate coal and iron mines, coking plants, furnaces, foundries and forges, rolling mills, and sometimes departments that turned out finished goods such as stoves, fenders, pipes, tools, machinery, or forgings, etc. The furnaces had a far greater capacity and *steam power was now in common use. In the 1830s a great advance in blast furnace design, allowing the use of hot blast at greater pressures in furnaces up to 60 feet high, increased output from less than 100 tons to more than 200 tons of iron a week. The development of a great variety of machine tools was of prime importance in the enormous expansion of the *engineering industry.

South Wales witnessed some of the greatest changes. The industry had grown steadily during the early 18th century and between 1759 and 1765 the famous names of Dowlais, Plymouth, Tredegar, and Cyfarthfa appeared. The application of the Cort puddling process in the 1780s ushered in a period of rapid expansion in the Welsh iron industry, 1790–1840. The Merthyr-Dowlais area alone had 44 furnaces by the 1840s, and by 1840 there were probably 150,000 people directly dependent on the various ironworks at the head of the valleys. The hey-day of the Welsh iron industry was during the first two decades of the Victorian era, when the traditional names continued to dominate. See Michael Atkinson and Colin Baber, *The Growth and Decline of the South Wales Iron Industry, 1760–1880* (1987).

The beginnings of the modern Scottish iron industry can be traced from 1759 with the establishment of the Carron Ironworks near Falkirk, the first Scottish concern to use coal in iron smelting. After 1830 the exploitation of the local coal and ironstone seams that outcropped in Monklands parish in North Lanarkshire brought about a major phase of blast-furnace construction. With the commercial application of the Neilson hot blast process of iron smelting, which brought considerable savings in fuel costs, the fortunes of the Scottish iron industry were transformed, but by the last third of the 19th century it was becoming obvious that the industry needed to adapt in face of foreign competition.

The south Staffordshire iron industry reached its peak in 1859, when it produced a total of 752,000 tons, that is some 22 per cent of British production. By that date 190 furnaces belonging to 55 firms were in blast. The north Staffordshire industry developed a little later, and by 1870, 30 furnaces were producing 303,378 tons of pig iron a year. Many of the new firms achieved their initial success by catering for the needs of civil engineering, especially the *railways, but also major projects such as the Crystal Palace and the great London bridges. They soon became noted for their great range and variety of manufactured articles. See W. K. Gale, *History of the Black Country Iron Industry* (1966).

The iron industry on the coal-measure sandstones of the West Riding of Yorkshire expanded on similar lines. On Teesside, the spectacular expansion of Middlesbrough, from four houses with 25 inhabitants in 1801 to a town of 91,302 people in 1901, was unrivalled elsewhere in Britain. In 1841 Henry Bolckow, an immigrant from Mecklenburg, established an ironworks on the banks of the Tees. At first he used imported ore, but from the 1850s he began to exploit the ironstone deposits in the Cleveland hills. By 1873 the north-eastern ironfield was producing over 2 million tons of pig iron per annum, about a third of the total British output. Meanwhile, at the other side of the Pennines, Barrow-in-Furness had grown from a fishing village of about 300 people in the 1840s to a town with over 40,000 inhabitants by 1878. Both Barrow and Middlesbrough were planned on grid patterns like many of the *medieval new towns. Both eventually became more reliant on steel. The 20th century has seen the decline and then the disappearance of most of the British iron industry.

Iron Age. The last of the prehistoric periods, from *c*.800 BC to the Roman invasion of AD 43, characterized by the use of iron tools and weapons, *hill forts, and farmhouses of roughly circular plan whose outlines are often revealed by *aerial archaeology. There was regular contact with the Continent of Europe during this period. The population was far greater than was once believed.

Irvingites. The followers of Edward Irving (1792–1834), the founder of the Holy Catholic Apostolic Church, which was based in London. Irving arrived in London from Scotland in 1822 and attracted large congregations by his eloquent preaching.

Issue Rolls. Records of payments made from Crown revenues, from 1240 to 1480 and from 1567 to 1700, kept at the *Public Record Office. Some have been published.

Italian immigrants. Although individual Italians had settled in Britain since the Middle Ages and Italian *Protestants had founded a church in London during the 16th century, it was only in the 19th century that a community was established in London, especially in Clerkenwell and Soho. Italian street performers and musicians became a feature of London streets; others made a living making plaster statuettes or as artisans and *pedlars. Many more Italians left their home country in the late 19th century. In London, numbers trebled from 3,500 in 1881 to 11,000 in 1901. Some worked as general labourers, but Italians became famous for their ice cream and other food businesses. Another wave of immigrants came in the 1950s and 1960s, at a time of unemployment in Italy and labour shortage in Britain. Italian restaurants and coffee bars became known in cities throughout the land.

J

Jacobites. Supporters of the deposed King James II and his descendants after the *'Glorious Revolution' of 1688, which placed William of Orange and his wife Mary on the throne. Armed conflict occurred in 1689–90 (culminating in James's defeat at the Battle of the Boyne, in northern Ireland, on 1 July 1690), in 1715 ('The Jacobite Rebellion'), and in 1745–6, ending in the battle of Culloden and the suppression of the Highland *clans. See B. Lenman, *The Jacobite Risings in Britain, 1689–1746* (1980), and F. McLynn, *The Jacobites* (1985).

jagger. A north country term for a man in charge of a team of *packhorses carrying *lead, *coal, etc. A number of Jagger Lanes survive and the occupation gave rise to a surname.

Jefferies, Richard (1848–87). Naturalist and novelist, whose letter to *The Times* in 1872 on the plight of the Wiltshire *agricultural labourer, and book *Hodge and His Masters* (1880), were based on detailed observations.

Jefferys, Thomas (d. 1771). Geographer to the King, London map engraver, and map seller. His map of Bedfordshire, published for the Society of Arts in 1765, was one of the first to use the Greenwich meridian. He published further maps for the Society of Arts: Huntingdonshire (1768), Oxfordshire (1768–9), and Yorkshire (1771–2). He and Thomas Kitchin published a *Small English Atlas* (1749), which ran into several editions up to 1787. Jefferys's *West Indies Atlas* (1775) and his *American Atlas* (1776) were published posthumously.

Jekyll, Gertrude (1843–1932). English garden designer. Her books *Wood and Garden* (1899), *Home and Garden* (1900), and *Old West Surrey* (1904) were enormously influential in emphasizing the informal planting of hardy plants, shrubs, and trees, so as to create colourful 'wild' or 'woodland' gardens with herbaceous borders, fitting for both large houses and small cottages. She advised on over 300 gardens.

Jesse window. A depiction in *stained glass of the Tree of Jesse, often in the east window of a church, showing Christ's descent from Jesse, the father of King David.

Jesuit. A member of the Society of Jesus, which was formed in Paris in 1534 by Ignatius Loyola as a body of scholars and missionaries dedicated to the aims of the Counter-*Reformation. Jesuit churches, notably the Gesu in Rome, where Loyola is buried, were richly ornamented in a *baroque style. English Jesuit priests, who were trained in France at Douai or Rheims for the English mission, were persecuted in the 16th century, particularly during the 1580s when a Spanish invasion to restore Catholicism appeared imminent. They were keen observers and reporters on the local scene, e.g. when they went to China; see Francesca Bray, *Science and Civilisation in China*, vi, 2 (1984). See also PRIEST HOLES.

Jewish immigrants. A small Jewish community settled in London after the *Norman Conquest at the invitation of William I. Medieval Christian laws against usury made Jews indispensable, but their financial dealings were sometimes resented. By the middle of the 12th century other English cities, e.g. King's Lynn and Norwich, had attracted Jewish moneylenders. Dominant figures such as Aaron of Lincoln and Josce of York offered *mortgages on 20-year terms and lent money to the king, nobles, religious communities, and other landowners. Anti-semitism broke out during the heightened emotions of the first *Crusade; by far the worst case was the massacre of the 40 households of Jews in York Castle on the night of 16 March 1190: see R. B. Dobson, *The Jews of Medieval York and the Massacre of March 1190* (1974). By 1218 England had 10 specially protected Jewish communities, with a total population of about 3,000, but their fortunes declined under Edward I and they were expelled in 1290.

These early settlers were *Sephardic Jews, whose name is derived from a Hebrew word meaning Spaniards. A small group resettled in London from 1541 onwards; by 1734 the number of English Jews had risen to about 6,000. Most of these were Sephardic Jews who had come from Portugal as traders; many were wealthy. They were followed by other Sephardic Jews from different parts of the Mediterranean, including Italy, Turkey, and Morocco, some of whom then moved on to distant parts of the British Empire. The ones who remained became integrated as Anglo-Jewry. See David S. Katz, *The Jews in the History of England, 1485–1850* (1994).

The other Jews who had settled in England by 1734 were from a different tradition. They were known as *Ashkenazic Jews from a Hebrew word meaning German, for they had once been concentrated in the Rhine valley before moving east into Poland, the Baltic States, and Russia. Their native language was Yiddish, a type of German written in Hebrew characters. Some had settled in London and other towns as skilled engravers, but most were poor people, many of them hawkers. Their numbers increased steadily after 1800, especially after the persecutions in Central and Eastern Europe of 1848–50 and 1863; then in the last two decades of the 19th century thousands of families from Russia, Poland, Lithuania, and other parts of the Russian Empire sought refuge in Britain after fleeing from the pogroms of Tsar Alexander III. The favourite destination was the East End of London, especially Stepney, followed by Leeds and Manchester. The Leylands district of Leeds was 85 per cent Jewish by the late 1880s, when Leeds had 6,000 Jews; by the eve of the First World War this number had risen to 20,000. In both London and Leeds these immigrants worked in a narrow range of jobs, especially the clothing trade, cabinet-making, boot-making, and retailing. (In 1884 Michael Marks opened his first Penny Bazaar in the covered market at Leeds and thus started the business that became Marks and Spencer's.) Many worked in 'sweated workshops', usually for their co-religionists. Concern over the number of immigrants led to an Act of 1905 which imposed severe restrictions. A further group of Jews, including a number of eminent intellectuals, settled in Britain in the 1930s to escape Nazi persecution.

The translation and Anglicization of Hebrew surnames causes great difficulties for the family historian. See E. R. Samuel's chapter on 'The Jews' in D. J. Steel (ed.), *Sources for Roman Catholic and Jewish Genealogy and Family History* (1974). Many synagogue records have been deposited in local *record offices. Most of these are an accurate record of marriages and burials, but the entries of birth are not comprehensive. The records of Ashkenazic congregations are very difficult to use because they are written in Hebrew or Yiddish in a difficult script, they note only Hebrew or synagogical names, which were not always the same as the names in everyday use, and they do not record surnames.

jointure. A fixed annual sum paid to a *widow out of her husband's *freehold estate until she remarried or died.

Josselin, Ralph (1616–83). Vicar of Earl's Colne (Essex), whose journal is a major source for 17th-century social historians. See Alan MacFarlane (ed.), *The Diary of Ralph Josselin, 1616–1683* (1976), and Alan MacFarlane, *The Family Life of Ralph Josselin, a Seventeenth-Century Clergyman* (1970).

journeyman. A *day labourer, often one who worked away from home; a man who had completed an *apprenticeship but had not set up as a master himself.

Julian calendar. The calendar in use since the time of Julius Caesar until the *Gregorian calendar was introduced into Catholic Europe in 1582 and into Britain in 1752. By the time that it was abandoned in Britain, the Julian calendar was 11 days out of line with the Gregorian.

jury. A body of 12 people sworn to give a verdict in a court of justice, manorial *court, coroner's court, etc. Jury service was dependent upon a property qualification defined in 1285 and extended in 1664 and 1692. From 1696 lists of eligible jurors (men aged 21–70 who possessed *freehold, *copyhold, or life-tenure property worth at least £10 a year) were presented by each *parish to meetings of the *quarter sessions and may now be consulted in county *record offices. From 1730 long-term *leaseholders of property valued at or above £20 were also eligible to serve. In 1825 jury service was restricted to those aged 21–60 and the property qualification was revised.

The Grand Jury was drawn from the ranks of the minor *gentry and substantial *yeomen who decided which cases should proceed to trial at the quarter sessions. Records of such proceedings are not well preserved; where they are extant, they are found with the records of quarter sessions at county record offices. The *assize judges gave the charge to the Grand Jury on their visits, otherwise the task fell to the chairman of the *Justices of the Peace. They spoke about the current issues and government preoccupations of the day. See Anthony Fletcher, *Reform in the Provinces: The Government of Stuart England* (1986).

jury of presentment. By ancient custom, confirmed in 1166, 12 men from each *hundred and four men from each *vill were liable for bringing suspects before the justices of the hundred court. These courts withered under the Tudors.

Justices of the Peace developed from the 'Keepers of the Peace' who were appointed by a commission under the *Great Seal in 1277 and 1287. They had acquired their name by 1361, when a statute gave them the power to try minor offenders. JPs were appointed by the Crown from the ranks of the major landowners of a county. They received no payment for the performance of their duties. They were expected to enforce the principal medieval statutes concerning the peace, to take sureties for good behaviour, and to imprison those who would or could give none. Serious felonies were tried at the *assizes. For a clear account of the evolution of the office see G. C. F. Forster, *The East Riding Justices of the Peace in the Seventeenth Century* (1973).

The duties of the JPs were greatly extended under the Tudors. The commission of peace by which justices were appointed was revised in 1590 to authorize them to hold regular sessions, to enquire by jury into a variety of offences, and to try cases upon indictment. By the end of Elizabeth I's reign no fewer than 309 statutes had imposed responsibilities of either a judicial or an administrative nature. The JPs had to try offenders and consign some of the guilty to gaols and *houses of correction, to oversee the operation of the *Poor Law and the laws concerning vagrancy, to attend to the regulation of *fairs and *markets, *wages and *prices, and *weights and measures, to see to the upkeep of *roads and *bridges, to license *Nonconformist meeting houses, *alehouses, playhouses, *badgers, *drovers, and *pedlars, and to levy rates. They were, in effect, the rulers of the counties of England and Wales from the Elizabethan period onwards, especially after the *Restoration of Charles II. Justices were also appointed to perform similar duties in some

*boroughs. Borough charters normally provided for a mayor to be *ex officio* justice during his year of office and for a year afterwards, so that there were always two justices at any one time in a borough.

Much of the business was humdrum and burdensome. Individual JPs varied from the casual and lazy to the energetic and conscientious. The role gave a justice important social standing. The meetings of the *quarter sessions were welcome occasions for tradesmen, for the justices expected to shop and be convivial. In some counties the quarter sessions were always held in the county town, but in others the JPs moved around; the West Riding of Yorkshire, for instance, had 10 different meeting-places. Some JPs had been trained in the law as young men; others gained experience from their obligation to attend the twice-yearly assizes and from legal handbooks. During the 17th century JPs became increasingly professional. New shire halls were built and records were kept in a more systematic way by a *clerk of the peace nominated by the *custos rotulorum. See Anthony Fletcher, *Reform in the Provinces: The Government of Stuart England* (1986), and Norma Landau, *The Justices of the Peace, 1679–1760* (1984), which is particularly concerned with Kent.

The JPs successfully adapted to changing requirements over the centuries. They began to lose their powers in 1888 when their administrative functions were transferred to elected councils in each county and large town. Responsibility for the police was divided between the JPs and the new councils through standing joint committees. The judicial and licensing powers were not affected, and quarter sessions continued to sit as criminal courts until 1971. The modern magistrates' courts, which have responsibility for petty crime and for licensing, have evolved from the ancient system.

juxta. A Latin word, meaning 'near', used in some place-names to mean 'by', e.g. Greensted-juxta-Ongar (Essex).

keep. The tower of a *castle, which contained the living quarters of the noble family and which acted as the ultimate place of defence. Some Norman *motte-and-bailey castles had wooden keeps on their mottes. The most important sites were converted to stone keeps in the 12th century, but the majority were abandoned. An early form of stone keep was the *shell keep, e.g. that at Lincoln Castle. Free-standing towers of a square plan were used from immediately after the *Norman Conquest, most famously the White Tower at London, and at Colchester and Chepstow. These relied on their own strength and height for defence. Over 60 square towers are known, two-thirds of them on new sites, the rest on converted *ringworks or reduced mottes. The stone keeps of the second half of the 12th century and the first quarter of the 13th century were often square, but from the 1170s experiments were made with cylindrical plans: the most notable surviving examples are at Orford (Suffolk) and Conisbrough (Yorkshire). Such keeps had a vaulted chamber for storage on the ground floor, then in increasing stages an entrance chamber with a staircase in the thickness of the wall, a great hall with a large chimney and glass windows, a *solar which served as a private apartment and which often had an adjoining chapel, and a roof-top walk with guard-house towers, *dovecotes, ovens, water tanks, etc. During the 1240s keeps went out of fashion, though occasional ones were built during the rest of the Middle Ages. They were replaced by hall blocks and by perimeter defences, such as those employed by the late 13th-century castles of Edward I.

kelp. Seaweed, used as a *manure and as an alkali in the *chemical industry. It was an important source of revenue for the *crofters in the Western Isles of Scotland until well into the 19th century.

Kennett, White (1660–1728). Clergyman and author of *Parochial Antiquities Attempted in the History of Ambrosden, Burcester and Other Adjacent Parts in the Counties of Oxford and Bucks* (1695), the first *parish history. In his preface he wrote: 'Next to the immediate discharge of my holy office, I know not how in any course of studies I could better have served my patron, my people and my successors than by preserving the memoirs of this parish.' He was the first of a long line of country parsons who wrote the history of their parish. His career culminated in his appointment as Bishop of Peterborough.

kerseys. Cheap, coarse cloths manufactured in many parts of medieval and early modern England. They formed the basis of the West Riding *woollen cloth industry. The belief that they were first made at Kersey (Suffolk) has been challenged.

Kilvert, Francis (1840–79). Clergyman and author of a diary (1870–9), kept while he was a curate, most famously at Clyro (Radnorshire). This was published in three volumes in 1938–40, and in an abridged version in 1944 (paperback 1977). His vivid, detailed picture of the mid-Victorian countryside and rural life is unmatched.

King, Gregory (1648–1712). Pioneer statistician and demographer. In his *Natural and Political Observations and Conclusions upon the State and Condition of England* (1696) he used taxation returns to analyse English society and to estimate the numbers in each social group, starting with 'Ranks, Degrees, Titles and Qualifications' and descending a social ladder via the merchants and professionals down to the humblest paupers. His table has been frequently reprinted, e.g. in J. Thirsk and J. P. Cooper (eds.), *Seventeenth-Century Economic Documents* (1972), or in Peter Laslett, *The World We Have Lost* (1965). At the top of the social pyramid were 161 temporal lords and an estimated 800 *baronets, 3,000 *esquires, and 12,000 gentlemen. King believed that at least half the population were scarcely able to maintain themselves. He estimated that at the bottom of society were some 364,000 families of labouring people and out-servants, 400,000 families of *cottagers and paupers, and 85,000 families of soldiers and sailors. At a guess, some 30,000 people were vagrants. Recent research has refined this picture, but King is still widely quoted. See Kevin Schurer and Tom Arkell (eds.), *Surveying the People: The Interpretation* *and Use of Document Sources for the Study of Population in the Later Seventeenth Century* (1992).

King's Bench, Court of. One of the three courts that had become separate from the *Curia Regis by the reign of Edward I (1272–1307). At first, it dealt with cases involving the king, but in time it tried both criminal and civil cases as the highest court of the realm other than Parliament. It was abolished in 1875 and merged into the High Court as the King's Bench Division. Records from the late 12th century onwards are kept at the *Public Record Office under KB. A number of early rolls have been published by the Record Commission, *Pipe Roll Society, and *Selden Society.

King's Evil. It was once popularly supposed that scrofula, a disease of the lymphatic glands, could be cured by a touch from the king or a reigning queen. The last monarch to attempt this cure was Queen Anne.

King's highway. Any public road, described in medieval and early modern records as *via regis*, or the king's highway.

kinship. T. M. Charles-Edwards, *Early Irish and Welsh Kinship* (1993), examines the subject in depth for the earliest periods. The value of kinship bonds in early modern England has been the subject of much debate, which is summarized in David Cressy, 'Kinship and Kinship Interaction in Early Modern England', *Past and Present*, 113 (1986). Little work has been done on other parts of Britain during the early modern period, but it is clear from studies of communities in later centuries that kinship ties were strongest in the remoter parts of Wales, Ireland, and Scotland: see, for example, Alwyn D. Rees, *Life in a Welsh Countryside* (1951), and David Jenkins, *The Agricultural Community in South-West Wales at the Turn of the Twentieth Century* (1971). See also CLANS, SCOTTISH; and Jenny Wormald, *Lords and Men in Scotland: Bonds of Manrent, 1442–1603* (1985). Mervyn James, *Family Lineage and Civil Society: A Study of Society, Politics and Mentality in the Durham Region, 1500–1640* (1974), suggested that complex family lineages had disappeared in lowland parishes but continued to survive in early modern highland societies. Alan MacFarlane rejects such a division in 'The Myth of the Peasantry: Family and Economy in a Northern Parish' in R. Smith (ed.), *Land, Kinship and Life Cycle* (1984). See also Ralph A. Houlbrooke, *The English Family, 1450–1700* (1984). Kinship ties differed in strength according to status and sex and from region to region among medieval and early modern English families. The study of kinship has been based largely on the analysis of *wills, which indicate that throughout England widows and children were usually chosen as executors. Sometimes, brothers or brothers-in-law acted in this capacity, but not other kin. Bequests were made to grandparents, uncles, aunts, nephews, nieces, and in-laws, but rarely to those kin beyond this inner circle. Cressy demonstrates the importance of the point in the life-cycle at which the will was made, in the effect on the range of kin who received bequests. A similar conclusion was reached by R. T. Vann, 'Wills and the Family in an English Town: Banbury, 1550–1800', *Journal of Family History*, 4 (1979). W. Coster, *Kinship and Inheritance in Early Modern England: Three Yorkshire Parishes* (Borthwick Paper, no. 83, 1993) examines these issues at local levels by studying wills in the context of other information for three contrasting parishes.

Wills may perhaps be too narrow a source for judging the strength of kinship bonds. See Amy Louise Erickson, *Women and Property in Early Modern England* (1993) on the use of *probate accounts. Family letters show that people approached a wider range of kin when help was required; these wider connections proved valuable in times of need, in borrowing money, securing jobs, and finding accommodation. At other times, people were little concerned with kin outside their immediate family circle. There were no firm rules or conventions about who should be recognized as kin: the choice differed from individual to individual. For a study that demonstrates the bonds of kinship and neighbourliness in a local community see Mary Prior, *Fisher Row: Fishermen, Bargemen and Canal Boatmen in Oxford, 1500–1900* (1982). Kinship bonds were not loosened by the *Industrial Revolution, but on the contrary were strengthened by the need to share accommodation and find work. See Michael Anderson, *Family Structure in Nineteenth-Century Lancashire* (1971), and, for the strength of these bonds in the 20th century, Richard Hoggart, *A Local Habitation: Life and Times, 1918–1940* (1988).

kitchen. The kitchens of *castles, *monasteries, and large *manor houses were originally detached buildings because of the scale of operations and the risk of fire. Some 40 medieval kitchens survive: the earliest have a square plan and a central hearth; from the 13th century onwards the more elaborate ones have fireplaces along side walls. The 13th-century abbot's kitchen at Glastonbury (Somerset) is an attractive building that rises to central octagons which are not just decorative features but act as louvres for the smoke. In the later Middle Ages kitchens began to be integrated with the main building, though they were separated from the communal *hall by a screen and were sometimes approached along a passage between the buttery and pantry, as at Haddon Hall (Derbyshire). In great households of the medieval and Tudor period the cooking was done by men and boys. See Mark Girouard, *Life in the English Country House* (1978).

In *vernacular buildings the kitchen was often regarded as an outbuilding well into the 17th century and beyond. The term was sometimes used for a brewhouse or a bakehouse, and so seems to have meant a room with a particular type of hearth and equipment. In some farmhouses the kitchen was an unheated lean-to for the preparation of food, which was then cooked on a hearth in the main living quarters.

knight. Originally the fighting men who accompanied William the Conqueror to England, their image was refined during the Age of Chivalry. William I rewarded them by grants of land (a *knight's fee) which they held in return for *knight service. This was gradually commuted to a money payment. The holder of a knight's fee did not necessarily take a knighthood (because of the expense) and thus remained an *esquire. Knighthood therefore became a personal rather than a hereditary honour. A register of knights has been kept at the College of *Arms since 1662.

knight bachelor. The lowest degree of knighthood. A knight bachelor commanded a small unit of personal retainers.

knight of the shire. A Member of Parliament who was elected to represent a county. The term survived from the Middle Ages into the 19th century, though by then county MPs rarely held a knighthood.

knight service. The military service owed to a feudal lord by a *knight in return for land. This involved bringing arms, armour, and horse for up to 40 days' active service per year. It was gradually commuted to a money payment and was abolished in 1662.

knight's fee. After the *Norman Conquest all the land in England was owned by William I, who by a process of *enfeoffment granted most of it (except the royal *demesnes) to *earls and *barons, who in turn granted it to *knights in return for *knight service. England had about 5,000–6,000 knights' fees.

knitting. During the late Elizabethan period the traditional country craft of hand-knitting was transformed into a flourishing rural industry when men's fashion changed and they wore short breeches and long hose that showed off the leg. Because knitting was not controlled by *guilds, it was chosen as work for the poor with the aim of reducing unemployment and at the same time making England less dependent on foreign imports. See Joan Thirsk, *Economic Policy and Projects: The Development of a Consumer Society in Early Modern England* (1978). The knitting of coarse, thick stockings was one of the most successful ventures. By the 1590s both Richmond and Doncaster were new centres of a knitting industry that provided employment for men, women, and children on small family farms. Every moment of spare time was spent in knitting: when travelling to market, tending sheep, or talking to neighbours. By 1664 over 2,000 dozen pairs of stockings per annum were shipped down the Tees from Stockton. See Marie Hartley and Joan Ingilby, *The Old Hand-Knitters of the Dales* (1951, reprinted 1969), and Roger Fieldhouse and Bernard Jennings, *A History of Richmond and Swaledale* (1978). Joan Thirsk has estimated that, as knitted stockings had become a standard item of clothing by the beginning of the 17th century, somewhere around 10 million pairs of stockings were needed each year to dress the whole population. As knitting was commonly a *by-employment it is reasonable to suppose that about 100,000 people were needed to meet this demand. In towns such as Leicester, Lincoln, and York knitting schools were founded to employ the poor. In *Barnabees Journal* (1638) Richard Braithwait noted that at Askrigg (Yorkshire), 'Here poor people live by knitting'. But the industry was mainly a rural one that provided welcome extra income to poor farming families and cottagers.

Other Elizabethan projects increased the production of caps, jerseys, silk stockings, etc. (See FRAMEWORK KNITTING.) The range of products had to be amended quickly to meet the changing quirks of fashion. See Joan Thirsk, 'The Fantastical Folly of Fashion: The English Stocking Knitting Industry, 1500–1700' in N. B. Harte and K. G. Ponting (eds.), *Textile History and Economic History* (1973).

Labourers, Statute of (1351). This Act attempted to hold *wages at their pre-*Black Death level by imposing severe penalties for infringement. The shortage of labour thwarted attempts to keep down wages, however, for demand was greater than supply.

labour history. 'Labour history' is an expression with three main meanings. It is the history of labour institutions and movements; the history of the working class; and a notion of labour history as a challenge to History Proper—a historical struggle, as it were, analogous to 'class struggle'. These strands are often separate, but the best work can combine them. It has been argued, for example, that it is difficult to write intelligible institutional history in the absence of a social history of the *class, because the latter contains the key to the former's successes and defeats.

The key terms 'labour', 'movement', and especially 'class' contain nuances which bring the historian into contact with the world of social science. The language within which labour history is discussed is important. The appropriate terms, and the reasoning which underlies them, changes as one moves through the various periods of labour's evolution.

Labour's experience can be divided into seven periods. The first is the 'primitive' stage, during which it is preferable to speak of 'the labouring people', for 'Labour' comes into existence in the modern sense with industrialization. Secondly, the first half of the 19th century was the period of the formation of the 'working class'. Thirdly, the third quarter of the 19th century witnessed industrial maturity and has inspired debate about the 'labour aristocracy'. Fourthly, the period of the rise of the Labour Movement with a distinctly modern character began with the revival of Socialism around 1883 and continued until the emergence by 1923 of Labour as the 'alternative governing party' of British politics. Fifthly, the First World War and the Russian Revolution were followed by a Labour minority government and the depression of the inter-war years. The sixth period was that of Labour majority government, including the wartime coalition, of 1939–1951.

The final period is that from 1951, in which labour experiences but loses 'full employment', and—politically—consensus.

Space allows no more than brief reference to issues or achievements of the historiography. The contemporary period is largely ignored, as is the 'primitive stage'. Attention is paid to local studies and biography and the main resources for further study are indicated. As work experience is ubiquitous, it will be readily acknowledged that 'labour history' is relevant to local and family historians: labour institutions and movements are found in many localities, and few families will have a member who was not, at some time, of that class dubbed 'working'.

The first great historians of labour institutions were Beatrice (1858–1943) and Sidney James (1859–1947) *Webb. As S. & B. Webb they produced the still valuable *The History of Trade Unionism* (1894, revised and extended edn. 1920). They illustrate labour history's engagement with social science through their indispensable work in political sociology, *Industrial Democracy* (1897, new edn. 1902). Historians and something more, their work was often informed by politics. Sidney was active in London municipal government before becoming a Labour Cabinet Minister; Beatrice was active in Poor Law reform: hence their scholarly *History of English Local Government* (10 vols., 1906–29). The subject here is not a labour institution, but the parish *vestries and the municipal councils were—or became—the theatre of much 'labour' activity.

The edifice of labour institutional history is now much developed. We have comprehensive general histories of *trade unionism; an introduction in Henry Pelling, *A History of British Trade Unionism* (3rd edn., 1976); and detailed studies more on the scale of the Webbs' work, notably H. A. Clegg, A. Fox, and A. F. Thompson, *A History of British Trade Unions since 1889*, i. *1889–1910* (1963), followed by H. A. Clegg's volume ii. *1911–1933* (1985), and iii. *1934–1951* (1994). The Trades Union Congress, founded in 1868, has no complete detailed history, but John Lovell and B. C. Roberts, *Short History of the TUC* (1968), serves as an introduction. Its erstwhile rival, founded in 1899, has been studied in Alice Prochaska, *History of the General Federation of Trade Unions 1899–1980* (1982); and local Trades Councils are treated on a national scale in Alan Clinton, *The Trade Union Rank and File* (1977).

The literature on narrower themes and individual unions is large. The best in terms of a combination of institutional and social history is Alan Campbell, *The Lanarkshire Miners: A Social History of their Trade Unions, 1775–1874* (1979). Mary Drake, *Women in Trade Unions* (1920, introduced by Noreen Branson in the 1984 edn.), is a pioneering study in the too-neglected but now vigorous area of women's involvement in labour history.

'Labour', prior to the creation of the welfare state, was involved in the provision of alternatives. Trade unions provided welfare benefits, but *friendly societies had many working-class members. Thus, P. H. J. H. Gosden, *The Friendly Societies in England 1815–1875* (1961), not normally seen as a product of labour history, is relevant. *Co-operative institutions were labour self-help organizations. No complete modern general history has been written, but see G. D. H. Cole (1889–1959), *A Century of Co-operation* (1944). Women's co-operation is treated in Jean Gaffin and David Thoms, *Caring and Sharing: The Centenary History of the Co-operative Women's Guild* (1983).

The political institutions of Labour belong to the late 19th and 20th centuries. The first were the socialist societies, which joined with the trade unions in the formation of the Labour Representation Committee in 1900, the *Labour Party, as it became in 1906. Family historians may prefer to approach the history of the Social Democratic Federation, formed in 1883, through biography; see Chushichi Tsuzuki, *H. M. Hyndman and British Socialism* (1961). The Webbs were involved in its more important parallel foundation, the Fabian Society; see A. M. McBriar, *Fabian Socialism and English Politics 1884–1918* (1966). The most important institution, founded in 1893, less London-based, more involved in the trade unions, and author of the successful 'labour alliance' strategy which uneasily united the unions and socialists to create the Labour Party, was the *Independent Labour Party. Here David Howell's exemplary *British Workers and the Independent Labour Party 1888–1906* (1983) should be consulted.

The ILP provided the Labour Party with its most prominent leader, Ramsay MacDonald. He has several biographers, but see David Marquand, *Ramsay MacDonald* (1977). MacDonald was connected with Leicester; see Bill Lancaster's fine local study, *Radicalism, Cooperation and Socialism: Leicester Working-Class Politics, 1860–1906* (1987). The Amalgamated Society of Railway Servants played a significant role in the formation of the Labour Party. Philip Bagwell's *The Railwaymen: The History of the National Union of Railwaymen* (1963) is excellent in all respects.

The starting-point for Labour Party history is Henry Pelling, *A Short History of the Labour Party* (1961; 8th edn. 1985). The indefatigable G. D. H. Cole provided *A History of the Labour Party from 1914* (1948) to 1945. The earlier period can be approached through K. D. Brown (ed.), *The First Labour Party 1906–1914* (1985), and the later through Kenneth O. Morgan, *Labour in Power 1945–1951* (1984). Much has been written on contemporary history, often in the tradition of Ralph Miliband, *Parliamentary Socialism: A Study in the Politics of Labour* (1961). This was an influential essay, but it is an exercise in applied politics rather than original history.

Despite an increasing amount of fine work, such as Kevin Morgan, *Harry Pollitt* (1993), much remains to be done on the historiography of the Communist Party and other left groups. L. J. MacFarlane, *The British Communist Party: Its Origin and Development until 1929* (1966) can be recommended. J. Callaghan treats *British Trotskyism* (1984).

The history of labour as the history of 'class' first appeared in relation to the second period, the late 18th to the mid-19th century. J(ohn) L(awrence Le Breton) and Barbara *Hammond were ardent Liberals, concerned with the impact of economic and technological changes upon the lives of the labouring classes. They pursued the theme in a trilogy: *The Village Labourer* (1911; 1978 edn. introduced by G. E. Mingay), *The Town Labourer* (1917; 1978 edn. introduced by John Lovell), and *The Skilled Labourer* (1919; 1979 edn. introduced by John Rule).

The bleak character of their interpretation proved more important than their focus upon labouring strata. It put their work firmly into the tradition of labour history as 'struggle' or interpretative challenge, since they became unwitting pioneers in a debate which flared through the work of Eric Hobsbawm (his British 'standard of living' essays, reprinted as chapters 5 to 7 of *Labouring Men: Studies in the History of Labour* (1964)) and still rumbles on. Yet their concern with class experience marked a different kind of departure.

They effectively commenced a journey continued by Asa Briggs and E(dward) P(almer)

*Thompson. Lord Briggs's strikingly original essay, 'The Language of "Class" in Early Nineteenth-Century England' in A. Briggs and J. Saville (eds.), *Essays in Labour History* (1960), showed how people came to speak of 'class' rather than 'classes', just as they had moved earlier from the notion of 'orders' and 'estates'. This linguistic shift involved a change of 'consciousness', which implied a changing experience of relationships. Thompson's more extended work, *The Making of the English Working Class* (1963, 2nd edn. 1968), which has become a great classic, takes up this point by treating relationships as central to the notion of 'class'. He sought to demonstrate, through marshalling experience as well as language, that broad masses of people were coming, by 1830, to an increased sense of identity of themselves as a 'working class', as having interests antagonistic and opposed to those of other classes. Despite questions about his conceptualization, this book placed upon the historian's agenda the issue of class 'formation'.

Family and local historians should approach 'class' with some caution. The 'working class' in this period can incorporate much that might not later be recognized as such. Numerous examples can be found of people of small property and production, employing labour, engaged in a gamut of activities from insurrection to more cautious appearances on the stage of political radicalism. 'Gentleman orators' appear; see, for instance, John Belchem, '*Orator' Hunt: Henry Hunt and English Working-Class Radicalism* (1985). G. D. H. Cole and Raymond Postgate's formulation, *The Common People 1746–1946* (1938; last revised in the 4th edn. of 1949), has been one way of avoiding some of the difficulties.

The argument for caution does not invalidate Thompson's insistence that a working class was being formed in the early 19th century. It does suggest need for care in characterization and the acquisition of some sophistication in the terms of social analysis. The complexities can be pursued through R. S. Neale, *Class in English History 1680–1850* (1981), and *History and Class: Essential Readings in Theory and Interpretation* (1983).

Two major reasons may be adduced for treating Thompson's argument with great respect. First, his proposition that there existed in the period, in Britain, an 'underground revolutionary movement', then controversial among historians, is now well attested. One example of a fine study is Iain McCalman, *Radical Underworld: Prophets, Revolutionaries, and Pornographers in London, 1795–1840* (1988). Second, one

cannot deny the sheer wealth of activity, or its temper. Five examples call for mention: on Welsh insurrectionism, see Gwyn A. Williams, *The Merthyr Rising* (1978); on illegal newspaper publishing, Patricia Hollis, *The Pauper Press: A Study in Working-Class Radicalism of the 1830's* (1970); and on 'English socialism', J. F. C. Harrison, *Robert Owen and the Owenites in Britain and America* (1969). On popular millenarianism and freethought, see J. F. C. Harrison, *The Second Coming. Popular Millenarianism, 1780–1850* (1979), and Edward Royle, *Victorian Infidels: The Origins of the British Secularist Movement, 1791–1866* (1974). For *Chartism, the democratic movement for universal male suffrage and vote by ballot, described as the first mass political mobilization of a working class in world history, see the large literature listed in Owen Ashton, Robert Fyson, and Stephen Roberts, *The Chartist Movement: A New Annotated Bibliography* (1995).

Iorwerth Prothero, *Artisans and Politics in Early Nineteenth-Century London: John Gast and His Times* (1979), acknowledges a 'general debt' to Thompson's classic, but he interprets the London working-class movements of the first four decades more in terms of an 'artisanate' than the broader class. A stratum, rather than a class, also dominates discussion of mid-Victorian labour.

The mid-Victorian stratum is the 'labour aristocracy', introduced by Eric Hobsbawm in his essay 'The Labour Aristocracy in Nineteenth-Century Britain', in *Labouring Men* (1964). Socially mobile upwards, but rigidly demarcated downwards, the stratum was invoked principally to explain the change in the character of working-class political activity in the third quarter of the 19th-century from an insurrectionary movement to one of a more peaceful, reformist, and class-collaborationist nature.

Hobsbawm's essay generated considerable discussion. He has returned to the subject on a number of occasions; see *Worlds of Labour: Further Studies in the History of Labour* (1984). His original treatment concentrated on economic delineation. It recognized social criteria, but left their pursuit to Geoffrey Crossick, *An Artisan Elite in Victorian Society: Kentish London 1840–1880* (1978). Another excellent example is Takao Matsumura, *The Labour Aristocracy Revisited: The Victorian Flint Glass Makers 1850–80* (1983), which largely concerns Stourbridge. This work shows that the importance of historical questions lies not so much in their epistemology (how we come to know), but in their ontology (what they reveal about the conditions of our being); for even if doubts about the validity of this social formation are well-founded, the concept has led to new information about 'respectability', occupational communities, and the inheritance of skill within families.

The necessarily local study of this social formation raises questions of *numeracy as well as literacy, since a principal method of investigation is through the analysis of marriage registers. The most sophisticated treatment, statistically and sociologically, is Roger Penn, *Skilled Workers in the Class Structure* (1984), a study of Rochdale.

Royden Harrison, Matsamura's supervisor, has made a different kind of contribution. His employment of the concept of a labour aristocracy in *Before the Socialists: Studies in Labour and Politics 1861–1881* (1965, reprinted 1994 with a new introduction) addresses such great political issues of British history as the passing of the Second Reform Act, 1867. The book brought labour history into direct conflict with History Proper and stimulated several responses. Maurice Cowling devoted *1867: Disraeli, Gladstone and Revolution: The Passing of the Second Reform Bill* (1967) to a refutation of the suggestion that the activity of the London trades could have had an impact upon Parliament. Another riposte was from Henry Pelling, who questioned the concept of labour aristocracy in an influential volume, *Popular Politics and Society in Late Victorian Britain* (1968). Pelling is not alone. Revisionism has been most recently expressed in Eugenio F. Biagini, *Liberty, Retrenchment and Reform: Popular Liberalism in the Age of Gladstone, 1860–1880* (1992). The argument is partly about the integrity of the labour aristocracy as a social formation, partly about the direction(s) of its behaviour. Suffice to say here, with Harrison, that despite the 'incoherence' of the concept of the labour aristocracy, other notions proposed are subject to just as great or greater intellectual difficulties.

If a debate which is almost as much about the historical understanding of social structure as about politics may not be of great concern to family historians, it is of some relevance to local historians, who have to be concerned with variation in local social structures.

Any question of a 'labour aristocracy' starts to be displaced within the 19th century's fourth quarter. Skill continues to be of interest (see Charles More, *Skill and the English Working Class, 1870–1914* (1980)), but as an attribute of the 'skilled workman'. The unskilled take their place within labour institutions, and upon the political stage, more forcefully now than before.

We see this in E. P. Thompson, 'Homage to Tom Maguire', the Leeds gasworkers' leader (1865–95), in *Essays in Labour History* (1960).

The great symbolic moment is the London Dock Strike of 1889, on which see John Lovell, *Stevedores and Dockers: A Study of Trade Unionism in the Port of London, 1870–1914* (1969). The strike brought forward the 'new unionism' of the unskilled, and new leaders. One example of the latter, selected here because of the role which contact with the subject's family played in allowing his biographer to solve the mystery of a period in Australia, is Chushichi Tsuzuki's *Tom Mann, 1856–1941* (1991). Industrial disputes, and associated entanglements with the courts, were important in the 'rise of labour', as is seen in John Saville's essay, 'Trade Unions and Free Labour: The Background to the Taff Vale Decision' in A. Briggs and J. Saville (eds.), *Essays in Labour History* (1960). The general story to 1900 was well told in Henry Pelling, *Origins of the Labour Party 1880–1900* (1965).

It is clear that, in terms of class formation, the working class of the late 19th century became a different animal from that of the early period: it can be seen in residential patterns (on which relevant, if not conventional labour history, is Richard Dennis, *English Industrial Cities of the Nineteenth Century: A Social Geography* (1984)); leisure activities (see, for example, Tony Mason, *Association Football and English Society, 1863–1915* (1980)), and 'culture' (for an introduction see Eric Hobsbawm, 'The Formation of British Working-Class Culture', in *Worlds of Labour* (1984)).

The working class became more 'solidaristic', as well as remaining jingoistic in this period. See, for example, Richard Price, *An Imperial War and the British Working Class: Working-Class Attitudes and Reactions to the Boer War 1899–1902* (1972). The labour movement remained insular. It did not adopt continental Marxism on any scale then or later, despite the existence of local pockets; see Ross McKibbin, 'Why Was There no Marxism in Great Britain?' in his *Ideologies of Class: Social Relations in Britain 1880–1950* (1990), and Stuart Macintyre, *Little Moscows: Communism and Working-Class Militancy in Inter-War Britain* (1980). But the 'woman question' came to the fore; on which notable studies have appeared, such as Jill Liddington and Jill Norris's *One Hand Tied Behind Us: The Rise of the Women's Suffrage Movement* (1978), or Carolyn Steedman's biography, *Childhood, Culture and Class in Britain: Margaret McMillan, 1860–1931* (1990). The large literature now available on working-class life in the period, including Robert Roberts's excellent account, *The Classic Slum: Salford Life in the First Quarter of the Century* (1971), partly based on family reminiscence, provide an adequate basis for assessing social factors in the rise of labour.

Debate between labour and other historians now centres on whether Labour's rise was inevitable, or arose out of mistakes on the part of the Liberal Party or the impact of the First World War. A recent and comprehensive treatment is in Duncan Tanner, *Political Change and the Labour Party, 1900–1918* (1990), while Keith Laybourn, *The Rise of Labour: The British Labour Party, 1890–1979* (1988) expresses a more traditional labour-history view. The First World War certainly had a major impact upon Labour's fortunes, as did the Second. This can be seen especially clearly through the activities of the 'labour' committee, treated in an account by Royden Harrison, 'The War Emergency: Workers' National Committee 1914–1920' in A. Briggs and J. Saville (eds.), *Essays in Labour History* (1971). The committee became the major channel for the expression of working-class grievances about living standards and other matters during the war.

The many other important studies include James Hinton, *The First Shop Stewards' Movement* (1973), Chris Wrigley's two books, *David Lloyd George and the British Labour Movement* (1976) and *Lloyd George and the Challenge of Labour: The Post-War Coalition, 1918–1922* (1990), and Ross McKibbin, *The Evolution of the Labour Party, 1910–1924* (1974). For events in London see Jill Bush, *Behind the Lines: East London Labour 1914–1919* (1984). The local consequence of the war is particularly well portrayed in Noreen Branson, *Poplarism 1919–1925: George Lansbury and the Councillors' Revolt* (1979).

The inter-war period is dominated by two episodes of minority Labour government, and by unemployment. The Russian Revolution of 1917 became a central point of reference for the labour movement. Fascism appeared as a major threat. The General Strike was a dramatic and traumatic episode. Christopher Farman provides a readable general account of the latter in *The General Strike: May 1926* (1972), but the subject lends itself to local investigation, as can be seen from the treatments of Battersea, Glasgow, Pontypridd, and Sheffield in Margaret Morris, *The General Strike* (1976). The most professional local treatment is A. Mason, *The General Strike in the North-East* (1970).

As to Russia, Bill Jones surveys the period 1917–48 in *The Russia Complex: The British Labour Party and the Soviet Union* (1977). A more detailed and specialized treatment of Labour's early inter-war years is in Stephen White, *Britain and the Bolshevik Revolution: A Study in the Politics of Diplomacy 1920–1924* (1979). These treatments are concerned with high politics and may seem of little concern to family and local historians, but such matters became inescapable for a party of government. They had an impact on the labour movement's local organizations and, in an age of radio and modern transport, touched individual lives.

Fascism touched one of Labour's most brilliant politicians, Sir Oswald Mosley. His son, Nicholas Mosley, demonstrates in *Rules of the Game: Sir Oswald and Lady Cynthia Mosley, 1896–1933* (1982), how an essay in family history can make a valuable contribution to labour history. Mosley's experience (his full biography is Robert Skidelsky, *Oswald Mosley* (1975)) was central to that of Labour government. A party of the working class gains its support, as Labour did throughout the 1920s, by raising aspirations and hope that something can be done about the major problems of people's lives. It is the cruel paradox of achieving government office that these hopes will be dashed. This occurred for some supporters during the first Labour government; the standard treatment is R. W. Lyman, *The First Labour Government 1924* (1957). The major problem was caused by the second Labour government's failure to deal with unemployment, rejecting Mosley's proposals. It is doubtful whether unemployment could have been treated successfully, though the matter might have been handled better politically. The issues are partly treated in Ross McKibbin's essay of 1979 in *Past and Present*, 'The Economic Policy of the Second Labour Government, 1929–1931', reprinted in *Ideologies of Class* (1990). For a general treatment see Robert Skidelsky, *Politicians and the Slump: The Labour Government of 1929–1931* (1967). There is no better way to catch the impact of the government's failure upon the labour movement than through Ray Challinor's portrait of the delightfully eccentric north-eastern Member of Parliament, *John S. Clarke: Parliamentarian, Poet, Lion Tamer* (1977).

The most general and best treatment of the unemployment question in the inter-war years is W. R. Garside, *British Unemployment 1919–1939: A Study in Public Policy* (1990). General economic history shades here into labour history. The agitation against unemployment is best represented by Richard Croucher, *We Refuse to Starve in Silence: A History of the National Unemployed Workers' Movement, 1920–1946* (1987). The voices of those who experienced unemployment and joined the marches against it are heard in Ian MacDougall (compiler), *Voices from the Hunger Marches: Personal Recollections by Scottish Hunger Marchers of the 1920's and 1930's*, i (1990), ii (1991).

After the collapse of the Labour Government in 1931, the leadership of the party eventually passed into the capable hands of Clement Attlee, whose elevation is well treated by John Shepherd, 'Labour and the Trade Unions: Lansbury, Ernest Bevin and the Leadership Crisis of 1935' in Chris Wrigley and John Shepherd (eds.), *On the Move: Essays in Labour and Transport History Presented to Philip Bagwell* (1991). Paul Addison, *The Road to 1945: British Politics and the Second World War* (1975) provided an influential account of the reasons for the formation of the first majority Labour government.

It remains to draw attention to a few significant works placed upon one side by the scheme of this essay, and to identify resources. The finest example of a local study of labour is still Sidney Pollard, *A History of Labour in Sheffield* (1959). Notable new local studies are appearing in some quantity. A relatively recent, widely admired example is Michael Savage, *The Dynamics of Working-Class Politics: The Labour Movement in Preston, 1880–1940* (1987). No place has been found here for discussion of the 18th century, but see ENCLOSURE, PARLIAMENTARY; COMMONS AND WASTES; and FOOD RIOTS. E. P. Thompson's essays, now collected in *Customs in Common* (1991), provide the most eloquent introduction, as startling in their impact as was *The Making of the English Working Class*.

The literature is immense. The best entry is through the annual bibliographies published in *Labour History Review*, the journal of the Society for the Study of Labour History (founded in 1960), appearing formerly as its *Bulletin*. The *Review*'s bibliography appears in 12 main sections, ranging from bibliography, methodology, and nature of the subject through biography, wages, and working conditions, to other (labour and left) organizations. The seventh section contains ten subdivisions and includes such topics as women and ethnic minorities. For the labour history of Wales, see the journal *Llafur*; for Ireland, *Saothar*; for Scotland, the *Journal of the Scottish Labour History Society*. North-west and north-east England also have Labour History Groups which produce journals.

The labour press, which has no general history, can be a valuable resource for many local and some family historians. Its riches can be approached through Royden Harrison, Gillian Woolven, and Robert Duncan (compilers), *The Warwick Guide to British Labour Periodicals 1790–1970: A Check List* (1977). Autobiographies of the working class have been studied by David Vincent, *Bread, Knowledge and Freedom: A Study of Nineteenth-Century Working Class Autobiography* (1981). For a full set of reference works see John Burnett, David Vincent, and David Mayall (eds.), *The Autobiography of the Working Class*, i. *An Annotated Critical Biography, 1790–1900* (1984); ii. *1900–1945* (1987); and iii. *A Supplement to the Annotated Critical Biography, 1790–1945* (1989). As to biography, G. D. H. Cole conceived the idea of a *Dictionary of Labour Biography* as an alternative to the *Dictionary of National Biography*. The idea was carried forward after Cole's death by John Saville, and nine volumes (1972–1993) of the *DLB* have now appeared, edited by Joyce M. Bellamy and John Saville. The volumes already contain some 857 entries.   JOHN L. HALSTEAD

labour party. The Labour Representation Committee, which was formed in 1900 as a loose federation of *trade unions and socialist societies, changed its name to the Labour Party upon winning 29 seats in the election of 1906. Its constitution was drawn up in 1918. The Labour Party formed minority governments in 1924 and 1929–31 and first achieved majority control in 1945–51. Since then, it has formed governments in 1964–70 and 1974–9.

labour services. The obligation of medieval peasants to work for certain periods on the *demesne of the *lord of the manor. (See BOON WORK.) The heaviest burden was borne by the peasants of East Anglia. In northern England, Kent, and Cornwall services were light. Lords had generally lightened their demands before the system was greatly weakened by the *Black Death. See John Hatcher, 'England in the Aftermath of the Black Death', *Past and Present*, 144 (1994). By the 16th century, labour services were a rare phenomenon.

lace-making was an Elizabethan project which took root in the south midlands and Devon. It survived as a handcraft ('pillow' lace-making) for females until the Victorian period in Bedfordshire, Buckinghamshire, Northamptonshire, and Devon. Machine-made lace originated in Nottingham in the late 18th century. The invention of the point-net frame in 1778 enabled the production of cheap lace, but the great growth of the Nottingham industry occurred after John Heathcote's invention of the bobbin net machine in 1808. Growth continued until the First World War, but demand for lace collapsed in the 1920s. See Linda Ballard, 'Irish Lace: Tradition or Commodity?', *Folk Life*, 31 (1993), H. J. Yallop, *The History of the Honiton Lace Industry* (1992), and Joanna Bourke, ' "I was always fond of my pillow": The Handmade Lace Industry in the United Kingdom, 1870–1914', *Rural History*, 5/1 (1994).

Lady chapels. *Chantry chapels in parish *churches dedicated to Our Lady, St Mary. Founders of chantries dedicated their chapels to a great variety of saints, but St Mary was the most popular choice. Chantry chapels were dissolved in 1547, but since Victorian times many of them have been restored as chapels for private prayer. Some of the restored 'Lady chapels' of today had a different dedication in the Middle Ages.

Lady Day. 25 March, the official start of the year until 1752. Rents were commonly paid twice a year, at Lady Day and *Michaelmas.

laithe houses. A term coined to distinguish a type of farmhouse found in northern England, especially on the Pennines, from the medieval *longhouse. The dwelling house and laithe (barn) are built on a long axis and share the same roof, but unlike the longhouse they have separate entrances and no internal connection. The earliest examples date from c.1650, but most laithe houses are 18th- and 19th-century. They are the characteristic farm buildings on the Yorkshire Pennines that were erected after the *enclosure of the wastes.

Lambarde, William (1536–1601). Author of *The Perambulation of Kent* (1576), the first county history, a work that was much concerned with the genealogies of the Kentish gentry as well as with topography. As a young man at Lincoln's Inn, Lambarde had studied Anglo-Saxon and other ancient manuscripts and had become interested in the meaning of *place-names and the ancient laws and customs of his county, particularly that of *gavelkind, whereby property was transmitted to all sons rather than the eldest alone. His writings reflect his interest in legal antiquarianism. In 1568 he published *Archaionomia*, a translation of Anglo-Saxon laws into Latin. In 1591 he completed *Archeion: Or a Discourse upon the High Courts of Justice in England*, which was published in 1635. His *Topographical Dictionary* circulated widely in manuscript but was not published until 1730. See Retha M. Warnicke, *William Lambarde* (1973).

Lambeth Palace Library. Founded in 1610 in a wing of the palace, this public library houses many of the documents of the Archbishopric of Canterbury, e.g. enquiries about *benefices, *tithes, buildings, etc., the *marriage licences of the Faculty Office and Vicar General's Office, and the *probate records of the Court of *Arches and certain *peculiar jurisdictions in London. The library is now administered by the Church Commissioners. Application to search the records should be made in writing to the Librarian, Lambeth Palace Library, London SE1 7JU.

Lammas grazing. Some enclosed lands, which formerly lay within the *open-fields of a *manor, were still grazed in common after the gathering of the harvest. Before 1752, Lammas Day was 1 August; after the change of the calendar it was 13 August. The derivation of the name and the nature of the harvested crop are disputed, but the date suggests that the crop was hay and that the name referred to a second, or later, mowing.

Lancaster, Duchy of. Created in 1351 when Henry, Earl of Lancaster, was made a duke, and revived in 1377 by a grant to John of Gaunt, the Duchy of Lancaster retained its distinctive judicial system and administrative structure after it reverted to the Crown in 1399. The dukedom had estates in almost every county of England and Wales. Its records are kept at the *Public Record Office; those for the county palatine of Lancaster have been listed in *Lists and Indexes* 40, those for other parts of the country in *Lists and Indexes* 14. More detailed listings of various classes of record include *Lists and Indexes* 6 (court rolls) and 25 (*rentals and *surveys). At the PRO other major classes of records include DL 10 (royal *charters for towns), DL 14 and 15 (*leases), DL 16 (presentations to *benefices), DL 25 to 27 (*deeds), DL 27 (*inquisitions post mortem), DL 29 (*ministers' accounts), DL 31 (*maps and plans), DL 32 (parliamentary surveys), DL 38 (*chantry certificates), DL 39 (*forest proceedings), DL 44 (special commissions), and DL 45 (*enclosure awards). The Duchy retained its common-law and criminal jurisdiction until 1873 and its chancery court until 1971. See R. Somerville, *History of the Duchy of Lancaster*, vol. i (1953).

landowners. British land is owned ultimately by the Crown, but most of it has been given, 'sold', or granted to private individuals or public bodies with an effective right of *freehold. Neither land registration nor national surveys have been popular in Britain, which means that there are few figures from which general trends can be assessed. Between the great *Domesday survey of 1086 and the late 19th century no national record was kept of transactions or ownership, although some major discontinuities in ownership are well known, particularly the turnover of land following the *Norman Conquest, and the transfer of land from the Church, initially to the Crown, and later into private hands, following the *Dissolution of the monasteries. The so-called New Domesday of 1876, in reality a *parliamentary paper based on information primarily culled from *rate books, gives an indication of ownership for the early 1870s by named individuals, but is known to be flawed. Information on the estates of the greater landowners was reassessed, and a more accurate statement of their property on a county basis was published as John Bateman, *The Great Landowners of Great Britain and Ireland* (1883). The work of the Inland Revenue in connection with Lloyd George's taxes on land levied as a result of the 1909 Budget produced another 'New Domesday', a property-by-property assessment of the whole country in 95,000 volumes (see VALUATION OFFICE). To date, the sheer bulk of the material has been too great for any easy analysis. Even today there is no complete record of land-ownership across the United Kingdom.

In the absence of good statistical material, any examination of land-ownership is bound to depend partly on informed speculation. From the evidence of a tax on land in 1436, it is estimated that the Crown and the Church together probably owned about one quarter of the total English landed income in the early 15th century, lay peers and others with incomes of £100 a year or more owned a further fifth, 30 per cent or so was in the hands of those with incomes of £5 to £99, and 26 per cent in the hands of those with incomes of £5 a year or less; see J. P. Cooper, 'The Social Distribution of Land and Men in England, 1436–1700', *Economic History Review*, 20 (1967). Over the following century this pattern is unlikely to have changed greatly, but the position was fundamentally altered by the transfer of monastic land into private ownership after 1536. By the late 17th century the best guess that we have suggests that the great majority of land was in private hands with between a quarter and a third owned by small proprietors, many of whom probably worked their own land.

From the late 17th century to at least the 1880s the general trend in the pattern of ownership was in favour of the large estate. This movement occurred for a number of reasons,

including the gradual squeezing of the small owner-occupier at the expense of the greater owners. The latter were aided by land laws which enabled them to hold their properties together over long periods of time, via a mechanism known as *entail, and to underwrite themselves financially, if needs be, by mortgaging their land. Some owners were able to run up substantial debts, among them the Dukes of Devonshire, but only seldom did this prove disastrous, as in 1848 when the second Duke of Buckingham was effectively bankrupted by his extravagances. Benjamin Disraeli found it all very mystifying, musing in the reminiscences which he wrote in the early 1860s on 'the difficulty of destroying a family rooted in the land'. The ability of the larger landowners to entail their property enabled them to resist the dispersion of their estates despite the demands of the *nouveaux riches* for land.

Much debate has surrounded the role of businessmen and *merchants. Contemporaries believed that every trader and manufacturer with money to spare was anxious to acquire a landed estate. Since buying a ready-made estate was increasingly difficult, a new pattern emerged by which rich families, looking to earn the social status carried by land, acquired small properties with a substantial house or the potential for building one. The initial trend was towards buying what came to be known as villa estates on the edge of large towns, a few acres which gave them the status of *gentry, and the land to build a suitable mansion. Daniel *Defoe noted this trend in the counties around London as early as the 1720s, and by the 19th century the pattern was repeated in the vicinity of more substantial provincial towns. Some families later moved further afield, acquiring a larger property at a greater distance from the place in which they had originally made their fortune and retiring to the countryside. Thus, Lancashire textile manufacturers settled in the Lake District, and London merchants in Lincolnshire. The desire to purchase land seems not to have faded—except perhaps in the case of some of the richest London merchants and financiers—even though the quantities acquired changed, which is why the proportion of land in gentry estates was still around 50 per cent of the whole in 1873. Although the case has been disputed, there seems to be little doubt that the flow of money from business into land continued at least until the late 19th-century *Agricultural Depression.

The people most clearly squeezed by this process were the owner-occupiers. From around 33 per cent of the landed acreage in

1688, their share declined to around 10 per cent in the 1870s. It was once argued that they had been dispossessed by the predatory greater owners in the years after 1530 and particularly after 1660. On this assumption it was believed that the great majority had been bought out by 1750, and any still left were swept away by parliamentary *enclosure. However, this belief now seems to be an exaggeration of the trend. In reality, two processes were at work. First, the expropriation of the smaller owner-occupier, the man (or woman) working the land that they owned. Many of these people either sold out altogether, or took to renting additional land in order to make a viable holding (see SMALLHOLDERS, DECLINE OF). Second, since the quantity of land in smallholdings by the 1870s was probably not much less than it had been in the 1690s, it is evident that a good deal of land—perhaps 10 to 15 per cent—came into the hands of non-farming owners. These people often turn out to have been pseudo-country gentlemen, petty landlords, rural tradesmen, publicans, absentees who had inherited land but no longer wished to work it, or small-scale investors, but their appearance in the countryside seems to have produced a new group of owners not readily identifiable prior to 1750.

Land-ownership in Scotland took a slightly different path from that of England and Wales, but there was a marked concentration of ownership in the 17th and 18th centuries. Landowners were a powerful social class in lowland Scotland, and historically ownership was concentrated. In the 1770s one-third or more of the valued rent was held by great landowners in a number of southern and lowland counties. The smaller proprietors held a greater proportion of land in the centre and west of Scotland, but by the early 19th century the country had about 7,500 owners. In the Highlands the 1820s and 1830s saw a rapid acceleration in the scale of property transfer, with many estates being acquired by Lowland and English commercial interests as the old élite was squeezed out by static rents and over-extended lifestyles. This was also one of the few areas in which a wealthy parvenu could still hope to acquire a large acreage relatively cheaply. By the 1870s, 90 per cent of Scottish land was owned by 1,500 people.

The pattern of ownership in Ireland had been partially determined by the upheavals of the 17th century, particularly the English *plantation policy which was designed to establish order and good government in Ireland. Particularly important was the Cromwellian policy which effectively altered the balance between

Protestant and recusant, with the former taking over not only land but also local government. The crisis of 1845 to 1850 in Ireland brought about a fundamental change in the law designed to simplify the transfer of landed property, which by then had been accumulated into the hands of about 10,000 proprietors. The greatest landowners included the Duke of Leinster with 73,000 acres in Kildare and Meath, the Marquess of Downship with 115,000 acres in five counties, and the Duke of Abercorn with 76,000 acres. By the 1870s over half the country was owned by fewer than 1,000 great landlords.

The consequences of these various trends across the United Kingdom were most clearly shown in the New Domesday of the 1870s. Intense debate surrounded the findings of the decennial *census of 1851 and 1861 which appeared to show that English land was owned by only a tiny minority of the population. The 1870s survey was intended to redress the balance of opinion, but it did precisely the opposite. Analysis of the returns showed that 7,000 owners controlled four-fifths of all the land in the United Kingdom, a concentration regarded by many as tantamount to a monopoly. The New Domesday added grist to the mill of the incipient campaign for a free trade in land, and across the British Isles the last quarter of the 19th century saw a sustained attack on 'landlordism', with land wars being fought in Ireland, Scotland (the Crofters' war), and Wales, and with considerable changes in the laws relating to land-ownership.

The position of the embattled owners was not helped by the fact that in the 1880s and 1890s many sections of British agriculture suffered severe depression. Landowners had to cope with falling rent rolls which reduced their disposable income, and falling land values, which reduced the security on which their mortgages were often secured. The introduction of death duties in 1894 was a symbolic turning-point for many owners. Some began seriously to consider selling property. Some were able to do so because of changes in the land laws in the 1880s, and by 1914 a number of large estates had come on to the market.

In the aftermath of the Armistice in 1918, estates across the country were put up for sale. Since the First World War there has, as a result, been a substantial change in the pattern of ownership. Large estates have often been broken up, with the land being sold to sitting tenants, or to institutions. As a result, the Forestry Commission is now the largest private landlord in Britain, and vast acreages are owned by the Ministry of Defence, the National Trust, and the electricity, water, and other utility companies. Pension funds and other investment groups including Oxford and Cambridge colleges and the *Church of England are also substantial owners, while at the other end of the social scale the growth of house owner-occupancy has greatly increased the number of people owning their own property. Yet while many of the great estates have been broken up and numerous country houses have either passed into other uses or been demolished, the great landlords have not disappeared entirely. The Duke of Westminster, with extensive estates in Cheshire as well as urban property in London, is still one of the wealthiest people in the country, and many of the greater owners remain on their (reduced) estates, among them the Dukes of Devonshire and Rutland. In Scotland, four of the top ten landowning families today, the Dukes of Buccleuch and Athol, the Countess of Sutherland, and Earl Seafield, were also among the greatest owners in the 1870s. See J. V. Beckett, *The Aristocracy in England, 1660–1914* (2nd edn., 1988), D. Cannadine, *The Decline and Fall of the British Aristocracy* (1990), and J. Habakkuk, *Marriage, Debt and the Estates System: English Landownership 1650–1950* (1994).   J. V. BECKETT

lands. The *strips or *selions of an *open-field. 'Lands' was the term most often used by farmers. See HEADLAND.

landscape history: the countryside. G. R. Elton described a 'large' historical subject as one which compels the historian to branch out widely and to consider many related topics. Landscape history is such a subject. A simple example—the decline of settlement in the 15th century to produce a *deserted village—will show what is meant by this. Some local historians will be interested in desertion from the viewpoint of social relations: as a village declined, what were the relative roles played by villagers and the *lord of the manor? Others may approach the topic from an economic angle, more concerned with the viability, in a period of changing patterns of demand, of the very different farming systems practised before and after desertion; yet others may approach it from the viewpoint of landscape, the changing appearance of the settlement and its fields as desertion took place. But from whichever of these three directions the topic is approached, the others cannot be neglected. The student of social relations cannot ignore the economic forces which influenced decisions made by dif-

ferent classes within the declining village, nor their differing and conflicting approaches to landscape management (e.g. to the maintenance of buildings and fields). The economic historian will need to understand the forces for inertia inherent in any human landscape or type of social structure, because the strength or weakness of those forces, as well as a changing external economy, affected the timing of desertion. The landscape historian will be reduced simply to contemplating and describing a lifeless artefact—the deserted village and its deserted fields—unless he or she understands both the decisions made by their owner and occupiers as the settlement dwindled and the economic and social repercussions of desertion. In this very simple example we should picture village desertion as a central point in an imaginary diagram, with paths of enquiry from several viewpoints all converging on the centre and tangling there. The researcher who seeks an understanding of the centre by treading any one of these paths cannot avoid being led out again along the others.

What W. G. *Hoskins wrote of *vernacular architecture is highly apposite to research in landscape history: 'We ought to place all types . . . in their *human* background and relate them to the social and economic history of their immediate surroundings. Without this . . . we can only dimly understand what we are looking at' (*Fieldwork in Local History*, 1967, 94). The human landscape (a telling term coined by geographers to distinguish those elements made by men and women from those made by nature) reflects past social relationships, population, economies, and culture. In the relationship between landscape and people another dimension helps us to explain as well as to appreciate: that approach concerns the human landscape (especially, but not exclusively, the pattern of settlement) as an influence on behaviour. A few examples will illustrate this point.

The first relates to the influence of village desertion on labour relations: where desertion during the 15th century left landscapes in which pools of village labour were fewer and more widely separated than in more robust countrysides, the boarding of servants on remote surviving farmsteads necessarily persisted long into the 19th century, when the practice nationally was on the decline. Thus a type of settlement pattern inherited from an earlier age continued to influence social relations of labour long afterwards. A second example relates to settlement pattern and aspects of *popular culture in the 17th century: in Wiltshire and adjoining counties it has been shown convincingly that inter-parochial *football matches and the practice of holding communal *church ales were best developed in regions of nucleated settlement and common-field farming, where there were strong traditions of co-operation within villages as well as periodic conflicts between communities over *boundaries and common pastures; in regions where more scattered settlement restricted parochial loyalties, such festivities tended to be absent. Then again, a very good case may be made for an association between, on the one hand, the type of dispersed settlement pattern which was established in regions colonized relatively late in the day (largely in the 200 years following the *Norman Conquest) and, on the other, well-developed personal freedom, sometimes engendering a notable resistance to authority; the stubbornness of 'people bred amongst woods' was noted by John *Norden in the 16th century and by many subsequent commentators. Historians have elaborated on the linkages, noting how personal independence tends to have been fostered by the distance of the new farmsteads from a manorial centre (which might be a distant 'parent' manor), by a tendency towards pastoral farming which involved relatively little co-operation between neighbours, and by the great size of some *parishes in late-colonized regions, which made parochial government difficult.

Quite complex relationships exist between the human landscape and demography. This may again be illustrated from regions where many villages were deserted and population declined severely during the 15th century, and where occupiers of surviving isolated farmsteads tended to employ living-in servants in husbandry rather than *day labourers. This practice may have depressed population even further, because farm-boarded servants tended to marry later than labourers with access to their own accommodation. The nature of the human landscape has a central place here: decline in population creates a particular type of settlement pattern, engendering a type of labour deployment conducive to further demographic decline. Another illustration may be drawn from our knowledge of *field systems. It is likely to have been pressure of population on the land which, among other factors, encouraged the people of some *townships to adopt the two-field system of cultivation, probably, we now think, in the 10th or 11th centuries. This was by no means the most productive type of medieval field system. Yet it was of a kind which, once introduced, was hard to modify, partly because *strips widely scattered over the face of a township made change very difficult; indeed, some historians now think that widespread scattering of strips (the system's expression in the landscape) was introduced as a conscious desire to prevent individuals pulling out of it through piecemeal *enclosure. The introduction of two-field systems may have curbed any large increase of population in the long term; regions in which many communities had adopted them tended to be relatively lightly populated (according to medieval sources) when compared with regions where more flexible and productive systems were practised. Finally, a clear and blatant illustration of the deliberate restructuring of landscape in order to curb population was the amalgamation of farms and destruction of *cottages by landlords in order to create 'closed' *villages with few people, few niches for immigrants, and, therefore, low poor rates.

In these examples the central, sometimes pivotal, role played by changes made by people to landscapes illustrates the heights of historical relevance to which landscape history can be elevated. Local historians may sometimes be asked to record and classify historic features in the present-day landscape, a task which is useful and above all enjoyable. But this is not landscape history, because history is about people; it is a type of surveying which requires historical skills, a technique, just as medieval archaeology or industrial archaeology are highly useful techniques which serve wider historical aims. Local historians with a fascination for landscapes should, rather, see themselves as students of past milieux and of the two-way relationship between those milieux and society: they were constantly being created, maintained, and modified, for economic, social, and cultural reasons, by people of all classes, sexes, and beliefs, while their character touched deeply upon the quality of life of those people. This approach alone is landscape history. It is an approach which locates the subject centrally within the history of the British people, ranking equally in importance with, say, the histories of social relations, *standards of living, or population.

The subject is relatively young. No historian would disagree with the claim that *The Making of the English Landscape* (1955) by W. G. Hoskins was the pioneer work. A few scholars (and it is a few) had previously touched upon particular aspects of the subject: here we might pick out the work of F. W. *Seebohm, W. Page, O. G. S. Crawford, H. C. Darby, M. R. G. Conzen, A. Raistrick, and H. Thorpe, all of whom were acknowledged by Hoskins. But it was Hoskins who pioneered the subject in the grand manner as is clear from the 1988 edition of his book, with a new introduction and commentary by C. Taylor.

It is useful, as an aid to disentangling the complexities of the subject, to think of British rural landscapes as belonging to three very broadly defined types. The first comprises what we may call village landscapes, typical of many parts of the English midlands, where nucleated villages and village communities (with all their internal divisions) were created towards the end of the *Anglo-Saxon period, beginning perhaps in the 9th century and continuing into the 11th. The second type comprises landscapes in which farmstead sites are dispersed, rather than nucleated, and which have had a continuity of occupance going back before the 9th century; these we may call landscapes of ancient dispersal. Finally, in some regions much of the dispersed settlement still apparent in the landscape was created relatively late, after nucleation had taken place in the village lands; these are landscapes of secondary dispersal. In this crude classification (many landscapes are intriguing complications and hybrids) the central variables are the type and date of origin of the settlements which we see today, for these tend to influence other variables in the texture of the landscape, such as patterns of lanes and fields.

Village landscapes cover large (though not all) parts of a great diagonal swathe of British countryside, stretching from mid-Somerset to the vicinity of the border with Scotland. As an example we shall take 25 square miles of Berkshire landscape in the vale of the infant River Ock, as shown on the first edition of the one-inch Ordnance Survey map. Within the square nine villages are shown, many of them with place-names in -ford (e.g. Stanford in the Vale), or -ey (such as Charney), recalling the importance of fords and streams in this gently undulating vale (the last element in Charney means 'island' in the sense of 'territory bounded by streams'). Settlements are few: nine villages; a very small number of isolated farms with old names (some of them along streams and with names ending in -wick, meaning a dairy farm and recalling the specialism in *cheese-making recorded here in the 11th century); and a few isolated farmsteads built proudly on *allotments made after parliamentary *enclosure, such as Eastfield Farm, which takes its name from one of the great *open-fields of Stanford. But the nine villages dominate the settlement pattern. Few settlements generate relatively few lanes, those which exist

in this landscape being, in origin, access tracks to the village fields with right-angle bends which once wove between the *furlongs. A consensus of opinion now suggests that in countrysides such as this most of the villages were created through nucleation of formerly dispersed settlement during a phase of vibrant social and economic development in the late Anglo-Saxon period (9th to 11th centuries). People in this period witnessed and participated in a coming-together in close proximity within villages of lords, dependent tenants, and labourers, and at the same time in the evolution of township-wide field systems, generally of the two-field or three-field variety, within whose agreed rhythms and intricately fragmented landscapes the village and villagers became locked. These developments in the landscape moulded social relations and standards of living in village countrysides for many centuries.

The mould was not easy to break, but broken it was in some villages when, from the late 14th century onwards, the social and physical fabric of settlements and their fields began to crumble away as demand for land and for the grains grown in the open-fields declined in the recession of the later Middle Ages; this process, in which tenants, labourers, and lords all played a role, gave some regional concentrations of depopulation, as on the Yorkshire Wolds, distant from urban markets, around the celebrated excavated site of Wharram Percy.

Another important divergence in the appearance and social composition of villages took place in the late 18th and 19th centuries (although there were earlier antecedents): this was the deliberate creation of 'closed' villages and the related spontaneous development of contrasted 'open' settlements. In closed villages landlords carefully controlled labour, destroyed surplus cottages, and renovated or reconstructed the building stock, as at Lockinge and Ardington, described in 1891 as a 'delightful Berkshire colony', though visibly steeped in deference and dependence. In open *villages no landlord or group of farmers could control immigration or building standards. Such villages came to have the appearance of the 'Alton Locke' of Charles Kingsley, 'a knot of thatched hovels all sinking and leaning every way but the right, which surrounded the beer shop'. The structure of land-ownership was responsible for this divergence, as was village size, for closure was easier in small and partially depopulated places; features inherited from a far earlier age had a profound influence on the fortunes of people and places in the 19th century. The same could be said of variations from place to place, and regionally, in the timing of enclosure of village fields, a movement which proceeded apace from the 15th century and petered out with the last enclosures sanctioned by Act of Parliament in Victoria's reign.

Landscapes of ancient dispersal, where parliamentary enclosure was rarely necessary, are Britain's 'antique lands'. The observant landscape historian can sometimes sense an old patina in their field surfaces, boundaries, and lanes. An example may be seen on another 25-mile square from the Ordnance Survey map, in Cornwall just to the south of Camelford, between the coast and the River Camel. The map is black with the names of settlements dispersed over the face of the land, a total of 75 farms and *hamlets in this small tract of countryside. The relatively few large clusters of buildings, e.g. St Kew, are service centres, recent in origin, rather than agricultural villages containing farmhouses. Patterns of lanes, determined in their direction and etched deep into the landscape, are noticeably denser than in the village lands; major field boundaries are more massive. *Lordship and Christian sites are also dispersed, the parish *church of Advent inaccessible except by footpaths and locked into an ancient pattern of fields. One clue to the antiquity of this landscape comes from the names of the settlements, for well over 90 per cent of them are purely Celtic. Another clue is provided by the very low frequency of place-names with elements denoting natural vegetation: the taming of the land took place so long ago (certainly before 1086, for the *Domesday Book records little *wood or pasture here) that its wild state is no longer remembered in its names. Ecclesiastical evidence provides further and firmer clues. A cult of St Kew flourished among the people of this landscape at least as early as AD 900, when a list of saints, a very rare survival, in all probability locates it here; a life of St Sampson of Dol, probably written in the 8th century, refers to this region as Tricurius, now Trigg. Just to the north of Camelford is a monument commemorating a Christian inhabitant of the area who, on the basis of the form of the inscription, is unlikely to have died much later than AD 700. For so early a period these facts are by no means slender evidence and testify to a landscape inhabited in the 8th century. It requires a leap of the imagination to conclude that the people who lived here then inhabited the same settlement sites which we still see today, but one is inevitably led to that conclusion by the apparent immovability of the landscape's bone-structure—its lanes and major field boundaries—and by a number of

place-names containing the Cornish element *hen*, meaning 'ancient', names which in all probability were coined before the Norman Conquest and testify to the antiquity even then of some of the sites.

Landscapes of secondary dispersal, by contrast, have a rougher, more youthful, less well-tamed air about them. Our third example from the one-inch Ordnance Survey map is a tract of country centred on the small town of Henley-in-Arden (Warwickshire). Arden is an ancient *pays name meaning 'steep' or 'high' (as in the continental Ardennes), and it was probably because of those characteristics that the region was still relatively lightly settled at the time of the Norman Conquest, to judge from the evidence of the Domesday Book. There is good documentary evidence from the 12th and 13th centuries of a vigorous colonization movement here in which both lords and their tenants participated, the latter anxious for new land in what was undoubtedly an age of population pressure. The evidence of the one-inch map adds new touches to this picture of activity. The generally dispersed nature of settlement (about 38 names in the 25-square-mile sample) matches the documentary evidence of 13th-century land grants relating to *assarts (clearings) in remote locations. The pattern made by the lanes is a tangled one with many loops which have no apparent rationale, a bequest perhaps from a pattern of haphazardly wandering tracks through *heath and wood. Many of the place-names tell of the wooded or heathy environments (a few ragged remnants of which still remain) into which settlements were first inserted by their pioneers. Reclamation here took place relatively recently, so that the landscape which preceded improvement is still recorded in the nomenclature of farms and hamlets. Of course we should not think of medieval colonization as a movement taking place in an unused 'wilderness'. It can be shown that the diverse resources of the woods and heaths of Arden were used by people from quite far afield long before the 13th century, seasonally occupied sites perhaps preceding permanent settlement. The same may be said of many moorland regions colonized at about the same time as Arden; examples include settlements on Bodmin Moor with the Cornish element *havos* ('summer dwelling') in their names, and sites in the significantly named Newlands Valley in the Lake District, where several farm-names contain the element *skali* ('temporary site'). Nor should we think of these relatively new settlements as particularly prone to desertion. Some contraction has taken place in landscapes of secondary dispersal (the hamlet is a 'pulsating' form, often growing out of a single farm, then contracting again) but in general the characteristics of independence and diversified economies created in regions of this type ensured a good deal of settlement survival.

It is clearly wrong to lump together all regions where settlements are dispersed rather than nucleated and to call them 'ancient countryside', as in some texts, for there are very great differences in landscape texture and in regional society between the Cornish and Warwickshire examples just given. It must be added that it is not always easy to make a case for the deep antiquity of settlement in some landscapes of dispersal and its relative freshness in others. In Wales, for example, a country once far more wooded than it is today, some farms and hamlets were still being newly created from woodland in the early modern period while others were undoubtedly already in existence by the 12th and 13th centuries, when dispersed settlement was described as the dominant type both by Giraldus Cambrensis (*Gerald of Wales), and by Archbishop Pecham, in a report to Edward I. If archaeologists could be persuaded to move away from a preoccupation with deserted sites and to incorporate living farms into their surveys, it may yet be shown that some of these farms have ancient, even prehistoric origins. By far the best guide to the problems and techniques of distinguishing between the two types—and the most ambitious and sustained essay in early landscape history to appear recently—is Alan Everitt, *Continuity and Colonization: The Evolution of Kentish Settlement* (1986), which convincingly argues, for Kent, that in some *pays* dispersed settlement may have ancient, pre-English roots, whereas in others, notably the Weald, it was of a secondary type, as in Arden.

Three advances in our knowledge since the publication of *The Making of the English Landscape* should be singled out for special attention. The first is the emerging consensus which places the origins of nucleated settlements in village landscapes towards the end of the Anglo-Saxon period, rather than at the beginning where Hoskins (and his contemporaries) placed them, believing that people of Anglo-Saxon stock 'swept all before them and built and planted afresh'. Archaeologists have found, in surveys from as far afield as the upper Trent Valley in Staffordshire and the Thames Valley in Oxfordshire, that in the early and middle Anglo-Saxon period the settlements from which people farmed were small and dispersed;

thus the early houses excavated near Sutton Courtenay (close to the tract of Berkshire countryside described above) formed part of a very diffuse arrangement of settlement. The demise of these scattered settlements—the obverse of the process of nucleation and clearly associated with it—took place in the 10th and 11th centuries (*not* the 12th, as is stated in some influential textbooks), to judge from datable sherd scatters and the occasional radiocarbon date. At about the same time we find our first references, in Anglo-Saxon charters, to what were almost certainly township-wide common-field systems, which is further confirmatory evidence for nucleation because such systems were inappropriate, both spatially and in terms of organization, for a pattern of dispersed settlement. Villages appear to have been created at this time through the small-scale migration of *husbandmen from peripheral settlements within a township towards a central or other suitable site, and through the coalescence of farms and hamlets already existing close to that spot, thus giving some villages a many-centred, rather formless appearance, which has been termed 'polyfocal' by C. C. Taylor in his acclaimed *Village and Farmstead* (1983). These processes constituted the single most important transformation ever to have taken place in the land of villages.

A second major advance has been the discovery that some villages were subjected to another, later transformation to produce a 'regular' plan. Two parallel rows of farmhouses facing each other across a street or *green, with *tofts of equal size stretching behind each row, is by far the most common type of regular plan, although there are many variants codified and discussed in B. K. Roberts, *The Making of the English Village* (1987), an important book for village-plan analysis generally. Regular villages are found in great numbers in Durham, where almost 70 per cent of surviving villages are regular, and in Yorkshire, and must surely have come about through a restructuring at a single point in time, for it is highly unlikely that such plans could have resulted from piecemeal additions. Roberts and others have equated them with a restructuring of settlement and resources (including human resources), necessary after the harrying of a rebellious North of England by William the Conqueror in 1069–70, an attractive idea (though not universally supported) because this is an explanation which equates a strongly 'northern' village type with a peculiarly northern episode in social history. The dating is strengthened by our knowledge that Norman lords used similar regular plans in founding new towns as well as in the 'plantation' of rural settlements in the newly conquered lands of Ireland and South Wales.

A third notable advance has been in our understanding of modifications to the landscape and their social repercussions towards the end of the Middle Ages, especially in the 13th, 14th, and 15th centuries. A masterpiece in the landscape history of this period, fully demonstrating the pivotal role of the human landscape in the evolution of a regional society, is H. E. Hallam, *New Lands of Elloe* (1954), which is concerned with reclamations made from marshes and fens; Hallam convincingly demonstrates the link between reclamation which was perforce communal (within and between communities), because of the scale of the task of keeping back the waters, and the development of an intense and enduring sense of regional identity. Colonization and reclamation in the 13th century (of which there have been many excellent local studies) were features of, and helped to fuel, an expanding economy which required new urban centres, exhaustively studied in M. W. Beresford, *New Towns of the Middle Ages* (1967). We are also now fairly clear about the main outlines of settlement contraction in the 14th and 15th centuries, thanks to the researches of M. W. Beresford, J. G. Hurst, and their collaborators (*Deserted Medieval Villages: Studies* (1971), updating M. W. Beresford, *Lost Villages of England* (1954)). Local studies have helped us to understand desertion and have explored the social disintegration which accompanied declining population and the shortages of labour, of services, perhaps even of women, which made living in a dwindling village very difficult.

Despite these advances, there are still glaring gaps in our appreciation of landscape history. One of the most serious of these concerns the character of the rural landscape in early Anglo-Saxon England (7th century and earlier), the problem being most acute in village landscapes where nucleation and, later, enclosure have swept so much away. How much continuity was there between the generally dispersed Romano-British settlement pattern and the similarly scattered early Anglo-Saxon one, matching a continuity in estate frameworks which has been argued for by G. R. J. Jones in a long and distinguished series of papers? (See *ESTATE, EARLY OR MULTIPLE.) How did *kinship fit into the dispersed pattern, and how much sharing of resources was there before nucleation took place? The answers to these and other questions will undoubtedly help us better to fill a second lacuna in our knowledge:

the process of nucleation in the late Anglo-Saxon period which, despite its long-term social implications, is still very imperfectly understood. There is little room for some of the vague notions encountered in the literature, ideas, for example, about the influence of a more centralized state, or of increased exactions from the peasantry, unless arguments can be put forward showing as precisely as possible how such developments would have been catalysts for nucleation. A link between adoption of nucleation and adoption of township-wide field systems is an attractive idea, because such systems seem to eat up, as it were, the old dispersed pattern of settlement which came to lie beneath them, and because locational analysis will show that a group of farmsteads at a more or less central site is the best way of serving a pattern of widely scattered strips. This idea, of course, simply throws the ball into another court, making us ask about the mainsprings of agricultural change, and ponder the question of whether the changes were set in motion by the cultivators themselves or by lords (and it is probable that many people experienced local, immediate lordship for the first time in the late Anglo-Saxon period). Intractable though some of the problems may seem, solutions may yet come from excavation, from detailed study of documentary evidence combined with landscape evidence in those parts of England where Anglo-Saxon charters survive in large numbers, and from examination of borderlands where village landscapes shade off into ancient dispersal.

A third gap is our limited appreciation of the history of enclosure landscapes in all their variety. Even for the era of parliamentary enclosure there have been no thorough studies of the socio-spatial redistribution of land-ownership which took place when a township was enclosed, a change which was just as important for the later character of the countryside as was the construction of the filigree quicksets and field walls about which Hoskins wrote in *The Making of the English Landscape*. Parliamentary enclosure affected only a small proportion of the English countryside, yet there are relatively few good studies of the faces of other types; of how these may be identified on the ground or on maps; of how they helped agricultural progress, or of how they later came to hinder it—the type of enclosed field which served the needs of one generation could hinder agricultural progress later, the landscape acting as a brake on improvement. At the more marginal level, *encroachments on to heaths and moorland by *squatters at all periods have not been properly studied, even though the cartographic evidence (especially on large-scale 18th-century county maps) is comprehensive, and often the most obvious starting-point for research, and though the very nature and location of these minute enclosures helped to breed and perpetuate a distinctive lifestyle rarely sung.

The practice of landscape history is exciting for being so difficult and therefore so challenging, and because the subject so often involves multi-period study. Medievalists become modernists as they strive to extrapolate back from the present landscape; modernists become medievalists as they seek to explore the forces for inertia in landscapes inherited from an earlier age. Difficulties and challenges also arise because the subject involves a multitude of types of evidence. Documents, where they exist, are vital, so that there is no logical division between approaches which are purely visual and those which are documentary. As we go back in time, *place-names come to be crucial for an understanding of the activities of people in landscapes; local historians will simply be staring at partially blank maps of the past if they are not brave enough to grapple with this ubiquitous type of evidence, with the help of the relevant glossaries and interpretative works.

The landscape provides its own evidence, though to advocate, for example, a study of parliamentary enclosure in a 19th-century township simply through an examination of existing *hedges or field-walls would be to suggest an approach which tells us very little that is not contained in the *enclosure award, and next to nothing about the social context of the event. Some landscape features (perhaps especially the most recent ones) impart little by way of novel evidence. However, we do not have to go back very far in time to find illustrations of landscape features that are more potent sources of evidence. For example, piecemeal enclosure of strips to produce narrow, strip-shaped closes—a process which was going on in many parts of England, particularly the west, between the 14th century and the 18th—is in many cases poorly recorded because the relevant documentation has not survived, so that historians must become adept at recognizing its traces in the landscape, and at extrapolating comparatively from places where the documentary evidence exists to those where it does not.

For an understanding of both landscape and society in even earlier periods (before and up to the 12th century) the controlled use of evidence surviving today in the living landscape (or shown on relatively recent maps) becomes very important indeed, so sparse are the written materials. The morphology of settlement patterns and of individual settlement sites, the courses taken by the boundaries of parishes, *manors, and townships, the siting of churches in relation to settlement (a subject which should be studied alongside church status and *church dedications), the networks traced by lanes: all of these convey important messages about the activities of people in landscapes in the past. Relationships between the different types of evidence should be searched for, because it is often found that they are all pointing towards the same conclusion. Inferences made from evidence in the landscape are no weaker than the inferences which historians are frequently forced to make from oblique or patchy documentary evidence, yet it must be added that they are still mistrusted in some circles, perhaps because some practitioners have erred on the wild side. That mistrust would be dispelled if we were able to construct a typological atlas of landscape evidence, explaining each category, its value, and the limits of the inferences which may be drawn from it.

The writing of landscape history also poses challenges. One poor type of writing is the catalogue. For example, an attempt is being made to illuminate the landscape of a moorland edge during the Middle Ages; the evidence, from place-names, parish boundaries, deserted sites, surviving sites, field patterns, documentary sources, and perhaps excavation is presented blow by blow as a catalogue; and readers are more or less left to form their own impression of medieval moorland-edge life. Lost here are the insights which often come from an examination of the interplay of the different types of evidence; writing of this kind, a catalogue of findings rather than a history, usually reflects poor research design in which the different types of evidence are considered in parallel, and illuminating lateral links (e.g. the relationships between boundaries and certain kinds of place-name) are ignored. Even worse, but very common, is what might be called landscape history as visual economic and social history with the difficult bits missed out. Changes taking place in the landscape of a region or county are recounted alongside 'explanations' for the changes drawn from a superficial knowledge of generalized national economic, demographic, and social developments; or changing landscapes are simply seen as 'reflections' of those developments. Such approaches are clearly inadequate, because entirely absent from the stage are the local actors, the inhabitants who made and lived in the landscapes, and because local socio-economic developments are often at variance with national trends.

Local historians as landscape historians have two fundamental contributions to make. First they may be called upon as technicians to contribute their local expertise to an assessment of landscape 'value' or 'quality' at some point in the planning process. They should be able to assist by providing more than a guide-book catalogue of when the individual items were inserted through offering an opinion about the overall texture of the region's landscape (relating the different features to one another by examining their function in the past) and the period, or usually periods, from which that texture largely dates. This first contribution quite clearly gives the work of landscape historians a direct and tangible 'relevance' which is denied to some other branches of history. The second contribution, discussed earlier, may be restated here more briefly: by researching and writing explicitly to explore the pivotal nature of human landscapes both as artefacts made by people and also as influences on behaviour—that is, the study of landscapes *in societies*—historians have a fundamental contribution to make to our appreciation of the history of the British people.   H. S. A. Fox

land tax was first imposed in England and Wales in 1693 and abolished in 1963. At first it took the form of a national poundage rate on both personal and real property, but in 1698 the direct poundage rate was replaced by a system of quotas, at county, *hundred, and *parish or *township level. During the 18th century the tax evolved into a true land tax, assessed on land, buildings, and various forms of rents. Relatively few records survive before 1780, but from that date until the Parliamentary Reform Act of 1832 annual copies or 'duplicates' of the assessments owed by each owner of real property and by each of his tenants were lodged at *quarter sessions in order to establish qualifications for the vote at county elections. These duplicates survive in bulk amongst the quarter sessions papers at county *record offices. The only return that covers almost all of England and Wales is that of 1798, which is kept in 121 volumes at the *Public Record Office in class IR 23.

The systematic geographical and chronological coverage of the duplicates for the half-century after 1780 makes the land tax a major source of evidence for landholding during the period of parliamentary *enclosure. Land tax assessments have therefore been central to the discussion of the effects of enclosure ever since Arthur Johnson's Ford lectures and their publication as *The Disappearance of the Small Landowner* (1909). Their reliability was placed under critical scrutiny by G. E. Mingay, 'The Land Tax Assessments and the Small Landowner', *Economic History Review*, 2nd ser., 17/2 (1965). See also J. V. Beckett, 'Land Tax or Excise: The Levying of Taxation in Seventeenth- and Eighteenth-Century England', *English History Review*, 100 (1985), and J. M. Neeson, *Commoners: Common Right, Enclosure and Social Change in England, 1700–1820* (1993). It is now widely accepted that land tax assessments cannot bear the weight of interpretation that has been placed upon them in the debate over small landowners. See the thorough study by Donald E. Ginter, *A Measure of Wealth: The English Land Tax in Historical Analysis* (1992). Ginter outlines the many problems that belie the superficial appearance of clarity and simplicity. Basically, the duplicates contain three categories of data, each arranged in a separate column: the name of each proprietor within the township; the names of the occupiers; and the amount of tax assessed. Some extra information is given in certain returns, e.g. in Cornwall from 1826 *field- and *place-names are recorded. However, 'very little in the duplicates is quite what it appears to be, nor do the duplicates say precisely what they appear to say to the uninitiated'. In practice, it is often difficult to identify holdings, owners, and tenants because land was scattered (even within a township), owners of certain properties were often tenants elsewhere, and common personal names prevent certainty of identification.

The main problem, however, is that huge proportions of smallholders are commonly and continually missing. Sometimes between 50 and 80 per cent of the smallholders of a township are not recorded. *Cottagers disappear in some assessments after 1798, only to reappear briefly when new arrangements for collecting the tax were made. Nor is the cut-off point in the valuation a consistent one. The tax values cannot be used for comparative analysis, nor can they be reliably transformed into *acres. It has become clear from much scholarly work that the duplicates do not provide accurate or even consistent counts, either in their tax entries or in the names they record, of the entire spectrum of the land-owning population. They cannot be used, therefore, to assess the impact of parliamentary enclosure on the small owner.

But they can still be used in other ways, especially if they are not treated in isolation and uncritically but form part of a wider study. Thus, they are useful in classifying townships as 'open' or 'close' according to landholding characteristics. A promising use for 'house repopulation' in small towns has been demonstrated by Adrian Henstock's research group at Ashbourne, whose findings were published in Michael Turner and Dennis Mills (eds.), *Land and Property: the English Land Tax, 1692–1832* (1986). The group have linked the personal names of both proprietors and occupiers with each individual property within this market town annually from 1780 to 1832 in the land-tax duplicates and then on the 1846 *tithe map. They have demonstrated that a great deal can be learned about the changing physical structure of a town, the rates and causes of change, and who was responsible for them.

The duplicates are also a useful source for family historians wishing to locate an ancestor in a difficult period before *census returns and *civil registration, and at a time when *parish registers are at their least reliable. For the whereabouts of the records see Jeremy Gibson and Dennis Mills (eds.), *Land Tax Assessments c.1690–c.1950* (1984). Few local returns have been printed, but see Roger Davey, *East Sussex Land Tax, 1785* (1991).

larceny. Stealing. Grand larceny, the theft of goods worth more than twelve pence from a person's house, was a *felony (therefore a capital offence) which was tried at the *assizes. Petty larceny was tried at the *quarter sessions. The distinction was abolished in 1827.

Latham, Richard. A Lancashire farmer who kept a detailed record of his expenditure, published as Lorna Weatherill (ed.), *The Account Book of Richard Latham, 1724–67* (1990).

lathe. An ancient Kentish division comparable with the Sussex *rape, comprising several *hundreds.

Latin, medieval. With the exception of the period 1651–60, Latin was the language of legal documents until 1733. It was also used in dog forms from time to time in other documents, e.g. *parish registers. In the Middle Ages and later, clerks had to coin Latin words for objects and ideas that were unknown to the classical world. They often wrote these words in an abbreviated form. See Eileen A. Gooder, *Latin for Local History* (1978), which translates the records most frequently consulted by local historians and provides a word list; also J. L.

Fisher, *A Medieval Farming Glossary of Latin and English Words* (1968), C. T. Martin, *The Record Interpreter* (1979), and R. E. Latham, *Revised Medieval Latin Word List* (1965), which notes non-classical meanings of words in English and Irish documents between the 5th and the 16th centuries. The genealogist is faced with only a few difficulties, e.g. the use of Latin forms of *Christian names in parish registers. See the list of Latin words and phrases found in parish registers in T. V. H. Fitzhugh, *The Dictionary of Genealogy* (1985).

lawn. Originally, a grassy plot in the wooded part of a medieval *deer park.

Laxton. The Nottinghamshire village famous for the unique survival of an *open-field system of communal agriculture regulated by a manorial *court. See J. V. Beckett, *Laxton: England's Last Open-Field Village* (1989).

lay brother. The *Cluniacs and other monastic orders had used lay brothers during the 11th century, but the idea was developed in a new way and on a much greater scale by the *Cistercians. Although all Cistercian monks were supposed to do physical work, the amount of time that was available after liturgical exercises and periods devoted to study was too limited for producing sufficient food for the monastic community. The order therefore decided to accept lay brothers and employ hired labour, both at the *monastery and at distant *granges. Lay brothers entered monastic life as adults, unlike the choir monks who were trained from childhood. Lay brothers were usually illiterate and took no part in the daily choral offices. They did, however, take monastic vows and wore the habit, though without the cowl worn by the choir monks. They provided both the skilled and the unskilled manual work, as farmers and craftsmen. They greatly outnumbered the choir monks. In 1167, for example, Rievaulx Abbey (Yorkshire) had 500 lay brothers to 140 choir monks. The two groups were kept physically separate for much of the time. The dormitory and refectory of the choir monks led straight into the choir of the monastic church, whereas the quarters of the lay brothers led into the nave. This arrangement can still be seen at Fountains Abbey (Yorkshire) where the dormitory and refectory of the lay brothers is exceptionally well preserved. The *choir of the church was separated from the *nave by a screen. Likewise, in the *cloister the lay brothers were confined to the walk on the west side, which was hidden from the view of the others by a wall. The lay brothers were recruited from local farming families. Large numbers of men were attracted to this life, through religious fervour and economic necessity at a time of *population growth before the *Black Death, but numbers declined subsequently.

lay subsidy. A tax for a specific purpose, e.g. to subsidize a foreign war, which was distinguished from taxes levied on the clergy. The lay subsidy rolls of 1290–1334 are a major medieval source for the local historian and for those who are interested in the origins of *surnames. The tax was commonly known as the Tenth and Fifteenth because it was levied on one-tenth of movable property in a town and one-fifteenth of similar property in the countryside. Movable property was chosen for the assessment because wealth was no longer concentrated in the ownership of land.

The records are held at the *Public Record Office under E 179. Some *county record societies have published their fullest returns. See, for example, A. M. Erskine (ed.), *The Devonshire Lay Subsidy of 1323* (1969), and Peter Franklin (ed.), *The Taxpayers of Medieval Gloucestershire: An Analysis of the 1327 Lay Subsidy Roll* (1993). The collectors arranged the returns by *hundred or *wapentake and then by *vill or *borough. The number of exempted poor and the amount of evasion are unknown, so the returns cannot be used for estimating the size of the population. They do, however, indicate the comparable wealth of different places and identify the prominent families. The 1334 assessment is particularly useful for comparative purposes, but it does not record personal names. It has been published as R. E. Glasscock (ed.), *The Lay Subsidy of 1334* (1975).

The lay subsidy fell out of use as a method of taxation, but was revived by Henry VIII. See Richard Hoyle, *Tudor Taxation Records: A Guide for Users* (PRO Readers' Guide, no. 5, 1994), which surveys the national scene and points out short cuts and pitfalls. The lay subsidy returns of 1524–5 have been used by W. G. Hoskins, *The Age of Plunder: The England of Henry VIII, 1500–1547* (1976) for a comparative study of the wealth and social structure of the counties of England. J. Cornwall (ed.), *Tudor Rutland: The County Community under Henry VIII* (1980) prints the return for England's smallest county. These Tudor assessments reverted to the old method of recording the taxpayers' names. In northern England the return of 1546 is fuller than that of 1524–5. See R. B. Smith, *Land and Politics in the England of Henry VIII* (1970). R. W. Hoyle (ed.), *Early Tudor Craven: Subsidies and Assessments, 1510–1547* (Yorkshire Archaeological Society Record Series, cxlv, 1987) demonstrates the range of assessments that are available for this period.

In 1513 the government attempted to tax wages as well as goods and land, but this was abandoned after 1525. Until then, most of the assessments made below £2 were on wages. Only a tiny handful of resident landowners were taxed on their land; the great majority of people were assessed on their goods. Fraud was not widespread, though there must have been some cases of avoidance, and large numbers were too poor to pay the tax. The returns show great inequalities of wealth. See C. V. Phythian-Adams, *Desolation of a City: Coventry and the Urban Crisis of the Late Middle Ages* (1979), which shows how the assessments can be used in a wider study of a community. The lay subsidy of 1546 is the last that is of use to local and family historians, though occasional assessments were made until 1623.

lead was mined and smelted during the Roman period. Pigs of lead with the names of Roman emperors stamped on them have been discovered in Derbyshire, the Yorkshire Dales, and the northern Pennines. The principal lead fields were in the carboniferous limestone parts of the Pennines and in the Mendips, with some production in the Lake District, Devon and Cornwall, north and central Wales, and southwest Scotland. The industry declined considerably with the lessening of demand for lead roofs, etc. upon the *dissolution of the monasteries, but it recovered from 1570 onwards until the Derbyshire lead field was the most productive in Europe. See David Kiernan, *The Derbyshire Lead Industry in the Sixteenth Century* (1989) for the way that the *bole hills of the medieval smelters were replaced by *water-powered sites in the wooded valleys, as the leading landowners of the region injected capital into the industry, and a new class of prosperous lead merchants emerged.

Before the sinking of deep mines, which required steam-driven pumps and winders and costly drainage 'soughs', lead was mined in long seams known as *rakes, whose overgrown trenches are now prominent landscape features. Small-scale partnerships of miner-farmers were typical in the Middle Ages and later, but with the great growth of the industry after 1570, particularly in the 17th century, large numbers of immigrants came into the lead fields as wage-labourers. Thus, a new community was established at Greenhow Hill (Yorkshire) at between

1,250 and 1,300 feet above sea level, and thousands of miners built cottages in existing villages or on new sites in the Derbyshire Peak District.

The ore was crushed by the use of a rotating stone worked by a horse and then was washed and sieved before being sent by *packhorse to the smelter. The smelting mills often lay several miles away from the mines, as bellows-blown hearths required water power and woods that could be converted into white coal. This method remained in use for two centuries after 1570 but was eventually replaced by the reverberatory coal-fired furnace known as a cupola. Pigs of lead were taken from the smelting sites to the nearest river ports, such as Bawtry or Yarm (both in Yorkshire), on two-wheeled vehicles known as wains (see WAGGONS AND WAINS).

The lead industry was a source of income for all sections of society. Great *landowners, such as the Cavendishes of Chatsworth and the Manners family of Haddon Hall, and *gentry such as the Gells of Hopton and the Eyres of Hassop, profited from rents and investments; new dynasties of *merchants arose; farmers found that the mining or carriage of lead was a useful by-employment; and *cottagers kept above the poverty line when trade prospered. The industry experienced boom conditions in the 1750s and 1760s and again from the late 1780s until 1796, but four years of depression followed. Derbyshire had 292 mines and 18 cupolas in 1809, but the quality of ore was generally inferior to that mined previously. The lead industry underwent prolonged periods of depression in 1816–18 and 1824–33, but recovered again before the lead fields became exhausted during the second half of the 19th century. The depression of 1880–2 signalled the end of mining in many districts and a dramatic emigration. In Swaledale, for instance, the population declined by nearly 50 per cent between 1871 and 1891. The Dales landscape contains far fewer houses and cottages now than it did in the first half of the 19th century. See Arthur Raistrick and Bernard Jennings, *A History of Lead Mining in the Pennines* (1965).

league. A measure longer than a mile that varied from one part of the country to another.

lease. The conversion of *copyhold tenure to *leasehold occurred over a long period, particularly from the mid-16th century onwards. The conditions attached to leases varied from *manor to manor but, as a generalization, in the western half of England the favoured method was a lease for three lives determinable upon 99 years. The lessee paid an entry fine and an annual rent and his lease held good as long as one of the entered names was still alive. It was common to enter the names of husband, wife, and eldest son, though any names could be chosen. Surviving leases of this kind are a useful source for genealogy. Given the high incidence of *infant mortality, there was no advantage in entering the names of young children. Fresh lives could usually be entered upon the payment of another entry fine. These fines were negotiable; during the first half of the 17th century lords usually managed to raise them to meet inflation. This method of holding property was obviously insecure, but on balance it was regarded as comparable with, and probably slightly better than, the method favoured in the eastern half of England, namely a lease for 21 years. Long leases, including some lasting 800 years or more, were offered on some estates; on the other hand, short terms, e.g. three years, could also be negotiated. *Estate records often include a good run of leases; *surveys of estates give an account of the various ways in which property was held.

lease and release. A method of transferring land from one party to another without the necessity of enrolling a deed. The purchaser first took a lease of the property for one year (thus avoiding the need to enrol), then on the following day the vendor conveyed to him the reversion of the lease. The records of the transaction consisted of two documents, the lease and the release. The method remained popular until 1845.

leasehold. Tenure by *lease, either for lives, or for a stated term, a method that began to replace *copyhold tenure in the early modern period and which was also used for *demesnes that a landowner did not wish to farm himself, but which he could recover at the end of the term.

leasow. A pasture, particularly in the West Midlands and Welsh Borders.

leather. The leather trades were important during the Middle Ages and the early modern period when garments, boots and shoes, bottles, belts, saddles, sheaths, etc. were made from tanned hides or dressed skins. Workers in leather formed a sizeable proportion of the work-force, especially in towns. See L. A. Clarkson, 'The Leather Crafts in Tudor and Stuart England', *Agricultural History Review*, 14/1 (1966). At that time, shoes were less substantial than they are today and not very durable;

shoemakers were also known as cordwainers and corvisers. By the time of the *Civil War Northampton had emerged as the main shoemaking centre; during the 18th and 19th centuries several Northamptonshire villages and small towns also became centres of production. However, most production remained on a small scale, each village having its shoemaker, until well into the 20th century. See also TANNING.

lectern. Medieval stone lecterns were normally fixed to the north wall of the *chancel of a parish *church. After the *Reformation detached wooden, brass, or latten lecterns were installed in the *nave. In three-decker pulpits the reading desk formed the middle tier. The Victorians reintroduced the late medieval practice of supporting the Bible by the outstretched wings of an eagle, the symbol of St John the Evangelist.

lecturer. In the 17th century private individuals endowed lectureships at parish *churches to encourage preaching. The idea was much favoured by *Puritans. The lecturer's salary often went to supplement the stipend of the incumbent, e.g. at Worsbrough (Yorkshire) the minister still receives £10 p.a. as the John Rainey lecturer.

Leicester University, Department of English Local History. Founded in 1948 with W. G. *Hoskins as reader and sole member, it quickly became a unique postgraduate department concerned with the comparative study of local history throughout the whole of England. As such, it is different from the various *centres of local history which have been set up at other English universities. Its subsequent heads have been H. P. R. *Finberg, Hoskins for a second term, Alan Everitt, and Charles Phythian-Adams. Other leading scholars in the subject, notably Joan Thirsk and Margaret Spufford, have been associated with it and it now has 100 postgraduates. Asa Briggs's reference to its members as 'The Leicester School of local historians, scattered though they are' was an acknowledgement of common approaches and interests which have led to considerable academic advances in the subject. The instrument for publicizing the new approaches was a series of occasional papers (1952–91) and monographs published by Leicester University Press. An important new venture in 1965 was the launch of The English Surnames Survey under Richard McKinley. A generous grant from the Marc Fitch Fund in 1989 allowed the purchase of Marc Fitch House in Salisbury Road, including an extensive and valuable library.

Leland, John (1506?–52). The first English topographer. In 1533 Leland was appointed the 'King's Antiquary'. Afterwards he was commissioned to search all the monastic, cathedral, and college libraries in the land so that 'the monumentes of auncient writers' might be 'brought owte of deadly darknes to lyvely lighte'. Leland spent nearly ten years touring the country and collecting materials. His notes of his journeys have been published as Lucy Toulmin Smith (ed.), *John Leland: The Itinerary*, 5 vols. (1907–10, repr. 1964). Leland became insane before he could rework his material in a form suitable for the ambitious publications he had in mind. The *Itinerary* is a rambling, disorganized compilation of the rough notes that he made on his travels. It was quarried by the Elizabethan antiquaries and is now of interest for its contemporary descriptions of places throughout the land.

Lent. The period of fasting and penitence from Ash Wednesday to Easter-eve, in commemoration of Christ's 40 days in the wilderness. A forbidden period for marriages.

lentils. A leguminous plant, closely related to the vetch, sometimes called 'tills'. It was valued as excellent fodder for calves and young cattle, and also for pigeons. They are referred to in farming *inventories, often in Kent but also on light soils in many other areas.

Letters and Papers (Foreign and Domestic), Henry VIII. A full *calendar for the years 1517–47 has been published in many volumes between 1864 and 1932. This includes papers from the *Public Record Office, the *British Library, and archives from abroad.

Levant Company. Founded in 1581 and known also as the Turkey Company. Its members, who until 1753 had to be Freemen of the City of London, acquired a virtual monopoly of trade in that area until 1825. The records are kept at the *Public Record Office, under SP 105.

levée en masse. Lists of men aged 17 to 55 who might form a reserve defence force in 1803–4 were drawn up by parish *constables. See MILITIA RECORDS.

Levellers. A group who advocated sweeping political reforms of a democratic nature in the 1640s and 1650s. See Christopher Hill, *The World Turned Upside Down: Radical Ideas during the English Revolution* (1972).

Lewis's *Topographical Dictionary*. Samuel Lewis published *A Topographical Dictionary of England* in seven editions between 1831 and 1848–9, the last edition being in 4 volumes and an atlas. He also published *A Topographical Dictionary of Wales* in 1833, 1844, and 1849, in 2 volumes and an atlas, *A Topographical Dictionary of Scotland* (1846), in 2 volumes and an atlas, and *A Topographical Dictionary of Ireland* (1846) in 2 volumes and an atlas. Brief historical details of each town and village were given and the civil and ecclesiastical arrangements noted.

leyerwite. A fine payable by a medieval *villein to the *lord of the manor upon his unmarried daughter becoming pregnant.

leys, grass. The *open-field system of farming was far more flexible than was once thought. Individual arable *strips were often converted to grass, on a temporary basis, in order to provide sufficient feed for livestock. These leys could last for varying periods, from two years to seven or eight years; if longer still, they seemed permanent.

Lhuyd, Edward (1660–1709). Welsh and Oxford antiquary, natural historian and philologist, who in 1684 succeeded Robert *Plot as keeper of the Ashmolean museum. He made a major contribution on Wales to Edmund *Gibson's revised edition of *Camden's *Britannia* (1695). He was celebrated for his great learning and wide interests. See Frank Emery, *Edward Lhuyd, 1660–1709* (1971).

Liberal Party. The mid-19th-century successor to the *Whig Party. It formed several governments in the Victorian period (when Gladstone was the dominant figure) and passed important social legislation in the Edwardian era. A split between groups led respectively by Asquith and Lloyd-George was a major cause of the decline of the party after the First World War. In 1988 the Liberals merged with a majority of the Social Democratic Party to form the Liberal Democrats.

Liberate Rolls. Writs authorizing royal officers to make payments on behalf of the Crown, from 1226 to 1426. The records are kept at the *Public Record Office. A *calendar has been published for the period up to 1272.

liberty. A *manor or group of manors, or other area, that lay outside a *sheriff's jurisdiction.

libraries, public. The first 'circulating libraries' were formed in Edinburgh (1729), London, and provincial cities, including Bath and Southampton, during the first half of the 18th century. The first parochial library was started in 1741 at Leadhills (Lanarkshire) by James Stirling of the Scots Mines Company. Today, the Association of Independent Libraries has 22 members, ranging in size from the London Library, in St James's Square, to the Tavistock Subscription Library (Devon). Public lending and reference libraries became widely available during the second half of the 19th century after an Act of Parliament of 1850 authorized local authorities to provide them. Many of the great civic public libraries date from this time, but some authorities did not take up their powers until the 1890s. The generosity of Andrew Carnegie (1835–1918), the Scots-born American multi-millionaire, allowed many small authorities throughout Britain to provide a 'free library'. Under the Public Libraries Act (1919) the Board of Education was made responsible for supervising the provision of libraries by Local Educational Authorities. It enabled the County Councils to form County Libraries. The local history reference library of a large authority usually forms a substantial section of the public library. These contain valuable collections of all the published works relating to a locality, together with *maps and plans, *photographs, *newspapers, *ephemera, and tape-recordings. Before the establishment of local *record offices, these local history libraries acted as record repositories. Some of the borough libraries in the large metropolitan districts still have an archive collection. See The Royal Commission on *Historical Manuscripts, *Record Repositories in Great Britain: A Geographical Directory* (1992), S. Guy, *English Local Studies Handbook* (1993), and W. A. Munford, *Penny Rate: Aspects of British Library History, 1850–1950* (1951).

licences. After the *Reformation schoolmasters, midwives, physicians, and surgeons had to prove that they conformed to the beliefs of the *Church of England and had attended communion. Licences to practice were then registered in the diocesan records. Identifying the names of schoolmasters from such records is a basic task when studying the local history of *education.

Licences to pass beyond the seas were an early form of *passport issued from the late Elizabethan period until 1677. The records, which are kept at the *Public Record Office under E 157, include registers of soldiers serving in the Low Countries, 1613–24; people going to Holland and other places, 1624–37; and passengers to the colonies, 1634–9 and 1677.

liege. The lord of whom a man held his principal property was his liege-lord, to whom he owed military service.

lighthouses are amongst the most unusual structures in Britain. The earliest survivors date from the 17th century, e.g. that constructed on Flamborough Head (Yorkshire) by Sir John Clayton in 1674. Many were erected by private individuals, public subscription, corporations, or groups of shipowners. By royal charter of 1514 and later grants, the Brethren of Trinity House were given control of pilotage on the river Thames. Part of their responsibilities was the provision of lighthouses around the coasts of England, Wales, and the Channel Islands. Separate authorities were created for Scotland and Ireland. St Catherine's Point (Isle of Wight) has two earlier structures—known as the Mustard Pot and the Pepper Pot—near to its present lighthouse. Before lighthouses were in general use, *beacons and lantern towers on churches, e.g. at Southwold (Suffolk), acted as guides. Electric arc lamps were used from the 1860s. Modern technology is making lighthouses redundant.

lime kilns. Ruined lime kilns are found in chalk and limestone districts, at coastal ports, and at *canal basins where limestone was brought as back-carriage. Some date from the 16th and 17th centuries, but most are from the 18th and 19th. Their chief use was to produce lime that farmers could spread on acid soils, but they were also a source of mortar and of quicklime for tanners. Kilns were often built into hillsides, which enabled them to be charged at a high level and to be drawn below. Some of the 19th-century kilns, especially those on the east coast of Scotland and the coast of Northumberland, where coal fuel was readily obtained, are massive structures, though smaller kilns probably remained more common. See R. J. Moore-Colyer, 'Coastal Limekilns in South-East Wales', *Folk Life*, 28 (1990).

linen. In the early modern period linen weaving for garments, sheets, tablecloths, and sailcloth was a widespread rural industry wherever *flax could be grown in the British Isles. It provided useful extra income for small farmers and poor cottagers. See Nesta Evans, *The East Anglian Linen Industry: Rural Industry and Local Economy, 1500–1850* (1985), and Patricia Baines, *Flax and Linen* (1985). The imposition of high tariffs on foreign linens from the late 17th century onwards encouraged the development of linen industries in various parts of England, Scotland, and Ireland. The Irish Linen Board was effective in promoting the growth of the industry between 1711 and 1828. See W. H. Crawford, 'The Evolution of the Linen Trade in Ulster before Industrialisation', *Irish Economic*

and Social History, 15 (1988), and Alastair J. Durie, *The Scottish Linen Industry in the Eighteenth Century* (1979). (See also SCOTCHMEN.)

The industry began to be mechanized in the late 18th century; John Marshall's first flax-spinning mill at Holbeck, Leeds, was built in 1792. See W. G. Rimmer, *Marshall's of Leeds, Flax Spinners, 1788–1886* (1960). The growth of Leeds as a centre of spinning stimulated the development of weaving in and around Barnsley to the south and Knaresborough to the north. Handloom weaving expanded in order to meet the production of the spinning mills. By the mid-19th century Scotland had about 70,000 handloom weavers of linens, mainly around Aberdeen, Dundee, and Dunfermline. Thereafter the number of English handloom weavers declined, but numbers in Scotland remained steady until the switch to power weaving in the 1870s. In Ulster the manufacture of linens continued to expand as spinning, weaving, and bleaching were transformed from a domestic to a factory-based industry, especially from the 1820s onwards. By the early 1850s Belfast had 28 flax mills, whereas the domestic industry was in decline. A few handloom weavers survived in parts of Ireland until the end of the century. See J. C. Beckett *et al.* (eds.), *Belfast: The Making of the City* (1983) for the ways in which Belfast became an industrialized Victorian city. Together with the other textile industries, the manufacture of linen declined sharply in the second half of the 20th century in face of foreign competition and the preference for non-creasing, mostly synthetic fabrics. See B. Messenger, *Picking Up the Linen Threads: A Study in Industrial Folklore* (1978).

liquorice. The cultivation of liquorice as a medicinal crop in garths and gardens probably originated in *monasteries. By the 17th century production was concentrated in and around Pontefract (Yorkshire), Worksop (Nottinghamshire), and Godalming (Surrey). The crop required plenty of dung, and as it took three summers for the roots to grow to full size, vegetables such as onions and lettuces were cultivated on the same plots.

List and Index Society. Established by readers and staff at the *Public Record Office to publish cheap finding-aids to records.

literary and philosophical societies. During the second half of the 18th century and the first half of the 19th, Britain's major towns founded 'lit. and phil.' societies to discuss the intellectual issues of the day and to sponsor cultural activities. A few survive, e.g. that in York.

livery and maintenance. The medieval practice of maintaining large numbers of retainers who wore their lord's badge and livery. These retainers were expected to respond to a call for military service in return for the lord's protection. The practice was widespread from the 14th to the 16th century, but from the reign of Henry VII it required a royal licence.

livery companies. The medieval *guilds of the City of London became known as livery companies from the distinctive dress worn by their senior officers. From the early 14th century it was the practice for all freemen of the City to be members of one of the guilds. By Elizabethan times the companies had become wealthy charitable institutions whose members did not necessarily follow the occupation given in the name of the guild. Many companies continue to support the schools which they founded. The records of most of the companies are kept at the *Guildhall Library, which also has a number of published histories; see the library's *Guide to the Archives of the Livery Companies and Related Organisations in Guildhall Library*.

local and regional history: modern approaches. The study of history was established on a professional basis during the second half of the 19th century. Some of the most distinguished historians of that era, notably F. W. *Maitland and P. *Vinogradoff, followed by Sir Frank *Stenton (who held a research fellowship in local history at the University of Reading between 1908 and 1912) were fully convinced of the value of local studies. The most important local histories of the inter-war period were written by scholars—G. H. *Tupling, J. D. *Chambers, and W. G. *Hoskins—whose interest in economic history led them to study a place or a region in depth over a limited period of time in order to make a contribution to the way that historians saw the development of the whole country. Hoskins went on to be the great popularizer of local history, but his influential book, *The Midland Peasant: The Economic and Social History of a Leicestershire Village* (1957), was intended as 'a study of the Midland peasant-farmer and of the open-field system . . . a contribution to English economic and social history, and not a history of the village as such'.

During the second half of the 20th century the academic debate on the purpose of the study of local history has revolved around two questions: how far should local studies be an end in themselves rather than an exploration of national themes at a local level?; and what is the appropriate unit of study for a local historian?

In his inaugural lecture at Leicester in 1952, H. P. R. *Finberg addressed the problem of the tension between the use of local history to illustrate general trends and local history *per se*. Insisting that local historians should be 'well grounded in the history of England', he offered the view that their principal concern should be with 'the origin, growth, and decline of local communities.' Community studies and the use of visual evidence were to become the hallmarks of what Asa Briggs referred to in a review of 1958 as the 'Leicester School' of historians, 'scattered though they are'. Local *communities were not considered in isolation, however, but were compared to and contrasted with other communities in different parts of the country. This approach was a novel one, but the distinction was blurred in practice, for both Hoskins and Finberg are best known for their contributions to general views of English history. In Finberg's case, his most influential work was his *Roman and Saxon Withington* (1956), a local study which caused a rethinking of the problem of continuity after the collapse of the Roman empire.

In 1956 Finberg gathered a group of scholars to launch *The *Agrarian History of England and Wales*, a multi-volume treatment of the subject from prehistoric times to the present day. In 1967 Volume iv, covering the period 1500 to 1640, appeared under the editorship of Joan Thirsk. In her occasional paper on *Fenland Farming in the Sixteenth Century* (1953), and her essay on 'Industries in the Countryside' in F. J. Fisher (ed.), *Essays in the Economic and Social History of Tudor and Stuart England in Honour of Professor R. H. Tawney* (1961), she had established some of the approaches and the framework of explanations that were to prove so fruitful in volumes iv and v of the *AHEW*. She placed a new emphasis on the comparison of different types of countryside, or *pays*, such as the *open-fields of the Midland Plain, the *wood pastures of the Kentish Weald, the *fens of Lincolnshire, the Pennine *moors, etc. The county (the typical unit of the early *antiquarians) was now considered to be a relevant area of study only in so far as it provided contrasts between its various *pays* (which in many cases were not confined within the county boundaries). A study of, for example, the sheep-and-corn country of Wiltshire was thought to benefit from a comparison with the similar farming economy of, say, the Yorkshire *Wolds. Moreover, the approach was not confined to studies of farming practices: each *pays* was thought of as having its distinctive characteristics in terms of manorial structure, settlement patterns, crafts, forms of religious observance, numbers of poor people, and so on.

It had become clear that each type of agrarian economy had its rationale and that pastoral communities were as worthy of study as were arable open-field villages. Local historians were thus provided with a way of linking their communities and regions to the wider social history of Britain. Alan Everitt, a contributor to volume iv, developed this approach in *The Pattern of Rural Dissent: The Nineteenth Century* (1972), and his subsequent writings, notably *Continuity and Colonization: The Evolution of Kentish Settlement* (1986), which emphasized the continuing importance of patterns that were established in the earliest periods for which we have evidence. The new approach was particularly influential in the study of rural communities in the early modern period, especially in Margaret Spufford, *Contrasting Communities: English Villagers in the Sixteenth and Seventeenth Centuries* (1974), a comparison of three very different Cambridgeshire parishes. Hoskins, Finberg, Thirsk, Everitt, and Spufford were, at one time or another, all members of the Department of English Local History at the University of *Leicester.

Meanwhile, the study of urban history had become a boom activity. At Leicester, H. J. *Dyos, the author of *Victorian Suburb: Camberwell* (1961), launched the *Urban History Newsletter*, the precursor of the journal *Urban History*, and in 1966 the first Urban History Conference. The great strides that were quickly made in the subject are evident in Dyos's posthumous Festschrift, Derek Fraser and Anthony Sutcliffe (eds.), *The Pursuit of Urban History* (1983), which sought to put into practice his vision of urban history as a 'central place' where 'an unusually large variety of disciplines, interests and tendencies could converge'. In contrast to the rural historians, the emphasis at first was on the 19th and 20th centuries, until a separate Early Towns Group was formed, and Peter Clark and Paul Slack edited *Crisis and Order in English Towns, 1500–1700* (1972), the first of a series of co-operative works on the Tudor and Stuart period. Whereas the older urban histories had concentrated on legal and constitutional issues, the emphasis was now on all sections of society, including the poor, and on the physical growth of towns. The approach was multi-disciplinary and comparative, for example in C. V. Phythian-Adams, *Desolation of a City: Coventry and the Urban Crisis of the Late Middle Ages* (1979) and Peter Borsay, *The English Urban Renaissance: Culture and Society in the Provincial Town,*

1660–1770 (1989). Several towns now have modern studies of particular periods of their history; and, in the cases of Birmingham, Leeds, Glasgow, Sheffield, and Nottingham, 'official histories' by groups of scholars have been published or are in preparation.

In recent years rural history and urban history have drifted apart. Although agrarian historians have acknowledged the leading role of the market and urban historians have looked beyond the suburbs to the hinterland, few attempts have been made to study both the urban and rural parts of local society and economy as an integrated whole. A notable exception is John Goodacre, *The Transformation of a Peasant Economy: Townspeople and Villagers in Lutterworth, 1500–1700* (1994). Some historians have avoided this difficulty by concentrating on a region, rather as the earliest chorographers wrote about a county. Indeed, the county has remained a flourishing unit of study. In his classic work, *Tudor Cornwall: Portrait of a Society* (1941), A. L. Rowse included religious and political as well as social and economic themes, to portray a provincial society as part of the national whole. County studies, starting with Alan Everitt, *The Community of Kent and the Great Rebellion, 1640–60* (1966), have proved particularly rewarding in reinterpreting the period of the *Civil War and *Commonwealth. Localized research has challenged the ways in which national history has been viewed. The county format was also used by the *Hodder and Stoughton series of landscape histories, under Hoskins's editorship. A purely practical reason for favouring the county unit was the establishment of county *record offices; the bulk of the archives, outside those of the major national collections, are housed together, whereas those of neighbouring counties are held in other county towns. Yet for many regional studies the county is not a satisfactory unit; for instance, the different *pays* often do not heed county boundaries and those towns which are sited on the borders have hinterlands that extend into other shires. Thus, the ancient county boundaries have little relevance to the historical study of, for example, the Birmingham district or of the economy of the Weald.

The problem of defining a region is one that has been much aired by historians and historical geographers. At the macro-level England cannot be divided satisfactorily into recognizable units based on former kingdoms or principalities, like those of France, Germany, or Italy. Few of the Anglo-Saxon tribal divisions had much meaning after England became a united country in the 11th century. Although the differences between one part of the country and another are clear for all to see, English regional identities are imprecise and no firm boundaries can be drawn. At the micro-level the problem of what actually constitutes a region has given rise to lively debate amongst the members of the *Conference of Regional and Local Historians. The boundaries of a region tend to move when viewed from different standpoints. It is clear, for example, that a farming region might not coincide with, say, a region defined by its speech or its *vernacular architecture. It is also clear that regional identities may vary over time, particularly when an area was transformed by industrialization. John Marshall has argued that: 'Whatever criteria one uses, a "region", in the rapidly developing world of modern history, can scarcely be seen as a fixed and static entity. It is, to say the least, a mass of overlapping and sometimes conflicting or interlocking economic and social relationships, influenced or shaped by occupation or workplace, by religious persuasion or organisation, by agrarian activities and customs, by population movements, by political bodies, by voluntary organisation of innumerable kinds, and by commercial activities almost as numerous. Relationships in each of these broad spheres tended to produce what were often self-conscious social groups within the region itself.' (J. D. Marshall and J. K. Walton, *The Lake Counties from 1830 to the Mid-Twentieth Century* (1981), p. ix.)

The universities, polytechnics, and colleges of higher education have provided the bulk of the membership of the Conference of Regional and Local Historians and the impetus for the study of regional history, through undergraduate, postgraduate, and extramural courses. Some universities—Nottingham, Lancaster, East Anglia, Keele, Hull—established *centres of local and regional history. From the universities came three journals devoted to the study of the wider regions of England. Volume i of *Northern History* was published in 1965 to review the history of the seven historic northern counties. It aimed to include 'both articles on topics treated regionally and articles on the history of particular topics . . . which make comparisons between different areas'. *Northern History* was soon followed by *Midland History* (1971), and then by *Southern History* (1979). Each of these journals has favoured an eclectic approach which has succeeded in focusing academic attention on the identity and concerns of three very different parts of England. As yet,

however, few attempts have been made to synthesize all this new work.

In 1986 the first of a projected 21-volume *Longman Regional History of England*, edited by Barry Cunliffe and David Hey, was published. This series divides the country into ten regions and covers all periods of time from prehistory to the present day. Each region has two volumes: before AD 1000, and from AD 1000, except that 'The Severn Valley and West Midlands' has two volumes for the post-AD 1000 period, and AD 1540 is the time division for the 'Lancashire and Cheshire' volumes. The boundaries are not regarded as being firm and unchanging, but as providing a framework for a synthesis of the enormous amount of new work that has been done at a local level in recent years. The authors have 'dwelt upon the diversity that can be found within a region as well as upon common characteristics in order to illustrate the local peculiarities of provincial life'. The approach is fundamentally different from that of the antiquarian tradition in being concerned with ordinary men and women and with everyday life in the past. The broad framework of the regional study is intended to provide a context for future research by local historians and at the same time to 'substantially enrich our understanding of the many histories which together make up the history of England'.

At the micro-level, Marie B. Rowlands, *Masters and Men in the Small Metalware Trades of the West Midlands* (1975), J. Obelkevich, *Religion and Rural Society: South Lindsey, 1825–1875* (1976), Victor Skipp, *Crisis and Development: An Ecological Case Study of the Forest of Arden, 1570–1674* (1978), and J. D. Marshall and J. K. Walton, *The Lake Counties from 1830 to the Mid-Twentieth Century* (1981) are amongst the best examples of histories which attempt to synthesize economic, agrarian, social, religious, and demographic history to reveal the peculiar nature of English regions. Such studies have contributed greatly to our understanding of the economic and social history of England as a whole. Meanwhile, the community approach has been favoured by, among others, David Hey, *An English Rural Community: Myddle under the Tudors and Stuarts* (1974), and David Levine and Keith Wrightson's two books, *Poverty and Piety in an English Village: Terling, 1525–1700* (1979), and *The Making of an Industrial Society: Whickham, 1560–1765* (1991).

The region remains an elusive concept, for it can be defined in so many different ways. The local historian is faced with the problem of identifying local societies that are wider than the town or village community but which are nevertheless real units of study. In *Re-thinking English Local History* (1987), Charles Phythian-Adams addressed the problem of the appropriate framework for academic local studies and the tension between the different approaches of 'national history localized' and 'local history *per se*'. He advocated an anthropological approach to the study of small-scale societies, whose membership and movements were not restricted by town or parish boundaries. The first task for the local historian is to identify these local societies, which, despite the mobility of recent generations, often survive to the present day. Genetic evidence, based on *blood groups and DNA samples, together with localized patterns of *surnames, revealed by an analysis of UK *telephone directories, show that Britain is still composed of numerous local societies with marked individual characteristics. Many of these are of ancient origin, though, of course, they have never been static. In Victorian times their identity was much stronger than it is now; it was even stronger before the coming of the *railways provided cheap transport to other parts of the land. The boundaries of local societies can be drawn around the districts within which people moved, worked, and married; the area which they thought of as being their '*country'; that neighbourhood of a 10- to 20-mile radius which was often centred on a market town. In a hierarchy of 'belonging' these local societies provide the link from urban or rural communities to broader regions and so to the nation as a whole.

This attempt to define a region socially takes account of the broadening of local historical concerns since the 1960s, when the emphasis was on economic activities. The modern explosion of interest in social history has directed the local historian towards the study of *population and *family, *kinship and neighbourhood, *education and religion, *crime and recreation, *civic ritual and superstition, as well as to *labour history, *oral history, and women's studies. Charles Phythian-Adams advocates a fourfold and interrelated approach to the study of local history. First and foremost should be the historical analysis of particular societies and their activities, studied as an entity and in relation to the wider world of their times; such societies must be understood in their geographic contexts. The second approach should be topographical: the study of landscapes and the interplay between man and his environment, revealed by both visual and documentary evidence. The third concern is with all the families that together constitute the local society that is being studied. The fourth is with

regional popular cultures, the *mentalité* of the various 'peoples' of Britain. In this way, the concerns of the social historian can be married to those of the economic historian and the topographer. A recent work which encompasses all these approaches is David Hey, *The Fiery Blades of Hallamshire: Sheffield and Its Neighbourhood, 1660–1740* (1991).

The relationship between local history and national history has been explored further by Charles Phythian-Adams in 'Local History and National History: The Quest for the Peoples of England', *Rural History: Economy, Society, Culture*, 2/1 (1991). He demonstrates the enduring combination of fundamental geographical considerations with persisting archaic arrangements in the formation and continuity of distinctive local societies. Using the example of Cumberland and Westmorland as an unambiguously distinct, ancient, and physically isolated area whose inhabitants form a local society, he explores the changing outlooks and relationships of Cumbrian people over time and emphasizes the alternating rhythms of alignment and realignment. The message is that, however distinctive a local society can appear, it needs to be studied in relationship to its neighbours in contexts that are constantly shifting. The context for such a study needs to be the entire British Isles.

Similar arguments are advanced in Charles Phythian-Adams (ed.), *Societies, Cultures and Kinship, 1580–1850: Cultural Provinces and English Local History* (1993), which suggests that English local history should be concerned with the entire English people in all the subdivisions of the country, not only for their own sakes but as interdependent parts of the wider whole. In his 'Introduction: An Agenda for English Local Historians' the editor divides the country into 14 cultural provinces that are larger than the spaces occupied by local societies yet of sufficiently limited geographical extent to form a meaningful context for their inhabitants, and which share a set of distinguishable cultural traits. With allowance made for overlap, the major river-drainage basins seem to have the necessary unifying characteristics that contribute to 'a broad commonality of culture'. The history of the people of particular places needs to be seen in an increasing circle of contexts, widening from community and local society to cultural province and the nation at large.

The great majority of local historians remain untouched by these academic debates, for they are amateurs who are concerned with the places where they live or work, or with particular topics, but who have little interest in abstract justifications of the subject. The growth of interest in local history amongst amateurs in the second half of the 20th century has been spectacular. In part, this is because of improved access to archives with the establishment of county *record offices in nearly every shire. It also owes much to the provision of courses by university extramural departments, the Workers' Educational Association (WEA), and other adult education bodies, and the formation of local history societies in every part of the land. The quarterly journal The *Local Historian, and the magazine *Local History cater for this readership. See also D. P. Dymond, Writing Local History (1981), and Kate Tiller, English Local History: An Introduction (1992).

The amateur and professional come together in *group projects organized by university extramural departments or the WEA. In the 1950s Bernard Jennings in Nidderdale and Lionel Munby in Hertfordshire independently developed this method of research. Their classes, and others that have followed them, have published some first-rate work. Group research has proved far more popular and productive with local history classes than with any other subject. See Joan Unwin, 'Local History Group Research Projects in Adult Continuing Education', The Local Historian, 24/1 (1994). Local history has also proved a popular choice for part-time qualification courses leading to a university certificate or a BA or MA degree. Local studies have increasingly formed the basis of M.Phil. or Ph.D. theses, either as local history per se or as case-studies of themes of national interest.

Meanwhile, interest in the many aspects of local history at a non-academic level has burgeoned. The variety of publications that pour off the presses or from desk-top computers is too rich and multi-faceted to summarize. Those authors who are influenced by the work of professional historians attempt a wider context or treat special themes or periods. Others are content to reproduce old photographs of trams or people, street scenes of then and now, picture postcards, anything that has a nostalgic appeal. Videos and visual displays for heritage centres offer other outlets for such activities. Some of it is excellent, much of it is worthy or commendable, part of it is poor. The demand at present seems insatiable. The pace of change has made people aware of the past at a time when the opportunities for research and publication are greater than ever before. At no time in British history has the study of local history at all levels of achievement been so popular.

A recent trend has been to integrate the study of local history with that of family history. See David Hey, Family History and Local History in England (1987), and C. D. Rogers and J. H. Smith, Local Family History in England (1992), together with the four volumes in the Open University series, Studying Family and Community History (1994), namely Ruth Finnegan and Michael Drake (eds.), From Family Tree to Family History, Rees Pryce (ed.), From Family History to Community History, John Golby (ed.), Communities and Families, and Ruth Finnegan, Michael Drake, and Jacqueline Eustace (eds.), Sources and Methods for Family and Community Historians: A Handbook. See also FAMILY HISTORY; IRISH LOCAL AND FAMILY HISTORY; SCOTTISH LOCAL AND FAMILY HISTORY; and WELSH LOCAL AND FAMILY HISTORY.

local government. As both a subject for historical study and a career, local government currently has a reputation for dullness. Nevertheless, some understanding of the evolution of local government is essential for the student who wishes to make sense of its records, and the history of local government itself is worthy of study for what it can tell us about the concerns and aspirations of individual *communities.

Several propositions concerning the history of local government may be quickly stated. Firstly, no universal, structured system of local government existed in England and Wales before 1888, rather a range of administrative and judicial institutions, each with distinct historical origins. Secondly, no clear distinction can be made between local government and the local administration of justice before 1888. Before this date the key individuals in local government were the *Justices of the Peace (collectively called the magistracy) who were primarily responsible for the indictment of crime. Indeed, JPs might use their power to indict as a means to secure administrative ends; for example, in 1809 the Oxfordshire JPs indicted *parishes for failures in the maintenance of *roads. As individuals, the JPs were also charged with other aspects of government, such as the collection of *taxation, and organization of the militia, which would not now be regarded as a part of local government. As a body, though, the magistracy were invariably concerned with the preservation of public order and social stability (and ultimately the protection of property) rather than the provision of public services. Thirdly, the connections between local and *central government before the 19th century were weak, and because they tended towards informality, are often ill-documented. Certainly JPs, particularly at times of social stress, were careful to inform central government of local problems. But the financial independence of local from central government allowed many of the formative developments in local government to arise out of local initiatives sanctioned by private Acts of Parliament. These were then adopted elsewhere by private Act before being incorporated in general Acts. Local government, in the modern form of agencies largely funded by central government and undertaking delegated tasks, is of fairly recent origin.

Local government developed out of a general expectation that the monarch, and the individual landowner, would provide justice. Whilst the range of central courts is considered elsewhere, by the beginning of the 13th century there existed an established system of hundredal and county courts presided over by the *sheriff. Although their business was essentially criminal or civil, these courts also dealt with matters of an administrative nature, including offences against the assize of bread and ale and nuisances. As the Bedfordshire roll of 1332–3 shows, the county could also make orders for the public good, in this case to repair a bridge. At the level of the individual rural community were the courts of each *manor. The origins of these courts are obscure: suffice it to say that, at the moment from which the first manorial court records survive (the mid-13th century), the courts have well-established procedures. Later jurists divided the court into the *court leet (which they considered to be a public court, with a delegated royal authority), and the lord's own court, the *court baron, which protected his seigneurial interests and profits.

Urban communities had their own systems of courts. Where the town had no corporate status, the court, whatever it might be called, was in effect the lord's manorial court. A corporate town invariably had a court presided over by its own officials and possibly courts held for individual wards. The essential business of both manorial and borough courts was the prosecution of *felonies and trespass, the settlement of civil disputes, the regulation of the lands of the manor (especially where they were *copyhold), and control over commons and grazing. But, like the *hundred courts, some of their functions were clearly administrative: the regulation of markets (including weights and measures and the sale of bread and ale) and the prosecution of nuisances, impassable roads, dunghills, pollution of waterways, the maintenance of fences and ditches, and so on. The courts appointed officers to watch over these areas.

These local institutions tended not to survive much beyond the end of the 16th century. A minority of court leets remained very active as, for instance, Prescot in Lancashire in the 18th century, but the majority of manorial courts, if they were held at all after 1650, dealt only with the transfer of copyhold lands. In part this appears to reflect changes in landholding and tenancy, but it also suggests the disinterest of landowners in the court leet, a lack of confidence within communities over their capacity for self-government, and most importantly the appearance of the JPs as the providers of a superior public justice.

Where the manor and its institutions disappeared, the parish remained the fundamental unit of local government out of which all else was built. It was the parish, through the meeting of its inhabitants or ratepayers, the *vestry, which was the sole body empowered to raise a rate. The vestry evolved; it had no statutory origins. It might be 'open' or 'select', in which case smaller groups acted in the name of the whole. (Select vestries quickly acquired a reputation for corruption.) Even where the vestry remained open, it was probably, in reality, an oligarchic meeting of the more substantial inhabitants. The vestry came to appoint the parochial officers and probably devised policy towards the poor. In theory the parish was self-sufficient in its support of the poor, and for this reason the majority of local government expenditure was raised and expended within the parish. Total county rates, which were levied by the parish on a magistrate's precept, were a much smaller charge nationally than total parochial expenditure (£0.3m against £2m in 1792 and £0.8m against £7m in 1832). Attempts were made to curb the scale of expenditure on the poor by altering the composition of the vestry. An act of 1818 instituted a system of plural voting for ratepayers with the aim of encouraging the domination of the vestry by minority of landholders or tenants. The power of the vestry to determine its own poor-relief policy was ended by the 1834 *Poor Law legislation, but the vestry itself survived and in 1894 it was transformed into the parish council.

Before 1834 the development of local government outside a few major *towns (and especially *London, which presents problems of its own) must be seen in terms of the evolution of the power and authority of the JPs. They were crown appointees named to a panel, the Commission of the Peace, for each county. By 1603, some 71 commissions were issued, 55 for English and Welsh counties (Wales receiving commissions only when shired in 1543), nine for *liberties, and seven for *boroughs. A number of towns were exempt from the county commissions, and were governed by their mayor and aldermen sitting *ex officio* as justices. Each commission was supported by a *clerk of the peace.

Magistrates were in the beginning, and always remained, unsalaried (although they were allowed certain expenses). They were also amateurs: whilst engaged in the exercise of the law, they were not bound to have any legal training (although they were expected to defer to their lawyer colleagues.) Membership of the commission was only open to men who met a minimum property qualification and who, until the Commission of the Peace was opened to men with 'commercial' wealth in the 1830s, were normally significant *landowners. (The exception to this rule were clerical justices.) They were largely unsupervised. In the 17th century, reports on the conduct of JPs might be made by the *assize justices, to whom the magistrates referred intractable legal or administrative questions. In the 18th century nomination to the bench came to rest in the hands of the *lord lieutenant, who might report on the adequacy of individuals.

The commission probably never met as a body. Indeed, some members of the commission, especially peers, were probably entirely honorific members who never sat, and not all the justices named in the commission could be guaranteed to swear their *dedimus protestatem* which allowed them to exercise the office. So whilst the Crown determined the membership of the commission, it could never be certain which of its nominees would offer themselves as active members. Even then, the functioning JPs rarely, if ever, met together. Some counties, from the 17th century, did have annual meetings of the bench, but for the most part the commission operated as a series of local benches with magistrates attending only the sessions which sat within their hundred and working entirely with their geographically proximate colleagues. The dangers inherent in this can be seen in the need for orders forbidding *alehouse keepers seeking licences from distant justices: the whole matter was formalized by the development of petty sessions.

The origins of the JPs' office may be found in the Keepers of the Peace, appointed from time to time in the late 13th century to undertake limited duties on behalf of the king. There then followed a period of experimentation in the early 14th century in which the keepers were given different sets of powers, especially the power to try crimes. By the 15th century the

general shape of their duties had been decided. They were to hold sessions quarterly (although they were also authorized to act out of sessions and, as individual justices, had the power to arrest, bail, and bind men on suspicion of a breach of the peace). At sessions, the late medieval justices heard presentments from jurors who would declare their knowledge of misdemeanours according to articles of enquiry read to them. One, apparently typical, 15th-century list asked for jurors to declare instances of 'various types of killing, robbery, arson, rape and those associated with them as receivers, maintainers, procurers and so on, those imprisoned on suspicion of felony, into trespasses, riots, giving liveries, taking oaths, forcible entries, disturbers of courts, extortion and oppression by officials, menaces, forced purveyance, buying goods on the way to market or forcing up the price before it had begun (i.e. regrating and forestalling), the malpractices of innkeepers and victuallers, breaches of the assize of bread and beer and weights and measures, a long list of breaches of labour regulations and into peace provisions such as whether watches and hue and cry were being carried out.' (A. L. Brown, *The Governance of Late Medieval England, 1272–1461* (1989), 124.)

This shows how the justice's administrative responsibilities were secondary to their criminal work. On the other hand, it is probably true to say that their regulatory responsibilities grew to a greater degree than any other of their duties, their control over labour being reiterated, for instance, by the Statute of *Artificers of 1563. When William *Lambarde published his manual for justices, *Eirenarcha*, in 1581, he was able to list 133 statutes enacted before 1485, and a further 176 after that date, which placed responsibilities on the JPs.

A listing of their statutory responsibilities fails to recognize the degree of discretion which they possessed. The great increase in the attentiveness of local government in the century or so after 1580 came not from any new legislative framework or instruction from the Crown, but as a magisterial response to social problems, especially the perceived growth in the numbers of the poor and the underemployed. This tended to take the form of the more active regulation of areas of life about which the justices had previously shown little concern, such as alehouses, drink, and sexual behaviour outside marriage. The whole process, which is well described for Essex and some towns, is known as the 'Reformation of Manners'.

The key to this new enthusiasm for regulation was the presentment system, whereby parish officers and selected inhabitants ('questmen') appeared at sessions (or before justices privately) and brought with them written presentments of misdemeanours within their parishes. The position of these officers was deeply ambiguous: they were representatives of their villages, but responsible for informing on the illicit affairs of their neighbours. Accordingly, the *constables tended to say less rather than more until pressed to do so by the magistrates (unless they were exceptionally well-motivated zealots for a reformation of society). Vigilant magistrates could make the system work through the careful use of their charge and individual interviews with constables, overseers, and questmen. Individual communities could and did petition the magistrates about behaviour which they found offensive; but the parish officers were the magistrates' eyes and ears.

Policy towards alehouses was typical in being driven by new magisterial concerns. Alehouses were viewed as morally dubious locations where the poor frittered away the little they had in the company of thieves and prostitutes. Whilst the framework for licensing had been laid down by statute of 1552, it was only in the late 16th century and more especially the early 17th that JPs began to implement the system vigorously with the aim of reducing the number of alehouses. Central government occasionally demanded that alehouses should be more tightly regulated, but a recent account argues that 'the gradual evolution of a comprehensive licensing system between 1600 and around 1680 does not bear any close relationship to the chronology of conciliar intervention' (A. Fletcher, *Reform in the Provinces: The Government of Stuart England* (1986), 241). Instead Fletcher identifies some counties which already held regular licensing sessions before the *Civil War, and others where their development was delayed until the 1670s. In the far north, magisterial authority over the sale of drink was only imposed in the last years of the century.

Whilst the licensing of alehouses was one of the ways in which the behaviour of the poor was regulated, the most obvious and direct way was through the administration of the Poor Law. The 1597 statute, with subsequent amendments, served to place developing local practice on a legal basis, but also compelled all parishes to adopt a uniform system of relief. Broadly, this obliged all parishes to levy rates for the support of the poor, to offer outdoor relief to poor persons in the form of a weekly dole, or to provide work. The responsibility for doing this

was placed on the parish and parish officers (the overseers of the *poor) appointed for that purpose. It was envisaged that the parish should normally be financially self-sufficient. The statute, however, provided for the justices to supervise at every turn: they were to nominate the overseers, hear their accounts at the end of their term of office, commit to prison those amongst the poor not willing to work, bind children to be apprentices, act as a court of appeal for aggrieved rate payers, and so on. Of course, the Poor Law was not implemented everywhere overnight. There are signs that the assize justices were trying to see it enforced in Lancashire in 1618 and later, and in a number of northern and Welsh counties the JPs apparently preferred to allow begging rather than court unpopularity by demanding that rates be levied. A mixture of magisterial pressure and the need for parishes to cope with the dearth years of 1630–1 and 1647–50 made for the near-universal establishment of parish relief by 1660. From this date, the duty of supervising the Poor Law in the parishes must have taken over a large part of an active magistrate's time.

But the Old Poor Law was essentially a system of *parish* relief, operated by overseers whose policy in the parish was determined by the vestry. The role of the county bench was that of the umpire: watching over the operation of parochial provision and hearing appeals (often from individual paupers who felt ill-treated by the overseers), but rarely determining policy. Nor did the magistracy handle the money expended on poor relief: they could not curb profligate expenditure by a parish (though they might instruct a parish to spend more than it wished).

So whilst the two centuries or so after 1600 may be considered the Golden Age of magisterial rule in the counties, it much be stressed how far removed were magistrates from being an executive authority. They enforced the law, administered justice, and undertook a range of miscellaneous regulatory functions. They did not support a *police force (though they did manage the county gaol). They oversaw parish government, but it was the responsibility of the parish, not the magistrates, to detect crime, repair roads, and make provision for the poor. As we saw earlier, the magistrates had very little money at their disposal. Their expenditure was small, only around £1,600–£2,000 per annum in mid-18th-century Cheshire, perhaps £1,000 in Wiltshire, but only £750 in Shropshire: that is, expenditure by individual counties was smaller than the income of a great many magistrates.

In one important respect the duties of the county bench diminished. Over the 18th century they lost control of the primary road system to *turnpike trusts, corporate bodies established by statute to take charge of the repair and improvement of specific lengths of road. The importance of the trusts was not only that they were administratively efficient, but that they could tax road-users and borrow on the security of future income. During the 18th century trusts proliferated, 562 being created between 1751 and 1815: the need for this to happen reveals the weakness of magisterial government.

The magistracy seems to have become much more professional in its approach to business in the 18th century. One indication of this is the appearance of the clerical magistrate. Clergy acting as justices were not new, but their profusion is indicative of a shortage of gentlemen willing to act as working magistrates. Membership of the 17th century bench conferred (or confirmed) status: membership in the 18th century exposed the active magistrate to a diet of petty sessions and alehouse licensing, and a stream of parish officers to his door to organize the prosecution of felons, the removal of paupers, the affiliation of bastards, and other local administrative minutiae. By the early 19th century large areas of Oxfordshire and Buckinghamshire were served entirely by clerical magistrates. The withdrawal from the bench of the status-conscious *gentry left the way open for the construction of a more committed and administratively active magistracy and the development of the latent authority of the bench. A further development was the practice of appointing standing chairmen of the commission, instead of annual chairmen or chairmen for individual sessions. The appearance of permanent chairmen (e.g. in Oxfordshire in 1771, Shropshire in 1785) permitted the appearance of capable administrators and administrative continuity. A number of county chairmen made reputations as innovators in organization of the commission with the establishment of subcommittees to act on specific areas of government. And rather like the zealous magistrates of the early 17th century, some chairmen set out to use their authority to reform society, often working under the influence of a revived movement for the reformation of manners. A new interest in *prisons developed, often coupled with schemes for rebuilding the county gaol along modern lines. Lancashire proceeded further than most counties by securing a statute in 1798 to constitute the magistracy into a Court of Annual General Sessions, in effect a proto-county council.

It was, however, the 1790s which offered the new activist magistracy both the challenge and the opportunity to create policy. Expenditure on poor rates had been rising, especially in the southern counties, from the 1770s: in 1793–5 the cost of relief soared as labourers faced high prices, food shortages, and unemployment. Overseers, therefore, found themselves trapped between growing poverty and heightened demands on the parish at a time when ratepayers themselves were hard pressed. It was in these circumstances that the magistracy of a number of counties (most famously Berkshire) met to lay down rules for the instruction of overseers which established minimum standards of relief related to the cost of victuals. In a sense this was merely an extension of the magistrate's power to set wages, but it also made for a shift in practical authority from the vestry to the magistracy. It was also the last moment at which independent magisterial action was allowed to fill a void left by government inactivity. The post-war depression, in which expenditure on relief again appeared to be running away in an unsustainable fashion, saw national legislation designed to cut the cost of relief by making the parish less generous.

Nineteenth-century policies tended to subtract areas of authority from the magistrates until the bench was left only with its primary duty of the indictment of criminal activity. It is clear that in an age of even limited democracy, an unelected magisterial élite could not command universal confidence. John Stuart Mill, writing in 1861, held that the *quarter sessions were 'obviously at variance with all the principles which are the foundation of representative government' (quoted in B. Keith-Lucas, *English Local Government in the Nineteenth and Twentieth Centuries* (1977), 20). It might be suggested that the magistracy survived as long as it did because, from the 1830s onwards, it was opened to men whose wealth was essentially commercial or professional. Clerical justices were the subject of much unfavourable comment in the early 1830s, and the influx of new talent allowed their disappearance from the bench.

The general pattern of local government which emerged after the 1830s may be described as one in which urban areas became increasingly closely governed under the control of elected boards and municipal authorities, whilst the countryside remained under the guidance of the magistrates and, in effect, continued to lack bodies recognizable as local government. The piecemeal development of local government was designed to cope with the essentially local problems of urban growth. Whilst their responsibility for government was increasingly restricted to non-urban areas, it would not be true to speak of any general attack on the magistracy, either as individuals or as a form of local government, until much later in the century. Indeed, they received new powers, being placed in charge of former turnpike roads in 1878, and this in turn prompted the further development of the staff employed by the magistracy, headed by the clerk of the peace.

This illustrates how the magistracy was central to the great expansion of local government in the mid-19th century. The first statute to alter materially the work of the magistracy was the Poor Law Amendment Act of 1834, which took the responsibility for the management of the Poor Law out of the hands of parishes and placed it in the hands of Poor Law unions managed by elected Boards of *Guardians (composed of magisterial and elected members) with salaried overseers. Each board was in turn responsible to the Poor Law Commission. The Municipal Incorporation Act of 1835 had obliged boroughs to organize police forces under the supervision of elected watch committees and not the magistracy. The Rural Constabulary Act of 1839 allowed the magistrates to launch rural police forces under their own supervision, but this was a rather timid and permissive statute, and in fact only a minority of counties chose to adopt it in full (22 by 1841). A further statue of 1842 permitted parishes to employ paid constables to supplement parish resources. This achieved some success with 368 parishes or unions adopting its provisions by 1846. In that year, however, only 2,817 paid constables were employed in England. That government chose to make advances in policing dependent on local initiative reflects the extreme sensitivity of the issue amongst conservative thinkers (who feared centralization and the appearance of a salaried magistracy). Making improvements in the quality of policing contingent on the decisions of an unelected élite was obviously unsatisfactory. In 1856 a further statute called into existence a uniform police force (although one which was still under the control of the county magistrates).

The birth of local government as a provider of local services must be located in both these statutes and the private Acts which preceded them. Turnpike Trusts, drainage boards, improvement or paving commissioners, or municipal water or gas companies were all created by private Act. Typically the statute would provide for the creation of a board of commissioners composed of *ex officio* and elected members. The statute conferred on them the authority to raise a rate to undertake limited tasks. Once adopted by one town, similar powers tended to be sought by others and might finally be incorporated into a general Act which other authorities could adopt if they wished. Obviously, this pattern of proceeding tended to result in authority being divided between the old municipal authorities and the new statutory boards, with every town possessing a unique range of powers.

In Manchester and Salford, the local government of the parishes was divided between the court leet which administered the market, the vestry which undertook the relief of the poor and the repair of highways, and the board created by a statute of 1792 which undertook a number of measures including street widening and, in 1817, established a municipal gasworks. The 1835 Act revised the charters of the existing boroughs and regulated their franchises: but it also permitted unincorporated towns (such as Manchester) to apply for incorporation into which the existing authorities could be merged. The progress of urban local government thus tended to depend on the enthusiasm of small groups of forward-looking individuals, and on the willingness of ratepayers to fund sometimes grandiose projects or to support applications for ever-increasing regulatory powers such as building regulation. As the municipal architecture of the period shows, this was the age of greatest civic pride, confidence, and independence from central government.

Government in 19th-century urban England remained uneven and was conducted by potentially overlapping elected boards and councils. Local government in rural England and Wales was barely embryonic. After the Highways Act of 1862 the magistrates joined parishes together as Highway Boards for the maintenance of roads, waged labour paid from the rates replacing the '*statute labour' days. Further statutes of 1873 and 1875 created an even system of urban and rural sanitary districts, piecemeal reform again establishing bodies for specific purposes rather than omni-competent local authorities. Nationally, in 1870 local administration in England and Wales was divided between 65 counties and 97 boroughs holding their own quarter sessions, 224 municipal borough councils, 667 Poor Law unions, 852 turnpike trusts, 117 improvement commissions, 637 Boards of Health, and 404 highway authorities (in rural areas), there being in all 27,000 different authorities (including parishes) entitled to levy one or more out of 18 different types of rate (D. N. Chester, *The English Administrative System* (1981), 347).

The role of the magistrates in local government was largely ended by the Local Government Act of 1888 which established *county councils and county boroughs. A proposal that the powers of quarter sessions should be transferred to a council comprised of magistrates and elected members had been made as long ago as 1835 in the report of the Royal Commission on County Rates. A bill to create county councils, without magisterial members, had been prepared by the Liberal government in 1886. It was left to Salisbury—rather against the inclination of his own party—to introduce a similar bill in 1888. Where this differed from the Liberal bill was in placing the police under the control of a joint committee of councillors and JPs. Rather to the surprise of many, a large number of magistrates secured election as councillors and in some counties the bench continued for the interim in a new guise. A further statute of 1894 established a second tier of local government in the *Urban and *Rural District Councils which took over the responsibilities of the sanitary boards.

Rather like the magistrates of the 16th and 17th centuries, the county councils gathered additional duties. In 1902 they took over the provision of *education from the School Boards which had been established in 1870. In 1930 they acquired the remaining functions of the Poor Law Unions, although they had been responsible for the provision of *asylums and other *public health services from their foundation. The proliferation of new statutory responsibilities placed on authorities, in housing, for instance, was accompanied by a growing level of grant aid from the central exchequer. This fatally undermined local authorities: by the 1970s it was widely believed that their spending needed to be restrained.

There remained a sense in which the county councils were responsible for that which was not urban. The tension here was partly that urban centres did not want to contribute to the provision of rural services. Nor did the predominantly rural magistrates wish to share power with radical urban councillors. The 1888 bill began by allowing ten boroughs to have county status: after amendment the Act came to create 61 county boroughs. Further towns sought this status. The separation of town from countryside made difficulties for the new county authorities (the 15 county boroughs in Lanca-

shire were called 'holes in the carpet') through the loss in rateable value, the more so in that urban growth prompted the boroughs to petition for boundary revisions to increase their extent. None the less, the system of counties, county boroughs, and urban and rural districts devised in 1888–94 remained in place until 1974 (although with many local adjustments, notably the merger of smaller districts). The local government reforms of 1972 tended to erase the distinction between county and town by abolishing the county boroughs while often making them the centres of mixed urban and rural authorities. Subsequent developments have tended to favour larger local authorities, often single-tier; with the loss of financial independence from central government over the 20th century, the possibilities for local innovation have diminished.

The history of local government in its heroic days of urban poverty, destitution, and disease in industrializing society is now well described in the literature. The less heroic history of the provision of elementary amenities by 20th-century councils—the revolution in living standards wrought by the provision of mains water and sewage or the spread of the tarmacadamed road, the rise or fall of municipal utility and transport companies—is less well known and provides fertile ground for the local historian. See D. Eastwood, *Governing Rural England: Tradition and Transformation in Local Government, 1780–1840* (1994), A. Fletcher, *Reform in the Provinces: The Government of Stuart England* (1986), B. Keith-Lucas, *English Local Government in the Nineteenth and Twentieth Centuries* (1977), N. Landau, *The Justices of the Peace, 1679–1760* (1984), and S. and B. Webb, *The Parish and the County* (1906) and *The Manor and the Borough* (1908).   R. W. HOYLE

Local Historian, The. Founded in 1952 as *The Amateur Historian*, its name was changed in 1968. Since 1961 it has been the official journal of the *Standing Conference for Local History and its successor, the *British Association for Local History. It is published quarterly and contains articles and reviews that are scholarly but accessible to a wider readership. As such, it is the principal journal for local historians.

Local History Magazine. A privately run national magazine for local historians, which has been published bi-monthly since 1984. It contains articles, reviews, and notices of events throughout the country.

Local Population Studies. A journal founded in 1968, devoted to the study of *population history. It contains articles, reviews, and news items. Occasional supplements on particular topics are published separately.

local societies. See COMMUNITIES AND LOCAL SOCIETIES.

lock-making. A West Midlands industry. Simple padlocks and chest locks were made on a large scale, but sophisticated locks of brass as well as iron were being made to individual order by the 16th century. Joseph Bramah (1749–1814) invented a famous thief-proof lock. The industry remained a handcraft until the second half of the 19th century.

Loder, Robert. Berkshire farmer whose farm accounts are an unusually detailed source for *agricultural history. See G. E. Fussell (ed.), *Robert Loder's Farm Accounts, 1610–1620* (Camden Society, 3rd ser., liii, 1936).

lodges. In the Middle Ages small and simple hunting lodges provided temporary accommodation for a lord and his party. Between the 16th and 18th centuries lodges were fashionable retreats set in a *park. Some were rebuildings of old hunting lodges, others were new structures of superior quality and unusual design, often on new sites.

lodgings. In the 14th and 15th centuries the provision of lodgings altered the plans of *palaces, *castles, and *manor houses. Whole new ranges were built to accommodate retainers as well as guests and their retinues. At the same time, urban terraces provided lodgings for *vicars-choral, *chantry priests, and students at universities. In the 19th century the word became associated with the rooms rented by migrant or unmarried workers in industrial towns.

Lollards. Followers of John Wycliffe (c.1329–84) who rejected the authority of priests and attacked abuses in the church, including the system of confession, penance, and indulgence. Wycliffe wrote popular religious tracts in English, translated the Bible, and organized a body of itinerant preachers who insisted on the importance of inward religion rather than the mechanical observance of established practices. His followers were persecuted from 1382, but his influence lasted down to the *Reformation.

London. Named by the Romans, London was the largest city in the British Isles by the time of the *Domesday Book. It has always been noted for its cultural diversity, attracting immigrants from distant parts in a way that no other British city could equal. See Roy Porter, *London: A Social History* (1994), and Nick Merriman (ed.), *The Peopling of London* (1993). London was unusual among capital cities in being not just the political and administrative centre but the country's major port and, until the 19th century, the greatest place of manufacture. Even in the Middle Ages London attracted people of every rank and occupation from many parts of the British Isles and abroad in large numbers. See Sylvia L. Thrupp, *The Merchant Class of Medieval London, 1300–1500* (1962).

London grew rapidly during the early modern period, until by 1750 it was the largest city in Europe and the fourth largest in the world. See A. L. Beier and Roger Finlay (eds.), *London, 1500–1700: The Making of the Metropolis* (1986). No other British town came anywhere near it in size and importance. It grew from an estimated population of 120,000 in 1550 to 200,000 in 1600, 375,000 in 1650, 490,000 in 1700, 675,000 in 1750, and 900,000 in 1800. At the beginning of Queen Elizabeth I's reign only about 4 per cent of the population of England and Wales were Londoners; by 1700 this proportion had risen to nearly 10 per cent. London accounted for half the increase in England's urban population during the 16th and 17th centuries. This growth was fuelled by immigration, for studies of *parish registers have shown that the numbers who died in London exceeded the numbers who were born there. Five major outbreaks of *plague occurred between 1563 and 1665, and other killer diseases kept the mortality rates high. It has been estimated that between 1650 and 1750 at least 8,000 immigrants a year were needed to explain how London's population rose to new levels. London was the great exception to the rule of short-distance *mobility, for it attracted immigrants from all parts of the country and abroad. Londoners were a unique mixture of people, with a significant minority coming from France, the Low Countries, and other parts of continental Europe. At any one time, only a minority of Londoners had been born there. The city was a youthful society, for most of the immigrants were in their late teens and early twenties, and an unusually mobile one, for many did not stay, but moved on or eventually returned home. On movement within London at this period, see Jeremy Boulton, 'Neighbourhood Migration in Early Modern England', in P. Clark and D. Souden (eds.), *Migration and Society in Early Modern England* (1987). See also Peter Earle, *The Making of the English Middle Class: Business, Society and Family Life in London, 1660–1730* (1989), Janet Barnes and Craig Spence, *An Atlas of London in the 1690s* (1994), which maps the city in social and economic terms, and John

Landers, *Death and the Metropolis: Studies in the Demographic History of London, 1670–1830* (1993).

The earliest surviving map of London shows the capital as it appeared at the accession of Queen Elizabeth I. Most of the City was still confined within the medieval walls, which followed the line of their Roman predecessor so as to enclose an area north of the river Thames, from the Tower in the east to the Strand in the west. Court and Parliament occupied the separate suburb of Westminster. Only one bridge crossed the river to the suburb of Southwark. See Felix Barker and Peter Jackson, *The History of London in Maps* (1990), and John Schofield (ed.), *The London Survey of Ralph Treswell* (1987), for a detailed collection of maps dating from 1585 to 1614. The Barker and Jackson collection also maps the rebuilding of the City after the fire of 1666 and the construction of Georgian squares, on which see Sir John Summerson, *Georgian London* (1962).

For an overview of 19th-century London, see Francis Sheppard, *London, 1808–1870: The Infernal Wen* (1971). Gavin Weightman and Steve Humphries, *The Making of Modern London, 1815–1914* (1983) examines the continued dominance of the City, the growth of affluent suburbs in the West End, the creation of an East End comprising Stepney, Poplar, Bethnal Green, and parts of Hackney (where thousands of unskilled immigrants came to work in the docks, the street markets, and sweated trades), and the influence of the transport system, from the horse to the railway, in the creation of *suburbs. (See LONDON UNDERGROUND.) For a family history that is related to the history of the local community, see P. Sanders, *The Simple Annals: The History of an Essex and East End Family* (1989). On the very different nature of the London boroughs, see two detailed local studies, F. M. L. Thompson, *Hampstead: Building a Borough, 1650–1964* (1974), and H. J. *Dyos, *Victorian Suburb: A Study of the Growth of Camberwell* (1961).

The study of Camberwell serves to illuminate the history of many of the boroughs that were transformed by rows upon rows of terraced houses. Before the reign of Victoria, Camberwell was a populous middle-class suburb, about $1\frac{1}{2}$ miles south of London Bridge. In 1841 it already had a population of 39,868. By the end of the century it was a metropolitan borough with a population of 259,339. The *census returns show that at any one time the majority of Camberwell's population had been born in London, but that many families had moved from a different district and that many others continued to move from street to street. Camberwell shared the general tendency for London's suburbs to deteriorate in status as the better-off families moved out and poorer families moved in.

Victorian London sprawled miles beyond the old limits of the medieval city. 'Greater London', a collective term for those suburbs that lay beyond the old county boundary, grew from about 414,000 inhabitants in 1861 to 2,045,000 at the turn of the century. Between 1881 and 1891 the most rapid population growth in the whole of Britain occurred in four London suburbs: Leyton (133.3 per cent), Willesden (121.9 per cent), Tottenham (95.1 per cent), and West Ham (58.9 per cent). By the end of the 19th century London's population was rising by an extra 100,000 inhabitants per annum to a total figure of over 4 million people. London had reached a size and complexity that was unparalleled in world history. It had become characterized by miles of Victorian terraced and semi-detached housing. The centre reflected London's role as an imperial capital, but it was never dominated by royalty or aristocracy. Rather, the capital city was essentially a commercial centre, with terrible contrasts between poverty and wealth. Meanwhile, some other British cities had expanded enormously, so that the proportion of the population that lived in the capital was less than before. Some of these cities, notably Manchester, took an independent line on many national issues. In the 20th century, however, London's leading role in politics and commerce, though not in manufacturing, has been strengthened. It remains by far the most cosmopolitan of British cities and continues to attract thousands of young migrants from far afield.

London Gazette. This official news sheet was first published in 1665 as *The Oxford Gazette*, but from number 24 onwards (5 February 1666) it bore the name of *The London Gazette*. At first it was published each Tuesday and Friday, but it now appears daily. It reached most parts of the country from its earliest years. A complete set is available in the *Guildhall Library. See P. M. Handover, *A History of the London Gazette, 1665–1965* (1965).

London Underground. The first underground railway in the world was the Metropolitan railway, which began to run between Paddington and Farringdon Street and then on to Moorgate in 1865. When it was extended into the Circle Line, around London's core, it ran into financial difficulties. The deep-tunnelling methods of the 1890s greatly extended the system and enabled men and women to travel quickly from the suburbs to their place of work. The Central Line connecting the West End and the City was opened in 1900, and the rest of central London's underground system—except for the later Victoria and Jubilee lines—was finished before the First World War. See T. C. Barker and Michael Robbins, *A History of London Transport*, vol. i. *The Nineteenth Century* (1963).

longhouse. A house with opposed entries and an unheated lower room which was once used for accommodating livestock or as a workshop or storage-place. The evidence for its former use for livestock is usually the presence of a drain or sump. Humans and animals entered the building via a common door and passage. The longhouse was a common form of farmhouse in the Middle Ages and later in southwest England, north-east England (Northumberland, Durham, and north-east Yorkshire), Cumbria, Herefordshire, south Wales, and some other areas, e.g. the chalk uplands of Wiltshire or the Yorkshire Wolds. Evidence comes from excavations, e.g. at Wharram Percy, the *deserted medieval village on the Yorkshire Wolds, and from standing structures. It is debatable whether the longhouse was once the normal type of farmhouse throughout Britain. In the early modern period livestock were removed from the lower ends of longhouses and the space was used instead for service rooms. New houses continued to be built on the old plan even though they never accommodated cattle. They are longer than they are wide, being only one room deep, and are readily distinguished by their off-centre entry with an axial chimney-stack to one side. See Barry Harrison and Barbara Hutton, *Vernacular Houses in North Yorkshire and Cleveland* (1984).

lord of misrule. During the twelve days of *Christmas the traditional social hierarchy in a *palace, *castle, or *manor house was turned upside down by the appointment of a lowly member of the household as lord of misrule, with licence to organize boisterous activities and to make fun of his social superiors. This short period of misrule served as a useful safety valve for the release of social tensions. See Ronald Hutton, *The Rise and Fall of Merry England: The Ritual Year, 1400–1700* (1994).

lord of the manor. *Manors varied considerably in size and their importance declined over the centuries. A lord of the manor could therefore be a medieval *baron, titled *landowner, or just a well-to-do local farmer, businessman, or *attorney. Lords frequently did not reside on their manors and left the administration of the manor court to a *steward.

lordship. The larger feudal territories, e.g. a *castellany. Some were compact estates, others consisted of scattered *manors.

lords lieutenant. In 1551 king's lieutenants were placed in charge of the county militias, with responsibility for *musters and *beacons. As they were noblemen, they came to be known as lords lieutenant. They became a valued means of passing on local news to the central government. Records of their activities (mostly from the second half of the 18th century and the early 19th century) are available at county *record offices. The duties of the office are now ceremonial.

lorimer. A maker of bits, spurs, and the metal parts of harness. The trade was a West Midlands one, concentrated in Walsall and characterized by extreme subdivision of labour.

Lowland zone. The concept of a Lowland zone was advanced in Sir Cyril Fox, *The Personality of Britain* (1932). It has greatly influenced historical geographers, archaeologists, and landscape historians. The populous, wealthier, and more advanced lowland areas, east and south of a line drawn from the Tees to the Exe, are contrasted with settlements in the *Highland zone. The concept has been refined by the study of *pays.

Lowside window. A low window on the south side of the *chancel of a parish *church, whose purpose is mysterious. Many appear to have been inserted into existing walls. The popular explanation that they enabled lepers to watch services is implausible. It is possible that they were inserted to enable a person outside the building to judge the right moment to ring the sanctum bell, so that those people who were excused attendance in order to work in the fields could bow their heads, but this explanation is not certain. The sanctum bell was a 13th-century innovation.

Lucas, John (1685?–1750). Leeds schoolmaster and author of a history of his native parish, Warton (Lancashire). This rambling work, compiled over three decades, contains much contemporary observation which is now of historical interest. For a condensed version see J. R. Ford and J. A. Fuller-Maitland (eds.), *John Lucas's History of Warton Parish (1710–40)* (1931).

lucerne. One of the artificial grasses imported from France during the later 17th and 18th centuries to diversify the native stock. In trials it was ranked alongside *clover and *sainfoin, and is superior to both in yield and its ability to nourish cattle. It survives drought better than other legumes because of its long root. But although grown in England, it became a far more important crop on the Continent. In England clover won the dominant place. See Mauro Ambrosoli, *The Sown and the Wild: Botany and Agriculture in Western Europe, 1350–1850* (1995).

Luddites. The machine-breaking activities of the Luddites occurred during 1811–12, with fresh outbreaks in 1814 and 1816. The first attacks in the *framework-knitting districts of Nottinghamshire were accompanied by warning letters and proclamations signed 'Ned Ludd', 'Captain Ludd', or 'General Ludd'. During 1812 Luddite activities spread to the woollen-manufacturing district of the West Riding of Yorkshire, where the skilled trade of cropping was threatened by the introduction of shearing frames and gig mills, and into the *cotton districts of Lancashire. The objectives of the machine-breakers were different in these three areas. The government sent 12,000 troops to restore order. The violence came to a head in the West Riding with the armed attack on Rawfold's Mill and the attempted murder of a mill-owner, William Horsfall. It is generally recognized that this was a turning-point that lost the Luddites much of the sympathy that they had previously enjoyed in their communities. Several Luddites were hanged at York.

The central records are kept at the *Public Record Office under HO 40. Local memories of events in the West Riding were collected in Frank Peel, *The Rising of the Luddites, Chartists and Plug-Drawers* (1880). See also J. A. Hargreaves, 'Methodism and Luddism in Yorkshire, 1812–1813', *Northern History*, 26 (1990). The debate amongst historians on how to interpret Luddism has centred upon whether or not Luddism was part of a more widespread agitation for parliamentary reform. E. P. *Thompson, *The Making of the English Working Class* (1963), quoting Peel, argues that in Yorkshire and Lancashire Luddism developed into an underground political movement that was linked to the activities of the Jacobins of the 1790s. M. I. Thomis, *The Luddites: Machine Breaking in Regency England* (1970) insists that Luddism was only an industrial movement. C. Calhoun, *The Question of Class Struggle: Social Foundations of Popular Radicalism during the Industrial Revolution* (1982) has played down class conflict and revolutionary aims and has stressed instead the importance of community as a basis for 'populist' action. J. Dinwiddy, 'Luddism and Politics in the Northern Counties', *Social History*, 4/1 (1979), accepts that there was a political dimension, but doubts whether the revolutionary underground movement was extensive.

lych-gate. A term coined by Victorian ecclesiologists from Old English *lich*, meaning corpse, for a roofed structure at the principal entrance to a *churchyard. Here priests met burial parties at 'the church style' to commence prayers for the dead. Most surviving examples date from the 18th and 19th centuries. They are generally timber-framed shelters with benches for seating.

lynchet. A landscape feature that is particularly noticeable on pasture land in limestone districts. Fields formed on slopes tended to have their upper and lower limits defined by scarps (lynchets) formed by the build-up of soil from ploughing. Lynchets vary in size and on the steepest slopes are very well defined. Some are prehistoric, but the type known as strip-lynchet is medieval. These represent the cultivation of former pasture at a time of *population growth and land hunger. Strip-lynchets are a series of stepped terraces running along a hillside, formed by the ploughing of *strips, as in *open-fields. With the decline of the population in the late Middle Ages most of these terraces were abandoned; they have survived as relict features where the land has remained as pasture ever since.

M

madder. A plant whose roots produce a red dye, introduced into *market gardens around London in the 1620s. Enthusiasm for growing it varied as prices for Dutch madder rose and fell. Madder takes three years to grow to maturity.

magic, belief in. The early Church was forced to adapt many pagan beliefs to Christian usage rather than attempt to stamp them out. Despite the efforts of its leaders, the medieval Church still had to cope with a popular perception that the working of miracles was the best proof of the truth of religion. The images of saints were widely regarded as possessing supernatural powers, holy water was thought of as having beneficial effects, the sacraments were treated as magical ceremonies, while priests were expected to act as conjurors and *wisemen. In *Religion and the Decline of Magic* (1971), a study of the systems of belief in 16th- and 17th-century England, Keith Thomas has shown that although most of the magical claims made for religion were parasitic on its teaching, the medieval Church had to make concessions to the reality of popular beliefs. The division between magic and religion was strongly emphasized by the propagandists of the Protestant *Reformation, and vigorous attempts were made to eliminate belief in magic by preaching from the *pulpit and through the discipline of church courts. The records of *ecclesiastical courts in the second half of the 16th century and the first half of the 17th are a prime source of evidence for the popular beliefs of this period. After the *Restoration the Church seems to have concluded that little time should henceforth be spent on denouncing the remnants of such beliefs.

Various magical beliefs were still widely accepted in later times, and mild superstitions survive to the present day. The novels, poems, and short stories of Thomas *Hardy consciously preserve customs and beliefs that were current in his parents' and grandparents' lifetimes. J. C. *Atkinson showed how tenacious were various beliefs amongst the country folk of the North York Moors in the Victorian period. George Ewart *Evans demonstrated the use of magic by Suffolk horsemen in *The Horse in the Furrow* (1960). For Irish tales, see George Ewart Evans and David Thompson, *The Leaping Hare* (1974). Well into the 19th century, wisemen or cunning men used charms or spells in their role as primitive vets, recoverers of stolen property, fortune tellers, and predictors of the weather and the harvest. See also FAIRIES, BELIEF IN; WITCHCRAFT; and KING'S EVIL.

Magna Carta. The great charter of 1215 by which King John, under pressure from his barons, conceded certain liberties, including the right of a freeman not to be imprisoned except by due process of law. It was much quoted in the constitutional struggles of the 17th century and came to be regarded as the foundation of English liberties.

mainprise. A writ requiring a *sheriff to obtain securities for the appearance of a defendant in court.

Maitland, F. W. (1850–1906). Cambridge historian and author of a *History of English Law* (1895), and the influential *Domesday Book and Beyond* (1897), which set rigorous standards for further enquiries.

majority, age at. The age at which a person is legally considered to be an adult was 21 until 1969, when it was lowered to 18. Before 1870 many marriage certificates did not record the ages of bride and groom, but simply noted that a person was 'of full age'. This did not imply an age of at least 21, for some registrars took 'full age' to mean the age of consent, which itself was variable until it was fixed at 16 in 1929.

malt. Until the development of 'common breweries' in the 18th and 19th centuries, malting was a small-scale business, and was usually carried on by women on a domestic scale in villages and towns. Larger enterprises were in men's hands and were often passed on to succeeding generations of a family. The production of malt required a drying-floor for the reduction of the moisture content of barley grains, a sprouting-floor where the grain germinated, and a steeping-tank. See BREWERIES.

Malthus, Thomas R. (1766–1834). Clergyman and economist, whose *Essay on the Principle of*

Population (1798; greatly enlarged in a new edition, 1803) argued that the natural tendency of *population was to increase faster than the means of subsistence. His arguments influenced Darwin and have remained relevant to current debates; the term 'Malthusian crisis' is used by demographers. He also wrote *An Inquiry into the Nature and Progress of Rent* (1815), anticipating Ricardo, and *Principles of Political Economy* (1820). See Michael Turner (ed.), *Malthus and His Time* (1986).

mandamus, writ of. An order to a public officer to carry out his duty. The term comes from the Latin 'We command'.

manners, reformation of. The term is used in a broad sense to mean the *Protestant, and more particularly the *Puritan, attempt to create a godly society in the late 16th and 17th centuries. See Ronald Hutton, *The Rise and Fall of Merry England: The Ritual Year, 1400–1700* (1994), ch. 4. It is also used, more specifically, to refer to the renewed concerns of clergymen and churchgoers, especially in towns, in the late 17th century. The matter was much debated in *newspapers and from *pulpits. Informers were used to prosecute wrongdoers, whose actions were then publicized and condemned. In 1691 a Society for the Reformation of Manners was founded in London. Its title was changed to the *Society for the Promotion of Christian Knowledge in 1698.

manor. The origins of the manor are uncertain, though they have been the subject of much debate since *Maitland and *Vinogradoff. See T. H. Aston, 'The Origins of the Manor in England with a Postscript' in T. H. Aston *et al.*, *Social Relations and Ideas: Essays in Honour of R. H. Hilton* (1983). By the time that the *Domesday Book was compiled the manorial system was established throughout most of England. It was subsequently imposed on other parts of the British Isles that came under Norman rule. E. A. Kosminsky, *Studies in the Agrarian History of England in the Thirteenth Century* (1956), which summarized articles that he had published since 1935, showed that there was no such thing as the 'typical manor'. Manors were 'deformed' or 'imperfectly formed', both in relation to the village, and internally in their components. He demonstrated the great diversity of manors at the time of the *Hundred Rolls (1279), when manors were just as untidy as they had been in 1086. Indeed, small manors were more numerous. In the former *Danelaw, coincidence between manor and *township, *parish, or village was extremely rare. (See also SUB-MANOR.)

A manor may be defined as a territorial unit that was originally held by *feudal tenure, by a landlord who was not necessarily noble, and who himself was a tenant either of the Crown or of a *mesne lord who held land directly of the Crown. In the Middle Ages the manor was an economic unit, which included the *demesne which the lord farmed himself (usually by paying wages and by *labour services or *boon work), and the rest of the land, which was farmed by tenants or used as common pasture and waste. *Villeins occupied their lands in return for certain defined services to the lord, while freemen paid a fixed (and often nominal) money rent. The two groups were not necessarily separate, for it was common practice for individuals to occupy lands by both types of tenure. There was much regional variety of practice; indeed, neighbouring manors differed in their customs. After the *Black Death the system of labour services decayed rapidly, to be replaced by tenures based wholly on money rents. Villein tenure evolved first into *copyhold tenure and then into *leasehold. The manor became less of an economic unit in the early modern period, but retained its legal functions. See COURT, MANORIAL; P. D. A. Harvey, *Manorial Records* (1984), Denis Stuart, *Manorial Records: An Introduction to their Transcription and Translation* (1992), and Mary Ellis, *Using Manorial Records* (*Public Record Office Readers' Guide, no. 6, 1994). The decline of the manorial system forced the Elizabethan central government to give civil responsibilities to townships and parishes, e.g. over the *poor or the *highways, or the maintenance of law and order. Some manorial courts continued to meet until the 20th century. Copyhold tenure was formally abolished in 1924.

manor house. The medieval manor house ranged considerably in size, for manors were many and varied. It has been estimated that there may have been between 25,000 and 50,000 manor houses, or halls as they were called in East Anglia and north of the Trent. The most common term in Kent is court. Manor houses were often surrounded by *moats, with the parish *church sited alongside: see, for example, Great Chalfield (Wiltshire). Many are *timber-framed, but some of the earliest examples, dating from the late 12th century, are of stone. Fewer than 100 surviving examples have been dated to before 1350. The stone-built manor houses, e.g. Boothby Pagnell (Lincolnshire) or Norbury (Derbyshire), are first-floor halls built over a vaulted undercroft. Although they are of modest size, they are similar in conception to those found in some *castles and *palaces.

The timber-framed manor houses were arranged around a ground-floor hall open to the rafters. The smoke from the central fire escaped from the hall via a louvre in the ceiling. In time, these *open halls were designed to a three-unit plan, with a service end separated from the open hall by a *screens passage, and a private set of rooms at the other end of the hall. The hall was used for communal dining, with the lord and his family and guests seated at a table on a slightly raised dais at the end adjoining his private quarters, facing the screen which masked from view the *kitchen, buttery, and pantry. Penshurst Place (Kent) is an outstanding mid-14th-century example. Most of these medieval arrangements are obscured by later additions and alterations. The 14th-century Haddon Hall (Derbyshire), for example, was turned into a courtyard manor during the 16th century and then extended in the Elizabethan period by a long *gallery.

The plans of medieval manor houses are seen to be remarkably uniform once later work has been discounted. The buildings look very different from one another partly because of variations in size, but largely because of their use of local building materials. The most substantial of the medieval manor houses were erected in the area south of a line running from the Wash to the Severn. The builders included old-established families such as the Vernons at Haddon, but also many men whose wealth was newly acquired. Stokesay Castle (Shropshire) was built by Lawrence of Ludlow, a clothier; Penshurst Place (Kent) by Sir John Poultney, a London merchant and financier; Great Chalfield (Wiltshire) by Thomas Tropnell, a clothier; and Athelhampton Hall (Dorset) by Sir William Martyn, a lord mayor of London. These manor houses are each in what was the richest part of the country at the time when they were built. Northern examples, such as Gainsborough Old Hall (Lincolnshire), are markedly rarer. See Maurice Barley, *Houses and History* (1986), M. E. Wood, *The English Medieval House* (1965), Mark Girouard, *Life in the English Countryside* (1978), and Peter Smith, *Houses of the Welsh Countryside* (1975).

manse. The residence of a *Nonconformist minister, e.g. a *Congregationalist or a Scottish *Presbyterian.

manures and fertilizers. Manuring was such a commonplace activity that it was not often recorded, though it is usual to find that dung (and occasionally other fertilizers such as *lime) was valued by the appraisers of probate *inventories. The shortage of manure was much commented upon by agricultural writers of the 16th, 17th, and 18th centuries. See Donald Woodward, ' "An Essay on Manures": Changing Attitudes to Fertilization in England, 1500–1800' in John Chartres and David Hey (eds.), *English Rural Society, 1500–1800: Essays in Honour of Joan Thirsk* (1990). Most farmers had to rely on the resources of their own farm—yard-muck, the products of the sheep-fold, ashes and other household refuse, pond mud, etc. In certain areas they had access to other fertilizers, such as *marl, lime, *kelp, silt, sand, and chalk, industrial by-products including crushed bones and woollen rags (which were valued for their water-retaining properties), or town muck (the products of urban stables, road sweepings, and 'night soil', i.e. human excrement). The *General Views of Agriculture* of the late 18th and early 19th centuries give many examples of regional and local practices. The provision of cheap transport by *canal or *railway reduced the old constraints. By the 1840s crushed bones and imported South American guano were being used on a much greater scale than before. They were followed by the products of the developing *chemical industries, such as phosphates and nitrates. Artificial fertilizers made a vast difference to *arable farming. The farmer no longer had to rely on his livestock for his manure.

manuscript. A document or book written by hand; abbreviated as MS, or MSS in the plural. *Parchment and *vellum were the chief manuscript medium in the Middle Ages. They were suitable for ornamentation, and so in the scriptoria of monastic houses the practice developed of illuminating manuscripts in colours and gold. These, notably the *Book of Kells* and the *Lindisfarne Gospels*, are great works of art; many other illustrations are important sources of information about *dress and everyday life.

maps and mapmakers, early. The first English map of the British Isles was drawn by Matthew Paris, a *Benedictine monk of St Albans, c.1250, followed about a century later by the anonymous 'Gough' map, so called because it later formed part of the collection of the 18th-century antiquary, Richard *Gough. By the beginning of the 15th century the principles of cartography were sufficiently understood for the making of maps to accompany local surveys, though they contained many inaccuracies. The earliest local map in the *Public Record Office is of Inclesmoor, on the southern border of Yorkshire, made in the winter of 1406–7. 'Town views' were made in the later 15th century, e.g. a view of Bristol was included in Robert Ricart's 'Mayor's Kalendar' of 1480. See R. A. Skelton and P. D. A. Harvey (eds.), *Local Maps and Plans from Medieval England* (1986).

The Italians were the first to excel at the surveying and engraving of maps and the drawing of architectural plans; from 1473 they published printed maps from engraved copper plates. But by the second half of the 16th century Dutch and Flemish cartographers led the world. In 1564 a wall-map of the British Isles, engraved on eight sheets, was published by the Flemish cartographer Gerard Mercator at Duisburg. In England, Lawrence Nowell engraved a map of the British Isles, c.1563. Interest in mapping the whole of England and Wales had begun in the 1540s, as a result of the improved skills and techniques of Henry VIII's military engineers, who drew topographical maps. By the 1570s some English surveyors understood the principles of triangulation and were using surveying instruments made by London craftsmen, some of whom were Flemish exiles. The main instrument for surveying was the plane table, which consisted of a rectangular board mounted on legs and fitted with an alidade, or ruler with sights. Theodolites and measuring rods and chains were also used in the late 16th century. The cartographer's skills included observation, measurement, drawing, and colouring. Elizabethan London became a centre of mapmaking and -publishing. See P. D. A. Harvey, *Maps in Tudor England* (1993).

During the 1570s maps of all the counties of England and Wales were made by Christopher *Saxton, servant to Thomas Seckford, master of the Court of Requests. Seckford's patronage was essential, for he financed the engraving and printing. His mottoes and *coat of arms are engraved on all 34 maps, which were republished as an atlas in 1579. The project also received the enthusiastic support of Lord Burghley, an avid collector of maps whose chief concern was to improve knowledge for the defence of the realm. The publication of the atlas and of an accompanying wall-map was unparalleled in contemporary Europe. Saxton's achievement provided the framework in which other topographers, such as John *Speed, John *Norden, and the Dutch mapmaker, Jan Blaeu, could work. Blaeu's *Theatrum Orbis Terrarum* (1654) included 46 maps of Scotland made earlier by Timothy Pont (1560–1630). See R. V. Tooley, *Maps and Mapmakers* (6th edn., 1978), D. G. Moir, *The Early Maps of Scotland to 1850*, i (1973) and ii (1983), and R. A. Skelton,

County Atlases of the British Isles: A Bibliography (1978).

During the late 16th and the 17th centuries written *surveys or descriptions of *manors or estates were often accompanied by a map. Thus, among the records of the Duchy of *Lancaster are over 60 manuscript local maps drawn before 1603 for many parts of England and Wales. Saxton and Norden obtained much work producing local maps and surveys. See Heather Lawrence, 'John Norden and His Colleagues: Surveyors of Crown Lands', *Cartographic Journal*, 22/1 (1985). Other notable land-surveyors from this period include John Walker, senior and junior, who worked mainly for Lord Petre and other Essex landowners, and William Senior, who worked chiefly for the Cavendishes of Chatsworth and Welbeck. See D. V. Fowkes and G. R. Potter, *William Senior's Survey of the Estates of the First and Second Earls of Devonshire, c.1600–28* (Derbyshire Record Society, 1988), A. Sarah Bendall, *Maps, Land and Society: A History with a Carto-Bibliography of Cambridgeshire Estate Maps, c.1600–1836* (1992), and Peter Eden, *Index of Land Surveyors of Great Britain and Ireland, 1550–1850* (1975). Such maps and surveys were concerned primarily with establishing ownership, *boundaries, *field-names, and, occasionally, land use. Their aims were to determine exactly what was owned and to provide accurate data to facilitate the efficient administration of the estate. The usual term for such maps was 'platt'.

During the later 17th century cartographic techniques improved. Robert *Morden was a prolific mapmaker, and John *Ogilby's *Britannia* (1675) pioneered a new approach by publishing 100 plates of strip-maps of the principal highways of the kingdom. Ogilby invented a 'wheel dimensurator' with which he measured each statute *mile. Emanuel *Bowen, *Britannia Depicta* or *Ogilby Improved* (1720) had 270 plates of road and county maps, while John Cary's *New and Correct English Atlas* (1787) and his *Traveller's Companion, or a Delineation of the Turnpike Roads of England and Wales* (1806) set new standards of accuracy and detailed information. In 1762 the London-based 'Society for the Encouragement of Arts, Manufactures, and Commerce' offered £100 prizes for the best county maps on the scale of one inch to the mile. This soon proved an important stimulus to cartography. Prizewinners included Peter Perez Burdett, whose map of Derbyshire appeared in 1767, and Thomas Jefferys, who published a map of Yorkshire in 1771–2. Meanwhile, the publication of town maps had grown apace since John Speed had included one or two town plans in the corners of his county maps of 1611. Most towns have at least one map from the 18th century, if not before.

The 19th century saw major advances in map-making. (See ORDNANCE SURVEY and GREENWOOD, CHARLES AND JAMES.) Samuel *Lewis published 'topographical dictionaries' of England, Wales, Scotland, and Ireland between 1831 and 1849. Every county *record office or the local studies departments of major public *libraries has collections of local maps, drawn for a variety of purposes, including *enclosure, *tithe commutation, and *valuations. The outstanding Fairbank collection of four generations of surveyors (1739–1850), held at Sheffield Archives, includes 4,650 local plans. At a national level, the *British Library holds large collections in its Map Library. See A. Campbell, *The Earliest Printed Maps, 1472–1500* (1988). The Public Record Office's published catalogue: *Maps and Plans in the Public Record Office: (1) British Isles* describes only a small portion of the maps available. See the information leaflets 'Maps in the Public Record Office' and 'The Map Room, Kew'. The Search Room at the *House of Lords Record Office has Indexes to Deposited Plans. Scotland, Wales, and Ireland have large collections of maps in their national libraries. John N. Moore, *The Mapping of Scotland: A Guide to the Literature of Scottish Cartography Prior to the Ordnance Survey* (1983).

General guides include Helen Wallis (ed.), *Historian's Guide to Early British Maps* (1994), J. B. Harley and C. W. Phillips, *The Historian's Guide to Ordnance Survey Maps* (1984), Brian Paul Hindle, *Maps for Local History* (1988), and D. Smith, *Maps and Plans for the Local Historian and Collector* (1988). The best introduction to the use of maps for historical fieldwork is M. W. Beresford, *History on the Ground* (1957).

march. Derived from the Old English *mearc*, meaning 'boundary', march denoted a tract of land along a border, notably the marches of Wales and Scotland. William I gave his marcher lords great powers. The numerous marcher lordships on the England–Wales frontier were abolished in 1536 by the Act of Union and the creation of the counties of Brecon, Denbigh, Monmouth, Montgomery, and Radnor. The *Council in the Marches of Wales, which Edward IV established in 1471, lasted as an administrative authority until 1689. In the 15th century the East, Middle, and West Marches of the Borders of Scotland were given administrative and judicial powers by the agreement of the kings of England and Scotland. The union of the crowns in 1603 resolved old border disputes.

mark. A metal unit of accountancy, worth 13s. 4d., two-thirds of a pound. The mark was much used by appraisers of probate *inventories.

market charter. At the *Quo Warranto enquiries of the late 13th century manorial lords often claimed a prescriptive right to hold *markets and fairs. The granting of royal charters for such foundations began in the late 12th century. A prescriptive right was one that dated from before that time, often going back to the early years of Norman rule, and sometimes into the *Anglo-Saxon era. In 1889 the *Royal Commission on Market Rights and Tolls*, i. 108–31 listed 2,713 grants of market and fair charters made between 1199 and 1483, records of which had been preserved in the *Public Record Office. This list needs to be treated cautiously, as many grants were confirmations or extensions of existing rights or translations to new sites, and some were to places overseas. It nevertheless provides a basis for further work. See *The *Agrarian History of England and Wales*, vols. iv and v, which map markets and fairs in existence between 1500 and 1750. The older county histories, the *Hodder and Stoughton series of landscape histories, and the topographical volumes of the *Victoria County History* note the charter evidence for markets and fairs. Charters normally date markets as being on the eve, day, and morrow of a *saint's day (usually the patronal saint of the local parish church). Fairs, too, were noted by the church calendar.

In thriving towns the ancient provision of one weekly market and a three-day annual fair became inadequate as the medieval population grew and trading activities increased. The owners of market rights and *tolls therefore sought by charter to add to their prescriptive rights, perhaps by holding a market on another day and by arranging an additional fair. Sometimes, these new times became more popular than the old ones; centuries later, a town's 'traditional' market day may not have been the original one. The granting of a market charter does not necessarily date the origin of market trading in a particular place.

In some places the original charter, or a record of its grant, is all the evidence that survives of market activity. Most of the smaller enterprises which tried to take advantage of expanding trade in the 13th and early 14th centuries ceased to function after the *Black Death and other pestilences had reduced the national population substantially. In some cases the charter can be matched with topographical evidence in the form of a *market cross or a significant space, but in the majority it is impossible to tell how long trading continued or even if the granting of a market charter managed to get the enterprise started.

market crosses are difficult to date for the most part. Some are probably the remnants of those set up at the time of the grant of a *market charter in the Middle Ages. Most of these are no longer in the form of a cross, but have been reduced to a stump. They are sometimes approached by steps, to give extra dignity, and are set in a base which, characteristically, has its four corners chamfered. Some have misleading legends attached to them; many are easily confused with crosses erected to mark *boundaries or to serve for varied Christian purposes, such as simple wayside crosses. After the *Reformation crosses took very different physical forms, though the generic word 'cross' continued in use. A 17th-century example at Hallaton (Leicestershire) is shaped like a conical pyramid with a ball on top. During the 18th century market 'crosses' came to resemble the classical structures that were normally found in the landscaped *park of a country house. Tickhill (Yorkshire) and Mountsorrel (Leicestershire) have rotundas raised on classical columns which are nevertheless known as market crosses. In the 19th century tall, slender pillars on a simple stone base were preferred, though by then market crosses had usually been replaced by *market halls.

market gardening. The growing of vegetables for sale was only a modest business in the Middle Ages. A market for selling surplus produce from the private gardens of large houses, *palaces, and institutions was in existence in London, near St Paul's, in the 14th century; Colchester had a well-established vegetable market by 1529. At this time, vegetables were grown on a much larger scale in the Low Countries, which had a higher density of population and a more advanced agriculture to meet the demands for food from the urban population and for dyes from the textile industry. Commercial gardening was introduced into southern and eastern England by *Protestant refugees from the Low Countries in the second half of the 16th century. Dutch gardeners soon made a significant contribution to food supplies in the markets of Norwich, Colchester, Sandwich, and the smaller towns of East Anglia, but it was in and around London that they made

their greatest impact. See Malcolm Thick, 'Root Crops and the Feeding of London's Poor in the Late Sixteenth and Early Seventeenth Centuries' in John Chartres and David Hey (eds.), *English Rural Society, 1500–1800: Essays in Honour of Joan Thirsk* (1990), and Malcolm Thick, 'Market Gardening in England and Wales', *The *Agrarian History of England and Wales*, v, pt 2, *1640–1750* (1985), ch. 18.

From the 1570s, *censuses and tax returns record the names of French and Dutch gardeners in the City of London and Southwark. These gardeners grew cabbages, cauliflowers, *turnips, carrots, parsnips, radishes, artichokes, onions, and other produce for summer salads. The dearth years of the 1590s brought a significant shift in attitude to what many people had considered inferior food. The poor had to eat vegetables simply in order to survive. The 1590s and the early 17th century saw an influx of foreign gardeners into London suburbs. Moreover, the demand from London was such that the foreigners who had settled in East Anglia could sell their carrots and other produce in the capital city.

Most gardens were small. They required intensive spadework and frequent manuring. By the early 17th century many East Anglian husbandmen had copied the foreigners by growing root crops. The farmers of this region eventually led the way in the cultivation of turnips as a field-crop for cattle fodder. (See also LIQUORICE.) The trades of seedsman and nurseryman did not emerge as distinct occupations until the mid-17th century. See John H. Harvey, *Early Nurserymen* (1974).

In the second half of the 17th century market gardening spread to new areas, well away from London and East Anglia. The soils around Evesham and in the Vale of Taunton Deane proved particularly favourable for the growing of carrots and other vegetables. By the middle of the 18th century most large towns and many smaller settlements were supplied with locally grown fresh vegetables, usually via the market stall. Continuing demand from the poor was by then matched by a change of fashion that no longer regarded garden produce as inferior.

market halls were originally timber-framed structures raised on pillars which provided shelter for certain trading activities at ground-floor level, such as the selling of butter and eggs from baskets, and a room on the upper floor which could be used as a meeting-place, school, or office. A fine example at Market Harborough (Leicestershire) was erected in 1614 by Robert Smythe, a local man who had become a London merchant. In his will he ordered that the building should 'stand upon posts or columns over a part of the market place to keep the market people dry in time of foul weather'; the upper chamber was used as a school.

In the later 17th and 18th centuries townspeople became increasingly conscious of the need to build better-quality public buildings. See Peter Borsay, *The English Urban Renaissance: Culture and Society in the Provincial Town, 1660–1770* (1989). This desire to improve facilities included the upgrading of market halls. Where a corporation was the owner of market rights and tolls, new market halls served a dual purpose as *town halls and public meetingplaces. In other cases, urban authorities and the owners of market rights joined together to erect a new building. The new town halls of the Victorian era had a separate function, and the official business of the market place was increasingly carried on in the new *corn exchanges.

market place. The market places of most British towns were laid out in the Middle Ages. In very many instances the original plan has been well preserved; in others it is obvious where encroachments have taken place. Some towns still have a few *timber-framed buildings in prominent positions; much more timber-framing is hidden from view behind later façades. In most cases, however, market places now have a Georgian or Victorian appearance, with *shops, banks, pubs, and *hotels arranged in a variety of building styles and materials around the cobbled pavements. They are a bustle of activity on market days, but are sometimes reduced to the status of car parks on others. They are much in evidence in old *photographs and in paintings depicting the stage-*coach era.

Early markets were often held in *churchyards, and market places are sometimes extensions of that space. An Act of 1285 banned the holding of markets in churchyards, but it was some time before this legislation could be enforced. In the planned *medieval new towns market places were made a central feature. They were normally square, rectangular, or triangular. The *burgage plots of the wealthiest townsmen were laid out from the sides of the market place and adjoining streets, with narrow frontages on to the prime trading positions. Shops and *inns occupied all sides, unless a prominent position was taken by the parish *church or *chapel-of-ease. The principal *roads of the neighbourhood, which converged on the market place, were often the scenes of

specialist market activities, commemorated in street names such as Roper Row, Horse Fair, Swine Market, or Goose Hill.

Such names are sometimes found at the heart of old market places where encroachments have occurred. The view from the top of Boston Stump, the medieval parish church of St Botolph, reveals how a corner of the original market place has been built on by shopkeepers whose predecessors were the owners of temporary stalls. Such encroachments characteristically have no gardens and are divided by narrow alleyways. Another good example is seen at St Albans. Such encroachments can sometimes be observed on early *maps; some have been cleared subsequently.

The whole history of market places from medieval times to the present day is exemplified by the experience of Chesterfield (Derbyshire). The street known as Saltergate, along which *salt was brought from Cheshire, bypasses the present market place and heads for what appears to have been the original site on the north side of the parish church. By the 1160s a new market place had been laid out on the present site, on what was then the western edge of the town. At the eastern side are a series of narrow alleyways enclosing shops and inns within the bounds of the market place. These may be encroachments, but the plan is so regular (and is shown as such on a map of the 1630s) that it must have originated as a single enterprise rather than by piecemeal encroachment, perhaps even at the foundation of the market. Only two timber-framed buildings survive, but the frontages of later buildings have not been allowed to encroach on the old space, so the outline of the Norman market place is well preserved. A huge brick Victorian market hall, with a tall tower, was built in the western part of the market place in 1857, but its brashness has mellowed with age. The market place survived the threat of conversion into a shopping centre in the 1970s and has kept its stalls for the sale of *fruit, vegetables, flowers, and cheap household goods. It also acts as a social space, free from traffic, in the centre of the town. Towns such as Leicester, which resisted the fashion to build permanent shops on their old market places, have realized that a thriving market place does not have merely a commercial benefit but helps to give places a distinctive character.

markets and fairs. Most British towns, with the exception of 19th-century boom-towns such as Middlesbrough, or 20th-century new towns, have a long history as market centres.

Industrial cities such as Leeds, Sheffield, Manchester, Liverpool, or Birmingham were small market towns in the early Middle Ages. Others, such as Oakham or Uppingham (Rutland), are still essentially local trading and social centres. In many other places, however, not only has the right to hold a weekly market and annual *fair disappeared, but the settlement itself has dwindled to the status of a village. There were many more market centres in medieval Britain than there are today.

To hold a market, and thus benefit from the *tolls that were charged, a manorial lord had to prove a prescriptive right or obtain a *market charter from the Crown. Some markets originated in *Anglo-Saxon times, if not before, but provision grew enormously as the *population expanded during the 12th and 13th centuries and continued up to the *Black Death. The subsequent decay of the national population led to the demise of most small markets. Some villages up and down the country still have the stump of an old market cross set in a space that can readily be imagined as a former market place, but trading activities have been abandoned there for centuries. Others decayed at the expense of rivals when communications improved, especially with the coming of the *railways. For these decayed markets see Alan Everitt, 'The Lost Towns of England', in *Landscape and Community in England* (1985).

For the nature and extent of market trading in the early modern period see The *Agrarian History of England and Wales*, vols. iv and v, which plot the distribution of markets and fairs. (See also MARKET PLACE and MARKET HALLS.) By the 18th century market activity in the larger towns had increased so much that new physical arrangements were having to be made. Livestock were removed from the central streets and new, larger market halls and *corn exchanges were built. During the last two centuries the market place has become associated with the selling of *fruit and vegetables, and of clothes and household goods at cheaper prices than in the surrounding *shops.

Some fairs may have very ancient origins, but again the main period of foundation was between the *Norman Conquest and the Black Death. For example, more than 90 fairs were founded in Somerset between 1066 and 1500. Fairs were generally held for two or three days once or twice a year, though the largest towns had more. Fairs frequently coincided with the *saint's day of the local parish *church. Cattle, sheep, and horse fairs attracted sellers and buyers over long distances. A few fairs, notably that at Stourbridge on the outskirts of Cam-

bridge, were nationally famous. See the various editions of William *Owen's *Book of Fairs* for the number of fairs in England and Wales in the late 18th century, their times of meeting, and their specialities. Fairs, too, declined with the arrival of the railways. See FUNFAIRS and HIRING FAIRS.

marl. A mixture of mud and *lime, which was dug out of pits and spread on fields to counteract acid soils and to improve the water retention of sandy soils, whether they were used for arable or grass. See W. M. Mathew, 'Marling in British Agriculture: A Case of Partial Identity', *Agricultural History Review*, 41/2 (1993). Marling also prevented reclaimed mosslands from shrinking, and so was described in the *General View of the Agriculture of Lancashire* (1795) as 'the great article of fertilization, and the foundation of the improvements in the agriculture of this county'. The use of marl was an ancient and widespread practice which retained an important role in improved farming through to the 19th century, when supplies of cheaply transportable lime became available. *The Great Diurnall of Nicholas Blundell of Little Crosby* (3 vols., 1968–72) recorded the customary festivities that were held on his estate in July 1712 when 14 marlers completed their work. The marl pit was dressed with garlands, eight sword-dancers performed to music in his barn, and the occasion was celebrated with feasting, dancing, and bull-baiting. Many former pits are now water-filled hollows.

marquess, marquis. The rank of nobility between *duke and *earl. The first man to receive the title was Robert de Vere, Earl of Oxford, who was made Marquess of Dublin in 1385. The French spelling 'marquis' is often preferred. The wife of a marquess is a marchioness. The heir to a dukedom sometimes has the courtesy title of marquis.

marriage. While it was a fairly common practice amongst the medieval and early modern *nobility to arrange marriages whilst the partners were children, the great majority of the people of Britain remained unmarried until their mid-twenties. The proportion of males and females who married before the age of 20 was always low. See R. B. Outhwaite, 'Age at Marriage in England from the Late Seventeenth to the Nineteenth Century', *Transactions of the Royal Historical Society*, 5th ser., 23 (1973), and R. I. Woods and P. R. A. Hinde, 'Nuptiality and Age at Marriage in Nineteenth-Century England', *Journal of Family History*, 10 (1985). The medieval evidence is inconclusive, but from the beginnings of parish registration in

1538 the pattern is clear. The detailed demographic studies that have been made indicate that in the early modern period the average bride was in her mid-twenties and her bridegroom was slightly older. The restrictions of service and *apprenticeship, and the necessity of saving enough money, prevented earlier marriages even if the wish was there. Economic considerations and social restraints delayed the timing of marriages. Moreover, a large number of people—at least one in six in the early modern period, sometimes rising to one in four—never married. In this, Britain fitted into the wider experience of north-west Europe. See Ralph A. Houlbrooke, *The English Family, 1450–1700* (1984), Lawrence Stone, *Uncertain Unions: Marriage in England, 1660–1753* (1992), and R. B. Outhwaite (ed.), *Marriage and Society* (1981).

The record of marriages in *parish registers indicates that the peak periods when people married coincided with the ending of annual service contracts, i.e. at springtime in pastoral farming districts and in the late autumn in arable regions. During the Middle Ages the Church had forbidden marriage during *Advent, *Lent, and *Rogationtide. Advent remained unpopular until the late 17th century and Lent stayed a prohibited period. Under ecclesiastical law a couple were supposed to marry in the parish in which one or both were resident. (See BANNS OF MARRIAGE and CLANDESTINE MARRIAGE.) The calling of banns could be avoided by obtaining a licence to marry from the diocesan consistory court. This method was often preferred by the rich, but many licences were issued to people of modest incomes. A licence might be preferred if, for example, the bride-to-be was pregnant and the forbidden season of Lent was approaching too quickly for banns to be called on three successive Sundays. The records of licences are kept at diocesan *record offices. They include the *allegations made by one of the parties, normally the bridegroom. Where a parish register has been lost or destroyed, or contains gaps, the grant of a licence may be the only surviving evidence that a marriage took place. Entries in marriage registers were not standardized until Lord Hardwicke's *Marriage Act came into force on 1 January 1754. (See also ROSE'S ACT (1812); BOYD'S MARRIAGE INDEX; and PALLOT'S INDEX OF MARRIAGES AND BIRTHS.)

In the 19th century marriages were recorded not only in Anglican and *Nonconformist registers, but (from 1 July 1837) by the process of *civil registration. As yet, only a few studies have been made of this data. (See POPULATION

LEVELS AND TRENDS for the way in which the age of marriage fell during the later 18th and early 19th centuries before reverting to its ancient pattern.) At the same time, fewer people remained unmarried. See F. M. L. Thompson, *The Rise of Respectable Society: A Social History of Victorian Britain, 1830–1900* (1988), ch. 3. The social and geographical range of partners conformed to old patterns. The upper and middle classes continued to choose marriage partners who were their social equals, and therefore extended their searches over a much wider area than the lower classes, who still found spouses from within their own neighbourhood or '*country'. The working classes not only married their social equals but showed a strong tendency to favour spouses from the same occupational groups.

Apart from the arranged marriages of the nobility, there is little evidence of parental interference in the choice of marriage partners. Quotations from literary sources usually underline the folly of parents in attempting to determine such choice. (See ROMANTIC LOVE.) In any case, by the time that children were old enough to marry, in the Middle Ages and the early modern period, many had lost one or both of their parents. It was usual for a bride to bring a marriage portion to the wedding, a sum of money which in rural Shropshire in the 17th century ranged from £30 to £100. Wealthier families dealt with the transfer of property through legal marriage settlements. The newly married couple was helped to set up home by presents brought to the marriage feast. (See BIDDING.) The custom for the bride to dress in white did not arise until late Victorian times. Wedding photographs show that even in the early years of the 20th century the practice had not become universal.

Marriage Act, Lord Hardwicke's (1753). An *Act for the Better Preventing of Clandestine Marriages*, which came into force on 25 March 1754 and was popularly named after the Lord Chancellor of the day, the first Earl of Hardwicke. Under this legislation marriage by the simple process of affirmation before witnesses was no longer recognized by the law. The Act required marriages to be performed in the churches and chapels of the *Church of England (except for *Quaker or *Jewish marriages) and to be registered in a prescribed form in books which were kept separate from the registers of baptisms and burials. The calling of *banns and the places of residence of bride and groom were recorded. Entries were signed by both parties and by witnesses.

Marriage Duty Act (1695). A tax on 'Marriages, Births and Burials and upon Bachelors and Widowers for the term of five years' lasted 11 years, from 1695 to 1706. The tax on vital events was charged as and when they occurred. Bachelors aged over 25 and childless widowers made an annual payment. Members of families in receipt of alms were exempt. A complete enumeration of the population was required for the efficient administration of this tax. A comprehensive listing of surviving returns by Christine Vialls is available at the *Institute of Heraldic and Genealogical Studies, Canterbury. See Jeremy Boulton, 'The Marriage Duty Act and Parochial Registration in London, 1695–1706' in Kevin Schurer and Tom Arkell (eds.), *Surveying the People: The Interpretation and Use of Document Sources for the Study of Population in the Later Seventeenth Century* (1992). From 1695 to 1706 marriage registers were very well kept. The effects in London were especially dramatic.

Marshall, William (1745–1818). Agricultural writer who produced a number of regional reports in his *Rural Economy* series between 1777 and 1796. These are regarded as being more authoritative than the similar writings of Arthur *Young. Marshall also wrote *On the Landed Property of England* (1804) and *The Review and Abstracts of the County Reports to the Board of Agriculture from the Several Agricultural Departments of England* (1818). His writings are quoted with approval by agricultural historians. See Pamela Horn, *William Marshall (1745–1818) and the Georgian Countryside* (1982).

marshlands. The low-lying, ill-drained lowlands near the coast, e.g. Romney Marsh (Kent and Sussex), were superficially like the *fens but had a distinctive farming economy that allowed many substantial peasant-farmers to prosper by not only fattening cattle and sheep and breeding horses, but by the growing of wheat, beans, and other *cereals for market. Marshland settlements were often nucleated, with *open-fields; rights on the *commons were important, and fishing and fowling were useful *by-employments. The *ings and carrs that were formed by frequent flooding were gradually reclaimed by drains and dykes, either as major projects by landowners (including some cathedral and monastic estates) or by the piecemeal efforts of villagers. See the publications of the Romney Marsh Research Trust, including Jill Eddison and Christopher Green (eds.), *Romney Marsh: Evolution, Occupation, Reclamation* (1988), and Jill Eddison (ed.), *Romney Marsh: The Debatable Ground* (1994).

Martello towers were built during the *Napoleonic wars on the eastern and southern coast of England, from Suffolk to Sussex, in a similar manner to the earlier Tudor coastal *forts. They were named after, and designed like, the Torre della Mortello, an impregnable Corsican fort. Of the 103 towers that were built between 1804 and 1812, 43 have survived.

maslin. A mixture of the two winter-sown *cereals, wheat and rye. The addition of rye was thought to keep bread more moist than purely wheaten bread.

masons' marks. Each mason had his own distinctive mark to indicate which stones he had dressed. Marks are of a variety of simple designs, usually about two inches long. Registers of marks were probably kept by masons' *guilds; some were passed on from father to son. The appearance of similar groups of marks on neighbouring buildings, particularly parish *churches, is sometimes an aid to dating and to the study of the spread of styles. A careful study has been made by the Royal Commission on *Historical Monuments of all the masons' marks in York Cathedral. It is thought that marks were made so that a supervisor could check workmanship and keep an account of what payment was owed. Other crafts, e.g. *cutlery, also had a system of individual marks.

masques. Costly and extravagant spectacles at court or a nobleman's house, either inside or in the open air, or a combination of both. Masques combined amateur dramatics and dancing with elaborate scenery, stage machines, lighting, and complex musical effects. They were much in favour at the court of Elizabeth I, James I, and Charles I. Ben Jonson and Inigo Jones frequently combined their talents in the production of such masques, which were used to bolster the prestige of the monarchy. See also TOURNAMENT.

Matins. Originally the office for the night, observed in *monasteries; now the service of Morning Prayer in the *Church of England.

Matrimonial Causes Act (1857). The Act, which came into force on 1 January 1858, cleared up the previous confused laws of *marriage and separation. Jurisdiction for matrimonial affairs was removed from the *ecclesiastical courts and placed under a new court headed by the Lord Chancellor. The Act did not make radical changes in procedure or in the legal basis of the grounds for *divorce, and the financial cost of divorce remained high. The Act did not apply to Ireland, where people who sought divorce still had to submit a private bill to Parliament. The records of the court established by the Act of 1857 are kept at the *Public Record Office under J 77 as the Principal Probate Registry Divorce Files, 1858 to 1937. These are indexed by the names of parties, subject to a 30-years closure rule.

Maundy Thursday. Christ's washing of the disciples' feet at the Last Supper is commemorated by the Maundy service on the day before Good Friday. At this service a royal personage performed a similar act and distributed clothing, food, or money to the poor. The ceremony survives as the distribution of specially minted money by the monarch to recipients whose number equals her age.

mausoleum. The marble tomb of Mausolus in Asia Minor was considered one of the seven wonders of the world. The sight of mausolea in Rome while on the Grand Tour inspired some English aristocrats to build their own in a similar style on their estates. Nicholas Hawksmoor's mausoleum for the third Earl of Carlisle at Castle Howard (Yorkshire), begun in 1731 on a hill-top site half a mile from the house, is the outstanding example, and possibly the earliest in Britain.

May Day. Originally the pagan festival of fertility which celebrated the arrival of spring, May Day remained a day of courtship and love-making for young unmarried people. Houses and halls were decorated with greenery and blossoms, and groups of young people paraded through the streets. See Charles Phythian-Adams, 'Milk and Soot: The Changing Vocabulary of a Popular Ritual in Stuart and Hanoverian London' in D. Fraser and A. Sutcliffe (eds.), *The Pursuit of Urban History* (1983).

The medieval church channelled some of this energy into fund-raising activities known as the May Games. These were largely suppressed at the *Reformation, though some survive (with later accretions) as picturesque *calendar customs, e.g. the Castleton Garland (Derbyshire). The *Puritans banned maypole dancing during the *Commonwealth, but the custom was revived upon the *Restoration. See Ronald Hutton, *The Rise and Fall of Merry England: The Ritual Year, 1400–1700* (1994). Many of the activities now associated with May Day, e.g. the election of a May Queen, originated in Victorian times. Thomas *Hardy's novels and short stories show, however, that many superstitions from earlier times were still half-believed in the late 19th century.

May Day is also celebrated in parts of the modern world as Labour Day, and is now a public *holiday in Britain.

meadow. Meadows for the growing of hay were a precious part of farming systems until the modern practice of cutting silage for storage in a silo became widespread. In *open-field systems meadows were divided into *doles, which were sometimes reallocated on an annual basis. Meadows were valued highly in *surveys. They were often sited adjacent to rivers, as they needed to be well-watered. During the 17th and 18th centuries artificial water-meadows were created, especially in Dorset and other parts of Wessex, so that in winter the grass was covered with a thin sheet of ice to protect it from frost and thus to encourage earlier and lusher growth. These 'floated' meadows had an elaborate system of weirs, hatches, channels, and drains to keep the water moving over the meadows. The remains of such systems can easily be identified. See J. H. Bettey, 'The Development of Water Meadows in Dorset during the Seventeenth Century', *Agricultural History Review*, 25/1 (1977).

measles. A children's disease, which often led to pneumonia and death before it was controlled in the 20th century.

Mechanics' Institutes. From the 1820s onwards mechanics' institutes were founded in most large towns and in many of the smaller ones. They represent the first serious efforts at adult working-class education. They were sponsored by enlightened middle-class groups, such as members of *literary and philosophical societies. When the Sheffield Mechanics' Institute was founded in 1832, the sponsors assured local businessmen that 'there was no danger that the increase of knowledge will cause those who possess it to show want of respect to their superiors or to disobey their masters'. Lectures were provided on 'Mechanics, Chemistry, and other branches of Natural or Moral Philosophy, and the Useful Arts: but, more especially, those which are immediately applicable to or connected with the different processes, of the Manufactures of this Town'. It was soon found, here and elsewhere, that large numbers of workers were not attracted by straightforward instruction and that a programme of a more appealing nature had to be provided.

The activities of mechanics' institutes were often reported in local *newspapers. Some institutes published annual reports, prospectuses, rules and regulations, etc. Their manuscript records, including minute books, committee reports, and account books, should be sought in local *record offices. In some towns the original building survives, but as educational institutions they did not outlast the 19th century.

medical treatment. Roy Porter, *Disease, Medicine and Society in England, 1550–1860* (1987) provides a short introduction to the impact of disease on society and responses to it, and reviews the literature. A recurring theme is how far progress was achieved through advances in medical science, and how far it was the result of state intervention, municipal enterprise, and philanthropy.

For the early modern period, see Charles Webster (ed.), *Health, Medicine and Mortality in the Sixteenth Century* (1978). (See also PLAGUE.) The medical profession consisted of physicians, surgeons, and *apothecaries, in that order, but much reliance was placed on traditional *herbal medicines, administered by numerous popular healers including 'wise women' and 'quacks'. Today, health is the normal expectation in Britain; in earlier times people were preoccupied with sickness and the possibility of death. *Diaries reveal a concern for healthy living, the steps that were taken to avoid sickness, the drinking of *spa water, and the use of bloodletting, purges, and emetics. Much thought was given to God's purpose for an individual, and illness was often regarded as divine punishment for wrongdoing. (See also WITCHCRAFT.)

Many *hospitals and infirmaries were founded in the 18th century through public or private charity. (See also DISPENSARIES.) D. Hamilton, *The Healers: A History of Medicine in Scotland* (1981) relates the special contribution of Scots doctors to British medicine, in particular the scientific education that was provided by Edinburgh and, later, Glasgow universities. Medical science made few advances during the 18th century (but see INOCULATION and VACCINATION against SMALLPOX). Ivan Waddington, *The Medical Profession in the Industrial Revolution* (1984) stresses that no simple theory of progress can be supported. M. J. Peterson, *The Medical Profession in Mid-Victorian London* (1978), emphasizes the importance of specialization, the foundation of teaching hospitals, and the rise of Harley Street. Anaesthetics and antiseptic procedures allowed major internal operations to be performed from the mid-19th century, and basic science eventually enabled medicine to combat bacteria and sepsis in the late 19th and 20th centuries. See F. F. Cartwright, *A Social History of Medicine* (1977) and, for the modern period, P. Thane, *The Foundations of the Welfare State* (1982).

Few detailed local studies are available, but see John V. Pickstone, *Medicine and Industrial Society: A History of Hospital Development in Manchester and Its Region, 1752–1946* (1985), an account of the role of voluntary and municipal hospitals in the life of a industrial community.

medieval architecture. John Harvey, *The Master Builders: Architecture in the Middle Ages* (1971) is an accessible introduction to the subject. Harvey stresses the western European context of Britain's great medieval *cathedrals, parish *churches, and *castles. New ideas, including most of the features of the *Romanesque and *Gothic styles, came from abroad, usually through France, though ultimately from much further afield. For example, hoisting machinery powered by a treadmill was introduced by Saracen prisoners captured in the *Crusades, Euclid's *Elements* (which provided the geometrical basis of the Gothic style) was made available in a 12th-century translation from the Arabic, and the ogee arch of 14th-century windows and doors came from the Middle East.

Each great building had one or more designers, known in the Middle Ages not as architects but as master masons. These men held a relatively high social position. From the beginning of the 12th century their status grew; and by the mid-13th century the names of the designers of many of the major buildings are known. See John Harvey, *English Medieval Architects: A Biographical Dictionary down to 1550* (2nd edn., 1984). A few architectural drawings in sketchbooks of the first half of the 13th century have a finished and highly sophisticated character. Geometrical designs survive as tracings on plaster floors at Wells and York cathedrals. (See ROSE WINDOW.) Ideas were spread through travel, whether military, diplomatic, or on pilgrimage.

Masons were often itinerant workers, but some found regular employment at a major site over much of their lifetime. The 17 castles built in north Wales for Edward I between 1277 and 1296 were erected by conscript labour. Masons were organized through lodges, which at major sites were permanent buildings but on smaller projects were temporary erections. They served as workshops and shelters: places where wages were paid, disputes settled, and ideas argued over. (See MASONS' MARKS.)

The *Norman Conquest brought an enormous amount of new building in stone on a much larger scale than before. By 1100 London and Colchester had castles that were far more massive and lofty than any Roman building in Britain. They were soon followed by the huge cathedrals with enormous roof-spans at Durham and Winchester, and the major *Benedictine abbey at Bury St Edmunds. By 1200 grand buildings in stone were a familiar sight in every part of Britain that was under Norman rule, and new parish churches had been built in their thousands. Regional variations in design, e.g. of *church towers, had already emerged. The master-builders of the Romanesque style relied on a modular treatment, repeating standard units in solid rhythms, and on massive, earth-bound columns to support their arches. A key invention was the use of *ashlar stone to give a smooth surface to rubble walls. Caen stone and *Purbeck marble were favoured in the grandest buildings, but transport costs prevented smaller projects from using anything but local materials.

The Gothic revolution in techniques began in the 12th century, with new ideas imported from France. A new sense of scale and an emphasis on individuality were now possible. In the later Middle Ages the English *Perpendicular style developed independently from Continental styles such as the Flamboyant. The mid-14th-century cathedral at Gloucester contains the earliest example of a large east window with Perpendicular tracery and, another English speciality, the fan vault. England also acquired a reputation for the ability of its designers and craftsmen to span huge roofs in secular buildings. The hammer-beam roof of Westminster Hall, designed by Hugh Herland and constructed between 1394 and 1400, is the finest in Europe. The Gothic style continued in favour under the Tudors. See PRODIGY-HOUSES for the long survival of the native tradition in the face of the new ideas of the Italian Renaissance.

medieval new towns. W. G. Hoskins, 'The Origin and Rise of Market Harborough' (1949, repr. in *Provincial England*, 1964) was a pioneering study of how a new town was deliberately planned on a virgin site, in this case on the Leicestershire–Northamptonshire border, in the *parish of Great Bowden. Hoskins noted the town's sudden appearance in the records, suggesting a foundation date in the 1160s or 1170s, and the significant topographical evidence including the absence of a churchyard around the fine medieval church (for the rectors of Great Bowden insisted on burials at the old parish centre). Local studies of such towns formed an important section of M. W. Beresford and J. K. St Joseph, *Medieval England: An Aerial Survey* (1958, 2nd edn. 1979), and the whole subject was examined at length in M. W.

Beresford, *New Towns of the Middle Ages: Town Plantation in England, Wales and Gascony* (1967), which made comparisons with French *bastides in an area still ruled by the kings of England in the 13th and 14th centuries. Studies of medieval new towns are also featured in the county volumes of the *Hodder and Stoughton series of landscape histories.

The fortified *burhs of the kings of *Wessex sometimes developed into towns. Wareham (Dorset) retains the earthen ramparts that surrounded the *Anglo-Saxon town. The majority of towns with the largest recorded populations in the *poll tax return of 1377 were already in existence before the *Norman Conquest. However, some of the most successful towns of later times originated as deliberate acts of plantation in the 12th, 13th, and early 14th centuries. The process came to a sudden end with the *Black Death.

These new towns were sometimes created by the king, but were often the result of decisions taken by mighty lay and ecclesiastical lords. Edward I was a great planter; for example, in 1293 he took over a small town known as Wyke, which had been founded by the Cistercian abbey of Meaux, and laid out the much larger settlement of Kingston-upon-Hull, or Hull as it became known for short. Place-names such as Kingston, Newtown, Newmarket, Newport, etc. are good indications of planned towns. Many of these new towns were associated with a *castle, and some had their own fortifications in the form of walls, ditches, and gates. A notable series of new towns dating from 1277 to 1296 were planted alongside Edward I's castles in north Wales, e.g. at Beaumaris, Caernarvon, Conway, Flint, and Harlech. The impact of planted new towns in Anglo-Norman Ireland was less dramatic. The most successful were the ones associated with powerful lords. See John Bradley, 'The Topography and Layout of Medieval Drogheda', *County Louth Archaeological and Historical Journal*, 19 (1978), and R. A. Butlin (ed.), *The Development of the Irish Town* (1977).

The new towns are characterized by a regular, compact plan. Often they were laid out on a grid pattern, with a central *market place, spaces for religious buildings, and symmetrical building-plots of a standard size. (See BURGAGE PLOTS.) Many were placed on fresh sites, e.g. the original settlement on the hill-top of Old Sarum was abandoned in favour of a new grid pattern alongside Salisbury Cathedral. A famous example is New Winchelsea (Sussex), which was founded in the 1280s after Old Winchelsea had disappeared under the sea. A rental of 1292 shows that the grid pattern that is still evident on the ground was already occupied by buildings. By the 16th century, however, the sea had retreated and the harbour had silted up. Winchelsea declined and is now smaller than it was in the 13th century. A number of other failed plantations have been identified.

Other new towns were grafted on to previous settlements. Holy Trinity church, Stratford-upon-Avon, stands in Old Town, where the Roman 'street' forded the river. In the 13th century the Bishop of Worcester, as lord of the manor, created a grid pattern of streets focused on a market place in a new town immediately to the east, forming what is now the centre of Stratford. At Bawtry (Yorkshire, but carved out of Nottinghamshire) the Great North Road was diverted into a new rectangular market place surrounded by burgage plots grafted on to an older, smaller settlement down by the river Idle, which was navigable up to that point; the church stands by the old wharf and cannot be seen from the market place. Such topographical clues often prompt lines of historical enquiry. Another such clue is that new towns often had tiny parishes or *chapelries and no surrounding *open-fields. Even some successful new towns, such as Hull, did not achieve parochial status in the Middle Ages. At the time of the *Domesday Book the tiny settlement later known as Old Barnsley (Yorkshire) lay at the eastern edge of Silkstone parish. When the market town of Barnsley was founded nearby in the 12th century, the ecclesiastical arrangements were not altered; Barnsley remained a *chapel-of-ease until the 19th century, long after it had outgrown the parochial centre.

The success of many new towns by the 14th century can be judged by the amount of tax paid by their inhabitants. The *lay subsidy of 1334 and the *poll tax returns of 1377–81 are particularly useful in this respect. Charters granting *markets, *fairs, and *borough status provide a rough indication of the period of foundation. The topographical evidence is regularly much more revealing than the surviving documentation, for although most of the original buildings have gone, property boundaries often remain intact and thus provide a clear indication of the original layout of the plantation.

See Susan Reynolds, *English Medieval Towns* (1977), Richard Holt and Gervase Rosser (eds.), *The Medieval Town, 1200–1540* (1990), Brian Paul Hindle, *Medieval Town Plans* (1990), and Jeremy Haslam, *Early Medieval Towns in Britain* (1985).

medieval peasant houses. It used to be thought that peasant houses of the 14th and 15th centuries were 'impermanent' structures that were built to last for decades rather than centuries, and that the techniques used in their construction were inferior to those employed in the early modern period. In fact, a remarkable number of late medieval houses belonging to people below the level of the *nobility survive in various parts of England and Wales. The new view has emerged from *dendrochronology, documentary research, and a reinterpretation of the archaeological evidence at excavated sites such as Wharram Percy (Yorkshire). See Stuart Wrathmell, 'Peasant Houses, Farmsteads and Villages in North-East England', in M. Aston, D. Austin, and C. Dyer (ed.), *The Rural Settlements of Medieval England: Studies Dedicated to Maurice Beresford and John Hurst* (1989).

The regional variation in the quality and survival of medieval peasant housing is striking. Few if any such houses survive in Ireland, Scotland, west Wales, Cornwall, the northern counties of England except Yorkshire, or the East Midlands. They are found in their thousands, however, in the south-east, particularly in Suffolk and Kent. Their present distribution reflects the contrasting wealth of the various regions in the two centuries following the *Black Death. Within each region, there are also marked differences between the various *pays; indeed, standards of building vary even in the same village, depending on the social status of the original owner.

The families for whom these houses were built cannot usually be identified, but they include *franklins and *yeomen, and the owners of small *manors. The poorer farmers and *cottagers lived in humbler dwellings which have long since disappeared. Numbers of surviving peasant houses increase with each succeeding century after 1350.

In part, the survival rate for medieval peasant houses depends on the materials used in building. The absence of suitable timber over much of the east midlands helps to explain why so little peasant housing survives there. In Wales and the Welsh Borders, by contrast, plentiful supplies of oak enabled carpenters to erect houses of good quality. See Peter Smith, *Houses of the Welsh Countryside* (1975). Devon houses have walls of granite or *cob and massive timber doors and roofs. In neighbouring Cornwall there was little timber, but readily available supplies of suitable stone; the virtual absence of surviving medieval small houses seems to reflect the relative poverty of the county at that time. Varying standards of wealth also explain the regional distributions of *cruck buildings as compared with the sturdier box frame. (See TIMBER-FRAMED BUILDINGS.)

The variety of building materials gives the buildings of each region a distinctive character, despite the similarity of basic plans. As with larger houses, the dwellings of the medieval peasantry were arranged around an *open hall of varying length but almost standard width. The entrance to the house was off-centre, along a cross passage, with a turn one way into the open hall and the other way into a service area, containing a *kitchen, etc. At the other side of the hall, the larger peasant houses had an inner room, or *parlour, sometimes with a *solar above. This basic plan of three units—kitchen, hall, parlour—continued to be used in the post-medieval period through to the 18th century. Such houses were normally only one room deep, though the better-quality buildings provided extra space through the use of aisles. The earliest peasant houses relied on a louvre rather than a chimney, as in contemporary *manor houses. Chimney-stacks were inserted later, either in the cross passage to form a lobby entrance, or in the open hall backing on to the passage. The relationship of the chimney to the passage can be readily spotted externally and often provides a first clue when examining a medieval building which has undergone alterations.

The largest houses of the medieval peasantry are found in the prosperous parts of south-east England. The finest are the Wealden houses, which date from the beginning of the 15th century until the 1530s. Kent alone has over 350 of them. They are standardized in form and plan, but vary in size and decoration. See Sarah Pearson, *Kentish Houses in the Later Middle Ages: An Historical Analysis* (1994). The open hall has elaborately carved crown posts. The two-storeyed wings at each side share the same hipped roof with the hall. These wings are jettied at the front, leaving the hall slightly recessed. The wall plate which stretches from end to end has therefore to be supported by arched braces springing from the jettied walls. *Aisled halls of a comparable size, but with less decorative carpentry, have been found in the West Riding of Yorkshire around Halifax. They date from the late 15th century and represent the wealth generated by the *woollen-cloth trade. They have all been altered subsequently. See Eric Mercer, *English Vernacular Houses* (1975).

The most enduring feature of medieval houses of all classes is the cross passage with opposed doorways at one end of the hall. At the level of the ordinary farmhouse, this passage often separated humans from their livestock. (See LONGHOUSE.) The low end was used for a number of purposes, which varied over time. As well as providing shelter for animals, it could accommodate workshops and act as a store for tools and equipment. (See also SHIELING; PELE-TOWERS; and VERNACULAR ARCHITECTURE.) Maurice Barley, *Houses and History* (1986), ch. 8, provides a general survey.

Memoranda Rolls. Financial accounts, especially of monies owing to the Crown, kept by the *Exchequer and the Lord Treasurer's Remembrancer. The rolls are housed at the *Public Record Office under E 159, 368, and 370. *Exchequer K. R. and L. T. R. Memoranda Rolls* have been published by the *List and Index Society, iv (1965).

memorial (heraldry). A formal application for a grant of arms.

merchant. The term used in the medieval and early modern periods for a businessman, especially one involved in overseas trade. Some specialized in the sale of particular commodities; others traded in whatever might make a profit. Merchants were normally based in towns and, indeed, the most prosperous were the leading figures in urban society. (See GUILD.) Others, however, were barely distinguishable from *chapmen and grocers. In the early modern period, a man described as, for example, a lead merchant might have been living in the countryside. London merchants dominated much of the commercial life of Britain. They were often the younger sons of landed families, and once they had acquired sufficient wealth they tended to retire to a country seat. Few merchant families remained in trade for more than two or three generations. See Sylvia L. Thrupp, *The Merchant Class of Medieval London, 1300–1500* (1962), and Peter Earle, *The Making of the English Middle Class: Business, Society and Family Life in London, 1660–1730* (1989). For a study of the merchants of a provincial town see R. G. Wilson, *Gentlemen Merchants: The Merchant Community in Leeds, 1700–1830* (1971).

merchant seamen. The Board of Trade records of men in the merchant service are kept at the *Public Record Office under BT. See the Public Record Office Information leaflet no. 5, 'Records of the Registrar General of Shipping and Seamen'. Ship's muster rolls (BT 98) list all members of the crew, from 1747 for Dartmouth vessels, but later for elsewhere, down to 1851. Four series of agreements and crew lists from 1835 onwards are held under BT 98 to 100, though they are far from being comprehensive. A register of all seamen from 1835 is kept under BT 112, 119, and 120. Register tickets, held by all seamen between 1844 and 1854, are contained under BT 113 to 116. Certificates of competency for masters and mates from 1845, and for engineers from 1862, are found under BT 112, 123 to 128, and 139 to 142. Records of *apprentices are kept under BT 150 to 152. Names and details of merchant seamen who died while at sea are given under BT 153 to 160. Other classes of record are outlined in the PRO leaflet. See also Stella Colwell, *Dictionary of Genealogical Sources in the Public Record Office* (1992).

The Registrar General of Shipping and Seamen, Block 2, Government Buildings, St Agnes Road, Gabalfa, Cardiff CF4 4YA, has full service records (under CRS 10) of seamen from 1939 to 1972, but it is necessary to know the name of at least one ship before a search can be made. For births, marriages, and deaths at sea, from 1 July 1837 to date, see the indexes of certificates in the Marine section of the *General Register Office, St Catherine's House, London. Other information is available at the *Guildhall Library and the National Maritime Museum. See C. T. and M. J. Watts, *My Ancestor Was a Merchant Seaman* (1987).

merchet. A payment from a *villein to his *lord of the manor upon the marriage of the villein's son or daughter. By some manorial customs the payment was made only if the marriage was to someone outside the manor.

Mercia. The kingdom of the Angles, which in the 7th century stretched south of the Humber and west of the Trent as far as the forests of the western midlands. The name means 'boundary folk'. Tamworth was the chief residence of its kings and Lichfield of its bishops. During the 7th century the Mercians began to expand under king Penda. From time to time they were in control of territories that normally lay within *Northumbria. Mercia was at its most powerful in the second half of the 8th century under Offa, who was supreme among English kings south of the Humber, and whose 70-mile-long dyke survives in part as the former border with Wales. Mercia was conquered by the Danes in 873. See Ann Dornier (ed.), *Mercian Studies* (1977).

mere. 1. A boundary, often commemorated in a place-name, e.g. Meersbrook, the stream that marked the ancient boundary between Derbyshire and Yorkshire.

2. A place-name element for a glacial lake or pool, e.g. Ellesmere (Shropshire).

Merton, Statute of (1235). This statute authorized lords to enclose part of the manorial wastes, provided they left sufficient pasture for their tenants.

mesne lord. A lord in the middle of the *feudal hierarchy, i.e. a *lord of a manor who held land from a superior lord and who let the land to a tenant.

Mesolithic. The middle period of the *Stone Age, c.10,000–5,000 BC, between the *Palaeolithic and the *Neolithic.

messuage. A term used in deed to signify a dwelling-house and the surrounding property, including outbuildings. A large residential property was referred to as a capital messuage.

Methodists. In 1738 John *Wesley (1703–91) and Charles Wesley (1707–88) began the movement which soon acquired the nickname of Methodism. The Methodist Society was founded two years later. In 1744 circuits for Wesleyan preachers were established and the first national conference was held. The Wesley brothers and George Whitefield (1714–70) travelled throughout Britain and in the USA, preaching in churches and chapels, private houses, and in the open air. The Wesleys' message was that salvation was possible for every believer, and that communion with God did not need the intervention of a priest; whereas George Whitefield offered hope of salvation only to a predestined elect. By 1747 Whitefield had established 31 separate societies. After his death, these Calvinistic Methodists mostly followed the Countess of *Huntingdon on a separate path from the Methodists; others joined the *Congregationalists. Meanwhile, a Calvinistic form of Methodism had been established in Wales in 1743 under the leadership of Howell Harris (1714–73).

The open-air meetings of the early Methodists often attracted hostile mobs. The visits of the famous preachers were rare highlights. The typical village-green meeting is well captured in George Eliot's novel *Adam Bede*. Progress was slow, and the Methodists did not break from the *Church of England until 1784. Their rapid expansion did not begin until the 19th century, with a particularly successful decade in the 1830s. They then overtook the older Dissenting sects in terms of membership, and by the time of the 1851 *ecclesiastical census were the chief rivals to the Church of England. See David Hempton, *Methodism and Politics in British Society, 1750–1850* (1984).

Meanwhile, several groups had broken away from the rule of the governing body, the Methodist Conference. In 1797 the Methodist New Connexion was formed from congregations that wished to have control over their own affairs. Their appeal was principally to the industrial poor, and their associations with political radicalism led to their being called 'Tom Paine Methodists'. The Primitive Methodists broke away in 1812 and soon became the second strongest of the Methodist sects. The 'Ranters', as they became known, were humble people, especially the farm labourers of eastern England, the urban poor, and the miners in the new pit-villages. By the 1870s the Primitives were associated with emergent agricultural trade unionism; Joseph Arch was typical in gaining experience of public speaking in the pulpit. See J. S. Werner, *The Primitive Methodist Connexion: Its Background and Early History* (1984), and R. W. Ambler, *Ranters, Revivalists and Reformers: Primitive Methodism and Rural Society, South Lincolnshire, 1817–1875* (1989). Smaller breakaway groups included the Independent Methodists, who left in 1807, the Bible Christians (O'Bryanites) of south-western England, who became independent in 1815, the Protestant Methodists, who became a separate body in 1827, and the Wesleyan Reform Movement, who set up a national headquarters in Sheffield in 1849. In the 20th century most of these groups have come together again. In 1907 the New Connexion joined with the United Free Methodist Churches to form the United Methodist Church. Then, in 1932, the Wesleyans joined the rest to form the Methodist Church in Great Britain. See R. Currie, *Methodism Divided: A Study in the Sociology of Ecumenicalism* (1968).

The early Methodists accepted Church of England baptism, marriage, and burial. Only a few Methodist registers survive before the 1790s. Most start in the second decade of the 19th century, and even then the majority recorded only baptisms. In 1837 these early registers were deposited at the *Public Record Office. Later ones are mostly kept in local *record offices. Each of the 31 Methodist administrative areas has an archivist. The decline of Methodism in the later 20th century has led to the closure of many *chapels and sometimes the loss of records.

metronymic. A surname derived from a mother, e.g. Marriott, Megson, or Maude.

Michaelmas. 29 September, the feast of St Michael the Archangel, the time when half-yearly rents were due.

Middle Ages. The term is used to mean the long period between the fall of the Roman Empire and the *Reformation. However, many British historians restrict its usage to the period after the *Norman Conquest. Earlier historians saw the Middle Ages as ending in 1485 with the accession of the Tudors, but the term is now used more loosely to cover the period up to the *dissolution of the monasteries and the events of the Reformation.

middle class. The term has been used by historians to refer to many different groups in widely contrasting periods. An old academic joke is that the middle classes were always rising. The term is used more precisely to refer to the emergence of a *bourgeois society. See Peter Earle, *The Making of the English Middle Class: Business, Society and Family Life in London, 1660–1730* (1989), which emphasizes the importance of London in the creation of a group that contemporaries described as the 'middle station' or the 'middling sort of people'. The term 'middle class' was not much used until the later 18th century. Such a group was not easy to define, but the majority were commercial or industrial capitalists and employers or professional men. See L. Davidoff and C. Hall, *Family Fortunes: Men and Women of the English Middle Class, 1780–1850* (1987). The term continues to be used as a convenient shorthand description, sometimes with a distinction made between upper-middle and lower-middle class.

Midland History. An annual journal, started at Birmingham University in 1971, which publishes articles, reviews, and bibliographies relating to the English midland counties south of Cheshire and Yorkshire.

Midsummer was turned from a pagan festival into the Christian feast of St John the Baptist but, as Thomas *Hardy showed in his stories and poems, old customs survived well into the 19th century.

migration, subsistence. A term coined by Peter Clark for the long-distance migration of poor people in the period between the *dissolution of the monasteries and the *Civil War, which was distinct from the 'betterment migration' of others. The large numbers of poor people who travelled long distances to London and other cities in the hope of employment declined considerably after the *Restoration. See P. Clark, 'Migration in England During the

Late Seventeenth and Early Eighteenth Centuries', *Past and Present*, 83 (1979).

miles, milestones. The statute mile of 1,760 yards was defined by Act of Parliament in 1593, but various customary miles long continued in use in most parts of Britain. The statute mile was first adopted on maps by John *Ogilby, *Britannia Depicta* (1675), and became usual in the 18th century both on maps and on the milestones erected by the *turnpike trusts. In earlier times, the customary measurements produced the short, middle, and long English miles. John Warburton's map of Yorkshire (1718–20) marks miles in both statute and customary measures. It is difficult to determine the exact length of customary miles. Warburton's map suggests that the Yorkshire mile may have been based on a pole of 7 yards instead of $5\frac{1}{2}$, giving a mile of 2,240 yards.

Nearly 100 Roman milestones have been located in Britain, though very few remain *in situ*. An Act of 1697 allowed *Justices of the Peace to order the erection of *guide stoops, some of which had customary miles inscribed on them. In the early 18th century some great estates, e.g. Wentworth Woodhouse (Yorkshire), or institutions, e.g. Trinity Hall, Cambridge, provided milestones in their localities. The turnpike milestones of the 18th and early 19th centuries used statute miles. At first these milestones were made of stone or were engraved in walls of buildings, but the later ones are of cast iron in a variety of attractive designs. They are adorned with the name of the turnpike trust and note distances to the nearest towns. A whimsical one in the centre of Alfreton (Derbyshire) records 'Alfreton 0 miles' on one of its sides. A good series of milestones is invaluable in tracing the route of a turnpike road, for most remain in their original positions.

military roads. No new roads were constructed in Britain between the fall of the Roman Empire and the military roads of the 18th century which were designed to help suppress the Highland *clans after the *Jacobite rebellions. General Wade, Commander-in-Chief of the British army in the Highlands, built new forts and roads from 1725 to the 1740s. Some of these have been abandoned, but many underlie modern roads. See William Taylor, *The Military Roads in Scotland* (1976).

militia records. (See MUSTER ROLLS for the Tudor and Stuart period, and LEVÉE EN MASSE.) The memory of the Jacobite rebellion of 1745–6, together with the threat of invasion by France, determined Parliament to re-establish the militia as a local defence force. An Act of 1757, modified by subsequent legislation, set out the procedures for raising the militia. From time to time *constables were ordered to draw up lists of all the able-bodied men of a certain age in their *parishes or *townships. A ballot was then held to decide which of these men should be called upon to serve or else pay for a replacement. The various local militias never saw active service, but the institution survived until the threat of invasion receded after the *Napoleonic wars.

Surviving militia lists are a rich source of evidence for local and family historians. They are found in the miscellaneous collections of local *record offices, and many have now been published by local or family history societies. See J. S. W. Gibson and M. Medlycott, *Militia Lists and Muster Rolls from 1757* (1989), and Garth Thomas, *Records of the Militia from 1757* (Public Record Office Guide no. 3, 1993). See also Ian Beckett, *The Amateur Military Tradition, 1558–1945* (1991).

The Act of 1757 instructed the constables of each township to list all men aged between 18 and 50, according to rank or occupation or incapacity, and to send their list to the *Lord Lieutenant of the county who supervised the ballot. In 1762 the age limit was reduced to 45. Those excused service included peers, clergymen, articled clerks, apprentices, seamen, soldiers, those who had served previously, and the constables. In some ballots judges, medical practitioners, *Quakers, and licensed teachers were also excused. Although the men in these exempted groups were supposed to be recorded by the constable when he drew up his return, this complete listing was not always carried out. Exemption from service was also granted on the grounds of infirmity or poverty, for it was held that, if such men were called to serve, their wives and children would have to be provided for out of the poor rates. The various Acts did not give precise definitions of 'infirm' or 'poor', but the constables were expected to write down their reasons for granting exemption. The lists were displayed in some public place, such as the church door, and objectors were informed of the place and time for the hearing of appeals.

The risk of putting families on poor relief by calling upon the breadwinner to serve in the militia was lessened by an Act of 1802 which divided the able-bodied into four classes, who would be called upon in order if the occasion arose: (1) men under 30 having no children; (2)

men above 30 having no children; (3) men aged between 18 and 45 with no children under 14; and (4) men aged between 18 and 45 having children under 14.

Militia returns do not cover the entire adult male work-force. Farmers, for example, tend to be under-recorded because of the cut-off point at the age of 45 or 50. The importance of dual occupations was not recognized by the compilers of the lists. Nevertheless, where they survive, militia returns provide the best occupational census that is available before the *census returns of the 19th century. See P. Glennie, 'Distinguishing Men's Trades': Occupational Sources and Debates for Pre-Census England (Historical Geography Research Series, 25, 1990). Militia returns provide strong evidence of the contrasting nature of neighbouring communities, such as estate *villages bordering on to industrial townships, and they help to identify regional characteristics such as the presence of certain rural industries. See, for instance, the contrasts between estate villages and rural centres of boot and shoe manufacture that are revealed by the Northamptonshire Militia Lists, 1777, edited by V. A. Hatley for the Northamptonshire Record Society (1973).

Militia returns are also useful for identifying individuals and for the study of regional patterns of *surnames. The county lists that survive differ greatly in their stock of surnames, many of which were still largely confined to certain regions in the 18th and early 19th centuries. Many counties have no surviving returns, but full collections exist for Cumberland, Dorset, Hertfordshire, Kent, Lincolnshire, Northamptonshire, and the city of Bristol, and for various *hundreds, *wapentakes, or parishes elsewhere. Those for Hertfordshire (1758–65) are a particularly fine set.

mills, water and wind. Water-powered corn mills had been installed in many parts of Britain before the *Norman Conquest; at least 6,000 English ones are recorded in the *Domesday Book. *Water power was also used for *fulling mills by the last quarter of the 12th century, the period when windmills made their first appearance. Windmills are thought to have been an English invention of c.1180, and they spread rapidly during the next half-century. See Richard Holt, The Mills of Medieval England (1988), and John Langdon, 'Water-Mills and Windmills in the West Midlands, 1086–1500', Economic History Review, 2nd ser., 44/3 (1991).

The sites of windmills are often marked by the mounds on which they were placed to gain extra height. These earthwork features are often misinterpreted. Windmills are also conspicuous in early illustrations and are often depicted on maps. The earliest type was the post mill, which could be turned round to face the wind by pivoting on a bearing on the top of the main post. These posts were massive uprights which were held in position by two or three crosstrees. A good example can be seen at Mountnessing (Essex). Post mills required constant attention, however, and so eventually the new smock and tower mills were generally preferred. The design of these new mills reduced the proportion of the structure that had to be turned to face the wind, their sails being mounted in rotating caps. Both types originated on the Continent in the Middle Ages, but it is not known when they were first built in Britain. Tower mills had been introduced before the end of the medieval period, but the first reference to a smock mill is not until 1588, at Holbeach (Lincolnshire). The smock mill may have been invented in the Low Countries; its British distribution is concentrated in eastern England. Tower and smock mills were used not just for corn-milling, but for working *drainage pumps. Smock mills had a wooden frame and are thought to have acquired their name from their resemblance to a man in a smock. A fine example, with four sails and a distinctive cap and fantail, survives at Cranbrook (Kent). More tower mills survive than any other type, if only as a shell, for they are more durable (being built of brick or stone) and have sometimes been put to other uses. One of the best examples, complete with sails, cap, and fantail, is at Burnham Overy (Norfolk). In western parts of Britain the tower mill was preferred for its strength and durability in exposed places. See Edward J. Kealey, Harvesting the Air (1987).

Corn mills usually had four or sometimes six sails. In the 18th century John Smeaton carried out many experiments with new designs and showed that five sails were the most efficient. Smeaton's designs were commonly used for industrial windmills in the late 18th and early 19th centuries before the triumph of steam power for purposes such as crushing oil out of linseed and *rape seed. An industrial windmill at Hessle, on the outskirts of Hull, is a rare survivor. Built between 1804 and 1812, it was used for crushing chalk so as to produce whitening for paint, putty, and cosmetics. Steam power did not replace wind power for corn-milling, but in the later 19th century the introduction of roller-milling in new works at the ports led to the rapid decline of windmills. They are now a relatively rare sight, but a few working examples have been restored by conservation societies, e.g. at Heckington (Lincolnshire).

When William *Cobbett approached Ipswich one day in 1830, he noted from a single vantage point no fewer than 17 windmills. He saw far fewer windmills when he travelled in western parts, where deep river valleys provided ample water power. Some water-powered corn mills, on sites in use since the Middle Ages, continued in operation until the third quarter of the 17th century. A few, such as Worsbrough (Yorkshire), where a mill was recorded in the Domesday Book, survived long enough to be converted into working museums. Water-powered mills were adapted to industrial uses long before the *Industrial Revolution. They were used particularly in the *iron industry during the early modern period, to provide the blast for *furnaces and to work the hammers of *forges, but they were also used in a variety of other industries, such as *paper making, the smelting of *lead, the crushing of oil seed, *tanning, the sawing of timber, the crushing of apples for *cider, and the manufacture of *gunpowder, long before they were used for spinning *silk, *cotton, and *wool. For a thorough survey of the archaeological and documentary evidence see David Crossley, *Post-Medieval Archaeology in Britain* (1990), ch. 6, which also discusses the technological problems associated with the use of races, ponds, and sluices, and overshot, breast, and undershot wheels, together with their pits and housing. See also Barrie Trinder, *The Blackwell Encyclopaedia of Industrial Archaeology* (1991).

Crossley observes that there can be few valleys in Britain where water power has not been used in the post-medieval centuries. Mills were recorded (by a symbol) on the 18th-century county maps that were produced for the *Royal Society of Arts. Thomas *Jefferys's map of Yorkshire (1767–71) shows the importance of water power in the Industrial Revolution in the West Riding of Yorkshire, but even in the lowlands the number of mills is remarkable. An exemplary survey, combining fieldwork and archives, is David Crossley (ed.), *Water Power on the Sheffield Rivers* (1989), a *group project that could serve as a model for similar research in other parts of Britain.

millstones. The hard carboniferous sandstones of the Pennines were so suited to the manufacture of millstones that 19th-century geologists named these measures the millstone grits. Large numbers of abandoned millstones can be found in parts of the Pennines, particularly on the Peak District escarpments near Hathersage, from where they were taken by sledges and wheeled vehicles to the nearest river ports and exported to many parts of England. This centuries-old industry came to an end between the two world wars. Its heyday was from the late 17th century to the 19th century. These 'Peak' or 'Grey' millstones, together with other millstones from small quarries elsewhere in Britain, were used for grinding the inferior grains: oats, barley, *peas, and beans. English millers ground their wheat either by Rhenish stones, known as 'Cullin' (from Cologne) or 'Dutch' (from Deutsch?), or by 'French burrs' from the Paris basin. In the 19th century composite millstones proved more efficient, and roller-milling replaced water and wind mills. The Peak District quarries turned to the manufacture of stones of various shapes and sizes for grinding paint, pulping wood, crushing *rape seed, or grinding animal feedstuffs. Large numbers of abandoned millstones can be found in the Peak District. Some were left when they were discovered to have flaws. Those which look fresh and complete were made in the 1920s but could not be sold. Cutlers' grindstones were made from the softer coal-measure sandstones.

ministers' accounts. The accounts of revenue and expenditure for Crown lands. They are kept at the *Public Record Office under SC 6 and have been indexed in *Lists and Indexes*, vols. 5, 8, and 34.

minster churches. The *Old English word *mynster* was derived from the Latin *monasterium*, for minster churches were served by communities of priests before the medieval system of *parishes was created. Although no set pattern can be discerned, many churches which were, and are, called 'minster', e.g. York Minster (the cathedral of the city of York) and the *collegiate church at Beverley, were ancient foundations, often going back to the origins of Christianity in Britain. They were either associated with royal strongholds or they stood at the centres of major lay or ecclesiastical estates. A number of place-names, especially in southern England, e.g. Westminster and Yetminster or Sturminster (Dorset), refer to former minster churches. St Mary's, Ecclesfield (Yorkshire) is still known locally as the 'Minster of the Moors', the name which Roger *Dodsworth recorded there in the early 17th century. Such churches were long-established and were regarded as 'mother churches' to which people over a large district paid dues. Their parishes remained significantly larger than neighbouring parishes, which had been carved from them.

However, it is difficult to prove that all minsters were ancient ecclesiastical centres. Although the common meaning of the word was 'church of superior status', by the late *Anglo-Saxon period it had acquired other meanings, including simply 'church building'. By then, minsters varied a good deal in size and wealth. Many were served by no more than two priests. The break-up of the great estates which they served often affected their position. Minsters were a feature of the Anglo-Saxon period for which little documentation survives. By the time that sufficient records are available the old pattern of ecclesiastical organization had largely disappeared, and can be reconstructed only tentatively. See Richard Morris, *Churches in the Landscape* (1989), ch. 3, and John Blair, 'Minster Churches in the Landscape' in Della Hooke (ed.), *Anglo-Saxon Settlement* (1988).

minstrels. In the Middle Ages and the Tudor period the court and great noblemen each kept a body of minstrels to perform music, tell stories, and act on special occasions. The *open halls of *palaces and *manor houses had a minstrels' gallery above the *screens passage. Other minstrels were itinerants, some of whom toured in companies. The laws that attempted to control the activities of wandering minstrels were largely ineffective.

misdemeanour. An indictable offence that is less serious than a *felony.

misericord. A wooden seat which can be tipped up to provide a rest for someone who appears to be standing. The name is derived from the Latin word *miserere*, meaning 'to have pity'. Misericords date from the later Middle Ages and are found in the *choirs of *cathedrals and monastic or *collegiate churches and the *chancels of some parish *churches. The underside of the seat (which is visible in its upright position) was carved with figures taken from *folklore, *bestiaries, and moral tales, or with heraldic devices. See M. Laird, *English Misericords* (1986).

missal. A book of devotions, often illuminated, containing the words and directions for the celebration of the mass.

mister, mistress, miss, ms. In *parish registers and other records of the early modern period most people were recorded only by their Christian name and surname. A 'Mr' was someone of at least minor *gentry status (though many did not possess a *coat of arms). Mistress or 'Mrs' was used for a woman of similar status, whether or not she was married. The use of 'Miss' for an unmarried woman came into use during the early 18th century. In the later 20th century 'Ms' has become increasingly popular as the female equivalent of 'Mr', which has been the style for any untitled adult male since the later 18th or early 19th century.

mistletoe. A plant sacred in pagan religion because its berries appear in the depth of winter. The belief that it could ward off evil spirits remained strong and was incorporated into Christmas-time traditions, e.g. the pre-*Reformation practice at York Minster of placing mistletoe on the high *altar.

moat. The digging of deep ditches, which were then usually filled with water, around *castles, *manor houses, and some smaller properties was a common medieval practice. The ditches had a minimum width of 15 feet and they formed an enclosure that was roughly rectangular in shape. The buildings within the enclosure did not differ from unenclosed buildings elsewhere.

E. V. Emery, 'Moated Settlements in England', *Geography*, 47 (1962) was the first discussion of the distribution and significance of moats, showing that they are found particularly on clay or drift deposits. H. E. Jean Le Patourel, *The Moated Sites of Yorkshire* (1973) was the first detailed investigation at the level of a single county. This proposed a classification by shape, while stressing that moats were subject to a process of continuous development while they were in use and to an even greater distortion when abandoned. Many moats have been filled in. Documentary and excavation evidence, coupled with an intensive field survey, showed that most moats were correlated with the existence of seignorial *demesne, whether in lay or ecclesiastical ownership, including monastic *granges. Most of the remaining sites (which did not form a large proportion) are likely to have been freemen's holdings, *assarted from woods and other uncultivated land. See David Wilson, *Moated Sites* (1985). For the distribution of Irish moats see B. J. Graham and L. J. Proudfoot, *An Historical Geography of Ireland* (1993), 75.

Moated sites of a 12th-century date are exceptional. Most date from the 13th and 14th centuries, particularly the period from 1250 to 1325. Security obviously played a part, but moats could act only as a temporary hindrance to a determined attacker. Prestige was the main reason for their construction, though they were also useful for keeping *fish. The continuity of use of moated sites for 16th- and 17th-century buildings suggests that they were still regarded as prestigious under the Tudors and Stuarts, though care was taken to improve standards of comfort. Some of the best-known (and most picturesque) sites, notably Little Moreton Hall (Cheshire) and Ightham Mote (Kent), contain both medieval and post-medieval buildings arranged around an internal *courtyard.

mobility, geographical. Even in the Middle Ages and the early modern period people moved from the place of their birth far more often than was once supposed. Demographers and social historians, using the evidence of manorial-*court records, *parish registers, *apprenticeship indentures, *freemen's admissions, depositions before civil and *ecclesiastical courts, etc., have shown beyond doubt that it was normal for single people and families to move around. Some travelled long distances, especially to *London, which was always a great magnet for people from most parts of Britain. (See MIGRATION, SUBSISTENCE.) Provincial cities such as Bristol and Norwich exerted a lesser pull. (See also EMIGRATION and IMMIGRATION.)

Studies of past and present distributions of *surnames, of the geographical range from which marriage partners were selected, and of the catchment area for *apprentices have shown that most of this mobility was restricted to the neighbourhood or '*country' in which a person was born. These districts contained groups of core *families who were resident there for several generations, and sometimes for centuries. The proportion of immigrants in a community at any one time was not large, except in unusual circumstances such as the settlement of French and Low-Country Protestant craftsmen in parts of southern and eastern England during the 16th century. Much of the geographical mobility that has been observed by historians was that of young servants and apprentices. The parish boundary was no deterrent, but movement was usually restricted to a 20 or 25-mile radius, often less, to a neighbourhood bounded by the nearest market towns.

In the 19th century *railways and steamships provided cheap travel over long distances. Individuals and whole families now ventured much further than the majority of their ancestors in search of work. *Agricultural labourers from the southern half of England and poor immigrants from Ireland sought jobs in the new *coal mines and *factories of northern and midland England, lowland Scotland, and south Wales, and great numbers left for a new life overseas. Some parts of the countryside saw a huge fall in population as families left for the burgeoning towns. Nevertheless, even at the height of the changes associated with the *Industrial Revolution, most movement was on a much more restricted scale. In 1885 E. G. *Ravenstein concluded from a study of information provided by the *census returns that most migration was purely local or over only short distances. His conclusions have been confirmed by recent studies. Individuals had a much greater choice of destination than before, but the old pattern of geographical mobility when studied over the population at large was not radically affected. Of course, the big rise in the total population meant that the actual numbers of long-distance migrants (as distinct from the proportion of the inhabitants) increased considerably. See David Hey, *The Oxford Guide to Family History* (1993), ch. 3.

mobility, social. The rise and fall of families is a constant theme in British history. After the *Norman Conquest, which replaced one élite with another, no major upheaval has occurred as a result of military victory. Rather, social change has been a continuous though gradual process. At the *dissolution of the monasteries, and at the time of the *plantations in *Ulster and other parts of Ireland, large estates changed hands. Some new families, like the Cavendishes, owed their rise to these opportunities, but the established *nobility also benefited. At other times, the acquisition of great wealth from trade or industry did not necessarily lead a man straight to the top of society, for the chances of buying the necessary landed estate did not always arise; often, the rise to the top was achieved only in the third generation. The surest way to rise spectacularly was in service to the Crown; Cardinal Wolsey, William and Robert Cecil, and (at a lower level) Samuel *Pepys are well-known examples.

Social climbing was, however, facilitated by the decline and sometimes the disappearance of many noble families. The failure of a male line allowed junior branches to rise, but often the failure was so complete that titles fell into abeyance. The rules of *primogeniture prevented the creation of a large nobility on Continental models, whereby junior members of the family had titles even though they did not have the wealth to match. Only 22 per cent of peers at the beginning of Victoria's reign had titles that went back in their families 150 years to the *Glorious Revolution, and only 5 per cent belonged to a line that had been ennobled two centuries further back, before the accession of the Tudors. Likewise, in 1928 it was calculated that only 24 per cent of *baronetcies created between 1611 and 1800 had survived; nearly 22 per cent had failed in the first generation. See J. V. Beckett, *The Aristocracy in England, 1660–1914* (1986).

The junior branches of noble families often descended the social scale rapidly. It is common to find that by the 18th and 19th centuries, when evidence of occupations becomes fuller than before, people who shared a common ancestor with an aristocratic family were performing humble tasks in order to earn their living. Newly risen families could decline just as rapidly. 'From clogs to clogs in three generations' was once a well-known saying.

Social mobility, both up and down, was equally marked amongst the ranks of the farmers and urban craftsmen. After the *Black Death many peasant families seized the opportunity to farm more land and to rise to the level of *yeomen and minor *gentry. The growth of industry and trade allowed middlemen to expand their businesses and become *merchants, and enterprising mechanics to become industrialists. But younger children found it hard to maintain their parents' standard of living and descended into the poorest ranks. Class distinctions in Britain have never prevented the rise or fall of individuals into different social groups, but the barriers to rapid movement, rather than up or down a notch or two, have been formidable.

modus. The conversion of a *tithe payment in kind (i.e. a tenth of produce) to a fixed sum of money.

moiety. A half. The term was used, for instance, when the right of *advowson was split between two heiresses.

monastery. The word 'monk' is derived from a Greek word meaning 'alone'. The first monks were solitaries, men who withdrew from society to pursue a lonely, ascetic, spiritual life in the deserts of Egypt, Palestine, and Syria in the later 3rd century. But as man is a social animal, the life of the desert hermit did not have wide appeal. St Basil of Caesarea represents the new type of monk of the mid-4th century. He was a highly educated man from a professional family who concluded that the organized communal way of life was better than the solitary existence of the *hermit.

By the 5th century the new monastic ideals had spread from the eastern Mediterranean to Italy and southern Gaul. St Martin of Tours (d. 397) was the first major figure in the Gallic monasticism that was to prove so influential in Britain. The Rule of St Benedict (*c*.480–550) provided what became the standard pattern of monastic observance throughout the medieval West. Little is known about the origins of the Rule of this obscure Italian abbot, but it was probably composed in his later years. His monastery was organized on the same lines as a Roman villa, with the abbot firmly in charge; obedience was the cardinal principle. Benedict provided a model of a well-organized community of ascetic, self-disciplined searchers after religious truth who followed a carefully planned routine of prayer, work, and study. The monks made vows of obedience, chastity, and poverty in order to conquer sensuality and self-will. All property was held in common. The monasteries were expected to own buildings and land, which they received from benefactors, but it is unlikely that Benedict foresaw how wealthy and influential the *Benedictine order would become. His monks were expected to do manual work, but it was accepted that most of the labour would be performed by tenants, so as to allow the monks to concentrate on spiritual matters. Each day they followed an ordered routine of eight offices that were recited in common at fixed hours. Communal worship began in the hours of darkness, at 2 a.m. or shortly after in winter, and at 3 a.m. or shortly after in summer, with the singing of the office of Vigils or Nocturns (later called Matins), the longest and most elaborate of the services. At first light Lauds were sung, followed at intervals by the shorter offices, sung at the first, third, sixth, and ninth hours, and then by the evening office of Vespers. The brief service of Compline was sung at sundown to end the day. Traces of this framework of worship are evident in church services of modern times, including those of many *Protestant churches. The remaining time was divided into periods of manual work and reading. The monks formed an educated élite in medieval society. Many, like *Bede, were child recruits who were reared in the monastery. In practice, adult recruitment was limited to the educated members of noble families. Some later orders, including the Cistercians, refused to accept children. The Fourth Lateran Council (1215) banned children from all monasteries.

Monastic life existed in Ireland, Wales, and Strathclyde by the 5th century, though how it began is not known. During the 6th century monasteries were founded in Ireland at Kildare, Cork, Clonard, Emly, Clonmacnoise, etc. Iona and Armagh became the two great ecclesiastical centres in the Irish world. The Irish monasteries attracted the rich and the powerful and were the regular residences of provincial kings and nobles. As such, they served as the spiritual homes of each tribe or kindred group. They became literary and artistic centres and bases for preaching to the pagans. An Irish monastery was enclosed by a rampart of earth and stones. Inside, the monks lived singly or in small groups in detached huts, made either of wattle or of stones and shaped in a characteristic beehive fashion. The crudity of the building technique imposed limitations of scale. Each monastery was autonomous, but monks moved freely between different establishments. The monastic traditions of the Celtic Church thus differed from those of the Romans, but both depended on powerful lay support, and in both the abbots were aristocrats. The Synod of Whitby (664) signalled the triumph of the Roman form of organization and checked the further development of the Celtic model.

Before then, the Celtic monks had vied with the Roman mission of St Augustine in converting the *Anglo-Saxons. Augustine obtained a base in Kent in 597, from which Paulinus converted the *Northumbrian royal family in 627, but northern monasticism owed much to the Celtic monks of Iona who sent Aidan to the island of Lindisfarne in 635. The first Benedictine monasteries in the North were founded by Wilfrid at Ripon and Hexham c.670, and by Benedict Biscop at Wearmouth and Jarrow in 674–85. These Northumbrian monasteries quickly gained a European reputation for their learning, but in the 9th century they and other British monasteries were destroyed by *Viking invaders.

The revival of English monasticism occurred in 10th- and 11th-century *Wessex, with the active support of the royal family and the determined efforts of St Dunstan, St Ethelwold, and St Oswald. By the year 1000 Benedictine houses had been founded or refounded at Glastonbury, Shaftesbury, Malmesbury, Abingdon, Winchester, and several other places, but at the time of the *Norman Conquest monasticism had still not been restored north of the river Trent. The Normans set about rebuilding the ruined Benedictine abbeys at Wearmouth, Jarrow, Whitby, and elsewhere, and founding new ones.

Much of the inspiration for the revival in Wessex came from the *Cluniac order which had been founded in Burgundy in 909. By the end of the 11th century Cluny was at the head of a huge international organization. The Clu-niacs had restored the strict Rule of the Benedictines. They taught that the monastic life was the only certain way to salvation in a sinful world. The first Cluniac house in Britain was that of Lewes Priory, endowed by William de Warenne, one of William I's mightiest barons. The Norman kings and magnates were liberal in their donations and the Cluniacs quickly became renowned for the splendour of their churches. Other orders, nearly all of which originated in France, were established during the 12th and later centuries. (See CISTERCIANS; AUGUSTINIANS; PREMONSTRATENSIANS; CARTHUSIANS; GILBERTINES; NUNNERY; and FRIARY.)

Monasteries were amongst the larger medieval settlements, bigger than most villages. In the mid-12th century Rievaulx Abbey had 140 monks and over 500 *lay brothers. But by about 1220 the great period of monastic growth in Britain had come to an end. The spread of monasticism had been remarkable; no place had escaped their influence, for the monks received numerous bequests of land and were often the owners of the *tithes of a *parish. The monasteries played an important part in the development of the agrarian economy. They were famed not only for their spiritual life but for the scale of their farming and industrial activities. (See GRANGE.) They owned *sheep runs that enabled them to graze thousands of sheep, whose fleeces they sold to Italian merchants, and they mined and smelted *iron and *lead on a scale that was rarely matched by lay lords.

The 14th century saw a decline in monasticism. The *Black Death caused severe losses: St Albans' Abbey alone lost 49 monks, including the abbot. But numbers also declined because the monks were anxious to preserve living standards and the reputation of their institution in the face of a sharp drop in endowments. Lay people began to favour their parish *churches and to construct *chantry chapels rather than leave their wealth to the monks. The decline in Britain fitted into a larger European pattern. By the beginning of the 16th century England's monastic population had dropped to about 10,000 monks and 2,000 nuns. The gap between a few rich establishments and the rest was a formidable one. Meanwhile, although scandal was rare, discipline had been relaxed. It was against this background that Henry VIII was able to close all the 650 monasteries in England and Wales in a brief five-year period between 1536 and 1540 and to confiscate their property. (See DISSOLUTION OF THE MONASTERIES.) The destruction was so complete that about a third of the monasteries have disappeared completely, and another third have only insubstantial remains.

See also C. H. Lawrence, *Medieval Monasticism* (1984), Lionel Butler and Chris Given-Wilson, *Medieval Monasteries of Great Britain* (1979), Dom David Knowles, *The Monastic Order in England* (1940) and *The Religious Orders in England* (3 vols., 1948–59), Glynn Coppack, *Abbeys and Priories* (1990), and Janet Burton, *Monastic and Religious Orders in Britain, 1000–1300* (1994). For the archaeological evidence see J. P. Greene, *Monastic Houses* (1989). A comprehensive catalogue of religious foundations is provided by Dom David Knowles and R. Neville Hadcock, *Medieval Religious Houses: England and Wales* (1971), and I. B. Cowan and D. E. Easson, *Medieval Religious Houses: Scotland* (1976). See the distribution map of medieval Irish monastic houses in B. J. Graham and L. J. Proudfoot, *An Historical Geography of Ireland* (1993), 78.

Monmouth's rebellion. The attempt in 1685 of the Duke of Monmouth to depose the new Catholic king, James II, was supported enthusiastically by Protestant craftsmen and labourers in Dorset and Somerset. Most of the local *gentry did not join the rebellion. Monmouth was proclaimed king in Taunton, but was defeated at the battle of Sedgemoor. Over 500 of his followers were killed in battle; many others were hanged or transported to the *West Indies in the terrible retribution that followed under Lord Chief Justice Jeffreys. The 'Bloody Assize' has remained etched in the folk memory of the south-west.

monogram. A character formed by interweaving two or more letters.

monumental inscriptions. See GRAVESTONES.

moors. Moorland is a distinctively British type of countryside. Over half of Scotland is moorland; almost one-fifth of Ireland is bogland. The word is applied in England not only to uncultivated high land, but to low-lying areas such as Sedgemoor (Somerset) or Inclesmoor (Yorkshire). See Oliver Rackham, *The History of the Countryside* (1986), ch. 14. For a detailed study of a moor over a long period of time, see Desmond Bonney (ed.), *Bodmin Moor: An Archaeological Survey*, i: *The Human Landscape to c.1800* (1994). Pollen analysis has shown that many of the present moors had a different character in *prehistoric times, when they were lightly wooded and attractive to settlers, whether permanent or seasonal. The gradual spread of *peat, at varied depths and at different paces, together with climatic change, pre-vented later settlement. A great deal of archaeological evidence therefore survives, particularly in the form of *Bronze Age burial and clearance cairns, *house platforms, and field boundaries.

Moors were primarily used in the Middle Ages for grazing livestock, *cattle as well as *sheep. Some *monasteries, e.g. Fountains Abbey, had very large flocks of sheep. Landowners often established *vaccaries for rearing young cattle. Peasant farmers also had common rights of grazing on the moors. The pressure of *population in the 12th and 13th centuries led to the moorland fringes being brought into cultivation and to the founding of small settlements, some of which were abandoned when the national population declined after the *Black Death. Hound Tor (Dartmoor) is one such site which has been excavated. The *Cistercians were responsible for many moorland *assarts. Increasing use of the moors led to disputes between neighbouring communities and the erection of boundary stones and way-markers, many of which survive *in situ*.

Another important common right was that of *turbary. The peat deposits on lowland moors, such as Thorne Moor (Yorkshire), were exploited on a large scale by monasteries and other bodies, who sold the peat in towns which could be reached by navigable rivers; but the peat on the upland moors was dug as fuel mostly by the local inhabitants. Shallow workings and accompanying *holloways are a common relict feature. There is also much surviving evidence of former industries, particularly the hewing of *millstones and the smelting of *lead. Transporting such heavy goods was difficult, but the moors retain ample evidence from the pre-turnpike era in the form of *guide stoops, *packhorse bridges, sunken tracks, etc., many of which were abandoned after the *turnpiking of the most important highways and the creation of new roads by the *enclosure commissioners.

Some moors, e.g. on Duchy of *Lancaster estates in the Peak District, were enclosed by agreement in the 17th century; but most remained unenclosed (though considerably reduced) until the era of parliamentary *enclosure. Most awards for enclosing moorland date from the first half of the 19th century. Upon enclosure much new land was brought into cultivation in rectangular fields, whose shapes contrast with the irregular appearance of earlier assarts nearby. A large number of farmhouses and *barns were erected on the newly converted land, and long boundary-walls were built even in the most inaccessible places. Parts of the remaining moors continued as sheepwalks, but the largest allotments now acquired a new character as reserves for rearing *grouse for the shooting season. Gamekeepers enforced the owners' instructions to stop people walking over the moors for recreation. In the Highlands of Scotland numerous families of *crofters were ejected in the *Clearances, when huge areas of moorland were turned over to sheep-grazing.

With the growth of rambling clubs in the early 20th century the right to roam over the moors became a fiercely fought issue. The battle for access was largely won in the second half of the 20th century, though some areas (including moors used for military purposes) remain restricted. Much moorland is now owned by the National Trust or the various National Parks. The management of moors has become a matter of lively discussion, for over-grazing by sheep and under-grazing by cattle (allowing bracken to spread), pollution from acid rain, and large-scale drainage schemes threaten to transform their character.

moot. An *Anglo-Saxon legislative assembly; hence, a moot-point is a subject for debate. The supreme council was the Witenagemot. Each *hundred and *borough also had its moot.

Moravians. A Protestant sect founded in Moravia and Bohemia by the followers of Jan Huss in the early 15th century. In 1728 Count Zinzendorf sent three missionaries from Saxony to London and Oxford. John and Charles *Wesley were early members. The earliest surviving register is that of the Fetter Lane congregation in London, beginning in 1741. The Moravians were soon overshadowed by the *Methodists, but societies established in the mid-18th century still flourish at Fulneck (Yorkshire), Ockbrook (Derbyshire), etc.

Morden, Robert (died 1703). London map- and globe-maker, whose county maps were used for Edmund Gibson's translation of *Camden's *Britannia* (1695). He is best known for *The New Description and State of England, containing the Maps of the Counties of England and Wales, in fifty-three copper plates* (1701, and later editions).

Mormon Branch Libraries. The *Mormons have established a number of branch libraries, attached to a local church, in various parts of Britain. Their aim is to foster genealogical research by the provision of microfiche, microfilm, etc. of records from all over Britain, and from other parts of the world. The basic source is the *International Genealogical Index, but a range of other records are made available in reproduction form, e.g. microfiche of the birth and marriage certificates of *civil registration and of the various British *census returns. The facilities are made available to all searchers, regardless of whether or not they are members of the Mormon Church, but the main purpose is to enable Mormons to trace their ancestors and to baptize them by proxy in the Mormon faith. A huge central computerized archive is kept at Salt Lake City in the USA.

Mormons. The Church of the Latter Day Saints of Jesus Christ, founded in the USA by Joseph Smith (1805–44). Members base their beliefs on the *Book of Mormon* (1830), claimed to have been written by a prophet of that name. The Mormons rapidly gained converts in the USA, though they also aroused great hostility. They eventually migrated west to the state of Utah and set up their headquarters in Salt Lake City. A few groups had been formed in Britain by the mid-19th century, but the major period of growth has been in the second half of the 20th century.

Morris, Joseph. Author of numerous topographical guides, including the series of 'Little Guides' to the counties of England, published by Black in the first third of the 20th century. These are now of historical interest for their contemporary descriptions.

morris dancing. Michael Heaney and John Forrest, *Annals of Early Morris* (1991) provided a database of references to morris dancing in the British Isles prior to 1751, under headings such as date, place, and source, together with a bibliography and brief analysis. See the same authors' article, 'Charting Early Morris', *Folk Music Journal*, 6/2 (1991). The references that they have collected take the form of factual descriptions, official documents, literary or dramatic texts, pictures, or pieces of music; the earliest date from the mid-15th century, so the origins of morris or 'Moorish', 'moresque', or 'morisco' dancing remain obscure. The pivotal role of the attitude of the Church is made clear; strong support was given until the 17th century, after which morris dancing declined in face of *Puritan clerical opposition. Early support also came from royal households and London *guilds; later references are heavily weighted towards performances in villages and private households. The dancers sometimes formed part of a pageant or annual festival, such as a *church ale; sometimes they performed on a stage, or around a maypole. The dancers were accompanied by standard characters such as the fool, a man dressed as a woman, a hobby horse, Robin Hood, Maid Marian, the Moor, etc. Little choreographic information survives. The usual musical instruments were the pipe and tabor, fiddle, and drum.

The supposed antiquity and continuity of morris dancing has a romantic appeal, which has led to a 20th-century revival and a spread of morris dancing into places for which there are no historical records. The supposed origins of the morris is a subject of much speculation, and more archival research is now needed to plot and explain regional patterns and variety. See Keith Chandler, 'Ribbons, Bells and Squeaking Fiddles': The Social History of Morris Dancing in the English South Midlands, 1660–1900 (1993). The University of Toronto has a major ongoing project on the records of Early English Drama of all forms.

mortality, bills of. During the 17th century the practice grew up in London and the major provincial cities of collating information on burials recorded in *parish registers. This allowed municipal authorities to keep a check on the progress of *plague and other diseases and enabled them to identify infected parishes. Bills of mortality were published for many towns in the 18th and 19th centuries, but the figures must be used with caution. See John Landers, Death and the Metropolis: Studies in the Demographic History of London, 1670–1830 (1993).

mortgage. In the early modern period obtaining a loan upon the mortgage of property was a common form of *credit. Large collections of *deeds relating to mortgages can be found in the various *registries of deeds and in local *record offices. See also BUILDING SOCIETIES.

Mortmain, Statute of (1279). This statute added to existing penalties for the transference of land to an ecclesiastical body without the lord's permission. The tenants of such land were free from the payment of *escheats and *reliefs, to the financial disadvantage of the lord.

mortuary. A fixed payment to the *rector or *vicar by a parishioner upon the death of a member of his or her *household. The poorest parishioners were exempt.

motte-and-bailey. An early type of *castle introduced by the Normans. Mottes were artificial mounds of stone and earth, which were round or oval at the base and flattened at the top so as to provide a look-out point and sometimes a temporary residence. Baileys varied enormously in size and shape, according to the scale of the enterprise and the restrictions imposed by the local topography. The bailey contained the outbuildings and was separated from the motte by a ditch. The whole complex was surrounded by a deep ditch and rampart, which was crossed by a removable wooden bridge. Some motte-and-baileys were temporary military camps; others were never more than look-out posts. The Normans are credited with their invention, for examples dating from the first half of the 11th century are known throughout Normandy, but they are also found widely in western Europe from Denmark to northern Spain. A few were erected in England before 1066, for there was much cultural exchange with Normandy during the reign of Edward the Confessor. The great majority, however, were constructed hastily, by forced labour, in the years immediately after the *Norman Conquest or during the civil wars of the reign of King Stephen (1135–54). In this poorly documented period it is impossible to establish a chronology. Some motte-and-baileys in the Welsh marches may have been built as late as the early 13th century. Those which were at the centre of important *lordships were converted into stone castles, but those which were in outlying positions were abandoned. About 750 are known in England and Wales, about 200 in Scotland, and about 270 in Ireland (90 per cent of which are in Ulster and Leinster), either from surviving earthworks or from documentary evidence and place-names.

mud walling. In areas where suitable building stone was unavailable mud was used from the Middle Ages to the 19th century in the construction of farmhouses and *cottages, *barns and other outbuildings, and field walls. In south-west England mud was mixed with straw, hair, gravel, flints, dung, etc. to form thick walls of *cob. Mud walls were given stone footings, sometimes coated with tar, to prevent rising damp, and a coat of lime and an overhanging thatched roof to keep off rainwater. In Leicestershire and other parts of midland England mud walls are often concealed behind a later skin of *brick, though mud is sometimes exposed in field walls. It was also commonly used as infilling in *timber-framed houses.

mummers. The local men who performed a traditional play at *Christmas in the larger houses of their parish. The characters included St George, the Turkish knight, Beelzebub (carrying a club and a frying pan), the Doctor, and the Fool. The *folklorists of the late 19th century recorded many surviving performances, but how far back in time the play goes is debatable. The play has been revived in many places in the later 20th century. See Alex Helm, *The English Mummers' Play* (1981).

municipal boroughs. The Municipal Corporations Act (1835) reformed the ancient constitutions of 178 *boroughs and provided for the incorporation of others. It ordered that councillors were to be elected every three years, by ratepayers who had been resident for at least three years, and that *aldermen should be elected by the councillors for six years. Later legislation gave these municipal boroughs responsibilities for *public health and law and order. The Municipal Corporations Act of 1882 revised and added to the Act of 1835. (See PARLIAMENTARY PAPERS.) Municipal corporations were abolished in 1974.

muniments. Title *deeds, etc. that confer rights and privileges. The term is used to refer to a collection of archives relating to an estate.

murrain. Infectious disease in cattle. Murrain played an important part in the agricultural crisis of 1315–22. Rinderpest affected large numbers of cattle in the 1740s. See John Broad, 'Cattle Plague in Eighteenth-Century England', *Agricultural History Review*, 28/2 (1980).

museums. The British tradition of collecting began in the 16th century with manuscripts, followed by coins, books, and, by the late 17th century, 'cabinets of curiosities' which included antiquities, contemporary artefacts, and specimens of the natural world, especially oddities. Two famous collections were those of Elias Ashmole (which became the basis of the Ashmolean Museum, Oxford) and Ralph *Thoresby. See R. W. Unwin, 'Cabinets of Curiosities', *The Historian*, 19 (1988).

The British Museum was founded in 1753. After the success of the *Great Exhibition, the South Kensington Museum was founded in 1852; by the end of the century it had developed into the separate Science Museum, Natural History Museum, Geological Museum, and the Victoria and Albert Museum. The Imperial War Museum moved from South Kensington in 1936. The National Maritime Museum was founded at Greenwich in 1937. The two major national museums of Scotland—the National Museum of Antiquities of Scotland and the Royal Scottish Museum, both based in Edinburgh—were amalgamated in 1985.

The civic museums which were created by municipal enterprise in the second half of the 19th century copied the national museums in the scope of their collections and in their style of presentation. The main subject areas were archaeology, natural history, and fine art, each of which was represented by exhibits from all over the world, especially from the British Empire. At first, local collections consisted largely of 'curiosities' or 'bygones', though eventually civic museums became important repositories of local material. See Gaynor Kavanagh, 'Mangles, Muck and Myths: Rural History Museums in Britain', *Rural History: Economy, Society, Culture*, 2/2 (1991).

The Scandinavian folk museums of the 1890s and 1900s were not imitated in Britain until after the Second World War. The first such 'open-air' museum was the Welsh Folk Museum at St Fagan's (1947). This was followed by the Museum of English Rural Life at the University of Reading (1951) and the Ulster Folk and Transport Museum (1958). In the park at St Fagan's, rural houses and craft buildings which were under threat of demolition were re-sited and refurnished in their original manner. During the 1960s and 1970s other open-air folk museums, such as the Weald and Downland Museum, Singleton (Sussex), the Museum of Lincolnshire Life, and the Acton Scott Working Farm Museum (Shropshire), were created along similar lines to that at St Fagan's. These museums were committed not only to reconstruction and preservation, but to fostering and demonstrating craft skills and rural practices and to pursuing an active research programme. Meanwhile, some of the most famous sites connected with the *Industrial Revolution, e.g. Coalbrookdale and Ironbridge Gorge, New Lanark, and Cromford, have become conservation areas incorporating open-air museums. Each of the basic industries also has its museum, e.g. Quarry Bank Mill at Styal (Cheshire), the Black Country Museum, the Gladstone Pottery (Stoke-on-Trent), and the Macclesfield Silk Mill. The North of England Open Air Museum at Beamish (County Durham) incorporates both industrial and agricultural sites and displays. See Kenneth Hudson, *Museums of Influence* (1987), and the annual publication, *Museums and Galleries in Great Britain and Ireland*.

The emphasis in many of these modern museums is on the social and economic history of ordinary people during the last two centuries. They are not only a focus for the display and interpretation of material culture, but also a research and publication facility. (See ORAL HISTORY.) York has 32 museums, and small towns and villages in many parts of Britain have their own museum or heritage centre devoted to the collection and display of local material.

music. Research into the performance of music at local levels has concentrated on *ballads and folk songs. Much remains to be done on church music, especially the influence of local composers, whose published works (prefaced by lists of subscribers) are housed at the *British Library. The tradition of the village choir and band in its dying days is observed in Thomas *Hardy, *Under the Greenwood Tree* (1872). The 'local carols' that are still sung in parts of Britain at Christmas time come from this tradition, before the musicians were banished from churches by the introduction of *organs and harmoniums.

Opportunities for communal music-making on a large scale increased enormously in the later 18th and 19th centuries, when churches, chapels, concert halls, and other public buildings, especially in the burgeoning industrial towns, provided adequate space and large numbers of amateur singers. The performance of oratorios became a widespread enthusiasm. The 19th century also saw the foundation of numerous *brass bands, local choirs and glee clubs, and amateur operatic societies. Meanwhile, the pianoforte became the most popular household musical instrument. Much research remains to be done on provincial music life, ranging from performances by symphony orchestras and philharmonic choirs to the popular music hall. See E. D. Mackerness, 'Sheffield's Cultural Life', in Clyde Binfield *et al.* (eds.), *The History of the City of Sheffield, 1843–1993* (3 vols., 1993).

muster rolls. The name given to *militia lists of the 16th and 17th centuries. All able-bodied men aged 16 to 60 were liable for military service, armed with their own weapons and armour according to their income. The government of Henry VIII became increasingly worried about the threat of invasion and therefore it called upon the *lords lieutenant of the various counties to hold frequent musters. Muster rolls or certificates of those present were drawn up and sent to the central government. These are now kept at the *Public Record Office, mostly in the *State Papers Domestic. See the Public Record Office Records Information leaflet no. 46, 'Militia Muster Rolls, 1522–1640'. Copies of muster rolls have often been preserved in local *record offices. See Jeremy Gibson and Alan Dell, *Tudor and Stuart Muster Rolls: A Directory of Holdings in the British Isles* (1989).

Muster rolls provide information about military organization and the types of arms in use, e.g. the replacement of the longbow by firearms. See L. Boynton, *The Elizabethan Militia,*

1558–1638 (1967). They are a useful source for family historians who are trying to locate an individual. They also provide a great deal of information about occupations and can be used in estimating population totals. A number of muster rolls have been published by local record societies. See, for instance, Nigel Lutt (ed.), *Bedfordshire Muster Lists* (1992), A. C. Chibnall (ed.), *The Certificates of Musters for Buckinghamshire in 1522* (1973), and Julian Cornwall (ed.), *Tudor Rutland: The County Community under Henry VIII* (1980), which includes the muster roll of 1522. The best-known muster roll is that published as J. Smith, *Men and Armour for Gloucestershire in 1608* (reprinted 1980), which records 19,402 men by name, approximate age, occupation, and parish. The occupations were analysed by A. J. and R. H. Tawney, 'An Occupational Census of the Seventeenth Century', *Economic History Review*, 5/1 (1934–5). See MILITIA RECORDS for similar lists in the 18th and 19th centuries.

mystery plays are so called because they were performed by the trade *guilds, or 'mysteries', of medieval towns. The best-known cycle of plays is that of York, for the text survives and performances have been revived since 1951 after a lapse of nearly four centuries. See J. S. Purvis, *The York Cycle of Mystery Plays* (1984 reprint). The York mystery plays are first recorded in 1376. They were performed at *Corpus Christi, a movable feast whose day depended upon that of Easter, and which fell between 21 May and 24 June. Each guild was responsible for financing, producing, and acting a particular scene. Sometimes the scene was particularly appropriate to the craft, e.g. the carpenters played the story of the building of Noah's ark, and the fishermen did the flood. Collectively, the plays told the Biblical story from the Creation to the Day of Judgement. The York cycle contained 56 short plays. These were performed on pageant waggons, which were wheeled about the streets, following a traditional route. In York the scenery was stored at Pageant Green near to the starting-point at Holy Trinity Church. The most important guild, the Mercers, performed the final play in the cycle, that of the Day of Judgement. The emphasis of the performances was verbal rather than scenic, given the restricted size of the pageant waggons. Surviving texts show the importance of alliteration, rhymes, and punchy rhythms. Female parts were played by men and boys, as in the later Elizabethan theatre. Certain *surnames are thought to originate from the association of actors with character roles.

The mystery plays were an important element in a vigorous popular culture which was destroyed at the *Reformation. Performances attracted large crowds from surrounding towns and villages. Such was their appeal that they survived until the mid-Elizabethan period. The York cycle was performed until 1570, that at Coventry until 1579. For the wider setting, see Charles Phythian-Adams, 'The Communal Year at Coventry, 1450–1550' in Peter Clark and Paul Slack (eds.), *Crisis and Order in English Towns, 1500–1700* (1972).

nail-making. The making of nails was an ancient handcraft in the industrial villages of the west midlands, south Yorkshire, north Derbyshire, and central Lancashire, which expanded greatly after the introduction of *slitting mills in the 17th century. Nailing was a part-time activity combined with farming until *population growth in the 18th and 19th centuries produced a class of landless workers. Nails were exported in large quantities to America during the 18th century, but the introduction of machine-made nails in the early 19th century rapidly turned the old handcraft into a depressed trade. See David Hey, *The Rural Metalworkers of the Sheffield Region* (1972), and Marie Rowlands, *Masters and Men in the Small Metalware Trades of the West Midlands* (1975).

Napoleonic wars. The initial enthusiasm for the French Revolution in some parts of Britain turned to hostility during the prolonged wars with France from 1793 to 1815. Napoleon I became First Consul of France in 1799 and Emperor in 1804. The threat of invasion was averted after the battle of Trafalgar (1805). The British army was involved in the Peninsular campaign in Spain (1808–14), and in the battle of Waterloo (1815), which ended the war.

narrow cloths. Cheap, coarse cloths, half the length and width of *broadcloths. The most famous example was the *kersey.

National Register of Archives. Founded in 1945 as a branch of the Royal Commission on *Historical Manuscripts, to collect and disseminate information about manuscript sources for British history outside the public records, the NRA aims to make this information available for public use as quickly and as widely as possible. Its coverage includes the papers of individuals of note, families and estates, businesses, churches, local authorities, societies, and other organizations. The Register may be consulted on Mondays to Fridays from 9.30 a.m. to 5 p.m. at The Royal Commission on Historical Manuscripts, Quality House, Quality Court, Chancery Lane, London WC2A 1HP. It consists of more than 35,500 unpublished lists and catalogues of manuscript collections. Computerized indexes provide access to a wide range of information. The Personal Index covers the correspondence and papers of over 30,000 men and women of importance in every field of British history. The Business Index notes the records of over 23,000 British businesses and enables searches to be made by reference to the name, location, and type of work of the firm, and the dates of the records. The Subject Index provides a classified arrangement of papers under 30 headings which reflect the archival origins of the material. The Locations File makes available up-to-date details of the addresses, telephone numbers, opening hours, reprographic and other facilities offered by over 1,500 national, local, specialist, and other repositories which contribute to the NRA. Copies of the reports on particular collections are sent to the owner of the archives, the local *record office, and national libraries.

naturalization. Applying for naturalization was a troublesome and costly business and many aliens did not bother, especially when they married an English woman, for their children then automatically became British nationals. Before 1844 naturalization could be accomplished only by private Act of Parliament; from 1844 it could be gained by a certificate from the Home Secretary. The records are kept in the *Public Record Office under HO.

nave. The public part of the parish *church, where parishioners congregate during services. Parishioners were responsible for the upkeep of the nave and its aisles, tower, and porch. Before the *Reformation the nave was separated from the *chancel by a *rood screen. As the church was usually the sole public building in a parish it was often used for secular purposes before the building of village halls, etc.

navvies. The 'navigators' who constructed the *canals and *railways. Many were itinerant labourers from Ireland. On major projects, e.g. the building of a long railway tunnel, special camps were erected to house these workers.

Navy records are kept at the *Public Record Office under the reference ADM (for Admiralty). See Nicholas Rodger, *Naval Records for*

Genealogists (1988). The systematic recording of naval service began in the 1660s, when Samuel *Pepys reorganized the administration. Nearly every class of naval records mentions individuals by name, but the chief sources are the Ships' Muster and the Ships' Pay Books. Ships' musters survive from 1667 under ADM 36–39, 41, 115, 119. From 1764 they sometimes give a man's age and place of birth. Description Books, particularly those of the 19th century, record a man's age, height, and complexion, and note any scars or tattoos. Ships' Pay Books from 1669 (ADM 31–35, 117) provide confirmation that a man served in a particular ship. Before the mid-19th century, however, documents concerning commissioned and warrant officers do not include comprehensive records of service, nor until 1856 was there any centralized record of ratings' services.

Various printed sources may be consulted in public reference libraries. The official *Navy List*, published quarterly from 1814 (preceded by Steele's *Navy List* from 1782), gives seniority lists of all officers and lists of ships of the Navy with the officers appointed to each. W. R. O'Byrn's *Naval Biographical Dictionary* gives the services of all commissioned officers alive in 1846. See also the *Commissioned Sea Officers' List*, a typescript issued by the National Maritime Museum in 1954, which gives a summary list of commissioned officers and their seniorities from 1660 to 1815.

The various service-records that should be searched for identifying warrant officers and ratings are listed in the Public Record Office Records Information leaflet no. 2, 'Admiralty Records as Sources for Biography and Genealogy'. They include service registers, certificates of service, passing certificates, and records relating to superannuation. The same leaflet also outlines naval records of births, marriages, and deaths, and other miscellaneous records, including those of the volunteer force, the Royal Navy Reserve, which was founded in 1862. See also SHIPS and MERCHANT SEAMAN, and Stella Colwell, *Dictionary of Genealogical Sources in the Public Record Office* (1992).

neatherd. The cowman who drove the cows of all villagers in one herd to the pastures.

needle-making. One of the Elizabethan projects designed to stimulate rural industries and to cut down on imports. Long Crendon (Buckinghamshire) and Hathersage (Derbyshire) were early centres, but Redditch and adjoining parts of Worcestershire and Warwickshire eventually captured most of the market.

negative proof. A term much used in genealogical research. It denotes the attempt to prove that a name found in a *parish register, etc. is the one being sought by searching all other records in the neighbourhood to make sure that no one else of that name is recorded.

Neolithic. The last phase (*c*.5000–2400 BC) of the *Stone Age, following the *Mesolithic.

nephew. Before the 18th century this could mean a descendant or kinsman and not just the son of a brother or sister.

New Draperies. In the 16th century the Tudor government sought to establish new industries, in both the towns and the countryside, to provide employment and to reduce England's dependency on foreign imports. Craftsmen from France and the Low Countries were invited to settle and practise their trade in southern and eastern England. The most successful of these projects was the enlargement of the cloth industry by the introduction of lighter-weight cloths, known collectively as the New Draperies, using innumerable combinations of long *wool, *silk, and *linen yarn. The first immigrants settled in Norwich; later groups settled in towns and villages all over Norfolk, Suffolk, and Essex. By the early 17th century some of the New Draperies had spread to other parts of the country. The new products went under a variety of names, such as bays, tufted taffeties, wrought velvets, and braunched satins. The history of these individual products is not well known, though the spectacular success of the New Draperies as a whole has been much commented on. See Eric Kerridge, *Textile Manufacturers in Early Modern England* (1992).

newspapers, local. The first newspapers were published in the 17th century. Large collections of early newspapers are kept at the newspaper library of the *British Library at Colindale, north London, and at the *Bodleian Library, Oxford. See R. T. Mitford and D. M. Sutherland, *Catalogue of English Newspapers and Periodicals in the Bodleian Library, 1622–1800* (1936). The larger provincial towns began to publish their own newspapers in the first half of the 18th century, but for many years they concentrated on national news. Local news began to feature prominently only in the later 18th century. The chief interest of local newspapers in the 18th century is often in the *advertisements, including those of businesses and of sales, and notifications of *bankruptcies. See G. R. Cranfield, *The Development of the Provincial Newspaper, 1700–1760* (1962). For a study of the influence of the provincial press in Leeds, Manchester, and Sheffield, see Donald Read, *Press and People, 1790–1850: Opinion in Three English Cities* (1993 reprint). For the history of a provincial newspaper see Stephen Caunce, 'Yorkshire Post Newspapers Ltd: Perseverance Rewarded' in John Chartres and Katrina Honeyman (eds.), *Leeds City Business, 1893–1993* (1993), ch. 2.

The first Scottish newspapers were published in the mid-17th century, but there was no continuity until the *Edinburgh Evening Courant* (1718) and the *Caledonian Mercury* (1720). These were national newspapers; the first Scottish papers to cater for a local readership were the *Glasgow Journal* (1741) and the *Aberdeen Journal* (1748). The first Scottish newspaper to include substantial local coverage was the *Glasgow Mercury* (1778). See R. M. W. Cowan, *The Newspaper in Scotland: A Study of its First Expansion, 1815–60* (1946).

Local newspapers can be consulted in local studies departments of public reference *libraries and sometimes in local *record offices. They are often available only on microfilm and have rarely been indexed. The British Library Newspaper Library at Colindale, north London, contains copies of English, Irish, Scottish, and Welsh provincial newspapers since 1690, and London and national newspapers since 1801, many of which are no longer available locally. See the British Library *Catalogue of the Newspaper Library*, 8 vols. (1975). See also J. P. S. Ferguson, *Directory of Scottish Newspapers* (1984).

Newspapers are a major source for local and family historians who are researching the 19th and 20th centuries. They provide a great amount of detailed information on a wide variety of topics, through their reports of local events and their consistent notification of births, marriages, and deaths (including *obituaries). See Michael Murphy, *Newspapers and Local History* (1991). The disappearance of most local newspapers in the later 20th century is a loss that is not adequately compensated for by the rise of free papers whose cost is covered by the advertisements.

New Zealand. Discovered by Tasman in 1642 and named after a province in the south-west Netherlands. The islands were visited by Captain Cook in the 1770s, after which they became a British colony. Official emigration figures are usually linked with those for Australia. Many British and Irish emigrants went on government-assisted passages. By 1840 only about 2,000 Europeans had settled in New Zealand, but during the next decade the number increased tenfold. New Zealand became self-governing in 1852 and achieved dominion status within the British Empire in 1907. See Rollo Arnold, *The Farthest Promised Land: English Villagers, New Zealand Immigrants of the 1870s* (1981). The *Public Record Office has lists, registers, correspondence, etc. concerning emigration to New Zealand, arranged under CO 208. See Stella Colwell, *Dictionary of Genealogical Sources at the Public Record Office* (1992).

Nichols, John (1779–1863). The second of three generations of editors of the *Gentleman's Magazine, publisher of county histories, and author of *The History and Antiquities of the County of Leicester*, 4 vols. (1795–1811). See ANTIQUARIAN TRADITION, THE.

nickname. The word is derived from 'an eke name', meaning an alternative. Nicknames are the most difficult group of *surnames to explain. The reasons for bestowing them were often ephemeral and whimsical and the expressions used were frequently colloquial or slang. Even those which sound straightforward, such as Short or Long, Savage or Wise, may have been bestowed ironically for the opposite characteristics. Pope, King, Knight, Squire, etc. were probably nicknames that were applied facetiously. Some words that were used as nicknames have changed their meaning over time; thus, Daft meant meek and Nice meant simple. Occasionally, names which sound like nicknames, e.g. Broadhead, are in fact from the names of places, and it is difficult to judge whether a name like Bacon is a nickname or occupational in origin. Even more puzzling is how such names became hereditary in preference to other forms of surnames.

The use of obscene language for some medieval nicknames (nearly all of which have long since been abandoned) suggests that they were bestowed by neighbours rather than the scribes who first recorded them in manorial or other records. Past and present distribution patterns of surnames suggest that some nicknames had a single-family origin. Mouse and Bunyan are Bedfordshire names, Speight (a woodpecker) and Verity come from the West Riding of Yorkshire. Some nicknames of multiple origin are characteristic of certain regions. Armstrong is associated with the counties on both sides of the Scottish border, whereas Yapp (meaning clever or crafty) is concentrated in the west midlands and the Welsh Borders. See P. H. Reaney, *The Origins of English Surnames* (1967), ch. 11.

niece. Until the 17th century this word was used in a wider sense than 'daughter of a brother or sister' to mean either a male or female descendant or a younger relative.

nobility. The term was originally applied to all ranks above commoners, so as to include *earls, *barons, *knights, and *esquires. The establishment of the House of Lords created a clear distinction between the hereditary nobility (the peerage) and lower ranks, but in the 17th century the *gentry were still thought of as noble. By the 19th century the exclusion of the gentry from the nobility led to the use of the inclusive term *aristocracy.

noble (coin). A gold coin worth 6s.8d., or half a *mark. It was first minted in 1351. See also ANGEL.

Nonconformity. A Nonconformist or Dissenter was originally one who refused to conform to the Acts of the 'Clarendon Code' passed after the *Restoration of Charles II, in particular the Act of Uniformity, which came into force on St Bartholomew's Day, 24 August 1662, and which required all English and Welsh clergy to consent to the entire contents of the *Book of Common Prayer. For refusing to conform, over 2,000 clergymen, about one-fifth of the entire body of ministers, were ejected from their livings. See A. G. Matthews, *Calamy Revised* (1934). Many of the ejected clergy were employed as private chaplains by *gentry families and were thus able to preach to small congregations, for many of their patrons were the *Justices of the Peace who were supposed to prosecute them. (See the records of QUARTER SESSIONS and ECCLESIASTICAL COURTS.) For short periods in 1669 and 1672 Nonconformist meetings were tolerated as 'licensed conventicles'. (See HEYWOOD, OLIVER, and COMPTON ECCLESIASTICAL CENSUS (1676), which estimated that 4 per cent of the population were Protestant Dissenters, with much higher proportions in various strongholds.)

In 1689, after the *Glorious Revolution, Protestant Nonconformists were allowed to license their meeting-houses for public worship at the quarter sessions, but they were still banned from holding public office and excluded from the universities. (See DISSENTING ACADEMIES.) A. Gordon, *Freedom After Ejection, 1690–2* (1917) provides contemporary information about preachers and meeting-houses. See also Dr *Williams's Library, especially John Evans's list of meeting-houses (1715), which provides an estimated figure of 300,000 Nonconformists in England and Wales; and M.

Mullett, *Sources for the History of English Nonconformity* (1991).

The term 'Nonconformist' was applied to groups of widely different beliefs. (See QUAKERS; ANABAPTISTS; FIFTH MONARCHY MEN; PRESBYTERIANS; INDEPENDENTS (CONGREGATIONALISTS); and BAPTISTS.) The distinctions between the last three denominations were loose, so that the labels for the same congregation varied from time to time. After toleration, many groups gradually abandoned their Calvinistic beliefs and some turned to *Unitarianism. Others faded away; the number of Dissenting congregations in England and Wales dropped from 1,107 in 1715 to 702 in 1772. The *Church of Scotland retained its Presbyterian beliefs and organization. (See also ULSTER.)

The early Nonconformist registers are mainly records of baptisms (but cf. QUAKERS). For marriages and burials (and often duplicate baptisms) Dissenters used the *Church of England. *Civil registration, from 1837, heralded a relaxation of the insistence that Church of England baptism was a necessary requirement for the holding of public office; Nonconformist registers deposited with the *Registrar-General (and now kept at the *Public Record Office) were allowed as legal evidence by the Non-Parochial Registers Act (1840).

The introspective nature of late 17th-century Nonconformity was unsuited to expansion. Dissenters gloried in their separateness and tenacity. The older Nonconformist sects were slow to respond to the *Evangelical revival of the 18th and 19th centuries, though eventually the Congregational (Independent) and Baptist denominations were transformed by it. This period saw the growth of the various *Methodist sects: the Wesleyans, the Primitives, the New Connexion, the Wesleyan Reform movement, and others. During the first half of the 19th century the Methodists outgrew the older Dissenting groups and began to rival the Church of England in many places. On Sunday 29 March 1851, the only time that a national census of religious attendance was ever made, the various Nonconformist denominations accounted for nearly half the church-going population. In no county of England and Wales did they number less than one-third. The census also revealed that, nation-wide, less than half of the population attended any form of service; in the new industrial cities the proportion was as small as one in 10. (See ECCLESIASTICAL CENSUSES.)

Between 1676 and 1851 Nonconformists had grown from 4 per cent of the population to nearly 50 per cent, and as this had happened at a time of unprecedented population growth the actual number of Nonconformists had multiplied enormously. Much of this growth had occurred in the second quarter of the 19th century. A large number of *chapels date from this period, though much new building and rebuilding took place in the Victorian and Edwardian era. The plain, square boxes and 'tin tabernacles' were gradually replaced by imposing classical buildings, and eventually even by some Gothic ones, in areas where congregations became increasingly middle-class. Many of them have become redundant during the last third of the 20th century as membership and attendance have declined.

Nonconformity was a major force in public life during the 19th and early 20th centuries. Many of the political battles of the time were fought over religious views, e.g. on the funding of *education. In many towns Nonconformists of various persuasions formed a political majority on the town council. Nonconformity was particularly associated with the *Liberal Party and with the early *Labour Party. Its strengths were uneven across the country. The shifting patterns of Nonconformity have attracted much attention from local historians: see the pioneering essay by Alan Everitt, *The Pattern of Rural Dissent: The Nineteenth Century* (1972), Margaret Spufford (ed.), *The World of Rural Dissenters, 1520–1725* (1995), and K. D. M. Snell, *Church and Chapel in the North Midlands: Religious Observance in the Nineteenth Century* (1991), and its bibliography. The subject lends itself to quantitative analysis as well as to the use of literary, documentary, and visual evidence. See James Obelkevich, *Religion and Rural Society: South Lindsey, 1825–1875* (1976), N. Virgoe and T. Williamson (eds.), *Religious Dissent in East Anglia: Historical Perspectives* (1993), and Clyde Binfield, 'Religion in Sheffield', in Binfield *et al.* (eds.), *The History of the City of Sheffield, 1843–1993*, vol. ii (1993) for exemplary rural and urban studies.

Norden, John (1548–1625?). Writer of county histories, surveyor and mapmaker, and author of devotional or religious works. Norden intended to follow *Camden and *Lambarde by writing a series of county chorographies illustrated by small maps. He called his project 'Speculum Britanniae'. He obtained the backing of Lord Burghley and in 1591 began a careful survey of more than a dozen counties. Only his descriptions of Middlesex (1593) and Hertfordshire (1598) were published during his lifetime. Posthumous editions cover North-amptonshire (1720), Cornwall (1728), Norfolk (1938), and Suffolk (1976). His project collapsed upon the death of Burghley in 1598. He is remembered today as an *antiquarian and cartographer and for his *The Surveyors Dialogue* (1607). See Heather Lawrence, 'John Norden and His Colleagues: Surveyors of Crown Lands', *Cartographic Journal*, 22/1 (1985), and Stan A. E. Mendyk, *'Speculum Britanniae': Regional Study, Antiquarianism, and Science in Britain to 1700* (1989), ch. 3.

Norman Conquest. On 25 September 1066 King Harold Godwinson defeated Earl Tostig and Harold Hardrada at Stamford Bridge, east of York, at what was to prove to be the last battle fought by the *Vikings on English soil. His army then marched southwards to combat a new threat, the arrival of the army of William, Duke of Normandy. On 14 October the Norman invaders were victorious at the battle of Hastings. William I was crowned King of England at Westminster on Christmas Day. It took another four years for the Normans to quell revolts, notably in the north of England. In 1072 William invaded Scotland and forced Malcolm to pay homage and to stop harbouring William's enemies, but Scotland did not come under Norman rule. William created large *castellanies in the border regions, delegating power to his *barons. Chester, Shrewsbury, and Ludlow were the centres of the marcher *lordships along the Welsh border. By the early 12th century the whole of south Wales was under Norman rule, but Welsh princes continued to enjoy some independence in the north until the building of Edward I's great *castles in the late 13th century. The Anglo-Norman military colonization of Ireland did not begin until 1169 and never reached large parts of the west.

The Norman forces constituted an army of occupation. They forced the native population to build *ringworks and *motte-and-bailey castles in the first stages of the conquest before massive stone castles were erected. The English aristocracy was almost entirely replaced by a new aristocracy of Norman origin. Only 19 of the commanders who fought alongside William at Hastings can be named, and four of these are doubtful. A descent in the male line can be proved only from William Mallet, and even there the early links have not been proved with certainty. The authenticity of the so-called Battle Abbey Roll has been rejected. See Anthony J. Camp, *My Ancestors Came With the Conqueror* (1990). Other Norman and Breton families crossed the Channel to become landowners shortly afterwards, but there was no large-scale immigration, as there had been with the Vikings. Britain has relatively few *place-names of French origin. See DOMESDAY BOOK; FEUDAL-ISM; CATHEDRALS; and CHURCHES, PARISH.

Northern History. An annual journal published by the History Department of the University of Leeds since 1965. It contains articles on the history of the seven historic counties of Northumberland, Durham, Cumberland, Westmorland, Lancashire, Cheshire, and Yorkshire, together with reviews and bibliographies.

Northumbria. The most northerly of the *Anglo-Saxon kingdoms. For more than two centuries, the Humber was the major division between the Anglo-Saxon peoples. The original Anglian migrants formed the two kingdoms of Bernicia (centred on Bamburgh) and Deira (in central and eastern Yorkshire). In the early 7th century Aethelfrith united the two territories into one kingdom, which remained intact until the Danish conquest of 865. In the 8th century Northumbria was famous throughout western Europe for the scholarship of its *monasteries. See BEDE, THE VENERABLE.

Norwich school of artists. The most famous of the provincial groups of artists in the late 18th and early 19th centuries. They concentrated on tranquil rural landscapes, mainly in Norfolk. Their best-known members were John Crome and John Sell Cotman. Their paintings and drawings are of interest to local historians for their accurate depictions of contemporary landscapes, seascapes, buildings, and antiquities. See Andrew W. Moore, *The Norwich School of Artists* (1985).

notary. A professional scribe and compiler of legal documents.

Notes and Queries. A periodical first published weekly in 1849, and now published quarterly by Oxford University Press. It contains much valuable information on all subjects, mostly supplied by readers in reply to other readers' queries. The main subjects are literary and historical, but much genealogy and local history are included. There are cumulative indexes, but not for the more recent volumes. It is available in most of the large public libraries.

novel disseisin. A medieval legal action for claiming recent dispossession.

numeracy. The 16th and 17th centuries saw a transformation in arithmetical calculation as roman numerals were replaced by arabic ones. The evidence for popular numeracy cannot easily be measured in the same way as that for literacy, but this period saw the beginning of calculations on paper, double-entry bookkeeping, the adoption of arithmetical signs, such as = for equals, and the beginnings of political arithmetic, e.g. the demographic calculations of Gregory *King. See Keith Thomas, 'Numeracy in Early Modern England', *Transactions of the Royal Historical Society*, 37 (1987).

nuncupative. A will made by word of mouth only, before 'credible witnesses' who later made sworn statements before a probate court.

nunnery. Double monastic houses under the rule of an abbess were a feature that was imported from Gaul in the 7th century. The most famous example was the abbey founded at Whitby in 657 by Hilda, who remained abbess until her death in 680. This and other houses were sacked by the *Vikings. Double houses were refounded in the 10th- and 11th-century revival in *Wessex, but after the *Norman Conquest separate nunneries were generally favoured. These were small religious houses, with usually only up to 12 nuns under a prioress. They catered for the daughters and widows of the *aristocracy, but they attracted few endowments and remained poor and insignificant. Their physical remains are insubstantial and have attracted little investigation. Most were founded in the 12th or 13th centuries, and show a peak period in the mid-12th century. See Eileen Power, *Medieval Religious Nunneries* (1922), S. Thompson, *Women Religious* (1991), and, for two regional studies, Janet E. Burton, *The Yorkshire Nunneries in the Twelfth and Thirteenth Centuries* (1979), and Roberta Gilchrist and Marilyn Oliva, *Religious Women in Medieval East Anglia* (1993). See GILBERTINES.

nuptiality. A measure of the extent to which women marry. See MARRIAGE.

O

oasthouses. Kilns for drying *hops in south-eastern England and the south-west midlands. Most surviving examples, with characteristic conical roofs, date from the 19th century; those with pyramidical roofs date from the 18th to the early 20th century. Hot air from a fire at ground level rose through a slatted floor to a drying room where hops were spread on horsehair cloths. Smoke escaped through an adjustable cowl at the top of the roof. Hops were cooled and packed on an upper floor. Many old oast-houses have been converted into domestic properties. A detailed study of surviving oast-houses, showing how much can be learned from them about changing drying-procedures, is Gwen Jones and John Bell, *Oasthouses in Sussex and Kent, their History and Development* (1992).

obelisk. Egyptian obelisks were copied in Rome and other parts of the ancient world and became a favourite feature of Italian Renaissance *gardens. In Britain they were used as eye-catchers in 18th- and 19th-century landscaped *parks and as memorials. The three obelisks at Wentworth Castle (Yorkshire), for example, commemorate Queen Anne (the patron of the owner of the estate) and Lady Mary Wortley-Montagu (who introduced *inoculation against *smallpox into the country, and who had local connections), and mark the point where the visitor left the *turnpike road to enter the estate. Small obelisks were also used in *funerary art.

obituaries in 19th- and 20th-century *newspapers have to be treated with caution, but they offer many clues to the family historian and often contain information that cannot be obtained elsewhere. They are particularly valuable for the first three-quarters of the 20th century, when local newspapers flourished and the coverage of obituaries was extensive.

Ogilby, John (1600–76). After a varied career, which included a spell as a dancing teacher, Ogilby became a London publisher and 'the king's cosmographer and geographic printer'. He is remembered best for his *Britannia Depicta* (1675), which contained 100 strip-maps of the 73 principal highways of the kingdom, the first set of road maps produced in Britain. He also engraved maps of Africa, America, and Asia.

old age pensions. Introduced from 1 January 1909 by David Lloyd-George, the Chancellor of the Exchequer of Asquith's Liberal Government. At first, the state pension was for people over 70, who at that time formed a smaller proportion of the population than that age-group does today. The introduction of state pensions was widely acclaimed for removing the fear of having to live in the *workhouse during old age.

Old English. 1. (linguistic). Term used to embrace all the dialects of the *Anglo-Saxons up to c.1150. These developed into Middle English (to c.1500) and Modern English.
2. (Irish). Term used to distinguish English people who settled in Ireland before the new settlers of the 16th and 17th centuries.

old style. The dating of days and months before the replacement of the *Julian by the *Gregorian calendar in 1752 and the change from 25 March to 1 January as the official start of a new year.

one hundred years' rule. The rule to preserve confidentiality of certain records, e.g. *census enumerators' returns, by prohibiting access before 100 years have passed. A 30-year rule applies to Cabinet papers.

One-Name Studies, Guild of. A group which encourages the registering of all available information about individuals sharing a particular *surname and which seeks to study past and present distributions of such names. The guild was founded in 1979, is based at the Society of *Genealogists, and holds regular meetings.

open-fields. The widespread system whereby the agricultural land of a *parish was farmed in large fields which were divided into *strips. The number and extent of the fields varied. They were normally farmed communally under regulations agreed at the manor *court. For their origins, distribution, and operation, see FIELD SYSTEMS. For their abolition, see ENCLOSURE, PARLIAMENTARY.

open hall. In the Middle Ages and after *manor houses were arranged around a central hall which was open to the rafters. Smoke from a central fire escaped through a louvre in the ceiling. The hall served as a communal dining-area and as sleeping accommodation for some of the servants. The lord's family and guests sat at a table on a raised dais at the end of the hall that had access to the private withdrawing rooms and chambers. The other end of the hall was shielded from the service rooms by a screen, which was often elaborately carved. Penshurst Place (Kent) has an outstanding 14th-century hall with all these features. The typical arrangements are preserved by many Oxford and Cambridge colleges.

oral history. Oral history is a term imported from the USA to describe a historical approach that is based on the use of personal reminiscences. Women like Charlotte Sophia Burne and Harriet Martineau were among the first in the 19th century to interrogate local inhabitants. Others include Diana Maria Mulock, *An Unsentimental Journey through Cornwall* (1884), and Maud F. Davies, *Life in an English Village: An Economic and Historical Survey of Corsley in Wiltshire* (1909). The recording of reminiscences is a very noticeable feature of the work of Ella Pontefract, Marie Hartley, and Joan Ingilby since the 1930s; see Hilary Dizper, *A Favoured Land, Yorkshire in Text and Image: The Work of Marie Hartley, Joan Ingilby and Ella Pontefract* (1994).

A more professional interest has been aroused in recent years by the pioneer work in Britain, *Ask the Fellows Who Cut the Hay* (1956) by George Ewart *Evans, who preferred to call his work folk-life studies or social anthropology. In this and subsequent books Evans established the value of personal testimony in providing an understanding of the old farming economy of the era of horse power and hand *tools. No written sources could match the wealth of detailed explanation of this former way of life. Indeed, documentary sources revealed very little about such everyday matters as the working practices and household arrangements of ordinary people. Evans established that personal memories could not be dismissed as 'mere hearsay', provided they had an internal consistency and that a large enough sample was taken so as to discover common strands and eliminate individual attitudes. He showed that oral evidence could be treated just as rigorously as evidence from other sources. Oral history has added a new dimension to the study of the recent past. It is emphatically not a marginal

activity that revels in nostalgia, but a method of gathering material, one type of approach among others.

Meanwhile, the School of Scottish Studies at Edinburgh University was pioneering a similar approach in Scotland. The early links with folk-life studies have remained strong. This is seen not only in Evans's later books, but in a series published by Dent, starting with Marie Hartley and Joan Ingilby, *Life and Tradition in the Yorkshire Dales* (1976), which combines oral recollections with the use of old photographs, material culture, and landscape to evoke a distinctive way of life in a particular region. The early folklorists ignored urban experience, but the way that personal life stories and communal memories can be blended together to produce a community history of a small town is well demonstrated by Melvyn Bragg, *Speak for England* (1976), a study of his Cumbrian birthplace, whose title suggests the wider implications of this local testimony.

An important step forward in focusing the varied activities of oral historians was taken in 1971 with the appearance of the first issue of *Oral History*, the annual journal of the Oral History Society. This contains articles, conference reports, and reviews; individual editions are often devoted to a particular topic. The oral approach has been basic to the study of women's history, notably in Elizabeth Roberts, *A Woman's Place: An Oral History of Working Class Women, 1890–1940* (1984), and Carl Chinn, *They Worked All Their Lives: Women of the Urban Poor in England, 1880–1939* (1988). See Maureen Sutton, 'The Problems, Difficulties and Advantages of Women's Oral History in Rural Society', *Rural History*, 5/2 (1994).

The academic credentials of the methodology of oral history have been established by Jan Vansina, *Oral History: A Study in Traditional Methodology* (1973), which is largely concerned with Africa, and by Paul Thompson, *The Voice of the Past: Oral History* (1978, 2nd edn., 1988), and Trevor Lummis, *Listening to History: The Authenticity of Oral Evidence* (1987). These books offer justifications of the approaches and methods of oral historians and provide advice on different types of project. Essex University has become the leading British academic centre for the study of oral history. A major survey into Edwardian life that has been conducted by Essex University historians led by Paul Thompson involved the interviewing of 500 people, who were selected by occupation and place of residence to represent the British population recorded in the census of 1911. This project resulted in the publication of Paul

Thompson, *The Edwardians: The Remaking of British Society* (1975).

Thompson and Lummis, together with Tony Wailey, have also written *Living the Fishing* (1983), in which extensive oral-history investigations were combined with all types of available documentary evidence to create a picture of the process of change in the fishing industry over the previous 150 years. Another good example of the way that oral testimony can be combined with other evidence is Alun Howkins, *Poor Labouring Men: Rural Radicalism in Norfolk, 1870–1923* (1985). These works show that oral history is not concerned simply with reminiscence and description, or with adding colour, but can deepen and widen an analysis of past societies.

Robert Perks, *Oral History, An Annotated Bibliography* (The British Library, 1990) lists 2,132 titles, including many foreign works. Lali Weerasinghe (ed.), *The Directory of Recorded Sound Resources in the United Kingdom* (The British Library National Sound Archive, 1989) lists most oral history collections of any size up to the year of publication. The recording of personal memories has attracted widespread interest among local and family historians, often working together in groups organized by museums, adult education classes, local history societies, and schools. It has also come to play an important role in hospitals as reminiscence therapy. The approach helps to break down subject barriers and has provided links with other disciplines, notably anthropology and sociology.

For practical guidance and a discussion of the value of the methodology, see Stephen Caunce, *Oral History for Local Historians* (1994).

orator. A plaintiff or petitioner, referred to in legal documents as 'your orator'.

oratory. A medieval *chapel which was licensed for private use. Upon toleration in the 19th century, a *Roman Catholic society of priests which was founded at Rome in 1564 built oratories for preaching and the holding of popular services, e.g. Brompton Oratory.

orchards. Medieval orchards were associated with manorial and monastic estates. Place-names such as Orchard Portman (Somerset), or several Applegarths, commemorate the cultivation of apples for cooking and *cider-making. A burst of fresh interest in *fruit-growing occurred in the 16th and 17th centuries, stimulated by court fashions and foreign influences. It brought new fruits and new varieties of old fruits (including apricots, cherries, nectarines,

peaches, plums, etc.) into orchards, along with more nut trees, and greatly enlarged their acreage in certain counties. Enthusiasm died away between 1750 and 1880, but then revived and launched another revolution, which now gave fresh fruit, and especially jam, a larger place than before in the *diet of all classes. See F. A. Roach, *Cultivated Fruits of Britain, Their Origin and History* (1985). Many new varieties of apple were developed in the 18th and 19th centuries, when orchards expanded in size to meet demand, especially those orchards that were sited near populous cities.

ordeal. Until 1212 legal suits could be decided by three types of ordeal; by combat for *knights, by fire for freemen, and by water for *villeins.

ordinary. 1. In *heraldry, a reference book that lists the heraldic descriptions of shields of arms, notably J. W. Papworth, *Ordinary of British Armorials* (1874).

2. In ecclesiastical law and administration, one having authority, e.g. a bishop.

Ordnance Survey. The maps of the Ordnance Survey appeared after a productive period in the later 18th century during which a series of county maps on the scale of one inch to one mile were prepared for the *Royal Society of Arts. The first military map made in Great Britain was that of the Highlands of Scotland, surveyed between 1747 and 1755 after the defeat of the Stuart rebellion. Schemes for an extension of the survey to the rest of Britain did not come to fruition until the threat of invasion from France in the late 18th century caused the Board of Ordnance, based at the Tower of London, to map the south coast of England on the scale of one inch to one mile. This grew into a series covering the whole of Britain. The survey aimed to produce military maps based on an accurate triangulation and to publish maps for general use. The first map published by the Ordnance Survey was William Faden's map of Kent (1801). See Col. Sir Charles Close, *The Early Years of the Ordnance Survey*, edited and introduced by J. B. Harley (1969), and W. A. Seymour (ed.), *A History of the Ordnance Survey* (1980). Work on the one-inch maps ceased between 1811 and 1817 and between 1824 and 1840 because the limited resources were diverted to a survey and valuation of Ireland. The first maps of Ireland were published in 1833.

The Ordnance Survey became a separate organization in 1841. Records before that date are kept at the *Public Record Office under WO 44, 47, and 55, with other material under T

1 and OS 3. Many of the oldest records of the Ordnance Survey were destroyed in a fire at the Tower of London in 1841. The original surveyors' drawings, at scales mostly of two inches, but also of three inches and six inches to one mile, and the accompanying revision sketches covering much of midland England, have been deposited at the *British Library Map Library, which also contains complete sets of sheets of all scales and editions. Similar sets are held at the other copyright libraries. The Public Record Office has large, though not complete, holdings of published sheets; a set each of both the Old Series and the New Series of one-inch maps is kept on open shelves in the Map Room at Kew. Local *record offices and public *libraries normally have good collections of local maps of various scales and editions.

The Ordnance Survey rapidly became a national service for government, military, and public use. A systematic survey of Scotland was begun in 1841; publication commenced in the early 1850s on the scale of six inches to one mile. The last sheet of the first national survey (known as the Old Series) was that of the Isle of Man, published in 1873, though a New Series had been started elsewhere in 1840. The larger-scale maps, which are such a prime source for local historians, also range widely in date from one part of the country to another. The six-inch series was started in 1840; the 25-inch maps covering all but the wildest areas date from 1853 to 1896. Large-scale maps for urban areas began with the five feet to one mile survey of the 1850s, which was abandoned in 1858 in favour of a 10 feet to the mile survey; this was discontinued in 1894. The latest series of 25-inch maps was begun in 1948 and completed in the early 1980s.

The delay between survey and the publication of individual sheets varied between a few years and 20 years. The New Series that gradually replaced the Old Series was not completed until the 1890s. Meanwhile, extra information, e.g. railway lines, was included in new issues of the Old Series. It is therefore often difficult to date 19th-century Ordnance Survey one-inch maps and to decide to which of the two series they belong. The David and Charles facsimile sets are of the post-1860 Old Series maps. After the First World War, government economies reduced the effectiveness of the Ordnance Survey, but a programme of expansion came into effect after the Second World War. By 1961 the seventh edition of the one-inch series was complete. During the 1970s this scale was gradually abandoned in favour of the metrical scale of 1:50,000.

The original surveys used white pillars (concrete tripods above trigonometrical points) and *bench marks carved on buildings, *milestones, and walls. Technological advance has been rapid in the last quarter of the 20th century, so that even aerial photography is now a dated technique. The Ordnance Survey has a collection of over half a million aerial photographs at its headquarters in Southampton, copies of which may be purchased by the public. Many other records were destroyed during air raids in the Second World War.

Ordnance Survey maps are a basic tool for the local historian. No other country is served so well by such high-quality maps. The Ordnance Survey has published specialist maps on Ancient Britain, Roman Britain, Dark Age Britain, Monastic Britain, etc. in several editions, for the interest of the Survey in antiquities has always been strong. A basic introduction to the use of maps for *landscape history is the Ordnance Survey's own publication, *Field Archaeology: Some Notes for Beginners* (several editions), a guide to the interpretation of minor features of the countryside.

From 1841 the Ordnance Survey was given responsibility for ascertaining and recording all the current public *boundaries in the United Kingdom. Some of these were new civil boundaries, but others were ancient. The old practice of perambulating boundaries and marking them by boundary stones was now no longer necessary. The boundaries were drawn on new editions of six-inch maps and given their administrative names. The records of this endeavour are kept in the Public Record Office in the Boundary Remark Book (OS 26), the Boundary Record Maps (OS 31 and 33), and the Parish Names Book (OS 23). Deposit Maps for England and Wales are held under OS 38 and OS 39. There are also several classes of correspondence relating to boundary changes. See the Public Record Office Records Information leaflet no. 93, 'Records of the Ordnance Survey'.

See also J. B. Harley, *Ordnance Survey Maps: A Descriptive Manual* (1975), J. B. Harley and C. W. Phillips, *Historian's Guide to Ordnance Survey Maps* (1964), and Richard Oliver, *Ordnance Survey Maps: A Concise Guide for Historians* (1993).

organs. Few parish *churches retain organs that predate the Act of Parliament of 1644 by which the *Puritans banned their use. Old Radnor has the oldest organ-case in Britain, one that dates from the reign of Henry VII (1485–1509). The most beautiful organ-cases were made in a *baroque style during the half-century after the *Restoration. Most church organs date from the *High Church movement of early Victorian times, when they were placed in a west gallery or installed in redundant spaces formerly occupied by *chantry chapels. Their introduction led to the displacement of the village bands that played in the west galleries of churches. The clash between the old and new provision is immortalized in Thomas Hardy, *Under the Greenwood Tree* (1872). See C. Clutton and A. Niland, *The British Organ* (1963).

orphans. From the 16th to the 19th centuries poor orphans were the responsibility of civil *parishes, whose overseers of the *poor apprenticed them to local householders. A notorious abuse was the apprenticing of poor orphans to *factory owners in distant places. (See also FOUNDLINGS.) After the *Poor Law Amendment Act (1834) Poor Law *guardians were responsible for orphanages. The records are kept at county *record offices. See also BARNARDO HOMES, DR, and WARDS AND LIVERIES, COURT OF.

Orwin, C. S. and C. S. Authors of *The Open Fields* (1938, 3rd edn., 1967), which used a practical approach to the problem of the origins of *open-fields, particularly in relation to the surviving system at Laxton (Nottinghamshire). Their contention was that the organization of large open-fields divided into *strips evolved from the practical demands of ploughing. 'Unfortunately historians are not all of them ploughmen', they remarked. The book has been very influential, even though most of their conclusions have now been discarded. See FIELD SYSTEMS.

outfangtheof. The right of a manorial lord to arrest a thief beyond the manorial estate and to hold the trial at his own court.

outlaw. One who had escaped custody or who had failed to appear before a court to answer criminal charges. After four summonses an absconder's goods were confiscated and he was declared beyond the protection of the law; therefore an outlaw could be legally killed by anyone who met him. Outlawry was not abolished until 1879.

ovens, common. In the Middle Ages and the early modern period many towns and villages had a common oven for the baking of bread. These were usually provided by manorial lords. That at Sheffield was probably typical of urban examples in being sited by the *market place.

Owen, William, *Book of Fairs*. The most popular of the 18th-century guides to *fairs, arranged under counties. First published in 1756, the sixth edition of 1770 is the fullest and most accessible. The entry for each place noted the dates (many of which were still in the *old style of the *Julian calendar) and the range of livestock and produce offered for sale. The days on which weekly *markets were held are also given. Thus, the entry for Chesterfield records the regular Saturday market, fairs for *cattle, *horses, and *pedlars on 25 January, 28 February, 3 April, 4 May, and 4 July, a fair for *cheese, onions, and pedlars on 25 September, and a fair for cattle, *sheep, and pedlars on 25 November.

oxen. In the late Anglo-Saxon and Norman periods an oxgang was a conventional unit based on the amount of land that a team of eight oxen could plough in a year. It is clear at this time that the ox, rather than the *horse, was the animal that was used to draw the *plough. In many regions oxen remained the choice for ploughing long after men started to prefer the horse for haulage and harrowing. The change to the quicker, more agile horse for both haulage and working the land was an extended process lasting from the Middle Ages to the 20th century. The arguments that were advanced in support of one or the other animal remained the same over the centuries. Oxen were admittedly slower and more cumbersome than horses, but they were stronger and had more stamina. Moreover, they were easier and cheaper to keep, less liable to succumb to disease, and they could be fattened and sold as meat at the end of their working lives. (See DURHAM OX.) On the other hand, they could not be used for riding. Horses were suitable for light soils, but oxen were preferred on stiff, heavy clays. The pace of change therefore varied considerably from one agricultural region to another. Regional preferences in the early modern period, which saw considerable movement away from the horse, are best revealed by a study of probate *inventories.

Oxford movement. An intellectual movement in the *Church of England, centred on Oxford University in the middle decades of the 19th century. It was concerned at first with doctrine and ecclesiastical authority, but soon became associated with the move to restore ritual in the Anglican church. The movement was inspired by a romantic medievalism, which led to many internal changes in parish *churches, involving *stained glass, screens, choir stalls, elevated chancel floors, etc. (See also HIGH CHURCH

MOVEMENT and CAMDEN SOCIETY.) For a local study, see Nigel Yates, *Kent and the Oxford Movement* (1983).

Oxford University archives. The archives of the University, including *wills proved at the court of the Chancellor of the University, are kept at the *Bodleian Library. The individual colleges have their own archives. As they are amongst the largest institutional *landowners in the country, their *estate records, including *surveys, *rentals, *maps, etc., form important collections for local historians in those districts where a college received grants of property. For example, see the comparison between the map of Padbury (Buckinghamshire) in 1591, belonging to All Souls College, and modern aerial photographs in M. W. Beresford and J.K. St Joseph, *Medieval England: An Aerial Survey* (2nd edn., 1979).

oxgang. See BOVATE.

oyer and terminer, commission of. In the Middle Ages and after, justices of the royal court were occasionally commissioned by the Crown to hear and determine specific cases of treason, murder, and other serious crimes within a particular county. The records are kept in the *Public Record Office under JUST 1. See also GAOL DELIVERY.

P

packhorses were used to carry a wide variety of goods over both short and long distances from time immemorial until the coming of *turnpike roads, *canals, and *railways gradually reduced this method to a minor activity in the hillier parts of Britain. It is customary to describe ancient routes, especially the ones that have declined in importance, as packhorse roads, but many of them were not confined to packhorse traffic; even in hilly districts small wheeled vehicles known as wains, and even the sturdier carts, were in common use. Trains of packhorses formed only part of the traffic on busy routes. Despite the disparaging comments of travellers, roads were passable (albeit slowly) and every part of the country was linked in a network of communications. Nor was land traffic in competition with water transport; the two systems should be seen not as rivals but as complementary.

Although specialist breeds of *horse were sometimes used, the term 'packhorse' was applied loosely to any horse that carried a pack. As most carriage was over relatively short distances and was undertaken during the summer months between the hay and the corn harvests, when the roads were dry and the farmers had less work than usual, the working horses (and *oxen) of the farm were used for carriage. The long-distance *carriers such as the 'Kendal men' probably preferred breeds such as the galloway or the Welsh pony, though it is difficult to find firm evidence. Surprisingly, local artists painted few pictures that included packhorse trains. Probate *inventories normally speak only of horses, mares, geldings, foals, and fillies. Most of the tracks that are now remembered as 'old packhorse roads' carried light traffic. Long trains of packhorses heading for the towns, inland *ports, and great country *fairs were a familiar sight only on certain routes. The approach of a long train of 10 to 40 packhorses was announced by the sound of the bells attached to the collars of the leading horses, for most roads were narrow and passing places were few.

The weight of the load varied according to the nature of the goods being carried and the distance to be covered. It probably increased over time as breeds of horses were improved. By the 18th century the normal weight of a pack of cloth was 240 lb. and the distance covered in a day was up to 30 miles, depending on the nature of the terrain. Coal and charcoal were stacked in panniers; other goods were carried in parcels strapped to a saddle or a rough pad known as a panel by means of cords, ropes, and belly-bands (wanteys or wantows). The fittings were as varied as were the animals that carried the load.

The packhorse era of road transport is poorly documented. The *quarter sessions records deal with the licensing of *drovers, *badgers, etc., and with complaints about the upkeep of highways and *bridges. Otherwise, the historian has to glean information from all the various sources (such as maps, *wills, and manorial *court records) that are available for any local study in the medieval and early modern periods. The first detailed set of records concern the turnpike roads, most of which were simply improved versions of older highways. The meagre documentation prior to the turnpike era has to be combined with the evidence of the landscape: the survival of packhorse bridges, *holloways, *guide stoops, and other waymarkers, and of *inns bearing names such as Packhorse or Woolpack. Clues to the lines of old routes are provided by minor place-names that commemorate distinctive travellers, such as Packman Lane, Saltersgate, Jaggers' Lane, or Hollowgate. See, for instance, David Hey, *Packmen, Carriers and Packhorse Roads: Trade and Communications in North Derbyshire and South Yorkshire* (1980).

The minor routes that are now thought of as 'old packhorse roads' were only part of the ancient system. The most important routes were turnpiked and remained the major roads of the country until the age of the motorway. The *enclosure commissioners of the late 18th and early 19th centuries incorporated many old packhorse routes into their new system of long, straight lanes over the former *commons and wastes. In considering the evidence of the landscape, it is therefore important to take account of modern roads as well as abandoned tracks.

pains. The regulations issued by the jury of a manorial *court leet, the breach of which incurred a fixed penalty. These regulations involved the organization of communal agriculture, the scouring of ditches, the use of public wells, the muzzling of mastiffs, etc.

palaces. Excavations of the palaces of the kings of *Northumbria at Yeavering, the kings of *Wessex at Cheddar, and the bishops of *East Anglia at North Elham have demonstrated how in *Anglo-Saxon times the most important building in such complexes was a long central hall raised on timber posts. The great halls of the post-Conquest era, when stone replaced timber, were often on the first floor. See Maurice Barley, *Houses and History* (1986) for a study of the substantial bishops' palaces of the Middle Ages, which stood alongside the *cathedrals. These were the greatest urban buildings of their time. Some bishops' palaces were built anew after the restoration of Charles II, e.g. that at Lichfield (1686–7). Royal palaces (as distinct from *castles) were built by the Tudor kings, Henry VII and VIII, in and near London, at Greenwich, Hampton Court, Richmond, Whitehall, etc. Like the bishops' palaces, they had both public and private functions, with a communal hall, elaborate suites, apartments, and an emphasis on ceremony and entertainment. Buckingham Palace, built for the Duke of Buckingham, was bought by George III in 1761 and converted into the major royal residence in London.

palaeography. The handwriting of documents from the 18th century onwards does not present too many difficulties in terms of unfamiliar forms and styles, though, as today, individual writers vary in their clarity. The script used in the 16th and 17th centuries was radically different, however, even if it was in English rather than Latin. Much practice is needed before such documents can be read. Understanding their form and knowing the sort of information they are likely to provide is an essential preparatory step. See, for instance, the typical examples set out in Denis Stuart, *Manorial Records* (1992), and E. A. Gooder, *Latin for Local History* (1978).

Several manuals provide guidance on how to read medieval Court Hand, the Secretary Hand of the Elizabethans, and the Italic Hand, which was introduced in the 16th century from Italy and which became general after the *Restoration and was the forerunner of modern styles. See, for example, L. C. Hector, *The Handwriting of English Documents* (1979), H. E. P. Grieve, *Examples of English Handwriting,* *1150–1750* (1978), C. T. Martin, *The Record Interpreter* (1982), F. G. Emmison, *How to Read Local Archives, 1500–1700* (1967), Lionel Munby, *Reading Tudor and Stuart Handwriting* (1987), and K. C. Newton, *Medieval Local Records: A Reading Aid* (1971). Many local *record offices have published similar reading aids, using examples of documents housed in their collections.

One of the greatest difficulties in reading old documents is caused by the use of abbreviations. These were developed in the Middle Ages, but long continued in use. At first, they consisted of various signs above the line to indicate the exact nature of the shortening, but by the 16th century they had often degenerated into dashes, flourishes, or squiggles. They cause particular problems when the declension of a Latin word is obscured by an abbreviated ending. The lack of punctuation, the indiscriminate use of capital letters, and idiosyncratic spellings of words, many of which are now archaic, add to the frustrations involved in deciphering a word, but also to the sense of achievement when the task is completed successfully.

Palaeolithic. The Old *Stone Age, the earliest period of human activity following the last Ice Age. Deposits in caves and scattered stone artefacts form the basis of archaeological investigation of this remote period.

palatine means 'pertaining to a palace'. Palatinates were huge lordships established for the defence of border regions. The Norman kings granted special powers to the Earls of Chester, Shrewsbury, and Hereford in the Welsh borders, and to the Prince Bishop of Durham in the Scottish borders. Durham, Cheshire, and Lancashire became known as the counties palatine. Their records are held in various collections in the *Public Record Office.

Pale. 1. A territory under a particular jurisdiction, e.g. the English Pale in the hinterland of Calais, or the Pale in Ireland over which the English had jurisdiction. This sense has given rise to the expression 'beyond the pale'.
2. A stake in a fence, e.g. around a *deer park.

palimpsest. A manuscript on which the original writing has been replaced by new. The word was recently used by W. G. *Hoskins to describe the successive layers of history that are revealed by a study of the landscape.

Palladian. The villas, churches, and other public buildings of Andrea Palladio (1508–80) in Vicenza, Venice, and the surrounding countryside, together with his *Four Books of Architecture*

(1570), were enormously influential in western European countries and their former colonies. Inigo Jones was Palladio's first champion in England, but as his buildings were associated with the Court circle they went out of fashion during the *Civil War. Young noblemen on the Grand Tour visited Italy and reintroduced the Palladian style (which was based on the strict proportions and decorative features of the major surviving buildings of ancient Greece and Rome) into Britain and Ireland during the second and third decades of the 18th century. The leading figure in this movement was the Earl of Burlington, who designed Chiswick House as a Palladian villa suitable as a meeting-place for the advancement of the arts. The great country houses built by the leading Whig families in the first half of the 18th century, e.g. Holkham Hall (Norfolk) and Wentworth Woodhouse (Yorkshire), were in this style. Strict Palladianism declined in popularity during the second half of the 18th century, but the general style remained in widespread use for public buildings for much of the 19th century, both in Britain and abroad.

Pallot's Index of Marriages and Births. An index begun in 1818 by a firm of record agents, whose successors included Messrs Pallot & Co. Much was destroyed in the Second World War, but the surviving part of the index includes the marriages of 101 of the 103 ancient *parishes of London and of many Middlesex parishes for the period 1800–37, with a smaller number from elsewhere, together with 30,000 baptisms. The index is now held (and catalogued) by the *Institute of Heraldic and Genealogical Studies, Canterbury.

palmer. One who wore a representation of a palm branch as a token of a pilgrimage to the Holy Land. The surname Palmer is derived in this way.

panelling. Oak wainscot was used from the 13th century onwards to line the interior walls of houses and public buildings so as to exclude draughts. Surviving examples are mostly in minor *gentry and *yeomen's homes of the 16th and 17th centuries. The wavy design known since Victorian times as linenfold was popular from the late 15th to the mid-16th century. Later examples incorporate Renaissance motifs.

pannage. The right to graze pigs on acorns and beech mast on the *commons of a *manor.

pantiles are the curving, orange-coloured roofing tiles which were introduced into eastern England from the Netherlands during the 17th century. 'Pan' is a Dutch word for tile. They were known at first as Dutch or Holland tiles, though they were made locally. They are particularly associated with *brick buildings in those parts of eastern England where good *building stones are absent.

paper-making. Wood pulp, woollen rags, and old ropes discarded by heavy industry and shipping were beaten by *water power for periods up to 36 hours to produce brown or white paper. The earliest-known paper mill was in production at Hertford in 1495, but the industry was insubstantial until the second half of the 17th century, when it was stimulated by technical improvements brought by *French immigrants and the high price of imported paper. Water power was used for beating until well into the 19th century, and some corn and other mills were adapted to this purpose. Additional water (of pure quality) was required for fermenting, washing, and pressing. Much paper was sold for wrapping goods, and many mills had specialities. See A. H. Shorter, *Paper Mills and Paper Makers in England* (1957) for the period before 1800, and D. C. Coleman, *The British Paper Industry, 1495–1860: A Study in Industrial Growth* (1958). For the range of sources that can be used in a local study see Tanya Schmoller, *Sheffield Papermakers: Three Centuries of Papermaking in the Sheffield Area* (1992).

parchment. Many old documents were written on both sides of the treated skins of sheep or goats. See also VELLUM.

pardoner. A seller of *indulgences.

pargeting. The decorative plasterwork on external walls of houses in Suffolk, Essex, and parts of adjacent counties. An extravagant example is Sparrowe's House, a former inn in Ipswich, where the pargeting dates from the reign of Charles II, but was much restored in 1850. Most examples have been restored from time to time.

paring and burning. A technique used to kill weeds and fertilize the land with potash before bringing it into cultivation. See ASSART.

parish. The majority of England's medieval parishes were formed by 1200. By that time some had been in existence for hundreds of years. (See MINSTER CHURCHES for the ways in which early ecclesiastical units were often coterminous with secular ones until the old framework disintegrated.) From the later 9th century onwards, local lords founded churches to serve their estates. The *boundaries of these estates were naturally used as the boundaries of the new parishes. Sometimes this process was agreed with the minsters, but in other cases disputes dragged on for years. Records of such disputes are often preserved in diocesan archives. A parish was not only a unit of pastoral care, but one that was expected to provide the resources to maintain its church and support its priest. Disputes therefore centred upon the payment of *tithes, offerings, dues, and fees. Burial rights were jealously guarded by the incumbents of churches, who were watchful over the claims of new *chapels-of-ease. During the 12th century arrangements began to stabilize as disputes were settled by agreement, or by royal or episcopal decree.

The antiquity of parish boundaries has been a matter of much debate. See D. Roffe, 'Pre-Conquest Estates and Parish Boundaries: A Discussion with Examples from Lincolnshire', in M. L. Faull (ed.), *Studies in Late Anglo-Saxon Settlement* (1984), and the overview in Richard Morris, *Churches in the Landscape* (1989). There was a natural tendency for parishes to follow convenient existing boundaries, some of which were ancient. Many parishes preserve the outline of pre-Conquest estates. As landholding was always in a state of transition, however, some of these estate boundaries may have been formed at the same time as parishes, or not long before. (See also DETACHED PORTION.) A cautious approach is needed, for the framework was not rigid and the evidence for the precise line of parish boundaries is often not forthcoming until after the Middle Ages. In some parts of the country, e.g. in much of Lincolnshire and Nottinghamshire, parishes were commonly formed from more than one *manor. The *Domesday Book notes many churches that were held jointly. The process is as obscure as that whereby parishes were formed from the amalgamation of territories upon the closure of churches. (See also PERAMBULATIONS.)

The shape and size of a parish varied from one part of the country to another. The contrast between the parishes on the Lincolnshire *Wolds and those in the neighbouring *fens is seen at a glance on the map. Shape was strongly influenced by variations of soil within the parish. In north Yorkshire, the Vale of Pickering parishes extended in long, narrow strips on to the moors for distances of up to 12 miles. Size was determined largely by *population levels and resources at the time of parish formation. In upland areas such as the Pennines or over much of Wales parishes were enormous. In northern England, where the *township or *vill formed the basic unit of local government, parishes such as Kendal (Westmorland) or

Halifax (West Riding) stretched for miles. In Cheshire, Great Budworth covered 35 townships and Malpas covered 24. By the early modern period, many a huge moorland or fenland parish had attracted a large population whose combined resources enabled the rebuilding of a fine parish *church. In contrast, many of the smaller parishes had become *deserted medieval villages whose churches lay in ruins.

The pattern of parishes in urban areas is markedly different from that in the countryside. London had over 100 parishes by the end of the Middle Ages, while leading provincial cities such as Norwich or York had over 40 each. The parishes enclosed tiny communities, whose boundaries wound along streets and the backs of gardens. On the other hand, the new industrial towns, such as Manchester or Sheffield, were served by single parishes which included large sections of the surrounding countryside. These huge urban parishes were not divided up into numerous new ones until the second and third quarters of the 19th century. Thus the medieval parish of Sheffield, which covered 22,370 acres, was divided into 23 new parishes in the early Victorian period.

The Tudor governments gave responsibilities for the poor, the highways, and for petty law and order to civil parishes, which often covered the same area as the ecclesiastical parishes. Where ecclesiastical parishes were large, their subdivisions (the townships, or groups of townships) became the civil parishes. The system was supervised by the *Justices of the Peace, meeting at *quarter sessions. Information on the size and shape of these civil parishes can be obtained from 19th-century *directories, the large-scale maps of the *Ordnance Survey, and the relevant volumes of the *Victoria County History. The Local Government Act (1894) divided England and Wales into some 14,000 parishes, whose boundaries generally followed those of the old civil parishes. Anomalies caused by divided parishes and detached portions were removed. The elected parish councils which were formed at that time survived the reorganization of local government in 1974.

Scotland had acquired a similar structure of ecclesiastical and civil parishes by the 16th century. See I. B. Cowan, *The Parishes of Medieval Scotland* (1967) and *The Parishes, Registers and Registrars of Scotland* (Scottish Association of Family History Societies, 1993). The medieval parishes of Ireland were often made redundant by the land reallocations of the 17th century. The parishes of the *Church of Ireland are usually amalgamations of the ancient parishes, but the Catholic Church had to create a new parish network in the 18th and 19th centuries. The wealthiest and most numerous parishes were formed in the south-east, in Leinster, and in east Munster, whereas in west Ulster and Connacht the poverty of the population delayed the process of parish formation until the mid-19th century. Ireland's 2,508 civil parishes are mapped in Brian Mitchell, *A New Genealogical Atlas of Ireland* (1986).

The rural parish has long been a natural unit of study for local historians, for in many parts of the British Isles it forms a locality to which people feel they belong, and many records were generated by ecclesiastical and civil parish administration. See ANTIQUARIAN TRADITION, THE, and COMMUNITIES AND LOCAL SOCIETIES.

parish churches. See CHURCHES, PARISH.

parish registers. In 1538 Thomas Cromwell ordered each *parish in England and Wales to keep a register of baptisms, marriages, and burials. At first the normal practice was to record such events on loose sheets, many of which have been lost or destroyed. In 1597 it was ordered that from the coming year each parish should keep a bound register and that older records should be entered into that register, the accuracy of the transcript being attested at the foot of each page by the minister and two churchwardens. Only a minority of parishes have records as far back as 1538; many parishes began their copies in 1558, the year that Elizabeth I came to the throne. The same Act of 1597 also ordered that in future a copy of all the events registered during the past year should be sent to the bishop's office. These *bishop's transcripts are now kept at diocesan *record offices. They sometimes cover gaps left by the destruction of original registers, but in general their survival rate is not as good.

Parishes varied enormously in size. Some were divided into *chapelries, which often registered some, or all, of their own events. See F. A. Youngs, Jr, *Guide to the Local Administrative Units of England* (2 vols., 1980–91), and C. Humphery-Smith (ed.), *The Phillimore Atlas and Index of Parish Registers* (2nd edn., 1994). Since 1979 (and in individual cases long before) parish registers have normally been deposited at the appropriate local record office, unless a church has adequate facilities to ensure their safe keeping. See the editorial in *Local Population Studies*, 50 (1993) on 'The Parochial Registers and Records Measure 1978, a New Guide'.

A great number of parish registers have been published, at least for their early years, sometimes privately, but more often by a county parish register society. Some counties have hundreds of registers in print, others relatively few. See the various (uncompleted) volumes of *The National Index of Parish Registers*, published by Phillimore. Local record offices commonly have a collection of registers or bishop's transcripts on microfilm. (See the INTERNATIONAL GENEALOGICAL INDEX of the Mormon Church.)

No standard form of entry was imposed on English and Welsh parish registers until Lord Hardwicke's *Marriage Act (1753) and *Rose's Act (1812). The style of entry therefore varies from place to place and over time. Often, only the barest details are given, i.e. the date of the event and the name of the person who was buried, or the names of the groom and bride, or the name of a baptized child with the name of the father. In the earliest registers this information is often recorded in simple Latin, e.g. Edwardus for Edward, or Margeria for Margery, and *baptizatus erat, nupti erat, sepultus erat* for baptized, married, and buried; *surnames are not affected by this practice. Sometimes the information is much fuller, with occupations and places of residence within the parish noted. A good run will allow the reconstruction of the occupational structure of the parish. See, for instance, David Hey, *An English Rural Community: Myddle Under the Tudors and Stuarts* (1974). Most registers have occasional gaps. The practice of some incumbents or clerks of not entering events immediately has led to their occasionally forgetting names and leaving blanks, and sometimes to their omitting events altogether. See J. T. Krause, 'The Changing Adequacy of English Registration' in D. V. Glass and D. E. C. Eversley (eds.), *Population in History* (1965), D. Levine, 'The Reliability of Parochial Registration and the Representativeness of Family Reconstitution', *Population Studies*, 30 (1976), and David Hey, *The Fiery Blades of Hallamshire: Sheffield and Its Neighbourhood, 1660–1740* (1991), App. I: 'Problems of Interpreting Registration Data'. Despite the failings of individual registers, sufficient demographic data survives in parish registers for historians to reconstruct the *population levels and trends of the nation before the *census returns of the 19th century. (See CAMPOP, and E. A. Wrigley and R. S. Schofield, *The Population History of England, 1541–1871: A Reconstruction* (1981).)

Until 1752, the custom was to begin a new year not at 1 January but at *Lady Day (25 March). The entries for each year therefore continue beyond 31 December until the following Lady Day. The normal practice (which was occasionally used at the time) is for family and local historians to note events that took place between 1 January and 25 March as, for example, 1677/8. This method of reckoning was abandoned in 1752 when Britain adopted the *Gregorian calendar, which had long been in use in the rest of Europe, in place of the old *Julian calendar, which was 11 days out by that time. The adjustment meant that 3 September 1752 was followed by 14 September. Some parish registers show that their incumbents or clerks did not quickly adapt to the new style.

Burials obviously took place within a day or two of death, but the gap between birth and baptism was often much wider. William *Camden noted that in the early 16th century baptism took place on the day of birth or the following day. The later practice was to hold the baptism ceremony within two or three days of birth, but many examples can be quoted of much longer intervals. It became the fashion in the late 17th and 18th centuries, particularly in London and amongst the *gentry, for baptismal ceremonies to be performed privately at home; these events were recorded as such in parish registers. (See MARRIAGE.)

An Act which came into force at *Michaelmas 1653 transferred responsibility for keeping the register to an elected official, known as the Parish Register [sic], though in practice the minister or clerk was often elected and the arrangements continued as before. The Act ordered the recording of births rather than baptisms, but this instruction was frequently ignored. See Dorothy McLaren, 'The Marriage Act of 1653: Its Influence on the Parish Registers', *Population Studies*, 28 (1974), and Donald Woodward, 'The Impact of the Commonwealth Act on Yorkshire Parish Registers', *Local Population Studies*, 14 (1975). Some parishes bought a new volume and the quality of the entries improved, but more often than not standards declined until the repeal of the Act upon the Restoration of Charles II in 1660.

During the later 17th and 18th centuries various attempts were made by central government or the bishops of some dioceses to improve the quality of registration. (See the MARRIAGE DUTY ACT, which was in force from 1696 to 1705.) Lord Hardwicke's Marriage Act (1753) imposed a standard form of entry for marriages, in an attempt to prevent *clandestine marriages. From the beginning of 1754 the record of marriage had to be signed by both parties and witnesses, in a bound volume of printed forms. Rose's Act (1812), which came into effect on 1 January 1813, insisted on standard entries in bound volumes for all events.

Henceforth, a baptismal entry noted the name of the child, the date of baptism, the full names of the parents, their place of residence, and the occupation of the father. Marriage entries recorded the names of both partners, their parishes, the date of the ceremony, and the names of witnesses. Burial entries noted the name and age of the deceased, his or her place of residence, and the date of the burial.

The growth of *Nonconformity in the late 18th and 19th centuries clearly affected the comprehensiveness of the Anglican registers. In earlier times, the problem was less acute, for although the *Quakers and some small sects eschewed the ceremonies of the *Church of England, other Dissenters were prepared to accept Anglican marriage and burial services and, to a lesser extent, baptism ceremonies. (See also CIVIL REGISTRATION, which began in England and Wales on 1 July 1837.)

In Scotland civil registration began in 1855. The older system of parish registration goes back to 1552, when the Church ordered baptisms and banns of marriage to be entered in a register, an order that was extended in 1565 to burials. Little was done to enforce this order, however, nor to respect the order of the Privy Council in 1616 that each parish should keep a register of baptisms, marriages, and burials. The quality of these registers was never as good as in England and Wales. The 4,000 or so registers that survive have been deposited in the Scottish General Register Office and have been microfilmed for the Mormon International Genealogical Index. They are listed in D. J. Steel (ed.), *The National Index of Parish Registers*, xii: *Sources for Scottish Genealogy and Family History* (1970).

In Ireland civil registration began in 1864. The earlier records of almost 1,000 parishes were destroyed by fire in 1922. However, transcripts survive for some parishes, and a number of original volumes are intact because they were not deposited centrally. The age of these records varies from parish to parish; in the wealthy towns a few go back to the late 17th century, but in the poor, rural districts most date only from the 19th century, when toleration allowed Catholic registers to be kept more openly. Microfilms of most Catholic registers are available at the National Library of Ireland.

park. The meaning of the word 'park' has changed considerably over time. It is derived from the *Old English *pearroc* 'an enclosed piece of land', a meaning which is retained in some *field-names. In the Middle Ages it was used exclusively for *deer park. The 18th century was the great age of landscaped parks, the 19th century of the municipal recreational park. See A. Taigel and T. Williamson, *Parks and Gardens* (1993).

The first county maps of *Saxton and *Speed mark the medieval deer parks that were still in existence in the reigns of Elizabeth I and James I. The hunting lodges that stood within them were sometimes rebuilt as country houses during this period, but other deer parks were converted into *coppice woods. Their outlines can often still be traced on the ground and on maps, or their sites identified by place-names. Some were altered out of recognition in the 18th century when landscaped parks replaced the earlier fashion for formal *gardens. (See BROWN, 'CAPABILITY' and REPTON, HUMPHRY.) The fashion that started in the 1720s was for rolling parkland, clumps of trees, and stretches of water, extending into the distance beyond a *ha-ha. The parks that surrounded the greatest country estates were adorned with classical and Gothic buildings, such as *temples, *mausolea, *obelisks, and bridges. In some cases, e.g. Milton Abbas (Dorset), entire villages were moved out of sight of the great house and rebuilt beyond the boundary of the park, which was approached by a lodge and a long, tree-lined drive. The earthworks of former *house platforms, the *holloways that were once the village streets and lanes, and the *ridge-and-furrow patterns of the former arable fields can often be seen in what is now rolling parkland. The *gentry imitated this fashion with more modest parks, enclosed by high walls and tall trees that made their halls more exclusive than in the past.

In Victorian times, local authorities and philanthropists created recreational parks with lawns, flower-beds, trees, shrubberies, pools and fountains, walks, bandstands, bowling greens, pitch-and-putt courses, tennis courts, cricket and football pitches, etc. In the 20th century many of the old landscaped parks have also been converted into recreational areas, especially into golf courses.

Parliament: the franchise. The right to vote at parliamentary elections was gradually extended by the Reform Acts of 1832, 1867, and 1884, until in 1918 all men over 21 and all women over 30 were enfranchised. In 1928 the age at which women were allowed to vote was lowered to 21. The age for both males and females was lowered to 18 in 1969. Voting was a public affair until the Secret Ballot Act (1872). See POLL BOOKS.

Parliamentary papers. The 'blue books' of the late 18th and 19th centuries, a comprehensive collection of which may be consulted at the *British Library. Reprints by the Irish Universities Press are available at major public and university *libraries. They are not always easy to trace because of their cumbersome titles and the different ways in which they are cited. See M. F. Bond, *Guide to the Records of Parliament* (1971).

The House of Commons sessional papers are the most valuable parliamentary papers for the local historian. They contain public bills; reports from committees and royal commissions; annual reports of inspectors, boards, etc.; and accounts and papers. Amongst the most useful volumes are those which enquire into particular industries, e.g. the *Report of the Select Committee on the Silk Trade* (1832), or into the employment of children and women in *factories and *coal mines; these contain a wealth of local detail. See the *Index to British Parliamentary Papers on Children's Employment* (Irish Universities Press, 1973). Other informative reports concerned *canals, charities, *churches, *education, *friendly societies, housing, *landownership, *municipal corporations, the *Poor Law, public libraries, public houses, *roads, sanitary conditions, the state of large towns, *theatres, *trade unions, etc. It has to be remembered that the recorded answers were often simple affirmatives to leading questions from commissioners who were determined reformers.

For Scotland, see J. A. Haythornthwaite, *Scotland in the Nineteenth Century: An Analytical Bibliography of Material relating to Scotland in Parliamentary Papers, 1800–1900* (1993).

parlour. A ground-floor sitting-room and bedroom, a private room beyond the main living-quarters. In many parts of Britain it remained the best bedroom into the 18th century, long after the introduction of upstairs chambers. The term is commonly found in probate *inventories. By the 19th century it had acquired the meaning of best front room.

parsonage. Most parsonages are either large Victorian houses or small modern residences, but some medieval and numerous early modern examples survive. They conform to the *vernacular styles of their locality, e.g. the vicar's *pele at Corbridge (Northumberland), or the Clergy House at Alfriston (Sussex), which is of Wealden design. See Maurice Barley, *Houses and History* (1986). *Glebe terriers from Elizabethan times onwards provide detailed information about parsonages, especially after 1660 when complete rebuilding rather than piece-meal improvements was favoured. Maurice Barley identified 62 parsons or rural parsonage houses in the *hearth tax returns for Notting-hamshire; see the account in the Introduction to W. F. Webster (ed.), *Nottinghamshire Hearth Tax, 1664: 1674* (Thoroton Society Record Series, xxxvii, 1988).

parterre. A level flower-bed in a formal *garden, especially one designed in the late 17th and early 18th centuries after French and Dutch examples.

partible inheritance. A system whereby all children, or in some cases all sons, received a share of an estate, in contrast to the system of *primogeniture. Particular types of partible inheritance included *Borough English and *gavelkind (or its Welsh equivalent *cyfran*). In Scotland and Ireland primogeniture operated unless there were no sons to inherit, in which case the estate was split between the daughters. In practice, in many areas where partible inher-itance was not formally recognized, all children nevertheless received part of the estate or (in the case of girls) a bequest of money. The system of partible inheritance led to consider-able splintering of some estates. It has been argued that this was one of the causes of the rise of rural industries as *by-employments.

passenger lists of emigrants to the colonies of the British Empire are incomplete. Most are kept in the *Public Record Office under BT 27. Some 17th-century lists survive for the ports of London, Sandwich, Southampton, Weymouth, Great Yarmouth, and Ipswich. The fullest give name, age, place of origin, occupation, and the family relationship of each passenger; but many are simply a list of names. Bristol Archives Office has a detailed register of passengers who embarked at Bristol for America between 1654 and 1679. See Peter Clark and David Souden (eds.), *Migration and Society in Early Modern England* (1987), and C. E. Banks and E. E. Brownell, *Topographical Dictionary of 2,885 English Emigrants to New England, 1620–1650* (1912).

The much greater scale of *emigration in the 19th century cannot be measured precisely by surviving passenger lists from Britain in the way that it can be done from Scandinavian coun-tries. See, however, Charlotte Erickson, 'Who Were the English and Scottish Emigrants in the 1880s?' in D. V. Glass and R. Revelle (eds.), *Population and Social Change* (1972), and 'The Use of Passenger Lists for the Study of British and Irish Immigration' in I. A. Glazier and L. De Rosa (eds.), *Migration Across Time and Distance: Population Mobility in Historical Con-text* (1986). The Fiscal Section, General Records Division, National Archives, Wash-ington DC, has lists of passengers to the United States compiled by the American Customs House between 1840 and 1870. From 1906 the Public Record Office has registers of passen-gers, under BT 32, arranged by port. Most British emigrants to America sailed from Liver-pool: see Peter Aughton, *Liverpool: A People's History* (1990).

passports. From the late 16th century to 1677 the government issued *licences to pass beyond the seas. A register of passports from 1795 onwards is kept at the *Public Record Office under FO 610. Indexes of names are available for 1851–62 and 1874–98 under FO 611. The modern type of passport with a description and photograph of the holder was introduced in 1921.

Past and Present. A quarterly journal founded in 1952, and based in Oxford, which publishes a wide variety of articles in the field of social history, dealing with countries throughout the world. A series of monographs similar in char-acter to the articles in the journal are published as *Past and Present Publications* by Cambridge University Press.

pastor. In Britain the word is used for a *Nonconformist minister.

patent. Patents are granted to individuals or companies, for new products or processes, or for improvements to existing ones. From 1617 the sovereign, *Privy Council, or Parliament granted the right to use an invention. The Patent Office for the *United Kingdom was established in 1852. The Science Reference Library (which is part of the *British Library) holds copies of all patents. The provincial pat-ent libraries also have large collections. A full list of patents granted between 1617 and the reconstruction of the patenting system in 1852 is contained in Bennet Woodcroft, *Alphabetical Index of Patentees and Inventions* (1854, reprinted 1969).

Patent rolls. The registered copies of Letters Patent issued by the Court of *Chancery from 1201 to 1946, kept at the *Public Record Office under C 66. The medieval and early modern rolls relate to much public business and to grants to individuals and corporations of land, privileges, licences, *denization, etc. They are rich in information, e.g. in James I's reign listing grants of patents and monopolies to individuals, and also excusing individuals from the operation of certain statutes. They are in

Latin up to 1733, but follow a standard form. Printed *Calendars* are available for 1216–1582 and 1584–7; those for 1509–47 are included in *Letters and Papers (Foreign and Domestic) of the Reign of Henry VIII.*

patronymic. A surname derived from a father, e.g. Robert, Roberts, Robson, Robertson.

pattern books. Local builders and other craftsmen obtained their knowledge of the latest styles through pattern books that were published in France, Italy, the Netherlands, etc. and in Britain from the 16th to the 19th centuries. Art historians have done much scholarly work in tracing influences derived in this way in the early modern period when Renaissance designs were imported directly from Italy, or via France and the Low Countries.

pavilions. The term had a specialist meaning in the 18th century to denote the balancing wings of a country house, which were sometimes one-storey structures containing a chapel and a library. They were much favoured, for instance, by the *Palladian architect James Paine.

pays. Joan Thirsk's work on fenland farming, rural industries, and the farming regions that she described in *The *Agrarian History of England and Wales,* iv: *1500–1640* (1957) offered a framework of explanation of social and economic development that was focused on distinctive countrysides, best described by the French word *pays.* The idea that such areas were not simply united by farming methods and specialities suited to the local soils and topography but had common social and economic features was developed by Alan Everitt in *The Pattern of Rural Dissent* (1971), and in essays subsequently collected in *Landscape and Community in England* (1985). Joan Thirsk's articles were collected together in *The Rural Economy of England* (1984).

This new emphasis shifted attention away from the country as a unit of study to its component parts. It stressed the value of studying comparative *pays* in other parts of the country and of identifying the nature of a particular *pays* by contrasting its history with that of its immediate neighbours. Thus, a study of the Weald would benefit by comparison with other woodland areas in Britain as well as by contrast with the marshes, downs, etc. nearby. A particular benefit of this approach was that it shifted attention away from *open-field England and brought out the significance of the pastoral areas, which previously had been largely neglected.

Although it was recognized that *pays* under-went change, studies have stressed the long continuity of major characteristics such as farming systems, land-ownership and manorial control, social structure, rural industries, and religious and political attitudes. Everitt's *Continuity and Colonization: The Evolution of Kentish Settlement* (1986) emphasizes the importance of patterns established in the earliest stages of settlement. His essay 'The Primary Towns of England' (in *Landscape and Community in England,* 1985) showed how distinctive urban features that were acquired at a very early period could influence the character and development of a town such as Banbury up to the present day.

The value of this approach was immediately recognized by agrarian historians and historical geographers and has remained influential.

peas were formerly grown as a fodder-crop for animals as well as for human consumption. They were sown with beans as a major crop in *open-fields during January and February. In clay districts such as Leicestershire an entire open-field was often devoted to peas and beans; in other places they were grown alongside a crop of oats. About a million acres of land in England and Wales was devoted to peas and beans in the late 18th century, especially in the midland shires. The canning of processed peas by such firms as Batchelors of Sheffield began in the inter-war period of the 20th century.

peasants. In France *paysan* is used to denote a small farmer, but in Britain the term has acquired derogatory connotations. The word was never in widespread use in the English language and some historians argue that the tenants of small family farms were very different from the peasants of continental Europe. Medieval historians still find the term an appropriate one, but early modern historians prefer the contemporary terms *husbandman and *yeoman. See J. M. Neeson, *Commoners: Common Right, Enclosure and Social Change in England, 1700–1820* (1993).

Peasants' Revolt (1381). The major uprising of the Middle Ages, also known as the English Rising, for it occurred in towns as well as in the countryside. The main area of revolt was southern and eastern England, i.e. the wealthiest parts of the country. It was sparked off by protest at the levying of a *poll tax in Essex and soon spread to Kent. The rebels marched on London, where they were joined by others from Surrey and Sussex. They pillaged *manor houses and *palaces and opened gaols. King Richard II conceded their demands and granted a free pardon to all the rebels, some of whom remained in London, where they burnt much property and murdered many Flemish immigrants. The authorities subsequently regained control and executed the leaders of the revolt. The names of John Ball, Jack Straw, and Wat Tyler have passed into communal memory for their part in leading the rising. See K. Webber, *The Peasants' Revolt* (1980), and R. H. Hilton and T. H. Aston (eds.), *The English Rising of 1381* (1984).

peat is formed by the pressure of the accumulated remains of centuries of dead plants. It varies in depth from one or two inches to many feet, on highland *moors and lowland *fens and bogs. Pollen analysis has shown that peat has often replaced earlier woodland, during periods which range from the prehistoric to the post-Roman. The digging of peat or turf for fuel was a common right on *manors with large moors or bogs. It was dug with spades that varied in type from one region to another to form pieces the size of bricks, which were then stacked to dry and brought home on a simple cart or sledge. See the illustration in George Walker, *The Costume of Yorkshire* (1814). Although its principal use was as domestic fuel, it was sometimes used in industrial kilns. Peat was often transported many miles along navigable rivers to towns and cities. The owners of medieval estates, including monastic ones, exploited their resources on a large scale. The Norfolk Broads were created when old pits from which huge quantities of peat had been extracted were flooded in the later Middle Ages.

Peat remained into the 20th century the principal domestic fuel in Ireland, the Highlands and Islands of Scotland, and those parts of England and Wales that had plentiful local supplies and which were located well away from the coalfields. In many places it continues in use to this day. A different demand for peat was at its height in the Victorian and Edwardian era, when it was used as bedding material for *horses. By 1889 a colony of about 100 Dutchmen had settled at Thorne Moorends (Yorkshire), bringing technical skills to exploit the peat deposits. In 1896 five companies amalgamated to form the British Peat Moss Litter Company. With the large-scale replacement of the horse by motor vehicles after the First World War demand declined, but a new demand grew for peat as a fertilizer. A desire to conserve both lowland and upland deposits of peat has grown in the later 20th century.

peculiar jurisdiction. For a variety of reasons, certain *parishes, *manors, and *liberties were exempt from the jurisdiction of the bishop and archdeacon in whose *diocese and *archdeaconry they were situated. They include the separate or 'peculiar' jurisdictions of another archbishop or bishop, the *dean and *chapter of a cathedral, the Knights *Templar and Knights *Hospitaller, and of chapels royal, e.g. St George's, Windsor. One such parish was Masham (Yorkshire), where Theakston's brewery produces the distinctive beer known as 'Old Peculier' (*sic*). A knowledge of such jurisdictions is necessary when searching for *wills and probate *inventories before 1858, when the state assumed responsibility for proving wills. In practice, the records of most peculiars are found in diocesan *record offices alongside those that were proved through the archdeaconry courts; but in some cases, e.g. when a manor of the Knights Templar passed to lay ownership, they are amongst manorial records in county record offices. Peculiar jurisdictions are mapped in C. Humphery-Smith, *The Phillimore Atlas and Index of Parish Registers* (2nd edn., 1994). Apart from the royal peculiars, most are now subject to the jurisdiction of the diocesan bishops.

pedigree. A genealogical table. The first collections of pedigrees were made in the 15th century. Pedigrees were a matter of aristocratic pride and of practical necessity for legal purposes. In the reigns of Elizabeth I, James I, and Charles I they were often displayed as colourful works of art.

pedlar. In the early modern period pedlars provided a distribution system that connected all parts of Britain. The character of Autolycus in Shakespeare's *The Winter's Tale* must have been familiar to audiences in the early 17th century. Various government attempts at a licensing system met with only partial success. Pedlars sold *ribbons, gloves, *lace, tape, points, *pins, thread, looking-glasses, necklaces, bracelets, brooches, hats, *ballads, *chapbooks, etc. See Margaret Spufford, *Small Books and Pleasant Histories: Popular Fiction and Its Readership in Seventeenth-Century England* (1981), and *The Great Reclothing of Rural England; Petty Chapmen and Their Wares in the Seventeenth Century* (1984).

pele-towers. Characteristic *tower houses found on both sides of the Scottish border, dating from the 14th to the 17th century, by which the typical arrangement of service-rooms, living-quarters, and bedrooms was expressed vertically rather than horizontally. Such buildings afforded short-term defence against marauders. They had thick walls, narrow windows, and crenellated roof-lines. Many were extended and adapted in more peaceful times, e.g. the vicar's pele at Houghton-le-Spring (County Durham). See H. G. Ramm *et al.*, *Shielings and Bastles* (1970).

penance. Primarily, one of the seven sacraments of the Church, by which sinners were reconciled to God and the Church. Secondarily, penance consists of the efforts of the sinner to make reparation for the sins forgiven—hence 'doing penance'. Thirdly and popularly, penance consists of the works of penance imposed upon the repentant sinner by the Church, e.g. the repetition of Paternosters and Ave Marias, almsgiving, pilgrimage, and personal austerity such as fasting and flagellation. Fourthly and by transference, penance consists of the sentences and penalties imposed by *ecclesiastical courts. At the *Reformation, penance was rejected as a sacrament by the Reformed Churches and the efficacy of good works denied; instead of having works of penance imposed, the guilty person was ordered to stand in the presence of the congregation at church, dressed in a white sheet, bare-headed, bare-legged, and bare-foot, carrying a wand, and to confess the fault, express penitence, and pray for forgiveness. The minister and churchwardens signed a certificate, which was sent to the bishop's office, to say that the penance had been performed. These certificates are kept at diocesan record offices. The practice fell into disuse in the later 17th century.

pence. Silver pennies were first minted in the 8th century, when they were known as *deniers* after the Roman *denarii*, hence the abbreviation *d*. Twelve old pence made one shilling, twenty shillings made one pound. Pence were often counted (and written down) in amounts up to two shillings, e.g. as 16*d.* or 20*d.* See COINAGE.

pens. The quill pen that was used until the 19th century was made from a goose feather, shaped by a penknife to form a nib. Metal nibs were first made in the mid-19th century and fountain pens from the end of the century. Penknives and pocket-knives with a spring became a speciality of Sheffield cutlers in Elizabeth I's reign. In *Writing Schoolmaster* (1590) Peter Bales advised: 'First, therefore, be the choice of your penknife, a right Sheffield knife is best.'

peppercorn rent. A nominal rent acknowledging the tenancy.

Pepys, Samuel (1633–1703). Best known for his famous diary of the 1660s, now handsomely edited by R. Latham and W. Matthews, 10 vols. (1970–83), Pepys was an outstanding administrator at the Navy Office and in 1684 was President of the *Royal Society. See Richard Ollard, *Pepys: A Biography* (1991 edn.). His collection of cheap books and *ballads (in the Pepys Library, Magdalene College, Cambridge) was used by Margaret Spufford in *Small Books and Pleasant Histories: Popular Fiction and Its Readership in Seventeenth-Century England* (1981).

perambulations. Until the *Ordnance Survey published large-scale maps which marked the *boundaries of *parishes, it was a common practice at *Rogationtide for groups of parishioners to walk their boundaries and to mark stones and trees. The *rector or *vicar usually led the perambulation and prayers were said at various points, which were commemorated by names such as Gospel Oak. In large parishes the perambulation was spread over a few days. In disputed areas, e.g. moorland, perambulations were sometimes also made of the boundaries of *manors. A number of written accounts of such perambulations have survived in manorial records, dating from the 16th to the 18th centuries, which record each boundary point in turn. These boundaries were sometimes disputed by neighbouring parishes, *townships, or manors. Written records of perambulations can be used to follow old boundaries on the ground.

perch. A square measure. 40 perches made one *rood (a quarter of an *acre). Old *maps and *surveys express measurements in the form of, e.g., '7 a[cres]. 3 r[oods]. 21 p[erches]'.

Perpendicular architecture. The last of the *Gothic styles of the Middle Ages and the only one to be peculiarly English. The east window of Gloucester Cathedral is an early example, predating the *Black Death. The style remained popular for another 200 years, until the *Reformation. It is distinguished by the straight mullions of the windows, by ranges of clerestorey windows surmounted by battlements and pinnacles, and by splendid *towers. See J. H. Harvey, *The Perpendicular Style, 1330–1485* (1978).

perpetual curate. A priest who was nominated by a lay *rector, and licensed by a bishop, to serve a *parish which did not have a *vicar. Once appointed, such a curate had lifelong tenure.

personalty. Personal estate that, under common law, did not pass to the heir upon the death of an owner but could be bequeathed by a *will.

petty sessions. Courts of summary jurisdiction held by two or more *Justices of the Peace or magistrates for trying lesser offences or to enquire into indictable offences. The proceedings of the 17th and 18th centuries are not well recorded. They are now sittings of magistrates' courts.

Pevsner, Sir Nikolaus (1902–83). Architectural historian. He emigrated from Germany to Britain when Hitler came to power. His *Pioneers of Modern Design* (1936) and *An Outline of European Architecture* (1942) were widely admired. He was Slade Professor of Fine Art at Cambridge, 1949–55, gave the Reith Lectures on the Englishness of English Art in 1955, and was knighted in 1969. His monumental series of county volumes on *The Buildings of England*, which was published between 1951 and 1974, changed public attitudes to historical buildings and inspired local historians to study the buildings of their localities with new understanding. The series has been revised and remains the starting-point for local studies and the appreciation of England's built environment.

pews were not widely used in the early Middle Ages, when most people stood during church services, or squatted on the floor. The 'weak went to the wall' to sit on a stone bench, such as that which survives in the *nave at Gaddesby (Leicestershire). Wooden benches were introduced into English churches during the 14th century. They became widespread during the 15th century, though they occupied only part of the available space. East Anglia and southwestern England have many fine examples, with carved *bench ends and backs, culminating in a poppy-head. The churches of Norfolk and Suffolk, and those of Somerset and Devon, have over a thousand each. Their comfort does not match their beauty. See Alec Clifton-Taylor, *English Parish Churches as Works of Art* (1974).

During the 17th century it became the fashion to fill the nave of a parish *church with box-pews. In rural parishes, in particular, the ownership of these pews passed with that of the farm or *cottage to which it belonged. The arrangement of the pews reflected the social structure of the parish, with the rich at the front, the middling sort in the centre, and the poor at the sides and the back. See Richard Gough, *The History of Myddle* (ed. David Hey, 1981). In corporate towns the mayor and corporation occupied the best pews. During the 18th century many churches became crammed with pews and galleries. Most of these were replaced during the Victorian period by new pews, usually made of pitch pine. Surviving Georgian interiors are catalogued, described, and illustrated in Mark Chatfield, *Churches the Victorians Forgot* (1979).

pewter. An alloy of *tin, *lead, and *brass, which was cast in moulds, then turned and hammered. Pewter goods were made in ancient times, e.g. by the Romans. From the early 14th to the 18th century pewter was widely used in Britain for plates, mugs, tankards, etc. The craft expanded enormously in the Tudor and Stuart era and was at its height in the late 17th century. Pewter was commonly recorded in probate *inventories, where it was often valued simply by its weight. The London *guild of pewterers was founded in 1348, but elsewhere the trade is poorly documented. It is known to have been widespread, especially in cities such as York and Bristol, and in smaller towns, notably Wigan, but as pewter was reused as scrap, it is rarely found in excavations. See John Hatcher and T. C. Barker, *A History of British Pewter* (1974).

pheasant shooting was a minority sport of the rich which became organized in a big way during the reign of Victoria. Thus, the game book of a Norfolk estate records that 39 pheasants were shot in 1821 and that 5,069 were shot in 1875. The rearing of pheasants made *landowners more concerned about stopping rights of way and preventing *poaching. It was a major cause of tension in the countryside. See GAME LAWS.

photographs. Photography was invented independently in France and England in the first half of the 19th century. Photographs become a major source of information for local and family historians in many parts of Britain in the 1840s and 1850s. Many places had their early enthusiasts who have left invaluable records. Most public reference *libraries or *museums have large collections of local photographs. For example, the *Rural History Centre at Reading has an important collection on rural life.

Many old photographs are undated, and few of those collected in family albums have been identified for future generations. Changing fashions, both in dress and in poses adopted for the photograph, help in dating. Photographers were listed in trade and commercial *directories, and as businesses often did not last very long, a photograph that bears the photographer's name might be dated within narrow limits from this source. See Don Steel and Lawrence Taylor, *Family History in Focus*

(1984), Robert Pols, *Dating Old Photographs* (1992), and George Oliver, *Using Old Photographs: A Guide for the Local Historian* (1989).

Old photographs need to be interpreted with caution. They are rarely accompanied with supporting evidence on why and when they were taken. Early photographers were attracted by unusual activities and by rare survivals of old costumes, crafts, and pastimes which were no longer typical of the time. It is necessary to distinguish between what was merely curious and what was commonplace. Even photographs which were consciously posed add a new dimension to local and family studies, however. Outstanding collections, such as those of Whitby and adjoining parts of north Yorkshire, which are published in Bill Eglon Shaw, *Frank Meadow Sutcliffe* (3 vols., 1974–90), provide vivid images that no other source can rival in the study of ordinary people and local places. Many local history societies and individual local historians have published collections of photographs of local scenes, some of them contrasted with modern views. Informative captions add a great deal to these images. See also AERIAL ARCHAEOLOGY and POSTCARDS.

Picts. During the *Roman occupation of Britain the *Picti* were hostile tribes north of the *Antonine wall. They were assimilated with the Scots in the 9th century.

piece halls. The *clothiers of the West Riding of Yorkshire brought their finished pieces of cloth to market at the close of each week. During the 18th century several clothing towns built halls to protect sellers and buyers from bad weather. Halifax had a piece hall by 1708, Wakefield by 1710, and Leeds by 1711. Much larger structures were built in the second half of the 18th century. The outstanding surviving example is the Halifax Piece Hall of 1779, which has 315 rooms arranged around a large central square.

piece work. The system by which a worker was paid by the 'piece', or finished good, rather than by a regular wage.

Piepoudre, Court of. Especially in the Middle Ages, the court by which the owner of the right to hold a *market or *fair settled disputes, regulated measures, and maintained order. The name came from French words for 'dusty feet' (Anglicized as 'pie powder') because they were frequented by *chapmen who travelled from fair to fair.

Piers Plowman. The great Middle English poem written by William Langland in the late 1370s, which *inter alia* provides much information about medieval agriculture.

pightle. A small, irregular shaped piece of land, usually at the edge of cultivation. The word was corrupted into various forms, e.g. pingle.

pigs. Many farmers throughout the ages have kept a pig or two, provided there was enough waste to scavenge. The value of the family pig, and the use to which every part of the animal was put, is vividly described in Flora Thompson, *Lark Rise to Candleford* (1945), an account of an Oxfordshire hamlet in the 1880s. Scavenging pigs were also a common sight in towns. In woodland areas the common right of *pannage allowed pigs to feed on acorns and beech mast (both unreliable crops, but highly valued for fattening in good years), in *dairying regions they fed on whey, and in arable zones on grain and pulses. Pork, ham, and bacon were an important ingredient of both the countryman's and the townsman's *diet.

Because pigs were kept on a domestic basis improved breeds did not appear as quickly as with *cattle, *sheep, and *horses. The chief improvements were made in the third quarter of the 18th century. Breeds such as the Tamworth or the Wessex Saddleback were developed as regional types, but a few, e.g. the Berkshire and the Large White, became widely used at this time. Cross-breeding with foreign (e.g. Neapolitan and Chinese) pigs has occurred, but is not well documented.

pilgrim. In the Middle Ages large numbers of people went on pilgrimages to *shrines at least once in their life. The motivation was religious, and pilgrimage was often prescribed as a *penance, but the event also served as a *holiday. Some pilgrims went all the way to the Holy Land, or to the shrine of St James at Santiago de Compostela in north-west Spain. The most famous shrines in the British Isles were those of St Thomas Becket at Canterbury and Our Lady of Walsingham (Norfolk). (See also HOLY WELL.) The suppression of shrines and relics at the *Reformation led to a considerable decline in pilgrimages. See Ronald C. Finucane, *Miracles and Pilgrims* (1977).

Pilgrimage of Grace (1536). A rebellion that began in Lincolnshire and the East Riding of Yorkshire and which quickly spread to other parts of the country. It was sparked off by opposition to the *dissolution of the monasteries, but its underlying causes were high prices and resentment directed against certain landlords. Commanded by Robert Aske, an army marched south from York, wearing badges that symbolized the Five Wounds of the Crucified Christ. At Doncaster the Duke of Norfolk, acting on the King's behalf, promised that their grievances would be discussed at a Parliament to be held in York. Upon hearing this assurance the rebels returned home. Further troubles gave Henry VIII an excuse to break his promise, and within a few months 200 of the rebels were executed.

The standard account remains M. H. Dodds and R. Dodds, *The Pilgrimage of Grace (1536–37) and the Exeter Conspiracy (1538)* (2 vols., 1915). Recent work has emphasized that the revolt started and ended as a series of regional uprisings and therefore needs to be studied on a regional basis. See M. L. Bush, 'The Richmondshire Uprising of October 1536 and the Pilgrimage of Grace', *Northern History*, 29 (1993).

pillboxes. In 1940 thousands of small concrete defences, from which Bren machine guns could be fired on all sides, were built under the threat of German invasion. Most were positioned so as to protect a coast, but some can be found in the most unlikely situations, e.g. on a hillside north of Grasmere (Cumbria).

pillory. Whereas the *stocks fastened an offender by the legs, the pillory secured a standing person by the neck and arms, thus leaving him vulnerable to objects thrown by spectators. Pillories stood in *market places and offenders were placed there by order of the *Justices of the Peace. The pillory was abolished in 1837.

pillow mounds. Long, raised banks of soft earth with artificial burrows were deliberately created for *rabbits by the keepers of *warrens, especially in the 16th century. They survive as earthworks which once puzzled archaeologists. See John Sheail, *Rabbits and Their History* (1971).

pinder. The manorial officer in charge of the *pinfold.

pineapples. The fruit was introduced from central and south America in the early 18th century. The 'pineapples' used in decorative carving in the 17th century were based on the cones of pine trees.

pinfold. A pound in which stray animals were locked. Manorial *court records record fines

and disputes. Surviving examples are usually at the edges of villages or by village greens; others are commemorated by minor place-names. As surviving features in the landscape, they are worthy of notice. See Philip Lyth, *The Pinfolds of Nottinghamshire: A Gazetteer* (1992).

pin-making. Pins made of iron had been made in Britain in the Middle Ages, but most pins were imported from the Netherlands. The government policy of encouraging domestic production so as to reduce the cost of imports led to the manufacture of brass pins in the third quarter of the 16th century. By the 1620s the industry was flourishing in Gloucestershire and London, in *workhouses such as that in Salisbury, and in small places such as Aberford (Yorkshire). At first, brass wire was imported from Sweden and Germany, but following a ban on imports in 1662 the home industry developed quickly. Brass plates were cut into strips, then drawn into wire, cut into pin-lengths, and ground. The heads were formed by two turns of wire, which were annealed and fitted to the shank, then finished by turning. See Joan Thirsk, *Economic Policy and Projects: The Development of A Consumer Society in Early Modern England* (1978). For the later history of the industry, see S. R. H. Jones, 'Price-Associations and Competition in the British Pin Industry, 1814–40', *Economic History Review*, 2nd ser., 26/2 (1973).

Pipe Rolls. The annual accounts of Crown revenues, which were sent by *sheriffs to the *Exchequer, where they were rolled around rods ('pipes') for storage. They are now housed in the *Public Record Office under E 372. They survive from 1130–1, with an almost continuous series from 1155–6 until 1832. Some have been published by the Pipe Roll Society.

piscary, right of. The common right to fish in the pools, etc. of a *manor.

piscina. The stone basin in which a priest washed his hands and the vessels after mass. They are normally set in the wall to the south of an *altar.

place-names. From the beginning of English historical writing authors have shown interest in the meaning of place-names. The Venerable *Bede sometimes renders *Old English names correctly into Latin (as *Insula uituli marini* for Selsey), but in many instances he displays the tendency shared by many modern philologists to rely overmuch on eponymous persons, as in his conjecture of a chieftain called *Hrof* to explain *Hrofesceaster* (modern Rochester). This tendency is even more marked in the men who compiled the *Anglo-Saxon Chronicle* in the late 9th century. They inferred the existence of chieftains such as *Port* from place-names like Portsmouth which do not contain personal names, and assigned to them roles in the conquest of southern Britain. In early times in Ireland place-name lore, or *dinnseanchas*, was a recognized branch of learning, but it was related to literature rather than to history, and it consisted of highly fanciful etymologies. In early medieval society there was probably so great a gap between the preoccupations of learned men and those of the peasant farmers among whom place-names arose that the conjectures of the former were bound to be wide of the mark.

Medieval chroniclers continued the tradition of occasional, random comments on place-names, and the great *antiquarian writers of the 16th and 17th centuries offer etymologies which vary between the sensible, frequently correct observations of *Dugdale on Warwickshire names and the totally fanciful, such as *Leland's reported explanation of Maidenhead in terms of 'a Hedde that they sayd was one of the xi thousand Virgines'. *Camden's frequent etymologies are occasionally lucky (as 'sheep island' for Sheppey), but mostly impossible. The place-name spellings offered by Leland and *Ogilby are particularly valuable because they represent spoken forms with little influence from earlier written ones.

The systematic study of English place-names has its origins in the late 19th century, when the potential value of the material attracted the attention of eminent historians and philologists. The honour of being considered the founding father of the discipline has sometimes been accorded to W. W. Skeat, but others, such as the philologist H. Bradley and the historian J. H. *Round, were also interested at this time in the application of 'scientific' method to the elucidation of place-names. The 'scientific' basis of the study was perceived to be the collection and examination of early spellings from all surviving written records; and this principle remains the fundamental one as regards English names, though in Celtic-speaking countries, where oral traditions are more reliable, the careful recording of local pronunciations is also important.

In 1899 J. H. Round published a plea for the study of English place-names county by county, a project which was taken up in 1922 by the institution of the Survey of English Place-Names. The following year saw the founding of the *English Place-Name Society, the object of which was to raise funding from subscribers for the production of a series of county volumes. These developments arose from the collaboration of a number of philologists and historians, most notably A. Mawer (the first Director of the Survey) and F. M. *Stenton. These two scholars were joint editors of the county surveys until Mawer's death in 1942. The Directorship of the Survey was held by Stenton till 1946, by B. Dickins till 1952, by A. H. Smith till 1967, by K. Cameron till 1993, and subsequently by V. Watts. The headquarters of the Survey was moved to Nottingham when Cameron became Director, and it remains in the English Department of that university. The work is funded by an annual grant from the British Academy, the subscriptions of members, and the sale of back volumes.

By 1922 the study of English place-names had attracted the attention of Swedish philologists, and their contributions, particularly those of E. *Ekwall, were of the utmost importance in the development of the subject. From 1922 up to the period of the Second World War the study took two main forms: the production of an annual English Place-Name Society regional volume, and the publication of Ekwall's great dictionaries, *The Concise Oxford Dictionary of English Place-Names* (1935, 4th edn. 1960) and *English River-Names* (1928). There were regional surveys by Swedish scholars (such as Ekwall's of Lancashire (1922), H. Kökeritz's of the Isle of Wight (1940), and K. Wallenberg's of Kent (1931, 1934), a great many papers in learned journals, and some important monographs on particular aspects, such as E. Tengstrand's *A Contribution to the Study of Genitival Composition in Old English Place-Names* (1942). During these years the basic assumptions of the founders of the English Place-Name Survey about the interpretation and significance of the material were seldom examined or questioned.

Production of the EPNS volumes ground to a halt in 1943, after the death of Sir Allen Mawer, and it was not until 1950 that the series was resumed with the publication of two volumes on Cumberland. The pause allowed space for reflection, and the series was seen to be deficient in two main respects. Insufficient use had been made of medieval records not available in printed editions or calendars, and insufficient attention had been paid to what were loosely designated 'field-names', i.e. names which occurred in documents but which could not be identified with items on Ordnance

Survey maps. The rectification of these deficiencies has caused post-Second World War volumes to be substantially different from earlier ones. It has also lengthened enormously the time required for the production of a county survey, to the extent that a large county in several volumes may now be considered an adequate life's work for a single scholar.

The less detailed pre-war surveys cover the counties of Bedfordshire, Buckinghamshire, Cambridgeshire, Devon, Essex, Hertfordshire, Huntingdonshire, Middlesex, Northamptonshire, Nottinghamshire, Surrey, Sussex, Warwickshire, Wiltshire, Worcestershire, and the East and North Ridings of Yorkshire. Post-war volumes deal with Berkshire, Cheshire, Cumberland, Derbyshire, Gloucestershire, Oxfordshire, Rutland, the West Riding, and Westmorland, and with parts of Dorset, Lincolnshire, Norfolk, Shropshire, and Staffordshire.

In addition to major changes in the scope of the county volumes, the post-war period saw the emergence of works of synthesis based on the enormous quantity of material which had been made available by English and Swedish scholars. In the 1960s and 1970s place-name studies were dramatically affected by the growth of interdisciplinary approaches to historical matters, and by changing currents in historical thinking. Particularly important were the conflicting opinions about the number of Anglo-Saxons who came to Britain in the 5th century, and the relationship of Anglo-Saxon settlement and administrative patterns to earlier ones.

Attempts to discern the course of events in Britain after the withdrawal of Roman government must take into account the evidence of place-names together with that of archaeology and historical records. Arguments about the ethnic composition of the English nation (to what extent Welsh, Anglo-Saxon, Viking) must also draw on place-names. The scholars who collaborated in the foundation of the English Place-Name Survey in 1922 were hoping for information on these topics, but it is perhaps fair to say that they were mainly looking for confirmation of views already formulated. There was little challenge to the 'clean-sweep' theory regarding the events of the *Dark Ages, by which it was assumed that the post-Roman inhabitants of most of England were numerically overwhelmed and politically subjugated by large numbers of immigrant Germanic people, and that the continuous history of England began with this immigration. Scientific place-name study rendered the most extreme 19th-century assumptions about the Anglo-Saxon conquest of Britain untenable, but the result was a modification rather than a total rejection of the earlier view. The most influential of the scholars who were involved in the use of place-name evidence before the 1960s were deeply committed to the 'clean-sweep' theory, and argued strongly that the replacement of most of the British place-names by English ones supported this. Because of the survival of some place-names which are in the British language it was recognized that some people who spoke the post-Roman form of that language must have coexisted with immigrants speaking the Germanic tongue which philologists call Old English; but Stenton and other historians and philologists, such as Dorothy Whitelock, underestimated the evidence provided by these names for continuity of settlement patterns. They stressed that British names adopted by English speakers were mostly those of rivers, hills, and forests, and that they contained no references to settlements. They failed to notice that the British names recorded from Roman Britain show that British people did not employ the equivalent of English names like Reading, Didcot, Birmingham, for British settlement-names were mostly derived from rivers or hills. Settlements such as Malvern, Penn, and Thame are likely to have had these names continuously from pre-English times. Some rivers with pre-English names, such as the Devon Clyst and the Gloucestershire Colne, have series of villages on their banks which are named from the river. Some names of proven pre-English origin, such as Penkridge, Staffordshire, from the Romano-British *Pennocrucium*, became the names of large, composite medieval estates. It is perverse to assume that all that was passed on to the English was the name of the hill or river and to deny the likely continuity of the pre-English settlement patterns at such places.

Place-name scholars of the generations which followed those of Stenton and Whitelock have worked conscientiously at the identification of pre-English names and at the evaluation of place-name evidence for the presence of British people and their institutions in the kingdoms of Anglo-Saxon England. There have been studies of English names which refer to Welsh people by the term *Walh* 'foreigner' (the plural is *Walas* and the adjective *Welisc*, hence Wales and Welsh), and attention has also been drawn to those, like Comberton and Comberford, which use the politer term *Cumbre*, adapted from Welsh. There have been studies of names containing *ecles*, which are considered to refer to Celtic Christian communities encountered by pagan Anglo-Saxons, and of the use of words derived from Latin. It has been shown that in Old English *wīchām* (modern Wickham, Wykeham etc.) the word *wīc* is used in a sense closely related to the Latin *vicus* from which it derives.

Philologists can now accept a greater degree of continuity than was conceded by Stenton and Whitelock, but the evidence of place-names nevertheless remains the main bulwark of argument against the opposite of the Stenton–Whitelock view. According to their opponents there was no Anglo-Saxon immigration, only a political take-over by a small new élite. Attempts by anti-immigrationists to explain away the overwhelmingly Old English nature of the name-stock which became established after the Roman period include the perennial suggestion that names which appear to be Old English are really adaptations of British ones which the Anglo-Saxons could not pronounce, and (more recently) a suggestion that the majority of settlements changed their sites in the 7th or 8th centuries and the new villages were named in English, that language having by then been adopted by people of British descent because of its social prestige. Neither argument will bear critical examination. There is no doubt that the place-names of most of England are overwhelmingly English, and this supports belief in the presence of a large number of Anglo-Saxon farmers. The change of name-stock happened, however, not only in the eastern half of England, where archaeology attests a large Anglo-Saxon presence in the early post-Roman centuries, but also in counties like Devon and Shropshire, where there is no pagan Anglo-Saxon archaeology, and where numerical swamping is highly unlikely. The place-names of Shropshire have recently been examined in detail, and it has been suggested that a clue to the change may lie in the extraordinary degree of repetition of some recurrent names ending in the commonest Old English place-name element *tūn* 'farm, estate'. Shropshire has ten Astons, eight Westons, seven Nortons, and eight Suttons, and there are five Uptons, four Middletons, and ten Newtons. Acton ('oak estate') occurs eight times, Eaton ('river estate') six, and Eyton ('island settlement') five. There are four instances of Hatton, Mor(e)ton, and Wootton (referring to heath, marsh, and wood). There are five Prestons (estates from which the revenues were devoted to the upkeep of a group of priests). Such names could have originated in the speech of Mercian administrators, who formed the habit of saying a settlement was the *ēa-tūn* of a particular composite estate (meaning, perhaps, that it provided a ferry), or the *prēosta tūn* of a minster church. Such appellatives might gradually come to be perceived as place-names, and so oust earlier British names.

The argument about the bearing of place-name evidence on the ethnic composition of the English nation continues and will continue. Place-names cannot provide universally acceptable answers to these intransigent problems, but the necessity for their evidence to be taken into account is one of the factors which have secured the subject a niche in academic life.

A similar long-running dispute concerns place-names of later origin which are in the language of the Danish and Norwegian Vikings whose incursions disrupted English history in the 9th and 10th centuries. Very important work by Kenneth Cameron has shown that the frequency of these names in some areas and the siting of the settlements to which they refer support the hypothesis of a peasant immigration from Denmark, made possible by the political control of parts of eastern England by Danish armies. The Danish equivalent of Old English *tūn* was *bý*, and the extraordinary line of -by names (Ferriby, Saxby, Bonby, Worlaby, Barnetby, Bigby, Somerby, Searby, Owmby, Grasby, Clixby, Audleby, Fonaby, Normanby, Claxby, Otby, Walesby, Rigby, Tealby) which runs along the western edge of the Lincolnshire Wolds, interspersed with sparse English names (Horkstow, Elsham, Caistor, Nettleton) can reasonably be seen as indicative of new settlements by Scandinavian speakers on land not fully exploited by the English. The climatically and geologically more comfortable area on the eastern side of the Wolds is occupied by villages which, with very few exceptions, have English names. Particularly telling for the hypothesis which equates Danish place-names with Danish immigration is the field-name material set out by Cameron in his volume on the Lincolnshire *wapentake of Yarborough (English Place-Name Society 64/65). In this part of Lincolnshire there are parishes in which a half or more of the *field-names in use in the 12th and 13th centuries are Scandinavian. Like the dispute over the likely number of post-Roman Anglo-Saxon immigrants, the argument over the relationship of Scandinavian place-names to Scandinavian settlement has become a perennial feature of early medieval studies, and there are wide divergences of opinion among historians and philologists.

With regard to the equation of place-names in a given language with immigration by people speaking that language, modern place-name studies are not totally at odds with the views expressed in the 1920s. There is, however, another aspect of early English history which the founders of the Survey considered capable of elucidation by place-name evidence, but on which their views have been almost totally rejected in more recent studies.

Historians of the Stenton generation were much interested in the chronology of the Anglo-Saxon settlement, and they believed that it was possible to identify place-names of certain types which could be plotted on maps and presented as the earliest sites occupied by the English. As the work of the Survey proceeded, however, it became increasingly apparent that many of the names highlighted by these scholars were in improbable situations for early settlements, and that there were serious discrepancies between their distribution and that of the sites where the earliest Anglo-Saxon archaeological material was found.

The first supposedly 'early' names to be subjected to critical examination were those which were considered to indicate sites of pagan religious practices. There are names which contain words (*hearg*, *wēoh*) which can be rendered 'heathen shrine', and others which contain names of the gods *Wōden* (*Wēden*), *Thunor*, *Tīw* and the goddess *Frīg*. In 1941 Stenton claimed to have found between 50 and 60 such names and predicted that more would come to light as the work of the Survey proceeded. This prediction was not fulfilled, however, and critical examinations of the Stenton corpus in 1960 and 1973 suggested that alternative etymologies were more likely for some of Stenton's examples. The distribution pattern of the items in the remaining corpus of about 40 names was shown to be incompatible with the claim that they indicated early Anglo-Saxon settlement, and it was suggested that they are more likely to indicate late conversion to Christianity. References to heathen practices would be particularly meaningful when they occurred in enclaves of resistance to the slow spread of Christianity in the 7th and 8th centuries. The cluster which surrounds Farnham in Surrey may be instanced. Here are Willey (which can be rendered 'sacred grove'), Thursley ('Thunor's grove') and Peper Harrow ('heathen temple of the pipers'). A monastery was founded at Farnham *c.*685, and the foundation charter mentions two more places with significant names, *Cusanweoh* ('heathen temple of Cusa') and *Besingahearh* ('heathen temple of the followers of Besa'), which were obviously in the vicinity. This wooded area, in land disputed by the kingdoms of Kent and *Wessex, is more likely to have seen late paganism than early settlement, and the monastery may have been placed there on that account.

The major upheaval in assumptions about 'early' English place-names was the challenge issued in 1966 by J. McN. Dodgson to the belief that names like Reading and Hastings (originally folk-names, 'followers of Rēad / Hæsta') were used as place-names by bands of immigrant Anglo-Saxons newly arrived from the Continent under the leadership of the man whose name formed the basis of the folk-name. This belief was deeply entrenched in Dark-Age studies. It had been put forward in 1849 by J. M. Kemble, and in a developed and refined form it held the field without serious questioning until after 1960, though the failure of such names to coincide with early Anglo-Saxon archaeological sites became more and more apparent as Anglo-Saxon archaeology became better understood. It is now believed that while the first immigrants may indeed have referred to themselves as *Hæstingas*, *Rēadingas* and the like, the use of the folk-names as settlement-names belongs to a later stage in the Anglicization of the place-name stock. In many cases these names will refer to places on tribal boundaries, rather than at the centre of a territory. The related formation, in which *hām* 'village' is added to the genitive of an *-ingas* name to give place-names of the Birmingham, Nottingham type, is now considered to be perhaps rather earlier than the *-ingas* type.

A further complication in the evaluation of *-ingas* names arises from the difficulty of distinguishing them from another type in which *-ing* (singular) is added to a word to give a meaning 'place characterized by x'. The distinction is clear when there are pre-Conquest spellings. Clavering in Essex and Docking in Norfolk, for instance, are recorded as *Clæfring* and *Doccynge* in the early 11th century, and there is no doubt that the correct etymologies are 'places characterised by clover / docks'. The spelling distinction between *-ing* and *-ingas* was not so scrupulously observed after the *Norman Conquest, however, and many names which now end in -ing cannot be definitively assigned to either category. This problem is acute in the case of Mucking in Essex, where the largest and earliest of all known Anglo-Saxon settlements has been excavated. Supporters of pre-1960 views have claimed Mucking as an *-ingas* name which gives confirmation of the postulated early context; but from careful study of the available spellings it is apparent that Mucking could equally well be an *-ing* name meaning 'muddy place', perhaps (since this type of formation is well evidenced in stream-names) referring to the creek at Mucking.

Both the -*ingas* and the -*ing* names are of special interest, but it is hazardous to put such material on distribution maps and to base on it theories about the progress of the Anglo-Saxon settlement.

The questioning in the 1960s of traditional assumptions about the nature of the earliest English place-names led to a fresh approach to the whole matter of relative chronology. The earliest surviving English records date from c.670, over 200 years later than the first settlements, which means that it will always be impossible to prove that any type of name was predominant in the earliest decades of the Anglo-Saxon era. But strong circumstantial evidence has been assembled by three methods: the analysis of names recorded between 670 and 730, the study of extant names in areas where the earliest archaeological evidence has been found, and the study of names which belong to places of major administrative importance. From these three lines of enquiry the probability emerges that the predominant type of settlement-name in the early years of the change to English speech was the so-called 'topographical' type, which defines a place by describing an aspect of its physical setting. It is noted above that such names, in the British language, predominate in records from the Romano-British period. The contrasting type of name, known as 'habitative', has as its main component (the 'generic') a word for a settlement. The two classes overlap, habitative generics being frequently qualified by topographical specifics (as in Clifton, Compton, Denton, Fencote, Fenwick, Saddleworth), but there is a clear distinction of method between the defining of a settlement solely by topography and the type of naming which involves a direct reference to buildings.

Habitative names may be very early, and topographical names may be very late, but the evidence points to a predominance of topographical over habitative in the period from 450 to 750.

The topographical type of settlement-name received less than its fair share of attention before this revision of place-name chronology, but since then studies of the enormous topographical vocabulary found in place-names have brought a new dimension to the subject. Place-names lend themselves to categorization, and the generics of topographical names can be divided into a number of categories. In a pioneering work of 1984 (Margaret Gelling, *Place-Names in the Landscape*), words were discussed under seven headings. These were: Rivers, Springs, Pools, and Lakes; Marsh, Moor, and Floodplain; River-Crossings and Landing-Places, Roads and Tracks; Valleys and Remote Places; Hills, Slopes, and Ridges; Trees, Forests, Woods, and Clearings; Ploughland and Pasture. Within each of these categories each of the most frequently used words was considered in relation to the landscape, and on a national, not a regional, basis. From this study emerged a new perception of the Old English topographical vocabulary as a subtle code, understanding of which would convey much more to the initiated than the basic fact that a settlement was on a hill, in a valley, by a ford, or near a marsh or wood. In the large groups of words which can be translated 'valley' or 'hill' there are few synonyms and not much overlap of meaning. A *denu* is a different sort of valley from a *cumb*, and a valley called *hop* has very special characteristics. A hill called *dūn* is different from one called *beorg*, and ridges called *hōh* are different from those called *ofer* or *ōra*. Exciting work has been done since the early 1980s on the relationship of some topographical names to ancient routeways, and the perceptions of the traveller can be shown to play a part in the evolution of settlement-names. This rewarding new study has developed rapidly since the basis was laid in 1984, but its potential is far from exhausted. The assembling of the material involves not only amalgamating the county surveys but also unscrambling the dictionaries. In English compound names the generic comes last, so the alphabetical order of place-name dictionaries gives no help. The exercise would be very much easier in Celtic-speaking countries, where the generic usually comes first in a compound.

Synthetic work on English place-names is possible because of the enormous quantity of material made available by the publications of the English Place-Name Society and the work of Swedish scholars. In Ireland, Scotland, and Wales the collection and publication of material is not so far advanced, though work is proceeding as swiftly as limited resources permit.

The first major work dealing with the interpretation of Irish place-names was P. W. Joyce's *The Origin and History of Irish Names of Places*, published in three volumes, 1869–1913. The high standard of Joyce's work has made him an authority to the present day, much more so than the contemporary work on English names, Isaac Taylor's *Words and Places*. The founding in 1952 of the Ulster Place-Name Society signalled the inception of more detailed work on Northern Ireland, and more recently the Northern Ireland Place-Name Project has been established at Queen's University, Belfast, with a commission to publish detailed regional volumes. The first publications in the series *Place-Names of Northern Ireland* are three volumes on County Down which appeared in 1992 and 1993.

In Wales, Professor Gwynedd Pierce observed in 1987 that 'not one county survey of the kind produced by the EPNS has ever appeared', and he regretted the fact that authoritative writings on Welsh names were so widely scattered in journals and occasional publications. These observations were made in the context of an eloquent plea for the setting up of a Place-Name Survey of Wales, a project which was initiated in 1988 under the sponsorship of the Board of Celtic Studies. Since then two outstanding regional surveys have appeared, dealing with Pembrokeshire and east Flintshire, and much work has been done on the computerization of the handwritten archive assembled by Melville Richards as the basis for a dictionary of Welsh place-names which he did not live to produce.

In Scotland, organized place-name research is housed at the School of Scottish Studies in the University of Edinburgh. Here there is an archive of early spellings and a collection of oral material from Gaelic-speaking areas. There is as yet no reliable dictionary, but W. F. H. Nicolaisen's *Scottish Place-Names* (1976) provides an overview, and an early work, W. J. Watson's *The History of the Celtic Place-Names of Scotland* (1926), remains of great value. There are good surveys of a few counties or parts of counties, but as regards comprehensive treatment the Northern Isles (with overwhelming predominance of Norse names) have fared best, due largely to the work of H. Marwick on Orkney and J. Jakobsen on Shetland.

The place-names of the Isle of Man have been subjected to intense scrutiny, and have been the cause of considerable controversy. The basic material was collected by J. J. Kneen and published in six parts between 1925 and 1929. This material was studied by a Norwegian scholar, C. J. S. Marstrander, in two publications of 1932 and 1934. As regards early documentation the Isle of Man occupies a position intermediate between England and the more sparsely documented parts of the Gaelic speech-area. There is a sufficient quantity of early spellings to attract the attention of scholars trained in the English and Scandinavian traditions, and the mixture of Norse, Gaelic, and English has given rise to lively discussions as to which language predominated in the medieval period. A new survey of Manx place-names was inaugurated in 1988 by the University of Mannheim, and the first two volumes, by Dr George Broderick, appeared in 1994 and 1995.

Dr Broderick's work on Manx place-name studies has included the systematic tape-recording of name pronunciations by elderly Manx people. As noted above, this type of recording plays an important role in Celtic-speaking countries, where oral traditions are on the whole less corrupt than in England. Local pronunciations of English place-names are a constant source of interest and surprise, but because they are not considered to be sound guides to etymology they have not been systematically studied by English toponymists. EPNS volumes give some indication of the local pronunciation of major names, but there is no archive of oral material and interpretation is based firmly on spellings.

Cornwall is included in the work of the English Place-Name Society. The foundations of the survey have been laid in O. J. Padel's *Cornish Place-Name Elements* (EPNS 56/7, 1985). The *Cornish language is less thoroughly known to scholars than the other Celtic languages of Britain, and it was therefore necessary to undertake this preliminary labour of establishing a toponymic vocabulary.

The characteristics of English and Norse place-names differ from those of names in the Celtic languages in certain important respects, one being that there is a much greater degree of transparency in the latter. Many Celtic place-names developed through the centuries in accordance with the development of the Celtic languages, and a high proportion of the words used in place-naming remained in the vocabulary. In England, for reasons not yet fully understood, place-names began to become separated from normal linguistic developments at about the time of the Norman Conquest. A very high proportion of the Old English and Old Norse toponymic vocabulary became obsolete, and as names became increasingly opaque to the people using them they became vulnerable to drastic distortion and confusion. Those which escaped this fate were likely to become fossilized in the forms which they had had in the late Anglo-Saxon period. A few English names, such as Nettlebed and Oxford, mean what they say in modern English, but the basic tenet of English place-name studies must always be that etymologies are based on early spellings, not on modern forms or pronunciations.

The failure to develop with the language

renders English names more amenable to chronological classification than Celtic names are. There is, of course a *terminus post quem* for English names, which can only date from after the English settlements, and for Norse names, which must be related to the Viking invasions. In addition to this it is possible to make estimates of the dates at which many toponymic words became obsolete in the spoken language. Even if names are not recorded until after the Norman Conquest it is frequently apparent from the vocabulary that they must have been coined in the Anglo-Saxon period. As regards Welsh, Cornish, and Gaelic names, however, there is no automatic *terminus post quem*, as the languages are of prehistoric antiquity in Britain, and there are not so many obsolete words. The structure of names of the 'phrase' type (e.g. Ardnamurchan, Pontardulais, and numerous Manx names like Cronk ny Arrhee Laa) must be relatively late, but there may be older names underlying them which have been remodelled in accordance with later syntactical practices. The manner of forming names in which the generic precedes the qualifier contrasts with that of Celtic names recorded during the Romano-British period, but here again refashioning, rather than total renaming, may be involved.

In spite of this uncertainty there are some large classes of Welsh, Cornish, and Gaelic names which can be definitely classified as newly coined in the Middle Ages. The conversion to Christianity and the building of churches caused the appearance of large numbers of new names referring to cemeteries (Welsh *llan*, Cornish *lan*), saints' graves (Welsh *merther*, Cornish *merthyr*), churches (Welsh *eglwys*, Cornish *eglos*, Irish *eaglais*, Irish *cill*, Manx *keeill*), and other ecclesiastical institutions. There are also numerous instances of the use as a settlement-name of the name of the saint to whom the church is dedicated. There is a contrast with England, where it was quite rare for new names to be formed referring to minsters or churches or saints. Norse *kirkja* is quite common, however, especially in the compound with *bý* which becomes Kirby or Kirkby; and in the adjacent parts of north-west England and south-west Scotland *kirk* became an English dialect word which was used by ecclesiastical authorities there and in the Isle of Man in the naming of parishes.

The ubiquitous settlement-term which gives Irish Bally-, Manx Balla- and Scottish Bal- has been the subject of much study, from which it emerges that it did not come into common use until the 12th or 13th centuries. It is possible that the absence of words for farms or villages in the recorded place-names of Roman Britain indicates that many habitative names, such as Welsh and Cornish formations with *tref* and *tre*, are of post-Roman date. Some are certainly medieval, because (as with Irish Bally- and Manx Balla- names) they have post-Norman-Conquest personal or family names as qualifiers.

In Celtic-speaking countries the establishment of distinctions between the earliest names and those of medieval origin is a fraught exercise which impinges on feelings about ethnic identity. Manx people, for instance, do not like to be told that many of their Gaelic names date from after rather than before the Viking period.

Other aspects of place-name research include the recovery of words which are not recorded in literary sources and the practical usefulness of place-name evidence to archaeologists. Perhaps the most important recent development is the compilation of databases. English place-name material is being computerized at Nottingham University under a generous grant from the Leverhulme Foundation, and scholars in Wales, Ireland, and Scotland are collaborating in the establishment of databases for name-material in those areas. Since the material lends itself to categorization and cries out for quantification, future generations of place-name scholars will benefit greatly from this work.

In 1990 place-name studies in the United Kingdom acquired a comprehensive bibliography: *A Reader's Guide to the Place-Names of the United Kingdom: A Bibliography of Publications (1920–89) on the Place-Names of Great Britain and Northern Ireland, The Isle of Man, and the Channel Islands*, compiled by J. Spittal and J. Field. This makes it possible to trace the growth and development of the study in great detail, and to assess the contributions of some 1600 or 1700 authors. The most widely used general books, apart from dictionaries, are Kenneth Cameron's *English Place-Names* (4th edn., 1988) and Margaret Gelling's *Signposts to the Past: Place-Names and the History of England* (2nd edn., 1988).   MARGARET GELLING

plague. Bubonic plague was a major killer disease that was transmitted to humans by fleas carried by rodents. The classic study is Paul Slack, *The Impact of Plague in Tudor and Stuart England* (1990). Plague was endemic in Britain from at least the *Black Death of 1348–50 until its mysterious disappearance after 1666. It erupted into major epidemics in London in 1563, 1603, and 1665 and accounted for high mortalities in provincial towns and rural *parishes at unpredictable times, like 1604 in York when a third of the population died. It was rarely absent from the British Isles during the 16th century and the first two-thirds of the 17th century. Major outbreaks, however, seem to have been the result of the importation of more virulent strains of the plague bacillus. Thus, the most serious epidemics in London followed those in Antwerp or Amsterdam, and the most general outbreaks coincided with plague years in Germany and the Low Countries. The south-eastern half of England was more prone to the disease than the north-west.

The rise and decline of an outbreak of plague can be traced through the record of burials in *parish registers, once they were introduced in 1538. Earlier evidence is more impressionistic and depends largely on *wills. Even the record in parish registers is likely to be incomplete, given the reluctance of parishes to contaminate their *churchyards, thus forcing the unregistered burial of victims in gardens and fields. Bubonic plague was identifiable by clear symptoms, buboes, and black, blue, or purple spots, but 'plague' was also used in a more general sense and it was not the only disease to cause heavy mortalities. Even when plague was not identified by marginal comments in the parish register, however, its course can often be followed by detecting the usual pattern of a surge in spring, leading to high mortalities in summer, and a dormant period in autumn and winter. The impact was greatest in the towns; it is much harder to assess the effects of plague on rural life.

Central government and local authorities took steps to try to control the spread of plague once an outbreak had been confirmed. The sick were isolated and supported from public funds. Severe restrictions were placed on their movements and on those who had recently visited them. *Justices of the Peace banned the movement of *carriers and other traders from infected places, and towns installed sentries to watch for travellers who attempted to enter. Nevertheless, those people with the means to do so usually fled from towns once an outbreak of plague became public knowledge. See Samuel *Pepys's diary for human reactions to the great plague of London of 1665.

Once the epidemic that began in 1665 had run its course, plague never returned to the British Isles, though there were recurrent scares, especially in 1720–2 when plague broke out in Marseilles. No satisfactory explanation for the disappearance of plague is available. Paul Slack concludes that the historian can never be certain whether it was good management or good fortune that prevented a serious outbreak of plague in any particular instance. However, quarantine procedures in European ports played an effective part in restricting the disease to the eastern Mediterranean after 1665. For the history of the last major outbreak of plague in the British Isles see L. Bradley, 'The Most Famous of All English Plagues: A Detailed Analysis of the Plague at Eyam, 1665–6', in *The Plague Reconsidered* (Local Population Studies Supplement, 1977).

Plantagenets. A family, French in origin, to which the Kings of England from 1154 (Henry II) to 1399 (Richard II) belonged.

Plantations. The new settlements in *Ulster and other parts of Ireland, *Virginia, New England, and the *West Indies in the late 16th and early 17th centuries. The government's aims in encouraging settlement differed between Ireland and the New World. Settlement in Ireland was seen as a method of stabilizing unrest by the imposition of English rule, law, religion, landholding systems, and commercial organization based on market towns. The earliest plantation schemes for Munster and Ulster date from the 1580s; those for parts of the midlands and the south-west came later. The schemes were easier to prepare than to implement. Thus, English farming systems were quickly abandoned in favour of the more profitable rearing of *cattle.

The transfer of land in the Irish plantations from the native Catholic families to Protestant immigrants was a gradual process, but one that produced the largest change of *land-ownership in any European country during the 17th century. The pattern was not uniform throughout the country, but the general trends are clear. In 1600 more than 80 per cent of Ireland was still held by Catholic owners, but by 1641 this figure had been reduced by the plantation policy to 59 per cent. After the Cromwellian wars and new settlements, Catholic ownership declined to 29 per cent. By 1703 only 14 per cent of the land remained in the hands of the old owners. See P. Robinson, *The Plantation of Ulster* (1994).

In contrast, the London government had no such direct interest in shaping settler society in the American colonies. Thus, the Virginia Company assumed the role of government in Virginia, and Lord Baltimore acquired almost absolute powers in Maryland. The London government was more interested in the commercial exploitation of its colonies and in establishing them in the face of competition from the other maritime powers of western Europe. In the New World the word 'plantation' came to mean the *tobacco plantations of Virginia and the *sugar plantations of the West Indies.

The main group of settlers in Ulster came from south-west Scotland, though others came from the western and south-western counties of England, and later from northern England. The earliest migrants to Virginia were mainly from south-western England via the port of Bristol. New England migrants were largely drawn from Norfolk, Suffolk, Essex, and Kent, with smaller numbers from Somerset, Dorset, and Wiltshire, and later from the north of England.

plashing. The formation of stock-proof hedges by skilful pruning and intertwining of branches. The management of such hedges by regular cutting was practised since at least Roman times. From the Tudor period, pleached trees such as hornbeam and lime became a decorative feature of formal *gardens.

plasterwork, decorative. The *nobility and leading members of the legal profession started the fashion for decorating ceilings and walls with plasterwork mouldings in the second half of the 16th century. The fashion spread to *gentry families and then to wealthy *yeomen. Pattern designs were drawn from *heraldry and Mannerist ornament, with new ideas imported by foreign craftsmen and through printed books, then spread by a network of family connections involving owners and patrons. In the later 17th and 18th centuries hanging pendants were abandoned in favour of more restrained motifs, culminating in the neo-classical designs of the 1760s onwards associated with Robert Adam. Pre-cast mouldings, e.g. a ceiling rose above a chandelier, were used from the middle of the 19th century onwards. Decorative plasterwork remained fashionable until the First World War.

playstow. A recreational area or playground, commemorated in minor place-names. See CAMPING CLOSES.

pleaching. See PLASHING.

Plea rolls. Records of actions brought under the common law in the courts of *Common Pleas, *Exchequer, *King's Bench, etc., from the late 12th century until 1873. A *Calendar of Pleas and Memoranda Rolls* is available for the early rolls down to 1482.

Plot, Robert (1640–96). Oxford scholar and first keeper of the Ashmolean museum, who was influential in moving the *antiquarian tradition of county studies in a new direction with his emphasis on natural history. His *Natural History of Oxfordshire* (1677) and *Natural History of Staffordshire* (1686) reflect the diverse interests of his fellow members of the *Royal Society. See Stan A. E. Mendyk, 'Speculum Britanniae': Regional Study, Antiquarianism, and Science in Britain to 1700 (1989), ch. 11, and Dennis Baker, 'A Kentish Pioneer in Natural History: Robert Plot of Borden, 1640–96', *Transactions of the Kent Field Club*, 3 (1971).

Plough Monday. The public holiday on the Monday following 6 January. In the Middle Ages farm-workers in eastern England raised money for the local parish *church by dragging a plough around the streets. The associated performance of a play involving song, dance, verse, and ad-libbing is not recorded before the 1760s, though it may have been earlier. See Ronald Hutton, *The Rise and Fall of Merry England: The Ritual Year, 1400–1700* (1994). In rural areas where the tradition survived into the late 19th century, e.g. Lincolnshire, the players toured the local farmhouses and were rewarded with food and drink. See Alun Howkins and Linda Merricks, 'The Ploughboy and the Plough Play', *Folk Music Journal*, 6/2 (1991).

ploughs. The design of ploughs was highly varied, since, until the late 18th century, most were made locally, were adapted to local soil conditions, and conformed to local preferences. See Eric Kerridge, *The Agricultural Revolution* (1967). For many illustrations, plus the text from encyclopaedia articles on the plough in the 19th century, see John Thompson, *Horse Drawn Farm Implements*, part I, *Ploughs: A Source Book* (1978). Wooden ploughs were often preferred to iron-tipped ones until the late 18th century, particularly on heavy claylands. Ploughing matches at agricultural shows did much to popularize new types, e.g. the Beverstone plough in the south-west, or the Rotherham plough in northern England. See G. Marshall, 'The Rotherham Plough', *Tools and Tillage*, 3 (1978). Small foundries in market towns were responsible for the rapid spread of iron ploughs in the 19th century.

plurality. The holding of more than one *benefice by a clergyman.

Plymouth Brethren. A *Nonconformist sect founded in Ireland in the late 1820s by The Revd J. N. Darby and established at Plymouth in 1830. It has no formal creed or ministers; each local church is autonomous. In 1849 the Open Brethren split from the Exclusive Brethren. The membership has remained small, but is widely distributed.

Plymouth colony. The *Puritan colony in Massachusetts which was founded in 1620 by emigrants who had crossed the Atlantic on the *Mayflower*. They named their new settlement after the port from which they had left England.

poaching. The poaching of game on the estates of the rich is an ancient activity. See Roger B. Manning, *Hunters and Poachers: A Social and Cultural History of Unlawful Hunting in England, 1485–1640* (1993), which deals primarily with deer stealing. (See GAME LAWS for the penalties imposed on poachers from the 17th to the 19th centuries.) Many of the poachers were young labourers, but organized gangs operated from some villages and towns. The growing number of bloody affrays between gamekeepers and poachers led to the passing of the Poaching Prevention Act (1862), which legalized the searching by police of working people on the road at night-time. See John E. Archer, *By a Flash and a Scare: Arson, Animal Maiming, and Poaching in East Anglia, 1815–1870* (1990), which attacks 'the myth of a serene countryside' and depicts the landed classes as being under constant threat. See also Garth Christian (ed.), *James Hawker's Journal: A Victorian Poacher* (1978).

Pococke, Dr Richard (1704–65). Irish bishop famous for his travel writings; the pioneer of Alpine travel. His account of his Scottish tours in 1747, 1750, and 1760 was edited by D. William Kemp and published by the Scottish Historical Society (1887), and that of his tours in England in the 1750s was edited by James J. Cartwright and published by the *Camden Society (1888–9). His account of his tour of Ireland was published in an edition of 1891. They contain much interesting observations on people and places.

police. The first police force was established at Bow Street, London, in the early 18th century. The 'Bow Street Runners' were under the control of a magistrate. In 1753, upon the recommendation of the magistrate and novelist Henry Fielding, more forces were created in London along these lines. In 1829 Sir Robert Peel, the Home Secretary, appointed police commissioners to take over responsibility from the magistrates; the nickname 'bobbies' is derived from his name. Other towns quickly followed the metropolitan example. In rural areas associations for the prevention of *crime supplemented the work of manorial and parish *constables and magistrates. An Act of 1839 allowed the *Justices of the Peace at *quarter sessions to create a county force of chief and petty constables. This was made compulsory in 1856 by an Act which sought to impose some uniformity. See David Foster, *The Rural Constabulary Act, 1839* (1982), which shows that 24 counties adopted the measure in the first two years and another 11 in the next 15 years.

The county and borough forces established in 1856 were responsible to the Home Office. Amongst the most useful of the records in the *Public Record Office are the registers of prisoners in county gaols, which give details of individual inmates from 1847 to 1866 (HO 23), and the statistical returns for local prisons for the 1860s (HO 24). An Act of 1877 placed all prisons under the control of a Prison Commission, whose records are under PCOM.

Polish immigrants. Many Polish *Jews emigrated to Britain in the late 19th century to escape Tsar Alexander III's pogroms. The main period of Polish immigration was during and immediately after the Second World War when German and Russian armies occupied Poland. The Polish immigrants of that period mostly settled in towns and coal-mining villages.

pollarding. The cropping of trees, especially oak, beech, elm, and hornbeam, at their heads (Norman French *poll*), in order to obtain poles for fencing, etc. The method is distinct from *coppicing at stool level, though both were designed to encourage new growth. Although the technique has been abandoned in most parts of the British Isles, old pollarded trees are easily recognized by the way that branches spring from the top of the trunk.

poll books. Until 1872 elections to Parliament were not held in secret. An Act of 1696, designed to prevent fraud on the part of returning officers, authorized the publication of copies of the poll, showing how each elector had voted. Returning officers soon afterwards allowed local printers to publish poll books of county elections as a commercial venture.

A uniform system of presentation was never adopted. The names of electors and their choice of candidate(s) are always recorded and sometimes the addresses and occupations of electors are given. The lists are normally arranged by *hundred or *wapentake and then in alphabetical order of *parish. The right to vote was restricted to men with certain property qualifications. (See PARLIAMENT: THE FRANCHISE.) Most large public libraries have collections of poll books; the best is at the *Institute of Historical Research, in the Senate House, the University of London. See J. R. Sims, *A Handlist of British Parliamentary Poll Books*

(1984). After the Parliamentary Reform Act of 1832 *electoral registers were printed.

Political historians have made much use of poll books. See J. R. Vincent, *Pollbooks: How Victorians Voted* (1967).

poll tax. A tax on heads, or polls, was first levied in England in 1377, the first year of the reign of Richard II. It was levied again in 1379 and 1381, but the hostility aroused by the tax caused the government to abandon it after the *Peasants' Revolt. The tax returns are kept in the *Public Record Office under E 179.

In 1377 the tax was levied at 4*d*. per head for all lay people over the age of 14; clergy paid a shilling. It is not clear how many people were exempt or under the age of 14 or who evaded payment, so different multipliers have been used to calculate population totals. The 1377 returns are considered to be the most complete, being less subject to the large-scale evasions of 1379 and 1381. The return of 1379 is useful, however, in grading the tax according to the wealth of people above the age of 16. The basic rate remained 4*d*., but many craftsmen and tradesmen paid 6*d*., 1*s*., or 2*s*., and the more substantial people paid higher rates, culminating in the £4 paid by an earl; clergy were now exempt.

The returns that record the names of the taxpayers are a basic source for the study of *surnames at a time when many were becoming fixed and hereditary. Unfortunately, the survival rate is patchy and few counties have returns in print. Despite these problems, the poll tax returns at least provide firm evidence that particular surnames were in existence by 1377–81. An edition of the national returns is being prepared by Richard Smith for publication by the British Academy.

The poll tax was reintroduced in 1641 and again upon the *Restoration of Charles II. It was levied on eight occasions between 1660 and 1697. Each was regarded as a specific, one-off measure. The early returns tend to be rural, while those which survive from the 1690s are mainly urban. Few returns survive in central records, but a number of local returns, e.g. that of 1660 for some of the *townships of Staincross *wapentake (Yorkshire), are housed in local *record offices, especially amongst the family papers of those who were *lords lieutenant at the time. The London returns for 1694 are in print. The format of surviving poll tax returns from this period is very variable. Some 17th-century returns list the names of all over the age of 16 who paid or were exempted on grounds of poverty, but in most cases the number of exempt is not known. Wives, children, and servants were often not named. The tax was graded according to wealth, the great majority paying the basic rate. That for Kettlewell Ward in King's Lynn (Norfolk) for the first quarter of 1692 gives the names of children and servants, and records the occupations and ages of those under 21. See Kevin Schurer and Tom Arkell (eds.), *Surveying the People: The Interpretation and Use of Document Sources for the Study of Population in the Later Seventeenth Century* (1992), part II.

In Scotland poll tax was levied on all adults except those in receipt of charity between 1693 and 1699. The records are incomplete, but some are found under E 70 at the *Scottish Record Office and others in a supplementary list there. The tax was collected by counties and parishes. Some name husband, wife, and children. The poll tax was revived briefly in Britain in the early 1990s.

polyfocal settlements. The old idea that the original *Anglo-Saxon settlers lived in villages has been discredited. It is now realized that villages arose in the late Anglo-Saxon / Scandinavian period either through a deliberate act of replanning or by the gradual coalescing of small settlements or isolated farms, which did not originally have a single focus. See Christopher Taylor, *Village and Farmstead: A History of Rural Settlement in England* (1983).

pontage. A toll levied at a bridge for its maintenance.

poor, overseer of. The officer chosen at a *vestry meeting of a *township or civil *parish to administer the *Poor Law for the ensuing year. Such officers were elected about Eastertime and their names were then submitted to the *Justices of the Peace for approval. A man who refused to serve was fined, for this role was expected to be performed by rotation. The overseer received no payment for this work, nor any recompense for loss of earnings. He was empowered to raise taxes ('assessments' or 'rates') in order to meet demands for poor relief. He had to submit his accounts at the end of his year of office for the approval of the vestry meeting and was himself expected to pay for anything that was not allowed by that meeting. He normally served for one year only, but on occasion he served for two. Some of the populous townships or parishes were served by two overseers at a time. The system started in Elizabeth's reign and was consolidated by the Poor Law Acts of 1597–1601. It lasted until the Poor Law Amendment Act (1834).

The overseer had the face-to-face responsibility of deciding the merits of appeals for poor relief. He had to temper mercy with the knowledge that the ratepayers of the parish would demand an explanation of his expenditure. At the same time, he knew that an aggrieved pauper could take his or her case to the JPs. He was therefore frequently faced with a dilemma. A large amount of his time was spent on checking the likelihood of incomers becoming a burden on the poor rates and on seeking their *removal to the parish in which they were legally settled. This involved the signing of certificates by JPs and sometimes attendance at *quarter sessions to argue a case. The overseer also had the duty of apprenticing poor orphans to local householders, a task that was rarely pleasant and which sometimes involved an appeal before a JP. The job of overseer was therefore onerous, but it was judged to be a local honour. Overseers tended to be middle-aged *yeomen, *husbandmen, and craftsmen, rather than labourers or *cottagers. Their records were kept in the parish chest and are now housed at local *record offices. Quarter sessions records in the form of depositions, indictment books, and order books are the other major source of information.

Poor Law. The history of poor relief in England and Wales is divided into two periods, separated by the Poor Law Amendment Act (1834). During the first period the civil *parish was the unit of administration. See Paul Slack, *The English Poor Law, 1531–1782* (1990), and Geoffrey Oxley, *Poor Relief in England and Wales, 1601–1834* (1974). The Acts of 1597 and 1601 ordered the annual election of overseers of the *poor, who were answerable to the parish *vestry and to the *Justices of the Peace. The overseers were empowered to raise revenue from local rates. This was supplemented by charities, some of which were administered on behalf of parishes by *feoffees. (See CHARITY BOARDS. See also WORKHOUSE and BADGING.) Some towns had public bodies which assisted the poor from monies obtained from rents. On the general background to the early period, see A. L. Beier, *The Problem of the Poor in Tudor and Early Stuart England* (1983), and Tom Arkell, 'The Incidence of Poverty in England in the Later Seventeenth Century', *Social History*, 12 (1987); for an account of the size of the problem in a leading city in the Elizabethan period see J. F. Pound, 'The Norwich Census of the Poor, 1570', *Norfolk Record Society*, 40 (1971).

The Act of *Settlement (1662) defined the ways in which a parish was responsible; this led to large numbers of cases being heard before the *quarter sessions. For the interpretation of the evidence of settlement certificates, which were issued from 1697 onwards, see K. D. M. Snell, *Annals of the Labouring Poor: Social Change and Agrarian England, 1660–1900* (1985), and 'Settlement, Poor Law and the Rural Historian: New Approaches and Opportunities', *Rural History: Economy, Society, Culture*, 3 (1992).

Expenditure on the poor rose considerably in the late 18th and early 19th centuries, as the national *population increased. See J. D. Marshall, *The Old Poor Law, 1795–1834* (1968), and M. E. Rose, *The English Poor Law, 1780–1930* (1971). (See also GILBERT'S ACT.) For a local study, see Jan Walmsley, 'Provision for the Non Able-bodied Poor in the Eighteenth and Early Nineteenth Centuries: Some Evidence from Three Bedfordshire Parishes', *The Local Historian*, 20/1 (1990). (See also SPEEN-HAMLAND SYSTEM and EDEN, SIR FREDERICK MORTON for accounts of workhouses in many parts of the country in the 1790s.) *Parliamentary papers give many details of local expenditure on the poor during the late 18th and early 19th centuries. In the *First Series of Sessional Papers*, ix (1774–1802), the return for 1777 (which deals with the years 1772–4) is particularly useful. In 1777 a detailed abstract was made of returns by overseers of the poor for the previous year. A similar abstract was made in 1787 for the years 1783–5. The *Abstract of the Answers and Returns Relative to the Poor* (1803–4), the *Reports of the Select Committee on the Poor Laws* (1817 and 1818), the *Report of the Lords Committee on the Poor Laws* (1818), and the *Abridgement of the Abstract of Returns Relative to the Poor* (1818) also provide detailed information on numerous parishes.

The Poor Law Amendment Act (1834) abolished the old system and introduced a new one based on unions of parishes, run by boards of elected *guardians. The new system met with much opposition in northern England. *Parliamentary Papers: Poor Law 10* (1834) contains a lot of information on parishes on the eve of the transition, including comments on *landownership, the labour force, and *wages, and on local attitudes and prejudices. After 1834 parliamentary papers continue to provide regular, detailed information on the operation of the Poor Law. These include the annual reports of the Poor Law Commission (1835–47), the Poor Law Board (1848–71), and the Local Government Board (from 1872); the annual returns on poor rates, relief, and paupers; and the reports of Royal Commissions of 1895 and 1909–10.

For the whereabouts of local records, see Jeremy Gibson, Colin Rogers, and Cliff Webb, *Poor Law Union Records, parts 1–4* (1992). For a local study, see Tydfil Thomas, *Poor Relief in Merthyr Tydfil Union in Victorian Times* (1992). For the 20th century, see David Vincent, *Poor Citizens: The State and the Poor in Twentieth Century Britain* (1991).

In Scotland, provision for the poor was on a parish basis. Responsibility lay with the *heritors and kirk session of each parish until the Poor Law (Scotland) Act (1845) established parochial boards to administer poor relief in each parish. Records from before and after 1845 are kept at the *Scottish Record Office. See R. A. Cage, *Scottish Poor Law, 1745–1845* (1981).

The Royal Commission of Enquiry into the Conditions of the Poorer Classes in Ireland, which was established in 1833, reported that 2,385,000 people were in need of relief from poverty. The report led to the passing of the 'Act for the More Effectual Relief of the Destitute Poor in Ireland' (1838), which divided Ireland into 130 (later, 163) unions, each of which had a workhouse run by an elected board of guardians on the English system. Some workhouses have detailed records, e.g. the minute books of Cork Union are contained in 133 volumes. A valuation of individual tenements, under the direction of Richard Griffith, Commissioner of Valuation, was made between 1844 and 1865 to form a basis for local taxation. This collection of over 200 volumes is a rich source for local and family historians in Ireland. See Tony McCarthy, *The Irish Roots Guide* (1991), ch. 5. Outdoor relief was authorized by the Poor Law Amendment Act (1847), which attempted to bring Ireland more in line with English practice.

popular culture. Popular culture—in crude terms, the culture of the 'people' as opposed to the 'polite' culture of the élite—has interested scholars, if only in passing, since the beginning of *antiquarian writing. It was not until John *Aubrey's unpublished 'The Remains of Gentilisme and Judaisme', and his *Miscellanies* (1696), however, that a more focused preoccupation, albeit largely with *customs and superstitions, became apparent. Thereafter the subject developed and widened in four broad stages.

It was with the work of Henry Bourne, whose *Antiquitates Vulgares; or the Antiquities of the Common People* (1725) was written condescendingly from the critical viewpoint of a churchman, that the subject first began to enlarge. This process was much accelerated by John Brand, who republished Bourne in 1777 with extensive additional commentary under the title *Observations on Popular Antiquities*, a further hugely expanded version of which, edited by Sir Henry Ellis, was published in 1813.

The first half of the 19th century thereafter witnessed a widening of interest and the beginnings of the serious, objective systematization of the subject outside England in particular. Pioneering work was accomplished, for example, on *Minstrelsy of the Scottish Border* (1802–3) by Walter Scott; with *Essays on the Superstitions of the Highlanders of Scotland* (1811) by Anne Grant; on urban *folklore—based on 'oral intelligence'—in *Traditions of Edinburgh* (1825) by Robert Chambers; on *The Fairy Mythology* (1828) by Thomas Keightley; and with *Nursery Rhymes of England* (1842) and *A Dictionary of Archaic and Provincial Words* (1847) by J. O. Halliwell-Phillips. Oral techniques were enlarged by John Campbell of Islay with his *Popular Tales of the West Highlands, Orally Collected* (1860–2) and by Patrick Kennedy, *The Bardic Stories of Ireland* (1871).

These developments, and those of the third stage, are usefully surveyed by Richard M. Dorson, *The British Folklorists: A History* (1968). 'Folk-lore' itself was a term coined as late as 1846, though it rapidly caught on. A great surge of activity, indeed, marked the years between the foundation of the Folklore Society itself in 1878 and the Great War. It was during this period, when Anglo-Saxon village folkmoots (see MOOT) were being seen as exhibiting the seeds of British democracy, that specific links were established between 'local history' and folklore, whether in the work of Laurence Gomme (e.g. *The Village Community* (1890)) or that of Charlotte Burne, whose new edition of *Shropshire Folk-Lore* (1883) gave an impetus to county studies. In a parallel development this period also saw the founding of the English Dialect Society (1873) by W. W. Skeat; the publication of A. J. Ellis's path-breaking survey covering Britain and part of Ireland, *On Early English Pronunciation*, v. *The Existing Phonology of English Dialects Compared with that of West Saxon Speech* (1889), and the appearance of Joseph *Wright's *English Dialect Dictionary* (1898–1905). It was no accident, therefore, that 1899 saw the first appearance of the *Journal of the Folk Song Society*, and 1907 the publication of Cecil Sharp's *English Folksongs: Some Conclusions*.

A fourth stage, since the First World War, was marked by that growing concern for understanding material culture—from housing to lobster pots—against relevant geographical backgrounds which must be traced back to the influential teaching of H. J. Fleure, professor of geography and anthropology at Aberystwyth. Now thought of—more inclusively—as 'Folk Life', this very different approach to the study of popular culture, which is associated with such leaders in the field as Iorweath Peate in Wales or Estyn *Evans in Ireland, has subsequently derived its main strength from specialized institutions. These include the National Museum of Antiquities of Scotland and the School of Scottish Studies (Edinburgh University); the Ulster Folk and Transport Museum and the Department of Irish Folklore (University College, Dublin); the Welsh Folk Museum; the Centre for English Cultural Tradition and Language (University of Sheffield); and the Museum of English Rural Life (now the *Rural History Centre) at Reading.

To sum up the achievement at the end of the 20th century, however, is also to recognize the degree to which current understanding of popular culture in the British Isles is now seriously fragmented. Most fundamental, perhaps, are underlying differences in approach and stress. At one extreme is the museum-led ethnological emphasis (especially in Celtic countries) that stems from the chronologically late survival within those regions of traditional cultures of work—both material and oral—and consequently an intellectual sensitivity to localized rural resources and contexts. At the other extreme is what will concern much of this article: the academic approach to social (and predominantly documentary) history of the last three decades with, especially in England, its national concentration on '*class' and, indeed, recreation. Few historians thus attempt to interrelate more than a scattering of disparate strands of popular culture, or more than either rural or urban contexts, or in many cases more even than one century at a time. Folklore tends to be ignored.

To find a way around this confusion involves treating popular culture as a continuously evolving whole, as a complex of elements that are constantly and variously interwoven. In that sense it might be defined as an interconnected pattern of widely observed ways of believing, communicating, and doing that is informally transmitted from generation to generation *within a society*. Popular culture cannot be imposed officially from above (though sometimes official precedents may be adopted to advantage). Its perpetuation is voluntary and collective. For most of its reconstructable history, therefore, popular culture might best be understood (1) as a collective memory store from which individuals or groups could choose different combinations of available beliefs or ways of doing (and which is therefore not now measurable by the incidence of any one idiom alone); (2) as geographically specific at the level of its realization; (3) as not restricted to any one 'class' (at its edges, popular culture was able to bind 'superiors' into obligation—and therefore participation—and even, when it suited them, into its defence); (4) as infinitely adaptable, but usually imperceptibly and in its own terms; and (5) as involving a perpetual, and often innovatory, interplay between rural and urban.

Down to the 19th century, at least, certainly both town and country tended to share all four of the underlying characteristics of 'traditional' cultural interaction. Each of these stemmed directly from the widely experienced coincidence of residence, work, and recreation in one local place. First was the public, predominantly open-air and daylight nature of culture, where privacy was minimal, and snooping, rumour, and (while Church courts were still active) delation were rife. Until the 19th century, punishment might be openly witnessed and was thus communally humiliating, as were shaming rituals like charivari (see ROUGH MUSIC). Street, *market place, and *churchyard were public arenas. Into all of them ritually came the pre-*Reformation church. Second, popular culture was participatory; it expressed the sharing of activities whether at home or at work (e.g. harvest time or market day) or on ritual occasions. Participants were 'incorporated' into special occasions by loud noise: from bell-ringing, to fairground organs, to the roar of the football crowd. On the other hand, in the context of ritual humiliation, they might be intimidated by the discordancy of 'rough music'. Often it was sound, then, that allowed popular cultural occasions to be claimed, to adapt E. P. *Thompson's words, as 'the people's own'. Third, other than speech in for what long remained an illiterate world for most of its inhabitants, interaction or communication was highly visual. People therefore were able to 'read' such signals. Body language, for example, for a long time involved more extreme modes of gesture than it does today, while those concerned seem to have been able to comprehend—probably instantly—an extraordinary range of identifying marks, signs, emblems, colour codes, *coats of arms, liveries, symbols, or trade banners. The fourth and last characteristic of popular interaction was its inevitable reflection of the harshness, roughness, and, frequently, the brutality of everyday reality. Verbal abuse was richer in its imagery, more metaphorical, more ferocious, and more personalized than it has since become (compare the current linguistic feebleness of 'shit off' with the impact of the medieval 'a turd in thy teeth'). Punishment could be barbaric: scolds' bridles and ducking-stools at one extreme; and in early periods, mutilation, branding, drawing (disembowelling), or burial alive, to quote only some, at the other. The later society which sent children down mines or up chimneys was also one which allowed pugilists voluntarily to fight themselves to defeat or exhaustion without protective gloves. Within very broad limits indeed, animal suffering—from baiting to burial alive to fend off brucellosis—was thus effectively disregarded. There is, however, no point in reading modern values into the past. Humankind itself lived with the uncertainties of destitution, dearth, or disease and hence with the ever-present apprehension of death and what might lie beyond it.

This collective, tough culture, which ramified into every corner of daily life (see, for example, Barry Reay (ed.), *Popular Culture in Seventeenth-Century England* (1985)), was for long informally 'codified', as it were, through constant repetition in terms of both knowledge and practice. Knowledge was of two kinds: what now tends to be called 'folklore' (and which much earlier might have been thought of as 'cunning' (an *Old English word for 'knowing'), a comprehensive spectrum of inherited esoteric beliefs and remedies; and 'craft', the traditional practical knowledge or art that comprised the hard-won (often secret) technical skills usually associated with specialized manual work. Current social practice, by contrast, was self-regulated through established precedent or 'custom'. Lore and custom were complementary. Lore 'defined' a proper place for everything and provided explanations if the pattern was disturbed. It embraced planets, trees, animals, humankind, minerals, and so on in a manner that integrated 'pagan' and popular Christian perceptions of the supernatural. It therefore also comprised the knowledge by which the potency inherent in all of nature might be harnessed by mankind for magical or medicinal purposes. Traditional popular culture, indeed, was entirely suffused with an awareness of the supernatural even to the point where specific charms, taboos, and saintly patrons might be associated with the manual work of a craft. If lore so 'ordered' the world and the heavens, the body of custom (from which specific *customs sprang) ordered society. Custom defined the internal practices of society, and the relation of it to the wider

context by ensuring—as a result of long local experiment—that through right-doing (and therefore, it was hoped, with the minimum of conflict) the members of society would themselves continue to occupy their own proper places in relation to each other as well as to the overall scheme of things. Lore and custom were linked publicly (and privately in the case of some superstitions) through constant rituals (or 'customs') in which few people failed to participate at some point or another in every year.

Lore and custom, however, were clearly never comprehended as whole 'systems', nor seen as requiring rational or scientific justification. Indeed, their content tended to be rehearsed or ritualized in a highly metaphorical and allusive, rather than direct, manner. Effectively, popular culture thus comprised a repertoire from which to draw as need arose, but which seems to have been articulated only in its parts by contemporaries. Folktales, *ballads, and rituals thus constantly rearranged motifs, symbols, and meanings in relation to each other and to circumstances in a kaleidoscope manner. Within its own frames of references, therefore, traditional popular culture was adaptable.

The essential genius of popular culture, however, was specifically local and regional. By their very natures, custom and craft were tailored to immediate landscapes. Indeed, it is in terms of culture in particular that the modern concept of the *pays is perhaps at its most enlightening. The soils, vegetation, wildlife, and topography of each farming region (to which may be added, as appropriate, the seaside) all combined to create localized cultural features: (1) building materials and the construction of the structures they determined; (2) varieties of farming (or fishing) practice and their reflection in farm layouts, field boundaries, the regulation of *field systems, and localized forms of agricultural implements or wheeled conveyances or boats; (3) crop and other products and their contribution to regionalized types of food like bread or cheese or feast-day specialities; (4) the separate subcultures of livestock supervision according to emphasis on cattle, sheep, or horses, for example; (5) the availability of certain minerals for extraction, or even differing species of wood that could be exploited to meet particularized market needs (like *coppice oak for *charcoal or alder for clog soles), and which might therefore predispose a region to a particular craft specialism; (6) the detailed cycles of the agricultural or seafaring years with their varying implications for the popular calendar of observances by which one community distinguished its annual rhythms from another. David Underdown, in his *Revel, Riot and Rebellion* (1985), has even seen contrasts between *pays* so far as the differential survival in the mid-17th century of popular feasts and recreation were concerned. Market towns between two adjacent *pays*, equally, would be influenced by the specialisms and cultural tendencies on either side of them.

Geography cannot wholly determine culture; it can only help to locate it. It is therefore the interrelationship between customary convention and the nature of an area that gives traditional popular culture its essentially spatial character. Probably every *township, for example, had some particularized sense of its own past: a myth of origin (usually associated specifically with either Britons, or Anglo-Saxons, or Scandinavians) or even a prehistoric landmark around which had gathered some legendary or superstitious association; see L. V. Grinsall, *The Folklore of Prehistoric Sites in Britain* (1976). Each local community, moreover, boasted its own annual cycle of *calendar customs that owed as much to cultural variables (like the earlier timing of parish wakes to coincide with the dedication feasts of the local church) as to physical contexts; while it was people, not objects, who were ritualized in the public rites of passage which regularly punctuated the life of any small society. Current work on the West Country is showing, moreover, that even in the 19th century local people shared mental 'maps' of their areas in terms of landscape features and *boundaries and their peculiarly local association with a range of supernatural or mythological perceptions. The marking of boundaries as transitional between two different worlds is, of course, very ancient, whether pagan shrines earlier or, for example, gate-chapels or bridge chapels later. *Rogation processions annually reiterated parish boundaries; summer often involved boundary tugs-of-war or some other sport, like 'foot' ball, between those living on either side of a dividing line.

More broadcast still were the associations or observances that were peculiar to entire regions. Twelfth-centruy miracles associated with St William of Norwich are recorded up to 50 miles from that city. Much of medieval north-east England looked to the protection of St Cuthbert, a relic of whom, stitched into 'his' banner, was brought out to rally the rebels on the *Pilgrimage of Grace. In Victoria's reign, by contrast, detailed work on the contrasted types of *'mummers' ' plays reveals heavily regionalized distributions of form and seasonal timing; see E. C. Cawte, Alex Helm, and N.

Peacock, *English Ritual Drama* (1967). Different types of supernatural being, varying beliefs about the character of certain 'sacred' birds like robins or wrens, and the range of terms for farm implements or flowers: all these exemplify the detailed ways in which popular culture was variously expressed across Britain so that those involved felt they 'belonged' to one district rather than to another.

Nothing illustrates this more than the often mutually incomprehensible languages, regional dialects, and pronunciations that used to characterize Britain: the early division of the Celtic linguistic traditions into Brythonic (*Cornish, *Welsh, Cumbric) and Goidelic (Irish, Scottish, and Isle of Man *Gaelic) on the one hand; and the evolution of separate English dialects (including lowland Scots), independently of Continental linguistic origins, on the other. The spatially concentrated, *regional* realities of these numerous popular linguistic divisions are therefore to be directly compared with the *internationally* inspired linguistic conventions of 'polite' culture: Latin as the language of the medieval church of Christendom, of law, of learning, and, through to the 18th century, of international diplomacy; Anglo-Norman French (and a European code of chivalry) as the language and culture of conquerors and courtiers down to the age of Chaucer. Even the new English of government (the later-14th-century 'Chancery standard') and the direct ancestor of today's standard English, 'southern English', evolved in a specifically restricted spatial sense, emanating from London, and by the late 16th century was described as confined to within a 60-mile radius of the capital; see Martyn F. Wakelin, *English Dialects* (1972). Culture, in both its popular and its élitist senses, therefore, is most accurately seen as comprising geographically variable expressions of different usages.

It was the *town (as an exceptional concentration of subcultures) that comprised the interface between rural and urban, popular and polite, and which, as a result, may be seen as the focus for regional culture; as at the forefront in adapting new practices; and thus as the prime mediator in any broad process of cultural change. The more important medieval towns with their calendars of *civic ritual which drew in crowds from the countryside, moreover, were sited in areas of relatively dense population that therefore also linked groups of neighbouring urban centres into identifiable regional networks. The towns comprising the core of each such network tended to concentrate towards the lower reaches of a major river-drainage basin; to look outwards along navigable rivers towards broadly the same external influences along the coast or from abroad; to straddle a whole series of *pays*; and to interlink several neighbouring counties. Each network was hierarchically structured, being headed normally by a substantial provincial centre (often a cathedral city). Usually dividing these networks and the areas they served from one another for most periods were belts of more sparsely populated, less urbanized countryside along the major watersheds. For these and other reasons, therefore, it has been suggested that—with due allowance paid to the identities of the constituent parts—such a cluster of interconnected counties (which might usefully be regarded as comprising a 'cultural province') could represent 'a realistically generalised cultural setting at its *maximal* localised extent'; see Charles Phythian-Adams (ed.), *Societies, Cultures and Kinship 1580–1850* (1993). The concept thus supplies an approximate way of defining the broad outer limits of separate regional cultures. Such combinations of old counties highlight and help to explain the cultural distinctiveness of, for example, Norfolk and Suffolk together, Devon with Cornwall, Lancashire (north and south of the Sands), together with south Westmorland and Cheshire; and perhaps Cardiganshire with Merioneth.

Change to both cultural and geographical patterns occurred piecemeal, cumulatively rather than suddenly, and in response to a whole range of causes. In the broadest possible terms it took 400 years, between *c*.1550 and *c*.1950, to extinguish the more traditional patterns that had continuously evolved over the previous millennium, and to replace them with wholly new modes. Change has therefore to be understood as the product of both erosive and innovative processes, as often a matter of adaption and survival rather than fundamental alteration, and as measurable ultimately in terms of the manner in which the new replaced the underlying characteristics, the essential idioms, and the spatial realities of the old.

The erosive processes of change may be swiftly summarized. Most subversive of the old was that long process of demystification by which all aspects of life in society (and especially social constructions of space and time) were gradually separated from supernatural associations and significances; see C. John Sommerville, *The Secularisation of Early Modern England* (1992). This process had begun even before the Reformation though, of course, it

accelerated with it (especially with the translation of the *Bible into English, and the targeting of festivals, relics, images, and the quasi-magical role of the *priest). There were, secondly, the varyingly successful *ad hoc* campaigns waged by the authorities (mistakenly treated by some historians as though they comprised a logical programme of reformation) to extirpate practices that they regarded as ungodly, idle, or dangerous to their own interests: the abolition of religious *guilds and great ceremonial occasions in towns at the Reformation; the *Puritan attack (backed up by some village élites) on sports and pastimes, like maypole dancing, on the Sabbath—the so-called 'reformation of manners'; the persecution of witches in the late 16th and 17th centuries (Christina Larner, *Enemies of God: The Witch Hunt in Scotland* (1981)); the 18th-century assertion of property rights over a spectrum of customary rights on pain of draconian statutory penalties; the campaign against blood-sports during the first 40 years of the 19th century (Robert W. Malcolmson, *Popular Recreation in English Society 1700–1850* (1973)); Victorian liturgical reform and the *temperance movement. Finally, and most destructive of all, however, was the disruption of traditional, collective farming routines (and the communal customs which punctuated them) as the product, first, of centuries of *enclosure (which incidentally also often involved the privatization and obliteration of both customary places for recreation and access to wildlife as food) and, second and eventually, of the mechanization of agriculture with the reduction in labour which that incurred.

None of these processes of erosion, however, was decisive in itself. It is worth emphasizing, indeed, that even putting aside the popular revivalism associated with the *Restoration, older modes often survived unscathed or were simply adapted. Londoners were still hanging horseshoes over their doors against *witchcraft in the late 17th century; people were consulting 'cunning' folk against witchcraft at Exeter, Leicester, and Newcastle in the 19th century; the 'magical' lore of the East Anglian horsemen has been passed through to the 20th. After the Reformation, the older pattern of calendrical observances was continued in reduced form through a growing multitude of *alehouses. Older modes of thought were often perpetuated even in print: in *chapbook tales, *almanacs, calendars, and ballads; see Bernard Capp, *Astrology and the Popular Press* (1979). Transposed into municipal or fair-time processions, something of the late medieval pattern of public ceremonial was projected through the London Lord Mayor's Show, or shows or processions at, for example, Norwich, Coventry, or Shrewsbury. Some calendrical observances were marked anew ('mummers'' plays) or taken over (*May Day) as occasions for licensed 'begging' by the less fortunate (farm labourers, milkmaids, or chimney sweeps, for example). For many, if the central rite of a former tradition ceased to be observed, the enjoyable ancillary activities—ritual foods, sports, dancing—nevertheless often survived. Private superstition lasted where public symbols were discarded.

What more definitively undermined the traditional pattern, therefore, were those forces for *innovation* that eventually subverted its regionalized basis. Leaving aside relevant and important considerations like population shifts between countryside and town and vastly improved communications, three specifically cultural factors are usually marshalled to account for this process.

One such was the role of the state, from *c.*1600 onwards, in changing and widening the significances of traditional calendars by promoting regular *national* celebrations (Guy Fawkes, the Defeat of the Armada), particular events like coronations or royal childbirths (David Cressy, *Bonfires and Bells* (1989)), and even by imposing the new *Gregorian calendar in 1752 and, later, new *holiday patterns (e.g. Bank Holidays) at the expense not only of local rhythms but also, with the (delayed) introduction in 1880 of Greenwich Mean Time, of local time itself. A corollary to this closer involvement of the state at local levels was the growing importance of popular elections, and the opportunities these provided for political 'theatre' and thus for localized participation in national controversies.

A second factor was the widening of consumer choice from the 16th and 17th centuries onwards: choice of housing (often in terms of rebuilding), decoration, furnishing, and utensils; choice of clothing or (with the spread of literacy) of reading matter with the ideas which might thus be publicized (Margaret Spufford, *The Great Reclothing of Rural England* (1984) and *Small Books and Pleasant Histories* (1981)). With that choice came products from far afield (including, eventually, both non-local building materials and cheaper factory-made products that undercut the old craft skills) and the influence of wider fashions (from increasing opportunities for gambling to addictive gindrinking) together with new opinions. Increasingly then, and especially in post-Restoration

towns, popular culture was affected by the growing presence, seductive influence, and—given funds—the ready imitability of the rival 'polite' culture (and the more sophisticated goods and recreations, like *horse racing, which it fostered), a manifestation which has been aptly dubbed, by Peter Borsay, 'the English Urban Renaissance'. A connected further development was the 'commercialisation of leisure' (J. H. Plumb (ed.), *The Commercialisation of Leisure in Eighteenth-Century England* (1973)), by which grew up a whole leisure industry for 'polite' society that, in turn, and in cheaper form, would later evolve a popular version of itself. The largely urban providers of leisure thus became outsiders to the local members of society who consumed it. In particular, the attraction of the capital for huge numbers of migrants and the expanding availability of special-purpose settlements at a distance from the home base—*spas or, still later, *seaside resorts—helped to widen hitherto spatially limited visions; see John K. Walton, *The English Seaside Resort* (1983).

The third and decisive factor was the emergence of mass urban societies and the distancing of humanity from 'wild' nature (though we do well to remember the continuing presence in towns of hens, pigs, cows, and horses—let alone *allotments eventually). By the mid-19th century, these vast built-up city areas, in so concentrating populations, may be seen as tending to supersede, in certain regions of Britain, the traditional urban networks that had acted formerly in the same vicinities as the vertebrae of the old cultural provinces. In the more successful and vibrant conurbations, nevertheless, a populist sense of urban-regional identity was newly expressed, most notably in widely circulated dialect literature and in the humorous local characterizations of popular theatre; see P. Joyce, *Visions of the People* (1991).

For a time, however, the more traditional popular culture appears to have been successfully adapted to a widespread displacement of the celebration of community customs by a developing emphasis instead on the wider values of inter-parochial neighbourhood, or even of broader areas, like Hallamshire, that could be individually characterized by contemporaries as an identifiable *'country'. The retimetabling of parish wakes by Henry VIII to the autumn season released neighbouring parishes to space their observances so that relatives could visit different celebrations in turn. The new non-conforming congregations—allowing choice in religion—were normally drawn from groups of proximate parishes. The drastic post-medieval decline in village markets focused attendance alternatively on those fewer, often small, market towns—so often also the vehicles for *Protestant preaching—that did survive the period of contraction. Craft regions surrounding other market centres ensured distinct geographical expressions of working culture, while the earlier stages of industrialization, at least, may well have intensified the regional observance of customary ways; see J. Langton, 'The Industrial Revolution and the Regional Geography of England', *Institute of British Geographers Transactions*, NS, 10/2 (1984). The continuing importance of county towns and cathedral cities, moreover, with their hierarchies of *inns (the equivalent of bus-stops for the rural *carriers), the regional circulation of their *newspapers, and their function as sites for *hiring fairs, similarly underlined the fact that even during the 19th century, in wide areas of Britain where mass urbanization did not take place (such as that idealized as *Hardy's *'Wessex') the former provincial patterns long survived.

It may well be, indeed, that instead of anticipating the ubiquitous and increasingly monolithic late 20th-century form of popular culture (backed as it currently is by the international mass media and advertising), historians of the 19th century should not underestimate the degree to which more traditional neighbourhood expressions of local popular culture might also be adapted (but in a more continuously connected fashion) to new mass urban conditions. It is certainly arguable that rather than thinking of a process of blending into something recognizable as a single, broad, 'working-class' culture, we should be considering instead a multiplication of popular subcultures in a spectrum of contrasted localized contexts. Social circumstances ranged from the variegated multitude of those whom Mayhew described as 'street folk' to the 'respectable' working class, and from the new ethnic blend of 'British' people—as opposed to natives—in the greater cities (with cultural concentrations of *Irish in English, Welsh, and Scottish towns, English in the south Wales conurbations and so on: Lynn Lees, *Exiles of Erin* (1979)) to the development of *Jewish or *Chinese ghettos. Types of neighbourhood might now vary in two ways. First was the relation of residence to place of work: from notable coincidences of the two (towns with small workshop traditions, mining settlements, mill or factory colonies, and perhaps former village cores that had been swamped by suburban expansion) to areas

wholly segregated from workplaces by the new transport systems. Second was the marked increase in social zoning. Mass urban society thus emphasized neighbourhoods of residence characterized by minute variation in class or ethnic origin at one extreme; and interest groups (associations, unions, chapels, etc.) of more widely dispersed individuals at the other.

It thus seems possible broadly to identify two contrasted spatial expressions of mass urban popular culture. On the one hand—and of course simplistically—where work (or ethnicity) and residence largely coincided, we seem to see highly localized neighbourhood areas sharing the cultures of work, survival, and leisure in ways that bear a recognizable relation to traditional modes (especially where manual skills predominated), but looking to new street-wise values—and often out-of-doors—with the pub as the local recreational outlet for men and, in the most impoverished cases, the pawn-shop as the focus of credit relationships for women (Melanie Tebbutt, *Making Ends Meet: Pawnbroking and Working-Class Credit* (1983)). It would mostly be in these areas, too, that communal recreational groups like choirs or *brass bands would be active of an evening or indoors.

On the other hand, there is a growing disjunction in the second type of neighbourhood between the individual, the area of residence, and the wider world, a disjunction which resolves itself into a new tension between what is public and what is private; see M. J. Daunton, 'Public Place and Private Space: The Victorian City and the Working-Class Household' in D. Fraser and A. Sutcliffe, (eds.), *The Pursuit of Urban History* (1983). In such forms of neighbourhood, communal and public participation, customary controls, traditional justifications for protest, local time and the collective marking of local space—all these now tended to be superseded by a growing concern for 'private' domestic space. 'Participation' here was becoming that of the anonymous individual or, in the case of seaside holidays, the family group in the crowd. An open-air, largely daylight culture was being increasingly displaced on the one hand by indoor work at a distance from home, often in disciplined numbers, and the growth of indoor entertainment (from music halls to the more sophisticated public houses); and on the other by slightly greater opportunities for personal privacy in upper-artisan and lower-middle-class homes with more rooms and, eventually, artificial lighting. In a parallel process of interiorization, if both *education and literacy (and thus consequently the sequential mode of reading) expanded hugely, the utility of visual metaphor, verbal imagery, and hence lateral skills of association probably dwindled, but in more complex ways than we had formerly suspected; see David Vincent, *Literacy and Popular Culture: England 1750–1914* (1989). Public, as opposed to family ritual, was replaced by commercialized recreation; see James Walvin, *Leisure and Society 1830–1950* (1978). The passivity of the reader, the spectator, the music-hall audience, or the worshipper confined to his or her pew was becoming the norm. The harshness and toughness of life could now be projected to some extent onto rival teams as urban *football, for example, became popular, rather than on to human and animal suffering. Newly organized sport, at venues for which it was necessary to travel beyond the home neighbourhood, involved other people's ritualized aggression; teams with which the spectator could identify, but at a distance; and a freshly developed sense of rival urban loyalties. Spectator sport, indeed, probably more than anything else, epitomizes the gulf that now divides what has become the predominantly urban, mass culture of today from the small-scale, participatory, provincial cultures of yesteryear. See J. M. Golby and A. W. Purdue, *The Civilisation of the Crowd: Popular Culture in England 1750–1900* (1984), and Alexander Fenton, *The Shape of the Past: Essays in Scottish Ethnology*, 2 vols. (1986).

CHARLES PHYTHIAN-ADAMS

population levels and trends. Interest in the study of demography began in an informed way in the late 17th century. An early attempt to calculate population totals was John Graunt, *Natural and Political Observations upon the Bills of Mortality* (1662). Sir William Petty, *Political Arithmetick* (1690) stressed the value of comparative statistics in a discussion of political economy. The outstanding work of this period was Gregory *King, *Natural and Political Observations and Conclusions upon the State and Condition of England* (1696), which used the *hearth tax and *poll tax returns of the previous decades to estimate population levels and analyse social structure. King's work is still discussed by historical demographers who study the late 17th century. Another early writer whose work is of lasting value was Thomas Short, a Scottish doctor based in Sheffield, who pioneered the use of *parish registers in the study of historical demography, in *New Observations . . . on City, Town and Country Bills of Mortality* (1750) and *A Comparative History of the Increase and Decrease of Mankind* (1767). The most influential of these earlier works, however, has undoubtedly been Thomas Robert *Malthus, *Essay on the Principle of Population* (1798, extended in a new edition, 1803), which argued that the natural tendency of population was to increase faster than the means of subsistence.

The study of disease attracted scholarly interest in the 19th century, when major advances in the control of certain diseases were made. The outstanding contribution was Charles Creighton, *A History of Epidemics in Britain* (2 vols., 1894). Another aspect of demography was the study of geographical *mobility, which was advanced by the publication of E. G. *Ravenstein, 'The Laws of Migration', *The Journal of the Royal Statistical Society*, 48 (1885), which categorized various stages of migration and emphasized that most people travelled relatively short distances. Ravenstein's model has proved of lasting worth.

Major advances in the study of historical demography have been made in the second half of the 20th century. An early attempt at an overall view of the population of the Middle Ages was J. C. Russell, *British Medieval Population* (1948). (See also POSTAN THESIS.) Establishing the level of population at various times in the past has become a major task for local historians. Two pioneering works were J. D. *Chambers, *The Vale of Trent, 1670–1800: A Regional Study of Economic Change* (*Economic History Review*, Supplement III, 1957), an examination of industrial development and population trends, and W. G. *Hoskins, 'The Population of an English Village, 1086–1801: A Study of Wigston Magna' (1957, repr. in *Provincial England*, 1963). Joan Thirsk, 'Sources of Information on Population', *Amateur Historian*, 4/4 and 5 (1959) outlined the problems of studying demographic history for the period 1500–1760, particularly for the years 1640–1700, stressing local variations and assessing sources such as parish registers, the *lay subsidy assessments of 1524 and 1525, the *ecclesiastical census returns of 1563 and 1603, the *Protestation returns of 1641–2, and the hearth tax returns of the 1660s and 1670s.

Meanwhile, French historians of the *Annales* school, notably Louis Henry and Pierre Goubert, were pioneering techniques for the study of parish registers in establishing demographic data for the early modern period. In 1964 their success inspired a group of historical demographers to form the Cambridge Group for the Study of Population and Social Structure (*CAMPOP), whereby a team of academics was assisted by amateur historians in many different parts of England in the transcription and analysis of numerous parish registers and involving the reconstituting of families. A leading member of the group, Peter Laslett, published *The World We Have Lost* (1965), which has been superseded by later findings but which was enormously stimulating in opening up new avenues of research, e.g. on the size and structure of *households and on whether the *peasants really starved. This was soon followed by an official publication of CAMPOP, E. A. Wrigley (ed.), *Introduction to English Historical Demography* (1966), which provided guidance on sources and method, e.g. the aggregative analysis of parish registers, *family reconstitution, and the recording of the impact of *harvest fluctuations. Similar guidance was provided by T. H. Hollingworth, *Historical Demography* (1969), which took a world view. See also J. T. Krause, 'The Changing Adequacy of English Registration, 1690–1837' in D. V. Glass and D. E. C. Eversley, *Population in History* (1965).

Amongst the detailed local studies of this period were D. E. C. Eversley, 'A Survey of Population in an Area of Worcestershire, 1660–1850', *Population Studies*, 10 (1957); Michael Drake, 'An Elementary Exercise in Parish Register Demography', *Economic History Review*, 2nd ser., 14/3 (1962), which dealt with certain West Riding parishes between 1540 and 1699; P. Laslett and J. Harrison, 'Clayworth and Cogenhoe' in H. E. Bell and R. L. Ollard, *Historical Essays Presented to David Ogg* (1962), which examined the social structure of two midland parishes from 17th-century listings; and E. A. Wrigley, 'Family Limitation in Pre-Industrial England', *Economic History Review*, 2nd ser., 19/1 (1966), which examined one Devon parish, Colyton. (See also the journal *Local Population Studies*.)

Further advances in the understanding of historical demography were made in the 1970s, starting with the overviews: M. W. Flinn, *British Population Growth, 1700–1850* (1970) and J. D. Chambers, *Population, Economy and Society in Pre-Industrial England* (1972). Local studies of wide general importance included M. Anderson, *Family Structure in Nineteenth-Century Lancashire* (1971), which was based on the *census returns for Preston, A. Gooder, 'The Population Crisis of 1727–30 in Warwickshire', *Midland History*, 1 (1972), A. B. Appleby, 'Disease or Famine? Mortality in Cumberland and Westmorland', *Economic History Review*, 2nd ser., 26/3 (1973), W. A. Armstrong, *Stability and Change in an English County Town: A Social Study of York, 1801–51* (1974), V. Skipp, *Crisis*

and Development: An Ecological Case Study of the Forest of Arden, 1570–1674 (1978), and C. V. Phythian-Adams, *Desolation of a City: Coventry and the Urban Crisis of the Late Middle Ages* (1979). Studies of particular aspects of demography included J. Cornwall, 'English Population in the Early Sixteenth Century', *Economic History Review*, 2nd ser., 23/1 (1970), P. Laslett and R. Wall (eds.), *Household and Family in Past Time* (1972), L. A. Clarkson, *Death, Disease and Famine in Pre-Industrial England* (1975), D. Levine, 'The Reliability of Parochial Registration and the Representativeness of Family Reconstitution', *Population Studies*, 30 (1976), J. Hatcher, *Plague, Population and the English Economy, 1348–1530* (1977), P. Laslett, *Family Life and Illicit Love in Earlier Generations* (1977), A. P. Appleby, *Famine in Tudor and Stuart England* (1978), and P. Clark, 'Migration in England During the Late Seventeenth and Early Eighteenth Centuries', *Past and Present*, 73 (1979).

The work of the Cambridge Group came to fruition with the publication of E. A. Wrigley and R. S. Schofield, *The Population History of England, 1541–1871: A Reconstruction* (1981). This magisterial work forms the basis of further studies at both the national and the local level. The paucity and inadequacy of demographic data for Scotland and Ireland, and to a lesser extent Wales, in the early modern period has prevented similar studies at the same depth. See, however, R. A. Houston, *The Population History of Britain and Ireland, 1500–1750* (1992), and J. G. Kyd (ed.), *Scottish Population Statistics, Including Webster's Analysis of Population, 1755* (Scottish History Society, 3rd ser., 44, 1952). Major contributions to the study of historical demography since the appearance of Wrigley and Schofield's book include L. Bonfield, R. Smith, and K. Wrightson (eds.), *The World We Have Gained: Histories of Population and Social Structure* (1986), P. Clark and D. Souden (eds.), *Migration and Society in Early Modern England* (1987), R. M. Smith (ed.), *Regional and Spatial Demographic Patterns in the Past* (1990), D. Levine and K. Wrightson, *The Making of An Industrial Society: Whickham, 1560–1765* (1991), and K. Schurer and T. Arkell, *Surveying the People: The Interpretation and Use of Document Sources for the Study of Population in the Later Seventeenth Century* (1992).

The work of the historical demographers has brought the sources that are commonly used for estimating population levels and analyzing social structure under intensive scrutiny. Far more is now known about the historical background of each source and the pitfalls in its interpretation. Historical demography is a highly technical subject that uses sophisticated statistical techniques. Given the dubious nature of the raw data, the results obtained by such techniques are bound to be controversial. A wide margin of error has to be allowed for. Even the 404 parishes chosen by Wrigley and Schofield because of the richness of their registration are only a small sample of the ancient parishes of England and Wales. The techniques of family reconstitution can be applied successfully to only a limited number of parish registers. Another criticism is that historical demographers often do not relate their findings to studies of *communities and local societies, but present them in isolation. It is clear that much work remains to be done on local and regional variations from the general picture outlined by the Cambridge Group. For example, not all parts of the country experienced stagnating population levels in the late 17th century.

Nevertheless, the achievements of CAMPOP are impressive. Local findings must certainly be set against the general trends that have emerged so clearly from the analysis of the 404 English parishes for the early modern period, leading into the modern. The local historian needs to grasp what seems to have been happening at the national level in order to understand whether the experience of his or her particular society was a common one or was exceptional. Establishing the level of population of a town or a rural parish at various points of time is a basic task for the local historian, even if he or she concludes that the records have too many imperfections to allow precision. The attempt must be made, and a working knowledge of the sources and their uses must be acquired. Likewise, the family historian needs to be familiar with current work on family size, age at marriage, expectancy of life, and all the other aspects of family life that have occupied social historians in the last third of the 20th century. It has been the considerable achievement of the historical demographers to establish the central importance of population levels and trends in the understanding of the history of local societies and the country at large.

The most difficult period for demographic study is the Middle Ages, before parish registers were first kept in 1538. The *Domesday Book, lay subsidies, and the poll tax returns of 1377–81 are poor guides to total population figures. Estimates of the population of England at the time of the Domesday Book vary from 1.5 to 2.25 million. It is accepted that population rose considerably in the 12th and 13th cen-

turies, to perhaps 5 or 6 million or more by 1300. Historians now place the level of the medieval population much higher than previous estimates. A lively area of debate concerns the question of how far the national population began to decline before the *Black Death (1348–50). See Bruce M. S. Campbell (ed.), *Before the Black Death: Studies in the 'Crisis' of the Early Fourteenth Century* (1991). The population in the second decade of the 14th century may have declined by 15 per cent or more, the severest decline ever recorded outside periods of bubonic plague. Old estimates of the death toll of the Black Death have been confirmed at a third, perhaps even a half of the population. Other major epidemics occurred in 1360–2 and 1369. Estimates based on the poll tax returns of 1377 suggest a national population of 2.2 to 3 million. The trend remained downwards for the next hundred years, so that by the third quarter of the 15th century the English population may have been reduced to barely 2 million. Recovery was slow, with only modest signs that the decline had been halted by the 1480s and 1490s. By 1500 England may have had only half the number of people that occupied the land 200 years previously. Even by the 1520s recovery had not gone far.

The earliest parish registers suggest that demographic recovery was well under way by the 1530s and 1540s, however. The whole of western Europe seems to have experienced moderately fast growth during the next hundred years. Wrigley and Schofield conclude that between 1540 and 1640 England's population rose from about 2.75 million to roughly 5 million. After 1640 the annual frequencies of both marriages and births fell, then oscillated until 1710, while burial frequencies continued to rise before flattening out about 1680. They estimate that England's population declined slightly between 1656 and 1686 and note that sustained population growth did not get under way until the 1740s, since when it has never stopped rising. However, the experiences of different regions must allow for considerable variation on this general pattern. Industrial regions, such as those centred on Birmingham and Sheffield, certainly experienced considerable population growth from c.1700, if not before; and certain non-industrial regions, e.g. Shropshire, witnessed steady growth throughout the 17th century.

The first national census to be taken in Britain was that of 1801. The population of England and Wales was counted at 8.9 million, which is usually adjusted for under-recording to

9.2 million. The second decade of the 19th century experienced the fastest rate of growth. By 1851 the population of England and Wales had almost doubled to 17.9 million, and by 1911 it had doubled again to 36.1 million. The 20th century has seen slower rates of growth. The old argument as to whether the great growth in the population was due more to increased births or to falling death rates has been settled. Wrigley and Schofield calculate that between 1750 and 1871 only about one-third of the growth of population can be accounted for by a reduced death rate, and that the remaining two-thirds of the growth was the result of rising fertility from earlier and more frequent marriages. From the late 1870s onwards, older patterns re-emerged, and at the same time *contraception techniques became widely available. Both the crude birth rate and the fertility rate therefore declined in the 1880s and 1890s, but the increased expectancy of life kept population totals rising.

Another old debate which has been largely resolved has been on the question of whether people starved to death as the result of *famine. England did not suffer as badly as did France in the early modern period. By the 17th century England's agricultural economy was sufficiently advanced to prevent dire consequences from bad harvests, other than in certain regions at exceptional times. Andrew Appleby demonstrated that in Cumbria heavy mortalities followed disastrous harvests in the 1580s, and that the bad harvests of 1622–3 caused considerable distress. Whether death was caused directly by starvation or by malnutrition which lowered resistance to infectious diseases such as *typhus is debatable. The relationship between malnutrition and individual diseases is complex. Wrigley and Schofield argue that English subsistence crises had a greater effect on fertility (particularly through delayed marriages) than on mortality, and that periods of high mortality were rarely related to economic conditions. Their explanation of exceptional numbers of burials is the independent and unpredictable visitations of infectious *disease. They demonstrate that in their sample of 404 parishes local crises were overwhelmingly of short duration, and that, although they occurred throughout the year, they were generally much more frequent in late summer and autumn. Diarrhoeal infections such as *dysentery seem to have been the major killers in the peak months of August and September. This pattern contrasts sharply with the normal peak of burials in the spring. This pattern is not universal, however. See David Hey, *The Fiery Blades of Hallamshire:*

Sheffield and Its Neighbourhood, 1660–1740 (1991), which demonstrates that in Sheffield summer and autumn epidemics were comparatively rare, that the pattern of epidemics bore little relation to that experienced in some of Wrigley and Schofield's 404 parishes, and that the peak months for mortalities were usually March, April, and May, even in abnormal years. The experience of local communities is very variable.

England is exceptional in having so many parish registers dating from the 16th and 17th centuries. Estimating earlier population levels and discerning trends is much more difficult in Wales, Scotland, and Ireland. The population of Wales has always been small, though it grew considerably in the south-east as the result of industrialization in the late 18th and 19th centuries. Estimates vary, but the population of Wales was probably around 200,000 in 1500, and perhaps 400,000 in 1700. By 1801 it had risen to 587,000, and by 1901 to 2,012,900. In 1976 it was recorded at 2,749,400. During the early modern period the inhabitants of Wales were spread fairly evenly between the various regions, but in the 19th century the south-east became dominant. In 1801 Glamorgan and Gwent accounted for 20 per cent of the Welsh population; by 1901 this proportion had risen to 57.5 per cent, and since the First World War it has varied between 60 and 65 per cent.

For Scotland, see M. Flinn *et al.* (eds.), *Scottish Population History from the Seventeenth Century to the 1930s* (1977), which used over 100 parish registers to identify the major periods of mortality. Three exceptional periods of crisis were recognized. That of 1623 was the result of the disastrous harvests of 1621–2; the crisis of 1645–8 was caused by bubonic *plague; and the third great crisis, which lasted for much of the 1690s, was again caused by seriously deficient harvests. Scotland experienced no similar crises during the 18th century, as the economy became more integrated, harvests did not fail for more than one year at a time, and measures to provide famine relief became more efficient. Scottish experience mirrors that of England until the *potato blight of 1836–7 and 1845–6 caused high mortalities in the western Highlands and Islands (though famine relief prevented disaster on the Irish scale). See T. M. Devine, *The Great Highland Famine* (1988). In the same period the larger towns suffered major epidemics, especially of water-borne diseases such as *cholera, dysentery, and *typhoid, and heavy mortalities from diseases such as *tuberculosis and typhus which spread in the slums.

Scottish mortality rates declined from the 1870s onwards.

The poor quality of Scottish parish registers has prevented systematic study of fertility, but the limited evidence suggests a pattern similar to that in England. See David Moody, *Scottish Family History* (1988), ch. 3, for a discussion of the records that are available for demographic analysis, and Helen Dingwall, *Late Seventeenth-Century Edinburgh: A Demographic Study* (1993). (See also EMIGRATION; IRISH EMIGRATION; CLEARANCES, HIGHLAND; and RURAL DEPOPULATION.) In 1755 Scotland's population was 1.25 million, by 1801 it had grown to more than 1.5 million, half a century later it had reached nearly 3 million, and by 1901 it was over 4.5 million. Whereas in 1755 only four Scottish towns had more than 10,000 inhabitants, by 1901 half the population lived in towns of at least that size. In the process of urbanization, Lowland Scotland closely followed the English model. Glasgow grew during the 19th century until it could claim to have become the 'Second City of the Empire'.

For an introduction to Irish demographic history, see Liam Kennedy and Leslie A. Clarkson, 'Birth, Death and Exile: Irish Population History, 1700–1921' in B. J. Graham and L. J. Proudfoot, *An Historical Geography of Ireland* (1993), ch. 5. Irish population growth in the 18th and and early 19th centuries was remarkable by European standards, for it was double that of France and at least equal to the rate of 0.8 per cent per annum of that of Britain. Population growth in Ireland clearly cannot be linked with the development of an industrial economy. It ended in the disaster of the Great Famine, on which see Mary E. Daly, *The Famine in Ireland* (1986), which provides a good introduction to the subject and a bibliography.

The first census of Ireland was taken in 1821. Estimates of the population in earlier periods are based on data that is far less reliable than the (imperfect) information that is available for England. Many places do not have surviving parish registers, and estimates of the national population based on hearth tax returns for 1687 vary from 1.7 million to 2.2 million. About a hundred years later, the population is thought to have reached somewhere between 4.2 and 4.8 million. The census of 1821 recorded 6.8 million. Twenty years later, this had risen to 8.2 million. The major difference between Ireland and the rest of the British Isles is that this population growth was not associated with rapid urbanization. The urban proportion rose sharply after the Famine as the rural population

migrated to the towns and overseas to Britain and North America. By 1901 Ireland's population had dropped to 4.5 million. It continued to decline in the first part of the 20th century.

See also BIRTH RATES; DEATH RATES; FERTILITY RATES; and LONDON.

port. 1. The place-name can mean either harbour, market town, or gate.

2. (See DOCKS, DOCKYARDS, and RIVER TRAFFIC.) The Exchequer port books, housed at the *Public Record Office under E 190, are an important source for the history of local overseas trade and of coastal traffic in the early modern period. They survive in large numbers for many ports for the period 1565–1799, though there are gaps in the *Civil War and *Commonwealth and for some ports the records cease in the mid-18th century. For a list of head ports and their subordinate ports, see N. J. Williams (ed.), *A Descriptive List of Exchequer, Queen's Remembrancer Port Books, 1565–1700* (1960). For the port books of 1701–98, see *List and Index Society Publications, vols. 58, 66, and 80 (1970–2). The overseas port books give details of trade with the colonies, Scotland, Ireland, and the Channel Isles. They name the ship and its master, note the tonnage, and record the date either of arrival or departure, or of the payment of duties. From 1660 onwards they increasingly record the name of the foreign port and give details of the goods that were being transported. Coastal trade was free from duties, but similar records were kept to ensure that the goods were taken no further than Britain. Historians are no longer as sceptical of the information in the port books as they were when it was believed that evasion was widespread through *smuggling and corruption.

Port books contain names of individuals who worked boats and those who had a commercial interest in the cargoes, but they provide this detailed information in an unsystematic manner and so they have rarely been studied in full. The University of Wolverhampton has created a computer database of the Gloucester port books between 1565 and 1765, which provide rich information on the trade of a major river-system. See M. D. G. Wanklyn, 'The Severn Navigation in the Seventeenth Century: Long Distance Trade of Shrewsbury Boats', *Midland History*, 13 (1988), and 'Urban Revival in Early-Modern England: Bridgnorth and the River Trade, 1660–1800', *Midland History*, 18 (1993), which uses some of this information in conjunction with other local sources. Port books may, however, distort the relative importance of towns or districts along a river. They record long-distance boats, but these may not have dominated the short-distance trade which may have been more important. See N. J. Williams, 'The London Port Books', *Transactions of the London and Middlesex Archaeological Society*, 18 (1955), D. M. Woodward, 'Port Books', *History*, 4 (1970), and W. B. Stephens, 'The Exchequer Port Books as a Source for the History of the English Cloth Trade', *Textile History*, 1 (1969).

portcullis. The heavy grating, made of iron or wood and iron, that defended the entrance of a medieval *castle, *manor house, or town. Few survive, but vertical grooves in the walls often indicate where a portcullis was raised and lowered.

Portland stone. The white oolitic limestone of the Isle of Portland (Dorset) was regarded by Sir Christopher Wren as the finest of building stones. It was shipped in large quantities to rebuild London after the Great Fire of 1666. The fashion was soon copied in other towns, e.g. Dublin. The huge quarries on the Isle testify to the importance of the industry through to the 20th century. 'Portland Cement' was patented in 1824 by Joseph Aspdin of Leeds, who thought his mixture of chalk and clay, fired at a high temperature and mixed with water, resembled Portland stone.

portraiture. The fashion for hanging portraits of family and friends developed in the reign of Elizabeth I. Few families have portraits of ancestors before the 18th and 19th centuries, however, when the fashion spread down the social scale to the middle classes.

Postan thesis. Sir Michael Postan's view of the demographic history of the English countryside before the *Black Death, expounded in M. M. Postan (ed.), *Cambridge Economic History of Europe*, i: *The Agrarian Life of the Middle Ages* (2nd edn., 1966), M. M. Postan, *The Medieval Economy and Society: An Economic History of Britain in the Middle Ages* (1972), and other works, was enormously influential, but from the late 1980s onwards has been increasingly challenged. See, for instance, Bruce M. S. Campbell (ed.), *Before the Black Death: Studies in the 'Crisis' of the Early Fourteenth Century* (1991), which reject Postan's *Malthusianism. The 'Postan thesis' was that the growing population in the 13th and 14th centuries was faced with land hunger, that smallholdings predominated, that land reclaimed from the edges of the fens, moors, woods, and marshes was of poor quality, that the fertility of soils declined, and

that the average expectation of life declined during the century after 1250. The series of crop and livestock disasters between 1315 and 1322 was seen as a Malthusian crisis. The enormous pressure of the population on the inadequate resources led to a declining standard of living until the pressure was dramatically eased with the Black Death. The thesis has been modified by demographic historians who have argued that the 1315–22 crisis was 'more than a mere fluctuation, but less than a turning point' and by agrarian historians who have argued that an adequate living could be earned even on the so-called margins. See Mark Bailey, *A Marginal Economy?: East Anglian Breckland in the Later Middle Ages* (1989).

postcards were used from about 1870 onwards. Picture-postcards with views of streets and rural scenes became popular towards the end of the 19th century and were used on a very large scale during the first 20 years of the 20th century. Local history societies and individual authors have reproduced collections of picture-postcards for many towns and villages, often comparing past and present scenes. Few attempts have yet been made to incorporate these and other old *photographs in a full study of a local community, however. See R. Carline, *Pictures in the Past: The Story of the Picture Postcard* (1971).

post-medieval archaeology. The archaeology of the centuries between 1500 and 1800. The importance of using archaeology to study this period has been increasingly recognized since the 1960s, with the publication of the annual journal *Post-Medieval Archaeology*. See David Crossley, *Post-Medieval Archaeology in Britain* (1990).

Post Office. The office of Postmaster of England was created by James I (1603–25), who in 1609 created a monopoly, the Royal Mail. By the middle of the 17th century towns throughout England and Wales were connected by a postal service. The system was subsequently extended to Scotland and to Ireland after unification. Letters were carried along the principal highways by horses which were changed at regular 'posts'. Mail coaches were used from 1784 onwards until they were superseded by the *railways. In 1840 a standard charge of one penny regardless of distance was introduced, using the famous 'Penny Black' stamp. A large number of Victorian post-boxes survive, the earliest being that at Holwell (Dorset), which dates from the mid-1850s. The Post Office has an Archives and Records Centre at Mount Pleasant House, London EC1A 1BB. The

Postal History Society has encouraged members to write local histories of the postal service.

potatoes. During the early 17th century the potato was introduced from America into Ireland and by the middle of the century was also successfully established in western Lancashire and Cumbria. See J. G. Hawkes, 'The History of the Potato', *Journal of the Royal Horticultural Society*, 92 (1967), which established that the potato needs a certain climate and a certain length of daylight hours to form decent tubers. They found a congenial home in the Irish climate from the outset, but not in the English until they were grown from seed and, over several generations, were selected for yield and earliness. The peaty soils of the reclaimed mosslands of Lancashire, coupled with the mild climate, were ideal. Soon, small plots of potatoes were a common sight in the fields as well as in gardens. By 1680 a specialized potato market had been established as far inland as Wigan. In the late 17th century the cultivation of the potato as a field crop was as far advanced on the Lancashire Plain as it was in most of the rest of England a hundred years later, though some other western areas, notably Cornwall, adopted the crop early. The potato was welcomed as a supplement to working-class diet, but it did not challenge bread as the staple food until cereal prices rose in the 1770s and 1780s. Its popularity increased when farmers found it could be a profitable cash crop when grown on the edge of towns, and when labourers began to cultivate it in their new *allotments. In the 19th century large parts of Ireland, and of the Highlands and Islands of Scotland, became dangerously dependent upon the potato crop, a dependency that ended in disastrous *famine when crops were ruined by blight. The potato was also used from the start as a fodder crop for livestock, especially cattle and *pigs. See R. N. Salaman, *The History and Social Influence of the Potato* (1949).

pottery. Establishing typologies of pottery is essential to archaeological research, for there is usually no better way of dating deposits closely. The range of vessel types made by medieval farmer-potters increased from the late 15th century onwards. During the next two centuries production became increasingly specialized as distant markets were reached. Staffordshire wares should not be dismissed (as Josiah Wedgwood's tombstone would have it) as a 'rude and inconsiderable manufacture' before Wedgwood revolutionized the industry in the later 18th century. See Lorna Weatherill, *The Pottery Trade and North Staffordshire, 1660–1760* (1971). Other potteries, e.g. the Rockingham in south Yorkshire, produced sophisticated wares in the late 18th and early 19th centuries, but traditional methods of production in small-scale units continued to be the norm; by 1829 the Potteries (the six towns of Stoke-on-Trent) had only seven large-scale integrated works compared with about 120 small works pursuing old techniques. Elsewhere, rural potters continued to manufacture traditional wares for local markets throughout the 18th and 19th centuries, and new centres, e.g. Leeds (Yorkshire) and Coalport (Shropshire), which had little or no ceramic tradition, began to prosper.

poultry. The keeping of poultry was traditionally regarded as the responsibility of the farmer's wife, the profits being used as spending money. For this reason poultry (or 'pullen') were often not recorded in probate *inventories. Sales took place to middlemen at the farm gate or to customers in the *market place. Production was geared to meet local needs until the 19th century, when two areas developed poultry-keeping for meat on a commercial scale for the London market: these were the Aylesbury area in Buckinghamshire and the Heathfield area in Sussex, where cramming was practised. See Brian Short, ' "The Art and Craft of Chicken Cramming": Poultry in the Weald of Sussex, 1850–1950', *Agricultural History Review*, 30/1 (1982). See GEESE and TURKEYS.

prebendary. A member of a *chapter of a *cathedral or *college, who held the revenues of a prebend, e.g. the *tithes and dues of a parish that formed a *peculiar jurisdiction.

precentor. The officer in charge of musical arrangements at a *cathedral.

precognition. In Scotland, the written report of the evidence of witnesses to a crime, taken in order to prepare a case before it comes to trial. These survive from 1812 onwards amongst the Lord Advocate's records at the *Scottish Record Office, under AD 14 and 15. The records are arranged within years by the name of the accused. A card index, arranged alphabetically, is available up to 1900.

prehistory. The prehistoric contribution to the present landscape is now considered to have been much more considerable than when W. G. *Hoskins wrote his pioneering book, *The Making of the English Landscape* (1955). Population levels are thought to have been much higher than was once supposed. Fieldwork, excavation, and *aerial archaeology have shown that much of the British Isles was being farmed long before the arrival of the Romans. See Richard Bradley, *The Prehistoric Settlement of Britain* (1978), T. C. Darvill, *Prehistoric Britain* (1987), Barry Cunliffe, *Iron Age Communities in Britain*, (3rd edn., 1991), and Barry Cunliffe (ed.), *The Oxford Illustrated History of Prehistoric Europe* (1994). See PALAEOLITHIC; MESOLITHIC; NEOLITHIC; BRONZE AGE; and IRON AGE.

Premonstratensians. An order of regular *canons, founded at Premontré, near Laon (France) in 1120. The first house in Britain was established at Newhouse (Lincolnshire) in 1143. Soon the Premonstratensians had 31 abbeys and three nunneries, mostly in remote places. The order was modelled on that of the *Cistercians, with regular inspections by visitors appointed by an annual general *chapter. This system ensured common standards of liturgy, dress, conduct, accommodation, food, etc. The heyday of the order was in the 12th century. Afterwards, there were few new foundations and little expansion of existing establishments. All were dissolved in the late 1530s. The largest houses included Bayham (Sussex), Dryburgh (near Melrose—the first and most important of the Premonstratensian houses in Scotland), Easby (Yorkshire), Egglestone (Durham), Leiston (Suffolk), Shap (Cumbria), and Titchfield (Hampshire).

prerogative courts. The probate courts of the Archbishops of Canterbury and York, which proved the *wills of testators who left considerable goods in more than one *diocese or *deanery. Wills proved in the Prerogative Court of Canterbury (the senior of the two) from 1383 to 1858 are kept at the *Public Record Office, under PROB 11 and 12. Indexes have been published down to 1700, and the Society of *Genealogists has a slip index for 1750–1800. Surviving probate *inventories are collected under PROB 2 to 5. During the years 1653–60 all wills in England and Wales were proved through this court. The probate records of the Prerogative Court of York are housed at the *Borthwick Institute of Historical Research, York, alongside the records of the *archdeaconry of York. The Yorkshire Archaeological Society Record Series has published indexes from the 1380s down to 1688; typewritten indexes are available for later periods.

Presbyterians. The Presbyterian Church rejected government by bishops in favour of a hierarchy of general assembly, synod, presbytery, and kirk session, on each of which sit ministers and elders of equal rank. The doctrines of the church were strongly influenced by Calvinism. At the *Reformation the *Church of Scotland became Presbyterian. See *Records of the Church of Scotland Preserved in the Scottish Record Office and General Register Office* (Scottish Record Society, 1967). In the 18th and 19th centuries the United Presbyterian Church, the Original Secession Church, and the Free Church of Scotland broke away from the official church but remained Presbyterian in organization. See Gordon Donaldson, *Scottish Church History* (1985).

The number of English Presbyterians grew in the 1570s and 1580s. They became one of the most influential *Puritan sects in the first half of the 17th century, but although bishops were removed from office during the *Civil War and *Commonwealth no organized national Presbyterian system was created to replace the old diocesan structure. After the *Restoration the Presbyterians became the most respectable *Nonconformist group, with an educated ministry and a prosperous membership. Presbyterian congregations were alternatively labelled '*Independent' in records of the late 17th and early 18th centuries. For the size of individual congregations, see John Evans's manuscript at the Dr *Williams's library. Some congregations gradually moved to a *Unitarian position. See C. B. Bolam *et al.*, *The English Presbyterians from Elizabethan Presbyterianism to Modern Unitarianism* (1968). In 1972 the Presbyterian Church of England joined with the Congregational Church of England and Wales to form the United Reformed Church.

presentment. A statement made on oath by a jury concerning matters within its knowledge, e.g. the ownership of property, or by a churchwarden at a bishop or archdeacon's visitation.

presents (by these). A formal start to a legal document, meaning 'by this document'.

press-gang. Once a man had accepted the 'King's shilling' from a recruiting party for the navy or army he was obliged to serve. Such payments did not entice enough volunteers, so military parties forcibly pressed others into service. The system was used sporadically from the 16th to the 19th centuries.

prices. Information about prices has to be gathered from miscellaneous sources. See the discussion in W. B. Stephens, *Sources for English Local History* (3rd edn., 1994), ch. 4. The starting point for price history was Thorold Rogers, *History of Agriculture and Prices in England* (7 vols., 1866–1902), but more recent work has produced new price series, mainly for foodstuffs, published in *The *Agrarian History of*

England and Wales. For the Middle Ages, see the statistical appendix in Edward Miller (ed.), vol. iii, *1348–1500* (1991); for 1500–1640, and 1640–1750, the appendices in vols. iv and v, ed. Joan Thirsk (1967, 1985); and for 1750–1850, the appendix in vol. vi (1989), ed. G. E. Mingay. Since continuous price series for individual commodities are not easily found, economists have lately preferred to compile tables showing the changing prices of 'a basket of consumables'. See E. H. Phelps-Brown and Sheila V. Hopkins, 'Seven Centuries of the Prices of Consumables Compared with Building Prices', *Economica*, 23 (1955). But severe criticism can be levelled at the contents ascribed to the basket of consumables over several centuries of changing diet. See Joan Thirsk, 'The Horticultural Revolution: A Cautionary Note on Prices' in Robert I. Rotberg and Theodore K. Rabb, *Hunger and History* (1983).

The national government rarely attempted to regulate prices. In the early modern period various books of rates gave the value of imported and exported goods, but they were formal, not current market valuations. See T. S. Willan (ed.), *A Tudor Book of Rates* (1962), which prints the book of 1552, and R. C. Jarvis, 'Books of Rates', *Journal of the Society of Archivists*, V (1977). Probate *inventories are a major source of information about prices in the early modern period and are thought to reflect current market values. See Lionel Munby, *How Much Is That Worth?* (1989). See also WAGES and STANDARD OF LIVING DEBATE.

priest. In Christian teaching, an ordained minister above the level of *deacon and below that of bishop, authorized to celebrate the mass and hear confession. After the *Reformation, use of the term declined within the Reformed Churches, being associated with the *Roman Catholic and Orthodox Churches, but in the *Church of England it was readopted in some parishes for clergymen associated with the *High Church movement.

priest holes. Secret hiding-places in the homes of *Roman Catholic families for protecting chaplains and itinerant priests from persecution during the late 16th and early 17th centuries. A good example in a National Trust property may be seen at Baddesley Clinton (Warwickshire). Worcestershire has a large number of cunningly constructed hides, e.g. at Harvingham Hall. A degree of scepticism is needed before accepting claims about priest holes.

Prime Ministers, lists of. See pp. 379–80.

primogeniture. The system of *inheritance whereby an estate passed to the eldest male heir. (See PARTIBLE INHERITANCE for alternative systems.) In practice, the distinctions were blurred, for younger children received some provision. See, however, ENTAIL.

priory. A *monastery or *nunnery headed by a prior or prioress, which was a lower rank than abbot or abbess. In practice, some priories were larger than some abbeys.

prise. The compulsory purchase of provisions for a royal household on the move and the requisition of means of transport. The Statute of Purveyors (1362) attempted to remedy abuses. See also PURVEYOR.

prison. Imprisonment as a punishment, as distinct from the confinement of those awaiting trial, was rarely used in the Middle Ages. During the 16th century *Justices of the Peace at *quarter sessions began to send offenders to *houses of correction, modelled on the London *Bridewell. Special debtors' prisons, notably the Fleet in London, were supervised by *sheriffs. The disgraceful state of prisons in the 18th century led John Howard to campaign for improvements. See his *State of the Prisons in England and Wales* (1777–80, 4th edn. 1792), which gives details of inmates. Uniform standards were not imposed until 1856, when the number of prisoners was increasing after the abolition of *transportation and a nation-wide system of policing had been established. In 1877 responsibility for prisons was transferred to the Home Secretary.

The *Public Record Office keeps records of prisoners from 1770 to 1894 under PCOM. These include registers, photographs, minute books, and visitors' books. From 1824 to 1876 quarterly prison returns record offence, date, place of conviction, and length of sentence. The PRO also has registers for the Fleet and King's Bench prisons and for Newgate Gaol (HO 10). A card index of people in debtors' prisons in London from 1775 can be consulted at the Corporation of London Record Office at the *Guildhall. Some county gaol records up to 1877 are retained amongst quarter sessions papers in county *record offices.

Privy Council. This group of royal advisers emerged in the 14th century and exercised great power during the 16th and 17th centuries, as the forerunner of the Cabinet. The council dealt with all matters of state, and members sat upon the bench at sessions of the courts of

Prime Ministers

Britain/United Kingdom

The term was first used in a mocking way about the person who held the post of First Lord of the Treasury.

SIR ROBERT WALPOLE	Whig	1721–42	BENJAMIN DISRAELI	Conservative	1874–80
EARL OF WILMINGTON	Whig	1742–3	WILLIAM EWART		
HENRY PELHAM	Whig	1743–54	GLADSTONE	Liberal	1880–5
DUKE OF NEWCASTLE	Whig	1754–6	MARQUIS OF SALISBURY	Conservative	1885–6
DUKE OF DEVONSHIRE	Whig	1756–7	WILLIAM EWART		
DUKE OF NEWCASTLE	Whig	1757–62	GLADSTONE	Liberal	1886
EARL OF BUTE	Tory	1762–3	MARQUIS OF SALISBURY	Conservative	1886–1892
GEORGE GRENVILLE	Whig	1763–5	WILLIAM EWART		
MARQUIS OF			GLADSTONE	Liberal	1892–4
ROCKINGHAM	Whig	1765–6	EARL OF ROSEBERY	Liberal	1894–5
EARL OF CHATHAM	Whig	1766–8	MARQUIS OF SALISBURY	Conservative	1895–1902
DUKE OF GRAFTON	Whig	1768–70	ARTHUR JAMES		
LORD NORTH	Tory	1770–82	BALFOUR	Conservative	1902–5
MARQUIS OF			SIR HENRY CAMPBELL-		
ROCKINGHAM	Whig	1782	BANNERMAN	Liberal	1905–8
EARL OF SHELBURNE	Whig	1782–3	HERBERT HENRY		
DUKE OF PORTLAND	coalition	1783	ASQUITH	Liberal	1908–16
WILLIAM PITT	Tory	1783–1801	DAVID LLOYD-GEORGE	coalition	1916–22
HENRY ADDINGTON	Tory	1801–4	ANDREW BONAR LAW	Conservative	1922–3
WILLIAM PITT	Tory	1804–6	STANLEY BALDWIN	Conservative	1923–4
LORD WILLIAM			JAMES RAMSAY		
GRENVILLE	Whig	1806–7	MACDONALD	Labour	1924
DUKE OF PORTLAND	Tory	1807–9	STANLEY BALDWIN	Conservative	1924–9
SPENCER PERCEVAL	Tory	1809–12	JAMES RAMSAY		
EARL OF LIVERPOOL	Tory	1812–27	MACDONALD	Labour	1929–31
GEORGE CANNING	Tory	1827	JAMES RAMSAY		
VISCOUNT GODERICH	Tory	1827–8	MACDONALD	coalition	1931–5
DUKE OF WELLINGTON	Tory	1828–30	STANLEY BALDWIN	Conservative	1935–7
EARL GREY	Whig	1830–4	NEVILLE CHAMBERLAIN	Conservative	1937–40
VISCOUNT MELBOURNE	Whig	1834	WINSTON SPENCER		
DUKE OF WELLINGTON	Tory	1834	CHURCHILL	coalition	1940–5
SIR ROBERT PEEL	Conservative	1834–5	CLEMENT RICHARD		
VISCOUNT MELBOURNE	Whig	1835–41	ATTLEE	Labour	1945–51
SIR ROBERT PEEL	Conservative	1841–6	SIR WINSTON SPENCER		
LORD JOHN RUSSELL	Whig	1846–52	CHURCHILL	Conservative	1951–5
EARL OF DERBY	Conservative	1852	SIR ANTHONY EDEN	Conservative	1955–7
EARL OF ABERDEEN	coalition	1852–5	HAROLD MACMILLAN	Conservative	1957–63
VISCOUNT PALMERSTON	Liberal	1855–8	SIR ALEC DOUGLAS-		
EARL OF DERBY	Conservative	1858–9	HOME	Conservative	1963–4
VISCOUNT PALMERSTON	Liberal	1859–65	HAROLD WILSON	Labour	1964–70
EARL RUSSELL	Liberal	1865–6	EDWARD HEATH	Conservative	1970–4
EARL OF DERBY	Conservative	1866–8	HAROLD WILSON	Labour	1974–6
BENJAMIN DISRAELI	Conservative	1868	JAMES CALLAGHAN	Labour	1976–9
WILLIAM EWART			MARGARET THATCHER	Conservative	1979–90
GLADSTONE	Liberal	1868–74	JOHN MAJOR	Conservative	1990–

Northern Ireland

SIR JAMES CRAIG (1927			TERENCE O'NEIL	Unionist	1963–9
VISCOUNT			JAMES CHICHESTER-		
CRAIGAVON)	Unionist	1921–40	CLARK	Unionist	1969–71
JOHN M. ANDREWS	Unionist	1940–3	BRIAN FAULKNER	Unionist	1971–2
SIR BASIL BROOKE					
(1952 VISCOUNT					
BROOKEBOROUGH)	Unionist	1943–63			

The office was suspended on 30 March 1972.

Republic of Ireland

William T. Cosgrave (1922–32) and Eamon De Valera (1932–7) held the office of President of the Executive Council of the Irish Free State. The term Prime Minister was used from 1937, under the remodelled constitution.

Many Irish governments have been coalitions; the political party noted here was that of the Prime Minister.

EAMON DE VALERA	Fianna Fáil	1937–48	CHARLES J. HAUGHEY	Fianna Fáil	1979–81
JOHN A. COSTELLO	Fine Gael	1948–51	DR GARRET		
EAMON DE VALERA	Fianna Fáil	1951–4	FITZGERALD	Fine Gael	1981–2
JOHN A. COSTELLO	Fine Gael	1954–7	CHARLES J. HAUGHEY	Fianna Fáil	1982
EAMON DE VALERA	Fianna Fáil	1957–9	DR GARRET		
SEAN LEMASS	Fianna Fáil	1959–66	FITZGERALD	Fine Gael	1982–7
JACK LYNCH	Fianna Fáil	1966–73	CHARLES J. HAUGHEY	Fianna Fáil	1987–92
LIAM COSGRAVE	Fine Gael	1973–7	ALBERT REYNOLDS	Fianna Fáil	1992–4
JACK LYNCH	Fianna Fáil	1977–9	JOHN BRUTON	Fine Gael	1994–

*Star Chamber, *Requests, and *High Commission. In Elizabeth I's reign, in particular, many local matters came to its attention. See *Acts of the Privy Council of England* (several vols., 1890–1964), which print the register from 1542 to 1631. The most important classes in the *Public Record Office are PC 1 and LIS 24 and 35.

Privy Seal. From the 12th century the clerks of the King's chamber attached a private seal to documents. By the 14th century the authority of this seal rivalled that of the *Great Seal.

probate accounts. About 30,000 probate accounts survive in various *record offices, but they have not received the attention they deserve. See Clare Gittings, 'Probate Accounts: A Neglected Source', *The Local Historian*, 21/2 (1991). A year or so after the death of a testator, accounts of the estate were submitted to an *ecclesiastical court by an executrix or executor, or by the person who had received letters of *administration in cases of intestacy. By that time, an inventory of the personal estate had been drawn up, debts had been paid, and expenses were known, leaving the residue to be divided according to the terms of the will or the wishes of the administratrix. Nearly three-quarters of all probate accounts were filed by women. These records therefore provide unique information on women's experience in handling property and the history of property relations between men and women. See Amy Louise Erickson, *Women and Property in Early Modern England* (1993).

probate courts. See WILLS; INVENTORIES, PROBATE; PROBATE ACCOUNTS; PREROGATIVE COURTS; PECULIAR JURISDICTION; and SOMERSET HOUSE. See also Philip Riden (ed.), *Probate Records and the Local Community* (1985).

prodigy-houses. The name for the huge country houses that were built in the Elizabethan and Jacobean age by the members of the government circle, e.g. Burghley House, near Stamford, or Hatfield House (Hertfordshire); members of the legal profession, e.g. Blickling Hall (Norfolk); or great landowners, e.g. Hardwick Hall (Derbyshire). Their style owed more to the native *Gothic tradition exemplified by

Hampton Court than to the influence of the Italian Renaissance. See Mark Girouard, *Robert Smythson and the Elizabethan Country House* (1983). Queen Elizabeth did not build new palaces herself, but spent much time progressing from one to another of her courtiers' great houses, at their expense.

professions. Many of the professions that were well established by the 19th century were created during the 16th and 17th centuries, particularly in the post-*Restoration period. See Geoffrey Holmes, *Augustan England: Professions, State and Society, 1680–1730* (1982). The law, the church, and medicine became profitable and respectable means of earning a livelihood, especially in the towns, in contrast with 'being in trade'.

proof of age. Before documentary evidence was available in the form of *parish registers, etc. proof of age, e.g. of a minor, was established by a sworn jury making a presentment. Records are kept in the *Public Record Office under C 132–42. See also the published volumes of *Calendars of Inquisitions*.

prospect towers. 18th- or 19th-century towers which commanded a prospect or distant view from a hill or a landscaped *park. Some commemorate historical events or characters.

Protectorate, the. The period 1653–60, when Oliver Cromwell, followed in 1658 by his son Richard, had the title of Lord Protector of the Commonwealth.

Protestant. Member of any of the churches that repudiated the supremacy of the pope at the *Reformation or which emerged later from that tradition.

Protestation returns. In 1642 Parliament ordered all males in England and Wales over the age of 18 to take an oath 'to live and die for the true Protestant religion, the liberties and rights of subjects, and the privilege of Parliaments'. One of the purposes of the protestation (which was read out in parish churches after services) was to identify *Roman Catholics. Lists were made by churchwardens and *constables of all who signed and of those who refused to sign. These lists are of great value to family historians who are trying to locate a particular ancestor just before the *Civil War, or who are interested in the geographical patterns of *surnames. They can be compared with the names of householders recorded in the *hearth tax returns of the 1660s and 1670s. Parish totals may also be converted into an estimate of the entire population of a parish.

The *Appendix* to the *5th Report of the Historical Manuscripts Commission* (1876), 120–34, notes all the areas for which returns survive in the *House of Lords Record Office. Some lists were entered into *parish registers. A number have been printed by local history or family history societies.

proto-industrialization. A concept advanced by F. F. Mendels, 'Proto-Industrialisation: The First Phase of the Industrialisation Process', *Journal of Economic History*, 32/1 (1972). Mendels argued that the origins of the *Industrial Revolution must be sought in rural industries which produced goods for external markets. The success of these industries provided economic opportunities for earlier marriages and therefore more children, and encouraged the rise of commercial agriculture, two necessary conditions for rapid industrial growth. Critics have pointed to the eventual failure of some flourishing rural industries and to the role of towns in the industrialization process. See D. C. Coleman, 'Proto-Industrialisation: A Concept Too Many?', *Economic History Review*, 2nd ser., 36/3 (1983), R. A. Houston and K. D. M. Snell, 'Proto-Industrialization?', *Historical Journal*, 27 (1984), Pat Hudson, 'Proto-Industrialization: The Case of the West Riding Textile Industry', *History Workshop*, 12 (1981), and Michael Zell, *Industry in the Countryside: Wealden Society in the Sixteenth Century* (1994). For the European context, see Sheilagh Ogilvie (ed.), *Proto-Industrialization in Europe* (1993).

province. See ARCHBISHOPRIC.

provost. **1.** In Scotland, the head of a municipal corporation or *burgh, cf. the English mayor.

2. In the *Church of England, the head of a *chapter of a *cathedral founded in the 19th or 20th century, cf. the *dean of older establishments.

3. The head of a *college.

Pryme, Abraham de la (1672–1704). Minister of Thorne (Yorkshire) and grandson of a Flemish settler who came with Vermuyden to drain Hatfield Chase. He wrote a manuscript history of the parish of Hatfield in the late 1690s (*British Library, Lansdowne MSS, 896), and a diary, published by the Surtees Society in 1870, but died young.

psalter. A written or printed book containing the Psalms.

pseudo-gentry. A term coined by Alan Everitt to describe those 17th-century townsmen who were as wealthy as the rural *gentry but who did not have a landed estate to support a claim to gentility.

public health. (For the early modern period, see DISEASE and PLAGUE.) Records concerning public health become much more voluminous in the 19th century. The Public Health Act (1848) established local boards which were responsible to the General Board of Health. The Public Health Act (1872) established urban and rural sanitary authorities, and the Public Health Act (1875) empowered local authorities to make by-laws governing the building of new houses and streets. Each of these authorities has extensive records, deposited in local *record offices. The reports by government inspectors on local conditions, which were published for about 300 places between 1848 and 1857, were often very detailed. The public libraries of major towns will normally have a copy of a local report and accompanying maps and plans. See H. J. Smith, 'Local Reports to the General Board of Health', *History*, 56 (1971). (See also PARLIA-MENTARY PAPERS.) The *Report on the Select Committee on the Health of Towns* (1840) and Edwin Chadwick's *Report on the Sanitary Condition of the Labouring Population of Great Britain* (1842), accompanied by *Local Reports, England and Wales* (1842) and *Local Reports, Scotland* (1842), contain a great deal of local information. The Royal Commission for Inquiry on the Sanitary State of Large Towns and Populous Districts published reports in 1844 and 1845. In 1858 the General Board of Health published *Papers Relating to the Sanitary State of the People of England*. Between 1868 and 1874 the Royal Sanitary Commission published three reports, and in 1848 and 1849 the General Board of Health reported on the recent *cholera epidemic. See also URBAN HOUSING and WATER SUPPLY.

Public Record Office. The Public Record Act (1838) established the Public Record Office as a central depository for 'all rolls, records, writs, books, proceedings, decrees, bills, warrants, accounts, papers, and documents whatsoever of a public nature, belonging to Her Majesty', together with those records previously deposited in the Tower of London, the Chapter House at Westminster, and elsewhere. In 1838 purpose-built premises in Chancery Lane, London, with reading space in the Round Room, the Long Room, and the Rolls Room, were opened to the public. See Jane Cox (ed.), *The Nation's Memory: A Pictorial Guide to the Public Record Office* (1994), and G. H. Martin and Peter Spufford (eds.), *The Records of the Nation: The Public Record Office, 1838–1988; The British Record Society, 1888–1988* (1990). In 1977 new

purpose-built premises were opened at Kew, with a main reading room, a microfilm room, and a room for large documents and maps. These rooms were provided with a new computerized system and mechanical delivery. In the 1990s an average of 800 people did research at Chancery Lane or Kew daily, particularly in the census rooms. Some 60 per cent of searchers at the PRO are family historians; 20 per cent are academics. The two buildings contain 93 miles of shelves, which hold central government records for England and Wales from the *Domesday Book to the present day. The Chancery Lane premises were scheduled to close late in 1995.

The various classes of records housed at the PRO are outlined in alphabetical order in this *Companion*. For general guidance, see Public Record Office, *Guide to the Contents of the Public Record Office* (3 vols., 1963–8; also available in microfiche). For family history, see Jane Cox, *Never Been Here Before? A First Time Guide for Family Historians at the Public Record Office* (1994), Stella Colwell, *Family Roots: Discovering the past in the Public Record Office* (1991), Stella Colwell, *Dictionary of Genealogical Sources in the Public Record Office* (1992), and A. Bevan and A. Duncan, *Tracing Your Ancestors in the Public Record Office* (1991). The PRO has also published a number of handbooks and information leaflets. Free reading aids to many classes of documents are available at Chancery Lane and Kew. (See also LIST AND INDEX SOCIETY.)

For Scotland, see the SCOTTISH RECORD OFFICE. The Public Record Office for the Republic of Ireland (now the National Archives) is housed at Bishop Street, Dublin. The Public Record Office of Northern Ireland is at 66 Balmoral Avenue, Belfast. For Ireland, see Alice Prochaska, *Irish History From 1700: A Guide to Sources in the Public Records* (1987).

Pugin, Augustus Welby (1812–52). Architect and writer, and the principal figure in the revival of *Gothic architecture. He was responsible for much of the decoration and sculpture of the new Houses of Parliament (1836–7) and for large houses, e.g. Alton Towers (Staffordshire); but after his conversion to Roman Catholicism about 1833, most of his designs were for Catholic churches, notably the Roman Catholic cathedral in Birmingham. Much of his work was completed by his son, Edward.

pulpits. Stone or wooden pulpits, with carved or painted figures, e.g. of the Four Evangelists, on traceried panels were introduced into the *naves of parish *churches in the 14th century. The *Reformation brought a greater emphasis on preaching and reading the *homilies, which was reflected in the prominent position given to the pulpit. The late 17th and 18th centuries was the age of the 'three-decker pulpit', with the clerk positioned below and the minister seated at the reading desk in the middle, until he ascended to the top tier to preach. A fine example can be seen at Kedington (Suffolk). During the *High Church movement of the Victorian period many of these 'three-deckers' were replaced by new pulpits designed in the medieval manner. In *Nonconformist chapels the pulpit is often the focal point, such is the importance attached to the 'Preaching of the Word'.

pumping-houses. The Victorian water authorities constructed some magnificent pumping-houses and water-towers in a *Gothic style with ornate detail. That at Ryhope (Tyne and Wear) is an outstanding example.

Purbeck marble. A dark limestone from the Isle of Purbeck (Dorset), used for columns in 13th- and 14th-century *cathedrals and *churches, e.g. Lincoln Cathedral, and for *funerary monuments. In later centuries much Purbeck marble was shipped from Poole and Swanage to London for roofing and paving. At the end of the 18th century some 400 men were employed in quarrying 50,000 tons of stone per annum.

Puritan. The word 'puritan' was in use in England by the late 1560s amongst both supporters and opponents. It came to mean a variety of things, but was originally a label for those radical *Protestants who were not content with the Elizabethan settlement of 1559. See Patrick Collinson, *The English Puritan Movement* (2nd edn., 1982). The lack of a precise definition has led some historians to abandon the term. Characteristics included a zeal for learning, albeit of a narrow kind, a belief in individual salvation, and a desire that everyone should have a personal 'calling' or vocation. Great emphasis was placed on listening to long sermons and reading theological works and on the 'godly' life that marked out the predestined elect from idle, sinful mankind. Opponents used the term 'puritan' in the sense of 'killjoy'. Before the 1630s Puritanism was not seen as separatist, anti-episcopalian, or revolutionary. Puritans were content to work for further reforms in the *Church of England, which they saw as having achieved many gains over previous *Roman Catholic practices. One major concern was to improve the standards of education and commitment of the clergy. (See

LECTURER.) That these clerical standards did increase enormously between 1559 and 1642 was largely due to Puritan influence. The Puritans were also concerned to improve standards of behaviour, which they were often in a position to do as *Justices of the Peace, or town or parish officers. (See ECCLESIASTICAL COURTS, where the Puritans attempted to enforce their moral standards.) Puritanism also led to fears of *witchcraft and increased prosecutions of alleged offenders.

The Puritans who were separatists were only a small group. Their numbers were kept low partly as a result of emigration to New England, where they founded 'godly commonwealths'. A challenge to the progress of Puritanism within the Established Church came in the reign of Charles I under Archbishop Laud. Fears of a return to Roman Catholicism strengthened the hand of the Puritans, who emerged as the main opponents of a despotic monarchy and an *Arminian episcopacy. The events of the *Civil War and the *Commonwealth have been labelled 'The Puritan Revolution', but by then the movement had splintered into different groups. Service in the New Model Army turned many to radical opinions. See Christopher Hill, *The World Turned Upside Down: Radical Ideology in the English Revolution* (1972), and J. F. McGregor and Barry Reay (eds.), *Radical Religion in the English Revolution* (1984). The 1640s and 1650s saw an outbreak of millenarian beliefs. (See FIFTH MONARCHY MEN.) Religious radicalism was also evident in the spread of *Quaker beliefs. Nevertheless, such groups remained small minorities of the national population. Upon the *Restoration, the former puritan sects formed the basis of *Nonconformity.

purlieu. Land on the edge of a *forest which had once formed part of that forest and which still came partly within its jurisdiction.

purpresture. An encroachment in a *forest or other royal land.

purveyor. One who purchased provisions for the Crown. The system caused resentment because of abuses.

putting-out system. A system by which manufacturers or middlemen sub-contracted work to pieceworkers, e.g. in the textile or *cutlery industries.

Pyne, W. H. (1769–1843). A painter of figures and landscapes, whose water-colours depicting rural scenes in various parts of the country are now an important source of historical information. His publications include *Microcosm, or a* *Picturesque Delineation of the Arts, Agriculture and Manufactures of Great Britain* (1806) and *The Costume of Great Britain* (1808).

Quakers. The popular name for members of a *Nonconformist sect. George Fox (1624–91), the son of a Leicestershire weaver and founder of the religious Society of Friends, began preaching in 1647. His followers, many of whom were young and radical in their conduct and beliefs, were known contemptuously as Quakers from the trembling and shaking that characterized their behaviour at early meetings. Quakers rejected formal church services and the sacraments (including baptism), paid ministers, and the authority of the scriptures, and emphasized instead the 'inner voice of God speaking to the soul'. They faced great hostility and much prosecution in *ecclesiastical courts (for interrupting church services and insulting clergymen and magistrates, for forming illegal *conventicles, and for non-payment of *tithes) and at *quarter sessions (for refusing oaths, military service, etc.) until the Toleration Act of 1689 allowed Nonconformists to worship in public.

Membership in England may have reached 35,000 to 40,000 by 1660. Early Quakers were often poor but, as the movement started to become more sober and respectable after the *Restoration, recruitment spread to the minor *gentry and *yeomen, to *husbandmen and craftsmen, and to manufacturers and urban shopkeepers. The early Quaker strongholds were in rural Westmorland, Lancashire, and Yorkshire, but the movement soon spread to London, Norwich, Bristol, and other parts of south-west England, and then to Scotland and Ireland. In the late 17th century the Society of Friends was the largest Nonconformist sect in the country, despite the emigration of hundreds of members to America, where they settled at first in New Jersey and then further west, when in 1681 the Quaker William Penn founded the colony of Pennsylvania.

Quaker meeting-houses are built in a simple, *vernacular style. Many examples date from the late 17th and early 18th centuries when the movement was at its height. At its peak in the second decade of the 18th century the membership in England and Wales stood at about 50,000. It then declined steadily and many gentry families returned to the *Church of England. However, certain families, notably the chocolate manufacturers and social reformers Fry, Cadbury, and Rowntree, stayed within the fold. The typical Quaker had become a quiet, respectable pillar of the community, very different from the young radicals of the 1650s.

The first yearly meeting was held in 1668, but a structure of monthly and quarterly meetings had been established by 1654. Records of births, marriages, and burials were normally kept by the monthly meetings, which may have been held many miles from the local meeting-house. For example, the early Sheffield Quakers attended monthly meetings at the small settlement of Balby, over 20 miles to the east. By 1670 most monthly meetings, and a few particular ones, were keeping registers. However, some Quakers were prepared to use the Church of England for some of their vital events, especially burials. The early Quaker meeting-houses had burial grounds, but the Society forbade the erection of *gravestones until the yearly meeting decided in 1850 that stones of a uniform size and design should be allowed.

The registers of births, marriages, and burials were not kept according to a standardized form until 1776. Another reform that was made at the same time ordered duplicate entries to be sent to the quarterly meetings. Searchers of these records need to be aware that the Society of Friends rejected the names of the days and months because these were derived from heathen gods; Sunday was therefore recorded as the First Day, January as the First Month, etc. Before the change to the *Gregorian calendar in 1752 the First Month was March. The Friends' Library, which was established in London in 1673, preserves many early records, but others have been deposited in local *record offices. It is rare to find a list of members before the late 18th century; many meetings did not make such lists until 1836. In the following year the registers of surviving Quaker meetings were copied for the *Registrar-General. They are now kept with other Nonconformist registers at the *Public Record Office.

quarantine. Upon the outbreak of bubonic *plague in the 16th and 17th centuries local authorities tried to confine the infection by prohibiting movement, e.g. ordering members of an infected household to remain indoors, or forbidding communication with London.

quarrying. The numerous small quarries that are found in many parts of Britain are usually badly recorded and so have not attracted much attention, even where they were once an important feature of the local economy. Sometimes *estate and *enclosure records (with maps) can be compared with the surviving visual evidence. Quarries often had specialities, e.g. *millstones, *grinding stones, roofing *slates, or *building stones. See Alec Clifton-Taylor, *The Pattern of English Building* (1972). For the medieval industry see David Parsons (ed.), *Stone: Quarrying and Building in England, AD 43–1525* (1990). The coming of *canals and *railways enabled the massive development of major enterprises, notably the Welsh slate quarries, which catered for wide markets. See Raphael Samuel (ed.), *Village Life and Labour* (1975), and *Miners, Quarrymen and Saltworkers* (1977), for studies of quarry workers at these large sites.

quarter sessions. The system of quarterly meetings of the *Justices of the Peace for each county and county *borough began in 1361. Under the Tudors the responsibilities of JPs were extended to include not only the enforcement of law and order but conformity to the established religion, the regulation of trade, commerce, and employment, the maintenance of the poor, and the upkeep of *roads and *bridges. See Anthony Fletcher, *Reform in the Provinces: The Government of Stuart England* (1986). The elected *county councils which were created in 1888 took over the administrative functions of the quarter sessions, but the judicial and licensing powers were retained, and until 1971 the quarter sessions continued to serve as a criminal court.

Surviving quarter-sessions records may be consulted at county *record offices. They date from the late 16th or 17th century and the more formal ones are written in Latin until 1733. Most counties have a series of indictment and order books, which record the cases under discussion and the decisions that were made. These form the basis of the quarter sessions records that have been published by various county record societies. Informal papers, including petitions and depositions, provide much more human detail where they survive. Associated documents include *jurors' lists,

*prison records, lists of licensed *brewsters (keepers of *inns and *alehouses) and of *badgers, *drovers, and other itinerant traders, together with *land tax assessments, and maps and plans associated with *enclosure awards, *turnpike roads, and other public works.

At the quarter sessions JPs tried crimes that were not capital offences, regulated *wages, enforced *apprenticeship regulations, licensed *Nonconformist meeting-houses and received *sacrament certificates, ordered the repair and rebuilding of 'county' bridges, and forced parishes to maintain their highways. A major part of their time, however, was spent on overseeing the operation of the *Poor Law, dealing with complaints from aggrieved parties, and judging *settlement disputes between contending parishes.

quarto. A quarter sheet, or a book consisting of such sheets.

Queen Anne's bounty. From 1704 the incomes of the poorer clergy of the *Church of England were supplemented by a fund which drew upon ecclesiastical revenues confiscated by Henry VIII and payments made by clergymen with larger incomes. The records are kept in the *Public Record Office under QAB 1; an index of parishes is available. In 1948 the scheme was taken over by the Church Commissioners. See G. F. A. Best, *Temporal Pillars: Queen Anne's Bounty, the Ecclesiastical Commissioners, and the Church of England* (1964).

querns. Stones for grinding corn by hand. They were used in the Romano-British period before the use of *millstones in water-powered mills. Probate *inventories show that they were used domestically at least into the 17th century.

Quia Emptores, Statute of (1290). A law ensuring that feudal obligations were preserved when a *mesne lord sold land for a nominal sum.

quit rent. A small fixed annual rent whose payment released a tenant from manorial services. Such payments were abolished in 1922.

Quo Warranto enquiries. From 1278 to 1294 the Crown made a series of enquiries into the privileges that lords claimed to hold, e.g. the right to hold a *market and fair, so as to ascertain by what warrant they were held. A statute of 1290 accepted undocumented rights that had been held since before the accession of Richard I in 1189. These have been published by the Record Commission. See D. W. Sutherland, *Quo Warranto Proceedings in the Reign of Edward I, 1278–1294* (1963).

R

rabbits. The rabbit was introduced into Britain by the Normans. Throughout the Middle Ages it was a rare and highly prized commodity, for both its meat and its fur. The word 'rabbit' was originally applied only to the young of the species; adult rabbits were known as *coneys, hence place-names such as Coney Garth. At first, rabbits had to be carefully reared in specially created *warrens until a hardier breed was able to withstand the damp British climate. It was not until the 18th century that rabbits successfully colonized the wild.

Rabbit warrens allowed the poorest soils, including the *breckland of East Anglia and the Wolds of Yorkshire and Lincolnshire, to become productive. Manorial *court rolls show that the legal right to take rabbits was guarded jealously, but that *poaching was hard to suppress in the remote areas that were typically used for breeding rabbits. Efficient and ruthless gangs of poachers were operating in the late Middle Ages. The later 14th and 15th centuries saw a great increase in the output of warren-bred rabbits in areas with ready access to markets, especially the London market, and some warrens remained important through to modern times.

Rabbits were notoriously destructive, but their value outweighed the damage that they caused. Some warrens were grubbed out after 1750, by which time the trade had peaked, but in East Anglia, Lincolnshire, and the East Riding of Yorkshire they remained till the 19th century. Supplies thereafter were obtained from the wild. See John Sheail, *Rabbits and Their History* (1971), and Mark Bailey, 'The Rabbit and the Medieval East Anglian Economy', *Agricultural History Review*, 36/1 (1988). See also PILLOW MOUNDS.

rack. Medieval and early modern instrument of torture by stretching to obtain a confession, e.g. that of Guy Fawkes.

rack rent. In the 18th and 19th centuries landowners increasingly tried to maximize their incomes by moving away from long leases to annual agreements with their tenants. Such 'rack rents' came to be regarded as extortionate, but in practice landowners were able to get only what the market would stand.

radio-carbon dating. A method of dating organic material from archaeological deposits, based on the knowledge that the radiocarbon content of dead animals and plants decays at a regular rate. However, radiocarbon years are not the same as calendar years and conversion formulae remain controversial. Dates arrived at by this method are only rough approximations.

railways. The earliest railways were horse-drawn wooden waggonways, which were used in the Northumberland and Durham coalfield in the 17th and 18th centuries to take coal from the pits to the wharves on the navigable rivers. See David Levine and Keith Wrightson, *The Making of an Industrial Society: Whickham, 1560–1765* (1991), ch. 1, M. J. T. Lewis, *Early Wooden Railways* (1974), and C. J. A. Robertson, *The Origins of the Scottish Railway System, 1722–1844* (1983). These waggonways occasionally required elaborate engineering, notably the Causey Arch, Tanfield (County Durham), a bridge with a span of 103 feet and a height of 60 feet, constructed in 1727. An elaborate system of waggonways was in operation in the north-eastern coalfield by the late 18th century.

Richard Trevithick, a Cornish engineer, built the first steam locomotive for a railway, in 1804. John Blenkinsop and William Hedley were other pioneers, who used steam locomotives to move coal. George Stephenson was part of this tradition. He built the engine *Locomotion* for the Stockton and Darlington railway, which was opened in 1825 for both passenger and goods traffic. However, this railway also used horses and stationary engines, and passenger traffic remained of minimal importance. Nevertheless, it attracted numerous visitors and inspired other schemes, the most important of which was the Manchester to Liverpool railway of 1830, which was the first to convey passengers and goods entirely by mechanical traction. Stephenson's *Rocket*, which won the famous Rainhill trials in 1829, was the first steam locomotive designed to pull passenger traffic quickly. The company which ran the Manchester to Liverpool railway was the prototype of the companies that were formed to build and run railways in many parts of Britain during the 'Railway Mania' of the late 1830s and 1840s.

The first important amalgamation occurred in 1844, when the Midland Railway Company was formed by Act of Parliament. This was largely the achievement of George Hudson, the 'Railway King' of York, the first man to make a fortune out of railways. His financial misdealings eventually brought about his downfall, but his energy and vision were vital to the formation of the other great railway companies of the 1840s, culminating in the Great Northern Railway of 1846. By 1852 nearly all the main lines of the modern railway system in England were authorized or completed; progress in Scotland, Wales, and Ireland was less rapid. The first *London Underground line was opened in 1863. The opening of the Great Central Line from Sheffield to London in 1899 meant that the railway system was largely complete by the end of the century. By Act of Parliament which came into effect on 1 January 1923 the nation's railways were amalgamated into four large companies: the Great Western; the London, Midland, and Scottish; the London and North Eastern; and the Southern. See C. Hamilton Ellis, *British Railway History, 1877–1947* (1954). These companies were nationalized as British Railways in 1948. See T. R. Gourvish, *British Railways, 1948–1973: A Business History* (1986).

The railways have attracted a vast literature. The best introduction remains Jack Simmons, *The Railways of Britain: An Historical Introduction* (3rd edn., 1986). For the ways in which railways affected settlements, see J. R. Kellett, *The Impact of the Railways on Victorian Cities* (1969), and Jack Simmons, *The Railway in Town and Country, 1830–1914* (1986). For a local study, see Diane Drummond, *Crewe: Railway Town, Company and People, 1840–1914* (1994). Local studies collections in public reference libraries contain numerous local and regional publications on railways. On the wider background, see also D. Brooke, *The Railway Navvy* (1983), G. R. S. Biddle, *Great Railway Stations of Britain* (1986), and Jack Simmons, *The Victorian Railway* (1991), which shows how railways expanded the horizons of ordinary people, allowing them to migrate long distances, to travel daily to a far-off place of work, and to take *holidays in *seaside resorts.

The *Public Record Office Records Information leaflet no. 32, 'Records Relating to Railways', outlines the national records of the former railway companies: these include maps and plans, reports and returns, *Parliamentary papers, minutes and accounts, staff records, etc. Important collections of railway records are also housed at the *House of Lords Record Office, the *Scottish Record Office, the Greater London Record Office, and the National Railway Museum, York. The Railway and Canal History Society, 51 Amberley Road, Enfield, EN1 2QZ has a large card index of documents held elsewhere. See also Tom Richards, *Was Your Grandfather A Railwayman? A Directory of Railway Archive Sources for Family Historians* (1989).

rake. A vein of lead. The term is often used in minor place-names in old lead fields, e.g. in the Peak District. Rakes run for hundreds of yards in straight, and rather narrow, lines. They are characterized by their irregular surfaces as a result of the surface deposit of spoil.

rapes. Ancient divisions of Sussex, comparable to the *lathes of Kent. The six Sussex rapes were adapted as castleries after the *Norman Conquest.

rape seed. The large expanses of yellow fields in springtime are a modern phenomenon, the result of European Community subsidies, but rape was once grown all down the eastern side of England. It was experimentally grown in the late Middle Ages and again in the second half of the 16th century, but spread more successfully on newly drained *fens in the 17th century. It was valued for its industrial oil and as fodder for sheep. The cultivation of rape required more labour than did grain, but it could be fitted into arable rotations at a slack time of the year. The seed was crushed at windmills or water *mills.

rate books. A few rate books, or assessments, survive amongst the records of the Old *Poor Law, naming householders and the rate paid. After the Poor Law Amendment Act (1834) the names of both owners and occupiers were recorded. Borough rate books from the 19th and 20th centuries are an important source of information about owner-occupiers and those who lived in rented properties. They are arranged in columns and typically list occupants and owners, then describe the property and name the street in which it was situated, and note the rental value and rate to be paid. Archivists have sometimes opted to preserve rate books only for selected years because of their bulk. See I. Darlington, 'Rate Books', *History*, 47 (1962).

Ravenstein, E. G. Former *Registrar-General and author of 'The Laws of Migration', *Journal of the Statistical Society*, 48/2 (1885), a pioneering article which identified five types of migrants and which concluded that most migration was over only short distances. See D. B. Grigg, 'E. G. Ravenstein and the Laws of Migration', *Journal of Historical Geography*, 3 (1977).

razor-making. Razors were one of the products made by cutlers until specialist razorsmiths first appeared in the late 17th century.

Reaney, P. H. Author of *A Dictionary of British Surnames* (1958) and *The Origins of English Surnames* (1967), whose later editions remain the standard introductions to the subject, and of studies of the place-names of Essex (1935) and Cambridgeshire (1943).

Rebecca riots. Riots in south Wales which formed the most dramatic and successful of the 19th-century rural protests. The name is derived from a passage in Genesis about Rebecca 'possessing the gates of those which hate them', for the protesters were principally concerned to remove the gates erected on the new *turnpike roads, and the leaders of the riots dressed in women's clothes. The riots began in 1839 and lasted until 1844. The targets of the rioters included the *workhouses of the New *Poor Law (which was applied widely in south Wales during 1837) and *Church of England clergymen who demanded the payment of *tithes. The government appointed a royal commission, which supported the demands of the rioters; these demands were strictly limited to reforms within the existing social and political framework. See David Williams, *The Rebecca Riots* (1955), and David J. V. Jones, *Rebecca's Children: A Study of Rural Society, Crime and Protest* (1989).

rebellions. The chief popular rebellion of the Middle Ages was the *Peasants' Revolt of 1381, now sometimes known as the English rising because of its urban as well as rural context. It took place in south-eastern England, which was also the scene of a mid-15th-century revolt against Henry VI: see I. M. W. Harvey, *Jack Cade's Rebellion of 1450* (1991). For an introduction to popular revolt in the Tudor era, see Anthony Fletcher, *Tudor Rebellions* (2nd edn., 1973), which deals with rebellions in Yorkshire (1489) and Cornwall (1497), the *Pilgrimage of Grace (1536), the Western Rebellion (1547–9), Kett's Rebellion (1549), Wyatt's Rebellion (1553–4), and the Northern Rebellion (1569–70). For the 17th century, see David Underdown, *Revel, Riot and Rebellion: Popular Politics and Culture in England, 1603–1660* (1985), a case study of Somerset, Dorset, and

Wiltshire, which relates unrest to the different *pays of those counties; Anthony Fletcher and John Stevenson (eds.), *Order and Disorder in Early Modern England* (1985); and Robin Clifton, *The Last Popular Rebellion: The Western Rising of 1685* (1984).

reclamation. See DRAINAGE; MARSHLANDS; and FENS.

recorder. The person who presided over *borough *quarter sessions.

record offices. The Royal Commission on *Historical Manuscripts, *Record Repositories in Great Britain: A Geographical Directory* (9th edn., 1992) is a complete guide, with opening hours, telephone numbers, and entrance requirements (if any). See Appendix for a list. See also LIBRARIES; MUSEUMS; GENERAL REGISTER OFFICE.

Recovery rolls. A fictional method of conveying property in use from the 15th century until 1833. The rolls are kept at the *Public Record Office under CP 43.

recto. The right-hand page of a book, the opposite of *verso. In folio numbering, the reader is guided by the use of the superscript 'r'.

rector. The person who was appointed to the *benefice of a *parish and who thus received the *tithes of the parishioners. At first, the rector was the incumbent who was responsible for the church services and the spiritual welfare of his parishioners, and for maintaining the *chancel of the parish *church. In time, many parishes were appropriated to *monasteries or *colleges, who kept the great tithes and spent the small tithes on the appointment of a *vicar to serve in their place. After the *dissolution of the monasteries the rector's rights were purchased by lay people. If a parish church is, or has been, served by a vicar, then its tithes must have been appropriated in the past.

reddle, ruddle, raddle. Red ochre dug out of pits and used for marking sheep, staining fences, etc. Diggory Venn, the reddleman, is an unforgettable character in Thomas *Hardy's *The Return of the Native* (1878). Former pits are often commemorated by minor place-names.

reeve. A man elected by his fellow tenants to act as intermediary with the *lord of the manor and to undertake certain customary duties. In some manors he was known as the greave or grave.

Reformation. The Protestant Reformation of the English Church began in 1534 with Henry VIII's decision to renounce papal supremacy and become head of the *Church of England.

This was soon followed by the *dissolution of the monasteries between 1536 and 1540 and the suppression of the cults of some local saints, which considerably reduced the number of minor holy days. These changes caused considerable resentment, culminating in some parts of the country in the *Pilgrimage of Grace, the largest *rebellion of the Tudor era.

In 1538 a new set of royal injunctions brought about the first major alteration in local worship at the parish *church. These injunctions ordered the churchwardens of every parish to purchase a Bible, to extinguish all lights in the church that were used for a religious purpose rather than for practical illumination, except for those on the *altar, in the *rood loft, and before the Easter sepulchre. The candles and lamps which had burned before the images of saints were extinguished, as were the 'plough lights' that had been maintained by *Plough Monday collections in Lincolnshire and other parts of eastern England. The injunctions also instructed churchwardens to remove any images which had been 'abused with pilgrimages or offerings', not to venerate holy relics, and to regard the surviving representations of saints simply as memorials. Heavy penalties ensured compliance with these orders. The cult of saints never recovered. Most of the traditional rituals and their associated ornaments remained untouched, however, during the last years of Henry's reign.

Meanwhile, in Scotland the Protestants were destroying most of the institutions and liturgy of the medieval Church and were establishing a new *Church of Scotland. See Gordon Donaldson, *The Scottish Reformation* (1960), and Michael Lynch, *Edinburgh and the Reformation* (1993 reprint).

Upon the death of Henry VIII and the accession of Edward VI the pace of change quickened considerably, as prominent ecclesiastics and laymen became converted to the views of the Protestant reformers of Germany and Switzerland: Luther, Calvin, and Zwingli. On 31 July 1547 the government of Lord Protector Somerset ordered the destruction of all shrines and pictures of saints, and of all images to which offerings had been made or before which candles had burned. They limited the number of lights in the church to two upon the high altar, they banned the blessing of wooden crosses, and they forbade processions in or around the church when mass was celebrated, thus cancelling one of the principal Palm Sunday ceremonies. They ordered churchwardens to buy the *Paraphrases* of Erasmus, a work much admired by the reformers. They enforced

these injunctions by dividing England into six circuits, with four to six visitors for each. These visitors were carefully selected for their commitment to the Protestant cause.

In the autumn of 1547 the government dissolved *chantry chapels, religious *guilds, and endowed masses known as perpetual obits, and confiscated their properties. The theological argument was that all these institutions dedicated prayers for the dead and that the falsity of the doctrine of Purgatory made such supplication unnecessary. About the same time, another change in liturgy allowed the laity to share the communion wine with the priest. On 6 February 1548 a royal proclamation forbade four of the major ceremonies of the religious year: the blessing of candles at *Candlemas, of ashes upon Ash Wednesday, and of foliage upon Palm Sunday, and 'Creeping to the Cross'. The dissolution of religious guilds meant the end of *Corpus Christi celebrations, which were a particular target of zealous Protestants. In mid-February 1548 the *Privy Council ordered the removal of all remaining images in parish churches. Together, these measures had a profound impact on religious observance at the local level. In its first 18 months of office, the government of Protector Somerset had demolished nearly all the seasonal rituals of the English Church and the ornaments and institutions that were a necessary part of them. In 1549 the *Book of Common Prayer set out the new liturgy: services were now held entirely in English, prayers to individual saints and for intercession on behalf of the dead were prohibited, and many old feast days and ceremonies were abolished. The *churchwardens' accounts which survive suggest that every parish obtained a copy of the book. Some parishes also purchased the *Book of Homilies*, an official collection of sermons upon important topics and doctrines which could be read to congregations by those clergy who were incapable of preaching.

The progress of the Protestant Reformation came to a sudden end in July 1553 with the death of Edward VI and the accession of the Catholic queen, Mary Tudor. Mary immediately declared a temporary tolerance of both creeds. Soon, the Edwardian statutes concerning altars and lights were repealed and seasonal processions and ceremonies allowed. Within nine months of her accession, the late medieval ecclesiastical year had been revived, except for the minor feasts that had been abolished in 1536. Churchwardens' accounts show that Catholic forms of worship were quickly restored, even though this put parishes to considerable expense. The Corpus Christi processions and *mystery plays were revived in the major urban centres, and *church ales and other seasonal festivities reappeared everywhere. Ronald Hutton, whose comprehensive survey *The Rise and Fall of Merry England: The Ritual Year, 1400–1700* (1994) is based upon an examination of all available churchwardens' accounts for that period, concludes that there were very many more professed Catholics in England at the end of Mary's reign than there had been Protestants at the death of Edward.

However, in November 1558 Mary died and her Protestant sister Elizabeth came to the throne. How far the Elizabethan church settlement of 1559 accorded with Elizabeth's wishes has been a matter of much debate. It was far from clear at the time that the settlement would be abiding. In April 1559 Parliament passed a statute prescribing the use of a new Protestant liturgy, based on that of 1552. The new injunctions were enforced by six teams of visitors who travelled to every part of the realm. The impact upon ritual was even swifter than that of Edward's measures, but the removal of the physical surroundings of Catholic worship was slower, churchwardens being naturally reluctant to destroy the images and fittings that had been paid for so recently and when the survival of the new regime was not certain. *Ecclesiastical visitation and court records and churchwardens' accounts show that many altars were not taken down until well into the 1560s.

The impact of the Reformation has long been a major concern of historians. The questions which continue to be debated are: was the Reformation imposed from above or was it popular? Were the changes the result of deliberate plans or did they come about through bungling confusion? Was the pace of change rapid or slow? Did it differ according to regions and localities? Evidence to answer these questions is hard to come by. One source of information is *wills, for historians have recognized that the formulae used by testators in bequeathing their souls varied according to whether they were Catholic or Protestant: see, for example, A. G. Dickens, *Lollards and Protestants in the Diocese of York, 1509–1558* (1959), and David Palliser, *Tudor York* (1979). The major sources for assessing the impact of changes at the local level are churchwardens' accounts and the records of *ecclesiastical courts and visitations. Dr Hutton notes that churchwardens' accounts reveal that parish representatives had repeatedly to entertain or attend upon agents of the Crown, bishops, or archdeacons, who instructed and cross-examined them. He concludes that the Tudor religious reforms and counter-reforms were not measures taken by a weak and remote central government, taking many years to filter through to the provinces, but were enforced rapidly and energetically at parish level. The question of whether they were imposed willingly or unwillingly upon parishioners is, however, a different and more difficult question. Robert Parkyn, the curate of Adwick-le-Street (Yorkshire), is one of the few provincial clergymen who recorded his (hostile) feelings; see A. G. Dickens, 'Robert Parkyn's Narrative of the Reformation', *English Historical Review*, 62 (1947).

The English Reformation has attracted new work during the 1980s and 1990s, much of it in the form of local studies, e.g. Christopher Haigh, *Reformation and Resistance in Tudor Lancashire* (1976), and Ronald Hutton, 'The Local Impact of the Tudor Reformations' in Christopher Haigh (ed.), *The English Reformation Revised* (1987). The conclusions of modern scholars are challenging and controversial. Thus, until recently, historians have generally accepted that the medieval Church was in need of reform, but Eamon Duffy, in *The Stripping of the Altars: Traditional Religion in England, 1400–1580* (1992), shows that late medieval Catholicism was vigorous and strong and that it stimulated the imagination and the loyalty of the great majority of people. He demonstrates the importance of liturgy in 15th-century England and the richness and complexity of the Catholic tradition. He argues that there was much popular discontent with the Protestant reforms.

Robert Whiting, *The Blind Devotion of the People: Popular Religion and the English Reformation* (1989) is concerned with the impact of the Reformation on ordinary people in south-west England. He concludes that for most of the population the Reformation should be seen not in terms of a change from Catholicism to Protestantism but rather as a decline in religious commitment, resulting in religious passivity, or even indifference. C. John Sommerville, *The Secularisation of Early Modern England: From Religious Culture to Religious Faith* (1992) argues that the dissolution of the monasteries and the demolition of shrines, the replacement of holy days with *holidays, and the destruction of the Catholic liturgy, produced a new culture of Prayer Book piety, preaching and teaching, and virulent anti-popery. Christopher Haigh, *English Reformations: Religion, Politics and Society under the Tudors* (1993) takes a different viewpoint in challenging the idea that there was a mass movement that can be called an English

Reformation. He sees the changes of the mid-16th century as a number of blundering Reformations, largely of a political nature, and he believes that well into Elizabeth's reign committed Protestants were a minority.

The trend of recent scholarship has been to stress the extent of popular conservatism in the English Reformation. The process is not seen as irresistible from the reign of Henry VIII onwards, but is thought of as a series of disparate and at the time reversible events, influenced as much, if not more, by political as by theological considerations. The excommunication of Elizabeth in 1570 and the defeat of the Spanish Armada were significant turning-points. Looking back, we can now see that Elizabeth's reign was a watershed. In the following century, the *Puritans were to push through further reforms, for to them the Elizabethan church settlement was an unsatisfactory compromise.

Regency. The term is applied to the period 1810–20, when the future George IV was Prince Regent during the final years of the reign of George III, who was ill, but it is also used to denote the Regency style of classical architecture which continued in use in the 1820s and 1830s. This style is seen at its best in the scheme devised for Regent's Park, London, by John Fordyce, Surveyor of Land Revenue, and the architect John Nash.

regional novels. The first regional novel was Maria Edgeworth's *Castle Rackrent* (1800), which is also acknowledged as the first historical novel in English, of the type soon to be developed by Sir Walter Scott. Relatively few regional novels were published in the first half of the 19th century, but they grew in popularity during the late Victorian and Edwardian periods. During the 20th century, such writing declined during both World Wars, but gained new impetus from the 1950s onwards. A survey of regional novels is being conducted by Dr Keith Snell of the Department of English Local History at *Leicester University.

Registrar-General. The civil servant in charge of the *General Register Office, created in 1836 to oversee the *civil registration of births, marriages, and deaths in England and Wales. From 1841 he has also been responsible for *census returns. In 1970 the department was remodelled as the Office of Population Censuses and Surveys. Scotland has its own Registrar-General, whose records are kept at the New Register House, Edinburgh, part of the *Scottish Record Office.

registries of deeds. Middlesex and the three Ridings of Yorkshire established registries of *deeds in the early 18th century, upon a voluntary basis. Deeds were copied in bound volumes and indexed by personal name and by place-name. These enormous collections are available for inspection. See C. A. Archer and R. K. Wilkinson, 'The Yorkshire Registries of Deeds as Sources on Housing Markets', *Urban History Yearbook* (1977), and F. Sheppard and V. Belcher, 'Deeds Registries of Yorkshire and Middlesex', *Journal of the Society of Archivists*, 6 (1980). See also Maurice Beresford, *East End, West End: The Face of Leeds during Industrialisation, 1684–1842* (1988) for the effective use of a collection of registered deeds.

regnal years. *See facing page.*

regrate. The buying of food and other goods outside the *market place. Market toll-owners frequently passed by-laws to prohibit this practice.

regular. A person bound by vows to a communal religious life (living 'by the rule').

relics. The venerated material remains or possessions of martyrs and other saints. The cult reached its peak during the *Crusades, when many spurious relics were brought back from the Holy Land. The relics were often kept in richly decorated reliquaries. (See SHRINES.) On the most important holy days the reliquaries were carried at the front of processions. Many superstitious beliefs were associated with them until their destruction at the *Reformation.

relict. Widow.

relief. 1. A customary payment to a *lord of the manor by an incoming *freeholder.

2. Payments to parish paupers by the overseers of the *poor.

remainder. The residue of an estate. The term is often used in title *deeds and *wills.

remarriage. The death of men and women in early adulthood or middle age was a common occurrence in medieval and early modern Britain. Many *widows and widowers remarried. *Wills commonly made provision for the children of a first marriage in the event of a woman remarrying and her estate passing to her new husband. Many *households contained step-parents and half-brothers and -sisters and foster children. See Miranda Chaytor, 'Household and Kinship: Ryton in the Late Sixteenth and Early Seventeenth Centuries', *History Workshop*, 10 (1980), and a rejoinder: Keith Wrightson, 'Critique: Household and Kinship in

Regnal years

WILLIAM I:	14 Oct. (crowned 25 Dec.) 1066–9 Sept. 1087
WILLIAM II:	26 Sept. 1087–2 Aug. 1100
HENRY I:	5 Aug. 1100–1 Dec. 1135
STEPHEN:	26 Dec. 1135–25 Oct. 1154
HENRY II:	19 Dec. 1154–6 July 1189
RICHARD I:	3 Sept. 1189–6 April 1199
JOHN:	27 May 1199–19 Oct. 1216
HENRY III:	28 Oct. 1216–16 Nov. 1272
EDWARD I:	20 Nov. 1272–7 July 1307
EDWARD II:	8 July 1307–20 Jan. 1327
EDWARD III:	25 Jan. 1327–21 June 1377
RICHARD II:	22 June 1377–29 Sept. 1399
HENRY IV:	30 Sept. 1399–20 March 1413
HENRY V:	21 March 1413–31 Aug. 1422
HENRY VI:	1 Sept. 1422–4 March 1461 (and 9 Oct. 1470–14 April 1471)
EDWARD IV:	4 March 1461–9 April 1483
EDWARD V:	9 April 1483–25 June 1483
RICHARD III:	26 June 1483–22 Aug. 1485
HENRY VII:	22 Aug. 1485–21 April 1509
HENRY VIII:	22 April 1509–28 Jan. 1547
EDWARD VI:	28 Jan. 1547–6 July 1553
MARY:	6 July 1553–24 July 1554
PHILIP AND MARY:	25 July 1554–17 Nov. 1558
ELIZABETH I:	17 Nov. 1558–24 March 1603
JAMES I:	24 March 1603–27 March 1625
CHARLES I:	27 March 1625–30 Jan. 1649
INTERREGNUM:	30 Jan. 1649–29 May 1660
CHARLES II:	29 May 1660–6 Feb. 1685 (but reckoned from 30 Jan. 1649)
JAMES II:	6 Feb. 1685–11 Dec. 1688
INTERREGNUM:	12 Dec. 1688–12 Feb. 1689
WILLIAM AND MARY:	13 Feb. 1689–27 Dec. 1694
WILLIAM III:	28 Dec. 1694–8 March 1702
ANNE:	8 March 1702–1 Aug. 1714
GEORGE I:	1 Aug. 1714–11 June 1727
GEORGE II:	11 June 1727–25 Oct. 1760
GEORGE III:	25 Oct. 1760–29 Jan. 1820
GEORGE IV:	29 Jan. 1820–26 June 1830
WILLIAM IV:	26 June 1830–20 June 1837
VICTORIA:	20 June 1837–22 Jan. 1901
EDWARD VII:	22 Jan. 1901–6 May 1910
GEORGE V:	6 May 1910–20 Jan. 1936
EDWARD VIII:	20 Jan. 1936–11 Dec. 1936
GEORGE VI:	11 Dec. 1936–6 Feb. 1952
ELIZABETH II:	6 Feb. 1952–

Sixteenth Century England', *History Workshop*, 12 (1981).

removals. Under the Act of *Settlement (1662) a person who needed poor relief was the responsibility of the *parish or *township in which he or she was legally settled. The overseers of the *poor of a parish or township could apply to the *Justices of the Peace for an order to remove such a person to the parish of settlement. Such orders were on printed forms with spaces in which the particular details of the case were filled. Removal orders survive amongst parish records deposited at local *record offices; they give the name(s) of the people removed, the names of the parishes involved, and the date of the order. Such cases were frequently disputed at *quarter sessions, where records survive in the form of indictment and order books and depositions.

rental. Manorial accounts and *estate records sometimes include details of rents collected each year, usually at *Lady Day and *Michaelmas, though sometimes at Christmas and Midsummer. These normally give only the tenants' names and the amounts of rent paid. It is often the case that the person who actually occupied the property was a *sub-tenant who is not recorded.

Repton, Humphry (1752–1818). Second in fame only to 'Capability' *Brown as a landscape gardener who created 'natural' *parks around country houses in place of the previous formal arrangements.

Requests, Court of. Court for the recovery of minor debts; abolished in 1642. The records are kept at the *Public Record Office under REQ 1–3. Details are given in *Lists and Indexes*, 21 and *Supplementary Lists and Indexes*, 7.

rescue archaeology. The pace of development, especially in towns and cities, where the deep foundations of modern buildings obliterate archaeological levels, has necessitated urgent excavations, partly funded by the developer. Sites that are not under threat are now rarely excavated.

reservoirs. In the 18th and 19th centuries private water companies constructed small reservoirs on the outskirts of towns to provide drinking water. Groups of millowners sometimes obtained private Acts of Parliament to build reservoirs to ensure a constant supply of water to turn the water wheels of their mills. Two of the greatest disasters of the reign of Victoria involved the bursting of reservoir embankments and the flooding of narrow Pennine valleys. On the night of 5 February 1852 the Bilberry reservoir, Holmfirth, burst its banks and 81 people were drowned. On the night of 11 March 1864 the Dale Dyke reservoir burst and 240 people and 693 animals were drowned in the 'Sheffield Flood'. In both cases, large numbers of buildings were destroyed or severely damaged.

During the Victorian period the demands for water from the growing industrial towns led to municipal authorities gradually taking over responsibility for the provision of water for drinking and for industrial purposes. Much larger impounding dams were constructed from the late 19th century onwards, and rank among the greatest engineering feats of modern times. See Brian Robinson, *Walls Across the Valley: The Building of the Howden and Derwent Dams* (1993), which describes and illustrates (with contemporary photographs) the preliminary plans and proposals, the political fights, the quarrying and transport by rail of stone, the building of temporary workers' villages, and the construction of dams which supply water to Derby, Leicester, Nottingham, and Sheffield. Water was piped long distances, e.g. from central Wales to Birmingham, or from the Lake District to Manchester. The effects on the landscape have been controversial, for small villages and farmhouses have been removed and the water authorities have favoured the planting of rigid lines of conifers around the reservoirs. Yet most reservoirs, including late 20th-century schemes such as Rutland Water, have mellowed into attractive landscape features.

resiants. The term used in the call lists of manorial *court rolls to describe those heads of *households who were not tenants. Resiants included *sub-tenants, ex-tenants who were still resident within the *manor, and some householders who eventually became tenants. Call lists of tenants and resiants cover most of the households within a manor, except the poorest ones. Some court rolls show that several men were admitted as resiants of the manor at the same time, suggesting that some were obliged to wait before they achieved this status. The resiant population was less stable than the tenant population.

residence, certificates of. The practice in the 16th and 17th centuries of issuing certificates to show that people who had paid their *lay subsidy and had then moved elsewhere should not be charged again. The certificates are kept in the *Public Record Office under E 115 and are calendared by surname.

Restoration. The restoration of the monarchy in 1660 after the *Civil War and *Commonwealth. Contemporary records date the start of the reign of Charles II not from 1660 but from the execution of his father, Charles I, in 1649. See the account of the events leading up to the Restoration in the diary of Samuel *Pepys.

Restoration houses. Country and town houses built in a classical style during the reign of Charles II (1660–85). These were greatly influenced by the houses in France and the Low Countries which had been visited by exiled Royalists during the *Civil War and *Commonwealth. Such houses ranged from grand country houses, e.g. Vaux-le-Vicomte, south of Paris, to compact town houses, e.g. the Mauritshuis in The Hague. The type was perfected in southern England by Sir Roger Pratt and Sir Hugh May. Ragley Hall (Warwickshire), designed in the late 1670s by Robert Hooke for Lord Conway, is a prime example. See Mark Girouard, *Life in the English Country House* (1978), ch. 5.

Restoration houses were formal and compact, with classical proportions and details. From the late 17th century their symmetrical appearance was improved by *sash windows. Gables were eliminated by the increased use of *lead for roofing and the development of the 'double pile' plan with a hipped roof and central lead flat. Such houses therefore saved space, walling, and other materials, and produced warm rooms. Internally, they were sumptuously decorated and richly furnished. At the rear of the large entrance hall was the chief ground-floor room known as the great parlour, above which was the finest room in the house, known as the saloon. A succession of withdrawing or antechambers led to bed-chambers and inner closets. Restoration houses were normally two storeys high, but sometimes had a semi-basement (of rusticated appearance) and an attic for the servants, who were expected to use the back staircase rather than the grand central one. This type of house continued to be built during the rest of the 17th century and into the 18th century, but at the highest social level it was replaced by the *baroque style.

retours. Scottish record of heirs, from about 1530 to the present day. Those dating before 1700 are summarized (in Latin) and indexed in *Inquisitionum Capellam Regis Retornatarum Abbreviatio* (3 vols., 1811–16). Original documents are kept with the Chancery records in the *Scottish Record Office, under C 22 (to 1847) and C28. They are indexed by the name of the heir.

ribbons and tapes. The manufacture of ribbons and tapes was one of the trades stimulated by foreign craftsmen in the 16th century, e.g. in Norwich, where it was associated with the *New Draperies. Such products were sold throughout the land by *pedlars. See Margaret Spufford, *The Great Reclothing of Rural England: Petty Chapmen and Their Wares in the Seventeenth Century* (1984).

Rickman, Thomas (1776–1841). Church architect whose *Styles of Architecture in England* (1817) was the first serious attempt at classifying successive styles. His terminology, e.g. *Early English, *Decorated, *Perpendicular, is still used.

rickyard. A farmyard where corn and hay were stacked after harvest. Ricks were built on platforms which were supported by staddle stones or brick arches and covered with *thatch (or from the late 19th century with tarpaulins), so as to provide protection from rodents and bad weather.

ridge-and-furrow. In many parts of Britain the evidence of former ploughing is preserved in patterns of ridge-and-furrow in fields now used for pasture. In some cases these patterns are a few hundred years old. In *Medieval England: An Aerial Survey* (2nd edn. 1979) M. W. Beresford and J. K. St Joseph showed that ridge-and-furrow on aerial photographs could be correlated with the *strips of *open-fields of 16th-century maps, in terms of length, breadth, and position.

Ridge-and-furrow patterns are particularly visible in the Midland Plain. They are rare in *wood-pasture regions which had only small open-fields. The ploughing of individual strips year after year built up ridges to the height of a foot or two, especially in areas of heavy soils. There are few signs of ridge-and-furrow in *chalklands, even though open-field systems were widespread; if such patterns ever developed here they could easily be ploughed out or lost by weathering.

The ridge-and-furrow patterns in former open-fields curve like an inverted S, to allow the *oxen team to turn as they reached the *headland. The furrows often appear greener than the ridges and in season are marked by buttercups or surface water. They did not simply mark the strip boundaries but were useful for drainage. They follow the lie of the land, with separate *furlongs going off in different directions. The hawthorn *hedges of parliamentary *enclosure often ignore the older pattern of ridge-and-furrow beneath, but enclosures by agreement created landscapes whereby the hedges or walls preserved the curving patterns.

Not all ridge-and-furrow is as old as this. Land taken in from the *commons and wastes by parliamentary enclosure, particularly during the period of the *Napoleonic wars, was newly ploughed with straight, narrow patterns of ridge-and-furrow. These patterns do not extend beyond the enclosing hedges or walls and can be readily distinguished from ancient ridge-and-furrow. These newer patterns are found, for example, on the edges of the Pennines. Much ridge-and-furrow of both sorts has been obliterated in the 20th century by deep ploughing. See also RUNRIG.

ridgeway. Ancient upland routes of *prehistoric origin. Most of their present names are modern inventions.

riding. A Viking word meaning 'a third part', used from the time of the *Danelaw until 1974 to divide Yorkshire into East, North, and West Ridings (with York separate from each). Lindsey, the northern division of Lincolnshire, was also divided into North, South, and West Ridings.

ringwork. An early Norman defensive earthwork in the form of a mound surrounded by a ditch. Some were adapted into *motte-and-bailey castles.

Riot Act (1715). A *constable or other figure of authority who was faced with 12 or more persons whom he considered to be gathered unlawfully or riotously was empowered to read a specified section of the Act, whereupon those who refused to disperse within an hour were considered to be felons.

riparian rights. Rights to river water and fish possessed by the owners of land bordering a river, above the tidal point.

rivers. River names are amongst the oldest *place-names, especially those in the west. The oldest names seem to be those of the greatest rivers, e.g. the Thames or Severn. These names are thought to include some pre-Celtic elements and are therefore amongst the oldest words in the present English language. They are often duplicated in other parts of the country, e.g. Avon, Don, or Ouse. Smaller rivers and streams have *Old English names whose modern forms end in -brook and -burn, or Scandinavian names such as -beck. Some names have disappeared as river names but have survived as the names of settlements, e.g. Colne (Gloucestershire) or Kennett (Wiltshire); however, some river names are back-formations from towns or villages, e.g. Chelmer from Chelmsford

(Essex). Rivers and streams often acted as *boundaries; some have names signifying this role, e.g. Meersbrook.

river traffic. Heavy, loose materials, such as *coal, clay, *lime, sand, gravel, *salt, and grain, and bulky goods such as pigs of *lead, were transported, wherever possible, by water rather than by land. Water transport was much cheaper than road transport, for a horse could tow up to 30 tons on a navigable river. Even in the Middle Ages, rivers were often navigable far inland, e.g. to Boroughbridge on the Ure, from where lead was exported from the northern Pennine fields, or to Reach, the medieval port for Cambridge, where a derelict hythe can still be observed. Many river ports, such as Bawtry (on the Yorkshire–Nottinghamshire boundary), were sited by the Great North Road. The road and water transport systems were complementary rather than rivals.

The navigability of the major rivers was improved by companies authorized by private Acts of Parliament during the 17th and early 18th centuries, during the period immediately before the great age of *canals. See T. S. Willan, *River Navigation in England, 1600–1750* (1936) for a general account, and for particular rivers, T. S. Willan, *The Early History of the Don Navigation* (1965), B. F. Duckham, *The Yorkshire Ouse: The History of a River Navigation* (1967), and M. D. G. Wanklyn, 'The Severn Navigation in the Seventeenth Century: Long Distance Trade of Shrewsbury Boats', *Midland History*, 13 (1988). By 1730 about 1,160 miles of English rivers were navigable for light craft. In Ireland, the major improvement scheme was the Shannon navigation, begun in 1715 and completed in 1769, with another phase in 1839–50. For a study of the people who lived and worked on the Thames, see Mary Prior, *Fisher Row: Fishermen, Bargemen and Canal Boatmen in Oxford, 1500–1900* (1982). (See also BOATMEN and PORT.) River traffic was seasonal because of summer droughts. The atmosphere of the Stour Navigation is captured in some of John Constable's most celebrated paintings.

roads. Many roads are *prehistoric in origin. Over 40 tracks constructed of logs, planks, and twigs have been discovered in the Somerset Levels and other *marshland areas, e.g. Thorne Moors (Yorkshire), and dated to the *Neolithic period. Processional ways are still evident on the ground near the major prehistoric sites in Wiltshire. It has long been claimed that *ridgeways are ancient thoroughfares, but revised upward estimates of the prehistoric population imply that many minor routes were also in use

before the Romans. Proving continuity of use is difficult, for the evidence has been obliterated by later traffic, but it is likely that once a way was established as the best route between two points it would continue to be used in later centuries. However, these ways must be thought of in terms of broad corridors rather than the narrow courses that have survived. The ones that are determined by the underlying geology, and which separate distinct areas of settlement, acted as later *boundaries over many miles. Other claims to antiquity need to be treated sceptically; the so-called 'Jurassic Way' is a modern invention, while the 'ley lines' of Alfred Watkins, *The Old Straight Track* (1925), are obvious nonsense. For general introductions see Christopher Taylor, *Roads and Tracks of Britain* (1979), Brian Paul Hindle, *Roads, Tracks and Their Interpretation* (1993), and Alexander Fenton and Geoffrey Stell (eds.), *Loads and Roads in Scotland and Beyond: Road Transport Over 6000 Years* (1984).

The Romans built many new roads for military purposes, but they also adapted older roads. Many of the minor roads and lanes of later times were probably in existence by the Romano-British period, given the high levels of population and the limitations imposed by the local topography. For instance, the *lead that was mined and smelted in the Peak District in Roman times was probably taken over land to the inland port of Bawtry (which was guarded by a Roman fort) along similar routes to those used in the early modern period. I. D. Margary's *Roman Roads in Britain* (2nd edn., 1967) is the foundation for modern research on Roman roads, though it is no longer possible to agree with his assertion that 'the roads were laid out as a carefully planned system'. The modern emphasis is on piecemeal development, specific roads being built at particular dates to meet new requirements. The military roads were only a small part of the network that was necessary to support the economy. The major roads can be traced in part by archaeological evidence (particularly in the form of raised *aggers), aerial photographs, and place-name evidence, particularly the use of 'street' in such forms as Ricknield Street, Old Street, and settlement names such as Stretton, Stretford, and Stratford. (See ROMAN ROADS.)

No further roads were planned until the 18th century. The medieval and early modern roads were partly ancient ones that continued in use and partly new ways that connected the medieval planned towns. The names of the traders in particular commodities are often attached to these routes, e.g. Salter's Lane. Others were 'church ways' or 'kirk gates' (see CORPSE WAY). The old words for such routes were the Anglo-Saxon 'way' and the Scandinavian 'gate', together with 'lane' and a variety of dialect words for minor tracks. The word 'road' was rarely used before the later 17th century. It occurs only once in the works of Shakespeare and once in the King James Bible. John *Ogilby's *Britannia Illustrata* (1675) was the first publication to popularize 'road'. During the following century this term became commonplace with the construction of *military roads in Scotland and *turnpike roads. The early turnpike authorities took over existing highways and improved them, sometimes with new diversions from the old course; entirely new roads were not constructed by such bodies until the end of the 18th century. See W. Taylor, *The Military Roads of Scotland* (1976), W. Albert, *The Turnpike Road System in England, 1663–1840* (1962), and E. Pawson, *Transport and Economy: The Turnpike Roads of Eighteenth Century Britain* (1977). (See also HIGHWAYS, OVERSEERS OF, and STATUTE LABOUR for the early modern method of road maintenance, and ENCLOSURE, PARLIAMENTARY, for the improvement of old roads and lanes and the laying out of new ones.)

The history of pre-turnpike roads is not an easy topic to research as there is no body of information other than that found in *quarter sessions records or scattered thinly amongst other archives. The documentary, map, and place-name evidence needs to be correlated with the evidence on the ground in the form of *holloways, *causeys, *bridges, *guide stoops, etc. Roads are best studied not simply as landscape features but in relation to the economy. See David Hey, *Packmen, Carriers and Packhorse Roads: Transport and Communication in North Derbyshire and South Yorkshire* (1980), Owen Silver, *The Roads of Fife* (1987), and L. A. Williams, *Road Transport in Cumbria in the Nineteenth Century* (1975). See also DROVERS; BADGER; and JAGGER.

Robin Hood. For explorations of the origins of the ballads and legends, in Barnsdale (Yorkshire) and Nottinghamshire, see J. C. Holt, *Robin Hood* (1982), and R. B. Dobson and J. Taylor, *Rymes of Robyn Hood* (1976).

Rogationtide. The Monday, Tuesday, and Wednesday before Ascension Day. Before the *Reformation this was a time of fasting and supplication for the coming harvest; afterwards it remained the time of year for the *perambulation of the parish boundaries by the parishioners.

Roman Britain. Recorded history begins in Britain with the Roman occupation. For an overview of the Roman period, see Peter Salway, *The Oxford Illustrated History of Roman Britain* (1993). The first Roman military expedition to Britain was that under Julius Caesar in 55 BC. Conquest began under Claudius from AD 43 and ended in AD 409. The whole of what later became England and Wales was conquered by Roman forces, and Lowland Scotland was occupied for a brief period, but Ireland and the Highlands and Islands of Scotland never came under Roman rule. (See ANTONINE WALL and HADRIAN'S WALL.) The area that was most intensively settled by the Romans lay south of the river Thames and the Bristol Channel. See Bari Jones and David Mattingly, *An Atlas of Roman Britain* (1990).

The debate over continuity of settlement from the time of the Roman Empire is a matter of interest for local historians, especially as the seminal work in opening up this debate was H. P. R. *Finberg, *Roman and Saxon Withington: A Study in Continuity* (1955). See also Christopher Taylor, *Dorset* (1970) in the *Hodder and Stoughton series of landscape histories, and the same author's *Fields in the English Landscape* (1975). On place-names, see Margaret Gelling, *Signposts to the Past* (1978), ch. 2. Some major medieval towns and cities grew on Roman foundations, notably London, York, Chester, Lincoln, Leicester, Gloucester, Colchester, Canterbury, Chichester, Winchester, Dorchester, and Exeter. Yet other important Roman sites, such as Silchester and Wroxeter, disappeared entirely. See B. C. Burnham and J. S. Wacher, *The 'Small Towns' of Roman Britain* (1990), A. S. Esmonde-Cleary, *Extra-Mural Areas of Romano-British Towns* (1987), R. Hingley, *Rural Settlement in Roman Britain* (1989), and J. Percival, *The Roman Villa: An Historical Introduction* (1976).

Estimates of the population of Roman Britain are speculative, but there is agreement that levels were much higher than was once thought, perhaps as high as that achieved in the 13th century. If this view is correct, the population must have fallen considerably after the withdrawal of the Romans, perhaps as a consequence of a major outbreak of bubonic *plague. Archaeological evidence, especially that provided by aerial photography, has confirmed that lowland Britain was farmed intensively during the Roman period. See, for example, C. W. Phillips (ed.), *The Fenland in Roman Times: Studies of a Major Area of Peasant Colonization, with a Gazetteer Covering All Known Sites and Finds* (1970).

The Roman period has long been of prime interest to archaeologists. Major excavated sites include the town of Verulamium (Hertfordshire), forts such as Wroxeter (Shropshire) and Housesteads on Hadrian's wall, the palace at Fishbourne (Sussex), important villas such as Chedworth (Gloucestershire) and Lullingstone (Kent), and the Roman baths at Bath. Many small sites, including farmsteads and small industrial complexes, e.g. for the manufacture of iron or pottery, have also been excavated. Much has also been learned from field-walking. The pattern of the main *Roman roads is well known. Some routes followed old *ridgeways, but others were new creations connecting forts. These military roads were the last planned roads to be made before the 18th century. If population totals in the Roman period did indeed approach or reach the same levels as those of the 13th century, the network of roads and lanes must have been comparable with that of later periods. It is likely that most of the highways and byways that were in existence before the era of *turnpike and *enclosure roads were Roman, if not prehistoric, in origin. See I. D. Margary, *Roman Roads in Britain* (2nd edn., 1967).

The possibility of continuity from Roman times is also raised by the study of early Christianity. (See CHURCH SITES.) For introductions to the subject, see M. E. Henig, *Religion in Roman Britain* (1984), and A. C. Thomas, *Christianity in Roman Britain to AD 500* (2nd edn., 1985).

Roman Catholicism. Until the *Reformation, people throughout the British Isles worshipped according to the rites of the Catholic Church. The thousands of medieval parish *churches which survive were built during the Catholic era, but have been much modified internally. During the reigns of Elizabeth I and James I, English Catholics formed only a small, persecuted minority. In certain rural areas, however, where local Catholic *gentry families provided leadership, they were stronger. Fears of a Catholic revival, inflamed by an association with foreign powers (France and Spain), arose from time to time, in the reigns of Charles I and II, and erupted in the *Glorious Revolution which deposed James II in 1688. (See JACOBITES.) The antagonism between the native Catholic Irish and the *Protestant settlers of *Ulster was exacerbated at this time, with lasting consequences.

In England and Wales, the fear of persecution meant that few Catholic registers were kept before the middle of the 18th century. Most Catholics opted for Anglican registration of their vital events. From 1791, more Catholic registers were kept, but most surviving ones date from the 19th century. Priests served large areas and often took the registers with them when they moved. In 1858 Catholic registers from Northumberland, Durham, Yorkshire, and some other places were deposited with the *Registrar-General and can now be consulted at the *Public Record Office, under RG 4. In recent years many Catholic registers have been deposited in local *record offices. For other central records see Stella Colwell, *Dictionary of Genealogical Sources in the Public Record Office* (1992). Occasional lists of 'Popish Recusants' are found in the records of *quarter sessions and *ecclesiastical courts, but many Anglican ministers turned a blind eye to the presence of Catholic families who worshipped privately. See John Bossy, *The English Catholic Community* (1975). (See also CATHOLIC RECORD SOCIETY, and the journal *Recusant History*.)

The English Catholic population was small before the 19th century: it probably amounted to about 250,000 in 1811. A number of Catholic chapels were opened between 1791 and 1814, particularly in the north of England. The formation of the *United Kingdom of Great Britain and Ireland in 1801 brought the question of penalties for Catholics to the fore; these were finally removed by the *Catholic Emancipation Act (1829), after which many more parish churches and a few cathedrals were built. See the *ecclesiastical census of 1851 for the numbers of people who attended Catholic services on census day. *Irish emigration brought a great rise in the numbers of Catholics living in England, Lowland Scotland, and parts of Wales. Very few present-day Catholics are descended from the Old Catholic families of the 16th-18th centuries; the great majority are descended from Irish or later immigrants, or are modern converts.

Roman roads. The Roman conquest began in AD 43 and by AD 80 Wales and northern England had been brought under control. The attempt to conquer Scotland proved unsuccessful. (See HADRIAN'S WALL and ANTONINE WALL for the northern frontier.) Most of the roads during the period of Roman occupation were ancient tracks, both thoroughfares and local lanes, but many new *military roads were constructed to link the forts which were established. These military roads are the ones that are thought of as 'Roman' and which have attracted most attention. See I. D. Margary, *Roman Roads in Britain* (2nd edn., 1967). Most local historical and archaeological journals contain articles on local Roman roads.

The Roman military roads went as straight as possible, with little regard to the landscape. Only the ones which followed the lines of earlier thoroughfares acted as *boundaries. See H. E. J. Le Patourel and others, *Yorkshire Boundaries* (1993). They vary a great deal in their present appearance, for local materials were used, but typical features include the *agger and drainage ditches at both sides. They are no longer regarded as being planned as part of an overall scheme drawn up in the 1st century, but as a piecemeal response to different needs. Despite the attention that has been paid to Roman roads, much work remains to be done, both in tracing routes on the ground and in searching for place-name clues amongst the mass of documentary and map evidence that is now available. Field-names containing the 'street' element are particularly suggestive. *Aerial archaeology occasionally reveals the unsuspected line of a Roman road through *crop marks. After the withdrawal of the Romans in the 5th century many of their military roads were abandoned, but others, e.g. the Fosse Way from Lincoln to Exeter, form the basis of modern routes. See Brian Paul Hindle, *Roads, Tracks and Their Interpretation* (1993), ch. 3, for ways of investigating Roman roads.

Romanesque. Architecture in the Roman manner. In Britain the style is divided into the Anglo-Saxon and the Norman, with a period of overlap in the 11th century. Surviving Romanesque buildings in Britain are all ecclesiastical.

Romanticism. A movement in European literature and art, from about 1770 to 1848, which asserted the importance of intense individual experience and valued a sense of the infinite. One of the lasting achievements of the movement was to bring an appreciation of untamed landscape to the fore.

romantic love. Lawrence Stone, in *The Family, Sex and Marriage in England, 1500–1800* (1979), argued that before 1600, and perhaps until 1700, people married for economic rather than emotional reasons. This view has been subject to much criticism. There is considerable evidence, e.g. from cases before *ecclesiastical courts, *ballads, and *diaries that romantic attachment was regarded as normal in the early modern period, and that it was a desirable precondition for marriage. Romantic love was not an invention of the 18th century.

rood. 1. (measure). A quarter of an *acre.

2. (ecclesiastical). The crucifix which was supported by a loft on top of the *rood screen that separated the *nave of a parish *church from the *chancel. The carved and painted figure of Christ on the cross was usually flanked by images of the Virgin Mary and St John the Evangelist. These figures were draped on Good Friday with white sheets which were removed on Easter Sunday. Most roods, with their lofts and screens, were removed at the *Reformation, under orders of 1547 and 1561, but new ones were installed in Victorian times under the influence of the *High Church movement. The former steps and opening on to the rood loft and the holes into which the screens were socketed into the chancel arch can still be seen in many parish churches.

In many parts of England, particularly in the south-west, East Anglia, and remote places, some fine medieval rood screens have survived. They were always highly coloured and often had painted panels depicting various saints with their personal symbols. That at Southwold (Suffolk) is a particularly fine example.

rope-making. Ropes were used particularly on sailing ships and in mining, so roperies were sited in ports or close to mines. An unusual one in the Derbyshire lead field occupied a cave at Castleton. *Hemp fibres were rotated by machine as men walked backwards along a ropewalk while releasing their supply. By this method the fibres were twisted into strands and the strands into ropes. Traditional roperies declined with mechanization in mills. In the 19th century Belfast became the major centre of rope production.

Rose's Act (1812). The Act which came into operation on 1 January 1813, by which the forms of entry of baptisms, marriages, and burials in Anglican churches were standardized in bound volumes.

rose window. A type of large, circular window found in medieval *Gothic cathedrals, with complex tracery and *stained glass. The fashion originated in 12th-century France. See Painton Cowen, *Rose Windows* (1979).

rotten borough. A *borough which still returned members to Parliament despite the decay of the settlement. Such boroughs, which were often controlled by a single landowner, were abolished by the Reform Act of 1832, which redistributed the seats to the growing industrial towns.

rough music. The use of a rude cacophony of sound and simple dramatic performance to ridicule or express hostility towards those who had offended against communal values and moral standards. See E. P. *Thompson, 'Rough Music' in *Customs in Common* (1991), ch. 8. Rough music was just one of the terms used for such activities; regional variations include '*skimmington' and 'riding the stang', and Continental historians use the term 'charivari'. A vivid picture of how rough music was used as a piece of street theatre to condemn individuals who did not conform to the moral standards of the community, together with its impact on those individuals, is provided by Thomas *Hardy's novel *The Mayor of Casterbridge* (1884). The rough music on such occasions came from pokers and tongs, tin kettles, warming pans, ram's horns, etc. The victim was often portrayed by an effigy supported upon a pole or donkey. The performance sometimes included mime and dance, lewd representations, and the reciting of verses. It was sometimes repeated on three successive nights. Cases are known from many different parts of Britain dating from the early modern period until well into the 19th century. Examples were collected by early folklorists and late cases were recorded in *newspapers.

The persons who were ridiculed were thought to have been guilty of one or more offences against the sexual code. Thus, the victim might be an adulterer, a wife-beater, a cuckold, or simply a masterful woman, virago, or scold. The ritual element in the performance shows the hold of rough music on folk memory, for the occasions on which people were ridiculed in this way were infrequent. Their purpose was not simply to mock but to uphold traditional values. Sometimes, the offending parties were driven away by the hostility that they had aroused.

Round, John Horace (1854–1928). Medieval historian and genealogist whose scathing attacks on fanciful claims to descent from medieval noble families helped to establish rigorous standards in genealogy. He was particularly dismissive about the 'errors, mis-statements and absurdities' of *Burke's *Peerage* in 1893. His collected writings were published as *Studies in Peerage and Family History* (1901), *Peerage and Pedigree* (2 vols., 1910), and *Family Origins and Other Studies* (ed. W. Page, 1930).

round tower. 1. Irish monastic bell-towers, probably designed as watch-towers and defences against *Viking raids. Some are over 100 feet high.

2. East Anglian *church towers of the late Saxon and Norman periods, constructed of *flint. The lack of adequate stone for quoins meant that a round form had to be used.

Royal Air Force. Formed in 1918 by combining the Royal Flying Corps and the Royal Navy Air Service. See the *Public Record Office Records Information leaflet no. 13, 'Air Records as Sources for Biography and Family History', and Eunice Wilson, *The Records of the Royal Air Force* (1991). The only complete muster list is that compiled on 1 April 1918 when the RAF was formed; it is kept in the PRO under AIR 1 and 10. *Air Force Lists* have been published regularly since then; a complete set is available at the PRO at Kew.

royal arms. Painted representations of the royal arms on square or lozenge-shaped boards were placed above the *chancel arch (upon the removal of *rood lofts and screens) to symbolize loyalty to the Crown as head of the *Church of England. Surviving Tudor ones are relatively rare; they can be distinguished by the Tudor griffin in place of the Stuart unicorn. Most date from after the *Restoration of Charles II. Where they survive, they are now found hanging in many different parts of a church.

Royal Institute of British Architects. The professional body for architects. Its library in Portland Place, London, houses an important historical collection of drawings of plans and elevations, e.g. those of Robert and John Smythson, the Elizabethan and Jacobean architects.

Royalist composition papers. In 1643 the Parliamentary Committee for the Sequestration of Delinquents' Estates was formed to confiscate the lands of those who fought on the Royalist side in the *Civil War. In 1653, after the war was ended, a new Committee for Compounding the Estates of Royalists and Delinquents was established. Those Royalists who pledged their loyalty to the new government were allowed to compound for their estates, i.e. pay a fine for their recovery, on scales depending upon the extent of their involvement in the war. The records of the two committees are kept at the *Public Record Office under SP 20 and 23. See Stella Colwell, *Dictionary of Genealogical Sources in the Public Record Office* (1992), and the *Calendar of Proceedings of the Committee for Compounding* (1889–92). Few of these voluminous records have been published. See J. W. Clay (ed.), 'Yorkshire Royalist Composition Papers', *Yorkshire Archaeological Society Record Series*, 15 (1893) and 17 (1895).

Royal Society. Founded in London in 1660 to promote the discussion of science, the Royal Society is the leading academic institution for scientists. Its published *Transactions* shed a flood of light on scientific discussions and experiments. From its earliest years, the society offered prizes for innovations, e.g. new crops.

Royal Society of Arts. The RSA grew from the London-based Society for the Encouragement of Arts, Manufactures, and Commerce. Its particular importance for local historians lies in its offer, made in 1762, of prizes for county surveys leading to the publication of *maps on the scale of one inch to one mile. See D. G. C. Allan, 'The Archives of the Royal Society of Arts, 1754–1847', *Archives*, 4 (1959–60). The RSA also played a useful role in setting syllabuses and examinations for schools of art and science.

Royal warrant. From Elizabethan times tradesmen who provided personal services to members of royal households (and from the 19th century those who provided particular products) advertised the fact that they operated 'By appointment to His [or Her] Majesty'.

rubble. Stones of different shapes and sizes, often uncut, used in *vernacular buildings. The term distinguishes such materials from *ashlar stone, but does not necessarily imply poor quality.

rugby. Named after the public school, where it is traditionally said to have originated, the game of rugby was taken up not only by the English middle classes, but from the 1870s by the working-class communities of south Wales. By the 1890s rugby had become the national sport of Wales. In other parts of the *United Kingdom association football (soccer) became the more popular working-class sport. The Northern Rugby Union, which was formed at Huddersfield in 1895, changed its name to the Rugby League in 1922.

runes. Letters used by *Anglo-Saxon and *Viking inscribers of *crosses and memorial stones.

runrig. In the Highlands and Islands of Scotland, and in parts of Ireland, the communal farmers of a permanent *infield and temporary outfields used *ridge-and-furrow for drainage, the patterns of which are still visible. The cultivated land was divided into a series of high-backed ridges, which were often as high as 6 feet from crown to foot and up to 20 feet in width. They were sinuous in form and were separated by *balks. Runrig is not, however, a synonym for infield / outfield, but an agrarian term which underwent an evolution of meaning. *Enclosure was facilitated by the Runrig Act (1695). See R. A. Dodgshon, 'The Removal

of Runrig in Roxburghshire and Berwickshire, 1680–1766', *Scottish Studies*, 16 (1972).

rural depopulation. The decline of the national *population in the late Middle Ages, as a consequence of the *Black Death and other *diseases, caused the rapid or gradual decay of many rural settlements. (See DESERTED MEDIEVAL VILLAGES.) Nevertheless, before the 19th century the population of the British Isles was overwhelmingly rural. *Famine in Ireland in the 1840s led to *emigration on an unprecedented scale and the evacuation of large parts of the countryside. The Highland *Clearances of the late 18th and 19th centuries depopulated many settlements in the Highlands and Islands of Scotland. During the 19th century large numbers of countryfolk throughout Britain migrated to the industrial towns in search of higher wages and a better standard of living. Large numbers emigrated overseas.

During the reign of Victoria, therefore, while the national population grew considerably, many rural areas experienced population decline. See W. A. Armstrong, 'The Flight from the Land' in G. E. Mingay (ed.), *The Victorian Countryside*, i (1981), which demonstrates that statistics relating to registration districts, rather than counties, show a persistent drain of people away from the countryside. The population of only three English counties (Cornwall, Huntingdon, and Rutland) and three Welsh counties (Cardigan, Montgomery, and Radnor) fell absolutely between 1841 and 1911, but in many other counties the growth of local towns obscures the extent of rural depopulation. The southern half of England experienced a considerable outflow as *agricultural labourers left the land in droves, particularly in the 1850s and the 1870s. In the north of England rural *wages were higher, as farmers tried to counter the pull of the towns and industrial villages, but many places in the rural north shrank in size during the later 19th century, especially during the 1880s. Employment opportunities were reduced by the disappearance of many old hand crafts and traditional industries. Thus, the exhaustion of the *lead seams in Swaledale caused the population there to decline by nearly 50 per cent between 1871 and 1891. The people most likely to leave were the young. Girls, in particular, sought employment as *domestic servants in the towns. See Bridget Hill, 'Rural–Urban Migration of Women and Their Employment in Towns', *Rural History*, 5/2 (1994). The net result of all this migration was that rural settlements commonly possessed fewer inhabitants in the mid-

Victorian era than they had in the early Middle Ages. The peaceful character of the sparsely populated countryside of much of the British Isles is largely a consequence of the rural depopulation of the 19th century.

Rural District Councils. Elected councils which were created in 1894, at the same time as *Urban District Councils. They took over the responsibilities of the old rural sanitary authorities, and later assumed responsibility for rural council housing. RDCs were abolished by local government reorganization in 1974. Minutes of the council and administrative records are kept at local *record offices.

Rural History: Economy, Society, Culture. First published in 1990, this journal uses interdisciplinary approaches with an emphasis on methodological innovation. Inspired by the French journals *Etudes Rurales* and *Annales, E.S.C.*, it aims to encourage the development of comparative approaches to local and regional culture. The articles are principally concerned with the British Isles, Continental Europe, America, and Canada.

Rural History Centre, University of Reading. Formerly the Institute of Agricultural History and the Museum of English Rural Life, a national centre for the study of the history of farming, food, and the countryside, particularly since 1750. Its library contains 30,000 books and periodicals, over 1 million photographs, numerous water-colours and drawings, and 40,000 computerized bibliographical references. See Raine Morgan, 'A Unique Data Source: The Classified Index of References on British Agrarian History', *The Local Historian*, 19/1 (1989). The archives contain the records of the Royal Agricultural Society of England, the National Farmers Union, the Council for the Protection of Rural England, and 2,500 businesses. The museum has permanent displays of farm tools, machinery, etc., and a large reserve collection.

rustication. A method used by the architects of the Italian Renaissance and widely adopted in Britain, at first by Inigo Jones and later by the *Palladians, by which the basement and ground storey of large houses were constructed of stones with deeply recessed joints to suggest that the building was emerging from the natural rock below. In contrast, the first floor (the *piano nobile* of the Italians) and upper storey were constructed in smoothly jointed stone.

Rylands, John, Library, Manchester. Set up by Mrs E. A. Rylands in memory of her husband, and opened in 1900, the library is in the custody of the University of Manchester. The collection started with the purchase of the famous Althorp library of Earl Spencer, containing 40,000 volumes. It has a considerable manuscript collection, including a wide range of charters and deeds, manorial records, and family muniments, particularly those of the landed families of Cheshire and Greater Manchester. See Peter McNiven and Dorothy Clayton, 'The John Rylands University Library of Manchester: A Resource for the Local Historian', *The Local Historian*, 19/2 (1989).

sacrament, certificate of. Amongst the provisions of the Test Act (1673), which excluded from civil or military employment all except members of the Church of England, was the requirement that a certificate, signed by a minister, churchwarden, and two witnesses, should be presented to *quarter sessions by the holder of a civil or public office to acknowledge that he had received communion in the *Church of England.

saffron, safflower. Saffron was grown as a dye, a condiment, medicine, and perfume in the 16th and 17th centuries, especially around Saffron Walden (Essex), Walsingham (Norfolk), and in Suffolk and Cambridgeshire, on a variety of soils. It was planted at midsummer, for harvesting in autumn, and in preparation for a crop of barley. It declined in use in the late 17th century and was almost extinct by 1750. Safflower was known as bastard saffron; it produced scarlet, pink, or rose-coloured dyes used in *silk manufacture. Most of it was imported from around Strasburg. It was first grown in England in the early 1670s, in Oxfordshire, and was tried without success in Ireland. It too had disappeared by the mid-18th century.

sainfoin. One of the new grasses, introduced from Normandy in the second quarter of the 17th century as a fodder crop. It appears in records under various spellings, e.g. St Foin. It was grown on many light soils by the 1670s and its cultivation gradually spread during the next century, especially on chalky soils, though it never seriously challenged *clover.

St Catherine's House. Home of the *General Register Office, which holds the records of *civil registration from 1 July 1837 to the present day. The address is 10 Kingsway, London WC2. It is open on weekdays from 8.30 a.m. to 4.30 p.m.

Saint John of Jerusalem, Order of. See TEMPLAR, KNIGHTS.

Saint Peter's Pence. Annual tribute by householders to the Papal See, stopped by Henry VIII in 1540, but still collected in Catholic churches.

Saints' Days, calendar of. Up to the 17th century documents were often dated by reference to saints' days. The major ones (and other Christian celebrations) are given below:

Saints' Days	
6 JANUARY:	Epiphany
2 FEBRUARY:	Candlemas (Purification of the Blessed Virgin Mary)
24 FEBRUARY:	St Matthias
1 MARCH:	St David
17 MARCH:	St Patrick
25 MARCH:	Lady Day (Annunciation of the Blessed Virgin Mary)
23 APRIL:	St George
25 APRIL:	St Mark
1 MAY:	St Philip and St James the Less
24 JUNE:	St John the Baptist (Midsummer)
29 JUNE:	St Peter
30 JUNE:	St Paul
25 JULY:	St James the Apostle
1 AUGUST:	Lammas Day (changed in 1752 to August 13)
24 AUGUST:	St Bartholomew
21 SEPTEMBER:	St Matthew
29 SEPTEMBER:	Michaelmas (St Michael and All Angels)
18 OCTOBER:	St Luke
28 OCTOBER:	St Simon and St Jude
1 NOVEMBER:	All Saints (All Hallows)
2 NOVEMBER:	All Souls
11 NOVEMBER:	Martinmas (St Martin)
30 NOVEMBER:	St Andrew and St Nicholas
21 DECEMBER:	St Thomas the Apostle
25 DECEMBER:	Christmas
26 DECEMBER:	St Stephen
27 DECEMBER:	St John the Evangelist
28 DECEMBER:	Holy Innocents
29 DECEMBER:	St Thomas Becket

For a fuller list, see David H. Farmer (ed.), *The Oxford Dictionary of Saints* (1978).

salt. The making of salt from sea water, or from the brine springs of Cheshire and Worcestershire, goes back to at least Roman times. Droitwich (Worcestershire) was the major centre at the time of the *Domesday Book, but the 'wiches' of Cheshire—Nantwich, Middlewich, and Northwich—grew in importance. Salt was also obtained at numerous coastal salterns by evaporation. See, for example, Sylvia Hallam, 'The Romano-British Salt Industry in South Lincolnshire', *Lincolnshire Architectural and Archaeological Society*, 9 (1961). Salt was important for preserving as well as flavouring food. See K. W. de Brisay and K. A. Evans (eds.), *Salt: The Study of an Ancient Industry* (1975). Numerous minor place-names, e.g. Saltergate, Salter Hill, Saltersford, indicate the routes of ancient *roads by which salt was carried to *market towns. Deep brine pits were in use at Droitwich and Nantwich in the Middle Ages and later. Rock salt was mined at Northwich, Middlewich, and Nantwich from the 1690s. See the leaflet on 'The Cheshire Salt Industry in Tudor and Stuart Times (1485–1714)' published by the Salt Museum at Northwich. Improved water transport from the Cheshire 'wiches' led to the decay of the coastal industry (which had expanded in west Scotland in the second half of the 17th century). See C. B. Phillips and J. H. Smith, *Lancashire and Cheshire from AD 1540* (1994).

Salt, William, Library. The library at 19 Eastgate Street, Stafford, which contains the antiquarian collection of William Salt, and forms part of the Staffordshire Record Office. See Catherine Bowden, 'The William Salt Library, Stafford', *The Local Historian*, 19/3 (1989).

sanctuary. The medieval right of sanctuary was claimed by fugitives from justice. The area of sanctuary was originally only around a bishop's throne, but it was later extended to include the whole of a church and an area around it defined by crosses. The fugitive had 40 days in which to appear before a coroner to confess his crime, to abjure the realm, and to accept banishment. In 1540 the privilege of sanctuary was restricted to seven towns. Sanctuary for those accused of crime was abolished in 1623 and for civil cases in 1773.

sarcophagus. A stone coffin from the Middle Ages, sometimes seen in *churchyards or church porches, shaped to take a body, and with a drainage hole.

sash windows. Derived from the French *chassis*, meaning 'frame', sashes were introduced from France and Holland in the 1670s. During the next half-century they replaced casement windows as the fashion spread down the social scale. The so-called Yorkshire sash, where the sashes slide sideways without the use of

weights, was also introduced in the late 17th century, and, despite its name, is found in many parts of Britain.

Sasines, Register of. In Scotland copies of legal transactions involving the ownership of hereditable property are registered in one of the registers of sasines. The Secretary's Register of 1599–1609 was the forerunner of the system inaugurated in 1617. Registers of sasines for royal *burghs were kept from 1681. The registers are kept in the *Scottish Record Office. Indexes up to 1780 have been published for most parts of Scotland. The registers are easier to search after 1780. Details are given in Cecil Sinclair, *Tracing Your Scottish Ancestors: A Guide to Ancestry Research in the Scottish Record Office* (1990).

saw-making. London was the early centre of tool manufacture, but by the early modern period saws were being made at *forges and by specialist smiths in the metalworking areas of the provinces. For example, saws made at Pleasley Forge (Derbyshire) in the 1660s were being exported to Barbados. Sheffield became the major centre of saw-making from the middle years of the 18th century onwards.

Saxo-Norman overlap. Churches built in the 11th century cannot usually be dated to either side of the *Norman Conquest, as techniques that had been developed by Saxon masons, e.g. the use of *herringbone masonry, continued in use.

Saxton, Christopher (*c*.1542–*c*.1611). The maker and publisher of the first atlas of England and Wales (1579) and the first wall map of England and Wales (1583). These were based on his series of county *maps which appeared individually between 1574 and 1579. Saxton served his apprenticeship with John Rudd, vicar of Dewsbury, prebendary of Durham Cathedral, and former royal chaplain, whose interest in map-making went back to the reign of Henry VIII. Saxton obtained a patron for his project in Thomas Seckford, a master of the Court of *Requests, and the support of William Cecil, Lord Burghley. His county maps formed the basis of other maps, e.g. John *Speed's, for the next two centuries, and his survey of the country was not superseded until after the foundation of the *Ordnance Survey in 1791. In later life, Saxton's main employment was in making estate maps, particularly in his native Yorkshire. See I. M. Evans and H. Lawrence, *Christopher Saxton: Elizabethan Map-Maker* (1979).

scagliola. Marble chips imported from Italy in the 18th and 19th centuries, which were cemented together to imitate true marble. The columns of many a great house have a hollow ring to them when rapped, for they are not of solid marble.

schools. See EDUCATION.

scissor-making. A trade well established in Sheffield by the 16th century. The scissorsmiths were founder members of the Cutlers' Company of Hallamshire in 1624.

scolding. Women who scolded their neighbours received rough justice in the form of the *cucking stool in the early modern period. Cases of scolding were sometimes brought before the *ecclesiastical courts or *quarter sessions. See D. E. Underdown, 'The Taming of the Scold: The Enforcement of Patriarchal Authority in Early Modern England' in A. Fletcher and J. Stevenson (eds.), *Order and Disorder in Early Modern England* (1985).

scot ale. A dinner given to tenants on the occasion when they paid their rents.

scot and lot. Parish rates; scot was collected for the poor, lot for church maintenance.

Scotch Baptists. The Scotch Baptists differed from the *Baptist church in their rejection of a trained or paid ministry. See Revd George Yuillie, *History of the Baptists in Scotland from Pre-Reformation Times* (n.d.), which traces their origins in the 1760s and their spread throughout Scotland and into parts of England during the next half-century. The separate congregations retained connections, e.g. intermarriage between members living as far apart as Fife, Lancashire, and Beverley (Yorkshire) was common. In the 19th century most congregations gradually merged with mainstream Baptism.

Scotchmen. In the 17th century Lowland Scots *pedlars hawked cheap *linen in many parts of England. Local authorities occasionally attempted to restrict the activities of such 'Scotchmen'. In time, the name was applied to any pedlar who specialized in linen, regardless of whether or not he originated from north of the border.

Scotland, National Library of. A copyright library occupying two sites in Edinburgh. The Department of Manuscripts and the Department of Printed Books are at George IV Bridge, Edinburgh EH1 1EW; the Map Room is at 137 Causewayside, Edinburgh EH9 1PH. The Department of Manuscripts inherited the collection of private papers in the Advocates' Library (dating from 1680), a catalogue of whose material has been published as the *Summary Catalogue of Advocates Manuscripts*. Five

catalogues of later holdings have also been published, but many other catalogues are not available in print. The collections are principally of *estate and *business papers; *trade union records are also strongly represented. The Map Room has collections of maps from the middle of the 16th century, including comprehensive holdings of all *Ordnance Survey series from the earliest surveys to the present day.

Scott, Sir George Gilbert (1811–78). The leading architect of the *Gothic revival of the 19th century, who was responsible for major public buildings such as the Albert Memorial, St Pancras station and hotel, Glasgow University, the Episcopal cathedral at Edinburgh, St George's church at Doncaster, the Martyrs' Memorial at Oxford, etc. He was instrumental in the founding of the Society for the Protection of Ancient Buildings. He was appointed Professor of Architecture at the Royal Academy (1868) and was knighted in 1872. His grandson, Sir Giles Gilbert Scott, was another noted architect, whose most famous work is the Anglican cathedral at Liverpool.

Scottish Episcopal Church. The Scottish church that retains the episcopal system of government, as in the *Church of England. The church's archives are kept at the *Scottish Record Office under CH 12. The SRO also has microfilm copies of Episcopal Church registers, arranged by diocese.

Scottish historical societies. Antiquarian societies began with the Spalding Club, Aberdeen (1841), and the Society of Antiquaries of Scotland, founded in Edinburgh by 1868. The major societies for the publication of historical texts are the Scottish Burgh Records Society (1868), the Scottish Text Society (1884), the Scottish History Society (1887), and the Scottish Record Society (1897). See David and Wendy B. Stevenson, *Scottish Texts and Calendars: An Analytical Guide to Serial Publications* (1987).

Scottish invasions of England. Sporadic warfare and cattle raids were regular features of the Borders during the Middle Ages, especially during the late 13th and early 14th centuries (see PELE-TOWERS). After their victory at Bannockburn (1314) Scots armies penetrated deep into the six northern English counties. An enquiry into the devastation they had caused in 1318 revealed that 140 of Knaresborough's 160 houses had been burnt. This was the most serious invasion before that of 1745. Henry VIII

(1509–47) waged several wars against the Scots. The defences of Berwick-on-Tweed were a major preoccupation throughout the 16th century. The union of the two crowns under James I of England and VI of Scotland in 1603 brought peace. The two countries were formally united in 1707, but Scottish support for the *Jacobite cause brought renewed tension, culminating in the invasion of Bonnie Prince Charlie's Highlanders in 1745 and their defeat at Culloden the following year. See Linda Colley, *Britons: Forging the Nation, 1707–1837* (1992).

Scottish local and family history Scottish local and family history differ markedly from English. If mythologies play a part in determining the agenda of historians, England provides a persuasive sense of continuity. In Scotland, such a picture is too far from reality.

There has been extreme poverty, starvation even; and villages hardly existed before the end of the 18th century. To find a domestic dwelling dating from earlier than 1800 is relatively rare, and much less than one per cent of Scotland's housing stock predates 1851. There is a shortage, too, of artefacts to support an artisanal vision: 18th-century *inventories of 'gear' of even the middling classes such as tenant farmers show a meagre stock—a few shirts, blankets, a bolster, chopins and noggins, perhaps a candlestick, a few pots and a smoothing iron, plus some linen and equipment for making butter and beer. The rude stone-and-turf homes where these bits and pieces were kept have long since gone, and with them any sense of continuity of community or of place.

Furthermore, the Scots had no stake in their land (without which what attachment to place is possible?). There were no rights to *commons to be fought over during *enclosure, for the Scots had no such rights; any more than they had any proprietorial stake in their Victorian tenement-flats (vividly described in Frank Worsdall, *The Tenement: A Way of Life* (1979)) or the estates of *council houses that have supplanted them. Scots have never been owner-occupiers in great numbers. All of which helps to explain why there is no equivalent of the *Victoria Histories of English counties and, until recently, weak provision of local *record offices.

Without a continuity of contentment to celebrate, Scots instead have looked to mythologies of bonding—the family, the *clan. Conveniently, too, they have had the focus of lost nationality to compensate for fugitive local attachment; which raises the question: 'Is Scottish history post-1707 in its entirety an aspect of local history?'. In terms of population and affiliations Scotland is no more and no less a region than, say, Lancashire. The dearth of local records has encouraged the tendency to plump for the national perspective.

Even working-class mythologies are different from England, as E. P. *Thompson recognized when deliberately excluding the Scots in his *Making of the English Working Class* (1963). Urbanization was even more rapid than in England, Scotland rising from ninth position in the European league in 1700 to second in 1850. *Emigration sent greater numbers away, and to a larger extent than in England the *Industrial Revolution was harnessed by the traditional *aristocracy. The proud equality of 'a man's a man for a' that' was proclaimed in a land half of whose extent and resources was controlled by under 200 men in Victorian times; and the gesture politics of the 1745 rebellion has seen many an action replay in the solidarity of Red Clydeside. In Scotland sentimentality and impotence have gone hand in hand.

Given this background, it is little wonder that the historiography of Scottish local and family studies is distinctive. There are other contributing factors too—the wholesale absence of local records from before the 17th century, the inhospitable nature of the terrain, with fertile straths separated by upland moors, the quite different structure and development of *local government, the radical principles of the established church (Presbyterians, it has been claimed, do not have the urge of Anglicans to ritualize the past), and the separate legal system which has maintained its independence.

The Society of Antiquaries of Scotland, founded in 1780, prophetically announced an agenda which has remained relevant. It proposed a programme of ethnographic surveys on a topographical basis, to include natural resources, population, language, and social customs—'in general, every thing that may tend to compare our antient with our modern attainments', in the words of the Earl of Buchan, prime mover of the Society. This instinct towards comparative studies was shared by many of the great figures of the Scottish Enlightenment: Adam Smith in economics; Adam Fergusson in anthropology (which science, of course, pioneered and led in Scotland, is fundamentally comparative in character); and James Hutton in geology. The rapid evolution of 18th-century Scotland, in which elements of pre-feudal clanship coexisted with both mercantilism and a nascent capitalism, helps to explain why Scots were so keen to compare past and present. Generally, the century had a passion for tabulating. Visitors from England, including Francis Grose, recorded whatever old buildings of historical interest they could find, revelling in their archaism, and came equally to experience the primitive and savage simplicity which they believed lay there. And at home, enthusiasm was similarly intense (partly because the Scots wanted to be more English than the English). One consequence was, and continues to be, the huge compilations on the music, folklore, beliefs, and customs of the highlands in particular. Scots have always been enthusiastic encyclopaedists. Note-sharing by underdogs is another aspect of the comparative tradition, and still proves fruitful, as in T. M. Devine and David Dickson (eds.), *Ireland and Scotland 1600–1850* (1983).

In their rush for modernity, the Scots were equally keen to record the 'modern attainments' praised by Buchan. Hugo Arnot, the 18th-century historian of Edinburgh, takes the trouble to tell us about the asparagus (not as good as London's), the pineapples, the green peas, and the strawberries (superior to those in England) to be had at the Edinburgh market. He was shortly to be followed among others by that most industrious of recorders, the 'political arithmetician, propagandist, and pathological pamphleteer' Sir John *Sinclair, who was responsible for the publication, in the 1790s, of a *statistical account* of every parish in the country. The surveys were in most cases made by the respective ministers, to a format suggested by Sinclair (to include situation and extent, state of agriculture with special reference to improvements, population, occupations, manufactures, state of the poor, schooling, roads, antiquities, plus observations on manners and morals). The watchword was progress, which, in the Calvinist ethos, became a tangible sign to serve as a substitute for election by grace. This particular current has run deep, for a *second* or new statistical account of each parish was soon to follow, in the 1830s; and then a *third* in the 1950s, of which the final volumes have recently appeared after many delays.

The ethnological impulse remains dominant to this day. The School of Scottish Studies, attached to Edinburgh University, was founded in 1951, and has pursued the study of folk customs and music, material culture, social organization, and literature. It has also made an impressive collection of *place-names and, since its amalgamation with the Linguistic Survey of Scotland, has produced the *third* volume of the *Linguistic Atlas of Scotland* (1975, 1977, and 1986). The School publishes an annual

journal, *Scottish Studies*, which reflects the breadth of its remit, and a more specialized journal, *Tocher*, consisting of transcripts of *oral-history recordings. The School has been the pioneer and leading exponent of oral history, and of folkways in particular since the 1950s, when few historians acknowledged their importance.

The Society of Antiquaries' own museum, the National Museum of Antiquities (now subsumed under the National Museums of Scotland), has played a leading role in the ethnological tradition, latterly under the leadership of James Fenton, author of several works on farming ways. Another legacy is the museum's Scottish Ethnological Archive in Edinburgh. The *Proceedings of the Society of Antiquaries of Scotland* have appeared annually since Victorian times and have recently been joined by an occasional serial, *Review of Scottish Culture*. Both journals delight in material culture: practical Scots, among whose numbers are many famous engineers, have an enduring interest in how things work, from the simplest tools of a peasant economy to the most complex machines of the Industrial Revolution; and they have an equally practical interest in the organization of work, typified in Adam Smith's lucid analysis of the efficient production of pins by division of labour. Thus these volumes are full of studies of such things as the layout of steadings, the workings of mill machinery, and the design of cradles. The Scottish Industrial Archaeological Unit, associated with the names of John Butt and John Hume, extended such work beyond the traditional agrarian economy.

The bias of Scottish historiography towards agrarian issues has indeed been remarked upon; as recently as 1983, G. Whittington and I. D. White in *An Historical Geography of Scotland* could note 'too unbalanced an involvement with agrarian and rural settlement features to the exclusion of most other topics . . . Industry, population and urbanism are topics still too little regarded'—this, in a country which became the second most urbanized in the world at around 1850.

The passion for agricultural improvement at the heart of Sir John Sinclair's activities galvanized subsequent activity, such as the county-based *General Views of Agriculture* straddling the start of the 19th century (two for each area) and the *Prize essays* and *Transactions of the Highland and Agricultural Society* (1799 to the present). A polemical spirit has also infused and often marred other Scottish writing. Labour and working-class history was rudely brought to general attention by Tom Johnston (later Secretary of State for Scotland) in his wayward and unscholarly *The History of the Working Class in Scotland* (2nd edn., 1929). Marxist interpretations have been influential with academics too, as Tony Dickson demonstrates in his *Scottish Capitalism* (1980).

The extent of prescriptive or polemical writing reflects the lack of a common ground among the Scots (taught English history as their own until recently) and the lack of a large academic establishment. Given this situation, most of the older amateur work, by an assortment of ministers, middle-class professionals, and the self-educated, would hardly be worth rescuing from the conflagration if more than a finger or two were to be scorched, though at best they too breathe with the vigour of progress, a pride in the building of the local gasworks, and other acts of progressive civic humanism. They are best, too, when the indefatigable urge to collect inconsequential snippets releases the James Boswell lurking in the Scots breast. If there are classics of Scottish local history, it would be romantic works such as Robert Chambers' *Traditions of Edinburgh* (3rd edn., 1868) with its intense delight in people and place; though it is guilty of introducing those couthie kailyard 'auld Tams' and their fellows, who went on to people innumerable local histories with their incomprehensible vernacular. Others fail in their inability to address locality as topography and community, viewing it instead as a backcloth on which the pageant of Scottish history unfolds—the visits of monarchs, the battles, the intrigues of the nobility.

Not polemics exactly, but a kindred passion has helped to drive the one programme that has come close to equalling those devoted to ethnology and traditional rural ways—economic history. G. C. Peden, in his 'Agenda for the Economic History of Twentieth-century Scotland', *Scottish Economic and Social History*, 13 (1993) described it as 'inverted-Whig history of terminal decline'; whilst R. H. Campbell, reminding us of the roots of Scottish economic history in moral philosophy, wrote in his *Rise and Fall of Scottish Industry 1707–1939* (1980) of his 'desire to provide a diagnosis of the present state of Scottish industry from the evidence of its historical evolution and so to provide a test of the effectiveness of remedies suggested for its present-day ills'—another instance of the Scots interest in practicality.

Work in the economic field began early in the century (already at this time there was a lectureship in economic history at Edinburgh University). James Mackinnon, Henry Hamilton, and Isabel F. Grant (also the author of marvellous books on Highland folk ways) contributed monographs. Post-war leadership has come as much from Glasgow, through S. G. Checkland, Edgar Lythe, John Butt, R. H. Campbell, and Anthony Slaven, and the subject has expanded in various directions. A statistical approach to historical problems encouraged research into food prices, wage rates, inflation levels, and boom and slump, though there are difficulties enough in disentangling Scottish data from British, let alone even more localized data. Some would argue that the effort is elusive anyway—a futile application of that comparative instinct in what is a national, if not an international, sphere.

Regional economic studies have explored the distinctive industrial character of different parts of Scotland, for example Anthony Slaven's *The Development of the West of Scotland 1750–1960* (1975); and the Highland *Clearances have received objective scrutiny from writers such as Malcolm Gray, A. J. Youngson, Eric Richards and Tom Devine. Philip Gaskell's *Morvern Transformed* (1968) is one of the few in-depth local studies. Aberdeen University's Centre for Scottish Studies publishes *Northern Scotland* as a forum for regional research in the north. Business history, in the words of G. C. Peden, has 'escaped from the confines of the boardroom' (with its anodyne commissioned and privately published histories) and there are now major studies of key industries—brewing by Iain Donnachie, *linen by Alastair Durie, *saltmaking by Christopher Whatley; and detailed work in banking history. Every area of Scottish studies also seems to have its classic of reportage: in the case of business it is David Bremner's *The Industries of Scotland: Their Rise and Progress* (1869) of which there was a centenary reprint. Business biography is a recent enthusiasm. The Centre for Business History in Scotland is at Stratchclyde University.

Leaving local history to local historians was always a bad idea. With the arrival of economic historians (and some maverick economists), local studies veered in a profitable direction, becoming the framework within which specific processes or events could be examined. The much-expanded academic community from the 1960s embraced such new approaches, one consequence being that academic interests, for good or ill, now dominate those of activists. *Labour history was taken out of the domain of manifesto by W. H. Marwick; and farming studies, having eschewed the cause of improvement, by means of detailed examination of estate papers and exchequer records have increased the knowledge of crop yields and organization of systems such as *runrig and *transhumance, though farming from the industrial age is still under-represented. Leading researchers are Robert A. Dodgshon, Ian D. Whyte, and T. M. Devine; while Ian Carter has brought a sociologist's perspective to the field.

Others of these specialists are in fact geographers, bringing with them a number of models on the uses of space. 'It is now widely accepted that geography and history are inter-related, wrote A. C. O'Dell and K. Walton in the introduction to their pioneering volume in the Nelson Regions of the British Isles series, *The Highlands and Islands of Scotland* (1962). More recent overviews are R. N. Millman, *The Making of the Scottish Landscape* (1975), which owes something to *Hoskins's classic study of the English landscape, and David Turnock, *The Historical Geography of Scotland since 1707* (1982).

Geographers' studies of the morphology of towns and suburbs are especially welcome after the noted preoccupation with rural pasts, and have prompted, for the first time, a significant use of *Sasine Registers (records of property transactions) and Dean of Guild registers in studies of housebuilding and the interrelationship of municipal and private capital. The works of R. G. Rodger capture these dynamics of urban development. Just as historical geography owes much to English initiatives, so urban history is indebted to the school of H. J. *Dyos at Leicester University. A recent establishment is Edinburgh University's Centre for Scottish Urban History. The subject, like local history, is difficult to pin down; and it is similarly effective when considered as a frame of reference in pursuing thematic ideas. Areas which have received attention in Scotland are public versus private policy, housing conditions, and suburban growth. The most comprehensive survey is that of Ian H. Adams, *The Making of Urban Scotland* (1978); other stimulating works include George Gordon and Brian Dicks (eds.), *Scottish Urban History* (1983), and George Gordon, *Perspectives of the Scottish City* (1985). Sources are outlined in David Moody, *Scottish Towns* (1992).

Strong Scottish contributions have also been made in urban archaeology. Archaeology, like geography, is crucial in a land of scanty records; and digs such as those under the aegis of the Scottish Urban Archaeological Trust have revolutionized views of urban development. Reports appear in journals such as the *Proceedings of the Society of Antiquaries of Scotland*, for the Society was a catalyst for the new archaeology. Michael Lynch is author of *The Early Modern Town in Scotland* (1987) and joint author with Michael Spearman and Geoffrey Stell of *The Scottish Medieval Town* (1988), which take account of the discoveries.

Current interdisciplinary vitality has fathered new journals such as *Scottish Industrial History* and *Scottish Social and Economic History* whilst the main academic journal, *Scottish History Review*, now leans much more towards social, economic, and local studies. The relative decline of interest in political and state history matches the erosion of the traditional Tory view of history (in Scotland, of course, Toryism has suffered dramatic decline). This has permitted the issue of quasi-nationhood to be bypassed; and by removing deference to an insecure centre, has released a new confidence in locality. If Scottish historical studies were once, as described in a recent review by Bruce Webster, 'riddled with localism', they are now, paradoxically, by liberating themselves from parochialism, able to take on the *parish with vigour and enthusiasm and respect. The new outlook has generated new-style local-history societies and an umbrella organization, the Scottish Local History Forum, which publishes its own journal, *Scottish Local History*. The traditional *antiquarian societies have also responded to these influences, and their journals, previously very antiquarian in tone, now display the same interdisciplinary range.

Mainstream antiquarianism (which suffers from a poor reputation now among some) has itself adapted. The splendid *Scottish Record Office encouraged the centralization of the nation's records, however local in character. Their content is examined in Cecil Sinclair, *Tracing Scottish Local History* (1994). Equivalents of the English county record offices appeared on a large scale after local government reorganization in 1974; some of these are regionally based, some district, more often than not attached to public libraries. Most of them hold local government records from recent centuries, and other records are being devolved from the Scottish Record Office. Holdings are listed in *Exploring Scottish History* (1992).

One major strand in the antiquarian tradition is the publishing of primary sources. The first of the dedicated societies, the Roxburghe, was founded in 1812, and the 19th century saw the publication of most of the meagre extant medieval records of *burgh and *monastery. Most of the societies are now defunct, but publication of primary sources is continued by the *Scottish History Society and the *Scottish Record

Society. A bibliography of all the published records is provided by David and Wendy Stevenson, *Scottish Texts and Calendars* (1987).

Antiquarian interest in buildings also remains strong. The (standing) Royal Commission on Ancient and Historical Monuments of Scotland is still only half-way through publishing its inventories of the monuments of each county, a programme which began at the start of the century. The most recent, for Argyll, has run to seven volumes. Historic Scotland, the government department in the Scottish Office responsible for monuments, has also recently embarked on a publication programme. In recent works, by writers such as Geoffrey Stell, the living context of buildings, be it military responses to new technology or the economics of maintaining a medieval castle's community, are now considered more prominently than once was the case.

Pot shots at antiquarianism have also come from another direction—the swashbuckling series of architectural histories published under the aegis of the Royal Incorporation of Architects in Scotland, with verbal demolitions of everything from medieval keeps to prefabricated factories. The *Pevsner series of architectural histories has penetrated into Scotland in a limited way only.

Scottish society has shown a resilient attachment to principles of *kinship. On the marginal lands in particular (highlands, borders), where the king's arm reached but weakly, clan-type societies persisted up to the end of the 18th century. In the highlands it was primarily an oral culture, and a *Gaelic one too, and the family historians were the sennachies who recited the genealogies of clan chiefs, as their equivalents in other oral cultures have done in many parts of the world. Gaeldom has its fair share of second sight, ghouls, and ghosties, plus a liberal helping of Celtic twilight—in all, too much for most Scottish (non-Gaelic-speaking) historians to come to terms with. History in Gaelic itself is of the Homeric variety; Derick Thomson is one of the authors to guide students through this minefield.

The demise of clan society triggered enormous romantic melancholy, collectively adopted by the nation in compensation for its lost nationhood and its commercial hardheadedness. The aristocracy played a leading part, financing a series of privately printed family histories written by Sir William Fraser over 40 Victorian years. James Balfour Paul, author of the nine-volume encyclopedia of the aristocracy, *The Scots Peerage* (1904), complained that Fraser 'seems afraid of wounding

the susceptibilities of his noble employees by narrating any but smooth and pleasant things about the family'. He also complained that the volumes were too heavy for comfortable reading.

It is a moot point to what extent family history, given the aristocratic domination of Scotland, was considered synonymous with the history of gentrified families. The 'clan' was and is still a complex set of ideas; and its members, however humble, considered themselves the children of the chief. Whole communities chose to emigrate together during the clearances and, for these exiles, family history, or the history of the clan, was a statement of belonging. Few clan histories build on the clarity found in Audrey Cunningham's *The Loyal Clans* (1932) until recently, with the work of E. R. Cregeen.

A pioneering work on family history was Hector McKechnie, *The Pursuit of Pedigree* (1928). McKechnie put his hat firmly in the egalitarian ring: 'It is but a poor creature which is not concerned as to its ancestry', he wrote, and this included the most humble stock 'who never had an acre from the Crown'. At this time the intellectual ambitions of family history were not extensive; for example, in the preface which Balfour Paul wrote for Margaret Stuart's dictionary of names and sources, *Scottish Family History* (1930), he suggests only four categories: the scientific (thorough and accurate but possibly dull); the historical (which must be of a family 'that had some influence on public affairs'); the small (the humble family again, whose story can best be told in a few pages): and the anecdotal (frequently, he delightfully suggests, the work of a lady).

The small family history of which Balfour Paul wrote has, within the last generation, become extraordinarily popular, beyond what would have been imagined 50 years ago, and among thousands of people who have had no other experience of historical research. Many are content with a purely genealogical search, and several textbooks giving detailed guidance have appeared, the best of the most recent being Cecil Sinclair, *Tracing Your Scottish Ancestors: A Guide to Ancestry Research in the Scottish Record Office* (1990). General help can also be found in Kathleen B. Cory, *Tracing your Scottish Ancestry* (1990) and Alwyn James, *Scottish Roots* (1981). The modern pursuit of genealogy appears to have no distinctively Scottish element, being shared by peoples throughout western Europe and the New World; though the fact that so many Scots emigrated to the latter has made Scotland a particular focus, with added associations of nostalgia for lost, imagined homelands. Given Scotland's poor crop of archives, however, few genealogies can be traced back further than the late 18th century.

The lives and experiences of emigrés have become an important theme among professional historians too. For, at the same time that family history began to inspire its dedicated following, academics began to look at areas barely noticed before. One of the seminal works in Scotland, edited by Michael Flinn, was *Scottish Population History* (1977), a study of the demography of the last 300 years based on registers of birth, marriage, and death, *census data, and tax rolls. Subsequent research by, among others, Malcolm Gray and R. A. Houston, has greatly strengthened the statistical backbone in areas such as mean distances of migration, fertility, and depopulation of uplands.

Family history has now become as much of an umbrella as local history, encompassing personal biography, work and leisure, culture, religion, and political activity; in short, all aspects of community life. And just as local studies have expanded to embrace academic disciplines other than history, so family studies are now felt worthy of a course in their own right in the Open University and at Stirling University.

One of the first of the more recent influences on family history was anthropology, which offered a structural analysis of kinship relationships as well as a comparative treasury for the study of rites of passage, marriage customs, and bonding. A good example of their use is Keith M. Brown, *Bloodfeud in Scotland, 1573–1625* (1986). Incidentally, this title, and many others cited here, were published by John Donald, a publisher who has made an outstanding contribution to promoting the new history in Scotland.

Sociology is another new influence, though a more problematic one. James Littlejohn, *Westrigg: The Sociology of a Cheviot Parish* (1963) falls into the tradition of contemporary recording rather than historical study (even the name of the parish is fictitious). The standard sociological practice when developing a thesis is to test it by means of experimental techniques such as surveys and controlled interviews. A good example is Lynn Jamieson and Claire Toynbee, *Country Bairns: Growing Up, 1900–1930* (1992). But of course one cannot interview the more distant past, and the surviving evidence is inevitably partial. The bravest effort to move down this road has been by Helen and Keith Kelsall in *Scottish Lifestyle 300*

Years Ago (1986) and subsequent work on the Home family, using family records of those few who have left us domestic archives of any scope. More widely used have been sociological concepts of power, where historians feel on more familiar ground. A dedicated collection is A. A. Maclaren (ed.), *Social Class in Scotland, Past and Present* (n.d.). Elites too have received attention, appropriately enough in a country with a Calvinist past. It is also a far cry from Fraser's monumental histories in which Balfour Paul lamented the absence of 'family scandals' to find studies of the mechanics of family aggrandizement on the public stage in works such as J. K. Stringer (ed.), *Essays on the Nobility of Medieval Scotland* (1985).

The rise of women's studies has, by the nature of former women's lives, a particular influence on perceptions of family history and the significance accorded to intimate domestic life. No doubt to the even greater horror of William Fraser's ghost, there have been studies of women's sexuality, led by those of Rosalind Mitchison and Leah Leneman. Women's political and social roles are being studied by Eleanor Gordon.

Such social studies are being pulled in two directions: on the one hand they are part of a corpus of social history which has tended to be viewed from a national perspective; on the other, they are influenced by a concept of community history. Social history is the much older discipline, though not one with a great appeal for academic historians until fairly recently. For a long time a few works stood alone, such as Henry Grey Graham, *The Social life of Scotland in the Eighteenth Century* (1899), another of those fascinating and erratic books, much reprinted, which pepper the semi-academic achievement of Scottish historical writing. 'He found endless delight in the detail and *minutiae* of daily life,' writes Eric Linklater in the introduction to the fifth edition. Graham was followed, at well-spaced intervals, by writers who shared his joy in the domestic, such as Marjorie Plant and Marion Lochhead. In fact, the tradition in which they worked was less one of history than of the perennial Scots impulse to record surroundings. Ramsay of Ochtertyre and Henry Mackenzie wrote in the same way of the 18th century, from personal memory; Graham and his followers projected themselves backwards in imagination.

Analytical social history was brought to centre stage by Rosalind Mitchison and T. C. Smout; the most recent synthesis is the three-volume *People and Society in Scotland: A Social History of Modern Scotland* (1988, 1990, and

1992). There are now many specialist branches: social welfare (Ian Levitt, Rosalind Mitchison), housing conditions (John Butt, Enid Gauldie), institutions (David Stevenson on freemasonry), sport, holidays (Alastair Durie), and domestic interiors (Ian Gow). The study of working lives has been extended beyond the macro-economic in order to consider the perspective of the workers themselves. Alan B. Campbell has done this for *The Lanarkshire Miners* (1979), Norman Murray for the *Scottish Hand-loom Weavers 1790–1850: A Social History* (1978). Politics also begin at the grass roots, following L. C. Wright, *Scottish Chartism* (1953). Leading historians in this field are W. Hamish Fraser and Ian Macdougall. There has been detailed work on discontent in the 18th century (Kenneth Logue) and on party affiliations (I. G. C. Hutchinson). The *Scottish Labour History Society Journal* gives a focus for this group. In cultural studies Scotland's educational system has been assailed in R. A. Houston, *Scottish Literacy and the Scottish Identity* (1985). Church studies too have exploded some assumptions, through the sociological approaches of C. Brown, *The Social History of Scottish Religion since 1730* (1987).

Historians, of course, are themselves part of history; and today's preoccupations would have been considered very odd 100 years ago. Our concern with 'the people' reflects our celebration of democracy, coupled with an attendant insecurity about lack of rankings. Aptly, the unsung book which launched the modern approach to history was Lawrence Saunders, *Scottish Democracy* (1950), which covered the key period from 1815 to 1840. The same is true of family history. The fascination with forebears is part of the democratic celebration, the assertion of the right of Everyman to claim a historical identity; but it is at the same time a reflection of a decline in allegiance to public rituals (when rituals fail, intimacy steps in), a decline in hierarchical social structures, and the rise (Tokyo being the leading example) of the disposable town, to be recycled every ten years or so like a plastic bottle. Family and community history provide alternative paradigms of belonging, where once had been paradigms of order.   DAVID MOODY

Scottish Record Office. HM General Register House, Edinburgh EH1 3YY has been the home of the Public Records of Scotland since the late 18th century. It was opened for public searches in 1847. The General Register House occupies a prime site at the east end of Princes Street and is open on Mondays to Fridays from 9 a.m. to 4.45 p.m. A second building, West Register House, in Charlotte Square a mile away, is also open during those hours. (The New Register House, which is adjacent to the General Register House, but is not part of the Scottish Record Office, serves as the *General Register Office for Scotland, housing the *civil registration records and *census returns. The names of these buildings are confusing!) See Cecil Sinclair, *Tracing Scottish Local History: A Guide to Local History Research in the Scottish Record Office* (1994), which details the contents of the Scottish Record Office, and Cecil Sinclair, *Tracing Your Scottish Ancestors . . . in the Scottish Record Office* (1990). Many calendars of the collections have been published by the Scottish Record Society, founded in 1897.

screens passage. Through passage, dividing the *open hall from the service end of a *manor house or other large building. The entry into the hall was through a screen, which was carved and decorated and sometimes supported a minstrels' gallery above.

scutage. The annual money payment by which military service that was owed by *knights to a feudal lord was commuted.

scythes were made in three main centres: Belbroughton and its neighbouring parishes in north Worcestershire, the north Derbyshire parish of Norton, and (later) parts of south-western England. By the 16th and 17th centuries the Belbroughton and Norton districts were exporting scythes to many parts of Britain and the New World. Scythes were forged from bars of iron around a cutting edge of steel. Scythe-grinding at a wheel worked by *water power was a specialist trade from at least the late 16th century until well into the 20th century. A widespread transition from reaping the wheat harvest with the *sickle to mowing with the scythe took place during the century after 1750, most of the change coming after 1830. The growing demand for scythes allowed businesses to expand. The Abbeydale Industrial Hamlet, Sheffield, is an open-air museum based on an old scythe works, dating from the 1780s, where water power was used for forging, plating, and grinding; the works eventually made its own crucible *steel.

seamen. See MERCHANT SEAMAN.

seaside resorts. The fashion for sea-bathing started with the *aristocracy and *gentry in the mid-18th century and soon spread to the middle classes. Resorts developed to meet the need for accommodation, as in *spa centres, which they rivalled. Scarborough, Margate, and

Brighton, the first resorts to be developed in the 1730s, attracted the same type of clientele as the spas. Sea-bathing was thought to be medically beneficial, as well as enjoyable. Horse-drawn bathing machines took people out to the sea, where they discreetly disrobed. The conversion of George III's court to sea-bathing at Weymouth between 1789 and 1805 established that town's reputation; meanwhile, the Prince of Wales did much to make Brighton fashionable in the late 18th century. Londoners travelled by steamboats and sailing packets, or by stage-*coaches, to resorts forming a wide arc from Southend to Weymouth. Some resorts, notably that laid out by the 7th Duke of Devonshire at Eastbourne, catered for the top end of the market, but most resorts quickly adapted to the day trippers and annual holidaymakers who came in great numbers once the *railways made travel cheap and quick. Skegness was described in 1791 by Viscount *Torrington as 'a vile, shabby bathing place'; in 1866 another visitor thought it 'a retired watering place . . . free from bustle', but after the railway arrived in 1873 the character of the place was transformed. The Earl of Scarbrough deliberately developed it to cater for the working classes of the east midlands. Blackpool, which became the greatest seaside attraction of all, owing to its proximity to the textile towns of Lancashire and the West Riding, was another small resort which was transformed by the railways. Nearly half a million visitors arrived at Blackpool by train in 1879; by the eve of the First World War this figure had risen to 4 million. See John K. Walton, *The Blackpool Landlady: A Social History* (1978). The growth of seaside resorts can be measured from the *population figures in the decennial *census returns, but as these figures were counted on census nights in the spring, they greatly underestimate the numbers resident during the summer season. See John K. Walton and Cliff O'Neill, 'Numbering the Holidaymakers: The Problems and Possibilities of the June Census of 1921 for Historians of Resorts', *The Local Historian*, 23/4 (1993).

Until the 1870s, and long afterwards in many places, the middle classes continued to account for the growth of the market. The appeal of the seaside changed from an emphasis on health to the provision of pleasure amongst all social groups. The golden years were those of the late Victorian and Edwardian era. Much of the surviving architecture in resorts dates from that period, including *hotels and boarding houses, churches, *shops, *theatres, promenades, and bandstands in public gardens. Some forms of entertainment were peculiar to the seaside.

Margate led the way in the late 18th century by providing donkey rides on the sands, Blackpool built its Tower and installed the Big Dipper, and most resorts built a pier that enabled visitors to promenade over the sea and spend their money at a variety of shows. The guide books to the various resorts, which were updated on a regular basis, are now a historical source that enables local historians to chart developments. Such places long remained a British, especially an English, phenomenon. See John K. Walton, *English Seaside Resorts: A Social History, 1750–1914* (1983), John Whyman, *Kentish Seaside Resorts Before 1900* (1970) and *The Early Kentish Seaside, 1736–1840* (1985), and Alastair J. Durie, 'The Development of the Scottish Coastal Resorts in the Central Lowlands, *c.*1770–1880', *The Local Historian*, 24/4 (1994).

Secretary hand. The style of handwriting of the 16th and 17th centuries. See PALAEOGRAPHY.

secularism. The doctrine propounded by G. J. Holyoake (1817–1906) that morality should be based not on a belief in God and the afterlife but on the well-being of mankind in the present life. This influenced debates such as that on whether religion should be taught in schools. See Edward Royle, *Victorian Infidels: The Origins of the British Secularist Movement, 1791–1866* (1974).

Seebohm, Frederic W. (1833–1912). A lawyer, banker, and historian. His early work, *The Oxford Reformers of 1498* (1867), is not now read, but his *The English Village Community* (1883) was enormously influential in the development of local agrarian studies. Using evidence from and around his home town of Hitchin (Hertfordshire), in particular a topographical study of Great Wymondley, he stressed the continuity between Roman settlement and English villages.

seed drills. Jethro Tull, the author of *The Horse-Hoeing Husbandry* (1733), invented the first seed drill, but its spread from his native Berkshire was slow. It did not begin to replace *broadcasting of seed in most districts until the 1830s and 1840s.

seigneurial borough. A *borough which did not have a mayor and corporation, but which had a measure of independence from the local *lord of the manor. The lord, however, remained a dominant figure in his *castle nearby; he often retained the right to the market tolls and exercised authority through his manorial *court.

seisin. Possession of property, as distinct from ownership.

Selden Society. A national record society founded in 1887 'to encourage the study and advance the knowledge of the history of English law' by annual publications.

select vestry. See VESTRY.

selion. A strip of arable land in an *open-field. This is the term usually favoured in documents.

Sephardic Jews. Those Jews whose ancestors lived in Spain became known as Sephardic from a medieval Hebrew word meaning Spaniard. Most of the 16th- and 17th-century Jewish migrants to England were Sephardic Jews, who came mostly from Portugal. During the following century others came from various Mediterranean countries, but the 19th-century Jewish immigrants were mainly of *Ashkenazic origin from central and eastern Europe.

sequestration (Scottish). The temporary possession of an estate or *benefice because of debt or vacancy. See Craig Young, 'An Assessment of Scottish Sequestrations as a Source in Historical Analysis', *Journal of the Society of Archivists* (1991), and Craig Young, 'The Content and Use of Scottish Sequestrations: Businesses in Lowland Perthshire, 1856–1913', *The Local Historian*, 24/1 (1994).

serf, serfdom. Serfs were the unfree peasants of the Middle Ages (see VILLEINS and BONDMAN). Their obligations to a *lord of the manor varied in detail from one *manor to another, but had a basic similarity. See Edward Miller and John Hatcher, *Medieval England: Rural Society and Economic Change, 1086–1348* (1978). Generally, they paid modest money rents and frequently some rents in kind, especially fowls at Christmas and eggs at Easter. (See also CHEVAGE and HERIOT.) They owed seasonal *boon works, which normally consisted of a few days' ploughing, harrowing, threshing, haymaking, and harvesting, and perhaps some carting, fencing, ditching, and cutting thatch. Their heaviest obligation in many places was 'week-work', a regular obligation to work the lord's land. The severity of these services was reduced considerably between the late Anglo-Saxon period and the 14th century. In many places services were commuted into money rents during the mid-12th century, only for serfs to face new exactions in the later 12th and 13th centuries, before a general relaxation again in the late 13th century. The great loss of population in the *Black Death created a situation in which such services were abolished once

and for all, though vestiges of serfdom survived into the early modern period.

sergeant-at-law. Member of a superior order of barristers which was abolished in 1880.

serjeantry. A type of medieval tenure by which land was held in return for various personal services below that of *knight service.

servant. See DOMESTIC SERVANT and FARM SERVANTS.

service rooms. The kitchen, dairy, etc., which in larger houses were separated by a *screens passage from the living and sleeping quarters.

Session, Court of. The highest civil court in Scotland. The arrangement of the records in the *Scottish Record Office is complicated and poorly indexed. See Cecil Sinclair, *Tracing Your Scottish Ancestors: A Guide to Ancestry Research in the Scottish Record Office* (1990) for the best procedure. The archives date from 1478 and include Registers and Acts of Decreets from 1542 to the present day, Minute Books from 1557, Register of Deeds from 1554, and Extracted and Unextracted Processes, by which claims and counter-claims were lodged.

settlement. 1. (landscape). See LANDSCAPE HISTORY: THE COUNTRYSIDE.

2. (legal). The complex arrangements for passing on property, adopted by the major landowning families after the *Restoration, are explained in Barbara English and John Saville, *Strict Settlement: A Guide for Historians* (1983).

Settlement, Act of (1662). The *Poor Law Acts of 1597–1601 established the *township or civil *parish as the unit of local government that was responsible for relieving the poor. The Act of 1662 set out the ways in which a poor person could claim to be legally settled. Anyone entering a township to occupy a property worth less than £10 per annum might be challenged by the overseers of the *poor within 40 days of arrival, and after an order from two *Justices of the Peace be removed by the *constable to the place where he or she was legally settled, unless security for indemnity against becoming chargeable to the parish could be provided. Children obtained settlement in the place where they were born, even if they were illegitimate; overseers were therefore anxious to remove pregnant, unmarried women before the birth of a child. A new settlement could be obtained through *apprenticeship, or through service for more than a year. Upon marriage, a wife took her husband's place of settlement.

The practice of issuing certificates, signed by churchwardens and overseers, and confirmed by JPs, whereby responsibility for an individual was acknowledged, began in 1691. Disputes about settlement occupied much of the business at *quarter sessions. The records of settlement examinations concerning applicants for poor relief, or of those thought liable to become a burden on the poor rates, may be found amongst parish records in local *record offices. They include much information about the length and conditions of service and about the movement of individuals. See K. D. M. Snell, *Annals of the Labouring Poor: Social Change and Agrarian England, 1660–1900* (1985). An Act of 1795 laid down that removal could take place only when a person became chargeable to the parish. The 1662 Act was repealed by the Poor Law Amendment Act (1834), which created unions of parishes as the responsible authorities.

severalty. Private possession of land. The term is used to describe enclosed lands beyond the *open-fields of a village.

Sewers, Commissioners of. An Act of 1531 authorized the appointment of commissioners charged with the drainage of low-lying land that was liable to floods. Courts of sewers conducted their administrative business in a judicial manner, before a jury. They were abolished in 1930, when their work was transferred to bodies which now form part of regional water authorities. Their records are to be found at local *record offices. See A. E. B. Owen, 'Records of Commissioners of Sewers', *History*, 53 (1967).

Shambles. The name was commonly applied to that part of a *market place or adjoining street where the *butchers (and sometimes the fishmongers) had their stalls or shops. The narrow medieval street in York called the Shambles was the place where the butchers lived and sold their meat. The word has come to mean chaos or mess, no doubt because of the scenes typically associated with such places.

sheep. For an introduction to the importance of sheep in the medieval economy, when *wool and woollen cloth were England's principal exports, see W. G. Hoskins, 'Sheep Farming in Saxon and Medieval England' in *Provincial England* (1963), ch. 1. The volumes of The *Agrarian History of England and Wales* provide a great deal of information about sheep farming and the marketing of wool and mutton from prehistoric times to the 20th century. M. L. Ryder's *Sheep and Man* (1983) is a monumental work of scholarship on the subject. Gregory *King estimated that England and Wales had

11 million sheep in the late 17th century, and in 1741 an anonymous writer estimated the sheep population of Great Britain at 16–17 million. Meanwhile, Ireland was exporting sheep to Britain. (See CLEARANCES, HIGHLAND, for the expansion of sheep farming in the Scottish Highlands during the 18th and 19th centuries.)

By the end of the 18th century most rough pastures and much of the improved grasslands were grazed by sheep. (See FOLDCOURSE for the practice of night-time folding of sheep brought down from the pastures to manure the arable.) See also the observations of Henry *Best, and W. H. Hudson, *A Shepherd's Life* (1910). Before 1750 sheep were reared principally for their wool, but breeders (starting with Robert Bakewell's development of the New Leicester) then began to produce an animal that not only had better wool but was increasingly valued also for its mutton. See the account by R. J. Moore-Colyer in G. E. Mingay (ed.), *The Agrarian History of England and Wales*, vi, *1750–1850* (1989). Mutton and fat lamb could be sold profitably to the growing urban population.

sheila-na-gig. A naked female figure, with legs wide open, which is incorporated in the decorative sculpture of some medieval churches and (in Ireland) secular buildings such as *castles and mills. The term is an Irish Gaelic expression for an immodest woman. About 70 images survive in both France and Ireland and about 40 in both Spain and England. They first appear in the British Isles amongst the *Romanesque carvings of 12th-century Herefordshire churches, where their purpose was to portray sin. See Ronald Hutton, *The Pagan Religions of the Ancient British Isles* (1991).

shell keep. A circular or polygonal stone enclosure, which in the later 12th century began to replace the wooden palisades on the tops of *mottes. They contained domestic quarters and were not strong defensive structures like the square and polygonal towers that often replaced them.

sheriff. The 'shire-reeve' was the chief official of a county after the *Norman Conquest. His legal responsibilities passed to the *Justices of the Peace in the 14th century and his responsibility for the *militia passed to the *lords lieutenant in the 16th century. The office is now ceremonial. See, for example, W. Croft Dickinson (ed.), 'The Sheriff Court Book of Fife, 1515–1522', *Scottish History Society*, 3rd ser., 12 (1928).

sherman. A sheep shearer.

shieling. A summer settlement for farmers practising *transhumance in Scotland and northern England, so as to rest their winter pastures. These men lived in stone or turf huts known as *bothies, and cultivated a small field of oats or rye, while tending their cattle and sheep. Place-names such as -erg, -scholes, and -sett commemorate these settlements. The Welsh 'hafod' and the Irish 'buaile' have the same meaning. Shielings also acted as territorial markers on disputed moorlands. See H. Ramm and others, *Shielings and Bastles* (1970), and Albert Bil, *The Shieling, 1600–1840: The Case of the Central Scottish Highlands* (1990).

shift work. The time-discipline imposed in the mills and *factories, including the practice of working night shifts, was a new feature of life in the late 18th century. See E. P. *Thompson, 'Time, Work-Discipline and Industrial Capitalism' in *Customs in Common* (1991), ch. 6.

shilling. A silver coin, introduced in 1504, bearing the portrait of Henry VII, and at first known as the testoon. It was worth 12 old pence; 20 shillings were worth £1.

shingles. Wooden tiles, usually of oak, were used for medieval roofs, especially in southern England. In domestic buildings, they were gradually replaced by clay tiles from the 16th century onwards, because of the fire risk, but they have continued in use on church spires, e.g. Stock (Essex).

ship money. The collection of a tax, based on the previous practice of raising money in time of war, but used in the 1630s by Charles I for other purposes without recourse to Parliament, was based on assessments levied on counties and towns. There are no detailed records naming individuals.

ships. The ship was such an important symbol in early times that some *Anglo-Saxon kings were ceremonially buried in one. The most famous site is that of Sutton Hoo (Suffolk). The *Viking long-boat is an equally powerful image. The construction of large warships was pursued by the Tudor monarchs, with considerable consequences for the economy of the Weald, which produced the necessary timbers and the iron for cannon. Knowledge of such ships, and of the merchant ships of the 17th and 18th centuries, has been considerably enhanced by under-water archaeology, starting with the *Mary Rose*, which sank off Spithead in 1545. The precision of dating that is available for many wrecks dates the artefacts discovered on board and thus helps to date those found elsewhere. See David Crossley, *Post-Medieval Archaeology in Britain* (1990), ch. 5. Contemporary paintings are another source of information, for ships were a favourite subject for artists. See also P. Mathias and A. W. H. Pearsall (eds.), *Shipping: A Survey of Historical Records* (1971).

The heyday of the wooden sailing ship was during the 18th and early 19th centuries, when the *East India Company and other companies traded with far-flung parts of the world. (See also TRADE, COASTING.) The challenge from steamships came first on the trans-Atlantic run. Steamships began to take passengers to Canada and America in the 1840s, but it was not until the 1860s that virtually all emigrants to the New World travelled that way. About two-thirds of them left from Liverpool. Shipyards became major employers in Liverpool, Belfast, Clydeside, London, etc. (See DOCKS, DOCKYARDS.) During the late 19th and early 20th centuries the manufacture of warships provided further employment in shipyards and the major centres of the *steel industry. In the decade before the First World War 60 per cent of the world's tonnage of ships was constructed in Britain: by the late 1930s this proportion had fallen to nearly 35 per cent. After the Second World War the British shipbuilding industry declined rapidly, so that by 1970 it was no longer significant.

shires. See COUNTIES, ORIGINS OF. In the kingdom of *Northumbria smaller units than counties were also known as 'shires', e.g. Blackburnshire, Hallamshire, Howdenshire; see ESTATE, EARLY.

shops. Gregory *King estimated that in the late 17th century England and Wales had about 40,000 shopkeepers. Most of these were based in towns, but a contemporary tract claimed that shops were also to be found 'in every country village'. This claim is supported by the evidence of *trade tokens and probate *inventories. See T. S. Willan, *The Inland Trade* (1976), and Lorna Weatherill, *Consumer Behaviour and Material Culture in Britain, 1660–1760* (1988). In towns, the best shops were found in the principal streets and around the *market place, for the market and shops were complementary, rather than rivals. Most shopkeepers were known as grocers, drapers, etc., but their inventories show that they sold anything they could and that shops were often general stores. In addition to the purely retail shops, towns had the workshops of craftsmen, which often had a retail as well as a manufacturing function. A surprising range of goods were on offer in provincial shops, including exotic groceries and medicines. See Ursula Priestley and Alayne Fenner, *Shops and Shopkeepers in Norwich, 1660–1730* (1985). See also J. D. Marshall (ed.), *The Autobiography of William Stout of Lancaster, 1665–1752* (1967) for the life of a provincial (and *Quaker) shopkeeper. For the later period, see David Alexander, *Retailing in England during the Industrial Revolution* (1970).

During the second half of the 19th century the centres of major towns and cities ceased to be residential areas and became retail and entertainment districts. The movement out of the centre of towns was aided by the provision of *tram and bus services. The process whereby shops replaced old houses can be followed in trade and commercial *directories and by the use of old *photographs. The lowly origins of such famous chains of shops as Boot's, Sainsbury's, and Marks and Spencer's can also be observed in 19th-century photographs. Many such departmental stores started in a small way in provincial cities, before moving to London. See Katrina Honeyman, 'Montague Burton Ltd: The Creators of Well-Dressed Men' in John Chartres and Katrina Honeyman (eds.), *Leeds City Business, 1893–1993* (1993). For an introductory account of the rise of the West End of London, see Gavin Weightman and Steve Humphries, *The Making of Modern London, 1815–1914* (1993), ch. 2. Some family firms remained rooted in the provinces, however, their names being locally famous until the later 20th century, when shops became increasingly part of national or international groups and the individual appearance of town centres gave way to uniform frontages. Shopping is no longer simply a necessity but a major leisure activity that is increasingly pursued in new shopping complexes on the edges of towns.

shot, shutt. A block of *strips in an *open-field, a *furlong.

shows, agricultural. Numerous local farmers' societies were founded in the late 18th and 19th centuries, especially from the 1830–1840s onwards. The highlight of their year was a show of livestock, produce, and machinery, which was intended to spread information about best practices and to award prizes for the best exhibits. These shows became local social institutions. The Royal Agricultural Society of England, founded in 1837, held its first national show in 1839.

shrines. The shrines of saints and martyrs attracted *pilgrims from the earliest days of Christianity in Britain. Some were the tombs of local saints to whom the church was dedicated, e.g. that of St Wystan at Repton (Derbyshire),

a major Anglo-Saxon church where the tomb is kept in a *crypt. Some churches claimed to hold relics brought back from the Holy Land, especially at the time of the *Crusades. It was widely believed that healing miracles could be performed by contact with such shrines. Shrines were also visited as an act of *penance or through simple curiosity over a place of repute. Pilgrims travelled long distances, often journeying abroad. See R. C. Finucane, *Miracles and Pilgrims: Popular Beliefs in Medieval England* (1977). The practice of visiting shrines declined rapidly with the *Reformation.

Shrove Tuesday. The day preceding Ash Wednesday, which together with the preceding two days forms Shrovetide, the period of confession before *Lent. Long after the *Reformation, Shrove Tuesday remained the day when *apprentices were boisterous in the streets (indulging in crude sports such as stoning cocks), and when traditional sports were held, e.g. the Ashbourne (Derbyshire) football match, or the Olney (Buckinghamshire) pancake race. The eating of pancakes survives as a muted version of the eating of large quantities of food before Lent.

shrunken settlements. Earthworks associated with *deserted medieval villages are often found at the edges of settlements which have shrunk rather than disappeared. They can, however, be confused with evidence for shifting settlement.

sickles were gradually replaced by *scythes for mowing the grain harvest during the period 1750–1850, especially in the 1830s and 1840s. The Moss Valley, in the north Derbyshire parish of Eckington, south-east of Sheffield, was the major centre of production from the late 16th to the late 19th centuries, as it had excellent facilities for *water-powered grinding. The sickle remained a gardening tool until it was replaced by the strimmer in the late 20th century.

silk. The silk stockings that were fashionable in Elizabethan times were sometimes made of Spanish silk, but were increasingly made from yarn produced by Flemish weavers working in London, especially Spitalfields. See Joan Thirsk, 'The Fantastical Folly of Fashion: The English Stocking Knitting Industry, 1500–1700' in *The Rural Economy of England: Collected Essays* (1984). Canterbury was another important silk weaving centre at the same period, accommodating French immigrants. The importation of French silks was banned in

1698, and of Indian and Chinese silks in 1701, in order to encourage the native industry.

Silk weaving was established as an industry in Coventry in the early 17th century and spread to nearby coalfield villages in the 18th century; coal was used for fuel to heat the dye vats. The first provincial silk spinning, or 'throwing', mill was that erected in 1702 on the river Derwent at Derby by Thomas Cotchett. This small mill was overshadowed by the one built alongside it in 1718–22 by Thomas Lombe, on an Italian model; both were designed by the engineer George Sorocold. Lombe's mill, which produced yarn of a superior quality, broke London's ancient monopoly. This mill (which was destroyed by fire in 1910 and was replaced by the building that now houses the Derby Industrial Museum) was the prototype of the textile mills of the *Industrial Revolution. By 1789 Derby had 12 silk spinning mills, which together employed 1,200 people, mainly women and children, who made silk for the *framework knitters, tapes, and *ribbons. Male silk weavers worked at home at domestic looms. Derby continued to grow as a centre of silk manufacturing, but declined in the Victorian period. Meanwhile, a silk-throwing mill had been built at Stockport in 1732, and by the 1750s Macclesfield and Congleton (Cheshire), and Leek (Staffordshire) had begun weaving by *water power; Sheffield, too, had a silk mill, built c.1760.

Luxury silk garments were worn by the wealthy in the 18th and 19th centuries, and the silk top hat became fashionable in the 1840s; in the first half of the 20th century silk garments became fashionable amongst wider sections of society. The Coventry silk ribbon trade was badly hit in the 1860s, when the restrictions on foreign imports were lifted, but the industry survived at a reduced level well into the 20th century. In Leek, the industry continued to thrive in steam-powered weaving mills and workshops. Macclesfield remained the centre of the British silk industry until the late 20th century and now has a Silk Museum. Associated with this is Paradise Silk Mill, built in 1820 and extended in 1860, which housed the last handloom silk weaving business until its closure in 1981 and conversion into a museum; it retains 26 Jacquard handlooms in their original setting.

silver. Most silver produced in Britain was not mined separately but was extracted from suitable *lead ores and was mostly confined to the north Pennines (around Alston) and north Devon (around Bere Alston). A 17th-century silver-mill site has been discovered near Aberystwyth.

simony. The buying or selling of a *benefice or other ecclesiastical office.

Sinclair, Sir John (1754–1835). Scottish politician and agricultural improver, created baronet in 1786. He established the *Board of Agriculture in 1793, and compiled a *Statistical Account of Scotland* between 1791 and 1799, a detailed economic and social record of parishes that was based on returns from the ministers of each parish. The information provided varies enormously in detail, but includes accounts of occupations, local trades and industries, prices, the names of major landowners, and recent agricultural improvements. The returns were published as they came in and so parishes are mixed indiscriminately in the 21 volumes which eventually appeared. This 'First or Old Statistical Account' inspired the New Statistical Account of the 1830s and the Third Statistical Account of the 1950s.

single-family surnames. The great variety of *surnames in England suggests the possibility that many are of single-family origin. This possibility is increased when a study of the distribution of a name from *telephone directories or the records of *civil registration shows that the name is rare and is concentrated in a particular region. When such a name is traced back through earlier records, its point of origin can sometimes be identified. This is particularly the case with surnames of the locative type, which are derived from individual farmsteads in areas of scattered settlement. See David Hey, *The Oxford Guide to Family History* (1993), ch. 2.

Names which at first sight appear to have had multiple origins sometimes turn out to descend from a single family. The name Widdowson has the straightforward meaning of 'son of the widow'. It is recorded in several widely scattered places in the Middle Ages. However, the distribution pattern of the surname in the 19th and 20th centuries shows a strong concentration in the Trent Valley of south Nottinghamshire and north Leicestershire, and the occurrence of the name in *parish registers points to the Nottinghamshire parish of Trowell as being the likely origin of the present-day Widdowsons; the other families which bore this surname in the Middle Ages must all have died out in the male line. Likewise, rare surnames that have been derived from occupations or nicknames can sometimes be shown to be very restricted in their distribution. Neat (the name of the man who looked after the cows, or the neat herd) is a north Wiltshire surname, the nicknames Bunyon and Mouse are from Bedfordshire, and Speight (a nickname from the green woodpecker) is a West Riding name found in and near Bradford.

Some names which appear rare and localized are merely variant spellings of other names. Some variations occurred when a family moved into a different district, where the name was unfamiliar. Thus, the surname Shufflebottom is derived from Shipperbottom in a valley in the Lancashire parish of Bury. Even within the district from which a surname has been derived, variant forms of the name are usual. Thus, the south Pennine farmstead which is marked on modern maps as Belle Clive, but which is still known locally by its original name Billcliff, is the home of the rare surname Billcliff and its variants Biltcliffe, Bintcliffe, Bincliff, etc. which are still found mainly within a few miles of their point of origin.

H. B. Guppy's *Homes of Family Names in Great Britain* (1890) was a pioneering attempt to locate the points of origin of surnames, but little further work on these lines was attempted until the creation of the English Surnames Survey under Richard McKinley at the Department of English Local History at *Leicester University. The etymologies proposed by linguists can often be shown to be wrong through detailed research undertaken by family and local historians. The technique is to establish the modern distribution pattern of the name through telephone directories and to work back through time by using the indexes of the civil registration records, which begin in 1837, and the *hearth tax returns of the 1660s–1670s. Having established that a name appears to have a local origin, genealogical techniques are then applied to parish registers (perhaps using the *International Genealogical Index), *wills, manorial records, etc. to trace the name as far back as possible. It is most unlikely that a firm link can be proved all the way back to the first holder of the name, but such research will home in to the point of origin and to the earliest recorded forms of the name, which in the case of locative names should be compared to the earliest forms of the place-name.

Sir. The title of *baronets and *knights, and, until the *Reformation, of a priest who was not a university graduate.

sister. The term was also used to mean sister-in-law.

skimmington ride. Public disapproval of an adulterous couple was expressed by the parading of effigies and *rough music, especially in the 18th and 19th centuries. The performance was also known as 'riding the stang'.

slate. In the 19th century geologists defined slate more narrowly than had been the customary usage, which included sandstone and limestone roofing 'slates'. The customary sense is preserved by builders and students of *vernacular architecture. It includes such regional specialities as Cumberland and Westmorland slate, the oolitic limestone 'slates', e.g. from Collyweston (Rutland), and the sandstone 'slates' which were the heaviest roofing material, thus requiring the roofs of Pennine houses and barns to have the lowest pitch of any traditional buildings. See Alec Clifton-Taylor, *The Pattern of English Building* (1972). (See also SWITHLAND SLATE.)

Welsh blue-slates were widely used when *canals, *shipping, and (especially) the *railways reduced transport costs to such an extent that Welsh quarries could compete effectively in distant markets. These small, light slates replaced traditional materials throughout Britain and were particularly associated with new, red-brick buildings. The north Wales slate industry expanded enormously in the 18th and 19th centuries, but declined quickly in the 20th century with the use of different materials for roofs. (See QUARRYING.) The major slate quarries were at Penrhyn (near Bethesda), Dyffryn Nantlle and Llanberis (Caernarvonshire), and Blaenau Ffestiniog (Merionethshire). For working conditions and industrial relations see Merfyn Jones, 'Y Chwarelwyr: The Slate Quarrymen of North Wales' in Raphael Samuel (ed.), *Miners, Quarrymen and Saltworkers* (1977).

slave trade. Many British merchants prospered from the trade in slaves from Africa to the *West Indies, *Virginia, and other parts of America in the 17th and 18th centuries. The shift of opinion in favour of abolition during the later 18th century led to Britain banning its inhabitants from any involvement in the trade in a series of measures passed in 1806–7. See Roger T. Anstey, *The Atlantic Slave Trade and British Abolition, 1760–1870* (1975), and Seymour Drescher, 'Whose Abolition? Popular Pressure and the Ending of the British Slave Trade', *Past and Present*, 143 (1994). Much material about the history of the slave trade is on display at the Wilberforce Museum, Hull.

slitting mill. *Water-powered mills for the slitting of iron into rods were introduced from the Continent into the west midlands by the 1620s. They were associated with *furnaces and *forges and were the source of supply of raw materials to local *nail-makers. By the second half of the 17th century they were becoming common in midland and northern England.

slubber. An occupation in the West Riding scribbling and *spinning mills, whereby loose cardings were drawn out and slightly twisted so that they could be wound on to bobbins. The man in charge of the 30 to 50 spindles of a 'slubbing billy' was one of the most highly paid craftsmen. He was assisted by two or three children who fed in the cardings by rubbing fresh ones on to the end of old ones.

smallholders, decline of. The decline, and in many places the disappearance, of smallholders has been hotly debated since the early years of the 20th century, when Gilbert Slater, *The English Peasantry and the Enclosure of the Common Fields* (1907), A. H. Johnson, *The Disappearance of the Small Landowner* (1909), and John and Barbara *Hammond, *The Village Labourer* (1911), argued that *enclosure was fatal to the small farmer, the *cottager, and the *squatter because of their loss of rights on the *commons. Much of the argument was based on analyses of *land tax assessments which have since been shown to be a flawed source. E. Davies, 'The Small Landowner, 1780–1832, in the Light of the Land Tax Assessments', *Economic History Review*, I/1 (1927) was the first to revise the conclusions of Slater, Johnson, and the Hammonds, arguing that enclosure did not adversely affect the small landowner and tenant farmer, whose numbers actually rose in many regions during the period of enclosure. See also J. A. Yelling, *Common Field and Enclosure in England, 1450–1850* (1977), and G. E. Mingay, *Enclosure and the Small Farmer in the Age of the Industrial Revolution* (1976). The debate has been reopened by J. M. Neeson, *Commoners: Common Right, Enclosure and Social Change in England, 1700–1820* (1993).

Recent arguments over the effects of enclosure have tended to concentrate on the *agricultural labourer and cottager rather than the small owner-occupier. The terms '*yeoman' and '*husbandman' gradually disappeared and the 19th century saw an increasing polarization between the larger owner-occupiers and the very small ones. Studies from Warwickshire, Lincolnshire, Westmorland, Suffolk, and Wiltshire confirm the widening gap between large and small tenant farmers during the late 18th and 19th centuries. (See VILLAGES, OPEN and CLOSE.) In old-enclosed parishes, especially those converted to pasture, the owner-occupier had almost ceased to exist by the late 18th century. However, many families continued to farm a smallholding, often with the assistance of another occupation (see DUAL ECONOMY). Indeed, hill-farmers and their lowland counterparts in the *fens continued to farm smallholdings in the traditional manner. See Adrian Hall, *Fenland Worker-Peasants: The Economy of Smallholders at Rippingale, Lincolnshire, 1791–1871 (Agricultural History Review* Supplement, i, 1992). Historians now stress the variety of the small owners' experience. The position of the smallholder weakened as the trend of the modern period has been towards large units, but in many parts of the British Isles the decline has not been such that he has disappeared. See Alun Howkins, 'Peasants, Servants and Labourers: The Marginal Workforce in British Agriculture, c.1870–1914', *Agricultural History Review*, 42/1 (1994).

smallpox was the major killer disease of the late 17th and 18th centuries. Survivors were disfigured by pock-marks on their skins. (See INOCULATION and VACCINATION.) Smallpox was believed to be eradicated throughout the world in 1977. See J. R. Smith, *The Speckled Monster: Smallpox in England, 1670–1970* (1987), which draws particularly on evidence from Essex.

smelting. In the Middle Ages *lead was smelted on the Pennines and Mendips in hearths situated on windy *bole hills. During the 16th century smelters abandoned this method in favour of bellows-blown ore hearths which were fuelled by kiln-dried wood known as white-coal; in the northern Pennines *peat was also used. The first changes took place in the Mendips in the mid-16th century. The bellows were operated by *water power, so the smelting industry became concentrated in valleys, near to *coppice woods. About 40 ore-hearth sites have been located in Derbyshire by intensive fieldwork. See D. Crossley and D. Kiernan, 'The Lead Smelting Mills of Derbyshire', *Derbyshire Archaeological Journal*, 112 (1992).

Experiments with the cupola, or reverberatory coal-fired furnace, began in the late 17th century (see also GLASS and STEEL). This method was not only more economic, but by isolating the fuel it reduced the risk of contaminating the smelted metal with sulphur. Operational difficulties prevented the method from spreading quickly, but from the mid-18th century it was widely adopted. Surviving cupolas date from this period. Smelters now abandoned the wooded valleys in favour of high moorland sites, away from settlements.

*Tin was smelted by water-powered *blowing houses from the Middle Ages to the 19th century. Reverberatory furnaces, similar to those used in the lead industry, were used in Cornwall from at least the early 18th century. The evidence for *copper smelting is uncertain, but the industry seems to have developed on similar lines. For a general survey of smelting, see David Crossley, *Post-Medieval Archaeology in Britain* (1990), ch. 8.

smithy. 1. The small forge of a blacksmith, cutler, nail-maker, etc.

2. A term used, often in the plural, in the 16th and 17th centuries for a much larger site for the forging of iron.

smoke-penny. An Easter due payable to the incumbent of a *parish by the occupier of a house with a fireplace.

smuggling. The duties charged on foreign imports such as *tobacco, wine, proof spirits, *tea, and *sugar from the 16th to the 19th centuries made smuggling a profitable if dangerous enterprise for the inhabitants of remote coastal communities. Smugglers have attracted a romantic literature, but so secret a trade has left little firm evidence. See CUSTOMS AND EXCISE.

soap was originally made from animal fats, vegetable oils, ashes, and lime, boiled in large pans. Its domestic use was rivalled by its use in the cloth industry. Soap-making was both an urban and a rural occupation, often combined with that of making candles. See M. Davies-Shiel, 'The Making of Potash for Soap in Lakeland', *Transactions of the Cumberland and Westmorland Archaeological and Antiquarian Society*, 72 (1972). Its content and manufacture underwent major changes in the 16th–17th centuries. Olive (Seville) oil used in the best quality soap gave way to *rape seed oil, and whale oil from the Greenland fisheries was also much used. Prices fell through the use of new ingredients, and the setting up of more commercial operations. Soaphouses in 1574 were said to be situated only in London, York, Hull, and Bristol. By the early 19th century Liverpool, Manchester, and Warrington were challenging London's supremacy as the major manufacturing centre. Merseyside could import vegetable oils and Scottish and Irish *kelp for alkali, had access to Cheshire *salt for the production of soda, and a ready market for soft soap in the nearby textile centres. Soap was one of the products of the Merseyside *chemical industry, which developed rapidly in the 19th century. In 1889 William Hesketh Lever moved his works from Warrington to Port Sunlight. By the 1920s Levers (later Unilever) owned 60 per cent of the industry. See A. E. Musson, *Enterprise in Soap and Chemicals* (1965).

socage. A form of *feudal tenure in which land was held not by service but by a money rent.

Society for the Promotion of Christian Knowledge. Founded in 1698 to reform manners and to encourage the provision of charity schools under the auspices of the *Church of England. The manuscript records of the society include letters and minutes from 1699 to 1729 (and later). Annual *Reports* were printed from 1705 to 1732. See W. E. Tate, 'S.P.C.K. Archives', *Archives*, III (1957).

Society of Genealogists. See GENEALOGISTS, SOCIETY OF.

sojourner. A temporary resident.

soke. Land in the *Danelaw which was held by free peasant tenants who owed suit of court and some minor customary dues to the *lord of the manor. They are recorded in the *Domesday Book. A soke was a dependent free territory scattered over many villages. By the end of the Middle Ages soke had come to mean simply an administrative division of a *lordship. The Soke of Peterborough, consisting of 32 *townships, was a separate county until 1974.

solar. A private chamber on the sunny side of a house.

Solemn League and Covenant. An agreement made by members of the House of Commons in 1643 to defend *Protestantism and the rights of Parliament, to which in the following year all males over 18 were expected to subscribe. A few lists survive in county *record offices.

Somerset House. The Principal Probate Registry, containing all *wills proved in England and Wales after 1858. Indexes may be consulted free. The address is Strand, London WC2. It is open on weekdays between 10.00 and 4.30.

son-in-law. The term was often used to mean 'stepson'. A 'son-in-law' was often referred to as 'son'.

South Africa. The Dutch East India Company was responsible for the first European settlers in the 17th and 18th centuries. The settlers lived in the Cape Colony, which by 1740 comprised about 4,000 free burghers and their families, of Dutch, German, Walloon, and *Huguenot descent, and about 1,500 Company servants and soldiers and their families. By 1800 Cape Colony contained about 16,000 people of European descent, 17,000 slaves, and an unknown number of Hottentots and Bushmen. The numbers of British settlers increased in the early 19th century, but by the 1820s the 8,000 British settlers were still heavily outnumbered by the 43,000 Dutch. By the middle of the 19th century the white population was probably about a quarter of the black. The number of Zulus and other black people increased subsequently. The new Dutch states of Natal, Orange Free State, and Transvaal, which were created after the Great Trek northwards, starting in 1836, were not reunited with the Cape until after the Boer War, with the creation of the Union of South Africa in 1910. The black population was enfranchised in 1994, when white minority rule came to an end.

Southern History. A journal founded in 1979, which publishes articles and reviews of books on the history of the southern counties of England.

South Sea bubble. The huge financial speculation, encouraged by the Government, which burst in September 1720 ruining many families. The South Sea Company of 1710 attracted thousands of investors as share prices rose rapidly until the bubble burst.

sovereign (coin). Introduced by Henry VII (1485–1509) at the value of 20 *shillings. During the second half of the 16th century it was worth 30s. Discontinued in the early 17th century, it was reintroduced from 1817 to 1917, when it was again valued at 20s.

spades. The catalogues of late 19th-century Sheffield firms show that an enormous variety of types and sizes of spades were on offer. One firm's products included a dozen different spades for digging out *rabbits. One of the earliest specialist spades was that used for digging *peat. The merits of spade cultivation in agriculture were much discussed in the 17th century, when *market gardening demonstrated how much more productive (per acre) was land so cultivated than when tilled by the plough. Spade cultivation increased during the 18th century, especially on *potato allotments in Ireland, and for the creation of lazy-beds in the Highlands and Islands of Scotland.

spas. The fashion of visiting spa centres for the supposed healing properties of sulphur and chalybeate springs was imported from Belgium, France, and Germany in the 16th and 17th centuries, but took a long time before it flourished in the 18th and 19th centuries. See Phyllis Hembry, *The English Spa, 1560–1815: A Social History* (1990). In the 1690s Celia *Fiennes wrote many observations on the new spas, some of which were still in a primitive condition. At that time, it was just becoming the custom not

only to drink the waters but to bathe in heated tubs. It therefore became necessary to provide accommodation for visitors. See, for example, Bernard Jennings, *The History of Harrogate and Knaresborough* (1970), which describes how a new site was gradually developed into a fashionable centre. For the growth of the most fashionable spa in Britain, see Barry Cunliffe, *The City of Bath* (1986). Spas such as Bath, Wells, and Epsom offered social activities out of the London season in addition to their medical facilities. For a sceptical view, see Tobias Smollett, *Humphry Clinker* (1771). Scarborough was unusual in being able to offer sea-bathing as well. (See SEASIDE RESORTS, and HYDROPATH.)

Many spa towns retain the pump rooms and baths, promenades, crescents, and squares of their hey-day. Thus, Tunbridge Wells has The Pantiles, which was first laid out in 1638, Buxton has The Crescent, which was designed by Carr of York about 1780, Leamington has The Parade of c.1815–33, and Cheltenham has The Promenade of c.1823 and the Pittville Pump Room of 1825–30. Cheltenham was formerly a small market town with a cold mineral spring. Its growth began modestly about 1740 as a cheaper resort than the more sophisticated Bath. The arrival of a *canal in 1792 meant that *building stone could be brought to the town at much cheaper rates. At the same time, several more mineral wells were discovered. After the end of the *Napoleonic wars in 1815 Cheltenham experienced a period of prosperity, with the development of Pittville to the north and Lansdown to the south of the town. From the 1840s it declined somewhat as Continental spas became more popular. Its story is a fairly typical one. In addition to the fashionable centres, many small places, including some remote ones, had sulphur or chalybeate springs. Some are commemorated in minor place-names.

speech. See DIALECTS AND ACCENTS.

Speed, John (1552–1629). Cartographer and antiquarian, and member of the Society of *Antiquaries. Between 1605 and 1610, with the financial backing of Sir Fulke Greville, he produced a new set of 54 maps of the counties of England and Wales, which remain popular to this day. In 1610 he published the six maps of the *Kingdome of Scotland*. The following year he published *Theatre of the Empire of Great Britaine*, a large folio volume that included all the county maps and a descriptive text. A particular feature of abiding interest was his insertion of town plans. The *Theatre* was accompanied by *The History of Great Britaine* (1611), a reworking of older histories in a decorative and expensive form, which went through various editions until 1650. See Nigel Nicholson (ed.), *The Counties of Britain by John Speed* (1988).

Speenhamland system. In 1795 the overseers of the *poor in the parish of Speenhamland (Berkshire) adopted a method of supplementing low *wages with an allowance paid for out of the rates. This allowance varied according to the cost of bread. The system was widely copied in southern England, but as local farmers deliberately kept wages low, in the knowledge that allowances would be given by the *parish, the number of people on poor relief actually rose. The system was discredited before the *Poor Law Amendment Act (1834).

spelling, phonetic. In documents of the Elizabethan period and later it is common to find the same word spelt in different ways only a line or two apart and to find that people spelt their own names in different ways as the spirit moved them. Spelling gradually became standardized during the 17th and 18th centuries as the amount of printed literature increased.

spice. Spices from the East came via the Mediterranean in the Middle Ages. The *East India Company was the major provider once a sea route around Africa was established. Household accounts and the probate *inventories of shopkeepers show that spices were widely available, even in places distant from the ports.

spinning. The spinning of yarn was traditionally a woman's domestic employment; hence the word 'spinster' for an unmarried woman. Spinning on the distaff was accelerated by spinning on the wheel, of which many examples survive in *museum collections. External spinning galleries are a feature of the *vernacular architecture of Westmorland and Cumberland. Spinning was mechanized during the late 18th century, long before *weaving. Women and children formed most of the work-force of the *water-powered *cotton and *woollen mills.

sport. For the sports that were popular before the age of mass spectator sports, see Robert W. Malcolmson, *Popular Recreations in English Society, 1700–1850* (1973), especially ch. 3 on *football, *cricket, wrestling, boxing, running, etc. The rise of professional sport in the second half of the 19th century has begun to attract the attention of historians. See Tony Mason, *Association Football and English Society, 1863–1915* (1980), David Brailsford, *Sport, Time and Society: The British at Play* (1991), and John Lowerson, *Sport and the English Middle Classes,*

1870–1914 (1993). For a study of the various sports in one locality, see Patrick Renshaw, 'Aspects of Sport and Recreation' in Clyde Binfield *et al.*, *History of the City of Sheffield, 1843–1993*, vol. ii (1993).

square panelling. The method of arranging the posts of *timber-framed buildings that was favoured in the western half of England. The external appearance of such buildings was of square patterns, ornamented in the better-quality houses. The style contrasts with the *close studding of eastern counties.

squarson. A word used in the 18th and 19th centuries for a clergyman (parson) who was also the *squire of his village.

squatters. The increase in the national *population in the late 16th and early 17th centuries meant that large numbers of families sought space on which to erect *cottages. They were attracted to the edges of *commons in *forests and *fens, and on the *moors. (See COTTAGES / COTTAGERS.) An Act of 1589 tried to ensure that new cottages had at least four acres of land attached, but this statute was enforced only sporadically. Some manorial lords allowed new settlements and obtained rents by the roundabout method of annual *fines for *encroachment. Squatting was tolerated where labour was needed on farms or in industries such as the mining of *lead, *coal, or ironstone, e.g. on the Clee Hills (Shropshire), or the lead-fields of Derbyshire. Many other squatters remained through the negligence of the authorities. Growing concern was expressed as resources dwindled during the population growth of the 18th century. The *enclosure of most of the remaining commons and wastes in the late 18th and early 19th centuries removed the opportunities for squatting and channelled the rural poor towards the towns.

squire. The dominant landowner in a *parish.

stables. Commodious stables first became an architectural feature of country houses during the 17th century. An early example is that built at Bolsover Castle in the mid-17th century for William Cavendish, Earl (later Duke) of Newcastle, a keen exponent of *haute-école*. An outstanding 18th-century example is that built at Chatsworth in 1762–3 to the designs of James Paine. Such stables indicate the value that was placed on *horses, as draught animals, for riding, for pulling carriages, and for hunting and racing. See also FARM, MODEL.

stained glass. Only small pieces of Anglo-Saxon stained glass survive, e.g. at St Paul's

Church, Jarrow (County Durham). During the late 12th and 13th centuries English churches adopted the designs and techniques used in French *grisaille and richly coloured glass. (See ROSE WINDOW.) For the rich variety of surviving medieval stained glass, see M. Archer, *English Stained Glass* (1985), and P. Cowan, *A Guide to Stained Glass in Britain* (1985). The *Reformation destroyed the living of many artists, but some, notably Henry Giles of York, found new patrons amongst the *aristocracy and *gentry for heraldic glass. Much medieval glass in churches was lost through deliberate destruction by *Puritan zealots and much more by neglect. William Peckitt and others kept the tradition of stained glass alive during the 18th century. The Victorian period saw a major revival under William Morris, Edward Burne-Jones, and C. E. Kempe. The later 20th century has seen another revival, notably with John Piper's great windows at Coventry and Liverpool (Catholic) cathedrals, and Marc Chagall's glass occupying all the windows of the parish *church at Tudeley (Kent).

staircases. Stone staircases are found in medieval *castles, *palaces, and *monasteries, both internally and externally. By the 15th century oak staircases, sometimes curving round a newel-post, had become common. The great houses of the early 17th century had elaborately carved wooden staircases ascending around a central 'well'. In the 18th and early 19th centuries lighter constructions were preferred, sometimes with stone steps, wrought-iron balusters, and mahogany handrails. Meanwhile, some *cottagers were still making do with ladders which could be raised and lowered at convenience.

staith. A wharf. The word is of Viking origin.

standard (tree). Many *coppice woods included a number of standard trees that were allowed to grow to a full height for timber. Legislation that tried to enforce a minimum number of standards per acre was difficult to enforce.

standard abbreviations (genealogy).

b.	born
bapt.	baptized
d.	died
d.unm.	died unmarried
d.s.p.	died without children
dau.	daughter
div.	divorced
l.	left descendants
s.	son
unm.	unmarried
=	married

standard of living debate. (See WAGES.) The debate is about whether the *Industrial Revolution raised or lowered the general standard of living. See A. J. Taylor (ed.), *The Standard of Living in Britain in the Industrial Revolution* (1975).

Standing Conference for Local History. Founded in 1948, under the aegis of the National Council for Social Service, the SCLH was the forerunner of the *British Association for Local History, and former publisher of *The *Amateur Historian*, later *The *Local Historian*.

Stannaries. The *tin-mining district of Cornwall, which was regulated through the Stannaries Court.

Star Chamber, Court of. So-called from the chamber at the royal palace of Westminster with painted stars on its ceiling, where the *Privy Council met in the 14th and 15th centuries. The court was revived by Henry VII in 1487 and at first was popular because it provided quick redress cheaply, but it was associated with the exercise of the royal prerogative under the early Stuarts and was abolished in 1641. Its records are kept at the *Public Record Office under STAC 1 to 9. See *Lists and Indexes* 13 and *Supplementary*, 4, part 1, for the period up to the accession of Elizabeth I in 1558, after which the records become much fuller. The court dealt with a number of local disputes and received lengthy depositions. Few cases have been printed by county record societies, but see W. Brown (ed.), 'Yorkshire Star Chamber Proceedings', *Yorkshire Archaeological Society Record Series*, 41 (1909).

State Papers Domestic. All the state papers from the accession of Edward VI (1547) to the second year of Queen Anne (1704) have been published in official *calendars. They are a rich mine of information on everything under the sun, and have reasonably, but not consistently, good indexes. The *List and Index Society has published a Calendar of State Papers (Domestic) for the reign of George I (1714–27). The term 'Home Office' was used for domestic, as distinct from foreign, affairs later in the century. See the *Calendar of Home Office Papers of the Reign of George II, 1760 to 1775*.

statute labour. An Act of 1555 ordered the annual election of overseers of the *highways for each *township or civil *parish, and obliged every householder to work under the supervision of the overseer for four days a year (or to pay for someone else to perform the work) on repairing and maintaining the local highways. An Act of 1563 increased this liability to six days a year. The better-off inhabitants were also obliged to provide carts and draught animals. In his *Description of England* (1577) William *Harrison wrote that this obligation was 'much evaded'. Nevertheless, 'statute labour' or 'the common days work' system formed the basis of road maintenance for the next three centuries. The system was not replaced by *turnpike roads (for statute labour was used to supplement the work-force there, and minor roads were not turnpiked).

steam engines. Few of the early steam engines of the late 17th and early 18th century remain, but some designed by Savery, Newcomen, and Trevithick are on display at the Science Museum, London. These were used for pumping water out of mines, and later for draining the *fens. They are marked on 18th-century county *maps as 'Fire Engine'. See L. T. C. Rolt and J. Allen, *The Steam Engine of Thomas Newcomen* (1977). A Newcomen-type beam engine erected at Elsecar (Yorkshire) in 1795 to drain Earl Fitzwilliam's *coal mines is the only one of its kind still *in situ*. Others are marked by ruined engine houses. Newcomen engines continued to be installed on the coalfield long after James Watt patented his separate condenser in 1769 because the high royalties charged by the firm of Boulton & Watt were more costly than the savings that could be made. Watt's single-action engine of 1769, his rotative engine of 1783, and other improvements made steam the principal source of power in many industries in the late 18th and 19th centuries, particularly in the blast *furnaces and the textile mills, though *water power remained the principal source for many others until well into the Victorian period. By 1795 the Boulton & Watt partnership had erected nearly 300 steam engines for use by a wide range of industries in many different parts of Britain and abroad. The installation, repair, and part renewal of steam engines is often noted in *business and *estate records. See Jennifer Tann, *Papers of Boulton and Watt*, vol. i: *The Steam Engine Partnership, 1775–1825* (1981). See also RAILWAYS.

steel. In the early modern period steel was imported from abroad, firstly from Bilbao, then via Cologne, or Danzig. The first steel to be made in England was in the Forest of Dean in the early 17th century. The technology had spread as far north as south Yorkshire before the *Civil War, but production was on a modest scale before the second half of the 18th century. The English cementation steel industry was largely dependent on imported Swedish ores. A purer form of steel was invented by Benjamin Huntsman in Sheffield *c*.1742. Huntsman reheated cementation steel in clay crucibles to a high temperature. By 1850, when the borough had about 1,250 crucible holes and 150 cementation furnaces, Sheffield had become the steel capital of the world. See K. C. Barraclough, *Steelmaking Before Bessemer*: vol. i: *Blister Steel: The Birth of An Industry*, and vol. ii: *Crucible Steel: The Growth of Technology* (1984). Very little physical evidence of this old industry survives, except in the crucible melting shop at the Abbeydale Industrial Hamlet. Sheffield now has only one intact cementation furnace.

A new stage of the steel industry began in 1856 when Henry Bessemer invented a convertor that could produce 800 times the output of a single crucible in a 30-minute period. The era of cheap steel started when he opened his own works in Sheffield two years later. Although Bessemer's steel was not of high quality, it proved better than iron for making *railway lines. During the second half of the 19th century Brown, Firth, Cammell, Hadfield, Vickers, and others built huge steel works at the east end of Sheffield, which produced castings for the engineering and shipbuilding industries, and then concentrated on armaments. By the end of the 19th century single items weighing up to 100 tons were being manufactured. Further advances were made by the Siemens open-hearth furnace, the James Nasmyth steam hammer, and the techniques of Robert Mushet and Robert Hadfield for making special steels. In 1912–13 Harry Brearley invented stainless steel, which eventually had particular application in the *cutlery industry. The steel works of the later 19th century employed large labour forces; by 1872 John Brown had 5,000 workers and Charles Cammell had 4,000. Many of these employees were immigrants who came to live in terraced houses close to the works.

Sheffield's dominance was not to last. Before the First World War British steel production had fallen behind that of the USA and Germany. It continued to decline in relative importance during the 1920s and 1930s and was badly hit by foreign competition during the 1980s. Automation meant that a large labour force was no longer required. Although Sheffield still makes as much steel as it did during the Second World War, the work-force has been reduced to a fraction of what it was in the 19th century.

Stenton, Sir F. M. Sir Frank Stenton is best remembered as the author of a classic work, *Anglo-Saxon England* (1943, 3rd edn. 1971). He was the leading Anglo-Saxon scholar of his day (see also PLACE-NAMES.) Stenton was Professor of Modern History in the University of Reading, where he had started his career as research fellow in Local History (1908–12).

steward. In the later 17th and early 18th centuries *landowners began to employ land stewards to supervise their estates during long periods of absence. These stewards became a highly professional group during the 18th and 19th centuries and were instrumental in the spread of agricultural improvement and efficiency, and in raising the profitability of an estate. See John Beckett, 'Estate Management in Eighteenth-Century England: The Lowther–Spedding Relationship in Cumberland' in John Chartres and David Hey (eds.), *English Rural Society, 1500–1800: Essays in Honour of Joan Thirsk* (1990), and G. E. Mingay, 'The Eighteenth-Century Land Steward' in E. L. Jones and G. E. Mingay (eds.), *Land, Labour, and Population in the Industrial Revolution* (1967).

stint. A share. The term was applied by manorial *courts to the amount of livestock that a tenant was allowed to graze on the *commons.

stocks. The stocks were an ancient punishment for petty offenders, who were subject to ridicule by having their feet locked in a wooden structure which was placed in some public space, such as a village green or market square. The use of the stocks died out during the middle years of the 19th century.

Stone Age. Popular term for the *Palaeolithic, *Mesolithic, and *Neolithic, the earliest periods of *prehistory.

Stout, William (1665–1757). Insights into the life and occupation of a 17th-century Quaker shopkeeper are provided in readable detail in J. D. Marshall, *The Autobiography of William Stout of Lancaster, 1665–1757* (1967).

Stow, John (1525–1605). Author of the famous *Survey of London and Westminster* (1598). An edition by C. L. Kingsford was published in two volumes in 1908, and an Everyman edition in 1955. Stow was a member of the Society of *Antiquaries and was inspired to write by the example of *Lambarde. His survey is still much quoted. He also published *Summary of English Chronicles* (1565), and *Annals, or a General Chronicle of England* (1580), and assisted in the preparation of *Holinshed's *Chronicles*.

strapwork. A fashionable ornamentation of the Elizabethan and Jacobean age, imported from the Netherlands for use on the roofs and garden walls of great houses, on chimney pieces and tombs, and in other decorative arts. The name came from the resemblance of the ornamentation to curved leather straps.

straw plaiting. The plaiting of straw hats, bonnets, and mats was a cottage industry for women and girls, especially in the south midlands. Luton and Dunstable were the main centres. The numbers employed declined rapidly in the last quarter of the 19th century with the introduction of cheaper goods from the Far East and a change of fashion. See Pamela Horn, 'Women's Cottage Industries' in G. E. Mingay (ed.), *The Victorian Countryside*, vol. i (1981), and Pamela Sharpe, 'The Women's Harvest: Straw-Plaiting and the Representation of Labouring Women's Employment, c.1793–1885', *Rural History*, 5/2 (1994).

strays. A term used by family historians for events that are recorded in unexpected places, e.g. a burial register might name the usual place of residence of a man who has died far from home. *Family history societies co-ordinate the recording of strays for mutual help.

street names. Many street names are medieval in origin, but others did not become fixed until Victorian times. Alternative forms can be found on successive maps. Once signs were erected, the names of streets became settled. The Victorians took this opportunity to rename streets which had offensive or lowly connotations. Locating streets named in early *directories, *census returns, etc. can be difficult because of these changes. Some names which sound ancient may be consciously archaic forms that were deliberately introduced in much later times. Old street names which can be identified on early maps are useful in identifying market activities or the location of certain trades. Some incorporate old *field-names and others help to date developments where streets are named after *landowners, contemporary national figures, and political events. Many remain inexplicable. For a local study, see R. N. G. Rowland, *The Street-Names of Acton, Middlesex* (1967).

street numbering. The early *census enumerators' returns and trade *directories show that in the mid-19th century the houses in most towns and nearly all villages were still not numbered. The fashion spread during the later 19th century, but it is common to find inconsistencies between one census return and the next, as houses were renumbered.

strips. The term used by agricultural historians to describe the long, narrow divisions of *open-fields that farmers usually called *lands. These had a sinuous, reverse-S shape to allow the plough-team to turn as they approached the *headland. Strips were individually owned, but initially the open-fields were farmed in common, allowing communal grazing over all the land after harvest. (See RIDGE-AND-FURROW.) The strip system of farming was abandoned at different periods, depending upon the timing of *enclosure.

stucco. The application of plaster to the exterior of a building to simulate stone. Stucco became fashionable during the *Regency period and was particularly associated with bowed frontages. Brighton has the best examples.

subinfeudation. The granting of a *fee by a *tenant-in-chief or *mesne lord to a *sub-tenant. (See QUIA EMPTORES, STATUTE OF.) It resulted in a considerable multiplication of manorial estates in the later Middle Ages (see SUB-MANOR).

sub-manor. The lords of large medieval *lordships sometimes granted favoured retainers the right to hold manorial *courts for small districts within their jurisdiction. In time, these sub-manors usually became completely independent, with their own manor houses, *deer parks, etc.

sub-tenant. *Surveys and *rentals usually record the name of the tenant but, as the matter was of no financial importance to the *landowner, they do not usually name any sub-tenants. A misleading picture of a local community may be drawn from such evidence, if much of the land was tenanted by absentees who sub-tenanted their properties to the men who actually farmed them. Usually, the historian is left in the dark about the extent of sub-tenanting. See C. J. Harrison, 'Elizabethan Village Surveys: A Comment', *Agricultural History Review*, 27/1 (1979).

suburbs. The major medieval and Tudor cities were largely confined within their walls. Early *maps, such as those of John *Speed, showed little extramural developments (see, however, LONDON). The early suburbs housed the poor immigrants. As towns became more crowded, so the middle classes moved out of the centres into spacious streets and squares at the edges. See C. W. Chalklin, *The Provincial Towns of Georgian England* (1974). This evacuation of town centres became a mass movement during the 19th century. See the studies of two contrasting London suburbs: H. J. Dyos, *Victorian Suburb: A Study of the Growth of Camberwell* (1961), and F. M. L. Thompson, *Hampstead: Building a Borough, 1650–1964* (1974). See also

David Pam, *A History of Enfield*, vol. i: *Before 1837* (1990), vol. ii: *1837–1914: A Victorian Suburb* (1992), and vol. iii: *1914–1938: A Desirable Neighbourhood* (1994). Relatively few studies have been made of the growth of middle-class suburbs on the edge of provincial towns. Such studies need to combine the architectural evidence in the form of housing and public buildings, the physical layout of planned and piecemeal developments, and the documentary evidence in the form of maps, *deeds, the archives of local firms of architects, *newspaper accounts, *rate books, *census returns, etc. (See *Builder, The*.) David Cannadine, *Lords and Landlords: The Aristocracy and the Towns, 1774–1967* (1980), and F. M. L. Thompson, *The Rise of Suburbia* (1982) provide general background and some local studies. (See also URBAN HOUSING, and FREEHOLD LAND SOCIETIES, for working-class housing in both the town centres and the suburbs.) In the 20th century various forms of public transport and the motor car have led to ribbon development on the edge of most towns and the spread of suburbs into the surrounding countryside, in both a planned and an unplanned fashion, until the creation of green belts. See GARDEN CITY MOVEMENT.

sugar. Sugar cane was imported from the Mediterranean from the 16th century. During the 17th century it became the major product of the new *plantations in the *West Indies. Sugar refineries were built in large ports such as Liverpool. In the 20th century a large supply has come from sugar beet.

suicide was held to be a crime by the *ecclesiastical courts. Those who had committed suicide were buried either in unconsecrated ground on the north side of a *churchyard or at cross-roads with a stake driven through the heart to destroy evil spirits. Suicide rates were low in the early modern period. For later times, see *coroners' inquests, and *newspaper reports.

sulung. A measure of land used in south-eastern England, about twice the size of a *hide.

summoner. An *apparitor who summoned people to appear before an *ecclesiastical court.

sumptuary laws. Medieval and early modern laws which attempted to restrict private expenditure on dress and to confine the use of certain materials to the *nobility. In England a series of Acts were passed from 1463 onwards. Until 1600 'excessive apparel' was controlled by seven Acts and ten proclamations. In 1566 four 'sad and discreet' persons were stationed at the gates of the City of London to watch for people who might be wearing prohibited styles of hose. See Joan Thirsk, 'The Fantastical Folly of Fashion: The English Stocking Knitting Industry, 1500–1700' (reprinted in *The Rural Economy of England: Collected Essays* (1984)), N. B. Harte, 'State Control of Dress and Social Change in Pre-Industrial England' in D. C. Coleman and A. H. John (eds.), *Trade, Government and Economy in Pre-Industrial England: Essays Presented to F. J. Fisher* (1976), and Frances Elizabeth Baldwin, *Sumptuary Legislation and Personal Regulation in England* (1926). Similar Acts were passed in Scotland up to 1621.

sundials. Parish *churches used sundials to enable clergymen to judge the times of services and for public use long before clocks were installed in *church towers. A few Saxon sundials survive, e.g. at St Gregory, Kildale (Yorkshire). In the Middle Ages 'scratch dials' were inscribed on a buttress or wall close to the porch of a parish church. Later sundials were mounted on stone posts in the *churchyard. From the 17th to the 19th centuries churchyard and private sundials became increasingly ornate. Many are inscribed with reminders of mortality.

superstition. See MAGIC, BELIEF IN, and ASTROLOGY.

surety. One who stood as security for the repayment of a *bond or for the proper performance of duties.

surnames. The fashion for families to have fixed, hereditary surnames began at the top level of society and spread slowly down the social scale. The reasons for this fashion remain mysterious, though the practice was adopted widely throughout western Europe in the Middle Ages. It may have started earlier in Ireland than it did in England, where before the *Norman Conquest people were known by their personal name and perhaps by a by-name which was not hereditary. The Norman barons took the name of their estate (either in England or in Normandy) as a surname. This link with property gave rise to the earliest form of hereditary surnames, a fashion that was gradually followed by others.

It is sometimes said that the narrow range of personal names favoured by the Normans was the major factor in the need for surnames which distinguished one person from another, but although this explains the reason for the use of by-names it does not explain why they became hereditary. The great increase in the use of written records during the 12th–14th centuries has perhaps something to do with the formation of hereditary surnames, so that continuity in the ownership of property could be established and disputes minimized. It is possible that the large numbers of locative surnames which are derived from farmsteads can be explained in this way. However, medieval scribes were content to record a man as 'John, the son of Robert' (usually in the Latin form, 'Johannes, filius Robertus'), rather than by a surname, so this is not the entire explanation. It also leaves us with the problem of why some hereditary surnames were formed from *nicknames (some of which were obscene and unlikely to have been coined by a scribe) or from occupations (many of which were not followed by the descendants of the man who first acquired a surname).

Many by-names in use during the 13th and 14th centuries never developed into hereditary surnames. Records from this period show that people were sometimes known by two or three by-names during their lifetime. The process by which surnames became fixed was prolonged and complicated. The fashion spread in southern England and East Anglia during the second half of the 13th century and the first half of the 14th century, but took another century to become widespread in northern England and Lowland Scotland. By the 15th century most English people had acquired fixed, hereditary surnames, but *Welsh names did not take an English form until the 16th century. (See also IRISH NAMES.) A concise introduction is available in R. A. McKinley, *A History of British Surnames* (1990).

Many of the surnames which were formed in the Middle Ages and which were recorded in the *lay subsidies and *poll tax returns of the 14th century have disappeared through the failure of the male line, especially those which had a *single-family origin. The stock of surnames has been partly replenished by immigrants, and the variety of surnames has been increased by the corruption of the original names into different forms, some of which now bear little resemblance to each other. Thus, Shimwell is derived from Shemeld, Answer from Edensor, and Capstick from Copestake. The use of phonetic spellings has added to the variety of forms that are now in use. Those people who insist that theirs is the correct spelling of a surname and that they have no connection with others who spell their name differently are mistaken.

British scholars lead the field in the study of

the etymology of surnames. The outstanding works are P. H. *Reaney, *The Origins of English Surnames* (1967), P. H. Reaney and R. M. Wilson, *A Dictionary of English Surnames* (3rd edn., 1991), P. Hanks and F. Hodges, *The Oxford Dictionary of Surnames* (1989), E. MacLysaght, *The Surnames of Ireland* (1980), R. Bell, *The Book of Ulster Surnames* (1980), G. F. Black, *The Surnames of Scotland, Their Origin, Meaning and History* (1946), and T. J. and P. Morgan, *Welsh Surnames* (1985). For France, see Marie-Thérèse Morlet, *Dictionnaire Etymologique des Noms de Famille* (1991). Surnames can be divided into broad classes in terms of origin: as well as nicknames, see SURNAMES OF RELATIONSHIP; SURNAMES, LOCATIVE AND TOPOGRAPHICAL; and SURNAMES, OCCUPATIONAL.

The explanations offered by linguists with necessary expertise in old languages are merely the starting-points for local and family historians who are interested in the origins, spread, and sometimes disappearance of surnames. The explanations offered by etymologists do not always fit the evidence provided by the past and present distributions of surnames, nor do the medieval references from different parts of the country quoted by Reaney take account of the disappearance of many male lines, leaving a much narrower distribution of the name at the present time. People bearing a rare name today may have a common ancestor, despite the evidence from the Middle Ages that the name was once more widespread, for other lines might have died out. Local and family historians have a great deal to contribute to the study of surnames. The English Surnames Survey at the Department of English Local History, *Leicester University, formerly directed by Richard McKinley, has published a number of county studies which are concerned not only with etymologies but with past and present distributions of surnames and with the ways in which some names have ramified over time. See George Redmonds, *Yorkshire, The West Riding: English Surnames Series* (1973), and R. A. McKinley's *Norfolk and Suffolk Surnames in the Middle Ages* (1975), *The Surnames of Oxfordshire* (1977), *The Surnames of Sussex* (1988), and *The Surnames of Lancashire* (1981).

One of the findings of the English Surnames Survey is that the decline in the number of different surnames in the late Middle Ages was followed during the period of population growth in the 16th and early 17th centuries by the spread of family names within a restricted neighbourhood, so that a surname that was once borne by a single family ramified to include several households by the time of the *hearth tax returns of the 1660s–1670s. These names did not migrate far, on the whole (though one always has to allow for individuals who moved away from their home district), so that in the early modern period certain surnames became characteristic of a restricted area. (See COUNTRY.) Despite the mobility of the 19th and 20th centuries, every part of Britain still retains its characteristic names. Surnames are therefore a useful tool in the study of population movement and the stability of groups of core *families. See also IMMIGRATION.

surnames, locative and topographical. In some parts of England surnames derived from places are very common; in Lancashire and the West Riding of Yorkshire the proportion rises to about half. See R. A. McKinley, *The Surnames of Lancashire* (1981), and George Redmonds, *Yorkshire, The West Riding: English Surnames Series* (1973). In Scotland and Ireland the proportion is very low, and in Wales it is insignificant, but in the other Celtic region—Cornwall—locative or topographical names beginning with Bos, Car, Lan, Pol, Pen, Ros, and Tre are prolific. See G. Pawley White, *A Handbook of Cornish Surnames* (1981).

Locative names are those derived from particular places. Some of these names arose when a man left his home town or village to live elsewhere at the period when surnames were becoming fixed and hereditary. Others were derived from the names of farmsteads where people were actually living at the time when surnames were being formed. In areas of scattered settlement such names are very common, but in regions characterized by nucleated villages they are rare. Locative surnames of this sort are still normally concentrated close to their point of origin, whereas those formed when a person travelled from a place at the period of surname formation may now be clustered a long way from the traveller's starting-point (but close to his destination). Locative names were amongst the first to be formed, for the Norman barons took their surnames from their estates in either Britain or Normandy.

Topographical names cannot usually be identified with the same precision, though they arose in the same way. They include such names as Brook, Green, Hill, Townend, and Wood, which clearly have multiple origins. However, Armitage is derived from a single hermitage near Huddersfield, and the Brooks, Greens, etc. of any one district may be descended from a single family which derived its name from a feature in that locality in the

Middle Ages. Names that are prefixed by a preposition, such as Atwood, Bywater, or Underhill, are topographical names, and so are many names that end in -er, such as Downer. Sussex is particularly rich in topographical names. See R. A. McKinley, *The Surnames of Sussex* (1988).

surnames, occupational. Occupations were used as by-names long before hereditary surnames were fixed. The most common occupational surnames—Smith, Wright, Tailor, Turner, etc.—became hereditary early in the process of surname formation. Most villages are likely to have had one craftsman pursuing each of such trades, but are unlikely to have had more, so the occupational surname was readily distinguishable. Some occupational surnames are derived from obscure trades which are no longer practised. Such names have as marked a geographical distribution pattern as the locative names; for example, Palliser (a maker of park pales) is a name that is largely confined to north Yorkshire and other parts of north-eastern England. The use of dialect words for the same trade also produces distinct regional patterns of surnames. For instance, the surname Fuller has the same derivation as the south-western Tucker and the northern Walker, and as the name Bowker, which was the usual form in south-eastern Lancashire.

This group of surnames includes those which were derived from offices, such as Chamberlain or Marshall. However, those which apparently denote a rank, such as Earl or Knight, are more likely to be *nicknames.

'Surnames', The. The *kinship groups of Northumberland and Cumberland which offered some measure of protection to their members and which had some affinity to Scottish *clans. They became an anachronism after the union of the English and Scottish crowns under James I and VI.

surnames of relationship. Some surnames are derived directly from the name of the father, e.g. John or Richard, but a much more common practice was to add -s or -son. The -s suffix was preferred in southern and midland England, and as it was popular in the border counties was the type that was widely imitated by Welsh surnames when they were formed in the English style in the 16th century. In northern England and Lowland Scotland the -son ending was preferred. As the practice of adopting hereditary surnames became common first in southern England, -son names were formed about a century later than those ending in -s. (See IRISH NAMES for those beginning with Ó

and Mac, and WELSH NAMES for the ab/ap form.)

*Old English and Scandinavian personal names declined rapidly in use after the *Norman Conquest, but some, e.g. Oddy and Gummer, nevertheless became surnames. The range of personal names favoured by the Normans was very restricted, so pet forms became common, often with the addition of -cock, -kin, -et, -ot, -mot, -on, or -in. Thus, families descended from a man whose father was called Richard acquired surnames as different as Richard, Richards, Richardson, Dickson, Hitchcock, Higgins, Ritson, etc. Surnames derived from mothers, e.g. Marriott, are relatively rare. They do not necessarily denote illegitimacy.

surrender. A document that extinguishes an owner's right in a property. Conditional surrender refers to the practice of mortgaging *copyhold land, for if the loan was not repaid the mortgagee could enter the property only if the *lord of the manor agreed to accept him as his tenant.

surrogate. A deputy presiding over a court.

Surtees Society. Founded in 1834, the society has published a wide range of records relating to County Durham and Yorkshire, in annual volumes.

survey. During the late 16th and 17th centuries *landowners often employed a land surveyor to make a survey of their estate, showing the extent of each property, the form of tenure by which it was held, and often the use to which it was put, i.e. arable, *meadow, pasture, or wood. The most detailed surveys also described each building, by its size (expressed as so many bays), purpose, and sometimes by its building materials. The entry *fines and rents and customary payments were always noted, sometimes with the 'improved rents'. Surveys were often made upon a change of ownership, with the intention of discovering the value of the estate in detail and of assessing ways in which the yield to the owner could be increased. The written survey was usually accompanied by a map, which is often the first large-scale map of the area. See, for example, D. V. Fowkes and G. R. Potter (eds.), *William Senior's Survey of the Estates of the First and Second Earls of Devonshire, c.1660–28* (Derbyshire Record Society, 1988). For instructions on measuring and the use of instruments, see Aaron Rathborne, *The Surveyor* (1616).

swaler. The alternative name in the north midlands for a *badger, i.e. a dealer in meal, corn, butter, and eggs.

sweating sickness. The name given by contemporaries to the epidemic of the late 1550s, which was probably a virulent form of *influenza.

Swing, Captain. The name given to the widespread rural incendiarism and destruction of *threshing machines of 1830–1, which started in Kent and spread over southern and eastern England. *Agricultural labourers demanded improved *wages, reductions in *tithe payments, and the removal of machinery which caused under-employment. Threatening letters were signed 'Captain Swing'. In some places, overseers of the *poor and *workhouses were attacked, but the characteristic acts of destruction were the breaking of threshing machines and the burning of barns and ricks. See E. J. Hobsbawm and George Rudé, *Captain Swing* (1969), which calculated that, in all, 1,976 prisoners were tried by 90 courts sitting in 34 counties. Of those found guilty, 19 were executed and 481 *transported to Australia. Alan Armstrong, *Farmworkers: A Social and Economic History, 1770–1980* (1988) stresses the economic causes of the troubles, for the labourers of southern England were poorer than their northern counterparts, having fewer chances of alternative work. Sixty per cent of all disturbances were concentrated in five counties (Berkshire 165, Hampshire 208, Kent 154, Sussex 145, Wiltshire 208). East Anglia had fewer incidents (Cambridge 17, Norfolk 88, Suffolk 40), while the south-west and the midlands were only marginally affected. Hobsbawm and Rudé note that riots occurred most frequently in open *villages, with large populations and numerous *artisans as well as labourers. Andrew Charlesworth, *Social Protest in a Rural Society: The Spatial Diffusion of the Captain Swing Disturbances of 1830–31* (1979) emphasizes the importance of the main routes of communication, especially the highways leading to London, in the spread of rioting. For a consideration of the Swing riots in a broader setting, see Andrew Charlesworth, 'The Spatial Diffusion of Riots: Popular Disturbances in England and Wales, 1750–1850', *Rural History: Economy, Society, Culture,* 5/1 (1994).

Swithland slate. The Swithland slate quarries of Charnwood Forest, Leicestershire, were worked from the Middle Ages until the late 19th century, when Welsh blue slates replaced the local products as roofing material. The *vernacular buildings of Leicestershire and adjoining counties retain many old roofs. The other major use was for *gravestones. The slate slabs were incised with flowing lettering and, sometimes, with representations of death; they are signed at the base with the name of the manufacturer. Some east midland *churchyards, e.g. at Breedon-on-the-Hill, are full of such stones. Further away, e.g. Bakewell (Derbyshire), only a few Swithland slate gravestones can be found scattered amongst the rest.

syke, sick. The steep slopes of land by streams were difficult to plough and were therefore not incorporated in *open-fields, but were used for hay which was auctioned to local farmers.

Synod of Whitby. The church synod of 664 which determined the outcome of the clash between English and Irish churchmen over the dating of Easter, a symbolic battle about whether the Roman or the Celtic form of Christianity would be the dominant one in Britain. The Roman form was triumphant.

syphilis. This contagious venereal disease was a particular concern in the 16th century, especially in Elizabethan London. Physicians attempted to treat it in St Bartholomew's, St Thomas's, and Christ's Hospitals and their 'outhouses' on the peripheries of the City at Southwark, Mile End, Hackney, Highgate, Knightsbridge, and Hammersmith. Other sufferers tried the mercurial ointments of the barber-surgeons. See Margaret Pelling, 'Appearance and Reality: Barber-Surgeons, the Body and Disease' in A. Beier and Roger Finlay (eds.), *London, 1500–1700: The Making of the Metropolis* (1986). The disease was generally known as the pox or the French pox. Many of the diagnostic symptoms were seen on the head and face, leading to loss of hair and voice, and unpleasant odours. For a personal account of treatment in the 18th century, see Frederick A. Pottle (ed.), *Boswell's London Journal, 1762–63* (1985).

T

tallage. A medieval tax, levied by a feudal lord upon his *villeins at *Michaelmas, by the king upon towns and his *demesne manors, or by a *borough upon its *burgesses. It was replaced by other taxes by the 14th century.

tally. A stick notched as a record of accounts and then split down the middle so that the two halves 'tallied'.

tanning. As the tanning of leather was a smelly process, tanneries were sited in the countryside or at the edges of towns. As a modest amount of capital had to be invested, tanning businesses tended to remain on the same sites, often in the ownership of the same families over the generations. Hides were soaked in a lime solution, then laid over a curved beam so that hair could be removed with a blunt scraper. After a further soaking and the subsequent removal of flesh and fat on the inner side of the hide by sharp knives, the hides were rinsed and cut into sections, then scoured in a pit containing water and dung and tanned in a series of pits filled with water and oak bark. The concentration of bark was increased in succeeding pits. After several months' soaking the hides were hung to dry, then dressed, and finished. See also LEATHER.

Tate, W. E. Former schoolteacher and lecturer in the history of education at the University of Leeds, he wrote two basic accounts of records for local historians: *The Parish Chest* (1946, and later editions), and *Domesday of Enclosure Acts and Awards* (ed. M. E. Turner, 1978).

Tawney, R. H. (1880–1962). Economic historian and socialist. Author of *The Agrarian Problem in the Sixteenth Century* (1912), *The Acquisitive Society* (1926), *Religion and the Rise of Capitalism* (1926), *Equality* (1931), *Business and Politics under James I: Lionel Cranfield as Merchant and Minister* (1958), and with Eileen Power (eds.), *Tudor Economic Documents*, 3 vols. (1924). He was Professor of Economic History at the London School of Economics, 1931–49, and had a lifelong involvement with the Workers' Educational Association.

Taxatio Ecclesiastica (1291). A tax valued at one-tenth, published by the Record Commission as *Taxatio Ecclesiastica Angliae et Walliae, auctoritate Papae Nicholai IV, c.1291* (1802). The values can be compared with those of the *Inquisition of the Ninths (1341).

taxation. Taxation is the means by which a state transfers from its subjects or citizens a part of their wealth for the support of the state and its purposes. It may be suggested (as one of the few iron rules of history) that taxpayers dislike and attempt to evade the payment of taxes, hence taxation is a constant tension between the state and its subjects. Because of this, the efficiency of individual taxation systems tend to decay over time as taxpayers learn to conceal their wealth, and the state is persistently forced either to reinvent forms of taxation or design new ones to tap new sources of wealth. Four broad types of taxable wealth or economic behaviour can be distinguished: wealth in the sense of capital assets including personalty; the rental value of land; income; and the consumption of goods or services. Of these, taxes on the value of land are the easiest to administer, land being hard to conceal, whilst taxes on income or consumption require complex administrative organizations.

Much ingenuity has gone into the devising of taxation systems, but most may be classified according to a series of simple dichotomies. Taxes may be either direct (levied on individuals) or indirect (*customs or excise levied on consumption). They may be progressive or regressive according to their comprehensiveness and the relative burden they place on the rich and the poor. Taxes may be levied either on behalf of the national state or by *local government. (The church's independent systems of taxation, notably *tithes, are excluded from consideration here.) A further distinction, relevant to taxes granted before 1640, is between those taxes which were levied by the monarch's authority or prerogative and those granted by parliamentary statute.

It must be stressed that before the *Civil War no regular taxation existed except for custom duties (tonnage and poundage), which were granted by parliament to each monarch for his life. Direct taxation was demanded only intermittently for the support of war; at some periods people were taxed heavily, at others barely at all. After 1660 taxation became a regular part of life, but periods of war again served both to increase the weight of taxation and (most crucially) to extend the range of taxes.

The capacity of the state to employ direct and indirect taxes in different proportions bears greatly on the records available to the historian. Edward I and his grandson funded their wars through a mixture of direct taxes (*lay subsidies charged on individuals) and indirect (customs duties, especially on wool). (The lay subsidies were so called to distinguish them from taxes on the clergy, clerical subsidies.) The method employed in the early subsidies was to assess each individual and then tax a proportion of their assessed value, so a ninth in 1297 and a fifteenth in 1301. Split tax-rates could be employed to differentiate between town and country. From 1334 the system was simplified (from the point of view of government) by charging each *vill with raising the sum returned in tax two years previously. The 1334 quotas, which came to be called the Tenth and Fifteenth after the tax rates, continued to be granted by parliament until 1623. But from 1334 the Exchequer ceased to receive lists of the individual taxpayers; the records of the fifteenth largely consist of repetitious details of the sums due from each tax unit. By the 1370s complaints were being made that the tax was regressive and a particular burden on the poor. In the 16th and early 17th century the fifteenth was charged as either a rate, or as a tax on cattle, or (in some towns) a graduated *poll tax according to local practice. The Poll Taxes of 1377–81 were, in their origins, an attempt to achieve a more equitable social and geographical spread of tax, but the widespread evasion of, and hostile reaction to, the Poll Tax of 1381 discouraged the use of direct taxation for more than a century. The anchor of English public finance in the 15th century was, by default, the customs.

By comparison, England in the 16th century saw a revival of direct taxation. The chief instrument of this was a refurbished parliamentary lay subsidy, devised incrementally during 1512–16. The chief features of the Tudor lay subsidy were threefold: that only taxpayers with more than a minimum amount of either land or goods were liable; that they paid on all their property, wherever it lay, at their normal place of residence; and that they paid on either lands or goods according to which brought the best profit to the Crown. For historians the most important development was the instruction, first contained in the 1523 statute, that the commissioners should return nominal listings of all those taxed to the Exchequer.

In addition, Henry VIII also made considerable use of prerogative taxation. In 1522 the government organized a joint muster / fiscal assessment, the surviving returns of which are generally now called the 'Military Surveys'. This was an ambitious (and unparalleled) attempt to compute the total wealth of the nation, to discover the manpower available for war, and to establish under whose control it fell. Sadly, relatively few returns survive and those which do vary considerably in the detail they contain. The military surveys were then employed to determine who could contribute to the forced loans demanded in 1522–4. Other forced loans were demanded in 1542 and 1544: all were retrospectively converted into grants. In 1545 Henry demanded a Benevolence, in effect a non-statutory subsidy, and in 1545 a 'free and loving contribution'. Whilst his daughters requested forced loans (in 1557, 1563, 1569–70, 1585–9, 1590–1, and 1597) the majority were repaid and neither Mary nor Elizabeth attempted to take other forms of prerogative taxation. Subsidies continued to be granted from time to time until the eve of the Civil War; the last forced loan was requested in 1626.

The 1640s appear to have been the pivotal decade in English taxation history, with the development of the parliamentary 'weekly assessment' and the excise. The *Restoration saw the enactment of the *hearth tax in 1662, at a rate of 1s. per hearth every six months. This was abolished in 1689 and replaced by the *land tax in 1692. Occasional recourse was made to poll taxes in the later 17th century (1641, 1660, 1667, 1678, 1689, 1690, 1692–4, and 1698) and duties on marriages and unmarried males between 1695 and 1706. Where their returns survive, they can be enormously helpful to historians, but financially they brought small rewards. The years after 1660 also saw a considerable expansion in the revenue drawn from the customs and excise, and whilst the land tax was the best yielding tax before 1714, it declined in importance thereafter. Generally, 18th-century government fought shy of direct taxation. The demands of war in the 1790s changed this, forcing the introduction of legacy duty in 1796 (the first of a whole range of inheritance taxes) and *income tax, first imposed in 1798, repealed in 1802, revived in 1803, repealed again in 1816, and then, from

1842, a constant feature of life. The *death duty registers have been exploited by historians concerned to establish an individual's wealth at death, but ought to be better known to local historians. Individual income tax returns have not been preserved.

The one 20th-century innovation in taxation which has produced records of interest to the historian was the land taxation introduced by the 1910 Finance Act, for the administration of which surveys and maps of ownership were prepared (see VALUATION OFFICE).

The local historian and genealogist is interested in taxation less for its economic importance than for the evidence it leaves of who was taxed and on what taxable wealth. Indirect taxation is usually unrewarding (although historians of *ports will find customs records a vital guide to their commercial activity). The most useful materials arise from direct taxes, the more regressive the better. For long periods—in the 15th century and in the 18th century—no satisfactory taxes were in operation. When direct taxes did operate, the appropriate records may not have been kept. Hence only a small number of nominal listings are extant for the subsidy before 1332, and virtually none for the early Tudor subsidies; nor for the hearth tax in the periods when it was administered by farmers; nor for the land tax before 1780 (after which returns had to be deposited with the *clerk of the peace for electoral purposes). The historian is forced to rely on a small number of oft-cited taxes: 1377–81, 1524–5, 1664, and the first extant land tax return.

Moreover, the returns which do survive vary considerably in their utility. This is especially true of the Henrician lay subsidies. Where some had low qualifying thresholds for inclusion (£2 in goods or wages in 1524–5, £1 in goods in 1543–5), in others the thresholds were much higher (£50 in 1526–7, £20 in 1535–6 and 1540–1). The utility of the hearth tax is much increased in those years when we have the names of those considered sufficiently poor to be exempt.

Nor does the mere availability of documents imply that useful material can be extracted from them. Tax returns are emphatically not census documents; with a few exceptions, we would not expect them to name the poor, dependent children, or servants resident in households. And, as we have already remarked, taxpayers had every reason to try and evade the payment of taxes and secure their undervaluation. It has been suggested that the pre-1334 lay subsidies which survive amongst the records of the *Exchequer do so because they were

called in upon suspicion of fraud. There have been doubts raised about the reliability of the 1524–5 returns from parts of northern England, and it would be generally accepted that the later lay subsidy returns, certainly after 1558, are so marked by evasion and under-assessment as to be useless for most purposes. Likewise, whilst we have large numbers of land tax assessments, historians have generally found them to be a difficult and unyielding source from which to draw useful results; certainly attempts to draw acreage equivalents have been largely unsuccessful.

In part, this reflects the personnel who administered taxation at the local level and who drew up the returns. Until the development of the excise, taxation was by the self-certification of the *township or *parish concerned. People were invited to declare their own and their neighbours' liability, and most declined to do so in full. The land tax was never a survey made by impartial or professional surveyors; it was therefore possible to throw its burden on to a minority of landowners. It was difficult for government to make independent checks on the reliability of the returns even if it was minded to do so; and it is no more possible for us to verify them now. Attempts to relate tax returns to other documentary sources have generally not been successful. Tax returns do not record the value of lands or goods in the form in which we might find them recorded elsewhere, for instance in *rentals, probate *inventories, or account books; rather they were prepared, often by estimation, using criteria which applied for taxation purposes only. It is probably best to think of the sum assessed for taxation purposes—of whatever sort—as not an absolute statement of wealth, but a relative description, to be viewed in comparison with that of contemporaries.

The majority of the surviving returns for the lay subsidies and the hearth taxes are in the *Public Record Office, E179. This is an artificial class containing a wide range of taxation documents of different periods and types. Access is through a typescript list arranged by counties which is more readily available as volumes 44, 54, 63, 75, and 87 of the *List and Index Society. Whilst very substantial numbers of returns survive, coverage is far from complete, and many are in poor condition. A few returns may be found in county *record offices. The land tax returns from 1780 are normally in the clerk of the peace's papers amongst the *quarter sessions records. Many lay subsidy and hearth tax returns have been published by county record societies and genealogical groups in editions of varying scholarship and reliability.

The most comprehensive history of taxes remains S. Dowell, *History of Taxes and Taxation in England* (2nd edn., 1884, repr. 1965). For the Tudor lay subsidies, see R. W. Hoyle, *Tudor Taxation Records: A Guide for Users* (Public Record Office, 1994), which includes a bibliography of records in print. For the hearth taxes, see K. Schurer and T. Arkell (eds.), *Surveying the People: The Interpretation and Use of Document Sources for the Study of Population in the Later Seventeenth Century* (1992). See also M. J. Braddick, *Parliamentary Taxation in Seventeenth-Century England* (1994), and M. Turner and D. Mills (eds.), *Land and Property; The English Land Tax, 1692–1832* (1986).

R. W. HOYLE

tea. Tea was brought from the Far East from the late 17th century, though at first it did not rival the popularity of coffee drunk in *coffee houses. It was sold by specialist dealers until it became part of the normal stock of grocers. Tea-making equipment was rarely found in London homes before the 1690s. The fashion spread gradually to other towns and then into the countryside. The annual consumption of tea per head of the population rose six- or sevenfold between 1725 and 1760 as the price fell. The British were becoming a nation of tea drinkers.

teasels. Plant with large prickly head, used for the finishing of cloth. Production in the 17th and 18th centuries was localized, notably in the Cheddar area of Somerset, parts of Gloucestershire, and Essex.

telecommunications. Before the Victorian period, the quickest means of communication was by hilltop telegraph stations whose adjustable wooden arms could send messages in semaphore. In 1837 the linking of Euston and Camden railway stations by electric telegraph was the first practical step towards a new age of telecommunications. The telegram became the usual means of business communication until the last quarter of the 19th century, when telephones became widely available. Underseas cables enabled messages to be transmitted in Morse Code to America and the British Empire. Alexander Graham Bell, a Scot who had emigrated to America, introduced his invention of the telephone to Britain, where the first telephone exchange was installed in 1879. Quick communication throughout Europe was established by the end of the century. In 1896 the Post Office acquired the monopoly of telephone and telegraphic communication in Brit-

ain; its first public telephone boxes were installed in 1921. Guglielmo Marconi's invention of the 'wireless telegraph' in 1896 revolutionized telecommunications. Marconi built a factory at Chelmsford to supply equipment for ships. In 1901 he transmitted a signal across the Atlantic from Poldhu (Cornwall). By 1912 he was able to transmit sounds other than the Morse Code. The British Broadcasting Corporation was established in 1927 and 'wirelesses' were soon installed in every home. John Logie Baird had successfully experimented with television pictures in the 1930s, but it was not until the 1950s that TV sets became widely available.

telephone directories are a prime source for establishing the modern distribution patterns of *surnames. By 1990 some 87 per cent of households had telephones, so the sample is a large one. It is no longer true that only the wealthier members of society have a telephone. The *United Kingdom is divided into 103 districts, so the geographical distribution of surnames is readily observable. Ideally, one should use a set of directories from the 1970s before the start of the modern practice of overlapping directories, but complete sets are hard to come by. The whole series from 1879 is available for consultation at The British Telecom Archives and Historical Information Centre, 2–4 Temple Avenue, London EC4Y OHL. Overlapping entries should be carefully eliminated. The increasing practice of using ex-directory numbers will make future directories a less reliable source.

Plotting the current distribution pattern of a surname provides strong clues to past distributions and the original homes of *single-family surnames. The data should be compared with those of the indexes of *civil registration records from 1837 onwards, and with those of the *hearth tax returns of the third quarter of the 17th century. See Colin D. Rogers, *The Surname Detective* (1995).

temperance movement. In the 19th century the social problem of hard drinking was at its worst in Scotland and parts of Ireland. The anti-spirits movement, which was started in Scotland and Ulster in the 1820s, spread to the textile towns of Lancashire and Yorkshire in the 1830s, and broadened into the temperance movement. The reforming zeal of the advocates of temperance was manifest at emotional mass meetings when reprobates signed the pledge that they would renounce alcoholic drink. *Nonconformist chapels often took the lead, e.g. in Wales in the 1850s. Many working-class leaders, especially those with a *Methodist background, were prominent teetotallers. See B. Harrison, *Drink and the Victorians* (1971), and W. R. Lambert, *Drink and Sobriety in Victorian Wales, c.1820–c.1895* (1983). For a local study, see B. Harrison and B. Trinder, 'Drink and Sobriety: An Early Victorian Country Town: Banbury, 1830–60', *English Historical Review*, supplement, 4 (1969). The temperance movement, with its Band of Hope, continued to crusade against alcoholic drink well into the 20th century, but its voice is now muted.

Templar, Knights. Founded in 1119 as the Order of the Poor Knights of Christ and of the Temple of Solomon to protect pilgrims in the Holy Land, the knights became established throughout Europe by the late 13th century. Opinion turned against them after their failure in 1291 to prevent the fall of the last Christian stronghold in the Holy Land. In 1312 their possessions were transferred to the Knights *Hospitaller. The Templars had about 50 preceptories in the British Isles, some of which are commemorated by place-names, e.g. Templecombe (Somerset) and Temple Newsam (Yorkshire). Their headquarters was the Temple Church, Fleet Street, London.

temples (in gardens). A feature of 18th-century landscape gardens, e.g. Stourhead (Wiltshire). At first, classical designs were used, but by the middle of the century *Gothick and Chinese temples also found favour, notably William Chambers's pagoda in Kew Gardens (1761).

temporalities. Ecclesiastical income that came from secular sources, e.g. rents, as distinct from spiritualities.

tenant-in-chief. Under the *feudal system a person who held land directly from the king. This was often written as 'tenant in *capite'. Such a person was usually the owner of many *manors, which he sub-let.

tenements. Originally, any rented property. In his account of Myddle (Shropshire) in 1700–2 Richard *Gough used the term to describe the holdings of *yeomen and *husbandmen, which were smaller than farms but larger than the properties of *cottagers. In the Victorian period the word was used to describe the working-class houses which were subdivided horizontally in the major industrial towns, e.g. Glasgow.

tenters. After a piece of woven cloth had returned from the *fulling mill, it was hung on frames known as tenters to be stretched and dried. The first edition of the six-inch *Ordnance Survey maps for the West Riding of Yorkshire shows large numbers of tenters in the

fields and *garths behind houses and *cottages. The phrase 'to be on tenterhooks' comes from this process.

tenure. See COPYHOLD TENURE; LEASEHOLD; FREEHOLD; CONVENTIONARY TENURE; FINES AND RENTS; RACK RENT; and SUB-TENANT.

terraces. 1. (housing). By the first half of the 19th century the typical accommodation of a working-class family was a two-storey house that formed part of a terrace. Such arrangements were found not only in the burgeoning towns but in the industrial villages. Terraced houses were built at first without much thought to town planning, often as speculative ventures by small builders. (See BACK-TO-BACK HOUSING.) They were sited as near as possible to factories and other places of employment. During the 1860s most municipal authorities began to regulate building standards, so terraces became more uniform according to favoured regional types.

2. (gardens). Terraced gardens were introduced into England and Wales during the reign of William III (1689–1702). The outstanding example is at Powis Castle, near Welshpool, where the steep hillside that had once been used for defence was transformed into a terraced garden c.1700.

testament. A testator began his last will and testament by bequeathing his soul to God and giving instructions for burial, before listing his legacies. The word was used in the same sense as the Old and New Testaments of the Bible.

textiles. See COTTON; WOOL; WORSTED; NEW DRAPERIES; LINEN; SILK; FRAMEWORK KNITTING; and KNITTING.

thane, thegn. An Anglo-Saxon landowner who held his land by charter in return for military service. King's thegns were substantial men, but petty thegns were hardly distinguishable from ordinary farmers.

thatch. The Old English word meant 'roof covering', hence 'thackstones', but the general sense is of roofing made from reeds, rushes, straw, ferns, etc. Such roofing was once widespread in Britain, but from the late 16th century onwards districts with suitable materials replaced thatch with *slates or *tiles. Norfolk water reed, which can last up to 80 years, is the chief source of thatch at present. Thatched roofs provide good insulation. They are steeply pitched to allow rainwater to run off quickly; they overhang to divert the rainwater from the walls and foundations of the building. See M. Billet, *Thatching and Thatched Buildings* (1981).

theatre. Drama was an integral part of the *civic ritual of the Middle Ages, but performances were not held in permanent theatres. (See MYSTERY PLAYS.) Travelling bands of actors are recorded in provincial towns and cities from the 1530s. The Vagabonds Act (1572) forced companies of travelling players to seek royal or aristocratic patronage and thus forced them to be based in London. Shakespeare was a member of the Lord Chamberlain's Men, later known as the King's Men. Other companies included those patronized by the Earls of Essex, Oxford, Sussex, Warwick, and Worcester. They frequently merged and changed their names. They played in some of the first theatres to be erected in Britain, e.g. the Swan, the Rose, and the Globe, whose sites are known. For an introduction to the Elizabethan theatre see Andrew Gurr, *Playgoing in Shakespeare's London* (1987). The London companies toured the provinces in summer. Records of performances indicate the use of great houses, college halls, inn yards, etc.

Theatres were banned by the *Puritans during the *Commonwealth, but were re-established in London after the *Restoration. Samuel *Pepys's diary is a major source for theatrical performances in the 1660s. During the next century provincial urban drama flourished as never before: see Peter Borsay, *The English Urban Renaissance: Culture and Society in the Provincial Town, 1660–1770* (1989). By the mid-18th century every self-respecting town had to have its playhouse, some of which survive, notably the small Georgian theatre at Richmond (Yorkshire). Others are known from illustrations and *photographs. Handbills, programmes, and *newspaper advertisements are often preserved in local studies libraries.

thirdborough. An alternative name for *headborough or *tithingman.

Thompson, E. P. (1924–93). Pioneer of the history of working-class men and women, whom he sought to rescue 'from the enormous condescension of posterity'. His *The Making of the English Working Class* (1963) was enormously influential and remains one of the most popular works of modern history, even though its conclusions about the formation of a working class have been much criticized (see LABOUR HISTORY). His early career was spent as an extramural lecturer at Leeds University, where he became interested in the themes that led to his most famous book. At Warwick University he founded the Centre for the Study of Social History and inspired a new generation of social historians. He wrote prolifically on historical

and political themes, notably in *Whigs and Hunters: The Origin of the Black Act* (1975), and his collection of essays, *Customs in Common* (1991). He was made a Fellow of the British Academy in 1993.

Thompson, Flora Jane (née Timms, 1876–1947). Author of a trilogy of books, reissued together as *Lark Rise to Candleford* (1945). The first of the three, *Lark Rise* (1939), an account of her childhood at Juniper Hill (Oxfordshire) in the 1880s, has won wide acclaim and is often quoted by social historians. A cautionary view has been expressed by Barbara English, 'Lark Rise and Juniper Hill: A Victorian Community in Literature and History', *Victorian Studies*, 29/1 (1985).

Thoresby, Ralph (1658–1725). The son of a *Puritan cloth merchant of Leeds, he acquired an early interest in the antiquities of his birthplace. His business activities allowed him to travel widely and to record inscriptions, transcribe documents, and compile lists and pedigrees. He became a noted numismatist and antiquary, whose collection of coins and curiosities were displayed in his private museum. Recognition came in his election to the *Royal Society and in an invitation to contribute to a new edition of *Camden's *Britannia*. His major works were *Ducatus Leodiensis* (1715), a topographical survey, and *Vicaria Leodiensis* (1724), part of a larger projected history. See G. C. F. Forster, 'The First Medievalist in Leeds: Ralph Thoresby, F.R.S., 1658–1725' in Ian S. Wood and Graham Loud (eds.), *Church and Chronicle in the Middle Ages: Essays Presented to John Taylor* (1991), ch. 17, and J. Hunter (ed.), *The Diary of Ralph Thoresby, F.R.S.*, 2 vols. (1830).

Thoroton, Robert (1623–78). Author of *The Antiquities of Nottinghamshire* (1677), which was modelled on *Dugdale's *Warwickshire*, but is largely genealogical and heraldic in character. His documentary researches were not supported by fieldwork. Thoroton was a country gentleman, physician, and JP.

threshing. Hand-threshing by *flail survived well into the 19th century, and later on the smallest holdings. Experiments with threshing machines had begun in the late 18th century, notably with Andrew Meikle's machine in Scotland (1786), but manufacture became a commercial proposition only during the labour shortages of the *Napoleonic wars. The earliest machines were large, fixed structures operated by horse, water, or wind. They were most common in southern Scotland and northern

England. Production fell with the return of peace and widespread agrarian riots. (See SWING, CAPTAIN.) Steam-powered threshing machines were made from the 1840s, and in 1842 Ransomes of Ipswich exhibited the first self-moving (traction) engine. The new technology rapidly gained acceptance, and agricultural engineers in many parts of the country, e.g. Fowlers of Leeds, established successful businesses.

tied housing. In the 19th century and later, farmers and other employers often provided rented accommodation for their work-force, whereby such housing was 'tied to the job'. If a worker left or was sacked he lost his accommodation. This seemed a reasonable system from the employer's point of view, but opponents complained of injustices and an attempt to create a docile work-force.

tiles. The Romans used baked clay roofing tiles but subsequently *thatch or wooden *shingles were preferred. Fire hazard persuaded the citizens of late 12th-century London to ban thatch in favour of tiles, shingles, and *slates. During the 13th century the practice spread widely in rural as well as urban *parishes. At the same time, baked clay floor tiles became widely used; surviving examples include the floors of the chapter house at Westminster Abbey and of the retro-choir of Winchester Cathedral. During the 17th century tiles replaced thatch as the roofing material for *vernacular buildings in many parts of Britain. (See PANTILES.) Tile-hanging as an external covering for walls became popular in south-east England during the 17th century, followed by the use of glazed brick tiles, known as mathematical tiles, during the later Georgian period. See Alec Clifton-Taylor, *The Pattern of English Building* (1972), ch. 10.

timber-framed buildings. Until the late 16th or 17th century the majority of *vernacular buildings were constructed with timber frames. In regions where wood was scarce, builders had to use local *rubble, *mud walling, or whatever was at hand, but wherever possible timber was preferred. Even those areas which became famous for the quality of their 16th- and 17th-century stone houses, such as the Cotswolds, used timber in earlier times. John *Leland's notes on his itineraries late in Henry VIII's reign confirm the use of timber in regions where stone was plentiful, as do surviving estate *surveys. Oak accounted for the majority of the frames that were constructed, though sweet chestnut was used for huge roof spans such as that of the great hall at Penshurst Place (Kent),

and elm and other woods were also favoured. Under normal conditions oak heartwood is beetle-proof. See R. W. Brunskill, *Timber Building in Britain* (2nd edn., 1994), J. R. Armstrong, *Traditional Buildings Accessible to the Public* (1979), and R. Harris, *Discovering Timber-Framed Buildings* (1978) for introductions to the subject.

*Dendrochronology has allowed the precise dating of numerous timbers. It is clear that many surviving timber-framed houses are medieval rather than Tudor, as was once thought. The earliest vernacular examples are 13th century; part of Sycamore Farm House, Long Crendon (Buckinghamshire) has been dated by dendrochronology to 1205. Oliver Rackham, 'Grundle House: On the Qualities of Timber in Certain East Anglian Buildings in Relation to Local Supplies', *Vernacular Architecture*, 3 (1972) showed that a small Suffolk manor house, with a hall and two cross-wings built about 1500, was constructed of some 300 trees, mostly oak, but 20 per cent elm. Rackham estimated that such a quantity might have been produced once in six years from 50 acres of managed woodland. About 40 of the trees were large, but the rest were less than 50 years old. At that time, the woods of West Suffolk were capable of producing 70 such houses each year. See also Oliver Rackham, *Trees and Woodland in the British Landscape* (1976), and *Ancient Woodland: Its History, Vegetation and Uses in England* (1980).

The study of timber-frame construction is highly technical. See C. A. Hewett, *English Historic Carpentry* (1980), N. W. Alcock (ed.), *Cruck Construction: An Introduction and Catalogue* (1982), Peter Smith, *Houses of the Welsh Countryside* (1975), and for an example of a regional study of types, P. F. Ryder, *Timber-Framed Buildings in South Yorkshire* (1978). See also the articles in the journals *Vernacular Architecture*, *Archaeological Journal*, and *Medieval Archaeology*, and in local transactions. (See also CLOSE STUDDING; SQUARE PANELLING; WATTLE AND DAUB; and CRUCKS.) There are marked regional variations in the types of framing employed, but these also reflect the social standing of the owner, and changing fashions. The use of certain features remains controversial. Jetties, for example, may have been constructed partly for technical advantages, but the desire to provide more space in an upper room is first evident in urban houses in France and Germany; it spread to terraced houses in English towns and then became fashionable in the countryside where space was no problem. The fashion for staining the external timbers black began in the Victorian period; previously, timbers had been left their natural colour, and in much of eastern England they had been protected by a coat of plaster. (See PARGET-ING.)

The timber-framed tradition came to an end partly because of changing fashion and partly because of the rising cost of timber, especially in those areas where the owners of woods found it more profitable to turn to the production of underwood. The change began at the *gentry and *yeoman level and gradually spread downwards. See GREAT REBUILDING.

time immemorial. From 1291 a person who had no *charter of authority for a franchise, e.g. the right to hold a *market or *fair, had his claim allowed if he could prove that he and his ancestors, or predecessors in his position, had held that right since 'time whereof the memory of man runneth not to the contrary'. This was known for short as 'time immemorial', or 'time out of mind', and was fixed as the period before the accession of Richard I in 1189.

tin was produced in Devon and Cornwall from prehistoric times in its alloy, bronze, and since at least Roman times in its alloy, *pewter. The industry came to an end in the late 20th century. Some early workings can be seen on the fringes of Dartmoor and Bodmin Moor, but the spoil heaps and engine houses of the deep mines of the 19th century have obliterated most evidence of earlier activities. The tin industry used *water power for *smelting by the end of the Middle Ages, i.e. earlier than in other industries. Water-powered blowing houses continued in use until the 19th century, though they were largely superseded from the beginning of the 18th century by reverberatory furnaces, as in the *lead industry.

From the Middle Ages onwards cooking utensils were 'tinned' inside to prevent corrosion from acid foods. Tinplate (thin, high-quality iron sheet) was first made in south Wales in the 1720s. The canning industry is a 20th-century development.

tithe awards and maps. The bureaucratic structure that was created in 1836 to solve the *tithe problem was closely modelled on the *Poor Law Commission established in 1834. The commissioners and assistant commissioners who were appointed to deal with tithes proceeded with commendable efficiency, without causing the great controversies associated with the contemporary work of the Poor Law Commission. Between 1836 and 1852 the Tithe Commission quietly brought about a major redistribution of English and Welsh property.

During that time they made apportionments for 11,395 districts (which were either *parishes or smaller *townships); in 7,147 cases (63 per cent) the agreements were made voluntarily. Only a few of the remaining cases dragged on, some until the 1880s.

The commissioners appointed surveyors to make large-scale maps and schedules. These were drawn up in triplicate: the copy made for the tithe office is now kept at the *Public Record Office; the ones for the parish clerk and the bishop of the diocese are normally kept at an appropriate county or diocesan *record office. The maps were not drawn to a uniform scale, but are nevertheless often the earliest surviving large-scale maps for a given area; they make interesting comparison with the first edition of the six-inch *Ordnance Survey maps and the *census returns of 1841 and 1851. The reference numbers on the tithe maps correspond to those in the accompanying tithe apportionment; in this way individual properties can be identified.

The tithe apportionment is often bound with the accompanying map. A preamble to the apportionment notes the extent and use of the arable land which was liable to tithe, the names of all tithe owners, and all customary payments which were made in lieu of tithe. After the preamble, the tithe apportionment lists all *landowners and tenants and their fields; it is therefore a principal source for the study of landownership and of *field-names. The apportionment goes on to note the land use of each field (usually as arable, meadow, or pasture, though sometimes in a more specific manner) and is thus of great value in a study of land use at that particular time. Unfortunately, not all surveys were entirely accurate, nor do they provide complete coverage, for some parishes had abolished tithes at the time of parliamentary *enclosure. Nevertheless, about 79 per cent of England and Wales is covered by tithe maps.

The tithe files in the Public Record Office consist for the most part of the working papers of the assistant commissioners. They were drastically weeded in the early years of the 20th century, but where they survive they provide information on farming methods, soil fertility, and levels of rent. The documentation associated with the operation of the Tithe Commutation Act is an enormous source of data for the agrarian historian. Two major books—Roger Kain and Hugh Prince, *The Tithe Surveys of England and Wales* (1985), and Roger Kain, *An Atlas and Index of the Tithe Files of Mid-Nineteenth Century England and Wales*

(1986)—are essential reference works. The *Atlas* provides a county-by-county survey of the process of commutation in all tithe districts of England and Wales. Its statistical place index refers the reader to the records of each tithe district in the Public Record Office and is a valuable guide to the type of evidence for land use—such as rotation practices, quality of pasture, and new crops—that is available for each district.

About half the civil parishes in Ireland were valued between 1823 and 1830; the rest were valued between 1832 and 1837. The valuers' notebooks, known as tithe applotment books, note the names of tenants and *townlands, and record the area, value, and tithe payable. Those for the counties in the Republic of Ireland, and copies of those from Northern Ireland, are kept at the Public Record Office in Dublin. The original note books for the six northern counties are at the Public Record Office of Northern Ireland. Microfilm and microfiche copies are available in some public libraries.

tithe barns. The collection of *tithes in kind by a *rector necessitated the construction of *barns which were large enough to store huge quantities of grain. Some of the largest barns that survive are known popularly as tithe barns but are in fact the barns of big estates, which needed similar storage space. Barns of both types survive in many parts of England, sometimes as working barns which have been subdivided between local farmers, but increasingly as museums. They are *timber-framed, using the most advanced carpentry techniques of their time, but they often have stone walls. The tithe barns at Bradford-upon-Avon (Wiltshire) and Abbotsbury (Dorset) are particularly fine examples.

tithes. The Biblical injunctions to Moses and Jacob to give one-tenth of all the produce of their land for the work of God had become a legal obligation in England by the 8th century. The great tithes of corn and hay, and the small tithes of livestock, wool, and non-cereal crops, went to the support of the *rector of a *parish, who in return maintained the *chancel of the church and saw to the provision of church worship. Where the resident minister was not the rector but an institution such as a *monastery or *college, or a layman, the small tithes were paid to the *vicar who served in the rector's place. Local customs varied greatly to complicate this general picture. At the *Reformation tithe-rights that belonged to monasteries were confiscated by the Crown and granted or sold to various owners known as lay

impropriators. From this time, about a third of all tithes became owned by lay people; moreover, some clergymen and ecclesiastical institutions leased the collection of tithes to laymen. This lay involvement created opposition to the payment of tithes. In the mid-17th century *Quakers and *Anabaptists refused to pay tithes to any owner. By the early 19th century the growth of *Nonconformity had increased opposition to the payment of tithes to the Established Church.

Originally, tithes were payable in kind: the rector or his appointee collected from each farm the tenth sheaf of corn, the tenth cow, sheep, or pig, the tenth pail of milk, etc. In most English parishes the precise customs to be followed in collecting tithes were set out in detail in *glebe terriers. In some parishes it had become the practice by the early modern period for farmers to pay a fixed *modus instead. After periods of inflation, tithe-owners frequently challenged the legality of such arrangements, either in diocesan courts (which tended to favour the tithe-owners) or in the equity courts of *Chancery and *Exchequer (which were expensive and dilatory). The records of such cases contain depositions which are often informative about local customs. Contests over the payment of tithes on new crops, e.g. *potatoes, indicate when such crops were first grown in a parish.

The ill-feeling created by the collection of tithes caused many owners to agree to a money payment. Parliamentary *enclosure provided an opportunity for ending strife by allotting land to the tithe-owners in lieu of tithe. Over 60 per cent of the 3,700 or so Acts passed between 1757 and 1835 dealt with tithes in this way. The question of commutation was not seriously discussed until the beginning of the 19th century, but then it became one of the great issues of the day as part of a general movement for reform. By the 1830s both *Whigs and *Tories accepted the need for reform, and the *Church of England, fearful of losing its established status, acquiesced in the passing of the Tithe Commutation Act of 1836, whereby tithes were converted into rent charge payments based on the prevailing price of grain. New Tithe Acts, notably those of 1891, 1925, and 1936, dealt with changed circumstances. Rent charges finally disappeared in 1936 when landowners began to pay an annuity over 60 years in order to redeem all tithe by 1996. See Eric J. Evans, *Tithes: Maps, Apportionments and the 1836 Act* (1993).

In Scotland, tithes were abolished at the *Reformation. In Ireland, opposition to tithes payable to the (Anglican) *Church of Ireland by all sections of the (mostly Roman Catholic) population came to a head in the 1820s and 1830s. An Act of 1823 allowed the voluntary commutation of tithes into a money payment; an Act of 1832 made commutation compulsory. In 1838 the tithe payment was reduced by 25 per cent and transferred from the tenant to the landowner. Tithes were abolished in Ireland in 1869.

tithing. The medieval system whereby groups of ten *households were responsible to the manorial *court leet for the good conduct of each member. See FRANKPLEDGE.

tithingman. The elected representative of each *tithing who was responsible for presenting the misdemeanours of his members or their families to the manor *court leet.

tobacco was a crop that was grown by the Native Americans, before the first European settlers arrived in America. It proved the mainstay of the settlements of *Virginia and Maryland. By the early 18th century 28 million lb. of tobacco per annum was grown on plantations there, mainly for export to Britain and Europe. Tobacco was introduced as a field crop in Winchcombe (Gloucestershire) in 1619, and despite government attempts to prohibit English production, by 1626 it was being grown in 39 places in Gloucestershire, 17 places in Worcestershire, and one in Wiltshire. Half a century later it was grown in 22 counties in England and Wales, and in the Channel Islands, but production had virtually disappeared by 1690. It was generally regarded as a poor man's crop that required hard labour. See Joan Thirsk, 'New Crops and Their Diffusion: Tobacco-Growing in Seventeenth-Century England', in C. W. Chalklin and M. A. Havinden (eds.), *Rural Change and Urban Growth, 1500–1800: Essays Presented to W. G. Hoskins* (1974).

toft. A plot of land to the rear of a building, often bounded at the rear by a *back lane. The regularity of tofts in some medieval villages suggests a planned settlement.

Toleration Act (1689). After the *Glorious Revolution of 1688 had ousted the Catholic King James II, congregations of Protestant *Nonconformists were allowed to worship openly provided they licensed their meeting houses at *quarter sessions.

tolls. The internal trade of the British Isles has been relatively free of passage tolls, when compared, for instance, with France, though some tolls were paid at *bridges and ports. Some toll books for *markets and fairs survive in local *record offices. See, for example, P. R. Edwards, *The Horse Trade of Tudor and Stuart England* (1988) and the report of the Royal Commission on Market Rights and Tolls, 1888. See also TURNPIKE ROADS.

Tolpuddle Martyrs. The six Dorset *agricultural labourers who were sentenced to *transportation to Australia in 1834 for being members of a secret society which aimed to improve their *wages. They subsequently became symbolic heroes of the *trade union movement.

tomb chest. A form of *funerary monument, dating from the 13th to the 17th century, and from the *Gothic revival of the 19th century. They can be dated from their use of decoration in styles similar to those used in contemporary church windows, etc. and from their *heraldry, which was formerly painted. The use of heraldry increased after the *Reformation. Renaissance forms became popular in the late 16th and 17th centuries. Tomb chests do not contain the mortal remains of the deceased but are merely memorials. Many are no longer in their original position.

tools, hand. Hand tools were not only the basis of the old agricultural economy, they shaped the modern industrial world. London was an ancient centre of tool manufacture (as in much else), but by the 16th century the metalworking districts centred on Birmingham and Sheffield, and to a lesser extent in south Lancashire, had already acquired wide reputations. (See SCYTHES, and SICKLES.) The production of tools for a world-wide market increased considerably during the 18th century and reached its peak in the Victorian period, when Sheffield was the world's major centre of tool production, manufacturing such tools as files, *saws, planes, hammers, *spades, etc. Meanwhile, other regions, especially south-western England, had emerged as centres of edge-tool production. During the second half of Victoria's reign the traditional handicraft basis of tool production gave way to mechanization.

See James M. Gaynor and Nancy L. Hagedorn, *Tools: Working Wood in Eighteenth-Century America* (1994), which reviews the English as well as the American evidence, concentrating on the material culture; W. L. Goodman, *History of Woodworking Tools* (1964), R. A. Salaman, *Dictionary of Woodworking Tools, c.1700–1970, and Tools of the Allied Trades* (1990), and Janet Barnes (ed.), *The Cutting Edge: An Exhibition of Sheffield Tools* (Ruskin Gallery, Sheffield, 1992). The Tool and Trades

History Society publishes an annual journal, *Tools and Trades*, and a quarterly newsletter. See also the journal *Tools and Tillage*. Manufacturers' trade catalogues are a prime source of evidence for the enormous variety of tools that were produced.

toot-hill. Look-out points used to watch for raiding armies in the *Anglo-Saxon and *Viking era. Place-names commonly preserve the memory of such observation posts.

topographical artists. The early histories in the *antiquarian tradition were often illustrated by prints. In the 17th century the fashion developed for commissioned drawings of country houses and views of London, particularly by Dutch artists. Knyff and Kip's bird's-eye views of country houses were gathered together for publication in *Britannia Illustrata* (1707). See Samuel and Nathaniel BUCK, who drew numerous 'prospects' of 18th-century towns and major buildings. Under the influence of *Romanticism, in the late 18th and early 19th centuries both professional and amateur artists sought picturesque views, which often incorporated historic buildings. Their usual medium was water-colours, which were particularly suited to working outdoors. Many of these artists were concerned to depict a building accurately, though artistic rather than historical purposes were paramount. They included such notable figures as John Buckler (1770–1851), John Chessell Buckler (1793–1894), and John Sell Cotman (1782–1842). (See NORWICH SCHOOL OF ARTISTS.) Paintings and drawings which aimed at accuracy are now a valuable historic source for buildings which have been demolished or altered; they are a particularly useful record of parish *churches before Victorian restoration or rebuilding. During the 19th century many local artists painted street scenes and depicted local industries and crafts; these, too, are an invaluable record before the age of *photography.

M. W. Barley, *A Guide to British Topographical Collections* (1974) lists many of the paintings, drawings, and prints that are now housed in national and local *record offices. The largest depository is the Manuscripts Department of the *British Library. See also M. Holloway, *A Bibliography of Nineteenth-Century British Topographical Books With Steel Engravings* (1977), and Ronald Russell, *Guide to British Topographical Prints* (1979).

topographical guides. The first topographical guides were published in the late 18th century to cater for the increasing numbers of visitors to the Lake District, Snowdonia, and the Highlands of Scotland. The first guide book to the Lake District was Thomas West's *A Guide to the Lakes* (1778), which ran into several editions until 1821. It was superseded by William Wordsworth's *Guide*, which went through five editions between 1810 and 1835; see Peter Bicknell (ed.), *The Illustrated Wordsworth's Guide to the Lakes* (1984). John Murray's *Handbooks for Travellers* began with Devon and Cornwall in 1851 and eventually covered every English county, some in a number of editions down to 1905. Single-volume handbooks for Scotland and Ireland were also published by Murray. Such guides contained much antiquarian information and their descriptions are now valuable as historical sources. They should be used alongside *travellers' accounts and the works of *topographical artists, as well as the imaginative literature of the period. See ROMANTICISM; see also MORRIS, JOSEPH.

toponymic. The term is used to describe the classes of surname that are derived from places. See SURNAMES, LOCATIVE AND TOPOGRAPHICAL.

Tories. The word (derived from an Irish word for 'outlaw') was first used as a nickname to distinguish a group of aristocratic politicians from their *Whig opponents in the late 17th century. The Tories were rarely in office until William Pitt the younger became *Prime Minister in 1783, but they then remained in power (except for a brief period in 1806–7) until 1830. They adopted the name *Conservative under Sir Robert Peel in the mid-1830s. 'Tory' remains an alternative word for 'Conservative'.

Torrington, Viscount. The Hon. John Byng, 5th Viscount Torrington, kept diaries of his tours through England and Wales between 1781 and 1794. These have been published as C. B. Andrews (ed.), *The Torrington Diaries*, 4 vols. (1935–6).

torture was commonly used in the Middle Ages and the early modern period to get a confession to a charge of treason. Common methods were to stretch suspects on a rack, or to press them with heavy weights on their chests, or to screw their thumbs. The use of torture by government declined during the 17th century.

total descent. A chart showing all ancestral lines, both male and female. In practice, such charts usually go back no further than the 16 great-great-grandparents.

tournament. Medieval tournaments were a mixture of sport and warfare, where rival groups of knights fought across open country, often with the loss of life and limb. The Tudor and Jacobean tournament was very different. It no longer served as a training ground for war, but was a carefully stage-managed public spectacle for political and cultural purposes, a major event in the court calendar that deliberately set out to revive the age of chivalry. The financial costs were enormous. See Alan Young, *Tudor and Jacobean Tournaments* (1987).

tower houses were built on both sides of the Scottish border in the 14th and 15th centuries to protect the occupants from raiders. The normal arrangement of the rooms of a medieval manor house was expressed horizontally, but in the tower house was treated vertically, with a vaulted basement and an internal staircase. About 150 tower houses have been identified in Cumberland and Northumberland. Some were added to later; e.g. Mortham Tower, the Teesdale seat of the Rokebys, was converted into a *courtyard manor house. See PELE-TOWERS, and BASTLE.

townfields. A term used in the north of England when referring to the *open-fields of a *township, particularly those relatively small open-fields of upland areas. See A. R. H. Baker and R. A. Butlin (eds.), *Studies of Field Systems in the British Isles* (1973).

town halls. The traditional town hall of the 16th and early 17th centuries consisted of a large room or rooms raised on columns above an open arcade. Such buildings served also as *market halls and sometimes as the meeting places of manorial *courts. They occupied sites in the centre of the town, often in an island of space. Peter Borsay, *The English Urban Renaissance: Culture and Society in the Provincial Town, 1660–1770* (1989) lists nearly 40 town halls constructed, rebuilt, or substantially modified in the century after the *Restoration, many of which still survive. Some were built in the old style, but others were compact and often striking classical buildings built to enhance the prestige of the town. A famous example is that at Abingdon (Oxfordshire), built in 1678–82.

Even more striking are the town halls of Britain's Victorian cities, which provided office space for staff as well as rooms and chambers for meetings and prestigious reception and dining areas. The architectural styles are eclectic and often incorporate both classical and *Gothic elements. Rivalry between neighbouring provincial cities caused councillors to commission buildings that reflected municipal grandeur. Outstanding examples include Cuthbert Brodrick's Leeds Town Hall (1853–8), which attracted international notice, Sir

Charles Barry's Halifax Town Hall (1859–63), and Lockwood and Mawson's Bradford Town Hall (1868–73), whose tower is modelled on that of Siena. The lesser halls of smaller towns are also worthy of attention. See Derek Linstrum, *West Yorkshire Architects and Architecture* (1978).

townland. The ancient and basic unit of local government in Ireland. The average size of the 60,462 townlands is 350 *acres; the range is from a little over 1 acre to over 7,000 acres. The names are often repeated; thus, there are 56 Kilmores and 47 Dromores. Townlands can be identified in *The General Alphabetical Index to the Townlands and Towns of Ireland* (1901), available in good reference libraries. This index locates townlands according to county, *barony, *parish, and *Poor Law union, and gives their *Ordnance Survey sheet number and the acreage.

towns. The British experience of towns has been unusual in a West European context, and its distinctive nature has coloured national attitudes down to the present day, as well as complicating the researches of local and family historians. Town life was an exotic importation from the Continent, both in Roman and in medieval times. Until the 18th century most British towns were small by Continental standards, and until the 19th century the majority of Britons still lived in rural settlements. Yet Britain then became the first country in the world to urbanize, rapidly outpacing its neighbours, and acting as a pioneer in developing new types of urban design such as *garden cities.

This historically very recent, but also decisive, change has had many effects upon British culture, including an ambivalent attitude to urban living. It has also made more difficult researches into family history, since the rapid growth of towns came about largely by mass migration from the countryside at the period when *parish registers were becoming less comprehensive and when *civil registration of births, marriages, and deaths was only just beginning.

Yet although townspeople were a minority of Britons until the last century, towns have long played a part in national life out of proportion to their size. Local migration was common as far back as the Middle Ages, and much of it consisted of movement from country to town. Indeed, many towns until the 18th century suffered a surplus of deaths over births, so that only immigration from the countryside could sustain their size, let alone permit them to grow. Furthermore, nearly everyone (at least in lowland England) was within easy reach of a market town by the 13th century, and visits to towns for trading were normal. Large towns, and above all *London, exercised an even greater pull. E. A. Wrigley has estimated that in the century 1650–1750 London grew as fast as it did only by absorbing as immigrants half of all the natural increase (surplus of births over deaths) of the rest of England, and many others made short or long visits to the capital without migrating there. Richard *Gough's accounts of all the families in Myddle (1701–2) reveal that one in six families in this distant Shropshire parish had at least one member who, at one time or another, had lived in London.

The study of urban history has been complicated by varying definitions of towns, and especially by the overlapping categories of *borough and town. A borough (*burgh in Scotland) gradually became a legal and constitutional term with particular reference to incorporated towns and to those towns represented in parliament. Some important towns, however, and many lesser towns, were not formally boroughs, and this is the difficulty about the best attempts so far at full catalogues of towns in the past, for they are really catalogues of boroughs: G. S. Pryde, *The Burghs of Scotland: A Critical List* (1965), and M. W. Beresford and H. P. R. Finberg, *English Medieval Boroughs: A Hand List* (1973). The word 'city', increasingly used in its North American sense as 'large town', is no more helpful: in England and Wales, historically, it means a cathedral town or a town given the title by royal charter as a mark of honour. The following discussion follows the definition that 'a town is a permanent human settlement with two chief and essential attributes. The first is that a significant proportion (but not necessarily a majority) of its population lives off trade, industry, administration, and other non-agricultural occupations . . . The second . . . is that it forms a social unit more or less distinct from the surrounding countryside' (Susan Reynolds, *An Introduction to the History of English Medieval Towns*, 1977, p. ix).

These problems of definition are especially acute for the earliest periods of British towns, down to the 12th century, for which written sources are scarce, and knowledge has to be derived largely from archaeology. There is evidence, for instance, for a significant number of nucleated settlements in the immediately pre-Roman *Iron Age, some of which have been claimed to represent 'the beginnings of urbanization' in Britain, and some of which were on or near sites which later became Roman and medieval towns (e.g. Colchester and St Albans). The first true towns, however, are usually taken to be those created by the Romans after AD 43.

Nearly a hundred towns have now been identified in *Roman Britain, the most privileged being chartered towns called *coloniae* or *municipia*, but the great majority described as *vici*; *vicus* was a broad term which could apply to a town or a village and which was used for most of the tribal capitals. These, however, were legal terms; in physical terms, using archaeological evidence, what can be distinguished are large towns with regular street-plans, major public buildings, and—increasingly from the 3rd century—earthwork or stone defences; and, in contrast, many small towns, often with an irregular street-plan and no defences. The larger towns had markets and workshops, and some smaller towns had specialized industrial functions, such as *Durobrivae* (Water Newton, Huntingdonshire) with its pottery manufacture. Almost all our knowledge of Romano-British towns is derived from archaeology and aerial photography, and most older works are quickly superseded. The best surveys are by John Wacher, *The Towns of Roman Britain* (1975), and B. C. Burnham and John Wacher, *The 'Small Towns' of Roman Britain* (1990), but both need supplementing by the annual summaries in the journal *Britannia*.

Three points should be especially stressed about Roman towns and their legacy to Britain. First, the Romans never occupied northern Britain or Ireland, and their urbanization was more restricted still: all the towns described by Wacher and Burnham lay south of Hadrian's Wall. In the rest of the British Isles the Iron Age pattern of settlement was unbroken. Second, towns were primarily social and administrative rather than economic centres; when imperial rule over Britain collapsed c.408–9, most towns quickly ceased to function. Third, however, though no 'continuity' has been proved between Roman and medieval town life anywhere in Britain, the Romans' legacy is not irrelevant. Their surveyors had a remarkable talent for spotting good sites, and nearly all their towns were reoccupied in the Middle Ages.

Until the 1950s it was possible to argue, from the documentary evidence, that towns in the economic sense did not reappear until late *Anglo-Saxon or even Norman times. However, archaeology has made it clear since the 1960s that towns reappeared in England as early as the 7th century. The earliest were apparently trading-centres on coasts and rivers (places called *wic* or *emporium* in contemporary documents), but others quickly developed as royal and ecclesiastical centres, notably the many small towns which originated around a *cathedral, *monastery, or major church ('*minster'). The period of *Viking invasions and conquests (*c.*835–954) saw a further stage, as established English towns were fortified, and new fortified towns (*burhs*) created. In northern and eastern England the Vikings stimulated commercial town life, especially in York and Lincoln, while Alfred and his successors created a network of *burhs*, first in Wessex and then in the Midlands, as they drove the Vikings back. Towns and markets proliferated in lowland England in the 10th and 11th centuries, and the proportion of English people living in towns by 1066 may have reached 10 per cent. By that time no true towns existed in Scotland and Wales, although both had important royal and ecclesiastical centres which can fairly be regarded as proto-urban settlements. In Ireland, where similar settlements had been founded in hill forts and round monasteries, there were also from the 9th century trading towns created by the Vikings, notably Dublin, which originated in their *longphorts* or fortified harbours.

The *Norman Conquest is no longer thought to represent a major change or starting-point in English town life, apart from the disruption caused by the building of *castles in the county towns and other important centres (though the Normans' subsequent conquest of South Wales from the 1070s led to the planting of castle-towns there, which were the start of Welsh urbanism). However, it was probably on the initiative of William the Conqueror that *Jewish immigrants first came to live in England—almost exclusively in the larger towns—and it was certainly on his orders that the *Domesday Book was compiled (*c.*1086), which allows us much more written evidence for towns in England than for anywhere else in north-west Europe for such an early date. It describes over 100 places as *burgi* (best translated as 'towns' rather than 'boroughs'), and gives enough information on about 50 of them to make clear that they were genuine towns of a largely non-agricultural character.

Between the Norman Conquest of England (1066) and the *Black Death (1348–50) towns proliferated in number and size throughout the British Isles, especially in lowland England (Scotland was the last country to develop true towns, though they were probably emerging by the late 11th century, a little earlier than the traditional dating from the reign of David I,

1124–53). What lay behind the expansion was the enormous growth of British (and indeed European) population in that period, leading to demand for more food and cultivated land, more markets, and a commercialized economy. Kings and lords realized that trade was profitable, and were generally quick to sponsor town growth, granting markets and *fairs, and equipping townsmen with burgage tenure, which meant that they held their properties by rent only (without any of the servile labour obligations of the countryside), and with the right to bequeath them freely to their children or other heirs. New towns were established by kings and private lords, whether grafted on to existing villages or laid out on virgin sites: M. W. Beresford's classic study, *New Towns of the Middle Ages* (1967), lists over 130 new towns created in England between 1100 and 1300, and at least 66 in Wales. Most of these towns were based around a *market-place, and a minority were regularly planned with street grids, including Salisbury; Edward I's conquest of North Wales involved his creation of a spectacular group of planned and fortified towns, including Conway and Caernarvon.

The growth of towns was achieved only by attracting immigrants, many of whom were men and women from the surrounding hinterlands. For some it was probably enough just to escape the burdens of villeinage and *labour services: some town charters from the 12th century expressly allowed that those who managed to enter the town and live there for a year and a day could remain without fear of pursuit from former lords. Others were tempted by the generous terms offered by lords, especially of new towns. The bishop of Worcester, founding a borough of Stratford-upon-Avon in the 1190s, allowed his new 'burgesses' quarter-acre housing plots for a shilling a year rent in lieu of all services, and freedom from tolls. A classic study by Eleanora Carus-Wilson, 'The First Half Century of the Borough of Stratford-on-Avon', *Economic History Review*, 2nd ser., 18/1 (1965), reprinted in R. Holt and G. Rosser (eds.), *The Medieval Town: A Reader* (1990), showed that by 1251–2, 234 burgesses had been attracted there, and it analysed those with place *surnames to suggest their origins. Some 90 per cent of them came, apparently, from villages and hamlets within a 16-mile radius. Large towns were able to attract immigrants from much greater distances. McClure's work on place surnames suggests that in the early 14th century over half of Nottingham's and Norwich's immigrants came from more than 15 miles away, while for York the equivalent threshold was 20 miles, and for London over 40 miles. London and a few other large towns were already attracting immigrants from overseas; and until 1290 (when they were expelled from the realm) several large English towns included a colony of Jews.

The period from the 12th to the 14th centuries was also one of growing urban autonomy. By the 12th century the *merchants and craftsmen in many towns formed themselves into an association (*guild merchant or hanse) to maintain and regulate a trading monopoly, and the leading guildsmen then usually tried to acquire political power as well. In England the decisive period was that of the reigns of Richard I and John (1189–1216), when two kings, short of money, were willing to sell chartered privileges. The royal towns (which included most of the more important English towns) were generally able to acquire their own elected officials (usually headed by a mayor), to free themselves from the control of *sheriffs and other royal officials, and effectively to become corporate towns, well before the formal age of charters of incorporation started in 1345. This meant that the town's officers and council could be treated as one 'body', able to hold property collectively and to sue and be sued at law. *Seigneurial towns (those held by lords other than the King) had more variable fortunes, however. Churchmen in particular took a conservative view of lordship, and towns controlled by a bishop or abbot were generally unsuccessful in acquiring much self-government.

So far the Church has been mentioned chiefly as an institution connected with the founding and governing of some towns, but it should also be remembered that it played a major role, and usually a very positive one, in the life of all medieval towns. Not all towns had a cathedral, monastery, *nunnery, or major church, but nearly all had one or more parish churches, and many had a wide array of other ecclesiastical institutions—chapels, *hospitals, and so on. In the 13th century, towns acquired *friaries, which were essentially urban-based religious orders and which clearly, to judge by their popularity, played a much wider role than the preaching and teaching for which they were intended.

By the early 14th century, British towns had reached their medieval peak, at least in terms of size. The proportion of the English population living in towns was perhaps 15 per cent, and London may have had 80,000 or even 100,000 inhabitants, making it one of the great European cities. No other British towns came anywhere near that in size, but Norwich and Dublin may each have reached 25,000 or so. The Black Death of 1348–50, and later epidemics, heavily reduced urban populations, though paradoxically some large towns (e.g. Coventry and York) rose to their largest medieval size about 1400, apparently because they could still attract rural immigrants. By the mid-15th century many English towns were complaining of 'decay' and seeking tax reductions, though a recent lively debate has left it unclear how far towns were poorer and how far simply smaller (see Alan Dyer, *Decline and Growth in English Towns 1400–1640* (1991) for a good guide to the controversy).

Certainly the 14th and 15th centuries were a time of development, and not merely problems, for British towns. Their trade and industry often increased (especially the textile industry in the larger English towns); they developed a rich urban culture of ceremonies and pageants, including the *Corpus Christi plays; and they developed more formal and elaborate structures of town government. Urban representatives became a regular part of the English and Scottish parliaments; the larger English towns acquired corporate status, and the very largest became counties corporate, which put them completely outside the control of county officials, with their mayors answerable directly to the King. And both in England and Scotland the popular element in municipal elections was being curbed in the 15th century with the approval of the Crown, to the point where some historians speak of a rise of urban oligarchies. Nevertheless, these proud towns were still small beer by Continental standards: around 1500 there were about 11 Italian cities each with over 40,000 inhabitants, but only one (London) in the British Isles. At the same period the largest English provincial towns (Norwich, Bristol, York, and Exeter) had only 8,000 or so inhabitants each, and probably no Scottish, Welsh, or Irish town matched even those modest totals, except Edinburgh and, just possibly, Dublin.

The 16th century was a watershed for British towns, particularly because of the impact of the *Reformation in all four countries. The end of Catholic ritual, and the suppression of religious houses (especially friaries), *chantries, and pilgrimages, had an enormous impact on urban life well beyond the sphere of worship. It also caused much hardship in towns heavily dependent on church landlords or on pilgrimage cults, such as Canterbury, Durham, and St Andrews, though in some towns the diverting of resources from the church may have been more beneficial. To make matters worse, the religious changes coincided, at least in England, with a period (c.1520–60) when the rural population was growing again, but most towns except London were still stagnant in size: this relatively short period may, more than most, justify the term 'urban crisis' in some hard-hit towns like Coventry.

In contrast, the period from about 1560 to 1700 saw a considerable growth in the size of many towns. Many, though not all, market towns flourished as the economy became more commercialized, and new towns of a specialist kind were growing, including *dockyard towns, industrial towns like Manchester and Birmingham, and even the first of what may be fairly called leisure towns (e.g. Tunbridge Wells and Bath). Old-established towns acquired new functions or new industries: thus Norwich prospered so well from the '*New Draperies' as to become the largest English town after London, while Bristol became a major Atlantic port. Above all, the capital cities expanded dramatically. London grew from about 60,000 people in the 1520s to about 500,000 by 1700, increasing its share of the English population from 2.5 per cent to nearly 10 per cent, and overtaking Paris to become the largest city in western Europe. Dublin's rise started later but was equally spectacular: it grew from perhaps 8,000 or so in 1600 to 70,000 by 1700, making it the second largest city in the British Isles (Edinburgh probably came third).

The growth of all these towns must have come primarily from immigration. Taking the freemen class—admittedly a minority of males, who may not have been typical in their experience—only 31 per cent of Cambridge entrants to the franchise in the 16th century were born in the town, and at Bristol and York the figure was only 28 per cent. In London, with its vastly greater pull, but for which a freemen's register survives only for the short period 1551–3, the proportion was as low as 17 per cent. *Parish registers, available from 1538, can give wider samples, but are difficult to analyse for large, multi-parish towns with much migration between parishes as well as between country and town. One London clergyman commented in the 1580s that every 12 years or so 'the most part of the parish changeth, as I by experience know, some going and some coming'—a situation, as Professor Stone comments on this extract, which resembles nothing so much as modern Los Angeles.

This summary of urban growth should not be taken to mean that all was improving. Some towns did decline in absolute or relative terms; and many endured short-term crises. The

*Civil War, or 'War of Three Kingdoms', was disruptive for many English towns, and disastrous for most Irish towns except Dublin. Epidemics and fires remained frequent scourges: the great London *plagues (1563, 1593, 1603, 1625, 1665) and fire (1666) were only the largest and most notorious. And although bubonic plague disappeared from Britain around 1670, epidemics of other types continued, and urban mortality was especially high between the 1670s and 1720s.

Nor should one forget the frequent disruptions brought about by clashes within urban ruling circles, or between the towns and central government. Many English and Irish borough charters concentrated formal power within fixed councils, often filled by co-option rather than election, but these councils were sometimes riven by feuds which became increasingly enmeshed into wider political and religious conflicts. Many English town councillors of the wrong persuasion were dismissed from office in the 1640s and 1660s; and between 1681 and 1688 the Stuart Kings ruthlessly remodelled borough corporations by calling in town charters and issuing new ones. At the same period some rapidly growing towns (e.g. Manchester and Birmingham) remained unincorporated, trying to govern their increasing populations within the inadequate machinery of manorial and parish government.

The period from 1688 to 1835, the 'long eighteenth century', marks a convenient phase in British urban history. The terminal dates are political, but the period makes sense as one in which Britain was developing the world's first modern urban society, while at the same time the political and administrative structure of towns was little changed. London continued to grow rapidly, with its new position as capital of Great Britain (1707), and also as the country's largest port and manufacturing town: it reached about 675,000 by 1750 and 960,000 by 1801. London apart, however, the *Industrial Revolution overturned the old hierarchy: the English provincial towns which had for centuries headed the league table (Norwich, York, Bristol, and so on) were overtaken by an enormous growth of the new industrial towns: London in 1801 was followed second by Manchester with 84,000 inhabitants, Liverpool, and Birmingham, though Bristol was still not far behind. Outside England, Dublin developed as a major Georgian capital; Edinburgh came to its peak as a social and intellectual, if no longer a political, centre; while Glasgow grew rapidly to rival Liverpool and Bristol in the Atlantic trade. And in all four countries, many smaller towns were growing rapidly. Urban growth was considerably aided by the spread of *brick and *tile construction, which at last brought to an end the perennial danger of major fires.

The usual view is that these major changes were not matched by appropriate improvements in urban government, and it is true that the state in 1688 restored the old pattern of chartered and unchartered towns in all their variety, and that no major changes were made until the 19th century. However, piecemeal improvements under acts of parliament were numerous, especially in the establishment of *improvement commissions from 1725; these enjoyed wide powers to raise money and to provide services, and in consequence corporate towns acquired a valuable supplementary authority, while unincorporated towns acquired a vital means of self-government. As a result, standards of paving, lighting, and street-widening improved in many places well before municipal reform. Besides these public bodies, many voluntary institutions—especially hospitals and schools—were created to fill the gaps left by urban government.

Nevertheless, the unreformed municipal corporations were, as Geoffrey Martin puts it, 'richly disgraceful', and as town populations and urban problems increased, the pressures for reform became overwhelming. The first reform was of the *parliamentary franchise: the First Reform Act of 1832 made sweeping changes to those boroughs represented in parliament, coupled with a widening of the qualifications for voting. The dangers of resisting reform had been made clear in 1831, when the Lords' rejection of the second Reform Bill had led to riots in several towns, including the burning of Nottingham Castle and the wrecking of Bristol's Mansion House. The reformed parliament then went on to pass the Municipal Reform Act of 1835, dissolving the corporations of nearly 200 English boroughs and replacing them by councils elected by ratepayers. Further reforms and reorganizations continued to widen the basis of urban local government, and to grant powers to the growing industrial towns: Birmingham and Manchester, for instance, both received charters of incorporation in 1838.

New powers and responsibilities were needed because urban growth continued to be rapid in England and Scotland (Ireland, by contrast, at least until 1845, experienced rapid population growth without urban growth). London doubled in size between 1801 and 1841, and Glasgow grew even faster, increasing by over 30 per cent in each of those four decades. Some industrial towns also grew very rapidly, such as Sheffield, which trebled in size between 1801 and 1851, and Belfast, an exception in Ireland. It is difficult to use the early censuses to measure total urban population because of varied local government areas, but it seems that the proportion of English and Welsh people living in towns rose from 33 per cent in 1801 to 54 per cent in 1851; for Scotland it is not possible to give a comparable figure for 1801, but by 1851 it was about 52 per cent. Towns were thus growing not only in absolute size but also as a proportion of the national population, and so one can say that by 1851, the year of the *Great Exhibition, Britain had become the first country in the world to urbanize.

This urbanization owed much to migration from country to towns and also, in the 1840s, to *emigration from Ireland (in 1851 22 per cent of Liverpool's population, 18 per cent of Glasgow's, and 13 per cent of Manchester's was Irish-born). Many towns were still very unhealthy, and could never have grown so fast by natural increase. Overcrowding and insanitary conditions were widespread, and the *cholera outbreaks of 1831–2 and later killed thousands through water infected by sewage. However, these outbreaks provoked a series of important sanitary measures, including the 1848 *Public Health Act and the institution of municipal sanitary inspectors in 1866. In 1875 another Public Health Act offered wide powers to all municipalities, and a Housing Act allowed them to clear and rebuild slums. A new spirit of municipal enterprise—seen strikingly, for instance, in Birmingham under Joseph Chamberlain—helped to improve urban conditions. Nevertheless, progress was for long very patchy.

Urban mortality was steadily reduced, but acute poverty long remained. The Revd Andrew Mearns, with *The Bitter Cry of Outcast London* (1883), helped to provoke parliamentary inquiries on working-class housing. More solidly, Charles *Booth demonstrated the poverty of the East End in immense statistical detail in his *Life and Labour of the People in London* (1889–1902), while his example inspired B. Seebohm Rowntree to do the same for York in *Poverty* (1901). Rowntree particularly provoked horror and demands for reform by showing that degrading poverty could be as acute and widespread in an ancient cathedral city as in the East End of London. Indeed, until the 1870s death rates in York were worse than the national average; and some industrial towns had rates much worse than York's.

Slums and overcrowding were an inevitable

consequence of rapid and largely uncontrolled urban growth, especially in the industrial towns. Bradford, to take an extreme case, grew by 52 per cent in 1831–41, by 55 per cent in 1841–51, and by 34 per cent in 1861–71. However, by the later 19th century such mushroom growth in the industrial towns was becoming the exception, as more people with the aid of better transport swelled the residential towns and *suburbs, and also boosted the *seaside resorts: some of the fastest urban growth rates between 1861 and 1911 were achieved by Bournemouth, Southend, and Blackpool. It should also be remembered, in fairness to the great industrial cities, that this was the period when they adorned themselves not only with magnificent *town halls, which could have been seen as wasteful status symbols, but also with many *museums, art galleries, *libraries, and other public buildings.

By the turn of the century, pressure was building up for urban planning rather than the *laissez-faire* individualism which was widely held to have degraded the urban environment. Two model communities started by industrialists in the 1890s, Bournville and Port Sunlight, pointed the way towards better conditions for factory workers. Ebenezer Howard went further in *Tomorrow* (1898: revised and reissued in 1902 as *Garden Cities of Tomorrow*) in advocating small, self-sufficient new towns with low-density housing. Howard himself initiated Letchworth (1903) and Welwyn Garden City (1920), and his ideas, coupled with those of the Scottish biologist Patrick Geddes, helped to develop the modern town-planning movement.

The period between the world wars, however, was ushered in by the 1919 Housing Act, which introduced state subsidies both for private houses and for local authorities' *council housing: and the 20 years following saw the building of four million new houses, many of them semi-detached, in sprawling new suburbs or in 'ribbon development' along main roads. These were the houses mocked by Osbert Lancaster as 'by-pass variegated', in which he invites us to admire 'the skill with which the houses are disposed, that insures that the largest possible area of countryside is ruined with the minimum of expense' (*Pillar to Post*, 1938, 68).

The reaction against this was compounded by the heavy damage sustained by many British cities in the Second World War: and the postwar Attlee government responded to a new mood for public planning, with its Town and Country Planning Act (1947), green belts around cities, and new towns. Under the New Towns Act of 1946 15 'new towns' were created, eight of them as satellites in a ring round London, and two for Glasgow, and reflecting many of Howard's ideas. Cumbernauld was added to the number in the 1950s, and the 1960s saw a further batch of 11 new towns in England and Scotland, including Telford and Milton Keynes. The major problem remained, however, of how to deal with existing towns with the spread of more affluence and especially of car ownership. The 1960s and 1970s saw what seems in retrospect a catastrophic phase of city centre redevelopment, road widenings, and high-rise construction which threatened to destroy the character of many British towns. It remains to be seen whether the more conservationist climate since then, with traffic-free zones, archaeological monitoring of development, and housing on a more human scale, will have turned the tide. See Geoffrey Martin, *The Town* ('A Visual History of Modern Britain' series, ed. Jack Simmons, 1961), and Stephen Porter, *Exploring Urban History: Sources for Local Historians* (1990). See also URBAN TOPOGRAPHY.   DAVID M. PALLISER

towns, ranking of. See W. G. *Hoskins, *Local History in England* (3rd edn., 1984), appendix 1, which uses taxation returns from 1334, 1377, 1523–7, and 1662, and the *census returns of 1801 and 1861, to list provincial English towns according to size of population.

township. The smallest unit of local government, and an ancient one, largely synonymous with *vill. In many parts of England *parishes formed a single township, but in districts where parishes were large, e.g. the Pennines, they were subdivided into townships. In the 16th century townships or civil parishes were given responsibility for the poor and the highways. They were also units of taxation. Townships survived until the creation of *Urban and *Rural District Councils in the late 19th century.

town walks and gardens. The formal provision of *gardens, *parks, and *avenues for public promenading began in England in the 17th century. London had landscaped walks at Moorfields and the *Inns of Court, and later in St James's Park. The Pantiles at Tunbridge Wells was first laid out in 1638, and Exeter had a formal walk on Northernhay before the Civil War. The provincial promenade was developed on a much wider scale from the 1690s. See Peter Borsay, *The English Urban Renaissance: Culture and Society in the Provincial Town, 1660–1770* (1989), ch. 6. Borsay lists 30 towns and *spas which by 1770 had public walks or gardens on their peripheries, often following the line of the city walls. Some promenades attracted superior residential accommodation, especially in the resorts. By the mid-18th century several provincial towns had followed the example of London in opening commercial pleasure gardens with facilities for breakfasting, bowling, and dancing. The local authority recreational gardens of today are largely 19th-century municipal enterprises in origin.

town walls. In the Middle Ages the major European towns were enclosed by great ditches and embankments surmounted by a wall. The City of London was thus enclosed on the north bank of the Thames. Very little of London's wall survives, but its outline is known from early maps and is commemorated by various place-names. Tracing the outline of a town wall by archaeological and historical methods is usually a local exercise in co-operation. The finest surviving town walls in Britain are those of York, Chester, Canterbury, and Southampton. Excavations at York have shown how the previous walls of the Romans, Vikings, and Normans underlie the present walls, which date largely from the 13th and early 14th centuries, though stretches have been substantially repaired in the 18th and 19th centuries. The walls were defended by four great bars, six posterns, and 44 towers. The bars, which formed the principal entrances to the town, remain largely intact, though only that at Walmgate retains its *barbican, the rest having been destroyed in the early 19th century to facilitate the movement of traffic. Important dignitaries were received by the mayor and corporation at one of the bars, and the heads of executed traitors were displayed from the battlements. Each bar had a *portcullis which was closed at night-time. The walls acted as an effective barrier against undesirable migrants and symbolized the importance of a town.

Most towns did not update their defences in the 16th century, but good examples of the improved techniques imported from Italy can be seen at Portsmouth and Berwick-on-Tweed, where the defence system was revised at every new crisis. See I. MacIvor, 'The Elizabethan Fortifications of Berwick-on-Tweed', *Antiquaries Journal*, 45 (1965), and A. D. Saunders, 'Hampshire Coastal Defences since the Introduction of Artillery', *Archaeological Journal*, 123 (1966). John *Speed's maps show that many towns were still largely contained within their medieval limits in the early 17th century. See SUBURBS.

toys. In the West Midlands the term referred to small fancy goods in metalware. The earliest reference is from 1710. By the 1750s Birmingham had 30 toymakers who between them took 68 apprentices. See Marie B. Rowlands, *Masters and Men in the Small Metalware Trades of the West Midlands* (1975).

trade. See INDUSTRY AND TRADE.

trade, coasting. Trade along the coasts of Britain in the medieval and early modern periods was largely an extension of river trade, even though goods were transhipped at the coastal ports. (See PORT.) The east coast of England was the busiest, in terms of both *exports and the conveyance of bulky goods of low value, such as *coal and grain, to London. The backcarriage of hides and groceries helped to make this trade viable. See T. S. Willan, *The English Coasting Trade, 1600–1750* (1967).

trade, export. See EXPORTS.

trade, inland. As the passage of goods in Britain was largely free of *tolls, the sources for the study of inland trade are scant compared with those available for the study of exports, so the subject has been comparatively neglected. See, however, T. S. Willan, *The Inland Trade* (1976), and J. A. Chartres, *Internal Trade in England, 1500–1700* (1977), which has an extensive bibliography. A research project at Wolverhampton University is exploring the history of trade on the river Severn. The subject is intimately connected with the manufacture, transportation, and marketing of consumer goods. Research has been concentrated on the early modern period, but is now attracting the interests of medievalists. The role of central government in stimulating trade and industry is examined in Joan Thirsk, *Economic Policy and Projects: The Development of Consumer Society in Early Modern England* (1978). For the role of middlemen, see Margaret Spufford, *The Great Re-Clothing of Rural England: Petty Chapmen and Their Wares in the Seventeenth Century* (1984). See MARKETS AND FAIRS; INNS; SHOPS; ROADS; RIVER TRAFFIC; PEDLAR; and CARRIER.

trade token. The shortage of coins in the early modern period led to shopkeepers and other traders issuing their own tokens. No fewer than 12,722 different tokens are listed in G. C. Williamson, *Trade Tokens Issued in the Seventeenth Century*, 3 vols. (1967); even so, the list is far from complete. Millions must have been produced until a royal proclamation of 1672 forbade their circulation after the introduction of copper *farthings and halfpennies. Williamson's list for England and Wales was analysed in T. S. Willan's *The Inland Trade* (1976) to show how widely distributed were 17th-century shopkeepers. He noted that tokens were issued by at least 2,151 shopkeepers in 1,534 places, which was twice as many as the number of contemporary market towns. Trade tokens prove the existence of *shops in quite small places.

trade unions. By the middle of the 18th century trade unionism was already well established among many groups of industrial workers. See C. R. Dobson, *Masters and Journeymen: A Pre-History of Industrial Relations* (1980). For overviews of how trade unionism developed, see Henry Pelling, *A History of British Trade Unionism* (3rd edn., 1976), John Rule (ed.), *British Trade Unionism, 1750–1850: The Formative Years* (1988), A. E. Musson, *British Trade Unionism, 1800–1875* (1972), and Keith Laybourn, *A History of British Trade Unionism, 1770–1990* (1992). S. and B. *Webb, *History of Trade Unionism* (revised and extended edn., 1920) is still useful in outlining the legislation affecting the formation and activities of trade unions. (See also COMBINATION ACTS, and FRIENDLY SOCIETIES.)

Histories of individual trade unions tend to be cast in the heroic mould. They nevertheless contain a great deal of information about local leaders and events, highlighting the struggles of the 19th and early 20th centuries. Much more information can be gained from local *newspaper accounts of strikes, meetings, and social events such as annual galas, and from the techniques of *oral history. (See LABOUR HISTORY for the ways in which trade union history needs to be seen as part of the wider history of working-class societies; a good example of this wider approach is Alun Howkins, *Poor Labouring Men: Rural Radicalism in Norfolk, 1870–1923* (1985).) For the use of oral history in recording modern events, see R. Samuel, B. Bloomfield, and G. Boanas (eds.), *The Enemy Within: Pit Villages and the Miners' Strike of 1984–5* (1986).

A starting-point for research is provided by R. and E. Frow and M. Katanka, *The History of British Trade Unionism: A Select Bibliography* (1969). The main collections of trade union records are those housed at Warwick University and Nuffield College, Oxford. See J. Druker and R. Storey, 'The Modern Records Centre at Warwick and the Local Historian', *The Local Historian*, 12/8 (1977). Many Scottish trade union records are kept at the Department of Manuscripts, the National Library of *Scotland. Some branches have deposited their archives at local *record offices, but much has

been lost. See also A. E. Musson, 'Writing Trade-Union History', *Amateur Historian*, 1/9 (1954), Sidney Pollard, 'Sources for Trade Union History', *Amateur Historian*, 4/5 (1960), E. J. Hobsbawm, 'Records of the Trade Union Movement', *Archives*, 4 (1960), and N. Scotland, 'Primary Sources for 19th-Century Agricultural Trade Unionism', *Local Historian*, 13/5 (1979).

trams and buses. Horse-drawn omnibuses were a Parisian invention, developed from the stage-*coach. They could carry 12–15 passengers over short distances, with frequent stops and cheap fares. London's first service was opened by George Shillibeer in 1829. The 1830s was a time of 'bus mania' in the capital as new companies competed fiercely. By the 1850s omnibuses were providing services to central London from the northern and western suburbs. Similar services were soon established in provincial towns. Old *photographs show how omnibuses originally had 'knife-board' seats on the upper deck, but these were gradually replaced by a central seat with 'decency boards' that preserved ladies' ankles from public view; these boards carried advertisements.

Horse-drawn trams, which ran on rails, were an American invention, which was introduced into London in 1870. They were cheaper than trains and could carry more passengers than an omnibus. They were soon replaced by electric trams, whose efficiency led to the decline of omnibus services except in suburbs where trams did not penetrate. Photographs show that by Edwardian times the driver and passengers on top were no longer exposed to the elements but enclosed by a glass front and a metal roof. Examples of historic trams can be seen at the Tram Museum, Crich (Derbyshire) and in Glasgow's Museum of Transport. Local transport gradually became a municipal responsibility during the late 19th and early 20th centuries; local authority records can be seen at local *record offices. The rapid expansion of cheap transport meant that working-class and lower middle-class *suburbs could be built away from the place of work. High Streets became shopping and entertainment centres. Trams and buses also took sports fans to *football and *cricket grounds at the edges of cities and towns. Some genteel suburbs managed to retain their character by preventing the extension of the tram network. The omnibus offered a fresh challenge to trams with the invention of the motor engine, and by the 1950s and 1960s trams were everywhere (except in Blackpool) in terminal decline. A new generation of 'super trams' was introduced in major cities such as Manchester and Sheffield in the 1990s.

transcript. An exact copy of the wording of a document. See BISHOPS' TRANSCRIPTS.

transhumance. The ancient practice whereby livestock that had been wintered in sheltered valleys were taken in summer to graze on upland or woodland pastures, accompanied by shepherds and cattle herders who lived in *shielings or similar structures.

transportation of convicts. In 1615 the *Privy Council authorized the transportation of criminals to America, particularly to *Virginia, as an alternative to hanging. On arrival, prisoners were sold to the highest bidders. See David T. Hawkings, *Criminal Ancestors: A Guide to Historical Criminal Records in England and Wales* (1992), ch. 12, for an account of records such as transportation bonds and transportation order books in local *record offices, and central sources in the *Public Record Office. Transportation to the American colonies continued until the War of Independence in 1776. By then, an estimated 40,000 convicts had been transported to America.

After 1776 British gaols began to get overcrowded. Parliament therefore authorized transportation to *Australia. The 'First Fleet' of 586 male and 192 female convicts, together with free settlers and seamen, set sail on 13 May 1787 and arrived the following January. New South Wales was formally declared a British colony on 26 January 1788. Transportation ceased in 1868, by which time it is estimated that about 162,000 convicts had been transported to the other side of the world. See David T. Hawkings, *Bound For Australia* (1987) for an account of the available records in Britain and Australia. The Public Record Office has convict transportation records arranged by ships (HO 11), contracts for the transportation of convicts who are named, with their place of trial and sentence noted (TS 18), lists of convicts on particular ships (PC 1), Privy Council registers (PC 2), lists of convicts at particular dates (HO 31/1), and thousands of petitions for release (HO 17). *Quarter sessions records are another major source of information. See, for example, Roger Davey (ed.), *East Sussex Sentences of Transportation at Quarter Sessions, 1790–1854* (1988).

travellers' accounts. Some discerning descriptions of England were written by early foreign travellers. See Walter B. Rye, *England as Seen by Foreigners* (1865), and a series covering the period 1597–1871, published by Caliban (1994 onwards). Many of the earliest travel diaries are little more than notes recording distances and expenses. Before the 17th century people rarely travelled for pleasure. A tour of the 'Wonders of the Peak', inspired by the writings of Thomas Hobbes, Isaak Walton, and Charles Cotton, was one of the first recognized itineraries. The celebrated account of the travels of Celia *Fiennes is exceptional, not only in its 17th-century date and in being written by a woman, but in its breadth of interest in contemporary matters. Such accounts were written as a private record or to entertain friends; most were not published until the 19th or 20th century and many remain in manuscript. Daniel *Defoe, *A Tour Through the Whole Island of Great Britain* (1724–6), the first attempt at a comprehensive account, was a compilation of observances made on journeys undertaken over many years, with additional information culled from other writers. The observations made by diarists on contemporary scenes are now of historical interest. Some of the best writers—*Thoresby, *Pococke, *Torrington—were informed also by a sense of history.

In the later 18th and early 19th centuries the fashion for travelling to remote places was at its height (see ROMANTICISM, and TOPOGRAPHICAL GUIDES.) Wales, the Lake District, and Scotland began to attract numerous visitors keen to record their impressions. The number of travel diaries that survive for this period is far in excess of earlier ones. Many travellers were also enticed by the spectacle of new industries in dramatic settings, such as Coalbrookdale (Shropshire), or Cromford (Derbyshire). The *Napoleonic wars made travel on the Continent difficult or impossible and forced travellers to search for enjoyment in their own land. The increasing use of post-chaises on *turnpike roads facilitated their journeys. Travel accounts from later periods are usually less valuable to historians, for other sources of historical information are then available, including *newspapers and *directories.

Few travel diaries have been published in full, but extracts have often appeared in the transactions of local *archaeological and historical societies. As most travel diaries contain information about places beyond the boundary of the county where the writer was living, locating such accounts is difficult. See, however, Robin Gard, *The Observant Traveller: Diaries of Travel in England, Wales and Scotland in the County Record Offices of England and Wales* (1989), which includes a catalogue of 608 diaries kept in various *record offices.

T.R.E. *Tempore regis Edwardi*, 'in the time of King Edward the Confessor', the *Domesday Book formula for the period before the *Norman Conquest.

treasure trove. Discovered hoards of gold or silver coins or other precious objects that have been deliberately hidden by unknown owners. Ownership is determined at a *coroner's inquest.

trefoil. One of the artificial grasses whose cultivation in pastures and in an arable rotation was introduced from the Continent in the 17th century. See LEYS, GRASS, or CONVERTIBLE HUSBANDRY.

Treswell, Ralph. One of the finest Elizabethan surveyors and mapmakers. His early works include panoramic representations of London buildings. During the three decades after 1580 he produced a series of scaled plans of the City, and occasional plans of other places. See J. Schofield (ed.), *The London Surveys of Ralph Treswell* (1987).

Tribal Hidage. A 7th- or possibly 8th-century document that appears to be a list of the tribute assessments paid to the kingdom of *Mercia by dependent peoples, some of whom are not known from other sources. See Steven Bassett (ed.), *The Origins of Anglo-Saxon Kingdoms* (1989).

Trinitarianism. Belief in the Holy Trinity, especially by 19th-century members of the *Church of England, in opposition to *Unitarianism.

trow. A term used in the 17th and 18th centuries for various kinds of boats or barges that conveyed goods on rivers or along the coast. The precise meaning varied considerably from region to region.

truck. The system by which employers paid part of an employee's wage by vouchers that could be used only at a shop or store belonging to the employer. The system was open to abuse and was forbidden by the Truck Act (1831), which insisted that wages (other than those of *domestic servants) should be paid in cash.

tuberculosis. Commonly known as consumption. A pulmonary disease which was often fatal, well into the 20th century. Isolation hospitals built in the Victorian and Edwardian era offered treatment.

Tudor and Stuart architecture. A large number of buildings, at both the 'polite' and the 'vernacular' level, survive from the Tudor and Stuart era in many parts of Britain, but their geographical distribution is uneven. See Malcolm Airs, *The Buildings of Britain, A Guide and Gazetteer: Tudor and Jacobean* (1982), and Richard Morrice, *The Buildings of Britain . . . Stuart and Baroque* (1982). The ideas of the Italian Renaissance were accepted only slowly and the native *Gothic tradition long remained influential. Architectural historians speak of the Tudor Court Gothic style, e.g. of Hampton Court, which continued to inspire provincial builders. New ideas from the Continent came via France and the Low Countries into the court circle, London, the universities of Oxford and Cambridge, and some ports, and were gradually diffused to other parts of the kingdom. British architecture emerged from its medieval past after the *Restoration, when it became more fully part of the western European tradition. On the greater houses, see Malcolm Airs, *The Making of the English Country House, 1500–1640* (1975), Maurice Howard, *The Early Tudor Country House: Architecture and Politics, 1490–1550* (1987), Mark Girouard, *Robert Smythson and the Elizabethan Country House* (1983), J. C. Dunbar, *The Historic Architecture of Scotland* (1966), and Peter Smith, *Houses of the Welsh Countryside* (1975). See also PRODIGY-HOUSES; VERNACULAR ARCHITECTURE; and GREAT REBUILDING.

tumulus. A term, favoured by the *Ordnance Survey, for a prehistoric burial site.

Tupling, G. H. One of the first to apply modern approaches to the study of local economic history, in *The Economic History of Rossendale* (1927) and in articles in the *Transactions of the Lancashire and Cheshire Antiquarian Society* on the early modern history of Lancashire *markets and fairs, early metal trades, and the beginnings of *engineering, etc.

turbary, right of. The right to dig *peat for fuel on the *commons and wastes.

turkeys. The bird was domesticated by the Aztec Indians in Mexico. From about 1540 it was imported into England by merchants of the *Levant Company, who were known as 'Turkey merchants'. King James I is credited with starting the fashion of having turkey for Christmas dinner instead of a goose. In the early 18th century, *Defoe commented on the rearing of large numbers of turkeys in Norfolk, from where they were walked to market in London. Norfolk has remained the major centre of turkey production.

turnips. An improved variety was introduced from the Low Countries as a vegetable, and became a *market garden crop in the later 16th century. By the end of that century they were much grown in gardens by the poor. Farmers learned in the 17th century to value them as fodder for cattle, sheep, and poultry. From the late 17th century onwards turnips were increasingly grown by farmers in *open-fields, on light soils but not on heavy clays. Their cultivation was much advocated by agricultural writers. By the second quarter of the 18th century, turnips were well established as a standard crop in the celebrated Norfolk rotation. Their cultivation cleaned the land, and they were much valued as fodder for sheep folded on the arable. Their use soon spread from Norfolk to the loams and sandy soils of Suffolk, Essex, and Hertfordshire. The crop had also become established as far away as Cornwall and Northumberland. By 1801 about 650,000 acres of land in England and Wales were devoted to turnip cultivation. Swedish turnips were introduced into Kent, via a Dutch seedsman, in 1767. Swedes were quickly adopted for late feeding in many parts of the country. The mangel, or mangold wurzel, was introduced from France in 1786. All these types of turnip were used essentially as winter fodder.

turnpike roads. Roads administered by trusts authorized by private Acts of Parliament, on which tolls were charged at gates. For an introduction to the subject, see G. N. Wright, *Turnpike Roads* (1992). The term 'turnpike' comes from an older practice whereby a pike that formed a barrier was turned to allow access. By the 18th century the amount of traffic on the roads was increasing so much that the statutory labour system whereby *parishes or *townships were responsible for the maintenance of highways could no longer cope. (See HIGHWAYS, OVERSEERS OF.) The answer was to form turnpike trusts which were empowered to levy tolls for the upkeep and improvement of named stretches of highway, and, it was hoped, would make a profit.

The first turnpike trust was established by private Act of Parliament in 1663 to repair and maintain a particularly badly worn 15-mile stretch of the Great North Road between Wadesmill and Royston in Hertfordshire and Cambridgeshire, but this pioneering enterprise was not imitated elsewhere until 1696. The number of new turnpike Acts rose steadily from four in the 1690s, to 10 in the 1700s, 22 in the 1710s, and 46 in the 1720s. By 1750 most of the major through routes in England had been turnpiked, though no turnpike roads had yet been authorized in Cornwall, Devon, Dorset, or Wales, and the movement had only just begun in Scotland, and had achieved only limited success in Ireland. The most active period for the formation of turnpike trusts was between 1751 and 1772, when 389 new Acts were passed. The 1790s was also a busy period. By 1820 over 1,000 turnpike trusts controlled about 22,000 miles of British roads and charged tolls at some 7,000 or more gates. The final turnpike to be created, in 1836, covered a stretch of less than two miles from Hastings to Hollington. See W. I. Albert, *The Turnpike Road System in England, 1663–1840* (1972), and E. Pawson, *Transport and Economy: The Turnpike Roads of Eighteenth-Century Britain* (1977).

The progress of a private bill through Parliament can be followed in the printed *Journals* of the *House of Commons and *House of Lords. Petitions normally began by claiming that the highway in question was in disrepair and could not be maintained by the ordinary laws of the realm unless tolls were levied to supplement local rates and the efforts of householders under the statutory labour system. Printed Acts, which name the trustees and outline their powers, are usually available at local studies libraries and local *record offices. A complete set of Acts is available in the *House of Lords Record Office, including renewal Acts which are available only in manuscript. The trustees were empowered to appoint surveyors, repair the roads (with the continued assistance of statutory labour), erect gates, and appoint toll collectors. They were allowed to mortgage the tolls and to elect new trustees. Powers were normally granted for 21 years, after which a renewal Act had to be sought. These renewal and amendment Acts often altered the mileage and sometimes part of the course of a road. Renewal was made automatic, if requested, in 1835.

The network of turnpike roads that became established in the 18th and 19th centuries was not planned by central government, but depended entirely on local initiatives. The petitioners were local landowners and tradesmen, who saw economic advantage in improved communications. Opponents sometimes managed to prevent a bill becoming law or protested by violent means. (See REBECCA RIOTS, which led to the abolition of Welsh turnpikes in 1844.)

The first turnpike trusts were concerned to improve existing highways, or relatively short stretches that were in great need of repair. Part of the explanation of why a highway was chosen for such treatment is the nature of the terrain, e.g. deep clays that made movement difficult in winter, but in general the dating of the turnpike

Acts reflects the comparative importance of the highway at that time. The names of some of the turnpike roads now seem quaint, e.g. Sheffield to Sparrowpit Gate, or Sheffield to Gander Lane, but the terminus was simply the point at which the road reached another major highway, which had already been improved. Brian Paul Hindle's *Roads, Tracks and Their Interpretation* (1993) makes the point that making a road into a turnpike was essentially a legal change, rather than a physical one; some Acts were never implemented, and others were only partially enforced. The amount of effort put into improving a turnpike road might vary considerably from one stretch of the road to another, depending upon the amount of traffic and the tolls generated. During the 18th century the repair of turnpikes was by traditional methods, i.e. the digging of drainage ditches, and the application of stones, cinders, etc. to the surface. The biggest difference was that turnpike roads were maintained more regularly and were widened to allow the passage of wheeled vehicles. This meant the building of new *bridges where *packhorse bridges had once sufficed. Some of the 18th-century trusts created new branches of existing roads, so as to avoid steep or otherwise difficult terrain, but on the whole they followed the old routes up hill and down dale. By the late 18th and early 19th centuries, however, new turnpike roads were being planned along routes which had not previously existed. The improvements in the techniques of road building are associated with John Metcalf ('Blind Jack of Knaresborough'), who was responsible for some 180 miles of turnpike roads in the second half of the 18th century, and Thomas Telford and John McAdam, the great road engineers of the early 19th century. Meanwhile, parishes remained responsible for local roads. (See also ENCLO-SURE ROADS.)

Telford crossed the mountains of Snowdonia with his London–Holyhead route and supervised the 'parliamentary roads' in the Highlands of Scotland, which the central government authorized to supplement its military roads and the private initiatives of the turnpike trusts. By 1713 a number of roads leading to Edinburgh had been turnpiked, but no other Scottish roads were improved in this manner until the 1750s. In Ireland, too, the turnpike roads which had been authorized from the 1730s to the 1750s had to be added to by a programme of road building paid for by the government. In 1765 County Grand Juries, composed of local landowners, were empowered to finance and oversee the improvement

and extension of roads and bridges in their part of Ireland, where private capital was not readily available. See J. H. Andrews, 'Road Planning in Ireland Before the Railway Age', *Irish Geography*, 15 (1963).

Turnpike roads are associated with the stage-*coach era. They ceased to be profitable with the coming of the *railways; tolls declined remorselessly as long-distance carriage was transferred to rail. During the 1850s and 1860s the condition of many turnpike roads deteriorated as trusts tried to pay off their debts. Most trusts were dissolved in the 1870s and 1880s, and in 1888 responsibility for main roads passed to the newly created *county councils. The final days of local toll bars are often captured in *photographs.

The private Acts which authorized the turnpiking of particular roads contain, in their preambles, statements on the type of traffic currently using the highway, and note the places where toll bars or gates were to be erected. Details are given of the proposed toll charges and the exemptions that were to be allowed. In addition to the information that can be gleaned from the various Acts and the collections in the House of Lords Record Office, much evidence of particular trusts can be found in local record offices: they include minute books, surveyors' reports, maps, and correspondence. See B. Duckham, 'Turnpike Records', *History*, 53 (1968). The county maps of the late 18th century are an accurate source for tracing the course of turnpike roads and for identifying toll bars (designated 'turnpikes'). Travellers' guides, notably John *Cary's *New Itinerary* (1798), are another prime source of information. This documentary evidence needs to be combined with the remaining visual evidence on the ground, in the form of *milestones, toll keepers' cottages, water troughs, bridges, and abandoned stretches of track. See C. Cox and N. Surry, 'The Archaeology of Turnpike Roads', *Journal of Industrial Archaeology*, 2 (1965). There are still plenty of opportunities for detailed local research. For examples of regional studies, see B. P. Hindle, *Roads and Trackways of the Lake District* (1984), G. N. Wright, *Roads and Trackways of the Yorkshire Dales* (1985), G. N. Wright, *Roads and Trackways of Wessex* (1988), Richard Colyer, *Roads and Trackways of Wales* (1984), and Owen Silver, *The Roads of Fife* (1987).

turves. See PEAT.

Tusser, Thomas (*c.*1520–80). East Anglian writer on agriculture, whose metrical *Five Hundrethe Pointes of Good Husbandrie* (1573), an enlarged version of his *A Hundreth Good Pointes of Husbandrie* (1557), went into numerous editions. Tusser's sound advice, expressed in a popular manner, ensured that he was widely read and memorized in the early modern period. His work is also of great interest to students of language.

twentieth century, the. The 20th century presents a paradox to the local historian which brings to mind the case of Mrs Jellyby in *Bleak House*, whose concern for the natives of Borrioboola-Gha precluded her interest in problems much nearer to home. The late Victorian and 20th-century state intervention in the many institutions of everyday life has generated vast resources of records, kept centrally or locally in ways which represented enormous improvements; yet, at the same time, as one approaches nearer to the present, so more and more documents will be found to be closed under the various clauses of the Public Records Act (1958) and its later 1967 version. Other sources have been seen as suspect or unreliable, and many local historians simply cannot come to terms with the 20th century. The result is a concentration on distant periods, rather than on the local history of the more immediate past.

Many local authorities now have well-established, modern records-management arrangements which deal only with the management of current and intermediate local authority records, all of which are normally closed to the public until they have been appraised and selected for permanent preservation as archives. A recent move to open up more records has changed some of this situation, but the 30-year rule is still normal, with a 50-year or even 75- (as with public records such as *coroners' records) or 100-year rule (as with such well-known public records as the *census enumerators' schedules) applied in sensitive cases. When local authority records have ceased to be current, there follows an intermediate period during which reviews of the sensitivity of the material can be undertaken, before the records truly can become archives, open to public inspection, or during which the decision can be taken to destroy them totally, retain them totally, or retain a sample. This records management is a service performed for the employing local authority with the twin aims of cost-saving efficiency and the selection of good archives.

East Sussex, for example, has 13,000 ft. of intermediate records, with about 2,000 ft. being destroyed each year. Of course, there are also deposited records which are less than 30 years old but which are accessible: modern *parish registers are deposited in those repositories which also act as diocesan *record offices.

Twentieth-century records can thus be thought of as falling into three categories: current, pre-archival, and archival. The first of these can be consulted only by special permission. Many are less than 30 years old, but initiating local authority departments may give permission for consultation, under certain circumstances and with appropriate safeguards. Pre-archival or intermediate records are in process of appraisal for retention or destruction but are frequently not old enough to be openly available. One is left with the archival material, which may be consulted by the public, and which forms the basis of the remainder of this section.

Despite these problems, the themes of the local and family historian working on the 20th century are innumerable. Urban and suburban growth and change can be plotted and analysed with materials unique to the 20th century. Work on rural land use, land-ownership, and changes in agriculture can similarly be initiated, using unique sources not available to students of the 19th century. The increasing levels of state intervention, leading up to the post-war nationalization programmes, have left records of bureaucracy yielding insights into local industrial and transport structures; whilst intervention in the fields of *education, *public health, and the structures of *local government similarly bring the potential for studies of local *communities in ways not open to those concentrating on earlier periods.

Of course, the nearer to the present day one is working, the more possibility there is also of using the improving methods of *oral history, or of other 20th-century archival material such as that of the Mass Observation Archive now housed at Sussex University, and dating back with individuals' *diaries to the later 1930s. Similar collections of reminiscences can now be found deposited in many local repositories, often springing from adult education classes or modern history workshops. Technological change has also given the possibilities of a wide range of visual material, which often finds expression in assemblages of surviving *photographs in local publications. Highly relevant secondary sources, but which contain the primary records of early 20th-century social investigators, can also be found in such volumes as H. Llewellyn Smith, *The New Survey of London Life and Labour* (1930–5) in the tradition of Charles *Booth's earlier work, and Seebohm Rowntree's three studies of York in *Poverty: A Study of Town Life* (1901), the co-authored *Poverty and Progress: A Second Survey of York* (1941), and *Poverty and the Welfare State: A Third Social Survey of York Dealing only with Economic Questions* (1951). G. C. M'Gonigle, *Poverty and Public Health* (1936), was based on a large sample of families at Stockton-on-Tees, a technique also employed in Ernest Simon, *Social Survey of Merseyside* (1934). In many ways, of course, books written earlier in the century can also be used as primary source materials for the light they shed on past factual interpretations and methodologies—Maude Davies, *Life in an English Village* (1909), a study of Corsley in Wiltshire, or Emrys Jones, *A Social Geography of Belfast* (1960), being contrasting but useful examples of locality studies. The Pike series of *Contemporary Biographies*, highlighting the county élites prior to the First World War, is also now an invaluable source.

For some material, whether national or local in origin, the 20th century merely represents a continuation of records which began in the 19th century. The runs of *directories, for example, continue through to the present day; whilst the 4th June Returns, which are still completed by farmers today, can now give insights into farming at the parish level for over 100 years from 1866, and are to be consulted at the *Public Record Office in MAF 68 (See AGRICULTURAL STATISTICS). The most recent parish-level statistics can be purchased from the Ministry of Agriculture's census branch at Guildford. By 1900 there were also about 15,000 6-inch and 51,000 25-inch, highly accurate *Ordnance Survey maps in existence; these have undergone 20th-century revisions at most scales, with the 25-inch (1:2500) plans being revised for many towns in the first two decades of the century, and again in the inter-war period, and with the 50-inch (1:1250) plans being introduced from 1911. For London, revisions to the 1:1056 series (5 ft. to the mile) date from 1906–9, when the series was extended into Surrey, Middlesex, and Kent. In the late 1930s the London County Council produced its own independent revision at this scale.

Some of this material improves in quality as one moves further into the 20th century, such as the quality and amount of photographs, or the size and local information content of local *newspapers, or perhaps sale catalogues; but, conversely, some declines. Because of the 100-year confidentiality rule on the decennial census, for example, information can be derived only at the abstracted level of the parish

or local authority unit, rather than at the level of the individual and household as now exists for the second half of the 19th century. Nevertheless, even at its abstracted level of information presented for local government units such as Urban and Rural Districts, the census remains a useful starting-point for much 20th-century work. The 1921 residence and workplace tables, for example, might be very useful in establishing socio-economic patterns for developing *suburbs, as would the 1951 social class and occupations tables.

Some material, such as that derived from oral history, cannot by its very nature now extend back to more than 80 or 90 years from the present. It may be as well to remind ourselves of E. H. Carr's caution about modern history: 'When I am tempted, as I sometimes am, to envy the extreme competence of colleagues engaged in writing ancient or medieval history, I find consolation in the reflexion that they are so competent mainly because they are so ignorant of their subject. The modern historian enjoys none of the advantages of this built-in ignorance' (*What is History?*, 1964 edn., 14). The modern historian, argues Carr, must sift the significant from the mass of insignificant material. Much depends on the questions being asked, and the degree to which the archivist or administrator has already made prior decisions about which material might or might not be worthwhile retaining.

Two classes of records that have become available since 1979 illustrate very well the points made above, as well as having enormous significance for the amount of information they release for local historical studies. These are the records of the *Valuation Office from c.1910, and the records of the National Farm Survey 1941–3, which will be examined in some detail.

Under the provisions of the Finance (1909–10) Act (1910), a full survey of landownership in the United Kingdom as of April 1909 was mounted. This has become known as the Lloyd George 'Domesday', forming one element of his well-known attack on the landed interest, and helping to create the political storm surrounding his 'People's Budget'. While many types of property were exempted from payment, all property was nevertheless to be surveyed, thereby infuriating landed interests, who felt that this might be the basis for future more swingeing taxation, or even land nationalization. Parts of the original Act were subsequently modified and landowners combined in organizations such as the Land Union to combat the valuation and duties. After a number of humiliating reverses in the courts and following the hiatus of war, most of the land duties of the Act were finally repealed in 1920.

The Inland Revenue had quickly recruited a huge staff; once they were in post, the large-format Valuation Books (sometimes referred to as 'Domesday Books') were filled in with the description of each property, together with names and addresses of owners and occupiers, and the figures for the extent of the property and its rateable value. These were copied in from the Rate Book or 'Schedule A' registers. Any unrated properties were also added, and each hereditament within the Income Tax Parish (a grouping of civil *parishes for Income Tax purposes) was given an identification number. Valuation Books survive for most areas, and (with the exceptions of books for the City of London and Westminster, Paddington, which are in the PRO) are to be found in the relevant local authority record office, or its equivalent.

Then landowners were sent the unpopular 'Form 4', on which they were to provide detailed information on every hereditament in their ownership. Most have now been destroyed, but contained owners' and occupiers' names and addresses, and much more detail. Valuers were then posted to different parts of the Districts, armed with Ordnance Survey maps and Field Books in which notes and calculations were made. Following inspection of the property a set of values was derived. No fewer than 95,000 volumes of the Field Books survive in the PRO as class IR 58. They are extant for most areas and contain the fullest information of any of the 1910 documents. The entry for each hereditament comprised four pages in the book, with each book containing information on up to 100 hereditaments. All of the information from Form 4 was transcribed onto the first page of the Field Book entry for the hereditament, and the second page included a description of the property which might include details of building materials, numbers and use of rooms, comments on repair and condition, as well as suitability for the purpose used, ancillary buildings and their condition, water supply and sanitary facilities, etc. Comments on the state of cultivation, drainage, land use, etc., are common for farms. On the third page, sketch plans of farmsteads or industrial premises traced from the Ordnance Survey sheets gave details of buildings and their uses, although as work began to fall behind schedule in 1912 the sketches were dispensed with. The lower half of the second page and the final page include figures for the complex and various

values demanded by the Finance Act. A statement of the provisional valuations was entered on Form 37, and a copy sent to the owner or owners of each hereditament and other interested parties. Forms 37 were made available by the Inland Revenue to local repositories in 1979, but not all archivists took up the offer and they were only sporadically transferred. The Forms include the hereditament number, a description of the property, its situation, the name of the occupier, and its extent. In addition they give the figures of each category of value and show how these were derived. On the reverse are the names and addresses of those persons to whom copies of the Provisional Valuation were issued.

Two sets of the largest-scale Ordnance Survey sheets were used (usually 1:2500, although 1:1250 or even 1:500 plans were used for built-up areas, and 1:10560 in many upland areas). One set was a working copy and the other a permanent record. The Ordnance Survey made some revisions for the valuation, especially where recent urban and industrial development had occurred. The permanent set of Record Plans, mounted on linen, has now been almost completely assembled in the PRO. The 'working copies', of uneven degrees of completeness and precision, generally contain less information than the Record Sheet Plans. They were offered to local repositories as long ago as 1968, where many still survive; but coverage is patchy.

The Record Sheet Plans are crucially important. They should show the boundaries of the Income Tax Parish in yellow, and the boundaries of each hereditament by a coloured edging or sometimes by an overall colour-wash. The number of each hereditament was entered onto the plan in red, with detached portions braced together. This number corresponds to the hereditament number in the Valuation Book, and is a key to finding the hereditament in the Field Books, through the PRO finding-aids.

The information to be found in the valuation documents presents numerous possibilities for the investigation of early 20th-century local society and economy. The fact that the valuers were specifically concerned to identify owners of land ensured the compilation of full data on owners' and occupiers' names and addresses, and land and property ownership, at a time in the late Edwardian period of great significance for the landed estates. Thus, the identification of individuals and the study of land-ownership are among the most obvious uses of the data. Indeed, the survey represents the most comprehensive set of property records ever compiled in the United Kingdom. With the addresses of owners given, it should be possible to make assessments as to the extent of owner-occupation of land and housing, absentee ownership, and possible family or *kinship linkages. Since the Valuation Books were primarily copies of the Rate Book they will also compensate for the often considerable gaps in coverage of the latter in rural areas. Each hereditament also has its boundaries delineated, and it follows that farm layout and fragmentation can be studied. Also of great importance is the study of tenure, the extent of *freehold ownership, *lease and *copyhold details, rents, and lengths of tenure.

There is much data on housing. The numbers and uses of rooms, house rents, sanitation and water supply, information on building materials, and details of stabling, pigsties, and other buildings, repair and general condition etc. should all be present, facilitating studies of living conditions prior to 1914 for all classes. Studies can also be made of land use in urban and rural areas, and it is sometimes possible to examine rural land use on a field-by-field basis, though this cannot be predicted for any one area without consulting the relevant documents. It is also possible to study the industrial and commercial structure of towns and cities. The frequently detailed information regarding buildings and equipment enhances our knowledge of industrial, domestic, and other buildings which have since been demolished or heavily altered. Most of these topics can also be studied over time, and there are many possibilities for comparative work with other 19th- and 20th-century documents, including the *tithe surveys, the census enumerators' books, *Kelly's Directories*, the 4th June Agricultural returns, the local rate revaluations of the 1920s and 1930s, and the National Farm Survey (1941-3) data. Researchers' ingenuity will uncover many more possibilities, and the development of computerized databases and analyses will prove indispensable.

The survey itself covered the entire United Kingdom. England and Wales were administered together, and documents relating to the Scottish valuation can be consulted in the *Scottish Record Office at Edinburgh. Here they form the three classes of Survey Books (IRS 88), which were on-site notebooks, Field Books (IRS 51-87), and Maps (IRS 101-133). The former were normally destroyed and none is known for England and Wales, but some covering the Dundee area have been retained. In Ireland the existence of the earlier Griffith Valuation, printed in 1849-65 and updated at intervals thereafter, avoided the necessity of another survey, except in urban areas, for which Field Books are available at the National Archives, Dublin. The survey and its constituent taxation served the needs of Imperial taxation, and should not be confused with local rating measures and rate-valuation lists, which were a regular feature of local authority income. One study, for example, has traced changes of tenure and ownership by combining the 1910 material together with successive 5-year interval-rating valuations for Bethnal Green through to the Second World War, and undoubtedly much more information awaits analysis in this way for most parts of England and Wales.

In 1992 the records of the National Farm Survey of England and Wales (1941-3) became available for inspection. They had previously been closed for 50 years because of the personally sensitive nature of some of the information relating to the farmers themselves. But with their unveiling, the records now become an extremely important source of information for those interested in mid-20th-century local rural conditions.

Once the wartime objective of increasing the cropped area had been initiated, arrangements were put in hand for a national farm survey which would provide comprehensive data for post-war planning purposes, as well as for the more immediate needs of the County War Agricultural Executive Committees. The survey, which began in 1941, consisted of five important components, all of which can be consulted at the PRO.

The first, referred to as *The Primary Farm Record*, was based on field visits to each farm by experienced farmers, whose notes were later written up to form the Record, providing detailed information for each farm under the main headings of tenure, acreage, condition of the farm, sources of water, and extent of electrification. Also included was the controversial assessment of the quality of farm management in terms of the ability of the farmer, given in terms of an A, B, or C grading, and reasons given for B or C grading, such as old age, lack of capital, or 'personal failings', with space for more detail in the case of the latter, allowing amplification on such issues as physical incapacity, lack of ambition, stupidity, laziness, or 'weaknesses of the flesh', such as drunkenness! Of the 300,000 holdings classified by the survey, 58 per cent (63 per cent of the area of crops and grass) were classified by as management grade A; 37 per cent (32 per cent area) as B, and 5 per cent by number and area as C. A report on the condition of the arable and pasture land

and the use of fertilizers was also included. This was followed by some general comments and a listing of the grass fields ploughed up in 1940 and in 1941.

The second component was the *4th June Return 1941* for each farm—the only year for which such information has been released on a farm-by-farm basis rather than as a parish summary. Complete land-use, livestock, and labour-input details are thus discernible. These were completed, as usual, by the farmers themselves. Thirdly came the *Supplementary 4th June Return: Small Fruit*, giving details on small-fruit types, vegetables, flowers, crops being grown under glass, and stocks of hay and straw. Fourthly, another Supplementary 4th June Return was prepared, this time giving more details on labour (regular and part-time, casual etc); on the motive power on the holding (tractors and stationary engines, with engine manufacturers' type and horsepower); rent (amount payable and whether the holding was part-owned and part-rented); and the length of occupation (in years) including parts occupied for different lengths of time.

Finally, maps were also used to plot the boundaries and fields of each holding. These constitute either the Ordnance Survey 1:2500 sheets reduced to half size at approximately 1:5000, or the 1:10560 sheets. Colour-wash over the whole farm area, or colouring of farm boundaries with the farm code reference in black ink, will be found.

This enormous amount of information covered all holdings of 5 acres or more, and 99 per cent of all agricultural land. An equivalent but independent survey was mounted in Scotland at the same time, and the Scottish Record Office in Edinburgh holds farm-boundary maps and records of the Scottish Agricultural Executive Committees. In its detail and coverage the National Farm Survey has no precise equal in Britain. It is more comprehensive in its spatial coverage than the *tithe surveys, though less so than the Lloyd George 'Domesday' of 1910, since the latter covered all hereditaments, urban and rural, irrespective of size. But its quality of information is far superior. Its use has been very limited to date, although the local authority planning departments who were charged with publishing Development Plans under the 1947 Town and Country Planning Act did make some use of it at that time.

Most importantly however, local studies of the earlier 20th century now have two incomparable benchmarks, both nationally and centrally organized and therefore relatively uniform, against which to measure local change.

The 20th-century local government system has also bequeathed a variety of records for the local and family historian, based primarily around the triad of poor relief, *public health, and *education. With the latter becoming a *county council or county *borough responsibility rather than one for individual school boards after the Education Act of 1902, and poor relief in 1929, many types of record are available. The central records of the correspondence of the Boards of *Guardians with the centralized *Poor Law Commission, Poor Law Board, and Local Government Board, prior to their abolition in 1929, were mostly destroyed in the Second World War, but some do remain at the PRO (MH 68). Series MH 48 and MH 52 contain correspondence from *c.*1900 to 1960 on matters of poor law, hospitals, and public health. Hospital management committees, regional hospital boards, and the governors of teaching hospitals have their correspondence with the Ministry of Health preserved since 1948, and local National Health Service records (including those of voluntary and poor law hospitals predating 1948) and hospital records are among the public records which may be held by recognized local repositories. Many local record offices are now very active in securing the transfer of such material, and this awaits full analysis by local and family historians. There also exist such potentially useful materials as lists of paid union officials (1837–1921) or plans of poor law unions. The work of the Medical Officers of Health can be profitably used in local studies: annual reports to local authorities give statistics and opinions on the environmental conditions at regular intervals. Public works committees and Distress Committees also occur sporadically across different local authorities, and the use of local charity records in early 20th-century urban areas is now being explored, although post-1929 social welfare / social services material is, as yet, under-utilized.

The fledgeling planning system has left various records for the 20th century, but in the absence of binding central legislation before 1947, these were sporadically distributed across different localities. Strategic planning before 1947 produced various *ad hoc* schemes of land use zoning and permitted uses. Development Plans were prepared after 1947, and many social and topographical surveys underpinned them which could be of great use for local studies. The use of building plans could shed a great deal of light on 20th-century development, but as yet few thematic studies on this vital data source for urban history have been made. The slum-clearance policies of the 1930s, sweeping away many of the older streets, have also left many potentially useful records, which chart the progress of bodies such as the Ecclesiastical Commissioners or the Duchy of *Cornwall in their building of flats and maisonettes by taking advantage of the grants available under the 1923–4 Housing Act. Useful too are the various deliberations of the many Finance, General Purposes, and Planning Committees of the 1920s and 1930s which can now be consulted locally. What does the modern historian make, for example, of the *en masse* approval of 1,500 houses in one set of Bexley Urban District Council minutes in September 1930?

Education, leaving more sources than any other local authority function at this time, is especially rich in local source material. A huge amount of information is stored at the PRO in Class ED, dealing with educational matters down to the level of individual schools, such as the 'Premises Survey' files of 1920–42 (ED 99) which included lists of schools with poor buildings. Individual secondary schools' files are to be found in ED 35, whilst their parent Local Education Authorities—the county and county borough councils—each have a file dating from 1902 through to reorganization of the archive after the 1944 Education Act (ED 53). Much of the education material is arranged at the PRO by LEA and is thus relatively easily accessible, although that for Wales is disappointing, owing to floods in Cardiff in 1960 that destroyed many of the records of the Welsh Department which had been established in 1907.

Education records kept at the local level mostly relate to the activities of the county and county borough education committees and their sub-committees after 1902, and records generated by individual schools are likely to be listed and accessible in the appropriate repository. Many records of great interest are still located at the relevant school itself where the fascinating school log books, sometimes accompanied by admission registers, frequently still act as a valuable educational resource, although the transfer of records is now actively encouraged by record offices, since the records are at risk from vandalism or even from losses due to 'loans' to local historians! The log books are well known as sources of information on the local society and economy as well as the life of the school. The admission registers record dates of children entering and leaving the school, with first destinations of employment sometimes given, such as farm work or domestic service. Any school closure should result in the deposition of such records at the archive.

Many records pertaining to secondary schools, whether under the aegis of the local authority or outside it as a privately funded school, still remain with the school itself. Some, as with Lancing College, Sussex—one of the Woodard group—have their own archivist, in the same way that chartered *livery companies such as the Mercers' Company, or hospitals such as the Royal London, also have their own archivists. Local authority records should also include those of the clerk's department, which give a good idea of local policies and the range of services provided by the authority: fire services, waterworks, gas and electricity companies, and police personnel departments (now much used by family historians), together with other miscellaneous police records which are useful for social history. Municipal trading records will also be available for many larger urban areas. Among a large body of other potentially useful material in local record offices, the family and local historian will find indexes of Second World War incidents which can be used to build up a picture of wartime living conditions, alongside local authority civil defence documents, and a plethora of souvenirs in local museums, etc.

The 20th-century central government system has also resulted in a large amount of material suitable for local studies, other than those discussed in more detail above. The Home Office records at the PRO contain many general topics listed under HO 45, where a list is arranged on a subject basis. Material to be found includes that relating to local government issues: *markets and fairs, justice, law and order, and prostitution, for example. The records of the Ministry of Home Security during the Second World War are also included under HO 207, and HO 199 contains reports on bomb damage. The records of the Board of Agriculture (est. 1889 and a Ministry from 1919) have been referred to above, but notice should also be taken of information on land *drainage and *water supply for each local authority, with maps and plans (MAF 77 and 49 respectively); local cattle markets (MAF 91); activities of local committees of the 1930's Wheat Commission (MAF 61); and the Women's Land Army (MAF 59). The Development Commission, established in 1909, has records which are open well into the post-war period (D4) and include records of the county Rural Community Councils and their various activities in promoting local rural welfare, economically through agriculture and rural industries at first, and then socially and culturally too.

The Forestry Commission was established in 1919, and Crown Woodland was transferred to its administration in 1924 as the Commissioners of Woods and Forests became the Commissioners of Crown Lands (becoming in 1956 the Crown Estate Commissioners). Files on each forest from the mid-19th century exist (F 313) and 'Forest Histories' are available from 1951, showing how the wood has been used. Woodland censuses were made in 1924, 1938, and 1942.

The records of the Ministry of Works (est. 1940; PRO WORK) can be useful in the study of individual properties, such as the public buildings belonging to the period of inter-war expansion, or royal palaces, statues, and memorials, ancient monuments, royal ordnance factories, and including maps and plans of the royal *dockyards. Local business history can be aided by reference to files on public and private companies in the Board of Trade papers at the PRO. Class BT 31 at Kew has companies listed chronologically with an index. *Bankruptcies and registrations can be traced through such papers, and firms operating in government 'Special Areas' or 'Development Areas' will have information of local interest. Nationalized companies after 1945 have records, such as those relating to the National Coal Board, which can shed light on individual collieries, although many such records have been transferred to the appropriate local record offices, as have those of former private iron and steel companies taken over as the British Steel Corporation. Private companies still in existence can be traced through files kept at Companies House, Cardiff.

Local transport history can be similarly helped by reference to central government records. The Ministry of Transport was established in 1919, and its own records (MT), together with those of the Board of Trade, contain vast amounts of locally significant material for almost every town and railway company in the country. The reports of the railway inspectorate on accidents up to 1930 are available (MT 29), as is information on inland waterways (MT 52), and on road transport after its nationalization into the British Transport Commission in 1947 (AN 68). The latter body assembled a great amount of information relating to inland transport and such matters as dock, harbour, river, and steamship companies (RAIL). Few *railway or *canal company records remained in local record offices after 1947.

The traumas ushered in during 1914 have all too frequently proved to be seen as appropriate end-points for local studies. And given the well-known antipathy of influential local historians such as W. G. *Hoskins to most things modern, the techniques and empirical information for mounting local studies after 1914 were simply not available. But 'Time's eternal motion' must inexorably bring the 20th century into the ambit of family and local historians, and the richness and variety of the records awaiting them will repay huge dividends.

See S. Caunce, *Oral History and the Local Historian* (1994), C. Cook and D. Waller, *The Longman Guide to Sources in Contemporary British History*, i (*Organisations and Societies*) and ii (*Individuals*) (1994), R. Oliver, *Ordnance Survey Maps: A Concise Guide for Historians* (1993), P. Riden, *Record Sources for Local History* (1987), and B. Short, *The Geography of England and Wales in 1910: An Evaluation of Lloyd George's 'Domesday' of Landownership* (Historical Geography Research Series 22, 1989).

BRIAN M. SHORT

Tyburn. The gallows, known as 'Tyburn tree', was the place of public execution in London until 1783. The site is now occupied by Marble Arch. The procession from Newgate Prison to Tyburn was staged as a public spectacle which attracted large crowds that came to hear the last confession of the condemned and to witness the hanging.

typhoid. An infectious disease, once thought to be a variety of *typhus, whose main characteristic is catarrhal inflammation of the intestines. See PUBLIC HEALTH.

typhus. A contagious fever transmitted to humans by body lice or rat fleas, and characterized by rose-coloured spots, prostration, and delirium. Outbreaks affected the urban poor and armies involved in siege warfare.

U

Ulster. The most northerly of the four provinces of Ireland (Ulster, Connacht, Leinster, and Munster). The ancient kingdom of Ulster became a medieval earldom. Its social and economic structure was transformed during the 17th century by the English government's policy of encouraging *plantations, whereby Scottish and English settlers acquired land, principally in Ulster. These settlers were mostly *Protestants, especially *Presbyterians from Lowland Scotland, whereas the prior inhabitants of Ulster were mostly *Roman Catholic. See P. Robinson, *The Plantation of Ulster* (1994). This sectarian division deepened at the time of the *Glorious Revolution of 1688. The armed forces of the new Protestant king William of Orange defeated the supporters of the deposed Catholic king James II at the Battle of the Boyne (1690), a victory still commemorated annually by the 'Orange Order', which was founded in 1795 at a time when the issue of *Catholic Emancipation was being argued.

In 1801 the whole of Ireland was united with Great Britain to form the *United Kingdom. During the 19th century Belfast grew rapidly to become Ireland's second city, its economy based on the *linen industry and the building of *ships. The sectarian divide between Protestants and Catholics was, and is, at its sharpest in industrial Belfast. The question of 'Home Rule for Ireland' was complicated by the refusal of the Protestant majority in Ulster to become part of an independent Ireland and by their insistence on retaining the Union with the rest of Great Britain. The Ulster Unionists were supported by the British *Conservatives, who became known as the Conservative and Unionist Party. When the Republic of Ireland became independent in 1922, six of the nine counties of Ulster did not join the new country, but formed the Northern Ireland part of Great Britain: these counties are Antrim, Armagh, Down, Fermanagh, Londonderry, and Tyrone.

ultimus haeres. Under Scottish law, if a person died without a known heir, the Crown was deemed the *ultimus haeres* (last heir). The records are kept in the *Scottish Record Office. Those dating before 1834 relate to the granting of *ultimus haeres* to petitioners. After 1834 fuller records are kept under E 851–870. See Cecil Sinclair, *Tracing Your Scottish Ancestors: A Guide to Ancestry Research in the Scottish Record Office* (1990).

uncle. In the early modern period the term had a wider meaning than brother of one's father or mother. It included more distant relatives and was used for an older man.

underdrainage. Although much land had been drained before the 19th century, the heavy clays could not be effectively drained until the invention of machine-made tiles *c.*1840 made the work cheaper and more efficient. See A. D. M. Phillips, *The Underdraining of Farmland in England during the Nineteenth Century* (1989).

Unitarians. A *Nonconformist denomination that denies the Holy Trinity and accepts the humanity of Christ. During the second decade of the 18th century *Presbyterian and *Independent congregations split on the issue of the Trinity. In some places the Unitarian majority retained possession of the chapel, elsewhere they left to erect new meeting houses. The old name Presbyterian was retained by both groups. Unitarianism became legal only in 1813 with the passing of the Trinity Act. See Graham and Judy Hague, *The Unitarian Heritage: An Architectural Survey of Chapels and Churches in the Unitarian Tradition in the British Isles* (1986), and the record publications of the Unitarian Historical Society.

United Kingdom. The United Kingdom of Great Britain and Ireland was formed in 1801. In 1922 southern Ireland became independent, since when the UK has consisted of England, Scotland, Wales, and Northern Ireland.

university archives. For the University of Oxford, see BODLEIAN LIBRARY. The University of Cambridge has a Department of Manuscripts and University Archives. The older colleges of these universities have their own archive collections, which are of interest to local historians of places where the colleges were landowners. Nuffield College, Oxford, and the University of Warwick have collections on *labour history. Some other universities have special collections, e.g. the University of Sheffield houses the 17th-century collection of Samuel Hartlib's papers. (See also the RURAL HISTORY CENTRE, University of Reading.) For addresses, details of access, etc., see Royal Commission on *Historical Manuscripts, *Record Repositories in Great Britain: A Geographical Directory* (9th edn., 1992).

up-and-down husbandry. See CONVERTIBLE HUSBANDRY.

urban archaeology. Much *rescue archaeology is concerned with urban sites because of the scale of redevelopment. Our knowledge of the topography and history of some major medieval cities, notably Norwich, York, Winchester, Southampton, London, and Dublin, has been deepened by the excavation programmes of the later 20th century; see, for example, C. Platt and R. Coleman Smith, *Excavations in Medieval Southampton*, 2 vols. (1975), and M. Biddle (ed.), *Winchester in the Early Middle Ages* (1976). These excavations have been accompanied by intensive archival research; see M. Biddle, 'The Study of Winchester: Archaeology and History in a British Town, 1961–1983', *Proceedings of the British Academy*, 69 (1983). Something of the street plans and buildings of many smaller medieval towns, e.g. Doncaster or Bawtry, has been recovered by a combination of archaeological and historical investigations. For a survey of a particular aspect of medieval urban history, based on excavation and archival research, see D. M. Palliser, 'The Topography of Monastic Houses in Yorkshire Towns' in Roberta Gilchrist and Harold Mytum (eds.), *Advances in Monastic Archaeology* (British Archaeological Reports, British Series 227, 1993).

Less excavation has been undertaken on post-medieval towns, but in compensation more standing structures and contemporary maps and plans survive. Post-medieval levels have often been destroyed by later building methods, including the 19th-century construction of *cellars. See David Crossley, *Post-Medieval Archaeology in Britain* (1990), ch. 2.

Urban District Councils. When county *borough councils were created in 1888, responsibility for the public health of towns with under 50,000 inhabitants remained with urban sanitary authorities. In 1894 these and other functions were taken over by elected urban district councils and their officers. UDCs were abolished under local government reorganization in 1974. Their minutes and other records have been deposited with local *record offices.

urban élites. Urban historians, particularly those of the medieval and early modern periods, have been concerned to identify the leading members of town society and to judge their political and socio-economic influence. Some corporations were difficult for newcomers to penetrate, but the industrial towns such as Birmingham and Sheffield were much more open. Historians have also examined the ways in which élites were linked through marriage, religion, and business connections by constructing detailed biographies: see, for instance, R. G. Wilson, *Gentlemen Merchants: The Merchant Community in Leeds, 1700–1830* (1971). They have also analysed the membership of governing bodies and have searched for evidence of clashes between élites and the governed. See P. Clark and P. Slack, *English Towns in Transition, 1500–1700* (1976), ch. 8.

Urban History. A journal published twice a year since 1992, the successor to *The Urban History Newsletter* and *The Urban History Yearbook*. It contains articles, reviews, bibliographies, conference reports, and historiographical and methodological surveys to provide an international overview of contemporary research.

urban housing. The earliest surviving town houses are the 12th-century stone buildings, notably two on Steep Hill, Lincoln, which had living accommodation on the first floor, with space at street level for a shop, workshop, or warehouse. Some had vaulted undercrofts. Such undercrofts remained popular in merchants' and craftsmen's houses later in the Middle Ages; Norwich has more than 60 dating from after c.1350. By then, the fashion for first-floor halls had long been replaced by halls on the ground floor, such as that which now forms the Bridewell Museum, Norwich. See Maurice Barley, *Houses and History* (1986), ch. 4, which notes that it is impossible to find a single town house whose ground-floor plan has not been altered at some time. For studies of single towns, see Vanessa Parker, *The Making of King's Lynn* (1971), and D. Lloyd, *Broad Street, Ludlow* (1979).

The houses of the prosperous townsmen fronted the principal streets or *market place and extended backwards along a *burgage plot. If the plots were sufficiently wide, the largest houses could be arranged around courtyards. Most plots were so narrow, however, that the plans of houses varied considerably. Narrow-fronted properties were usually entered by a passage which led under the front range of building and along one side of the plot to an open space at the rear. As in contemporary rural houses, the principal room was in the form of an *open hall. Smaller houses were arranged in terraces along the streets which had no burgage plots, sometimes filling in spaces such as market places and the edges of *churchyards. A group in Lady Row, Goodramgate, York, which were begun in 1316 and remain as the oldest *timber-framed houses in the city, provided simple accommodation consisting of a ground-floor room and a chamber above. They, and similar medieval terraces, have left no trace of heating arrangements. The houses of the very poor have long since gone.

The improved standards of housing that have been noted in the countryside during the 16th and 17th centuries were matched in the towns. (See GREAT REBUILDING.) The open hall, with its central fireplace and clay floor, disappeared as houses were reconstructed or entirely rebuilt. D. Portman, *Exeter Houses* (1966) showed how new features such as jettied upper floors and brick chimney stacks were added to old houses or incorporated in the new. *Brick was used increasingly in the framework of the house, especially in eastern parts of England, in order to reduce the risk of fire. A. D. Dyer, 'Urban Housing: A Documentary Study of Four Midland Towns, 1530–1700', *Post-Medieval Archaeology*, 15 (1981) used probate *inventories to study the use of rooms in houses in Birmingham, Coventry, Derby, and Worcester. The most detailed study of inventory material for this purpose is U. Priestley, P. J. Corfield, and H. Sutermeister, 'Rooms and Room-Use in Norwich Housing, 1580–1730', *Post-Medieval Archaeology*, 16 (1982), which shows how the city's housing stock was used increasingly intensively during this period, with subdivisions into smaller units and the acquisition of more floors. See also Michael Laithwaite, 'Totnes Houses, 1500–1800' in Peter Clark (ed.), *The Transformation of English Provincial Towns* (1984), and the survey of recent archaeological and historical investigations in David Crossley, *Post-Medieval Archaeology in Britain* (1990). As with the Middle Ages, there is little evidence of the houses of the poorest sections of the urban community.

After the *Restoration the prosperous members of towns and cities throughout the land built brick or stone houses to classical designs to match those of the new public buildings. See Peter Borsay, *The English Urban Renaissance: Culture and Society in the Provincial Town,*

1660–1770 (1989). (See also GEORGIAN ARCHITECTURE, and REGENCY.) The overall quality of a town's housing in this period is increasingly obvious from *topographical prints, and can be assessed from *hearth tax returns. See Sir John Summerson, *Georgian London* (1945), C. W. Chalklin, *The Provincial Towns of Georgian England: A Study of the Building Process, 1740–1820* (1974), and for an exemplary study of a provincial city, Maurice Beresford, *East End, West End: The Face of Leeds during Urbanisation, 1684–1842* (1988).

During the 19th century the middle classes left the old centres of towns for detached and semi-detached houses in the *suburbs. These houses were of many different styles and sizes and were normally rented. All the major cities had acquired middle-class suburbs by the 1830s and 1840s. Few detailed studies of such developments have been made: see F. M. L. Thompson (ed.), *The Rise of Suburbia* (1982), and David Cannadine, *Lords and Landlords: The Aristocracy and the Towns, 1774–1967* (1980). For two very different London suburbs, see F. M. L. Thompson, *Hampstead: Building a Borough, 1650–1964* (1974), and H. J. Dyos, *Victorian Suburb: A Study of the Growth of Camberwell* (1961). For the late Victorian and Edwardian period, see S. M. Gaskell, 'Housing the Lower Middle Class, 1870–1914' in Geoffrey Cossick (ed.), *The Lower Middle Class in Britain, 1870–1914* (1977).

In 19th-century cities the contrast between middle-class and working-class districts was marked, but the houses of working-class families varied considerably in standards of comfort and amenities. Until the coming of electric *trams working-class families lived close to the place of work. During the first half of the 19th century such families usually rented a two-storey dwelling that formed part of a terrace, consisting of two rooms, sometimes with a small pantry, or a cellar. Cheaper accommodation was available in some towns in single-room cellar dwellings, which were built below a cottage and reached by descending a flight of steps, and in other towns in *tenements. (See also BACK-TO-BACK HOUSING; BUILDING SOCIETIES; and FREEHOLD LAND SOCIETIES.) For general views, see S. D. Chapman (ed.), *History of Working-Class Housing: A Symposium* (1971), Anthony Sutcliffe (ed.), *Multi-Storey Living: The British Working Class Experience* (1974), Enid Gauldie, *Cruel Habitations: A History of Working-Class Housing, 1780–1918* (1974), and M. Daunton, *House and Home in the Victorian City: Working Class Housing, 1850–1914* (1983). For regional studies, see Lucy Caffyn, *Workers'*

Housing in West Yorkshire, 1750–1920 (1986), and J. G. Timmins, *Handloom Weavers' Cottages in Lancashire* (1977). For the 20th century, see COUNCIL HOUSING.

urban renaissance. A term coined by Peter Borsay, in *The English Urban Renaissance: Culture and Society in the Provincial Town, 1660–1770* (1989), to chart the rise of provincial urban society after the *Restoration, together with the great improvement of the built environment, and the provision of leisure and intellectual activities on an unprecedented scale. This activity was modest when compared with the urban achievements of the Italian Renaissance, but it brought about a significant improvement in many spheres. A new wave of prosperity financed the improvements, and town authorities began to see that pleasant surroundings and ample facilities drew in the local *gentry and fostered trade. Many gentry families began to build town houses in their local urban centre, as well as heading for the seasons at London and Bath. Their presence at certain times of the year was encouraged by *horse-racing weeks and annual musical and dramatic events, and by an all-round attempt to improve facilities.

Disastrous fires, such as those which destroyed large parts of Warwick (1694) and Blandford Forum (1731), allowed replanning and rebuilding in a classical style. Other towns built new squares and crescents on vacant sites at the edges of settlement. In other cases, old buildings were torn down to make way for urban spaces and more regular plans. The livestock markets which had long occupied the central streets were moved to the outskirts of towns. Traditional *vernacular architecture was abandoned in favour of symmetrical, classical façades, and *timber-framing was rejected for *brick or stone. Sometimes, as at Ludlow (Shropshire) or Totnes (Devon), earlier, timber-framed buildings were hidden behind new façades, but many townsmen preferred to build anew in the new materials. Stamford is an outstanding example of a fine medieval town which entered into an even greater period of prosperity in the 18th century, resulting in numerous Georgian houses and public buildings.

London, of course, was at the forefront of this development, with its many new squares and notable streets, and Dublin and Edinburgh were largely rebuilt in *Georgian style and refashioned into handsome cities. The movement was slower to gather pace in the provinces, but few towns remained unaffected by the second half of the 18th century. Provincial towns became social as well as commercial centres. Every self-respecting town of even modest pretension had to have its *assembly room, *theatre, concert hall, racecourse (with grandstand), *town hall, new *churches and *chapels, squares and crescents, walks and gardens. Operas, oratorios, and chamber music were performed at public venues, and great musical events, notably the Three Choirs Festival, attracted large audiences. Old centres, such as York or Norwich, moved with the times, new *spa centres tried to emulate Bath, and even industrial towns such as Birmingham or Sheffield followed the new fashions, if somewhat belatedly.

The new pride in the provincial urban environment is reflected in the commissioning of maps and prospects of the town by the local authorities, by the establishment of provincial *newspapers, local printers, and firms of publishers, by the wrting of local histories, and by the foundation of clubs and societies.

urban topography. British local history has its roots in the countryside, and it is significant that the historical study of *towns as physical places has often used rural metaphors without any sense of incongruity. In his pioneering chapter in *The Making of the English Landscape* (1955), W. G. *Hoskins wrote of 'the landscape of towns' rather than 'townscape', and he and others have also written of 'urban fieldwork'. A broader term popularized in the past 30 years is 'urban topography', an interdisciplinary study of the form, fabric, and layout of towns, drawing on documentary history, cartography, historical geography, town planning, architectural history, and archaeology. Geographers often refer to it as urban morphology, or more simply as urban form.

The study of urban topography in Britain can be traced back to the 16th century, when John *Stow adopted a ward-by-ward approach in his *Survey of London*, and was able to make use of the first large-scale plan of the city by Wyngaerde. Since the 19th century, topographical studies have been revolutionized by, among other things, accurate and large-scale town plans, and careful reconstructions from documentary evidence. H. E. Salter, for instance, was able to plot virtually every tenement in central Oxford and to trace its ownership, occupation, and use from the Middle Ages onwards, thus pioneering a technique which has since been used in other towns and which has been described as 'total plot history'. More recently, such empirical work has been enriched by M. R. G. Conzen, who brought to

Britain the German approach to urban morphology. His studies of the plans of Alnwick (1960) and Newcastle-upon-Tyne (1962), followed by his chapter on 'The Use of Town Plans in the Study of Urban History' in H. J. Dyos (ed.), *The Study of Urban History* (1968), have been very influential.

The traditional introductory method in studying the topography of a particular town is that generally called by geographers 'site and situation', in which a successful town is perceived as having to adapt to its environment, in terms of its hinterland, its precise site, and the way its shape developed. Clearly all of this needs to be taken into account. It is striking, for instance, how nearly all major towns before the *canal age were sited on or near the coast, or on a navigable river at a point where it could be forded or bridged; and M. W. Beresford's *New Towns of the Middle Ages* (1967) provides many object lessons of towns sponsored as commercial ventures but with very variable success, often depending on their siting. However, historical geographers stress the need for more depth and subtlety in analysing sites and plans; and both they and historians give much weight to the conscious human decisions behind town origins and development. Towns, after all, do not 'grow' at suitable locations, they are built.

The same increasingly sophisticated approach is now evident in discussions of town plans and layout. Many *Roman towns were regularly planned, and similar planning has been well known as a revived tradition in Italy since the Renaissance, with examples in Britain starting with new estates (London's Covent Garden in the 1630s is the first) and then being used for whole new towns (e.g. Whitehaven from as early as the 1680s). However, many older towns seem superficially unplanned, and a long tradition classifies most British towns between the Romans and the 18th century as 'organic', implying that they grew from villages, with little or no overall control. Beresford's *New Towns*, however, demonstrated that a substantial minority of towns in England and Wales between 1066 and 1350 were planned as a whole, though he and Hoskins believed that there were no post-Roman planned towns before the *Norman Conquest. Since then the identification of deliberately planned settlements has been pushed steadily backwards. Biddle and Hill showed that most of the *burhs or fortified towns laid out by Alfred and his successors were planned; Biddle and Vince later extended this category to include London; Haslam has suggested planned burhs in Mercia in the 8th century which may have inspired

Alfred; and the earliest clearly planned post-Roman town is now identified as Hamwic (Southampton) as early as about 700; see R. Hodges and B. Hobley (eds.), *The Rebirth of Towns in the West, AD 700–1050* (Council for British Archaeology Research Report, 68, 1988).

These were all towns planned as a whole: but the conclusion from much recent work is that the sharp distinction between 'organic' and 'planned' towns should be abandoned. Most towns of most periods are now seen as 'composite', with no single overall plan, but rather with a series of plan units, some consciously planned and some built piecemeal. The analysis of such towns depends on identifying such plan units and working out their chronology and relationships, a technique pioneered in Britain by Conzen. In the 1980s T. R. Slater developed techniques of metrological analysis by which *burgage plots are measured to discover regular patterns, which help to identify the units. It seems, from examples of towns in different English regions, that the statute *perch and the statute *acre were the usual units of measurement employed by the medieval surveyors.

Urban morphology of this type marks a great advance on most earlier work, which at best analysed the street plan and major features such as defences. It requires the identification of 'primary plot boundaries', and within them individual burgage plots, to relate ideal planning principles to the framework of existing features. However, it can only suggest solutions, since it requires working backwards from 19th- and 20th-century plans and measurements. Where the documentary sources are rich enough, Salter's total-plot-history method can be employed, as has been done with great success for Winchester. Where records are lacking, and for pre-documentary periods, archaeological excavation is the only method of proof, and numerous urban excavations since the 1960s have been able to establish the age and identity of street lines and house-plot boundaries. At York, for instance, some plots proved to have been first laid out c.900, and were still unchanged at the time of the first *Ordnance Survey plans.

Urban growth since the 17th century is relatively well documented, and is studied with a different range of techniques and sources from those employed for pre-industrial towns. H. J. Dyos, *Victorian Suburb: A Study of the Growth of Camberwell* (1961) initiated a series of documentary studies which have enabled us to see, often in great detail, how *suburbs were financed and laid out. More recently Maurice Beresford, in *East End, West End* (1988), has shown how a huge range of sources can be drawn on to illuminate the development of an entire city (Leeds). Nevertheless, the urban historian should not neglect the insights offered by geographers. Conzen's concepts of the burgage cycle, by which burgage plots are filled up and then redeveloped, and of 'fringe belts' of peripheral land utilization, have great importance for older towns as they have grown in more recent times.

The urban form is, however, only a part of urban topography, which is concerned also with the changing components of plans as the needs of townspeople, or their rulers, change over time. Of these, the most stable is usually the framework of streets and lanes, since it was generally difficult before the 20th century (given the multiplicity of landowners) to divert, close, or open up streets. Even after the Great Fire of London (1666), when Wren and others submitted designs for rebuilding on wholly new street-lines, the plans remained paper exercises because of the urgency of rebuilding. The origins and early land-use of urban streets can often be deduced from their names, though it must be remembered that many streets have been renamed. Likewise, though many old streets preserve their original alignments, many have been widened for traffic or public-health reasons over the past two centuries. Archaeologists, when excavating down to medieval levels, frequently find that they uncover only the rear portions of house foundations and backyards; the fronts often lie beneath pavements and roads.

Building-plot boundaries also tend to remain unchanged over long periods, for similar reasons. Burgage analysis shows that piecemeal amalgamation and subdivision of individual plots has always been common, but that the framework of blocks of plots is generally stable. The buildings on those plots, however, are replaced frequently. For one thing, variable pressures of space have demanded rebuilding: increased demand often called for more room, either on the street frontage (through rebuilding to incorporate *cellars, or extra storeys above) or in the *yards behind. For another, buildings were often replaced either through accident, fashion, or decay. Substantial medieval, 16th- and even 17th-century houses were predominantly *timber-framed (while '*cottages' or poorer houses were often of flimsier materials), and were often roofed in *thatch, and always vulnerable to fire. This building stock was largely replaced in *brick between the

17th and 19th centuries (or, in many Scottish towns, by stone), while more recent pressures (including slum clearance, war damage, and central redevelopment) have caused further replacements. Consequently, most towns of any age have built fabrics above ground which are predominantly post-1700. For instance, *Pevsner could note correctly that while 'in the popular view Chester is the English medieval city *par excellence*', in reality 'Chester is not a medieval, it is a Victorian city'. (N. Pevsner and E. Hubbard, *The Buildings of England: Cheshire*, 1971, 130–1).

This development has been linked to two others: the change of use of historic centres, and the growth of suburbs. Until the 17th and 18th centuries, rich townspeople tended to live in town centres, often literally 'above the shop' or workshop, and with warehousing behind; the poor lived either crammed into alleys and courts behind the main streets, or on the town fringes. However, successive improvements in private and public transport enabled the well-to-do to move out to new suburbs, and later to dormitory villages, leaving centres increasingly as business districts and (until slum clearance) as subdivided housing for the poor. As towns expanded in this way, town walls (where they existed) were often demolished as obstructions, and the old physical boundary between centre and suburbs was obliterated.

The greater part of urban areas has always been accounted for by public space (especially the streets and lanes), private housing, and business premises, but public buildings have also played a role out of proportion to their numbers. Until the 16th century the most numerous and prominent public buildings were churches, especially parish *churches. These were numerous in those large English towns which developed by the 12th century (London had over 100 at its peak, Norwich about 60, and Winchester 54), but towns founded after *c.*1200 usually had only one or two, while Scottish towns were all single-parish *burghs until the 1590s. In addition, there were *cathedrals in the episcopal centres, monastic houses, *nunneries, and friaries in many towns, and *chapels and *hospitals everywhere. Secular public buildings, however, were few in the Middle Ages: they were confined largely to *bridges, *town halls, and guildhalls, and especially town defences. Town walls dominate our image of the medieval town, but in general only the larger English towns had circuits of stone walls; many English and Scottish towns were without them, though they were more common in Wales and Ireland.

The 16th century saw the closure and demolition of many ecclesiastical buildings, and little that was dominant was put in their place; but since the 17th century there has been a great increase in the numbers of public buildings of all kinds (see URBAN RENAISSANCE). For one thing, religious pluralism and the growth of urban populations produced a huge rise in the numbers of churches and chapels, reaching a peak in the 19th century. For another, the increase of organized leisure activities resulted in many new buildings and structures, such as *assembly rooms, *theatres, racecourses, *parks, and promenades, followed by *museums, art galleries, *cinemas, and sports centres. And finally, overlapping with this, the development of *local government and public services resulted in town halls, court rooms, *prisons, *market halls, schools, *libraries, waterworks, and so on: in industrial town centres, a 19th-century town hall is often still the dominant accent. See Michael Aston and James Bond, *The Landscape of Towns* (1976), T. R. Slater, 'The Analysis of Burgage Patterns in Medieval Towns', *Area*, 13 (1981), Dietrich Denecke and Gareth Shaw, eds, *Urban Historical Geography: Recent Progress in Britain and Germany* (1988), and T. R. Slater, ed., *The Built Form of Western Cities: Essays for M. R. G. Conzen* (1990). DAVID M. PALLISER

vaccary. A place for rearing *cattle in hilly or moorland districts. In the medieval *manor of Wakefield, for instance, farms with 24–30 acres of grazing land for upwards of 40 cattle were created high on the Pennines to rear *oxen suitable as draught beasts. Vaccaries can sometimes be identified by place-names ending in Old Danish *booth* or *Old English *stall*. Many of the Peak District farms in Edale, for example, incorporate *booth* in their names.

vaccination against *smallpox was introduced by Edward Jenner (1749–1823), a physician from Berkeley (Gloucestershire). Previous attempts to combat the disease had been by *inoculation. In 1775 Jenner began to examine the traditional belief that cowpox offered protection against smallpox, but the experiment that proved the worth of vaccination (injecting a mild form of smallpox into humans) was not carried out until 1796. After initial hostility, the method was quickly adopted both in Britain and abroad. Smallpox was eradicated throughout the world in 1977. See J. R. Smith, *The Speckled Monster: Smallpox in England, 1670–1970* (1987).

vagabond. The Elizabethan *Poor Law Acts of 1597–1601 dealt harshly with sturdy *beggars, rogues, and vagabonds, whose numbers were greatly exaggerated by the government and commentators. Most vagrants were single men, who travelled alone or in twos, rather than in the gangs that worried the writers of pamphlets. After the *Restoration their numbers fell and they ceased to be a matter of national concern.

Valor Ecclesiasticus. An Act of 1535 impropriated the 'first fruits' and imposed an annual tax of one-tenth of the net income of all ecclesiastical *benefices. As a result, a detailed and exact valuation of church wealth was made. This has been published in six volumes as J. Caley and J. Hunter (eds.), *Valor Ecclesiasticus* (Record Commission, 1810–34). The survey gives details of the income of all parish *churches, together with many *chapels, *guilds, and *chantry chapels. The full report is missing for some counties, but summaries of incomes survive. The valuation is a major

source for the study of church wealth on the eve of the *Reformation.

Valuation Office. The Finance Act (1910) proposed a tax on land values. Although this was never implemented, the Board of Inland Revenue was required to ascertain the site value of all land in England and Wales. The valuation survey that was carried out between 1910 and 1915 describes and assesses the value of land and buildings in both an urban and a rural context. Information on each unit of property was recorded in Valuation Office Field Books, which are now housed in the *Public Record Office under IR 58, and in the accompanying forms of return which were filled in by owners. The properties referred to in the Field Books can be identified from accompanying *Ordnance Survey sheets. Parish indexes are available in the Map Room at the Public Record Office, where a detailed finding sheet is available. The survey is a major source for the study of property throughout England and Wales just before the First World War. See Brian Short, *The Geography of England and Wales in 1910: An Evaluation of Lloyd George's 'Domesday' of Landownership* (1989), Brian Short, *The Lloyd George Finance Act Material* (Historical Association, Short Guides to Records, no. 36, 1994), and for a parish study, Charles Rawding and Brian Short, 'Binbrook in 1910: The Use of the Finance (1909–10) Act Records', *Lincolnshire History and Archaeology*, 28 (1993). See also TWENTIETH CENTURY, THE.

vassal. Under the *feudal system, a person who held land of a lord in return for sworn homage.

Vatican records. The medieval papacy received a constant stream of letters petitioning for privileges, confirming appointments, and dealing with disputes. The Vatican houses a mass of documentation of an administrative and legal nature that is of use to local historians who are concerned with the Middle Ages; e.g., between 1153 and 1261 the papal curia wrote 497 letters to people in Ireland. See A. Theiner-Vetera, *Monumenta Hibernorum et Scotorum* (1864), for the period 1201–1547, and M. P. Sheehy, *Pontificia Hibernica: Medieval Papal*

Chancery Documents Concerning Ireland, 640–1261, 2 vols. (1962). For Scotland, see *Calendar of Scottish Supplications to Rome, 1418–47* (4 vols., 1934–83), and I. B. Cowan, 'The Vatican Archives: A Report on Pre-Reformation Material', *Scottish Historical Review*, 48 (1969). See also the *Public Record Office *Calendar of Papal Registers Relating to Great Britain and Ireland* and the *Calendar of Petitions to the Pope*.

vellum. A fine type of parchment made from the skin of young calves and kids.

verderer. The medieval official who administered the *vert and venison of a *forest. Each forest had four verderers, who were elected by the *freeholders who had rights in the forest. The Verderers' Court of the Forest of Dean still meets to settle disputes; its records date from the 17th century and are kept at the *Public Record Office under F 16.

vernacular architecture. The term 'vernacular architecture' has been used by architects, historians, and archaeologists since at least 1839 to describe the minor buildings of town and countryside, but it is only in the second half of the 20th century that the term has been widely employed to define an area of interest that has attracted much scholarly and amateur study. The Vernacular Architecture Group was founded in 1954 to bring together the widely scattered interests of the architectural historians of the Royal Commission on *Historical Monuments, archaeologists, local and regional historians, and museum curators. Since 1970 the group has published an annual journal, *Vernacular Architecture*. Amateur interest has been catered for by University Extramural Departments and the Workers' Educational Association, and by local history societies. Public interest in old buildings has been strengthened by the conservation movement.

Scholarly interest in minor buildings was awakened in the late 19th century as part of a wider interest in folk-life studies. The first classic account was S. O. *Addy, *The Evolution of the English House* (1898, revised edn. 1933). Addy was a folklorist and local historian who was interested in combining visual and documentary evidence in interpreting the past. The next work, by the architect and amateur historian C. F. Innocent, *The Development of English Building Construction* (1916, new edn. 1971), was mainly concerned with the same parts of north Derbyshire and south Yorkshire that had provided so many of Addy's examples. See also Louis Ambler, *Old Halls and Manor Houses of Yorkshire* (1913).

Interest in the rural houses of ordinary farmers and craftsmen has been a major concern of scholars working in Wales, starting with I. C. Peate, *The Welsh House* (1940), and continuing with Sir Cyril Fox and Lord Raglan, *Monmouthshire Houses*, 3 vols. (1951–4), and Peter Smith, *Houses of the Welsh Countryside* (1975, 2nd edn. 1988). A thorough survey of nearly all the old houses of Breconshire by Stanley Jones and John Smith was published as 'The Houses of Breconshire', parts 1 to 5, in issues of *Brycheiniog* from 1963 onwards. The Royal Commission on the Ancient and Historical Monuments of Wales has published *Glamorgan Farmhouses and Cottages: Glamorgan Inventory*, iv, pt 2 (1988).

The publication of W. G. *Hoskins, 'The Rebuilding of Rural England, 1570–1640' in *Past and Present*, 4 (1953) came just before the founding of the Vernacular Architecture Group. Hoskins's concept of a *Great Rebuilding was enormously influential, though his ideas have subsequently been refined, both by the discovery that *medieval peasant housing was more substantial than had been thought, and by the realization that in parts of the country rebuilding occurred at much later periods, e.g. 1670–1720 in the four northern counties of England, and even later in Scotland, Ireland, and much of Wales. Maurice Barley, *The English Farmhouse and Cottage* (1961) was the first of the new general surveys to combine documentary evidence, especially probate *inventories and manorial *surveys, with the study of surviving structures. R. B. Wood-Jones, *Traditional Domestic Architecture of the Banbury Region* (1963) remained for over 20 years the most comprehensive regional study published in England. Eric Mercer, *English Vernacular Houses* (1975) provided a series of essays which summarized current knowledge and formed the basis for future research.

Since then, a number of fine local and regional studies have been published. The RCHM has been responsible for Sarah Pearson, *Rural Houses of the Lancashire Pennines, 1560–1760* (1985), Colum Giles, *Rural Houses of West Yorkshire, 1400–1830* (1986), and D. W. Black, R. M. Butler, I. H. Goodall, and I. R. Pattison, *Houses of the North York Moors* (1987). Barry Harrison and Barbara Hutton, *Vernacular Houses in North Yorkshire and Cleveland* (1984) is a similar comprehensive survey. N. W. Alcock, *People at Home: Living in a Warwickshire Village, 1500–1800* (1993) integrates the information provided by over 400 probate inventories and the records of the Stoneleigh Abbey estate with some 50 *timber-framed buildings in the most detailed local study that has ever been undertaken.

The subject now has an extensive technical literature, not only in *Vernacular Architecture* but in other academic journals, chiefly *The Archaeological Journal*, *Folk Life*, *Medieval Archaeology*, and *Post-Medieval Archaeology*. General views are provided by R. W. Brunskill, *Traditional Buildings of Britain: An Introduction to Vernacular Architecture* (2nd edn., 1994), and the same author's technical introduction, *Illustrated Handbook of Vernacular Architecture* (1987), which contains a useful bibliography. See also M. W. Barley, *Houses and History* (1986), which combines the study of both 'polite' and 'vernacular' architecture, and Anthony Quiney's two books, *House and Home: A History of the Smaller English House* (1986) and *The Traditional Buildings of England* (1990). For urban houses see Vanessa Parker, *The Making of King's Lynn* (1971), the series of papers on houses in Ludlow published by the Ludlow Research Group, and the RCHM's volume *Beverley: An Archaeological and Architectural Study* (1982). For Scotland, see A. Fenton and B. Walker, *The Rural Architecture of Scotland* (1981), and R. S. Morton, *Traditional Farm Architecture in Scotland* (1976); for Ireland, Alan Gailey, *Rural Houses of the North of Ireland* (1984).

The concept of a 'vernacular architecture' distinct from the building traditions of 'polite' architecture has been criticized for being too exclusive, for it is clear that many elements of local traditions were derived from the examples of great houses in the vicinity. Moreover, most *manor houses and *gentry halls had some features that were purely local in character. The contrast between 'polite' and 'vernacular' is similar to that in speech. The division is not a sharp one, and the two styles should be seen as overlapping and as influencing each other. With this caveat in mind, 'vernacular architecture' seems to be an appropriate shorthand term for the simple, unpretentious houses, farm outbuildings, workshops, etc. of the past. The term is best thought of as a broad one that can include small *churches and *chapels and some gentry halls as well as the buildings of the peasantry, despite some attempts to define the subject narrowly.

One of the most striking characteristics of vernacular architecture is the use of local building materials. Before the age of *canals and *railways it was expensive to transport *building stones and *bricks over long distances, unless a navigable river or the sea provided a direct link. Britain (especially England) is so varied geologically that even over very short distances the traveller moves from one building region to the next. Where no adequate stone was available and the soils were unsuitable for making bricks, builders had to make do with mud, straw, *flints, and cobbles. These humble materials continued in use for cottages, outbuildings, and field walls long after the *yeomen and *husbandmen had turned to imported stone or brick. See Alec Clifton-Taylor, *The Pattern of English Building* (1972). The picturesque appearance of much vernacular building is enhanced by the choice of local roofing materials.

A basic distinction in vernacular architecture divides houses built of mass construction (with walls of stone, flint, cobble, brick, and earth) from those which are timber-framed. Even where stone was locally abundant, timber was usually preferred in the Middle Ages. The timber frame of an earlier house is often masked by the walls and roof of later rebuilding. A great deal of the energy that has gone into the study of vernacular architecture has been devoted to the study of carpentry techniques and to establishing the distribution of different types. (See CRUCKS.) *Dendrochronology is now providing accurate dating for timbers. The timber-frame tradition came to an end in the 17th century in most parts of England, but continued in Scotland for another 100 years. During the same period, thatch was replaced in regions where tiles or stone flags could be manufactured economically.

The study of vernacular architecture is concerned as much with plans as with elevations. Plans of the foundations of excavated houses in *deserted medieval villages have been highly informative (though their true meaning has been much debated) in the understanding of the evolution of house types. The use of local materials disguises the fact that small houses were built to a number of standard plans, with only minor variations or additions. For example, the standard yeoman's house throughout much of England was based on three units— one for cooking, one for living in, and one for sleeping—originally open to the rafters, but then chambered over, with a lobby entrance leading on to a chimney stack dividing two of the rooms. Smoke-blackened timbers often reveal how a house has had a chimney and chambers inserted during the Great Rebuilding. (See OPEN HALL; AISLED HALL; LONGHOUSE; and LAITHE HOUSES.)

Regional variety is also expressed in the use of ornamentation, e.g. the group of houses at the top of the vernacular scale in the Halifax district which have porches framed by classical columns and lit by *rose windows. Town houses have, of necessity, different plans from those in the countryside. But most distinctions between houses of a similar period are explained by the contrasting wealth and social status of the original owner. The local gentry and yeomen were not only the first to adopt new styles and to abandon the old, but their sturdier buildings have survived from much earlier periods. A fruitful concept is that of the 'vernacular threshold', which allows for the survival of medieval buildings from the top end of the social scale but not for the houses of ordinary farmers and labourers, and which points to the numerous examples of 16th- to 18th-century farmhouses, but the rarity of *cottages before *c*.1800. This framework must not be accepted too rigidly, however, for in western England a number of 16th- and 17th-century timber-framed cottages have now been recognized. A complicating factor is that many houses which started off as substantial yeoman homes may have been divided into cottages two or three centuries later (and sometimes restored to their original function in the late 20th century). The history of a building can be unravelled only by combining the techniques of the social historian with those of vernacular architecture.

verso. The left-hand page of an open book, the opposite of *recto. In folio numbering, the reader is guided by the use of the superscript 'v'.

vert and venison. In a *forest, vert referred to the trees and shrubs which bore green leaves and thus provided food and shelter for livestock; venison referred originally to all livestock, not just deer.

vestry. A room attached to the *chancel of a church which is used for the keeping of vestments, etc. The vestry is now usually reserved for the minister, but it was originally the room where parish meetings were held. Membership of the vestry comprised the minister, churchwardens, and leading parishioners, who were either co-opted (under a 'close' or 'select' vestry system) or elected ('open vestry'). In the 16th and 17th centuries the vestry assumed many of the old functions of the manor *court, e.g. appointing the *constable, as well as taking on new responsibilities for the *poor and the *highways. The vestry lost these responsibilities during the 19th century, and in 1894 the civil functions of parishes were transferred to parish councils and parish meetings.

vicar. Originally, the minister who was appointed by an absentee *rector, e.g. a *monastery or *college. The vicar received the small *tithes, whereas a resident rector received all the tithes. Parishes which today are served by a vicar must have paid their tithes to a religious institution such as a monastery in the Middle Ages.

vicars-choral. The body of choristers in a cathedral. The 36 vicars-choral at York were self-governing from 1252 and incorporated as a *college in 1421. At Wells the street of identical houses, which provided domestic accommodation, a common hall, and a library, all of which were built upon the founding of the College of the Vicars-Choral in 1348, survives intact on the north side of the Cathedral.

vicinage, common of. Rights on *commons claimed by owners of adjacent properties.

Victoria County History, The. The *Victoria History of the Counties of England* was founded in 1899 as a private enterprise by Laurence Gomme and Arthur Doubleday, with a subsidy of £20,000 and a list of subscribers, the first of whom was Queen Victoria. A century later, new volumes are still 'Inscribed to the memory of her late majesty Queen Victoria who graciously gave the title to and accepted the dedication of this history'. At the launch, it was confidently predicted that a series of 160 volumes would be completed in six years and would produce a profit of £250,000. Over 200 volumes have so far been published, but no one will now predict when and if the series will be completed and all talk of profitability has been abandoned.

The *VCH*, as the series is popularly known, was designed to be 'a scholarly and comprehensive encyclopaedia of English local history in all periods, a repository of essential information and the starting point for further research'. After a promising start, the enterprise faltered after 1910 and had to be rescued in 1933, when it was transferred to the *Institute of Historical Research of the University of London, where it is still based. The present method of financing, in partnership with the respective local authorities, began in 1948. The county councils who enter such a partnership employ full-time professional historians to do the research, writing, and editing, while the Institute of Historical Research provides supervision and technical expertise, guarantees the quality of the work, and looks after printing and publication. The cost of printing is met out of revenue from sales.

The series is divided into sets for each of the historic counties and, within each county set, into general and topographical volumes. The general volumes deal with natural history, *prehistory, the *Roman and *Anglo-Saxon periods, the *Domesday Book, political and administrative history, ecclesiastical history and religious houses, social and economic history, *forests, endowed schools, and *sport. The topographical volumes are arranged by *hundred or *wapentake, subdivided into *parishes and *townships, or by *towns. The history of each township is traced by a general description, followed by sections on *manors and other estates, economic history, *local government, church, *Nonconformity, *education, and charities for the poor. The *Handbook for Editors and Authors* ensures that texts are comparable throughout the country. Readers of the *VCH* are assumed to be familiar with the main outlines of English history. The volumes are planned not only as general surveys but as starting-points for further research; they therefore include numerous footnotes quoting sources of information.

The *VCH* is recognized as a storehouse of knowledge, but it has been much criticized for its inflexibility and for an old-fashioned approach. The scheme that was conceived at the beginning of the enterprise is not well suited to take account of new approaches. Some of the general volumes which were written at the beginning of the 20th century are now woefully out of date and limited in scope because they were written long before the collection of copious archives in county *record offices. The sections on *agricultural history, for example, were mostly written before serious attention was paid to the subject. Volume iv of the Shropshire *VCH*, published in 1989, is a world apart in its treatment of the subject from accounts written for other counties before the First World War. These criticisms have been partly met by the volumes that deal with the histories of towns (where the format can be changed more readily), by an increased attention to *vernacular architecture, and by the encouragement given to some county staff, e.g. in Shropshire, to write popular but scholarly works based on their researches for the topographical volumes. The original plan was for each parish history to have 800–900 words: the average length is now 10,000 words. Less emphasis is now placed on churches, country houses, and the *coats of arms of the *nobility and *gentry, and more attention is paid to the modern period. The number and character of illustrations and map and line drawings have

changed, for the improved quality of photographs has meant that less reliance has had to be placed on impressionistic drawings.

Only a few counties have a complete set of histories, and in Northumberland, Westmorland, and the West Riding of Yorkshire the project never got started. Work is continuing in about a dozen counties. Topographical volumes have formed most of the output of the *VCH* in more recent years, amounting to 74 of the 98 volumes published between 1950 and 1992. The compilation of the topographical volumes, so as to provide each town and parish with a comprehensive systematic account of its landscape, settlement, buildings, landownership, agriculture, trade and industry, local government, church and chapel, schools, and endowed charities, is the chief priority for the *VCH*. The principal aim remains the production of a coherent series, which serves as a comprehensive work of reference with a systematic approach and arrangement. The *VCH* is of particular use in those parts of the country which have no adequate county history in the *antiquarian tradition. The topographical volumes do the basic spadework, e.g. on manorial descents, that is necessary for the furtherance of much local history.

See the *General Introduction* to the *VCH* (1970) for a fuller account, and its *Supplement, 1970–1990* (1990).

Victorian cities. The 19th century witnessed a huge rise in *population and the phenomenal growth not only of London, but of industrial cities such as Belfast, Birmingham, Glasgow, Leeds, Liverpool, Manchester, and Sheffield, and many other towns in northern and midland England. The problems of *urban housing and *public health were enormous, but these cities also provided new recreational and intellectual opportunities as civic pride was expressed in *town and city halls, *theatres, concert halls, *museums and art galleries, *parks and squares, and civic universities. Victorian cities were also the scene of great political struggles. See Asa Briggs, *Victorian Cities* (1963), H. J. Dyos and M. Wolff (eds.), *The Victorian City: Images and Realities*, 2 vols. (1973), Peter Sanders, *English Industrial Cities of the Nineteenth Century* (1984), and for a comprehensive study of one large city, Clyde Binfield et al., *The History of the City of Sheffield, 1843–1993*, 3 vols. (1993).

Vikings. Scandinavian invaders, settlers, and traders who spread throughout northern Europe between the 8th and the 11th centuries. They came to Britain as two groups: the Norwegians, who settled in the Orkney and Shetland Islands, the Hebrides and west Scotland, north-west England, the Isle of Man, and the eastern coast of Ireland; and the Danes, who settled in what became the *Danelaw in north-eastern and eastern England.

The first settlers were peaceful farmers in the Orkney and Shetland Islands, where numerous archaeological monuments and sites survive. They were followed from the late 8th century onwards by bands of warriors looking for plunder. The development of speedy longships made the Vikings exceptionally mobile and took them as far away as Russia, where they sailed the length of the Dnieper and Volga, and across the Atlantic to Greenland and America. The first raids on England, Scotland, Ireland, and France came in the last decade of the 8th century, beginning with the sack of the *monastery at Lindisfarne in 793, and continuing over the next few decades. The raids became more intense in the 830s, then in 865 Halfdan's great army arrived in England and soon conquered *East Anglia, *Northumbria, and eastern *Mercia. Only *Wessex held out against them.

Once they had achieved military control, the armies settled peacefully: in Yorkshire in 876, in eastern Mercia in 877, and in East Anglia in 879. There they were joined by later settlers, as the numerous Viking place-names and the large body of Scandinavian words which have been incorporated into the English language testify. Their capital, Jorvik (modern York), became a major Viking trading city, the chief place of contact with Scandinavia, and one of the most important mercantile cities in western Europe. The Coppergate excavation in York in the 1970s transformed our understanding of the Vikings, with an emphasis on peaceful commerce rather than the violence committed in the name of Thor's hammer and Odin's raven and commemorated as heroism in the sagas. The Vikings brought new art forms, founded market towns, and developed new forms of administration and justice. The parliament of the Isle of Man is still known as the Tynwald from the Viking open-air assembly, while the *ridings of Yorkshire and Lindsey (Lincolnshire) survived until 1974.

Other Vikings wintered at Dublin for the first time in 841–2, but they never took over entire kingdoms as the Danes did in England. A further wave of Vikings arrived in Ireland in the second decade of the 10th century, but no Irish monastery was destroyed, nor did the Vikings settle in large numbers beyond the coastal trading forts that they established at Dublin, Waterford, Wexford, Wicklow, and Limerick. In Ireland the Vikings became merchants and seamen, in Scotland they became farmers and fishermen; no Viking cities were founded in Scotland, and no coins were minted there.

From the arrival of Halfdan in 865 to the downfall of Eric Bloodaxe in 954 the Vikings controlled northern England, Scotland, and Ireland from their major bases in Dublin and York. Wessex then became the dominant power in England, but during the late 10th and early 11th centuries Viking attacks were renewed. Svein Fork-Beard was king of England in all but name when he died in 1014, and two years later his son Cnut was undisputed king. Upon his death in 1035 Cnut was ruler of Denmark, Norway, Scotland, and England. Viking power was at its height, but it quickly crumbled and in 1042 the Englishman Edward the Confessor became king. Once William the Conqueror had driven the remaining Vikings out of Yorkshire in the late 1060s the Viking era, as far as it affected England, was over, except that numerous families that were now well settled were descended from Viking stock, as indeed were the new Norman rulers. See Magnus Magnusson, *Vikings!* (1980) for a readable and sound introduction.

vill. A term often found in medieval records, e.g. central government taxation returns, for a *township.

villages, close. A term coined by the *Poor Law Commissioners to denote those villages where all the land was owned by a *squire, or a small group of landowners, from which poor immigrants were excluded in order to keep the poor rates at a minimum. Such villages tended to be neat in appearance, and the public houses that were allowed were usually named after the chief landowners. Unless the squire was himself a religious dissenter, *Nonconformist chapels were usually absent. (See, in contrast, VILLAGES, OPEN.) See also B. A. Holderness, ' "Open" and "Close" Parishes in England in the Eighteenth and Nineteenth Centuries', *Agricultural History Review*, 20/2 (1972).

villages, estate. During the 18th and 19th centuries great landowners and country squires redesigned and rebuilt villages in an aesthetically pleasing manner. To do this they had to own all the properties. Some, e.g. Milton Abbas (Dorset), were resited outside the landscaped *park of the great house. They were often built in *vernacular styles, especially the Tudor or Jacobean, using traditional materials for walls and roofs. At Edensor (Derbyshire), on the Chatsworth estate, a variety of designs were chosen from *pattern books to make every house individual. In some counties estate villages are thick on the ground; in Northamptonshire, for example, two out of every three villages were owned by a single landowner or a small group of farmers. Elsewhere, an estate village stands out as being exceptional.

villages, open. A term coined by the *Poor Law Commissioners to describe villages that were not dominated by a *squire, or a small group of farmers, and where control of movement, building, and religious and social preferences was therefore lax. Such villages were populous and contained large numbers of poor people. Many were industrial villages. Labourers from open villages often walked to work on the farms of neighbouring 'close' villages. The Poor Law Amendment Act (1834) created unions of parishes to spread the burden of the poor rates more evenly. See D. R. Mills, *Lord and Peasant in Nineteenth-Century Britain* (1980), and Sarah Banks, 'Nineteenth-Century Scandal or Twentieth-Century Model?: A New Look at "Open" and "Close" Parishes', *Economic History Review*, 2nd ser., 41/1 (1988), which questions the usefulness of 'open' and 'close' as predictive models.

villeins. An unfree tenant of manorial land under the *feudal system. A villein held his land by agricultural services, by working on the *demesne, and by *boon work. The term was introduced by the Normans and gradually fell into disuse after the consequences of the *Black Death had altered the supply of labour.

vineyards. Viticulture was practised in southern England and the south midlands by the Romans and later under the Normans, mostly on monastic estates. *William of Malmesbury refers to vineyards in Gloucestershire. Few medieval vineyards survived the *dissolution of the monasteries, but interest revived intermittently thereafter, and in the late 20th century viticulture has been revived on a commercial basis in many parts of southern Britain.

Vinogradoff, Paul, Sir (1854–1925). Russian historian and former professor at Moscow, who settled in England and became Professor of Jurisprudence at Oxford University in 1903. He was one of the great pioneers of British agrarian history. His major works were *Villeinage in England* (1892), *The Growth of the Manor* (1905), and *English Society in the Eleventh Century* (1908). He emphasized the use of Celtic and Roman evidence in tracing the development of the *manor and other later institutions. He was knighted in 1917.

virgate. A standard holding of arable land in the Middle Ages, of up to 30 *acres, scattered amongst the *open-fields of a *manor, with accompanying rights on the *commons.

Virginia. The permanent settlement of America by Europeans dates from 1607, when three ships belonging to the Virginia Company of London arrived in *Chesapeake Bay. The new colony was named after the virgin Queen Elizabeth; the first settlement was named Jamestown after King James I. Only 38 of the original 105 settlers survived the first two years. The colony eventually prospered through the cultivation of the Native American crop, *tobacco. Young people from central and southern England, who went to work there as indentured servants for a fixed term before obtaining their freedom, formed the majority of the workforce. Expansion was checked by high mortalities and large numbers of people returning to Britain. Nevertheless, the population of Virginia had reached 100,000 or so by 1700. The names of 75 per cent of the 17th-century settlers are known from the records of the Land Office at Richmond, Virginia, but few of these have been traced to their points of origin in England. See, however, Eric Gethyn-Jones, *George Thorpe and the Berkeley Company* (1982), which reveals the Gloucestershire origins of the first settlers in Jamestown.

viscount. The rank of the peerage between *earl and *baron, created in 1440.

Vitruvius Britannicus. The publication in 1715 by Colen Campbell, under the sponsorship of the Earl of Burlington, of two volumes of plans and elevations of contemporary country houses in Britain, to inspire others to follow best practice. It signalled the beginning of the *Palladian movement in Britain. Vitruvius was the greatest architect in ancient Rome. A further three volumes were subsequently published.

wages. Firm information on the levels of real wages before the later 19th century is hard to come by. Wages varied not only over time but from region to region, and some of those regions which offered low wages at one period provided some of the highest payments at another. Even when money wages were recorded in estate accounts or business records the full picture is not necessarily revealed. Some men were able to gain extra employment elsewhere, some had a garden or *allotment, others received part of their wages in kind. The family budget might benefit from the wife taking in washing or sewing, or from children's employment. On the other hand, men who were paid on piece-rates suffered from seasonal unemployment and irregular lay-offs. Finally, trends in money wages need to be compared with those for foodstuffs and rents to see whether the standard of living was rising or falling, or staying the same.

The problem of shortage of data is particularly acute before the late 18th century and does not improve until well into the 19th century. The basis of all modern work is Thorold Rogers, *History of Agriculture and Prices in England*, 7 vols. (1866–1902), which deals with the medieval and early modern periods down to 1797, but his references are widely scattered and do not form part of a continuous series. See also W. H. Beveridge and others, *Prices and Wages in England from the Twelfth to the Nineteenth Century* (1939). Revised tables showing long-term trends have been published, for agricultural wages in *The *Agrarian History of England and Wales*, iii, pp. 471, 475, 479; iv, pp. 864–5; and v, pt 2, pp. 876–9; and for building workers in E. H. Phelps Brown and S. V. Hopkins, 'Seven Centuries of the Prices of Consumables Compared with Builders' Wage-Rates' in E. M. Carus-Wilson (ed.), *Essays in Economic History*, ii (1962). The Statute of Labourers in 1351 and the Statute of *Artificers in 1563 attempted to enforce standard wages, but this was not usually practicable. Information is available for the rates paid to labourers and builders, but rarely for other craftsmen. See Donald Woodward, 'The Determination of Wage Rates in the Early Modern North of England', *Economic History Review*, 2nd ser., 47/1 (1994), and W. B. Stephens, *Sources for English Local History* (3rd edn., 1994), ch. 4 for the sources which may (with difficulty) be used to extract information on wages and *prices.

For the period 1750–1850, G. E. Mingay (ed.), *The Agrarian History of England and Wales*, vi, *1750–1850* (1989), ch. 7 gives an account of current knowledge. Arthur *Young often noted wages on his tours of 1768–71, but his data were collected unsystematically. Sir F. M. *Eden's *The State of the Poor* (1795) is more consistent and systematic in its coverage. For agricultural wages in the second quarter of the 19th century there are the Parliamentary enquiries of 1824 and the mid-1830s, followed by the much more thorough survey by James Caird, published as *English Agriculture in 1850–51* (1852). Caird found that the highest individual wage level was the 15s. paid in Lancashire, and that the lowest was the 6s. obtainable in south Wiltshire. On average, weekly wages in the counties of northern England amounted to 11s. 6d., whereas in the south they stood at 8s. 5d. Agricultural wage levels in the north had to come reasonably close to those offered in industry if men were to continue working on farms, but there were no such constraints on the bargaining power of farmers in the south. This regional pattern was the reverse of what it had been in earlier centuries, and what it became again in the 20th century, under different conditions. The impressionistic evidence offered by Arthur Young suggests that the new pattern was already beginning to emerge by c.1770.

The question of whether the *Industrial Revolution improved or lowered the standard of living of working people continues to be debated. The timing of the long-term upward trend in industrial wages is also a matter for debate. See M. W. Flinn, 'Trends in Real Wages', *Economic History Review*, 2nd ser., 27/3 (1974), and E. H. Hunt, *Regional Wage Variations in Britain, 1850–1914* (1974). F. W. Botham and E. H. Hunt, 'Wages in Britain during the Industrial Revolution', *Economic History Review*, 2nd ser., 40/3 (1987) demonstrate that the fragile statistics that can be gathered for north Staffordshire suggest that in 1750 money wages were less than one shilling a day, but by 1788–92 they had risen to 1s. 6d. As with agricultural wages, the upward trend had already begun.

waggons and wains. The Old English word 'wain' and the Dutch word 'waggon' have a common root. They were translated as *plaustrum* in medieval Latin documents. The lighter, two-wheeled wain was in common use, even in highland Britain, in the Middle Ages. Thus, the *Domesday Book records that the inhabitants of the Peak District parish of Hope paid five wain-loads of *lead as a tribute to their manorial lord. Wains are recorded far more commonly than the sturdier cart in 16th-century probate *inventories. They were simple vehicles, far less substantial than John Constable's famous 'Hay Wain' (which was the name given to the picture by an art dealer). See Stephen Porter, 'Farm Transport in Huntingdonshire, 1610–1749', *Journal of Transport History*, 3rd ser., 3 (1982) for an analysis of the appearance of waggons on farms, as revealed by the evidence of probate inventories.

John *Stow observed that 'long waggons' which brought goods and passengers to London from Canterbury, Norwich, Ipswich, Gloucester, etc., began to operate about 1564. This heavy, four-wheeled vehicle was introduced from the Low Countries. Its use was long confined to southern England. By the middle of the 17th century larger waggons, with a swivelling front axle, had been introduced. Concern was frequently expressed about the way that such waggons ruined the surface of roads. In 1618 the legal draught for waggons was limited to five horses. In 1662 the draught was increased to seven horses or eight *oxen, but loads were limited to 30 hundredweight in summer and to 20 hundredweight in winter. In 1696 a further horse was allowed. In 1708 *Justices of the Peace were authorized to issue licences allowing greater numbers of horses or oxen to draw vehicles uphill in difficult terrain.

Waggons were used only where the roads were passable and demand for carriage and back-carriage was substantial. They were preferred to *packhorses for conveying heavy and bulky goods over short and middle distances, especially by the London carriers. The coming of *turnpike roads allowed the expansion of waggon services to London and major provincial centres. Local *newspapers carried *advertisements offering quick services by 'stage-waggons' and 'flying-waggons'; by 1742,

for example, the 'Derby Flying Waggon' set off for London every Wednesday morning and arrived at the capital early on Saturday. See Dorian Gerhold, 'Packhorses and Wheeled Vehicles in England, 1550–1800', *Journal of Transport History*, 3rd ser., 14/1 (1993).

waits, town. Musicians employed by urban authorities to play on ceremonial and other occasions, e.g. accompanying the watch at fair times. Extra employment was obtained by playing at weddings and other private gatherings. Waits appear in town records from the Middle Ages to the 18th century upon their appointment and upon the provision of cloaks, ribbons, badges, etc. Payments were also made for musical instruments, such as fiddles, bass viols, hauteboys, and bassoons.

Wales, National Library of. The National Library of Wales houses valuable collections which are extensively used by family and local historians. Founded by royal charter in 1907, and sited at Aberystwyth, the Library collects a wide range of manuscript, printed, cartographic, visual, sound, and moving-image material relating to Wales and the Celtic peoples, and similar material which furthers the aims of higher education, and literary and scientific research. The collections are held in three curatorial departments: Printed Books, Manuscripts and Records, and Pictures and Maps.

The Library is one of the six legal deposit libraries in the United Kingdom and Ireland, and thereby has the right to claim almost all British and Irish publications. This privilege, together with purchases of foreign material, has resulted in the development of significant collections of books and periodicals in most subject areas, and of cartographic material.

The Department of Printed Books is responsible for the collections of printed books, periodicals, *newspapers, and other print-based materials. Publications relevant for the study of family and local history are listed in *Bibliotheca Celtica* (1911–85), *Llyfryddiaeth Cymru / Bibliography of Wales* (1985–6, 1987–8, 1989–90), *Subject Index to Welsh Periodicals* (1931–55, 1968–84), and *A Bibliography of Welsh Periodicals, 1735–1850* (1953). Newspapers published in Wales, and those published outside Wales in the Welsh language, have been systematically collected, and the Library played an active role in the Newsplan Wales conservation project for the microfilming of newspapers.

Important genealogical manuscripts including those compiled in the 16th century by Gruffudd Hiraethog and Lewys Dwnn are held in the Department of Manuscripts and Records. Handwritten *pedigrees are described in the *Handlist of Manuscripts in the National Library of Wales*. Public records include the records of the Court of Great Sessions, established by the Second Act of Union 1542 and functioning until 1830. The extensive collections of *estate records, including correspondence, account books, *deeds, and *rentals, and associated manorial records, together with a wide range of ecclesiastical records, are valuable sources. The records of the Welsh *dioceses, the Presbyterian Church of Wales (previously Welsh Calvinistic Methodists), and other *Nonconformist churches have been deposited at the Library. Of particular importance are *bishops' transcripts, *parish registers, probate records, membership lists, and annual reports. A computer index to the pre-1858 probate records is available, as also is the post-1858 Calendar of Grants. Microform copies of the *census returns for the whole of Wales (1841–1991), the *General Register Office's indexes (1837–1983), and the 1988 edition of the *International Genealogical Index may be consulted in the microfilm reading area.

An indication of the various categories of surveys held at the Library is presented in the exhibition catalogue, *Domesday 1086–1836–1986* (1986). These include *tithe apportionment maps and schedules, which were formerly held in the Welsh diocesan registries, but are now housed in the Department of Pictures and Maps. The cartographic collection also includes antiquarian maps, 'historic' *Ordnance Survey maps, *railway and public utility plans, and manuscript farm and estate maps relating to Wales: the volumes of estate maps were listed in *Estate Maps of Wales 1600–1836: An Exhibition Catalogue* (1982). Large and important collections of topographical pictures and portraits, in various media—paintings, drawings, prints, sculpture, posters, *photographs, and *postcards—illustrate the country and people of Wales. Artists represented include John 'Warwick' Smith, Sir Richard Colt *Hoare, Thomas Rowlandson, and Moses Griffith. The photographic collection, the largest and most valuable in Wales, includes the work of John Thomas, Geoff Charles, and the Francis Frith Company. The Sound and Moving Image Collection contains sound and video recordings, films, and recorded radio and television programmes; the Library is a designated archive for off-air recordings.

The Journal of the National Library of Wales has been published since 1939 and contains scholarly articles and notes based upon the collections. Volumes recently published by the Library include *Cofrestri Plwyf i Cymru / Parish Registers of Wales*, eds. C. J. Williams and J. Watts-Williams (1986), and *Cofrestri Anghydffurfiol Cymru / Nonconformist Registers of Wales*, ed. Dafydd Ifans (1994).   D. Huw Owen

wall painting. The interiors of medieval parish *churches were a blaze of colour, very different from the bare stonework or whitened walls of today. Wall paintings of scenes from the Bible and lives of saints were used as visual aids. *Doom paintings over the *chancel arch depicted the weighing of souls at the Day of Judgement. At the *Reformation it was ordered that these paintings should be destroyed or covered with whitewash. Many have been recovered during the 19th and 20th centuries. About 200 British churches have paintings in a good state of preservation and very many more have fragments.

The finest collection of Norman wall paintings is at Chaldon (Surrey). On the western wall is a representation of 'the ladder of salvation', showing the causes and wages of sin and the triumph of Christ and the blessed. The largest collection is that of the 15th-century frescoes at Pickering (Yorkshire), discovered in 1851. Those on the north wall of the nave include the coronation of the Virgin, Herod's feast (with Salome dancing and the head of St John Baptist on a plate), the martyrdoms of Becket and St Edmund, St George and the Dragon, and St Christopher carrying the Christ child across a river. Characteristically, St Christopher is placed opposite the main door on the south side of the nave, for a popular superstition held that anyone who saw such an image would not die unprepared that day. See A. Caiger-Smith, *English Medieval Mural Paintings* (1963).

wall paper. The earliest British wall papers, dating from Tudor times, were printed from wood-blocks to imitate fabric designs. Wall paper became fashionable in the late 17th century. The standard roll size of that time, 36 feet long and 22 inches wide, remains in use to this day. From the 1690s until the 19th century Chinese hand-painted papers were particularly popular in great houses; as they were imported from China by the *East India Company, they were often known as 'Indian' papers. Those at Nostell Priory (Yorkshire), which depict many different kinds of birds in brilliant blues, pinks, and greens, were purchased in 1771. Duty was imposed on rolls from 1712 to 1860. Machine-made papers were first produced in the 1830s. William Morris and other members of the

Victorian 'Art and Craft Movement' produced some memorable designs for wall papers, which revived in popularity in the late 20th century. A Wallpaper History Society is based at the Victoria and Albert Museum.

Walter of Henley. 13th-century author of a treatise on husbandry, which provided practical advice for owners of estates of moderate size and for squires farming their own land. The treatise advocated careful supervision and attention to detail. See Dorothea Oschinsky (ed.), *Walter of Henley and Other Treatises on Estate Management and Accounting* (1971).

wapentake. The *Danelaw equivalent of the Anglo-Saxon *hundred, i.e. a subdivision of a county for administrative and judicial purposes. The original meeting-places were open-air sites, often at river crossings or near major highways. Wapentakes survived as taxation districts (combining a number of *townships) into the early modern period and for calling out the *militia in the *Napoleonic wars, and did not finally disappear until the reorganization of *local government in 1974.

ward. A division in the four northern counties of England and in some of the southern counties of Scotland. Many are named from river valleys, others from *castles or *manors. They appear to have arisen after the *Norman Conquest. East Ward and West Ward (Westmorland), and Castle Ward (Northumberland), survived as the names of *civil registration districts.

Wards and Liveries, Court of. The court that administered funds received by the monarch for rights of *wardship, marriage, and livery. Established in 1541, it was abolished in 1660. Its records are kept at the *Public Record Office under WARD 1 to 7.

wardship. The right of the Crown to hold and administer the estates of heirs of *tenants-in-chief until they reached the age of 21, or 14 for an heiress. During this period the Crown received the revenues of the estate and could determine the marriage of the heir or heiress. These rights were enforced from Henry VII's reign (1485–1509) until the abolition of feudal tenures in 1660. (See WARDS AND LIVERIES, COURT OF.) Wardships were frequently sold to *nobility and *gentry, and were, of course, lucrative assets. Often wards were married off to a child of the person who got wardship; sometimes relations got wardship. See J. Hurstfield, 'Lord Burghley as Master of the Court of Wards, 1561–98', *Transactions of the Royal Historical Society*, 4th ser., 31 (1949).

war memorials. Memorials listing the dead, as distinct from earlier monuments commemorating victories or peace, were first placed in public places after the Crimean War. A number survive from the Boer War, but it was only after the First World War that monuments were erected by public subscription in every town and parochial centre, by *churchyards, in *market places, at crossroads, or in *parks, as focal points for annual memorial services, and on plaques and boards in *churches, *chapels, and halls. They list the deceased in alphabetical order and give their ranks. The names of those who died in the Second World War are normally inscribed on the same memorial. See Alan Borg, *War Memorials* (1991), and Catherine Moriarty, 'The National Inventory of War Memorials', *The Local Historian*, 20/3 (1990). For the Commonwealth War Graves Commission, see WORLD WARS, RECORDS OF.

War Office records. The appointment of a Secretary at War upon the *Restoration in 1660 led to the keeping of more systematic records. These are now kept in the *Public Record Office under WO. See ARMY RECORDS and the PRO Readers' Guide, *Army Records for Family Historians*. The returns of accommodation for men and horses at *inns and *alehouses in 1686 (WO 30) provide statistical information about such provision for each settlement in England and Wales.

warrens. In the Middle Ages royal grants of *free warren allowed feudal lords to hunt small game in defined areas. Warrens which were enclosed for the rearing of *rabbits were widely established, on *heaths, sandy wastes, and other land that was fit for little else, in the medieval and early modern periods. Some are known from their perimeter rampart and ditch, others are commemorated only by minor place-names such as Coneygarth. (See PILLOW MOUNDS.) Skill was required to rear a colony of rabbits that were sturdy enough to survive in the wild. Rabbits were killed from six weeks for their meat and their skins used as furs. Warrens formed a major part of the economy of the Brecklands of Norfolk and Suffolk. See Mark Bailey, *A Marginal Economy? East Anglian Breckland in the Later Middle Ages* (1989). The warreners' lodge on the Prior of Thetford's estate is a two-storey, stone-built, fortified structure of the 15th century which resembles a small castle.

wars, foreign. The first major foreign war in English experience was the prolonged war with France, begun by Edward III (1327–77), and known as the Hundred Years' War. It came to a temporary end in 1382, but was revived under Henry V (1413–22). By the mid-15th century the English retained no interest in France, except for Calais. Henry VIII conducted three expensive and inconclusive campaigns in France (1511–14, 1522–5, and 1542–6), and waged war against the Scots. During the second half of the 16th century the Continental balance of power changed and Spain became the major threat to England, until the defeat of the Armada in 1588. Another war with Spain lasted from 1656 to 1659. From the reign of Elizabeth I (1558–1603) onwards, the English were concerned to create and extend an empire, starting with Ireland, and then *Virginia. This led not only to conflict with the Irish and the Native Americans, but to frequent skirmishes, and eventually to full-scale wars, with other western European powers engaged in similar activity. Three wars were fought against the Dutch (1652–4, 1665–7, and 1672–4), and two long wars were fought against the France of Louis XIV (1689–97 and 1701–14, the latter being known as the War of Spanish Succession).

In the 18th century the Union with Scotland (1707) and the defeat of the *Jacobite rebellions of 1715 and 1745 brought an end to wars between England and Scotland, but renewed struggle with the Catholic countries of Europe brought the War of Jenkins' Ear (1739), the War of Austrian Succession (1740–8), and the Seven Years' War (1756–63). Military activity took place not only in Europe, but in Brazil, the Caribbean, New England, Africa, and India. See Linda Colley, *Britons: Forging the Nation, 1707–1837* (1992). The American colonies were lost as a result of the War of Independence (1775–83). The major and prolonged conflict known as the French Revolutionary and *Napoleonic wars lasted from 1793 to 1815. France subsequently ceased to be the traditional enemy of the English and fought with the British against the Russians in the Crimean War (1854–6). British military activity was thereafter largely concentrated on consolidating an empire in India and Africa, culminating in the Boer War (1899–1902). (See ARMY RECORDS; NAVY RECORDS; and the records of the two WORLD WARS (1914–18 and 1939–45).) The Korean War (1949–51), the Suez Campaign (1956), and the Falklands War (1982) have been the major wars involving British troops in the second half of the 20th century.

Wars of the Roses. A struggle for power between the rival aristocratic factions headed by the houses of Lancaster and York, both of which descended from Edward III (1327–77)

and therefore claimed rights to the throne. Several battles were fought between 1455 and 1461, notably those at St Albans, Blore Heath, Northampton, Wakefield, Mortimer's Cross, and Towton. The Yorkist victory at Towton led to the crowning of Edward IV as king of England in 1461. See Charles Ross, *The Wars of the Roses* (1986).

'waste' in the Domesday Book. After valuing a *manor as it had been in the time of Edward the Confessor, the *Domesday Book often concludes 'and now it is waste'. The frequency of this expression in entries for the north of England has led to the belief that such manors were laid to waste by William I's army during the 'Harrying of the North'. Such views are now largely discredited, despite the reality of the 'harrying'. See W. E. Wightman, 'The Significance of "Waste" in the Yorkshire Domesday', *Northern History*, 10 (1975), and David Palliser, 'Domesday Book and the "Harrying of the North" ', *Northern History*, 29 (1993). 'Waste' seems to have meant land from which no tax was forthcoming, for whatever reasons. No fewer than 128 Yorkshire manors in the Domesday Book were described as 'waste', even though some had resources, population, or value recorded.

watch and ward. The medieval and early modern system whereby the security of towns was preserved by patrols. The watch kept a lookout at night, the ward was responsible for daytime security. Membership of the watch and ward was a duty for all male citizens by rotation.

water closet. The first water closet used in Britain was invented in the Elizabethan period by Sir John Harrington, who lived near Bath, but it was not until the late 17th century that water closets became installed in country houses, as part of an elaborate system of water works in the house and gardens. When Celia *Fiennes visited Windsor, she observed 'a little place with a seat of easement of marble with sluices of water to wash all down'. At least ten water closets were installed at Chatsworth in the early 1690s; they were made of cedar, with brass fittings and *alabaster bowls, except those of the duke and duchess, which were made of marble.

The first patent for a water closet was taken out in 1755 by Alexander Cummings, a watchmaker. Rapid progress came with Joseph Bramah's water closet, patented in 1778. By 1797 Bramah claimed to have made 6,000 closets. Water closets were in common, though not universal, use in country houses by the beginning of Victoria's reign, but the servants still had to make do with outside earth closets. The lack of an adequate supply of water was the major constraint. By the 1870s water closets had been installed in many middle-class homes. Ceramic pans replaced metal ones, and more efficient flushing systems had been introduced, notably the S bend, which prevented odours from rising. The *council houses of the 20th century led the way in introducing water closets into working-class homes, but earth closets remained in use in rural areas long after the Second World War, into the 1960s.

water power. (See MILLS, WATER AND WIND.) For a survey of the archaeological evidence, see David Crossley, *Post-Medieval Archaeology in Britain* (1990), ch. 6, and John Shaw, *Water Power in Scotland, 1550–1870* (1984). For a local study that combines fieldwork with documentary evidence, see David Crossley (ed.), *Water Power on the Sheffield Rivers* (1989).

water supply. Manor *court rolls contain many references to the need to keep public wells free from contamination. Many rural settlements remained dependent on such wells, or on simple pumps, into the 20th century. Aqueducts were used by the Romans to bring water to towns and forts; that which partly survives at Dorchester was 12 miles long. Similar aqueducts were constructed in the 16th and 17th centuries to supply towns, including Plymouth and Cambridge. Many medieval and early modern towns had conduits by which water was brought through pipes. The most ambitious scheme was that of the New River Company, which between 1609 and 1614 constructed a pipeline to London from Hertfordshire. Under such schemes, householders who were connected to the water main paid a water rate. The poorest families became dependent on communal standpipes paid for by their landlords.

Private companies continued to provide water well into the Victorian period, but the Public Health Act (1848) authorized local authorities to provide such a service. The rapid growth of industrial towns in the 19th century posed considerable problems for those responsible for providing a constant supply of water. Domestic consumption rose rapidly as the population increased and higher standards of health were attained, and at the same time demand from industry increased enormously. In the late 19th and 20th centuries *reservoirs were constructed in moorland areas to supply the major centres of population. Manchester had to go as far as the Lake District for its water, and Birmingham to Wales.

For a local study, see Jean Cass, 'Water Supply' in Clyde Binfield et al. (eds.), *The History of the City of Sheffield, 1843–1993* (1993), which is based on the records of the city council and the Water Authority, combined with fieldwork.

wattle and daub. One of the principal ways of filling in the spaces between the posts of a *timber-framed building. The wattle came from *coppice wood, the daub was made from clay, cow dung, animal hair, straw, etc. and was usually whitened to improve the appearance.

weatherboard. Timber cladding used to protect the external walls of houses, *mills, church towers, etc. in eastern and southern England.

weather cocks / vanes. Weather cocks are revolving metal structures on the tops of *church towers and spires, which indicate the direction of the wind. The cockerel shape was preferred as the tails are well suited to catch the wind, but the emblems of patron saints were also favoured, as were idiosyncratic designs. Most examples are difficult to date, and in any case have probably been replaced frequently. The use of weather vanes is thought to have originated in France. The first in England were heraldic devices (the word is derived from *fane*, meaning banner), placed on domestic buildings, especially of the Tudor period. Pre-Victorian vanes were usually painted.

weaving was a major source of employment in the Middle Ages and the early modern period, in both the towns and the countryside. Early weavers are commonly referred to as websters, the feminine form of the word, suggesting that the first weavers were women, but that the activity was taken over by men once it became a commercial business. Webster has become a common surname. The urban weavers were often members of *guilds; those in the countryside were usually smallholders who combined their craft with running a small farm. (See DUAL ECONOMY.) Weaving did not become mechanized as quickly as spinning, so when *woollen and *worsted *spinning mills were erected in the late 18th and early 19th centuries the increased amount of yarn was produced continued to be woven at handlooms in *cottages. The characteristic weavers' cottages that survive in parts of the Pennines mostly date from this time. They are distinguished by their row of windows on the second or top floor, which allow the maximum amount of light to fall on the looms. By this time, weaving was normally a full-time occupation. Weaving became mechanized from the 1820s and 1830s, and hand-weaving disappeared during Victoria's reign. See Geoffrey Timmins, *The Last Shift: The Decline of Handloom Weaving in Nineteenth-Century Lancashire* (1993). See also COTTON; LINEN; NEW DRAPERIES; and SILK.

Webb, Sidney and Beatrice. Sidney Webb, Baron Passfield (1859–1947) and his wife Beatrice, née Potter (1858–1943) were social reformers whose writings on economic and social history were enormously influential in the late 19th century and the first half of the 20th century. They were prominent members of the Fabian Society, helped to found the London School of Economics (1895), and began the *New Statesman* (1913). Sidney Webb was Labour MP for Seaham (1992–9) and President of the Board of Trade (1924). As Baron Passfield he was Colonial Secretary (1929–31). The Webbs' monumental work, *English Local Government* (10 vols., 1906–29), remains a basic source of information on this subject. Beatrice Webb was an early investigator in the east end of London for Charles *Booth's survey of life and labour; see Rosemary O'Day, 'Before the Webbs: Beatrice Potter's Early Investigations for Charles Booth's Inquiry', *History*, 78 (1993). The other major works of the Webbs included *The History of Trade Unionism* (1894, revised and extended 1920), and *Industrial Democracy* (1897, 2nd edn. 1902).

weights and measures. There was much regional variety in the use of customary weights and measures. See F. G. Skinner, *Weights and Measures* (1967); Giles V. Harrison, 'Agricultural Weights and Measures' in Joan Thirsk (ed.), *The *Agrarian History of England and Wales*, v, pt 2, *1640–1750* (1985), pp. 815–25; G. E. Mingay (ed.), *The Agrarian History of England and Wales*, vi, *1750–1850* (1989), for the statistical appendix by A. H. John, which provides an index of terms and measures used in different parts of England and Wales in the early 19th century; and J. Geoffrey Dent, 'Aspects of Change: Evolution and Revolution in Weights and Measures', *Folk Life*, 31 (1993).

weld. A crop that produced a yellow dye, hence its alternative name of 'dyer's weed'. It was grown on warm, dry soils, and as it did not flower until the second year, it was sown with an intermediate crop of barley or oats. The chief area of production in the early modern period was the chalklands of Kent, especially around Canterbury and Wye.

Wellcome Institute for the History of Medicine. An archive and research centre at 183 Euston Road, London NW1 2BN. The members of the Wellcome Unit for the History of Medicine in the University of Oxford have published numerous books and articles on medical history.

Welsh History Review. A journal founded in 1960 to publish articles and reviews on all aspects of Welsh history.

Welsh language. The Union of Wales and England under Henry VIII did not lead to an immediate change in the use of Welsh as the normal medium of communication. The Welsh language survived remarkably well throughout the early modern period, even amongst the wealthiest sections of society. Perhaps 80 or 90 per cent of the population used Welsh as their first language well into the 19th century. The remoter communities in the hills spoke only Welsh. In 1891 the first linguistic census suggested that the number of Welsh speakers was about 1 million, or half the population. Some 16 per cent were monoglot Welsh speakers. Twenty years later, the number of Welsh speakers was unchanged, but population growth meant that the proportion of the population of Wales who spoke Welsh was only 40 per cent. The decline in the speaking of Welsh was particularly noticeable in the industrial southeast, which was close to England and subject to much immigration. Since 1945 each subsequent census has shown that the Welsh language is declining in use at the national level, and is less commonly spoken by younger age-groups. The areas of Wales where at least 70 per cent of the population are Welsh-speaking are now confined to the western coastal strip and Anglesey. See Philip Jenkins, *A History of Modern Wales, 1536–1990* (1992), and John Aitchison and Harold Carter, 'Rural Wales and the Welsh Language', *Rural History: Economy, Society, Culture*, 2/1 (1991).

Welsh local and family history. Interest in local and family history has been a consistent feature of Welsh life from an early date. An intense attachment and allegiance to one's family and locality reflected social and political conditions in early medieval Wales. The kindred grouping occupied a crucial element in Welsh law, and *Gerald of Wales, in the late 12th century, emphasized the importance to the ordinary individual of a knowledge of one's family background. The significance of genealogy and of *heraldry in medieval and early modern Wales have been examined respectively by P. C. Bartrum in *Early Welsh Genealogical Tracts* (1966), *Welsh Genealogies 300–1400* (1974), and *Welsh Genealogies 1400–1500* (1983), and by Michael P. Siddons in *The Development of Welsh Heraldry*, vol. i (1991), vols. ii and iii (1993).

Medieval poets praised noble ancestry and, in the 16th century, Gruffudd Hiraethog (d. 1564) and Lewys Dwnn (*fl.* 1568–1616), both of whom were professionally trained bards, served as deputy heralds appointed by the king of arms, visiting all parts of Wales. By this time the study of genealogy and of the local community was of increasing interest to *antiquarian scholars in Wales as in England. A network of contacts linked together Lewys Dwnn with George Owen of Henllys (1552–1613), whose map of Pembrokeshire, drawn in 1602, was published by his friend William *Camden in the 1607 edition of *Britannia*. *Morganiae Archaiographia, A Book of the Antiquities of Glamorganshire*, compiled by Rice Merrick (*c.*1520–1586/7) during the period 1578–1584, ed. B. Ll. James (1983), was influenced both by contemporary antiquarian scholars and also by the Welsh bardic tradition, with hospitality provided for itinerant poets at Merrick's home, Cottrell, in the parish of St Nicholas, Glamorgan.

Antiquarian scholars also contributed to the production of the early printed *maps of Wales, which contained detailed topographical information. Humphrey Llwyd (*c.*1527–1568), one of the leading Renaissance scholars of Wales, drew the earliest printed map of Wales, *Cambriae Typus*. This map, and also his map of England and Wales, were incorporated in the *Additamentum* (1573), the supplement to *Theatrum Orbis Terrarum* (1570). This was the first modern geographical atlas, compiled and edited by Abraham Ortelius, who lived and worked in Antwerp. Christopher *Saxton's map of Wales (*c.*1580), the relevant sections of his atlas of England and Wales (1579), and his wall map (1583) constitute valuable sources for students interested in *place- and river-names, and in the topography of Wales. The second volume of John *Speed's *Theatre of the Empire of Great Britaine* (1611), featuring Wales, was influenced by the writings of Llwyd and Saxton's maps, but Speed himself was responsible for the town-plans which accompanied the county maps, and the 16 town-views which accompanied his map of Wales: one for each of the four episcopal centres and the main town in 12 shires.

The members of the North Wales gentry who provided John Speed with additional information for a revised version of the *Theatre* probably included Sir John Wynn of Gwydir near Llanrwst (1553–1627). He had collected material from Welsh *chronicles and English administrative records for his *History of the Gwydir Family* (1770) [*The History of the Gwydir Family and Memoirs*, ed. J. Gwynfor Jones (1990)], and he depended on the Welsh poet and herald, Siôn Tudur, for genealogical information. Also, Wynn was influenced by Philemon Holland's English translation of *Britannia* in 1610. Camden's work also motivated Edward *Lhuyd, of Llanforda, Oswestry. He contributed sections on Wales to Edmund *Gibson's new translation and edition, printed in 1695. In 1697 he distributed four thousand copies of his 'Parochial Queries', containing questions on antiquities, place-names, customs, and natural history, and he toured Wales systematically in the following three years. His manuscripts illustrate his wide-ranging antiquarian, archaeological, philological, and scientific interests. Camden's influence continued into the second half of the 18th century, with Thomas Pennant (1726–98), born at Downing, in the parish of Whitford, Clwyd, contributing to Richard *Gough's translation and edition of *Britannia* (1789). Pennant was mainly interested in antiquarianism, geology, and natural history. He began to publish his *Tours in Wales* in 1788, and the text was illustrated by the drawings of his servant Moses Griffith (1747–1819). Pennant's *Tours* covered north Wales, but information on south Wales was provided by Benjamin Heath Malkin, who travelled throughout the region in 1803, and published *The Scenery, Antiquities and Biography of South Wales* in 1804.

At this time, also, Sir Richard Colt *Hoare and Richard Fenton (1747–1821) travelled extensively in Wales. Hoare encouraged his friend to collect and publish, and in 1811 Fenton's *A Historical Tour through Pembrokeshire* appeared. This followed the publication of other county histories, with Theophilus Jones (1759–1812) responsible for the comprehensive *History of the County of Brecknock* (2 vols., 1805, 1809), and Samuel Rush Meyrick (1783–1848) for the *History and Antiquities of the County of Cardigan* (1809–10). An edition of Fenton's manuscripts was published in the volume *Tours in Wales 1804–13* (1917). Whilst living in London, he was a member of influential literary and cultural societies. One of these was the Gwyneddigion, and other prominent members included the lexicographer William Owen Pughe (1759–1835), who edited the three volumes of the periodical *The Cambrian Register* (1795, 1796, 1818) which contained articles on biography, history, and topography; and the remarkable Edward Williams, 'Iolo Morganwg' (1747–1826), whose over-zealous promotion of the significance of the bardic tradition, and also of his native Glamorgan, resulted in a fabrication of historical sources. Pughe and Iolo Morganwg were closely involved in the production of *The Myvyrian Archaiology of Wales* (1801–07). Another London-based cultural and patriotic society was the Honourable Society of Cymmrodorion, founded in 1751, revived in 1820, and again in 1873. The society has promoted and published scholarly works, including significant studies in genealogy and local history. It published the journal *Y Cymmrodor* from 1877 to 1951, the *Dictionary of Welsh Biography* (1953, 1959), and from 1893 the *Transactions*, which continue to appear regularly. The society was also responsible for the *Cymmrodorion Record Series* with 13 volumes published from 1899 to 1936. These included *The Description of Penbrokeshire, by George Owen of Henllys*, edited by Henry Owen in four volumes from 1902 to 1936.

The study of local and family history in Wales also benefited from record publishing ventures in England. *The Record of Caernarvon*, edited by Henry Ellis (1838), and Aneurin Owen's edition of the *Ancient Laws and Institutes of Wales* (1841) were published in the *Record Commission* series. The publications in the *Rolls Series* included the *Annales Cambriae*, edited by John Williams (*ab Ithel*), and J. Gwenogvryn Evans's *Report on Manuscripts in the Welsh Language* (1898–1910) was published by the *Historical Manuscripts Commission. Material relating to Wales in repositories in England, especially the *British Library and the *Public Record Office, explains the importance to Welsh scholars of these collections and associated finding-aids and publications. A wide range of documents illustrating the history of Glamorgan from 447 to 1721, and housed in these two repositories as well as in private collections, were presented in G. T. Clark's *Cartae et Alia Munimenta quae ad Dominium de Glamorgan Pertinent* (6 vols., 2nd edn., 1910). J. H. Matthews's *Records of the County Borough of Cardiff* (1888–1911) also appeared in six volumes. Large-scale, multi-volume histories of the Welsh *dioceses, and of the *Nonconformist denominations, together with biographies of the leaders, were published in the second half of the 19th century and the early 20th century. In spite of their bulk, and in some cases intimidating appearance, valuable information is often contained in these works, and also in more recent studies, including D. Walker's *A History of the Church in Wales* (1976); T. M. Bassett, *Bedyddwyr Cymru / The Welsh Baptists* (1966), R. Tudur Jones, *Hanes Annibynwyr Cymru*

(1966) [Welsh Independents]; Gomer M. Roberts (ed.), *Hanes Methodistiaeth Galfinaidd Cymru*, 1 (1974), 2 (1978) [Welsh Calvinistic Methodists, Presbyterian Church of Wales], and Eric Edwards, *Yr Eglwys Fethodistaidd* (1980) [Statistical Survey of Welsh Methodism].

Historical societies within the main churches of Wales publish journals annually, and these promote an awareness of records which are frequently of considerable relevance for family and local historians. The transactions of the Historical Society of the Welsh Baptists have been published since 1906. The corresponding publications of other religious historical societies include those of the Presbyterian Church of Wales (1916), the Welsh Independents (1923), the Methodist Church in Wales (1946), and the Church of Wales (1949). More recent developments in this field have been the publication of the *Journal of Welsh Ecclesiastical History*, which first appeared in 1984, and also the Newsletter and information leaflets produced by *CAPEL*, the Chapels Heritage Society. This society was established in 1986 to encourage the study and preservation of the Nonconformist heritage of Wales. An awareness of the threat presented to distinctive features of the landscape and history of Wales was also responsible for the foundation in 1970 of *Llafur*, the Society for the Study of Welsh Labour History, which has fostered research into, and the teaching of, the history of the working class in Wales. The society has published, since 1972, an annual volume of transactions, which contains scholarly articles and reports on meetings and activities organized by and involving the society. The contraction of the *coal industry had led to the closure and dispersal of many miners' institute libraries, but since 1973 the South Wales Miners' Library, located in Swansea, has collected a wide range of material, including books from miners' institute libraries, pamphlets and printed ephemera, *photographs, tapes, and miners' banners.

The earliest scholarly society in Wales, and one which continues to flourish, is the Cambrian Archaeological Association, founded in 1846 for the study and the preservation of the antiquities of Wales. Its journal, *Archaeologia Cambrensis*, contains material on genealogy, heraldry, toponomy, *folklore, and literature, and also reports on the society's excavations. Each one of the historic counties of Wales has a county history society, of which the earliest series is *The Montgomeryshire Collections*, the journal of the Powysland Club, published since 1868. Other local historical journals established in the 19th century and containing material of Welsh interest include the *Journal of the Chester and North Wales Archaeological and Historic Society* (1849), the *Transactions of the Woolhope Naturalists' Field Club* (1851), the *Report and Transactions of the Cardiff Naturalists' Society* (1867), and the *Transactions of the Caradoc and Severn Valley Field Club* (1893). The journals of the county history societies established in the 20th century were those of Carmarthenshire (1905), Cardiganshire (1909–39, 1950), Anglesey (1913), Brecknock (1928–9), Radnorshire (1931), Caernarfonshire (1939), Merioneth (1950), Denbighshire (1952), Flintshire (1952), Monmouthshire (1954), Glamorgan (1957), and Pembrokeshire (1959). Other journals produced by well-established local societies include the *Transactions of the Neath Antiquarian Society* (1930) and *Gower* (1950).

The various proceedings of these societies include scholarly articles examining various aspects of local history over an extended period of time. These are accompanied by illustrative material which, in some recent instances, is presented in colour. The cover of *Ceredigion*, 12/1 (1993) featured a colour reproduction of a painting of Aberystwyth harbour by Alfred Worthington. Colour illustrations effectively contribute to an appreciation of the recording of Glamorgan by artists, in *Morgannwg*, 36 (1992); stained glass windows in St Margaret's Church, in the mining village of Crynant, in *Morgannwg*, 37 (1993); and the survey of the structure of Powis Castle in *The Montgomeryshire Collections*, 81 (1993). The 'Powisiana' section in this journal contains references to recent publications relating to the history and archaeology of Montgomeryshire. Book reviews appear in most of the journals, and attention is also drawn to publications with which the society has been involved. These include A. D. Carr, *Medieval Anglesey* (1982) and Helen Ramage, *Portraits of an Island: Eighteenth Century Anglesey* (1987) [Anglesey Antiquarian Society and Field Club]; Francis Jones, *Historic Carmarthenshire Homes and their Families* (1987) and Heather James (ed.), *Sir Gâr: Studies in Carmarthenshire History* (Carmarthenshire Antiquarian Society, 1991; and J. L. Davies and D. P. Kirby (ed.), *Cardiganshire County History*, i (Ceredigion Antiquarian Society, 1994).

Other regular features include archaeological reports and information on local museums and record offices; for example, *Brycheiniog*, 26 (1992–3) contains an account of the activities of the Clwyd-Powys Archaeological Trust in Brecknockshire, the Powys County Archives Office, and Brecknock Museum. In *Mor-* *gannwg*, 37 (1993), a series of archaeological notes, prepared by members of the Glamorgan-Gwent Archaeological Trust, the National Museum of Wales, and Wessex Archaeology are followed by reports from the Glamorgan Record Office and the West Glamorgan County Archives Service. Information is provided on the membership and activities of the local society, with reports of lectures, meetings, and field excursions arranged during the year.

Specific projects sponsored by a society include the Carmarthenshire Place-Name Survey. Details are also given of local societies within the county, and the *Transactions of the Caernarfonshire History Society* frequently contain accounts of the activities of the local societies based at Aberconwy, Dyffryn Nantlle, Llandygái and Llanllechid, Llandudno and District, Llanfairfechan, Penmaenmawr, and Trefor. Indexes to the contents of the journals appear at periodic intervals; thus, a cumulative title index to volumes 1–31 of the *Transactions of the Denbighshire Historical Society* was presented in volume 32 (1983). A comprehensive index, compiled by Andrew Green, and listing authors, persons, places, objects, and topics mentioned in the publications of the Carmarthenshire Antiquarian Society from 1905 to 1977, was published by the society in 1981.

County history societies have also been responsible for publishing record sources which are relevant for family and local historians. The publications of the *Flintshire Historical Society Record Series* include *Flint Pleas, 1283–5*, ed. J. G. Edwards (1921), and *Flintshire Ministers' Accounts*, ed. D. L. Evans (1929). Several volumes were published in the *West Wales Historical Records* series (1910–29). The tradition established by the *South Wales and Monmouth Record Society Publications* (1932 ff.) has been maintained by the South Wales Record Society, which was established in 1982 to publish editions of historical records relating to the history of south Wales. Publications include *Morganiae Archaiographia*, compiled by Rice Merrick, ed. B. Ll. James (1983), Joseph Bradney, *A History of Monmouthshire*, v. *The Hundred of Newport*, ed. M. Grey (1993), and *Glamorgan Hearth Tax Assessment of 1670*, ed. Elizabeth Parkinson (1994).

The latter volume is especially valuable for family historians. At present there are six active family-history societies in Wales, covering Glamorgan, Clwyd, Gwynedd, Powys, Dyfed, and Gwent. Meetings are held regularly, and research projects include the transcription of monumental inscriptions in churches and graveyards, the transcription and indexing of *parish registers, and the preparation of *census indices. The Clwyd Family History Society opened its Centre at Ruthin in 1988, and provides access to a range of family and local history sources. The Association co-operates fully with the *Federation of Family History Societies, and the two bodies jointly published *Welsh Family History: A Guide to Research*, ed. John Rowlands *et al.* (1993). A proposed volume on Welsh *surnames, to be published by the Federation, will be geared to the needs of family historians and will consider the subject from both statistical and historical perspectives. The numerous publications of the Federation, including the official journal, *Family History News and Digest*, provide valuable information and guidance for Welsh family historians.

Similarly, the activities and publications of the *British Association for Local History, and, before that, of the *Standing Conference for Local History, have assisted Welsh as well as English local historians, as both organizations have sought to encourage the study of local history in Wales and provide services necessary for its furtherance. The quarterly journal *The *Local Historian* occasionally publishes articles and book reviews of specific Welsh interest, and Brian Howells provided an admirable survey of 'Local History in Wales' in 1973 (10/8). This journal, and other publications of the BALH and the *Historical Association, including the journal *History*, have succeeded in drawing attention to research work undertaken in other localities and also to the availability and value of source-material. Other journals, whose scope is not confined to Wales but which at times contain material of specific Welsh interest, include The *Agricultural History Review, Antiquity*, The *Archaeological Journal, Folk Life*, and *History Workshop Journal*. The involvement of Welsh historians in co-operative ventures, for instance The *Agrarian History of England and Wales*, has proved fruitful.

D. Walker's *Medieval Wales* (1990), published in the *Cambridge Medieval Textbooks* series, provided an introduction to the main political developments of medieval Wales. The major publications of the Oxford University Press, which again facilitate the work of Welsh family and local historians, include W. Rees, *South Wales and the March* (1924), and R. R. Davies, *Lordship and Society in the March of Wales* (1978). The Press has also co-operated with the University of Wales Press to publish, in six volumes, the authoritative history of Wales. Volume vi, K. O. Morgan, *Rebirth of a Nation, Wales 1880–1980*, was published in 1981, and volumes ii, iii and iv in 1987, namely R. R.

Davies, *Conquest, Coexistence and Change, Wales 1066–1485*; Glanmor Williams, *Recovery, Reorientation and Reformation, Wales c. 1415–1642*; and G. H. Jenkins, *The Foundations of Modern Wales, Wales 1642–1780*.

The University of Wales has made an immense contribution to scholarship in Wales, and has promoted the study of family and local history in many ways. The University of Wales Press, established in 1922, has published a large number of significant monographs and texts. These include A. D. Rees, *Life in a Welsh Countryside* (1950), David Williams, *The Rebecca Riots* (1955), H. Carter, *The Towns of Wales* (1965), David Jenkins, *The Agricultural Community in South West Wales at the Turn of the Twentieth Century* (1971), C. A. Gresham, *Eifionydd, A Study in Landownership from the Medieval Period to the Present Day* (1973); R. A. Griffiths (ed.), *Boroughs of Medieval Wales* (1978), and T. J. Morgan and Prys Morgan, *Welsh Surnames* (1985). The University's Board of Celtic Studies has been responsible for several important series of publications, with the History and Law Committee publishing major groups of historical records, such as *The Merioneth Lay Subsidy Roll 1292–3*, ed. K. Williams-Jones (1976), *The Religious Census of 1851*, i: *South Wales*, eds. Ieuan Gwynedd Jones and David Williams (1976), and ii: *North Wales*, ed. Ieuan Gwynedd Jones (1981). The *Studies in Welsh History* series of monographs includes John Davies, *Cardiff and the Marquesses of Bute* (1981) and R. Merfyn Jones, *The North Wales Quarrymen 1874–1922* (1981). The biennial journal *Welsh History Review* has been published since 1960 and includes, every year, a list of periodical articles relating to Welsh history in a preceding year. The *Bulletin of the Board of Celtic Studies* has been published since 1921, and the Social Studies Committee published the *National Atlas of Wales*, ed. H. Carter, in 1988.

The University has encouraged and fostered adult education, and local history has featured prominently in the subjects studied by classes organized by the Departments of Extra-Mural Studies or Departments of Continuing Education in the constituent colleges. The Workers' Educational Association, the voluntary organization designated as a provider of adult education, has also promoted the study of local history in many localities. Four lectures delivered under the auspices of the WEA in Merthyr Tydfil were published by the University of Wales Press in the volume *Merthyr Politics: The Making of a Working-Class Tradition*, ed. Glanmor Williams (1966). One of the most active branches in Wales of the Workers' Educational Association is the one based at Llanelli, where classes on a wide range of subjects, including local history, have been organized since 1914. Articles on the history of the Llanelli area have appeared in *Amrywiaeth Llanelli Miscellany*, published annually since 1986 by the local branch which was also responsible for the volume *Footprints of Faith*, a series of lectures on 'The Anglican Church and Nonconformity in Llanelli' which was delivered to classes organized by the WEA in 1987–8.

Local authorities have supported ambitious ventures to publish official county histories. The publication of *Glamorgan County History*, vi: *Glamorgan Society, 1780–1980*, ed. Prys Morgan (1988) completed an enterprise launched in 1930 to publish a six-volume history of the county. Joseph Bradney had published his four-volume *A History of Monmouthshire* (1904–33), and A. H. Dodd outlined *A History of Caernarfonshire, 1284–1900* (1968). J. E. Lloyd's *A History of Carmarthenshire* appeared in two volumes (1935, 1939) and the first volume of the *History of Merioneth*, ed. E. D. Jones, was published in 1967. Two volumes of the *Pembrokeshire County History* have appeared: iii: *Early Modern Pembrokeshire 1536–1815*, ed. B. E. Howells (1987), and iv:, *Modern Pembrokeshire, 1815–1974*, ed. David W. Howell (1993). Studies of towns and cities include A. H. Dodd, *A History of Wrexham* (1957), W. Rees, *Cardiff: A History of the City* (1969), Ieuan Gwynedd Jones, *Aberystwyth 1277–1977* (1977) and *Swansea, An Illustrated History*, ed. Glanmor Williams (1990). The *Glamorgan Historian* series, vols. 1–12 (1963–81), together with four other volumes on Glamorgan (1959–62) and a number of publications including collections of photographs illustrating various towns and districts, represent the remarkable contribution of an individual, Stewart Williams, to the historiography of local studies in Wales.

A number of institutions, such as the National Library of *Wales and the National Museum of Wales, both of which were founded by royal charters in 1907, have also proved to be of critical importance on account of their extensive and valuable collections and associated publications. The first galleries of the National Museum and Galleries of Wales were opened in Cathays Park, Cardiff in 1927. Permanent exhibitions now include 'The Evolution of Wales', which narrates the combined physical and biological evolution of Wales from the earliest geological eras up to the end of the last Ice Age. The 'Natural History of Wales' exhibition links the processes of biological evolution with the development of the landscape, and attention is focused on the marine and woodland environments of modern Wales. The new art galleries display Welsh art in its international context. The Museum of Welsh Life, at St Fagans near Cardiff, the Welsh Industrial and Maritime Museum in the Cardiff Bay area, and the Snowdonia Museum, Llanberis, Caernarfonshire are integral parts of the National Museum, as also are the smaller specialist *museums and galleries in various parts of Wales, including the Museum of the Welsh Woollen Industry at Dre-fach Felindre; the Welsh Slate Museum, Llanberis; the Roman Legionary Museum, Caerleon; Segontium Roman Fort Museum, Caerleon; and also the Turner House Gallery at Penarth, and the Graham Sutherland Gallery at Picton Castle, Dyfed. At the Museum of Welsh Life buildings which are typical features of Welsh communities have been re-erected, and the collections of material culture are accompanied by surveys of oral traditions in Wales. Publications by members of the staff of the Museum include I. C. Peate, *The Welsh House* (1946), V. E. Nash-Williams, *Early Christian Monuments of Wales* (1950), Cyril Fox, *The Personality of Britain* (1951), Geraint Jenkins, *The Welsh Woollen Industry* (1969), D. Morgan Rees, *The Industrial Archaeology of Wales* (1975), and Eurwyn Wiliam, *Farm Buildings of North-East Wales, 1550–1900* (1982). The *Bulletin* of the National Museum appeared between 1969 and 1976 and the journal *Amgueddfa* has been published since 1969.

The Royal Commission on Ancient Monuments for Wales was established in 1908 to make an inventory of the ancient and historical monuments of Wales and Monmouthshire. It has published, since 1911, inventories covering a number of the historic Welsh counties, including several volumes on Caernarfonshire (1956, 1960, and 1964) and Glamorgan (1976, 1981, 1982, 1988, and 1991). These handsome volumes contain an abundance of illustrative material with colour and monochrome plates and sequences of line-drawings, plans, and sections explaining and expanding upon the detailed descriptions of distinctive internal features, and of the external appearance of a wide range of buildings and settlements, including *hill forts, *castles, platform houses, monastic *granges, *deserted villages, gentry houses, farmhouses, and *cottages. *The Houses of the Welsh Countryside* (1975) was written by Peter Smith, the former Secretary of the Commission. By a Royal Warrant of 1992 the Commission has been empowered to survey, record, publish, and maintain a database of ancient and historical sites, structures, and landscapes in Wales. In 1964 the records of the Royal Commission were amalgamated with the Welsh section of the National Buildings Record to form the National Monuments Record of Wales, which is also based in Aberystwyth. The NMR seeks to collect, maintain, and make available a comprehensive record of the archaeological, architectural, and historical monuments of Wales, and extensive collections have been assembled of photographs, drawings, and surveys, together with documents, maps, databases, and a small library.

Welsh Historic Monuments, *Cadw*, was established in 1984 with a statutory responsibility for protecting, conserving, and presenting the ancient monuments and historic buildings of Wales. Revised guides to Welsh historical sites have been published, including Arnold Taylor, *Caernarfon Castle* (1989), and Jeremy K. Knight, *Chepstow Castle and Port Wall* (1991). These attractive, informative, and popular publications have numerous illustrations which effectively depict the architectural detail presented in the text. Other volumes which successfully interpret the heritage of Wales include Elizabeth Whittle, *The Historic Gardens of Wales* (1992). Sian Rees, *Dyfed* (1992) and Elizabeth Whittle, *Glamorgan and Gwent* (1992) launched a series of regional guides. Conferences are organized, and the papers presented to the third Cadw Archaeological Conference held at Cardiff in 1986 were published in *Welsh Industrial Heritage: A Review*, ed. C. Stephen Briggs (1992) [CBA Research Report no. 79].

Four archaeological trusts have been established in Wales to cover the counties of Clwyd-Powys, Glamorgan-Gwent, Gwynedd, and Dyfed. Publications which result directly from the work of the trusts include E. G. T. James, *Carmarthen: An Archaeological and Topographical Survey* (1980) and D. M. Robinson, *South Glamorgan's Heritage* (1985). Archivists were appointed in Monmouthshire in 1938 and in Glamorgan in 1939, but most of the county *record offices were established after the Second World War, as in Caernarfonshire (1948), Flintshire (1951), Merioneth (1952), and Carmarthenshire (1959). An archive service was established in Powys in 1984, and in 1992 the West Glamorgan Record Office was founded, with the Glamorgan Archive Service thereby serving the counties of Mid and South Glamorgan. The collections held include the *quarter sessions records, covering all aspects of local administration before the creation of *county councils in 1889. The earliest series are those of

Caernarfonshire, which survive from 1541, and their value was emphasized in the *Calendar of the Caernarvonshire Quarter Sessions Records, i: 1541–58*, ed. W. Ogwen Williams (1956), and in the *Denbighshire Quarter Session Records*, ed. A. G. Veysey (1991). These records include *land tax assessments, *enclosure awards, *poll books, and *electoral registers (after 1832). Other records which are frequently consulted include *rate books, *parish and nonconformist *registers, family and estate papers, a wide range of educational, industrial, and business records, and, especially in the Gwynedd Archives Service, a large collection of maritime records. Published guides to county record offices include W. Ogwen Williams, *Guide to the Caernarvonshire Record Office* (1952) and A. G. Veysey, *Guide to the Flintshire Record Office* (1974). The latter was published at the time of the reorganization of local government which resulted in the creation of the county of Clwyd in north-east Wales. In the same year, Swansea City Archives was established, and its collections include electoral registers, poll books, *freeman's records, and rare books from the 19th and 20th centuries.

The record offices have been responsible for a wide range of publications in addition to the detailed annual reports. These include Donald Moore, *The Earliest Views of Glamorgan* (1978) and *A Catalogue of Glamorgan Estate Maps*, compiled by Hilary M. Thomas (1992), both of which were published by the Glamorgan Archives Service. The series 'Studies in Swansea's History' was launched with the publication, sponsored by Swansea City Council and edited by the City Archivist, Dr. John Alban, of R. T. Price, *Little Ireland, Aspects of the Irish and Greenhill, Swansea* (1992) and N. A. Robins, *Home for Heroes: Early Twentieth-Century Housing in the County Borough of Swansea* (1992). Volumes published by the Gwynedd Archives and Museum Service include M. Elis-Williams, *Bangor, Port of Beaumaris* (1988) and Eric Jones and David Gwyn, *Dolgarrog, An Industrial History*, (1989); the journal *Cymru a'r Môr / Maritime Wales*, has been published since 1976. The recently established Friends of the Clwyd Record Office have taken over the responsibility for the *Clwyd Historian: Hanes Bro Clwyd*, which was first published in 1977 by the Clwyd Local History council, and edited at the Clwyd County Record Office.

Archival material, together with maps, *newspapers, photographs, and audio-visual material, are held in some of the public and academic *libraries of Wales. The oldest public libraries are the South Glamorgan Library, founded in 1862 as the Cardiff Free Library, and the West Glamorgan Library at Swansea, established in 1870; and both institutions have over the years collected a wide range of material. A number of public libraries have supported publishing ventures. The Local History Research Group, based at the Llanelli Public Library, has published a series of monographs, including M. V. Symons, *Coal Mining in the Llanelli Area*, i. *16th Century to 1829* (1979), and D. Q. Bowen, *The Llanelli Landscape* (1980). Facsimile editions of works published by library authorities include E. Humphrey's *Reminiscences of Briton Ferry and Baglan* (1898) and John Lewis, *The Swansea Guide* (1851), reprinted respectively in 1982 and 1989 by the West Glamorgan County Council Library and Information Service. University libraries also contain important collections, such as those relating to north Wales estates, mines, and quarries, housed at the University of Wales, Bangor. *Trade union, political, and private records associated with the south Wales coalfield, and genealogical material previously held in the Royal Institution of South Wales, are now housed at the University of Wales, Swansea.

The Royal Institution, founded in 1834, continues to operate as an independent voluntary learned society. It supports and helps to promote the Swansea Museum, which, built in 1835 to house the Institution's growing collections, is the oldest public museum in Wales. A number of museums effectively interpret the localities in which they are sited. Specialized museums concerned with specific subjects include the Gwent Rural Life Museum, Usk; the Lloyd George Museum, Llanystumdwy; and the Seiont 11 Maritime Museum, Caernarfon. J. Geraint Jenkins, *Exploring Museums, Wales* (1990), a Museums Association Guide, describes the collections and facilities of 131 museums and galleries in Wales. The Gomer Press, Llandysul, Christopher Davies, Swansea, and Gee and Son, Denbigh have been responsible over an extended period of time for a number of significant volumes in both the English and Welsh languages. Recent publications include W. S. K. Thomas, *Brecon 1093–1660: An Illustrated History* (1991) and Malcolm Seaborne, *Schools in Wales 1500–1900: A Social and Architectural History* (1992). In recent years there has also been a proliferation of publishing houses in Wales and the researches of J. B. Sinclair and R. W. D. Fenn into aspects of Radnorshire history have been published by Cadoc Books (*Marching to Zion:*

Radnorshire Chapels (1990)) and by Mid-Border Books (*The Facility of Locomotion: The Kington Railways* (1991)). Welsh family and local historians have also benefited from volumes published in England. These include Philip Riden, *Local History, A Handbook for Beginners* (1983), Ian Soulsby, *The Towns of Medieval Wales* (1983), and Philip Jenkins, *A History of Modern Wales, 1536–1990* (1992), together with books on particular topics, such as Paul R. Davis and Susan Lloyd-Fern, *Lost Churches of Wales and the Marches* (1990) and M. R. C. Price, *The Llanelly and Mynydd Mawr Railway* (1992). John Davies, *Hanes Cymru* (1990) and an English translation, *A History of Wales* (1993), a comprehensive one-volume history of Wales from the earliest period to the late 1950s were published by Allan Lane: the Penguin Press. R. Haslam, *Powys* (1979), and E. Hubbard, *Clwyd* (1986) appeared in Penguin's 'The Buildings of Wales' series.

Relevant bibliographical information is available in *A Bibliography of the History of Wales* (1962), with supplements for the period 1959–71 in the *Bulletin of the Board of Celtic Studies* (1963, 1966, 1969, and 1972). Also, in *A Bibliography of the History of Wales*, ed. Philip Henry Jones (microfiche, 1988) and in *Llyfryddiaeth Cymru / Bibliography of Wales* (1985–6, 1987–8, 1989–90). Comments on a wide range of publications are presented by Gwyn A. Williams, in *When was Wales?* (1985) and also in *A People and a Proletariat*, ed. David Smith (1980). There is a select bibliography in *Settlement and Society in Wales*, ed. D. Huw Owen (1989), a collection of essays examining various aspects of the development of the landscape, settlement patterns, and social framework of Wales, and containing Glanmor Williams's survey of the long and honourable tradition of local history studies in Wales.

A proposed bibliography of family history sources by Jill Barber and Derryan Paul is based upon a research project at the Department of Information and Library Studies, University of Wales at Aberystwyth. Research work and courses on local history and archive administration offered by the Department provide future archivists and librarians with an enhanced awareness of relevant sources. Research projects at the University of Wales Centre for Advanced Welsh and Celtic Studies, also based at Aberystwyth, include 'The Social History of the Welsh Language' and 'The Visual Culture of Wales'.

An awareness of the benefits of the use of personal *computers is illustrated by Gareth Evans, *Dunvant, Portrait of a Community* (1992), produced on the author's Apple Macintosh, using Aldus Pagemaker. The application of new technology is likely to increase in the future, enabling family and local historians to take advantage of innovations which will improve facilities for both research and publishing ventures.

See Glanmor Williams, 'Local and National History in Wales', in *Settlement and Society in Wales*, ed. D. Huw Owen (1989), and John Rowlands et al. (eds.), *Welsh Family History, A Guide to Research* (1993).   D. HUW OWEN

Welsh names. The use of fixed, hereditary surnames was a much later development in Wales than in England. Until the union of the two countries under Henry VIII, a person was generally distinguished by the use of ab or ap, meaning 'son of', e.g. Hywel ap Llewelyn, or Einion ab Owen. Many old Welsh names which are still in use as first names, e.g. Branwen, Geraint, and Iorwerth, are found in the *Mabinogi*, a medieval collection of ancient legends. The princes who led resistance to foreign invasion, especially Llewelyn and Glyndwr, were another source of inspiration for names. Names such as Gareth and Trevor are Anglicizations of Celtic names. Other first names have been derived from the Bible, notably David, the patron saint of Wales, in the Welsh forms Dafydd and Dewi, which have produced the surnames Davies, Davis, Davy, Dackyn, Dakin, etc. In the 20th century many old Welsh names have been consciously revived and some new names, such as Glenda or Dyfed, have been formed from Celtic words. See T. J. Morgan and Prys Morgan, *Welsh Surnames* (1985) for a historical introduction to the subject and a dictionary of names.

The ancient stock of Celtic names was supplemented in the 11th and 12th centuries by Norman ones favoured by kings and barons: William, Henry, Robert, Richard, Roger, John, Edward, etc. When hereditary surnames in the English manner came to be formed in the 16th century the widespread popularity of these first names restricted the choice of surnames, particularly as most of them were formed from patronymics. At first, the Welsh had difficulty pronouncing these foreign names; thus, Richard occasionally became Rhisiart, and Roger became Rosser or Rhoser. On the other hand, some native Welsh names were replaced by English translations or their nearest equivalents, e.g. Lewis for Llewelyn, Hugh for Hywell, Edward for Iorwerth. These changes began long before the adoption of English-type surnames in the 16th century. The naming pattern was complicated (as in other parts of Europe) by the use of pet forms of first names. Thus, the many names derived from John (including some versions imported from England) include Evan, Ievan, Ifan, Jack, Jankin, Jeavon(s), Jenkins, Jennings, John(s), Jones, Sion, and others. Celtic names had their own pet forms, which have given rise to surnames: for example, Gittings is derived from a pet form of Gruffydd and therefore has a similar etymology to Griffiths.

Migrants from Wales to England adopted the new style of surnames long before the 16th century. Many migrants acquired surnames from their place of origin, but, in marked contrast to England, this type of surname never became popular within Wales. Early Welsh surnames are also found in Ireland, where Welsh settlement occurred in the 12th century under the Earl of Pembroke, the Norman lord who was nicknamed Strongbow. For example, Wogan was imported from Pembrokeshire, and Walsh is an Irish pronunciation of Welsh, from Strongbow's time.

The lack of a large body of early records makes it difficult to identify the period when the new style of fixed surnames began, but it started with the *gentry in the border regions, even though such families remained Welsh speakers. The main movement towards the English style came under the Tudors, and by the 17th century most of Wales had adopted it. However, some pockets of resistance were found in remoter parts of the country during the 18th century.

The type of surname that was favoured overwhelmingly was the patronymic. Sometimes, this was done simply by adopting the father's name as a surname, e.g. Anthony, John, Richard, but more commonly the use of the suffix -s was preferred, no doubt because this was the system in widespread use in those English counties which lay just across the border. Because of this, and because of the rather narrow choice of male first names at the time of surname formation, Wales acquired a stock of surnames that was far more uniform than in other parts of Britain. The ab/ap element was dropped entirely if the father's name had no grip for the b/p sound, as in names such as Gruffydd or Morgan. Where the father's name began with a vowel or 'r', however, the ab or ap was joined to that name to produce what are now common Welsh surnames such as Bevan,

Bowen, Powell, or Pritchard. However, in many instances the ab/ap was omitted before Owen, Evan, Harry, Rhydderch, Robert, etc., leaving just the father's name or an -s ending. It is now impossible to say why some people chose Bevan as their surname while others preferred Evans.

The Celtic first name Einion, which was once one of the commonest names in Wales, illustrates how a patronymic might produce a variety of surname forms. Anion, En(n)ion, In(n)ion, Onion(s), Onian, Oynions, etc. are the most obvious ones, with additional forms where a final 'm' has replaced the 'n', but Benyon is also derived from this name.

Occupational names, place-names, and *nicknames, although used colloquially in Wales as much as in England, as additional names to distinguish individuals, were rarely used to form hereditary surnames. Across the border in England a variety of surnames derived from these Welsh epithets can be found, often in corrupted or misspelt forms. Welsh place-names were occasionally used as surnames when a person moved to another district, but although a person was commonly known by the name of the farm where he lived (or had once lived) this custom did not produce fixed, hereditary surnames as it did in England.

An examination of the *civil registration records of births, marriages, and deaths from 1 July 1837 onwards reveals how Welsh surnames remained concentrated in Wales and the Welsh Borders, though they were spreading to the nearest industrial towns, such as Birmingham and Liverpool, as well as to the older destination: London. Even some of the commonest Welsh surnames were not spread evenly over Wales, however. Roberts is seen from these records to be a name concentrated in north Wales. A further complication is that it had arisen independently in the West Riding of Yorkshire, and perhaps elsewhere. It must not be assumed that names such as Roberts, Edwards, or Richards are invariably Welsh in origin. Ellis is another example of a name that was used in many parts of England in the Middle Ages. Even such a name as Lloyd, which is derived from the Celtic word *llwyd*, meaning 'grey', was commonly found in English counties on the Welsh Borders in the Middle Ages. On the other hand, Hopkin(s), a diminutive of Hob, which in turn is a pet form of Robert, has been used in Wales since the 13th century, particularly in Glamorgan and parts of north Cardiganshire.

wergild. The *Anglo-Saxon system of compensation for murder or malicious injury, payable by the malefactor or his family to the family of the murdered or injured person. Payments were on a scale according to a man's social position.

Wesley, John and Charles. John Wesley (1703–91) and Charles Wesley (1707–88) were the sons of the rector of Epworth (Lincolnshire) and students at Oxford University, where they formed (in 1729) the small group nicknamed the Holy Club or Methodists. They were joined by George Whitefield in their strict devotions and evangelism. (See also MORAVIANS.) The brothers spent some time as missionaries in Georgia (America) in the mid-1730s. Upon their return, they found pulpits closed to them and so began open-air preaching, at Bristol in 1739, where the first Methodist chapel was founded. The ruined Foundry at Moorfields, London, became their headquarters. The brothers spent the rest of their lives as indefatigable travellers and preachers, often in the face of great hostility. John travelled 250,000 miles and preached 40,000 sermons during his ministry. Charles wrote over 5,500 hymns, many of which remain popular. John's *Journal* was published in 8 volumes between 1909 and 1916, edited by N. Curnock. *Methodism remained a movement within the Anglican church during the brothers' lifetime, but broke away after their deaths.

Wessex. The kingdom of the West Saxons, which became pre-eminent in *Anglo-Saxon England. During the period 685–840 Wessex became dominant in southern England, alongside the kingdoms of *Mercia and *East Anglia to the north. Under Alfred (871–99), Wessex successfully resisted the Danes. During the 10th century Alfred's descendants recovered much of England from the Danes. In 973 Edgar was crowned king of England at Bath (near the border of Wessex and Mercia) by the Archbishops of York and Canterbury. Winchester was the capital of Wessex and its ecclesiastical centre. During the 10th century many fortified towns and *monasteries were created. Fresh Viking attacks culminated in a Danish victory and the crowning of Cnut as king of England in 1016. The name 'Wessex' was revived in the 19th century by the Dorset poet William Barnes, and by Thomas *Hardy.

Western Rebellion. A *rebellion in Cornwall and Devon during 1547–9 against the Edwardian *Reformation. See Anthony Fletcher, *Tudor Rebellions* (1973), ch. 5.

West Indies. The first European settlers in the West Indies were from Spain. They were followed in the 17th century by French, English, and Dutch colonists. In 1624 Thomas Warner founded the first permanent English settlement at St Kitts. His company prospered by growing *sugar on plantations, which were organized on similar lines to the *tobacco plantations of *Virginia. At first, the work-force was English. Transported convicts were sent to the West Indies until 1718 and young indentured *domestic servants were given free passage, their board and keep, and a sum of money upon obtaining their freedom. The expansion of the sugar plantations and the high rate of mortality ensured that job opportunities were available for all who came in these ways.

By 1640 the population of St Kitts and Nevis had reached at least 20,000, and that of Barbados 30,000 or more. Thereafter, the white population declined and the number of black slaves imported from Africa as forced labour on the plantations rose dramatically. Barbados had only a few hundred black African slaves in 1640, but by 1645 it had over 6,000. By the mid-1660s the white population had dropped sharply from 40,000 to 12,000. A similar development occurred in the Leeward Islands. Some white settlers returned to Britain; others moved from Barbados to Jamaica, which was settled from 1664, for here were opportunities to acquire large estates of between 150 and 5,000 acres. By 1673 Jamaica had 7,700 whites and 9,500 blacks. The number of whites remained constant during the next 50 years, but the number of black slaves increased to 74,000. Throughout the islands of the West Indies black African slaves formed the great majority of the population by the early 18th century.

wet-nursing. The employment of women to breast-feed the infants of the upper classes was an old custom that continued to flourish in the early modern period, but which had become unfashionable by the mid-19th century. Wet-nurses were also regularly needed for orphans and abandoned babies, and the practice has been called 'a forgotten cottage industry'. Some rural villages around London specialized in providing wet-nurses. Recent local research has identified some of these places, as well as using the evidence to discuss the relationship of breast-feeding and ovulation. See Valerie Fildes, *Wet Nursing: A History from Antiquity to the Present* (1988), and the bibliography therein.

wheelhouses. Horse-mills under permanent cover. These are built in a semi-circular shape, one storey high with a sloping roof, against the wall of a barn in which machinery was housed. A horse walked round and round to power a gin for *threshing, cutting turnips and chaff, crushing *gorse for animal feed, etc. More than 1,300 surviving wheelhouses have been recorded in England, Scotland, and Wales. See K. Hutton, 'The Distribution of Wheel-Houses in the British Isles', *Agricultural History Review*, 24/1 (1976). They date from 1770 to 1870 and perhaps accompanied the spread southwards of threshing machines, patented in Scotland by Meikle. They fell into disuse with the adoption of traction engines for threshing.

Whigs. A nickname of uncertain origin applied to the aristocratic political party that was formed after the *Glorious Revolution of 1688 to keep a check on royal power. The Whigs supported the Hanoverian succession after the death of Queen Anne in 1714, and from that time formed most of the ministries until 1783. They were responsible for passing the Parliamentary Reform Act (1832), but in the 1850s were succeeded by the *Liberal Party.

whipping. The whipping of men and women, who were tied to a post or fastened to the tail of a cart which was led through the streets, was a punishment for criminals, *vagabonds, and *beggars until well into the 18th century. Whipping was also used to maintain discipline in the army and navy.

whisky. Whisky *distilling was a traditional Scottish industry, which expanded in the mid-16th century, with the introduction of the worm still. See T. M. Devine, *Clanship to Crofters' War: The Social Transformation of the Scottish Highlands* (1994), ch. 9, on the rapid growth of illicit whisky-making in the Highlands, 1760–1840, before the government was able to enforce licensing under legislation of 1823. The Highlands malt whisky industry is centred upon Speyside, Argyll, and Islay; the Lowlands industry uses blended grain spirit. The production of whisky is Scotland's leading export industry, but a comparatively small labour force is employed. See M. S. Moss and J. R. Hume, *The Making of Scotch Whisky* (1981). The Irish whiskey industry has always been on a smaller scale, despite the fame of distilleries such as Bushmills.

White, Gilbert (1720–93). Clergyman and naturalist, internationally famous for his *Natural History and Antiquities of Selborne* (1789), his observations on his Hampshire parish. The *Antiquities* is usually omitted from modern editions—unfortunately so, for White took great pains over his antiquarian research and was a Fellow of the Society of *Antiquaries. The publication of his book was delayed for many years while he studied medieval manuscripts held by Magdalene College, Oxford, relating to Selborne Priory. His antiquarian writings should be seen as an essential part of his parochial studies, though they lack the freshness and vitality of his observations on natural history.

whitesmith. A worker in tin; also, a polisher and finisher of metalware.

Whitsuntide sings. A tradition which grew up in the Victorian period, especially in Lancashire and the West Riding of Yorkshire, and remained popular until the 1960s, since when it has declined considerably. The members of each church or chapel walked behind a banner bearing the name and foundation date of the Sunday School and a large religious picture. At selected points, they would be joined by other congregations in prayers and the singing of hymns, until all the members of churches and chapels in the locality met together in some public place—a park or market square—for the main celebration, led by a conductor and *brass band and the various ministers. Special programmes were printed for the event. This was an occasion for new clothes and the return of the native-born. The hymn-singing and prayers were followed by teas and sports at the respective churches. There was much mild rivalry to assemble the largest congregation and put on the best show. In some Lancashire towns the Protestants and Catholics paraded on different days; elsewhere, the occasion was ecumenical.

widow. The harshness of life for poor widows cannot be doubted. They appear regularly in the accounts of the *Poor Law overseers and local charities. *Hearth tax returns suggest that widows frequently lived alone after their children had grown up and left home. They are recorded in such lists not by their Christian names, but as 'Widow'. However, not all widows were poor; see B. A. Holderness, 'Widows in Pre-Industrial Society: An Essay upon Their Economic Functions' in R. M. Smith (ed.), *Land, Kinship and Life Cycle* (1984) for their role in supplying *credit and in continuing to run businesses. Many women did not remain widows long, but remarried. See Mary Prior (ed.), *Women in English Society, 1500–1800* (1985). In the early modern period an average of about 20 per cent of householders were widowed at any one time; widows greatly outnumbered widowers. *Wills usually specified the rights of widows to accommodation, furni-

ture, and income. Local customs varied, but until the late 17th century widows commonly enjoyed at least a third of the estate of their deceased husband. In some places, this customary provision was much more generous. On some *manors, a widow's rights were relinquished when her eldest son came of age, but on others the rights lasted during her lifetime. Women were commonly appointed executrixes and guardians of their children. From the late Middle Ages onwards the wealthier families agreed at marriage to a 'jointure', by which property was held jointly by the husband and wife, and after the death of the husband by the widow. Bess of Hardwick is a remarkable example of a woman whose wealth and social status rose considerably during the 16th century after the deaths of four husbands.

wife-selling. The 'poor man's divorce' of the 18th and early 19th centuries. Some 400 examples are known from *newspapers, etc. from every region of England, but few are recorded in Wales, and only one case is known from Scotland. The sale was conducted according to recognized procedures: the venue was the *market place or other public space, the event was sometimes preceded by a public announcement and was conducted by an auctioneer, the woman was led in by a halter round her neck to signify that she was the property of her husband, a nominal purchase price was agreed, and the woman left with her purchaser, who was her accepted lover (not a casual passer-by, as in *Hardy's novel *The Mayor of Casterbridge*). The ritual was thus a form of divorce and remarriage. See E. P. *Thompson, 'The Sale of Wives' in *Customs in Common* (1991), ch. 7.

William of Malmesbury (*c*.1090–1143). *Benedictine monk and historian. His *Gesta Regum Anglorum*, a history of the kings of England from the *Anglo-Saxon invasions to 1126, was followed by the *Historia Novella*, which continued the story to 1142, and the *Gesta Pontificum*, an account of the bishops and chief *monasteries of England to 1123. He also wrote lives of St Dunstan and St Wulfstan and a history of the church at Glastonbury.

William of Worcester (1415–82). Physician and secretary to Sir John Fastolf of Caister (Norfolk) until 1459, when he returned to his native Bristol. A man of wide interests, between 1478 and 1480 he travelled through Norfolk, Bristol, and the south-west collecting *antiquarian information for a projected description of Britain. This was never completed, but his *Itineraries*, containing antiquarian notes and everyday accounts of his journeys and conversations (edited and translated by John Harvey in 1969), make interesting reading.

Williams's, Dr, Library, 14 Gordon Square, London. A library and archive of *Nonconformity. Of particular use is John Evans's list of dissenting congregations (1715), MS 34-4, which gives the numerical strengths of meetings throughout England and Wales. A voluntary General Register of Births for Dissenters was opened on 1 January 1743. This contains entries from many parts of Britain, but particularly for London, until the introduction of *civil registration in 1837.

wills. The practice of making a will goes back to *Anglo-Saxon times, but was originally restricted to the wealthiest groups. In some *dioceses large numbers of wills of people of more modest incomes were registered in the later Middle Ages, but the custom was not widely adopted by farmers and urban craftsmen until the 16th century. Labourers and other poor people rarely made wills, even in later times. Will-making was always a minority concern, even amongst the middling groups, for the transmission of property was usually a straightforward business, regulated by local custom. (See INHERITANCE CUSTOMS.) The various studies that have compared the numbers of adult males who made a will with those whose deaths are recorded in *parish registers usually show that the figure was about 1 in 3 or 1 in 4. Nevertheless, wills survive in their tens of thousands and are a major source for the local and family historian.

The ancient responsibility for proving a will lay with the church. Wills normally began: 'In the Name of God, Amen', followed by the testator committing his or her soul to Almighty God and asking for Christian burial in the *church or *churchyard, and in the Middle Ages often by a bequest towards the church fabric or an *altar. Most wills are therefore kept at the *record offices of the ancient dioceses. The name of the relevant diocese is not always immediately apparent, e.g. north Derbyshire was in the diocese of Coventry and Lichfield and so its wills must be sought at the Lichfield Joint Record Office. During the *Commonwealth (1653–60) all wills in England and Wales were proved in the *Prerogative Court of Canterbury and are now kept at the *Public Record Office. Indexes of all PCC wills from 1383 to 1700 have been compiled by the *British Record Society. A 'Provisional Guide to the Records of the PCC' is available at the Public Record Office and a handbook is in preparation. Some indexes of wills proved elsewhere

have also been published, but many other indexes are available at record offices only in handwritten form.

A. J. Camp, *Wills and Their Whereabouts* (4th edn., 1974) and J. S. W. Gibson, *Wills and Where to Find Them* (1974) are the standard guides. Most wills were proved in an archdeacon's court, but a general principle was adopted that a testator with property in more than one jurisdiction had to use a higher court. People with land in two or more *archdeaconries had to use a bishop's court, testators with property in two or more bishoprics went to a prerogative court, and those with land in the two provinces went to the Prerogative Court of Canterbury. (See PROBATE ACCOUNTS, and PECULIAR JURISDICTION.) On 12 January 1858 the state took over responsibility for proving wills. Since then, they have been kept at the Principal Registry of the Family Division, *Somerset House, The Strand, London. Other copies of wills survive in family papers and solicitors' collections deposited at local record offices, and in *registries of deeds.

The ancient Scottish system of proving wills was through one of the 22 *commissary courts, and after 1823 in sheriff's courts. The records are kept at the *Scottish Record Office and indexes of all records up to 1800 have been published by the Scottish Record Society; typescript indexes are available for 1800–23. Maps of the areas covered by the commissary courts have been published by the *Institute of Heraldic and Genealogical Studies, Northgate, Canterbury. See Cecil Sinclair, *Tracing Your Scottish Ancestors: A Guide to Ancestry Research in the Scottish Record Office* (1990). From 1876 to 1959 an annual series of volumes called *Calendar of Confirmations and Inventories* is available.

In Ireland the system was similar to that in England and Wales, being based on church dioceses until 1858, when responsibility for proving wills passed to a new Principal Registry in Dublin whose records were destroyed by fire in 1922, though the indexes were saved. A miscellaneous collection of wills and will-substitutes, e.g. notebook copies made before the fire, is housed at the National Archives, Dublin. Few wills survive from before 1780. Other collections are housed at the National Library, the Genealogical Office, the Registry of Deeds, and the Land Commission. The Public Record Office of Northern Ireland also has a large collection of wills.

Most wills have a long preamble which usually follows one of the formats recommended in books of advice on how to draw up a will. The choice of phrasing can nevertheless indicate a person's religious beliefs, especially in the 16th century, when references to 'Our Lady and all the Holy Company of Heaven' identify *Roman Catholics. See, for example, Margaret Spufford, *Contrasting Communities: English Villagers in the Sixteenth and Seventeenth Centuries* (1974), and David Palliser, *Tudor York* (1979) for rural and urban studies.

After the disposal of religious matters, the testator arranged for the payment of all debts and funeral expenses and then shared out his or her worldly goods. Executors were appointed and friends called in to sign as witnesses. Last wills and testaments were often made shortly before death to annul all previous wills. (See NUNCUPATIVE.) Family historians will find many wills invaluable in detailing relationships (but see BROTHER; SISTER; and NEPHEW). However, wills were not the only method of transmitting property, and not all descendants are necessarily named. For instance, adult children may already have been provided for at marriage. A common provision safeguarded the interests of children if a widow should remarry, for otherwise the property might pass to the new husband. Widows and spinsters made wills, but very few wives did so, as they were supposed to require the consent of their husbands. See Mary Prior, 'Wives and Wills, 1558–1700' in John Chartres and David Hey (eds.), *English Rural Society, 1500–1800: Essays in Honour of Joan Thirsk* (1990).

windows. Except in the largest buildings, Saxon and Norman windows were usually narrow slits, splayed on the inside, with horn often serving as a substitute for glass. *Gothic ecclesiastical and secular buildings used a variety of elaborate tracery forms, whose styles help to date the windows. In the late Middle Ages windows of *churches and *cathedrals were enlarged until they almost filled entire walls. In contemporary houses, oriel windows were a sign of superior status. The Elizabethan *prodigy-houses displayed as much glass as possible, but windows continued to be divided by mullions and transomes, and the glass was arranged in small pieces held together by lattice work. Casements allowed such windows to be opened, but from the last quarter of the 17th century they were gradually replaced by *sash windows. Meanwhile, smaller domestic houses were made much lighter from the 16th century onwards by the widespread adoption of windows.

window tax. Introduced in 1697, after the abolition of the *hearth tax. The occupier of every house was taxed at the rate of two shillings a year, with an additional payment of eight shillings for a house with over 10 windows. In 1709 the rates were increased for larger houses, but those who were too poor to pay church or poor rates were exempt. From the mid-18th century the rates paid by those with over 10 windows were frequently increased. From 1825 occupiers with fewer than eight windows were exempt. The tax was abolished in 1851. The number of windows that were blocked up to avoid paying the tax is often exaggerated; windows were blocked for other reasons, particularly because of the changing uses of rooms. Unlike the hearth tax, few returns have survived. They should be sought at county *record offices. See W. R. Ward, *The Administration of the Window and Assessed Taxes, 1696–1798* (1963).

winnowing. Probate *inventories of the early modern period often record 'winnowing fans' and sheets for separating grain from chaff. Winnowing took place in *barns, in the area between the large doors, which were opened so as to allow a gentle breeze to assist the process.

wire-making. Water-powered wire drawing was introduced from Germany in 1567, when the Mineral and Battery Company was given a monopoly of brass manufacture. The failure to make satisfactory brass led to a concentration on iron wire, e.g. in the Tintern area. Wire-making long continued as a manual process in small workshops, however, e.g. at Barnsley (Yorkshire). By the turning of a handle, red-hot iron or steel was pulled through tapering holes in an iron or steel plate known as a wortle, and gradually reduced to thin wire.

wiseman. A conjuror or wizard who performed 'white' magic which was generally regarded as being beneficial, e.g. the healing of sick people and animals, the recovery of stolen property, and forecasting the weather. Numbers in the early modern period are difficult to assess as such figures were tolerated and did not often appear before the secular courts, though they were frequently prosecuted by the ecclesiastical authorities before the *Restoration. See Keith Thomas, *Religion and the Decline of Magic* (1971). A striking portrait of a 19th-century wiseman is that of John Wrightson of Stokesley (north Yorkshire) in J. C. *Atkinson, *Forty Years in a Moorland Parish* (1891). Wrightson dressed in strange garb and had a network of informers to bolster his reputation as a man with magical powers. Customers often travelled several miles to consult him.

witchcraft. The best introductions to the study of witchcraft are Keith Thomas, *Religion and the Decline of Magic* (1971), and Alan MacFarlane, *Witchcraft in Tudor and Stuart England: A Regional and Comparative Study* (1970). See also the summary in J. A. Sharpe, *Early Modern England: A Social History* (1987). British experience was very different from that of the various witch crazes on the Continent. In the Middle Ages prosecutions were few and punishments light. In 1542, probably as a result of plots against Henry VIII, an Act made conjuration, witchcraft, sorcery, and enchantment punishable by death, but this was repealed five years later. Witchcraft became a felony again in 1563, after the return of Marian exiles imbued with Continental ideas of witchcraft. The death penalty was carried out on those who were found guilty of causing death by witchcraft, and lesser offenders were imprisoned. Serious cases were tried at the *assizes, minor offences at the *ecclesiastical courts. Prosecutions rose from 1563 to a peak during the last two decades of the 16th century. They fell away markedly during the 17th century, except for the craze that affected East Anglia and south-eastern England in 1645-7.

Witchcraft was not primarily associated with the worship and service of the Devil, but with the supposed power to do harm. It offered an explanation of individual misfortunes which could be linked to the malice of a neighbour. The assize records are not well preserved, but the cases brought before the ecclesiastical courts suggest that most accusations followed quarrels between neighbours, which were accompanied by threats and curses. The typical person accused of witchcraft was a woman who was both old and poor. Most accusations were brought by slightly wealthier neighbours, and it has been argued that such cases represent a breakdown in former traditions of neighbourly help and charity. By far the greatest number of recorded cases come from Essex, one of the richer counties. However, even there, only a minority of those found guilty of witchcraft were sentenced to death. Between 1559 and 1736, only 112 of the 513 Essex people who were found guilty of witchcraft were hanged. In Sussex during the same period a mere 17 people were tried, of whom only one was hanged. Essex was also at the centre of the witch craze led by 'Witch Finder General' Matthew Hopkins in 1645-7, which took in neighbouring counties, especially Suffolk. In other parts of the country witchcraft was not a major concern. P. Tyler, 'The Church Courts at York and Witchcraft Prosecutions, 1567-1640', *Northern History*, 4 (1969) noted 117 cases of witchcraft and sorcery; 62 of these cases were unspecified, 18 were concerned with casting or lifting spells on cattle, and a further 18 with similar activities concerning human beings. The majority of cases that came before such courts were concerned with 'white' witchcraft that involved spells, magic healing, the recovery of stolen property, etc. by *wisemen or conjurors rather than 'black' witchcraft that was thought to be the cause of illness and sometimes death. The number of cases tried at the assizes and church courts dropped in the first part of the 17th century. Occasional crazes flared up later, e.g. at Pendle (Lancashire) in 1612. The last known execution for witchcraft was at Exeter in 1682; the last case to be tried before the assizes was in 1712; the laws were repealed in 1736. Belief in witchcraft lingered on into the 19th century.

woad. The leaves of this plant afforded the essential dye in the colouring of blue, black, and purple cloth until the demand was partially satisfied, from the 16th century onwards, by imports of indigo. Even then dyers mixed woad with indigo, and woad continued in use on cheaper *woollen cloth and on *linen. Toulouse became the leading supplier of woad to English dyers in the 16th century (in the Middle Ages it came from Erfurt, Tuscany, and Piedmont), but supplies were interrupted by the French wars of religion, and so the plant began to be grown on a large scale by English farmers. It proved highly profitable and large numbers of women and children were employed for up to four months a year in its cultivation and harvest, for the leaves were picked two or three times in the course of a summer. In 1591 and 1592 Sir Francis Willoughby of Wollaton Hall (Nottinghamshire) employed 300-400 pickers a day from Nottingham and surrounding villages. See Joan Thirsk, *Economic Policy and Projects: The Development of a Consumer Society in Early Modern England* (1978). It could be grown by all classes of farmers, on small or large acreages, but a demountable woadmill had to be available locally to handle the leaves when picked, and this service came to be rendered by itinerant woadmen; gradually, the necessity for contracts with woadmen made it a crop grown by larger farmers. By the 18th and 19th centuries woad growing had become much more localized, but it did not die out until 1932 when it ceased to be grown in Lincolnshire.

wolds. The wolds as a special type of *pays* was first discussed by Alan Everitt, 'River and Wold: Reflections on the Historical Origins of Regions and *Pays*' in *Landscape and Community in England* (1985), ch. 3. This stressed the influence of early settlement and exploitation on later characteristics. The general history of wolds landscapes was considered by H. S. A. Fox, 'The People of the Wolds in English Settlement History' in M. Aston, D. Austin, and C. Dyer (eds.), *The Rural Settlements of Medieval England: Studies Dedicated to Maurice Beresford and John Hurst* (1989). *Wold* is derived from *wald*, and originally described a tract of countryside characterized by isolated strands of wood, perhaps amidst pasture and some cultivated land. The high density of Scandinavian place-names in areas of wold suggests new colonization from the 9th to the 11th century, when the last of the old *wood pastures were brought under the plough. By the 12th century the arable fields of the wolds were not much different from those overlying the days of midland England. In the later Middle Ages many wolds settlements suffered from depopulation and the land was used for sheep grazing. Much land returned under the plough after parliamentary *enclosure during the 18th and 19th centuries. The wolds landscape typically has many estate *villages, shrunken or deserted settlements, and little rural industry.

wolves are commemorated in place-names, but were generally extinct by the end of the Middle Ages. The last recorded sighting in the Highlands of Scotland was in 1743 and in Ireland in 1786.

women local and family historians. It is not usual to distinguish the work of women historians from those of men, though it is always instructive to do so. Their different lives make for different viewpoints and yield different insights; hence, in practice, they frequently choose distinctive themes for investigation, have their own styles in research and presentation, and rank their objectives and priorities differently. In the fields of local and family history especially, their insights are likely to be original and influential, since much of women's energy is devoted to creating and maintaining families and sustaining local communities. But other signs of their individuality are likely to stem from their stronger sympathy for animate creatures than for inanimate things, and their keen observation of social relationships. These themes feature prominently in local and family history, though they are not, of course, the whole agenda of the subject. In so far as they are accepted nowadays as standard topics, the contribution of women historians in putting them there calls for recognition.

Identifying the originality of women authors is not easy for, in the ugly phrasing of the scientists, they have suffered 'obliteration by incorporation'. Their themes have been absorbed into the mainstream, and their pioneering role in many directions has been forgotten. In the realm of fiction, in contrast, the originality of women has not been consigned to oblivion. Maria Edgeworth is recognized as the first writer of a historical novel, *Castle Rackrent* (1800), to whom Sir Walter Scott acknowledged his debt; Jane Austen is appreciated for her mastery in depicting manners, and Mary Russell Mitford in depicting landscape.

But local and family history has forgotten its women. To identify them requires a search in every county of the kingdom, and considerable ingenuity and local knowledge. Both in the 19th century and earlier, women authors were trained to seek obscurity, writing anonymously, signing with initials which concealed their gender, or collaborating with husbands. In this brief essay only a first attempt can be made to open up a large subject. Its main purpose must be to encourage local and family historians to search out women's contributions more thoroughly, analyse their content, assess their quality and originality, and give them equal recognition alongside the men.

Local and family history cannot be written without access to libraries and archives. So the first women authors of whom we have any record came from upper-class families, which possessed such facilities, and had the accommodation for, and the tradition of, preserving archives. Even then, such work was more likely to lie in manuscript until discovered and published in the 19th century. Thus appeared in 1806 Lucy Hutchinson's contribution to *family* history, even though its main concern was her husband's career during the Civil War, and so it was entitled *Memoirs of the Life of Colonel Hutchinson*. Another work which now ranks as a most valuable local history, though it was written to describe the contemporary scene between 1687 and 1702, is Celia *Fiennes's account of her travels through England on a side-saddle. It too lay in manuscript until it came into the possession of Baron Saye and Sele, when his daughter, the Hon. Mrs Emily Griffiths, edited it for publication (1888).

It is likely that much more writing by women exists in local archives, remaining to be reread and appraised afresh. The newly established journal, *Women's Writing* (1994–), should perform the much-needed role of bringing some of it to light. In its first issue Bridget Hill rescued from oblivion Catherine Hutton, an observant traveller, who did not consider herself a historian (though her father was the historian of Birmingham), but whose lively social comment, colourful descriptions of landscape, regional customs, food, and dress, and perceptive summaries of people serve as local history today ('Catherine Hutton (1756–1846): A Forgotten Letter-Writer', *Women's Writing*, 1/1 (1994). Though much of Hutton's writing survived in letters, she also wrote 60 articles anonymously for such periodicals as *The *Gentleman's Magazine*, and one of her descriptions of a living person, a Derbyshire yeoman, can be shown to have been incorporated, with slight changes, in her novel *Oakwood Hall* (1819).

Eighteenth-century magazines, especially *The Lady's Magazine*, may well contain local history written by women: a summary search reveals some flat historical descriptions of places, intended to encourage travellers to visit, but others, still anonymously, show personal intimacy with the place described, and score some success, despite their brevity, in evoking the atmosphere of place and people.

In the course of the 19th century many more middle-class women came to prominence as authors, thriving in family circumstances which enabled and encouraged them to read widely, write freely, and get their work published. A remarkable number produced something of everything: poems, novels, short stories for adults and for children, history, biography, and translations. They were helped by an increasing number of documents in print, and by a world not yet sufficiently professionalized to impose restrictive, academic conventions on content. Hence, writers on local and family history, both men and women, were relatively untrammelled and unconfined. They followed their own interests and adopted their own style, often using a fictional format to give faithful portraits of local society, which can now be termed local history. In that genre of writing John Galt is much cited for his scenes of Scottish country life (see *Annals of the Parish* (1821)). He desired that his fiction be regarded as 'theoretical histories'; that is a purpose and achievement that may fairly be ascribed to the women authors as well.

The list of women writers surveying a local scene is long, and runs far beyond Mrs Gaskell, George Eliot, and the Brontës. Among precursors of this celebrated trio, and following several different strands of womanly interest,

was Mary Leadbeater (see *Cottage Dialogues among the Irish Peasantry* (1811) and *Cottage Biography, being a Collection of Lives of the Irish Peasantry* (1822)). She was commended by Maria Edgeworth for her 'exact representation of the manner of being of the lower Irish and a literal transcription of their language'. A later author was Margaret E. Poole, whose *Pictures of Cottage Life in the West of England* (1870) comprise tales which, as she explains in the Preface, are drawn from life, though the plots and characters were fictitious. They were deliberately written to illustrate the character, traditions, and superstitions of the West Country, and especially of Somerset people, and she wrote in dialect in order to preserve it from being totally lost. She was, in short, a local historian, finding her own preferred way.

Poole's interest in dialect highlights a special interest of women in local speech and vocabulary, and signals their role in making a place for this subject in local history. An early collector was Sarah Sophia Banks, sister of Sir Joseph Banks, who compiled glossaries in Lincolnshire dialect between 1778 and 1783, and continued to add more until 1814. Her work is a manuscript in the *British Library (BL Add. MS 32,640), and although it was not mentioned by Joseph *Wright when he compiled the *English Dialect Dictionary* (1898–1905), in fact, she collected about 300 words more than did Wright and two other Lincolnshire collectors of his generation. An example of her feminine slant of interest may be noticed in her care, under the word 'Goose', to list the local names given to individual geese, and the owner's explanations. It proves not to be an eccentric concern, for one name uncovers a legend about John of Gaunt giving East and West Fens to the poor of the Soke of Bolingbroke. (Eileen Elder, 'Sarah Sophia Banks, sister of Sir Joseph Banks', *Lincolnshire Past and Present*, 13 (1993)). Another distinguished collector of dialect in Shropshire was Georgina F. Jackson, who started in 1870, and published in 1879, *Shropshire Word-Book, A Glossary of Archaic and Provincial Words . . . used in the County* (1879).

Georgina Jackson's work further illustrates another distinctive slant of women's interests: they were intent on gathering as much information as possible by talking to local people. Nowadays, it is called *oral history, and is rated as a distinct branch of history. Then it was an obvious and favoured routine in women's procedures, calling for the keen attention of their eyes and ears, and compensating for their meagre access to books and documents. Jackson's search for dialect depended essentially on talking to people, and it is still more explicitly demonstrated by Dinah Maria Mulock (Mrs Craik), author of a best-selling novel, *John Halifax Gentleman* (1856), who made no claim to be a local historian, yet wrote *An Unsentimental Journey through Cornwall* (1884) which contains much discerning local history. She wrote vividly of its distinctive landscape, expressing her strong feeling of Cornwall being an 'old country'; and in reporting her conversations with local people, she strove to uncover the distinctive qualities of Cornish folk. That same strategy has shown again powerfully in this century in the work of Ella Pontefract, Marie Hartley, and Joan Ingilby, writing from the 1930s up to the present, starting from visits to remote Swaledale before many visitors had found it (see Hilary Diaper (ed.), *A Favoured Land: Yorkshire in Text and Image: The Work of Marie Hartley, Joan Ingilby, and Ella Pontefract* (1994)). Oral history has now risen still higher in esteem, and is much valued for recording women's life-stories (Elizabeth Roberts, *A Woman's Place: An Oral History of Working Class Women, 1890–1940* (1984)). Yet it is still worth reading Charlotte Burne's practical advice on the best way of collecting information when arriving as a stranger in an unfamiliar place (C. S. Burne, 'The collection of English folklore', *Folklore*, 3 (1890)).

Since conversations with local people elicited much *folklore, this came to be regarded as women's special concern. Georgina Jackson gathered a great store when collecting dialect, and when she met Charlotte Sophia Burne, who was exploring folklore in the Severn valley, she handed over her material to her, and Burne published it in two volumes (*Shropshire Folklore: A Sheaf of Gleanings* (1883)). Its themes include some aspects of local history that are routinely studied nowadays and would not be defined as folklore, like inscriptions on *gravestones, while other topics have been studied with fresh interest in recent years, like local ceremonies, wakes, feasts, well-worship, local sports, and the dates and ceremonial of servant hirings, giving this book a modern look. But, judging by a small incident in the life of Harriet Martineau, women were being typecast as folklorists by the middle 19th century. (Compare also Jessie M. E. Saxby on Shetland folklore in *Foys and Fanteens: Shetland Feasts and Fasts* (1915), even though she wrote much else on Shetland's local history.) Martineau already enjoyed fame for her writing on economics for the layman, and for her political advice to eminent politicians. But when she went to live in the Lake District, and *The History and Topog-*

raphy of the Counties of Cumberland and Westmoreland (sic) was planned (ed. William Whellan (1860)), folklore, customs, and superstition were the subjects on which she was asked to write. The resulting chapter silently proclaimed her resistance to this constraint, for she started with landscape, archaeological remains of the past in the present, settlement history, local industries, household economies, local lifestyles, and diet, before turning to folklore. Like many other women, she wished to build up a whole local picture, incorporating landscape and people in one view.

Folklore was given a high place in women's research for sound, well-argued reasons. Charlotte Burne regarded it not as the quaint stories of ignorant peasants, but as insights into past codes of morals and 'living principles of action', surviving from a time before written record. It also revealed fine local differences, to which women have always paid sensitive attention. While generalizing, then, Burne insisted on paying as much regard to regional differences as to likenesses. She reflected deeply on the significance of *boundaries separating the customs of different regions in the light of early settlement history. Thus she opened to full view (in 1883, be it noted) the wide canvas against which local history must be set, if all aspects of human activity in the past are to be seen, and explained as a connected whole. But 'I do not attempt to form any theory', she emphasized, exemplifying the characteristic caution of women in generalizing prematurely. Her task was to map the existing situation accurately and comprehensively, though she did compose a list of practical questions, arising out of personal experiences and observation, showing her sharp eye and ear for detail.

Setting the scene thoroughly, painting a local canvas with as much delicacy of detail as possible were prime objectives among women. Harriet Martineau set this quality at the centre of her commendations of Jane Austen and Mary Russell Mitford: they rescued us from 'slovenly indefiniteness in delineation', she said. Edmund Gosse in 1921 repeated this judgement on Mitford, calling her 'the creator of a new mode of writing . . . rural delineation'. She was 'minutely picturesque'; no one had done it before her, but after *Our Village* appeared (published serially from 1824) 'everybody has been able to do it' (Edmund Gosse, *Books on the Table* (1921), 160). In the 20th century, the classic work in the same vein is Flora *Thompson, *Lark Rise to Candleford* (1939), sympathetically appraised by John Fowles for its 'telling detail and the detailed telling' (*New Statesman*, 3 August 1973, 154).

Attention to detail of yet another kind is exemplified in Charlotte Burne's work, in her resolve to compile her history of Shropshire 'from every shred and scrap of evidence which I could accumulate'. Women regularly scoured the realm (and those who wrote on national history showed the same resolution in scouring Europe) for all the documents they could find. They were indefatigable in assembling a mass of documents, and this made them ideal editors of texts for publication, a task in which they were further assisted by their command of foreign languages. Thus, in the later 19th century, some became distinguished editors of texts for local history.

Lucy Toulmin Smith edited *The Itinerary of John Leland* (1906), Mary Bateson, *Records of the Borough of Leicester* (1899) and *Cambridge Gild Records* (1903), and Maud Sellers, a *York Memorandum Book* (1912) and manuscripts of *The York Mercers and Merchant Aventurers, 1356–1917* (1918). Other women, increasingly after 1900, became editors of single volumes for local record societies (see E. L. C. Mullins, *Texts and Calendars, an Analytical Guide to Serial Publications* (Royal Historical Society, 1958)). Some women were almost certainly effective agitators for the setting up of county record societies; one can suspect this in cases where the editor of the first volume in the series is a woman (as in the case of Rose Graham and the Oxfordshire Record Society, 1919; Madeleine Hope Dodds and the Newcastle upon Tyne Records Committee Publications, 1920; and Joan Wake, certainly, in the case of the Northamptonshire Record Society, 1924).

A lively general debate on the content of history in the 1880s and 1890s distinguished between the 'painters' of epic events and those who wanted to solve problems, explain phases of national growth, and trace chains of cause and effect (Mark Reid, 'Our Young Historians', *Macmillans Magazine*, 67 (1892–3)). In the opinion of another writer (W. Whellan, *History and Topography of the Counties of Cumberland and Westmoreland*, 1860) this meant that local history ceased 'to possess any general interest' since 'the multiplicity of separate independencies were absorbed in the centralisation of power'. In fact, this shift in central objectives did not lead to the death of local history, but history generally did undergo change, losing some of its earlier freedom to range widely. Conventions hardened, causing professional scholars to focus much attention on political history, which was of more interest to men than

women. Women were deemed slow to throw themselves into 'the severer study of history' (Augustus Jessop, 'Women as Historians, II', *Literature*, 4 (1899)), though the more likely explanation is that political history did not engage women's sympathy. In fact, a more attractive opening came into view when economic history emerged as a distinct branch of study. Since more than a few women with a scholarly bent were now receiving a university training, they perceived the relationship of economic history with social history, and its potential for advancing local history. Hence, the women moving between Cambridge and the London School of Economics were much influenced by William Cunningham and others to combine economic and administrative history, and explore both on the local scene. This is well illustrated in Eleanor Trotter's *Seventeenth-Century Life in the Country Parish with special Reference to Local Government* (1919), in which thanks are given to the help of William Cunningham, the *Webbs, and William Ashley. Women's own style, nevertheless, survived in M. F. Davies, *Life in an English Village* (1909), describing Corsley, Wiltshire. It examined one village from multiple viewpoints, depicting its distinctive landscape and its diversity of settlement forms in village, hamlet, and single farms, tracing parish boundaries, dwelling on the significance of the Hundred Oak Tree as a meeting place, and locating it physically, and concluding with a survey of the inhabitants in 1905–6, collected in a house-to-house enquiry that was intended to find out how village families got their living, and which included family budgets and daily diet. It is a classic local history, structured in accordance with women's preferences, and building up a picture of both landscape and people viewed from many angles.

Scholarly women with the same central interests found another congenial niche around the turn of the century as transcribers of documents and writers of parish histories for the *Victoria County History, started in 1899. It has recently been described as 'a history for gentlemen, largely researched by ladies' (Christopher Lewis, *Particular Places* (1989)). In 1904, indeed, its women workers in the Public Record Office were deemed so numerous by the Secretary as to be 'a great inconvenience to the general public'. The *VCH* passed through mixed fortunes, but it still holds a key position in furthering local history, having since 1950 broadened the scope of its subject so that it satisfies the interests of both women and men. Its range includes landscape, population, economic development, education, religion, charities, as well as landholding and manorial descents; some of its editors since the 1950s have been and are women. Yet another satisfying career for women in local history in the early decades of this century has been as archivists; in fact, they are the anonymous authors of innumerable *calendars of documents in our *record offices.

Outside the academic world, freelance women local historians pursued their own paths. Mrs Bryan (Mary Ann) Stapleton gathered innumerable documents for her *Three Oxfordshire Parishes: A History of Kidlington, Yarnton, and Begbroke* (Oxfordshire Hist. Soc., 24 (1893)), not weaving them into a continuous narrative, but relating separate documents to evidence on the ground, dwelling on lively detail, and every now and then linking separated facts to conjure up a fresh view of a living scene. As a Catholic, she went on to gather systematically documents about Catholic families throughout the county, assembling some highly suggestive clues to a network of like-minded families, which links firmly with present-day interests in networks (*A History of Post Reformation Catholic Missions in Oxfordshire* (1908)). Two children shared her expeditions to read tombstones, gather fossils, and study local botany, and both showed that influence in their own later books: See Mary W. F. Stapleton, *Reminiscences* (1938).

Another Oxfordshire local historian with her own distinctive style was Mary Sturge Henderson, later Gretton, whose accounts of Cotswold places was much enlivened by her combings through 19th-century newspapers, her talks with local people, and her attention to seemingly fanciful oral traditions which were subsequently validated by the documents. 'When, I wonder, will history be taught in our village schools from the local end, as surely it should be?' she wrote in exasperation in 1914 (*A Corner of the Cotswolds* (1914). See also *Three Centuries in North Oxfordshire* (1902), and *Oxfordshire Justices of the Peace in the Seventeenth Century*, Oxfordshire Record Society, 16 (1934)). Pride in an urban and industrial past prodded Mary Walton to make a first attempt to portray the history of Sheffield in *Sheffield, Its Story and Its Achievements* (1948), but it is noticeable in this case how the conventions of urban history plainly laid a restraining hand on her inclination to give more personal detail.

Women generally have given careful attention to schools and to local industries, showing a sensitive understanding of the way handicrafts were a mainstay of local economies. This is most conspicuous in some impressively researched studies of local industries, such as that of Fanny Bury Palliser, *History of Lace* (1865), which was then much enlarged by Margaret Jourdain and Alice Dryden in 1902; Emily Nevill Jackson, *History of Lace* (1865); *A History of Hand made Lace* (1900); and Jessie M. E. Saxby, *Shetland Knitting* (a 3d. pamphlet, n.d.). Their successors in this century include Marie Hartley and Joan Ingilby, *The Old Hand-Knitters of the Dales* (1951), on stocking knitting in Yorkshire; Helen Bennett, on *Scottish Knitting* (1985); Kirstie Buckland, making as well as writing on Monmouth caps in *Costume*, 13 (1979); and Peta Lewis, mastering the workings of William Lee's stocking frame, and explaining it in *Textile History*, 17/2 (1986).

Women often express a lively interest in people of the past when they view, or live in, old buildings (see Frederica St John Orlebar, below), and this imaginative stimulus may well explain their notable contribution since 1900 to the history of buildings. Usually they favour buildings on a domestic, rather than monumental, scale though Ella Sophia Armitage's *Early Norman Castles of the British Isles* (1912) deserves to head the list for another reason, displaying as it does women's determination to make a thorough search of the documentary records. Margaret Wood's *The English Mediaeval House* (1965) was the first study for over a century to serve the interests of the general reader in tracing the evolution of houses, while Sarah Pearson's *Medieval Houses of Kent* (1994) counts as the most recent, striving also to link existing buildings to the social classes who built them. In the interval, women have made thorough-going local inventories of vernacular buildings, sometimes highly technical in their examination of constructional detail, like that for North Yorkshire and Cleveland (Barbara Hutton), for Surrey (Joan Harding), and for Wiltshire (Pamela Slocombe).

In the inter-war years, in unobtrusive ways, women forged important links between amateur and academic historians which have been greatly strengthened, to the advantage of both, since 1950. Joan Wake was an early pioneer. She had attended LSE courses in 1913, when Eileen Power was her tutor; she became the founder of the Northants Record Society, and then county archivist. Mary Dormer Harris also straddled two worlds. She was highly respected for her profound knowledge of documents and the architecture of Warwickshire. Her main scholarly book, taking 10 years to complete, was a transcript of the *Coventry Leet Book* (Early English Text Society, 4 vols. (1907–13)), but her popular reputation rested on regular articles in the *Coventry Herald* and lectures in local history for Birmingham University. Less celebrated were women like Mary S. Holgate, who edited one volume for the Sussex Record Society of *Inquisitions post mortem (33 (1927)), but whose remaining work concentrated on exploring every corner of her own parish, and writing on its boundaries, fields, roads, houses, and inhabitants in the parish magazine of Ardingly, *From Generation to Generation: Notes for the History of Ardingly* (1925), and *The Place Names of Ardingly* (1934).

The role of women in local history societies is a large subject waiting to be fully measured. Until 1945 most societies, though not all, embraced whole counties. Afterwards, a large number of local (parish) societies were formed. Kent alone has over 70 (co-ordinated by the Kent History Federation), and they are an arena in which women generally enjoy numerical equality with men. How many such societies existed between the wars is not crystal clear (although see Sara E. Harcup, *Historical, Archaeological and Kindred Societies in the British Isles: A List* (1968), who gives the foundation dates of most of them), but women upheld an active interest in local history through the Women's Institutes. Joan Wake's book (1924) *How to compile a History and Present Day Record of Village Life* (repr. 1925, 1935), was written for the Northamptonshire Federation of Women's Institutes. Then in the 1930s local history committees were set up under their county's Council of Social Service (that for Kent was formed in 1935, and the county archivist, Irene Churchill, was a prime mover). Finally, the National Council for Social Service in London set up a *Standing Conference for Local History in 1948, thus indirectly associating and formalizing the connection of women with local history.

Since the 1960s, when local history has won a larger place in academic syllabuses, many women teach the subject, especially in extramural departments of universities and the Open University. Amateurs in local classes, many of whom are women, have been encouraged to produce attractive histories; see, for example, Joan Wayne (ed.), *A Foot on Three Daisies: Pirton's Story* (Herts., 1987). Whatever the occasion for their writing, women are likely to show a strong desire to bring people into the picture, whether into buildings, into landscapes, or to illustrate in a personal way general historical developments.

As historians of the family, much women's work falls equally appropriately into the category of local history (see above) and of literature. Women have left considerable family records in letters, memoirs, and diaries, and a voluminous list of their writings and editorial work is found in the *Cambridge Bibliography of English Literature*. Until recently, women wrote no guides to family history, and no woman author appears in the article on *family history in this *Companion*. Discursive writing which paints portraits of individuals and family groups in a social setting enlists women's enthusiasm more readily than compiling *pedigrees: see, for example, the Darwin family depicted in Gwen Raverat, *Period Piece: A Cambridge Childhood* (1960). This is not perhaps surprising, since it was customary among genealogists to cut short the family trees of women and concentrate on descent in the male line. However, the Cambridge Group for the History of Population and Social Structure (*CAMPOP) has successfully enlisted women voluntarily to transcribe *parish registers, in order to reconstruct whole families and analyse their experience of nuptiality, fertility, and mortality. Some of the uses of this material bring individuals into a more lifelike social context (see, for example, the connection between women's fertility and breastfeeding), and puts flesh onto a skeleton of names. In more recent years women, searching their own family trees, have firmly incorporated the women's side in the descent.

A fresh examination of women's contributions to family history is needed, illuminated by the proposition that their themes and style are unlikely to be severely genealogical. An engaging example, beautifully illustrated (almost certainly by the author herself), came from the pen of Frederica St John Orlebar, after a systematic search of family papers 'in the lumber room' of the family home at Hinwick, Bedfordshire. She started some time after 1870, but her book was only published in 1930, two years after her death in her ninetieth year in 1928. It is a most vivid and sympathetic evocation of a place and its local families, houses, and interiors, infused with an imaginative power for putting people into a landscape (*The Orlebar Chronicles in Bedfordshire and Northamptonshire, 1553–1733, or the Children of the Manorhouse* [sic] *and their Posterity* (1930)). Practicalities were characteristically in the forefront of her mind, causing her often to cast 'a lingering thought after the old family when I move about their kitchen'. Another remarkable example of a pedigree, showing determination to breathe life into bare names, is that of the Tempest family of Broughton, Craven, Yorks., by Eleanor Blanche Tempest. On every large page of the family tree, documents are summarized in minuscule handwriting beside the names (British Library, Add. MS 40670).

Women have frequently skirted around sources studied by men, and have fastened on neglected aspects of the local scene. Thus Sheila Macbeth Mitchell between 1950 and 1980 recorded all pre-1855 family graves in central Scotland, and with her husband, John Mitchell, published 12 volumes of *Monumental Inscriptions* for eight Scottish counties (1966–75). Their son and daughter continue their work. The systematic listing of portraits is another women's interest, strongly pursued in Kent at present, where it is co-ordinated by Julia Page. Children's games, folk-songs, and folk-dances were the special interest of Alice Gomme, née Merck (1853–1938), and she is thought by some of her contemporaries to have inspired Cecil Sharp to collect folk-songs (Gillian Thomas, *A Position to Command Respect* (1992), 32, 170).

Under the headings of both local and family history women follow lines of investigation that are often distinctive, but are then absorbed into the mainstream. Their preferences are variously explained, by links with their own experience, by the opportunity to work in an uncrowded field, by the demands of the subject for manifold detail which brings it to life in some practical or vivid way. They frequently choose to build up large pictures of a local scene, inserting scenery, buildings, plants, and people, and anchoring them all in their distinctive cultural setting. In a study confined to the country house and literature, Malcolm Kelsall writes: 'The apprehension of the spirit of the place, house, and land is the role of those who lovingly preserve and understand, and that function falls especially to women' (*The Great Good Place: The Country House and English Literature* (1993), 175). In this account, the verdict is much the same, but it adds people. It also suggests that because women were long exempt from professionalizing influences their experimental flair was not curbed, and so women's 'heterodoxy and experimentation' have undoubtedly broadened and enriched the scope of local and family history.

See Bonnie G. Smith, 'The Contribution of Women to Modern Historiography in Great Britain, France, and the United States, 1750–1940', *American Historical Review*, 89 (1984), and Joan Thirsk, 'The History Women' in Mary O'Dowd and S. Wichert (eds.), *Chattel, Servant, or Citizen. Women's Status in Church, State, and Society* (1995).

JOAN THIRSK

women's names. After the *Norman Conquest the personal names that had been popular with the *Anglo-Saxons and the *Vikings fell out of favour. Some of the names favoured by the Normans were female equivalents of male names, e.g. Joan, Jane, Janet from John, or Patricia, Petra, and Paula from Patrick, Peter, and Paul. Others were biblical names or the names of saints. Joan and Agnes were first recorded in England in 1189, Catherine in 1196, Mary in 1203, Elizabeth in 1205, and Anne in 1218. Folk culture widely accepted that Anne was the mother of St Mary, though the New Testament is silent on the matter. The influence of the *mystery plays helps to explain why Old Testament names such as Eve, Hester, Judith, Sarah, and Susanna became popular in the Middle Ages. Rebecca, Ruth, and Deborah are other Old Testament names which are still in use, while the New Testament was the source of such names as Julia and Lydia, which remain popular, of Lois, Priscilla, and Rhoda, which now sound old-fashioned, and of Berenice, Dorcas, and Drusilla, which are now hardly used at all, if ever. Some biblical names, including Abigail, were revived by 19th-century fundamentalists. The 19th century also saw a revival of 17th-century Puritan names such as Faith, Hope, Charity, Joy, Patience, and Prudence. The names of martyred saints that were once common include Agatha, Agnes, Anastasia, Lucilla, and Lucia. The mystic Teresa and the Lourdes girl Bernadette remain popular models for Catholic families.

In the 18th century a fashion arose for Latin forms of women's names, e.g. Anna or Maria, especially among the upper class. Some medieval names such as Alice, Amy, Edith, Emma, Mabel, or Matilda were revived in the 18th and 19th centuries, particularly under the influence of the Romantics, Tennyson, and the Pre-Raphaelites. The influence of literature is seen in such Shakespearian names as Juliet and Rosalind, while novels and films have been the main source of such names as Pamela, Amelia, Justine, Shirley, Janice, Tracy, and Kylie. In the 19th and early 20th centuries the range of sources was extended to include precious stones (Beryl and Ruby), flowers (Daisy and Primrose), and former pet names (Peggy and Sally), which became first names in their own right. The family historian should note that in early *parish registers names such as Anne and Agnes, Hester and Esther, Joan and Jane were used interchangeably, and that in Victorian times pet forms such as Nancy for Anne or Polly for Mary may not be immediately obvious.

The 20th century has seen the adoption of foreign names, such as the Russian Natasha and Tanya, or the Swedish Astrid and Ingrid, and the introduction of many new names by immigrants. Meanwhile, *Gaelic and *Welsh names have been consciously preserved and many have undergone a revival. See Patrick Hanks and Flavia Hodges, *A Dictionary of First Names* (1990), which deals with names from all over the world, and E. G. Withycombe, *The Oxford Dictionary of English Christian Names* (1977).

wong. A strip in a shared meadow.

wood pasture. The term used to describe those agricultural districts where the farming economy was significantly different from *champion land which was farmed on the *open-field system. Such districts often had only small areas devoted to open-fields; instead most of the land was in *closes and used for pastoral activities, such as the rearing of cattle or *dairying. The neighbouring *woods were often extensive and were a source of grazing rights on the *commons. Settlement was not confined to nucleated villages, but was scattered in hamlets and isolated farmsteads. Wood-pasture districts often had specific social characteristics, notably light manorial control, numerous freeholders, and sometimes a predilection for religious and political dissent, and for rural industry. See Joan Thirsk (ed.), *The Agrarian History of England and Wales*, iv, *1500–1640* (1967).

woods. The earliest evidence for woodmanship comes from the *Neolithic trackways that have been found in the Somerset Levels. Woodland management was practised by both prehistoric peoples and the Romans. Large areas of wildwood were cleared during the *Iron Age and the *Roman period. The importance of woodland in the local economy of the *Anglo-Saxon period is demonstrated by the large number of words that were used to denote different types of wood. See, for instance, Alan Everitt, *Continuity and Colonization: The Evolution of Kentish Settlement* (1986). By the time of the *Norman Conquest many parts of England were without woods. The interpretation of the woodland entries in the *Domesday Book remains controversial, but it is clear that the surviving woods had to be carefully managed as an economic asset, mostly as *coppice or spring-woods, that is, trees which were felled just above ground level, allowing regeneration through young shoots. The alternative method of *pollarding involved the lopping of branches about 7–18 feet above the ground. *Hedges

were also a source of wood from early times. A strong tradition of woodland conservation developed long before woodland management became well recorded in the late medieval and early modern periods.

The recent study of the history of woods by a botanist begins with Oliver Rackham's two books, *Trees and Woodland in the British Landscape* (1976), and *Ancient Woodland: Its History, Vegetation and Uses in England* (1980). Rackham shows that, historically, woods should be regarded as sources of fuel and energy rather than timber. Although some trees were grown to their full height to produce timber, the regular and most important product was underwood, which was sold in bundles known as cordwood to be used as fuel by the charcoal *iron industry and for smelting *lead, as well as for pit props, fences, hurdles, poles, gates, ladders, handles, furniture, logs, faggots, etc. See Thomas Hardy's novel *The Woodlanders* (1887). The bark from underwood was stripped for use in *tanning, while the twigs and other bits left over (known as rammel in the north midlands) were used for kindling fires. Holly was grown in special 'haggs' as winter fodder for sheep and deer: see Martin Spray, 'Holly as a Fodder in England', *Agricultural History Review*, 29/2 (1981).

Concern over supplies of timber for shipbuilding led to the passing of an Act of 1543 'for the preservacion of woods', which required all woods to contain a minimum of 12 'standards' (i.e. full-grown trees) per acre. It is unlikely that the legislation had much effect. In 1664 John *Evelyn, concerned about the lack of adequate supplies of timber, published *Sylva: A Discourse on Forest Trees* (ed. A. Hunter, 1801), which quoted the information of correspondents from all over England on the felling of huge oaks. Fears were expressed that the ironmasters were destroying woods, but in fact they frequently took good care to conserve their resources. The complaints might have been more realistically directed against the lack of standard trees, for wood owners found it more profitable to sell underwood.

In the Middle Ages almost all buildings below the level of the *manor house had been built of timber, but from Elizabethan times onwards timber was abandoned in favour of stone or *brick. (See TIMBER-FRAMED BUILDINGS.) The majority of medieval building timbers are oak. Large numbers of small oak trees were required, together with hazel, etc. for the infilling of panels. Rackham has estimated that a typical 15th-century Suffolk farmhouse (which was rather larger than average) was made from some 330 trees. Of these, only three trees were as much as 18 inches in diameter, half were less than 9 inches, and one in ten was as small as 6 inches. Such sizes are typical of medieval houses, barns, colleges, and the less grand church roofs. Outsize timbers, which were often brought considerable distances, were used in large, prestigious buildings, such as royal *castles or *cathedrals. Pine was imported from Norway and the Baltic, even in the Middle Ages.

Most woods were privately owned, often by the *lord of the manor, but others were shared. *Surveys show that farms sometimes included parts of a neighbouring wood. The manorial woods were frequently subject to grazing rights on the *commons for cattle and pigs, once the young shoots had become established. Woods have often retained their shape and size for centuries, largely because their boundaries were carefully defined by a surrounding ditch and bank, usually topped by a hedge, fence, or wall. This prevented encroachment and stopped livestock from feeding off the young shoots. The boundary ditches typically follow a sinuous course. Banks and ditches were also used to mark the internal divisions of woods, for different areas followed separate felling cycles and were often leased to different people. These internal ditches are difficult to distinguish from those constructed for drainage; perhaps some served both purposes.

Many medieval Welsh woods have been identified, but relatively little topographical investigation has been undertaken. See William Linnard, *Welsh Woods and Forests: History and Utilisation* (1982), which relates their documentary history. Scotland has fewer types of native woodland than England and the area devoted to woodland was smaller. Most of the surviving Scottish woods are in the Highlands, for which the documentary evidence is sparse. The evidence for ancient woodland in Ireland is even thinner and very little fieldwork has been attempted. In the 17th century Ireland had less than a third as much woodland as England in relation to its area, but the distribution was uneven. See Oliver Rackham, *The History of the Countryside* (1986), ch. 5.

The ancient tradition of coppicing began to decline in the late 19th century, in face of competition from foreign imports, and was largely abandoned after the First World War. Many deciduous woods have not been coppiced since the first decade of the 20th century and so now look very different from when they were managed carefully. Rackham has estimated that between 1946 and 1976 about 30

per cent of Britain's ancient broad-leaved woods were destroyed by agricultural expansion or by replacement with conifers. The conservation movement of the late 20th century has drawn public attention to the need to preserve woods and to maintain them regularly, and now, for other reasons, coppicing is returning. Most surviving broad-leaved woodlands have a continuous history from at least the late Middle Ages. A knowledge of that history adds to the more immediate appeal of woods as places of beauty and wildlife.

wool. The woollen industry was pre-eminent in the economy of the British Isles during the Middle Ages and the early modern period. The manufacture of cloth was unrivalled as England's principal medieval industry, in both the towns and the countryside. (See FULLING MILLS, and CLOTHIERS.) By the mid-15th century cloth had outstripped wool as the major export. Sales of both wool and cloth expanded considerably in the late 15th and early 16th centuries. The fine *Perpendicular churches of East Anglia and south-west England were paid for out of the profits of this trade, before the recession of the mid-1520s onwards. The industry revived in the later 16th century with the introduction of *New Draperies. See Eric Kerridge, *Textile Manufacturers in Early Modern England* (1992). Despite periodic depressions and crises, the woollen industry remained the nation's major industrial employer before the *Industrial Revolution. See Peter Bowden, *The Wool Trade in Tudor and Stuart England* (1962), and G. D. Ramsay, *The English Woollen Industry* (1982). (See COTTON, for the growth to pre-eminence of another textile industry.)

The woollen industry has long attracted regional studies. See, for example, Herbert Heaton, *The Yorkshire Woollen and Worsted Industry* (1920), W. B. Crump and Gertrude Ghorbal, *History of the Huddersfield Woollen Industry* (1935), G. D. Ramsay, *The Wiltshire Woollen Industry in the Sixteenth and Seventeenth Centuries* (1943), Julia de L. Mann, *The Cloth Industry of the West of England from 1640 to 1850* (1971), K. G. Ponting, *The Woollen Industry of South-West England* (1971), and C. Gulvin, *The Tweedmakers: A History of the Scottish Fancy Woollen Industry, 1600–1914* (1973). See also articles in the journal *Textile History*. The manufacture of woollen cloth in East Anglia, the Cotswolds, and other regions declined in face of West Riding competition during the 18th and 19th centuries. The settlement pattern of the West Riding was transformed by the use of *water power from the 1770s onwards, when workers' houses were built around the *mills in the valley bottoms. See D. T. Jenkins, *The West Riding Wool Textile Industry, 1770–1835* (1975), and Lucy Caffyn, *Workers' Housing in West Yorkshire, 1750–1920* (1986). The preparation and spinning processes were mechanized long before *weaving. The domestic production of woollen cloth remained more important than factory output until the second quarter of the 19th century. Even then, small mills and workshops remained more typical than larger units. The mills have attracted the attention of industrial archaeologists in the later 20th century as the industry has declined in face of Asian competition.

woollen industry. See WOOL.

workhouse. A few workhouses for the able-bodied poor were founded, from the late 17th century onwards, by local Acts. More were established under the Acts of 1722 and 1782. From 1722 parishes were allowed to farm out their responsibility for the poor to a contractor at a fixed fee. *Gilbert's Act (1782) allowed parishes to join forces in the erection of a workhouse, in an arrangement by which each *parish paid the cost of maintaining its own poor but achieved savings by sharing the premises. The establishment of these 18th-century workhouses is noted in the accounts of the overseers of the *poor, but detailed records usually do not survive, since the operation was often let to contractors. (See, however, EDEN, SIR F. M.)

By the *Poor Law Amendment Act of 1834 the whole of England and Wales was divided into unions of parishes, in each of which a board of guardians was elected to administer poor relief. These unions were often centred on a market town, and they sometimes stretched beyond county boundaries. (See CIVIL REGISTRATION.) The new Poor Law met with considerable opposition in the north of England. Each union built a workhouse to house those people who were in receipt of relief. Some unions merely took over existing workhouses, and others were slow to build their own. Contrary to the intention of the Act, the guardians often continued to pay relief to people who lived in their own houses. Workhouses gradually evolved into orphanages and hospitals, especially for the feeble-minded, the aged, and the infirm. Recent studies have stressed continuity with the old system and the way in which medical services soon came to be a very important part of the provision of workhouses. In the mid-19th century some workhouses established schools for the children in their care, until local

board schools were built in the 1870s. Children were finally removed from the workhouse in 1908. *County and district councils took over responsibility for workhouses from the guardians in 1894. The system was replaced in 1948 upon the creation of the National Health Service.

In Ireland, the same system of Poor Law unions, elected guardians, and union workhouses began in 1838. In Scotland, the *heritors and kirk session of each parish were responsible for the poor until the Poor Law Act (1845) established parochial boards to administer poor relief in each parish. From 1845 poor houses were established more widely than before. Here, too, the old system was replaced in 1894 when responsibility passed to elected parish councils, which were replaced in turn by district councils in 1929, until the reorganization of local government in 1974.

The best-known workhouse records are the master's accounts. Some admission registers survive, together with guardians' minute books and general ledgers. These will be found in local *record offices. *Census returns list the inmates of workhouses on census night. See Felix Driver, *Power and Pauperism: The Workhouse System, 1834–1864* (1993), M. E. Rose, *The Relief of Poverty, 1834–1914* (1972), Jane M. Coleman, 'Guardians' Minute Books', *History*, 48 (1963), P. Grey, 'Parish Workhouses and Poorhouses', *The Local Historian*, 10/2 (1972–3), and R. M. Gutchen, 'Paupers in Union Workhouses: Computer Analysis of Admissions and Discharges', *The Local Historian*, 11/8 (1974–5).

World Wars, records of. Regimental museums have lists of soldiers who served in the First and Second World Wars, and much background information, including *photographs. Many rolls of honour for the dead in the two World Wars have been published by regiments, schools, and professional bodies. (See also WAR MEMORIALS.) The Commonwealth War Graves Commission, 2 Marlow Road, Maidenhead, Berkshire SL6 7DX, has details of servicemen who died overseas and on ships during the two World Wars.

*The *London Gazette* published despatches, campaign reports, casualty lists, and citations for awards and decorations. The *Public Record Office has First World War records of military tribunals (MH 47), medical and discharge papers (MH 106), and records of pensions and allowances (PIN 15 and 26, PMG 42–47). The PRO's records of the Second World War include the Army Roll of Honour, which lists servicemen and servicewomen who died, noting their rank, regiment, birthplace, residence, and place of death (WO 304), and war pensions paid to widows (PMG 10). Other war records are noted in Stella Colwell, *Dictionary of Genealogical Sources in the Public Record Office* (1992).

The Imperial War Museum has published *Officers Who Died in the Great War* (1921), and *Soldiers Who Died in the Great War* (1921–2). See also N. Holding, *World War One Army Ancestry* (1982), and *More Sources of World War One Army Ancestry* (1986).

worsted. A type of cloth, using long wools, that was originally made in Worstead, Norfolk, but which became a speciality of the upper Calder and Aire valleys in the West Riding of Yorkshire from the later 17th century onwards. The construction of the Aire and Calder Nav-

igation from 1699 substantially reduced the cost of importing long wools from Lincolnshire and Leicestershire. By 1770 output in the district centred on Halifax (where worsted manufacture had replaced the traditional *kerseys) had reached the same level as that of Norwich. The transition to factory production in the early 19th century was rapid and the centre of the West Riding industry moved eastwards to Bradford. See WOOL.

Wright, Joseph (1855–1930). Professor of Comparative Philology at the University of Oxford, best known for his work as editor of *The English Dialect Dictionary*, 6 vols. (1898–1905), which despite its title covers Ireland, Scotland, and Wales as well as England.

writ. A written and sealed command from a court, ordering or forbidding an act by the person to whom it is addressed.

Y

yard. A word meaning enclosed ground, as in the sense of back yard, courtyard, farmyard, etc. The Americans use 'yard' for 'garden'. (See GARTH.) Some of the worst working-class housing in the industrial towns of the 19th century fronted on to badly lit communal yards, with middens and earth closets close by. This form of high-density housing resulted from the infilling of inn yards, gardens, orchards, and other vacant spaces in the centres of towns, which had been abandoned by the middle classes who had sought instead new housing in the residential suburbs. The plans of such yards were irregular, the houses in effect lining the interior walls of the former properties. They therefore had no back doors and often no back windows. The names of some yards and courts have been preserved, but the buildings have mostly been demolished. They may be identified from large-scale 19th-century *Ordnance Survey maps.

yardland. A *virgate, a typical peasant holding in the Middle Ages, often dispersed in *strips in the *open-fields. The acreage of yardlands varied considerably (e.g. in Northamptonshire it ranged from 14 to 80 acres), but as a fiscal unit it often remained consistent over long periods of time (though not in the west midlands).

yeomanry. The local volunteer force of the Victorian and Edwardian era, who were mounted on their own horses and were therefore distinct from the foot soldiers of the *militia.

yeomen. The term has changed its meaning over time. In the 13th-15th centuries it was principally applied to a *knight's servants or retainers, though in the royal household the minor officials under the Chamberlain were known as the Yeomen of the King's Chamber. Geoffrey Chaucer was once a yeoman in this sense. Under the Tudors the use of the term was gradually widened to include the prosperous working farmers below the rank of the *gentry, the class formerly known as *franklins. They worked their own land, but did not necessarily have to be freeholders. Yeomen increasingly held their land by a variety of tenures: *freehold, *copyhold, and *leasehold. The term had no legal precision, but was used informally to distinguish a farmer who was more prosperous than the average *husbandman. The wealth that was needed for a farmer to be judged a yeoman by his neighbours varied from region to region and over time. The term is commonly found in the *wills and *inventories of the early modern period, but during the 18th and 19th centuries both 'yeoman' and 'husbandman' were gradually abandoned in favour of the all-embracing 'farmer'.

yoke. A piece of wood curved round the necks of two *oxen, or other animals, by which they were harnessed to a plough or vehicle. Yokes were also used by people, e.g. milkmaids carrying pails.

Young, Arthur (1741–1820). Writer on agriculture. His major works include *A Tour through the Southern Counties* (1768), *A Tour through the North of England* (1771), *The Farmer's Tour through the East of England* (1770–1), *Tour in Ireland* (1780), *Travels in France during 1787–88–89–90* (1792–4), *The Farmer's Kalendar* (which went into 215 editions by 1862), and reports on seven counties published in the *General Views of Agriculture* series of the *Board of Agriculture, where he was Secretary from 1793. He also edited *The Annals of Agriculture* (1784–1815), to which he contributed many papers. His writings are a major source for agricultural historians, though it is recognized that his opinions are not always reliable. See G. E. Mingay (ed.), *Arthur Young and His Times* (1975).

APPENDIX

I. The national record offices are as follows:

Public Record Office, Ruskin Avenue, Kew, Richmond TW9 4DU
British Library, Manuscript Collection, Great Russell Street, London WCIB 3DG
House of Lords Record Office, House of Lords, London SWIA OPW
National Library of Wales, Department of Manuscripts and Records,
    Aberystwyth SY23 3BU
Scottish Record Office, HM General Register House, Edinburgh EHI 3YY
National Library of Scotland, Department of Manuscripts, George IV
    Bridge, Edinburgh EHI IEW
The National Archives [Republic of Ireland], Bishop Street, Dublin 7
Public Record Office of Northern Ireland, 66 Balmoral Avenue, Belfast BT9 6NY

2. The major county and local record offices, arranged by modern counties, are:

England

Avon	Bath City Record Office, Guildhall, Bath BAI 5AW
	Bristol Record Office, 'B' Bond Warehouse, Smeaton Road, Bristol BSI 6XN
Bedfordshire	Bedfordshire Record Office, County Hall, Cauldwell Street, Bedford MK42 9AP
Berkshire	Berkshire Record Office, Shire Hall, Shinfield Park, Reading RG2 9XD
Buckinghamshire	Buckinghamshire Record Office, County Hall, Aylesbury HP20 IUA
Cambridgeshire	County Record Office, Cambridge, Shire Hall, Cambridge CB3 OAP
	County Record Office, Huntingdon, Grammar School Walk, Huntingdon PEI8 6LF
Cheshire	Cheshire Record Office, Duke Street, Chester, CHI IRL
	Chester City Record Office, Town Hall, Chester CHI 2HJ
Cleveland	Cleveland Archives Section, Exchange House, 6 Marton Road, Middlesbrough TSI IDB
Cornwall	Cornwall Record Office, Truro, TRI 3AY
Cumbria	Cumbria Record Office, Carlisle, The Castle, Carlisle CA3 8UR
	Cumbria Record Office, Kendal, County Offices, Kendal LA9 4RQ
	Cumbria Record Office, Barrow, 140 Duke Street, Barrow-in-Furness, LAI4 IXW
Derbyshire	Derbyshire Record Office, New Street, Matlock (correspondence to County Education Department, County Offices, Matlock DE4 3AG)

Devon	Devon Record Office, Castle Street, Exeter EX4 3PU
	North Devon Record Office, Tuly Street, Barnstaple EX32 7EJ
	West Devon Area Record Office, Unit 3, Clare Place, Coxside, Plymouth PL4 0JW
Dorset	Dorset Record Office, Bridport Road, Dorchester DT1 1RP
Durham	Durham County Record Office, County Hall, Durham DH1 5UK
Essex	Essex Record Office, PO Box 11, County Hall, Chelmsford CM1 1LX
	Essex Record Office, Colchester and North-East Essex Branch, Stanwell House, Stanwell Street, Colchester CO2 7DL
	Essex Record Office, Southend Branch, Central Library, Victoria Avenue, Southend-on-Sea SS2 6EX
Gloucestershire	Gloucestershire Record Office, Clarence Row, Alvin Street, Gloucester GL1 3DW
Hampshire	Hampshire Record Office, 20 Southgate Street, Winchester SO23 9EF
	Portsmouth City Records Office, 3 Museum Road, Portsmouth PO1 2LE
	Southampton City Records Office, Civic Centre, Southampton SO9 4XR
Hereford and Worcester	Hereford and Worcester Record Office, County Hall, Spetchley Road, Worcester WR5 2NP
	Hereford Record Office, The Old Barracks, Harold Street, Hereford HR1 2QX
	Worcester (St Helen's) Record Office, Fish Street, Worcester WR1 2HN
Hertfordshire	Hertfordshire Record Office, County Hall, Hertford SG13 8DE
Humberside	Humberside County Archive Office, County Hall, Beverley HU17 9BA
	South Humberside Area Archive Office, Town Hall Square, Grimsby DN31 1HX
	Kingston upon Hull City Record Office, 79 Lowgate, Kingston upon Hull HU1 2AA
Kent	Centre for Kentish Studies, County Hall, Maidstone ME14 1XQ
	Canterbury City and Cathedral Archives, The Precincts, Canterbury CT1 2EG
	Shepway Branch Archives Office, Central Library, Grace Hill, Folkestone CT20 1HD
	Thanet Branch Archives Office, Ramsgate Library, Guildford Lawn, Ramsgate CT11 9AI
	Medway Area Archives Office, Civic Centre, Strood, Rochester ME2 4AW
	Sevenoaks Branch Archives Office, Central Library, Buckhurst Lane, Sevenoaks TN13 1LQ
Lancashire	Lancashire Record Office, Bow Lane, Preston PR1 2RE
Leicestershire	Leicestershire Record Office, 57 New Walk, Leicester LE1 7JB
Lincolnshire	Lincolnshire Archives, St Rumbold Street, Lincoln LN2 5AB
Greater London	Greater London Record Office and History Library, 40 Northampton Road, London EC1R 0HB

Corporation of London Records Office, PO Box 270, Guildhall, London EC2P 2EJ

Guildhall Library, Aldermansbury, London EC2P 2EJ

Barnet Archives and Local Studies Centre, Hendon Catholic Social Centre, Chapel Walk, Egerton Gardens, London NW4 4BE

Bexley Libraries and Museums Department, Local Studies Centre, Hall Place, Bourne Road, Bexley DA5 1PQ

Bromley Public Libraries, Archives Section, Central Library, High Street, Bromley BR1 1EX

Camden Leisure Services, Swiss Cottage Library, Local Studies Library, 88 Avenue Road, London NW3 3HA

Camden Leisure Services, Holborn Library, Local Studies Library, 32-38 Theobalds Road, London WC1X 8PA

Greenwich Local History Library, Woodlands, 90 Mycenae Road, Blackheath, London SE3 7SE

Hackney Archives Department, Rose Lipman Library, De Beauvoir Road, London N1 5SQ

Hammersmith and Fulham Archives, The Lilla Huset, 191 Talgarth Road, London W6 8BJ

Haringey Community Information, Bruce Castle Museum, Lordship, London N17 8NU

Kensington and Chelsea Libraries and Arts Service, Central Library, Phillimore Walk, London W8 7RX

Lambeth Archives Department, Minet Library, 52 Knatchbull Road, London SE5 9QY

Lewisham Local History Centre, The Manor House, Old Road, Lee, London SE13 5SY

Redbridge Central Library, Local History Room, Clements Road, Ilford IG1 1EA

Southwark Local Studies Library, 211 Borough High Street, London SE1 1JA

Tower Hamlets Local History Library and Archives, Central Library, 277 Bancroft Road, London E1 4DQ

Waltham Forest Archives, Vestry House Museum, Vestry Road, Walthamstow, London E17 9NH

Westminster City Archives, Victoria Library, 160 Buckingham Palace Road, London SW1W 9UD

Westminster City Archives, Marylebone Library, Marylebone Road, London NW1 5PS

Greater Manchester

Greater Manchester County Record Office, 56 Marshall Street, New Cross, Manchester M4 5FU

Bolton Archive Service, Central Library, Civic Centre, Le Mans Crescent, Bolton BL1 1SE

Bury Archive Service, Derby Hall Annexe, Edwin Street, Bury BL9 0AS

Manchester Central Library, Local Studies Unit, St Peter's Square, Manchester M2 5PD

Rochdale Libraries, Local Studies Department, Area Central Library, Esplanade, Rochdale OL16 1AS

	Salford Archives Centre, 658-662 Liverpool Road, Irlam, Manchester M30 5AD
	Stockport Archive Service, Central Library, Wellington Road South, Stockport SK1 3RS
	Tameside Archive Service, Tameside Local Studies Library, Astley Cheetham Public Library, Trinity Street, Stalybridge SK15 2BN
	Wigan Archives Service, Wigan Record Office, Town Hall, Leigh WN7 2DY
Merseyside	Merseyside Record Office, Cunard Building (4th Floor), Pier Head, Liverpool L3 1EG
	Liverpool Record Office, City Libraries, William Brown Street, Liverpool L3 8EW
	St Helens Local History and Archives Library, Central Library, Gamble Institute, Victoria Square, St Helens WA10 1DY
	Wirral Archives Service, Birkenhead Reference Library, Borough Road, Birkenhead L41 2XB
West Midlands	Birmingham Central Library, Archives Division, Chamberlain Square, Birmingham B3 3HQ
	Coventry City Record Office, Mandela House, Bayley Lane, Coventry CV1 5RG
	Dudley Archives and Local History Service, Mount Pleasant Street, Coseley, Dudley WV14 9JR
	Sandwell District Libraries, Local Studies Centre, Smethwick Library, High Street, Smethwick, Warley B66 1AB
	Walsall Archives Service, Local History Centre, Essex Street, Walsall WS2 7AS
	Wolverhampton Borough Archives, Central Library, Snow Hill, Wolverhampton WV1 3AX
Norfolk	Norfolk Record Office, Central Library, Norwich NR2 1NJ
Northamptonshire	Northamptonshire Record Office, Wootton Hall Park, Northampton NN4 9BQ
Northumberland	Northumberland Record Office, Melton Park, North Gosforth, Newcastle upon Tyne NE3 5QX
	Berwick upon Tweed Record Office, Council Offices, Wallace Green, Berwick upon Tweed TD15 1ED
Nottinghamshire	Nottinghamshire Archives Office, County House, Castle Meadow Road, Nottingham NG2 1AG
Oxfordshire	Oxfordshire Archives, County Hall, New Road, Oxford OX1 1ND
Shropshire	Shropshire Record Office, Shirehall, Abbey Foregate, Shrewsbury SY2 6ND
	Shropshire Local Studies Library, Castle Gates, Shrewsbury SY1 2AS
Somerset	Somerset Archive and Record Service, Obridge Road, Taunton TA2 7PU
Staffordshire	Staffordshire Record Office, County Buildings, Eastgate Street, Stafford ST16 2LZ
	William Salt Library, Eastgate Street, Stafford ST16 2LZ
	Lichfield Joint Record Office, Lichfield Library, The Friary, Lichfield WS13 6QG

Suffolk	Suffolk Record Office, Ipswich Branch, Gatacre Road, Ipswich IP1 2LQ
	Suffolk Record Office, Bury St Edmunds Branch, Raingate Street, Bury St Edmunds IP33 IRX
	Suffolk Record Office, Lowestoft Branch, Central Library, Clapham Road, Lowestoft NR32 IDR
Surrey	Surrey Record Office, County Hall, Penrhyn Road, Kingston upon Thames KT1 2DN
	Surrey Record Office, Guildford Muniment Room, Castle Arch, Guildford GU1 3SX
East Sussex	East Sussex Record Office, The Maltings, Castle Precincts, Lewes BN7 1YT
West Sussex	West Sussex Record Office, Sherburne House, 3 Orchard Street, Chichester (correspondence to County Hall,Chichester PO19 IRN)
Tyne and Wear	Tyne and Wear Archives Service, Blandford House, Blandford Square, Newcastle upon Tyne NE1 4JA
	Gateshead Central Library, Local Studies Collection, Prince Consort Road, Gateshead NE8 4LN
Warwickshire	Warwickshire County Record Office, Priory Park, Cape Road, Warwick CV34 4JS
Isle of Wight	Isle of Wight County Record Office, 26 Hillside, Newport PO30 2EB
Wiltshire	Wiltshire Record Office, County Hall, Trowbridge BA14 8JG
North Yorkshire	Borthwick Institute of Historical Research, St Anthony's Hall, York YO1 2PW
	North Yorkshire County Record Office, Malpas Road, Northallerton DL7 8TB
	York City Archives Department, Art Gallery Building, Exhibition Square, York YO1 2EW
	York Minster Archives, Dean's Park, York YO1 2JD
South Yorkshire	Barnsley Archive Service, Central Library, Shambles Street, Barnsley S70 2JF
	Doncaster Archives Department, King Edward Road, Balby, Doncaster DN4 0NA
	Rotherham Archives and Local Studies Section, Brian O'Malley Central Library, Walker Place, Rotherham S65 IJH
	Sheffield Archives, 52 Shoreham Street, Sheffield S1 4SP
West Yorkshire	West Yorkshire Archive Service, Wakefield Headquarters, Registry of Deeds, Newstead Road, Wakefield WF1 2DE
	West Yorkshire Archive Service, Bradford, 15 Canal Road, Bradford BD1 4AT
	West Yorkshire Archive Service, Calderdale, Central Library, Northgate House, Halifax HX1 1UN
	West Yorkshire Archive Service, Kirklees, Central Library, Princess Alexandra Walk, Huddersfield HD1 2SU
	West Yorkshire Archive Service, Leeds, Chapeltown Road, Sheepscar, Leeds LS7 3AP
	West Yorkshire Archive Service, Yorkshire Archaeological Society, Claremont, 23 Clarendon Road, Leeds LS2 9NZ

Wales

Clwyd	Clwyd Record Office, Hawarden Branch, The Old Rectory, Hawarden, Deeside CH5 3NR Clwyd Record Office, Ruthin Branch, 46 Clwyd Street, Ruthin LL15 1HP
Dyfed	Dyfed Archives Service, Carmarthenshire Area Record Office, County Hall, Carmarthen SA31 1JP Dyfed Archives Service, Cardiganshire Area Record Office, County Office, Marine Terrace, Aberystwyth, SY23 2DE Dyfed Archive Service, Pembrokeshire Area Record Office, The Castle, Haverfordwest SA61 2EF
Mid and South Glamorgan	Glamorgan Record Office, County Hall, Cathays Park, Cardiff CF1 3NE
West Glamorgan	West Glamorgan Record Office, County Hall, Oystermouth Road, Swansea SA1 3SN
Gwent	Gwent County Record Office, County Hall, Cwmbran NP44L 2XH
Gwynedd	Gwynedd Archives, Caernarfon Area Record Office,Victoria Dock, Caernarfon (correspondence to County Offices, Shirehall Street, Caernarfon LL55 1SH) Gwynedd Archives, Dolgellau Area Record Office, Cae Penarlag, Dolgellau LL40 2YB Gwynedd Archives, Llangefni Area Record Office, Shire Hall, Llangefni LL77 7TW
Powys	Powys County Archives Office, County Hall, Llandrindod Wells LD1 5LD

Scotland

Borders	Borders Region Archive and Local History Centre, Regional Library Headquarters, St Mary's Mill, Selkirk TD7 5EW
Central	Central Regional Council Archives Department, Unit 6, Burghmuir Industrial Estate, Stirling FK7 7PY
Dumfries and Galloway	Dumfries and Galloway Regional Library Service, Ewart Public Library, Catherine Street, Dumfries DG1 1JB Dumfries Archive Centre, 33 Burns Street, Dumfries DG1 2PS
Grampian	Grampian Regional Archives, Old Aberdeen House, Dunbar Street, Aberdeen AB2 1UE Moray District Record Office, Tolbooth, High Street, Forres IV36 0AB Aberdeen City Archives, The Charter Room, The Town House, Aberdeen AB9 1AQ
Highland	Highland Regional Archive, Inverness Branch Library, Farraline Park, Inverness IV1 1NH
Lothian	City of Edinburgh District Council Archives, Department of Administration, City Chambers, High Street, Edinburgh EH1 1YJ
Orkney	Orkney Archives, Orkney Library, Laing Street, Kirkwall, KW15 1NW
Shetland	Shetland Archives, 44 King Harald Street, Lerwick ZE1 0EQ

Strathclyde	Strathclyde Regional Archives, Mitchell Library, North Street, Glasgow G3 7DN
	Argyll and Bute District Archives, Kilmory, Lochgilphead PA31 8RT
Tayside	Dundee District Archive and Record Centre, 14 City Square, Dundee DDI 3BY
	Perth and Kinross District Archive, Sandeman Library, 16 Kinnoul Street, Perth PHI 5ET

3. Special collections of national interest are housed at the following:

Centre for Rural History, University of Reading, Whiteknights Park, PO Box 229, Reading RG6 2AG

Cambridge University Library, Department of Manuscripts and University Archives, West Road, Cambridge CB3 9DR

British Architectural Library, Royal Institute of British Architects, Manuscripts and Archives Collection, 66 Portland Place, London WIN 4AD

Dr Williams's Library, 14 Gordon Square, London WCIH OAG

Bodleian Library, Department of Western Manuscripts, Broad Street, Oxford OXI 3BG

Further information is available in Jeremy Gibson and Pamela Peskett, *Record Offices: How to Find Them* (1985), Jean Cole and Rosemary Church, *In and Around Record Offices in Great Britain* (1990), J. Foster and J. Shepherd, *British Archives: A Guide to Archive Resources in the United Kingdom* (2nd edn., 1989), and A. Morton and G. Donaldson, *British National Archives and the Local Historian* (1983), which is a guide to official record publications.

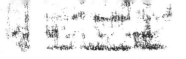
DATE DUE
